W9-BLH-276

Visual Basic® 2010

PROGRAMMER'S REFERENCE

Visual Basic® 2010

PROGRAMMER'S REFERENCE

Rod Stephens

Wiley Publishing, Inc.

Visual Basic® 2010 Programmer's Reference

Published by
Wiley Publishing, Inc.
10475 Crosspoint Boulevard
Indianapolis, IN 46256
www.wiley.com

Copyright © 2010 by Wiley Publishing, Inc., Indianapolis, Indiana

Published simultaneously in Canada

ISBN: 978-0-470-49983-2

Manufactured in the United States of America

10 9 8 7 6 5 4 3 2 1

Library of Congress Control Number: 2009942303

ABOUT THE AUTHOR

 **ROD STEPHENS** started out as a mathematician, but while studying at MIT, discovered the joys of programming and has been programming professionally ever since. During his career, he has worked on an eclectic assortment of applications in such fields as telephone switching, billing, repair dispatching, tax processing, wastewater treatment, concert ticket sales, cartography, and training for professional football players.

Rod is a Microsoft Visual Basic Most Valuable Professional (MVP) and ITT adjunct instructor. He has written more than 20 books that have been translated into languages from all over the world, and more than 250 magazine articles covering Visual Basic, C#, Visual Basic for Applications, Delphi, and Java. He is currently a regular contributor to DevX (www.DevX.com).

Rod's popular *VB Helper* web site www.vb-helper.com receives several million hits per month and contains thousands of pages of tips, tricks, and example code for Visual Basic programmers, as well as example code for this book.

CREDITS

EXECUTIVE EDITOR
Robert Elliott

PROJECT EDITOR
Adaobi Obi Tulton

TECHNICAL EDITOR
John Mueller

PRODUCTION EDITOR
Eric Charbonneau

COPY EDITOR
Kim Cofer

EDITORIAL DIRECTOR
Robyn B. Siesky

EDITORIAL MANAGER
Mary Beth Wakefield

PRODUCTION MANAGER
Tim Tate

VICE PRESIDENT AND EXECUTIVE GROUP PUBLISHER
Richard Swadley

VICE PRESIDENT AND EXECUTIVE PUBLISHER
Barry Pruett

ASSOCIATE PUBLISHER
Jim Minatel

PROJECT COORDINATOR, COVER
Lynsey Stanford

PROOFREADER
Nancy Bell

INDEXER
Jack Lewis

COVER IMAGE
© Erik Isakson / Tetra images/ Jupiter Images

COVER DESIGNER
Michael Trent

ACKNOWLEDGMENTS

THANKS TO BOB ELLIOTT, Adaobi Obi Tulton, Kristin Vorce, Kim Cofer, and all of the others who worked so hard to make this book possible.

Thanks also to John Mueller for giving me another perspective and the benefit of his extensive expertise. Visit `www.mwt.net/~jmueller` to learn about John's books and to sign up for his free newsletter .NET Tips, Trends & Technology eXTRA.

CONTENTS

CONTENTS

INTRODUCTION

It has been said that Sir Isaac Newton was the last person to know everything. He was an accomplished physicist (his three laws of motion were the basis of classical mechanics, which defined astrophysics for three centuries), mathematician (he was one of the inventors of calculus and developed Newton's Method for finding roots of equations), astronomer, natural philosopher, and alchemist (okay, maybe the last one was a mistake). He invented the reflecting telescope, a theory of color, a law of cooling, and studied the speed of sound.

Just as important, he was born before relativity, quantum mechanics, gene sequencing, thermodynamics, parallel computation, and a swarm of other extremely difficult branches of science.

If you ever used Visual Basic 3, you too could have known everything. Visual Basic 3 was a reasonably small but powerful language. Visual Basic 4 added classes to the language and made Visual Basic much more complicated. Versions 4, 5, and 6 added more support for database programming and other topics such as custom controls, but Visual Basic was still a fairly understandable language, and if you took the time you could become an expert in just about all of it.

Visual Basic .NET changed the language in much more fundamental ways and made it much harder to understand every last detail of Visual Basic. The .NET Framework added powerful new tools to Visual Basic, but those tools came at the cost of increased complexity. Associated technologies have been added to the language at an ever-increasing rate, so today it is impossible for anyone to be an expert on every topic that deals with Visual Basic.

To cover every nook and cranny in Visual Basic you would need an in-depth understanding of database technologies, custom controls, custom property editors, XML, cryptography, serialization, two- and three-dimensional graphics, multi-threading, reflection, the code document object model (DOM), diagnostics, globalization, Web Services, inter-process communication, work flow, Office, ASP, Windows Forms, WPF, and much more.

This book doesn't even attempt to cover all of these topics. Instead, it provides a broad, solid understanding of essential Visual Basic topics. It explains the powerful development environment that makes Visual Basic such a productive language. It describes the Visual Basic language itself and explains how to use it to perform a host of important development tasks.

It also explains the forms, controls, and other objects that Visual Basic provides for building applications in a modern windowing environment.

This book may not cover every possible topic related to Visual Basic, but it does cover the majority of the technologies that developers need to build sophisticated applications.

SHOULD YOU USE VISUAL BASIC 2010?

Software engineers talk about five generations of languages (so far). A *first-generation language* (*1GL*) is *machine language*: 0s and 1s. For example, the binary command 00110010 00001110 00010010 00000000 might mean to combine the register CL with the value at address 12H by using the exclusive-or (XOR) operation. Pretty incomprehensible, right? You actually had to program some early computers by painstakingly toggling switches to enter 0s and 1s!

A *second-generation language* (*2GL*) is an *assembly language* that provides terse mnemonics for machine instructions. It provides few additional tools beyond an easier way to write machine code. In assembly language, the previous XOR command might look like XOR CL, [12H]. It's a lot better than assembly language but it's still pretty hard to read.

Third-generation languages (*3GLs*) are higher-level languages such as Pascal and FORTRAN. They provide much more sophisticated language elements such as subroutines, loops, and data structures. In Visual Basic, the previous example might look something like total = total Xor value.

WHERE DID THE REGISTER GO?

Higher-level languages generally don't directly use registers or memory addresses. Instead they work with variables such as total and value. The language's compiler figures out when a value should be placed in a register or other location.

Fourth-generation languages (*4GLs*) are "*natural languages*," such as SQL. They let developers use a language that is sort of similar to a human language to execute programming tasks. For example, the SQL statement "SELECT * FROM Customers WHERE Balance > 50" tells the database to return information about customers that owe more than $50.

Fifth-generation languages (*5GLs*) provide powerful, highly graphical development environments to allow developers to use the underlying language in more sophisticated ways. The emphasis is more on the development environment than the language itself.

The Visual Studio development environment is an extremely powerful fifth-generation tool. It provides graphical editors to make building forms and editing properties easy and intuitive; IntelliSense to help developers remember what to type next; auto-completion so developers can use meaningful variable names without needing to waste time typing them completely by hand; tools that show call hierarchies indicating which routines call which others; and breakpoints, watches, and other advanced debugging tools that make building applications easier.

Visual Studio is so powerful that the answer to the question of whether you should use it is practically obvious: if you want to write powerful applications that run in a Windows operating system, you should use Visual Studio.

Visual Basic is not the only language that uses Visual Studio. The C# language does, too, so now the question is, should you use Visual Basic or C#?

LOTS OF LANGUAGES

Visual Studio also supports a few other languages including Visual C++, Visual J#, and Visual F#, and in theory it could support others in the future. Visual Studio originally built for Visual Basic and C# was designed to work with Visual Studio so Visual Studio provides the most support for these.

A Visual Basic programmer's joke asks, "What's the difference between Visual Basic .NET and C#? About three months!" The implication is that Visual Basic .NET syntax is easier to understand and building applications with it is faster. Similarly, C# programmers have their jokes about Visual Basic .NET, implying that C# is more powerful.

In fact, Visual Basic .NET is *not* a whole lot easier to use than C#, and C# is *not* significantly more powerful. The basic form of the two languages is very similar. Aside from a few stylistic differences (Visual Basic is line-oriented; C# uses lots of braces and semicolons), the languages are comparable. Both use the Visual Studio development environment, both provide access to the .NET Framework of support classes and tools, and both provide similar syntax for performing basic programming tasks.

The main difference between these languages is one of style. If you have experience with previous versions of Visual Basic, you will probably find Visual Basic 2010 easier to get used to. If you have experience with C++ or Java, you will probably find C# (or Visual C++ or Visual J#) easy to learn.

Visual Basic does have some ties with other Microsoft products that increase its value. For example, *Active Server Pages* (*ASP*) and ASP.NET use Visual Basic to create interactive web pages. Microsoft Office applications (Word, Excel, PowerPoint, and so forth) and many third-party tools use *Visual Basic for Applications* (*VBA*) as a macro programming language. If you know Visual Basic, you have a big head start in using these other languages. ASP and VBA are based on pre-.NET versions of Visual Basic, so you won't instantly know how to use them, but you'll have an advantage if you need to learn ASP or VBA.

If you are new to programming, either Visual Basic 2010 or C# is a good choice. I think Visual Basic 2010 is a little easier to learn, but I may be slightly biased because I've been using Visual Basic since long before C# was invented. You won't be making a big mistake either way, and you can easily switch later, if necessary.

WHO SHOULD READ THIS BOOK

This book is intended for programmers of all levels. It describes the Visual Basic 2010 language from scratch, so you don't need experience with previous versions of the language. The book also covers many intermediate and advanced topics. It covers topics in enough depth that even experienced developers will discover new tips, tricks, and language details. After you have mastered the language, you may still find useful tidbits throughout the book, and the reference appendixes will help you look up easily forgotten details.

The chapters move quickly through the more introductory material. If you have never programmed before and are intimidated by computers, you might want to read a more introductory book first. If you are a beginner who's not afraid of the computer, you should have few problems learning Visual Basic 2010 from this book.

If you have programmed in any other language, fundamentals such as variable declarations, data types, and arrays should be familiar to you, so you should have no problem with this book. The index and reference appendixes should be particularly useful in helping you translate from the languages you already know into the corresponding Visual Basic syntax.

HOW THIS BOOK IS ORGANIZED

The chapters in this book are divided into five parts plus appendixes. The chapters in each part are described here. If you are an experienced programmer, you can use these descriptions to decide which chapters to skim and which to read in detail.

Part I: IDE

The chapters in this part of the book describe the Visual Studio *integrated development environment* (*IDE*) from a Visual Basic developer's point of view. The IDE is mostly the same for C# and other developers, but a few differences exist, such as which keyboard shortcuts perform which tasks.

Chapter 1, "Introduction to the IDE," explains how to get started using the Visual Studio integrated development environment. It tells how to configure the IDE for different kinds of development. It defines and describes Visual Basic projects and solutions, and shows how to create, run, and save a new project.

Chapter 2, "Menus, Toolbars, and Windows," describes the most useful and important commands available in the IDE's menus and toolbars. The IDE's menus and toolbars include hundreds of commands, so this chapter covers only those that are the most useful.

Chapter 3, "Customization," explains how to customize the IDE. It tells how you can create, hide, and rearrange menus and toolbars to make it easy to use the tools that you find most useful.

Chapter 4, "Windows Forms Designer," describes the designer you can use to build Windows Forms. It explains how to create, size, move, and copy controls. It tells how to set control properties and add code to respond to control events. It also explains how to use handy designer tools such as smart tags and command verbs.

Chapter 5, "WPF Designer," explains how to use the Windows Presentation Foundation (WPF) form designer. This chapter is similar to Chapter 4 except that it covers WPF forms instead of Windows Forms.

Chapter 6, "Visual Basic Code Editor," describes one of the most important windows used by developers: the code editor. It explains how to write code, set breakpoints, use code snippets, and get the most out of IntelliSense.

Chapter 7, "Debugging," explains debugging tools provided by Visual Studio. It describes the debugging windows and explains techniques such as setting complex breakpoints to locate bugs.

Part II: Getting Started

The chapters in this part of the book explain the bulk of the Visual Basic language and the objects that support it. They explain the forms, controls, and other objects that a program uses to build a user interface, and they tell how you can put code behind those objects to implement the program's functionality.

Chapter 8, "Selecting Windows Forms Controls," provides an overview of the Windows Forms controls that you can put on a form. It groups the controls by category to help you find the controls you can use for a particular purpose.

Chapter 9, "Using Windows Forms Controls," gives more detail about how you can use Windows Forms controls. It explains how you can create controls at design time or runtime, how to set complex property values, and how to use useful properties that are common to many different kinds of controls. It explains how to add event handlers to process control events and how to validate user-entered data.

Chapter 10, "Windows Forms," describes the forms you use in a Windows Forms application. Technically, forms are just another kind of control, but their unique position in the application's architecture means they have some special properties, and this chapter describes them.

Chapter 11, "Selecting WPF Controls," provides an overview of WPF controls. It groups the controls by category to help you find the controls you can use for a particular purpose. This chapter is similar to Chapter 8 except it covers WPF controls instead of Windows Forms controls.

Chapter 12, "Using WPF Controls," gives more detail about how you can use WPF controls. This chapter is similar to Chapter 9 except it deals with WPF controls instead of Windows Forms controls.

Chapter 13, "WPF Windows," describes the windows that WPF applications use in place of Windows forms. This chapter is similar to Chapter 10 except it deals with WPF windows instead of Windows forms.

Chapter 14, "Program and Module Structure," describes the most important files that make up a Visual Basic project. It describes some of the hidden files that projects contain and explains some of the structure that you can give to code within a module, such as code regions and conditionally compiled code.

Chapter 15, "Data Types, Variables, and Constants," explains the standard data types provided by Visual Basic. It shows how to declare and initialize variables and constants, and explains variable scope. It discusses technical topics, such as value and reference types, passing parameters by value or reference, and creating parameter variables on the fly. It also explains how to create and initialize arrays, enumerated types, and structures.

Chapter 16, "Operators," describes the operators a program uses to perform calculations. These include mathematical operators (+, *, \), string operators (&), and Boolean operators (And, Or). The chapter explains operator precedence and potentially confusing type conversion issues that arise when an expression combines more than one type of operator (for example, arithmetic and Boolean).

Chapter 17, "Subroutines and Functions," explains how you can use subroutines and functions to break a program into manageable pieces. It describes routine overloading and scope. It also describes lambda functions and relaxed delegates.

Chapter 18, "Program Control Statements," describes the statements that a Visual Basic program uses to control code execution. These include decision statements, such as If, Then, or Else and looping statements, such as For and Next.

Chapter 19, "Error Handling," explains error handling and debugging techniques. It describes the Try Catch structured error handler, in addition to the older On Error statement inherited from early versions of Visual Basic. It discusses typical actions a program might take when it catches an error. It also describes important techniques for preventing errors and making errors more obvious when they do occur.

Chapter 20, "Database Controls and Objects," explains how to use the standard Visual Basic database controls. These include database connection components that manage connections to a database, DataSet components that hold data within an application, and data adapter controls that move data between databases and DataSets.

Chapter 21, "LINQ," describes language integrated query (LINQ) features. It explains how you can write SQL-like queries to select data from or into objects, XML, or database objects. It also explains PLINQ, a parallel version of LINQ that can provide improved performance on multi-core systems.

Chapter 22, "Custom Controls," explains how to build your own customized controls that you can then use in other applications. It covers the three main methods for creating a custom control: derivation, composition, and building from scratch. This chapter also provides several examples that you can use as starting points for controls of your own.

Chapter 23, "Drag and Drop, and the Clipboard," explains how a Visual Basic program can support drag-and-drop operations. It tells how your program can start a drag to another application, respond to drag operations started by another application, and receive a drop from another application. This chapter also explains how you can copy data to and from the clipboard. Using the clipboard is similar to certain types of drag-and-drop operations, so these topics fit naturally in one chapter.

Chapter 24, "UAC Security," describes the User Account Control (UAC) security model used by the Vista and Windows 7 operating systems. With UAC security, all users run with reduced "normal" user privileges. If a program must perform tasks requiring administrator permissions, a UAC dialog box allows you to elevate the application's privilege level. This chapter describes UAC security and explains how you can mark a program for privilege elevation.

Part III: Object-Oriented Programming

This part explains fundamental concepts in object-oriented programming (OOP) with Visual Basic. It also describes some of the more important classes and objects that you can use when building an application.

Chapter 25, "OOP Concepts," explains the fundamental ideas behind object-oriented programming (OOP). It describes the three main features of OOP: encapsulation, polymorphism, and inheritance. It explains the benefits of these features, and tells how you can take advantage of them in Visual Basic.

Chapter 26, "Classes and Structures," explains how to declare and use classes and structures. It explains what classes and structures are, and it describes their differences. It shows the basic declaration syntax and tells how to create instances of classes and structures. It also explains some of the trickier class issues such as private class scope, declaring events, and shared variables and methods.

Chapter 27, "Namespaces," explains namespaces. It discusses how Visual Studio uses namespaces to categorize code and to prevent name collisions. It describes a project's root namespace, tells how Visual Basic uses namespaces to resolve names (such as function and class names), and demonstrates how you can add namespaces to an application yourself.

Chapter 28, "Collection Classes," explains classes included in Visual Studio that you can use to hold groups of objects. It describes the various collection, dictionary, queue, and stack classes; tells how to make strongly typed versions of those classes; and gives some guidance on deciding which class to use under different circumstances.

Chapter 29, "Generics," explains templates you can use to build new classes designed to work with specific data types. For example, you can build a generic binary tree, and then later use it to build classes to represent binary trees of customer orders, employees, or work items.

Part IV: Graphics

The chapters in this part of the book describe graphics in Visual Basic 2010. They explain the Graphics Device Interface+ (GDI+) routines that programs use to draw images in Visual Basic. They explain how to draw lines and text; how to draw and fill circles and other shapes; and how to load, manipulate, and save bitmap images. This part also explains how to generate printed output and how to send reports to the screen or to the printer.

Chapter 30, "Drawing Basics," explains the fundamentals of drawing graphics in Visual Basic 2010. It describes the graphics namespaces and the classes they contain. It describes the most important of these classes, Graphics, in detail. It also describes the Paint event handler and other events that a program should use to keep its graphics up to date.

Chapter 31, "Brushes, Pens, and Paths," explains the most important graphics classes after Graphics: Pen and Brush. It tells how you can use Pens to draw solid lines, dashed lines, lines with custom dash patterns, and lines with custom lengthwise stripe patterns. It tells how to use Brushes to fill areas with colors, hatch patterns, linear color gradients, color gradients that follow a path, and tiled images. This chapter also describes the GraphicsPath class, which represents a series of lines, shapes, curves, and text.

Chapter 32, "Text," explains how to draw strings of text. It shows how to create different kinds of fonts, determine exactly how big text will be when drawn in a particular font, and use GDI+ functions to make positioning text simple. It shows how to use a StringFormat object to determine how text is aligned, wrapped, and trimmed, and how to read and define tab stops.

Chapter 33, "Image Processing," explains how to load, modify, and save image files. It shows how to read and write the pixels in an image, and how to save the result in different file formats such as BMP, GIF, and JPEG. It tells how to use images to provide auto-redraw features, and how to manipulate an image pixel-by-pixel, both using a Bitmap's GetPixel and SetPixel methods and using "unsafe" access techniques that make pixel manipulation much faster than is possible with normal GDI+ methods.

Chapter 34, "Printing," explains different ways that a program can send output to the printer. It shows how you can use the PrintDocument object to generate printout data. You can then use the PrintDocument to print the data immediately, use a PrintDialog control to let the user select the printer and set its characteristics, or use a PrintPreviewDialog control to let the user preview the results before printing.

Part V: Interacting with the Environment

The chapters in this part of the book explain how an application can interact with its environment. They show how the program can save and load data in external sources (such as the System Registry, resource files, and text files); work with the computer's screen, keyboard, and mouse; and interact with the user through standard dialog controls.

Chapter 35, "Configuration and Resources," describes some of the ways that a Visual Basic program can store configuration and resource values for use at runtime. Some of the most useful of these include environment variables, the Registry, configuration files, and resource files.

Chapter 36, "Streams," explains the classes that a Visual Basic application can use to work with stream data. Some of these classes are FileStream, MemoryStream, BufferedStream, TextReader, and TextWriter.

Chapter 37, "File-System Objects," describes classes that let a Visual Basic application interact with the file system. These include classes such as Directory, DirectoryInfo, File, and FileInfo that make it easy to create, examine, move, rename, and delete directories and files.

Chapter 38, "Windows Communication Foundation," describes the Windows Communication Foundation (WCF), a library and set of tools that make building service-oriented applications easier. This chapter explains how to use new WCF attributes to easily define a service, how to use configuration files to configure the service, and how to use WCF tools to consume the service.

Chapter 39, "Useful Namespaces," describes some of the more useful namespaces defined by the .NET Framework. It provides a brief overview of some of the most important System namespaces and gives more detailed examples that demonstrate regular expressions, XML, cryptography, reflection, threading, parallel programming, and Direct3D.

Part VI: Appendixes

The book's appendixes provide a categorized reference of the Visual Basic 2010 language. You can use them to quickly review the syntax of a particular command or refresh your memory of what a particular class can do. The chapters earlier in the book give more context, explaining how to perform specific tasks and why one approach might be better than another.

Appendix A, "Useful Control Properties, Methods, and Events," describes properties, methods, and events that are useful with many different kinds of controls.

Appendix B, "Variable Declarations and Data Types," summarizes the syntax for declaring variables. It also gives the sizes and ranges of allowed values for the fundamental data types.

Appendix C, "Operators," summarizes the standard operators such as +, <<, OrElse, and Like. It also gives the syntax for operator overloading.

Appendix D, "Subroutine and Function Declarations," summarizes the syntax for subroutine, function, and property procedure declarations. It also summarizes the syntax for using lambda functions and statements (subroutines).

Appendix E, "Control Statements," summarizes statements that control program flow, such as If Then, Select Case, and looping statements.

Appendix F, "Error Handling," summarizes both structured and classic error handling. It describes some useful exception classes and gives an example showing how to build a custom exception class.

Appendix G, "Windows Forms Controls and Components," summarizes standard Windows Forms controls and components provided by Visual Basic 2010. It explains the properties, methods, and events that I have found most useful when working with these components.

Appendix H, "WPF Controls," summarizes the most useful WPF controls.

Appendix I, "Visual Basic Power Packs," lists some additional tools that you can download to make Visual Basic development easier. This appendix describes some Visual Basic 6 compatibility tools provided by Microsoft, and some GotDotNet Power Packs that contain useful controls built in Visual Basic 2003.

Appendix J, "Form Objects," describes forms. In a very real sense, forms are just another type of control, but they play such a key role in Visual Basic applications that they deserve special attention in their own appendix.

Appendix K, "Classes and Structures," summarizes the syntax for declaring classes and structures, and defining their constructors and events.

Appendix L, "LINQ," summarizes LINQ and PLINQ syntax.

Appendix M, "Generics," summarizes the syntax for declaring generic classes.

Appendix N, "Graphics," summarizes the objects used to generate graphics in Visual Basic 2010. It covers the most useful graphics namespaces.

Appendix O, "Useful Exception Classes," lists some of the more useful exception classes defined by Visual Basic. You may want to throw these exceptions in your own code.

Appendix P, "Date and Time Format Specifiers," summarizes specifier characters that you can use to format dates and times. For example, they let you display a time using a 12-hour or 24-hour clock.

Appendix Q, "Other Format Specifiers," summarizes formatting for numbers and enumerated types.

Appendix R, "The Application Class," summarizes the Application class that provides properties and methods for controlling the current application.

Appendix S, "The My Namespace," describes the My namespace, which provides shortcuts to useful features scattered around other parts of the .NET Framework. It provides shortcuts for working with the application, computer hardware, application forms, resources, and the current user.

Appendix T, "Streams," summarizes the Visual Basic stream classes such as Stream, FileStream, MemoryStream, TextReader, CryptoStream, and so forth.

Appendix U, "File-System Classes," summarizes methods that an application can use to learn about and manipulate the file system. It explains classic Visual Basic methods such as FreeFile, WriteLine, and ChDir, as well as newer .NET Framework classes such as FileSystem, Directory, and File.

Appendix V, "Index of Examples," briefly describes the more than 400 example programs that are available for download on the book's web site. You can use this list to see which programs demonstrate particular techniques.

BONUS CHAPTERS

Occasionally I will post bonus chapters on the book's web site to cover topics that didn't fit into this book (despite its size) or to cover new technologies and techniques.

In particular, Crystal Reports is a useful reporting tool that Visual Basic developers have used for years. Unfortunately, Crystal Reports 2010 won't be ready until after Visual Studio 2010 is released and that will be too late for this book. Rather than using the older version of Crystal Reports and including a chapter that will become obsolete almost immediately, I'm going to provide that chapter online when Crystal Reports 2010 is available. (Hopefully a free edition of Crystal Reports for Visual Studio users should be available sometime in the second quarter of 2010.)

To learn when bonus chapters are available, check the book's web site or email me at RodStephens@ vb-helper.com. If you'd like more information about some other topic, feel free to drop me a note. If I think others will find the information useful, I may be able to write another bonus chapter or some examples. I can at least give you some hints and pointers that you may find helpful.

HOW TO USE THIS BOOK

If you are an experienced Visual Basic .NET programmer, you may want to skim the language basics covered in the first parts of the book. You may find a few new features that have appeared in Visual Basic 2010, so you probably shouldn't skip these chapters entirely, but most of the basic language features are the same as in previous versions.

Intermediate programmers and those with less experience with Visual Basic .NET should take these chapters a bit more slowly. The chapters in Part III, "Object-Oriented Programming," cover particularly tricky topics. Learning all the variations on inheritance and interfaces can be rather confusing.

Beginners should spend more time on these first chapters because they set the stage for the material that follows. It will be a lot easier for you to follow a discussion of file management or regular expressions if you are not confused by the error-handling code that the examples take for granted.

Programming is a skill best learned by doing. You can pick up the book and read through it quickly if you like (well, as quickly as you can given how long it is), but the information is more likely to stick if you open the development environment and experiment with some programs of your own.

Learning by doing may encourage you to skip sections of the book. For example, Chapter 1 covers the IDE in detail. After you've read for a while, you may want to skip some sections and start experimenting with the environment on your own. I encourage you to do so. Lessons learned by doing last longer than those learned by reading. Later, when you have some experience with the development environment, you can go back and examine Chapter 1 in more detail to see if you missed anything during your experimentation.

The final part of the book is a Visual Basic 2010 reference. These appendixes present more concise, categorized information about the language. You can use these appendixes to recall the details of specific operations. For example, you can read Chapter 8 to learn which controls are useful for different purposes. Then use Appendix G to learn about specific controls' properties, methods, and events.

Throughout your work, you can also refer to the appendixes to get information on specific classes, controls, and syntax. For example, you can quickly find the syntax for declaring a generic class in Appendix M. If you need more information on generics, you can find it in Chapter 29 or the online help. If you just need to refresh your memory of the basic syntax, however, scanning Appendix M will be faster.

NECESSARY EQUIPMENT

To read this book and understand the examples, you will need no special equipment. To use Visual Basic 2010 and to run the examples found on the book's web page, you need any computer that can reasonably run Visual Basic 2010. That means a reasonably modern, fast computer with a lot of memory. See the Visual Basic 2010 documentation for Microsoft's exact requirements and recommendations. (I use a dual-core 1.83 GHz Intel Core 2CPU system with 2 GB of memory and 100 GB of hard disk space running Windows 7 Ultimate. It's a nice system but I wouldn't say it's overkill.)

To build Visual Basic 2010 programs, you will also need a copy of Visual Basic 2010. Don't bother trying to run the examples shown here if you have a pre-.NET version of Visual Basic such as Visual Basic 6. The changes between Visual Basic 6 and Visual Basic .NET are huge, and many Visual Basic .NET concepts don't translate well into Visual Basic 6. With some experience in C#, it would be much easier to translate programs into that language.

Much of the Visual Basic 2010 release is compatible with Visual Basic 2008 and earlier versions of Visual Basic .NET, however, so you can make many of the examples work with earlier versions of Visual Basic .NET. You will not be able to load the example programs downloaded from the book's web site, however. You will need to open the source code files in an editor such as WordPad and copy and paste the significant portions of the code into your version of Visual Basic.

To use UAC security, you must have UAC security installed on your computer. UAC is installed and activated by default in the Windows Vista and Windows 7 operating systems.

CONVENTIONS

To help you get the most from the text and keep track of what's happening, a number of conventions have been used throughout the book.

As for styles in the text:

➤ Important words are *highlighted* when they are introduced.

➤ Keyboard strokes are shown like this: Ctrl+A.

➤ File names, URLs, and code within the text are shown like this: `persistence.properties`.

➤ Code is presented in the following two different ways:

```
We use a monofont type for most code examples.
We use bolded type to emphasize code that's particularly important in the
present context.
```

SOURCE CODE

As you work through the examples in this book, you may choose either to type in all the code manually or to use the source code files that accompany the book. Many of the examples show only the code that is relevant to the current topic and may be missing some of the extra details that you need to make the example work properly.

All of the source code used in this book is available for download at www.wrox.com. Once at the site, simply locate the book's title (either by using the Search box or by using one of the title lists) and click the Download Code link on the book's detail page to obtain all the source code for the book.

FIND IT FAST

Because many books have similar titles, you may find it easiest to locate the book by its ISBN: 978-0-470-49983-2.

Once you download the code, just decompress it with your favorite compression tool. Alternatively, you can go to the main Wrox code download page at `www.wrox.com/dynamic/books/download.aspx` to see the code available for this book and all other Wrox books.

You can also download the book's source code from its web page on my VB Helper web site `www.vb-helper.com/vb_prog_ref.htm`. That page allows you to download all of the book's code in one big chunk or by individual chapter.

ERRATA

We make every effort to ensure that there are no errors in the text or in the code. However, no one is perfect, and mistakes do occur. If you find an error in one of my books, like a spelling mistake or faulty piece of code, I would be very grateful for your feedback. By sending in errata you may save another reader hours of frustration and at the same time you will be helping me provide even higher quality information.

To find the errata page for this book, go to `www.wrox.com` and locate the title using the Search box or one of the title lists. Then, on the book details page, click the Book Errata link. On this page you can view all errata that have been submitted for this book and posted by Wrox editors. A complete book list including links to each book's errata is also available at `www.wrox.com/misc-pages/booklist.shtml`.

If you don't spot "your" error on the Book Errata page, go to `www.wrox.com/contact/techsupport.shtml` and complete the form there to send us the error you have found. We'll check the information and, if appropriate, post a message to the book's errata page and fix the problem in subsequent editions of the book.

P2P.WROX.COM

For author and peer discussion, join the P2P forums at `p2p.wrox.com`. The forums are a Web-based system for you to post messages relating to Wrox books and related technologies and interact with other readers and technology users. The forums offer a subscription feature to e-mail you topics of interest of your choosing when new posts are made to the forums. Wrox authors, editors, other industry experts, and your fellow readers are present on these forums.

At p2p.wrox.com you will find a number of different forums that will help you not only as you read this book, but also as you develop your own applications. To join the forums, just follow these steps:

1. Go to p2p.wrox.com and click the Register link.

2. Read the terms of use and click Agree.

3. Complete the required information to join as well as any optional information you wish to provide and click Submit.

4. You will receive an e-mail with information describing how to verify your account and complete the joining process.

> **JOIN THE FUN**
>
> You can read messages in the forums without joining P2P, but in order to post your own messages, you must join.

Once you join, you can post new messages and respond to messages other users post. You can read messages at any time on the Web. If you would like to have new messages from a particular forum e-mailed to you, click the Subscribe to this Forum icon by the forum name in the forum listing.

For more information about how to use the Wrox P2P, be sure to read the P2P FAQs for answers to questions about how the forum software works as well as many common questions specific to P2P and Wrox books. To read the FAQs, click the FAQ link on any P2P page.

Using the P2P forums allows other readers to benefit from your questions and any answers they generate. I monitor my book's forums and respond whenever I can help.

If you have other comments, suggestions, or questions that you don't want to post to the forums, feel free to e-mail me at RodStephens@vb-helper.com with your comments, suggestion, or questions. I can't promise to solve every problem but I'll try to help you out if I can.

IMPORTANT URLs

Here's a summary of important URLs:

➤ www.vb-helper.com — My VB Helper web site. Contains thousands of tips, tricks, and examples for Visual Basic developers.

➤ www.vb-helper.com/vb_prog_reg.htm — This book's web page on my VB Helper web site. Includes basic information, code downloads, errata, and more.

➤ p2p.wrox.com — Wrox P2P forums.

➤ www.wrox.com — The Wrox web site. Contains code downloads, errata, and other information. Search for the book by title or ISBN.

➤ RodStephens@vb-helper.com — My e-mail address. I hope to hear from you!

PART I
IDE

1

Introduction to the IDE

The chapters in the first part of this book describe the Visual Studio integrated development environment (IDE). They explain the most important windows, menus, and toolbars that make up the environment, and show how to customize them to suit your needs. They explain some of the tools that provide help while you are writing Visual Basic applications and how to use the IDE to debug programs.

Even if you are an experienced Visual Basic programmer, you should at least skim this material. The IDE is *extremely* complex and provides hundreds (if not thousands) of commands, menus, toolbars, windows, context menus, and other tools for editing, running, and debugging Visual Basic projects. Even if you have used the IDE for a long time, there are sure to be some features that you have overlooked.

SNEAKY SHORTCUTS

When I teach Visual Basic, for example, I cover the IDE's keyboard shortcuts (such as Alt+Space to open IntelliSense, and Ctrl+C, Ctrl+X, and Ctrl+V to copy, cut, and paste) early in the class. The students don't really write enough code to take full advantage of these tools for several weeks, however, so we revisit the topic later.

These chapters describe some of the most important of those features, and you may discover something useful that you've never noticed before.

Even after you've read these chapters, you should periodically spend some time wandering through the IDE to see what you've missed. Every month or so, spend a few minutes exploring little-used menus and right-clicking things to see what their context menus contain. As you become a more proficient Visual Basic programmer, you will find uses for tools that you may have dismissed or not understood before.

It's also useful to save links to tips you discover online. You can make a Visual Basic Tips folder in your browser's favorites list to make finding the tips again later easier.

This chapter explains how to get started using the IDE. It tells how to configure the IDE for different kinds of development. It explains Visual Basic projects and solutions, and shows how to create, run, and save new projects. This chapter is mostly an introduction to the chapters that follow. The other chapters in this part of the book provide much more detail about particular tasks, such as using the IDE's menus, customizing menus and toolbars, and using the Windows Forms Designer to build forms.

DIFFERENT IDE APPEARANCES

Before you start reading about the IDE and viewing screen shots, it's important to understand that the Visual Studio IDE is *extremely* customizable. You can move, hide, or modify the menus, toolbars, and windows; create your own toolbars; dock, undock, or rearrange the toolbars and windows; and change the behavior of the built-in text editors (change their indentation, colors for different kinds of text, and so forth).

These chapters describe the basic Visual Studio development environment as it is initially installed. After you've moved things around to suit your needs, your IDE may look nothing like the pictures in this book. If a figure doesn't look exactly like what you see on your computer, don't worry too much about it.

To avoid confusion, you should probably not customize the IDE's basic menus and toolbars too much. Removing the help commands from the Help menu and adding them to the Edit menu will only cause confusion later. Moving or removing commands will also make it more difficult to follow the examples in this and other books, and will make it more difficult to follow instructions given by others who might be able to help you when you have problems.

Instead of making drastic changes to the default menus and toolbars, hide the menus and toolbars that you don't want and create new customized toolbars to suit your needs. Then you can find the original standard toolbars if you decide you need them later. Chapter 3, "Customization," has more to say about rearranging the IDE's components.

The screens shown in this book may not look exactly like the ones on your system for several other reasons as well. Visual Studio looks different on different operating systems. The figures in this book were taken on a computer running Windows 7 so they display the Windows 7 look and feel. You may see a different appearance, even if you are using Windows 7 and you have selected another style. Additionally, some commands may not behave exactly the same way on different operating systems.

SECURITY OBSCURITY

Windows Vista and Windows 7 use the User Account Control (UAC) security model. When you first log on, all accounts get a *normal* level of user privileges. Later, when you try to run certain applications that require increased permissions, a UAC privilege elevation dialog box appears where you can enter an administrator password. The examples in this book were tested using a normal user account, so you should not see that dialog while running them, but you may see it if you use other development tools. Chapter 24, "UAC Security," provides more details about UAC.

Visual Studio will also look different depending on which version you have installed. The free Visual Basic 2010 Express Edition product has fewer tools than other editions such as the high-end Team Suite. The figures in this book were captured while using Team Suite, so if you have another version, you may not see all of the tools shown here. Menu items, toolbars, and other details may also be slightly different for different versions. Usually you can find moved items with a little digging through the menus and customizations.

FOR MORE INFORMATION

You can learn about Visual Studio's free Express editions at `www.microsoft.com/express`. Learn about Visual Basic in general at the Visual Basic home page `msdn.microsoft.com/vbasic`.

Finally, you may be using different configuration settings from the ones used while writing this book. You can configure Visual Studio to use settings customized for developing projects using Visual Basic, C#, Web tools, and other technologies. This book assumes your installation is configured for Visual Basic development and the screen shots may look different if you have selected a different configuration. The following section says more about different IDE configurations and tells how you can select a particular configuration.

IDE CONFIGURATIONS

When you install it, Visual Studio asks you what kind of development settings you want to use. The most obvious choice for a Visual Basic developer is Visual Basic Development Settings. This choice customizes Visual Studio to work more easily with Visual Basic, and is a good selection if you will focus on Visual Basic development.

Another reasonable choice is General Development Settings. This option makes Visual Studio behave more like Visual Studio 2003. It's a good choice if you're used to Visual Studio 2003, or if you expect to use other Visual Studio languages, such as C#, somewhat regularly because these settings are fairly effective for C# development as well as Visual Basic development.

This book assumes that you have configured Visual Studio for Visual Basic development. If you have chosen a different configuration, some of the figures in this book may look different from what you see on your screen. Some of the menu items available may be slightly different, or may appear in a different order. Usually, the items are available somewhere, but you may have to search a bit to find them.

If you later decide that you want to switch configurations, open the Tools menu and select Import and Export Settings to display the Import and Export Settings Wizard. Select the "Reset all settings" option button and click Next. On the second page, tell the wizard whether to save your current settings and click Next. On the wizard's final page (shown in Figure 1-1), select the type of configuration you want and click Finish. When the wizard is done, click Close.

FIGURE 1-1: Use the Tools menu's Import and Export Settings command to change the Visual Studio configuration.

PROJECTS AND SOLUTIONS

Before you can understand how to use the IDE effectively to manage Visual Basic projects and solutions, you should know what projects and solutions are.

A *project* is a group of files that produces some specific output. This output may be a compiled executable program, a dynamic-link library (DLL) of classes for use by other projects, or a control library for use on other Windows forms.

A *solution* is a group of one or more projects that should be managed together. For example, suppose that you are building a server application that provides access to your customer order database. You are also building a client program that each of your sales representatives will use to query the server application. Because these two projects are closely related, it might make sense to manage them in a single solution. When you open the solution, you get instant access to all the files in both projects.

Both projects and solutions can include associated files that are useful for building the application but that do not become part of a final compiled product. For example, a project might include the application's proposal and architecture documents. These are not included in the compiled code, but it is useful to associate them with the project so they are easy to find, open, and edit while working on the project.

When you open the project, Visual Studio lists those documents along with the program files. If you double-click one of these documents, Visual Studio opens the file using an appropriate application. For example, if you double-click a file with a .doc, .docm, or .docx extension, Visual Studio normally opens it with Microsoft Word.

To associate one of these files with a project or solution, right-click the project file at the top of the Solution Explorer (more on the Solution Explorer shortly). Select the Add command's New Item entry, and use the resulting dialog box to select the file you want to add.

CUT OUT CLUTTER

Although you can add any file to a project or solution, it's not a good idea to cram dozens of unrelated files into the same project. Although you may sometimes want to refer to an unrelated file while working on a project, the extra clutter brings additional chances for confusion. It will be less confusing to shrink the Visual Basic IDE to an icon and open the file using an external editor such as Word or WordPad. If you won't use a file very often with the project, don't add it.

STARTING THE IDE

When you launch Visual Studio, it initially displays the Start Page shown in Figure 1-2 by default. The Start Page's Recent Projects section lists projects that you have worked on recently and provides links that let you open an existing project or web site, or create a new project or web site. The Get Started tab contains links to help topics that may be useful to beginners.

The Get Started tab is further divided into sub-topics such as Welcome, Windows, Web, Cloud, and so forth. Click on those sub-topics for more specific information.

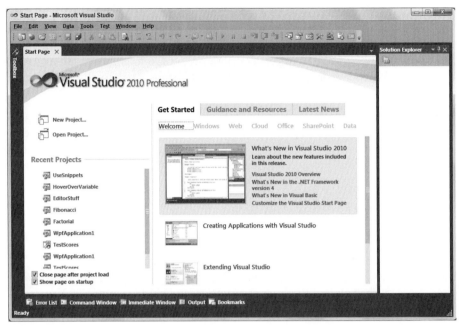

FIGURE 1-2: By default, Visual Studio initially displays the Start Page.

Click on the Guidance and Resources tab to see general development topics such as those shown in Figure 1-3. Use the MSDN Resources sub-topic to learn more about MSDN subscriptions and downloads. Use the Additional Tools sub-topic to learn more about additional extensions to Visual Studio.

Click on the Latest News tab to see the RSS feed shown in Figure 1-3. This feed lists current articles and stories about Visual Studio development. To change the feed, simply enter a new URL in the textbox.

Use the links on the left to open or create new projects. Click New Project to start a new project. Click Open Project to browse for a project to open. Click one of the Recent Project links to quickly open a project that you have recently edited.

Instead of displaying the Start Page, Visual Studio can take one of several other actions when it starts. To change the startup action, open the Tools menu and select Options. Then select the

"Show all settings" check box so you can see all of the options and open the Environment folder's Startup item. In the "At startup" dropdown, you can select one of the following options:

➤ Open Home Page

➤ Load last loaded solution

➤ Show Open Project dialog box

➤ Show New Project dialog box

➤ Show empty environment

➤ Show Start Page

Pick one and click OK.

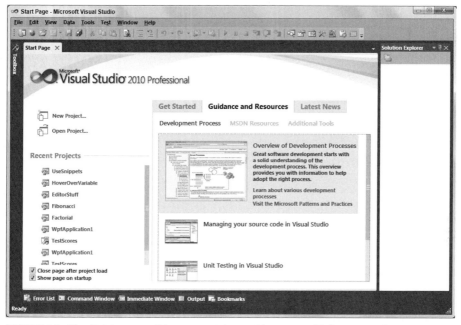

FIGURE 1-3: The Guidance and Resources tab provides general information about development with Visual Studio.

CREATING A PROJECT

After you open Visual Studio, you can use the Start Page's New Project link (see Figure 1-4) or the File menu's New Project command to open the New Project dialog shown in Figure 1-5.

FIGURE 1-4: The Latest News tab shows current articles and information from a Microsoft RSS feed.

FIGURE 1-5: The New Project dialog lets you start a new project.

Use the Project Types tree view on the left to select the project category that you want. Then select a specific project type on the right. In Figure 1-5, the Windows Forms Application project type is selected. Enter a name for the new project in the text box at the bottom.

After you fill in the new project's information, click OK to create the project.

 Visual Studio initially creates the project in a temporary directory. If you close the project without saving it, it is discarded.

Figure 1-6 shows the IDE immediately after starting a new Windows Forms Application project. Remember that the IDE is extremely configurable, so it may not look much like Figure 1-6 after you have rearranged things to your liking (and I've arrange things to my liking here).

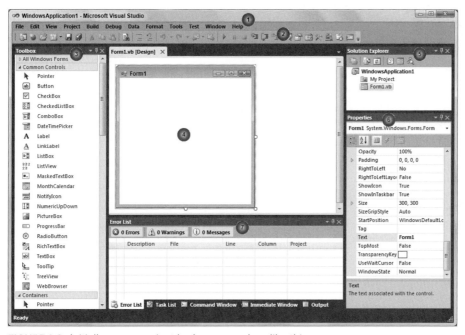

FIGURE 1-6: Initially a new project looks more or less like this.

The key pieces of the IDE are labeled with numbers in Figure 1-6. The following list briefly describes each of these pieces:

1. *Menus* — The menus contain standard Visual Studio commands. These generally manipulate the current solution and the modules it contains, although you can customize the menus as needed. Visual Studio changes the menus and their contents depending on the object you currently have selected. In Figure 1-6, a Form Designer (marked with the number 4) is open so the IDE is displaying the menus for editing forms.

2. *Toolbars* — Toolbars contain tools that you can use to perform frequently needed actions. The same commands may be available in menus, but they are easier and faster to use in toolbars. The IDE defines several standard toolbars such as Formatting, Debug, and Image Editor. You can also build your own custom toolbars to hold your favorite tools. Visual Studio changes the toolbars displayed to match the object you currently have selected.

3. *Toolbox* — The Toolbox contains tools appropriate for the item that you currently have selected and for the project type that you are working on. In Figure 1-6, a Form Designer is selected in a Windows Forms application so the Toolbox contains tools appropriate for a Form Designer. These include Windows Forms controls and components, plus tools in the other Toolbox tabs.

4. *Form Designer* — A Form Designer lets you modify the graphical design of a form. Select a control tool from the Toolbox, and click and drag to place an instance of the control on the form. Use the Properties window (marked with the number 6) to change the new control's properties. In Figure 1-6, no control is selected, so the Properties window shows the form's properties rather than a control's.

5. *Solution Explorer* — The Solution Explorer lets you manage the files associated with the current solution. For example, in Figure 1-6, you could select Form1.vb in the Project Explorer and then click the View Code button (the third icon from the right at the top of the Solution Explorer) to open the form's code editor. You can also right-click an object in the Solution Explorer to get a list of appropriate commands for that object.

6. *Properties* — The Properties window lets you change an object's properties at design time. When you select an object in a Form Designer or in the Solution Explorer, the Properties window displays that object's properties. To change a property's value, simply click the property and enter the new value.

7. *Error List* — The Error List window shows errors and warnings in the current project. For example, if a variable is used but not declared, this list will say so.

If you look at the bottom of Figure 1-6, you'll notice that the Error List window has a series of tabs. The Task List tab displays items flagged for further action such as To Do items. The Command window lets you execute Visual Studio commands, such as those invoked by menu items. The Immediate window lets you type and execute Visual Basic commands, possibly while a program is running, but paused.

The Output tab shows output printed by the application. Usually an application interacts with the user through its forms and dialog boxes, but it can display information here, usually to help you debug the code. The Output window also shows informational messages generated by the IDE. For example, when you compile an application, the IDE sends messages here to tell you what it is doing and whether it succeeded.

> **WHAT WINDOWS?**
>
> If you don't see the Error List, Task List, and other windows, they are probably hidden. You can display many of them by selecting the appropriate item in the View menu. Commands to display some of the more exotic windows are located in other menus, such as the View menu's Other Windows submenu and the Debug menu's Windows submenu.

As soon as you create a new project, it is ready to run. If you open the Debug menu and select Start Debugging, the program will run. It displays only an empty form containing no controls, but the form automatically handles a multitude of mundane windowing tasks for you.

> **READY TO RUN**
>
> If you're using the Visual Basic environment settings, you can simply press F5 to start the program.

Before you write a single line of code, the form lets the user resize, minimize, restore, maximize, and close the form. The form draws its title bar, borders, and system menu, and repaints itself as needed when it is covered and restored. The operating system also automatically handles many tasks such as displaying the form in the Windows taskbar and Task Manager. Vista automatically generates thumbnail previews for its Flip and Flip 3D tools that you display by pressing Alt+Tab or Windows+Tab, respectively. Visual Basic and the operating system do a ton of work for you before you even touch the project!

The form contains no controls, can't open files, doesn't process data, in fact doesn't really do anything unique but a lot of the setup is done for you. It handles the windowing chores for you so you can focus on your particular problem.

SAVING A PROJECT

Later chapters explain in depth how to add controls to a form and how to write code to interact with the form. For now, suppose you have built a project complete with controls and code.

If you try to close Visual Studio or start a new project, the dialog shown in Figure 1-7 appears. Click Save to make the Save Project dialog shown in Figure 1-8 appear. Click Discard to throw away the existing project and start a new one. Click Cancel to continue editing the current project.

As you work with the new project, Visual Studio saves its form definitions and code in a temporary location. Each time you run the program, Visual Studio updates the files so it doesn't lose everything if it crashes. The files are still temporary, however.

FIGURE 1-7: Before closing Visual Studio or starting a new project, you must decide what to do with the previous project.

When you are ready to make the new project permanent, open the File menu and select Save All to display the Save Project dialog shown in Figure 1-8.

The Name field shows the name that you originally gave the project when you created it. Verify that the name is okay or change it.

Next, enter the location where you want the project saved. The default location is similar to the rather non-intuitive value shown in Figure 1-8. (This image was taken while I was logged in as the user named Developer. When you save a project, the "Developer" part of the location would be replaced with your user name.)

Be sure to pick a good location before you click Save. The next time you build a project, the default will be the location you specify now so you won't need to be quite as careful in the future, assuming you want to build a lot of projects in the same directory.

If you check the "Create directory for solution" box, Visual Studio enables the Solution Name text box and adds an extra directory above the project directory to hold the solution. This is most useful when you want to include more than one project in a single solution. For example, you might want several projects in the same solution to sit in a common solution directory.

After you have entered the project name and location, and optionally specified a separate solution directory, click Save.

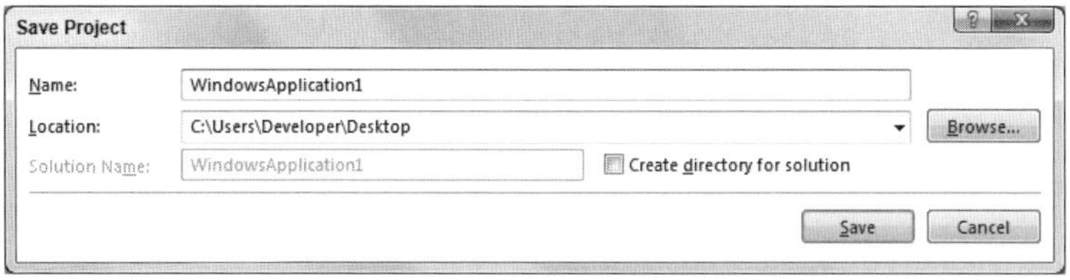

Save Project	
Name:	WindowsApplication1
Location:	C:\Users\Developer\Desktop Browse...
Solution Name:	WindowsApplication1 ☐ Create directory for solution
	Save Cancel

FIGURE 1-8: Use this dialog to save a new project.

> **"SAVE AS" SURVIVAL SKILLS**
>
> The File menu's Save As commands let you save particular pieces of the solution in new files. For example, if you have a project named OfficeArrangerMain selected in Project Explorer, the File menu contains a command named "Save OfficeArrangerMain As." This command lets you save the project file with a new name. Unfortunately it doesn't make a new copy of the whole project; it just makes a copy of the project file. That file contains information about the project on a high level such as references used by the project, files imported by the project, and the names of the forms included in the project. It does not contain the forms themselves.
>
> Many beginners try to use the File menu's Save As commands to make copies of a project or a solution but it doesn't work. Instead, use Windows Explorer to find the directory containing the whole project or solution and make a copy of the entire directory.
>
> Similarly, if you want to back up a project or send someone a copy of a project, you need to use the entire solution directory, not just one or two of the many files that Visual Studio creates.

SUMMARY

This chapter explains how to get started using the Visual Studio integrated development environment. It shows how to configure the IDE for different kinds of development and explains that different configurations might make your version of Visual Studio look different from the screen shots shown in this book. It explains what Visual Basic projects and solutions are, and shows how to create, run, and save a new project.

The next few chapters describe parts of the IDE in greater detail. Chapter 2, "Menus, Toolbars, and Windows," describes the commands available in the IDE and the menus, toolbars, and secondary windows that hold them.

Menus, Toolbars, and Windows

The Visual Studio IDE is incredibly powerful and provides hundreds of tools for building and modifying projects. The price you pay for all of these powerful tools is extra complexity. Because so many tools are available, it can take some digging to find the tool you want, even if you know exactly what you need.

This chapter describes the menus, toolbars, and windows that contain the tools provided by the IDE. It explains some of the most useful tools provided by the IDE and tells where to find them, provided you haven't moved them while customizing the IDE.

This chapter also tells how you can customize the menus and toolbars to give you easy access to the commands that you use most frequently and how to hide those that you don't need.

MENUS

The IDE's menus contain standard Visual Studio commands. These are generally commands that manipulate the project and the modules it contains. Some of the concepts are similar to those used by any Windows application (File ⇨ New, File ⇨ Save, Help ⇨ Contents), but many of the details are specific to Visual Studio programming, so the following sections describe them in a bit more detail.

The menus are customizable, so you can add, remove, and rearrange the menus and the items they contain. This can be quite confusing, however, if you later need to find a command that you have removed from its normal place in the menus. Some developers place extra commands in standard menus, particularly the Tools menu, but it is generally risky to remove standard menu items. Usually it is safest to leave the standard menus alone and make custom menus and toolbars to hold customizations. For more information on this, see Chapter 3, "Customization."

Many of the menus' most useful commands are also available in other ways. Many provide keyboard shortcuts that make using them quick and easy. For example, Ctrl+N opens the New Project dialog box just as if you had selected the File ⇨ New Project menu command. (If you are using the C# or General Development settings, the shortcut is Ctrl+Shift+N.) If you find yourself using the same command very frequently, look in the menu and learn its keyboard shortcut to save time later.

Many menu commands are also available in standard toolbars. For example, the Debug toolbar contains many of the same commands that are in the Debug menu. If you use a set of menu commands frequently, you may want to display the corresponding toolbar to make using the commands easier.

Visual Studio also provides many commands through context menus. For example, if you right-click a project in the Solution Explorer, the context menu includes an Add Reference command that displays the Add Reference dialog box just as if you had invoked Project ⇨ Add Reference. Often it is easier to find a command by right-clicking an object related to whatever you want to do than it is to wander through the menus.

The following sections describe the general layout of the standard menus and briefly explain their most important commands. You might want to open the menus in Visual Studio as you read these sections, so you can follow along.

> **MOVING MENUS**
>
> Visual Studio displays different menus and different commands in menus depending on what editor is active. For example, when you have a form open in the Windows Forms Designer, Visual Studio displays a Format menu that you can use to arrange controls on the form. When you have a code editor open, the Format menu is hidden because it doesn't apply to code.

File

The File menu contains commands that deal with creating, opening, saving, and closing projects and project files. The following list describes the most important commands contained in the File menu and its submenus:

➤ **New Project** — This command displays the dialog box shown in Figure 2-1. This dialog box lets you create new Windows applications, class libraries, console applications, control libraries, and more. Select the type of project yo want to start, enter a project name, and click OK.

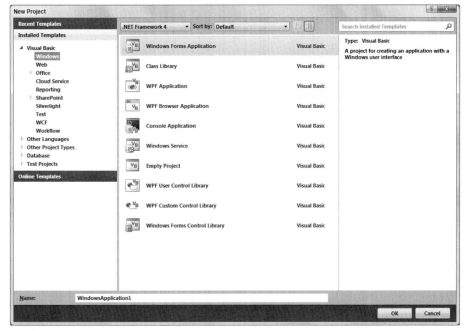

FIGURE 2-1: The New Project dialog box lets you start various kinds of new projects.

➤ **New Web Site** — This command lets you start a new web site project. It displays a dialog box where you can select the type of web site to create from among choices such as ASP .NET Web Site, ASP.NET Web Service, and Empty Web Site.

➤ **Open Project** — This command lets you open an existing project.

➤ **Open Web Site** — This command lets you open an existing web site project.

➤ **Open File** — This command displays the dialog box shown in Figure 2-2 and lets you select a file to open. The IDE uses integrated editors to let you edit the new file. For example, a simple bitmap editor lets you set a bitmap's size, change its number of colors, and draw on it. When you close the file, Visual Studio asks if you want to save it. Note that this doesn't automatically add the file to your current project. You can save the file and use the Project ➪ Add Existing Item command if you want to do that.

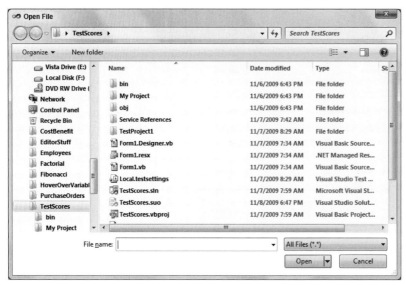

FIGURE 2-2: The Open File dialog box lets you select files to view
and edit.

➤ **Add** — This submenu lets you add new items to the current solution. This submenu's most useful commands for Visual Basic developers are New Project and Existing Project, which add a new or existing Visual Basic project to the current solution.

➤ **Close** — This command closes the current editor. For example, if you were editing a form in the Windows Forms Designer, this command closes the Designer.

➤ **Close Project** — This command closes the entire project and all of the files it contains. If you have a solution open, this command is labeled Close Solution and it closes the entire solution.

➤ **Save Form1.vb** — This command saves the currently open file, in this example, Form1.vb.

➤ **Save Form1.vb As** — This command lets you save the currently open file in a new file.

➤ **Save All** — This command saves all modified files. When you start a new project, the files are initially stored in a temporary location. This command allows you to pick a directory where the project should be saved permanently.

➤ **Export Template** — The *Export Template* command displays the dialog box shown in Figure 2-3. The Export Template Wizard enables you to create project or item templates that you can use later when making a new project.

FIGURE 2-3: The File/Export Template command displays this dialog box to help you create project or items templates that you can easily use in other projects.

➤ **Page Setup and Print** — The Page Setup and Print commands let you configure printer settings and print the current document. These commands are enabled only when it makes sense to print the current file. For example, they let you print if you have a code editor open because the code is text but they are disabled while you are using a Windows Forms Designer.

➤ **Recent Files and Recent Projects and Solutions** — The Recent Files and Recent Projects and Solutions submenus let you quickly reopen files, projects, and solutions that you have used recently.

Edit

The Edit menu contains commands that deal with manipulating text and other objects. These include standard commands such as the Undo, Redo, Cut, Copy, Paste, and Delete commands that you've seen in other Windows applications.

The following list describes other important commands contained in the Edit menu:

➤ **Find Symbol** — The *Find Symbol* command lets you search the application for a program symbol rather than a simple string. You can search for such items as namespaces, types, interfaces, properties, methods, constants, and variables.

➤ **Quick Find** — This command displays a find dialog box where you can search the project for specific text. A drop-down menu lets you indicate whether the search should include the current document, the currently selected text, all open documents, the current project, or the current solution. Options let you determine such things as whether the text must match case or whole words.

➤ **Quick Replace** — This command displays the same dialog box as the Quick Find command except with some extra controls. It includes a text box where you can specify replacement text, and buttons that let you replace the currently found text or all occurrences of the text.

REGRETFUL REPLACEMENT

Be careful when using Quick Replace. Often it gets carried away and replaces substrings of larger strings so they don't make sense anymore. For example, suppose you want to replace the variable name "hand" with "handed." If you let Quick Replace run, it will change Handles clauses into "handedles" clauses, which will confuse Visual Basic. To reduce the chances of this type of error, keep the scope of the replacement as small as possible and check the result for weird side effects.

➤ **Go To** — This command lets you jump to a particular line number in the current file.

➤ **Insert File As Text** — This command lets you select a file and insert its text into the current location. This can be useful if the file contains a code snippet.

➤ **Advanced** — The Advanced submenu contains commands for performing more complex document formatting such as converting text to upper- or lowercase, controlling word wrap, and commenting and uncommenting code.

➤ **Bookmarks** — The Bookmarks submenu lets you add, remove, and clear bookmarks, and move to the next or previous bookmark. You can use bookmarks to move quickly to specific pieces of code that you have previously marked.

➤ **Outlining** — The Outlining submenu lets you expand or collapse sections of code, and turn outlining on and off. Collapsing code that you are not currently editing can make the rest of the code easier to read.

➤ **IntelliSense** — The IntelliSense submenu gives access to IntelliSense features. For example, its List Members command makes IntelliSense display the current object's properties, methods, and events.

➤ **Next Method/Previous Method** — The Next Method and Previous Method commands move to the next or previous method or class in the current document.

View

The View menu contains commands that let you hide or display different windows and toolbars in the Visual Studio IDE. The following list describes the View menu's most useful commands:

- ➤ **Code** — The Code command opens the selected file in a code editor window. For example, to edit a form's code, you can click the form in the Solution Explorer and then select View ➪ Code.

- ➤ **Designer** — The Designer command opens the selected file in a graphical editor if one is defined for that type of file. For example, if the file is a form, this command opens the form in a graphical form editor. If the file is a class or a code module, the View menu hides this command because Visual Studio doesn't have a graphical editor for those file types.

- ➤ **Standard windows** — The next several commands in this menu list some explorers, Object Browser, Error List, Properties window, and Toolbox. These commands restore a previously hidden window.

- ➤ **Other Windows** — The Other Windows submenu lists other standard menus that are not listed in the View menu itself. These include the Bookmark window, Class View, Command window, Document Outline, Output, Task List, Macro Explorer, and many others. Like the standard windows commands, these commands are useful for recovering lost or hidden windows.

- ➤ **Tab Order** — If the currently visible document is a Windows Form that contains controls, the Tab Order command displays the tab order on top of each control. You can click the controls in the order you want them to have to set their tab orders quickly and easily. (If you are working with a WPF form, you must set the controls' TabIndex properties to set their tab order.)

- ➤ **Toolbars** — The Toolbars submenu lets you hide or display the currently defined toolbars. This submenu lists the standard toolbars in addition to any custom toolbars you have created.

- ➤ **Full Screen** — The Full Screen command hides all toolbars and windows except for any editor windows that you currently have open. It also hides the Windows taskbar so that the IDE occupies as much space as possible. This gives you the most space possible for working with the files you have open. The command adds a small box to the title bar containing a Full Screen button that you can click to end full-screen mode.

- ➤ **Property Pages** — This command displays the current item's property pages. For example, if you select an application in the Solution Explorer, this command displays the application's property pages similar to those shown in Figure 2-4.

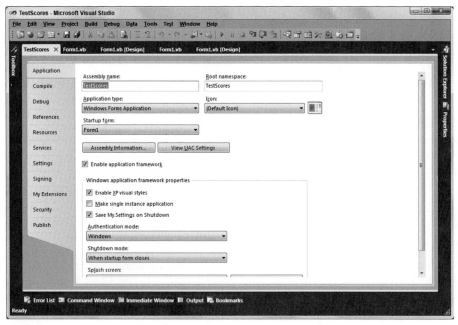

FIGURE 2-4: The View menu's Property Pages command displays an application's property pages.

Project

The Project menu contains commands that let you add and remove items to and from the project. Which commands are available depends on the currently selected item.

The following list describes the most important commands on the Project menu:

➤ **New items** — The first several commands let you add new items to the project. These commands are fairly self-explanatory. For example, the Add Class command adds a new class module to the project. Later chapters explain how to use each of these file types.

➤ **Add New Item** — The Add New Item command displays the dialog shown in Figure 2-5. The dialog lets you select from a wide assortment of items such as about boxes, text files, bitmap files, and class modules.

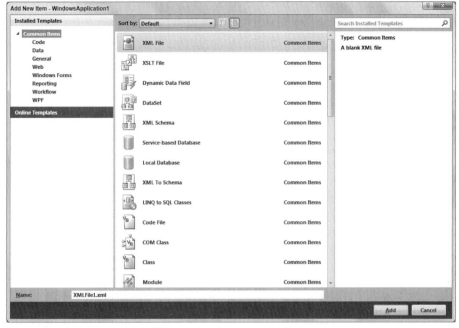

FIGURE 2-5: The Project menu's Add New Item command lets you add a wide variety of items to the project.

EASY ICONS

You can build an icon, cursor, or other graphical file right inside Visual Studio. Use the Add New Item command to add the new file. Visual Studio's built-in editors let you draw these files, give them transparent backgrounds, and even set a cursor's hotspot. (The hotspot is the pixel that determines where the cursor is pointing. For example, an arrow cursor's hotspot is the tip of the arrow.)

➤ **Add Existing Item** — The Add Existing Item command lets you browse for a file and add it to the project. This may be a Visual Basic file (such as a module, form, or class), or some other related file (such as a related document or image file).

➤ **Exclude From Project** — This command removes the currently selected item from the project. Note that this does not delete the file; it just removes it from the project.

➤ **Show All Files** — The Show All Files command makes Solution Explorer list files that are normally hidden. These include resource files used by forms, and hidden partial classes such as designer-generated form code. Normally, you don't need to work with these files, so they are hidden. Select this command to show them. Select the command again to hide them again.

➤ **Add Reference** — The Add Reference command displays the dialog shown in Figure 2-6. Select the category of the external object, class, or library that you want to find. For a .NET component, select the .NET tab. This is what you'll want most of the time. For a Component Object Model (COM) component such as an ActiveX library or control built using Visual Basic 6, select the COM tab. Select the Projects tab to add a reference to another Visual Studio project. Click the Browse tab to manually locate the file you want to reference.

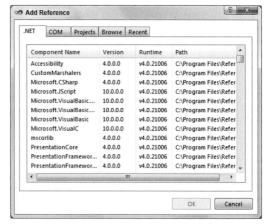

FIGURE 2-6: Use the Add Reference dialog box to add references to libraries.

Scroll through the list of references until you find the one you want and select it. You can use Shift+Click and Ctrl+Click to select more than one library at the same time. When you have made your selections, click OK to add the references to the project. After you have added a reference to the project, your code can refer to the reference's public objects. For example, if the file MyMathLibrary.dll defines a class named MathTools and that class defines a public function Fibonacci, a project with a reference to this DLL could use the following code:

```
Dim math_tools As New MyMathLibrary.MathTools
MessageBox.Show("Fib(5) = " & math_tools.Fibonacci(5))
```

➤ **Add Service Reference** — The Add Service Reference command displays the dialog shown in Figure 2-7. You can use this dialog to find Web Services and add references to them so your project can invoke them across the Internet. Figure 2-7 shows a service reference for the TerraServer map and aerial photography service. For more information, go to terraserver .microsoft.com.

➤ **WindowsApplication1 Properties** — This command displays the application's property pages shown in Figure 2-4.

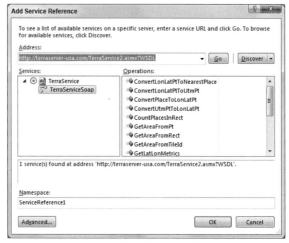

FIGURE 2-7: Use the Add Service Reference dialog to add references to Web Services.

Use the tabs on the left of the application's property pages to view and modify different types of application settings. You can leave many of the property values at their default values and many can be set in ways other than the property pages. For example, by default, the Assembly name and Root namespace values shown in Figure 2-4 are set to the name of the project when you first create it. For more projects, that's fine.

Figure 2-8 shows the Compile property page. This page holds four properties that deserve special mention.

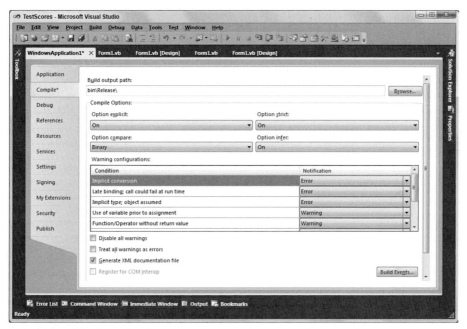

FIGURE 2-8: The Compile tab contains important properties for controlling code generation.

First, *Option Explicit* determines whether Visual Basic requires you to declare all variables before using them. Leaving this option turned off can sometimes lead to subtle bugs. For example, the following code is intended to print a list of even numbers between 0 and 10. Unfortunately, a typographical error makes the Debug.WriteLine statement print the value of the variable j not i. Because j is never initialized, the code prints out a bunch of blank values. If you set Option Explicit to On, the compiler complains that the variable j is not declared and the problem is easy to fix.

```
For i = 1 To 10
    If i Mod 2 = 0 Then Debug.WriteLine(j)
Next i
```

The second compiler option is *Option Strict*. When this option is turned off, Visual Studio allows your code to implicitly convert from one data type to another, even if the types are not always compatible. For example, Visual Basic will allow the following code to try to copy the string s into the integer i. If the value in the string happens to be a number, as in the first case, this works. If the string is not a number, as in the second case, this fails at runtime.

```
Dim i As Integer
Dim s As String
s = "10"
i = s ' This works.
s = "Hello"
i = s ' This Fails.
```

If you set Option Strict to On, the IDE warns you at compile time that the two data types are incompatible, so you can easily resolve the problem while you are writing the code. You can still use conversion functions such as CInt, Int, and Integer.Parse to convert a string into an Integer, but you must take explicit action to do so. This makes you think about the code and reduces the chances that the conversion is just an accident. This also helps you use the correct data types and avoid unnecessary conversions that may make your program slower.

The third compiler directive, *Option Compare*, can take the values Binary or Text. If you set Option Compare to Binary, Visual Basic compares strings using their binary representations. If you set Option Compare to Text, Visual Basic compares strings using a case-insensitive method that depends on your computer's localization settings. Option Compare Binary is faster, but may not always produce the result you want.

The final compiler directive, *Option Infer*, determines whether you can omit the data type when declaring a variable and let Visual Basic deduce its data type from the context. For example, the first statement in the following code declares the variable x, explicitly declaring it as a Single. The second statement declares variable y without specifying a data type. Because y's initialization value looks like a Double, Visual Basic infers that the variable should be a Double.

```
Dim x As Single
Dim y = 3.14159265
```

The problem with inferred data types is that it is not obvious from the code what data type Visual Basic should use. In the preceding code, you need to know Visual Basic's inference rules to know whether variable y is a Single, Double, or Decimal.

You can use an Option statement to set the values for each of these options at the top of a code module. For example, the following code turns Option Explicit On and Option Infer Off for a module:

```
Option Explicit On
Option Infer Off
```

Instead of using Option statements in a file, you can use the property page shown in Figure 2-8 to set these options for all of the files in the application.

OPTION RECOMMENDATIONS

To avoid confusion and long debugging sessions, I recommend that you use the Compile property page to set Option Explicit On, Option Strict On, and Option Infer Off to make Visual Basic as restrictive as possible. Then if you must loosen these restrictions in a particular file, you can add an Option statement at the top of the file. For example, you may need to set Option Infer On for a module that uses LINQ. See Chapter 21, "LINQ," for more information about LINQ.

A final item on this tab that deserves special mention is the "Generate XML documentation file" checkbox near the bottom. If you check this box, then when you build the application Visual Studio creates an XML document containing any XML comments you have included in the code. For more information about XML comments, see the section "XML Comments" in Chapter 14, "Program and Module Structure."

Build

The Build menu contains commands that let you compile projects within a solution. The following list describes the most useful commands contained in the Build menu:

➤ **Build WindowsApplication1** — This command compiles the currently selected project, in this case the project WindowsApplication1. Visual Studio examines the project's files to see if any have changed since the last time it compiled the project. If any of the files have changed, Visual Studio saves and recompiles them.

➤ **Rebuild WindowsApplication1** — This command recompiles the currently selected project from scratch. It recompiles every file even if it has not been modified since the last time it was compiled.

➤ **Clean WindowsApplication1** — This command removes temporary and intermediate files that were created while building the application, leaving only the source files and the final result .exe and .dll files.

➤ **Publish WindowsApplication1** — This command displays the Publish Wizard shown in Figure 2-9. It can walk you through the process of making your application available for distribution in a local file, file share, FTP site, or web site.

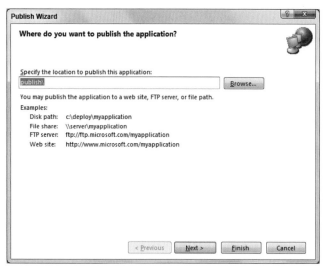

FIGURE 2-9: The Publish Wizard helps you deploy an application.

If your solution contains more than one application, then the Build menu also contains the solution-related commands Build Solution, Rebuild Solution, and Clean Solution. These are similar to their application counterparts except they apply to every application in the solution.

Debug

The Debug menu contains commands that help you debug a program. These commands help you run the program in the debugger, move through the code, set and clear breakpoints, and generally follow the code's execution to see what it's doing and hopefully what it's doing wrong.

For more information about the Debug menu and debugging Visual Basic code, see Chapter 7, "Debugging."

Data

The Data menu contains commands that deal with data and data sources. Some of the commands in this menu are only visible and enabled if you are designing a form and that form contains the proper data objects.

The following list describes the most useful Data menu commands:

➤ **Show Data Sources** — This command displays the Data Sources window, where you can work with the program's data sources. For example, you can drag and drop tables and fields from this window onto a form to create controls bound to the data source.

➤ **Preview Data** — This command displays a dialog box that lets you load data into a DataSet and view it at design time.

➤ **Add New Data Source** — This command displays the Data Source Configuration Wizard, which walks you through the process of adding a data source to the project.

➤ **Add Query** — This command is available when you are designing a form and have selected a data-bound control such as a DataGridView or bound TextBox. This command opens a dialog where you can specify a query to add to the form. This places a ToolStrip on the form containing ToolStripButtons that populate the bound control by executing the query.

Format

The Format menu contains commands that arrange controls on a form. The commands are grouped into submenus containing related commands. The following list describes the Format menu's submenus:

➤ **Align** — This submenu contains commands that align the controls you have selected in various ways. It contains the commands Lefts, Centers, Rights, Tops, Middles, Bottoms, and to Grid. For example, the Lefts command aligns the controls so their left edges line up nicely. The to Grid command snaps the controls to the nearest grid position.

➤ **Make Same Size** — This submenu contains commands that makes the dimensions of the controls you have selected the same. It contains the commands Width, Height, and Both. The Size to Grid command adjusts the selected controls' widths so that they are a multiple of the alignment grid size. (This command is disabled unless the Windows Forms Designer's LayoutMode is set to SnapToGrid. To set this, open the Tools menu, select the Options command, go to the Windows Forms Designer tab, open the General sub-tab, and set the LayoutMode property.)

➤ **Horizontal Spacing** — This submenu contains commands that change the horizontal spacing between the controls you have selected. It contains the commands Make Equal, Increase, Decrease, and Remove.

➤ **Vertical Spacing** — This submenu contains the same commands as the Horizontal Spacing submenu except it adjusts the controls' vertical spacing.

➤ **Center in Form** — This submenu contains the commands Horizontally and Vertically that center the selected controls on the form either horizontally or vertically.

➤ **Order** — This submenu contains the commands Bring to Front and Send to Back, which move the selected controls to the top or bottom of the stacking order.

➤ **Lock Controls** — This command locks all of the controls on the form so that you cannot move or resize them by clicking and dragging, although you can still move and resize the controls by changing their Location and Size properties in the Properties window. Invoking this command again unlocks the controls.

Tools

The Tools menu contains miscellaneous tools that do not fit particularly well in the other menus. It also contains a few duplicates of commands in other menus and commands that modify the IDE itself.

The following list describes the Tools menu's most useful commands. Note that some of these commands only appear when a particular type of editor is open.

➤ **Attach to Process** — This command displays a dialog box to let you attach the debugger to a running process.

➤ **Connect to Database** — This command displays the Connection Properties dialog box, where you can define a database connection. The connection is added to the Server Explorer window. You can later use the connection to define data adapters and other objects that use a database connection.

➤ **Connect to Server** — This command displays a dialog box that lets you connect to a database server.

➤ **Code Snippets Manager** — This command displays the Code Snippets Manager, which you can use to add and remove code snippets.

➤ **Choose Toolbox Items** — This command displays a dialog box that lets you select the tools displayed in the Toolbox. For instance, some controls are not included in the Toolbox by default. You can use this command to add them if you will use them frequently.

➤ **Add-in Manager** — This command displays the Add-in Manager, which lists the add-in projects registered on the computer. You can use the Add-in Manager to enable or disable these add-ins.

➤ **Macros** — The Macros submenu contains commands that help you create, edit, and execute macros. See the section "Macros" later in this chapter for details.

➤ **Extension Manager** — This command displays an Extension Manager dialog that lets you find Visual Studio extensions online and install them.

➤ **External Tools** — This command displays a dialog box that lets you add and remove commands from the Tools menu. For example, you could add a command to launch WordPad, MS Paint, WinZip, and other handy utilities from the Tools menu.

➤ **Import/Export Settings** — This command displays a dialog box that you can use to save, restore, or reset your Visual Studio IDE settings. Use this dialog box to configure your development environment for general development, project management, team test, Visual Basic, C#, C++, or Web development.

➤ **Customize** — This command allows you to customize the Visual Studio IDE. See Chapter 3, "Customization," for details.

➤ **Options** — This command allows you to specify options for the Visual Studio IDE. See the "Options" section later in this chapter for details.

Macros

The *Macros* submenu provides commands that help you create, edit, and execute macros that automate repetitive Visual Studio programming chores. If you must perform a series of actions many times, you can record a macro that performs them. Then you can call the macro repeatedly to perform the actions rather than executing them manually.

Some examples of macros that I've used in the past include code that:

➤ Arranges controls in unusual ways, such as spacing picture boxes around the edge of a circle.

➤ Generates a long series of statements that does the same thing to a bunch of text values (for example, makes Select Case statements for a series of text values).

➤ Sets up a new dialog box by creating the OK and Cancel buttons, positioning them, setting their DialogResult properties, and setting the form's AcceptButton and CancelButton properties.

➤ Building a name and address form with labels and text boxes that have appropriate Anchor properties.

Author John Mueller (`www.mwt.net/~jmueller`) uses similar macros to set up dialog boxes, create standard menus, and build standard event handlers. You have other ways to do these things, such as saving a pre-built dialog box for use as a template, or by using code snippets described later in this chapter, but macros are quick and easy.

After you have recorded a macro, you can edit the macro's code and make changes. For example, if you want to run the code a certain number of times, you can include it in a For loop. Often, a quick inspection of the code lets you figure out how to modify the macro to perform actions similar to (but not exactly the same as) the actions you originally recorded.

Most of the commands in the Macros submenu are self-explanatory. Use the Record TemporaryMacro command to record a macro for quick temporary use. When you select this command, a small window pops up that contains buttons you can click to suspend, finish, or cancel recording. Visual Studio saves the commands you execute in a macro named TemporaryMacro.

Select Run TemporaryMacro to run this macro. If you record a new TemporaryMacro, it overwrites the existing one without warning you. Select the Save TemporaryMacro command to rename the macro so you can record a new TemporaryMacro without destroying the previous one.

Select the Macro Explorer command to display the window shown in Figure 2-10. If you right-click a macro, the resulting pop-up menu lets you run, edit, rename, or delete the macro. Notice the Macro Explorer's predefined Samples section, which contains example macros that you can use or modify for your own use.

FIGURE 2-10: The Macro Explorer lets you edit, run, and delete macros.

Sometimes when you perform a series of programming tasks many times, you have better ways to approach the problem than writing a macro. For example, you may be able to make your program repeat the steps inside a loop. Or you may be able to extract the common code into a subroutine and then call it repeatedly rather than repeating the code many times. In these cases, your application doesn't need to contain a long sequence of repetitive code that may be hard to debug and maintain.

Macros are generally most useful when you must write similar pieces of code that cannot be easily extracted into a routine and shared by different parts of the application. For example, suppose that you need to write event handlers for several dozen TextBox controls. You could record a macro while you write one of them. Then you could edit the macro to make it generate the others in a loop using different control names for each event handler. You could place the bulk of the event-handling code in a separate subroutine that each event handler would call. That would avoid the need for extensive duplicated code. (In fact, you could even use the AddHandler statement or a Handles clause to make all the controls use the same event handler.)

Macros are also useful for manipulating the IDE and performing IDE-related tasks. For example, you can write macros to show and hide your favorite toolbars, or to change whether the current file is opened read-only.

Options

The Tools menu's Options command displays the dialog box shown in Figure 2-11. This dialog box contains a huge number of pages of options that configure the Visual Studio IDE.

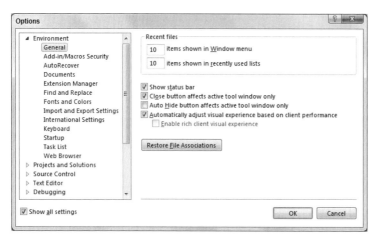

FIGURE 2-11: The Options dialog box lets you specify IDE options.

The following list describes the Options dialog box's most important categories:

➤ **Environment** — Contains general IDE settings such as whether the IDE uses tabs or multiple windows to display documents, the number of items shown in the most recently used file lists, and how often the IDE saves AutoRecover information. The Fonts and Colors subsection lets you determine the colors used by the editors for different types of text. For example, comments are shown in green by default, but you can change this color.

➤ **Projects and Solutions** — Contains the default settings for Option Explicit, Option Strict, and Option Compare.

➤ **Source Control** — Contains entries that deal with the source code control system (for example, Visual SourceSafe). These systems provide file locking and differencing tools that let multiple developers work on the same project without interfering with each other.

➤ **Text Editor** — Contains entries that specify the text editor's features. For example, you can use these pages to determine whether delimiters are highlighted, whether long lines are automatically wrapped, whether line numbers are displayed, and whether the editor provides smart indentation. The Basic ➪ VB Specific subsection lets you specify options such as whether the editor uses outlining, displays procedure separators, and suggests corrections for errors.

➤ **Debugging** — Contains debugging settings such as whether the debugger displays messages as modules are loaded and unloaded, whether it should make you confirm when deleting all breakpoints, and whether it should allow Edit-and-Continue.

➤ **Database Tools** — Contains database parameters such as default lengths for fields of various types.

➤ **HTML Designer** — Contains options for configuring HTML Designer. These options determine such settings as whether the designer starts in source or design view, and whether it displays Smart Tags for controls in design view.

➤ **Office Tools** — Contains settings that specify how the keyboard should work when you use Excel or Word files within Visual Studio.

➤ **Test Tools** — Contains settings that determine how testing tools behave.

➤ **Windows Forms Designer** — Contains settings that control the Windows Forms Designer. For example, this section lets you determine whether the designer uses a snap-to grid or snap lines and how far apart grid points are.

Test

The Test menu contains commands that control the Visual Studio testing tools. These tools let you perform such actions as coverage testing (to see if every line of code is executed), regression testing (to see if changes to the code broke anything), and load testing (to see how the application performs with a lot of simulated users running at the same time).

The following list briefly describes the Test menu's commands:

➤ **New Test** — Displays a dialog box that lets you create various kinds of tests for the application.

➤ **Load Metadata File** — Lets you load a test metadata file. These XML files describe test lists, each of which can contain tests. This command lets you load test lists into different projects.

➤ **Create New Test List** — Lets you make a new test list. Test lists let you group related tests so that you can execute them together. For example, you might have test lists for user interface testing, print tests, database tests, and so forth.

➤ **Run** — Starts executing the currently active test project without the debugger.

➤ **Debug** — Starts executing the currently active test project with the debugger.

➤ **Windows** — Displays test-related windows including Test View, Test List Editor, Test Results, and Test Runs.

The Window menu contains commands that control Visual Studio's windows. Which commands are enabled depends on the type of window that has the focus. For example, if focus is on a code editor, the Split command is enabled and the Float, Dock, and Dock as Tabbed Document commands are disabled, but when the Solution Explorer window has the focus, the opposite is true.

The following list briefly describes the most useful of these commands:

➤ **Split** — Splits a code window into two panes that can display different parts of the code at the same time. This command changes to Remove Split when you use it.

➤ **Float, Dock, Dock as Tabbed Document** — Secondary windows such as the Toolbox, Solution Explorer, and Properties windows can be displayed as dockable, floating, or tabbed documents. A dockable window can be attached to the edges of the IDE or docked with other secondary windows. A floating window stays in its own independent window even if you drag it to a position where it would normally dock. A tabbed document window is displayed in the main editing area in the center of the IDE with the forms, classes, and other project files.

➤ **Auto Hide** — Puts a secondary window in Auto Hide mode. The window disappears, and its title is displayed at the IDE's nearest edge. When you click the title or hover over it, the window reappears so that you can use it. If you click another window, this window hides itself again automatically.

➤ **Hide** — Removes the window.

➤ **Auto Hide All** — Makes all secondary windows enter Auto Hide mode.

➤ **New Horizontal Tab Group** — Splits the main document window horizontally so that you can view two different documents at the same time.

➤ **New Vertical Tab Group** — Splits the main document window vertically so that you can view two different documents at the same time.

➤ **Close All Documents** — Closes all documents.

➤ **Reset Window Layout** — Resets the window layout to a default configuration.

➤ **Form1.vb** — The bottom part of the Window menu lists open documents such as form, code, and bitmap editors. The menu displays a checkmark next to the currently active document. You can select one of these entries to quickly view the corresponding document.

➤ **Windows** — If you have too many open documents to display in the Window menu, select this command to see a list of the windows in a dialog. This dialog box lets you switch to another document, close one or more documents, or save documents. By pressing Ctrl+Click or Shift+Click you can select more than one document and quickly close them.

Help

The Help menu displays the usual assortment of help commands. You should be familiar with most of these from previous experience. The following list summarizes some of the more interesting non-standard commands:

➤ **Visual Studio Documentation** — Opens Visual Studio documentation in a web browser.

➤ **MSDN Forums** — Opens an MSDN community forums web page where you can post and search for answers to questions.

➤ **Report a Bug** — Opens the Microsoft Developer Division Feedback Center where you can report bugs, make suggestions, and look for hot fixes for known problems.

➤ **Samples** — Opens a Microsoft web page containing links to Visual Studio documentation and samples.

➤ **Customer Feedback Options** — Displays a dialog that lets you indicate whether you want to participate in Microsoft's anonymous Customer Experience Improvement Program. If you join, Microsoft collects anonymous information about your system configuration and how you use its software.

➤ **Check for Updates** — Check online for Visual Studio updates.

➤ **Technical Support** — Opens a help page describing various support options. The page includes phone numbers and links to more information.

TOOLBARS

The Visual Studio toolbars are easy to rearrange. Simply grab the four gray dots on a toolbar's left or upper edge and drag the toolbar to its new position. If you drag a toolbar to one of the IDE's edges, it will dock there either horizontally (on the IDE's top or bottom edge) or vertically (on the IDE's left or right edge). If you drop a toolbar away from the IDE's edges, it becomes a floating window not docked to the IDE.

You can use the IDE's menu commands to determine which toolbars are visible, to determine what they contain, and to make custom toolbars of your own. See Chapter 3, "Customization," for more details.

Many menu commands are also available in standard toolbars. For example, the Debug toolbar contains many of the same commands that are in the Debug menu. If you use a set of menu commands frequently, you may want to display the corresponding toolbar to make using the commands easier. Alternatively, you can make your own custom toolbar and fill it with your favorite commands.

SECONDARY WINDOWS

You can rearrange secondary windows such as the Toolbox and Solution Explorer almost as easily as you can rearrange toolbars. Click and drag the window's title bar to move it. As the window moves, the IDE displays little blue icons to help you dock the window, as shown in Figure 2-12. This figure probably looks somewhat confusing, but it's fairly easy to use.

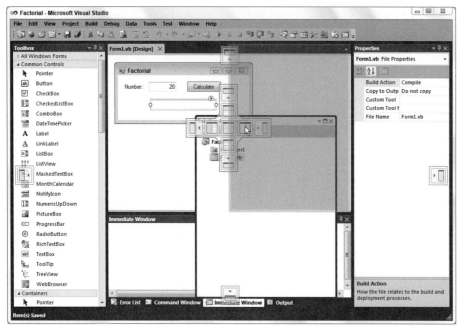

FIGURE 2-12: Use the IDE's docking icons to help you dock windows.

When you drag the window over another window, the IDE displays docking icons for the other window. In Figure 2-12, these are the five center most icons. The four icons on the sides dock the window to the corresponding edge of the other window.

The center icon places the dropped window in a tab within the other window.

When you drag the mouse over one of the docking icons, the IDE displays a pale blue rectangle to give you an idea of where the window will land if you drop it. In Figure 2-12, the mouse is over the main document window's right docking icon, so the blue rectangle shows the dropped window taking up the right half of the main document window.

If you drop a window somewhere other than on a docking icon, the window becomes free-floating.

When you drop a window on the main document area, it becomes a tabbed document within that area, and you cannot later pull it out. To free the window, select it and use the Window menu's Dock or Float command.

Sometimes the IDE is so cluttered with windows that it's hard to figure out exactly where the window will be dropped. It's usually fairly easy to just move the mouse around a bit and watch the pale blue rectangle to see what's happening.

The windows in the Microsoft Document Explorer used by the MSDN Library and other external help files provide the same arranging and docking tools for managing its subwindows such as Index, Contents, Help Favorites, Index Results, and Search Results.

This section describes some of the general features of the IDE's secondary windows. The following sections describe two of the most important of those secondary windows: the Toolbox and the Properties window.

Toolbox

The *Toolbox* window displays tools that you can use with the currently active document. The tools are available when you are editing a Windows Form, WPF Form, UserControl, web page, or other item that can contain objects such as controls and components.

The tools are grouped into sections called *tabs*, although they don't look much like the tabs on most documents. The Toolbox in Figure 2-13 displays tools for the Windows Forms Designer. The All Windows Forms section is showing its tools as icons whereas the Data section is listing its tools by name. Other tabs are hidden. In this figure, the Toolbox was enlarged greatly to show most of its contents. Most developers keep this window much smaller and docked to the left edge of the IDE.

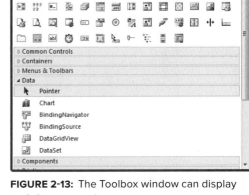

You can customize the Toolbox by right-clicking a tab and selecting one of the commands in the context menu. The following list briefly describes the most useful of these commands:

FIGURE 2-13: The Toolbox window can display tools by name or icon.

➤ **List View** — Toggles the current tab to display tools either as a list of names (as in the Data section in Figure 2-13) or a series of icons (as in the All Windows Forms section in Figure 2-13).

➤ **Show All** — Shows or hides less commonly used tool tabs such as XML Schema, Dialog Editor, DataSet, Login, WPF Interoperability, Windows Workflow, Device Controls, and many others.

➤ **Choose Items** — Displays the dialog box shown in Figure 2-14. Use the .NET Framework Components tab to select .NET tools, and use the COM Components tab to select COM tools. Click the Browse button to locate tools that are not in either list.

➤ **Sort Items Alphabetically** — Sorts the items within a Toolbox tab alphabetically.

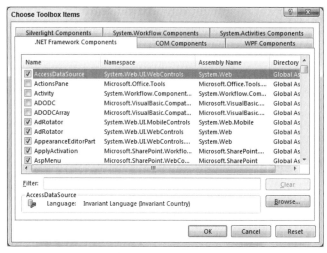

FIGURE 2-14: Use the Choose Toolbox Items dialog box to select the tools in the Toolbox.

➤ **Reset Toolbox** — Restores the Toolbox to a default configuration. This removes any items you may have added by using the Choose Items command.

➤ **Add Tab** — Creates a new tab where you can place your favorite tools. You can drag tools from one tab to another. Hold down the Ctrl key while dragging to add a copy of the tool to the new tab without removing it from the old tab.

➤ **Delete Tab** — Deletes a tab.

➤ **Rename Tab** — Lets you rename a tab.

➤ **Move Up, Move Down** — Moves the clicked tab up or down in the Toolbox. You can also click and drag the tabs to new positions.

If you right-click a tool in the Toolbox, the context menu *contains most of these commands plus Cut, Copy, Paste, Delete, and Rename Item.

Properties Window

When you are designing a form, the *Properties window* allows you to view and modify the properties of the form and of the controls that it contains. Figure 2-15 shows the Properties window displaying properties for a Button control named btnCalculate. You can see in the figure that the control's Text property is "Calculate" so that's what the button displays to the user.

Figure 2-15 shows some important features of the Properties window that deserve special mention. At the top of the window is a drop-down list that holds the names of all of the controls on the

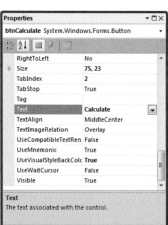

FIGURE 2-15: The Properties window lets you view and modify control properties.

form. To select a control, you can either click it on the Windows Forms Designer or select it from this list.

The buttons in the row below the dropdown determine what items are displayed in the window and how they are arranged. If you click the leftmost button, the window lists properties grouped by category. For example, the Appearance category contains properties that affect the control's appearance such as BackColor, Font, and Image. If you click the second icon that holds the letters A and Z, the window lists the control's properties alphabetically.

Arranging properties alphabetically makes finding properties easier for many developers.

The third icon makes the window display the control's properties and the fourth icon (which displays a lightning bolt) makes the window display the control's events instead. (Yes, it's a little odd that the Properties window displays either properties or events, but there is no Events window.)

For more information on using the Properties window to edit properties and create event handlers in the Windows Forms Designer, see Chapter 4, "Windows Forms Designer."

SUMMARY

The Visual Studio integrated development environment provides a huge number of tools for manipulating projects. Menus and toolbars contain hundreds if not thousands of commands for creating, loading, saving, and editing different kinds of projects and files.

This chapter describes the most useful and important commands available in the IDE's menus and toolbars. The kinds of menus, toolbars, and commands that are available depend on the type of window that currently has focus, in addition to the project's current state. For example, the Format menu contains commands that arrange controls on a form so it is only available when you are using a Windows Forms Designer.

Chapter 3, "Customization," explains in greater detail how you can rearrange Visual Studio's toolbars and menus to meet your needs. It explains how you can make your own toolbars and menus and fill them with the commands that you find most useful during your day-to-day development.

3

Customization

The Visual Studio IDE is packed with thousands of tools that are available through toolbar and menu commands. So many tools are available that the IDE would be practically useless if every tool were displayed at the same time. In the interests of usability, the IDE displays only the tools that the Microsoft Visual Studio developers thought would be most useful when you were performing a particular task.

Unfortunately, the Microsoft developers didn't know exactly what you would be doing while developing applications, so they made their best guesses about which tools you would need. Under some circumstances, you may find that a completely different set of tools would be more useful. In those cases, you should customize the IDE to make using those tools easier and faster.

This chapter explains how you can customize the IDE. It explains how to make new toolbars and menus, add commands to them, and determine the commands' appearances. It also tells how you can define keyboard shortcuts to make the commands you use most often really easy to access.

ADDING COMMANDS

The Tools menu's Customize command displays the dialog box shown in Figure 3-1. On the Toolbars tab, select the check boxes next to the toolbars that you want to be visible. Click New to create a new toolbar where you can add your favorite tools. You can leave the toolbar floating or drag it to the edge of the IDE and dock it. If you drag it to the top, it joins the other toolbars.

FIGURE 3-1: The Customize dialog box's Toolbars tab lets you determine which toolbars are visible.

Click the Commands tab and select a menu. Then click the Add Command button to see the dialog shown in Figure 3-2. Select a command in the dialog and click OK to add it to the menu you originally selected.

FIGURE 3-2: The Add Command dialog lets you add commands to toolbars and menus.

To make a command that executes a macro you have created, select the Macros category in the list on the left. Find the macro you want to use in the list on the right, and drag it onto a toolbar or menu.

To create a new menu, click the Customize dialog's Add New Menu button.

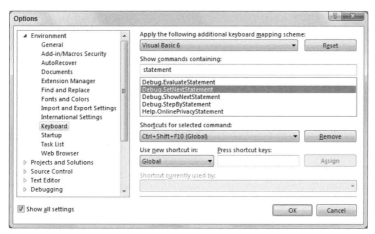

FIGURE 3-3: The Options dialog's Keyboard section lets you view and modify keyboard shortcuts.

MAKING KEYBOARD SHORTCUTS

Keyboard shortcuts let you quickly invoke a command by pressing a key combination. For example, in most applications including Visual Studio, Ctrl+S invokes the save command.

The Keyboard button at the bottom of the Customize dialog displays the dialog box shown in Figure 3-3. You can use this dialog to view and edit keyboard shortcuts.

Enter words in the "Show commands containing" text box to filter the commands. When you click a command, the dialog box displays any keyboard shortcuts associated with it.

To make a new shortcut, click the "Press shortcut keys" text box and press the keys that you want to use as a shortcut. The "Shortcuts for selected command" drop-down list displays any commands that already use the shortcut you entered. To make the assignment, click the Assign button.

CONFUSING SHORTCUTS

To avoid confusion, don't use standard shortcuts for non-standard commands. For example, Ctrl+S normally makes the IDE save the currently selected items (for example, the file you are editing). Changing the meaning of Ctrl+S so it runs a macro that builds a sales form could be very confusing later.

When you type a new shortcut sequence in the "Press shortcut keys" box, look in the "Shortcut currently used by" list to see if that combination of keys is already assigned to another command. If the combination is in use, try something different.

SUMMARY

The Visual Studio IDE comes with a huge assortment of tools. Initially the IDE's menus and toolbars are arranged to make it easy to access the tools that developers use most often, but if you need to use some other tool frequently, you are not limited to the IDE's initial layout. This chapter explains how you can create, hide, and rearrange menus and toolbars to make it easy to use the tools that you find most useful.

In addition to its many menus and toolbars, the IDE contains dozens of windows that contain tools or that allow you to view and modify different aspects of an application. Of all the windows displayed by the IDE, one of the first that Visual Basic developers use when building a new application is the Windows Forms Designer. This window allows you to add controls to a form, arrange them to create a user interface, and set their properties to determine their appearances and behaviors.

Chapter 4, "Windows Forms Designer," explains how to use the Windows Forms Designer to build the forms that make up most Windows applications.

Windows Forms Designer

The *Windows Forms Designer* allows you to design forms for typical Windows applications. It lets you add, size, and move controls on a form. Together with the Properties window, it also lets you change a control's properties to determine its appearance and behavior.

This chapter provides an introduction to the Windows Forms Designer. It explains how to add controls to a form, move and size controls, set control properties, and add code to respond to control events. It also describes tips and tricks that make working with controls easier.

SETTING DESIGNER OPTIONS

When you first install Visual Studio, the Windows Forms Designer is configured to be quite usable. You can immediately open a form and use the Toolbox to place controls on it. You can use the mouse to move and resize controls. You can use the Format menu to arrange and size controls. Overall the Windows Forms Designer provides a first-class intuitive *WYSIWYG* ("what you see is what you get") experience.

Behind the scenes, however, there are a few configuration options that control the Designer's behavior and that you should know about to get the most out of the Designer.

To view the Designer's options, open the Tools menu, select Options, open the Windows Forms Designer branch, and select the General page to display the dialog shown in Figure 4-1.

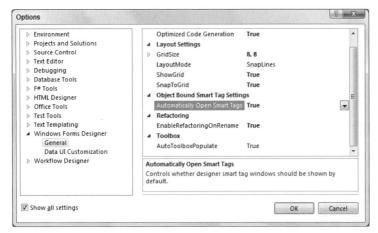

FIGURE 4-1: This dialog lets you control the Windows Forms Designer's behavior.

The following list describes the most important of these settings.

➤ **Optimized Code Generation** — Determines whether Visual Studio generates optimized code. This setting is here instead of some more code-oriented part of the Options dialog because some controls may be incompatible with code optimization.

➤ **Grid Size** — Determines the horizontal and vertical dimensions of the sizing grid for use when LayoutMode is SnapToGrid.

➤ **LayoutMode** — Determines whether Visual Studio uses *snap-to-grid* or *snap lines*. If this is SnapToGrid, objects automatically snap to the nearest grid point when you drag or resize them. When this is SnapLines, resized controls automatically snap to lines that align with the edges or centers of other controls, or with the form's margins. Both of these options make it easy to build controls that are consistently sized and that align along their edges. The two options have a very different feel, however, so you might want to experiment with both to see which one you like best.

➤ **Automatically Open Smart Tags** — Determines whether Visual Studio displays smart tags by default.

➤ **EnableRefactoringOnRename** — Determines whether Visual Studio performs refactoring when you rename a control. (*Refactoring* is the process of restructuring the code, hopefully to make it better.) If this setting is True and you change a control's name, Visual Studio updates any code that uses that control so it uses the new name. If this setting is False and you rename a control, any code that refers to the control still uses its old name, so the code will no longer work.

➤ **AutoToolboxPopulate** — Determines whether Visual Studio adds components built by the solution to the Toolbox window.

USEFUL OPTIONS

Which LayoutMode you should use is a matter of preference. I know many developers who use each style. The EnableRefactoringOnRename option can save you a lot of trouble when you rename controls so it's almost always worth leaving True.

ADDING CONTROLS

The Windows Forms Designer allows you to add controls to a form in several ways.

First, if you double-click a control on the Toolbox, Visual Studio places an instance of the control on the form in a default location and at a default size. You can then use the mouse to move and resize the control.

When you use this method, the new control is placed inside the currently selected container on the form. If the currently selected control is a GroupBox, the new control is placed inside the GroupBox. If the currently selected control is a TextBox that is inside a Panel, the new control is placed inside the Panel.

Second, if you click a control in the Toolbox, the mouse cursor changes while the mouse is over the form. The new cursor looks like a plus sign with a small image of the control's Toolbox icon next to it. If you click the form, Visual Studio adds a control at that location with a default size. Instead of just clicking, you can click and drag to specify the new control's location and size. After you place the new control, the mouse returns to a pointer cursor so you can click existing controls to select them.

If you hold down the Control key when you click or drag on the form, the Designer adds the new control to the form and keeps the control's Toolbox tool selected so you can add another instance of the control. For example, suppose you need to create a series of TextBoxes to hold a user's name, street, city, state, and ZIP code. Select the TextBox tool in the Toolbox. Then you can quickly use Ctrl+Click five times to create the TextBoxes. Press the Escape key to stop adding TextBoxes and then drag them into their correct positions.

SELECTING CONTROLS

When you first create a control, the Designer selects it. The Designer indicates that the control is selected by surrounding it with white boxes. In Figure 4-2, the Button2 control is selected.

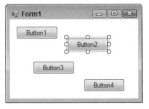

FIGURE 4-2: The Designer surrounds a selected control with white boxes.

To select a control on the Designer later, simply click it.

You can click and drag to select a group of controls. As you drag the mouse, the Designer displays a rectangle so you can tell which controls will be selected. When you release the mouse button, all of the controls that overlap the rectangle at least partly are selected.

When you select a group of controls, the Designer surrounds most of them with black boxes. It surrounds a special "master" control with white boxes. In Figure 4-3, four buttons are selected. Button1 is the "master" control so it is surrounded by white boxes.

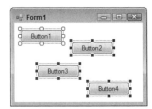

FIGURE 4-3: The selection's "master" control is surrounded by white boxes.

The Designer uses the "master" control to adjust the others if you use the Format menu's commands. For example, if you use the Format ⇨ Make Same Size ⇨ Height command, the Designer gives the "black box" controls the same height as the "master" control. Similarly the Format ⇨ Align ⇨ Tops command moves the "black box" controls so their tops are the same as the top of the "master" control.

To change the "master" control, simply click the control that you want to use as the "master."

After you have selected some controls, you can Shift+Click or Ctrl+Click to add and remove single controls from the selection. You can Shift+Click-and-drag or Ctrl+Click-and-drag to add and remove groups of controls from the selection.

TRICKY CLICKS

Under some circumstances, the Designer will not remove its selection even if you click the form off of the selected controls. To deselect all of the controls, either click a control that is not selected or press the Escape key.

COPYING CONTROLS

A particularly useful technique for building a series of similar controls is to build one and then use copy and paste to make others.

For example, to build the name, street, city, state, and ZIP code TextBoxes described in the previous section, you could start by adding the Name TextBox to the form. Next, set all of the properties for the control that will be shared by the other controls. For example, you may want to adjust the

TextBox's width, set its MaxLength property to 20, and set its Anchor property to "Top, Left, Right" so it resizes horizontally when its container resizes. Now select the control on the Designer and press Ctrl+C to copy it. Then press Ctrl+V repeatedly to make copies for the other controls. Drag the controls into position and you have quickly built all of the controls with their shared properties already set.

CONTAINER CONFUSION

When you paste a copied control, the new control is placed inside whatever container is currently selected on the form. This can be confusing if you quickly copy and paste a container. For example, suppose you want to make three GroupBoxes. You build one and size it the way you want it. Then you press Ctrl+C, Ctrl+V, Ctrl+V. The first GroupBox is copied and the first copy is pasted inside the original GroupBox. Then the second copy is also placed inside the first copy. The result is somewhat confusing and you'll probably need to drag the copies out onto the form before you can place them where you want.

You can also use copy and paste to copy a group of controls. For example, suppose you want to make name, street, city, state, and ZIP code TextBoxes but you also want Label controls to the left of the TextBoxes. First create the name Label and TextBox, set their properties, and position them so they are lined up vertically and the Label is to the left of the TextBox as desired. Click and drag to select both controls and then press Ctrl+C to copy them both. Now when you press Ctrl+V, the Designer makes a copy of the Label and the TextBox. The copies are lined up vertically and the Label is to the left of the TextBox as in the originals. The new controls are even both selected so you can use the mouse to grab them both and drag them into position.

MOVING AND SIZING CONTROLS

Moving a control in the Windows Forms Designer is easy. Simply click and drag the control to its new position.

To move a group of controls, select the controls that you want. Then click one of the controls and drag to move the whole group.

Note that you can drag controls in and out of container controls such as the FlowLayoutPanel, GroupBox, Panel, and PictureBox. When you drag a control into a new container, the mouse cursor acquires a little fuzzy rectangle on the lower right. If you are dragging a control and you see this appear, you know that dropping the control at the current position will move it into a new container. The new container indicator appears if you are dragging a control from the form into a container, from a container onto the form, or from one container to another.

Resizing a control is almost as easy as moving one. Click a control to select it. Then click and drag one of the white boxes surrounding the control to change its size.

To resize a group of controls, select the group. Then click and drag one of the boxes surrounding one of the controls. When you drag the mouse, the control beside the box you picked is resized as if it were the only control selected. The other selected controls resize in the same manner. For example, if you widen the clicked control by eight pixels, all of the other controls widen by eight pixels, too.

ARRANGING CONTROLS

The Format menu contains several submenus that hold tools that make arranging controls easier. For example, the Format menu's Align submenu contains commands that let you align controls vertically and horizontally along their edges or centers.

For a description of this menu's commands, see the section "Format" in Chapter 2, "Menus, Toolbars, and Windows." (Or just experiment with these commands — they aren't too complicated.)

For more information about how the selection's "white box master" control determines how other controls are adjusted, see the section "Selecting Controls" earlier in this chapter.

SETTING PROPERTIES

When you select a control, the Properties window allows you to view and edit the control's properties. For most properties, you can simply click the property and type a new value for the control. Some properties are more complex than others and provide drop-down lists or special dialogs to set the property's value. Most of the editors provided for setting property values are fairly self-explanatory, so they are not described in detail here.

In addition to using the Properties window to set a single control's properties one at a time, you can quickly set property values for groups of controls in a couple of ways. The following sections describe some of the most useful of these techniques.

Setting Group Properties

If you select a group of controls, you can sometimes use the Properties window to give all of the controls the same property value all at once. For example, suppose you select a group of TextBoxes. Then you can use the Properties window to give them the same values for their Anchor, Text, MultiLine, Font, and other properties simultaneously.

Sometimes, this even works when you select different kinds of controls at the same time. For example, if you select some TextBoxes and some Labels, you can set all of the controls' Text properties at the same time. You cannot set the TextBoxes' MultiLine properties because the Labels do not have a MultiLine property.

BLANKING TEXT

One handy use for this technique is to set the Text property to a blank string for a group of TextBox controls. Unfortunately, if the selected TextBoxes have different Text values, the Properties window displays a blank value for the Text property. If you then try to make the property blank, the Properties window doesn't think you've changed the value, so it doesn't blank the controls' Text properties.

To work around this restriction, first set the Text property to any non-blank value ("x" will do) to give all of the controls the same value. Then delete the Text value to blank all of the controls' Text values.

Setting Different Properties for Several Controls

When you select a control on the Windows Forms Designer, the Properties window initially selects a property for the control. The property selected depends on the kind of control you select and on the property currently selected in the Properties window.

If the newly selected and previously selected controls both have the currently selected property, the Properties window keeps that property selected. Otherwise the Properties window selects the default property for the newly selected control.

For example, suppose you select a Label control on the Designer and then click the TabIndex property in the Properties window. Now suppose you select a TextBox in the Designer. Because the TextBox also has a TabIndex property, that property remains selected in the Properties window.

In contrast, suppose you select a Button and click the Text property. Now suppose you click on a ListBox. The ListBox control doesn't have a Text property so the Properties window selects its default property (which is Items).

Because the Properties window tries to keep the same property selected, you can easily give a series of controls different values for the same property. For example, suppose you copy and paste to make a series of TextBoxes, and you want to give them good names. Select one TextBox, click its Name property in the Properties window, and type the new name (for example, txtName). Now click a different TextBox on the Windows Forms Designer. The Name property is still selected in the Properties window. If you immediately type this control's name (for example, txtStreet), the Properties window assigns the control the new name. You can repeat this process of selecting a new TextBox and typing its name very quickly.

WPF WANTING

Unfortunately, the WPF Designer is missing this feature (and many others). You need to click the Name property each time you want to change a control's name. Hopefully this designer will catch up with the Windows Forms Designer some day.

Using Smart Tags

Many controls display a *smart tag* when you select them on the Designer. The smart tag looks like a little box containing a right-pointing triangle. When you click the smart tag, a small dialog appears to let you perform common tasks for the control quickly and easily.

FIGURE 4-4: The PictureBox control's smart tag lets you choose an image, set the control's SizeMode, or dock the control in its container.

Figure 4-4 shows a PictureBox with the smart tag expanded. Because the smart tag's dialog is visible, the smart tag indicator shows a left-pointing triangle. If you click this, the dialog disappears.

The PictureBox control's smart tag dialog lets you choose an image for the control, set the control's SizeMode, or dock the control in its container. These actions set the control's Image, SizeMode, and Dock properties.

Many controls, particularly the more complicated kinds, provide smart tags to let you perform common actions without using the Properties window.

ADDING CODE TO CONTROLS

After you have added the appropriate controls to a form and set their properties, the next step is to add code to the form that responds to control events and that manipulates the controls.

You use the code editor to write code that responds to control events. The code editor is described in Chapter 6, "Visual Basic Code Editor," but you can open the code editor from the Windows Forms Designer.

An *event handler* is a code routine that catches an event raised by a control and takes some action. Almost all program action is started from an event handler. Even actions started automatically by a timer begin when an event handler catches a timer's events.

If you double-click a control on the Windows Forms Designer, Visual Studio creates an empty event handler to handle the control's default event and it opens the event handler in the code editor. For example, the following code shows the event handler the IDE built for a Button control named Button1. The default event for a Button is Click so this code is a Click event handler. (Note that I added the line continuation in the first line so it would fit in the book. Visual Studio makes that all one long line.)

```
Private Sub Button1_Click(ByVal sender As System.Object, _
    ByVal e As System.EventArgs) Handles Button1.Click

End Sub
```

RELAX, DON'T WORRY

Relaxed delegates let you remove the parameters from the event handler's declaration if you don't need them. For example, if you use separate event handlers for each button, you probably don't need the parameters to figure out what's happening. If the user clicks the button named btnExit, the btnExit_Click event handler executes and the program can exit.

In this case, you can remove the parameters to simplify the code. The following code shows the simplified btnExit_Click event handler (without any code in it):

```
Private Sub btnExit_Click() Handles btnExit.Click

End Sub
```

Another way to build an event handler and open the code editor is to select the control on the Windows Forms Designer. Then click the Events icon (the lightning bolt) near the top of the Properties window to make the window show a list of events for the control as shown in Figure 4-5. Double-click an event in the window to create an event handler for it and to open it in the code editor.

If you select more than one control in the Windows Forms Designer and then double-click an event, Visual Studio makes an event handler that catches the event for all of the selected controls. To create the following event handler, I selected three Buttons and double-clicked their Click event:

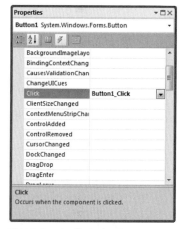

FIGURE 4-5: Click the Events icon to make the Properties window display a control's events.

```
Private Sub Button2_Click(ByVal sender As System.
Object, _
  ByVal e As System.EventArgs) _
  Handles Button3.Click, Button2.Click, Button1.Click

End Sub
```

The event handler's name is Button2_Click instead of Button1_Click or some other name because Button2 was the "white box master" control for the selected controls. See the section "Selecting Controls" earlier in this chapter for more information about a selection's "master" control.

TOO MANY HANDLERS

If you select a group of controls and then double-click them, Visual Studio makes a separate event handler for each control. If you want the same event handler to catch events from all of the controls, click the event handler button (the lightning bolt) on the Properties window and then double-click the event name there.

SUMMARY

The Windows Forms Designer allows you to build forms for use in Windows applications. It lets you add controls to a form, and resize and move the controls. Together with the Properties window, it lets you view and modify control properties, and create event handlers to interact with the controls.

This chapter introduces the Windows Forms Designer and explains how you can take advantage of its features. Future chapters provide much more of the detail necessary for building forms. Chapter 8, "Selecting Windows Forms Controls," and Chapter 9, "Using Windows Forms Controls," provide more information about the kinds of controls you can use with the Windows Forms Designer. Chapter 10, "Windows Forms," says a lot more about how Windows Forms work and what you can do with them.

Chapter 5, "WPF Designer," describes the designer that you use to build Windows Presentation Foundation forms. In some ways it is similar to the Windows Forms Designer. For example, you use the Toolbox to place controls on the form, and you use the Properties window to view and edit control properties much as you do when using the Windows Forms Designer.

5

WPF Designer

The *WPF* (*Windows Presentation Foundation*) Designer allows you to build WPF windows interactively much as the Windows Forms Designer lets you build Windows Forms. It provides a WYSIWYG (what you see is what you get) surface where you can add controls to a window. If you select one or more controls on the designer's surface, the Properties window displays the objects' properties and lets you edit many of them.

In addition to the WYSIWYG design surface, the designer provides an XAML (Extensible Application Markup Language) code editor. Here you can view and edit the XAML code that defines the user interface. This lets you edit properties and arrange controls in ways that are impossible using the WYSIWYG designer.

This chapter provides an introduction to the WPF Designer. It explains how to add controls to a window, move and size controls, set control properties, and add code to respond to control events.

FOR MORE INFORMATION

Windows Presentation Foundation is quite large and complex, requiring you to learn about a whole new set of controls, objects, properties, animations, and other items. It even uses a whole new system for properties and events that isn't used by Windows Forms.

The chapters in this book cover WPF in enough detail to get you started and let you build an effective application, but there's much more to WPF. For more details, see my book *WPF Programmer's Reference: Windows Presentation Foundation with C# 2010 and .NET 4.0* (Stephens, Wrox, 2009). Some of the code examples use C# but most of the code uses XAML code, which is described by the book. You can learn more and download the book's example code in C# and Visual Basic versions on the book's web page www.vb-helper.com/wpf.htm.

EDITOR WEAKNESSES

Visual Studio's Windows Forms Designer has been around for a long time and over the years it has become extremely powerful. In contrast, the WPF Designer is relatively new and lacks many of the features included in its more mature cousin.

Although the WPF Designer is a WYSIWYG tool, it has a lot of weak spots. A small sampling of these weaknesses includes:

- ➤ You cannot graphically put controls inside controls that are not primarily used as containers. For example, you cannot graphically put a Grid control inside a Button. You need to resort to XAML to do this.

- ➤ The Properties window does not provide editors for many types of objects, and many of the editors it does provide are incomplete. For example, the Properties window provides no tools for recording property animations and no tools for building styles or templates.

- ➤ The Properties window provides no descriptions for the selected property, so you must look in the documentation for help. Even the tooltips are weak, saying things like ClickMode: ClickMode.

- ➤ The designer surface has no snap-to-grid mode.

- ➤ The XAML code editor's IntelliSense is incomplete and doesn't provide help in many places where it would be useful (although it's much better than nothing).

The WYSIWYG designer has enough weaknesses that it is often easier to build parts of a user interface by using the XAML code editor. For example, the designer provides no methods for making resources, styles, and templates, three items that are essential for building a maintainable interface. Fortunately, these things are not too difficult to build in the XAML code editor.

In all fairness, the WPF Designer has improved greatly since its first version and includes several enhancements added since the previous version, including better enumerated property support and primitive brush editors. It also crashes much less often and gets confused about how to draw its controls much less frequently. Hopefully it will catch up with the Windows Forms Designer some day.

All of these issues aside, the WPF Designer is a powerful tool. It lets you quickly build the basic structures of a WPF window and layout controls. You may need to rearrange controls somewhat and build additional elements such as resources and styles in the XAML editor, but the WYSIWYG surface can get you started.

Though the XAML editor also has shortcomings, it does provide the tools you need to fine-tune the user interface initially built by the designer surface. Together the two pieces of the WPF Designer give you everything you need to build aesthetically pleasing and compelling WPF user interfaces.

BUILDING WITH BLEND

Microsoft's Expression Blend product provides some of the features that are missing from the WPF Designer. For example, it provides better tools for creating styles and templates, better brush editors, and the ability to record property animations.

It still has its drawbacks (one being the fact that there is no free version) but it complements Visual Studio's WPF Designer nicely. Learn more about Expression Blend or download a 30-day trial copy at www.microsoft.com/expression/products/Overview.aspx?key=blend.

RECOGNIZING DESIGNER WINDOWS

Figure 5-1 shows the Visual Studio IDE displaying the WPF Designer. You can rearrange the IDE's windows, but normally the Toolbox is on the left and the Properties window is on the right, below Solution Explorer. The WPF Designer is shown in the middle with its WYSIWYG design surface on top and its XAML code editor on the bottom.

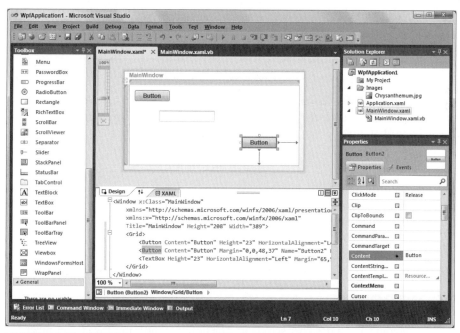

FIGURE 5-1: The WPF Designer includes a WYSIWYG design surface and an XAML code editor.

You can click the up and down arrow label between the WYSIWYG designer and the XAML editor to make the two switch panes. This is useful if you make one pane large and the other small. Then you can quickly switch back and forth, moving the one you want into the bigger pane as you move from using the WYSIWYG designer to the XAML editor.

If there is an error in the XAML code, the designer may display a message at its top indicating that there are errors. You can click that label to open the Error list to see the types of errors. You can then fix them in the XAML editor and refresh the designer.

ADDING CONTROLS

The WPF Designer allows you to add controls to a form in several ways that are similar to those provided by the Windows Forms Designer. If you are familiar with that topic you might want to skip this section.

First, if you double-click a control on the Toolbox, Visual Studio places an instance of the control on the window in a default location and at a default size. You can then use the mouse to move and resize the control.

CONTAINER CONFUSION

When you use this method, the new control is placed inside the currently selected container on the window. If the currently selected control is a StackPanel, the new control is placed inside the StackPanel. If the currently selected control is a TextBox that is inside a Grid, the new control is placed inside the Grid.

Second, if you click a control in the Toolbox, the mouse cursor changes to a crosshair while the mouse is over the window. If you click the window, Visual Studio adds a control at that location with a default size. Instead of just clicking, you can click and drag to specify the new control's location and size.

If you hold down the Ctrl key when you select a tool from the Toolbox, that tool remains selected even after you create a control on the window so you can add another instance of the control. For example, suppose you need to create a series of TextBoxes to hold a user's name, street, city, state, and ZIP code. Hold the Ctrl key and click the TextBox tool in the Toolbox. Then you can quickly click five times to create the TextBoxes. Click another tool or the arrow tool in the Toolbox to stop adding TextBoxes.

SELECTING CONTROLS

When you first create a control, the designer selects it. The designer indicates that the control is selected by surrounding it with light gray boxes. In Figure 5-1, the button in the lower right is selected.

To select a control on the designer later, simply click it. You can also click and drag to select a group of controls. As you drag the mouse, the designer displays a rectangle so you can tell which controls will be selected. When you release the mouse button, all of the controls that overlap the rectangle at least partly are selected.

When you select a group of controls, the designer surrounds them with little marks that look like crop marks or frame marks. In Figure 5-2, the text box and the lower-right button are selected.

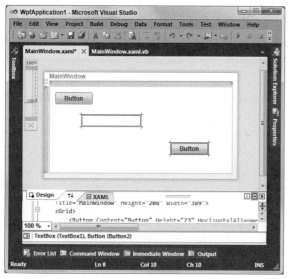

FIGURE 5-2: Selected controls are surrounded by frame marks.

After you have selected some controls, you can Shift+Click to add new controls to the selection or Ctrl+Click to toggle a control's membership in the selection. You can also Shift+Click-and-drag or Ctrl+Click-and-drag to add or toggle groups of controls from the selection.

 You can quickly deselect all controls by pressing the Escape key.

COPYING CONTROLS

A particularly useful technique for building a series of similar controls is to build one and then use copy and paste to make others.

For example, suppose you want to build a contact form with fields for name, street, city, state, and ZIP code. You could build a Label control that contains the text "Name" and a TextBox next to it. You can set the TextBox's properties such as its size, MaxLength, and MaxLines properties. Then you can click and drag to select both controls, press Ctrl+C to copy them to the clipboard, and press Ctrl+V to paste new copies of the controls onto the window. The new TextBox will have the same size, MaxLength, and MaxLines properties as the original TextBox, and will be next to the new Label. You can then drag the two controls into position and paste again to make two more.

MOVING AND SIZING CONTROLS

Moving most controls in the WPF Designer is easy. Simply click and drag the control to its new position.

Container controls work slightly differently. When you select a container such as a Grid, StackPanel, or WrapPanel, the designer displays a drag handle above and to the left of the control. This handle looks like a small box containing arrows pointing up, down, left, and right. Click and drag this handle to move the container and the controls it holds.

To move a group of controls, select the controls that you want. Then click one of the controls and drag to move the whole group. If one of the controls is a container, you can click and drag its move handle to reposition the group.

Note that you can drag controls in and out of container controls such as the Grid or StackPanel. When you drag a control over a new container, the cursor acquires a little curvy arrow and the designer grays out the rest of the window's controls so only the new container is white and you can see where the control will land if you drop it.

As you drag a control, the designer displays snap lines to show how the control lines up with other controls. It displays lines when the control's edges align with another control's edges. For some controls, it displays lines when the control's text baseline aligns with the text baseline of other controls.

Figure 5-3 shows the designer dragging the lower button. Four snap lines show that this control's edges line up with the left and right edges of the upper button, the left edge of the GroupBox control at the bottom, and the upper edge of the Ellipse control to the right. Numbers on each snap line show the distance between the moving control and the controls with which it is aligned.

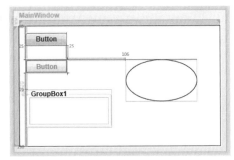

FIGURE 5-3: Snap lines show how moving controls align with other controls.

Resizing a control is almost as easy as moving one. Click a control to select it. Then click and drag one of its edges or one of the light gray boxes surrounding the control to change its size.

WPF controls provide a fairly complex set of properties to determine how they are anchored to their containers. Fortunately, the WPF Designer provides aids to make understanding control anchoring easier.

When you select a control, the designer displays symbols next to the control's edges showing how it is anchored. An arrow from the control's edge to the corresponding container edge means the control's edge remains the same distance from the container's edge even when the container resizes. In Figure 5-1, the selected button's lower and right edges are connected to its container's lower and right edges. When the window resizes, the button moves to stay the same distance from those edges.

A circle near the selected control's edge means that edge remains the same distance from the control's opposite edge. In Figure 5-1, the circles mean the selected button's left and top edges move when its lower and right edges move, so the control stays the same width and height.

If the button's left and top edges were also connected to the container with arrows, the button would grow when the container grew.

> **ATTACHMENT ANXIETY**
>
> The designer will not allow you to remove the attachment from all of a control's edges (so they display circles). If you remove an arrow, the designer changes the opposite side's anchor symbol to a circle if it isn't one already.

You can easily change a control's edge anchors by simply clicking the symbol. If you click a circle, the designer changes that anchor to an arrow and vice versa.

SETTING PROPERTIES

When you select a control, the Properties window allows you to view and edit the control's properties. For Boolean properties, the Properties window displays a box that you can check or uncheck to indicate whether the property's value should be True or False.

For many other properties, you can simply click the property and type a new value for the control in a text box. Unfortunately, the Properties window doesn't give you much help, and you need to know what to type.

For example, you can set a control's Margin property to a blank string to indicate no margins; to a single number to make its left, top, right, and bottom margins the same; to two numbers separated by commas to set the control's left/right and top/bottom margins; or to four numbers separated by commas to set the control's left, top, right, and bottom margins, respectively. You cannot set this property to three numbers or more than four numbers, but the Properties window doesn't give you any hints that this is the case.

SETTING GROUP PROPERTIES

If you select a group of controls, you can sometimes use the Properties window to give all of the controls the same property value all at once. For example, suppose you select a group of TextBoxes. Then you can use the Properties window to give them the same values for their Width, Height, Margin, MaxLength, and many other properties.

Sometimes, this even works if you select different kinds of controls at the same time. For example, if you select some TextBoxes and some Labels, you can set all of the controls' Width, Height, and Margin properties at the same time. You cannot set the controls' MaxLength properties because the Labels do not have a MaxLength property.

ADDING CODE TO CONTROLS

After you have added the appropriate controls to a form and set their properties, the next step is to add code to the form that responds to control events and manipulates the controls.

You can add some kinds of code declaratively in the XAML editor. For example, you can make a trigger respond to a change in a control's property or to a control's event.

You can also write Visual Basic source code to respond to control events just as you would in a Windows Forms application. If you double-click a control on the WPF Designer, Visual Studio creates an empty event handler to catch the control's default event, and it opens the event handler in the code editor.

For example, the following code shows the event handler the IDE built for a Button control. The default event for a Button is Click so this code is a Click event handler. Note that I added the line continuation in the first line so that it would fit in the book. Visual Studio makes that all one long line.

```
Private Sub Button1_Click(ByVal sender As System.Object, _
    ByVal e As System.Windows.RoutedEventArgs) Handles Button1.Click

End Sub
```

> ### SIT BACK AND RELAX
>
> As is the case with Windows Forms, you can use relaxed delegates to remove unneeded parameters from event handlers. For example, the following code shows an event handler with no parameters that catches the btnExit button's Click event:

```
Private Sub btnExit_Click() Handles btnExit.Click

End Sub
```

Another way to build an event handler and open the code editor is to select the control on the WPF Designer. Then click the Events icon (the lightning bolt) near the top of the Properties window to make the window show a list of events for the control. Double-click an event in the window to open a new event handler for it in the code editor.

You can also create a new event handler within the code editor. The upper-left part of the code editor displays a dropdown listing the window's controls. If you select a control from the list, you can then pick an event for that control from a second dropdown in the code editor's upper right. If you select an event, the code editor makes a corresponding empty event handler.

SUMMARY

The WPF Designer allows you to build windows for use in WPF applications. It lets you add controls to the window, and to resize and move the controls. Together with the Properties window, it lets you view and modify control properties, and create event handlers to interact with the controls.

This chapter introduces the WPF Designer and explains how you can take advantage of its features. Other chapters provide much more of the detail that is necessary for building windows. Chapter 11, "Selecting WPF Controls," and Chapter 12, "Using WPF Controls," provide more information about the kinds of controls you can use with the WPF Designer. Chapter 13, "WPF Windows," says more about WPF windows and pages.

Chapter 6, "Visual Basic Code Editor," describes the code editor that you can use to edit the code that sits behind Windows Forms and WPF control events. Later chapters explain the Visual Basic language that you use within the code editor.

Visual Basic Code Editor

The Visual Studio IDE includes editors for many different kinds of documents, including several different kinds of code. For example, it has Hypertext Markup Language (HTML), Extensible Markup Language (XML), Extensible Application Markup Language (XAML), and Visual Basic editors. These editors share some common features, such as displaying comments and keywords in different colors.

As a Visual Basic developer, you will use the Visual Basic code editor frequently, so you should spend a few minutes learning about its specialized features. The most obvious feature of the code editor is that it lets you type code into a module, but the code editor is far more than a simple text editor such as Notepad. It provides many features to make writing correct Visual Basic code easier.

This chapter describes some of the most important of these features. Many of these tools are invaluable for understanding and navigating through the code so, even if you have worked with Visual Studio before, you should take some time to read through this chapter and experiment with the tools it describes.

> **FANTASTIC FEATURES**
>
> The Visual Basic code editor provides many features that are not provided by other Visual Studio editors. For example, the HTML, XML, and XAML editors do not provide breakpoints or features that let you step through executing code. Even the C# code editor is missing some of the features in the Visual Basic editor, such as immediately updated error indicators as you type.

Figure 6-1 shows the code editor displaying some Visual Basic code at runtime. To make referring to the code lines easier, this figure displays line numbers. To display line numbers, invoke the Tools menu's Options command, navigate to the Text Editor ⇨ Basic ⇨ General page, and check the Line Numbers box.

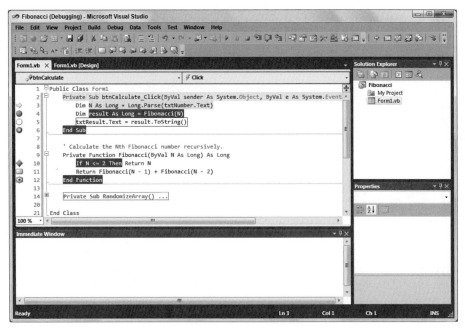

FIGURE 6-1: The Visual Basic code editor provides many features, including line numbers and icons that indicate breakpoints and bookmarks.

MARGIN ICONS

The gray margin to the left of the line numbers contains icons giving information about the corresponding lines of code. The following table describes the icons on lines 3 through 11.

LINE	ICON	MEANING
3	Yellow arrow	Indicates that execution is paused at this line
4	Red circle	Indicates a breakpoint
5	Hollow red circle	Indicates a disabled breakpoint
6	Red circle with plus sign	Indicates a breakpoint with a condition or hit count test
10	Red diamond	Indicates a breakpoint that executes an action when reached
11	Blue and white rectangle	Indicates a bookmark

BREAK TIME

A *breakpoint* is a line of code that you have flagged to stop execution so you can test and debug the program. When you run the program in the IDE, the program stops at the breakpoint and lets you see what routines called what other routines, examine variable values, change variables, and so forth to figure out what's happening. For more information on breakpoints and debugging, see Chapter 7, "Debugging."

These icons can combine to indicate more than one condition. For example, line 12 shows a blue and white rectangle to indicate a bookmark, a hollow red diamond to indicate a disabled breakpoint that performs an action, and a plus sign to indicate that the breakpoint has a condition or hit count test.

Note that the editor marks some of these lines in other ways than just an icon. It highlights the currently executing line with a yellow background. It marks lines that hold enabled breakpoints with white text on a red background.

To add or remove a simple breakpoint, click in the gray margin.

To make a more complex breakpoint, click in the margin to create a simple breakpoint. Then right-click the breakpoint icon and select one of the context menu's commands. The following list describes these commands:

- ➤ **Delete Breakpoint** — Removes the breakpoint.

- ➤ **Disable Breakpoint** — Disables the breakpoint. When the breakpoint is disabled, this command changes to Enable Breakpoint.

- ➤ **Location** — Lets you change the breakpoint's line number. Usually it is easier to click in the margin to remove the old breakpoint and then create a new one.

- ➤ **Condition** — Lets you place a condition on the breakpoint. For example, you can make the breakpoint stop execution only when the variable num_employees has a value greater than 100.

- ➤ **Hit Count** — Lets you set a hit count condition on the breakpoint. For example, you can make the breakpoint stop execution when it has been reached a certain number of times.

- ➤ **Filter** — Lets you restrict the breakpoint so it is only set in certain processes or threads.

- ➤ **When Hit** — Lets you specify the action that the breakpoint performs when it triggers. For example, it might display a message in the Output window or run a macro.

➤ **Edit Labels** — Lets you add labels to a breakpoint. Later you can select this option to view, change, or remove the breakpoint's labels.

➤ **Export** — Lets you export information about the breakpoint into an XML file.

To add or remove a bookmark, place the cursor on a line and then click the Toggle Bookmark tool. You can find this tool, which looks like the blue and white bookmark icon, in the Text Editor toolbar (under the mouse in Figure 6-1) and at the top of the Bookmarks window. Other bookmark tools let you move to the next or previous bookmark, the next or previous bookmark in the current folder, or the next or previous bookmark in the current document. Others let you disable all bookmarks and delete a bookmark.

OUTLINING

By default, the code editor displays an outline view of code. If you look at the first line in Figure 6-1, you'll see a box with a minus sign in it just to the right of the line number. That box represents the outlining for the Form1 class. If you click this box, the editor collapses the class's definition and displays it as a box containing a plus sign. If you then click the new box, the editor expands the class's definition again.

The gray line leading down from the box leads to other code items that are outlined, and that you can expand or collapse to give you the least cluttered view of the code you want to examine. Near the bottom of Figure 6-1, you can see that the RandomizeArray subroutine has been collapsed. The ellipsis and rectangle around the routine name provide an extra indication that this code is hidden.

The editor automatically creates outlining entries for namespaces, classes and their methods, and modules and their methods. You can also use the Region statement to group a section of code for outlining. For example, you can place several related subroutines in a region so you can collapse and expand the routines as a group.

Figure 6-2 shows more examples of outlining. Line 36 begins a region named Randomization Functions that contains three collapsed subroutines. Notice that the corresponding End Region statement includes a comment that I added giving the region's name. This is not required but it makes the code easier to understand when you are looking at the end of a region.

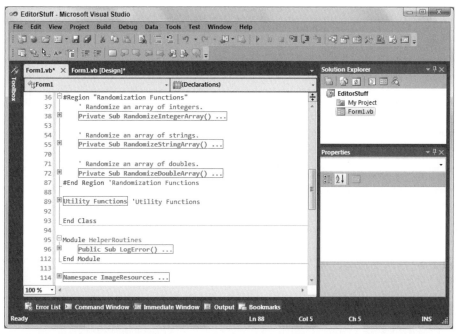

FIGURE 6-2: The code editor outlines namespaces, classes and their methods, modules and their methods, and regions.

Line 89 contains a collapsed region named Utility Functions.

Line 95 starts a module named HelperRoutines that contains one collapsed subroutine.

Finally, line 114 holds the collapsed ImageResources namespace.

Notice that the line numbers skip values for any collapsed lines. For example, the RandomizeIntegerArray subroutine is collapsed on line 38. This subroutine contains 15 lines (including the Sub statement), so the next visible line is labeled 53.

COLLAPSED CODE COMMENTS

Notice that comments before a subroutine are not collapsed with the subroutine. You can make reading collapsed code easier by placing a short descriptive comment before each routine.

TOOLTIPS

If you hover the mouse over a variable at design time, the editor displays a tooltip describing the variable. For example, if you hover over an integer variable named `num_actions`, the tooltip displays "Dim num_actions As Integer."

If you hover over a subroutine or function call (not the routine's definition, but a call to it), the tooltip displays information about that routine. For example, if you hover over the RandomizeArray subroutine (which takes an array of integers as a parameter), the tooltip reads, "Private Sub RandomizeArray(arr() As Integer)."

At runtime, if you hover over a variable, the tooltip displays the variable's value. If the variable is complex (such as an array or structure), the tooltip displays the variable's name and a plus sign. If you click or hover over the plus sign, the tooltip expands to show the variable's members.

In Figure 6-3, the mouse hovered over variable `arr`. The editor displayed a plus sign and the text `arr {Length = 100}`. When the mouse hovered over the plus sign, the editor displayed the values shown in the figure. Moving the mouse over the up and down arrows at the top and bottom of the list makes the values scroll.

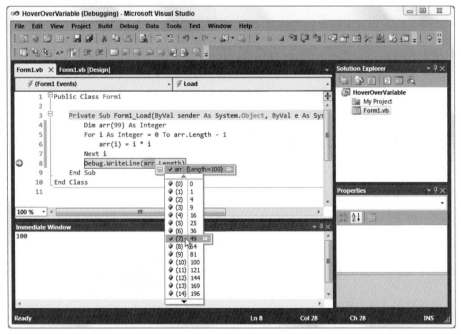

FIGURE 6-3: You can hover the mouse over a variable at runtime to see its value.

If a variable has properties that are references to other objects, you can hover over their plus signs to expand those objects. You can continue following the plus signs to drill into the variable's object hierarchy as deeply as you like.

INTELLISENSE

If you start typing a line of code, the editor tries to anticipate what you will type. For example, if you typed "Me." the editor would know that you are about to use one of the current object's properties or methods.

IntelliSense displays a list of the properties and methods that you might be trying to select. As you type more of the property or method, IntelliSense scrolls to show the choices that match what you have typed.

In Figure 6-4, the code includes the text "Me.Set", so IntelliSense is displaying the current object's methods that begin with the string "Set."

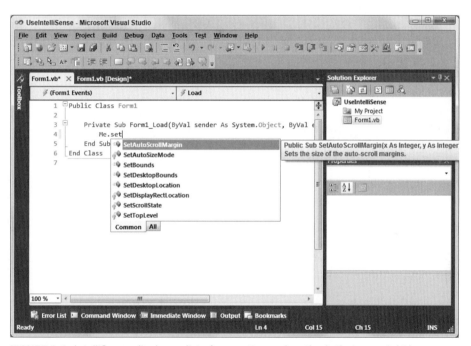

FIGURE 6-4: IntelliSense displays a list of properties and methods that you might be trying to type.

While the IntelliSense window is visible, you can use the up and down arrows to scroll through the list. While IntelliSense is displaying the item that you want to use, you can press the Tab key to accept that item and make IntelliSense type it for you. Press the Escape key to close the IntelliSense window and type the rest manually.

After you finish typing a method and its opening parenthesis, IntelliSense displays information about the method's parameters. Figure 6-5 shows parameter information for a form object's SetBounds method. This method takes four parameters: x, y, width, and height.

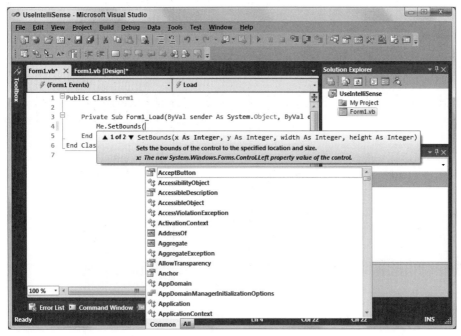

FIGURE 6-5: IntelliSense displays information about a method's parameters.

IntelliSense shows a brief description of the current parameter *x*. As you enter parameter values, IntelliSense moves on to describe the other parameters.

IntelliSense also indicates whether overloaded versions of the method exist. In Figure 6-5, IntelliSense is describing the first version of two available versions. You can use the up and down arrows on the left to move through the list of overloaded versions.

CODE COLORING AND HIGHLIGHTING

The code editor displays different types of code items in different colors (although they all appear black in this book). You can change the colors used for different items by selecting the Tools menu's Options command and opening the Environment ➪ Fonts and Colors option page.

COLOR CONFUSION

To avoid confusion, you should probably leave the editor's colors alone unless you have a good reason to change them.

The following table describes some of the default colors that the code editor uses to highlight different code elements.

ITEM	HIGHLIGHTING
Comment	Green text
Compiler error	Underlined with a wavy blue underline
Keyword	Blue text
Other error	Underlined with a wavy purple underline
Preprocessor keyword	Blue text
Read-only region	Light gray background
Stale code	Purple text
User types	Navy text
Warning	Underlined with a wavy green underline

A few other items that may sometimes be worth changing have white backgrounds and black text by default. These include identifiers (variable names, types, object properties and methods, namespace names, and so forth), numbers, and strings.

When the code editor finds an error in your code, it highlights the error with a wavy underline. If you hover over the underline, the editor displays a tooltip describing the error. If Visual Studio can guess what you are trying to do, it adds a small flat rectangle to the end of the wavy error line to indicate that it may have useful suggestions.

The assignment statement `i = "12"` shown in Figure 6-6 has an error because it tried to assign a string value to an integer variable and that violates the Option Strict On setting. The editor displays the wavy error underline and a suggestion indicator because it knows a way to fix this error. The Error List window at the bottom also shows a description of the error.

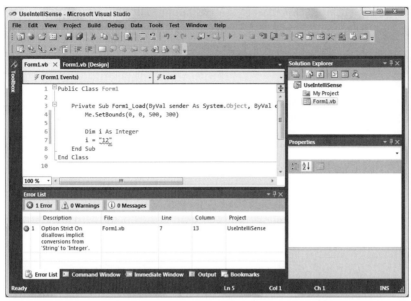

FIGURE 6-6: If the code editor thinks it can figure out what's wrong, it displays a suggestion indicator.

If you hover over the suggestion indicator, the editor displays a tooltip describing the problem and an error icon. If you click the icon, Visual Studio displays a dialog box describing the error and listing the actions that you may want to take. Figure 6-7 shows the suggestion dialog box for the error in Figure 6-6. If you click the text over the revised sample code, or if you double-click the sample code, the editor makes the change.

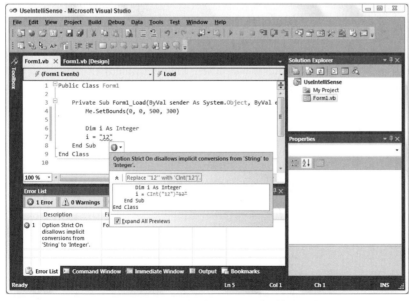

FIGURE 6-7: The error suggestion dialog box proposes likely solutions to an error.

CODE SNIPPETS

A code snippet is a piece of code that you might find useful in many applications. It is stored in a snippet library so that you can quickly insert it into a new application.

Visual Studio comes with hundreds of snippets for performing standard tasks. Before you start working on a complicated piece of code, you should glance at the snippets that are already available to you. In fact, it would be worth your time to use the Snippet Manager available from the Tools menu to take a good look at the available snippets right now before you start a new project. There's little point in reinventing methods for calculating statistical values if someone has already done it and given you the code.

Snippets are stored in simple text files with XML tags, so it is easy to share snippets with other developers. Go to the book's supplemental web page, www.vb-helper.com/vb_prog_ref.htm, to contribute snippets and to download snippets contributed by others.

The following sections explain how to use snippets in your applications and how to create new snippets.

Using Snippets

To insert a snippet, right-click where you want to insert the code and select Insert Snippet to make the editor display a list of snippet categories. Double-click a category to find the kinds of snippets that you want. If you select a snippet, a tooltip pops up to describe it. Figure 6-8 shows the editor preparing to insert the snippet named "Create a public property" from the "VB Prog Ref Snippets" category.

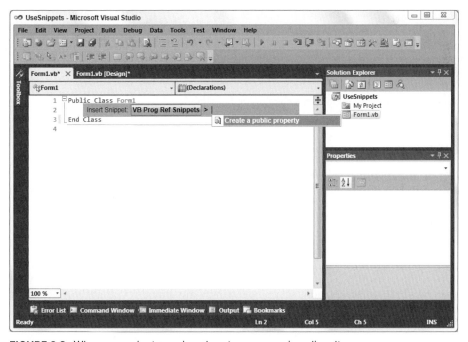

FIGURE 6-8: When you select a code snippet, a pop-up describes it.

Double-click the snippet to insert it into your code.

The snippet may include values that you should replace in your code. These replacement values are highlighted with a light green background, and the first value is initially selected. If you hover the mouse over one of these values, a tooltip appears to describe the value. You can use the Tab key to jump between replacement values.

Figure 6-9 shows the inserted code for this example. The text "An Integer Property" is highlighted and selected. Other selected text includes "Integer," "0," and "MyProperty." The mouse is hovering over the value "An Integer Property," so the tooltip explains that value's purpose.

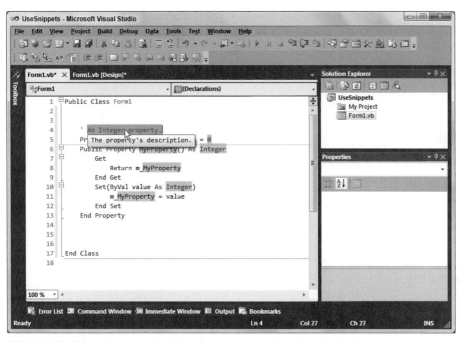

FIGURE 6-9: Values that you should replace in a snippet are highlighted.

Creating Snippets

To create a new snippet, you need to build an XML file containing the property tags to define the snippet and any replacements that the user should make. To tell Visual Studio that the file contains a snippet, save it with a ".snippet" extension.

The following code shows the "Create a public property" snippet used in the previous section. The outer CodeSnippets and CodeSnippet tags are standard and you should not change them.

Use the Title tag in the Header section to describe the snippet.

Inside the Snippet tag, build a Declarations section describing any literal text that the user should replace. This example defines DataType, Description, DefaultValue, and PropertyName symbols. Each literal definition includes an ID, and can include a ToolTip and Description.

After the declarations, the Code tag contains the snippet's source code. The syntax
<![CDATA[. . .]]> tells XML processors to include any characters including carriage returns
between the <![CDATA[and the]]> in the enclosing tag.

```xml
<CodeSnippets xmlns="http://schemas.microsoft.com/VisualStudio/2005/CodeSnippet">
    <CodeSnippet Format="1.0.0">
        <Header>
            <Title>Create a public property</Title>
        </Header>
        <Snippet>
            <Declarations>
                <Literal>
                    <ID>DataType</ID>
                    <ToolTip>The property's data type.</ToolTip>
                    <Default>Integer</Default>
                </Literal>
                <Literal>
                    <ID>Description</ID>
                    <ToolTip>The property's description.</ToolTip>
                    <Default>An Integer property.</Default>
                </Literal>
                <Literal>
                    <ID>DefaultValue</ID>
                    <ToolTip>The property's default value.</ToolTip>
                    <Default>0</Default>
                </Literal>
                <Literal>
                    <ID>PropertyName</ID>
                    <ToolTip>The property's name.</ToolTip>
                    <Default>MyProperty</Default>
                </Literal>
            </Declarations>
            <Code Language="VB">
                <![CDATA[
' $Description$
Private m_$PropertyName$ As $DataType$ = $DefaultValue$
Public Property $PropertyName$() As $DataType$
    Get
        Return m_$PropertyName$
    End Get
    Set(ByVal value As $DataType$)
        m_$PropertyName$ = value
    End Set
End Property
]]>
            </Code>
        </Snippet>
    </CodeSnippet>
</CodeSnippets>
```

Create a directory to hold snippets and save the snippet's XML definition there. To tell Visual
Studio where to look for your snippets, select the Tools menu's Code Snippets Manager command
to display the tool shown in Figure 6-10. In the Language dropdown, select Visual Basic. Then click
the Add button, browse to your snippet directory, and click OK. Now the directory and the snippets
that it contains will be available in the Insert Snippet pop-ups.

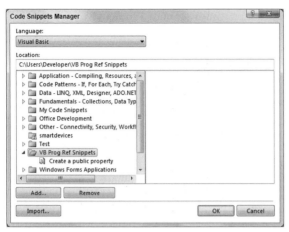

FIGURE 6-10: The Code Snippets Manager lets you add and remove snippet directories.

ARCHITECTURAL TOOLS

The code editor provides several powerful new tools in Visual Basic 2010 that can help you understand the structure of your code and how to navigate through its pieces. They can give you a better understanding of how the pieces of the program fit together, and they can help you track down important code snippets, such as where a variable or type is defined and where one piece of code is called by others.

The following sections describe the most useful of these kinds of architectural tools and explain how to invoke them.

Rename

If you right-click the definition or occurrence of a symbol, such as a variable, subroutine, function, or class, and select Rename, Visual Studio displays a dialog where you can enter a new name for the item. If you enter a name and click OK, Visual Studio updates all references to that symbol. If the symbol is a variable, it changes all references to the variable so they use the new name.

This is much safer than using a simple textual find-and-replace, which can wreak havoc with strings that contain your target string. For example, if you textually replace the variable name "factor" with "issue," your Factorial function becomes Issueial. In contrast, if you right-click the "factor" variable, select Rename, and set the new name to "issue," Visual Studio only updates references to the variable.

CORRUPTED COMMENTS

Unfortunately, Rename still leaves any comments that discuss the factor variable unchanged. You'll have to search the comments to fix them.

Go To Definition

If you right-click a symbol or type, such as a variable, function, or class, and select Go To Definition, the code editor jumps to the location where the symbol is defined. For example, it would jump to a variable's declaration or a function's definition.

If the symbol you clicked is defined by Visual Basic or a library rather than your code, Visual Studio opens the Object Browser and displays the symbol's definition there.

Go To Type Definition

If you right-click a variable and click Go To Type Definition, the code editor jumps to the location where the symbol's data type is defined. For example, if you right-click a variable of type Employee, the editor would jump to the definition of the Employee class.

If you click a variable that has one of the pre-defined data types such as Integer, Double, or String, the editor displays the Object Browser entry for that type.

> **UNEXPECTED DEFINITIONS**
>
> If you right-click a function call and select Go To Type Definition, the editor goes to the definition of the data type that the function returns. This can be fairly confusing. You will probably learn more by using the Go To Definition command instead.

Highlight References

As of Visual Studio 2010, whenever the cursor sits on a symbol, the code editor highlights all references to that symbol by giving them a light gray background. It's a subtle effect, so you may not even notice it unless you know to look for it.

Reference highlighting makes it easier to see where a symbol such as a variable or subroutine is used, although it only really works locally. If a subroutine is called from many pieces of code that are far apart, you'll only see the ones that are currently visible in the code editor's window.

When you have a reference highlighted, you can use Ctrl+Shift+Up Arrow and Ctrl+Shift+Down Arrow to move to the next or previous reference.

To learn more about references to a symbol that are farther away, use the Find All References command described next.

Find All References

If you right-click a symbol such as a subroutine or variable and select "Find All References," Visual Studio displays a list of everywhere in the program that uses that symbol.

For example, if you right-click a call to a function named Fibonacci, the list includes all calls to that function and the function's definition.

You can double-click any of the listed references to make the code editor quickly jump to that reference.

Generate From Usage

As of Visual Studio 2010, the code editor can provide methods for automatically generating pieces of code. These come in the form of suggested error corrections.

For example, suppose you have not defined a Person class but you type the following code:

```
Dim new_student As New Person()
```

The code editor correctly flags this as an error because the Person class doesn't exist. It underlines the word Person with a blue squiggly line and displays a short red rectangle near it. If you hover over the rectangle, you'll see an error icon. If you then click the icon, Visual Studio displays a list of suggested corrections that include:

➤ Change Person to Version

➤ Generate 'Class Person'

➤ Generate new type

The first choice assumes you have made a simple spelling error.

The second choice creates a new empty class named Person. You can fill in its properties and methods later.

The third choice displays the dialog shown in Figure 6-11 so you can make Person another data type that might make sense such as an Enum or Structure. The dialog lets you set the type's access to Default, Friend, or Public, and to specify the file where Visual Studio should create the new type.

Now suppose you type the following code:

```
new_student.FirstName = "Zaphod"
```

The code editor also flags this statement as an error. If you click the error icon this time, the suggested solution says:

Generate a property stub for 'FirstName' in 'WindowsApplication1.Person'

If you click this text, Visual Studio adds the following simple property to the Person class:

```
Property FirstName As String
```

FIGURE 6-11: The New Type dialog lets you create a new Class, Enum, or Structure.

The code editor can also generate a constructor for the class if you enter the following code:

```
Dim another_person As New Person("Trillian")
```

This code is flagged as an error because no constructor is defined that takes a parameter. The error suggestions can make a constructor for you, although you'll need to edit it to give it code that handles the parameter.

This also causes a new error because the class now has a constructor that takes a single parameter, but not one that takes no parameters, so the earlier statement `Dim new_student As New Person()` is flagged as an error.

By now you can probably guess what's coming: if you click the error icon, the suggestions can make a constructor for this case, too.

Similarly, you can use the error suggestions to generate stubs for subroutines and functions. Simply use the new items as if they already exist, use the error suggestions to build stubs, and then fill in the appropriate code.

THE CODE EDITOR AT RUNTIME

The code editor behaves slightly differently at runtime and design time. Many of its design-time features still work. Breakpoints, bookmarks, IntelliSense, and snippets still work.

At runtime, the editor adds new tools for controlling the program's execution. Right-click a value and select Add Watch or QuickWatch to examine and monitor the value. Use the Step Into, Step Over, and Step Out commands on the Debug menu or toolbar to make the program walk through the code. Hover the mouse over a variable to see a tooltip giving the variable's value (see the section "Tooltips" earlier in this chapter for more information).

ESSENTIAL SHORTCUTS

Some very handy runtime shortcuts are F5 (Start Debugging), F8 (Step Into), and Shift+F8 (Step Over). Some particularly handy code editing shortcuts are F9 (Toggle Breakpoint) and Shift+Space (Open IntelliSense). You might want to write down these and any others that you use frequently.

(Note that some shortcuts are different if you don't have Visual Studio set up for Visual Basic development. If the IDE is customized for C# or general development, Step Over is F10 and Step Into is F11.)

Right-click a statement and select Show Next Statement to move the cursor to the next statement that the program will execute. Select Run To Cursor to make the program continue running until it reaches the cursor's current line.

Right-click and select Set Next Statement to make the program skip to a new location. You can also drag the yellow arrow indicating the next statement to a new location in the left margin.

REPOSITION RESTRICTIONS

Some restrictions exist as to where you can move the execution position. For example, you cannot jump out of one routine and into another.

By using all of these runtime features, you can walk through the code while it executes and learn exactly what it is doing at each step. You can see the values of variables, follow paths of execution through If Then statements, step in and out of routines, and run until particular conditions are met.

For more information on the Debug menu and its submenus, see the section "Debug" in Chapter 2, "Menus, Toolbars, and Windows." For more information on debugging techniques, see Chapter 7, "Debugging."

You can discover other runtime features by exploring the editor at runtime. Right-click different parts of the editor to see which commands are available in that mode.

SUMMARY

The Visual Basic code editor is one of the most important IDE windows for Visual Basic developers. Though you can use the Windows Forms Designer alone to place controls on a form, the form can't do much without code behind those controls.

The Visual Basic code editor lets you type code into a module, but it also does much more. It provides tooltips that let you view variable values; outlining that lets you expand and collapse code, so you can focus on your current task; IntelliSense that helps you remember what methods are available and what their parameters are; code coloring and highlighting that immediately flags errors; and code snippets that let you save and reuse complex pieces of code that perform frequent tasks. Architectural tools let you quickly find symbol and type definitions, jump to specific pieces of code, and easily see where a symbol is being used in the currently visible code. The code editor can even automatically generate stubs for classes, constructors, properties, and methods.

Many of these tools help you understand how the code works as you write it. Chapter 7, "Debugging," explains IDE tools that help you understand the code when it runs. Those tools let you walk through the code as it executes to see exactly what it is doing and what it is doing wrong.

7

Debugging

The Visual Basic code editor described in Chapter 6, "Visual Basic Code Editor," provides tools that make writing Visual Basic applications relatively easy. Features such as error indicators, tooltips, and IntelliSense help you write code that obeys the rules of Visual Basic syntax.

No code editor or any other tool can guarantee that the code you write actually does what you want it to do. Debugging is the process of modifying the code to make it run and produce correct results.

NUNIT NOTE

Testing tools such as NUnit (www.nunit.org) can do a lot to ensure that your code runs correctly, but they only work if the code you write does the right things. If you need a billing system but write an inventory application, no tool will save you.

Depending on the application's complexity, debugging can be extremely difficult. Although Visual Studio cannot do your debugging for you, it does include features that make debugging easier. It allows you to stop execution while the program is running so you can examine and modify variables, explore data structures, and step through the code to follow its execution path.

This chapter explains Visual Basic's most important debugging tools. It describes the tools available in the Debug menu and the other IDE windows that are most useful for debugging.

THE DEBUG MENU

The Debug menu contains commands that help you debug a program. These commands help you run the program in the debugger, move through the code, set and clear breakpoints, and generally follow the code's execution to see what it's doing and hopefully what it's doing wrong.

GIVE ME A BREAK

A breakpoint is a line of code that is marked to temporarily stop execution so you can test the code and figure out what's happening. The section "The Breakpoints Window" later in this chapter says a lot more about how to use breakpoints but breakpoints are mentioned a lot between now and then so it's useful to have some idea of what they are now.

Effectively using these debugging tools can make finding problems in the code much easier, so you should spend some time learning how to use them. They can mean the difference between finding a tricky error in minutes, hours, or days.

The commands visible in the Debug window change depending on several conditions, such as the type of file you have open, whether the program is running, the line of code that contains the cursor, and whether that line contains a breakpoint. The following list briefly describes the most important menu items available while execution is stopped at a line of code that contains a breakpoint:

➤ **Windows** — This submenu's commands display other debugging-related windows. This submenu is described in more detail in the following section, "The Debug ➪ Windows Submenu."

➤ **Continue** — This command resumes program execution. The program runs until it finishes, it reaches another breakpoint, it encounters an error, or you stop it.

➤ **Break All** — This command stops execution of all programs running within the debugger. This may include more than one program if you are debugging more than one application at the same time. This can be useful, for example, if two programs work closely together.

➤ **Stop Debugging** — This command halts the program's execution and ends its debugging session. The program stops immediately, so it does not get a chance to execute any cleanup code that it may contain.

➤ **Step Into** — This command makes the debugger execute the current line of code. If that code invokes a function, subroutine, or some other procedure, the point of execution moves into that procedure. It is not always obvious whether a line of code invokes a procedure. For example, a line of code that sets an object's property may be simply setting a value or it may be invoking a property procedure.

➤ **Step Over** — This command makes the debugger execute the current line of code. If that code invokes a function, subroutine, or some other procedure, the debugger calls that routine but does not step into it, so you don't need to step through its code. However, if a breakpoint is set inside that routine, execution will stop at the breakpoint.

➤ **Step Out** — This command makes the debugger run until it leaves the routine it is currently executing. Execution pauses when the program reaches the line of code that called this routine.

➤ **QuickWatch** — This command displays a dialog box that gives information about the selected code object. Figure 7-1 shows the dialog box displaying information about a TextBox control named txtDirectory. If you look closely, you can see some of the control's properties including TabIndex, TabStop, Tag, and Text.

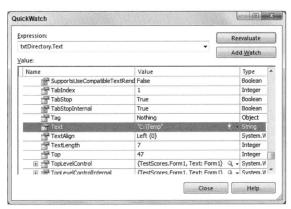

FIGURE 7-1: The QuickWatch dialog box lets you examine an object's properties and optionally set a new watch on it.

If you right-click a property's value and select Edit Value, you can change it within the dialog box. If you click the Add Watch button, the debugger adds the expression to the Watch window shown in Figure 7-2. You can also highlight a variable's name in the code and drag and drop it into a Watch window to create a watch very quickly. Right-click a watch in this window and select Delete Watch to remove it.

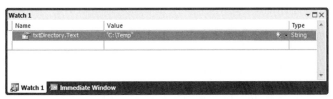

FIGURE 7-2: The Watch window lets you easily track expression values.

➤ **Exceptions** — This command displays the dialog box shown in Figure 7-3. When you select a Thrown check box, the debugger stops whenever the selected type of error occurs. If you select a User-unhandled check box, the debugger stops when the selected type of error occurs and the program does not catch it with error-handling code.

For example, suppose that your code calls a subroutine that causes a divide-by-zero exception. Use the dialog box to select Common Language Runtime Exceptions/System/System.

DivideByZeroException (use the Find button to find it quickly). When you select the Thrown check box, the debugger stops in the subroutine when the divide-by-zero exception occurs, even if the code is protected by an error handler. When you select the User-unhandled check box, the debugger stops only if no error handler is active when the error occurs.

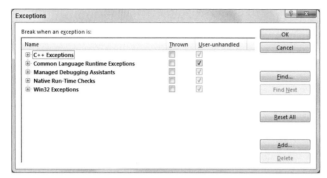

FIGURE 7-3: The Exceptions dialog box lets you determine how Visual Basic handles uncaught exceptions.

➤ **Toggle Breakpoint** — This command toggles whether the current code line contains a breakpoint. When execution reaches a line with an active breakpoint, execution pauses so you can examine the code and program variables. You can also toggle a line's breakpoint by clicking the margin to the left of the line in the code editor or by placing the cursor in the line of code and pressing F9.

➤ **New Breakpoint** — This submenu contains the Break At Function command. This command displays a dialog box that lets you specify a function where the program should break.

➤ **Delete All Breakpoints** — This command removes all breakpoints from the entire solution.

THE DEBUG ⇨ WINDOWS SUBMENU

The Debug menu's Windows submenu contains commands that display debugging-related windows. The following list briefly describes the most useful of these commands. The two sections that follow this one provide more detail about the Breakpoints, Command, and Immediate windows.

➤ **Immediate** — This command displays the Immediate window, where you can type and execute ad hoc Visual Basic statements. The section "The Command and Immediate Windows" later in this chapter describes this window in a bit more detail.

➤ **Locals** — This command displays the Locals window shown in Figure 7-4. The Locals window displays the values of variables defined in the local context. To change a value, click it and enter the new value. Click the plus and minus signs to the left of a value to expand or collapse it. For example, the Me entry shown in Figure 7-4 is an object with lots of properties that have their own values. Click the plus sign to expand the object's entry and view its properties. Those properties may also be objects, so you may be able to expand them further.

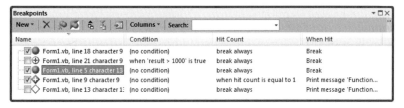

Locals		
Name	Value	Type
⊞ ◆ Me	{TestScores.Form1, Text: Form1} 🔍 ▾	TestScore
⊞ ◆ base_rate	{Length=12}	Decimal()
⊞ ◆ e	{X = 45 Y = 15 Button = Left {1048576}}	System.E
◆ i	0	Integer
◆ j	287	Integer
⊞ ◆ sender	{Text = "Button1"}	Object
◆ txt	"C:\Temp" 🔍 ▾	String
⊟ ◆ values	{Length=6}	Integer()
◆ (0)	8237	Integer
◆ (1)	4376	Integer
◆ (2)	901987	Integer
◆ (3)	3287	Integer
◆ (4)	17843	Integer
◆ (5)	328797	Integer
◆ x	365.2136	Double
◆ y	-1.3278E+16	Double

FIGURE 7-4: The Locals window displays the values of variables defined in the local context.

➤ **Breakpoints** — This command displays the Breakpoints window shown in Figure 7-5. This dialog box shows the breakpoints, their locations, and their conditions. Select or clear the check boxes on the left to enable or disable breakpoints. Right-click a breakpoint to edit its location, condition, hit count, and action.

Use the dialog box's toolbar to create a new function breakpoint, delete a breakpoint, delete all breakpoints, enable or disable all breakpoints, go to a breakpoint's source code, and change the columns displayed by the dialog. Right-click a breakpoint to change its condition (a condition that determines whether the breakpoint is activated), hit count (a count that determines whether the breakpoint is activated), and When Hit (action to take when activated). See the section "The Breakpoints Window" later in this chapter for more detail.

Breakpoints			
New ▾ ✕ 🔍 📁 📑 📑 ⤵ Columns ▾ Search: ▾			
Name	Condition	Hit Count	When Hit
☑● Form1.vb, line 18 character 9	(no condition)	break always	Break
☐⊕ Form1.vb, line 21 character 9	when 'result > 1000' is true	break always	Break
☑● Form1.vb, line 5 character 13	(no condition)	break always	Break
☑◇ Form1.vb, line 9 character 9	(no condition)	when hit count is equal to 1	Print message 'Function...
☐◇ Form1.vb, line 13 character 1:	(no condition)	break always	Print message 'Function...

FIGURE 7-5: The Breakpoints window helps you manage breakpoints.

➤ **Output** — This command displays the Output window. This window displays compilation results and output produced by Debug and Trace statements.

➤ **Autos** — This command displays the Autos window shown in Figure 7-6. This window displays the values of local and global variables used in the current line of code and in the previous line.

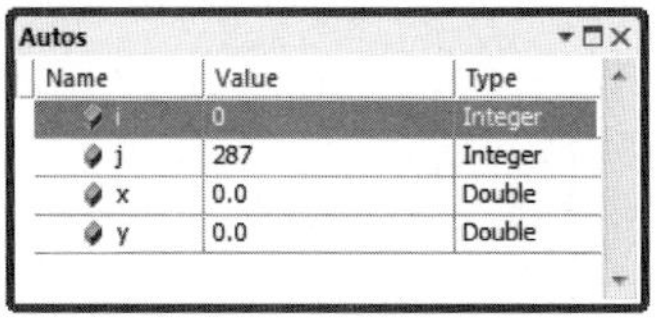

Autos			▼ □ ×
Name	Value	Type	
⏺ i	0	Integer	
⏺ j	287	Integer	
⏺ x	0.0	Double	
⏺ y	0.0	Double	

FIGURE 7-6: The Autos window displays the variables used in the current code statement and the three statements before and the three after.

➤ **Call Stack** — This command displays the Call Stack window shown in Figure 7-7. This window lists the routines that have called other routines to reach the program's current point of execution. In Figure 7-7 the program is at line 49 in the function FindEmployee. That function was called by function SearchDatabase at line 36, and that function was called by the btnLocals_Click event handler.

Double-click a line to jump to the corresponding code in the program's call stack. This technique lets you move up the call stack to examine the code that called the routines that are running.

➤ **Threads** — This command displays the Threads window shown in Figure 7-8. A *thread* is a separate execution path that is running. A *multi-threaded application* can have several

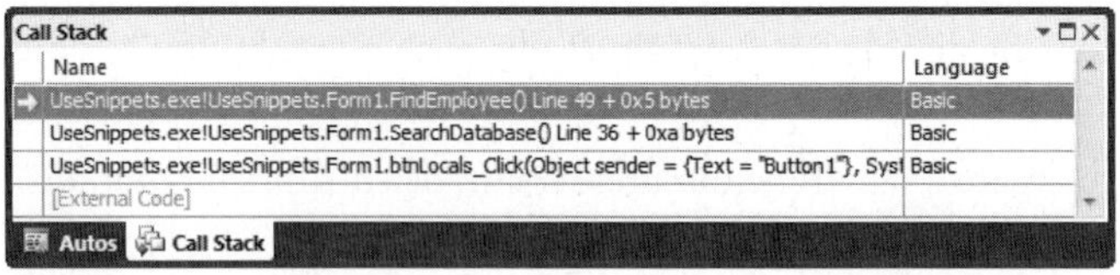

Call Stack		▼ □ ×
Name	Language	
➡ UseSnippets.exe!UseSnippets.Form1.FindEmployee() Line 49 + 0x5 bytes	Basic	
UseSnippets.exe!UseSnippets.Form1.SearchDatabase() Line 36 + 0xa bytes	Basic	
UseSnippets.exe!UseSnippets.Form1.btnLocals_Click(Object sender = {Text = "Button1"}, Sys Basic		
[External Code]		

🖼 Autos 🔧 Call Stack

FIGURE 7-7: The Call Stack window shows which routines have called which to get to the program's current point of execution.

threads running to perform more than one task at the same time. The Threads window lets you control the threads' priority and suspended status.

The last line in Figure 7-8 has the location WindowsApplication1.Form1.FindEmployee, indicating that this thread is executing the FindEmployee routine in the Form1 module in program WindowsApplication1. The arrow on the left indicates that this is the currently active thread.

Right-click a thread and select Freeze to suspend it. Right-click the thread again and select Thaw to make it resume execution. Double-click a thread or right-click it and select Switch To Thread to activate that thread.

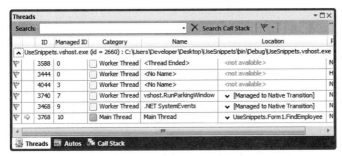

FIGURE 7-8: The Threads window displays information about the program's threads of execution.

➤ Parallel Tasks — This command lists all of the application's running tasks. This is useful for debugging parallel applications.

➤ Parallel Stacks — This command shows the call stacks for tasks running in parallel.

➤ Watch — The Watch submenu contains the commands Watch 1, Watch 2, Watch 3, and Watch 4. These commands display four different watch windows that let you easily keep track of variable values. When you create a watch using the Debug menu's QuickWatch command described earlier, the new watch is placed in the Watch 1 window (shown in Figure 7-2). You can click and drag watches from one watch window to another to make a copy of the watch in the second window.

You can also click the Name column in the empty line at the bottom of a watch window and enter an expression to watch.

WONDERFUL WATCHES

A useful IDE trick is to drag Watch windows 2, 3, and 4 onto Watch 1 so that they all become tabs on the same window. Then you can easily use the tabs to group and examine four sets of watches.

➤ Modules — This command displays the Modules window shown in Figure 7-9. This window displays information about the DLL and EXE files used by the program. It shows each module's file name and path. It indicates whether the module is optimized, whether it is your code (rather than an installed library), and whether debugging symbols are loaded. The window shows each module's load order (lower-numbered modules are loaded first), the version, and timestamp. Click a column to sort the modules by that column.

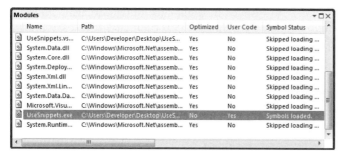

FIGURE 7-9: The Modules window displays information about the modules used by the program.

➤ **Processes** — This window lists processes that are attached to the Visual Studio session. This includes any programs launched by Visual Studio and processes that you attached to using the Debug menu's Attach to Process command.

Usually, when these debug windows are visible at runtime, they occupy separate tabs in the same area at the bottom of the IDE. That lets you switch between them quickly and easily without them taking up too much space.

THE BREAKPOINTS WINDOW

A *breakpoint* is a line of code that you have flagged to stop execution. When the program reaches that line, execution stops and Visual Studio displays the code in a code editor window. This lets you examine or set variables, see which routine called the one containing the code, and otherwise try to figure out what the code is doing.

The Breakpoints window lists all the breakpoints you have defined for the program. This is useful for a couple of reasons. First, if you define a lot of breakpoints, it can be hard to find them all later. Although other commands let you disable, enable, or remove all of the breakpoints at once, there are times when you may need to find a particular breakpoint.

A common debugging strategy is to comment out broken code, add new code, and set a breakpoint near the modification so that you can see how the new code works. When you have finished testing the code, you probably want to remove either the old or new code, so you don't want to blindly remove all of the program's breakpoints.

The Breakpoints window lists all of the breakpoints and, if you double-click a breakpoint in the list, you can easily jump to the code that holds it.

Source code control systems such as Visual SourceSafe track the entire change history of your code. Later, if you find a problem with the code, you can compare the current version to previous versions to see what has changed. In the worst case, you can back out the changes and recover an earlier version. This can be a lot easier than manually trying to remember and remove the changes.

The Breakpoints window also lets you modify the breakpoints you have defined. Select or clear the boxes on the left to enable or disable breakpoints. Use the dialog's toolbar to enable or disable all breakpoints, clear all breakpoints, or jump to a breakpoint's location in the source code.

Right-click a breakpoint and select Condition to display the dialog shown in Figure 7-10. By default, a breakpoint stops execution whenever it is reached. You can use this dialog box to add an additional condition that determines whether the breakpoint activates when reached. In this example, the breakpoint stops execution only if the expression (i = j) And (i > 20) is True when the code reaches the breakpoint.

FIGURE 7-10: The Breakpoint Condition dialog box lets you specify a condition that determines whether Visual Studio stops at the breakpoint.

PERFORMANCE ISSUE

Note that specifying a breakpoint condition can slow execution considerably because Visual Basic must evaluate the condition frequently.

Right-click a breakpoint and select Hit Count to display the Breakpoint Hit Count dialog box shown in Figure 7-11. Each time the code reaches a breakpoint, it increments the breakpoint's hit count. You can use this dialog box to make the breakpoint's activation depend on the hit count's value.

From the drop-down list you can select one of the following options:

FIGURE 7-11: The Breakpoint Hit Count dialog box lets you make a breakpoint's activation depend on the number of times the code has reached it.

➤ break always

➤ break when the hit count is equal to

➤ break when the hit count is a multiple of

➤ break when the hit count is greater than or equal to

If you select any but the first option, you can enter a value in the text box and the program will pause execution when the breakpoint has been reached the appropriate number of times. For example, if you select the option "break when the hit count is a multiple of" and enter 2 into the text box, execution will pause every second time it reaches the breakpoint.

Right-click a breakpoint and select When Hit to display the When Breakpoint Is Hit dialog box shown in Figure 7-12. This dialog box lets you specify the actions that Visual Basic takes when the breakpoint is activated. Select the "Print a message" check box to make the program display a message in the Output window. Select the "Run a macro" check box to make the program execute a VBA macro. Select the "Continue execution" check box to make the program continue running without stopping.

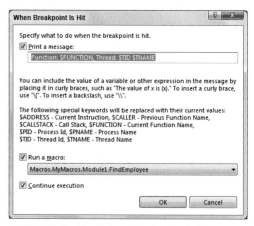

FIGURE 7-12: The When Breakpoint Is Hit dialog box lets you determine what actions Visual Basic takes when the breakpoint is activated.

THE COMMAND AND IMMEDIATE WINDOWS

The Command and Immediate windows enable you to execute commands while the program is stopped in the debugger. One of the more useful commands in each of these windows is the `Debug` `.Print` statement. For example, the command `Debug.Print x` displays the value of the variable x.

You can use a question mark as an abbreviation for `Debug.Print`. The following text shows how the command might appear in the Command window. Here the > symbol is the command prompt provided by the window and `123` is the result: the value of variable x. In the Immediate window, the statement would not include the > character.

```
>? x
123
```

The command `>immed` tells the Command window to open the Immediate window. Conversely, the command `>cmd` (you need to type the > in the Immediate window) tells the Immediate window to open the Command window.

Although there is some overlap between these two windows, they serve two mostly different purposes. The Command window can issue commands to the Visual Studio IDE. Typically, these are commands that appear in menus or toolbars, or that could appear in menus and toolbars. For example, the following command uses the Debug menu's QuickWatch command to open a QuickWatch window for the variable `first_name`:

```
>Debug.QuickWatch first_name
```

One particularly useful command is `Tools.Alias`. This command lists command aliases defined by the IDE. For example, it indicates that `?` is the alias for `Debug.Print` and that `??` is the alias for `Debug.QuickWatch`.

The Command window includes some IntelliSense support. If you type the name of a menu, for example Debug or Tools, IntelliSense will display the commands available within that menu.

While the Command window issues commands to the IDE, the Immediate window executes Visual Basic statements. For example, suppose that you have written a subroutine named `CheckPrinter`. Then the following statement in the Immediate window executes that subroutine:

```
CheckPrinter
```

You can execute subroutines in the Immediate window to quickly and easily test routines without writing user interface code to handle all possible situations. You can call a subroutine or function, passing it different parameters to see what happens. If you set breakpoints within the routine, the debugger will pause there.

You can also set the values of global variables and then call routines that use them. The following Immediate window commands set the value of the `m_PrinterName` variable and then call the `CheckPrinter` subroutine:

```
m_PrinterName = "LP_REMOTE"
CheckPrinter
```

You can execute much more complex statements in the Command and Immediate windows. For example, suppose that your program uses the following statement to open a file for reading:

```
Dim fs As FileStream = File.OpenRead( _
  "C:\Program Files\Customer Orders\Summary" & _
  DateTime.Now().ToString("yymmdd") & ".dat")
```

Suppose that the program is failing because some other part of the program is deleting the file. You can type the following code (all on one line) into the Immediate window to see if the file exists. As you step through different pieces of the code, you can use this statement again to see if the file has been deleted.

```
?System.IO.File.Exists("C:\Program Files\Customer Orders\Summary" &
  DateTime.Now().ToString("yymmdd") & ".dat")
```

The window evaluates the complicated string expression to produce a file name. It then uses the System.IO.File.Exists command to determine whether the file exists and displays True or False accordingly.

SUMMARY

Although Visual Basic cannot debug your applications for you, it provides all of the tools you need to get the job done. By using the tools in the Debug menu and the IDE's debugging-related windows, you can get a good idea about what your program is doing or doing wrong.

The chapters in the first part of the book describe the basic pieces of the development environment. They describe the windows, menus, and toolbars that you use to build and debug Visual Basic applications.

The next part of the book provides more detail about the steps you follow to build an application before you debug it. Chapter 8, "Selecting Windows Forms Controls," describes the most common controls that you can use to build Windows Forms applications.

PART II
Getting Started

Selecting Windows Forms Controls

A *control* is a programming entity that has a graphical component. A control sits on a form and interacts with the user, providing information and possibly allowing the user to manipulate it. Text boxes, labels, buttons, scroll bars, drop-down lists, menu items, toolstrips, and just about everything else that you can see and interact with in a Windows application is a control.

Controls are an extremely important part of any interactive application. They give information to the user (Label, ToolTip, TreeView, PictureBox) and organize the information so that it's easier to understand (GroupBox, Panel, TabControl). They enable the user to enter data (TextBox, RichTextBox, ComboBox, MonthCalendar), select options (RadioButton, CheckBox, ListBox), tell the application to take action (Button, MenuStrip, ContextMenuStrip), and interact with objects outside of the application (OpenFileDialog, SaveFileDialog, PrintDocument, PrintPreviewDialog). Some controls also provide support for other controls (ImageList, ToolTip, ContextMenuStrip, ErrorProvider).

This chapter provides only a very brief description of the standard Windows Forms controls together with some tips that can help you decide which control to use for different purposes. Appendix G, "Windows Forms Controls and Components," covers the controls in much greater detail, describing each control's most useful properties, methods, and events.

FIGURE 8-1: Visual Basic provides a large number of standard controls for Windows Forms.

CONTROLS OVERVIEW

Figure 8-1 shows the Visual Basic Toolbox displaying the standard Windows Forms controls. Because you can add and remove controls on the Toolbox, you may see a slightly different selection of tools on your computer.

The following table briefly describes the controls shown in Figure 8-1 in the order in which they appear in the figure (starting at the top, or row 1, and reading from left to right).

CONTROL	PURPOSE
Row 1	
Pointer	This is the pointer tool, not a control. Click this tool to deselect any selected controls on a form. Then you can select new controls.
BackgroundWorker	Executes a task asynchronously and notifies the main program when it is finished.
BindingNavigator	Provides a user interface for navigating through a data source. For example, it provides buttons that let the user move back and forth through the data, add records, delete records, and so forth.
BindingSource	Encapsulates a form's data source and provides methods for navigating through the data.
Button	A simple push button. When the user clicks it, the program can perform some action.
CheckBox	A box that the user can check and clear.
CheckedListBox	A list of items with check boxes that the user can check and clear.
ColorDialog	Lets the user pick a standard or custom color.
ComboBox	A text box with an attached list or drop-down list that the user can use to enter or select a textual value.
ContextMenuStrip	A menu that appears when the user right-clicks a control. You set a control's ContextMenuStrip property to this control, and the rest is automatic.
Row 2	
DataGridView	A powerful grid control that lets you display large amounts of complex data with hierarchical or Web-like relationships relatively easily.
DataSet	An in-memory store of data with properties similar to those of a relational database. It holds objects representing tables containing rows and columns, and can represent many database concepts such as indexes and foreign key relationships.
DateTimePicker	Lets the user select a date and time in one of several styles.
DirectoryEntry	Represents a node in an Active Directory hierarchy.
DirectorySearcher	Performs searches of an Active Directory hierarchy.

CONTROL	PURPOSE
DomainUpDown	Lets the user scroll through a list of choices by clicking up-arrow and down-arrow buttons.
ErrorProvider	Displays an error indicator next to a control that is associated with an error.
EventLog	Provides access to Windows event logs.
FileSystemWatcher	Notifies the application of changes to a directory or file.
FlowLayoutPanel	Displays the controls it contains in rows or columns. For example, when laying out rows, it places controls next to each other horizontally in a row until it runs out of room and then it starts a new row.
Row 3	
FolderBrowserDialog	Lets the user select a folder.
FontDialog	Lets the user specify a font's characteristics (name, size, boldness, and so forth).
GroupBox	Groups related controls for clarity. It also defines a default *RadioButton* group for any RadioButtons that it contains.
HelpProvider	Displays help for controls that have help if the user sets focus on the control and presses F1.
HScrollBar	A horizontal scroll bar.
ImageList	Contains a series of images that other controls can use. For example, the images that a TabControl displays on its tabs are stored in an associated *ImageList* control. Your code can also pull images from an ImageList for its own use.
Label	Displays text that the user cannot modify or select by clicking and dragging.
LinkLabel	Displays a label, parts of which may be hyperlinks. When the user clicks a hyperlink, the program can take some action.
ListBox	Displays a list of items that the user can select. Depending on the control's properties, the user can select one or several items.
ListView	Displays a list of items in one of four possible views: LargeIcon, SmallIcon, List, and Details.

continues

(continued)

CONTROL	PURPOSE
Row 4	
MaskedTextBox	A text box that requires the input to match a specific format (such as a phone number or ZIP code format).
MenuStrip	Represents the form's main menus, submenus, and menu items.
MessageQueue	Provides communication between different applications.
MonthCalendar	Displays a calendar that allows the user to select a range of dates.
NotifyIcon	Displays an icon in the system tray or status area.
NumericUpDown	Lets the user change a number by clicking up-arrow and down-arrow buttons.
OpenFileDialog	Lets the user select a file for opening.
PageSetupDialog	Lets the user specify properties for printed pages. For example, it lets the user specify the printer's paper tray, page size, margins, and orientation (portrait or landscape).
Panel	A control container. Using the control's Anchor and Dock properties, you can make the control resize itself so that its child controls resize themselves in turn. The control can automatically provide scroll bars and defines a RadioButton group for any RadioButtons that it contains.
PerformanceCounter	Provides access to Windows performance counters.
Row 5	
PictureBox	Displays a picture. Also provides a useful drawing surface.
PrintDialog	Displays a standard print dialog box. The user can select the printer, pages to print, and printer settings.
PrintDocument	Represents output to be sent to the printer. A program can use this object to print and display print previews.
PrintPreviewControl	Displays a print preview within one of the application's forms.
PrintPreviewDialog	Displays a print preview in a standard dialog box.
Process	Allows the program to interact with processes, and to start and stop them.
ProgressBar	Displays a series of colored bars to show the progress of a long operation.

CONTROL	PURPOSE
PropertyGrid	Displays information about an object in a format similar to the one used by the Properties window at design time.
RadioButton	Represents one of an exclusive set of options. When the user selects a RadioButton, Visual Basic deselects all other RadioButton controls in the same group. Groups are defined by GroupBox and Panels controls and the Form class.
RichTextBox	A text box that supports Rich Text extensions. The control can display different pieces of text with different font names, sizes, bolding, and so forth. It also provides paragraph-level formatting for justification, bullets, hanging indentation, and more.
Row 6	
SaveFileDialog	Lets the user select the name of a file where the program will save data.
SerialPort	Represents a serial port and provides methods for controlling, reading, and writing it.
ServiceController	Represents a Windows service and lets you manipulate services.
SplitContainer	Lets the user drag a divider vertically or horizontally to split available space between two areas within the control.
Splitter	Provides a divider that the user can drag to split available space between two controls. The Dock properties and stacking orders of the controls and the Splitter determine how the controls are arranged and resized. The *SplitContainer* control automatically provides a Splitter between two containers, so it is usually easier and less confusing to use.
StatusStrip	Provides an area (usually at the bottom of the form) where the application can display status messages, small pictures, and other indicators of the application's state.
TabControl	Displays a series of tabs attached to pages that contain their own controls. The user clicks a tab to display the associated page.
TableLayoutPanel	Displays the controls it contains in a grid.
TextBox	Displays some text that the user can edit.
Timer	Triggers an event periodically. The program can take action when the event occurs.

continues

(continued)

CONTROL	PURPOSE
Row 7	
ToolStrip	Displays a series of buttons, dropdowns, and other tools that let the user control the application.
ToolStripContainer	A container that allows a ToolStrip control to dock to some or all of its edges. You might dock a ToolStripContainer to a form to allow the user to dock a ToolStrip to each of the form's edges.
ToolTip	Displays a tooltip if the user hovers the mouse over an associated control.
TrackBar	Allows the user to drag a pointer along a bar to select a numeric value.
TreeView	Displays hierarchical data in a graphical, tree-like form.
VScrollBar	A vertical scroll bar.
WebBrowser	A web browser in a control. You can place this control on a form and use its methods to navigate to a web page. The control displays the results exactly as if the user were using a standalone browser. One handy use for this control is displaying Web-based help.

Example program UseToolStripContainer, which is available for download on the book's web site, contains a ToolStripContainer that holds two ToolStrip controls that you can drag and dock to the sides of the ToolStripContainer.

See Appendix G for detailed descriptions of the controls.

CHOOSING CONTROLS

Keeping all of the intricacies of each of these controls in mind at once is a daunting task. With so many powerful tools to choose from, it's not always easy to pick the one that's best for a particular situation.

To simplify error-handling code, you should generally pick the most restrictive control that can accomplish a given task, because more restrictive controls give the user fewer options for entering invalid data.

For example, suppose that the user must pick from the choices Small, Medium, and Large. The application could let the user type a value in a TextBox control, but then the user could type Weasel. The program would need to verify that the user typed one of the valid choices and display an error message if the text was invalid. The program might also need to use precious screen real estate to list the choices so that the user can remember what to type.

A better idea would be to use a group of three RadioButton controls or a ComboBox with DropDownStyle set to DropDownList. Then the user can easily see the choices available and can only select a valid choice. If the program initializes the controls with a default value rather than leaving them initially undefined, it knows that there is always a valid choice selected.

> **COMMON SENSE DEFENSE**
>
> Restrictive controls also make the application more secure. By presenting users with a list of choices rather than letting them type in whatever they like, the program can protect itself from attack. For example, two of the most common attacks on web sites are buffer overflow attacks, in which the attacker enters far more text than intended in a text box, and SQL injection attacks, in which the attacker enters carefully designed gibberish into a text box to confuse a database. Requiring the user to select options rather than typing defuses both of these attacks.

The following sections summarize different categories of controls and provide some tips about when to use each.

Containing and Arranging Controls

These controls contain, group, and help arrange other controls. These controls include FlowLayoutPanel, TableLayoutPanel, GroupBox, Panel, TabControl, and SplitContainer.

The FlowLayoutPanel arranges the controls it contains in rows or columns. For example, when its FlowDirection property is LeftToRight, the control arranges its contents in rows from left to right. It positions its contents in a row until it runs out of room and then it starts a new row. FlowLayoutPanel is particularly useful for toolboxes and other situations where the goal is to display as many of the contained controls as possible at one time, and the exact arrangement of the controls isn't too important.

The TableLayoutPanel control displays its contents in a grid. All the cells in a particular row have the same height, and all the cells in a particular column have the same width. In contrast, the FlowLayoutPanel control simply places controls next to each other until it fills a row and then starts a new one. Example program LayoutPanels, which is available for download on the book's web site, is shown in Figure 8-2 displaying these two controls side by side.

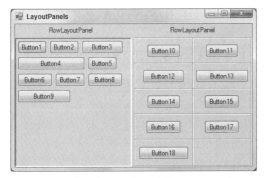

FIGURE 8-2: FlowLayoutPanel places controls close together. TableLayoutPanel arranges controls in a grid.

A GroupBox control is good for grouping related controls or the RadioButton controls in a RadioButton group. (The RadioButton control is discussed later in this chapter in the section "Making Selections.") It provides a visible border and caption so that it can help the user make sense out of a very complicated form.

GREAT GROUPS

The rule of thumb in user interface design is that a user can evaluate around seven items (plus or minus two) at any given time. A list of five or six choices is manageable, but a list containing dozens of options can be confusing.

By placing choices into categories visibly separated in GroupBox controls, you can make the interface much easier for the user to understand. Rather than trying to keep dozens of options straight all at once, the user can mentally break the problem into smaller pieces and consider each group of options separately.

The Panel control can also contain the RadioButton controls in a RadioButton group. Unlike a GroupBox control, the Panel control doesn't display a visible border, so you must use some other method to ensure that the user can tell that the buttons form a group. For example, you could use several Panels in a row, each containing a column of RadioButton controls. Then the user would select one option from each column.

One of the Panel control's more powerful features is its ability to automatically display scroll bars. If you set a Panel control's AutoScroll property to True and the Panel resizes so all of its contents cannot fit, it automatically displays the scroll bars so the user can still see all of the content. Scrolling back and forth can be cumbersome for the user, however, so this is not the best way to display data if the user must view it all frequently. If the user must jump back and forth between different controls inside a scrolling Panel, it may be better to use a TabControl.

TabControl displays data grouped by pages. The tabs enable the user to quickly jump from page to page. The control can display scroll bars if necessary, although that makes using the control much more awkward. TabControl works well if the data falls into natural groupings that you can use for the tab pages. It doesn't work as well if the user must frequently compare values on one page with those on another, forcing the user to jump back and forth.

The SplitContainer control allows the user to divide an area between two adjacent regions. SplitContainer contains two Panel controls in which you can place your own controls. When the user drags the splitter between the two panels, the control resizes the panels accordingly. You can set the Panels' AutoScroll properties to True to make them automatically provide scroll bars when necessary.

SplitContainer is helpful when the form isn't big enough to hold all the data the program must display, and the user can trade area in one part of the form for area in another. It is particularly useful when the user must compare values in the two areas by viewing them at the same time.

Though you can nest SplitContainers inside other SplitContainers, they are easiest to use when they separate only two areas. Large groups of SplitContainers separating many areas are usually clumsy and confusing.

Example program UseSplitter, which is available for download on the book's web site, uses a Splitter control to divide its form into two regions covered by Panel controls. To make the Splitter work, the program contains a Panel with Dock = Left at the bottom of the stacking order, the Splitter next in the stacking order, and then another Panel with Dock = Fill at the top of the stacking order.

Example program UseSplitContainer, which is also available for download, uses a SplitContainer control to divide its form into two regions. The SplitContainer includes two Panel controls and a Splitter so it's all set to divide an area into two regions. Because you don't need to worry about Dock properties and stacking order as you do with a Splitter control, the SplitContainer is easier to use.

These container controls help arrange the controls they contain. The Anchor and Dock properties of any controls inside the containers work relative to the containers. For example, suppose you place a series of buttons with Anchor = Top,Left,Right inside a SplitContainer so that they are as wide as the Panel containing them. When you drag the splitter, the buttons automatically resize to fit the width of their Panel.

Making Selections

Selection controls enable the user to choose values. If you use them carefully, you can reduce the chances of the user making an invalid selection, so you can reduce the amount of error-handling code you need to write.

These controls include CheckBox, CheckedListBox, ComboBox, ListBox, RadioButton, DateTimePicker, MonthCalendar, DomainUpDown, NumericUpDown, TrackBar, HScrollBar, and VScrollBar.

CheckBox enables the user to select an option or not, independently of all other selections. If you want the user to select only one of a series of options, use a RadioButton instead. If a form requires more than, say, five to seven CheckBox controls that have related purposes, consider using a CheckedListBox instead.

The CheckedListBox control enables the user to select among several independent options. It is basically a series of CheckBox controls arranged in a list that provides scroll bars if necessary.

The ComboBox control enables the user to make one brief selection. This control is particularly useful when its DropDownStyle property is set to DropDownList because then the user must pick a value from a list. If you want to allow the user to select a value or enter one that is not on the list, set the control's DropDownStyle to Simple or DropDown. This control does roughly the same things as a simple ListBox but takes less space.

The ListBox control displays a list of items that the user can select. You can configure the control to let the user select one or more items. A ListBox takes more room than a ComboBox but can be easier to use if the list is very long.

LONG LISTS

If you have a long list and want to allow the user to select many items, it is relatively easy for the user to accidentally deselect all of the previous selections by clicking a new item. To make things easier for the user, you should consider using a CheckedListBox, which doesn't cause that problem.

The RadioButton control lets the user pick one of a set of options. For example, three RadioButton controls might represent the choices Small, Medium, and Large. If the user selects one, Visual Basic automatically deselects the others. This control is useful when the list of choices is relatively small, and there is a benefit to allowing the user to see all the choices at the same time. If the list of choices is long, consider using a ListBox or ComboBox.

The DateTimePicker and MonthCalendar controls enable the user to select dates and times. They validate the user's selections, so they are generally better than other controls for selecting dates and times. For example, if you use a TextBox to let the user enter month, date, and year, you must write extra validation code to ensure that the user doesn't enter February 29, 2013.

The DomainUpDown and NumericUpDown controls let the user scroll through a list of values. If the list is relatively short, a ListBox or ComboBox may be easier for the user. The DomainUpDown and NumericUpDown controls take very little space, however, so they may be helpful on very crowded forms. By holding down one of the controls' arrow buttons, the user can scroll very quickly through the values, so these controls can also be useful when they represent a long list of choices.

The TrackBar control lets the user drag a pointer to select an integer value. This is usually a more intuitive way to select a value than a NumericUpDown control, although it takes a lot more space on the form. It also requires some dexterity if the range of values allowed is large.

The HScrollBar and VScrollBar controls let the user drag a "thumb" across a bar to select an integral value much as the TrackBar does. HScrollBar, VScrollBar, and TrackBar even have similar properties. The main difference is in the controls' appearances. On one hand, the two scroll bar controls allow more flexible sizing (the TrackBar has definite ideas about how tall it should be for a given width), and they may seem more elegant to some users. On the other hand, users are familiar with the scroll bars' normal purpose of scrolling an area on the form, so using them as numeric selection bars may sometimes be confusing.

Entering Data

Sometimes it is impractical to use the selection controls described in the previous section. For example, the user cannot reasonably enter a long work history or comments using a ComboBox or RadioButton.

The RichTextBox, TextBox, and MaskedTextBox controls let the user enter text with few restrictions. These controls are most useful when the user must enter a large amount of textual data that doesn't require any validation.

The TextBox control is less complex and easier to use than the RichTextBox control, so you may want to use it unless you need the RichTextBox control's extra features. If you need those features (such as multiple fonts, indentation, paragraph alignment, superscripting and subscripting, multiple colors, more than one level of undo/redo, and so forth), you need to use a RichTextBox.

The MaskedTextBox control is a TextBox control that requires the user to enter data in a particular format. For example, it can help the user enter a phone number of the form 234-567-8901. This is useful only for short fields where the format is tightly constrained. In those cases, however, it reduces the chances of the user making mistakes.

Displaying Data

These controls display data to the user: Label, DataGridView, ListView, TreeView, and PropertyGrid.

The Label control displays a simple piece of text that the user can view but not select or modify. Because you cannot select the text, you cannot copy it to the clipboard. If the text contains a value that you think the user might want to copy to the clipboard and paste into another application (for example, serial numbers, phone numbers, e-mail addresses, web URLs, and so forth), you can use a TextBox control with its ReadOnly property set to True to allow the user to select and copy the text.

The DataGridView control can display table-like data. The control can also display several tables linked with master/detail relationships and the user can quickly navigate through the data. You can also configure this control to allow the user to update the data.

The ListView control displays data that is naturally viewed as a series of icons or as a list of values with columns providing extra detail. With a little extra work, you can sort the data by item or by detail columns.

The TreeView control displays hierarchical data in a tree-like format similar to the directory display provided by Windows Explorer. You can determine whether the control allows the user to edit the nodes' labels.

The PropertyGrid control displays information about an object in a format similar to the one used by the Properties window at design time. The control enables the user to organize the properties alphabetically or by category and lets the user edit the property values. Example program EmployeePropertyGrid, which is available for download on the book's web site, is shown in Figure 8-3 displaying information about an Employee object in a PropertyGrid control.

FIGURE 8-3: The PropertyGrid control displays an object's properties.

Providing Feedback

These controls provide feedback to the user: ToolTip, HelpProvider, ErrorProvider, NotifyIcon, StatusStrip, and ProgressBar. Their general goal is to tell the user what is going on without becoming so obtrusive that the user cannot continue doing other things. For example, the ErrorProvider flags a field as incorrect but doesn't prevent the user from continuing to enter data in other fields.

DISRUPTIVE VALIDATION

You can force users to fix errors by using a TextBox's Validating event handler. For example, if the event handler determines that a TextBox's value is invalid, it can set its e.Cancel parameter to True to prevent the user from moving out of the TextBox or closing the application.

I don't recommend this approach, however, particularly if the users are performing "heads down" data entry, because it interrupts their flow of work. Instead I recommend using an ErrorProvider to flag the error and letting the user fix the problem when it's convenient.

For more information on validation events, see the section "Validation Events" in Chapter 9.

The ToolTip control provides the user with a brief hint about a control's purpose when the user hovers the mouse over it. The HelpProvider gives the user more detailed help about a control's purpose when the user sets focus to the control and presses F1. A high-quality application provides both tooltips and F1 help for every control. These features are unobtrusive and appear only if the user needs them, so it is better to err on the side of providing too much help rather than not enough.

TOO MANY TOOLTIPS?

It may seem silly to place tooltips on every single control. For example, does it really make sense to place a tooltip on a text box that sits next to a label that says "Phone Number?" Surprisingly the answer is yes. It turns out that some screen reader applications for the visually impaired get important cues from tooltips. Giving that text box a tooltip can help some users figure out what belongs in it. The ErrorProvider control flags a control as containing invalid data. It is better to use selection controls that do not allow the user to enter invalid data, but this control is useful when that is not possible.

The NotifyIcon control can display a small icon in the taskbar notification area to let the user easily learn the application's status. This is particularly useful for applications that run in the background without the user's constant attention. If the application needs immediate action from the user, it should display a dialog or message box rather than relying on a NotifyIcon.

> **WHAT'S THE TRAY?**
>
> The *taskbar notification area*, also called the *Windows system tray*, is the small area in the taskbar, usually on the right, that displays the current time and icons indicating the status of various running applications.

The StatusStrip control displays an area (usually at the bottom of the form) where the program can give the user some information about its state. This information can be in the form of small images or short text messages. It can contain a lot more information than a NotifyIcon, although it is visible only when the form is displayed.

The ProgressBar indicates how much of a long task has been completed. Usually, the task is performed synchronously, so the user is left staring at the form while it completes. The ProgressBar lets the user know that the operation is not stuck.

Initiating Action

Every kind of control responds to events, so every control can initiate an action. Nevertheless, users only expect certain kinds of controls to perform significant actions. For example, users expect pushing a button to start an action, but they don't expect clicking a label or check box to start a long process.

To prevent confusion, you should start actions from the controls most often used to start actions. These controls include Button, MenuStrip, ContextMenuStrip, ToolStrip, LinkLabel, TrackBar, HScrollBar, VScrollBar, and Timer. All except the Timer control let the user initiate the action.

All of these controls interact with the program through event handlers. For example, the Button control's Click event handler normally makes the program perform some action when the user clicks the button.

Other controls also provide events that can initiate action. For example, the CheckBox control provides CheckChanged and Click events that you could use to perform some action. By catching the proper events, you can use almost any control to initiate an action. Because the main intent of those controls is not to execute code, they are not listed in this section.

The Button control allows the user to tell the program to execute a particular function. A button is normally always visible on its form, so it is most useful when the user must perform the action frequently or the action is part of the program's central purpose. For actions less frequently performed, use a MenuStrip or ContextMenuStrip control.

Items in a MenuStrip control also enable the user to make the program perform an action. You must perform more steps to open the menu, find the item, and select it than you must to click a button, so a Button control is faster and easier. On the other hand, menus take up less form real estate than buttons. You can also assign keyboard shortcuts (such as F5 or Ctrl+S) to frequently used menu items, making them even easier to invoke than buttons.

A ContextMenuStrip control provides the same advantages and disadvantages as a MenuStrip control. ContextMenuStrip is available only from certain controls on the form, however, so it is useful for commands that are appropriate only within specific contexts. For example, a Save command applies to all the data loaded by a program, so it makes sense to put it in a MenuStrip. A command that deletes a particular object in a drawing only applies to that object. By placing the command in a ContextMenuStrip control attached to the object, the program keeps the command hidden when the user is working on other things. It also makes the relationship between the action (delete) and the object clear to both the user and the program.

The ToolStrip control combines some of the best features of menus and buttons. It displays a series of buttons so they are easy to use without navigating through a menu. The buttons are small and grouped at the top of the form, so they don't take up as much space as a series of larger buttons.

It is common to place buttons or ToolStrip buttons on a form to duplicate frequently used menu commands. The menu commands provide keyboard shortcuts for more advanced users, and the buttons make it easy to invoke the commands for less-experienced users.

The LinkLabel control displays text much as a Label control does. It also displays some text in blue with an underline, displays a special cursor when the user moves over that text, and raises an event if the user clicks the text. That makes the control appropriate when clicking a piece of text should perform some action. For example, on a web page, clicking a link typically navigates to the link's web page.

The TrackBar, HScrollBar, and VScrollBar controls let the user drag a "thumb" across a bar to select an integral value. As mentioned in the section "Making Selections" earlier in this chapter, you can use these controls to let the user select a numeric value. However, they can also be used to perform some action interactively. For example, the scroll bars are often used to scroll an area on the form. More generally, they are used to make the program take action based on some new value. For example, you could use a scroll bar to let the user select new red, green, and blue color components for an image. As the user changed a scroll bar's value, the program would update the image's colors.

The Timer control triggers some action at a regular interval. When the Timer control raises its Timer event, the program takes action.

Displaying Graphics

These controls display graphics, either on the screen or on a printout: Form, PictureBox, PrintPreviewControl, PrintDocument, and PrintPreviewDialog.

A Form (which can also display graphics) provides methods for drawing, but it's often better to draw in a PictureBox control instead of the form itself. That makes it easier to move the drawing if you later need to redesign the form. For example, if you decide that the picture might be too big, it is easy to move a PictureBox control into a scrolling Panel control. It would be much harder to rewrite the code to move the drawing from the Form into a PictureBox control later.

PrintPreviewControl displays a print preview for a PrintDocument object. The program responds to events raised by the PrintDocument object. PrintPreviewControl displays the results within a control on one of the program's forms.

The PrintPreviewDialog control displays graphics from a PrintDocument object much as a PrintPreviewControl does, but it provides its own dialog box. Unless you need to arrange the print preview in some special way, it is easier to use a PrintPreviewDialog rather than build your own preview dialog box with a PrintPreviewControl. The PrintPreviewDialog control provides many features that enable the user to zoom, scroll, and move through the pages of the preview document. Implementing those features yourself would be a lot of work.

Displaying Dialog Boxes

Visual Basic provides a rich assortment of dialog boxes that enable the user to make standard selections. Figuring out which of these dialog boxes to use is usually easy because each has a very specific purpose. The following table lists the dialog boxes and their purposes.

DIALOG	PURPOSE
ColorDialog	Select a color.
FolderBrowserDialog	Select a folder (directory).
FontDialog	Select a font.
OpenFileDialog	Select a file to open.
PageSetupDialog	Specify page set up for printing.
PrintDialog	Print a document.
PrintPreviewDialog	Display a print preview.
SaveFileDialog	Select a file for saving.

Example program UseDialogs, which is available for download on the book's web site, demonstrates each of these dialogs.

Supporting Other Controls

Many of the Visual Basic controls require the support of other controls. The two controls used most by other controls are ImageList and PrintDocument. These controls also include DataConnector and DataNavigator.

The ImageList control holds images for other controls to display. Your code can also take images from an ImageList control to use in whatever way it needs.

The PrintDocument control provides support for printing and print previewing. It generates the graphics sent to the printer, PrintPreviewDialog, or PrintPreviewControl.

The DataConnector control provides a link between a data source and controls bound to the connector. The program can use the DataConnector's methods to navigate, sort, filter, and update the data, and the control updates its bound controls appropriately.

The DataNavigator control provides methods for navigating through a data source such as DataConnector.

THIRD-PARTY CONTROLS

Visual Basic comes with a large number of useful controls ready to go, but many other controls are available that you can use if you need them. If you right-click the Toolbox and select Choose Items, you can select from a huge list of .NET Framework and COM components available on your system.

You can also obtain other controls provided by other companies and available for purchase and sometimes for free on the Web. Many of these controls perform specialized tasks such as generating bar codes, making shaped forms, warping images, and providing special graphical effects.

Other controls extend the standard controls to provide more power or flexibility. Several controls are available that draw two- and three-dimensional charts and graphs. Other controls provide more powerful reporting services than those provided by Visual Studio's own tools.

If you use any major web search engine to search for "windows forms controls," you will find lots of web sites where you can download controls for free or for a fee. A few places you might like to explore include:

- ➤ MVPs.org (www.mvps.org), a site leading to resources provided by people related to Microsoft's Most Valuable Professional (MVP) program. The Common Controls Replacement Project (ccrp.mvps.org) provides controls that duplicate and enhance standard Visual Basic 6 controls. Development on this project has stopped but some of the old Visual Basic 6 controls may give you some ideas for building controls of your own. MVPs .org is also a good general resource.

- ➤ Windows Forms .NET (windowsclient.net), Microsoft's official WPF and Windows Forms .NET community.

- ➤ ASP.NET (www.asp.net), Microsoft's official ASP.NET community.

- ➤ Download.com (www.download.com).

- ➤ Shareware.com (www.shareware.com).

- ➤ Shareware Connection (www.sharewareconnection.com).

You should use these as a starting point for your own search, not as a definitive list. You can download controls from hundreds (if not thousands) of web sites.

CONTROL CHAOS

You should also show some restraint in downloading third-party controls and products in general. Every time you add another control to a project, you make the project depend on that control. If you later move the project to a newer version of Visual Basic, you must ensure that the control works with that version. Similarly, if the vendor makes a new version of the control, you must find out if it works with your version of Visual Basic. If it doesn't, you may be stuck using an older, unsupported version of the control.

If controls and tools interact with each other, the problem becomes much more difficult. If anything changes, you must find a set of versions for all of the tools that can work correctly together.

I try to keep my use of third-party controls to a bare minimum because, when I write a book, I generally cannot assume that you have a particular third-party control. I use tools such as WinZip (`www.WinZip.com`) and Internet Download Manager (`www.InternetDownloadManager.com`) outside of projects, but nothing inside them.

Use a third-party control if it will save you a lot of work. But, before you do, ask yourself how much work would it be to do without the control and how much work it will be to replace it if you need to move to a new version of Visual Basic.

And of course, if you download a control from a source that isn't trustworthy, you could be downloading a virus.

SUMMARY

Controls form the main connection between the user and the application. They allow the application to give information to the user, and they allow the user to control the application. Controls are everywhere in practically every Windows application. Only a tiny percentage of applications that run completely in the background can do without controls.

This chapter briefly describes purposes of the standard Visual Basic controls and provides a few tips for selecting the controls appropriate for different purposes. Appendix G describes the controls in much greater detail.

Even knowing all about the controls doesn't guarantee that you can produce an adequate user interface. There's a whole science to designing user interfaces that are intuitive and easy to use. A good design enables the user to get a job done naturally and with a minimum of wasted work. A bad interface can encumber the user and turn even a simple job into an exercise in beating the application into submission.

For more information on building usable applications, read some books on user-interface design. They explain standard interface issues and solutions. You can also learn a lot by studying other successful applications. Look at the layout of their forms and dialog boxes. You shouldn't steal their designs outright, but you can try to understand why they arrange their controls in the way they do. Look at applications that you like and find particularly easy to use. Compare them with applications that you find awkward and confusing.

This chapter provided an introduction to Windows Forms controls to help you decide which controls to use for different purposes. Chapter 9, "Using Windows Forms Controls," explains in greater detail how you can use the controls you select. It tells how to add a control to a form at design time or runtime, and explains how to use a control's properties, methods, and events.

Using Windows Forms Controls

As Chapter 8 mentions, a *control* is a programming entity that has a graphical component. Text boxes, labels, list boxes, check boxes, menus, and practically everything else that you see in a Windows application is a control.

A *component* is similar to a control, except it is not visible at runtime. When you add a component to a form at design time, it appears in the *component tray* below the bottom of the form. You can select the co mponent and use the Properties window to view and change its properties. At runtime, the component is invisible to the user, although it may display a visible object such as a menu, dialog box, or status icon.

This chapter explains controls and components in general terms. It describes different kinds of controls and components. It explains how your program can use them at design time and runtime to give the user information and to allow the user to control your application. It also explains in general terms how a control's properties, methods, and events work, and it lists some of the most useful properties, methods, and events provided by the Control class. Other controls that are derived from this class inherit those properties, methods, and events unless they are explicitly overridden.

Appendix G, "Windows Forms Controls and Components," describes some of the most commonly used controls in greater detail.

CONTROLS AND COMPONENTS

Controls are graphic by nature. Buttons, text boxes, and labels provide graphical input and feedback for the user. They display data and let the user trigger program actions. Some controls (such as grid controls, tree view controls, and calendar controls) are quite powerful and provide a rich variety of tools for interacting with the user.

In contrast, components are represented by graphical icons at design time and are hidden at runtime. They may display some other object (such as a dialog box, menu, or graphical indicator), but the component itself is hidden from the user.

Many components display information to the user. Others provide information needed by graphical controls. For example, a program can use connection, data adapter, and data set components to define data that should be selected from a database. Then a grid control could display the data to the user. Because the connection, data adapter, and data set objects are components, you can define their properties at design time without writing code.

Figure 9-1 shows a form at design time that contains several components. The components appear in the component tray at the bottom of the form, not on the form's graphical surface.

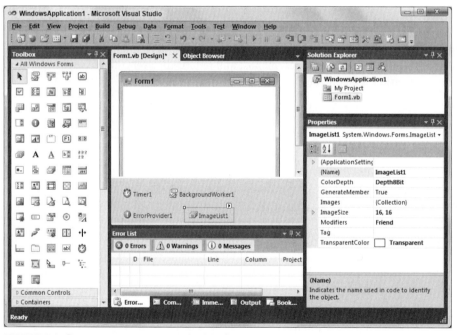

FIGURE 9-1: Some components provide data for graphical controls.

This example contains four components. Timer1 fires an event periodically so the program can take some action at specified time intervals. ErrorProvider1 displays an error icon and error messages for certain controls on the form such as TextBoxes. BackgroundWorker1 performs tasks asynchronously while the main program works independently. ImageList1 contains a series of images for use by another control. Usually an ImageList is associated with a control such as a Button, ListView, or TreeView, and provides images for that control. For example, a ListView control can use the images in an ImageList to display icons for the items it contains.

Aside from the lack of a graphical component on the form, working with components is very similar to working with controls. You use the Properties window to set components' properties, the code editor to define event handlers, and code to call their methods. The rest of this chapter focuses on controls, but the same concepts apply just as well to components.

CREATING CONTROLS

Usually you add controls to a form graphically at design time. In some cases, however, you may want to add new controls to a form when the program is running. This gives you a bit more flexibility so that you can change the program's appearance at runtime in response to the program's needs or the user's commands.

For example, suppose an application might need between 1 and 100 text boxes. Most of the time it needs only a few, but depending on the user's input, it might need a lot. You could give the form 100 text boxes and then hide the ones it didn't need, but that would be a waste of memory most of the time. By creating only the number of text boxes actually needed, you can conserve memory in the most common cases.

The following sections explain how to create controls both at design time and at runtime.

Creating Controls at Design Time

To create a control at design time, double-click a form in Solution Explorer to open it in the form editor. Decide which control you want to use from the Toolbox. If the Toolbox tab you are using is in List View mode, it displays the controls' names. If the tab displays only control icons, you can hover the mouse over a tool to see a tooltip that gives the control's name and a brief description. For example, Figure 9-2 shows the Button control's tooltip.

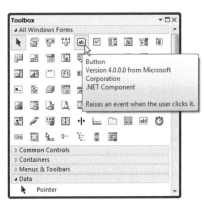

FIGURE 9-2: Tools summarize controls.

After you have chosen a control, you have several ways to add it to the form. First, you can double-click the tool to place an instance of the control on the form at a default size in a default location. After adding the control to the form, the IDE deselects the tool and selects the pointer tool (the upper leftmost tool in the Toolbox's current tab).

Second, you can select the tool in the Toolbox, and then click and drag to place it on the form. If you click the form without dragging, the IDE adds a new control at that position with a default size. After you add the control, the IDE deselects the tool and selects the pointer tool.

Third, if you click and drag a tool from the Toolbox onto the form, Visual Basic makes a new control with a default size at the position where you dropped the tool.

Fourth, if you plan to add many copies of the same type of control to the form, hold down the Ctrl key and click the tool. Now the tool remains selected even after you add a control to the form. When you click and drag on the form, the IDE creates a new control at that position and keeps the tool selected so that you can immediately create another control. When you click the form without dragging the mouse, the IDE adds a new control at that position with a default size. When you are finished adding instances of that control type, click the pointer tool to stop adding new controls.

Adding Controls to Containers

Some controls can contain other controls. For example, the GroupBox and Panel controls can hold other controls.

You can place a control in a container in several ways. If you select the container and then double-click a control's tool in the Toolbox, Visual Basic places the new control inside the container.

When you select a tool and click and drag inside a container, Visual Basic also places the new control inside the container, whether or not it is selected.

You can also click and drag a Toolbox tool onto the container, or click and drag controls from one part of the form onto the container. If you hold down the Ctrl key when you drop the controls, Visual Basic makes new copies of the controls instead of moving the existing controls.

Two common mistakes programmers make with containers are placing a control *above* a container when they want it *inside* the container, and vice versa. For example, you can place groups of controls inside different Panel controls and then hide or display the Panels to show different controls at different times. If a control lies above a Panel but is not inside it, the control remains visible even if the Panel is not.

To tell if a control is inside a container, move the container slightly. If the control also moves, it is inside the container. If the control doesn't move, it is above the container but not inside it. (When you're finished with this test, you can press Ctrl+Z or use the Edit menu's Undo command to undo the move and put the container back where it was.)

Creating Controls at Runtime

Normally, you create controls interactively at design time. Sometimes, however, it's more convenient to create new controls at runtime. For example, you may not know how many pieces of data you will need to display until runtime. Sometimes you can display unknown amounts of data using a list, grid, or other control that can hold a variable number of items, but other times you might like to display the data in a series of labels or text boxes. In cases such as these, you need to create new controls at runtime.

The following code shows how a program might create a new Label control. First it declares a variable of type Label and initializes it with the New keyword. It uses the label's SetBounds method to position the label and sets its Text property to "Hello World!" The code then adds the label to the current form's Controls collection.

```
Dim lbl As New Label
lbl.SetBounds(10, 50, 100, 25)
lbl.Text = "Hello World!"
Me.Controls.Add(lbl)
```

CHANGING CONTAINERS

To place a control inside a container other than the form, add the control to
the container's Controls collection. For example, to add the previous Label to a
GroupBox named grpLabels, you would use the statement `grpLabels.Controls`
`.Add(lbl)`.

Usually, a label just displays a message so you don't need to catch its events. Other controls such as
buttons and scroll bars, however, are not very useful if the program cannot respond to their events.

You can take two approaches to catching a new control's events. First, you can use the WithEvents
keyword when you declare the control's variable. Then you can open the form in the code editor,
select the variable's name from the left drop-down list, and select an event from the right
drop-down list to give the control an event handler.

The following code demonstrates this approach. It declares a class-level variable btnHi using the
WithEvents keyword. When you click the btnMakeHiButton button, its event handler initializes the
variable. It sets the control's position and text, and adds it to the form's Controls collection. When
the user clicks this button, the btnHi_Click event handler executes and displays a message.

**Available for
download on
Wrox.com**

```
' Declare the btnHi button WithEvents.
Private WithEvents btnHi As Button

' Make the new btnHi button.
Private Sub btnMakeHiButton_Click() Handles btnMakeHiButton.Click
    btnHi = New Button
    btnHi.SetBounds(16, 16, 80, 23)
    btnHi.Text = "Say Hi"
    Me.Controls.Add(btnHi)
End Sub

' The user clicked the btnHi button.
Private Sub btnHi_Click() Handles btnHi.Click
    MessageBox.Show("Hi")
End Sub
```

code snippet MakeButtons

This first approach works if you know the number and types of the controls you will need. Then
you can define variables for them all using the WithEvents keyword. If you don't know how many

controls you need to create, however, this isn't practical. For example, suppose that you want to create a button for each file in a directory. When the user clicks a button, the file should open. If you don't know how many files the directory will hold, you don't know how many variables you'll need.

One solution to this dilemma is to use the AddHandler statement to add event handlers to the new controls. The following code demonstrates this approach. When you click the btnMakeHelloButton button, its Click event handler creates a new Button object, storing it in a locally declared variable. It sets the button's position and text and adds it to the form's `Controls` collection as before. Next, the program uses the `AddHandler` statement to make subroutine Hello_Click an event handler for the button's Click event. When the user clicks the new button, subroutine Hello_Click displays a message.

```
' Make a new Hello button.
Private Sub btnMakeHelloButton_Click() Handles btnMakeHelloButton.Click
    ' Make the button.
    Dim btnHello As New Button
    btnHello.SetBounds(240, 64, 80, 23)
    btnHello.Text = "Say Hello"
    Me.Controls.Add(btnHello)

    ' Add a Click event handler to the button.
    AddHandler btnHello.Click, AddressOf Hello_Click
End Sub

' The user clicked the Hello button.
Private Sub Hello_Click()
    MessageBox.Show("Hello")
End Sub
```

code snippet MakeButtons

TAG, YOU'RE IT

When you build controls at runtime, particularly if you don't know how many controls you may create, the Tag property can be very useful. You can place something in a new control's Tag property to help identify it. For example, you might store a control number in each new control's Tag property and make them all use the same event handlers. The event handlers can check the Tag property to see which control raised the event.

You can use the same routine as an event handler for more than one button. In that case, the code can convert the sender parameter into a Button object and use the button's Name, Text, and other properties to determine which button was pressed.

To remove a control from the form, simply remove it from the form's Controls collection. To free the resources associated with the control, set any variables that refer to it to Nothing. For example, the following code removes the btnHi control created by the first example:

```
Me.Controls.Remove(btnHi)
btnHi = Nothing
```

This code can remove controls that you created interactively at design time, as well as controls you create during runtime.

Example program MakeButtons, available on the book's web site, demonstrates techniques for adding and removing buttons.

CODE ON THE RUN

In addition to creating new controls at runtime, you can actually create code! You can build a string containing Visual Basic code that holds subroutines, functions, variables declarations, and so forth just as if you had typed it into the code editor. Your program can then compile and execute the code.

This is an interesting and fun exercise but it's very advanced so it's not covered in detail here. My book *Expert One-on-One Visual Basic 2005 Design and Development* (Wrox, Stephens, 2007) has a chapter on scripting that you may find useful. For more information and some brief tutorials, try these web pages:

➤ www.vb-helper.com/talk_vsa.html

➤ www.vb-helper.com/howto_net_use_vsa.html

➤ www.codeproject.com/KB/dotnet/dynacodgen.aspx

➤ www.codeguru.com/columns/dotnet/article.php/c10729

➤ www.codeproject.com/KB/dotnet/VBRunNET.aspx

PROPERTIES

A *property* is some value associated with a control. Often, a property corresponds in an obvious way to the control's appearance or behavior. For example, the Text property represents the text that the control displays, BackColor represents the control's background color, Top and Left represent the control's position, and so forth.

Many properties, including Text, BackColor, Top, and Left, apply to many kinds of controls. Other properties work only with certain specific types of controls. For example, the ToolStrip control has an ImageList property that indicates the ImageList control containing the images the ToolStrip should display. Only a few controls such as the ToolStrip have an ImageList property.

The following sections explain how you can manipulate a control's properties interactively at design time or using code at runtime.

Properties at Design Time

To modify a control's properties at design time, open its form in the Windows Forms Designer and click the control. The Properties window displays the control's properties. Figure 9-3 shows the Properties window displaying a Button control's properties. For example, the control's Text property has the value "Make Hi Button," and its TextAlign property (which determines where the button displays its text) is set to MiddleCenter.

The drop-down list at the top of the Properties window, just below the Properties title, indicates that this control is named btnMakeHiButton and that it is of the System.Windows .Forms.Button class.

FIGURE 9-3: The Properties window lets you change a control's properties at design time.

You can set many properties by clicking a property's value in the Properties window and then typing the new value. This works with simple string and numeric values such as the controls' Name and Text properties, and it works with some other properties where typing a value makes some sense.

For example, the HScrollBar control (horizontal scrollbar) has Minimum, Maximum, and Value properties that determine the control's minimum, maximum, and current values. You can click those properties in the Properties window and enter new values. When you press the Enter key or move to another property, the control validates the value you typed. If you entered a value that doesn't make sense (for example, if you typed ABC instead of a numeric value), the IDE reports the error and lets you fix it.

Compound Properties

A few properties have compound values. The Location property includes the X and Y coordinates of the control's upper-left corner. The Size property contains the control's width and height. The Font property is an object that has its own font name, size, boldness, and other font properties.

The Properties window displays these properties with a plus sign on the left. When you click the plus sign, the window expands the property to show the values that it contains. Figure 9-4 shows the same Properties window shown in Figure 9-3 with the Font property expanded. You can click the Font property's subvalues and set them independently just as you can set any other property value.

When you expand a compound property, a minus sign appears to the left (see the Font property in Figure 9-4). Click this minus sign to collapse the property and hide its members.

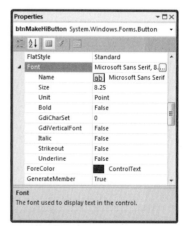

FIGURE 9-4: The Properties window lets you change complex properties at design time.

Some compound properties provide more sophisticated methods for setting the property's values. If you click the ellipsis button to the right of the Font property shown in Figure 9-4, the IDE presents a font selection dialog that lets you set many of the font's properties.

Restricted Properties

Some properties allow more restricted values. For example, the Visible property is a Boolean, so it can only take the values True and False. When you click the property, a drop-down arrow appears on the right. When you click this arrow, a drop-down list lets you select one of the choices, True or False.

Many properties have enumerated values. The Button control's FlatStyle property allows the values Flat, Popup, Standard, and System. When you click the drop-down arrow to the right of this property, a drop-down list appears to let you select one of those values.

You can also double-click the property to cycle through its allowed values. After you select a property, you can use the up and down arrows to move through the values.

Some properties allow different values at different times. For example, some properties contain references to other controls. The Button control's ImageList property is a reference to an ImageList component that contains the picture that the Button should display. If you click the drop-down arrow to the right of this value, the Properties window displays a list of the ImageList components on the form that you might use for this property. This list also contains the entry (none), which you can select to remove any previous control reference in the property.

Many properties take very specialized values and provide specialized property editors to let you select values easily. For example, the Anchor property lets you anchor a control's edges to the edges of its container. Normally, a control is anchored to the top and left edges of the container so that it remains in the same position even if the container is resized. If you also anchor the control on the right, its right edge moves in or out as the container gets wider or narrower. This lets you make controls that resize with their containers in certain useful ways.

If you select the Anchor property and click the drop-down arrow on the right, the Properties window displays the small graphical editor shown in Figure 9-5. Click the skinny rectangles on the left, top, right, or bottom to anchor or unanchor (sometimes called *float*) the control on those sides. Press the Enter key to accept your choices or press Escape to cancel them.

Other complex properties may provide other editors. These are generally self-explanatory. Click the ellipsis or drop-down arrow to the right of a property value to open the editor, and experiment to see how these editors work.

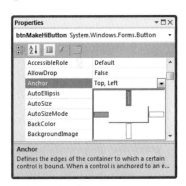

FIGURE 9-5: Some properties, such as Anchor, provide specialized editors to let you select their values.

You can right-click any property's name and select Reset to reset the property to a default value. Many complex properties can take the value "(none)," and for those properties, selecting Reset usually sets the value to "(none)."

Collection Properties

Some properties represent collections of objects. For example, the ListBox control displays a list of items. Its Items property is a collection containing those items. The Properties window displays the value of this property as "(Collection)." If you select this property and click the ellipsis to the right, the Properties window displays a simple dialog box where you can edit the text displayed by the control's items. This dialog box is quite straightforward: Enter the items' text on separate lines and click OK.

Other properties are much more complex. For example, to create a TabControl that displays images on its tabs, you must also create an ImageList component. Select the ImageList component's Images property, and click the ellipsis to the right to display the dialog box shown in Figure 9-6. When you click the Add button, the dialog box displays a file selection dialog box that lets you add an image file to the control. The list on the left shows you the images you have loaded and includes a small thumbnail picture of each image. The values on the right show you the images' properties.

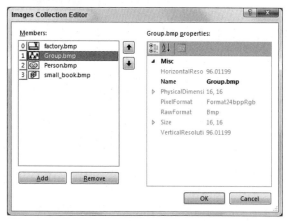

FIGURE 9-6: This dialog box lets you load images into an ImageList control at design time.

After you add pictures to the ImageList control, create a TabControl. Select its ImageList property, click the drop-down arrow on the right, and select the ImageList control you created. Next, select the TabControl's TabPages property, and click the ellipsis on the right to see the dialog box shown in Figure 9-7.

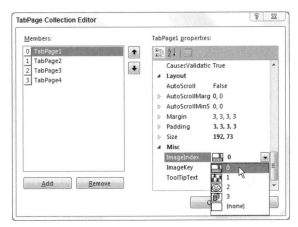

FIGURE 9-7: This dialog box lets you edit a TabControl's tab pages.

Use the Add button to add tab pages to the control. Select a tab page, click its ImageIndex property, click the drop-down arrow to the right, and pick the number of the image in the ImageList that you want to use for this tab. Figure 9-8 shows the resulting ImageTabs example program, which is available for download on the book's web site.

Some properties even contain a collection of objects, each of which contains a collection of objects. For example, the ListView control has an Items property that is a collection. Each item in that collection is an object that has a SubItems property, which is itself a collection. When you display the ListView control as a list with details, an object in the Items collection represents a row in the view and its SubItems values represent the secondary values in the row.

FIGURE 9-8: A TabControl displays the images stored in an ImageList component on its tabs.

To set these values at design time, select the ListView control and click the ellipsis to the right of the control's Items property in the Properties window. Create an item in the editor, and click the ellipsis to the right of the item's SubItems property.

Other complicated properties provide similarly complex editors. Although they may implement involved relationships among various controls and components, they are usually easy enough to figure out with a little experimentation.

Properties at Runtime

Visual Basic lets you set most control properties at design time, but often you will need to get and modify property values at runtime. For example, you might need to change a label's text to tell the user that something has changed, disable a button because it is not applicable at a particular moment, or read the value selected by the user from a list.

As far as your code is concerned, a property is just like any other public variable defined by an object. You get or set a property by using the name of the control, followed by a dot, followed by the name of the property. For example, the following code examines the text in the TextBox named txtPath. If the text doesn't end with a / character, the code adds one. This code both reads and sets the Text property:

```
If Not txtPath.Text.EndsWith("/") Then txtPath.Text &= "/"
```

If a property contains a reference to an object, you can use the object's properties and methods in your code. The following code displays a message box indicating whether the txtPath control's font is bold. It examines the TextBox control's Font property. That property returns a reference to a Font object that has a Bold property.

```
If txtPath.Font.Bold Then
    MessageBox.Show("Bold")
Else
    MessageBox.Show("Not Bold")
End If
```

> **FINALIZED FONTS**
>
> A Font object's properties are read-only, so the code cannot set the value of txtPath.Font.Bold. To change the TextBox control's font, the code would need to create a new font as in the statement:
>
> ```
> txtPath.Font = New Font(txtPath.Font, FontStyle.Bold)
> ```
>
> This code passes the Font object's constructor a copy of the TextBox control's current font to use as a template, and a value indicating that the new font should be bold.

If a property represents a collection or array, you can loop through or iterate over the property just as if it were declared as a normal collection or array. The following code lists the items the user has selected in the ListBox control named lstChoices:

```
For Each selected_item As Object In lstChoices.SelectedItems()
    Debug.WriteLine(selected_item.ToString())
Next selected_item
```

A few properties are read-only at runtime, so your code can examine them but not change their values. For example, a Panel control's Controls property returns a collection holding references to the controls inside the Panel. This property is read-only at runtime so you cannot set it equal to a new collection. (The collection provides methods for adding and removing controls so you don't really need to replace the whole collection; you can change the controls that it contains instead.)

Note also that at design time, this collection doesn't appear in the Properties window. Instead of explicitly working with the collection, you add and remove controls interactively by moving them in and out of the Panel control.

A control's Bottom property is also read-only and not shown in the Properties window. It represents the distance between the top of the control's container and the control's bottom edge. This value is really just the control's Top property plus its Height property (control.Bottom = control.Top + control.Height), so you can modify it using those properties instead of setting the Bottom property directly.

THE ELUSIVE WRITE-ONLY PROPERTY

In theory, a property can also be write-only at runtime. Such a property is really more like a subroutine than a property, however, so most controls use a subroutine instead. In practice, read-only properties are uncommon and write-only properties are extremely rare.

Useful Control Properties

This section describes some of the most useful properties provided by the Control class. Appendix A, "Useful Control Properties, Methods, and Events," summarizes these and other Control properties for quick reference. Appendix A doesn't cover every property, just those that are most useful.

All controls (including the Form control) inherit directly or indirectly from the Control class. That means they inherit the Control class's properties, methods, and events (unless they take explicit action to override the Control class's behavior).

Although these properties are available to all controls that inherit from the Control class, many are considered advanced, so they are not shown by the IntelliSense pop-up's Common tab. For example, a program is intended to set a control's position by using its Location property not its Left and Top properties, so Location is in the Common tab whereas Left and Top are only in the Advanced tab.

Figure 9-9 shows the Common tab on the IntelliSense pop-up for a Label control. It shows the Location property but not the Left property. If you click the All tab, you can see Left and the other advanced properties.

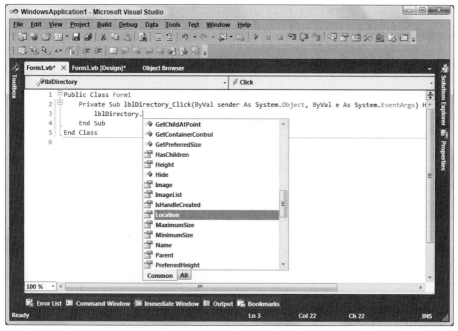

FIGURE 9-9: The Location property is on the IntelliSense Common tab but the Left property is not.

When you type the control's name and enough of the string Left to differentiate it from the Location property (in this case "lblDirectory.Le"), the pop-up automatically switches to show a smaller version of the IntelliSense pop-up listing only properties that contain "Le" such as Left, RightToLeft, and TopLevelControl.

Many of the Control class's properties are straightforward, but a few deserve special attention. The following sections describe some of the more confusing properties in greater detail.

Anchor

The Anchor property allows a control to automatically resize itself when its container is resized. Anchor determines which of the control's edges should remain a fixed distance from the corresponding edges of the container.

For example, normally a control's Anchor property is set to Top, Left. That means the control's top and left positions remain fixed when the container resizes. If the control's upper-left corner is at the point (8, 16) initially, it remains at the position (8, 16) when you resize the container. This is the normal control behavior, and it makes the control appear fixed on the container.

For another example, suppose that you set a control's Anchor property to Top, Right, and you place the control in the container's upper-right corner. When you resize the container, the control moves, so it remains in the upper-right corner.

If you set two opposite Anchor values, the control resizes itself to satisfy them both. For example, suppose that you make a button that starts 8 pixels from its container's left, right, and top edges. Then suppose that you set the control's Anchor property to Top, Left, Right. When you resize the container, the control resizes itself so that it is always 8 pixels from the container's left, right, and top edges.

In a more common scenario, you can place Label controls on the left with Anchor set to Top, Left so they remain fixed on the form. On the right, you can place TextBoxes and other controls with Anchor set to Top, Left, Right, so they resize themselves to take advantage of the resizing form's new width.

Similarly, you can make controls that stretch vertically as the form resizes. For example, if you set a ListBox control's Anchor property to Top, Left, Bottom, the control stretches vertically to take advantage of the form's height and display as much of its list of items as possible.

If you do not provide any Anchor value for either the vertical or horizontal directions, the control anchors its center to the container's center. For example, suppose you position a button in the bottom middle of the form and you set its Anchor property to Bottom only. Because you placed the control in the middle of the form, the control's center coincides with the form's center. When you resize the form, the control moves so it remains centered horizontally.

If you place other controls on either side of the centered one, they will all move so they remain together centered as a group as the form resizes. You may want to experiment with this property to see the effect.

At runtime, you can set a control's Anchor property to AnchorStyles.None or to a Boolean combination of the values AnchorStyles.Top, AnchorStyles.Bottom, AnchorStyles.Left, and AnchorStyles .Right. For example, Example program AnchorButton, available for download on the book's web site, uses the following code to move the btnAnchored control to the form's lower-right corner and set its Anchor property to Bottom, Right, so it stays there:

Available for download on Wrox.com

```
Private Sub Form1_Load() Handles MyBase.Load
    btnAnchored.Location = New Point( _
        Me.ClientRectangle.Width - Button1.Width, _
        Me.ClientRectangle.Height - Button1.Height)
    btnAnchored.Anchor = AnchorStyles.Bottom Or AnchorStyles.Right
End Sub
```

code snippet AnchoredButtons

Dock

The Dock property determines whether a control attaches itself to one or more of its container's sides. For example, if you set a control's Dock property to Top, the control docks to the top of its container. It fills the container from left to right and is flush with the top of the container. If the container is resized, the control remains at the top, keeps its height, and resizes itself to fill the container's width. This is how a typical toolbar behaves. The effect is similar to placing the control at the top of the container so that it fills the container's width and then setting its Anchor property to Top, Left, Right.

You can set a control's Dock property to Top, Bottom, Left, Right, Fill, or None. The value Fill makes the control dock to all of its container's remaining interior space. If it is the only control in the container, it fills the whole container.

If the container holds more than one control with Dock set to a value other than None, the controls are arranged according to their stacking order (also called the Z-order). The control that is first in the stacking order (would normally be drawn first at the back) is positioned first using its Dock value. The control that comes next in the stacking order is arranged second, and so on until all of the controls are positioned.

Figure 9-10 shows example program Docking, which is available for download on the book's web site. It contains four TextBoxes with Dock set to different values. The first in the stacking order has Dock set to Left so it occupies the left edge of the form. The next control has Dock set to Top, so it occupies the top edge of the form's remaining area. The third control has Dock set to Right, so it occupies the right edge of the form's remaining area. Finally, the last control has Dock set to Fill so it fills the rest of the form.

FIGURE 9-10: Docked controls are arranged according to their stacking order.

Controls docked to an edge resize to fill the container in one dimension. For example, a control with Dock set to Top fills whatever width the container has available. A control with Dock set to Fill resizes to fill all of the form's available space.

Other than that, the Dock property does not arrange controls very intelligently when you resize the container. For example, suppose that you have two controls, one above the other. The first has Dock set to Top and the second has Dock set to Fill. You can arrange the controls so that they evenly divide the form vertically. When you make the form taller, however, the second control, with Dock set to Fill, takes up all of the new space, and the other control remains the same size.

You cannot use the Dock property to make the controls divide the form evenly when it is resized. You cannot use the Anchor property to evenly divide the form either. Instead, you need to use code similar to the following. When the form resizes, this code moves and sizes the two controls TextBox1 and TextBox2 to fill the form, evenly dividing it vertically.

```
Private Sub Form1_Load() Handles Me.Load
    ArrangeTextBoxes()
End Sub
Private Sub Form1_Resize() Handles Me.Resize
    ArrangeTextBoxes()
End Sub
Private Sub ArrangeTextBoxes()
    Dim wid As Integer = Me.ClientRectangle.Width
    Dim hgt1 As Integer = Me.ClientRectangle.Height \ 2
    Dim hgt2 As Integer = Me.ClientRectangle.Height - hgt1
    txtTop.SetBounds(0, 0, wid, hgt1)
    txtBottom.SetBounds(0, hgt1, wid, hgt2)
End Sub
```

code snippet DivideForm

Example program DivideForm, available for download on the book's web site, uses similar code to divide its form between two text boxes.

When you want to divide a form, the SplitterContainer control can also be useful. The SplitterContainer contains two panels that can hold other controls. The user can drag the divider between the two panels to adjust the size allocated to each.

Position and Size Properties

Controls contain many position and size properties, and the differences among them can be confusing. Some of the more bewildering aspects of controls are client area, non-client area, and display area.

A control's *client area* is the area inside the control where you can draw things or place other controls. A control's *non-client area* is everything else. In a typical form, the borders and title bar are the non-client area. The client area is the space inside the borders and below the title bar where you can place controls or draw graphics.

MENUS AND CLIENT AREA

A form's menus can make the client and non-client areas a bit confusing. Logically, you might think of the menus as part of the non-client area because you normally place controls below them. Nevertheless, the menus are themselves controls and you can even place other controls above or below the menus (although that would be very strange and confusing to the user), so they are really contained in the client area.

A control's *display area* is the client area minus any internal decoration. For example, a GroupBox control displays an internal border and a title. Although you can place controls over these, you normally wouldn't. The display area contains the space inside the GroupBox's borders and below the space where the title sits.

The following table summarizes properties related to the control's size and position.

PROPERTY	DATA TYPE	READ/WRITE	PURPOSE
Bounds	Rectangle	Read/Write	The control's size and position within its container including non-client areas.
ClientRectangle	Rectangle	Read	The size and position of the client area within the control.
ClientSize	Size	Read/Write	The size of the client area. If you set this value, the control adjusts its size to make room for the non-client area, while giving you this client size.
DisplayRectangle	Rectangle	Read	The size and position of the area within the control where you would normally draw or place other controls.
Location	Point	Read/Write	The position of the control's upper-left corner within its container.
Size	Point	Read/Write	The control's size including non-client areas.
Left, Top, Width, Height	Integer	Read/Write	The control's size and position within its container including non-client areas.
Bottom, Right	Integer	Read	The position of the control's lower-right corner within its container.

METHODS

A *method* executes code associated with a control. The method can be a function that returns a value or a subroutine that does something without returning a value.

Because methods execute code, you cannot invoke them at design time. You can only invoke them by using code at runtime.

Appendix A summarizes the Control class's most useful methods. Controls that inherit from the Control class also inherit these methods unless they have overridden the Control class's behavior.

EVENTS

A control or other object *raises* an *event* to let the program know about some change in circumstances. Sometimes raising an event is also called *firing* or *throwing* the event. Specific control classes provide events that are relevant to their special purposes. For example, the Button control provides a Click event to let the program know when the user clicks the button.

The program responds to an event by creating an event handler that *catches* the event and takes whatever action is appropriate. Each event defines its own event-handler format and determines the parameters that the event handler will receive. Often, these parameters give additional information about the event.

For example, when part of the form is covered and exposed, the form raises its Paint event. The Paint event handler takes as a parameter an object of type PaintEventArgs named e. That object's Graphics property is a reference to a Graphics object that the program can use to redraw the form's contents.

Some event handlers take parameters that are used to send information about the event back to the object that raised it. For example, the Form class's FormClosing event handler has a parameter of type FormClosingEventArgs. That parameter is an object that has a property named Cancel. If the program sets Cancel to True, the Form cancels the FormClosing event and remains open. For example, the event handler can verify that the data entered by the user was properly formatted. If the values didn't make sense, the program can display an error message and keep the form open.

Although many of a control's most useful events are specific to the control type, controls do inherit some common events from the Control class. Appendix A summarizes the Control class's most important events. Controls that inherit from the Control class also inherit these events unless they have overridden the Control class's behavior.

Creating Event Handlers at Design Time

You can create an event handler at design time in a couple of ways. If you open a form in the Windows Forms Designer and double-click a control, the code editor opens and displays the control's default event handler. For example, a TextBox control opens its TextChanged event handler, a Button control opens its Click event handler, and the form itself opens its Load event handler.

To create some other non-default event handler for a control, select the control and then click the Properties window's Events button (which looks like a lightning bolt). This makes the Properties window list the control's most commonly used events. If you have defined event handlers already, possibly for other controls, you can select them from the events' drop-down lists. Double-click an event's entry to create a new event handler.

To create other non-default event handlers or to create event handlers inside the code editor, open the code window, select the control from the left drop-down list, and then select the event handler from the right drop-down list, as shown in Figure 9-11. To create an even handler for the form itself, select "(Form1 Events)" from the left dropdown and then select an event from the right dropdown.

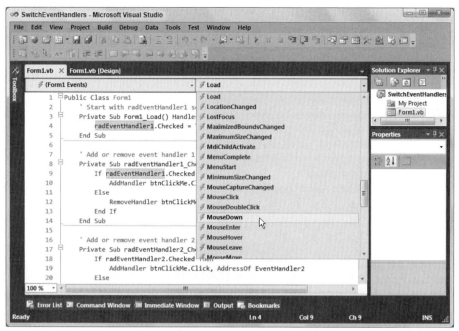

FIGURE 9-11: To create an event handler in the code window, select a control from the left dropdown, and then select an event from the right dropdown.

The code window creates an event handler with the correct parameters and return value. For example, the following code shows an empty TextBox control's Click event handler (note that the first two lines are wrapped in this text but appear on one line in the code editor). Now you just need to fill in the code that you want to execute when the event occurs.

```
Private Sub TextBox1_Click(ByVal sender As Object, _
 ByVal e As System.EventArgs) Handles TextBox1.Click
End Sub
```

RELAX

Because Visual Basic supports relaxed delegates, you can omit the parameters from the event handler's declaration if you don't need to use them. To make the code easier to read, this book omits these parameters wherever they are not needed. For example, the following code shows a relaxed version of the previous TextBox_Click event handler:

```
Private Sub TextBox1_Click() Handles TextBox1.Click
End Sub
```

WithEvents Event Handlers

If you declare an object variable using the WithEvents keyword, you can catch its events. After you declare the variable, you can select it in the code designer's left dropdown, just as you can select any other control. Then you can pick one of the object's events from the right dropdown.

When the code assigns an instance of an object to the variable, any event handlers defined for the variable receive the object's events. Later, if you set the variable to Nothing, the event handlers no longer receive events.

Usually, you don't need to create WithEvents variables for controls because Visual Basic does it for you. However, using a variable declared WithEvents lets you enable and disable events quickly and easily. For example, suppose a program wants to track a PictureBox's mouse events at some times, but not at others. It declares a PictureBox variable as shown in the following code:

```
Private WithEvents m_Canvas As PictureBox
```

When the program wants to receive events, it sets this variable equal to its PictureBox control as in the following code. Now the variable's event handlers such as m_Canvas_MouseDown, m_Canvas_MouseMove, and m_Canvas_MouseUp are enabled.

```
m_Canvas = PictureBox1
```

When it no longer wants to receive these events, the program sets m_Canvas to Nothing as in the following statement. While m_Canvas is Nothing, it has no associated control to generate events for it.

```
m_Canvas = Nothing
```

Setting Event Handlers at Runtime

Not only can you create event handlers at design time, but you can also assign them at runtime. First create the event handler. You must get the routine's parameters exactly correct for the type of event handler you want to create. For example, a TextBox control's Click event handler must take two parameters with types System.Object and System.EventArgs.

EASY EVENT PARAMETERS

To ensure that you get the details right, you can start by creating an event handler for a normal control at design time. Select the control from the code designer's left dropdown, and then select the event from the right. Change the resulting event handler's name to something more appropriate (for example, you might change Button1_Click to ToolClicked) and remove the Handles statement that ties the event handler to the control. You can also delete the original control if you don't need it for anything else.

After you build the event handler, you can use the AddHandler and RemoveHandler statements to add and remove the event handler from a control. The following code shows how example program SwitchEventHandlers switches the event handler that a button executes when it is clicked:

```
' Add or remove event handler 1.
Private Sub radEventHandler1_CheckedChanged() _
 Handles radEventHandler1.CheckedChanged
    If radEventHandler1.Checked Then
        AddHandler btnClickMe.Click, AddressOf EventHandler1
    Else
        RemoveHandler btnClickMe.Click, AddressOf EventHandler1
    End If
End Sub

' Add or remove event handler 2.
Private Sub radEventHandler2_CheckedChanged() _
 Handles radEventHandler2.CheckedChanged
    If radEventHandler2.Checked Then
        AddHandler btnClickMe.Click, AddressOf EventHandler2
    Else
        RemoveHandler btnClickMe.Click, AddressOf EventHandler2
    End If
End Sub

' Display a message telling which event handler this is.
Private Sub EventHandler1(ByVal sender As System.Object, _
 ByVal e As System.EventArgs)
    MessageBox.Show("EventHandler1")
End Sub

Private Sub EventHandler2(ByVal sender As System.Object, _
 ByVal e As System.EventArgs)
    MessageBox.Show("EventHandler2")
End Sub
```

code snippet SwitchEventHandlers

When the user selects or clears radio button radEventHandler1, the control's CheckedChanged event handler adds or removes the EventHandler1 event handler from the btnClickMe control's Click event. Similarly, when the user selects or clears radEventHandler2, its CheckedChanged event handler adds or removes the EventHandler2 event handler from the btnClickMe control's Click event.

The EventHandler1 and EventHandler2 event handlers simply display a message telling you which is executing.

AddHandler and RemoveHandler allow you to switch one or two events relatively easily. If you must switch many event handlers for the same control all at once, however, it may be easier to use a variable declared using the WithEvents keyword.

Control Array Events

Visual Basic 6 and earlier versions allowed you to use control arrays. A *control array* was an array of controls with the same name that shared the same event handlers. A parameter to the event handlers gave the index of the control in the array that fired the event. If the controls perform closely related tasks, the common event handler may be able to share a lot of code for all of the controls.

Visual Basic .NET does not support control arrays, but you can get similar effects in a couple of ways.

First, suppose that you add a control to a form and give it event handlers. Then you copy and paste the control to make other controls on the form. By default, all of these controls share the event handlers that you created for the first control. If you look at the event handlers' code, you'll see the Handles statements list all of the copied controls. You can also modify an event handler's Handles clause manually to attach it to more than one control.

Another way to make controls share event handlers is to attach them to the controls by using the AddHandler statement.

An event handler's first parameter is a variable of the type System.Object that contains a reference to the object that raised the event. The program can use this object and its properties (for example, its Name or Text property) to determine which control raised the event and take appropriate action.

Validation Events

Data validation is an important part of many applications. Visual Basic provides two events to make validating data easier: Validating and Validated. The following sections describe three approaches to using those events to validate data.

Integrated Validation

The Validating event fires when the code should validate a control's data. This happens when the control has the input focus and the form tries to close, or when focus moves from the control to another control that has its CausesValidation property set to True. Integrated validation uses the Validating event to perform all validation.

The Validating event handler can verify that the data in a control has a legal value and take appropriate action if it doesn't. For example, consider the FiveDigits example program, which is shown in Figure 9-12. The first TextBox control's Validating event handler checks that the control's value contains exactly five digits. If the value does not contain five digits, as is the case in the figure,

the program uses an ErrorProvider control to flag the TextBox's value as being in error and moves the input focus back to the TextBox. The ErrorProvider displays the little exclamation mark icon to the right of the control and makes the icon blink several times to get the user's attention. When the user hovers the mouse over the icon, the ErrorProvider displays the error text in a tooltip.

FIGURE 9-12: The Validating event fires when the focus moves to a control that has CausesValidation set to True.

The second TextBox control in this example has a CausesValidation property value of False. When the user moves from the first TextBox control to the second one, the Validating event does not fire and the TextBox control is not flagged. The third TextBox control has CausesValidation set to True, so when the user moves into that TextBox control, the first TextBox's Validating event fires, and the value is flagged if it is invalid. The Validating event also fires if the user tries to close the form.

The following code shows the Validating event handler used by this example. Notice that the Handles clause lists all three TextBoxes' Validating events so this event handler catches the Validating event for all three controls.

```vb
' Validate the TextBox's contents.
Private Sub txtNumber_Validating(ByVal sender As Object, _
 ByVal e As System.ComponentModel.CancelEventArgs) _
 Handles txtNumber1.Validating, txtNumber2.Validating, txtNumber3.Validating
    ' Get the TextBox.
    Dim text_box As TextBox = DirectCast(sender, TextBox)

    ' Validate the control's value.
    ValidateFiveDigits(text_box, e.Cancel)
End Sub

' Verify that the TextBox contains five digits.
Private Sub ValidateFiveDigits(ByVal text_box As TextBox, _
 ByRef cancel_event As Boolean)
    If text_box.Text.Length = 0 Then
        ' Allow a zero-length string.
        cancel_event = False
    Else
        ' Allow five digits.
        cancel_event = Not (text_box.Text Like "#####")
    End If

    ' See if we're going to cancel the event.
    If cancel_event Then
        ' Invalid. Set an error.
        errBadDigits.SetError(text_box, _
            text_box.Name & " must contain exactly five digits")
    Else
        ' Valid. Clear any error.
        errBadDigits.SetError(text_box, "")
    End If
End Sub
```

code snippet FiveDigits

The event handler receives the control that raised the event in its sender parameter. It uses DirectCast to convert that generic Object into a TextBox object and passes it to the ValidateFiveDigits subroutine to do all of the interesting work. It also passes the e.Cancel parameter, so the subroutine can cancel the action that caused the event if necessary.

ValidateFiveDigits checks the TextBox control's contents and sets its cancel_event parameter to True if the text has nonzero length and is not exactly five digits. This parameter is passed by reference, so this changes the original value of e.Cancel in the calling event handler. That will restore focus to the TextBox that raised the event and that contains the invalid data.

If cancel_event is True, the value is invalid, so the program uses the ErrorProvider component named errBadDigits to assign an error message to the TextBox control.

If cancel_event is False, the value is valid so the program blanks the ErrorProvider component's error message for the TextBox.

Separated Validation

A control's Validated event fires after the focus successfully leaves the control, either to another control with CausesValidation set to True or when the form closes. The control should have already validated its contents in its Validating event, hence the event name Validated.

This event doesn't really have anything directly to do with validation, however, and it fires whether or not the code has a Validating event handler and even if the control's value is invalid. The only time it will not execute is if the validation does not complete. That happens if the Validating event handler cancels the event causing the validation.

The previous section shows how to set or clear a control's error in its Validating event handler. An alternative strategy is to set errors in the Validating event handler and clear them in the Validated event handler, as shown in the following code. If the control's value is invalid, the Validating event handler cancels the event causing the validation so the Validated event does not occur. If the control's value is valid, the Validating event handler does not cancel the event and the Validated event handler executes, clearing any previous error.

```
' Validate the TextBox's contents.
Private Sub txtNumber_Validating(ByVal sender As Object, _
 ByVal e As System.ComponentModel.CancelEventArgs) _
 Handles txtNumber1.Validating, txtNumber2.Validating, txtNumber3.Validating
    ' Validate the control's value.
    ValidateFiveDigits(DirectCast(sender, TextBox), e.Cancel)
End Sub

' Verify that the TextBox contains five digits.
Private Sub ValidateFiveDigits(ByVal text_box As TextBox, _
 ByRef cancel_event As Boolean)
    ' Cancel if nonzero length and not five digits.
    cancel_event = (text_box.Text.Length <> 0) And _
        Not (text_box.Text Like "#####")
    ' See if we're going to cancel the event.
    If cancel_event Then
        ' Invalid. Set an error.
        ErrorProvider1.SetError(text_box, _
            text_box.Name & " must contain exactly five digits")
    End If
End Sub

' Validation succeeded. Clear any error.
```

```
Private Sub txtNumber_Validated(ByVal sender As Object, _
 ByVal e As System.EventArgs) _
 Handles txtNumber1.Validated, txtNumber2.Validated, txtNumber3.Validated
    ' Valid. Clear any error.
    ErrorProvider1.SetError(DirectCast(sender, TextBox), "")
End Sub
```

code snippet FiveDigitsSeparate

Example program FiveDigitsSeparate, available for download on the book's web site, demonstrates this approach.

Deferred Validation

By keeping focus in the control that contains the error, the previous approaches force the user to fix problems as soon as possible. In some applications, it may be better to let the user continue filling out other fields and fix the problems later. For example, a user who is touch-typing data into several fields may not look up to see the error until much later, after entering a series of invalid values in the first field and wasting a lot of time.

The following code shows one way to let the user continue entering values in other fields:

```
' Validate the TextBox's contents.
Private Sub txtNumber_Validating(ByVal sender As Object, _
 ByVal e As System.ComponentModel.CancelEventArgs) _
 Handles txtNumber1.Validating, txtNumber2.Validating, txtNumber3.Validating
    ' Validate the control's value.
    ValidateFiveDigits(DirectCast(sender, TextBox))
End Sub

' Verify that the TextBox contains five digits.
Private Sub ValidateFiveDigits(ByVal text_box As TextBox)
    ' See if the data is valid.
    If (text_box.Text.Length <> 0) And _
       Not (text_box.Text Like "#####") _
    Then
        ' Invalid. Set an error.
        errBadDigits.SetError(text_box, _
            text_box.Name & " must contain exactly five digits")
    Else
        ' Valid. Clear the error.
        errBadDigits.SetError(text_box, "")
    End If
End Sub

' See if any fields have error messages.
Private Sub Form1_FormClosing(ByVal sender As Object, _
 ByVal e As System.Windows.Forms.FormClosingEventArgs) _
 Handles Me.FormClosing
    ' Assume we will cancel the close.
    e.Cancel = True
```

```
    ' Check for errors.
    If IsInvalidField(txtNumber1) Then Exit Sub
    If IsInvalidField(txtNumber3) Then Exit Sub

    ' If we got this far, the data's okay.
    e.Cancel = False
End Sub


' If this control has an error message assigned to it,
' display the message, set focus to the control,
' and return True.
Private Function IsInvalidField(ByVal ctl As Control) As Boolean
    ' See if the control has an associated error message.
    If errBadDigits.GetError(ctl).Length = 0 Then
        ' No error message.
        Return False
    Else
        ' There is an error message.
        ' Display the message.
        MessageBox.Show(errBadDigits.GetError(ctl))

        ' Set focus to the control.
        ctl.Focus()
        Return True
    End If
End Function
```

code snippet FiveDigitsDeferred

The Validating event handler calls the ValidateFiveDigits subroutine much as before, but this time ValidateFiveDigits does not take the cancel_event parameter. If the TextBox object's value has an error, the routine uses the ErrorProvider to assign an error message to it and exits.

When the user tries to close the form, the FormClosing event handler executes. This routine assumes that some field contains invalid data, so it sets e.Cancel to True. It then calls the function IsInvalidField for each of the controls that it wants to validate. If any call to IsInvalidField returns True, the event handler exits, e.Cancel remains True, and the form refuses to close. If all of the fields pass validation, the event handler sets e.Cancel to False, and the form closes.

The function IsInvalidField uses the ErrorProvider's GetError method to get a control's assigned error message. If the message is blank, the function returns False to indicate that the control's data is valid. If the message is not blank, the function displays it in a message box, sets focus to the control, and returns True to indicate that the form's data is invalid.

If the focus is in a TextBox when the form tries to close, its Validating event fires before the form's FormClosing event so the TextBox control has a chance to validate its contents before the FormClosing event fires.

Example program FiveDigitsDeferred, available for download on the book's web site, demonstrates this approach.

VALIDATING BUTTONS

If the form is a dialog, you could validate the form's data in an OK button's Click event handler instead of in the form's FormClosing event.

Similarly, you may want to validate the data when the user clicks some other button. On a New Order form, you might validate all of the fields when the user clicks the Submit button.

SUMMARY

This chapter describes controls, components, and objects in general terms. It tells how to create controls and how to use their properties, methods, and events. It spends some extra time explaining how to add and remove event handlers, and data-validation events and strategies.

Appendix A, "Useful Control Properties, Methods, and Events," describes the most useful properties, methods, and events provided by the Control class. All controls that inherit from this class also inherit these properties, methods, and events, unless they take action to override the Control class's behavior.

Appendix G, "Windows Forms Controls and Components," describes the standard Windows controls and components in greater detail. This appendix can help you understand the controls to get the most out of them.

The Form class inherits from the Control class all of that class's properties, methods, and events. In some sense a Form is just another control, but it does have special needs and provides special features that are not shared with other controls. To help you use these objects effectively, Chapter 10, "Windows Forms," describes the Form class in greater detail.

10

Windows Forms

The Visual Basic Windows Form class is a descendant of the Control class. The inheritance trail is Control ⇨ ScrollableControl ⇨ ContainerControl ⇨ Form. That means a form *is* a type of control. Except where overridden, it inherits the properties, methods, and events defined by the Control class. In many ways, a form is just another kind of control (like a TextBox or ComboBox).

At the same time, Forms have their own special features that set them apart from other kinds of controls. You usually place controls inside a form, but you rarely place a form inside another form. Forms also play a very central role in most Visual Basic applications. They are the largest graphical unit with which the user interacts directly. The user can minimize, restore, maximize, and close forms. They package the content provided by the other controls so that the user can manage them in a meaningful way.

This chapter describes some of the special features of Windows Forms not provided by other objects. It focuses on different ways that typical applications use forms. For example, it explains how to build multiple-document interface (MDI) applications, custom dialogs, and splash screens.

MDI VERSUS SDI

An MDI application displays more than one document at a time in separate windows within a larger MDI parent form. MDI applications usually provide tools for managing the child forms they contain. For example, commands in the Window menu may let the user minimize child forms, arrange the icons for the minimized forms, tile the parent form's area with the child forms, and so on. Visual Studio can display many windows (form designers, code editors, bitmap editors, and so forth) all within its main form, so it is an MDI application.

A single-document interface (SDI) application displays only one document in each form. For example, Microsoft Paint can manage only one picture at a time, so it is an SDI application. Some SDI applications can display more than one document at a time, but each has its own separate form.

The chapter covers the Form object's properties, methods, and events only in passing. For a detailed description of specific Form properties, methods, and events, see Appendix J, "Form Objects."

TRANSPARENCY

The Form object provides a couple of properties that you can use to make a form partially transparent. Opacity determines the form's opaqueness. At design time, the Properties window shows Opacity as a percentage where 100% means the form is completely opaque, and 0% means that the form is completely transparent. At runtime, your program must treat Opacity as a floating-point value between 0 (completely transparent) and 1 (completely opaque).

A program can use an Opacity value less than 100% to let the user see what lies below the form. For example, you might build a partially transparent Search dialog box so the user could see the underlying document as a search progresses.

Figure 10-1 shows example program SemiTransparent, which is available for download at the book's web page. The program contains a form with Opacity set to 66%. You can still see the form's borders, title bar, system menus, menu bar, and button, but you can also see the Visual Basic IDE showing through from behind.

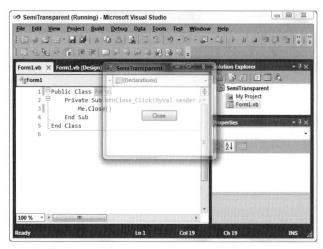

FIGURE 10-1: A form with Opacity set to 66% allows the Visual Basic IDE to show through.

If Opacity is greater than 0%, the form behaves normally aside from its ghostlike appearance. The user can click it, interact with its controls, minimize and maximize it, and grab its borders to resize it.

If Opacity is 0%, the form is completely transparent and the user can only interact with the form through the keyboard. For example, the user can press the Tab key to move between the form's controls, type text, press the Spacebar to invoke a button that has the focus, and press Escape or

Cancel to fire the form's Accept and Cancel buttons; however, the form and its controls will not detect mouse clicks. The user also cannot see the form (obviously), so figuring out which control has the focus can be next to impossible.

TOO MUCH TRANSLUCENCY

Many developers don't see a great need for translucent forms. A well-designed application allows the user to move windows around so they don't obscure each other. Translucent forms can be confusing, may create extra confusion for users with special needs, and incur a performance penalty. They're an interesting special effect but not everyone thinks they are necessary.

Example program TransparentForm, available for download on the book's web site, has a form with Opacity = 0 so you cannot see it while it is running. You can still use the Tab key to move between its controls, and you can use the Space key to make its buttons execute.

If Opacity is 2%, the form is still invisible, but it recognizes mouse clicks, so it can obscure the windows below. Example program CoverAll, also available for download, displays a maximized form with Opacity set to 2%.

OPTIMAL OPACITY

Normally, you should set a form's Opacity high enough that the user can see the form. It can be useful to have toolbars, property grids, and other secondary windows float translucently above the main form to provide information without completely obscuring the main form. In cases such as those, Opacity less than 50% makes it hard to read the secondary form, whereas Opacity greater than 75% makes it hard to see the main form. A value around 66% seems to provide a reasonable balance.

A second property that helps determine the form's transparency is TransparencyKey. This property is a color that tells Visual Basic which parts of the form should be completely transparent. When the form is rendered, any areas with this color as their background colors are not drawn.

Figure 10-2 shows example program Hole, which is available for download at the book's web page. The program's form has TransparencyKey set to red. Both the form and the Hole label have red backgrounds so they are transparent. The label's ForeColor property is black so its text is visible. The form's Paint event handler draws a black ellipse around the inside of the form.

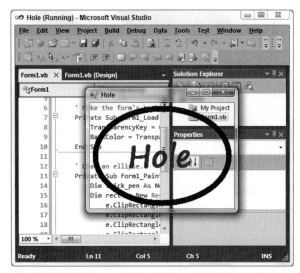

FIGURE 10-2: A form's TransparencyKey property lets you make shaped forms such as this one with a hole in it.

Example program GhostForm, also available for download, also uses a transparent background so only its borders and controls are visible when it runs.

The most common use for TransparencyKey is to create shaped forms or skins. Set the form's FormBorderStyle property to None to remove the borders, title bar, and system buttons. Set the form's BackColor and TransparencyKey properties to a color that you don't want to appear on the form. Then draw the shape you want the form to have in some other color.

Figure 10-3 shows the Smiley example program, which has a form shaped like a smiley face. The form's Paint event handler draws the image from a bitmap file. These sorts of forms make interesting splash screens and About dialog boxes, although they are often too distracting for use in a program's main user interface.

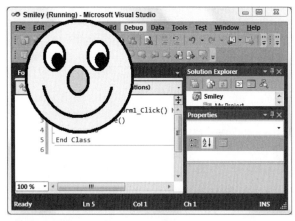

FIGURE 10-3: The TransparencyKey property lets you make shaped forms such as this one.

CONCEALED CONTROL

Note that the form in Figure 10-3 has no title bar, borders, or system buttons, so the user cannot move, resize, minimize, maximize, or close it. To use this form as a splash screen, add a Timer control to make the form disappear after a few seconds. To use it as an About dialog or some other kind of dialog, add a button that closes it.

If you use Opacity and TransparencyKey together, pixels that match TransparencyKey are completely removed and any remaining pixels are shown according to the Opacity value.

ABOUT, SPLASH, AND LOGIN FORMS

The TransparencyKey and Opacity properties enable you to build forms with unusual and interesting shapes. Although these would be distracting if used for the bulk of a business application, they can add a little interest to About dialog boxes, splash screens, and login forms.

These three kinds of forms have quite a bit in common. Usually, they all display the application's name, version number, copyright information, trademarks, and so forth. They may also display a serial number, the name of the registered user, and a web site or phone number where the user can get customer support.

The main difference between these forms is in how the user dismisses them. A splash screen automatically disappears after a few seconds. The user closes an About dialog box by clicking an OK button. A login form closes when the user enters a valid user name and password and then clicks OK. It also closes if the user clicks Cancel, although then it doesn't display the main application.

REMOVING THE SPLASH

Sometimes a splash screen is displayed while the application initializes, loads needed data, and otherwise prepares itself for work. In that case, the application removes the splash screen after initialization is complete or a few seconds have passed, whichever comes second.

The forms also differ slightly in the controls they contain. A splash screen needs a Timer control to determine when it's time to close the form. An About dialog box needs a single OK button. A login form needs TextBoxes to hold the user name and password, two Labels to identify them, and OK and Cancel buttons.

Splash screens and login forms greet the user, so there's no need to provide both. However, that still leaves you with the task of building two nearly identical forms: splash and About, or login and About. With a little planning, you can use a single form as a splash screen, About dialog box, and login form. At runtime, you can add whichever set of controls is appropriate to the form's use.

Alternatively, you can build the form with all three sets of controls at design time and then hide the ones you don't need for a particular purpose.

The following code shows how example program SplashScreen displays a form either as a splash screen or as an About dialog:

```
' Display as a splash screen.
Public Sub ShowSplash()
    Me.tmrUnload.Enabled = True ' The Timer close the dialog.
    Me.TopMost = True           ' Keep on top of main form.
    Me.Show()                   ' Show non-modally.
End Sub

' Unload the splash screen.
Private Sub tmrUnload_Tick()  Handles tmrUnload.Tick
    Me.Close()
End Sub

' Display as an About dialog.
Public Sub ShowAbout()
    btnOK.Visible = True      ' The OK button closes the dialog.
    Me.ShowDialog()           ' Show modally.
End Sub

' Close the About dialog.
Private Sub btnOK_Click() Handles btnOK.Click
    Me.Close()
End Sub
```

code snippet SplashScreen

The form contains both a Timer named tmrUnload and an OK button named btnAboutOk. The form's ShowSplash method enables the tmrUnload Timer control and calls Show to display the form. The Timer control's Interval property was set to 3,000 milliseconds at design time, so its Timer event fires after three seconds and closes the form.

The ShowAbout method makes the btnOk button visible and calls ShowDialog to display the form modally. A *modal* form holds the application's focus so the user cannot interact with other parts of the application until the modal form is dismissed. When the user clicks the button, the button's Click event handler closes the form.

MOUSE CURSORS

A form's Cursor property determines the kind of mouse cursor the form displays. The Form class inherits the Cursor property from the Control class, so other controls have a Cursor property, too. If you want to give a particular control a special cursor, you can set its Cursor property. For example, if you use a Label control as a hyperlink, you could make it display a pointing hand similar to those displayed by web browsers to let the user know that the control is a hyperlink.

The Cursors class provides several standard cursors as shared values. For example, the following statement sets a form's cursor to the system default cursor (normally an arrow pointing up and to the left):

```
Me.Cursor = Cursors.Default
```

Figure 10-4 shows example program ShowCursors, which is available for download on the book's web site, displaying the names and images of the standard cursors defined by the Cursors class in Windows 7. In previous versions of Windows, the AppStarting and WaitCursor values display hourglasses instead of animated circles.

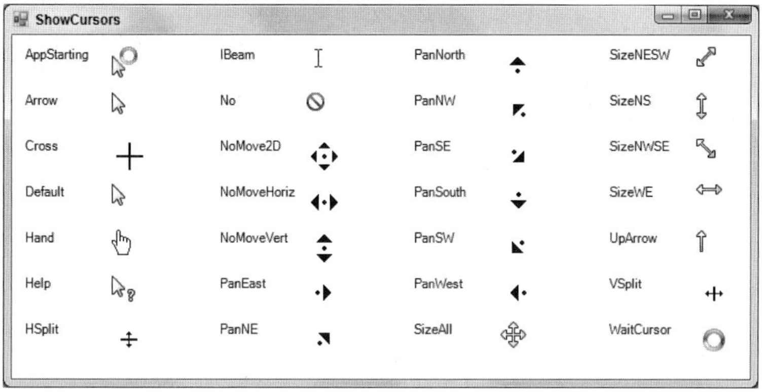

ShowCursors						
AppStarting		IBeam		PanNorth		SizeNESW
Arrow		No		PanNW		SizeNS
Cross		NoMove2D		PanSE		SizeNWSE
Default		NoMoveHoriz		PanSouth		SizeWE
Hand		NoMoveVert		PanSW		UpArrow
Help		PanEast		PanWest		VSplit
HSplit		PanNE		SizeAll		WaitCursor

FIGURE 10-4: The Cursors class defines standard cursors.

Unless a control explicitly sets its own cursor, it inherits the cursor of its container. If the control is placed directly on the form, it displays whatever cursor the form is currently displaying. That means you can set the cursor for a form and all of its controls in a single step by setting the form's cursor.

Similarly, if a control is contained within a GroupBox, Panel, or other container control, it inherits the container's cursor. You can set the cursor for all the controls within a container by setting the cursor for the container.

One common use for cursors is to give the user a hint when the application is busy. The program sets its cursor to Cursors.WaitCursor when it begins a long task and then sets it back to Cursors.Default when it finishes. The following code shows an example:

Available for
download on
Wrox.com

```
Me.Cursor = Cursors.WaitCursor
' Perform the long task.
...
Me.Cursor = Cursors.Default
```

code snippet UseWaitCursor

Example program UseWaitCursor displays a wait cursor when you click its button.

If the program displays more than one form, it must set the cursors for each form individually. It can set the cursors manually, or it can loop through the My.Application.OpenForms collection. The SetAllCursors subroutine shown in the following code makes setting the cursor for all forms a bit easier:

```
Private Sub SetAllCursors(ByVal the_cursor As Cursor)
    For Each frm As Form In My.Application.OpenForms
        frm.Cursor = the_cursor
    Next frm
End Sub
```

code snippet UseMultipleWaitCursors

The following code uses the SetAllCursors subroutine while performing a long task:

```
SetAllCursors(Cursors.WaitCursor)
' Perform the long task.
...
SetAllCursors(Cursors.Default)
```

Example program UseMultipleWaitCursors uses the SetAllCursors subroutine to display a wait cursor on each of its forms when you click its button.

To use a custom cursor, create a new Cursor object using a file or resource containing cursor or icon data. Then assign the new object to the form's Cursor property. The following code sets a form's cursor to the program resource named SmileIcon.ico:

```
Me.Cursor = New Cursor(My.Resources.SmileIcon.Handle)
```

Example program SmileCursor, also available for download, uses this code to display a custom cursor.

ICONS

Each form in a Visual Basic application has its own icon. A form's icon is displayed on the left side of its title bar, in the system's taskbar, and by applications such as the Task Manager and Windows Explorer.

Some of these applications display icons at different sizes. For example, Windows Explorer uses 32 × 32 pixel icons for its Large Icons view and 16 × 16 pixel icons for its other views. Toolbar icons come in 16 × 16, 24 × 24, and 32 × 32 pixel sizes. Windows uses still other sizes for different purposes. For more information on various pixel sizes used by Windows Vista, see `msdn2.microsoft` `.com/aa511280.aspx`.

If an icon file doesn't provide whatever size Windows needs, the system shrinks or enlarges an existing image to fit. That may produce an ugly result. To get the best appearance, you should ensure that icon files include at least 16 × 16 and 32 × 32 pixel sizes. Depending on the characteristics of your system, you may also want to include other sizes.

The integrated Visual Studio icon editor enables you to define images for various color models ranging from monochrome to 24-bit color, and sizes ranging from 16 × 16 to 256 × 256 pixels. It even lets you build icon images with custom sizes such as 32 × 48 pixels, although it is unlikely that Windows will need to use those.

To use this editor, open Solution Explorer and double-click the My Project entry to open the Project Properties window. Select the Resources tab, open the Add dropdown, and select New Icon. Use the drawing tools to build the icons. Right-click the icon and use the Current Icon Image Types submenu to work with icons of different sizes.

ICON-A-THON

The integrated icons editor works and is free but it's fairly cumbersome. Many developers use other icon editors such as IconForge (`www.cursorarts.com/ca_if` `.html`), IconEdit (`www.iconedit.com`), IconEdit 2 (no relation between this and IconEdit, `www.iconedit2.com`), and RealWorld Cursor Editor (`www.rw-designer` `.com/cursor-maker`). Note that I don't endorse one over the others.

To assign an icon to a form at design time, open the Windows Forms Designer and select the Icon property in the Properties window. Click the ellipsis button on the right and select the icon file that you want to use.

To assign an icon to a form at runtime, set the form's Icon property to an Icon object. The following code sets the form's Icon property to an icon resource named MainFormIcon:

```
Me.Icon = My.Resources.MainFormIcon
```

Some applications change their icons to provide an indication of their status. For example, a process-monitoring program might turn its icon red when it detects an error. It could even switch back and forth between two icons to make the icon blink in the taskbar.

Application Icons

Windows displays a form's icon in the form's title bar, in the taskbar, and in the Task Manager. Applications (such as Windows Explorer) that look at the application as a whole rather than at its individual forms display an icon assigned to the application, not to a particular form. To set the application's icon, open Solution Explorer and double-click the My Project entry to open the Project Properties window. On the Application tab, open the Icon drop-down list, and select the icon file that you want to use or select <Browse . . . > to look for the file you want to use.

> *To set the icon for a form, open the form in the Windows Forms Designer. In the Properties window, select the Icon property, click the ellipsis to the right, and select the icon file you want to use.*

Note that these different purposes display icons at different sizes. For example, the icon in the form's title bar is very small, whereas the one displayed by Task Manager is relatively large. As the previous section mentions, the integrated Visual Studio icon editor enables you to define images for various color models and sizes in the same icon file.

Notification Icons

Visual Basic applications can display one other kind of icon by using the NotifyIcon control. This control can display an icon in the system tray. The *system tray* (also called the *status area*) is the little area holding small icons that is usually placed in the lower-left part of the taskbar.

FIGURE 10-5: An application can use a NotifyIcon control to display status icons in the system tray.

Figure 10-5 shows example program UseNotifyIcon, which is available for download on the book's web page, and its notification icon. The little stop light near the mouse pointer is an icon displayed by a NotifyIcon control. Hovering the mouse over the icon makes it display a tooltip showing its text, in this case Stopped. The program also sets its form icon to match the icon shown in the NotifyIcon control.

The control's Icon property determines the icon that it displays. A typical application will change this icon to give information about the program's status. For example, a program that monitors the system's load could use its system tray icon to give the user an idea of the current load. Notification icons are particularly useful for programs that have no user interface or that run in the background so that the user isn't usually looking at the program's forms.

Notification icons also often include a context menu that appears when the user right-clicks the icon. The items in the menu enable the user to control the application. If the program has no other visible interface, this may be the only way the user can control it.

Appendix G, "Windows Forms Controls and Components," describes the NotifyIcon control in greater detail.

PROPERTIES ADOPTED BY CHILD CONTROLS

Some properties are adopted by many of the child controls contained in a parent control or in a form. For example, by default, a Label control uses the same background color as the form that contains it. If you change the form's BackColor property, its Label controls change to display the same color. Similarly if a GroupBox contains a Label and you change the GroupBox's BackColor property, its Label changes to match.

Some properties adopted by a form's controls include BackColor, ContextMenu, Cursor, Enabled, Font, and ForeColor. Not all controls use all of these properties, however. For example, a TextBox only matches its form's Enabled and Font properties.

If you explicitly set one of these properties for a control, its value takes precedence over the form's settings. For example, if you set a Label control's BackColor property to red, the control keeps its red background even if you change the Form's BackColor property.

Some of these properties are also not tremendously useful to the Form object itself, but they give guidance to the form's controls. For example, a form doesn't automatically display text on its surface, so it never really uses its Font property. Its Label, TextBox, ComboBox, List, RadioButton, CheckBox, and many other controls adopt the value of this property, however, so the form's Font property serves as a central location to define the font for all of these controls. If you change the form's Font property, even at runtime, all of the form's controls change to match. The change applies to all of the form's controls, even those contained within GroupBoxes, Panels, and other container controls, so that they do not sit directly on the form.

These properties can also help your application remain consistent both with the controls on the form and with other parts of the application. For example, the following code draws the string "Hello World!" on the form whenever the form needs to be repainted. This code explicitly creates the Comic Sans MS font.

```
Private Sub Form1_Paint(ByVal sender As Object, _
  ByVal e As System.Windows.Forms.PaintEventArgs) Handles Me.Paint
    Dim new_font As New Font("Comic Sans MS", 20)
    e.Graphics.DrawString("Hello World!", _
        new_font, Brushes.Black, 10, 10)
    new_font.Dispose()
End Sub
```

Rather than making different parts of the program build their own fonts, you can use the forms' Font properties as shown in the following code. This makes the code simpler and ensures that different pieces of code use the same font.

```
Private Sub Form1_Paint(ByVal sender As Object, _
  ByVal e As System.Windows.Forms.PaintEventArgs) Handles Me.Paint
    e.Graphics.DrawString("Hello World!", Me.Font, Brushes.Black, 10, 100)
End Sub
```

As a nice bonus, changing the form's Font property raises a Paint event, so, if the form's font changes, this code automatically runs again and redraws the text using the new font.

Example program ChangeFormFont, available for download on the book's web page, contains three radio buttons and a label. When you click a radio button, the form's font changes and the label's font automatically changes to match.

PROPERTY RESET METHODS

The Form class provides several methods that reset certain property values to their defaults. The most useful of those methods are ResetBackColor, ResetCursor, ResetFont, ResetForeColor, and ResetText.

If you change one of the corresponding form properties, either at design time or at runtime, these methods restore them to their default values. The default values may vary from system to system, but currently on my computer BackColor is reset to Control, Cursor is reset to Default, Font is reset to 8-point regular (not bold or italic) Microsoft Sans Serif, ForeColor is reset to ControlText, and Text is reset to an empty string.

Because the controls on a form adopt many of these properties (all except Text), these methods also reset the controls on the form.

OVERRIDING WNDPROC

The Windows operating system sends all sorts of messages to applications that tell them about changes in the Windows environment. Messages tell forms to draw, move, resize, hide, minimize, close, respond to changes in the Windows environment, and do just about everything else related to Windows.

All Windows applications have a subroutine tucked away somewhere that responds to those messages. That routine is traditionally called a WindowProc. A Visual Basic .NET form processes these messages in a routine named WndProc. You can override that routine to take special actions when the form receives certain messages.

Example program FixedAspectRatio, available on the book's web page, looks for WM_SIZING messages. When it finds those messages, it adjusts the form's new width and height so they always have the same aspect ratio (ratio of height to width).

WNDPROC WARNING

When you override the WndProc method, it is very important that the new method calls the base class's version of WndProc as shown in the following statement:

```
MyBase.WndProc(m)
```

If the program doesn't do this, it won't respond properly to events. For example, the form won't be able to draw itself correctly, resize or move itself, or even create itself properly.

When you override the WndProc method, you must also figure out what messages to intercept, what parameters those messages take, and what you can do to affect them safely. One way to learn about messages is to insert the following WndProc and then perform the action that you want to study (resizing the form, in this example):

Available for
download on
Wrox.com

```
Protected Overrides Sub WndProc(ByRef m As System.Windows.Forms.Message)
    Debug.WriteLine(m.ToString)
    MyBase.WndProc(m)
End Sub
```

code snippet ViewWindowMessages

Example program ViewWindowsMessages uses this code to display information about the messages it receives.

The following statement shows the result for the WM_SIZING message sent to the form while the user resizes it. It at least shows the message name (WM_SIZING) and its numeric value (hexadecimal 0x214).

```
msg=0x214 (WM_SIZING) hwnd=0x30b8c wparam=0x2 lparam=0x590e29c result=0x0
```

Searching for the message name on the Microsoft web site and on other programming sites usually gives you the other information you need to know (such as what m.WParam and m.LParam mean).

Note also that the Form class inherits the WndProc subroutine from the Control class, so all other Windows Forms controls inherit it as well. That means you can override their WndProc routines to change their behaviors.

For example, the following code shows how the NoCtxMnuTextBox class works. This control is derived from the TextBox control. Its WndProc subroutine checks for WM_CONTEXTMENU messages and calls the base class's WndProc for all other messages. By failing to process the WM_CONTEXTMENU message, the control prevents itself from displaying the TextBox control's normal Copy/Cut/Paste context menu when you right-click it.

```
Public Class NoCtxMnuTextBox
    Inherits System.Windows.Forms.TextBox

    Protected Overrides Sub WndProc(ByRef m As System.Windows.Forms.Message)
        Const WM_CONTEXTMENU As Integer = &H7B

        If m.Msg <> WM_CONTEXTMENU Then
            MyBase.WndProc(m)
        End If
    End Sub
End Class
```

code snippet NoContextMenu

Example program NoContextMenu uses similar code to display a text box that does not display a context menu when you right-click it.

SDI AND MDI

A *single-document interface* (*SDI*) application displays a single document in each form. Here, a *document* can be an actual disk file, or it can be a group of related items such as those on an order, employee record, or architectural drawing. For example, Microsoft Paint and Notepad are both SDI applications. Figure 10-6 shows an SDI application showing three files in separate forms. Example program SDIEdit, which is available for download on the book's web page, is a simple SDI application.

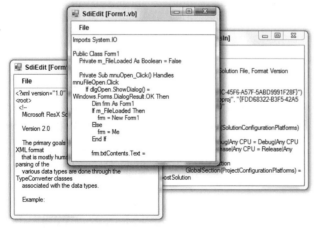

FIGURE 10-6: An SDI application displays separate documents in separate forms.

In contrast, a *multiple-document interface (MDI)* application displays its documents in their own forms, but then places the forms inside a container form. For example, Visual Studio can act either as an MDI application or it can display its child forms (form designers, code editors, and so forth) using tabs. The individual document windows are called *MDI child forms* and the container form is called the *MDI container* or *MDI parent* form. Figure 10-7 shows an MDI application with three MDI child forms. Example program MDIEdit, which is also available for download, is a simple MDI application.

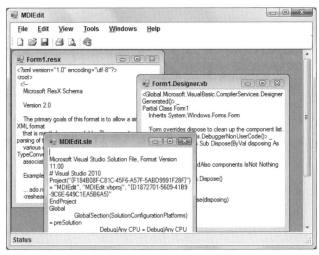

FIGURE 10-7: An MDI application displays documents in forms contained within an MDI container form.

The following sections describe some of the features provided by MDI forms and discuss reasons you might want to use an MDI or SDI application style.

MDI Features

The MDI container form provides several services for its child forms. It contains the forms and keeps them all together so that they are easy to find. If you move a form so that it won't fit within the container, the container automatically displays scroll bars so you can view it.

The program displays an icon in the taskbar and Task Manager for the MDI container, but not for the child forms. If you minimize the MDI container, all of the forms it contains are hidden with it. If you minimize a child form, its icon is displayed within the container, not separately in the taskbar. If you maximize an MDI child, it fills the parent form and its caption becomes part of the parent's. For example, if the MDI parent form's caption is Parent and the child's caption is Child, then when you maximize the child, the parent's caption becomes Parent - [Child].

The MDI container also provides some methods for arranging its child forms. The following code shows how an MDI container's code can cascade the children so that they overlap nicely, tile the children vertically or horizontally, and arrange the icons of any minimized child forms:

```
Private Sub mnuWinCascade_Click() Handles mnuWinCascade.Click
    Me.LayoutMdi(MdiLayout.Cascade)
End Sub

Private Sub mnuWinTileVertical_Click() Handles mnuWinTileVertical.Click
    Me.LayoutMdi(MdiLayout.TileVertical)
End Sub

Private Sub mnuWinTileHorizontal_Click() Handles mnuWinTileHorizontal.Click
    Me.LayoutMdi(MdiLayout.TileHorizontal)
End Sub

Private Sub mnuWinArrangeIcons_Click() Handles mnuWinArrangeIcons.Click
    Me.LayoutMdi(MdiLayout.ArrangeIcons)
End Sub
```

code snippet MDIEdit

Some other useful commands that you can add to an MDI application include Minimize All, Restore All, Maximize All, and Close All. You can implement these commands by looping through the MDI container's MdiChildren collection, as shown in the following code:

```
Private Sub mnuWinMinimizeAll_Click() Handles mnuWinMinimizeAll.Click
    For Each frm As Form In Me.MdiChildren
        frm.WindowState = FormWindowState.Minimized
    Next frm
End Sub

Private Sub mnuWinRestoreAll_Click() Handles mnuWinRestoreAll.Click
    For Each frm As Form In Me.MdiChildren
        frm.WindowState = FormWindowState.Normal
    Next frm
End Sub

Private Sub mnuWinMaximizeAll_Click() Handles mnuWinMaximizeAll.Click
    For Each frm As Form In Me.MdiChildren
        frm.WindowState = FormWindowState.Maximized
    Next frm
End Sub

Private Sub mnuWinCloseAll_Click() Handles mnuWinCloseAll.Click
    For Each frm As Form In Me.MdiChildren
    frm.Close()
    Next
End Sub
```

code snippet MDIEdit

Depending on your application, you might also provide commands that operate on subsets of the child forms. Suppose that a program displays a main order record and its many related order items in MDI child forms. You might want to let the user close all the order items, while keeping the main order form open.

Many MDI programs include a Window menu that displays a list of the MDI child forms that are open. You can select one of these menu items to move that form to the top of the others.

Building an MDI child list is easy in Visual Basic. Select the main MenuStrip control. Then in the Properties window, set the control's MdiWindowListItem property to the menu that you want to hold the child list. When you open and close child windows, Visual Basic automatically updates the list.

Figure 10-8 shows a menu displaying an MDI child list. The form with the caption MDIEdit .sln (behind the menu) currently has the focus, so the list displays a check mark next to that form's entry.

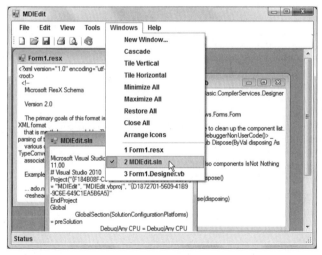

FIGURE 10-8: The MenuStrip's MdiWindowListItem property determines which menu item displays an MDI child list.

Most regular Visual Basic applications use SDI and when you create a new application, you get SDI by default. To build an MDI application, start a new application as usual. Then set the startup form's IsMdiContainer property to True. In the Windows Forms Designer, this form will change appearance, so it's obvious that it is an MDI parent form.

Alternatively, you can select the Project menu's Add Windows Form command. In the Add New Item form dialog that appears, select MDI Parent Form, give the form a reasonable name, and click Add. Visual Basic adds a new MDI parent form and gives it an assortment of standard controls that you might like it to have including a menu strip containing standard menus (File, Edit, View, and so forth) and a toolbar with standard tools (new, open, save, and so forth).

At design time, an MDI child form looks just like any other form. To make the child form sit inside the MDI container, you must set its MdiParent property to the MDI container form at runtime.

The following code shows how the MDI parent form in Figure 10-7 creates new MDI children. When the user selects the File menu's Open command or the toolbar's Open tool, this event handler executes and displays an open file dialog. If the user selects a file and clicks OK, the code creates a new Form1 object. It loads the selected file into the form's txtContents TextBox, sets the form's caption to the file's name (without the path), sets the form's MdiParent property to Me (the MDI parent form), and displays the form. The form is automatically shown in the MDI container and added to the MDI child list.

```
Private Sub OpenFile() Handles mnuFileOpen.Click, toolOpen.Click
    If dlgOpen.ShowDialog(Me) = Windows.Forms.DialogResult.OK Then
        Dim frm As New Form1
        frm.FileName = dlgOpen.FileName
        frm.txtContents.Text = _
            My.Computer.FileSystem.ReadAllText(dlgOpen.FileName)
        frm.txtContents.Select(0, 0)
        frm.Text = New FileInfo(dlgOpen.FileName).Name
        frm.MdiParent = Me
        frm.Show()
    End If
End Sub
```

code snippet MDIEdit

Normally, the system menu in the left of a form's title area includes a Close command with the shortcut Alt+F4. This command closes the form. An MDI child's system menu also contains a Close command, but this one's shortcut is Ctrl+F4. If you select this command or invoke its shortcut, the application closes the MDI child form but not the MDI container.

The MDI child's system menu also includes a Next command that moves the focus to the MDI container's next MDI child. The menu shows this command's shortcut as Ctrl+F6. However, Ctrl+Tab works as well. Ctrl+Tab may be a bit easier to remember because it is more similar to the Alt+Tab shortcut that moves to the next application on the desktop. This is also more consistent with the shortcuts for closing forms: Alt+F4 closes a top-level form, whereas Ctrl+F4 closes an MDI child; Alt+Tab moves to the next desktop application, whereas Ctrl+Tab moves to the next MDI child form.

MDI Events

Events for an MDI child form generally occur before the corresponding MDI parent's events. For example, if you try to close an MDI form, the child forms all receive FormClosing events before the MDI parent receives its FormClosing event. Next, the MDI child forms receive FormClosed events, and finally the MDI parent receives its FormClosed event.

Note that MDI child forms also receive these events if only the child form is closing. If the user closes an MDI child form, it receives a FormClosing event followed by its FormClosed event.

If a form's FormClosing event handler sets its e.Cancel parameter to True, the close is canceled and the form remains open. The form can use this to guarantee that its data is consistent and has been saved.

For example, the following code checks the txtContents control's Modified property to see if the form's data has been modified since it was loaded. The program sets this property to False when the file is opened or created from scratch, and sets it to True when the user changes the form's text. If this property is True, the program displays a message box asking if it should save the changes.

```
' See if it's safe to close the form.
Private Sub mdiChild_FormClosing(ByVal sender As Object, _
 ByVal e As System.Windows.Forms.FormClosingEventArgs) Handles Me.FormClosing
    If txtContents.Modified Then
        ' There are unsaved changes.
        ' Ask the user if we should save them.
        Select Case MessageBox.Show( _
            "The data has changed. Save the changes?", _
            "Save Changes?", _
            MessageBoxButtons.YesNoCancel, _
            MessageBoxIcon.Question)
          Case Windows.Forms.DialogResult.Yes
              ' Save the changes.
              SaveFile()

              ' See if we succeeded.
              e.Cancel = txtContents.Modified
          Case Windows.Forms.DialogResult.No
              ' Discard the changes.
              ' Leave e.Cancel = False.
          Case Windows.Forms.DialogResult.Cancel
              ' Cancel the close.
              e.Cancel = True
        End Select
    End If
End Sub
```

code snippet MDIEdit2

If the user clicks the Yes button, the code calls subroutine SaveFile to save the changes. This routine saves the data and sets the txtContents control's Modified property to False if it is successful. If SaveFile fails (for example, if the data file is locked), it leaves the Modified property set to True.

If the user clicks No to indicate that the program should discard the changes, the FormClosing event handler leaves e.Cancel equal to False so the form closes normally.

If the user clicks the Cancel button to indicate that the form should not be closed after all, the event handler sets e.Cancel to True to keep the form open.

If the user tries to close the MDI container and *any* of the MDI child forms' FormClosing event handlers sets e.Cancel to True, the close is canceled for *all* the child forms. Any child forms that have not yet received a FormClosing event do not get one. All of the children remain open, even those that set e.Cancel = False.

After the children process their FormClosing events, the MDI parent form still gets the final word. It receives a FormClosing event with its e.Cancel value set to True if *any* of the child forms set it to True. The e.Cancel value is False if all of the child forms left it False.

The MDI parent can leave the e.Cancel alone to accept whatever value the child forms selected, or it can override the value and force the program to exit or not as it desires.

The child forms still have one chance to save their data in their FormClosed events. At this point, they will close, however, so they had better take action if they need to save their data.

MDI versus SDI

MDI and SDI applications both have their advantages. In an SDI application, building and understanding the menus is simpler. A menu applies to exactly one form, and there is no merging and swapping of menus as the user changes MDI child forms.

SDI applications work particularly well when the program works with only one document at a time. Notepad, Microsoft Paint, and similar applications that only let the user work with one file at a time are SDI applications. These programs are light enough in weight that the user can easily run more than one instance of the program to view more than one file at a time if necessary.

MDI applications help the user display many related files at once without cluttering up the desktop. For example, Visual Studio can use an MDI interface to let you examine all of the files in a project side by side. Displaying all of a project's form designers, code editors, resource editors, and other files in separate windows might bury the desktop under forms and fill the taskbar with icons. Putting all of these forms inside an MDI container makes using the application easier. It lets the system represent the Visual Studio program with a single container form and a single icon. The Window menu provides an MDI child list that makes it easier to find a particular form.

You can also build a hybrid application that displays several MDI containers, each holding any number of MDI child forms. For example, each MDI container might hold all the forms related to a particular order: customer data, order items, and so forth. This would keep these related items together. It would also enable the user to display information about more than one order at a time in separate MDI containers.

In practice, examples of this kind of hybrid application are often cumbersome and poorly designed. It would generally be simpler to build this application as a standard MDI application and let the user launch multiple instances to display more than one order's data at once, but there may be times when it is easier to build a single multiple-MDI application. For example, if the program must work with a password-protected database, the program would need only to prompt the user for a user name and password once, and all the MDI containers could share the same database connection. Often, you can avoid the need for multiple forms (and hence an MDI format) by using other controls to fit more information on a single form. For example, ComboBox, ListBox, TreeView, SplitterContainer, and many other controls can display large amounts of data in a limited space, providing scroll bars as necessary.

The TabControl lets an application display many pages of data on a single form. For example, you might use different tabs to display the different pages that are relevant to an order: customer data, the order itself, order items, shipping and billing addresses, and so forth. This type of tabbed form placed inside an MDI container can make a very powerful application that enables the user to easily manage and understand huge amounts of information.

One drawback to many of these controls is that they make it more difficult to perform side-by-side comparisons of values. For example, suppose that a single form displays different addresses (billing, shipping, contact, and so forth) on different tabs. Then it would be difficult for the user to compare two addresses to see if they are identical. If you know that the user may want to compare two pieces of data, try to arrange them so they can both be visible at the same time.

WHITHER MDI?

The more recent versions of Visual Studio seem to be providing less and less support for MDI applications. MDI parent forms don't merge child menus as automatically as they did back in the good old days and WPF windows don't even have a concept of MDI. With Microsoft's ever-increasing focus on the Internet and applications that use Web-like navigation styles, it's unlikely that MDI will get much attention in the future.

MRU LISTS

MDI and SDI interfaces provide different ways to manage documents. Another tool that helps users manage documents is a *Most Recently Used list (MRU)*. The MRU list is a series of menu items (usually at the bottom of an application's File menu) that displays the files most recently accessed by the user. If the user clicks one of these menu items, the program reopens the corresponding file. Figure 10-9 shows an MRU list in a simple editing application.

By convention, these menu items begin with the accelerator characters 1, 2, 3, and so forth. If you opened the File menu shown in Figure 10-9 and pressed 2, for example, the program would reopen the file SDIEdit.sln.

When the user opens a new file or saves a file with a new name, that file is placed at the top of the list. Most applications display up to four items in the MRU list and, if the list ever contains more items, the oldest are removed.

FIGURE 10-9: An MRU list makes it easier for users to reopen the files they have used most recently.

Most applications remove a file from the MRU list if the applications try to open it and fail. For example, if the user selects an MRU menu item but the corresponding file has been removed from the system, the program removes the file's menu item.

Building an MRU list isn't too difficult in Visual Basic. The MruList example program shown in Figure 10-9 and available for download on the book's web site uses the MruList class to manage its MRU list. This class manages a menu that you want to use as an MRU list and updates the menu as the user opens and closes files. For example, if you configure the class to allow four MRU list entries and the user opens a fifth file, the class removes the oldest entry and adds the new one.

The class saves and restores the MRU list in the system's Registry. When the user selects a file from the MRU list, the class raises an event so the main program's code can open the corresponding file. The class also provides an Add method that the main program can use to add new files to the MRU list when the user opens a new file. Download the example and look at its code for more details.

The following code shows how the main MruList program uses the MruList class. This program is a simple text viewer that lets the user open and view files.

This program declares an MruList variable named m_MruList. It uses the WithEvents keyword so that it is easy to catch the object's OpenFile event.

The form's New event handler initializes the MruList object, passing it the application's name, the File menu, and the number of items the MRU list should hold.

When the user selects the File menu's Open command, the program displays an open file dialog box. If the user selects a file and clicks OK, the program calls subroutine OpenFile, passing it the name of the selected file.

If the user selects a file from the MRU list, the m_MruList_OpenFile event handler executes and calls subroutine OpenFile, passing it the name of the selected file.

Subroutine OpenFile loads the file's contents into the txtContents TextBox control. It then calls the MruList object's Add method, passing it the file's name. It finishes by setting the form's caption to the file's name without its directory path.

```
Imports System.IO

Public Class Form1
    Private WithEvents m_MruList As MruList

    ' Initialize the MRU list.
    Private Sub Form1_Load() Handles Me.Load
        m_MruList = New MruList("SdiMruList", mnuFile, 4)
    End Sub

    ' Let the user open a file.
    Private Sub mnuFileOpen_Click() Handles mnuFileOpen.Click
        If dlgOpen.ShowDialog() = Windows.Forms.DialogResult.OK Then
            OpenFile(dlgOpen.FileName)
        End If
    End Sub

    ' Open a file selected from the MRU list.
    Private Sub m_MruList_OpenFile(ByVal file_name As String) _
     Handles m_MruList.OpenFile
        OpenFile(file_name)
    End Sub

    ' Open a file and add it to the MRU list.
    Private Sub OpenFile(ByVal file_name As String)
        txtContents.Text = File.ReadAll(file_name)
```

```
                txtContents.Select(0, 0)
                m_MruList.Add(file_name)
                Me.Text = "[" & New FileInfo(file_name).Name & "]"
        End Sub
    End Class
```

You could easily convert the MruList class into a component. If you give the component ApplicationName, FileMenu, and MaxEntries properties, you can set those values at design time. For more information about building components, see Chapter 22, "Custom Controls."

DIALOG BOXES

Using a form as a dialog box is easy. Create the form and give it whatever controls it needs to do its job. Add one or more buttons to let the user dismiss the dialog. Many dialog boxes use OK and Cancel buttons, but you can also use Yes, No, Retry, and others.

You may also want to set the form's FormBorderStyle property to FixedDialog to make the form non-resizable, although that's not mandatory.

Set the form's AcceptButton property to the button you want to invoke if the user presses the Enter key. Set its CancelButton property to the button you want to invoke when the user presses the Escape key.

The form's DialogResult property indicates the dialog box's return value. If the main program displays the dialog box by using its ShowDialog method, ShowDialog returns the DialogResult value.

The following code shows how the main program can display a dialog box and react to its result. It creates a new instance of the dlgEmployee form and displays it by calling its ShowDialog method. If the user clicks OK, ShowDialog returns DialogResult.OK and the program displays the employee's name entered on the dialog. If the user clicks the Cancel button, ShowDialog returns DialogResult. Cancel and the program displays the message "Canceled."

```
Private Sub btnShowDialog_Click() Handles btnShowDialog.Click
    Dim dlg As New dlgEmployee
    If dlg.ShowDialog() = Windows.Forms.DialogResult.OK Then
        MessageBox.Show( _
            dlg.txtFirstName.Text & " " & _
            dlg.txtLastName.Text)
    Else
        MessageBox.Show("Canceled")
    End If
End Sub
```

If the user clicks the Cancel button or closes the form by using the system menu (or the little "X" in the upper-right corner), the form automatically sets its DialogResult property to Cancel and closes the form.

If the user clicks some other button, your event handler should set DialogResult to an appropriate value. Setting this value automatically closes the form.

 You can also set a button's DialogResult property to indicate the value that the dialog box should return when the user clicks that button. When the user clicks the button, Visual Basic sets the form's DialogResult property automatically.

The following code shows how the employee form reacts when the user clicks the OK button. It sees if the first and last name TextBox controls contain non-blank values. If either value is blank, the event handler displays an error message and returns without setting the form's DialogResult property. If both values are non-blank, the code sets DialogResult to OK, and setting DialogResult closes the form.

Available for download on Wrox.com

```vb
Private Sub btnOk_Click() Handles btnOk.Click
    ' Verify that the first name is present.
    If txtFirstName.Text.Length = 0 Then
        MessageBox.Show( _
            "Please enter a First Name", _
            "First Name Required", _
            MessageBoxButtons.OK, _
            MessageBoxIcon.Exclamation)
        txtFirstName.Select()
        Exit Sub
    End If

    ' Verify that the last name is present.
    If txtLastName.Text.Length = 0 Then
        MessageBox.Show( _
            "Please enter a Last Name", _
            "Last Name Required", _
            MessageBoxButtons.OK, _
            MessageBoxIcon.Exclamation)
        txtLastName.Select()
        Exit Sub
    End If

    ' Accept the dialog.
    Me.DialogResult = Windows.Forms.DialogResult.OK
End Sub
```

code snippet CustomDialog

CANCEL WITHOUT EVENTS

Note that the dialog box doesn't need an event handler for the Cancel button. If you set the form's CancelButton property to the button and if the user clicks it, Visual Basic automatically sets the form's DialogResult to Cancel and closes the form.

Example program CustomDialog demonstrates this kind of dialog.

Many dialog boxes provide OK and Cancel buttons, so they usually set DialogResult to OK or Cancel. However, you can also set DialogResult to Abort, Ignore, No, None, Retry, and Yes if that makes sense for your program. The main program can use an If Then or Select Case statement to see which value was set.

WIZARDS

One common type of dialog box is called a wizard. A *wizard* is a form that guides the user through a series of steps to do something. For example, building a database connection is complicated, so Visual Basic provides a data connection configuration wizard that helps the user enter the correct information for different kinds of databases. When it finishes, the wizard adds a connection object to the current form.

Figure 10-10 shows a typical wizard. The user enters data on each tab and then moves on to the next one. This wizard asks the user to enter an employee's name, identification (Social Security number and Employee ID), address and phone number, office location and extension, and privileges. Many tabbed wizards also include Next and Previous buttons to help you move from one tab to another.

FIGURE 10-10: A wizard guides the user through the steps of some complicated task.

When the user has filled in all the fields, the wizard enables the OK button. When the user clicks the OK or Cancel button, control returns to the main program, which handles the result just as it handles any other dialog box.

Figure 10-11 shows a different style of wizard. Instead of tabs, it uses buttons to let the user move through its pages of fields. The wizard only enables a button when the user has filled in the necessary information on the previous page. In Figure 10-11, the Office button is disabled because the user has not filled in all the fields on the Address page.

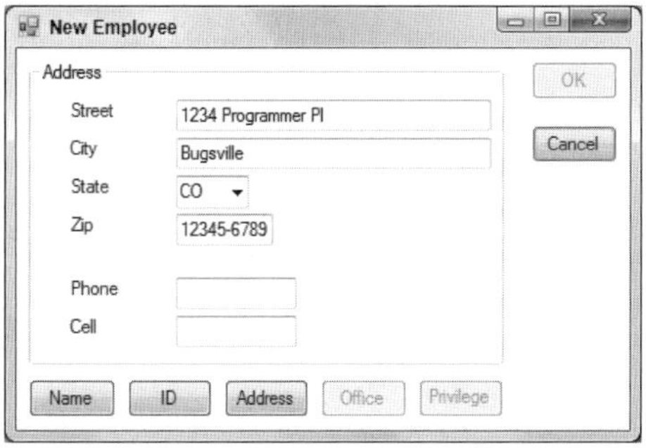

The button style is sometimes better at helping the user fill in all of the required fields because the user must finish filling in one page before moving on to the next. In a tabbed wizard, the user might leave a required field blank or use an incorrect format (for example, an invalid phone number) on the first tab and not realize it until clicking the OK button.

FIGURE 10-11: This wizard uses buttons instead of tabs to move through its pages of data.

SUMMARY

Although forms are just one kind of control, they have some very special characteristics. They form the basic pieces of an application that sit on the desktop, and they have many properties, methods, and events that set them apart from other controls. Appendix J provides more information about form properties, methods, and events.

This chapter describes some of the more typical uses of forms. It explains how to build About, splash, and login forms; manage a form's mouse cursor and icon; override WndProc to intercept a form's Windows messages; build MDI applications and tools that help the user manage MDI child forms; and make dialog boxes and wizards. After you master these tasks, you can build the forms that implement the large-scale pieces of an application.

Chapters 8, 9, and 10 describe Windows Forms controls and the Form class. The next three chapters provide corresponding information for Windows Presentation Foundation (WPF) controls and forms. Chapter 11, "Selecting WPF Controls," starts by providing an overview of WPF controls and giving tips on which you might like to use for given purposes, much as Chapter 8 does for Windows Forms controls.

11

Selecting WPF Controls

Windows Presentation Foundation (*WPF*) provides a whole new method for building user interfaces. Although it bears a superficial resemblance to Windows Forms, WPF provides new controls, a new event architecture, and a new foundation for building and interacting with properties.

WPF also provides tools for separating the user interface from the code behind the interface so that the two pieces can potentially be built by separate user interface designers and Visual Basic developers. It includes a new *Extensible Application Markup Language* (*XAML*, pronounced "zammel") that lets you build a user interface by using declarative statements rather than executable code. XAML lets you determine the size, position, and other properties of the WPF controls on a form. It lets you define styles that can be shared among many controls, and it lets you define transformations and animations that affect the controls.

As is the case in Windows Forms applications, controls play a central role in WPF applications. Different kinds of controls give information to the user (Label, StatusBar, TreeView, ListView, Image) and organize the information so that it's easy to understand (Border, StackPanel, DockPanel, TabControl). They enable the user to enter data (TextBox, TextBlock, ComboBox, PasswordBox), select options (RadioButton, CheckBox, ListBox), and control the application (Button, Menu, Slider).

To make an application as effective as possible, you should match controls with your application's needs. Though it is often possible to use many controls to perform a particular task, some controls usually work better than others. For example, you could display status information by changing a button's caption, but that's not really what buttons do best. A label in a status bar is usually a better way to give the user status information because the user will expect and understand it. Users generally don't expect to see status information in a button with changing text.

This chapter briefly describes the most common WPF controls so you can understand which controls work best for different purposes. To help you find the controls you need, the sections later in this chapter group controls by their general function. For example, if you need to display status to the user, look in the section "Providing Feedback."

I provide only brief descriptions of the WPF controls in this chapter, and some tips that can help you decide which control to use for different purposes. The following chapter, "Using WPF Controls," covers the controls in much greater detail, describing each control's most useful properties, methods, and events.

FOR MORE INFORMATION

This chapter and those that follow provide only the briefest glance at WPF. They explain enough to get you started but for greater detail and more in-depth information, see a book about WPF such as my book *WPF Programmer's Reference: Windows Presentation Foundation with C# 2010 and .NET 4.0* (Wrox, Stephens, 2009, www.amazon.com/exec/obidos/ASIN/0470477229/vbhelper).

CONTROLS OVERVIEW

You can group WPF controls into several categories. Some of these correspond naturally to the purposes of Windows Forms controls. Other categories play a more important role in WPF than they do in Windows Forms applications.

In particular, WPF controls rely heavily on layout controls that arrange and organize the controls that they contain. Windows Forms developers often simply arrange controls on a form with their desired sizes and positions. A WPF application is more likely to arrange the controls in a hierarchy of StackPanel and Grid controls and let those controls arrange their contents.

The following sections describe the main categories of WPF controls. The example programs for this chapter, which are available on the book's web site, demonstrate many of the controls' basic uses.

CONCEALED CONTROLS

Not all of the controls described here are available by default when you create a new WPF application. You need to add some of these controls to the Toolbox before you can use them. To add a control that is missing, right-click a Toolbox section and select Choose Items. On the Choose Toolbox Items dialog, select the WPF Components tab, check the boxes next to the controls that you want, and click OK.

Note, also, that some additional controls may be available in the Choose Toolbox Items dialog that are not described here. The following sections describe only the most commonly used controls.

CONTAINING AND ARRANGING CONTROLS

Layout controls determine the arrangement of the controls that they contain. For example, they may arrange controls vertically, horizontally, or in rows and columns.

The preferred style for WPF control arrangement is to make container controls determine the positions of their children and let the children take advantage of whatever space is allowed. This can be particularly useful for localized applications where you cannot easily predict how much space a control will need in a particular language.

For example, suppose a form contains a StackPanel control. The StackPanel contains several buttons that launch application dialogs. If you remove the buttons' Width properties, the buttons automatically size themselves to fit the StackPanel horizontally. Now if you need to make the buttons wider to hold text for a new language, you can simply widen the form. The StackPanel widens to fill the form and the buttons widen to fit the StackPanel.

Example program ResizingButtons, which is available for download on the book's web site, demonstrates buttons with fixed heights but widths that resize when their container resizes.

 In a Windows Forms application, you can achieve a similar effect by using Anchor and Dock properties.

Layout controls are also important because they can hold lots of other controls. Some of the WPF controls can hold only a single content item. For example, an Expander can hold only a single item. However, if you place another layout control such as a StackPanel inside the Expander, you can then place lots of other controls inside the StackPanel.

The following table briefly describes the WPF controls that are intended mainly to contain and arrange other controls.

CONTROL	PURPOSE
Border[1]	Provides a visible border or background to the contents.
BulletDecorator[2]	Contains two children. The first is used as a bullet and the second is aligned with the first. For example, you can use this to align bullet images next to labels. (See example program UseBulletDecorator, available for download on the book's web site.)
Canvas	Creates an area in which you can explicitly position children by specifying their Width, Height, Canvas.Left, and Canvas.Top properties. (See example program UseCanvas, available for download on the book's web site.)
DockPanel	Docks its children to its left, right, top, or bottom much as the Dock property does in a Windows Forms application. If the control's LastChildFill property is True, the control makes its last child control fill the remaining space. (See example program UseDockPanel, available for download on the book's web site.)

continues

(continued)

CONTROL	PURPOSE
Expander[1]	Displays a header with an expanded/collapsed indicator. The user can click the header or indicator to expand or collapse the control's single content item. (See example program UseExpander, available for download on the book's web site.)
Grid	Displays children in rows and columns. This is somewhat similar to the Windows Forms TableLayoutPanel control. Grid is one of the most useful container controls.
GridSplitter	Allows the user to resize two rows or columns in a Grid control.
GridView	Displays data in columns within a ListView control.
GroupBox[1]	Displays a border and caption much as a Windows Forms GroupBox control does.
Panel	Panel is the parent class for Canvas, DockPanel, Grid, TabPanel, ToolbarOverflowPanel, UniformGrid, StackPanel, VirtualizingPanel, and WrapPanel. Usually you should use one of those classes instead of Panel, but you can use Panel to implement your own custom panel controls.
ScrollViewer[1]	Provides vertical and horizontal scroll bars for a single content element. (See example program UseScrollViewer, available for download on the book's web site.)
Separator	Separates two controls inside a layout control. (See example program UseSeparator, available for download on the book's web site.)
StackPanel	Arranges children in a single row or column. If there are too many controls, those that don't fit are clipped. StackPanel is one of the most useful container controls.
TabControl	Arranges children in tabs. TabItem controls contain the items that should be displayed in the tabs. (See example program UseTabControl, available for download on the book's web site.)
TabItem[1]	Holds the content for one TabControl tab.
Viewbox[1]	Stretches its single child to fill the Viewbox. The Stretch property determines whether the control stretches its child uniformly (without changing the width-to-height ratio). (See example program UseViewbox, available for download on the book's web site.)

CONTROL	PURPOSE
VirtualizingStackPanel	Generates child items to hold items that can fit in the available area. For example, when working with a ListBox bound to a data source, the VirtualizingStackPanel generates only the items that will fit within the ListBox. If the control is not bound to a data source, this control behaves like a StackPanel.
WrapPanel	Arranges children in rows/columns depending on its Orientation property. When a row/column is full, the next child moves to a new row/column. This is similar to the Windows Forms FlowLayoutPanel control. (See example program UseWrapPanel, available for download on the book's web site.)

[1]This control can hold only a single child.
[2]This control should hold exactly two children. Controls with no footnote can hold any number of children.

Many of the layout controls have the ability to resize their children if you let them. For example, if you place a Button inside a Grid control's first row and column, by default the Button resizes when its row and column resize. The control's Margin property determines how far from the cell's edges the Button's edges lie.

If a child control explicitly defines its Width and Height properties, those properties override the parent's arrangement policy. For example, if you set Width and Height for a Button inside a Grid, the Button does not resize when its Grid cell does.

To get the effect that you want, consider how the control's Margin, Width, and Height properties interact with the parent layout control.

MAKING SELECTIONS

Selection controls enable the user to choose values. If you use them carefully, you can reduce the chances of the user making an invalid selection, so you can reduce the amount of error-handling code you need to write.

The following table briefly describes the WPF controls that allow the user to select choices.

CONTROL	PURPOSE
CheckBox	Lets the user select an item or not. Each CheckBox choice is independent of all others.
ComboBox	Displays items in a drop-down list. ComboBoxItem controls contain the items displayed in the list. (See example program UseComboBox, available for download on the book's web site.)
ComboBoxItem[1]	Holds the content for one ComboBox item.

continues

(continued)

CONTROL	PURPOSE
ListBox	Displays items in a list. ListBoxItem controls contain the items displayed in the list. The control automatically displays scroll bars when needed. (See example program UseListBox, available for download on the book's web site.)
ListBoxItem[1]	Holds the content for one ListBox item.
RadioButton	Lets the user pick from among a set of options. If the user checks one RadioButton, all others with the same parent become unchecked. (See example program UseRadioButtons, available for download on the book's web site.)
ScrollBar	Allows the user to drag a "thumb" to select a numeric value. Usually scroll bars are used internally by other controls such as the ScrollViewer and your applications should use a Slider instead. (See example program UseScrollBar, available for download on the book's web site.)
Slider	Allows the user to drag a "thumb" to select a numeric value. Similar to the Windows Forms TrackBar control. (See example program UseSlider, available for download on the book's web site.)

[1]This control can hold only a single child.

ENTERING DATA

Sometimes, it is impractical to use the selection controls described in the previous section. For example, the user cannot reasonably enter biographical data or comments using a ComboBox or RadioButton. In those cases, you can provide a text control where the user can type information.

The following table briefly describes the WPF controls that allow the user to enter text.

CONTROL	PURPOSE
PasswordBox	Similar to a TextBox but displays a mask character instead of the characters that the user types. (See example program UsePasswordBox, available for download on the book's web site.)
RichTextBox	Similar to a TextBox but contains text in the form of a document object. See the section "Managing Documents" later in this chapter for more information on documents.
TextBox	Allows the user to enter simple text. Optionally can allow carriage returns and tabs, and can wrap text.

DISPLAYING DATA

These controls are used primarily to display data to the user. The following table briefly describes these WPF controls.

CONTROL	PURPOSE
Label	Displays non-editable text.
TextBlock	Displays more complex non-editable text. This control's contents can include inline tags to indicate special formatting. Tags can include AnchoredBlock, Bold, Hyperlink, InlineUIContainer, Italic, LineBreak, Run, Span, and Underline.
TreeView	Displays hierarchical data in a tree-like format similar to the directory display provided by Windows Explorer.

PROVIDING FEEDBACK

The following controls provide feedback to the user. Like the controls that display data in the previous section, these controls are intended to give information to the user and not interact with the user. The following table briefly describes these WPF controls.

CONTROL	PURPOSE
Popup	Displays content in a window above another control. Usually you can use the Tooltip and ContextMenu controls instead of a Popup. (See example program UsePopup, available for download on the book's web site.)
ProgressBar	Indicates the fraction of a long task that has been completed. Usually, the task is performed synchronously, so the user is left staring at the form while it completes. The ProgressBar lets the user know that the operation is not stuck. (See example program UseProgressBar, available for download on the book's web site.)
StatusBar	Displays a container at the bottom of the form where you can place controls holding status information. Though you can place anything inside a StatusBar, this control is intended to hold summary status information, not tools. Generally, menus, combo boxes, buttons, toolbars, and other controls that let the user manipulate the application do not belong in a SatusBar. (See example program UseStatusBar, available for download on the book's web site.)
StatusBarItem[1]	Holds the content for one StatusBar item.
ToolTip	Displays a tooltip. To give a control a simple textual tooltip, set its Tooltip property. Use the Tooltip control to build more complex tooltips. For example, a Tooltip control might contain a StackPanel that holds other controls. (See example program UseToolTip, available for download on the book's web site.)

[1]This control can hold only a single child.

INITIATING ACTION

Every kind of control responds to events, so every control can initiate an action. In practice, however, users only expect certain kinds of controls to perform actions. For example, they generally don't expect the application to launch into a time-consuming calculation when they double-click a label.

The following table summarizes controls that normally initiate action.

CONTROL	PURPOSE
Button[1]	Raises a Click event that the program can catch to perform an action. (See example program UseButtonRepeatButton, available for download on the book's web site.)
ContextMenu	Displays a context menu for other controls. Normally the ContextMenu contains MenuItem controls. (See example program UseMenuContextMenu, available for download on the book's web site.)
Menu	Displays a menu for the form. Normally, the Menu contains MenuItem controls representing the top-level menus. Those items contain other MenuItem controls representing commands. (See example program UseMenuContextMenu, available for download on the book's web site.)
MenuItem	Contains an item in a ContextMenu or Menu.
PrintDialog	Displays a standard Windows print dialog. You shouldn't place a PrintDialog on a window. Instead use code to build and display the PrintDialog. (See example program UsePrintDialog, available for download on the book's web site.)
RepeatButton[1]	Acts as a Button that raises its Click event repeatedly when it is pressed and held down. (See example program UseButtonRepeatButton, available for download on the book's web site.)
ToolBar	Contains items. Normally, the control sits across the top of the form and contains command items such as buttons and combo boxes. (See example program UseToolBar, available for download on the book's web site.)
ToolBarTray	Contains ToolBars and allows the user to drag them into new positions. (See example program UseToolBar, available for download on the book's web site.)

[1]This control can hold only a single child.

PRESENTING GRAPHICS AND MEDIA

Any control can display an image. The following XAML code makes an ImageBrush and then uses it to fill a Grid control's background:

```
<Window x:Class="Window1"
    xmlns="http://schemas.microsoft.com/winfx/2006/xaml/presentation"
    xmlns:x="http://schemas.microsoft.com/winfx/2006/xaml" Title="FormImage"
    Height="300" Width="300">
    <Window.Resources>
        <ImageBrush ImageSource="smile.bmp" x:Key="brSmile" />
    </Window.Resources>
    <Grid Background="{StaticResource brSmile}">

    </Grid>
</Window>
```

code snippet FormImage

Example program FormImage displays an image in a Grid control's background.

Though a Grid control can display an image or other graphic, its real purpose is to arrange other controls. The following table describes controls whose main purpose is to present graphics and media.

CONTROL	PURPOSE
Ellipse	Displays an ellipse.
Image	Displays a bitmap image, for example, from a .bmp, .jpg, or .png file. Can optionally stretch the image with or without distortion.
Line	Draws a line segment.
MediaElement	Presents audio and video. To let you control the media, it provides Play, Pause, and Stop methods, and Volume and SpeedRatio properties. (See example program UseMediaElement, available for download on the book's web site.)
Path	Draws a series of drawing instructions.
Polygon	Draws a closed polygon.
Polyline	Draws a series of connected line segments.
Rectangle	Draws a rectangle, optionally with rounded corners.

The shape drawing objects (Ellipse, Line, Path, Polygon, Polyline, and Rectangle) all provide Stroke, StrokeThickness, and Fill properties to let you control their appearance. Although these controls are primarily intended to draw simple (or not so simple) shapes, like any other control they provide a full assortment of events. For example, they provide an IsMouseOver property and a MouseUp event that you can use to make these objects behave like simple buttons.

Example program DrawingShapes, which is available for download on the book's web site, demonstrates several of these shape controls. Program EllipseClick, which is also available for download, uses triggers to change the color of an Ellipse when the mouse is over it, and displays a message when you click the Ellipse.

PROVIDING NAVIGATION

The Frame control provides support for navigation through external web sites or the application's pages. Use the control's Navigate method to display a web page or XAML page. The Frame provides back and forward arrows to let the user navigate through the pages visited.

Example program UseFrame, which is available for download on the book's web site, uses a Frame control to provide navigation between two Page objects.

MANAGING DOCUMENTS

WPF includes three different kinds of documents: flow documents, fixed documents, and XPS documents. These different kinds of documents provide support for high-end text viewing and printing.

> ### XPS EXPLAINED
>
> XPS (XML Paper Specification) is a Microsoft standard that defines fixed-format documents similar to PDF files. An XPS reader can view an XPS file but will not reformat it as a web browser might rearrange the text on a web page. For more information, see the section "XPS Documents" in Chapter 12, "Using WPF Controls."

The following table summarizes the controls that WPF provides for viewing these kinds of documents.

CONTROL	PURPOSE
DocumentViewer	Displays fixed documents page-by-page.
FlowDocumentPageViewer	Displays a flow document one page at a time. If the control is wide enough, it may display multiple columns although it still only displays one page at a time.
FlowDocumentReader	Displays flow documents in one of three modes. When in *single page mode*, it acts as a FlowDocumentReader. When in *scrolling mode*, it acts as a FlowDocumentScrollViewer. In *book reading mode*, it displays two pages side-by-side much as a real book does.
FlowDocumentScollViewer	Displays an entire flow document in a single long scrolling page and provides scroll bars to let the user move through the document.

DIGITAL INK

Digital ink controls provide support for stylus input from tablet PCs (where you use a plastic stylus similar to a pen to draw right on a tablet PC's touch screen). Normally you would only use digital ink in a tablet PC application where the user is expected to enter data by drawing on the screen with a stylus. These applications usually provide text recognition to understand what the user is writing. They also use the stylus to perform the same operations they would perform with the mouse on a desktop system. For example, they let you tap to click buttons, and tap and drag to move items. For more information on tablet PCs and mobile PC development, see `msdn.microsoft.com/windows/aa905027.aspx`.

Though ink controls are most useful for tablet PCs, WPF includes two ink controls that you can use in any Visual Basic application.

CONTROL	PURPOSE
InkCanvas	Displays or captures ink strokes.
InkPresenter	Displays ink strokes.

SUMMARY

Controls are the link between the user and the application. They allow the application to give information to the user and they allow the user to control the application.

This chapter briefly describes the WPF controls grouped by category. You can use the categories to help you decide which controls to use. If the user must select an item, consider the controls in the "Making Selections" section. If the application needs to display status information, look at the controls in the "Providing Feedback" section.

This chapter gives only a brief introduction to the WPF controls and provides some hints about each control's purpose. Chapter 12, "Using WPF Controls," describes the controls in greater detail. It explains the most important properties, methods, and events provided by the most useful WPF controls.

12

Using WPF Controls

The code behind WPF controls is the same as the code behind Windows Forms controls. That means that everything the earlier chapters have explained about applications, forms, controls, Visual Basic code, error handling, drawing, printing, reports, and so forth, still work almost exactly as before.

Chapter 11, "Selecting WPF Controls," briefly describes the most common WPF controls, grouped by category to help you pick the control that best suits a particular task. This chapter provides more detail about WPF. It explains some of the more important concepts that underlie WPF. It also gives more detail about how particular controls work and tells how you can use them in your applications.

WPF is a huge topic. It basically reproduces all of the functionality of Windows Forms programming, and then some. This chapter cannot hope to cover all of the concepts, tools, and techniques used by WPF. Instead, it introduces some of the more important concepts and explains how to build basic WPF forms.

WPF CONCEPTS

WPF applications are similar in concept to Windows Forms applications in many respects. Both display a form or window that contains controls. Controls in both systems provide properties, methods, and events that determine the control's appearance and behavior.

Windows Forms applications use a set of controls provided by the System.Windows .Forms namespace. WPF applications use a different set of controls in the System.Windows .Controls namespace. Many of these controls serve similar functions to those used by Windows Forms applications, but they provide a different set of capabilities. For example, both namespaces have buttons, labels, combo boxes, and check boxes, but their appearances and abilities are different.

WPF uses these similar, but different, controls for two main reasons:

➤ To take better advantage of the graphics capabilities of modern computer hardware and software. The new controls can more easily provide graphical effects such as transparent or translucent backgrounds, gradient shading, rotation, two- and three-dimensional appearance, multimedia, and other effects.

➤ To provide a greater separation between the user interface and the code behind it. The following sections describe this idea and some of the other key WPF concepts in greater detail.

Separation of User Interface and Code

The idea of separating the user interface from the code isn't new. Visual Basic developers have been building *thin user interface* applications for years. Here, the user interface contains as little code as possible, and calls routines written in libraries to do most of the work.

Unfortunately, the code that calls those libraries sits inside the same file that defines the user interface, at least in Windows Forms applications. That means you cannot completely separate the code from the user interface. For example, if one developer wants to modify the user interface, another developer cannot simultaneously modify the code behind it.

WPF separates the user interface from the code more completely. The program stores the user interface definition in a XAML file.

Associated with a XAML file is a code file containing Visual Basic code. It contains any code you write to respond to events and manipulate the controls much as Windows Forms code can. Unlike the case with Windows Forms, WPF keeps the user interface definition and the code behind it in two separate files so, in theory at least, different developers can work on the user interface and the code at the same time. For example, a graphics designer can use the Expression Blend design tool to build the user interface, defining the forms' labels, menus, buttons, and other controls. Then a Visual Basic developer can attach code to handle the controls' events.

> *Though it isn't a free product, Expression Blend provides some useful tools that are missing from Visual Studio such as tools to record animations. If you frequently need to build property animations, I highly recommend that you give it a try.*
>
> *You can learn more about Expression Blend and download a trial version at* `www.microsoft.com/expression/products/Overview.aspx?key=blend`.

Because the user interface definition is separate from the code behind it, the graphic designer can later edit the XAML to rearrange controls, change their appearance, and otherwise modify the user interface while the code behind it should still work unchanged.

DEVELOPERS DIVIDED

It's not yet clear whether this scenario will actually play out as envisioned by Microsoft. At a Visual Studio users group meeting, a Microsoft representative said that Expression Blend would not be included with MSDN subscriptions. The group greeted this statement with a rousing chorus of boos. Of the 100 or so people in the room, none thought that their companies would have the desire or budget to provide separate graphics designers and developers. They felt that the developers would be building user interfaces much as they do today.

The separation between the user interface file and the code behind also it isn't as great as Microsoft would like. While you can work on the two files separately, they are tied closely together. For example, the user interface file defines event handlers that the code-behind must implement. If the code-behind doesn't implement them yet, then the graphic designer cannot test the interface by running it.

I suspect there's still some room for adjustment in Microsoft's plan, however. Some of the features of Expression Blend have moved into the latest Visual Studio release. For example, the previous version of Visual Studio didn't include any brush editors but the latest version does. It is possible that Visual Studio will gain at least some new features in future releases, although it is likely that Expression Blend will always include at least some tools that are missing from Visual Studio.

You can also implement these features by using XAML code or Visual Basic code, although that will be more difficult than using built-in design tools. If using the new features is too difficult, developers simply won't bother.

WPF Control Hierarchies

In a WPF application, the Window class plays a role similar to the one played by a Form in a Windows Forms application. Whereas a Form can contain any number of controls, a Window can contain only one. If you want a WPF form to display more than one control, you must first give it some kind of container control, and then place other controls inside that one.

For example, when you create a WPF application, its Window initially contains a Grid control that can hold any number of other controls, optionally arranged in rows and columns. Other container controls include Canvas, DockPanel, DocumentViewer, Frame, StackPanel, and TabControl.

The result is a tree-like control hierarchy with a single Window object serving as the root element. This matches the hierarchical nature of XAML. Because XAML is a form of XML, and XML files must have a single root element, XAML files must also have a single root element. When you look at XAML files later in this chapter, you will find that they begin with a Window element that contains all other elements.

Many non-container controls can hold only a single element, and that element is determined by the control's Content property. For example, you can set a Button control's Content property to the text that you want to display.

A control's Content property can only have a single value, but that value does not need to be something simple such as text. For example, Figure 12-1 shows a Button containing a Grid control that holds three labels.

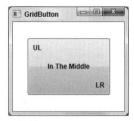

FIGURE 12-1: This Button contains a Grid that holds three labels.

WPF IN THE IDE

The Visual Studio IDE includes editors for manipulating WPF Window classes and controls. Although many of the details are different, the basic operation of the IDE is the same whether you are building a Windows Forms application or a WPF application. For example, you can use the WPF Window Designer to edit a WPF window. You can select controls from the Toolbox and place them on the window much as you place controls on a Windows Form.

Despite their broad similarities, the Windows Forms Designer and the WPF Window Designer differ in detail. Although the Properties window displays properties for WPF controls much as it does for Windows Forms controls, many of the property values are not displayed in similar ways.

The window represents many Boolean properties with check boxes. It represents other properties that take enumerated values with combo boxes where you can select a value or type one in (if you know the allowed values). The window represents some object properties with the objects' type names and doesn't allow you to select objects as the Properties window does in the Windows Forms Designer.

Future Visual Studio releases may make Expression Blend more consistent with Visual Studio, although some more advanced features (such as animation recording) are likely to remain only in Expression Blend to encourage developers to buy it.

Though some of these property editors are inconvenient or missing, it is important to note that the editors merely build the XAML code that defines the user interface. You can always edit the XAML manually to achieve effects that the Properties window does not support directly.

The following sections explain how to write XAML code and the Visual Basic code behind it.

Editing XAML

Figure 12-2 shows the IDE displaying a new WPF project. Most of the areas should look familiar from Windows Forms development. The Toolbox on the left contains tools that you can place on the window in the middle area. Solution Explorer on the right shows the files used by the application. The Properties window shows property values for the currently selected control in the middle. The selected object in Figure 12-2 is the main Window, so the top of the Properties window shows its type: System.Windows.Window.

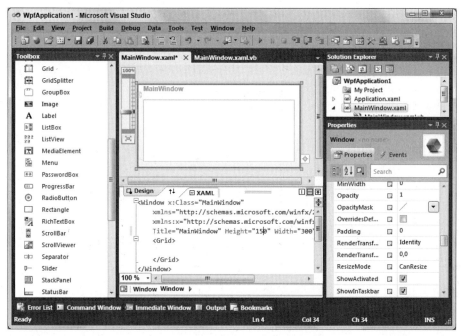

FIGURE 12-2: The IDE looks almost the same for Windows Forms and WPF applications.

One large difference between the IDE's appearance when building a WPF application versus a Windows Forms application is the central editor. In a Windows Forms application, you edit a form with the Windows Forms Designer. In a WPF application, you use the graphical XAML editor shown in Figure 12-2 to edit a Window object's XAML code. The upper half of this area shows a graphical editor where you can drag controls from the Toolbox much as you design a Windows Form. The lower part of the editor shows the resulting XAML code.

If you look closely at Figure 12-2, you can see the Window element that includes the rest of the file. When you first build an application, the Window object's element contains a single Grid control.

Usually, it is easiest to build WPF Window objects by using the graphical editor and the Toolbox. When you select a control in the graphical editor, you can view and modify many of its properties in the Properties window. Unfortunately, the Properties window does not give you access to all of the controls' features. Some properties are read-only in the Properties window or represent values that you cannot enter in the Properties window.

For example, a control's LayoutTransform property determines how the control is moved, scaled, rotated, and skewed before it is positioned and drawn. In the Properties window, this property appears as "Identity" if you have not defined a transformation, or the name of a class such as "System.Windows.Media.RotateTransform" if the transform rotates the control. Unfortunately, the

Properties window does not provide any tools for setting the LayoutTransform property's value. If you want to set this property, you must type it into the XAML code by hand.

Figure 12-3 shows a Window containing a Button that is rotated 20 degrees. Notice that the LayoutTransform property in the Properties window displays the RotateTransform's class name System.Windows.Media.RotateTransform. The XAML code in the bottom left defines the control's LayoutTransform property.

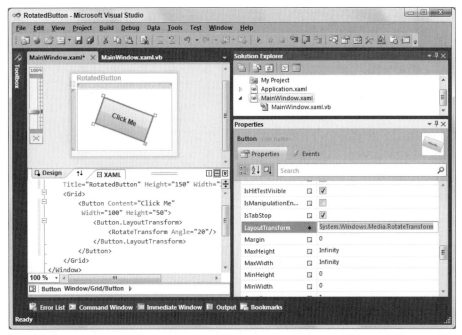

FIGURE 12-3: XAML code can make a LayoutTransform but the Properties window cannot.

Example program RotatedButton, which is available for download on the book's web site, uses the code shown in Figure 12-3 to display a rotated button.

Expression Blend provides additional tools for editing XAML. For example, it includes editors that let you define layout transformations interactively. Although the Visual Studio IDE doesn't provide similar tools, you can build these by hand with XAML code.

Similarly, the Properties window doesn't give you an easy way to set a non-container control's Content property to another control, but you can do this easily with XAML code. For example, to place a Grid inside a Button control, simply type the Grid control's definition between the Button control's start and end tags.

Example program GridButton uses the following XAML code to build a Button containing a Grid similar to the one shown in Figure 12-1:

```
<Window x:Class="Window1"
  xmlns="http://schemas.microsoft.com/winfx/2006/xaml/presentation"
  xmlns:x="http://schemas.microsoft.com/winfx/2006/xaml" Title="XamlGridButton"
  Height="193" Width="219">
    <Grid>
      <Button Name="btnGrid" Height="100" Width="150">
        <Grid Height="90" Width="140">
          <Grid.RowDefinitions>
            <RowDefinition Height="33*" />
            <RowDefinition Height="33*" />
            <RowDefinition Height="33*" />
          </Grid.RowDefinitions>
          <Grid.ColumnDefinitions>
            <ColumnDefinition Width="33*" />
            <ColumnDefinition Width="33*" />
            <ColumnDefinition Width="33*" />
          </Grid.ColumnDefinitions>
          <Label Content="UL" Grid.Row="0" Grid.Column="0" />
          <Label Content="In The Middle" Grid.Row="1"
           Grid.Column="0" Grid.ColumnSpan="3"
           VerticalAlignment="Center" HorizontalAlignment="Center" />
          <Label Content="LR" Grid.Row="2" Grid.Column="2"
           VerticalAlignment="Bottom"
           HorizontalAlignment="Right" />
        </Grid>
      </Button>
    </Grid>
</Window>
```

code snippet GridButton

The top-level Window element contains a Grid control that holds a single Button. The Button contains a second Grid control. Grid.Row and Grid.Column elements define the grid's row and column sizes.

The inner Grid contains three Label controls. The first displays the text UL, is aligned to the upper left (by default), and is contained in the grid's upper-left cell (row 0, column 0).

The second Label displays the text In the Middle, is aligned in the center, and is contained in grid's second row (row 1), first column (column 0). Its ColumnSpan property is 3, so it spans all three cells in the second row.

The final Label displays the text LR, is aligned to the lower right, and is in the grid's lower-right cell (row 2, column 2).

The graphical editor and the Properties window don't give you access to all of XAML's features, but they do let you build a basic user interface for WPF applications. Once you have defined the window's basic structure, you can use XAML to fine-tune the result (for example, by adding gradient backgrounds).

Editing Visual Basic Code

Each XAML file is associated with a Visual Basic code file. When you first create a WPF project, that file is opened by default. If you look closely at the central designer in Figure 12-3, you'll see that the XAML file Window1.xaml is open and visible in the designer. Another tab contains the corresponding Visual Basic file Window1.xaml.vb. Click that tab to view the Visual Basic source code.

The following text shows the Visual Basic source code initially created for a XAML file:

```
Class Window1

End Class
```

You can add event handlers to this file just as you can add event handlers to Windows Forms code. Use the left dropdown to select a control or Window1 Events. Then use the right drop-down list to select an event for that object.

You can also double-click a WPF control on the WPF Window Designer to create an event handler for that control's default event. This doesn't work with every control (such as Grid, Label, and StackPanel) but it works for those that are most likely to need event handlers (such as Button, CheckBox, ComboBox, RadioButton, and TextBox).

You can also add non-event handler subroutines and functions as you can in any other Visual Basic code file.

Inside the Visual Basic code file, you can get and set control properties and call control methods, just as you can in a Windows Forms project. The only differences are in the features the WPF controls provide. Those differences generally correspond to the XAML commands that define controls.

For example, the following Visual Basic code builds the same Button containing a Grid holding three Labels shown in Figure 12-1. The previous section, "Editing XAML," shows XAML code that builds this button.

Available for
download on
Wrox.com

```
Class Window1
    Private Sub Window1_Loaded() Handles Me.Loaded
        ' Make a grid.
        Dim grd As New Grid()
        grd.Width = btnGrid.Width - 10
        grd.Height = btnGrid.Height - 10

        ' Add rows and columns.
        AddRow(grd, New GridLength(33, GridUnitType.Star))
        AddRow(grd, New GridLength(33, GridUnitType.Star))
        AddRow(grd, New GridLength(33, GridUnitType.Star))
```

```
      AddCol(grd, New GridLength(33, GridUnitType.Star))
      AddCol(grd, New GridLength(33, GridUnitType.Star))
      AddCol(grd, New GridLength(33, GridUnitType.Star))

      ' Put things inside the grid.
      Dim lbl1 As New Label()
      lbl1.Content = "UL"
      lbl1.HorizontalAlignment = Windows.HorizontalAlignment.Left
      lbl1.VerticalAlignment = Windows.VerticalAlignment.Top
      lbl1.SetValue(Grid.RowProperty, 0)
      lbl1.SetValue(Grid.ColumnProperty, 0)
      grd.Children.Add(lbl1)

      Dim lbl2 As New Label()
      lbl2.Content = "In the Middle"
      lbl2.HorizontalAlignment = Windows.HorizontalAlignment.Center
      lbl2.VerticalAlignment = Windows.VerticalAlignment.Center
      lbl2.SetValue(Grid.RowProperty, 1)
      lbl2.SetValue(Grid.ColumnProperty, 0)
      lbl2.SetValue(Grid.ColumnSpanProperty, 3)
      grd.Children.Add(lbl2)

      Dim lbl3 As New Label()
      lbl3.Content = "LR"
      lbl3.HorizontalAlignment = Windows.HorizontalAlignment.Right
      lbl3.VerticalAlignment = Windows.VerticalAlignment.Bottom
      lbl3.SetValue(Grid.RowProperty, 2)
      lbl3.SetValue(Grid.ColumnProperty, 2)
      grd.Children.Add(lbl3)

      ' Put the grid inside the button.
      btnGrid.Content = grd
  End Sub

  ' Add a row of the indicated height to the grid.
  Private Sub AddRow(ByVal my_grid As System.Windows.Controls.Grid, _
   ByVal height As GridLength)
      Dim row_def As New RowDefinition()
      row_def.Height = height
      my_grid.RowDefinitions.Add(row_def)
  End Sub

  ' Add a column of the indicated width to the grid.
  Private Sub AddCol(ByVal my_grid As System.Windows.Controls.Grid, _
   ByVal width As GridLength)
     Dim col_def As New ColumnDefinition()
     col_def.Width = width

     my_grid.ColumnDefinitions.Add(col_def)
  End Sub
```

```
Private Sub btnGrid_Click() Handles btnGrid.Click
   MessageBox.Show("Clicked!", "Clicked", _
      MessageBoxButton.OK, _
      MessageBoxImage.Information)
End Sub
End Class
```

code snippet GridButtonCode

The main Window class's Loaded event handler fires when the form is loaded. The code starts by creating a Grid control and setting its width and height.

Next, the code calls subroutines AddRow and AddCol to make three rows and columns. These routines make building rows and columns easier, and are described shortly.

The code then creates three Label controls and sets their properties. Some properties, such as HorizontalAlignment and Content, are fairly straightforward. Other properties, such as Grid .RowProperty, Grid.ColumnProperty, and Grid.ColumnSpan, are a little trickier. Those properties only make sense when the Label controls are contained in a Grid, so they are not really properties of the Label controls. Instead they are properties added by the Grid control's SetValue method, much as an ExtenderProvider adds properties to a control. If you place a Button inside a StackPanel, the Properties window doesn't show these properties.

After it initializes each Label, the code uses the Grid control's Children.Add method to put the Label inside the Grid.

After it finishes creating all of the controls, the code sets the Button control's Content property to the new grid.

Subroutine AddRow creates a new RowDefinition object to represent a Grid's row. It sets the object's Height and adds the object to the Grid control's RowDefinitions collection. Subroutine AddCol uses similar methods to make a new Grid column.

The last piece of code in this example is a Click event handler for the btnGrid button. When you click the button, this code displays a message box.

Anything you can do declaratively with XAML you can also do procedurally with Visual Basic. The following section, "XAML Features," describes some of the things that you can do with XAML and shows examples. The section "Procedural WPF" later in this chapter explains how you can implement some of the same features with Visual Basic code instead of XAML.

XAML FEATURES

XAML is a form of XML that defines certain allowed combinations of XML elements. For example, a XAML file should have a single root element that represents a Window. That object can have a single child element that is normally a container. The container can hold several children with specifically defined properties such as Width and Height.

XAML is a very complicated language, and many of its features are available only in certain places within the file. For example, inside a Button element you can place attributes such as Background, BorderThickness, Margin, Width, Height, and Content. The XAML text editor provides IntelliSense that makes figuring out what is allowed in different places easier, but building a XAML file can still be quite challenging.

One good way to learn XAML is to go online and search for examples. The Microsoft web site has lots of examples, as do several other sites. Although the documentation isn't always easy to use, the examples can help you learn specific techniques. Some good places to start include the XAML overview at msdn2.microsoft.com/ms752059.aspx *and the Windows Presentation Foundation development page at* msdn2.microsoft.com/ms754130.aspx. *My book* WPF Programmer's Reference *(Wrox, Stephens, 2010,* www.amazon.com/exec/obidos/ASIN/0470477229/vbhelper*) also provides lots of examples of useful techniques. If you discover other sources of good examples, email me at* RodStephens@vb-helper.com *and I'll post them on the book's web site.*

The following sections describe some of the basic building blocks of a XAML application. They explain how to build objects; how to use resources, styles, and templates to make objects consistent and easier to modify; and how to use transformations and animations to make objects interactive. The section "Procedural WPF" later in this chapter explains how to do these things in Visual Basic code instead of XAML.

Objects

WPF objects are represented by XML elements in the XAML file. Their properties are represented either by attributes within the base elements or as separate elements within the main element.

For example, the following XAML code shows a Window containing a Grid object. The Grid element contains a Background attribute that makes the object's background red.

```
<Window x:Class="Window1"
  xmlns="http://schemas.microsoft.com/winfx/2006/xaml/presentation"
  xmlns:x="http://schemas.microsoft.com/winfx/2006/xaml" Title="WindowsApplication1"
  Height="235" Width="300">
    <Grid Background="Red">

    </Grid>
</Window>
```

More complicated properties must be set in their own sub-elements. The following code shows a similar Grid that has a linear gradient background:

```
<Window x:Class="Window1"
 xmlns="http://schemas.microsoft.com/winfx/2006/xaml/presentation"
 xmlns:x="http://schemas.microsoft.com/winfx/2006/xaml" Title="WindowsApplication1"
 Height="235" Width="300">
    <Grid>
      <Grid.Background>
        <LinearGradientBrush StartPoint="0,0" EndPoint="1,1">
        <GradientStop Color="Red" Offset="0.0" />
        <GradientStop Color="White" Offset="0.5" />
        <GradientStop Color="Blue" Offset="1.0" />
      </LinearGradientBrush>
    </Grid.Background>
  </Grid>
</Window>
```

code snippet GradientBackground

Instead of using a Background attribute, the Grid element contains a Grid.Background element. That, in turn, contains a LinearGradientBrush element that defines the background. The StartPoint and EndPoint attributes indicate that the gradient should start at the upper-left corner of the grid (0, 0) and end at the lower right (1, 1). The GradientStop elements inside the brush's definition set the colors that the brush should display at different fractions of the way through the gradient. In this example, the gradient starts red, changes to white halfway through, and changes to blue at the end.

 You cannot define an object's Background property more than once. If you include a Background attribute and a Grid.Background element for the same grid, the XAML editor complains.

Object elements often contain other elements that further define the object. The following code defines a grid that has two rows and three columns. (From now on I'm leaving out the Window element to save space.) The rows each occupy 50 percent of the grid's height. The first column is 50 pixels wide and the other two columns each take up 50 percent of the remaining width.

```
<Grid >
  <Grid.RowDefinitions>
    <RowDefinition Height="50*" />
    <RowDefinition Height="50*" />
  </Grid.RowDefinitions>
  <Grid.ColumnDefinitions>
    <ColumnDefinition Width="50" />
    <ColumnDefinition Width="50*" />
    <ColumnDefinition Width="50*" />
  </Grid.ColumnDefinitions>
</Grid>
```

When you use a * in measurements, the control divides its height or width proportionally among items that contain a *. For example, if a grid has two rows with height 50*, they each get half of the control's height. If the two rows had heights 10* and 20*, the first would be half as tall as the second.

If the control also contains items without a *, their space is taken out first. For example, suppose a grid defines rows with heights 10, 20*, and 30*. Then the first row has height 10, the second row gets 20/50 of the remaining height, and the third row gets the rest.

 Most of the examples in this chapter use values that are at least close to percentages because they're easier to understand.

An object element's body can also contain content for the object. In some cases, the content is simple text. The following example defines a Button object that has the caption Click Me:

```
<Button Margin="2,2,2,2" Name="btnClickMe">Click Me</Button>
```

An object's content may also contain other objects. The following code defines a grid with three rows and three columns holding nine buttons:

Available for
download on
Wrox.com

```
<Grid>
  <Grid.RowDefinitions>
    <RowDefinition Height="33*" />
    <RowDefinition Height="33*" />
    <RowDefinition Height="33*" />
  </Grid.RowDefinitions>
  <Grid.ColumnDefinitions>
   <ColumnDefinition Width="33*" />
   <ColumnDefinition Width="33*" />
   <ColumnDefinition Width="33*" />
  </Grid.ColumnDefinitions>
  <Button Grid.Row="0" Grid.Column="0" Margin="5">0,0</Button>
  <Button Grid.Row="0" Grid.Column="1" Margin="5">0,1</Button>
  <Button Grid.Row="0" Grid.Column="2" Margin="5">0,2</Button>
  <Button Grid.Row="1" Grid.Column="0" Margin="5">1,0</Button>
  <Button Grid.Row="1" Grid.Column="1" Margin="5">1,1</Button>
  <Button Grid.Row="1" Grid.Column="2" Margin="5">1,2</Button>
  <Button Grid.Row="2" Grid.Column="0" Margin="5">2,0</Button>
  <Button Grid.Row="2" Grid.Column="1" Margin="5">2,1</Button>
  <Button Grid.Row="2" Grid.Column="2" Margin="5">2,2</Button>
</Grid>
```

code snippet NineButtons

Usually, it is easiest to start building a Window by using the graphical XAML editor, but you may eventually want to look at the XAML code to see what the editor has done. It often produces almost but not quite what you want. For example, if you size and position a control by using click and drag, the editor may set its Margin property to 10,10,11,9 when you really want 10,10,10,10 (or just 10).

It can also sometimes be hard to place controls exactly where you want them. You can fix some of these values in the Properties window, but sometimes it's just easier to edit the XAML code directly.

Resources

Example program Calculator, which is available for download on the book's web site, is shown in Figure 12-4. This program contains three groups of buttons that use radial gradient backgrounds with similar colors. The number buttons, +/-, and the decimal point have yellow backgrounds drawn with RadialGradientBrush objects. The CE, C, and = buttons have blue backgrounds, and the operator buttons have green backgrounds.

FIGURE 12-4: This program uses resources to simplify maintenance.

You could build each button separately, including the appropriate RadialGradientBrush objects to give each button the correct background. Suppose, however, you decide to change the color of all of the number buttons from yellow to red. You would have to edit each of their 12 RadialGradientBrush objects to give them their new colors. In addition to being a lot of work, those changes would give you plenty of chances to make mistakes. The changes would be even harder if you decide to change the numbers of colors used by the brushes (perhaps having the brush shade from yellow to red to orange), or if you want to use a completely different brush for the buttons such as a LinearGradientBrush.

One of the ways XAML makes maintaining projects easier is by letting you define resources. You can then use the resources when defining objects. In this example, you can define resources to represent button backgrounds, and then use those resources to set each button's Background property. If you later need to change the background, you only need to update the resources.

The following code shows how the calculator application shown in Figure 12-4 creates a LinearGradientBrush resource called brResult, which the program uses to draw the result text box at the top. Ellipses show where code has been omitted to make it easier to read.

```
<Window x:Class="Window1"
  xmlns="http://schemas.microsoft.com/winfx/2006/xaml/presentation"
  xmlns:x="http://schemas.microsoft.com/winfx/2006/xaml" Title="XamlCalculator"
  Height="292" Width="227" Focusable="True">
  <Window.Resources>
    ...
    <LinearGradientBrush x:Key="brResult" StartPoint="0,0" EndPoint="1,1">
      <GradientStop Color="LightBlue" Offset="0.0" />
      <GradientStop Color="AliceBlue" Offset="1.0" />
    </LinearGradientBrush>
    ...
  </Window.Resources>
  ...
</Window>
```

code snippet Calculator

The Window element contains a Window.Resources tag that contains the resource definitions. The LinearGradientBrush element defines the brush. One of this element's more important attributes is x:Key, which identifies the brush for later use.

The following code shows how the calculator program defines the Label that displays calculation results. The Background attribute refers to the resource brNumber.

```
<Label Name="lblResult"
  Background="{StaticResource brResult}"
  Grid.ColumnSpan="4"
  Margin="2,2,2,2"
  HorizontalContentAlignment="Right"
  VerticalContentAlignment="Center">0</Label>
```

code snippet Calculator

Later if you decide to change the background color for the result label, you only need to change the definition of the brResult resource. This example only uses that resource for one label so you don't save a huge amount of work by defining a resource. The program's buttons, however, reuse the same resources many times. Instead of reusing the background resources directly, however, the buttons use styles as described in the next section.

Styles

Resources make it easy to create many controls that share an attribute such as a background. Styles take attributes a step further by allowing you to bundle multiple attributes into one package. For example, you could define a style that includes background, width, height, and font properties. Then you could use the style to help define controls.

You can also use styles to define other styles. For example, you can make a base style to be applied to every button in an application. Then you can derive other styles for different kinds of buttons from the base style.

The following example defines a style named styAllButtons. It contains Setter elements that set controls' properties. This style sets a control's Focusable property to False and its Margin property to 2,2,2,2.

```
<Style x:Key="styAllButtons">
  <Setter Property="Control.Focusable" Value="false" />
  <Setter Property="Control.Margin" Value="2,2,2,2" />
</Style>
```

code snippet Calculator

The following code defines a style named styClear for the calculator's C, CE, and = buttons:

```
<Style x:Key="styClear" BasedOn="{StaticResource styAllButtons}">
    <Setter Property="Control.Background" Value="{StaticResource brClear}" />
    <Setter Property="Grid.Row" Value="1" />
    <Setter Property="Control.Margin" Value="2,20,2,2" />
</Style>
```

code snippet Calculator

The BasedOn attribute makes the new style start with the properties defined by styAllButtons. The new style then uses two Setter elements to add new values for the Background (set to the brush resource brClear) and Grid.Row properties (these buttons are all in row 1 in the calculator). It then overrides the styAllButtons style's value for the Margin property to increase the margin above these buttons.

The following code shows how the program defines its C button. By setting the button's style to styClear, the code sets most of the button's properties with a single statement. It then sets the button's Grid.Column property (those values are different for the C, CE, and = buttons) and its content.

```
<Button Name="btnC"
    Style="{StaticResource styClear}"
    Grid.Column="1">C</Button>
```

code snippet Calculator

Styles let the program keep all of the common properties for a set of controls in a single location. Now if you decided to change the color of the C, CE, and = buttons, you would only need to change the definition of the brClear brush. If you wanted to change the brushes' margins, you would only need to change the styClear style.

As the previous code shows, styles also keep the controls' definitions very simple.

Styles also let you easily change the controls' properties later. For example, if you later decide to specify the font family and font size for the calculator's C, CE, and = buttons, you only need to add the appropriate Setter elements to styClear instead of adding a new property to every button. If you want to set the font for every button in the program, you simply add the appropriate Setter elements to styAllButtons and the other styles automatically pick up the changes.

Templates

Templates determine how controls are drawn and how they behave by default. For example, the default button template makes buttons turn light blue when the mouse hovers over them. When you press the button down, it grows slightly darker and shows a thin shadow along its upper and left edges. By using Template elements, you can override these default behaviors.

The following code contained in the Window.Resources section defines a button template:

Available for
download on
Wrox.com

```xaml
<Style TargetType="Button">
  <Setter Property="Margin" Value="2,2,2,2" />
  <Setter Property="Template">
   <Setter.Value>
      <ControlTemplate TargetType="{x:Type Button}">
      <Grid>
        <Polygon x:Name="pgnBorder"
          Stroke="Purple"
          StrokeThickness="5"
          Points="0.2,0 0.8,0 1,0.2 1,0.8 0.8,1 0.2,1 0,0.8 0,0.2"
          Stretch="Fill"
          Fill="{StaticResource brOctagonUp}">
        </Polygon>
        <ContentPresenter HorizontalAlignment="Center" VerticalAlignment="Center" />
      </Grid>

      <!-- Triggers -->
      <ControlTemplate.Triggers>
        <Trigger Property="IsMouseOver" Value="true">
          <Setter TargetName="pgnBorder" Property="Stroke" Value="Black" />
          <Setter TargetName="pgnBorder" Property="Fill"
              Value="{StaticResource brOctagonOver}" />
        </Trigger>
      </ControlTemplate.Triggers>
    </ControlTemplate>
   </Setter.Value>
  </Setter>
</Style>
```

code snippet ButtonTemplate

The code begins with a Style element that contains two Setter elements. The first Setter sets a button's Margin property to 2,2,2,2. The second Setter sets a Template property. The Setter's value is a ControlTemplate element targeted at Buttons.

The ControlTemplate contains a Grid that it uses to hold other elements. In this example, the Grid holds a Polygon element named pgnBorder. The Points attribute lists the points used to draw the polygon. Because the polygon's Fill attribute is set to Stretch, the polygon is stretched to fill its parent area, and Points coordinates are on a 0.0 to 1.0 scale within this area. The polygon's Fill attribute is set to the brOctagonUp brush defined elsewhere in the Window.Resources section and not shown here. This is a RadialGradientBrush that shades from white in the center to red at the edges.

The ControlTemplate element also contains a Triggers section. The single Trigger element in this section executes when the button's IsMouseOver condition is true. When that happens, a Setter changes the pgnBorder polygon's Stroke property to Black. A second Setter sets the polygon's Fill property to another brush named brOctagonOver. This brush (which also isn't shown here) shades from red in the center to white at the edges.

Because this style does not have an x:Key attribute, it applies to any button in the Window that doesn't have a Style set explicitly.

Example program ButtonTemplate uses the following code to create its controls:

```
<Grid>
  <Grid.ColumnDefinitions>
    <ColumnDefinition Width="0.25*" />
    <ColumnDefinition Width="0.25*" />
    <ColumnDefinition Width="0.25*" />
    <ColumnDefinition Width="0.25*" />
  </Grid.ColumnDefinitions>
  <Grid.RowDefinitions>
    <RowDefinition Height="0.50*" />
    <RowDefinition Height="0.50*" />
  </Grid.RowDefinitions>
  <Button Name="btnOne" Content="One" Grid.Row="1" Grid.Column="0" />
  <Button Name="btnTwo" Content="Two" Grid.Row="1" Grid.Column="1" />
  <Button Name="btnThree" Content="Three" Grid.Row="1" Grid.Column="2" />
  <Button Name="btnFour" Content="Four" Grid.Row="1" Grid.Column="3" />

  <Button Name="btnClickMe" Content="Click Me"
    Style="{StaticResource styYellowButton}" />
  <Button Name="btnYellow" Content="I'm Yellow"
    Style="{StaticResource styYellowButton}" Grid.Column="2" Grid.Row="0" />
</Grid>
```

code snippet ButtonTemplate

The Window contains a Grid that holds six buttons. The first four buttons do not explicitly set their Style, so they use the previously defined octagonal style.

The final buttons set their Style attributes to styYellowButton (also defined in the Windows .Resources section, but not shown here) so they display a yellow background. That style also positions the button's text in the upper center. When you hover the mouse over these buttons, they switch to an orange background. If you press the mouse down on these buttons, they change to a red background with white text that says "Pushed!"

Example program ButtonTemplate demonstrates this code. Download the example to see how the triggers work.

Figure 12-5 shows the result. The mouse is hovering over the second button, so it displays the black border and its background shades from red in the center to white at the edges.

FIGURE 12-5: Templates let you change the appearance and behavior of objects such as buttons.

TAME TEMPLATES

You can use templates to change the appearance and behavior of XAML objects to give your applications distinctive appearances, but you probably shouldn't get too carried away. Although you can make buttons radically change their colors, shapes, captions, and other characteristics when the user interacts with them, doing so may be very distracting. Use templates to make your applications distinctive, but not overwhelming.

Also be careful not to make controls hard for those with accessibility issues. For example, if you use subtle color differences to distinguish button states, users with impaired color vision or those who have trouble seeing small items may have trouble using your program. Similarly using sounds to indicate state won't help hearing impaired users (and may annoy people sitting at nearby desks).

Transformations

Properties determine a control's basic appearance, but you can further modify that appearance by using a RenderTransform element. The following code creates a button that has been rotated 270 degrees. The Button.RenderTransform element contains a RotateTransform element that represents the rotation.

Available for download on Wrox.com

```
<Button Name="btnSideways"
  Content="Sideways"
  Background="{StaticResource brButton}"
  Margin="-6,-6.5,0,0"
  Height="43"
  HorizontalAlignment="Left"
  VerticalAlignment="Top"
  Width="94">
  <Button.RenderTransform>
    <RotateTransform Angle="270" CenterX="75" CenterY="50" />
  </Button.RenderTransform>
</Button>
```

code snippet RotatedButtons

XAML also provides TranslateTransform and ScaleTransform elements that let you translate and scale an object. Example program RotatedButton, which is available for download on the book's web site and shown in Figure 12-6, uses transformations to draw several buttons that have been rotated and scaled vertically and horizontally.

XAML also defines a TransformGroup element that you can use to perform a series of transformations on an object. For example, a TransformGroup would let you translate, scale, rotate, and then translate an object again.

FIGURE 12-6: Buttons can be rotated and scaled vertically and horizontally by using RotateTransform and ScaleTransform.

Animations

The section "Templates" earlier in this chapter shows how to use Triggers to make an object change its appearance in response to events. For example, it shows how to make a button change its background and border color when the mouse moves over it.

XAML also provides methods for scripting more complicated actions that take place over a defined period of time. For example, you can make a button spin slowly for two seconds when the user clicks it.

You use a trigger to start the animation and a Storyboard object to control it. A Storyboard contains information about the state the animation should have at various times during the animation.

The SpinButton example program uses the following code to make a button rotate around its center when it is clicked:

```
<Button Name="btnSpinMe" Content="Spin Me"
  Width="150" Height="100">
  <Button.Background>
    <RadialGradientBrush
      Center="0.5,0.5"
      RadiusX="1.0" RadiusY="1.0">
      <GradientStop Color="Yellow" Offset="0.0" />
      <GradientStop Color="Orange" Offset="1.0" />
    </RadialGradientBrush>
  </Button.Background>
  <Button.RenderTransform>
    <RotateTransform x:Name="rotButton" Angle="0" CenterX="75" CenterY="50" />
  </Button.RenderTransform>
  <Button.Triggers>
    <EventTrigger RoutedEvent="Button.Click">
     <EventTrigger.Actions>
      <BeginStoryboard>
       <Storyboard
         Storyboard.TargetName="rotButton"
         Storyboard.TargetProperty="(RotateTransform.Angle)">
         <DoubleAnimationUsingKeyFrames>
         <SplineDoubleKeyFrame KeyTime="0:0:00.0" Value="0.0" />
         <SplineDoubleKeyFrame KeyTime="0:0:00.2" Value="30.0" />
         <SplineDoubleKeyFrame KeyTime="0:0:00.8" Value="330.0" />
```

```
        <SplineDoubleKeyFrame KeyTime="0:0:01.0" Value="360.0" />
      </DoubleAnimationUsingKeyFrames>
    </Storyboard>
  </BeginStoryboard>
</EventTrigger.Actions>
</EventTrigger>
</Button.Triggers>
</Button>
```

code snippet SpinButton

Much of this code should seem familiar by now. The Button element's attributes set its name, contents, and size. A Background element fills the button with a RadialGradientBrush.

The Button element contains a RenderTransform element similar to the ones described in the previous section. In this case, the transform is a RotateTransform with angle of rotation initially set to 0 so that the button appears in its normal orientation. Its center is set to the middle of the button. The transform is named rotButton so that other code can refer to it later.

After the transform element, the code contains a Triggers section. This section holds an EventTrigger element that responds to the Button.Click routed event.

A *routed event* is a new kind of event developed for WPF. Routed events travel up and down through a WPF application's hierarchy of controls so interested controls can catch and process the events. For simple purposes, however, a routed event behaves much like a Windows Forms event does and you can catch it with a normal Visual Basic event handler. When the user clicks the button, the Button.Click event fires and this trigger springs into action.

The trigger's Actions element contains the tasks that the trigger should perform when it runs. In this example, the trigger performs the BeginStoryboard action. Inside the BeginStoryboard element is a Storyboard element that represents the things that the storyboard should do.

STORYBOARD START

When I see "BeginStoryboard," I think of the beginning of a storyboard. Actually, this element more properly means "start the storyboard." When this element executes, it starts the storyboard running. (The name "ExecuteStoryboard" or "PlayStoryboard" might have been more intuitive.)

The Storyboard element's TargetName attribute gives the target object on which the storyboard should act, in this case the RotateTransform object named rotButton. The TargetProperty attribute tells what property of the target button the storyboard should manipulate, in this example the object's Angle property.

The Storyboard element contains a DoubleAnimationUsingKeyFrames element. A *key frame* is specific point in an animation sequence with known values. The program calculates values between the key frame values to make the animation smooth.

This DoubleAnimationUsingKeyFrames element holds a collection of SplineDoubleKeyFrame elements that define the animation's key values. Each key frame gives its time in the animation in hours, minutes, and seconds, and the value that the controlled property should have at that point in the animation. In this example, the rotation transformation's angle should have a value of 0 when the storyboard starts, a value of 30 when the animation is 20 percent complete, a value of 330 when the storyboard is 80 percent complete, and a value of 360 when the storyboard finishes. The result is that the button rotates slowly for the first 0.2 seconds, spins relatively quickly for the next 0.6 seconds, and then finishes rotating at a more leisurely pace.

Example program SpinButton animates a single property, the button's angle of rotation, but you can animate more than one property at the same time if you like. Program SpinAndGrowButton simultaneously animates a button's angle of rotation and size. This example has two key differences from program SpinButton.

First, the new button's RenderTransform element contains a TransformGroup that contains two transformations, one that determines the button's angle of rotation and one that determines its scaling:

```
<Button.RenderTransform>
    <TransformGroup>
        <RotateTransform x:Name="rotButton" Angle="0" CenterX="50" CenterY="25" />
        <ScaleTransform x:Name="scaButton" ScaleX="1" ScaleY="1"
        CenterX="50" CenterY="25" />
    </TransformGroup>
</Button.RenderTransform>
```

code snippet SpinAndGrowButton

The second difference is in the new button's Storyboard. The following code omits the animation's TargetName and TargetProperty from the Storyboard element's attributes. It includes three DoubleAnimationUsingKeyFrame elements inside the Storyboard, and it is there that it sets the TargetName and TargetProperty. The three animations update the button's angle of rotation, horizontal scale, and vertical scale.

```
<Storyboard>
  <!-- Rotate -->
  <DoubleAnimationUsingKeyFrames
      Storyboard.TargetName="rotButton"
      Storyboard.TargetProperty="(RotateTransform.Angle)">
      <SplineDoubleKeyFrame KeyTime="0:0:00.0" Value="0.0" />
      <SplineDoubleKeyFrame KeyTime="0:0:01.0" Value="360.0" />
  </DoubleAnimationUsingKeyFrames>

  <!-- ScaleX -->
  <DoubleAnimationUsingKeyFrames
      Storyboard.TargetName="scaButton"
      Storyboard.TargetProperty="(ScaleTransform.ScaleX)">
      <SplineDoubleKeyFrame KeyTime="0:0:00.0" Value="1.0" />
      <SplineDoubleKeyFrame KeyTime="0:0:00.5" Value="2.0" />
```

```
      <SplineDoubleKeyFrame KeyTime="0:0:01.0" Value="1.0" />
    </DoubleAnimationUsingKeyFrames>

    <!-- ScaleY -->
    <DoubleAnimationUsingKeyFrames
      Storyboard.TargetName="scaButton"
      Storyboard.TargetProperty="(ScaleTransform.ScaleY)">
      <SplineDoubleKeyFrame KeyTime="0:0:00.0" Value="1.0" />
      <SplineDoubleKeyFrame KeyTime="0:0:00.5" Value="2.0" />
      <SplineDoubleKeyFrame KeyTime="0:0:01.0" Value="1.0" />
    </DoubleAnimationUsingKeyFrames>
  </Storyboard>
```

code snippet SpinAndGrowButton

By using XAML Storyboards, you can build complex animations that run when certain events occur. As with templates, however, you should use some restraint when building storyboard animations. A few small animations can make an application more interesting, but too many large animations can distract and annoy the user.

Drawing Objects

WPF provides several objects for drawing two-dimensional shapes. The following sections summarize the most useful of these objects: Line, Ellipse, Rectangle, Polygon, Polyline, and Path.

Line

The *Line* object draws a straight line between two points. The X1, Y1, X2, and Y2 attributes determine the line's endpoints. The following code draws a line from (10, 10) to (90, 90) and another from (90, 10) to (10, 90):

```
<Line X1="10" Y1="10" X2="90" Y2="90"
  Grid.Column="0" Grid.Row="1"
  Stroke="Blue" StrokeThickness="10"
  StrokeStartLineCap="Round" StrokeEndLineCap="Round" />
<Line X1="90" Y1="10" X2="10" Y2="90"
  Grid.Column="0"
  Grid.Row="1" Stroke="Blue" StrokeThickness="10"
  StrokeStartLineCap="Round" StrokeEndLineCap="Round" />
```

code snippet Shapes

The Stroke and StrokeThickness attributes determine the lines' color and thickness.

The StrokeStartLineCap and StrokeEndLineCap attributes determine the appearance of the lines' start and end points. This example draws rounded end caps.

Ellipse

The *Ellipse* object draws an ellipse. The following code draws an ellipse filled with a LinearGradientBrush:

```
<Ellipse Margin="2,20,2,20"
  Grid.Column="2" Grid.Row="0"
  Stroke="Orange" StrokeThickness="5">
  <Ellipse.Fill>
   <LinearGradientBrush
     StartPoint="0,0"
     EndPoint="1,0">
     <GradientStop Color="Green" Offset="0.0" />
     <GradientStop Color="White" Offset="0.5" />
     <GradientStop Color="Green" Offset="1.0" />
   </LinearGradientBrush>
  </Ellipse.Fill>
</Ellipse>
```

code snippet Shapes

Rectangle

The *Rectangle* object draws a rectangle. The syntax is similar to that used to draw ellipses. The following code draws a rectangle filled with a LinearGradientBrush:

```
<Rectangle Margin="2,20,2,20"
  Grid.Column="2" Grid.Row="0"
  Stroke="Orange" StrokeThickness="5">
  <Rectangle.Fill>
   <LinearGradientBrush
     StartPoint="0,0"
     EndPoint="1,0">
     <GradientStop Color="Green" Offset="0.0" />
     <GradientStop Color="White" Offset="0.5" />
     <GradientStop Color="Green" Offset="1.0" />
   </LinearGradientBrush>
  </Rectangle.Fill>
</Rectangle>
```

This code is exactly the same as the ellipse code except it uses the keyword Rectangle instead of Ellipse.

Polygon

The *Polygon* object draws a closed polygon. Its Points attribute lists the points that should be connected. The Polygon object automatically closes its figure by connecting the final point to the first point.

The following code draws the four-pointed star:

```
<Polygon Margin="0,0,0,0"
  Grid.Column="0" Grid.Row="0"
  Points="10,10 50,40 90,10 60,50 90,90 50,60 10,90 40,50"
  Fill="LightBlue"
  Stroke="Red" StrokeThickness="3" />
```

code snippet Shapes

Polyline

The Polyline object is similar to the Polygon object, except that it does not automatically close the drawing by connecting the final point to the first point.

The following code draws a series of four dashed lines:

```
<Polyline Margin="0,0,0,0"
  Grid.Column="1" Grid.Row="0"
  Points="20,20 40,40 60,30 90,90 30,70"
  Stroke="Black" StrokeLineJoin="Round"
  StrokeThickness="3"
  StrokeDashArray="2,1,2,3" />
<Ellipse Margin="2,20,2,20"
  Grid.Column="2" Grid.Row="0"
  Stroke="Orange" StrokeThickness="5">
  <Ellipse.Fill>
    <LinearGradientBrush
      StartPoint="0,0"
      EndPoint="1,0">
      <GradientStop Color="Green" Offset="0.0" />
      <GradientStop Color="White" Offset="0.5" />
      <GradientStop Color="Green" Offset="1.0" />
    </LinearGradientBrush>
  </Ellipse.Fill>
</Ellipse>
```

code snippet Shapes

This code demonstrates a few additional features of line drawing in general. The StrokeLine Join attribute determines how lines are connected. In this example, the lines are joined with rounded corners.

The StrokeDashArray attribute determines the lines' dash pattern. The numbers indicate the number of units the line draws and skips. In this example, the value 2,1,2,3 means the line draws 2 units, skips 1 unit, draws 2 units, and skips 3 units. Each unit represents the line's width.

Path

The *Path* object draws a series of shapes such as lines, arcs, and curves. A Path object can be incredibly complex, and can include any of the other drawing objects plus a few others that draw smooth curves.

You can define a Path object in two ways. First, you can make the Path element contain other elements (Line, Ellipse, and so forth) that define objects drawn by the path.

The second (and more concise) method is to use the Path element's Data attribute. This is a text attribute that contains a series of coded commands for drawing shapes. For example, the following code makes the Path move to the point (20, 20), and then draw to connect the following points (80, 20), (50, 60), (90, 100), and (50, 120):

```
<Path Stroke="Gray" StrokeThickness="5" Grid.Column="1" Grid.Row="1"
   Data="M 20,20 L 80,20 50,60 90,100 50,120" />
```

You can use spaces or commas to separate point coordinates. To make it easier to read the code, you may want to use commas between a point's X and Y coordinates and spaces between points, as in the previous example.

Some commands allow both uppercase and lowercase command letters. For those commands, the lowercase version means that the following points' coordinates are relative to the previous points' coordinates. For example, the following data makes the object move to the point (10, 20) and then draws to the absolute coordinates (30, 40):

```
Data="M 10,20 L 30,40"
```

In contrast, the following data moves to the point (10, 20) as before, but then moves distance (30, 40) relative to the current position. The result is that the line ends at point (10 + 30, 20 + 40) = (40, 60).

```
Data="M 10,20 l 30,40"
```

There isn't enough room for a complete discussion of the Path object, but the following table summarizes the commands that you can include in the Data attribute.

COMMAND	RESULT	EXAMPLE
F0	Sets the fill rule to the odd/even rule.	F0
F1	Sets the fill rule to the non-zero rule.	F1
M or m	Moves to the following point without drawing.	M 10,10
L or l	Draws a line to the following point(s).	L 10,10 20,20 30,10
H or h	Draws a horizontal line from the current point to the given X coordinate.	h 50
V or v	Draws a vertical line from the current point to the given Y coordinate.	v 30
C or c	Draws a cubic Bezier curve. This command takes three points as parameters: two control points and an endpoint. The curve starts at the current point moving toward the first control point. It ends at the endpoint, coming from the direction of the second control point.	C 20,20 60,0 50,50

COMMAND	RESULT	EXAMPLE
S or s.	Draws a smooth cubic Bezier curve. This command takes two points as parameters: a control point and an endpoint. The curve defines an initial control point by reflecting the second control point used by the previous S command, and then uses it plus its two points to draw a cubic Bezier curve. This makes a series of Bezier curves join smoothly.	S 60,0 50,50 S 80,60 50,70
Q or q	Draws a quadratic Bezier curve. This command takes two points as parameters: a control point and an endpoint. The curve starts at the current point moving toward the control point. It ends at the endpoint, coming from the direction of the control point.	Q 80,20 50,60
T or t	Draws a smooth cubic Bezier curve. This command takes one point as a parameter: an endpoint. The curve defines a control point by reflecting the control point used by the previous T command, and then uses it to draw a quadratic Bezier curve. The result is a smooth curve that passes through each of the points given as parameters to successive T commands.	T 80,20 T 50,60 T 90,100
A or a	Draws an elliptical arc. This command takes five parameters:	A 50,20 0 1 0 60,80
	size — The X and Y radii of the arc	
	rotation_angle — The ellipse's angle of rotation	
	large_angle — 0 if the arc should span less than 180; 1 if the arc should span 180 degrees or more	
	sweep_direction — 0 if the arc should sweep counterclockwise; 1 if it should sweep clockwise	
	end_point — The point where the arc should end	
Z or z	Closes the figure by drawing a line from the current point to the Path's starting point.	Z

Example program Shapes, which is available for download on the book's web site, demonstrates several different Path objects.

Example program BezierCurves, shown in Figure 12-7, shows examples of the four different kinds of Bezier curves. This program also draws a gray polyline to show the curves' parameters.

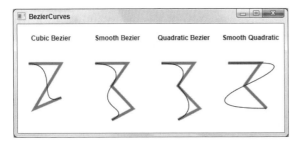

FIGURE 12-7: The Path object can draw Bezier curves.

The cubic Bezier curve on the left connects the two endpoints using the two middle points to determine the curve's direction at the endpoints.

The smooth cubic Bezier curve shown next passes through the first, third, and fifth points. The second point determines the curve's direction as it leaves the first point and as it enters the third point. The curve automatically defines a control point to determine the direction leaving the third point, so the curve passes through the point smoothly. Finally, the fourth point determines the curve's direction as it ends at the fifth point.

The next curve shows two quadratic Bezier curves. The first curve connects the first and third points with the second point determining the curve's direction at both points. The second curve connects the third and fifth points, using the fourth to determine its direction.

The final curve in Figure 12-7 uses an M command to move to the point (20, 20). It then uses three smooth quadratic Bezier curves to connect the following three points. The curve automatically defines the control points it needs to connect the points smoothly.

With all of these drawing objects at your disposal, particularly the powerful Path object, you can draw just about anything you need. The graphical XAML editor does not provide interactive tools for drawing shapes, but you can draw them by using the XAML text editor. It may help to sketch out what you want to draw on graph paper first.

PROCEDURAL WPF

The previous sections explain how to use XAML to build WPF windows. By using XAML, you can define controls, resources, styles, templates, transformations, and even animations.

Behind the scenes, an application reads the XAML code, and then builds corresponding controls and other objects to make the user interface. Often, it's easiest to build forms by using the XAML editor, but if necessary, your Visual Basic code can build exactly the same objects.

KEEP YOUR DISTANCE

Usually you should build the interface with XAML to increase the separation between the user interface and the code. However, it may sometimes be easier to build dynamic elements in code (for example, in response to data loaded at run-time, inputs from the user, or in response to errors).

For example, the following Visual Basic code adds a button to a WPF form:

```
' The button we will build.
Private WithEvents btnClickMe As Button

' Build the user interface.
Private Sub Window1_Loaded() Handles Me.Loaded
 ' Get the window's default Grid.
    Dim grd As Grid = DirectCast(Me.Content, Grid)

    ' Add a Button.
    btnClickMe = New Button()
    btnClickMe.Content = "Click Me"
    btnClickMe.Margin = New Thickness(5)
    grd.Children.Add(btnClickMe)
End Sub

' The user clicked the button.
Private Sub btnClickMe_Click() Handles btnClickMe.Click
    MessageBox.Show("Clicked!")
End Sub
```

The code starts by converting the window's Content property into a Grid object. It then creates a Button, sets a couple of properties for it, and adds it to the Grid control's Children collection.

The Button control's variable is declared at the module level and includes the WithEvents keyword so it is easy to catch the button's Click event.

Example program ProceduralAnimatedButton uses Visual Basic code to implement several of the techniques described earlier using XAML code. It creates a brush object and uses it to define a Style for buttons. It then creates three Buttons using that Style.

When the mouse moves over a button, the program's code builds and plays an animation to enlarge the button. When the mouse moves off of the button, the code restores the button to its original size.

The following code builds the user interface objects when the program's window loads:

```
Private WithEvents btnCenter As Button
Private Const BIG_SCALE As Double = 1.5

Private Sub Window1_Loaded() Handles Me.Loaded
    ' Make a style for the buttons.
    Dim br_button As New RadialGradientBrush( _
        Colors.HotPink, Colors.Red)
    br_button.Center = New Point(0.5, 0.5)
    br_button.RadiusX = 1
    br_button.RadiusY = 1

    Dim style_button As New Style(GetType(Button))
    style_button.Setters.Add(New Setter(Control.BackgroundProperty, _
        br_button))
    style_button.Setters.Add(New Setter(Control.WidthProperty, CDbl(70)))
    style_button.Setters.Add(New Setter(Control.HeightProperty, CDbl(40)))
    style_button.Setters.Add(New Setter(Control.MarginProperty, _
        New Thickness(5)))

    ' Set the transform origin to (0.5, 0.5).
    style_button.Setters.Add(New Setter( _
        Control.RenderTransformOriginProperty, New Point(0.5, 0.5)))

    ' Make a StackPanel to hold the buttons.
    Dim stack_panel As New StackPanel()
    stack_panel.Margin = New Thickness(20)

    ' Add the Left button.
    Dim btn_left As Button
    btn_left = New Button()
    btn_left.Style = style_button
    btn_left.Content = "Left"
    btn_left.RenderTransform = New ScaleTransform(1, 1)
    btn_left.SetValue( _
        StackPanel.HorizontalAlignmentProperty, _
        Windows.HorizontalAlignment.Left)
    AddHandler btn_left.MouseEnter, AddressOf btn_MouseEnter
    AddHandler btn_left.MouseLeave, AddressOf btn_MouseLeave
    stack_panel.Children.Add(btn_left)

    ' Make the Center button.
    btnCenter = New Button()
    btnCenter.Style = style_button
    btnCenter.Content = "Center"
    btnCenter.RenderTransform = New ScaleTransform(1, 1)
    btnCenter.SetValue( _
        StackPanel.HorizontalAlignmentProperty, _
        Windows.HorizontalAlignment.Center)
    AddHandler btnCenter.MouseEnter, AddressOf btn_MouseEnter
    AddHandler btnCenter.MouseLeave, AddressOf btn_MouseLeave
    stack_panel.Children.Add(btnCenter)
```

```
    ' Make the Right button.
    Dim btn_right As New Button
    btn_right.Style = style_button
    btn_right.Content = "Right"
    btn_right.RenderTransform = New ScaleTransform(1, 1)
    btn_right.SetValue( _
        StackPanel.HorizontalAlignmentProperty, _
        Windows.HorizontalAlignment.Right)
    AddHandler btn_right.MouseEnter, AddressOf btn_MouseEnter
    AddHandler btn_right.MouseLeave, AddressOf btn_MouseLeave
    Stack_panel.Children.Add(btn_right)

    Me.Content = stack_panel
End Sub
```

code snippet ProcedurallyAnimatedButton

This code starts by declaring a Button control using the WithEvents keyword. The program makes three buttons, but only catches the Click event for this one. The code also defines a constant that determines how large the button will grow when it enlarges.

When the window loads, the code creates a RadialGradientBrush and defines its properties. It then creates a Style object that can apply to Button objects. It adds several Setter objects to the Style to set a Button control's Background, Width, Height, Margin, and RenderTransformOrigin properties.

Next, the code creates a StackPanel object. This will be the window's main control and will replace the Grid control that Visual Studio creates by default.

The program then makes three Button objects. It sets various Button properties, including setting the Style property to the Style object created earlier. It also sets each Button control's RenderTransform property to a ScaleTransform object that initially scales the Button by a factor of 1 vertically and horizontally. It will later use this transformation to make the Button grow and shrink.

The code uses each Button control's SetValue method to set its HorizontalAlignment property for the StackPanel. The code uses AddHandler to give each Button an event handler for its MouseEnter and MouseLeave events. Finally, the code adds the Button controls to the StackPanel's Children collection.

The window's Loaded event handler finishes by setting the window's Content property to the new StackPanel containing the Button controls.

The following code shows how the program responds when the mouse moves over a Button:

Available for download on Wrox.com

```
    ' The mouse moved over the button.
    ' Make it larger.
    Private Sub btn_MouseEnter(ByVal btn As Button, _
     ByVal e As System.Windows.Input.MouseEventArgs)
        ' Get the button's transformation.
        Dim scale_transform As ScaleTransform = _
            DirectCast(btn.RenderTransform, ScaleTransform)

        ' Create a DoubleAnimation.
```

```
        Dim ani As New DoubleAnimation(1, BIG_SCALE, _
            New Duration(TimeSpan.FromSeconds(0.15)))

        ' Create a clock for the animation.
        Dim ani_clock As AnimationClock = ani.CreateClock()

        ' Associate the clock with the transform's
        ' ScaleX and ScaleY properties.
        scale_transform.ApplyAnimationClock( _
            ScaleTransform.ScaleXProperty, ani_clock)
        scale_transform.ApplyAnimationClock( _
            ScaleTransform.ScaleYProperty, ani_clock)
    End Sub
```

code snippet ProcedurallyAnimatedButton

This code first gets the button's ScaleTransform object. It then creates a DoubleAnimation object to change a value from 1 to the BIG_SCALE value (defined as 1.5 in the earlier Const statement) over a period of 0.15 seconds. It uses the object's CreateClock statement to make an AnimationClock to control the animation. Finally, the code calls the ScaleTransformation object's ApplyAnimationClock method twice, once for its horizontal and vertical scales. The result is that the Button control's ScaleTransform object increases the Button control's scale vertically and horizontally.

The btn_MouseLeave event handler is very similar, except that it animates the Button controls' scale values shrinking from BIG_SCALE to 1.

Example program GrowingButtons uses a similar technique to enlarge and shrink Button controls. Instead of using a simple DoubleAnimation to enlarge the Button controls, however, it uses DoubleAnimationUsingKeyFrames. This object lets you define a series of values that the animation should visit.

The following code shows how this program's MouseEnter event handler works:

```
Private Const BIG_SCALE As Double = 1.75
Private Const END_SCALE As Double = 1.5

Private Sub btn_MouseEnter(ByVal btn As Button, _
    ByVal e As System.Windows.Input.MouseEventArgs)
        ' Get the button's transformation.
        Dim scale_transform As ScaleTransform = _
            DirectCast(btn.RenderTransform, ScaleTransform)

        ' Create a DoubleAnimation that first
        ' makes the button extra big and then
        ' shrinks it to the "normal" big size.
        Dim ani As New DoubleAnimationUsingKeyFrames()
        Dim fr1 As New SplineDoubleKeyFrame(1.0, KeyTime.FromPercent(0.0))
        Dim fr2 As New SplineDoubleKeyFrame(BIG_SCALE, KeyTime.FromPercent(0.5))
        Dim fr3 As New SplineDoubleKeyFrame(END_SCALE, KeyTime.FromPercent(1.0))
        ani.KeyFrames.Add(fr1)
        ani.KeyFrames.Add(fr2)
```

```
      ani.KeyFrames.Add(fr3)
      ani.Duration = New Duration(TimeSpan.FromSeconds(0.33))

      ' Create a clock for the animation.
      Dim ani_clock As AnimationClock = ani.CreateClock()
      'Dim ani_clock As AnimationClock = ani.CreateClock()

      ' Associate the clock with the transform's
      ' ScaleX and ScaleY properties.
      scale_transform.ApplyAnimationClock( _
         ScaleTransform.ScaleXProperty, ani_clock)
      scale_transform.ApplyAnimationClock( _
         ScaleTransform.ScaleYProperty, ani_clock)

      ' Pop the button to the top of the stacking order.
      grdMain.Children.Remove(btn)
      grdMain.Children.Add(btn)
   End Sub
```

code snippet GrowingButtons

Instead of simply growing the Button's scale factors from 1 to 1.5, the animation first makes the Button grow by a factor of 1.75, and then shrink to a growth factor of 1.5. This overshoot gives the Button a cartoon-like style that is popular in some user interfaces.

After it finishes animating the Button, the code removes the Button from the main Grid control's Children collection, and then re-adds it to the collection to make the Button appear above the other Buttons so it covers parts of its neighbors.

Figure 12-8 shows example program GrowingButtons in action with the mouse resting over the Tuesday button.

FIGURE 12-8: Program GrowingButtons uses Visual Basic code to animate buttons.

Other examples available for download on the book's web site demonstrate other procedural WPF techniques. For example, program ProceduralCalculator builds a calculator similar to the one shown in Figure 12-4, but it builds its user interface in Visual Basic code. Example program GridButtonCode uses Visual Basic code to build a button that holds a grid similar to the one shown in Figure 12-1.

DOCUMENTS

WPF includes three different kinds of documents: flow documents, fixed documents, and *XPS* (*XML Paper Specification*) documents. These different kinds of documents provide support for high-end text and printing capabilities.

For example, fixed documents allow you to generate a document that keeps the same layout whether it is viewed on a monitor, printed at low-resolution, or printed at a very high-resolution. On each device, the document uses the features available on that device to give the best result possible.

Each of these three kinds of documents is quite complex so there isn't room to do them justice here. However, the following three sections provide an overview and give brief examples.

Flow Documents

Flow documents are designed to display as much data as possible in the best way possible, depending on runtime constraints such as the size of the control displaying the document. If the control grows, the document rearranges its contents to take advantage of the new available space. If the control shrinks, the document again rearranges its contents to fit the available space. The effect sort of mimics the way a web browser behaves, rearranging the objects it displays as it is resized.

The WPF FlowDocument control represents a flow document. The FlowDocument can contain four basic content elements: List, Section, Paragraph, and Table. These have rather obvious purposes: to display data in a list, group data in a section, group data in a paragraph, or display data in a table.

Although the main emphasis of these elements is on text, they can contain other objects. For example, a Paragraph can contain controls such as Button, Label, TextBox, and Grid controls. It can also contain shapes such as Polygon, Ellipse, and Path.

A fifth content element, BlockUIElement, can hold user interface controls such a Button, Label, and TextBox. A BlockUIElement can hold only one child, but if that child is a container such as a Grid or StackPanel it may contain other controls.

WMF provides three types of objects for displaying FlowDocuments: FlowDocumentReader, FlowDocumentPageViewer, and FlowDocumentScrollViewer.

The *FlowDocumentReader* lets the user pick from three different viewing modes: single page, book reading, and scrolling. In *single page mode*, the reader displays the document one page at a time. The object determines how big to make a page based on its size. If the reader is wide enough, it will display the FlowDocument in two or more columns, although it still considers its surface to hold a single page at a time, even if that page uses several columns.

In *book reading mode*, the reader displays two pages at a time. The object divides its surface into left and right halves, and fills each with a "page" of data. The reader always displays two pages, no matter how big or small it is.

In *scrolling mode*, the reader displays all of the document's contents in a single long page, and it provides a scroll bar to allow the user to scroll down through the document. This is similar to the way web browsers handle a very tall web page.

Example program UseFlowDocumentReader, shown in Figure 12-9 and available for download on the book's web site, shows a FlowDocumentReader object displaying a document in book reading mode. The program's View menu lets you change the viewing mode.

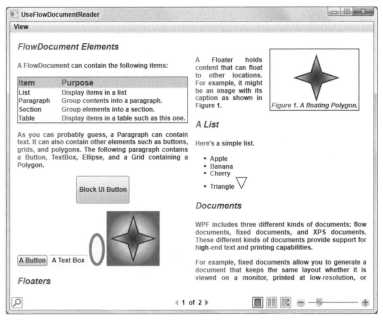

FIGURE 12-9: This FlowDocumentReader is using book reading mode.

This program demonstrates several useful features of FlowDocument objects. The section headers are contained in Paragraph objects that use a Style that defines their font. If you wanted to change the appearance of all of the headers, you would only need to change the Style.

The FlowDocument uses a LinearGradientBrush that shades from black to gray as the text moves left to right. (The effect is more striking on a monitor if you use a colored gradient.)

The document contains a table in its first section, Button and TextBox controls, an Ellipse, and a Grid that holds a Polygon. It uses the Floater element to allow another Grid containing a Polygon and a text caption to float to a position where it will fit nicely in the display. The document also holds a list, one item of which contains a Polygon drawing a triangle.

The bottom of the FlowDocumentReader displays a toolbar. If you click the magnifying glass button on the left, a search text box appears next to it. You can enter text to search for, and the reader will let you scroll back and forth through any matches.

In the middle of the toolbar, the reader displays the current page number and the total number of pages. The three buttons to the right let the user select the single page, book reading, and scrolling views. Finally, the slider on the lower right lets the user adjust the document's scale to zoom in or out.

The *FlowDocumentPageViewer* and *FlowDocumentScrollViewer* objects behave as the FlowDocumentReader does in its single page and scrolling modes, respectively. (The big difference is that FlowDocumentReader can display documents in several modes while the others use only one. If you want to allow the reader more options, use FlowDocumentReader. If you want to restrict the view available, use one of the other kinds of viewers.)

Example programs UseFlow DocumentPageViewer and UseFlowDocumentScrollViewer, which are available for download on the book's web site, demonstrate these controls.

 If you display a FlowDocument element itself, it acts as a FlowDocumentReader. See example program UseFlowDocument, which is available for download on the book's web site.

Fixed Documents

A *FixedDocument* represents a document that should always be displayed exactly as it was originally composed. Whereas a FlowDocument rearranges its content to take advantage of its current size, all of the content in a FixedDocument remains where it was originally placed. If a FlowDocument is similar to a web browser, then a FixedDocument is similar to an Adobe Acrobat PDF document.

The FixedDocument object contains one or more PageContent objects, each containing a FixedPage object. It is in the FixedPage object that you place your content. You can use the usual assortment of containers to arrange controls and other objects inside the FixedPage object.

A program can use a *DocumentViewer* to display a FixedDocument. The DocumentViewer provides tools to let the user print, zoom in and out, size the document to fit the viewer, display the document in one- or two-page modes, and search for text within the document.

Example program UseFixedDocument, which is available for download on the book's web site, displays a FixedDocument inside a DocumentViewer.

XPS Documents

In addition to flow documents and fixed documents, WPF also defines a third kind of document called *XML Paper Specification (XPS)* documents. XPS is an XML-based open standard used to represent fixed documents.

An XPS document is stored in a file called a *package*. The package is made up of pieces called *parts*. Physically, the parts are arranged as files and folders. When you save the document to disk, it is stored as a ZIP-compressed collection of these physical files and folders. If you change the file's extension from .xps to .zip, you can read the files using any ZIP-enabled viewer. For example, Windows Explorer will let you browse through the ZIP file.

Logically, the document's parts form a hierarchical representation of the document. (Remember that the document uses an XML format, and XML is hierarchical, so the document is also hierarchical.) The document itself may contain a FixedDocumentSequence object that contains one or more

FixedDocument objects. The FixedDocument objects are similar to the ones described in the previous section, so they can hold container controls that contain any number of objects arranged in a hierarchical way.

In addition to the features provided by FixedDocuments, XPS documents also allow you to digitally sign the package. That tells others that you signed it, gives them the time and date that you signed it, and ensures that the document has not been modified since then. A document can contain more than one signature and you can provide different levels of security on different parts of the document. For example, you could prevent others from changing the document's body, but allow them to add annotations.

Like the other new WPF document objects, XPS documents are quite complex, and there isn't room to do them justice here. See Microsoft's online help (`msdn2.microsoft.com/system.windows.xps` and `www.microsoft.com/whdc/xps/xpsspec.mspx` are good places to start) and search the Web for more detailed information and examples.

 Note that many of the WPF examples scattered around the Web were written in early betas and no longer work exactly as they were originally posted. You may need to perform some conversions to make them work properly.

SUMMARY

One of the main goals of WPF is to separate the user interface more completely from the code behind it. XAML lets you declaratively build a user interface, and then later add code to handle the events that any Windows application needs to perform. Because the user interface is separate from the code, you can assign different developers to work on each of them. You can have a graphics designer use a graphical XAML editor to build the user interface, and have a Visual Basic developer write the underlying code. Later, the graphical designer can modify the user interface without forcing you to rewrite the code.

WPF also includes hundreds of new objects for defining user interfaces. These objects let you build windows that take advantage of modern computer graphics hardware, and can provide advanced features such as translucency and rotated controls. New drawing objects produce complex graphics in two and three dimensions.

Resources and styles let you customize objects so that they are easy to change in a central location. Triggers, animations, and storyboards let the interface interact with the user at a very high level, so the bulk of your code doesn't need to handle these more cosmetic chores.

New document objects let you display information that can flow to take best advantage of the available space, or that remain in fixed positions on any display device. Powerful document viewers let users scroll through documents, zoom in and out, print, and copy data to the clipboard.

WPF provides a huge number of powerful new features, and this chapter barely scratches the surface.

In Windows Forms applications, Form objects play a special role. They represent the top-level user interface components in which all other controls reside.

In a WPF application, the situation is a little less obvious. A top-level object in a WPF application can be a Window, which roughly corresponds to a Form, but it can also be a Page, PageFunction, or FlowDocument. Chapter 13, "WPF Windows," describes the Windows class and these other top-level classes, and explains their special roles in WPF applications.

13

WPF Windows

In Windows Forms applications, Form objects play a special role. They represent the top-level user interface components in which all other controls reside. Ignoring behind-the-scenes chores such as parsing command-line arguments and messing with the operating system, a typical Windows Forms application starts by displaying a Form object. That Form may provide buttons, menus, and other controls that open other Form objects, but all of the controls are contained in Form objects.

In WPF applications, you can display controls on a Window, an object that is basically the WPF version of a Form. Alternatively you can display controls in a Page. A Page is a lot like a Window without decorations such as borders, title bar, and system menus (maximize, minimize, restore, close, and so forth). A Page must be hosted inside another object that provides these decorations. Usually, a Page is displayed in a web browser, but the WPF Frame control can also display Page objects.

This chapter explains how you can use these top-level objects, Window and Page, in your WPF applications. It explains how a program can display and manage multiple Window and Page objects, and provides some examples showing simple navigation schemes.

WINDOW APPLICATIONS

A typical desktop WPF application displays its controls in Window objects. To create this type of application, select the File menu's New Project command to display the New Project dialog. On the Visual Basic ⇨ Windows tab, select WPF Application, enter a project name, and click OK.

The new application begins with a single Window class named Window1. Open the Solution Explorer and double-click the Window1.xaml entry to edit the Window's controls. Double-click the Window1.xaml.vb entry to edit the Visual Basic code behind the Window.

> **CODE-BEHIND**
>
> The code behind a Window is called its *code-behind*. It's not a very imaginative term, but it's easy to remember.

To add other Window classes, open the Project menu and select Add Window. Enter a name for the class and click OK.

To display a window in code, create a variable that refers to a new instance of the window. Call its `Show` method to display the window non-modally, or call its `ShowDialog` method to display the window modally. The following code creates a new window of type Window2 and displays it modally:

```
Dim win2 As New Window2
win2.ShowDialog()
```

Although several similarities exist between the way a program uses a Window and the way it uses a Form, there are many significant differences.

For example, both classes have a DialogResult property that indicates how the user closed the form. Both classes' ShowDialog methods return this result, so the code can easily determine the form's DialogResult value. In a Form, the DialogResult property is a value of type DialogResult, an enumerated type that provides values such as OK, Cancel, Yes, and No to indicate which button the user clicked to close the form. If the code sets this value, the form automatically hides, so the calling ShowDialog method returns.

In contrast, a WPF Window's DialogResult value is a Boolean intended to indicate whether the user accepted or canceled the dialog. If you need more detail (did the user click Yes, No, or Cancel?), you'll need to provide code in the dialog to remember which button the user clicked. If the code sets DialogResult, the window automatically closes so the calling ShowDialog method returns. Unfortunately, the window closes rather than hides so you cannot display the dialog again (you cannot display a window after it has closed). If you want to remember which button the user clicked and then hide the window without closing it, you'll need to implement your own property rather than DialogResult, and you'll need to hide the window explicitly.

The Windows Forms and WPF Button classes also both have properties that you can use to define a dialog's default and cancel buttons, but they work in different ways.

You can set a Windows Forms Button object's DialogResult property to the value you want the button to give to the form's DialogResult property. If the user clicks the button, it assigns the form's DialogResult value and hides the form so the calling ShowDialog method returns that value.

In a WPF application, you can set a button's IsCancel property to True to indicate that the button is the form's cancel button. If the user presses the Escape key or clicks the button, the button sets the form's DialogResult property and closes the form so the calling ShowDialog method returns. Unfortunately, the button closes the form rather than merely hiding it so, as before, you cannot display the dialog again.

You can also set a WPF button's IsDefault property to indicate that it should fire if the user presses the Enter key. Unfortunately, this does not automatically set the form's DialogResult property and does not close the dialog.

Example program UseDialog shows one approach to solving this problem. The dialog class Window2 contains three buttons labeled Yes, No, and Cancel.

The following code shows how the dialog handles button clicks. The single `btn_Click` event handler fires for all three of the buttons. It saves the button's text in the public variable `UserClicked` and then closes the form.

```
Partial Public Class Window2
    Public UserClicked As String = "Cancel"

    Private Sub btn_Click(ByVal btn As Button, _
     ByVal e As System.Windows.RoutedEventArgs) _
     Handles btnYes.Click, btnNo.Click, btnCancel.Click
        UserClicked = btn.Content
        Me.Close()
    End Sub
End Class
```

code snippet UseDialog

The following code shows how the program's main window displays the dialog and checks the result. When you click the Show Dialog button, the program creates a new dialog window and displays it modally. It then checks the dialog's `UserClicked` property to see which button the user clicked.

```
Private Sub btnShowDialog_Click() Handles btnShowDialog.Click
    Dim win2 As New Window2
    win2.ShowDialog()
    Select Case win2.UserClicked
        Case "Yes"
            MessageBox.Show("You clicked Yes", "Yes", MessageBoxButton.OK)
        Case "No"
            MessageBox.Show("You clicked No", "No", MessageBoxButton.OK)
        Case "Cancel"
            MessageBox.Show("You clicked Cancel", "Cancel", _
                MessageBoxButton.OK)
    End Select
End Sub
```

code snippet UseDialog

Most of the things that you can do with a Form you can do with a Window. For example, you can:

➤   Create new instances of Window classes.

➤   Display Windows modally or non-modally.

➤   Close or hide Windows.

➤   View and manipulate the properties of one Window from within the code of another Window.

Nevertheless, the details between Form and Window operations may be different. You may need to use slightly different properties, and you may need to take a slightly different approach, but Window is a fairly powerful class and with some perseverance you should be able to build usable interfaces with it.

A BLAST FROM THE PAST

In many ways, the Window class seems like a primitive version of the Form class, somewhat like those used in early versions of Visual Basic. Hopefully future versions of WPF will give us a more powerful and consistent control that provides the features we've grown used to in the Form class.

PAGE APPLICATIONS

A Page is similar to a borderless Window. It doesn't provide its own decorations (border, title bar, and so forth), but instead relies on its container to provide those elements.

Often a Page is hosted by a web browser, although the WPF Frame control can also display Page objects.

The following sections explain how you can use Page objects to build WPF applications.

Browser Applications

To make a XAML Browser Application (XBAP, pronounced *ex-bap*), select the File menu's New Project command to display the New Project dialog. On the Visual Basic ➪ Windows tab, select WPF Browser Application, enter a project name, and click OK.

EXCITING XBAPS

For an interesting site that has lots of information about XBAPs including a FAQ, tutorial, and samples, see XBap.org (`www.xbap.org`).

The new application begins with a single Page class named Page1. You can view and edit this Page exactly as you would view and edit a Window. Open the Solution Explorer and double-click the Page1.xaml entry to edit the Window's controls. Double-click the Window1.xaml.vb entry to edit the Visual Basic code behind the Window.

To run the application, open the Debug menu and select Start Debugging. Internet Explorer should open and display the initial Page. Visual Studio is nicely integrated with this instance of Internet

Explorer so you can set breakpoints in the code to stop execution and debug the code just as you can debug a Windows Forms application or a WPF Window application.

To add other Page classes to the application, open the Project menu and select Add Page. Enter a name for the class and click OK.

To display a Page in code, create a variable that refers to a new instance of the Page. Then use the current Page's NavigationService object's Navigate method to display the new Page.

The following code creates a new page of type Page2, and then uses the NavigationService object to display it:

```
Dim p2 As New Page2
NavigationService.Navigate(p2)
```

Because the application is hosted inside a browser, several differences exist in the ways in which the user will interact with the application. Rather than displaying new forms and dialogs, the application will generally display new material within the same browser.

This design has several consequences. For example, the previous code creates a new instance of the Page2 class and displays it. If the user were to execute this same code later, it would create a second instance of the class and display it. Because these are two instances of the class, they do not have the same controls, so any changes the user makes (entering text, checking radio buttons, and so forth) are not shared between the two pages. When the second instance appears, the user may wonder where all of the previous selections have gone.

The program can prevent this confusion by using a single application-global variable to hold references to the Page2 instance. Every time the program needs to show this page, it can display the same instance. That instance will display the same control values so the user's selections are preserved.

That approach solves one problem but leads to another. Because the application runs inside a browser, the browser's navigation and history tools work with it. If you press the browser's Back button, it will display the previous page. That part works relatively transparently, but every time the application uses NavigationService.Navigate to display a Page, that Page is added to the browser's history.

To see why this is an issue, suppose the application has an initial Page that contains a button leading to a second Page. That Page has a button that navigates back to the first page. If the user moves back and forth several times, the browser's history will be cluttered with entries such as Page 1, Page 2, Page 1, Page 2, Page 2, and so forth. Although this represents the user's actual path through the Pages, it isn't very useful.

You can reduce clutter in the browser's history by using the NavigationService object's GoForward and GoBack methods whenever it makes sense. In this example, it would probably make sense for the second Page to use the GoBack method to return to the main page. Instead of creating a new entry in the history as the Navigate method does, GoBack moves back one position in the existing history. After several trips between the two Pages, the history will contain only those two Pages, one possibly available via the browser's Back button and one possibly available via the browser's Next button.

Example program BrowserApp demonstrates this technique. The program uses two Pages that provide buttons to navigate to each other. Both Pages also contain a text box where you can enter some text, just to verify that the values are preserved when you navigate between the pages.

The following code shows how the main Page navigates to the second Page. If the NavigationService can go forward, the code calls its `GoForward` method. If the NavigationService cannot go forward, the code uses its `Navigate` method to visit a new `Page2` object.

```
Private Sub btnPage2_Click() Handles btnPage2.Click
    If NavigationService.CanGoForward Then
        NavigationService.GoForward()
    Else
        NavigationService.Navigate(New Page2)
    End If
End Sub
```

code snippet BrowserApp

The following code shows how the second Page returns to the first. This code simply calls the NavigationService object's `GoBack` method.

```
Private Sub btnBack_Click() Handles btnBack.Click
    Me.NavigationService.GoBack()
End Sub
```

Once you've built an XBAP, you can run it by pointing a web browser at the compiled xbap file. When I built the previous example program, the file BrowserApp.xbap was created in the project's bin/Debug directory and the file successfully loaded in either Internet Explorer or Firefox.

Building a Page class is almost exactly the same as building a Window class. You use the same XAML editor and Visual Basic code behind the scenes. The main difference is in how you navigate between the application's forms. In a WPF application, you create Window objects and use their Show or ShowDialog methods. In an XBAP, you create Page objects and use the NavigationService object's navigation methods.

Frame Applications

Though Page objects normally sit inside a browser, the WPF Frame control can also host them. The program simply navigates the Frame control to a Page and the rest works exactly as it does for an XBAP.

Example program FrameApp, which is available for download on the book's web page and shown in Figure 13-1, uses the following code to load a `Page1` object into its Frame control:

```
fraPages.Navigate(New Page1)
```

This example contains the same Page1 and Page2 classes used by the BrowserApp example program described in the previous section.

If an XBAP runs so easily in a browser, why would you want to host pages in a Frame control?

One reason is that you can place multiple frames within a Window to let the user view different pieces of information or perform different tasks at the same time. For example, you can display help in a separate frame, possibly in a separate Window.

If you build each frame's contents in a separate XBAP, you can load the frames at runtime. That makes replacing XBAPs to upgrade or change their contents easy.

FIGURE 13-1: The Frame control provides navigation between Page objects.

The Frame control also provides simple browser-style navigation that uses Next and Back buttons and that may be easier for users to navigate in some situations. Microsoft's web page "Top Rules for the Windows Vista User Experience" at msdn2.microsoft.com/Aa511327.aspx lists as Rule 7 "Use Windows Explorer-hosted, navigation-based user interfaces, provide a Back button." That page argues that this style of interaction simplifies navigation even in traditional applications.

> ### STRENGTH OR WEAKNESS?
>
> Personally I think Microsoft is claiming a weakness as a strength. Web browsers use this type of navigation because they have no context to provide more organized navigation other than the hyperlinks provided by Web pages. There are certainly cases where this style of navigation is reasonable (for example, in wizards that lead the user through a series of steps) but many desktop applications are more natural if the user can open separate windows for different tasks. Let me know what you think at RodStephens@vb-helper.com.

The Frame control gives you more control than a browser does. For example, it provides easier access to Page history. You can also determine a Frame control's size whereas you have no control over a browser's size and position.

Displaying Page objects within a Frame control won't make sense for every application, but for some it can be a useful technique.

PageFunction Applications

Microsoft's documentation says that a PageFunction is "a special type of page that allows you to treat navigation to a page in a similar fashion to calling a method." This is a fairly misleading statement. Navigating to a PageFunction is actually similar to navigating to any other Page object. What is different is that a PageFunction is intended to take parameters when it is displayed and to return a result when it finishes.

The PageFunction does not perform these tasks in the same way that a method call performs them. The program "passes parameters" to the object by including them in the PageFunction's constructor. It receives a "return value" by catching the PageFunction's Return event and examining a parameter passed to that event.

Example program UsePageFunction, which is shown in Figure 13-2, demonstrates the PageFunction class. This program is an XBAP that contains a startup Page and a PageFunction. The startup Page contains two text boxes: one for an initial value and one for a return value. Type some text into the Initial Value text box and click the "Go to Page 2" button.

FIGURE 13-2: The PageFunction class simplifies passing parameters and return values to pages.

The second Page displays the text you typed on the first Page in a text box to show that the code successfully passed your text into the PageFunction. If you modify the text and click the Return button, the first Page displays the modified text to show that it successfully received the PageFunction object's return value.

The following code shows how the PageFunction works. Notice that the class inherits from PageFunction(Of String). That indicates that this is a PageFunction class and that its "parameter" and "return value" are strings. The wizard example described in the following section shows how a PageFunction can use a different data type.

```
Partial Public Class PageFunction1
    Inherits PageFunction(Of String)

    ' Start with the input value.
    Public Sub New(ByVal initial_value As String)
        Me.InitializeComponent()

        txtValue.Text = initial_value
    End Sub
```

```
    ' Return the current text.
    Private Sub btnReturn_Click() Handles btnReturn.Click
        OnReturn(New ReturnEventArgs(Of String)(txtValue.Text))
    End Sub
End Class
```

code snippet UsePageFunction

The PageFunction's constructor takes a string as a parameter. It calls its InitializeComponent method to prepare its controls for use and saves the string value in the page's text box.

When you click the Return button, the `btnReturn_Click` event handler calls the PageFunction's `OnReturn` method, passing it a new ReturnEventArgs(Of String) object. That object becomes the return result that the first page receives. The code passes this object's constructor the string that it wants to return. In this example, the result is the text you modified in the text box.

The following code shows how the startup Page works:

Available for download on Wrox.com

```
Class Page1
    Private WithEvents page2 As PageFunction1

    Private Sub btnPage2_Click() Handles btnPage2.Click
        page2 = New PageFunction1(txtInitialValue.Text)
        NavigationService.Navigate(page2)
    End Sub

    ' Catch the Return event and process the result.
    Private Sub page2_Return(ByVal sender As Object, _
     ByVal e As System.Windows.Navigation.ReturnEventArgs(Of String)) _
     Handles page2.Return
        txtReturnedValue.Text = e.Result
    End Sub
End Class
```

code snippet UsePageFunction

This code starts by declaring a variable named `Page2` of type PageFunction1. The code uses the `WithEvents` keyword, so it is easy to catch the object's events.

When you click the Page's Go to Page 2 button, the `btnPage2_Click` event handler creates a new PageFunction1 and saves it in the variable `Page2` so it can catch that object's events. It then navigates to the new object.

When the PageFunction calls its OnReturn method, this Page catches the object's Return event. The event handler receives a parameter e that contains the return value in its `Result` property. The code displays the result in the `txtReturnedValue` text box.

This isn't exactly the way a method call works, but it does allow the application to pass a value to the PageFunction and receive a result. The next section describes a more complicated PageFunction example.

Wizard Applications

Although PageFunction objects, or XBAPs in general for that matter, are not appropriate for all situations, they work well for building wizards. A typical wizard walks the user through a series of steps one at a time until the user finishes the final step.

The BrowserWizard example program is an XBAP that uses PageFunction objects to build a simplistic dinner selection wizard.

The initial Page is a Page object that displays a Start Wizard button and a list of final selections made by the wizard (initially these are blank). When the user clicks the button, the program displays the wizard's first step.

The first step is displayed by a PageFunction that contains a combo box where the user can select an appetizer and a check box that lets the user select salad (or not). After making selections, the user can click the Next button to move to the wizard's second step. The user can also click the Cancel button to close the wizard.

The second step is another PageFunction that contains two combo boxes where the user can select an entrée and a drink. This step enables its Next button only after the user selects an entrée. This step also contains a Prev button that lets the user move back to the first step and a Cancel button that lets the user cancel the wizard.

The wizard's final step is also implemented with a PageFunction object. It contains a combo box that lets the user select a dessert. It provides Prev and Cancel buttons similar to those on the second page. Instead of a Next button, it displays a Finish button that ends the wizard. Control returns to the initial Page and that Page displays the user's choices.

This application passes an object of type WizardData to each of its steps. This class, shown in the following code, keeps track of the user's selections as the wizard walks through its steps:

```vb
Public Enum DessertType
    None
    IceCream
    Cake
    Pie
    Cookie
End Enum

' This is the data that the user will fill in.
' We set default values here.
Public Class WizardData
    Public Canceled As Boolean = True
    Public Appetizer As String = ""
    Public Entree As String = ""
    Public Salad As Boolean = False
    Public Drink As String = ""
    Public Dessert As DessertType = DessertType.None
End Class
```

code snippet BrowserWizard

In addition to fields to store the user's appetizer, entrée, salad, drink, and dessert selections, the WizardData class also defines a Canceled field to keep track of whether the user clicked the Cancel button at any stage.

The following code shows how the initial Page works:

```
Class WizardStart
    Private WithEvents m_Page1 As WizardPage1

    ' Display page 1.
    Private Sub btnPage1_Click() Handles btnPage1.Click
        m_Page1 = New WizardPage1(New WizardData)
        NavigationService.Navigate(m_Page1)
    End Sub

    ' Page 1 returned.
    Private Sub m_Page1_Return(ByVal sender As Object, _
     ByVal e As System.Windows.Navigation.ReturnEventArgs(Of WizardData)) _
     Handles m_Page1.Return
        Dim wiz_data As WizardData = e.Result

        ' See if the user canceled.
        If wiz_data.Canceled Then
            lblAppetizer.Content = ""
            lblEntree.Content = ""
            lblSalad.Content = ""
            lblDrink.Content = ""
            lblDessert.Content = ""
        Else
            lblAppetizer.Content = wiz_data.Appetizer
            lblEntree.Content = wiz_data.Entree
            lblSalad.Content = wiz_data.Salad.ToString
            lblDrink.Content = wiz_data.Drink
            lblDessert.Content = wiz_data.Dessert.ToString
        End If
    End Sub
End Class
```

code snippet BrowserWizard

This Page declares a variable of type WizardPage1, using the WithEvents keyword so it is easy to catch the object's Return event. When the user clicks the Start Wizard button, the btnPage1_Click event handler creates a new WizardPage1 object passing its constructor a new WizardData object and navigates to the new page.

When the WizardPage1 object returns, the start page catches its Return event. If the returned WizardData object's Canceled value is True, the code clears all of the start page's menu choice controls. If Canceled is False, the program displays the menu selections in the initial Page's controls.

The following code shows how the wizard's first step begins. Notice that this class inherits from PageFunction(Of WizardData) so its constructor and OnReturn method take WizardData objects as parameters.

```
Inherits PageFunction(Of WizardData)

Private m_WizardData As WizardData
Private WithEvents m_Page2 As WizardPage2

' Save the WizardData object.
Public Sub New(ByVal wizard_data As WizardData)
    InitializeComponent()

    m_WizardData = wizard_data
End Sub
```

code snippet BrowserWizard

The code declares a private WizardData variable to hold information about the user's current menu selections. The class's constructor initializes its controls and then saves the WizardData object it is passed in this variable.

The code also creates a variable of type WizardPage2. It displays this object when the user clicks this page's Next button.

When that step returns, the following code catches its Return event and calls this Page's OnReturn method passing it the same event parameter that it received. This forwards the results of the following step back to the initial Page.

```
' The next page returned. Return its result.
Private Sub m_Page2_Return(ByVal sender As Object, _
 ByVal e As System.Windows.Navigation.ReturnEventArgs(Of WizardData)) _
 Handles m_Page2.Return
    OnReturn(e)
End Sub
```

code snippet BrowserWizard

The following code shows the first Page's navigation code:

```
' Open the next page.
Public Sub btnNext_Click() Handles btnNext.Click
    If NavigationService.CanGoForward Then
        NavigationService.GoForward()
    Else
        m_Page2 = New WizardPage2(m_WizardData)
        NavigationService.Navigate(m_Page2)
    End If
End Sub

' Return a result indicating that we canceled.
Private Sub btnCancel_Click() Handles btnCancel.Click
    m_WizardData.Canceled = True
    OnReturn(New ReturnEventArgs(Of WizardData)(m_WizardData))
End Sub
```

code snippet BrowserWizard

When the user clicks the Next button, the btnNext_Click event handler checks whether the NavigationService can go forward. This object's CanGoForward property will be True if the user went to the next page and then came back to this one. In that case, the program shouldn't create a new Page object. Instead it calls NavigationService object's GoForward method to display the same object again.

If NavigationService.CanGoForward is False, the code has not displayed the second Page yet. The code creates a new WizardPage2 object, passing its constructor the WizardData object that holds the information about the user's current menu selections. It then navigates to the new Page.

If the user clicks the Cancel button, the btnCancel_Click event handler sets the WizardData object's Canceled property to True and then calls the page's OnReturn method, passing it the WizardData. Control returns to the start page where that page catches the Return event and sees that the WizardData object's Canceled property is True.

The following code records the user's appetizer and salad selections:

```
' Save the selection.
Private Sub cboAppetizer_SelectionChanged() _
 Handles cboAppetizer.SelectionChanged
    ' The ComboBox's Text property isn't updated yet.
    If cboAppetizer.SelectedIndex < 0 Then
        m_WizardData.Appetizer = ""
    Else
        m_WizardData.Appetizer = _
            cboAppetizer.Items(cboAppetizer.SelectedIndex).Content
    End If
End Sub

' Save the selection.
Private Sub chkSalad_Checked() _
 Handles chkSalad.Checked, chkSalad.Unchecked
    m_WizardData.Salad = chkSalad.IsChecked
End Sub
```

code snippet BrowserWizard

When the user selects an appetizer, the `cboAppetizer_SelectionChanged` event handler saves the user's new choice in the WizardData object's Appetizer field. Similarly, if the user checks or unchecks the Salad check box, the `chkSalad_Checked` event handler saves the user's new selection.

The second and third wizard pages are similar to the first except for two issues.

First, the user can navigate back to wizard steps that come before these steps. The following code shows how these steps move to the previous step when the user clicks the Prev button:

```
' Go back to the previous page.
Private Sub btnPrev_Click() Handles btnPrev.Click
    NavigationService.GoBack()
End Sub
```

code snippet BrowserWizard

Second, the final step does not navigate to a next step when the user clicked a Next button. Instead when the user clicks the Finish button, the following code executes:

```
' Finish.
Public Sub btnFinish_Click() Handles btnFinish.Click
    M_WizardData.Canceled = False
    OnReturn(New ReturnEventArgs(Of WizardData)(m_WizardData))
End Sub
```

code snippet BrowserWizard

This code sets the WizardData object's Canceled field to False to indicate that the user did not cancel. The code then calls the PageFunction's OnReturn method, passing it a new ReturnEventArgs object that contains the WizardData.

At this point, control cascades back through the navigations. The second Page catches this Page's Return event and calls its own OnReturn method. Next, the first Page catches the second Page's Return event and calls its own OnReturn method. Finally the initial Page catches the first wizard Page's Return event and displays the results contained in the returned WizardData object.

PageFunction classes are not necessary in every application, but they can simplify wizards such as this one and other applications that pass information back and forth through a series of Pages.

SUMMARY

In a Windows Forms application, everything is contained in Form objects. Some of those Form classes may be dialogs or derived from the Form class, but ultimately everything is contained in a form.

In a WPF application, controls may be contained in Window objects or in Page objects. Window objects sit on the desktop much as Windows Forms do. Page objects must be hosted inside something else, usually a browser or a Frame control in a Window. The PageFunction class provides a modified version of a Page that makes it easier to pass values back and forth between coordinated Pages.

Chapters 8 through 13 give useful background on working with controls. They explain how to select and use both Windows Forms and WPF controls. They also explain the top-level user interface classes: Form for Windows Forms applications, and Window, Page, and PageFunction for WPF applications.

Although these are huge topics, there's even more to building a Visual Basic application than just controls. You also need to understand the code behind the Form or Window that lets the program take the controls' values, manipulate those values, and display a result in other controls. The next several chapters cover these topics in detail. Chapter 14, "Program and Module Structure," starts the process by explaining the files that make up a Visual Basic project and the structure contained within code files.

14

Program and Module Structure

A Visual Basic *solution* contains one or more related projects. A *project* contains files related to some topic. Usually, a project produces some kind compiled output (such as an executable program, class library, control library, and so forth). The project includes all the files related to the output, including source code files, resource files, documentation files, and whatever other kinds of files you decide to add to it.

This chapter describes the basic structure of a Visual Basic project. It explains the functions of some of the most common files and tells how you can use them to manage your applications.

This chapter also explains the basic structure of source code files. It explains regions, namespaces, and modules. It describes some simple typographic features provided by Visual Basic such as comments, line continuation, and line labels. These features do not execute programming commands themselves, but they are an important part of how you can structure your code.

HIDDEN FILES

Figure 14-1 shows the Solution Explorer window for a solution that contains two projects. The solution named MySolution contains two projects named WindowsApplication1 and WindowsApplication2. Each project contains a My Project item that represents the project's properties, various files containing project configuration settings, and a form named Form1.

In WindowsApplication2, the Show All Files button has been clicked (the second button from the left with the box around it) so that you can see all the project's files. WindowsApplication1 has similar files, but they are hidden by default.

These files are generated by Visual Basic for various purposes. For example, Resources.resx contains resources used by the project and Settings.settings contains project settings.

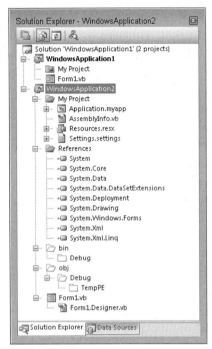

FIGURE 14-1: A solution contains one or more projects that contain files.

RESOURCES AND SETTINGS

Resources are chunks of data that are distributed with the application but are not intended to be modified by the program. These might include prompt strings, error message strings, icons, and sound files. For example, resources are commonly used for customizing applications for different languages. You build different resource files for different languages, and the program loads its prompts and error messages from the appropriate resource file. Chapter 36, "Configuration and Resources," has more to say about resources. (Technically, you can change resource values, but then they are acting more as settings than resources, so I won't cover that here. In fact, changing resources in a strongly named resource file raises an alarm indicating that someone may have tampered with the file.)

Settings are values that control the execution of the application. These might include flags telling the program what options to display or how to perform certain tasks. For example, you could build different profiles to provide settings that make the program run in a restricted demo mode or in a fully licensed mode. Normally, settings for .NET applications are stored in .config files, although an application can also store settings in the Registry, XML, or .ini files. For example, this article discusses savings in XML files: www.devsource .com/c/a/Techniques/XML-Serialization-Better-than-the-Registry.

The following list describes the files contained in WindowsApplication2 and shown in Figure 14-1. The exact files you see may be different from those shown here, but this list should give you an idea of what's involved in building a project. Note that some of these files are generated automatically by Visual Studio and you shouldn't edit them manually. If you change them directly, you are likely to lose your changes when Visual Studio rebuilds them and you may even confuse Visual Studio.

➤ WindowsApplication2 — This folder represents the entire project. You can expand or collapse it to show and hide the project's details.

➤ My Project — This folder represents the project's assembly information, application-level events, resources, and configuration settings. Double-click the My Project entry to view and edit these values.

➤ Application.myapp — This XML file defines application properties (such as whether it's a single instance program and whether its shutdown mode is AfterMainFormCloses or AfterAllFormsClose).

➤ Application.Designer.vb — This file contains code that works with the values defined in Application.myapp.

➤ AssemblyInfo.vb — This file contains information about the application's assembly such as copyright information, company name, trademark information, and assembly version.

➤ Resources.resx — This resource file contains project's resources.

➤ Resources.Designer.vb — This file contains Visual Basic code for manipulating resources defined in Resources.resx. For example, if you define a string resource named Greeting in Resources.resx, Visual Basic adds a read-only property to this module so you can read the value of Greeting as shown in the following code:

```
MessageBox.Show(My.Resources.Greeting)
```

➤ Settings.settings — This file contains settings that you can define to control the application.

➤ Settings.Designer.vb — This file contains Visual Basic code for manipulating settings defined in Settings.settings, much as Resources.Designer.vb contains code for working with Resources.resx. For example, the following code uses the UserMode setting:

```
If My.Settings.UserMode = "Clerk" Then ...
```

➤ References — This folder lists references to external components such as DLLs and COM components.

➤ bin — This folder is used to build the application before it is executed. It contains the compiled .exe file.

➤ obj — This folder is used to build the application before it is executed.

➤ ApplicationEvents.vb — This code file contains application-level event handlers for the MyApplication object. For example, it contains the application's Startup, Shutdown, and NetworkAvailabilityChanged event handlers.

➤ Form1.vb — This is a form file. It contains the code you write for the form, its controls, their event handlers, and so forth.

➤ Form1.Designer.vb — This file contains designer-generated Visual Basic code that builds the form. It initializes the form when it is created, adds the controls you placed on the form, and defines variables with the WithEvents keyword for the controls so that you can easily catch their events.

Some projects may have other hidden files. For example, when you add controls to a form, the designer adds a resource file to the form to hold any resources needed by the controls.

Normally, you do not need to work directly with the hidden files and doing so can mess up your application. At best, the changes you make will be lost. At worst, you may confuse Visual Studio so it can no longer load your project.

You can use other tools to modify hidden files indirectly. For example, the files Resources.Designer .vb, Settings.Designer.vb, and Form1.Designer.vb are automatically generated when you modify their corresponding source files Resources.resx, Settings.settings, and Form1.vb.

You don't even need to work with all of these source files directly. For example, if you double-click the My Project item in Solution Explorer, the property pages shown in Figure 14-2 appear. The Application tab shown in this figure lets you set high-level application settings. The View Application Events button at the bottom of the figure lets you edit the application-level events stored in ApplicationEvents.vb.

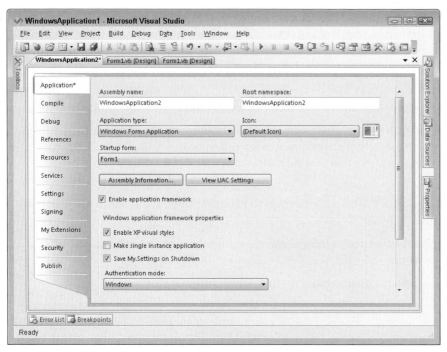

FIGURE 14-2: These property pages let you define the project's resources, settings, and general configuration.

The References tab shown in Figure 14-2 lets you view, add, and remove project references. As you can probably guess, the Resources and Settings tabs let you edit the project's resources and settings.

A particularly important section hidden away in these tabs is the assembly information. When you click the Assembly Information button shown in Figure 14-2, the dialog box shown in Figure 14-3 appears.

Many of the items in this dialog box, such as the application's title and description, are self-explanatory. They are simply strings that the assembly carries around for identification. The assembly and file versions are used by the Visual Studio runtime to verify compatibility between an application's components. The GUID (which stands for "globally unique identifier" and is pronounced to rhyme with "squid") uniquely identifies the assembly and is generated by Visual Studio. The "Make assembly COM-Visible" check box lets you determine whether

FIGURE 14-3: The Assembly Information dialog box lets you define basic project information such as title, copyright, and version number.

the assembly should make types defined in the assembly visible to COM applications. For more information on this dialog box, see `msdn2.microsoft.com//1h52t681.aspx`.

An assembly is the fundamental unit of deployment and version control in Visual Studio .NET. An assembly can contain an executable application, a DLL (dynamic-link library), or a control library. Usually a project is contained in a single assembly.

The Assembly Information dialog box lets you define information that should be associated with the assembly, including the assembly's company name, description, copyright, trademark, name, product name, title, and version (which includes major, minor, revision, and build values).

The My.Application.AssemblyInfo namespace provides easy access to these values at runtime. Example program ShowAssemblyInfo uses the following code to display this information in a series of labels when it starts:

```
Private Sub Form1_Load() Handles MyBase.Load
    lblCompanyName.Text = My.Application.Info.CompanyName
    lblDescription.Text = My.Application.Info.Description
    lblCopyright.Text = My.Application.Info.Copyright
    lblTrademark.Text = My.Application.Info.Trademark
    lblDirectoryPath.Text = My.Application.Info.DirectoryPath
    lblProductName.Text = My.Application.Info.ProductName
    lblTitle.Text = My.Application.Info.Title
    lblVersion.Text = My.Application.Info.Version.ToString
End Sub
```

code snippet ShowAssemblyInfo

CODE FILE STRUCTURE

A form, class, or code module should contain the following sections in this order (if they are present — you can omit some):

➤ Option statements — Option Explicit, Option Strict, Option Compare, or Option Infer. By default, Option Explicit is on, Option Strict is off, Option Compare is binary, and Option Infer is on.

➤ Imports statements — These declare namespaces that the module will use.

➤ A Main subroutine — The routine that starts execution when the program runs.

➤ Class, Module, and Namespace statements — As needed.

DEBUGGING OPTIONS

To uncover potentially annoying and sometimes elusive bugs, turn Option Explicit on, Option Strict on, and Option Infer off. The section "Project" in Chapter 2 describes these options.

Some of these items may be missing. For example, Option and Imports statements are optional. Note that an executable Windows program can start from a Main subroutine or it can start by displaying a form, in which case it doesn't need a Main subroutine. (In that case, the program starts with the automatically generated New subroutine in the file Application.Designer.vb.) Classes and code modules don't need Main subroutines.

The following code shows a simple code module. It sets Option Explicit On (so variables must be declared before used), Option Strict On (so implicit type conversions cause an error), and Option Infer Off (so you must give variables explicit data types). It imports the System.IO namespace so the program can easily use classes defined there. It then defines the Employee class.

```
Option Explicit On
Option Strict On
Option Infer Off

Imports System.IO

Public Class Employee
    ...
End Class
```

Usually, you put each class or module in a separate file, but you can add multiple Class or Module statements to the same file if you like.

Class and Module statements define top-level nodes in the code hierarchy. Click the minus sign to the left of one of these statements in the code editor to collapse the code it contains. When the code is collapsed, click the plus sign to the left of it to expand the code.

The project can freely refer to any public class, or to any public variable or routine in a module. If two modules contain a variable or routine with the same name, the program can select the version it wants by prefixing the name with the module's name. For example, if the AccountingTools and BillingTools modules both have a subroutine named ConnectToDatabase, the following statement executes the version in the BillingTools module:

```
BillingTools.ConnectToDatabase()
```

Code Regions

Class and Module statements define regions of code that you can expand or collapse to make the code easier to understand. Subroutines and functions also define collapsible code sections. In addition to these, you can use the Region statement to create your own collapsible sections of code. You can place subroutines that have a common purpose in a region so you can collapse and expand the code as needed. The following code shows a simple region:

```
#Region "Drawing Routines"
    ...
#End Region
```

Note that the IDE's search-and-replace features normally work only on expanded regions. If you collapse a region and make a global search-and-replace in the current document or the current selection, the collapsed code remains unchanged. If you make a global replace throughout the whole project, the replacement occurs within collapsed regions as well.

> ### RENAME, DON'T REPLACE
>
> Instead of using a global find and replace to rename a variable, class, or other programming entity, use Visual Basic's renaming feature. Right-click the entity you want to rename and select Rename. Enter the new name and click OK. Visual Basic will change all occurrences of the entity in every module as needed.
>
> Using rename instead of global replace makes it easier to rename one variable while not renaming other variables with the same name in different scopes. It also prevents annoying replacement errors. For example, if you use global replace to change "man" to "person," you may accidentally change "manager" to "personager" and "command" to "compersond."

By itself, the End Region statement does not tell you which region it is ending. You can make your code easier to understand, particularly if you have many regions in the same module, by adding a comment after the End Region statement giving the name of the region, as shown in the following code:

```
#Region "Drawing Routines"
    ...
#End Region ' Drawing Routines
```

REAL-LIFE REGIONS

I use regions extensively in my code. They make it easy to collapse code that I'm not working on and they group related code into meaningful sections. Just building the regions helps you put related material together and makes reading the code easier.

Sometimes it may be easier to move related pieces of code into separate files. The Partial keyword allows you to place parts of a class in different files. For example, you could move a form's code for loading and saving data into a separate file and use the Partial keyword to indicate that the code was part of the form. Chapter 26, "Classes and Structures," describes the Partial keyword in detail.

However, you cannot use the Partial keyword with modules so a module's code must all go in one file. In that case, you can use regions to similarly separate a group of related routines and make the code easier to read.

Conditional Compilation

Conditional compilation statements allow you to include or exclude code from the program's compilation. The basic conditional compilation statement is similar to a multiline If Then Else statement. The following code shows a typical statement. If the value *condition1* is True, the code in *code_block_1* is included in the compiled program. If that value is False but the value *condition2* is True, the code in *code_block_2* becomes part of the compiled program. If neither condition is True, the code in *code_block_3* is included in the program.

```
#If condition1 Then
    code_block_1 ...
#ElseIf condition2 Then
    code_block_2 ...
#Else
    code_block_3 ...
#End if
```

It is important to understand that the code not included by the conditional compilation statements is *completely* omitted from the executable program. At compile time, Visual Studio decides whether or not a block of code should be included. That means any code that is omitted does not take up space in the executable program. It also means that you cannot set the execution statement to omitted lines in the debugger because those lines are not present.

In contrast, a normal `If Then Else` statement includes all the code in every code block in the executable program, and then decides which code to execute at runtime.

Because the conditional compilation statement evaluates its conditions at compile time, those conditions must be expressions that can be evaluated at compile time. For example, they can be expressions containing values that you have defined using compiler directives (described shortly). They cannot include values generated at runtime (such as the values of variables).

In fact, a conditional compilation statement evaluates its conditions at design time, so it can give feedback while you are writing the code. For example, if Option Explicit is set to On, Visual Basic flags the following assignment statement as an error. Because the first condition is True, the variable X is declared as a string. Option Explicit On disallows implicit conversion from an integer to a string, so the IDE flags the statement as an error.

```
#If True Then
    Dim X As String
#Else
    Dim X As Integer
#End If

    X = 10
```

That much makes sense, but it's also important to realize that the code not included in the compilation is *not* evaluated by the IDE. If the first condition in the previous code were False, the code would work properly because variable X would be declared as an integer. The IDE doesn't evaluate the other code, so it doesn't notice that there is an error if the condition is False. You probably won't notice the error until you try to actually use the other code.

You can set conditional compilation constants in two main ways: in code and in the project's compilation settings.

Setting Constants in Code

To set conditional compilation constants explicitly in your program, use a `#Const` statement, as shown in the following code:

```
#Const UserType = "Clerk"

#If UserType = "Clerk" Then
    ' Do stuff appropriate for clerks ...
    ...
#ElseIf UserType = "Supervisor" Then
    ' Do stuff appropriate for supervisors ...
```

```
    ...
#Else
    ' Do stuff appropriate for others ...
    ...
#End if
```

Note that these constants are defined only after the point at which they appear in the code. If you use a constant before it is defined, its value is False (unfortunately Option Explicit doesn't apply to these constants). That means the following code displays the value Slow followed by the value Fast:

```
#If UseFastAlgorithm Then
    MessageBox.Show("Fast")
#Else
    MessageBox.Show("Slow")
#End If

#Const UseFastAlgorithm = True

#If UseFastAlgorithm Then
    MessageBox.Show("Fast")
#Else
    MessageBox.Show("Slow")
#End if
```

To avoid possible confusion, many programmers define these constants at the beginning of the file so they don't need to worry about using a variable before it is defined.

Also note that your code can redefine a constant using a new #Const statement later. That means these are not really constants in the sense that their values are unchangeable.

Setting Constants with the Project's Compilation Settings

To set constants with the project's compilation settings, open Solution Explorer and double-click My Project. Select the Compile tab and click its Advanced Compile Options button to open the Advanced Compiler Settings dialog box shown in Figure 14-4. Enter the names and values of the constants in the "Custom constants" text box. Enter each value in the form ConstantName=Value, separating multiple constants with commas.

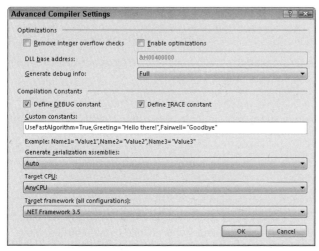

FIGURE 14-4: Use the Advanced Compiler Settings dialog box to define compilation constants.

Constants that you specify on the Advanced Compiler Settings dialog box are available everywhere in the project. However, your code can redefine the constant using a #Const directive. The constant has the new value until the end of the file or until you redefine it again.

Example program CompilerConstantsSettings, which is available for download on the book's web site, includes constants set on this dialog and code to check their values.

Predefined Constants

Visual Basic automatically defines several conditional compilation constants that you can use to determine the code that your application compiles. The following table describes these constants.

> **CONSTANT CASE**
>
> Compilation constant values are case-sensitive. For example, you should compare CONFIG to "Debug" not "debug" or "DEBUG."

CONSTANT	MEANING
CONFIG	A string that gives the name of the current build. Typically, this will be "Debug" or "Release."
DEBUG	A Boolean that indicates whether this is a debug build. By default, this value is True when you build a project's Debug configuration.

continues

(continued)

CONSTANT	MEANING
PLATFORM	A string that tells you the target platform for the application's current configuration. Unless you change this, the value is "AnyCPU."
TARGET	A string that tells the kind of application the project builds. This can be winexe (Windows Form or WPF application), exe (console application), library (class library), or module (code module).
TRACE	A Boolean that indicates whether the Trace object should generate output in the Output window.
VBC_VER	A number giving Visual Basic's major and minor version numbers. The value for Visual Basic 2005 is 8.0 and the value for Visual Basic 2008 is 9.0. The value for Visual Basic 2010 should logically be 10.0, but it was still 9.0 in late beta versions.
_MyType	A string that tells what kind of application this is. Typical values are "Console" for a console application, "Windows" for a class or Windows control library, and "WindowsForms" for a Windows Forms application.

MORE ON _MYTYPE

For more information on _MyType and how it relates to other special compilation constants, see `msdn2.microsoft.com/ms233781.aspx`.

Example program CompilerConstantsInCode, which is available for download on the book's web site, shows how a program can check these compiler constants. Example program WpfCompilerConstantsInCode, which is also available for download, is a WPF version of the same program.

The following sections describe the DEBUG, TRACE, and CONFIG constants and their normal uses in more detail.

DEBUG

Normally when you make a debug build, Visual Basic sets the DEBUG constant to True. When you compile a release build, Visual Basic sets DEBUG to False. The Configuration Manager lets you select the Debug build, the Release build, or other builds that you define yourself.

After you have activated the Configuration Manager, you can open it by clicking the project in the Solution Explorer and then selecting the Build menu's Configuration Manager command. Figure 14-5 shows the Configuration Manager. Select Debug or Release from the drop-down list, and click Close.

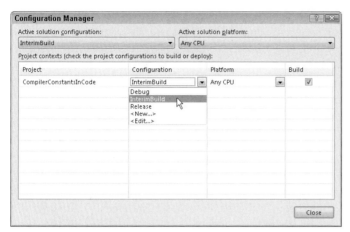

FIGURE 14-5: Use the Configuration Manager to select a Debug or Release build.

THE MISSING MANAGER MYSTERY

If the Configuration Manager is not available in the Build menu, open the Tools menu and select the Options command. Open the Projects and Solutions node's General entry, and select the "Show advanced build configurations" check box.

When the DEBUG constant is True, the Debug object's methods send output to the Output window. When the DEBUG constant is not True, the Debug object's methods do not generate any code, so the object doesn't produce any output. This makes the Debug object useful for displaying diagnostic messages during development and then hiding the messages in release builds sent to customers.

The following sections describe some of the Debug object's most useful properties and methods.

Assert

The Debug.Assert method evaluates a Boolean expression and, if the expression is False, displays an error message. This method can optionally take as parameters an error message and a detailed message to display. The following code shows how a program might use Debug.Assert to verify that the variable NumEmployees is greater than zero:

```
Debug.Assert(NumEmployees > 0, _
    "The number of employees must be greater than zero.", _
    "The program cannot generate timesheets if no employees are defined")
```

Example program EmployeeAssert, which is available for download on the book's web site, demonstrates this Debug.Assert statement.

If NumEmployees is zero, this statement displays an error dialog that shows the error message and the detailed message. It also displays a long stack dump that shows exactly what code called what other code to reach this point of execution. Only the first few entries will make sense to practically anyone because the stack dump quickly moves out of the application's code and into the supporting Visual Basic libraries that execute the program.

The dialog also displays three buttons labeled Abort, Retry, and Ignore. If you click the Abort button, the program immediately halts. If you click Retry, the program breaks into the debugger, so you can examine the code. If you click Ignore, the program continues as if the Assert statement's condition was True.

A good use for the Assert method is to verify that a routine's parameters or other variable values are reasonable before starting calculations. For example, suppose that the AssignJob subroutine assigns a repairperson to a job. The routine could begin with a series of Assert statements that verify that the person exists, the job exists, the person has the skills necessary to perform the job, and so forth. It is usually easier to fix code if you catch these sorts of errors before starting a long calculation or database modification that may later fail because, for example, the repairperson doesn't have the right kind of truck to perform the job.

If the DEBUG constant is not True, the Assert method does nothing. This lets you automatically remove these rather obscure error messages from the compiled executable that you send to customers. The dialog with its messages and stack dump is so technical that it would terrify many users anyway, so there's no point inflicting it on them.

You should take some care when deciding what tests should be placed in Assert statements so that they are removed from the compiled executable. For example, suppose you use Assert to verify that a string entered by the user contains a valid value. When you run the compiled executable, this test is removed, so the program does not protect itself from bad data. When you use Assert to verify a condition, you must be certain that the program can run safely if the Assert statement is removed and the condition fails.

If the program cannot run safely when the condition fails, you should also add code to protect it even in the final compiled version.

Fail

The Debug.Fail method displays an error message just as Debug.Assert does when its Boolean condition parameter is False.

IndentSize, Indent, Unindent, and IndentLevel

These properties and methods determine the amount of indentation used when the Debug object writes into the Output window. You can use them to indent the output in subroutines to show the program's structure more clearly.

The IndentSize property indicates the number of spaces that should be used for each level of indentation. The IndentLevel property determines the current indentation level. For example, if IndentSize is 4 and IndentLevel is 2, output is indented by eight spaces.

The Indent and Unindent methods increase and decrease the indentation level by one.

Write, WriteLine, WriteIf, and WriteLineIf

These routines send output to the Output window. The Write method prints text and stops without starting a new line. WriteLine prints text and follows it with a new line.

The WriteIf and WriteLineIf methods take a Boolean parameter and act the same as Write and WriteLine if the parameter's value is True.

TRACE

The Trace object is very similar to the Debug object and provides the same set of properties and methods. The difference is that it generates output when the TRACE constant is defined rather than when the DEBUG constant is defined.

Normally, the TRACE constant is defined for both debug and release builds so Trace.Assert and other Trace object methods work in both builds. By default, DEBUG is defined only for debug builds, so you get Debug messages for debug builds.

You can add *listener* objects to the Trace object (or the Debug object) to perform different actions on any Trace output. For example, a listener could write the Trace output into a log file.

CONFIG

The CONFIG constant's value is the name of the type of build. Normally, this is either Debug or Release, but you can also create your own build configurations. You can use these for interim builds, point releases, alpha and beta releases, or any other release category you can think of.

To create a new build type, click the project in the Solution Explorer and then select the Build menu's Configuration Manager command to display the dialog box shown in Figure 14-5. Select <New ... > from the drop-down list to display the New Project Configuration dialog box. Enter a name for the new configuration, select the existing configuration from which the new one should initially copy its settings, and click OK.

The following code shows how to use the CONFIG compiler constant to determine which build is being made and take different actions accordingly:

```
#If CONFIG = "Debug" Then
    ' Do stuff for a Debug build ...
#ElseIf CONFIG = "Release" Then
    ' Do stuff for a Release build ...
#ElseIf CONFIG = "InterimBuild" Then
    ' Do stuff for a custom InterimBuild ...
#Else
    MessageBox.Show("Unknown build type")
#End if
```

One reason you might want to make different configurations is to handle variations among operating systems. Your code can decide which configuration is in effect and then execute the appropriate code to handle the target operating system. For example, it might need to work around the reduced privileges that are granted by default on Vista.

Debugging Level Constants

Sometimes it is helpful to be able to easily adjust the level of diagnostic output a program generates. You could define the constant DEBUG_LEVEL and then send data to the Output window, depending on its value. For example, you might place level 1 Debug statements in major subroutines, level 2 statements in secondary routines, and level 3 statements throughout important routines to provide step-by-step information. Then you can define the DEBUG_LEVEL constant to quickly give you the amount of information you want.

The following code shows a small example. The IsPhoneNumberValid function determines whether its parameter looks like a valid 7- or 10-digit U.S. phone number. If DEBUG_LEVEL is at least 1, the function displays messages when it starts and when it exits. It also indents the output when it starts and unindents the output before it exits. If DEBUG_LEVEL is at least 2, the function also displays statements telling when it is about to check for 7- and 10-digit phone numbers.

```
#Const DEBUG_LEVEL = 2

    Private Function IsPhoneNumberValid(ByVal phone_number As String) As Boolean
#If DEBUG_LEVEL >= 1 Then
        Debug.WriteLine("Entering IsPhoneNumberValid(" & phone_number & ")")
        Debug.Indent()
#End If

        ' Check for a 7-digit phone number.
#If DEBUG_LEVEL >= 2 Then
        Debug.WriteLine("Checking for 7-digit phone number")
#End If
        Dim is_valid As Boolean = _
            phone_number Like "###-####"

        If Not is_valid Then
#If DEBUG_LEVEL >= 2 Then
            Debug.WriteLine("Checking for 10-digit phone number")
#End If
            is_valid = phone_number Like "###-###-####"
        End If

#If DEBUG_LEVEL >= 1 Then
        Debug.Unindent()
        Debug.WriteLine("Leaving IsPhoneNumberValid, returning " & is_valid)
#End If
        Return is_valid
    End Function
```

code snippet DebugLevel

The following text shows the results in the Output window when DEBUG_LEVEL is set to 2:

```
Entering IsPhoneNumberValid(123-4567)
    Checking for 7-digit phone number
Leaving IsPhoneNumberValid, returning True
```

From this output, you can tell that the function examined the string 123-4567, did not need to check for a 10-digit phone number, and returned True.

Example program DebugLevel, which is available for download on the book's web site, uses this strategy to provide different levels of debugging output.

For more information on debugging Visual Basic applications, see Chapter 19, "Error Handling."

Namespaces

Visual Studio uses *namespaces* to categorize code. A namespace can contain other namespaces, which can contain others, forming a hierarchy of namespaces.

You can define your own namespaces to help categorize your code. By placing different routines in separate namespaces, you can allow pieces of code to include only the namespaces they are actually using. That makes it easier to ignore the routines that the program isn't using. It also allows more than one namespace to define items that have the same names.

For example, you could define an Accounting namespace that contains the AccountsReceivable and AccountsPayable namespaces. Each of those might contain a subroutine named ListOutstandingInvoices. The program could select one version or the other by calling either Accounting.AccountsReceivable.ListOutstandingInvoices or Accounting.AccountsPayable .ListOutstandingInvoices.

You can only use the Namespace statement at the file level or inside another namespace, not within a class or module. Within a namespace, you can define nested namespaces, classes, or modules.

The following example defines the AccountingModules namespace. That namespace contains the two classes PayableItem and ReceivableItem, the module AccountingRoutines, and the nested namespace OrderEntryModules. The AccountingRoutines module defines the PayInvoice subroutine. All the classes, modules, and namespaces may define other items.

```
Namespace AccountingModules
    Public Class PayableItem
        ...
    End Class

    Public Class ReceivableItem
        ...
    End Class

    Module AccountingRoutines
        Public Sub PayInvoice(ByVal invoice_number As Long)
```

```
            . . .
        End Sub
        . . .
    End Module

    Namespace OrderEntryModules
        Public Class OrderEntryClerk
            . . .
        End Class
        . . .
    End Namespace
End Namespace
```

Code using a module's namespace does not need to explicitly identify the module. If a module defines a variable or routine that has a unique name, you do not need to specify the module's name to use that item. In this example, there is only one subroutine named `PayInvoice`, so the code can invoke it as `AccountingModules.PayInvoice`. If the `AccountingModules` namespace contained another module that defined a `PayInvoice` subroutine, the code would need to indicate which version to use as in `AccountingModules.AccountingRoutines.PayInvoice`.

Although modules are transparent within their namespaces, nested namespaces are not. Because the nested `OrderEntryModules` namespace defines the `OrderEntryClerk` class, the code must specify the full namespace path to the class, as in the following code:

```
Dim oe_clerk As New AccountingModules.OrderEntryModules.OrderEntryClerk
```

NORMAL NAMESPACES

Note that a Visual Basic project defines its own namespace that contains everything else in the project. Normally, the namespace has the same name as the project. To view or modify this root namespace, double-click the Solution Explorer's My Project entry to open the project's property pages, and select the Application tab. Enter the new root namespace name in the text box labeled "Root namespace" in the upper right.

You can use an Imports statement to simplify access to a namespace inside a file. For example, suppose that you are working on the GeneralAccounting project that has the root namespace GeneralAccounting. The first statement in the following code allows the program to use items defined in the AccountingModules namespace without prefixing them with AccountingModules. The second statement lets the program use items defined in the AccountingModules nested namespace OrderEntryModules. The last two lines of code declare variables using classes defined in those namespaces.

```
Imports GeneralAccounting.AccountingModules
Imports GeneralAccounting.AccountingModules.OrderEntryModules
...
Private m_OverdueItem As PayableItem    ' In the AccountingModules namespace.
Private m_ThisClerk As OrderEntryClerk  ' In the namespace
                                        ' AccountingModules.OrderEntryModules.
```

TYPOGRAPHIC CODE ELEMENTS

A few typographic code elements can make a program's structure a bit easier to understand. They do not execute programming commands themselves, but they are an important part of how you can structure your code. These elements include comments, line continuation and joining characters, and line labels.

Comments

Comments can help other developers (or you at a later date) understand the program's purpose, structure, and method. You start a comment by typing a single quotation mark (') that is not inside a quoted string. All of the characters starting at the quote and continuing until the end of the line are part of the comment and are ignored by Visual Basic.

If a line with a comment ends with a line continuation character (described shortly), Visual Basic ignores that character. That means the line is *not* continued onto the next line, so the comment ends with the current line. In other words, you cannot use line continuation characters to make a multi-line comment.

In the following code, the first declaration is followed by a comment. The comment ends with a line continuation character so you might expect the second declaration to be part of the comment. That is not the case. Because this can be misleading, you should not end comments with a line continuation character. The second statement declares and initializes a string using a value that contains a single quote. Because the quote is inside a quoted string, it becomes part of the string and does not start a comment. The next single quotation mark outside of the string begins a new comment.

```
Dim num_customers As Integer    ' The number of customers. _
                                This doesn't work as a continued comment!
Dim product_name As String = "Bob's Miracle Code Fixer" ' The program's name.
```

If you want to continue a comment on the following line, you must use another comment character, as in the following example:

```
' Return True if the address is valid. This function checks the address
' format to see that it makes sense. It also looks up the ZIP code and
' verifies that the city is valid for that ZIP code. It does not verify
' that the street and street number exist.
Private Function IsAddressValid(ByVal address_text As String) As Boolean
    ...
```

To quickly comment or uncomment a large block of code, click and drag to select it using the mouse and then open the Edit menu's Advanced submenu. Select the Comment Selection command to comment out the selection or select Uncomment Selection to remove the comment characters from the front of the selection. Those commands are also available more conveniently as buttons in the Text Editor toolbar. Use the View menu's Toolbars submenu's Text Editor command to show or hide this toolbar.

Another way to quickly remove a chunk of code from the program is to surround it with compiler directives, as in the following code:

```
#If False Then
    Dim A As Integer
    Dim B As Integer
    Dim C As Integer
#End if
```

Use comments to make your code clear. Comments do not slow the executable program down (some superstitious developers think they must slow the code because they make the file bigger), so there's no good reason to exclude them.

XML Comments

A normal comment is just a piece of text that gives information to a developer trying to read your code. XML comments let you add some context to a comment. For example, you can mark a comment as a summary describing a subroutine.

Visual Studio automatically extracts XML comments to build an XML file describing the project. This file displays the hierarchical shape of the project, showing comments for the project's modules, namespaces, classes, and other elements.

The result is not particularly easy to read, but you can use it to automatically generate more useful documentation such as reports or web pages.

You can place a block of XML comments before code elements that are not contained in methods. Generally, you use them to describe a module, class, variable, property, method, or event.

To begin a comment block, place the cursor on the line before the element you want to describe and type three single quotes (' ' '). Visual Studio automatically inserts a template for an XML comment block. If the element that follows takes parameters, it includes sections describing the parameters, so it is in your best interest to completely define the parameters before you create the XML comment block. (Otherwise you'll need to add the appropriate comment sections by hand.)

The following code shows the XML comment block created for a simple subroutine. It includes a summary area to describe the subroutine, two `param` sections to describe the subroutine's parameters, and a `remarks` section to provide additional detail.

```
''' <summary>
'''
''' </summary>
''' <param name="jobs"></param>
''' <param name="employees"></param>
''' <remarks></remarks>
Public Sub AssignJobs(ByVal jobs() As Job, ByVal employees() As Employee)

End Sub
```

Note that XML elements can span multiple lines, as the summary element does in this example.

You can add more XML comment sections to the block simply by typing them, following the convention that they should begin with three single quotes. For example, the following code adds some content for the comments in the previous code and an extra WrittenBy element that contains a date attribute:

```
''' <summary>
''' Assigns jobs to employees, maximizing the total value of jobs assigned.
''' </summary>
''' <param name="jobs">The array of Jobs to assign.</param>
''' <param name="employees">The array of Employees to assign.</param>
''' <remarks>The full assignment is not guaranteed to be unique.</remarks>
''' <WrittenBy date="7/24/10">Rod Stephens</WrittenBy>
Public Sub AssignJobs(ByVal jobs() As Job, ByVal employees() As Employee)

End Sub
```

COMMENT CONVENTIONS

Note that I just made up the WrittenBy element and its date attribute — they're not part of some XML comment standard. You can put anything you want in there, although the comments will be easiest to use if you use standard elements such as param and remarks whenever possible.

These XML comments are somewhat bulky and hard to read. In the previous example, it isn't easy to pick out the subroutine's most important summary information with a quick glance at the code. To make reading XML comments easier, Visual Basic defines an outlining section for each XML comment block. If you click the minus sign to the left of the first line in the block, the whole block collapses and shows only the summary information. If you then click the plus sign to the left of the summary, Visual Studio expands the comments to show them all.

The following code shows the beginning of an application that assigns jobs to employees. The project contains two files, a form named Form1.vb and a code module named Module1.vb. The form contains very little code. The code module defines the Job and Employee classes and the AssignJobs subroutine. Each of these has an XML comment block.

```
Public Class Form1
    Private m_Jobs() As Job
    Private m_Employees() As Employee
End Class

Module Module1
    Public Class Job
        Public JobNumber As Integer
        ''' <summary>
        ''' A list of skills required to perform this job.
        ''' </summary>
        ''' <remarks>Represent required equipment as skills.</remarks>
        Public SkillsRequired As New Collection
        ''' <summary>
        ''' The value of this job.
        ''' </summary>
        ''' <remarks>Higher numbers indicate more priority.</remarks>
         Public Priority As Integer
    End Class

Public Class Employee
    Public FirstName As String
    Public LastName As String
    ''' <summary>
    ''' A list of skills this employee has.
    ''' </summary>
    ''' <remarks>Represent special equipment as skills.</remarks>
    Public Skills As New Collection
    End Class

    ''' <summary>
    ''' Assigns jobs to employees.
    ''' </summary>
    ''' <param name="jobs">Array of Jobs to assign.</param>
    ''' <param name="employees">Array of Employees to assign jobs.</param>
    ''' <remarks>Maximizes total value of jobs assigned.</remarks>
    ''' <WrittenBy date="7/26/04">Rod Stephens</WrittenBy>
    Public Sub AssignJobs(ByVal jobs() As Job, ByVal employees() As Employee)

    End Sub
End Module
```

code snippet AssignJobs

In addition to providing documentation for your use, XML comments let the Object Browser provide additional information about your code. Figure 14-6 shows the Object Browser describing the Job class's SkillsRequired property. The area on the lower right shows the property's XML summary and remarks sections. This project's name is AssignJobs, its root namespace is AssignJobs, and the Job class is contained in the JobStuff module, so the complete path to the Job class shown in the tree view on the left is AssignJobs (project) ⇨ AssignJobs (root namespace) ⇨ JobStuff.Job (module and class).

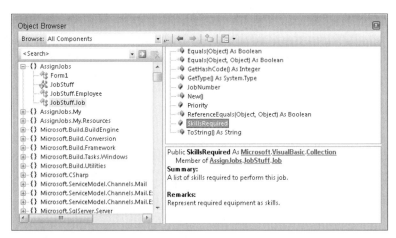

FIGURE 14-6: The Object Browser displays an item's XML summary and remarks sections.

When you compile the application, Visual Studio extracts the XML comments and places them in an XML file with the same name as the executable file in the project's bin\Debug directory. The following text shows the result. If you look through the document carefully, you can pick out the XML comments.

```
<?xml version="1.0"?>
<doc>
<assembly>
<name>
AssignJobs
</name>
</assembly>
<members>
<member name="F:AssignJobs.JobStuff.Job.SkillsRequired">
    <summary>
 A list of skills required to perform this job.
 </summary>
    <remarks>Represent required equipment as skills.</remarks>
</member><member name="F:AssignJobs.JobStuff.Job.Priority">
    <summary>
 The value of this job.
 </summary>
```

```
    <remarks>Higher numbers indicate more priority.</remarks>
</member><member name="F:AssignJobs.JobStuff.Employee.Skills">
    <summary>
 A list of skills this employee has.
 </summary>
    <remarks>Represent special equipment as skills.</remarks>
</member><member name="M:AssignJobs.JobStuff.AssignJobs(
AssignJobs.JobStuff.Job[],AssignJobs.JobStuff.Employee[])">
    <summary>
 Assigns jobs to employees.
 </summary>
    <param name="jobs">Array of Jobs to assign.</param>
    <param name="employees">Array of Employees to assign jobs.</param>
    <remarks>The assignment maximizes total value of jobs assigned.</remarks>
    <WrittenBy date="1/13/07">Rod Stephens</WrittenBy>
</member>
</members>
</doc>
```

Example program AssignJobs, which is available for download on the book's web site, defines job assignment classes that you can view with the Object Browser. If you compile the program (which actually doesn't do any job assignment, it just defines the classes), you can examine its XML documentation.

Line Continuation

Line continuation characters let you break long lines across multiple shorter lines so that they are easier to read. To continue a line, end it with a space followed by an underscore (_). Visual Basic treats the following code as if it were all on one long line:

```
Dim background_color As Color = _
    Color.FromName( _
        My.Resources.ResourceManager.GetString( _
            "MainFormBackgroundColor"))
```

As the previous section explains, you cannot continue comments. A comment includes any space and underscore at the end of its line so the comment does not apply to the following line.

You can break a line just about anywhere that a space is allowed and between program elements. For example, you can break a line after the opening parenthesis in a parameter list, as shown in the following code:

```
AReallyReallyLongSubroutineNameThatTakesFiveParameters( _
    parameter1, parameter2, parameter3, parameter4, parameter5)
```

You cannot break a line inside a quoted string. If you want to break a string, end the string and restart it on the next line, as in the following example:

```
Dim txt As String = "To break a long string across multiple lines, " & _
    "end the string, add the line continuation character " & _
    "(space + underscore) " & _
    "and restart the string on the next line."
```

Visual Basic does not enforce its usual indentation rules on continued lines, so you can indent the lines in any way you like to make the code's structure more clear. For example, many programmers align parameters in long subroutine calls:

```
DoSomething( _
    parameter1, _
    parameter2, _
    parameter3)
```

Implicit Line Continuation

Visual Basic can also guess where you are continuing a line even if you don't use the line continuation character, at least sometimes. For example, Visual Basic can figure out that the statement shown in the following code isn't complete until the final line so it treats all of this code as if it were written on a single long line.

```
Dim background_color As Color =
    Color.FromName(
        My.Resources.ResourceManager.GetString(
            "MainFormBackgroundColor"
        )
    )
```

CONVENTIONAL CONTINUATION

Implicit line continuation is a new feature in Visual Basic 2010 and is not supported by previous versions. If you use it, then you won't be able to copy and paste your code into older versions of Visual Basic. That may not be a big problem if you don't plan to go back to Visual Basic 2008 but, because missing line continuation characters look like typos, you may confuse some people in online discussions and forums.

To avoid potential confusion, at least some developers plan to not use this new feature.

Visual Basic does not allow implicit line continuation in all cases, however. For example, in the following code the "Next i" statement is split across two lines. Because a Next statement's variable name is optional, Visual Basic doesn't know that the following i is required so it doesn't look for it.

```
For i As Integer = 1 To 10

Next
    i
```

In fact, you can't break the statement "For i As Integer = 1 To 10" at any point without a line continuation character or Visual Basic gets confused.

Some places that Visual Basic *does* allow implicit line continuation include:

➤ After an equals sign

➤ After a binary operator such as + or *

➤ After commas

➤ After opening parentheses or brackets and before closing parentheses or brackets

The following code shows a few examples:

```
<
    ComClass()
>
Public Class Employee
    Public Function CalculateStuff(
        ByVal v1 As Integer,
        ByVal v2 As Integer
    )

        Dim a As Integer =
            Math.Max(
                v1,
                v2 +
                12
            )
        Return a
    End Function

    ...
End Class
```

IMPLICIT CONFUSION

Implicit line continuation has great potential for causing confusion so use it carefully. Use proper indentation to show the structure and make it easier to see that the parts of the continued line belong together as in the previous example.

Also, don't assume that implicit line continuation automatically makes the code easier to understand. Use it to break very long lines or to show nested structure but sometimes a statement is easier to read in one piece. For example, the following code is easier to read than the previous version.

```
a = Math.Max(b, c + d)
```

Line Joining

Not only can you break a long statement across multiple lines, but you can also join short statements on a single line. To use two statements on a single line, separate them with a colon (:). The following line of code contains three statements that store the red, green, and blue components of a form's background color in the variables r, g, and b:

```
r = BackColor.R : g = BackColor.G : b = BackColor.B
```

Line joining is most useful when you have many lines in a row that all have a very similar structure. By scanning down the lines, you can tell if there are differences that may indicate a bug.

Use line joining with some caution. If the statements are long, or if you have a series of joined lines with dissimilar structure, combining lots of statements on a single line can make the code harder to read. If the code is easier to read with each statement on a separate line, write the code that way. Using more lines doesn't cost extra or make the code run any slower.

Line Labels

You can place a label to the left of any line of code. The label can be either a name or a number, followed by a colon. The following code defines three labels. The first is named DeclareX and marks the declaration of the variable x. The second has value 10 and is located on a line containing a comment. The third label, named Done, labels a blank line.

```
DeclareX: Dim X As Single
10:       ' Do something here.
Done:
```

You must label a line if you will later want to jump to that line. For example, the GoTo, On Error GoTo, and Resume statements can make code jump to a labeled line. These are less useful in Visual Basic .NET than they were in Visual Basic 6 and previous versions that didn't have structured error handling (the Try Catch block), but they are still available.

SUMMARY

A Visual Studio solution contains a hierarchical arrangement of items. At the top level, it contains one or more projects. Each project contains several standard items such as My Project (that represents the project as a whole), References (that records information about references to external objects), the bin and obj items (that are used by Visual Studio when building the application), and app.config (that holds configuration information). Projects also contain form, class, and other code modules.

Normally, many of these files are hidden and you do not need to edit them directly. Instead, you can double-click Solution Explorer's My Project entry and use the project's Properties pages to view and modify application values. Other hidden files store code and resources that determine a form's appearance, and you can modify them by altering the form with the Form Designer.

Within a code module, you can use modules, classes, regions, and namespaces to group related code into blocks. You can use conditional compilation statements and conditional compilation constants to easily add or remove code to or from the compiled application. The Debug and Trace objects let you generate messages and alerts, depending on whether certain predefined constants are defined.

Finally, typographic elements such as comments, line continuation, and line joining let you format the code so that it is easier to read and understand. XML comments provide additional information that is useful to the Object Browser and that you can use to automatically generate more complete documentation.

Although all of these components are not required by Visual Basic, they can make the difference between understanding the code quickly and completely, and not understanding it at all. Over an application's lifetime of development, debugging, upgrading, and maintenance, this can determine a project's success.

This chapter describes structural elements that make up code files. Within those elements, you can place the code that gathers, manipulates, stores, and displays data. Chapter 15, "Data Types, Variables, and Constants," describes the variables that a program uses to hold data values. It explains how to declare variables, what types of data they can hold, and how Visual Basic converts from one data type to another.

15

Data Types, Variables, and Constants

Variables are among the most fundamental building blocks of a program. A *variable* is a program object that stores a value. The value can be a number, letter, string, date, structure containing other values, or an object representing both data and related actions.

When a variable contains a value, the program can manipulate it. It can perform arithmetic operations on numbers, string operations on strings (concatenation, calculating substrings, finding a target within a string), date operations (find the difference between two dates, add a time period to a date), and so forth.

Four factors determine a variable's exact behavior:

- ➤ **Data type** determines the kind of the data (integer, character, string, and so forth).

- ➤ **Scope** defines the code that can access the variable. For example, if you declare a variable inside a For loop, only other code inside the For loop can use the variable. If you declare a variable at the top of a subroutine, all the code in the subroutine can use the variable.

- ➤ **Accessibility** determines what code in other modules can access the variable. If you declare a variable at the module level (outside of any subroutine in the module) and you use the Private keyword, only the code in the module can use the variable. If you use the Public keyword, code in other modules can use the variable as well.

- ➤ **Lifetime** determines how long the variable's value is valid. A variable inside a subroutine that is declared with a normal Dim statement is created when the subroutine begins and is destroyed when it exits. If the subroutine runs again, it creates a new copy of the variable and its value is reset. If the variable is declared with the Static keyword, however, the same instance of the variable is used whenever the subroutine runs. That means the variable's value is preserved between calls to the subroutine.

For example, a variable declared within a subroutine has scope equal to the subroutine. Code outside of the subroutine cannot access the variable. If a variable is declared on a module level outside any subroutine, it has module scope. If it is declared with the Private keyword, it is accessible only to code within the module. If it is declared with the Public keyword, then it is also accessible to code outside of the module.

Visibility is a concept that combines scope, accessibility, and lifetime. It determines whether a certain piece of code can use a variable. If the variable is accessible to the code, the code is within the variable's scope, and the variable is within its lifetime (has been created and not yet destroyed), the variable is visible to the code.

This chapter explains the syntax for declaring variables in Visual Basic. It explains how you can use different declarations to determine a variable's data type, scope, accessibility, and lifetime. It discusses some of the issues you should consider when selecting a type of declaration, and describes some newer variable concepts such as anonymous and nullable types, which can complicate variable declarations. This chapter also explains ways you can initialize objects, arrays, and collections quickly and easily.

Constants, parameters, and property procedures all have concepts of scope and data type that are similar to those of variables, so they are also described here.

The chapter finishes with a brief explanation of naming conventions. Which naming rules you adopt isn't as important as the fact that you adopt some. This chapter discusses where you can find the conventions used by Microsoft Consulting Services. From those, you can build your own coding conventions.

DATA TYPES

The following table summarizes Visual Basic's elementary data types.

TYPE	SIZE	VALUES
Boolean	2 bytes	True or False
Byte	1 byte	0 to 255 (unsigned byte)
SByte	1 byte	−128 to 127 (signed byte)
Char	2 bytes	0 to 65,535 (unsigned character)
Short	2 bytes	−32,768 to 32,767
UShort	2 bytes	0 through 65,535 (unsigned short)
Integer	4 bytes	−2,147,483,648 to 2,147,483,647
UInteger	4 bytes	0 through 4,294,967,295 (unsigned integer)
Long	8 bytes	−9,223,372,036,854,775,808 to 9,223,372,036,854,775,807

TYPE	SIZE	VALUES
ULong	8 bytes	0 through 18,446,744,073,709,551,615 (unsigned long)
Decimal	16 bytes	0 to +/−79,228,162,514,264,337,593,543,950,335 with no decimal point. 0 to +/−7.9228162514264337593543950335 with 28 places to the right of the decimal place.
Single	4 bytes	−3.4028235E+38 to −1.401298E-45 (negative values) 1.401298E-45 to 3.4028235E+38 (positive values)
Double	8 bytes	−1.79769313486231570E+308 to −4.94065645841246544E-324 (negative values) 4.94065645841246544E-324 to 1.79769313486231570E+308 (positive values)
String	variable	Depending on the platform, a string can hold approximately 0 to 2 billion Unicode characters
Date	8 bytes	January 1, 0001 0:0:00 to December 31, 9999 11:59:59 pm
Object	4 bytes	Points to any type of data
Structure	Variable	Structure members have their own ranges.

The System namespace also provides integer data types that specify their number of bits explicitly. For example, Int32 represents a 32-bit integer. Using these values instead of Integer emphasizes the fact that the variable uses 32 bits. That can sometimes make code clearer. For example, suppose that you need to call an application programming interface (API) function that takes a 32-bit integer as a parameter. In Visual Basic 6, a Long uses 32 bits but in Visual Basic .NET, an Integer uses 32 bits. You can make it obvious that you are using a 32-bit integer by giving the parameter the Int32 type.

The data types that explicitly give their sizes are Int16, Int32, Int64, UInt16, UInt32, and UInt64.

The Integer data type is usually the fastest of the integral types. You will generally get better performance using Integers than you will with the Char, Byte, Short, Long, or Decimal data types. You should stick with the Integer data type unless you need the extra range provided by Long and Decimal, or you need to save space with the smaller Char and Byte data types. In many cases, the space savings you will get using the Char and Byte data types isn't worth the extra time and effort, unless you are working with a very large array of values.

Note that you cannot safely assume that a variable's storage requirements are exactly the same as its size. In some cases, the program may move a variable so that it begins on a boundary that is natural for the hardware platform. For example, if you make a structure containing several Short (2-byte) variables, the program may insert 2 extra bytes between them so they can all start on 4-byte boundaries because that may be more efficient for the hardware. For more information on structures, see Chapter 26, "Classes and Structures."

ALIGNMENT ATTRIBUTES

Actually, you can use the StructLayout attribute to change the way Visual Basic allocates the memory for a structure. In that case you may be able to determine exactly how the structure is laid out. This is a fairly advanced topic and is not covered in this book. For more information, see `msdn.microsoft.com/system .runtime.interopservices.structlayoutattribute.aspx`.

Some data types also come with some additional overhead. For example, an array stores some extra information about each of its dimensions.

TYPE CHARACTERS

Data type characters identify a value's data type. The following table lists the data type characters of Visual Basic.

CHARACTER	DATA TYPE
%	Integer
&	Long
@	Decimal
!	Single
#	Double
$	String

You can specify a variable's data type by adding a data type character after a variable's name when you declare it. When you use the variable later, you can omit the data type character if you like. For example, the following code declares variable `num_desserts` as a Long and `satisfaction_quotient` as a Double. It then assigns values to these variables.

```
Dim num_desserts&
Dim satisfaction_quotient#

num_desserts = 100
satisfaction_quotient# = 1.23
```

If you have Option Explicit turned off, you can include a data type character the first time you use the variable to determine its data type. If you omit the character, Visual Basic picks a default data type based on the value you assign to the variable.

If the value you assign is an integral value that will fit in an Integer, Visual Basic makes the variable an Integer. If the value is too big for an Integer, Visual Basic makes the variable a Long. If the value contains a decimal point, Visual Basic makes the variable a Double.

The following code shows the first use of three variables (Option Explicit is off). The first statement sets the variable `an_integer` equal to the value 100. This value fits in an Integer, so Visual Basic makes the variable an Integer. The second statement sets `a_long` equal to 10000000000. That value is too big to fit in an Integer, so Visual Basic makes it a Long. The third statement sets `a_double` to 1.0. That value contains a decimal point, so Visual Basic makes the variable a Double.

```
an_integer = 100
a_long = 10000000000
a_double = 1.0
```

If you set a variable equal to a True or False, Visual Basic makes it a Boolean.

In Visual Basic, you surround date values with # characters. If you assign a variable to a date value, Visual Basic gives the variable the Date data type. The following code assigns Boolean and Date variables:

```
a_boolean = True
a_date = #12/31/2007#
```

In addition to data type characters, Visual Basic provides a set of *literal type characters* that determine the data type of literal values. These are values that you explicitly type into your code in statements such as assignment and initialization statements. The following table lists the literal type characters of Visual Basic.

CHARACTER	DATA TYPE
S	Short
US	UShort
I	Integer
UI	UInteger
L	Long
UL	ULong
D	Decimal
F	Single (F for *floating point*)
R	Double (R for *real*)
c	Char (note lowercase c)

A literal type character determines the data type of a literal value in your code and may indirectly determine the data type of a variable assigned to it. For example, suppose that the following code is the first use of the variables i and ch (with Option Explicit turned off).

```
i = 123L
ch = "X"c
```

Normally, Visual Basic would make i an Integer, because the value 123 fits in an Integer. Because the literal value 123 ends with the L character, however, the value is a Long, so the variable i is also a Long.

Similarly, Visual Basic would normally make variable ch a String because the value "X" looks like a string. The c following the value tells Visual Basic to make this a Char variable instead.

Visual Basic also lets you precede a literal integer value with &H to indicate that it is hexadecimal (base 16) or &O to indicate that it is octal (base 8). For example, the following three statements set the variable flags to the same value. The first statement uses the decimal value 100, the second uses the hexadecimal value &H64, and the third uses the octal value &O144.

```
flags = 100      ' Decimal 100.
flags = &H64  ' Hexadecimal &H64 = 6 * 16 + 4 = 96 + 4 = 100.
flags = &O144 ' Octal &O144 = 1 * 64 + 4 * 8 + 4 = 64 + 32 + 4 = 100.
```

BASE CONVERSIONS

The Hex and Oct functions let you convert numeric values into hexadecimal and octal strings, respectively. In some sense, this is the opposite of what the &H and &O codes do: make Visual Basic interpret a string literal as hexadecimal or octal number.

The following code displays the value of the variable flags in decimal, hexadecimal, and octal:

```
Debug.WriteLine(flags)         ' Decimal.
Debug.WriteLine(Hex(flags))  ' Hexadecimal.
Debug.WriteLine(Oct(flags))  ' Octal.
```

Sometimes you must use literal type characters to make a value match a variable's data type. For example, consider the following code:

```
Dim ch As Char
ch = "X"  ' Error because "X" is a String.
ch = "X"c ' Okay because "X"c is a Char.

Dim amount As Decimal
amount = 12.34  ' Error because 12.34 is a Double.
amount = 12.34D ' Okay because 12.34D is a Decimal.
```

The first assignment tries to assign the value "X" to a Char variable. This throws an error because "X" is a String value so it won't fit in a Char variable. Although it is obvious to a programmer that this code is trying to assign the character X to the variable, Visual Basic thinks the types don't match.

The second assignment statement works because it assigns the Char value "X"c to the variable. The next assignment fails when it tries to assign the Double value 12.34 to a Decimal variable. The final assignment works because the value 12.34D is a Decimal literal.

The following code shows another way to accomplish these assignments. This version uses the data type conversion functions CChar and CDec to convert the values into the proper data types. The following section, "Data Type Conversion," has more to say about data type conversion functions.

```
ch = CChar("X")
amount = CDec(12.34)
```

Using data type characters, literal type characters, and the Visual Basic default data type assignments can lead to very confusing code. You cannot expect every programmer to notice that a particular variable is a Single because it is followed by ! in its first use, but not in others. You can make your code less confusing by using variable declarations that include explicit data types.

DATA TYPE CONVERSION

Normally, you assign a value to a variable that has the same data type as the value. For example, you assign a string value to a String variable, you assign an integer value to an Integer variable, and so forth. Whether you can assign a value of one type to a variable of another type depends on whether the conversion is a narrowing or widening conversion.

Narrowing Conversions

A *narrowing conversion* is one where data is converted from one type to another type that cannot hold all of the possible values allowed by the original data type. For example, the following code copies the value from a Long variable into an Integer variable. A Long value can hold values that are too big to fit in an Integer, so this is a narrowing conversion. The value contained in the Long variable may or may not fit in the Integer.

```
Dim an_integer As Integer
Dim a_long As Long
...
an_integer = a_long
```

The following code shows a less obvious example. Here the code assigns the value in a String variable to an Integer variable. If the string happens to contain a number (for example "10" or "1.23"), the assignment works. If the string contains a non-numeric value (such as "Hello"), however, the assignment fails with an error.

```
Dim an_integer As Integer
Dim a_string As String
...
an_integer = a_string
```

Another non-obvious narrowing conversion is from a class to a derived class. Suppose that the Employee class inherits from the Person class. Then setting an Employee variable equal to a Person object, as shown in the following code, is a narrowing conversion because you cannot know without additional information whether the Person is a valid Employee. All Employees are Persons, but not all Persons are Employees.

```
Dim an_employee As Employee
Dim a_person As Person
...
an_employee = a_person
```

If you have Option Strict turned on, Visual Basic will not allow implicit narrowing conversions. If Option Strict is off, Visual Basic will attempt an implicit narrowing conversion and throw an error if the conversion fails (for example, if you try to copy the Integer value 900 into a Byte variable).

To make a narrowing conversion with Option Strict turned on, you must explicitly use a data type conversion function. Visual Basic will attempt the conversion and throw an error if it fails. The CByte function converts a numeric value into a Byte value, so you could use the following code to copy an Integer value into a Byte variable:

```
Dim an_integer As Integer
Dim a_byte As Byte
...
a_byte = CByte(an_integer)
```

If the Integer variable contains a value less than 0 or greater than 255, the value will not fit in a Byte variable so CByte throws an error.

The following table lists the data type conversion functions of Visual Basic.

FUNCTION	CONVERTS TO
CBool	Boolean
CByte	Byte
CChar	Char
CDate	Date
CDbl	Double
CDec	Decimal
CInt	Integer
CLng	Long
CObj	Object
CSByte	SByte
CShort	Short
CSng	Single
CStr	String
CUInt	UInteger
CULng	ULong
CUShort	UShort

The CInt and CLng functions round fractional values off to the nearest whole number. If the fractional part of a number is exactly .5, the functions round to the nearest even whole number. For example, 0.5 rounds to 0, 0.6 rounds to 1, and 1.5 rounds to 2.

In contrast, the Fix and Int functions truncate fractional values. Fix truncates toward zero, so Fix(−0.9) is 0 and Fix(0.9) is 0. Int truncates downward, so Int(−0.9) is −1 and Int(0.9) is 0.

Fix and Int also differ from CInt and CLng because they return the same data type they are passed. CInt always returns an Integer no matter what type of value you pass it. If you pass a Long into Fix, Fix returns a Long. In fact, if you pass a Double into Fix, Fix returns a Double.

The CType function takes as parameters a value and a data type, and it converts the value into that type if possible. For example, the following code uses CType to perform a narrowing conversion from a Long to an Integer. Because the value of a_long can fit within an integer, the conversion succeeds.

```
Dim an_integer As Integer
Dim a_long As Long = 100
an_integer = Ctype(a_long, Integer)
```

The DirectCast statement changes value types much as CType does, except that it only works when the variable it is converting implements or inherits from the new type. For example, suppose the variable `dessert_obj` has the generic type Object and you know that it points to an object of type Dessert. Then the following code converts the generic Object into the specific Dessert type:

```
Dim dessert_obj As Object = New Dessert("Ice Cream")
Dim my_dessert As Dessert
my_dessert = DirectCast(dessert_obj, Dessert)
```

DirectCast throws an error if you try to use it to change the object's data type. For example, the following code doesn't work, even though converting an Integer into a Long is a narrowing conversion:

```
Dim an_integer As Integer = 100
Dim a_long As Long
a_long = DirectCast(an_integer, Long)
```

The TryCast statement converts data types much as DirectCast does, except that it returns Nothing if there is an error, rather than throwing an error.

Data Type Parsing Methods

Each of the fundamental data types (except for String) has a Parse method that attempts to convert a string into the variable type. For example, the following two statements both try to convert the string value `txt_entered` into an Integer:

```
Dim txt_entered As String = "112358"
Dim num_entered As Integer
...
num_entered = CInt(txt_entered) ' Use CInt.
num_entered = Integer.Parse(txt_entered) ' Use Integer.Parse.
```

Some of these parsing methods can take additional parameters to control the conversion. For example, the numeric methods can take a parameter that gives the international number style the string should have.

The class parsing methods have a more object-oriented feel than the conversion functions. They are also a bit faster. They only parse strings, however, so if you want to convert from a Long to an Integer, you need to use CInt rather than Integer.Parse or Int32.Parse.

Widening Conversions

In contrast to a narrowing conversion, a *widening conversion* is one where the new data type is always big enough to hold the old data type's values. For example, a Long is big enough to hold any Integer value, so copying an Integer value into a Long variable is a widening conversion.

Visual Basic allows widening conversions. Note that some widening conversions can still result in a loss of data. For example, a Decimal variable can store more significant digits than a Single variable can. A Single can hold any value that a Decimal can but not with the same precision. If you assign a Decimal value to a Single variable, you may lose some precision.

The Convert Class

The Convert class provides an assortment of methods for converting a value from one data type to another. For example, the following code uses the ToInt32 method to convert the string "17" into a 32-bit integer:

```
Dim i As Integer = Convert.ToInt32("17")
```

These methods are easy to understand so they make code simple to read. Unfortunately they work with particular data type sizes such as 16- or 32-bit integer rather than with the system's default integer size so they may require editing in the future. For example, if a later version of Visual Basic assumes 64-bit integers, then you may need to update your calls to Convert methods.

ToString

The ToString method is a conversion function that is so useful it deserves special mention. Every object has a ToString method that returns a string representation of the object. For example, the following code converts the integer value num_employees into a string:

```
Dim txt As String = num_employees.ToString()
```

Exactly what value ToString returns depends on the object. For example, a double's ToString method returns the double formatted as a string. More complicated objects tend to return their class names rather than their values (although you can change that behavior by overriding their ToString methods).

ToString can take as a parameter a format string to change the way it formats its result. For example, the following code displays the value of the double angle with two digits after the decimal point:

```
MessageBox.Show(angle.ToString("0.00"))
```

Appendix P, "Date and Time Format Specifiers," and Appendix Q, "Other Format Specifiers," describe format specifiers in greater detail.

VARIABLE DECLARATIONS

The complete syntax for a variable declaration is as follows:

```
[attribute_list] [accessibility] [Shared] [Shadows] [ReadOnly] _
Dim [WithEvents] name [(bounds_list)] [As [New] type] _
[= initialization_expression]
```

All declarations have only one thing in common: They contain a variable's name. Other than the name, different declarations may have nothing in common. Variable declarations with different forms can use or omit any other piece of the general declaration syntax. For example, the following two declarations don't share a single keyword:

```
Dim i = 1           ' Declare private Integer named i. (Option Explicit Off)
Public j As Integer ' Declare public Integer named j.
```

The many variations supported by a variable declaration make the general syntax rather intimidating. In most cases, however, declarations are straightforward. The previous two declarations are fairly easy to understand.

The following sections describe the pieces of the general declaration in detail.

Attribute_List

The optional attribute list is a comma-separated list of attributes that apply to the variable. An attribute further refines the definition of a variable to give more information to the compiler and the runtime system.

Attributes are rather specialized and address issues that arise when you perform very specific programming tasks. For example, when you write code to serialize and de-serialize data, you can use serialization attributes to gain more control over the process.

The following code defines the OrderItem class. This class declares three public variables: ItemName, Quantity, and Price. It uses attributes on its three variables to indicate that ItemName should be stored as text, Price should be stored as an attribute named Cost, and Quantity should be stored as an attribute with its default name, Quantity.

```
Public Class OrderItem
    <XmlText()>
    Public ItemName As String

    <XmlAttributeAttribute(AttributeName:="Cost")>
    Public Price As Decimal

    <XmlAttributeAttribute()>
    Public Quantity As Integer
End Class
```

The following code shows the XML serialization of an OrderItem object:

```
<OrderItem Cost="1.25" Quantity="12">Cookie</OrderItem>
```

Because attributes are so specialized, they are not described in more detail here. For more information, see the sections in the online help related to the tasks you need to perform. For more information on XML serialization attributes, for example, search for "System.Xml. Serialization Namespace," or look at these web pages:

➤   XML Serialization in the .NET Framework, msdn.microsoft.com/ms950721.aspx.

➤   Controlling XML Serialization Using Attributes, msdn.microsoft.com/2baksw0z(VS.71) .aspx.

➤   Attributes That Control XML Serialization, msdn.microsoft.com/83y7df3e (VS.71).aspx.

For more information on attributes in general, see the "Attributes" section of the Visual Basic Language Reference or go to msdn.microsoft.com/39967861.aspx.

For a list of attributes you can use to modify variable declarations, search the online help for "Attribute Hierarchy," or see these web pages:

➤   Attributes Used in Visual Basic, msdn.microsoft.com/f51fe7sf.aspx.

➤   Attribute Class, msdn.microsoft.com/system.attribute.aspx. (Look for the "Inheritance Hierarchy" section to see what attributes inherit from the Attribute class.)

Accessibility

A variable declaration's *accessibility* clause can take one of the following values:

➤   Public – You can use the Public keyword only for variables declared at the module, class, structure, namespace, or file level but not inside a subroutine. Public indicates that the variable should be available to all code inside or outside of the variable's module. This allows the most access to the variable.

➤   Protected – You can use the Protected keyword only at the class level, not inside a module or inside a routine within a class. Protected indicates that the variable should be accessible only to code within the same class or a derived class. The variable is available to code in the same or a derived class, even if the instance of the class is different from the one containing the variable. For example, one Employee object can access a Protected variable inside another Employee object.

➤   Friend – You can use the Friend keyword only for variables declared at the module, class, namespace, or file level, not inside a subroutine. Friend indicates that the variable should be available to all code inside or outside of the variable's module within the same project. The difference between this and Public is that Public allows code outside of the project to access the variable. This is generally only an issue for code and control libraries. For example, suppose that you build a code library containing dozens of routines and then you write a program that uses the library. If the library declares a variable with the Public keyword, the code in the library and the code in the main program can use the variable. In contrast, if the library declares a variable with the Friend keyword, only the code in the library can access the variable, not the code in the main program.

➤ `Protected Friend` — You can use Protected Friend only at the class level, not inside a module or inside a routine within a class. Protected Friend is the union of the Protected and Friend keywords. A variable declared Protected Friend is accessible only to code within the same class or a derived class and only within the same project.

➤ `Private` — You can use the Private keyword only for variables declared at the module, class, or structure, not inside a subroutine. A variable declared Private is accessible only to code in the same module, class, or structure. If the variable is in a class or structure, it is available to other instances of the class or structure. For example, one Customer object can access a Private variable inside another Customer object.

➤ `Static` — You can use the Static keyword only for variables declared within a subroutine or a block within a subroutine (for example, a For loop or Try Catch block). You cannot use Static with Shared or Shadows. A variable declared Static keeps its value between lifetimes. For example, if a subroutine sets a Static variable to 27 before it exits, the variable begins with the value 27 the next time the subroutine executes. The value is stored in memory, so it is not retained if you exit and restart the whole program. Use a database, the System Registry, or some other means of permanent storage if you need to save values between program runs.

Shared

You can use the Shared keyword at the module, class, structure, namespace, or file level, not within a subroutine. This keyword means that all instances of the class or structure containing the variable share the same variable.

For example, suppose that the Order class declares the Shared variable NumOrders to represent the total number of orders in the application. Then all instances of the Order class share the same NumOrders variable. If one instance of an Order sets NumOrders to 10, all instances of Order see NumOrders equal 10.

You can access a Shared variable either by using a specific class instance or by using the class itself. For example, the following code uses the order1 object's NumOrders variable to set the value of NumOrders to 100. It then displays this value by using order1 and another Order object named order2. Next, it uses the class itself to set the value of NumOrders and uses the class to display the result.

```
order1.NumOrders = 100             ' Use order1 to set NumOrders = 100.
MessageBox.Show(order1.NumOrders)  ' Use order1 to display 100.
MessageBox.Show(order2.NumOrders)  ' Use a different Order to Display 100.
Order.NumOrders = 101              ' Use the class to set NumOrders = 101.
MessageBox.Show(Order.NumOrders)   ' Use the class to display 101.
```

You cannot use the Shared keyword with the Static keyword. This makes sense because a Shared variable is in some fashion static to the class or structure that contains it. If one instance of the class modifies the variable, the value is available to all other instances. In fact, even if you destroy every instance of the class or never create any instances at all, the class itself still keeps the variable's value safe. That provides a persistence similar to that given by the Static keyword.

Shadows

You can use the Shadows keyword only for variables declared at the module, class, structure, namespace, or file level, not inside a subroutine. Shadows indicates that the variable hides a variable with the same name in a base class. In a typical example, a subclass provides a variable with the same name as a variable declared in one of its ancestor classes.

Example program ShadowTest, which is available for download on the book's web site, uses the following code to demonstrate the Shadows keyword:

Available for download on Wrox.com

```
Public Class Person
    Public LastName As String
    Public EmployeeId As String
End Class

Public Class Employee
    Inherits Person
    Public Shadows EmployeeId As Long
End Class

Public Class Manager
    Inherits Employee
    Public Shadows LastName As String
End Class

Private Sub TestShadows()
    Dim txt As String = ""

    Dim mgr As New Manager
    mgr.LastName = "Manager Last Name"
    mgr.EmployeeId = 1

    Dim emp As Employee = CType(mgr, Employee)
    emp.LastName = "Employee Last Name"
    emp.EmployeeId = 2

    Dim per As Person = CType(mgr, Person)
    per.LastName = "Person Last Name"
    per.EmployeeId = "A"

    txt &= "Manager: " & mgr.EmployeeId & ": " & mgr.LastName & vbCrLf
    txt &= "Employee: " & emp.EmployeeId & ": " & emp.LastName & vbCrLf
    txt &= "Person: " & per.EmployeeId & ": " & per.LastName & vbCrLf

    txtResults.Text = txt
    txtResults.Select(0, 0)
End Sub
```

code snippet ShadowTest

The code defines a Person class that contains public String variables `LastName` and `EmployeeId`. The Employee class inherits from Person and declares its own version of the `EmployeeId` variable. It uses the Shadows keyword so this version covers the version defined by the Person class. Note that Shadows works here even though the two versions of `EmployeeId` have different data types: Long versus String. An Employee object gets the Long version, and a Person object gets the String version.

The Manager class inherits from the Employee class and defines its own version of the `LastName` variable. A Manager object uses this version, and an Employee or Person object uses the version defined by the Person class.

Having defined these three classes, the program works with them to demonstrate shadowing. First it creates a Manager object, and sets its `LastName` variable to "Manager Last Name" and its `EmployeeId` variable to 1. The `LastName` value is stored in the Manager class's version of the variable declared with the Shadows keyword. The `EmployeeId` value is stored in the `EmployeeId` variable declared with the Shadows keyword in the Employee class.

The program then creates an Employee variable and makes it point to the Manager object. This makes sense because Manager inherits from Employee. A Manager is a type of Employee so an Employee variable can point to a Manager object. The program sets the Employee object's LastName variable to "Employee Last Name" and its `EmployeeId` variable to 2. The `LastName` value is stored in the Person class's version of the variable. The `EmployeeId` value is stored in the `EmployeeId` variable declared with the Shadows keyword in the Employee class. Because the Manager class does not override this declaration with its own shadowing declaration of `EmployeeId`, this value overwrites the value stored by the Manager object.

Next, the program creates a Person variable and makes it point to the same Manager object. Again this makes sense because a Manager is a type of Person so a Person variable can point to a Manager object. The program sets the Person object's `LastName` variable to "Person Last Name" and its `EmployeeId` variable to "A." The Person class does not inherit, so the program stores the values in the versions of the variables defined by the Person class. Because the Employee class does not override the Person class's declaration of `LastName` with its own shadowing declaration, this value overwrites the value stored by the Employee object.

Finally, the program prints the values of the `EmployeeId` and `LastName` variables for each of the objects.

The following output shows the program's results. Notice that the Employee object's value for `EmployeeId` (2) overwrote the value saved by the Manager object (1) and that the Person object's value for `LastName` (Person Last Name) overwrote the value saved by the `Employee` object (Employee Last Name).

```
Manager: 2: Manager Last Name
Employee: 2: Person Last Name
Person: A: Person Last Name
```

Normally, you don't need to access shadowed versions of a variable. If you declare a version of `LastName` in the Employee class that shadows a declaration in the Person class, you presumably did it for a good reason (unlike in the previous example, which does it just to show how it's done), and you don't need to access the shadowed version directly.

However, if you really do need to access the shadowed version, you can use variables from ancestor classes to do so. For example, the previous example creates Employee and Person objects pointing to a Manager object to access that object's shadowed variables.

Within a class, you can similarly cast the `Me` object to an ancestor class. For example, the following code in the Manager class makes a Person variable pointing to the same object and sets its `LastName` value:

```
Public Sub SetPersonEmployeeId(ByVal employee_id As String)
    Dim per As Person = CType(Me, Person)
    per.EmployeeId = employee_id
End Sub
```

Code in a class can also use the `MyBase` keyword to access the variables defined by the parent class. The following code in the Manager class sets the object's `LastName` variable declared by the Employee parent class:

```
Public Sub SetManagerLastName(ByVal last_name As String)
    MyBase.LastName = last_name
End Sub
```

ReadOnly

You can use the ReadOnly keyword only for variables declared at the module, class, structure, namespace, or file level, not inside a subroutine. ReadOnly indicates that the program can read, but not modify, the variable's value.

You can initialize the variable in one of two ways. First, you can include an initialization statement in the variable's declaration, as shown in the following code:

```
Public Class EmployeeCollection
    Public ReadOnly MaxEmployees As Integer = 100
    ...
End Class
```

Second, you can initialize the variable in the object's constructors. The following code declares the ReadOnly variable `MaxEmployees`. The empty constructor sets this variable to `100`. A second constructor takes an integer parameter and sets the `MaxEmployees` to its value.

```
Public Class EmployeeCollection
    Public ReadOnly MaxEmployees As Integer

    Public Sub New()
        MaxEmployees = 100
    End Sub

    Public Sub New(ByVal max_employees As Integer)
        MaxEmployees = max_employees
    End Sub
    ...
End Class
```

After the object is initialized, the program cannot modify the ReadOnly variable. This restriction applies to code inside the module that declared the variable, as well as code in other modules. If you want to allow code inside the same module to modify the value but want to prevent code in other modules from modifying the value, you should use a property procedure instead. See the section, "Property Procedures," later in this chapter for more information.

Dim

The Dim keyword officially tells Visual Basic that you want to create a variable.

You can omit the Dim keyword if you specify Public, Protected, Friend, Protected Friend, Private, Static, or ReadOnly. In fact, if you include one of these keywords, the Visual Basic editor automatically removes the Dim keyword if you include it.

If you do not specify otherwise, variables you declare using a Dim statement are Private. The following two statements are equivalent:

```
Dim num_people As Integer
Private num_people As Integer
```

> **CERTAIN SCOPE**
>
> For certainty's sake, many programmers (including me) explicitly specify Private to declare private variables. Using Private means that programmers don't need to remember that the Dim keyword gives a private variable by default.

One place where the Dim keyword is common is when declaring variables inside subroutines. You cannot use the Private keyword inside a subroutine (or Public, Protected, Friend, Protected Friend, or ReadOnly, for that matter), so you must use either Static or Dim.

WithEvents

The WithEvents keyword tells Visual Basic that the variable is of a specific object type that may raise events that you will want to catch. For example, the following code declares the variable `Face` as a PictureBox object that may raise events you want to catch:

```
Private WithEvents Face As PictureBox
```

When you declare a variable with the WithEvents keyword, Visual Basic creates an entry for it in the left drop-down list in the module's code window, as shown in Figure 15-1.

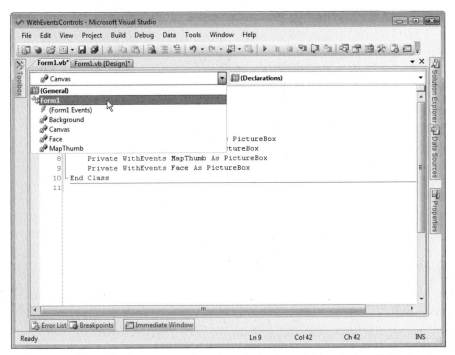

FIGURE 15-1: Visual Basic creates a drop-down entry for variables declared WithEvents.

If you select the object in the left drop-down list, Visual Basic fills the right drop-down list with the object's events that you might want to catch, as shown in Figure 15-2.

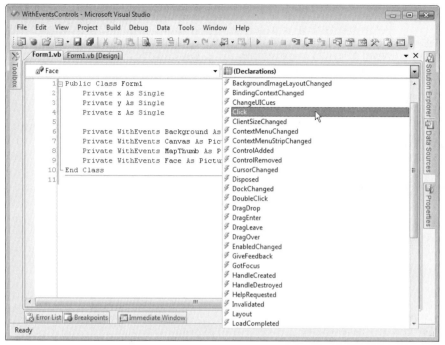

FIGURE 15-2: When you select an object declared WithEvents in the left drop-down list, Visual Basic fills the right drop-down list with events you might want to catch.

If you select an event, Visual Basic creates a corresponding empty event handler. Letting Visual Basic automatically generate the event handler in this way is easier and safer than trying to type the event handler yourself, creating all of the required parameters by hand.

Declaring variables using the WithEvents keyword is a powerful technique. You can make the variable point to an object to catch its events. Later, if you want to process events from some other object using the same event handlers, you can set the variable to point to the new object. If you no longer want to receive any events, you can set the variable to Nothing.

Unfortunately, you cannot declare an array using the WithEvents keyword. That means you cannot use a simple declaration to allow the same event handlers to process events from more than one object. However, you can achieve this by using the AddHandler method to explicitly set the event handler routines for a series of objects. For more information on this technique, see the section "Catching Events" in Chapter 26.

Name

A declaration's *name* clause gives the name of the variable. This must be a valid Visual Basic identifier. The rules for valid identifiers are a bit confusing, but generally an identifier should begin with a letter or underscore, followed by any number of letters, digits, or underscores.

If the identifier begins with an underscore (which is unusual), it must contain at least one other valid character (letter, digit, or underscore) so that Visual Basic doesn't confuse it with a line continuation character.

Identifier names cannot contain special characters such as &, %, #, and $, although some of these may be used as data type characters.

Here are some examples:

`num_employees`	Valid
`NumEmployees`	Valid
`_manager`	Valid (but unusual)
`_`	Invalid (contains only a single underscore)
`__`	Valid (two underscores is valid but could be very confusing)
`1st_employee`	Invalid (doesn't begin with a letter or underscore)
`#employees`	Invalid (contains the special character #)

Normal identifiers cannot be the same as a Visual Basic keyword. However, you can *escape* an identifier (mark it to give it a special meaning) by enclosing it in square brackets. If you escape an identifier, you can give it the same name as a Visual Basic keyword. For example, in the following code, the `ParseString` subroutine takes a single parameter named `String` of type String:

```
Public Sub ParseString(ByVal [String] As String)
    Dim values() As String = Split([String])
    ...
End Sub
```

If you begin writing a call to this subroutine in the code editor, the IntelliSense pop-up describes this routine as ParseString(String As String).

These rules let you come up with some strange and potentially confusing identifier names. For example, you can make escaped variables named String, Boolean, ElseIf, and Case. Depending on your system's settings, underscores may be hard to read either on the screen or in printouts. That may make variables such as __ (two underscores) seem to vanish and may make it hard to tell the difference between _Name and Name.

Although these identifiers are all legal, they can be extremely confusing and may lead to long, frustrating debugging sessions. To avoid confusion, use escaped identifiers and identifiers beginning with an underscore sparingly.

Bounds_List

A variable declaration's *bounds_list* clause specifies bounds for an array. This should be a comma-separated list of non-negative integers that give the upper bounds for the array's dimensions. All dimensions have a lower bound of zero. You can optionally specify the lower bound, but it must always be zero.

> **LIMITED LOWER BOUNDS**
>
> Henry Ford once said, "Any customer can have a car painted any color that he wants so long as it is black." A similar rule applies here: you can specify any lower bound for an array as long as it's zero.

The following code declares two arrays in two different ways. The first statement declares a one-dimensional array of 101 Customer objects with indexes ranging from 0 to 100. The second statement defines a two-dimensional array of Order objects. The first dimension has bounds ranging from 0 to 100 and the second dimension has bounds ranging from 0 to 10. The array's entries are those between orders(0, 0) and orders(100, 10) giving a total of 101 * 11 = 1111 entries. The last two statements define similar arrays, while explicitly declaring the arrays' lower bounds.

```
Private customers(100) As Customer
Private orders(100, 10) As Order
Private customers2(0 To 100) As Customer
Private orders2(0 To 100, 0 To 10) As Order
```

You may find that specifying the lower bound makes the code easier to read because it gives the lower bound explicitly rather than requiring you to remember that lower bounds are always 0. It can be particularly helpful for those who have used Visual Basic 6 and earlier versions because those versions of Visual Basic allowed arrays to have lower bounds other than 0.

Note that declarations of this sort that use an object data type do not instantiate the objects. For example, the first declaration in the previous example defines 101 array entries that all point to Nothing. They do not initially point to instances of the Customer class. After this declaration, the program would need to create each object reference individually, as shown in the following code:

```
Private customers(100) As Customer
For i As Integer = 0 To 100
    customers(i) = New Customer
Next i
```

Alternatively, the program can use an initialization statement to declare and initialize the objects in a single step. See the section Initialization_Expression coming up shortly for more information on initializing arrays in their declarations.

If you provide parentheses but no *bounds_list*, Visual Basic defines the array, but doesn't create it with specific bounds. Later, you can use the ReDim statement to give it bounds. Note that you can also use ReDim to change the bounds of an array that you initially give bounds. The following example declares two arrays named a1 and a2. Initially, the program allocates 11 items for array a1 but no items for array a2. The program then uses ReDim to allocate 21 entries for both arrays.

```
Dim a1(10) As Integer
Dim a2() As Integer

ReDim a1(20)
ReDim a2(0 To 20)
```

The ReDim statement cannot change the number of bounds in an array. If you want to declare but not initialize a multidimensional array, include commas as if you were defining the bounds. The following code declares a three-dimensional array and initializes its separate steps:

```
Dim a1(,,) As Integer

ReDim a1(10, 20, 30)
```

New

If you are declaring an object variable, the New keyword tells Visual Basic to create a new instance of the object. Without this keyword, Visual Basic makes an object variable that doesn't yet hold a reference to any object. It initially holds Nothing.

For example, the first line in the following code declares an Employee object variable named emp1. After that line, the variable is defined, but it doesn't point to anything. If you examine the variable, you will find that it has the value Nothing. The second line sets emp1 equal to a new Employee object. The last line creates an Employee object variable named emp2 and assigns it to a new Employee object. This does the same thing as the first and second line but in a single statement.

```
Dim emp1 As Employee
emp1 = New Employee

Dim emp2 As New Manager
```

If the object's class has constructors that take parameters, you can include the parameters after the class name. For example, suppose that the Employee class has two constructors: an empty constructor (one that takes no parameters) and a constructor that takes first and last name strings as parameters. Then the following code creates two Employee objects using the different constructors:

```
Dim emp1 As New Employee
Dim emp2 As New Employee("Rod", "Stephens")
```

Note that you must provide parameters that match some constructor. If the class does not have a constructor that takes no arguments, you cannot use the New keyword without specifying parameters. If the Employee class didn't have an empty constructor, the first line in the previous example would be illegal.

As Type and Inferred Types

The As clause tells Visual Basic what kind of variable you are declaring. For example, the following As statement indicates that the variable `cx` has type Single:

```
Dim cx As Single
```

If Option Infer is on, you do not need to declare a local variable's data type. If you omit the As clause, Visual Basic infers the variable's data type from the value that you assign to it. For example, the following code declares a variable named `message`. Because the code assigns a string value to the variable, Visual Basic infers that the variable should be a String.

```
Dim message = "Hello!"
```

Unfortunately, inferred data types make the code harder to understand later. You can figure out that the previous declaration makes a variable that is a String, but it is much more obvious if you explicitly include the As String clause. In this example, type inference only saves you a few keystrokes and makes the code slightly harder to understand. Now, consider the following statement:

```
Dim x = 1.234
```

Does this statement make variable `x` a Single, Double, Decimal, or some other data type? In this case, it's much less obvious what data type Visual Basic will decide to use. (It makes `x` a Double.)

MINIMIZE CONFUSION

To avoid confusion and make the code as easy to read as possible, I recommend that you turn Option Infer off. Then you can use an Option Infer statement at the top of any module where type inference would be helpful. Even in those modules, I recommend that you explicitly give variables data types whenever possible.

The only times when type inference is helpful is when you cannot easily figure out the type needed by a variable. For example, LINQ lets a program generate results that have confusing data types, so type inference can be very handy when working with LINQ. For more information on LINQ, see Chapter 21, "LINQ."

INOFFENSIVE INFERENCE

When you create a new project, Option Infer is on by default. To restrict its scope, turn it off for the project as a whole and then turn it on only in the files that need it.

Initialization_Expression

The *initialization_expression* clause gives data that Visual Basic should use to initialize the variable. The most straightforward form of initialization assigns a simple value to a variable. The following code declares the variable num_employees and assigns it the initial value zero:

```
Dim num_employees As Integer = 0
```

More complicated data types may require more complex initialization clauses. If the declaration declares an object variable, you can use the New keyword to initialize the variable. For example, the first line in the following code declares an Employee variable named emp1 and sets it equal to a new Employee object. The second statement uses the As New form of declaration to do the same thing without a separate initialization clause. This version is slightly more compact, but you can use whichever version seems most natural to you.

```
Dim emp1 As Employee = New Employee("Rod", "Stephens")
Dim emp2 As New Employee("Rod", "Stephens")
```

The With keyword allows you to initialize an object without using a special constructor. This statement lets you assign values to an object's public properties and variables right after the object is created. The following code creates a new Employee object and sets its FirstName and LastName values much as the previous statements do:

```
Dim emp3 As New Employee With {.FirstName = "Rod", .LastName = "Stephens"}
```

Initializing Arrays

Arrays have their own special initialization syntax. To declare and initialize an array in one statement, you must omit the array's bounds. Visual Basic uses the initialization data to discover the bounds.

Place the array's values inside curly braces separated by commas. The following code initializes a one-dimensional array of integers:

```
Dim fibonacci() As Integer = {1, 1, 2, 3, 5, 8, 13, 21, 33, 54, 87}
```

If you have Option Infer on, you can omit the array's data type and Visual Basic will try to deduce it from the values that you use to initialize it. For example, the following code creates three arrays. Visual Basic can infer that the first contains Integers and the second contains Strings. The third array contains Strings, Integers, and Doubles so Visual Basic makes it an array of Objects.

```
Dim numbers() = {1, 2, 3}
Dim strings() = {"A", "B", "C"}
Dim objects() = {"A", 12, 1.23}
```

TYPES OF THE TIMES

Inferring array type is a new feature in Visual Basic 2010. In earlier versions, Visual Basic always created arrays without explicit data types as arrays of Objects.

For a multidimensional array, put commas in the variable's parentheses to indicate the number of dimensions. Use curly braces to surround the array data. Nest each dimension of data inside the previous one, enclosing each dimension's data with braces and separating entries with commas.

This probably makes the most sense if you think of a multidimensional array as an array of arrays. For example, a three-dimensional array is an array of two-dimensional arrays. Each of the two-dimensional arrays is an array of one-dimensional arrays. You can use line continuation and indentation to make the array's structure more obvious.

The following code declares and initializes a two-dimensional array of integers and then prints the values:

```
Dim int_values(,) As Integer =
{
    {1, 2, 3},
    {4, 5, 6}
}
Dim txt As String = ""
For i As Integer = 0 To 1
    For j As Integer = 0 To 2
        txt &= int_values(i, j)
    Next j
    txt &= vbCrLf
Next i
```

The following shows this code's output:

```
123
456
```

The following code declares and initializes a three-dimensional array of strings. The text for each value gives its position in the array. For example, the value str_values(0, 1, 1) is "011." Notice how the code uses indentation to make the data a bit easier to understand. Items in the first dimension are indented one level and items in the second dimension are indented two levels. The final level is basically a one-dimensional array, which is fairly easy to understand with just commas separating its values. After initializing the array, the code loops through its entries and prints them.

```
Dim str_values(,,) As String =
{
    {
        {"000", "001", "002"},
        {"010", "011", "012"}
    },
    {
        {"100", "101", "102"},
        {"110", "111", "112"}
    }
}
Dim txt As String = ""
For i As Integer = 0 To 1
    For j As Integer = 0 To 1
        txt &= "[ "
        For k As Integer = 0 To 2
            txt &= str_values(i, j, k) & " "
        Next k
        txt &= "] "
    Next j
    txt &= vbCrLf
Next i
```

The following text shows this code's output:

```
[ 000 001 002 ] [ 010 011 012 ]
[ 100 101 102 ] [ 110 111 112 ]
```

Example program InitializeArrays, which is available for download on the book's web site, uses similar code to demonstrate array initialization.

Note that you must provide the correct number of items for each of the array's dimensions. For example, the following declaration is invalid because the array's second row contains fewer elements than its first row:

```
Dim int_values(,) As Integer =
{
    {1, 2, 3},
    {4, 5}
}
```

Initializing Object Arrays

The basic syntax for initializing an array of objects is similar to the syntax you use to initialize any other array. You still omit the array bounds from the declaration and then include values inside curly braces. The values you use to initialize the array, however, are different because object variables do not take simple values such as 12 and "Test" that you would use to initialize integer or string arrays.

If you create an array of objects without an initialization clause, Visual Basic creates the object variables but does not create objects for them. Initially, all of the array's entries are Nothing.

The following code creates an array containing 11 references to Employee objects. Initially, all of the references are set to Nothing.

```
Dim employees(0 To 10) As Employee
```

If you want to initialize the objects, you must initialize each object in the array separately using Nothing or the class's constructors. Optionally, you can add a With statement to set public properties and variables after creating the object. The following code declares an array of Employee objects. It initializes two entries using an Employee object constructor that takes as parameters the employees' first and last names, two entries with an empty constructor and a With statement, two with an empty constructor only, and two final entries with the value Nothing.

```
Dim employees() As Employee =
{
    New Employee("Alice", "Andrews"),
    New Employee("Bart", "Brin"),
    New Employee With {.FirstName = "Cindy", .LastName="Cant"},
    New Employee With {.FirstName = "Dan", .LastName="Diver"},
    New Employee,
    New Employee,
    Nothing,
    Nothing
}
```

To initialize higher-dimensional arrays of objects, use the syntax described in the previous section. Use Nothing or the New keyword and object constructors to initialize each array entry individually.

Initializing XML Variables

To initialize an XElement object, declare the XElement variable and set it equal to properly formatted XML code. The XML code must begin on the same logical line as the variable assignment, although, as usual, you can use line continuation characters to start the actual XML code on the following line. Visual Basic reads the data's opening tag and then reads XML data until it reaches a corresponding closing tag so the XML data can include whitespace just as an XML document can. In particular, it can span multiple lines without line continuation characters.

XML CONTINUED

In fact, if you use line continuation characters within the XML, the underscore characters become part of the XML data, which is probably not what you want.

For example, the following code declares a variable named `book_node` that contains XML data representing a book:

```
Dim book_node As XElement =
    <Book>
        <Title>The Bug That Was</Title>
        <Year>2010</Year>
        <Pages>376</Pages>
    </Book>
```

This type of declaration and initialization makes it easy to build XML data directly into your Visual Basic applications.

You can initialize XML literal values with much more complicated expressions. For example, you can use LINQ to select values from relational data sources and build results in the form of an XML document. For more information on LINQ, see Chapter 21.

INITIALIZING COLLECTIONS

Starting with Visual Basic 2010, collection classes that provide an Add method such as List, Dictionary, and SortedDictionary have their own initialization syntax. Instead of using an equals sign as you would with an array initializer, use the From keyword followed by the values that should be added to the collection surrounded by curly braces.

For example, the following code initializes a new List(Of String):

```
Dim pies As New List(Of String) From {
    "Apple", "Banana", "Cherry", "Coconut Cream"
}
```

The items inside the braces must include all of the values needed by the collection's Add method. For example, the Dictionary class's Add method takes two parameters giving the key and value that should be added.

The following code initializes a Dictionary(Of String, String). The parameters to the class's Add method are an item's key and value so, for example, the value 940-283-1298 has the key Alice Artz.

Later you could look up Alice's phone number by searching the Dictionary for the item with key "Alice Artz."

```
Dim phone_numbers As New Dictionary(Of String, String) From {
    {"Alice Artz", "940-283-1298"},
    {"Bill Bland", "940-237-3827"},
    {"Carla Careful", "940-237-1983"}
}
```

ADDING ADD

Some collection classes such as Stack and Queue don't have an Add method, so From won't work for them. Fortunately, you can use extension methods (described in the "Extension Methods" section in Chapter 17, "Subroutines and Functions") to add one. The following code adds a simple extension method to the Stack(Of String) class:

```
<Extension()>
Sub Add(ByVal the_stack As Stack(Of String), ByRef value As String)
    the_stack.Push(value)
End Sub
```

Now the program can initialize a Stack(Of String) as in the following code:

```
Dim orders As New Stack(Of String) From {
    "Art", "Beatrice", "Chuck"
}
```

Multiple Variable Declarations

Visual Basic .NET allows you to declare more than one variable in a single declaration statement. For example, the following statement declares two Integer variables named num_employees and num_customers:

```
Private num_employees, num_customers As Integer
```

You can place accessibility keywords (Private, Public, and so on), Shared, Shadows, and ReadOnly only at the beginning of the declaration and they apply to all of the variables in the declaration. In the preceding statement, both num_employees and num_customers are Private.

You can declare variables with different data types by including more than one As clause separated by commas. The following statement declares two Integer variables and one String variable:

```
Private emps, custs As Integer, cust As String
```

You cannot use an initialization statement if multiple variables share the same As clause, but you can include an initialization statement for variables that have their own As clause. In the preceding example, you cannot initialize the two Integer variables, but you can initialize the String variable as shown in the following statement:

```
Private emps, custs As Integer, cust As String = "Cozmo"
```

To initialize all three variables, you would need to give them each their own As clauses, as shown in the following example:

```
Private emps As Integer = 5, custs As Integer = 10, cust As String = "Cozmo"
```

You can also declare and initialize multiple objects, arrays, and arrays of objects all in the same statement.

Although all of these combinations are legal, they quickly become too confusing to be of much practical use. Even the relatively simple statement that follows can lead to later misunderstandings. Quickly glancing at this statement, the programmer may think that all three variables are declared as Long.

```
Private num_employees, num_customers As Integer, num_orders As Long
```

You can reduce the possibility of confusion by using one As clause per declaration. Then a programmer can easily understand how the variables are defined by looking at the beginning and ending of the declaration. The beginning tells the programmer the variables' accessibility and whether they are shared, shadowing other variables, or read-only. The end gives the variables' data type.

You can also keep the code simple by giving variables with initialization statements their own declarations. Then a programmer reading the code won't need to decide whether an initialization statement applies to one or all of the variables.

There's nothing particularly wrong with declaring a series of relatively short variables in a single statement, as long as you don't find the code confusing. The following statements declare five Integer variables and three Single variables. Breaking this into eight separate Dim statements would not make it much clearer.

```
Dim i, j, k, R, C As Integer
Dim X, Y, Z As Single
```

OPTION EXPLICIT AND OPTION STRICT

The Option Explicit and Option Strict compiler options play an important role in variable declarations.

When Option Explicit is set to On, you must declare all variables before you use them. If Option Explicit is Off, Visual Basic automatically creates a new variable whenever it sees a variable that it has not yet encountered. For example, the following code doesn't explicitly declare any variables. As it executes the code, Visual Basic sees the first statement, num_managers = 0. It doesn't recognize the variable num_managers, so it creates it. Similarly, it creates the variable i when it sees it in the For loop.

```
Option Explicit Off
Option Strict Off

Public Class Form1
    ...
    Public Sub CountManagers()
        num_managers = 0
        For i = 0 To m_Employees.GetUpperBound(0)
            If m_Employees(i).IsManager Then num_managrs += 1
        Next i

        MessageBox.Show(num_managers)
    End Sub
    ...
End Class
```

Keeping Option Explicit turned off can lead to two very bad problems. First, it silently hides typographical errors. If you look closely at the preceding code, you'll see that the statement inside the For loop increments the misspelled variable num_managrs instead of the correctly spelled variable num_managers. Because Option Explicit is off, Visual Basic assumes that you want to use a new variable, so it creates num_managrs. After the loop finishes, the program displays the value of num_managers, which is zero because it was never incremented.

The second problem that occurs when Option Explicit is off is that Visual Basic doesn't really know what you will want to do with the variables it creates for you. It doesn't know whether you will use a variable as an Integer, Double, String, or PictureBox. Even after you assign a value to the variable (say, an Integer), Visual Basic doesn't know whether you will always use the variable as an Integer or whether you might later want to save a String in it.

To keep its options open, Visual Basic creates undeclared variables as generic objects. Then it can fill the variable with just about anything. Unfortunately, this can make the code much less efficient than it needs to be. For example, programs are much better at manipulating integers than they are at manipulating objects. If you are going to use a variable as an integer, creating it as an object makes the program run much slower.

IMPRECISE INFERENCE

If Option Infer is on, Visual Basic may be able to deduce an explicit data type for a variable declared without a type. In that case, the program may not incur a performance penalty. It won't be clear from the code whether that's the case, however, so it could lead to some confusion.

In more advanced terms, integers are value types, whereas objects are reference types. A reference type is really a fancy pointer that represents the location of the actual object in memory. When you treat a value type as a reference type, Visual Basic performs an operation called *boxing*, where it wraps the value in an object so it can use references to the boxed value. If you then perform an operation involving two boxed values, Visual Basic must unbox them, perform the operation, and then possibly box the result to store it in another reference variable. All of this boxing and unboxing has a significant overhead.

Example program TimeGenericObjects, which is available for download on the book's web site, uses the following code to demonstrate the difference in speed between using variables with explicit types and variables of the generic Object type:

```
Dim num_trials As Integer = Integer.Parse(txtNumTrials.Text)

Dim start_time As DateTime
Dim stop_time As DateTime
Dim elapsed_time As TimeSpan

start_time = Now
For i As Integer = 1 To num_trials

Next i
stop_time = Now
elapsed_time = stop_time.Subtract(start_time)
lblIntegers.Text = elapsed_time.TotalSeconds.ToString("0.000000")
Refresh()

start_time = Now
For j = 1 To num_trials

Next j
stop_time = Now
elapsed_time = stop_time.Subtract(start_time)
lblObjects.Text = elapsed_time.TotalSeconds.ToString("0.000000")
```

code snippet TimeGenericObjects

The code executes two For loops. In the first loop, it explicitly declares its looping variable to be of type Integer. In the second loop, the code doesn't declare its looping variable, so Visual Basic automatically makes it an Object when it is needed. In one test, the second loop took more than 60 times as long as the first loop.

The second compiler directive that influences variable declaration is Option Strict. When Option Strict is turned off, Visual Basic silently converts values from one data type to another, even if the types are not very compatible. For example, Visual Basic will allow the following code to try to copy the string s into the integer i. If the value in the string happens to be a number (as in the first case), this works. If the string is not a number (as in the second case), this throws an error at runtime.

```
Dim i As Integer
Dim s As String
s = "10"
i = s          ' This works.
s = "Hello"
i = s          ' This Fails.
```

If you turn Option Strict on, Visual Basic warns you of possibly illegal conversions at compile time. You can still use conversion functions such as CInt, Int, and Integer.Parse to convert a string into an Integer, but you must take explicit action to do so.

To avoid confusion and ensure total control of your variable declarations, you should always turn on Option Explicit and Option Strict.

For more information on Option Explicit and Option Strict (including instructions for turning these options on), see the "Project" section in Chapter 2, "Menus, Toolbars, and Windows."

SCOPE

A variable's *scope* tells which other pieces of code can access it. For example, if you declare a variable inside a subroutine, only code within that subroutine can access the variable. The four possible levels of scope are (in increasing size of scope) block, procedure, module, and namespace.

Block Scope

A *block* is a series of statements enclosed in a construct that ends with some sort of End, Else, Loop, or Next statement. If you declare a variable within a block of code, the variable has block scope, and only other code within that block can access the variable. Furthermore, only code that appears after the variable's declaration can see the variable.

Variables declared in the block's opening statement are also part of the block. Note that a variable is visible within any sub-block contained within the variable's scope.

The following example uses a For loop with the looping variable i declared in the For statement. The scope of variable i is block-defined by the For loop. Code inside the loop can see variable i, but code outside of the loop cannot.

Inside the loop, the code declares variable j. This variable's scope is also the For loop's block.

If i equals j, the program declares variable M and uses it. This variable's scope includes only the two lines between the If and Else statements.

If i doesn't equal j, the code declares variable N. This variable's scope includes only the two lines between the Else and End If statements.

The program then declares variable k. This variable also has block scope, but it is available only after it is declared, so the code could not have accessed it earlier in the For loop.

```
For i As Integer = 1 To 5
    Dim j As Integer = 3
    If i = j Then
        Dim M As Integer = i + j
        Debug.WriteLine("M: " & M)
    Else
        Dim N As Integer = i * j
        Debug.WriteLine("N: " & N)
    End If

    Dim k As Integer = 123
    Debug.WriteLine("k: " & k)
Next i
```

Other code constructs that define blocks include the following:

➤ Select Case statements — Each Case has its own block.

➤ Try Catch statements — The Try section and each Exception statement defines a block. Note also that the exception variable defined in each Exception statement is in its own block; for example, they can all have the same name.

```
Try
    Dim i As Integer = CInt("bad value")
Catch ex As InvalidCastException
    Dim txt As String = "InvalidCastException"
    MessageBox.Show(txt)
Catch ex As Exception
    Dim txt As String = "Exception"
    MessageBox.Show(txt)
End Try
```

➤ Single-Line `If Then` statements — These are strange and confusing enough that you should avoid them, but the following code *is* legal:

```
If manager Then Dim txt As String = "M" : MessageBox.Show(txt) Else _
    Dim txt As String = "E" : MessageBox.Show(txt)
```

➤ `While` loops — Variables declared inside the loop are local to the loop.

➤ `Using` statements — Resources acquired by the block and variables declared inside the block are local to the block. The Using statement in the following code defines two Employee objects and a Pen object within its block. Those variables are visible only within the block.

```
Using _
  emp1 As New Employee("Ann", "Archer"),
  emp2 As New Employee("Bob", "Beagle"),
  the_pen As New Pen(Color.Red)
    ...
End Using
```

Because block scope is the most restrictive, you should use it whenever possible to reduce the chances for confusion. The section "Restricting Scope" later in this chapter discusses more about restricting variable scope.

Procedure Scope

If you declare a variable inside a subroutine, function, or other procedure, but not within a block, the variable is visible in any code inside the procedure that follows the declaration. The variable is not visible outside of the procedure. In a sense, the variable has block scope where the block is the procedure.

A procedure's parameters also have procedure scope. For example, in the following code, the scope of the `order_object` and `order_item` parameters is the `AddOrderItem` subroutine:

```
Public Sub AddOrderItem(ByVal order_object As Order, ByVal order_item As OrderItem)
    order_object.OrderItems.Add(order_item)
End Sub
```

Module Scope

A variable with module scope is available to all code in its code module, class, or structure, even if the code appears before the variable's declaration. For example, the following code works even though the `DisplayLoanAmount` subroutine is declared before the `m_LoanAmount` variable that it displays:

```
Private Class Lender
    Public Sub DisplayLoanAmount()
        MessageBox.Show(m_LoanAmount)
    End Sub

    Private m_LoanAmount As Decimal
    ...
End Class
```

To give a variable module scope, you should declare it with the Private, Protected, or Protected Friend keyword. If you declare the variable Private, it is visible only to code within the same module.

If you declare the variable Protected, it is accessible only to code in its class or a derived class. Remember that you can only use the Protected keyword in a class.

A Protected Friend variable is both Protected and Friend. That means it is available only to code that is inside the variable's class or a derived class (Protected), and that is within the same project (Friend).

These keywords apply to both variable and procedure declarations. For example, you can declare a subroutine, function, or property procedure Private, Protected, or Protected Friend.

For more information on accessibility keywords, see the section "Accessibility" earlier in this chapter.

Example program ScopeTest, which is available for download on the book's web site, demonstrates module and procedure scope.

Namespace Scope

By default, a project defines a namespace that includes all the project's variables and code. However, you can use Namespace statements to create other namespaces if you like. This may be useful to help categorize the code in your application.

If you declare a variable with the Public keyword, it has namespace scope and is available to all code in its namespace, whether inside the project or in another project. It is also available to code in any namespaces nested inside the variable's namespace. If you do not create any namespaces of your own, the whole project lies in a single namespace, so you can think of Public variables as having global scope.

If you declare a variable with the Friend keyword, it has namespace scope and is available to all code in its namespace within the same project. It is also available to code in any namespaces nested inside the variable's namespace within the project. If you do not create any namespaces of your own, the whole project lies in a single namespace so you can think of Friend variables as having project scope.

For more information on the Public and Friend keywords, see the section "Accessibility" earlier in this chapter.

Restricting Scope

There are several reasons why you should give variables the most restrictive scope possible that still lets them do their jobs.

Limited scope keeps the variable localized so that programmers cannot use the variable incorrectly in far off code that is unrelated to the variable's main purpose.

Having fewer variables with global scope means programmers have less to remember when they are working on the code. They can concentrate on their current work, rather than worrying about whether variables r and c are declared globally and whether the current code will interfere with them.

Limiting scope keeps variables closer to their declarations, so it's easier for programmers to check the declaration. One of the best examples of this situation is when a For loop declares its looping variable right in the For statement. A programmer can easily see that the looping variable is an integer without scrolling to the top of the subroutine hunting for its declaration. It is also easy to see that the variable has block scope, so other variables with the same names can be used outside of the loop.

Limited scope means a programmer doesn't need to worry about whether a variable's old value will interfere with the current code, or whether the final value after the current code will later interfere with some other code. This is particularly true for looping variables. If a program declares variable i at the top of a subroutine, and then uses it many times in various loops, you might need to do a little thinking to be sure the variable's past values won't interfere with new loops. If you declare i separately in each For statement, each loop has its own version of i, so there's no way they can interfere with each other.

Finally, variables with larger scope tend to be allocated more often, so they take up memory more often. For example, block variables and non-static variables declared with procedure scope are allocated when they are needed and are destroyed when their scope ends, freeing their memory. A variable declared Static or with module or namespace scope is not freed until your application exits. If those variables are large arrays, they may take up a lot of memory the entire time your application is running.

PARAMETER DECLARATIONS

A *parameter declaration* for a subroutine, function, or property procedure defines the names and types of the parameters passed into it. Parameter declarations always have non-static procedure scope. Visual Basic creates parameter variables when a procedure begins and destroys them when the procedure ends. The subroutine's code can access the parameters, but code outside of the routine cannot.

For example, the following subroutine takes an integer as a parameter. The subroutine calls this value `employee_id`. Code within the subroutine can access `employee_id`, whereas code outside of the subroutine cannot.

```
Public Sub DisplayEmployee(ByVal employee_id As Integer)
    ...
End Sub
```

Whereas a parameter's basic scope is straightforward (non-static procedure scope), parameters have some special features that complicate the situation. Although this isn't exactly a scoping issue, it's related closely enough to scope that it's worth covering here.

You can declare a parameter ByRef or ByVal (ByVal is the default if you use neither keyword). If you declare the variable ByVal, the routine makes its own local parameter variable with procedure scope just as you would expect.

If you declare a parameter with the ByRef keyword, the routine does not create a separate copy of the parameter variable. Instead, it uses a reference to the parameter you pass in, and any changes the routine makes to the value are reflected in the calling subroutine.

For example, the following code includes two routines that double their parameters. Subroutine `DoubleItByVal` declares its parameter with the ByVal keyword. This routine makes a new variable named X and copies the value of its parameter into that variable. The parameter X is available within the subroutine, the routine multiplies it by 2, and then exits. At that point, the parameter variable goes out of scope and is destroyed.

Subroutine `DoubleItByRef` declares its parameter with the ByRef keyword. This routine's variable X is a reference to the variable passed into the routine. The subroutine doubles X and that doubles the variable in the calling code.

Subroutine `TestParameters` calls each of these routines. It declares a variable named `value`, passes it to subroutine `DoubleItByVal`, and displays the result after `DoubleItByVal` returns. Because `DoubleItByVal` declares its parameter ByVal, the variable value is not changed so the result is 10.

Subroutine `TestParameters` then calls subroutine `DoubleItByRef` and displays the result after the call returns. Subroutine `DoubleItByRef` declares its parameter ByRef so the variable `value` is changed to 20.

```
Sub DoubleItByVal(ByVal X As Single)
    X*= 2
End Sub
Sub DoubleItByRef(ByRef X As Single)
    X*= 2
End Sub
Sub TestParameters()
    Dim value As Single

    value = 10
    DoubleItByVal(value)
    Debug.WriteLine(value)

    value = 10
    DoubleItByRef(value)
    Debug.WriteLine(value)
End Sub
```

Even this more complex view of how procedures handle parameters has exceptions. If you pass a literal value or the result of an expression into a procedure, there is no variable to pass by reference, so Visual Basic must create its own temporary variable. In that case, any changes made to a ByRef parameter are not returned to the calling routine, because that code did not pass a variable into the procedure. The following code shows statements that pass a literal expression and the result of an expression into the `DoubleItByRef` subroutine:

```
DoubleItByRef(12)     ' Literal expression.
DoubleItByRef(X + Y) ' Result of an expression.
```

Another case where a ByRef parameter does not modify a variable in the calling code is when you omit an optional parameter. For example, the following subroutine takes an optional ByRef parameter. If you call this routine and omit the parameter, Visual Basic creates the `employee_id` parameter from scratch so the subroutine can use it in its calculations. Because you called the routine without passing it a variable, the subroutine does not update a variable.

```
Sub UpdateEmployee(Optional ByRef employee_id As Integer = 0)
    ...
End Sub
```

Probably the sneakiest way a ByRef variable can fail to update a variable in the calling routine is if you enclose the variable in parentheses. The parentheses tell Visual Basic to evaluate their contents as an expression, so Visual Basic creates a temporary variable to hold the result of the expression. It then passes the temporary variable into the procedure. If the procedure's parameter is declared ByRef, it updates the temporary variable, but not the original variable, so the calling routine doesn't see any change to its value.

The following code calls subroutine `DoubleItByRef`, passing the variable `value` into the routine surrounded with parentheses. The `DoubleItByRef` subroutine doubles the temporary variable Visual Basic creates, leaving `value` unchanged.

```
DoubleItByRef((value))
```

Keep these issues in mind when you work with parameters. Parameters have non-static procedure scope but the ByRef keyword can sometimes carry their values outside of the routine.

For more information on routines and their parameters, see Chapter 17.

PROPERTY PROCEDURES

Property procedures are routines that can represent a variable-like value. To other pieces of the program, property procedures look just like variables, so they deserve mention in this chapter.

The following code shows property procedures that implement a `Name` property. The Property Get procedure simply returns the value in the private variable `m_Name`. The Property Set procedure saves a new value in the `m_Name` variable.

```
    Private m_Name As String

    Property Name() As String
        Get
            Return m_Name
        End Get
        Set(ByVal Value As String)
            m_Name = Value
        End Set
    End Property
```

A program could use these procedures exactly as if there were a single public Name variable. For example, if this code is in the Employee class, the following code shows how a program could set and then get the Name value for the Employee object named emp:

```
emp.Name = "Rod Stephens"
MessageBox.Show(emp.Name)
```

You might want to use property procedures rather than a public variable for several reasons. First, the routines give you extra control over the getting and setting of the value. For example, you could use code to validate the value before saving it in the variable. The code could verify that a postal code or phone number has the proper format and throw an error if the value is badly formatted.

You can set breakpoints in property procedures. Suppose that your program is crashing because a piece of code is setting an incorrect value in a variable. If you implement the variable with property procedures, you can set a breakpoint in the Property Set procedure and stop whenever the program sets the value. This can help you find the problem relatively quickly.

Property procedures let you set and get values in formats other than those you want to actually use to store the value. For example, the following code defines Name property procedures that save a name in m_FirstName and m_LastName variables. If your code would often need to use the last and first names separately, you could also provide property procedures to give access to those values separately.

```
    Private m_LastName As String
    Private m_FirstName As String

    Property MyName() As String
        Get
            Return m_FirstName & " " & m_LastName
        End Get
        Set(ByVal Value As String)
            m_FirstName = Value.Split(" "c)(0)
            m_LastName = Value.Split(" "c)(1)
        End Set
    End Property
```

Finally, you can use property procedures to create read-only and write-only variables. The following code shows how to make a read-only `NumEmployees` property procedure and a write-only `NumCustomers` property procedure. (Write-only property procedures are unusual but legal.)

```
Public ReadOnly Property NumEmployees() As Integer
    Get
        ...
    End Get
End Property

Public WriteOnly Property NumCustomers() As Integer
    Set(ByVal Value As Integer)
        ...
    End Set
End Property
```

You don't need to remember all of the syntax for property procedures. If you type the first line and press Enter, Visual Basic fills in the rest of the empty property procedures. If you use the keyword ReadOnly or WriteOnly, Visual Basic only includes the appropriate procedure.

Visual Basic 2010 introduced auto-implemented properties. These are simple properties that do not have separate property procedures. You declare the property's name and Visual Basic automatically creates the necessary backing variables and property procedures behind the scenes.

The following code shows a simple `FirstName` property:

```
Public Property FirstName As String
```

You can give a property a default value as in the following code:

```
Public Property FirstName As String = "<missing>"
```

You cannot use the ReadOnly or WriteOnly keywords with auto-implemented properties. If you want to make a read-only or write-only property, you need to write Get and Set procedures as described earlier.

The advantage of auto-implemented properties is that you don't need to write as much code. The disadvantage is that you can't set breakpoints in the property procedures.

PROPERTY PROCEDURES AS YOU NEED THEM

To get the best of both worlds, you can initially use auto-implemented properties. Later if you need to set breakpoints in the property procedures, you can redefine the property to include them.

ENUMERATED DATA TYPES

An *enumerated type* is a discrete list of specific values. You define the enumerated type and the values allowed. Later, if you declare a variable of that data type, it can take only those values.

For example, suppose that you are building a large application where users can have one of three access levels: clerk, supervisor, and administrator. You could define an enumerated type named AccessLevel that allows the values Clerk, Supervisor, and Administrator. Now, if you declare a variable to be of type AccessLevel, Visual Basic will only allow the variable to take those values.

The following code shows a simple example. It defines the AccessLevel type and declares the variable m_AccessLevel using the type. Later the MakeSupervisor subroutine sets m_AccessLevel to the value AccessLevel.Supervisor. Note that the value is prefixed with the enumerated type's name.

```
Public Enum AccessLevel
    Clerk
    Supervisor
    Administrator
End Enum

Private m_AccessLevel As AccessLevel ' The user's access level.

' Set supervisor access level.
Public Sub MakeSupervisor()
    m_AccessLevel = AccessLevel.Supervisor
End Sub
```

The syntax for declaring an enumerated type is as follows:

```
[attribute_list] [accessibility] [Shadows] Enum name [As type]
    [attribute_list] value_name [= initialization_expression]
    [attribute_list] value_name [= initialization_expression]
    ...
End Enum
```

Most of these terms, including *attribute_list* and *accessibility*, are similar to those used by variable declarations. See the section "Variable Declarations" earlier in this chapter for more information.

The *type* value must be an integral type and can be Byte, Short, Integer, or Long. If you omit this value, Visual Basic stores the enumerated type values as integers.

The *value_name* pieces are the names you want to allow the enumerated type to have. You can include an *initialization_expression* for each value if you like. This value must be compatible with the underlying data type (Byte, Short, Integer, or Long). If you omit a value's initialization expression, the value is set to one greater than the previous value. The first value is zero by default.

In the previous example, Clerk = 0, Supervisor = 1, and Administrator = 2. The following code changes the default assignments so Clerk = 10, Supervisor = 11, and Administrator = –1:

```
Public Enum AccessLevel
    Clerk = 10
    Supervisor
    Administrator = -1
End Enum
```

Usually, all that's important about an enumerated type is that its values are unique, so you don't need to explicitly initialize the values.

Note that you can give enumerated values the same integer value either explicitly or implicitly. For example, the following code defines several equivalent AccessLevel values. The first three values, Clerk, Supervisor, and Administrator, default to 0, 1, and 2, respectively. The code explicitly sets User to 0, so it is the same as Clerk. The values Manager and SysAdmin then default to the next two values, 1 and 2 (the same as Supervisor and Administrator, respectively). Finally, the code explicitly sets Superuser = SysAdmin.

```
Public Enum AccessLevel
    Clerk
    Supervisor
    Administrator
    User = 0
    Manager
    SysAdmin
    Superuser = SysAdmin
End Enum
```

This code is somewhat confusing. The following version makes it more obvious that some values are synonyms for others:

```
Public Enum AccessLevel
    Clerk
    Supervisor
    Administrator

    User = Clerk
    Manager = Supervisor
    SysAdmin = Administrator
    Superuser = Administrator
End Enum
```

code snippet AccessLevelEnum

You can get an effect similar to enumerated types using integer variables and constants, as shown in the following code. This code does roughly the same thing as the previous examples.

```
Public Const Clerk As Integer = 0
Public Const Supervisor As Integer = 1
Public Const Administrator As Intger = 2

Private m_AccessLevel As Integer ' The user's access level.

' Set supervisor access level.
Public Sub MakeSupervisor()
    m_AccessLevel = Supervisor
End Sub
```

Declaring an enumerated type has a couple of advantages over using integers and constants, however. First, it prevents you from assigning nonsense values to the variable. In the previous code, you could set m_AccessLevel to 10, which wouldn't make any sense.

Using an enumerated data type allows Visual Basic to verify that the value you are assigning to the variable makes sense. You can only set the variable equal to one of the values in the enumerated type or to the value stored in another variable of the same enumerated type.

If you really need to set an enumerated variable to a calculated value for some reason, you can use the CType function to convert an integer value into the enumerated type. For example, the following statement uses the value in the variable integer_value to set the value of the variable m_AccessLevel. Making you use CType to perform this type of conversion makes it less likely that you will set an enumerated value accidentally.

```
m_AccessLevel = CType(integer_value, AccessLevel)
```

Another benefit of enumerated types is that they allow Visual Basic to provide IntelliSense help. If you type m_AccessLevel =, Visual Basic provides a list of the allowed AccessLevel values.

A final benefit of enumerated types is that they provide a ToString method that returns the textual name of the value. For example, the following code displays the message "Clerk":

```
Dim access_level As AccessLevel = Clerk
MessageBox.Show(access_level.ToString())
```

Example program AccessLevelEnum, which is available for download on the book's web site, makes an AccessLevel Enum and then displays the results returned by calling ToString for each of its values.

If you have a value that can take only a fixed number of values, you should probably make it an enumerated type. Also, if you discover that you have defined a series of constants to represent related values, you should consider converting them into an enumerated type. Then you can gain the benefits of the improved Visual Basic type checking and IntelliSense.

ANONYMOUS TYPES

An *anonymous type* is an object data type that is built automatically by Visual Basic and never given a name for the program to use. The type is used implicitly by the code that needs it and is then discarded.

The following code uses LINQ to select data from an array of BookInfo objects named m_BookInfo. It begins by using a LINQ query to fill variable book_query with the selected books. It then iterates through the results stored in book_query, adding information about the selected books to a string. It finishes by displaying the string in a text box.

```
Dim book_query =
    From book In m_BookInfo
    Where book.Year > 1999
    Select book.Title, book.Pages, book.Year
    Order By Year

Dim txt As String = ""
For Each book In book_query
    txt &= book.Title & " (" & book.Year & ", " &
        book.Pages & " pages)" & ControlChars.CrLf
Next book
txtResult.Text = txt
```

The book_query variable is an ordered sequence containing objects that hold the data selected by the query: Title, Pages, and Year. This type of object doesn't have an explicit definition; it is an anonymous type created by Visual Basic to hold the selected values Title, Pages, and Year. If you hover the mouse over the book_query variable in the code editor, a tooltip appears giving the variable's data type as:

```
System.Linq.IOrderedSequence(Of <anonymous type>)
```

Later, the code uses a For Each loop to enumerate the objects in book_query. The looping variable book must have the same type as the items in the sequence. The code does not explicitly give the variable's data type, so Visual Basic can infer it. If you hover the mouse over the book variable in the code editor, a tooltip appears giving the variable's data type as:

```
<anonymous type>
```

You are not really intended to use anonymous types explicitly. For example, you shouldn't need to declare a new object of the anonymous type. They are intended to support LINQ. Although you won't use anonymous types explicitly, it's still helpful to understand what they are.

> **IMPORTANT INFERENCE**
>
> In this example, Visual Basic infers the data types for the `book_query` and `book` variables. This is important because they must use an anonymous type, so you cannot explicitly give them a type. Because these data types are inferred, the code will only work if Option Infer is on.

For more information on LINQ, see Chapter 21.

NULLABLE TYPES

Most relational databases have a concept of a null data value. A null value indicates that a field does not contain any data. It lets the database distinguish between valid zero or blank values and non-existing values. For example, a null value in a text field means there is no data in the field and a blank value means the field contains a value that happens to be blank.

You can create a nullable variable in Visual Basic by adding a question mark either to the variable's name or after its data type. You can also declare the variable to be of type Nullable(Of *type*). For example, the following code declares three nullable integers:

```
Dim i As Integer?
Dim j? As Integer
Dim k As Nullable(Of Integer)
```

To make a nullable variable "null," set it equal to Nothing. The following code makes variable `num_choices` null:

```
num_choices = Nothing
```

To see if a nullable variable contains a value, use the Is operator to compare it to Nothing. The following code determines whether the nullable variable `num_choices` contains a value. If the variable contains a value, the code increments it. Otherwise the code sets the value to 1.

```
If num_choices IsNot Nothing Then
    num_choices += 1
Else
    num_choices = 1
End If
```

Calculations with nullable variables use "null-propagation" rules to ensure that the result makes sense. For example, if a nullable integer contains no value, it probably doesn't make sense to add another number to it. (What is null plus three?)

If one or more operands in an expression contains a null value, the result is a null value. For example, if `num_choices` in the previous example contains a null value, then `num_choices + 1` is also a null value. (That's why the previous code checks explicitly to see whether `num_choices` is null before incrementing its value.)

Example program NullableTypes, which is available for download on the book's web site, demonstrates nullable types.

CONSTANTS

In many respects, a constant is a lot like a read-only variable. Both variable and constant declarations may have attributes, accessibility keywords, and initialization expressions. Both read-only variables and constants represent a value that the code cannot change after it is assigned.

The syntax for declaring a constant is as follows:

```
[attribute_list] [accessibility] [Shadows] _
Const name [As type] = initialization_expression
```

For the general meanings of the various parts of a constant declaration, see the section "Variable Declarations" earlier in this chapter. The following sections describe differences between read-only variable and constant declarations.

Accessibility

When you declare a variable, you can omit the Dim keyword if you use any of the keywords Public, Protected, Friend, Protected Friend, Private, Static, or ReadOnly. You cannot omit the Const keyword when you declare a constant, because it tells Visual Basic that you are declaring a constant rather than a variable.

You cannot use the Static, ReadOnly, or Shared keywords in a constant declaration. Static implies that the value will change over time, and the value should be retained when the enclosing routine starts and stops. Because the code cannot change a constant's value, that doesn't make sense.

The ReadOnly keyword would be redundant because you already cannot change a constant's value.

You use the Shared keyword in a variable declaration within a class to indicate that the variable's value is shared by all instances of the class. If one object changes the value, all objects see the changed value. Because the program cannot change a constant's value, the value need not be shared. All objects have the same version of the constant at all times. You can think of a constant as always shared.

You can use the other accessibility keywords in a constant declaration: Public, Protected, Friend, Protected Friend, and Private.

As Type

If you have Option Strict turned on, you must include the constant's data type. A constant can only be an intrinsic type (Boolean, Byte, Short, Integer, Long, Decimal, Single, Double, Char, String, Date, or Object) or the name of an enumerated type. You cannot declare a constant that is a class, structure, or array.

If you declare the constant with the Object data type, the *initialization_expression* must set the object equal to Nothing. If you want a constant that represents some other object, or a class, structure, or array, use a read-only variable instead.

Because the generic Object class doesn't raise any events, and because you cannot make a constant of some other class type, it doesn't make sense to use the WithEvents keyword in a constant declaration.

> **INFER REQUIRED**
>
> Though Visual Basic has inferred types for local variables, it does not infer types of constants. If you have Option Strict on, you must explicitly give all constants a data type.

Initialization_Expression

The *initialization_expression* assigns the constant its never-changing value. You cannot use variables in the *initialization_expression*, but you can use conversion functions such as CInt. You can also use the values of previously defined constants and enumeration values. The expression can include type characters such as # or &H, and if the declaration doesn't include a type statement (and Option Explicit is off), the type of the value determines the type of the constant.

The following code demonstrates these capabilities. The first statement uses the CInt function to convert the value 123.45 into an integer constant. The second and third statements set the values of two Long constants to hexadecimal values. The next statement combines the values defined in the previous two using a bitwise Or. The final statement sets a constant to a value defined by the enumerated type AccessLevel.

```
Private Const MAX_VALUES As Integer = CInt(123.45)
Private Const MASK_READ As Long = &H1000&
Private Const MASK_WRITE As Long = &H2000&
Private Const MASK_READ_WRITE As Long = MASK_READ Or MASK_WRITE
Private Const MAX_ACCESS_LEVEL As AccessLevel = AccessLevel.SuperUser
```

DELEGATES

A *delegate* is an object that refers to a subroutine, function, or other method. The method can be an instance method provided by an object, a class's shared method, or a method defined in a code module. A delegate variable acts as a pointer to a subroutine or function. Delegate variables are sometimes called *type-safe function pointers*.

The Delegate keyword defines a delegate class and specifies the parameters and return type of the method to which the delegate will refer.

The following code uses a Delegate statement to declare the `StringDisplayerType` to be a delegate to a subroutine that takes a string as a parameter. Next, the code declares the variable `m_DisplayStringRoutine` to be of this type. This variable can hold a reference to a subroutine that takes a string parameter. The code then sets the variable equal to the `ShowStringInOutputWindow` subroutine. Finally, the code invokes the delegate's subroutine, passing it a string.

```
' Define a StringDisplayerType delegate to be a pointer to a subroutine
' that has a string parameter.
Private Delegate Sub StringDisplayerType(ByVal str As String)

' Declare a StringDisplayerType variable.
Dim m_DisplayStringRoutine As StringDisplayerType

' Assign the variable to a subroutine.
m_DisplayStringRoutine = AddressOf ShowStringInOutputWindow

' Invoke the delegate's subroutine.
m_DisplayStringRoutine("Hello world")
```

The delegate in the preceding example holds a reference to a subroutine defined in a code module. A delegate can also hold the address of a class's shared method or an instance method. For example, suppose the Employee class defines the shared function GetNumEmployees that returns the number of employees loaded. Suppose that it also defines the instance function ToString that returns an Employee object's first and last names.

Example program UseDelegates, which is available for download on the book's web site, uses the following code to demonstrate delegates for both of these functions:

```
Dim emp As New Employee("Rod", "Stephens")

' Use a delegate pointing to a shared class method.
Private Delegate Function NumEmployeesDelegate() As Integer

Private Sub btnShared_Click() Handles btnShared.Click
    Dim show_num As NumEmployeesDelegate
    show_num = AddressOf Employee.GetNumEmployees
    MessageBox.Show(show_num().ToString, "# Employees")
End Sub

' Use a delegate pointing to a class instance method.
Private Delegate Function GetNameDelegate() As String
Private Sub btnInstance_Click() Handles btnInstance.Click
    Dim show_name As GetNameDelegate
    show_name = AddressOf emp.ToString
    MessageBox.Show(show_name(), "Name")
End Sub
```

code snippet UseDelegates

First, it declares and initializes an Employee object named `emp`. It then defines a delegate named `NumEmployeesDelegate`, which is a pointer to a function that returns an integer. The `btnShared_Click` event handler declares a variable of this type, sets it to the address of the Employee class's shared `GetNumEmployees` function, and calls the function. Then the code defines a delegate named `GetNameDelegate`, which is a pointer to a function that returns a string. The `btnInstance_Click` event handler declares a variable of this type, sets it to the address of the `emp` object's ToString function, and then calls the function.

These examples are somewhat contrived because the code could easily invoke the subroutines and functions directly without delegates, but they show how a program can save a delegate pointing to a subroutine or function and then call it later. A real application might set the delegate variable's value and only use it much later.

A particular delegate variable could hold references to different methods, depending on the program's situation. For example, different subroutines might generate output on a form, on the printer, or into a bitmap file. The program could set a delegate variable to any of these routines. Later, the program could invoke the variable's routine without needing to know which routine will actually execute.

Another useful technique is to pass a delegate variable into a subroutine or function. For example, suppose that you are writing a subroutine that sorts an array of Customer objects. This routine could take as a parameter a delegate variable that references the function to use when comparing the objects in the array. By passing different functions into the routine, you could make it sort customers by company name, contact name, customer ID, total past sales, or anything else you can imagine.

Delegates are particularly confusing to many programmers, but understanding them is worth a little extra effort. They can add an extra dimension to your programming by essentially allowing you to manipulate subroutines and functions as if they were data.

NAMING CONVENTIONS

Many development teams adopt naming conventions to make their code more consistent and easier to read. Different groups have developed their own conventions, and you cannot really say that one of them is best. It doesn't really matter which convention you adopt. What is important is that you develop some coding style that you use consistently.

One rather simple convention is to use `lowercase_letters_with_underscores` for variables with routine scope, `MixedCaseLetters` for variables with module and global scope, and `ALL_CAPS` for constants of any scope. Use the prefixes `m_` and `g_` to differentiate between module and global scope, and an abbreviation to give an object's data type. For example, the following statement defines a module-scope PictureBox variable:

```
Private m_picCanvas As PictureBox
```

Routine names are generally `MixedCase`.

Many developers carry these rules a bit further and add type prefix abbreviations to all variables, not just objects. For example, this statement declares an integer variable:

```
Dim iNumEmployees As Integer
```

If you apply these rules strictly enough, you should never need to assign one variable to another variable's value, unless the two have the same type abbreviation. If you see a statement that mixes variable types, you should examine the code more closely to see if there is a real data type mismatch problem. For example, the following statement should make the developer suspicious because it's assigning an Integer value to a Long variable:

```
mlngNumEmployees = intNumAbsent + intNumPresent
```

Some developers extend the rules to cover all programming objects, including functions and subroutines. For example, a global function that returns a string might be named `gstrGetWebmasterName`.

Generally, this scope and type information is more important the farther you are from a variable's declaration. If you declare a variable inside a subroutine, a developer can usually remember the variable's data type. If there is any doubt, it's easy to scroll up and review the variable's declaration.

In contrast, if a variable is declared globally in an obscure code module that developers rarely need to read, a programmer may have trouble remembering the variable's scope and data type. In that case, using prefixes to help the developers' memory can be important.

No matter which convention you use, the most important piece of a name is the descriptive part. The name `mblnDL` tells you that the value is a module-scope Boolean, but it doesn't tell you what the value means (and variables with such terrible names are all too common). The name `mblnDataIsLoaded` is much more descriptive.

WHAT'S IN A NAME?

I have never seen a project that suffered because it lacked variable prefixes such as `mbln`. However, I have seen developers waste huge amounts of time because the descriptive parts of variable names were confusing. Take a few seconds to think of a good, meaningful name.

Building an all-encompassing naming convention that defines abbreviations for every conceivable type of data, control, object, database component, menu, constant, and routine name takes a lot of time and more space than it's worth in a book such as this. For an article that describes the conventions used by Microsoft Consulting Services, go to `support.microsoft.com/kb/110264`. It explains everything, including data type abbreviations, making the first part of a function name contain a verb (`GetUserName` rather than `UserName`), and commenting conventions.

Naming and coding conventions make it easier for other programmers to read your code. Look over the Microsoft Consulting Services conventions or search the Web for others. Select the features that you think make the most sense and ignore the others. It's more important that you write consistent code than that you follow a particular set of rules.

SUMMARY

Two of the most important things you control with a variable declaration are its data type and its visibility. Visibility combines scope (the piece of code that contains the variable such as a For loop, subroutine, or module), accessibility (the code that is allowed to access the variable determined by keywords such as Private, Public, and Friend), and lifetime (when the variable has been created and not yet destroyed).

To avoid confusion, explicitly declare the data type whenever possible and use the most limited scope possible for the variable's purpose. Turn Option Explicit and Option Strict on to allow the IDE to help you spot potential scope and type errors before they become a problem.

Code that uses LINQ complicates matters somewhat. When you use LINQ, it is generally not possible to declare explicitly every variable's data type. A LINQ query returns a sequence of objects that have an anonymous type. If you enumerate over the sequence, the looping variable will be of the same anonymous type. In those cases, when you cannot explicitly declare a variable's type, use extra caution to make the code easy to understand so you can fix and maintain it later. For more information on LINQ, see Chapter 21.

Parameters, property procedures, and constants have similar data types and scope issues. Once you become comfortable with variable declarations, they should give you little trouble.

One of the most important steps you can take to make your code easier to debug and maintain is to make your code consistent. A good naming convention can help. Review the guidelines used by Microsoft Consulting Services, and adopt the pieces that make the most sense to you.

When you know how to declare variables, you are ready to learn how to combine them. Chapter 16, "Operators," explains the symbols (such as +, 2, and ^) that you can use to combine variables to produce new results.

16

Operators

An *operator* is a basic code element that performs some operation on one or more values to create a result. The values the operator acts upon are called *operands*. For example, in the following statement, the operator is + (addition), the operands are B and C, and the result is assigned to the variable A:

```
A = B + C
```

The Visual Basic operators fall into five categories: arithmetic, concatenation, comparison, logical, and bitwise. This chapter first explains these categories and the operators they contain, and then discusses other operator issues such as precedence, assignment operators, and operator overloading. Also included are discussions of some specialized issues that arise when you work with strings and dates.

ARITHMETIC OPERATORS

The following table lists the arithmetic operators provided by Visual Basic. Most programmers should be very familiar with most of them. The four operators that may need a little extra explanation are \, Mod, <<, and >>.

OPERATOR	PURPOSE	EXAMPLE	RESULT
^	Exponentiation	2 ^ 3	(2 to the power 3) = 2 * 2 * 2 = 8
–	Negation	-2	-2
*	Multiplication	2 * 3	6
/	Division	3 / 2	1.5

continues

(continued)

OPERATOR	PURPOSE	EXAMPLE	RESULT
\	Integer division	17 \ 5	3
Mod	Modulus	17 Mod 5	2
+	Addition	2 + 3	5
2	Subtraction	3 - 2	1
<<	Bit left shift	10110111 << 1	01101110
>>	Bit right shift	10110111 >> 1	01011011

The \ operator performs integer division. It returns the result of dividing its first operand by the second, dropping any remainder. It's important to understand that the result is truncated toward zero, not rounded. For example, 7 \ 4 = 1 and –7 \ 4 = –1 rather than 2 and –2 as you might expect.

The Mod operator returns the remainder after dividing its first operand by its second. For example, 17 Mod 5 = 2 because 17 = 3 * 5 + 2.

The << operator shifts the bits of an Integer value to the left, padding the empty bits on the right with zeros. For example, the byte value with bits 10110111 shifted 1 bit to the left gives 01101110. Shifting 10110111 2 bits to the left gives 11011100.

The >> operator shifts the bits of a value to the right, padding the empty bits on the left with zeros. For example, the byte value with bits 10110111 shifted 1 bit to the right gives 01011011. Shifting 10110111 2 bits to the right gives 00101101.

Unfortunately, Visual Basic doesn't work easily with bit values, so you cannot use a binary value such as 10110111 in your code. Instead, you must write this value as the hexadecimal value &HB7 or the decimal value 183. The last two entries in the table show the values in binary, so it is easier to understand how the shifts work.

CALCULATOR CLEVERNESS

The Calculator application that comes with Windows lets you easily convert between binary, octal, hexadecimal, and decimal. To start the Calculator, open the Start menu and select Run. Type calc and click OK. Open the View menu and select Scientific. Now you can click the Bin, Oct, Dec, or Hex radio buttons to select a base, enter a value, and select another base to convert the value.

CONCATENATION OPERATORS

Visual Basic provides two concatenation operators: + and &. Both join two strings together. Because the + symbol also represents an arithmetic operator, your code will be easier to read if you use the & symbol for concatenation. Using & can also make your code faster and lead to fewer problems because it lets Visual Basic know that the operands are strings.

COMPARISON OPERATORS

Comparison operators compare one value to another and return a Boolean value (True or False), depending on the result. The following table lists the comparison operators provided by Visual Basic. The first six (=, <>, <, <=, >, and >=) are relatively straightforward. Note that the Not operator is not a comparison operator, so it is not listed here. It is described in the next section, "Logical Operators."

OPERATOR	PURPOSE	EXAMPLE	RESULT
=	Equals	A = B	True if A equals B
<>	Not equals	A <> B	True if A does not equal B
<	Less than	A < B	True if A is less than B
<=	Less than or equal to	A <= B	True if A is less than or equal to B
>	Greater than	A > B	True if A is greater than B
>=	Greater than or equal to	A >= B	True if A is greater than or equal to B
Is	Equality of two objects	emp Is mgr	True if emp and mgr refer to the same object
IsNot	Inequality of two objects	emp IsNot mgr	True if emp and mgr refer to different objects
TypeOf ... Is	Object is of a certain type	TypeOf(obj) Is Manager	True if obj points to a Manager object
Like	Matches a text pattern	A Like "###-####"	True if A contains three digits, a dash, and four digits

The Is operator returns True if its two operands refer to the same object. For example, if you create an Order object and make two different variables, A and B, point to it, the expression A Is B is True. Note that Is returns False if the two operands point to different Order objects that happen to have the same property values.

The IsNot operator is simply shorthand for a more awkward Not . . . Is construction. For example, the statement A IsNot Nothing is equivalent to Not (A Is Nothing).

The value *Nothing* is a special value that means *not an object*. If you have an object variable, you can use the Is or IsNot operator to compare it to Nothing to see if it represents anything. Note that you cannot use Is or IsNot to compare an object variable to 0 or some other numeric value. Is and IsNot only work with objects such as those stored in variables and the special value Nothing.

The TypeOf operator returns True if its operand is of a certain type. This operator is particularly useful when a subroutine takes a parameter that could be of more than one object type. It can use TypeOf to see which type of object it has.

The Like operator returns True if its first operand matches a pattern specified by its second operand. Where the pattern includes normal characters, the string must match those characters exactly. The pattern can also include several special character sequences summarized in the following table.

CHARACTER(S)	MEANING
?	Matches any single character
*	Matches any zero or more characters
#	Matches any single digit
[characters]	Matches any of the characters between the brackets
[!characters]	Matches any character not between the brackets
A-Z	When inside brackets, matches any character in the range A to Z

You can combine ranges of characters and individual characters inside brackets. For example, the pattern [a-zA-Z] matches any letter between a and z or between A and Z. The following table lists some useful patterns for use with the Like operator.

PATTERN	MEANING
[2-9]##-####	Seven-digit U.S. phone number
[2-9]##-[2-9]##-####	Ten-digit phone number, including area code
1-[2-9]##-[2-9]##-####	Eleven-digit phone number, beginning with 1 and area code
#####	Five-digit ZIP code
#####-####	Nine-digit ZIP + 4 code
?*@?*.?*	E-mail address

For example, the following code checks whether the text box txtPhone contains something that looks like a 10-digit phone number:

```
If Not (txtPhone.Text Like "[2-9]##-[2-9]##-####") Then
    MessageBox.Show("Please enter a valid pohone number")
End If
```

These patterns are not completely foolproof. For example, the e-mail address pattern verifies that the string contains at least one character, an @ character, at least one other character, a dot, and at least one more character. For example, it allows RodStephens@vb-helper.com. However, it does not verify that the extension makes sense, so it also allows `RodStephens@vb-helper.commercial`, and it allows more than one @ character, as in `RodStephens@vb-helper.com@bad_value`.

Regular expressions provide much more powerful pattern-matching capabilities. The section "Regular Expressions" in Chapter 40, "Useful Namespaces," contains more information about regular expressions.

LOGICAL OPERATORS

Logical operators combine two Boolean values and return True or False, depending on the result. The following table summarizes Visual Basic's logical operators.

OPERATOR	PURPOSE	EXAMPLE	RESULT
Not	Logical or bitwise negation	Not A	True if A is false
And	Logical or bitwise And	A And B	True if A and B are both true
Or	Logical or bitwise Or	A Or B	True if A or B or both are true
Xor	Logical or bitwise exclusive Or	A Xor B	True if A or B but not both is true
AndAlso	Logical or bitwise And with short-circuit evaluation	A AndAlso B	True if A and B are both true (see the following notes)
OrElse	Logical or bitwise Or with short-circuit evaluation	A OrElse B	True if A or B or both are true (see notes)

The operators Not, And, and Or are relatively straightforward.

"Xor" stands for "exclusive or," and the Xor operator returns True if one but not both of its operands is true. The expression A Xor B is true if A is true or B is true but both are not true.

Xor is useful for situations where exactly one of two things should be true. For example, suppose you're running a small software conference with two tracks so two talks are going on at any given time. Each attendee should sign up for one talk in each time slot but cannot sign up for both because they're at the same time. Then you might use code similar to the following to check whether an attendee has signed up for either talk 1a or talk 1b but not both.

```
If talk1a Xor talk1b Then
    ' This is okay
    ...
End If
```

The AndAlso and OrElse operators are similar to the And and Or operators, except that they provide short-circuit evaluation. In *short-circuit evaluation*, Visual Basic is allowed to stop evaluating operands if it can deduce the final result without them. For example, consider the expression A AndAlso B. If Visual Basic evaluates the value A and discovers that it is false, the program knows that the expression A AndAlso B is also false no matter what value B has, so it doesn't need to evaluate B.

Whether the program evaluates both operands doesn't matter much if A and B are simple Boolean variables. However, assume that they are time-consuming functions in the following code. For example, the TimeConsumingFunction function might need to look up values in a database or download data from a web site. In that case, not evaluating the second operand might save a lot of time.

```
If TimeConsumingFunction("A") AndAlso TimeConsumingFunction("B") Then ...
```

Just as AndAlso can stop evaluation if it discovers one of its operands is False, the OrElse operand can stop evaluating if it discovers that one of its operands is True. The expression A OrElse B is True if either A or B is True. If the program finds that A is True, it doesn't need to evaluate B.

Because AndAlso and OrElse do the same thing as And and Or but sometimes faster, you might wonder why you would ever use And and Or. The main reason is that the operands may have side effects. A *side effect* is some action a routine performs that is not obviously part of the routine. For example, suppose that the NumEmployees function opens an employee database and returns the number of employee records, leaving the database open. The fact that this function leaves the database open is a side effect.

Now, suppose that the NumCustomers function similarly opens the customer database, and then consider the following statement:

```
If (NumEmployees() > 0) AndAlso (NumCustomers() > 0) Then ...
```

After this code executes, you cannot be certain which databases are open. If NumEmployees returns 0, the AndAlso operator's first operand is False, so it doesn't evaluate the NumCustomers function and that function doesn't open the customer database.

The AndAlso and OrElse operators can improve application performance under some circumstances. However, to avoid possible confusion and long debugging sessions, do not use AndAlso or OrElse with operands that have side effects.

BITWISE OPERATORS

Bitwise operators work much like logical operators do, except they compare values one bit at a time. The bitwise negation operator Not flips the bits in its operand from 1 to 0 and vice versa. The following shows an example:

```
          10110111
      Not 01001000
```

The And operator places a 1 in a result bit if both of the operands have a 1 in that position. The following shows the results of combining two binary values by using the bitwise And operator:

```
          10101010
      And 00110110
          00100010
```

The bitwise Or operator places a 1 bit in the result if either of its operands has a 1 in the corresponding position. The following shows an example:

```
          10101010
      Or  00110110
          10111110
```

The bitwise Xor operator places a 1 bit in the result if exactly one of its operands, but not both, has a 1 in the corresponding position. The following shows an example:

```
          10101010
      Xor 00110110
          10011100
```

There are no bitwise equivalents for the AndAlso and OrElse operators.

OPERATOR PRECEDENCE

When Visual Basic evaluates a complex expression, it must decide the order in which to evaluate operators. For example, consider the expression 1 + 2 * 3 / 4 + 2. The following text shows three orders in which you might evaluate this expression to get three different results:

```
1 + (2 * 3) / (4 + 2) = 1 + 6 / 6 = 2
1 + (2 * 3 / 4) + 2 = 1 + 1.5 + 2 = 4.5
(1 + 2) * 3 / (4 + 2) = 3 * 3 / 6 = 1.5
```

Precedence determines which operator Visual Basic executes first. For example, the Visual Basic precedence rules say the program should evaluate multiplication and division before addition, so the second equation is correct.

The following table lists the operators in order of precedence. When evaluating an expression, the program evaluates an operator before it evaluates those lower than it in the list.

OPERATOR	DESCRIPTION
( )	Grouping (parentheses)
^	Exponentiation
-	Negation
*, /	Multiplication and division
\	Integer division
Mod	Modulus
+, -, +	Addition, subtraction, and concatenation
&	Concatenation
<<, >>	Bit shift
=, <>, <, <=, >, >=, Like, Is, IsNot, TypeOf ... Is	All comparisons
Not	Logical and bitwise negation
And, AndAlso	Logical and bitwise And with and without short-circuit evaluation
Xor, Or, OrElse	Logical and bitwise Xor, and Or with and without short-circuit evaluation

When operators are on the same line in the table, or if an expression contains more than one instance of the same operator, the program evaluates them in left-to-right order. For example, * and / are on the same line in the table so in the expression 12 * 4 / 20 Visual Basic would perform the multiplication first. (Of course, it wouldn't matter much in this example because the result should be the same either way, at least within the limits of the computer's precision.)

Parentheses are not really operators, but they do have a higher precedence than the true operators, so they're listed to make the table complete. You can always use parentheses to explicitly dictate the order in which Visual Basic will perform an evaluation.

If there's the slightest doubt about how Visual Basic will handle an expression, add parentheses to make it obvious. Even if you can easily figure out what an expression means, parentheses often make the code even easier to read and understand. There's no extra charge for using parentheses, and they may avoid some unnecessary confusion.

ASSIGNMENT OPERATORS

Visual Basic has always had the simple assignment operator =. Visual Basic .NET added several new assignment operators to handle some common statements where a value was set equal to itself combined with some other value. For example, the following two statements both add the value 10 to the variable iterations:

```
iterations = iterations + 10 ' Original syntax.
iterations += 10 ' New syntax.
```

All the other assignment operators work similarly by adding an equals sign to an arithmetic operator. For example, the statement A ^= B is equivalent to A = A ^ B.

You can still use the original syntax if you like. However, the new syntax sometimes gives you better performance. If the left-hand side of the assignment is not a simple variable, Visual Basic may be able to save time by evaluating it only once. For example, the following code adds 0.1 to a customer order's discount value. By using +=, the code allows Visual Basic to find the location of this value only once.

```
Customers(cust_num).Orders(order_num).Discount += 0.1
```

PERFORMANCE ANXIETY

In most applications, performance is usually adequate whether you use += or the older syntax. Usually, you are best off if you use whichever version seems most natural and easiest to understand and only worry about performance when you are sure you have a problem.

The complete list of assignment operators is: =, ^=, *=, /=, \=, +=, -=, &=, <<=, and >>=.

If you have Option Strict set to On, the variables must have the appropriate data types. For example, /= returns a Double, so you cannot use that operator with an Integer, as in the following code:

```
Dim i As Integer = 100
i /= 2                      ' Not allowed.
```

To perform this operation, you must explicitly convert the result into an Integer, as shown in the following statement:

```
i = CInt(i / 2)
```

This makes sense because you are trying to assign the value of floating-point division to an Integer. It's less obvious why the following code is also illegal. Here the code is trying to assign an Integer result to a Single variable, so you might think it should work. After all, an Integer value will fit in a Single variable.

```
Dim x As Single
x \= 10                     ' Not allowed.
```

The problem isn't in the assignment, but in performing the calculation. The following statement is equivalent to the previous one, and it is also illegal:

```
x = x \ 10                  ' Not allowed.
```

The problem with both of these statements is that the \ operator takes as arguments two Integers. If Option Strict is on, the program will not automatically convert a floating-point variable into an Integer for the \ operator. To make this statement work, you must manually convert the variable into an Integer data type, as shown in the following example:

```
x = CLng(x) \ 10 ' Allowed.
```

The += and &= operators both combine strings but &= is less ambiguous, so you should use it whenever possible. It may also give you better performance because it explicitly tells Visual Basic that the operands are strings.

THE STRINGBUILDER CLASS

The & and &= operators are useful for concatenating a few strings together. However, if you must combine a large number of strings, you may get better performance using the StringBuilder class. This class is optimized for performing long sequences of concatenations to build big strings.

For small pieces of code, the difference between using a String and a StringBuilder is not noticeable. If you need only to concatenate a dozen or so strings once, using a StringBuilder won't make much difference in runtime and may even slow performance slightly.

However, if you make huge strings built up in pieces, or if you build simpler strings but many times in a loop, StringBuilder may make your program run faster.

Example program StringBuilderTest1, which is available for download on the book's web site, uses the following code to compare the speeds of building a long string with and without the StringBuilder class:

Available for download on Wrox.com

```
Private Sub btnGo_Click() Handles btnGo.Click
    Const ADD_STRING As String = "1234567890"
    Dim num_trials As Long = Long.Parse(txtNumTrials.Text)
    Dim start_time As DateTime
    Dim stop_time As DateTime
    Dim elapsed_time As TimeSpan
    Dim txt As String
    Dim string_builder As New StringBuilder

    lblString.Text = ""
    lblStringBuilder.Text = ""
    Application.DoEvents()

    txt = ""
    start_time = Now
    For i As Long = 1 To num_trials
        txt = txt & ADD_STRING
    Next i
    stop_time = Now
    elapsed_time = stop_time.Subtract(start_time)
    lblString.Text = elapsed_time.TotalSeconds.ToString("0.000000")
```

```
    txt = ""
    start_time = Now
    For i As Long = 1 To num_trials
        string_builder.Append(ADD_STRING)
    Next i
    txt = string_builder.ToString()
    stop_time = Now
    elapsed_time = stop_time.Subtract(start_time)
    lblStringBuilder.Text = elapsed_time.TotalSeconds.ToString("0.000000")
End Sub
```

code snippet StringBuilderTest1

The code concatenates the string `1234567890` a large number of times, first using a String variable and then using a StringBuilder. In one test that performed the concatenation 10,000 times to build strings 100,000 characters long, using a String took roughly 1.6 seconds. Using a StringBuilder, the program was able to build the string in roughly 0.001 seconds.

Admittedly, building such enormous strings is not a common programming task. Even when the strings are shorter, you can sometimes see a noticeable difference in performance, particularly if you must build a large number of such strings.

Example program StringBuilderTest2, which is also available for download, uses the following code to concatenate the string `1234567890` to itself 100 times, making a string 1,000 characters long. It builds the string repeatedly for a certain number of trials. In one test building the 1,000-character string 10,000 times, using a String took around 0.95 seconds, whereas using a StringBuilder took about 0.06 seconds.

```
Private Sub btnGo_Click() Handles btnGo.Click
    Const ADD_STRING As String = "1234567890"
    Dim num_trials As Long = Long.Parse(txtNumTrials.Text)
    Dim start_time As DateTime
    Dim stop_time As DateTime
    Dim elapsed_time As TimeSpan
    Dim txt As String
    Dim string_builder As New StringBuilder

    lblString.Text = ""
    lblStringBuilder.Text = ""
    Application.DoEvents()

    start_time = Now
    For i As Long = 1 To num_trials
        txt = ""
        For j As Long = 1 To 100
            txt = txt & ADD_STRING
        Next j
    Next i
    stop_time = Now
    elapsed_time = stop_time.Subtract(start_time)
    lblString.Text = elapsed_time.TotalSeconds.ToString("0.000000")
```

```
        txt = ""
        start_time = Now
        For i As Long = 1 To num_trials
            string_builder = New StringBuilder
            For j As Long = 1 To 100
                string_builder.Append(ADD_STRING)
            Next j
            txt = string_builder.ToString()
        Next i
        stop_time = Now
        elapsed_time = stop_time.Subtract(start_time)
        lblStringBuilder.Text = elapsed_time.TotalSeconds.ToString("0.000000")
    End Sub
```

code snippet StringBuilderTest2

Strings and string operations are a bit more intuitive than the StringBuilder class, so your code will usually be easier to read if you use String variables when performance isn't a big issue. If you are building enormous strings, or are building long strings a huge number of times, the performance edge given by the StringBuilder class may be worth slightly more complicated-looking code.

DATE AND TIMESPAN OPERATIONS

The Date data type is fundamentally different from other data types. When you perform an operation on most data types, you get a result that has the same data type or that is at least of some compatible data type. For example, if you subtract two Integer variables, the result is an Integer. If you divide two Integers using the / operator, the result is a Double. That's not another Integer, but it is a compatible numeric data type used because an Integer cannot always hold the result of a division.

If you subtract two Date variables, however, the result is not a Date. For example, what's August 7 minus July 20? It doesn't make sense to think of the result as a Date. Instead, Visual Basic defines the difference between two Dates as a TimeSpan. A TimeSpan measures the elapsed time between two Dates. In this example, August 7 minus July 20 is 18 days. (And yes, TimeSpans know all about leap years.)

The following equations define the arithmetic of Dates and TimeSpans:

➤ Date – Date = TimeSpan

➤ Date + TimeSpan = Date

➤ TimeSpan + TimeSpan = TimeSpan

➤ TimeSpan – TimeSpan = TimeSpan

The TimeSpan class also defines unary negation (`ts2 = -ts1`), but other operations (such as multiplying a TimeSpan by a number) are not defined. However, in some cases, you can still perform the calculation if you must.

Example program MultiplyTimeSpan, which is available for download on the book's web site, uses the following statement to make the TimeSpan `ts2` equal to 12 times the duration of TimeSpan `ts1`:

```
ts2 = New TimeSpan(ts1.Ticks * 12)
```

Starting with Visual Basic 2005, the +, –, <, >, <=, >=, <>, and = operators are defined for Dates and TimeSpans. Previous versions did not define these operators, but the Date class did provide equivalent operator methods. For example, the Date class's op_Subtraction method subtracts two Dates and returns a TimeSpan.

These operator methods are still available and you may want to use them if you find using the normal operator symbols less clear. The following table lists the Date operator methods. Note that the Common Language Runtime name for the Date data type is DateTime, so you need to look for DateTime in the online help for more information on these methods.

SYNTAX	MEANING
`result_date = Date.op_Addition(date1, timespan1)`	Returns `date1` plus `timespan1`
`result_boolean = Date.op_Equality(date1, date2)`	True if `date1>date2`
`result_boolean = Date.op_GreaterThan(date1, date2)`	True if `date1>date2`
`result_boolean = Date.op_GreaterThanOrEqual(date1, date2)`	True if `date1>= date2`
`result_boolean = Date.op_Inequality(date1, date2)`	True if `date1<>date2`
`result_boolean = Date.op_LessThan(date1, date2)`	True if `date1<date2`
`result_boolean = Date.op_LessThanOrEqual(date1, date2)`	True if `date1<= date2`
`result_timespan = Date.op_Subtraction(date1, date2)`	Returns the TimeSpan between `date1` and `date2`
`result = Date.Compare(date1, date2)`	Returns a value indicating whether `date1` is greater than, less than, or equal to `date2`

The Compare method is a bit different from the others, returning an Integer rather than a Boolean or Date. Its value is less than zero if date1 < date2, greater than zero if date1 > date2, and equal to zero if date1 = date2.

These are shared methods, so you do not need to use a specific instance of the Date data type to use them. For example, the following code displays the number of days between July 20 and August 7:

```
Dim date1 As Date = #7/20/04#
Dim date2 As Date = #8/7/04#
Dim elapsed_time As TimeSpan

    elapsed_time = Date.op_Subtraction(date2, date1)
    Debug.WriteLine(elapsed_time.Days)
```

These operators are a bit cumbersome. To make these kinds of calculations easier, the Date data type provides other methods for performing common operations that are a bit easier to read. Whereas the operator methods take both operands as parameters, these methods take a single operand as one parameter and use the current object as the other. For example, a Date object's Add method adds a TimeSpan to the date and returns the resulting date. The following table summarizes these methods.

SYNTAX	MEANING
`result_date = date1.Add(timespan1)`	Returns `date1` plus `timespan1`
`result_date = date1.AddYears(num_years)`	Returns the date plus the indicated number of years
`result_date = date1.AddMonths(num_months)`	Returns the date plus the indicated number of months
`result_date = date1.AddDays (num_days)`	Returns the date plus the indicated number of days
`result_date = date1.AddHours(num_hours)`	Returns the date plus the indicated number of hours
`result_date = date1.AddMinutes(num_minutes)`	Returns the date plus the indicated number of minutes
`result_date = date1.AddSeconds(num_seconds)`	Returns the date plus the indicated number of seconds
`result_date = date1.AddMilliseconds(num_milliseconds)`	Returns the date plus the indicated number of milliseconds
`result_date = date1.AddTicks (num_ticks)`	Returns the date plus the indicated number of ticks (100-nanosecond units)
`result_timespan = date1.Subtract (date2)`	Returns the time span between `date2` and `date1`
`result_integer = date1.CompareTo (date2)`	Returns a value indicating whether `date1` is greater than, less than, or equal to `date2`
`result_boolean = date1.Equals(date2)`	Returns `True` if `date1` equals `date2`

The CompareTo method returns a value less than zero if date1 < date2, greater than zero if date1 > date2, and equal to zero if date1 = date2.

OPERATOR OVERLOADING

Visual Basic defines operators for expressions that use standard data types such as Integers and Boolean values. It defines a few operators such as Is and IsNot for objects, but operators such as * and Mod don't make sense for objects in general.

Nevertheless, you can also define those operators for your structures and classes, if you like, by using the Operator statement. This is a more advanced topic, so if you're new to Visual Basic, you may want to skip this section and come back to it later, perhaps after you have read Chapter 26, "Classes and Structures."

The general syntax for operator overloading is:

```
[ <attributes> ] Public [ Overloads ] Shared [ Shadows ] _
[ Widening | Narrowing ] Operator symbol ( operands ) As type
    ...
End Operator
```

The parts of this declaration are:

➤ *attributes* — Attributes for the operator.

➤ Public — All operators must be Public Shared.

➤ Overloads — You can only use this if the operator takes two parameters that are from a base class and a derived class as its two operators. In that case, it means the operator overrides the operator defined in the base class.

➤ Shared — All operators must be Public Shared.

➤ Shadows — The operator replaces a similar operator defined in the base class.

➤ Widening — Indicates that the operator defines a widening conversion that always succeeds at runtime. For example, an Integer always fits in a Single, so storing an Integer in a Single is a widening operation. This operator must catch and handle all errors. The CType operator must include either the Widening or Narrowing keyword.

➤ Narrowing — Indicates that the operator defines a narrowing conversion that may fail at runtime. For example, a Single does not necessarily fit in an Integer, so storing a Single in an Integer is a narrowing operation. The CType operator must include either the Widening or Narrowing keyword.

➤ *symbol* — The operator's symbol. This can be +, − , *, /, \, ^, &, <<, >>, =, <>, <, >, <=, >=, Mod, Not, And, Or, Xor, Like, IsTrue, IsFalse, or CType.

➤ *operands* — Declarations of the objects to be manipulated by the operator. The unary operators +, − , Not, IsTrue, and IsFalse take a single operand. The binary operators +, − , *, /, \, ^, &, <<, >>, =, <>, <, >, <=, >=, Mod, And, Or, Xor, Like, and CType take two operands.

➤ *type* — All operators must have a return type and must return a value by using a Return statement.

Operator overloading is subject to several constraints:

➤ Some operands come in pairs, and if you define one you must define the other. The pairs are = and <>, < and >, <= and >=, and IsTrue and IsFalse.

➤ For the standard unary or binary operators, the class or structure that defines the operator must appear in an operand. For the CType conversion operator, the class or structure must appear in the operand or return type.

➤ The IsTrue and IsFalse operators must return Boolean values.

➤ The second operands for the << and >> operators must be Integers.

If you define an operator, Visual Basic automatically provides the corresponding assignment operator. For example, if you define the + operator, Visual Basic provides the += assignment operator.

Though you cannot use the IsTrue and IsFalse operators directly, you can use them indirectly. If you define IsTrue for a class, Visual Basic uses it to determine whether an object should be treated as True in a Boolean expression. For example, the following statement uses the IsTrue operator to decide whether the object c1 should be considered True:

```
if c1 Then ...
```

If you define the And and IsFalse operators, Visual Basic uses them to handle the AndAlso operator as well. For this to work, the And operator must return the same type of class or structure where you define it. For example, suppose you have defined And and IsFalse for the Composite class and suppose variables c1, c2, and c3 are all instances of this class. Then consider the following statement:

```
c3 = c1 AndAlso c2
```

Visual Basic uses IsFalse to evaluate c1. If IsFalse returns True, the program doesn't bother to evaluate c2. Instead it assumes the whole statement is False and returns a False value. Because IsFalse returned True for c1, Visual Basic knows that c1 is a False value, so it sets c3 equal to c1.

This is pretty confusing. It may make more sense if you think about how Visual Basic evaluates Boolean expressions that use the normal AndAlso operator.

Similarly, if you define the Or and IsTrue operators, Visual Basic automatically provides the OrElse operator.

Although you generally cannot make two versions of a function in Visual Basic that differ only in their return types, you can do that for CType conversion operators. When the program tries to make a conversion, Visual Basic can tell by the type of the result which conversion operator to use.

Example program ComplexNumbers, which is available for download on the book's web site, uses the following code to define a Complex class that represents a complex number. It defines +, -, and * operators to implement normal addition, subtraction, and multiplication on complex numbers. It also defines =, <>, and unary negation operators, and a conversion operator that converts a Complex object into a Double by returning its magnitude.

```
Public Class Complex
    Public Re As Double
    Public Im As Double

    ' Constructors.
    Public Sub New()
    End Sub
    Public Sub New(ByVal real_part As Double, ByVal imaginary_part As Double)
        Re = real_part
        Im = imaginary_part
    End Sub

    ' ToString.
    Public Overrides Function ToString() As String
        Dim txt As String = Re.ToString
        If Im < 0 Then
            txt &= " - " & Math.Abs(Im).ToString
        Else
            txt &= " + " & Im.ToString
        End If
        Return txt & "i"
    End Function

    ' Operators.
    Public Shared Operator *(ByVal c1 As Complex, ByVal c2 As Complex) _
     As Complex
        Return New Complex(
            c1.Re * c2.Re - c1.Im * c2.Im,
            c1.Re * c2.Im + c1.Im * c2.Re)
    End Operator
    Public Shared Operator +(ByVal c1 As Complex, ByVal c2 As Complex) _
     As Complex
        Return New Complex(
            c1.Re + c2.Re,
            c1.Im + c2.Im)
    End Operator
    Public Shared Operator -(ByVal c1 As Complex, ByVal c2 As Complex) _
     As Complex
        Return New Complex(
            c1.Re - c2.Re,
            c1.Im - c2.Im)
    End Operator
    Public Shared Operator =(ByVal c1 As Complex, ByVal c2 As Complex) _
```

```
      As Boolean
          Return (c1.Re = c2.Re) AndAlso (c1.Im = c2.Im)
      End Operator
      Public Shared Operator <>(ByVal c1 As Complex, ByVal c2 As Complex) _
       As Boolean
          Return (c1.Re <> c2.Re) OrElse (c1.Im <> c2.Im)
      End Operator
      Public Shared Operator -(ByVal c1 As Complex) As Complex
          Return New Complex(-c1.Re, -c1.Im)
      End Operator
      Public Shared Narrowing Operator CType(ByVal c1 As Complex) As Double
          Return System.Math.Sqrt(c1.Re * c1.Re + c1.Im * c1.Im)
      End Operator
  End Class
```

code snippet ComplexNumbers

It is easy to get carried away with operator overloading. Just because you can define an operator for a class doesn't mean you should. For example, you might be able to concoct some meaning for addition with the Employee class, but it would probably be a counterintuitive operation. You would probably be better off writing a subroutine or function with a meaningful name instead of using an ambiguous operator such as + or >>.

OPERATORS WITH NULLABLE TYPES

Chapter 15, "Data Types, Variables, and Constants," describes nullable types. A variable declared as nullable can distinguish between holding zero, blank, and other "trivial" values and holding no data at all. For example, if you declare the variable x as a nullable Integer, you can set it to the special value Nothing to indicate that it doesn't contain any data.

If all of the operands in an expression contain actual values rather than Nothing, then arithmetic, comparison, logical, or bitwise operations return the values you would expect. If one or more nullable variables in an expression contains the special value Nothing, Visual Basic uses special "null-propagation" rules for evaluating the expression.

If one or more of the operands in an arithmetic, comparison, logical, or bitwise operation is Nothing, the result is also Nothing. For example, if x and y are nullable and x contains no value, the following expressions, and just about any other expression containing x, have the value Nothing.

```
-x
x + y
x * y
x ^ y
x >> y
```

For more information about nullable types, see Chapter 15.

SUMMARY

A program uses operators to manipulate variables, constants, and literal values to produce new results. The Visual Basic operators fall into five categories: arithmetic, concatenation, comparison, logical, and bitwise. In most cases, using operators is straightforward and intuitive.

Operator precedence determines the order in which Visual Basic applies operators when evaluating an expression. In cases where an expression's operator precedence is unclear, add parentheses to make the order obvious. Even if you don't change the way that Visual Basic handles the statement, you can make the code more understandable and avoid possibly time-consuming bugs.

The String data type has its own special needs. String manipulation plays a big role in many applications, so Visual Basic provides a StringBuilder class for manipulating strings more efficiently. On the one hand, if your program only works with a few short strings, it probably doesn't need to use a StringBuilder, and using the String data type will probably make your code easier to understand. On the other hand, if your application builds enormous strings or concatenates a huge number of strings, you may be able to save a noticeable amount of time using the StringBuilder class.

The Date data type also behaves differently from other data types. The normal operators such as + and – have different meanings here from other data types. For example, a Date minus a Date gives a TimeSpan, not another Date. These operations generally make sense if you think carefully about what dates and time spans are.

Just as addition, subtraction, and the other operators have special meaning for Dates and TimeSpans, you can use operator overloading to define operators for your classes. Defining division or exponentiation may not make much sense for Employees, Customer, or Orders, but in some cases custom operators can make your code more readable. For example, you might imagine the following statement adding an OrderItem to a CustomerOrder:

```
the_order += new_item
```

This chapter explains how to use operators to combine variables to calculate new results. A typical program may perform the same set of calculations many times for different variable values. Although you might be able to perform those calculations in a long series, the resulting code would be cumbersome and hard to maintain. Chapter 17, "Subroutines and Functions," explains how you can use subroutines and functions to break a program into manageable pieces that you can then reuse to make performing the calculations easier and more uniform.

17

Subroutines and Functions

Subroutines and functions enable you to break an otherwise unwieldy chunk of code into manageable pieces. They allow you to extract code that you may need to use under more than one circumstance and place it in one location where you can call it as needed. This not only reduces repetition within your code; it also enables you to maintain and update the code in a single location.

A *subroutine* performs a task for the code that invokes it. A *function* performs a task and then returns some value. The value may be the result of a calculation, or a status code indicating whether the function succeeded or failed.

Together, subroutines and functions are sometimes called *routines* or *procedures*. They are also sometimes called *methods*, particularly when they are subroutines or functions belonging to a class. Subroutines are also occasionally called *sub procedures* or less formally *subs*.

This chapter describes subroutines and functions. It explains the syntax for declaring and using each in a Visual Basic application. It also provides some tips for making routines more maintainable.

SUBROUTINES

A Sub statement defines the subroutine's name. It declares the parameters that the subroutine takes as arguments and defines the parameters' data types. Code between the Sub statement and an End Sub statement determines what the subroutine does when it runs.

The syntax for defining a subroutine is as follows:

```
[attribute_list] [inheritance_mode] [accessibility] _
Sub subroutine_name([parameters]) [ Implements interface.subroutine ]
    [ statements ]
End Sub
```

The following sections describe the pieces of this declaration.

Attribute_List

The optional attribute list is a comma-separated list of attributes that apply to the subroutine. An attribute further refines the definition of a class, method, variable, or other item to give more information to the compiler and the runtime system.

DELIGHTFUL DECORATIONS

Applying an attribute to a class, variable, method, or other code entity is sometimes called *decorating* the entity.

Attributes are specialized and address issues that arise when you perform very specific programming tasks. For example, the Conditional attribute means the subroutine is conditional upon the definition of some compiler constant. Example program AttributeConditional uses the following code to demonstrate the Conditional attribute:

Available for download on Wrox.com

```
#Const DEBUG_LIST_CUSTOMERS = True
' #Const DEBUG_LIST_EMPLOYEES = True

Private Sub Form1_Load() Handles MyBase.Load
    ListCustomers()
    ListEmployees()

    txtResults.Select(0, 0)
End Sub

<Conditional("DEBUG_LIST_CUSTOMERS")>
Private Sub ListCustomers()
    txtResults.Text &= "ListCustomers" & vbCrLf
End Sub

<Conditional("DEBUG_LIST_EMPLOYEES")>
Private Sub ListEmployees()
    txtResults.Text &= "ListEmployees" & vbCrLf
End Sub
```

code snippet AttributeConditional

The code defines the compiler constant DEBUG_LIST_CUSTOMERS. The value DEBUG_LIST_EMPLOYEES is not defined because it is commented out.

This program's Form1_Load event handler calls subroutines ListCustomers and ListEmployees. ListCustomers is defined using the Conditional attribute with parameter DEBUG_LIST_CUSTOMERS. That tells the compiler to generate code for the routine only if DEBUG_LIST_CUSTOMERS is defined. Because that constant is defined, the compiler generates code for this subroutine.

Subroutine `ListEmployees` is defined using the Conditional attribute with parameter `DEBUG_LIST_EMPLOYEES`. Because that constant is not defined, the compiler does not generate code for this subroutine and, when `Form1_Load` calls it, the subroutine call is ignored.

The following text shows the output from this program:

```
ListCustomers
```

Visual Basic 2010 defines more than 400 attributes. Many have very specialized purposes that won't interest you most of the time, but some are pretty useful. For example, the Browsable attribute determines whether a property or event should be listed in the Properties window. It is fairly general and useful, so it's described shortly. In contrast, the System.EnterpriseServices.ApplicationQueuing attribute enables queuing for an assembly and allows it to read method calls from message queues. This attribute is only useful in very specialized circumstances, so it isn't described here.

Many attributes give metadata for editors and the IDE, so you will often see their effects only when you view an object in an editor or the IDE. If you are building a control or component, you can put one on a form and then see its properties in the Properties window. In that case, many kinds of attributes will be useful. If you're building an Employee class that's used only in code, fewer attributes are useful in any obvious way.

However, Visual Basic comes with a powerful PropertyGrid control that lets you display an object's properties on a form much as the Properties window displays them to a developer. That control honors all of the property-related attributes and gives them a whole new level of usefulness.

The following list describes some of the most useful attributes. Most of them are in the System .ComponentModel namespace. Check the online help to find the namespaces for the others and to learn about each attribute's parameters. Even these most useful attributes are fairly specialized and advanced so you may not immediately see their usefulness. If one of them doesn't make sense, skip it and scan the list again after you have more experience with such topics as building custom controls.

- ➤ `AttributeUsage` — You can build your own custom attributes by inheriting from the Attribute class. You can give your attribute class the AttributeUsage attribute to specify how your attribute can be used. You can determine whether an item can have multiple instances of your attribute, whether your attribute can be inherited by a derived class, and the kinds of things that can have your attribute (assembly, class, method, and so forth).

- ➤ `Browsable` — This indicates whether a property or event should be displayed in an editor such as the Properties window. If you pass the attribute's constructor the value False, the Properties window does not display the property.

- ➤ `Category` — This indicates the grouping that should hold the property or event in a visual designer such as the Properties window. For example, if the user clicks the Categorized button in the Properties window, the window groups the properties by category. This attribute tells which category should hold the property. Note that the category names are not magic. You can use any string you like and the Properties window will make a new category for you if necessary.

➤ `DefaultEvent` — This gives a class's default event name. If the class is a control or component and you double-click it in a form, the code editor opens to this event. For example, the default event for a Button is Click, so when you double-click a Button at design time, the code editor opens the control's Click event handler.

➤ `DefaultProperty` — This gives a class's default property name. Suppose that the Employee component has LastName set as its default property. Then suppose that you select the form and click the FormBorderStyle property in the Properties window. Now you click an Employee. Because Employee doesn't have a FormBorderStyle property, the Properties window displays its default property: LastName.

➤ `DefaultValue` — This gives a property a default value. If you right-click the property in the Properties window and select Reset, the property is reset to this value. Be sure to use a valid value. For example, don't set this to the string "unknown" if the property is an Integer.

➤ `Description` — This gives a description of the item. If a property has a Description and you select the property in the Properties window, the window displays the description text at the bottom.

Visual Basic carries this one step further and also allows you to use XML comments to provide a description of routines and their parameters for use by IntelliSense. For more information, see the section "XML Comments" in Chapter 14, "Program and Module Structure."

➤ `Localizable` — This determines whether a property should be localizable so you can easily store different versions of the property for different languages and locales. If this is True, localized values are automatically stored in the appropriate resource files for different locales and automatically loaded at startup based on the user's computer settings. If this is False (the default), all locales share the same property value.

To try this out, set the form's Localizable property to True and enter a value for the property. Then set the form's Language property to another language and give the localizable property a new value. Visual Basic automatically applies the right value for the user's locale when it runs the program.

➤ `MergableProperty` — This indicates whether or not the property can be merged with the same property provided by other components in the Properties window. If this is False and you select more than one instance of a control with the property, the Properties window does not display the property.

If this is True and you select more than one control with the property, the Properties window displays the value if the controls all have the same value. If you enter a new value, all of the controls are updated. This is the way the Text property works for TextBox, Label, and many other kinds of controls.

➤ `ParenthesizePropertyName` — This indicates whether editors such as the Properties window should display parentheses around the property's name. If the name has parentheses, the Properties window moves it to the top of the list when displaying properties alphabetically or to the top of its category when displaying properties by category.

➤ `ReadOnly` — This indicates whether designers should treat this property as read-only. For example, the Properties window displays the property grayed out and doesn't let the user change its value. This attribute is a little strange in practice because ReadOnly is a Visual Basic keyword. If you enter just the attribute name ReadOnly, Visual Basic gets confused. Either use the full name System.ComponentModel.ReadOnly or enclose the name in square brackets as in <[ReadOnly](True)>. . . .

➤ `RecommendedAsConfigurable` — This indicates that a property should be tied to the configuration file. When you select the object at design time and expand the "(Dynamic Properties)" item, the property is listed. If you click the ellipsis to the right, a dialog appears that lets you map the property to a key in the configuration file.

➤ `RefreshProperties` — This indicates how an editor should refresh the object's *other* properties if *this* property is changed. The value can be Default (do not refresh the other properties), Repaint (refresh all other properties), or All (re-query and refresh all properties).

➤ `Conditional` — This indicates that the method is callable if a compile-time constant such as DEBUG or MY_CONSTANT is defined. If the constant is not defined, code for the method is still generated and parameters in the method call are checked against the parameter types used by the method, but calls to the method are ignored at runtime. If the method has more than one Conditional attribute, the method is callable if any of the specified compile-time constants is defined.

Note that the constant must be defined in the main program, not in the component if you are building a component. Select the main program, open the Project menu, select the Properties item at the bottom, open the Configuration Properties folder, click Build, and in the Custom constants text box enter a value such as IS_DEFINED=True.

You can also use the compiler directive #If to exclude code completely from compilation. However, if you eliminate a method in this way, any calls to the routine will generate compile-time errors because the method doesn't exist. The Conditional attribute lets you hide a method while still allowing the code to contain calls to it.

➤ `DebuggerHidden` — This tells debuggers whether a method should be debuggable. If DebuggerHidden is True, the IDE skips over the method and will not stop at breakpoints inside it.

➤ `DebuggerStepThrough` — This tells debuggers whether to let the developer step through a method in the debugger. If DebuggerStepThrough is True, the IDE will not step through the method, although it will stop at any breakpoints inside it.

➤ `ToolboxBitmap` — This tells the IDE where to find a control or component's Toolbox bitmap. This can be a file, or it can be a type in an assembly that contains the bitmap and the bitmap's name in the assembly. It's awkward but essential if you're developing controls or components.

➤ `NonSerializedAttribute` — This indicates that a member of a serializable class should not be serialized. This is useful for excluding values that need not be serialized.

➤ `Obsolete` — This indicates that the item (class, method, property, or whatever) is obsolete. Optionally, you can specify the message that the code editor should display to the developer if code uses the item (for example, "Use the NewMethod instead"). You can also indicate whether the IDE should treat using this item as a warning or an error.

➤ `Serializable` — This indicates that a class is serializable. All public and private fields are serialized by default. Note that some routines require a class to be serializable even though you don't use the serialization yourself. Also note that attributes in the System.Xml .Serialization namespace can provide a lot of control over serializations.

➤ `ThreadStaticAttribute` — This indicates that a Shared class variable should not be shared across threads. Different threads get their own copies of the variable and all instances of the class within each thread share the thread's copy.

FINDING ATTRIBUTES

Finding the attributes that you need for a particular task can be tricky. It helps to realize that attribute classes inherit either directly or indirectly from the Attribute class. You can get information about the Attribute class at `msdn2.microsoft.com/ system.attribute.aspx`. You can see a list of classes that inherit from System .Attribute at `msdn2.microsoft.com/2e39z096.aspx`.

Inheritance_Mode

The *inheritance_mode* can be one of the values Overloads, Overrides, Overridable, NotOverridable, MustOverride, Shadows, or Shared. These values determine how a subroutine declared within a class inherits from the parent class or how it allows inheritance in derived classes. The following list explains the meanings of these keywords:

➤ `Overloads` — Indicates that the subroutine has the same name as another subroutine defined for this class. The parameter list must be different in the different versions so that Visual Basic can tell them apart (if they are the same, this works just like Overrides described next). If you are overloading a subroutine defined in a parent class, you must use this keyword. If you are overloading only subroutines in the same class, you can omit the keyword. If you use the keyword in any of the overloaded subroutines, however, you must include it for them all.

➤ `Overrides` — Indicates that this subroutine replaces a subroutine in the parent class that has the same name and parameters.

➤ `Overridable` — Indicates that a derived class can override this subroutine. This is the default for a subroutine that overrides another one.

➤ `NotOverridable` — Indicates that a derived class cannot override this subroutine. You can only use this with a subroutine that overrides another one.

➤ `MustOverride` — Indicates that any derived classes must override this subroutine. When you use this keyword, you omit all subroutine code and the End Sub statement, as in the following code:

```
MustOverride Sub Draw()
MustOverride Sub MoveMap(ByVal X As Integer, ByVal Y As Integer)
MustOverride Sub Delete()
...
```

If a class contains a subroutine declared MustOverride, you must declare the class using the MustInherit keyword. Otherwise, Visual Basic won't know what to do if you call this subroutine, because it contains no code.

MustOverride is handy for defining a subroutine that derived classes must implement, but for which a default implementation in the parent class doesn't make sense. For example, suppose that you make a Drawable class that represents a shape that can be drawn and that you will derive specific shape classes such as Rectangle, Ellipse, Line, and so forth. To let the program draw a generic shape, the Drawable class defines the Draw subroutine. Because Drawable doesn't have a particular shape, it cannot provide a default implementation of that subroutine. To require the derived classes to implement Draw, the Drawable class declares it MustOverride.

➤ `Shadows` — Indicates that this subroutine replaces an item (probably a subroutine) in the parent class that has the same name, but not necessarily the same parameters. If the parent class contains more than one overloaded version of the subroutine, this subroutine shadows them all. If the derived class defines more than one overloaded version of the subroutine, they must all be declared with the Shadows keyword.

➤ `Shared` — Indicates that this subroutine is associated with the class itself, rather than with a specific instance of the class. You can invoke it using the class's name (ClassName. SharedSub) or using a specific instance (class_instance.SharedSub). Because the subroutine is not associated with a specific class instance, it cannot use any properties or methods that are provided by a specific instance. The subroutine can only use other Shared properties and methods, as well as globally available variables.

Accessibility

A subroutine's *accessibility* clause can take one of these values: Public, Protected, Friend, Protected Friend, or Private. These values determine which pieces of code can invoke the subroutine. The following list explains these keywords:

➤ `Public` — Indicates that there are no restrictions on the subroutine. Code inside or outside of the subroutine's class or module can call it.

➤ `Protected` — Indicates that the subroutine is accessible only to code in the same class or in a derived class. You can only use the Protected keyword with subroutines declared inside a class.

➤ `Friend` — Indicates that the subroutine is available to all code inside or outside of the subroutine's module within the same project. The difference between this and Public is that Public allows code outside of the project to access the subroutine. This is generally only an issue for code libraries (DLLs) and control libraries. For example, suppose that you build a code library containing dozens of routines and then you write a program that uses the library. If the library declares a subroutine with the Public keyword, the code in the library and the code in the main program can use the subroutine. In contrast, if the library declares a subroutine with the Friend keyword, only the code in the library can access the subroutine, not the code in the main program.

➤ `Protected Friend` — Indicates that the subroutine has both Protected and Friend status. The subroutine is available only within the same project and within the same class or a derived class.

➤ `Private` — Indicates that the subroutine is available only within the class or module that contains it.

To reduce the amount of information that developers must remember, you should generally declare subroutines with the most restricted accessibility that allows them to do their jobs. If you can, declare the subroutine Private. Then, developers working on other parts of the application don't even need to know that the subroutine exists. They can create other routines with the same name if necessary and won't accidentally misuse the subroutine.

Later, if you discover that you need to use the subroutine outside of its class or module, you can change its declaration to allow greater accessibility.

Subroutine_Name

The subroutine's name must be a valid Visual Basic identifier. That means it should begin with a letter or an underscore. It can then contain zero or more letters, numbers, and underscores. If the name begins with an underscore, it must include at least one other character so that Visual Basic can tell it apart from a line continuation character.

Many developers use *camel case* when naming subroutines so a subroutine's name consists of several descriptive words with their first letters capitalized. A good method for generating subroutine names is to use a short phrase beginning with a verb and describing what the subroutine does. Some examples include LoadData, SaveNetworkConfiguration, and PrintExpenseReport.

Subroutine names with leading underscores can be hard to read, so you should either save them for special purposes or avoid them entirely. Names such as _1 and __ (two underscores) are particularly confusing.

Parameters

The *parameters* section of the subroutine declaration defines the arguments that the subroutine takes as parameters. The parameter declarations define the numbers and types of the parameters. This section also gives the names by which the subroutine will know the values.

Declaring parameters is very similar to declaring variables. See Chapter 15, "Data Types, Variables, and Constants," for information on variable declarations, data types, and other related topics.

The following sections describe some of the more important details related to subroutine parameter declarations.

ByVal

If you include the optional ByVal keyword before a parameter's declaration, the subroutine makes its own local copy of the parameter with procedure scope. The subroutine can modify this value all it wants and the corresponding value in the calling procedure isn't changed.

For example, consider the following code. The main program initializes the variable A and prints its value in the Output window. It then calls subroutine DisplayDouble, which declares its parameter X with the ByVal keyword. It doubles X and displays the new value. Because the parameter X is declared ByVal, the subroutine has its own local copy of the variable, so doubling it doesn't change the value of the variable A in the main program. When the subroutine ends and the main program resumes, it displays the value of variable A.

```
Private Sub Main()
    Dim A As Integer = 12
    Debug.WriteLine("Main: " & A)
    DisplayDouble(A)
    Debug.WriteLine("Main: " & A)
End Sub

Private Sub DisplayDouble(ByVal X As Integer)
    X *= 2
    Debug.WriteLine("DisplayDouble: " & X)
End Sub
```

The following text shows the results:

```
Main: 12
DisplayDouble: 24
Main: 12
```

ByRef

If you declare a parameter with the ByRef keyword, the subroutine does not create a separate copy of the parameter variable. Instead, it uses a reference to the original parameter passed into the subroutine and any changes the subroutine makes to the value are reflected in the calling subroutine.

Consider the following code. This code is the same as the previous example except that the DisplayDouble subroutine declares its parameter using the ByRef keyword. As before, the main program initializes the variable A and prints its value in the Output window. It then calls subroutine DisplayDouble, which doubles its parameter X and displays the new value. Because X is declared ByRef, this doubles the value of the variable A that was passed by the main program into the subroutine. When the subroutine ends and the main program resumes, it displays the new doubled value of variable A.

```
Private Sub Main()
    Dim A As Integer = 12
    Debug.WriteLine("Main: " & A)
    DisplayDouble(A)
    Debug.WriteLine("Main: " & A)
End Sub

Private Sub DisplayDouble(ByRef X As Integer)
    X *= 2
    Debug.WriteLine("DisplayDouble: " & X)
End Sub
```

The following shows the results:

```
Main: 12
DisplayDouble: 24
Main: 24
```

Arrays Declared ByVal and ByRef

If you declare an array parameter using ByVal or ByRef, those keywords apply to the array itself, not to the array's values. In either case, the subroutine can modify the values inside the array.

The `DoubleArrayValues` subroutine shown in the following code has a parameter named `arr`. This parameter is an array of integers and is declared ByVal. The routine loops through the array, doubling each of its values. It then loops through the array, displaying the new values. Next, the subroutine assigns the variable `arr` to a new array of integers. It loops through the array, again displaying the new values.

```
Private Sub DoubleArrayValues(ByVal arr() As Integer)
    ' Double the values.
    For i As Integer = arr.GetLowerBound(0) To arr.GetUpperBound(0)
        arr(i) *= 2
    Next i

    ' Display the values.
    For i As Integer = arr.GetLowerBound(0) To arr.GetUpperBound(0)
        Debug.WriteLine(arr(i))
    Next i
    Debug.WriteLine("----------")

    ' Create a new array of values.
    arr = New Integer() {-1, -2}

    ' Display the values.
    For i As Integer = arr.GetLowerBound(0) To arr.GetUpperBound(0)
        Debug.WriteLine(arr(i))
    Next i
    Debug.WriteLine("----------")
End Sub
```

The following code declares an array of integers containing the values 1, 2, and 3. It invokes the subroutine `DoubleArrayValues` and then loops through the array, displaying the values after `DoubleArrayValues` returns.

```
Dim the_values() As Integer = {1, 2, 3}
DoubleArrayValues(the_values)

For i As Integer = the_values.GetLowerBound(0) To the_values.GetUpperBound(0)
    Debug.WriteLine(the_values(i))
Next i
```

The following text shows the results. The `DoubleArrayValues` subroutine lists the array's doubled values 2, 4, 6, assigns a new array to its local variable `arr`, and then displays the new values -1 and -2. When `DoubleArrayValues` returns, the main program displays its version of the values. Notice that the values were updated by `DoubleArrayValues` but that the subroutine's assignment of its `arr` variable to a new array had no effect on the main program's array `the_values`.

```
2
4
6
----------
-1
-2
----------
2
4
6
```

Now suppose that the subroutine `DoubleArrayValues` was declared with the following statement:

```
Private Sub DoubleArrayValues(ByRef arr() As Integer)
```

In this case, when `DoubleArrayValues` assigns a new array to its `arr` variable, the calling routine sees the change, so the `the_values` array receives the new array. The following text shows the new results:

```
2
4
6
----------
-1
-2
----------
-1
-2
```

Parenthesized Parameters

A subroutine can fail to update a parameter declared using the ByRef keyword in a couple ways. The most confusing occurs if you enclose a variable in parentheses when you pass it to the subroutine. Parentheses tell Visual Basic to evaluate their contents as an expression. Visual Basic creates a temporary variable to hold the result of the expression and then passes the temporary variable into the procedure. If the procedure's parameter is declared ByRef, the subroutine updates the temporary variable but not the original variable, so the calling routine doesn't see any change to its value.

The following code calls subroutine `DisplayDouble`, passing it the variable A surrounded by parentheses. Subroutine `DisplayDouble` modifies its parameter's value, but the result doesn't get back to the variable A.

```
Private Sub Main()
    Dim A As Integer = 12
    Debug.WriteLine("Main: " & A)
    DisplayDouble((A))
    Debug.WriteLine("Main: " & A)
End Sub

Private Sub DisplayDouble(ByRef X As Integer)
    X *= 2
    Debug.WriteLine("DisplayDouble: " & X)
End Sub
```

The following text shows the results:

```
Main: 12
DisplayDouble: 24
Main: 12
```

Chapter 15 has more to say about parameters declared with the ByVal and ByRef keywords.

Optional

If you declare a parameter with the Optional keyword, the code that uses it may omit that parameter. When you declare an optional parameter, you must give it a default value for the subroutine to use if the parameter is omitted by the calling routine.

The `DisplayError` subroutine in the following code takes an optional string parameter. If the calling routine provides this parameter, the subroutine displays it. If the calling routine leaves this parameter out, `DisplayError` displays its default message "An error occurred." The `PlaceOrder` subroutine checks its `the_customer` parameter. If this parameter is Nothing, `PlaceOrder` calls `DisplayError` to show the message "Customer is Nothing in subroutine PlaceOrder." Next, subroutine `PlaceOrder` calls `the_customer`'s `IsValid` function. If `IsValid` returns False, the subroutine calls `DisplayError`. This time it omits the parameter so `DisplayError` presents its default message.

```
Private Sub DisplayError(Optional ByVal error_message As String = _
 "An error occurred")
    MessageBox.Show(error_message)
End Sub

Private Sub PlaceOrder(ByVal the_customer As Customer,
 ByVal order_items() As OrderItem)
    ' See if the_customer exists.
    If the_customer Is Nothing Then
        DisplayError("Customer is Nothing in subroutine PlaceOrder")
        Exit Sub
    End If

    ' See if the_customer is valid.
    If Not the_customer.IsValid() Then
        DisplayError()
        Exit Sub
    End If

    ' Generate the order.
    ...
End Sub
```

Optional parameters must go at the end of the parameter list. If one parameter uses the Optional keyword, all of the following parameters must use it, too.

OPTIONAL AND NULLABLE

A new feature in Visual Basic 2010 allows nullable parameters to also be optional. For example, the following code defines three subroutines that each take an optional nullable parameter. The first two give the parameter the default value Nothing, and the third uses the default value 0.

```
Public Sub Sub1(Optional ByVal x? As Integer = Nothing)
    ...
End Sub

Public Sub Sub2(Optional ByVal x As Integer? = Nothing)
    ...
End Sub

Public Sub Sub3(Optional ByVal x As Nullable(Of Integer) = 0)
    ...
End Sub
```

Optional parameters are particularly useful for initializing values in a class's constructor. The following code shows a DrawableRectangle class. Its constructor takes as parameters the rectangle's position and size. All the parameters are optional, so the main program can omit them if it desires. Because each parameter has default values, the constructor always knows it will have the four values, so it can always initialize the object's Bounds variable.

```
Public Class DrawableRectangle
    Public Bounds As Rectangle

    Public Sub New(
      Optional ByVal X As Integer = 0,
      Optional ByVal Y As Integer = 0,
      Optional ByVal Width As Integer = 100,
      Optional ByVal Height As Integer = 100
    )
        Bounds = New Rectangle(X, Y, Width, Height)
    End Sub
    ...
End Class
```

Note that overloaded subroutines cannot differ only in optional parameters. If a call to the subroutine omitted the optional parameters, Visual Basic would be unable to tell which version of the subroutine to use.

Optional versus Overloading

Different developers have varying opinions on whether you should use optional parameters or overloaded routines under various circumstances. For example, suppose that the FireEmployee method could take one or two parameters giving either the employee's name or the name and reason for dismissal. You could make this a subroutine with the reason parameter optional, or you could make one overloaded version of the FireEmployee method for each possible parameter list.

One argument in favor of optional parameters is that overloaded methods might duplicate a lot of code. However, it is easy to make each version of the method call another version that allows more parameters, passing in default values. For example, in the following code the first version of the FireEmployee method simply invokes the second version:

```
Public Sub FireEmployee(ByVal employee_name As String)
    FireEmployee(employee_name, "Unknown reason")
End Sub

Public Sub FireEmployee(ByVal employee_name As String, ByVal reason As String)
    ...
End Sub
```

Method overloading is generally superior when the different versions of the routine need to do something different. You might be able to make a single routine with optional parameters take different actions based on the values of its optional parameters, but separating the code into overloaded routines will probably produce a cleaner solution.

Parameter Arrays

Sometimes it is convenient to allow a subroutine to take a variable number of parameters. For example, a subroutine might take as parameters the addresses of people who should receive e-mail. It would loop through the names to send each a message.

One approach is to include a long list of optional parameters. For example, the e-mail subroutine might set the default value for each of its parameters to an empty string. Then it would need to send e-mail to every address parameter that was not empty.

Unfortunately, this type of subroutine would need to include code to deal with each optional parameter separately. This would also place an upper limit on the number of parameters the subroutine can take (however many you are willing to type in the subroutine's parameter list).

A better solution is to use the ParamArray keyword to make the subroutine's final argument a parameter array. A *parameter array* contains an arbitrary number of parameter values. At runtime, the subroutine can loop through the array to process the parameter values.

The DisplayAverage subroutine shown in the following code takes a parameter array named values. It checks the array's bounds to make sure it contains at least one value. If the array isn't empty, the subroutine adds the values it contains and divides by the number of values to calculate the average.

```
' Display the average of a series of values.
Private Sub DisplayAverage(ByVal ParamArray values()As Double)
    ' Do nothing if there are no parameters.
    If values Is Nothing Then Exit Sub
    If values.Length < 1 Then Exit Sub

    ' Calculate the average.
    Dim total As Double = 0
    For i As Integer = LBound(values) To UBound(values)
        total += values(i)
    Next i

    ' Display the result.
    MessageBox.Show((total / values.Length).ToString)
End Sub
```

The following code shows one way the program could use this subroutine. In this example, DisplayAverage would display the average of the integers 1 through 7, which is 4.

```
DisplayAverage(1, 2, 3, 4, 5, 6, 7)
```

Parameter arrays are subject to the following restrictions:

➤ A subroutine can have only one parameter array, and it must come last in the parameter list.

➤ All other parameters in the parameter list must *not* be optional.

➤ All parameter lists are declared ByVal, so any changes the subroutine makes to the array's contents do not affect the calling routine.

➤ Parameter array values are implicitly optional, so the calling routine can provide any number of values (including zero) for the array. However, you cannot use the Optional keyword when you declare the parameter array.

➤ All the items in the parameter array must have the same data type. However, you can use an array that contains the generic Object data type and then it can hold just about anything. The downside is you may need to convert the items into a more specific type (for example, using DirectCast or CInt) to use their features.

The calling routine can pass any number of values (including zero) for the parameter array. It can also pass the value Nothing, in which case the subroutine's parameter array has value Nothing.

The program can also pass an array of the appropriate data type in place of the parameter array values. The following two calls to the DisplayAverage subroutine produce the same result inside the DisplayAverage subroutine:

```
DisplayAverage(1, 2, 3, 4, 5, 6, 7)

Dim values() As Double = {1, 2, 3, 4, 5, 6, 7}
DisplayAverage(values)
```

Implements interface.subroutine

An *interface* defines a set of properties, methods, and events that a class implementing the interface must provide. An interface is a lot like a class with all of its properties, methods, and events declared with the MustOverride keyword. Any class that inherits from the base class must provide implementations of those properties, methods, and events.

The IDrawable interface shown in the following code defines a Draw subroutine, a Bounds function, and a property named IsVisible. The DrawableRectangle class begins with the statement Implements IDrawable. That tells Visual Basic that the class will implement the IDrawable interface. If you make the class declaration, type the Implements statement, and then press the Enter key, Visual Basic automatically fills in the declarations you need to satisfy the interface. In this example, it creates the empty Bounds function, Draw subroutine, and IsVisible property procedures shown here. All you need to do is fill in the details.

```
Public Interface IDrawable
    Sub Draw(ByVal gr As Graphics)
    Function Bounds() As Rectangle
    Property IsVisible() As Boolean
End Interface

Public Class DrawableRectangle
    Implements IDrawable

    Public Function Bounds() As System.Drawing.Rectangle _
     Implements IDrawable.Bounds

    End Function

    Public Sub Draw(ByVal gr As System.Drawing.Graphics) _
     Implements IDrawable.Draw

    End Sub

    Public Property IsVisible() As Boolean Implements IDrawable.IsVisible
        Get

        End Get
        Set(ByVal Value As Boolean)

        End Set
    End Property
End Class
```

If you look at the preceding code, you can see where the subroutine declaration's Implements interface.subroutine clause comes into play. In this case, the `Draw` subroutine implements the `IDrawable` interface's `Draw` method.

When you type the Implements statement and press the Enter key, Visual Basic generates empty routines to satisfy the interface; then you don't need to type the Implements interface.subroutine clause yourself. Visual Basic enters this for you.

The only time you should need to modify this statement is if you change the interface's name or subroutine name or you want to use some other subroutine to satisfy the interface. For example, you could give the DrawableRectangle class a DrawRectangle method and add `Implements IDrawable` `.Draw` to its declaration. Visual Basic doesn't care what you call the routine, as long as *some* routine implements `IDrawable.Draw`.

Statements

A subroutine's *statements* section contains whatever Visual Basic code is needed to get the routine's job done. This can include all the usual variable declarations, For loops, Try blocks, and other Visual Basic paraphernalia.

The subroutine's body cannot include module, class, subroutine, function, structure, enumerated type, or other file-level statements. For example, you cannot define a subroutine within another subroutine.

One new statement that you can use within a subroutine is Exit Sub. This command makes the subroutine immediately exit and return control to the calling routine. Within a subroutine, the Return statement is equivalent to Exit Sub.

You can use Exit Sub or Return as many times as you like to allow the subroutine to exit under different conditions. For example, the following subroutine checks whether a phone number has a 10-digit or 7-digit format. If the phone number matches a 10-digit format, the subroutine exits. Then if the phone number matches a 7-digit format, the subroutine exits. If the number doesn't match either format, the subroutine displays an error message to the user.

```
Private Sub ValidatePhoneNumber(ByVal phone_number As String)
    ' Check for a 10-digit phone number.
    If phone_number Like "###-###-####" Then Exit Sub

    ' Check for a 7-digit phone number.
    If phone_number Like "###-####" Then Return

    ' The phone number is invalid.
    MessageBox.Show("Invalid phone number " & phone_number)
End Sub
```

FUNCTIONS

Functions are basically the same as subroutines, except that they return some sort of value. The syntax for defining a function is as follows:

```
[attribute_list] [inheritance_mode] [accessibility] _
Function function_name([parameters]) [As return_type] [ Implements interface.
function ]
    [ statements ]
End function
```

This is almost the same as the syntax for defining a subroutine. See the section, "Subroutines," earlier in this chapter for information about most of this declaration's clauses.

One difference is that a function ends with the End Function statement rather than End Sub. Similarly, a function can exit before reaching its end using Exit Function rather than Exit Sub.

The one nontrivial difference between subroutine and function declarations is the clause As return_type that comes after the function's parameter list. This tells Visual Basic the type of value that the function returns.

The function can set its return value in one of two ways. First, it can set its name equal to the value it wants to return. The Factorial function shown in the following code calculates the factorial of a number. Written N!, the factorial of N is N * (N21) * (N22) . . .* 1. The function initializes its result variable to 1, and then loops over the values between 1 and the number parameter, multiplying these values to the result. It finishes by setting its name, Factorial, equal to the result value that it should return.

```
Private Function Factorial(ByVal number As Integer) As Double
    Dim result As Double = 1

    For i As Integer = 2 To number
        result *= i
    Next i

    Factorial = result
End function
```

A function can assign and reassign its return value as many times as it wants to before it returns. Whatever value is assigned last becomes the function's return value.

The second way a function can assign its return value is to use the Return keyword followed by the value that the function should return. The following code shows the Factorial function rewritten to use the Return statement:

```
Private Function Factorial(ByVal number As Integer) As Double
    Dim result As Double = 1

    For i As Integer = 2 To number
        result *= i
    Next i

    Return result
End function
```

The Return statement is roughly equivalent to setting the function's name equal to the return value, and then immediately using an Exit Function statement. The Return statement may allow the compiler to perform extra optimizations, however, so it is generally preferred to setting the function's name equal to the return value. (Return is also the more modern syntax and has become so common that some developers don't even recognize the other syntax anymore.)

PROPERTY PROCEDURES

Property procedures are routines that can represent a property value for a class. The simplest kind of property is an *auto-implemented property*. Simply add the Property keyword to a variable declaration as shown in the following code:

```
Public Property LastName As String
```

If you want, you can give the property a default value as in the following code:

```
Public Property LastName As String = "<missing>"
```

Behind the scenes, Visual Basic makes a hidden variable to hold the property's value. When other parts of the program get or set the value, Visual Basic uses the hidden variable.

This type of property is easy to make but it has few advantages over a simple variable. You can make the property more powerful if you write your own procedures to get and set the property's value. If you write your own procedures you can add validation code, perform complex calculations, save and restore values in a database, set breakpoints, and add other extras to the property.

A normal read-write property procedure contains a function for returning the property's value and a subroutine for assigning it.

The following code shows property procedures that implement a Value property. The Property Get procedure is a function that returns the value in the private variable m_Value. The Property Set subroutine saves a new value in the m_Value variable.

```
Private m_Value As Single

Property Value() As Single
    Get
        Return m_Value
    End Get
    Set(ByVal Value As Single)
        m_Value = Value
    End Set
End Property
```

Although the property is implemented as a pair of property procedures, the program could treat the value as a simple property. For example, suppose that the OrderItem class contains the preceding code. Then the following code sets the Value property for the OrderItem object named paper_item:

```
paper_item.Value = 19.95
```

You can add property procedures to any type of object module. For example, you can use property procedures to implement a property for a form or for a class of your own.

It's less obvious that you can also use property procedures in a code module. The property procedures look like an ordinary variable to the routines that use them. If you place the previous example in a code module, the program could act as if there were a variable named `Value` defined in the module.

For more information on property procedures, see the section "Property Procedures" in Chapter 15.

EXTENSION METHODS

Extension methods allow you to add a new method to an existing class without rewriting it or deriving a new class from it. To make an extension method, decorate the method declaration with the Extension attribute. Then make a normal subroutine or function that takes one or more parameters. The first parameter determines the class that the method extends. The method can use that parameter to learn about the item for which the method was called. The other parameters are passed into the method so it can use them to perform its chores.

> **EASIER EXTENSIONS**
>
> The Extension attribute is defined in the System.Runtime.CompilerServices namespace. Using an Imports statement to import that namespace makes it easier to write extensions.

For example, the following code adds a MatchesRegexp subroutine to the String class. The Extension attribute tells Visual Basic that this is an extension method. The method's first parameter is a String so this method extends the String class. The second parameter is a regular expression. The method returns True if the String matches the regular expression.

```
' Return True if a String matches a regular expression.
<Extension()>
Public Function MatchesRegexp(ByVal the_string As String,
 ByVal regular_expression As String) As Boolean
    Dim reg_exp As New Regex(regular_expression)
    Return reg_exp.IsMatch(the_string)
End function
```

The following code shows how a program might use this method to decide whether the string stored in variable `phone_number` looks like a valid 7-digit United States phone number:

```
if Not phone_number.MatchesRegexp("^[2-9]\d{2}-\d{4}$") Then
    MessageBox.Show("Not a valid phone number")
End if
```

Example program ValidatePhone demonstrates the MatchesRegexp extension method. It also uses the MatchesRegexp method to define the following three additional extension methods that determine whether a string looks like a valid 7- or 10-digit United States phone number. These methods simply call the MatchesRegexp method, passing it appropriate regular expressions.

```
' Return True if a String looks like a 7-digit US phone number.
<Extension()>
Public Function IsValidPhoneNumber7digit(ByVal the_string As String) As Boolean
    Return the_string.MatchesRegexp("^[2-9]\d{2}-\d{4}$")
End Function

' Return True if a String looks like a 10-digit US phone number.
<Extension()>
Public Function IsValidPhoneNumber10digit(ByVal the_string As String) As Boolean
    Return the_string.MatchesRegexp("^([2-9]\d{2}-){2}\d{4}$")
End Function

' Return True if a String looks like a 7- or 10-digit US phone number.
<Extension()>
Public Function IsValidPhoneNumberUS(ByVal the_string As String) As Boolean
    Return IsValidPhoneNumber7digit(the_string) OrElse
            IsValidPhoneNumber10digit(the_string)
End function
```

code snippet ValidatePhone

If you build a class and later need to change its features, it's usually easiest to modify its code directly. That will cause less confusion than extension methods, which may lie in some obscure module that seems unrelated to the original class. If you need to add methods to existing classes that you cannot modify, such as String and other classes defined by Visual Basic and the .NET Framework, extension methods can be extremely useful.

LAMBDA FUNCTIONS

Lambda functions are functions that are defined within the flow of the program's code. Often they are defined, used, and forgotten in a single statement without ever being given a name.

To define a lambda function for later use, start with the Function keyword. Add the function's name and any parameters that it requires, followed by a single statement that evaluates to the value that the function should return.

Next include either (1) a single statement that evaluates to the value that the function should return, or (2) a function body that ends with an End Function statement.

The following code fragment shows examples of both of these styles. First the program creates a lambda function named square_it that takes parameter n and returns n * n. It then creates a multiline lambda function named factorial that calculates and returns a number's factorial. The code finishes by calling both functions and displaying their results.

```
Dim square_it = Function(n As Integer) n * n
Dim factorial = Function(n As Integer) As Integer
                    Dim result As Integer = 1
                    For i As Integer = 2 To n
                        result *= i
                    Next i
                    Return result
                End Function

Debug.WriteLine(square_it(5))
Debug.WriteLine(factorial(5))
```

Example program LambdaFunction contains the following code fragment:

```
' Define a lambda function that adds two integers.
Dim plus = Function(i1 As Integer, i2 As Integer) i1 + i2

' Get A and B.
Dim A As Integer = Integer.Parse(txtA.Text)
Dim B As Integer = Integer.Parse(txtB.Text)

' Call the lambda function to calculate the result.
txtResult.Text = plus(A, B).ToString
```

code snippet LambdaFunction

This code starts by defining a variable named `plus`. This variable holds a reference to a lambda function that takes two integers as parameters and returns their sum. The code then gets input values from text boxes and calls the `plus` function, passing it those values. It converts the result into a string and displays it in the `txtResult` text box.

This example creates a variable to hold a reference to a lambda function and then invokes the function by using that variable. It could just as easily have invoked the lambda function itself while defining it.

Example program InlineFunction, which is also available for download on the book's web site, demonstrates this in the following line of code. This line defines the function and invokes it without ever saving a reference to it.

```
txtResult.Text =
    (Function(i1 As Integer, i2 As Integer) i1 + i2)(A, B).ToString
```

Because lambda functions are declared in a single line of code, they are also called *inline functions*. A lambda function defined inside a subroutine or function is also sometimes called a *nested function*.

LAMBDA OR INLINE?

To the extent that anyone distinguishes between lambda and inline functions, the preceding example is more properly called an inline function because the function is contained within the line that uses it and is never given a name. The examples before that one are more properly called lambda functions because they create named functions (square_it, factorial, and plus).

No matter which method the program uses to define a lambda function, it could then pass the function to another routine that will later call the function. For example, suppose subroutine PerformCalculations takes as a parameter the function it should use to perform its calculations. The following code shows how a program could call subroutine PerformCalculations while passing it the previous lambda functions:

```
' Define the plus function.
Dim plus = Function(i1 As Integer, i2 As Integer) i1 + i2

' Call PerformCalculations passing it the lambda function.
PerformCalculations(plus)

' Call PerformCalculations passing it an inline lambda function.
PerformCalculations(Function(i1 As Integer, i2 As Integer) i1 + i2)
```

Inline functions were invented for use by LINQ and are most often used with LINQ. For more information about LINQ, see Chapter 21, "LINQ."

Visual Basic 2010 also adds the ability to write lambda subroutines that are similar to lambda functions except they don't return a value.

The following code defines two named lambda subroutines. The first does all of its work on a single line whereas the second uses the multiline format. After defining the subroutines, the code invokes them to display two messages.

```
Dim write_msg = Sub(ByRef msg As String) Debug.WriteLine("write_msg: " & msg)
Dim show_msg = Sub(ByRef msg As String)
                    MessageBox.Show("show_msg: " & msg)
               End Sub

write_msg("Hi")
show_msg("Hi again")
```

As with lambda functions, you can build and pass a lambda subroutine into another routine as a parameter as shown in the following code:

```
Delegate Sub MsgFunc(ByVal m As String)

Private Sub DisplayMessage(ByVal msg As String, ByVal msg_func As MsgFunc)
    msg_func(msg)
End Sub

Private Sub TestSub()
    DisplayMessage("Hello?", Sub(m As String) MessageBox.Show(m))
End Sub
```

The code first declares a delegate type named MsgFunc that represents a subroutine that takes a String parameter.

Subroutine DisplayMessage takes as parameters a String and a subroutine of type MsgFunc. It calls the subroutine, passing it the String parameter.

The test subroutine TestSub calls DisplayMessage passing it a String and a lambda subroutine created inline.

RELAXED DELEGATES

If you assign a variable to the value in a variable of a different type, Visual Basic automatically converts the value into the correct type under some circumstances. If you set a Single variable equal to an Integer variable, Visual Basic automatically converts the Integer into a Single.

If Option Strict is off, you can also do the reverse: if you assign an Integer variable equal to a Single variable, Visual Basic converts the Single into an Integer (if it can).

In a similar manner, relaxed delegates let Visual Basic convert method parameters from one data type to another under certain circumstances. If the code invokes a subroutine by using a delegate, Visual Basic tries to convert parameters when it can. Probably the easiest way to understand how this works is to consider an example.

The following code declares a delegate type named `TestDelegate`. Methods that match this delegate should be subroutines that take a Control as a parameter.

```
' Declare the delegate type.
Private Delegate Sub TestDelegate(ByVal ctl As Control)
```

The following code defines three subroutines that take parameters of different types. The first takes an Object as a parameter, the second takes a TextBox, and the third takes no parameters. Note that the first subroutine cannot work if Option Strict is on. Option Strict disallows late binding, so the code cannot use a Text property provided by a generic Object.

```
' A more general parameter type.
Private Sub Test1(ByVal obj As Object)
    obj.Text = "Test1" ' Needs Option Strict off.
End Sub

' A more specific parameter type.
Private Sub Test2(ByVal text_box As TextBox)
    text_box.Text = "Test2"
End Sub

' Parameter omitted.
Private Sub Test3()
    txtField3.Text = "Test3"
End Sub
```

The following code declares three variables of the TestDelegate type and sets them equal to the addresses of the three test subroutines:

```
' Make variables of the delegate type
' hold references to the subroutines.
Private Sub1 As TestDelegate = AddressOf Test1
Private Sub2 As TestDelegate = AddressOf Test2 ' Needs Option Strict off.
Private Sub3 As TestDelegate = AddressOf Test3
```

The first assignment works even though subroutine Test1 does not exactly match the delegate type. Subroutine Test1 takes an Object as a parameter and TestDelegate takes a Control as a parameter. When Visual Basic invokes the Sub1 variable, it will pass the subroutine a Control object as a parameter because Sub1 has type TestDelegate, and that type takes a Control as a parameter. A Control is a type of Object, so Visual Basic can safely pass a Control in place of an Object parameter. That allows the code assigning Sub1 to the address of subroutine Test1 to work.

The second line of code that assigns variable Sub2 to subroutine Test2 works only if Option Strict is off. When Visual Basic invokes the Sub2 variable, it will pass the subroutine a Control object as a parameter because Sub1 has type TestDelegate, and that type takes a Control as a parameter. Subroutine Test2 takes a TextBox as a parameter, and not every Control is a TextBox. That means at design time Visual Basic cannot tell whether it can safely invoke the Sub2 delegate so, if Option Strict is on, Visual Basic flags this assignment as an error. If Option Strict is off, Visual Basic allows the assignment, although the program will crash if it tries to pass a control that is not a TextBox into Sub2 at runtime.

STRICTLY SPEAKING

This is similar to setting a TextBox variable equal to the value in a Control variable. If Option Strict is on, Visual Basic will not allow that assignment.

The final assignment sets variable Sub3 to the address of subroutine Test3. Subroutine Test3 takes no parameters. This is a special case that Visual Basic allows: if the method does not need to use the parameters specified by the delegate, it can omit its parameters. Note that the method must omit all or none of the parameters; it cannot omit some and not others.

The following code invokes the subroutines pointed to by the three TestDelegate variables, passing each a reference to a different TextBox. Sub1 treats `txtField1` as an Object, Sub2 treats `txtField2` as a TextBox, and Sub3 ignores its parameter completely.

```
Sub1(txtField1)
Sub2(txtField2)
Sub3(txtField3)
' Test3(txtField3) ' This doesn't work.
```

The final line of code, that invokes subroutine Test3 directly, doesn't work. Omitting the parameter list from a method only works if you access the method from a delegate. If you call the method directly, the parameter list must match the one declared for the method.

Example program RelaxedDelegates, which is available for download on the book's web site, demonstrates this code.

All of these relaxed delegate rules are somewhat confusing. They give you a little more flexibility, but they can make the code a lot more confusing. You may wonder why you should bother. In fact, if you use delegates such as those shown in this example, you might want to avoid using relaxed delegates to keep the code easier to understand.

These rules also apply to event handlers, and in that context they are fairly useful. They let you change an event handler's parameter types to make them more general or more specific, or to omit them.

The following code shows a simple, standard Button Click event handler. It takes two parameters of types Object and EventArgs. In this example, the code reads a text file into a text box.

```
Private Sub btnLoad_Click(ByVal sender As System.Object,
  ByVal e As System.EventArgs) Handles btnLoad.Click
    txtContents.Text = System.IO.File.ReadAllText(txtFile.Text)
End Sub
```

Many event handlers must deal explicitly with the control that raised their event. In that case, the first thing the event handler usually does is convert the generic `sender` parameter from an Object into a more specific control type.

The following code defines a Button Click event handler similar to the previous one but this one declares its `sender` parameter to be of type Button. This works as long as the event is actually raised by a Button, so the `sender` parameter really is a button. If you were to attach this event handler to a TextBox's TextChanged event, the program would crash when Visual Basic tries to convert the TextBox into a Button when it raises the event.

```
' Needs Option Strict off.
Private Sub btnLoad2_Click(ByVal btn As Button,
 ByVal e As Object) Handles btnLoad2.Click
    txtContents.Text = System.IO.File.ReadAllText(txtFile.Text)
End Sub
```

Note that this version requires Option Strict off. If Option Strict is on, Visual Basic will not allow this subroutine to handle a Button's Click event. This is similar to the way Option Strict prevents you from setting a Button variable equal to a generic Object variable.

The previous code declares its parameters to have a more restrictive type than those passed into it by the control raising the event. You can also make the parameters more general. You could declare the e parameter to be of type Object instead of EventArgs. Usually, that doesn't help you much. It could be useful if you want to use the same event handler to catch different kinds of events that provide different types of arguments, but it's hard to imagine a really good example where that wouldn't be confusing.

A more common situation is where the event handler ignores its parameters completely. Usually each Button has its own Click event handler so you don't need to look at the parameters to figure out which button was clicked.

The following code defines a Button Click event handler that takes no parameters. When the user clicks the btnLoad3 Button, Visual Basic doesn't pass the event handler any parameters. This code is easier to read than the previous versions, partly because the Sub statement fits all on one line.

```
Private Sub btnLoad3_Click() Handles btnLoad3.Click
    txtContents.Text = System.IO.File.ReadAllText(txtFile.Text)
End Sub
```

Example program RelaxedEventHandlers, which is available for download on the book's web site, demonstrates relaxed event handlers.

Relaxed delegates may add more confusion than they're worth if you use delegate variables, but they can be useful for simplifying event handlers. Declaring parameters with a more specific type (for example, Button instead of Object) can make the code easier to write and understand, although it has the large drawback of requiring Option Strict off. Omitting parameters when you don't need them is an even better technique. It simplifies the code without forcing you to turn Option Strict off.

PARTIAL METHODS

A *partial method* is a private subroutine that is declared in one place and implemented in another. The code includes a subroutine declaration that uses the Partial keyword and that has an empty body. Another part of the class declares the method again, this time without the Partial keyword and providing a method body.

What's the point? Partial methods were invented for the convenience of code generators. The details are somewhat technical and not relevant for developers at this point so they are only briefly considered here.

Partial methods were designed as a more efficient alternative to events. Rather than raising an event for a class to catch, the generated code can call a partial method. If the method has no body, the compiler optimizes the call away and nothing happens, much as would be the case if an object did not catch an event.

The following list summarizes the differences between event handlers and partial methods:

➤ An event can be caught by any number of event handlers, but a partial method has only one body.

➤ An event can be declared Public, Private, or Friend, but a partial method must be Private.

➤ Raising an event requires some overhead even if no event handlers catch it. If a partial method has no body, the compiler ignores calls to it so there's no overhead.

➤ A program can add and remove event handlers at runtime, but a partial method is given a body or not at design time.

➤ Just about any piece of code can catch an object's events, but only that object can see its partial method (because it's private).

Partial methods are really intended for use by code generators, but it's conceivable that you might find a use for them. It's also worth knowing about them so you know what's going on if you see them in automatically generated code.

Example program PartialMethods uses the following code to define the TestMethod subroutine:

```
Public Class Form1
    ' Define the TestMethod subroutine without a method body.
    Partial Private Sub TestMethod(ByVal msg As String)

    End Sub

    ' Other code omitted ...
End Class
```

code snippet PartialMethods

The example uses the following code in a separate module to define the method's body:

```
Partial Public Class Form1
    ' Define the implementation for TestMethod.
    Private Sub TestMethod(ByVal msg As String)
        MessageBox.Show(msg)
    End Sub
End Class
```

code snippet PartialMethods

When you click the program's button, the code calls subroutine TestMethod, passing it a string to display. If you comment out the method's body definition, the program ignores this call.

You can achieve results similar to methods without using partial methods in a couple of ways. First, you can make a class raise an event. If no code catches the event, the event is essentially ignored much as a partial method call is ignored if you have not defined the method body.

A second approach is to decorate a method with the Conditional attribute. In that case, Visual Basic removes the method and any calls to it from the code if the condition is not satisfied. The AttributeConditional example program, which is available for download on the book's web site, demonstrates this approach. For more information about that example, see the section "Attribute_ List" earlier in this chapter.

Partial methods are also somewhat similar to interfaces, which also define a method's signature but don't provide an implementation.

Finally, partial methods are similar to classes with overridable methods. Any derived classes can override the overridable methods to give them method bodies. If the parent class gives the method a body, the child class can leave it alone and inherit the parent's version as a default.

Partial methods are really intended for use by code generators, but you can use them if you wish.

SUMMARY

Subroutines and functions let you break an application into manageable, reusable pieces. A subroutine performs a series of commands. A function performs a series of commands and returns a value.

Property procedures use paired functions and subroutines to provide the behavior of a simple property using routines.

These form the fundamental building blocks of the procedural part of an application. Chapters 25 through 29 explain the other half of an application's structure: the objects that encapsulate the application's behavior. Together, the program's objects and its procedural subroutines and functions define the application.

This chapter explains how to break an otherwise unwieldy expanse of code into subroutines and functions of manageable size. It also explains techniques related to subroutines and functions, such as extension methods and relaxed delegates, that let you use existing classes and events in new ways.

The chapters so far do not explain how to write anything other than straight-line code that executes one statement after another with no deviation. Most programs need to follow more complex paths of execution, performing some statements only under certain conditions and repeating others a given number of times. Chapter 18, "Program Control Statements," describes the statements that a Visual Basic program uses to control the flow of code execution. These include decision statements (If Then Else, Select Case, IIF, Choose) and looping statements (For Next, For Each, Do While, While Do, Repeat Until).

18

Program Control Statements

Program control statements tell an application which other statements to execute under a particular set of circumstances. They control the path that execution takes through the code. They include commands that tell the program to execute some statements but not others and to execute certain statements repeatedly.

The two main categories of control statements are *decision statements* (or *conditional statements*) and *looping statements*. The following sections describe in detail the decision and looping statements provided by Visual Basic .NET.

DECISION STATEMENTS

A decision or conditional statement represents a branch in the program. It marks a place where the program can execute one set of statements or another, or possibly no statements at all, depending on some condition. These include If, Choose, and Select Case statements.

Single-Line If Then

The single-line If Then statement has two basic forms. The first allows the program to execute a single statement if some condition is true. The syntax is as follows:

```
If condition Then statement
```

If the condition is true, the program executes the statement. In the most common form of single-line If Then statement, the statement is a single simple command (such as assigning a value to a variable or calling a subroutine).

The following example checks the emp object's IsManager property. If IsManager is True, the statement sets the emp object's Salary property to 90,000.

```
If emp.IsManager Then emp.Salary = 90000
```

The second form of the single-line If Then statement is more confusing and generally harder to debug and maintain. To prevent unnecessary confusion, many programmers switch to the multiline If Then statement described in the next section when the simple single-statement version won't work.

The second form of single-line If Then statement uses the Else keyword. The syntax is as follows:

```
If condition Then statement1 Else statement2
```

If the condition is true, the code executes the first statement. If the condition is false, the code executes the second statement. The decision about which statement to execute is an either-or decision; the code executes one statement or the other, but not both.

This type of single-line If Then Else statement can be confusing if it is too long to easily see in the code editor. For longer statements, a multiline If Then Else statement is easier to understand and debug. The performance of single-line and multiline If Then Else statements is comparable (in one test, the multiline version took only about 80 percent as long), so you should use the one that is easiest for you to read.

The statements executed by a single-line If Then statement can be simple commands (such as assigning a value to a variable). They can also be a series of simple statements separated by colons on the same line. For example, the following code tests the value of the Boolean variable is_new_customer. If is_new_customer is true, the program calls the customer object's Initialize method and then calls its Welcome method.

```
If is_new_customer Then customer.Initialize(): customer.Welcome()
```

Using more than one simple statement separated by colons like this can be perplexing. It gets even worse if you use single-line If Then Else, as shown here:

```
If order.Valid() Then order.Save(): order.Post() Else order.order.Delete()
```

The single-line If Then statement can also include Else If clauses. For example, the following code examines the variable x. If x is 1, the program sets variable txt to "One." If x has the value 2, the program sets txt to "Two." If x is not 1 or 2, the program sets txt to a question mark.

```
Dim txt As String
If X = 1 Then txt = "One" Else If X = 2 Then txt = "Two" Else txt = "?"
```

The code can include as many Else If clauses as you like, and each execution statement can be composed of multiple simple statements separated by colons. However, confusing code such as these examples can lead to puzzling bugs that are easy to avoid if you use multiline If Then statements instead.

In summary, if you can write a simple single-line If Then statement with no Else If or Else clauses, and the whole thing fits nicely on the line so that it's easy to see the whole thing without confusion, go ahead. If the statement is too long to read easily, contains Else If or Else clauses, or executes a series of statements separated by colons, you are usually better off using a multiline If Then statement. It may take more lines of code, but the code will be easier to read, debug, and maintain later.

Multiline If Then

A multiline If Then statement can execute more than one line of code when a condition is true. The syntax for the simplest form of multiline If Then statement is as follows:

```
If condition Then
    statements ...
End If
```

If the condition is true, the program executes all the commands that come before the End If statement.

Like the single-line If Then statement, the multiline version can include Else If and Else clauses. For possibly historical reasons, ElseIf is spelled as a single word in the multiline If Then statement. The syntax is as follows:

```
If condition1 Then
    statements1 ...
ElseIf condition2
    statements2 ...
Else
    statements3 ...
End If
```

If the first condition is true, the program executes the first set of statements. If the first condition is false, the code examines the second condition and, if that one is true, the code executes the second set of statements. The program continues checking conditions until it finds one that is true and it executes the corresponding code.

If the program reaches an Else statement, it executes the corresponding code. If the program reaches the End If statement without finding a true condition or an Else clause, it doesn't execute any of the statement blocks.

It is important to understand that the program exits the If Then construction immediately after it has executed any block of statements. It does not examine the other conditions. This saves the program some time and is particularly important if the conditions involve functions. If each test calls a relatively slow function, skipping these later tests can save the program a significant amount of time.

Select Case

The Select Case statement lets a program execute one of several pieces of code depending on a single value. The basic syntax is as follows:

```
Select Case test_value
    Case comparison_expression1
        statements1
    Case comparison_expression2
        statements2
    Case comparison_expression3
        statements3
    ...
    Case Else
        else_statements
End Select
```

If `test_value` matches `comparison_expression1`, the program executes the statements in the block `statements1`. If `test_value` matches `comparison_expression2`, the program executes the statements in the block `statements2`. The program continues checking the expressions in the Case statements in order until it matches one, or it runs out of Case statements.

If `test_value` doesn't match any of the expressions in the Case statements, the program executes the code in the `else_statements` block. Note that you can omit the Case Else section. In that case, the program executes no code if `test_value` doesn't match any of the expressions.

Select Case is functionally equivalent to an If Then Else statement. The following code does the same thing as the previous Select Case code:

```
If test_value = comparison_expression1 Then
    statements1
ElseIf test_value = comparison_expression2 Then
    statements2
ElseIf test_value = comparison_expression3 Then
    statements3
...
Else
    else_statements
End If
```

Select Case is sometimes easier to understand than a long If Then Else statement. It is often faster as well, largely because Select Case doesn't need to reevaluate `test_value` for every Case statement. If `test_value` is a simple variable, the difference is insignificant, but if `test_value` represents a slow function call, the difference can be important. For example, suppose `test_value` represents a function that opens a database and looks up a value. The Select Case version will find the value once and use it in each comparison, whereas the If Then version would reopen the database for each comparison.

The previous If Then example assumes the comparison expressions are constants. A comparison expression can also specify ranges using the To and Is keywords, and include a comma-separated list of expressions. These forms are described in the following sections. The final section describing Select Case discusses using enumerated values to control Select Case statements.

To

The To keyword specifies a range of values that `test_value` should match. The following code examines the variable `num_items`. If `num_items` is between 1 and 10, the program calls subroutine `ProcessSmallOrder`. If `num_items` is between 11 and 100, the program calls subroutine `ProcessLargeOrder`. If `num_items` is less than 1 or greater than 100, the program beeps.

```
Select Case num_items
    Case 1 To 10
        ProcessSmallOrder()
    Case 11 To 100
        ProcessLargeOrder()
    Case Else
        Beep()
End Select
```

Is

The Is keyword lets you perform logical comparisons using the test value. The word Is takes the place of the test value in the comparison expression. For example, the following code does almost the same things as the previous version. If the value num_items is less than or equal to 10, the program calls subroutine ProcessSmallOrder. If the first Case clause doesn't apply and num_items is less than or equal to 100, the program calls subroutine ProcessLargeOrder. If neither of these cases applies, the program beeps.

```
Select Case num_items
    Case Is <= 10
        ProcessSmallOrder()
    Case Is <= 100
        ProcessLargeOrder()
    Case Else
        Beep()
End Select
```

This version is slightly different from the previous one. If num_items is less than 1, this code calls subroutine ProcessSmallOrder whereas the previous version beeps.

You can use the operators =, <>, <, <=, >, and >= in an Is clause. (In fact, if you use a simple value in a Case clause as in Case 7, you are implicitly using Is = as in Case Is = 7.)

Comma-Separated Expressions

A comparison expression can include a series of expressions separated by commas. If the test value matches any of the comparison values, the program executes the corresponding code.

For example, the following code examines the department_name variable. If department_name is "R & D," "Test," or "Computer Operations," the code adds the text "Building 10" to the address_text string. If department_name is "Finance," "Purchasing," or "Accounting," the code adds "Building 7" to the address. More Case clauses could check for other department_name values and the code could include an Else statement.

```
Select Case department_name
    Case "R & D", "Test", "Computer Operations"
        address_text &= "Building 10"
    Case "Finance", "Purchasing", "Accounting"
        address_text &= "Building 7"
    ...
End Select
```

Note that you cannot use comma-separated expressions in a Case Else clause. For example, the following code doesn't work:

```
Case Else, "Corporate" ' This doesn't work.
```

You can mix and match constants, To, and Is expressions in a single Case clause, as shown in the following example. This code checks the variable `item_code` and calls subroutine `DoSomething` if the value is less than 10, between 30 and 40 inclusive, exactly equal to 100, or greater than 200.

```
Select Case item_code
    Case Is < 10, 30 To 40, 100, Is > 200
        DoSomething()
    ...
End Select
```

Complex comparison expressions are sometimes difficult to read. If an expression is too complicated, you should consider rewriting the code to make it easier to understand. Storing values in temporary variables can help. The following code shows a version of the preceding code that's a bit easier to understand:

```
Select Case item_code
    Case Is < 10
        DoSomething()
    Case 30 To 40
        DoSomething()
    Case 100
        DoSomething()
    Case Is > 200
        DoSomething()
    ...
End Select
```

While this version is easier to understand, it is more verbose and uses duplicated code (repeated calls to DoSomething). The following version uses a temporary variable to make the code easy to read without the duplication.

```
' See if we must do something.
Dim must_do_something As Boolean = False
If item_code < 10 Then must_do_something = True
If (item_code >= 30) AndAlso (item_code <= 40) Then must_do_something = True
If item_code = 100 Then must_do_something = True
If item_code > 200 Then must_do_something = True

If must_do_something Then
    ...
End If
```

Enumerated Values

Select Case statements work very naturally with lists of discrete values. You can have a separate Case statement for each value, or you can list multiple values for one Case statement in a comma-separated list.

Enumerated types defined by the Enum statement also work with discrete values, so they work well with Select Case statements. The enumerated type defines the values and the Select Case statement uses them, as shown in the following code fragment:

```
Private Enum JobStates
    Pending
    Assigned
    InProgress
    ReadyToTest
    Tested
    Released
End Enum
Private m_JobState As JobStates
...
Select Case m_JobState
    Case Pending
        ...
    Case Assigned
        ...
    Case InProgress
        ...
    Case ReadyToTest
        ...
    Case Tested
        ...
    Case Released
        ...
End Select
```

To catch bugs when changing an enumerated type, many developers include a Case Else statement that throws an exception. If you later add a new value to the enumerated type but forget to add corresponding code to the Select Case statement, the Select Case statement throws an error when it sees the new value, so you can fix the code.

For more information on enumerated types, see the section "Enumerated Data Types" in Chapter 15, "Data Types, Variables, and Constants."

IIf

The IIf statement evaluates a Boolean expression and then returns one of two values, depending on whether the expression is true or false. This statement may look more like an assignment statement or a function call than a decision statement such as If Then.

The syntax is as follows:

```
variable = IIf(condition, value_if_true, value_if_false)
```

For example, the following code examines an Employee object's `IsManager` property. If `IsManager` is True, the code sets the employee's `Salary` to 90,000. If `IsManager` is False, the code sets the employee's `Salary` to 10,000.

```
emp.Salary = IIf(emp.IsManager, 90000, 10000)
```

Note that the IIf statement returns an Object data type. If you have Option Strict turned on, Visual Basic will not allow this statement, because it assigns a result of type Object to an Integer variable. To satisfy Visual Basic, you must explicitly convert the value into an Integer, as in the following code:

```
emp.Salary = CInt(IIf(emp.IsManager, 90000, 10000))
```

The IIf statement has several drawbacks. First, it is confusing. When you type an IIf statement, IntelliSense will remind you that its parameters give a condition, a True value, and a False value. When you are reading the code, however, you must remember what the different parts of the statement mean. If you use IIf in some other statement, the chances for confusion increase. For example, consider the following code:

```
For i = 1 To CType(IIf(employees_loaded, num_employees, 0), Integer)
    ' Process employee i.
    ...
Next i
```

Code is generally much easier to understand if you replace IIf with an appropriate If Then statement.

Another drawback to IIf is that it evaluates both the True and False values whether the condition is true or false. For example, consider the following code. If the Boolean `use_groups` is True, the code sets `num_objects` to the result of the `CountGroups` function. If `use_groups` is False, the code sets `num_objects` to the result of the `CountIndividuals` function. IIf evaluates both functions no matter which value it actually needs. If the functions are time-consuming or executed inside a large loop, using IIf can waste a lot of time.

```
num_objects = CType(
    IIf(use_groups,
        CountGroups(),
        CountIndividuals()),
    Integer)
```

For an even more dangerous example, consider the following code. If `data_loaded` is True, this statement sets `num_loaded = num_employees`. If `data_loaded` is False, the code sets `num_loaded` to the value returned by the `LoadEmployees` function (which loads the employees and returns the number of employees it loaded).

```
num_loaded = CType(IIf(data_loaded, num_employees, LoadEmployees()), Integer)
```

IIf evaluates both the value num_employees and the value LoadEmployees() no matter what. If the employees are already loaded, IIf calls LoadEmployees() to load the employees again, ignores the returned result, and sets num_loaded = num_employees. LoadEmployees may waste quite a lot of time loading the data that is already loaded. Even worse, the program may not be able to handle loading the data when it is already loaded.

A final drawback to IIf is that it is slower than a comparable If Then Else statement. In one test, IIf took roughly twice as long as a comparable If Then statement.

One case where you can argue that IIf is easier to understand is when you have a long series of very simple statements. In that case, IIf statements may allow you to easily see the common features in the code and notice if anything looks wrong. For example, the following code initializes several text boxes using strings. It uses an IIf statement to set a text box's value to <Missing> if the string is not yet initialized.

```
txtLastName.Text = IIf(last_name Is Nothing, "<Missing>", last_name)
txtFirstName.Text = IIf(first_name Is Nothing, "<Missing>", first_name)
txtStreet.Text = IIf(street Is Nothing, "<Missing>", street)
txtCity.Text = IIf(city Is Nothing, "<Missing>", city)
txtState.Text = IIf(state Is Nothing, "<Missing>", state)
txtZip.Text = IIf(zip Is Nothing, "<Missing>", zip)
```

To avoid confusing side effects, use IIf only if it makes the code easier to understand.

If

The If statement resolves some of the problems with the IIf statement. It evaluates a Boolean expression and then returns one of two values, depending on whether the expression is true or false, as IIf does. The difference is that If only evaluates the return value that it actually returns.

For example, the following code examines an Employee object's IsManager property. If IsManager is True, the code sets the employee's Salary to the result returned by the GetManagerSalary function and never calls function GetEmployeeSalary. If IsManager is False, the code sets the employee's Salary to the result of the GetEmployeeSalary function and never calls function GetManagerSalary. This is different from the way IIf works because IIf would call both functions no matter which value it was going to return. If the functions are time-consuming, using If can make the code more efficient.

```
emp.Salary = If(emp.IsManager, GetManagerSalary(), GetEmployeeSalary())
```

Other than the fact that If doesn't evaluate both of its possible return values, it behaves just as IIf does. For more information, see the previous section.

Choose

The IIf statement uses a Boolean expression to pick between two values. The Choose statement uses an integer to decide among any number of options. The syntax is as follows:

```
variable = Choose(index, value1, value2, value3, value4, ... )
```

If the index parameter is 1, Choose returns the first value, value1; if index is 2, Choose returns value2; and so forth. If index is less than 1 or greater than the number of values in the parameter list, Choose returns Nothing.

This statement has the same drawbacks as IIf. Choose evaluates all of the result values no matter which one is selected, so it can slow performance. It can be particularly confusing if the values are functions with side effects.

Often Choose is more confusing than a comparable Select Case statement. If the values look dissimilar (mixing integers, objects, function calls, and so forth), involve complicated functions, or are wrapped across multiple lines, a Select Case statement may be easier to read.

However, if the Choose statement's values are short and easy to understand, and the statement contains many values, the Choose statement may be easier to read. For example, the following Choose and Select Case statements do the same thing. Because the Choose statement's values are short and easy to understand, this statement is easy to read. The Select Case statement is rather long. If the program had more choices, the Select Case statement would be even longer, making it more difficult to read.

```
fruit = Choose(index, "apple", "banana", "cherry", "date")

Select Case index
    Case 1
        fruit = "apple"
    Case 2
        fruit = "banana"
    Case 3
        fruit = "cherry"
    Case 4
        fruit = "date"
End Select
```

Although it's not always clear whether a Choose statement or a Select Case statement will be easier to read, Select Case is certainly faster. In one test, Choose took more than five times as long as Select Case. If the code lies inside a frequently executed loop, the speed difference may be an issue.

Choose and Select Case are not your only options. You can also store the program's choices in an array, and then use the index to pick an item from the array. For example, the following code stores the strings from the previous example in the values array. It then uses the index to pick the right choice from the array.

```
Dim fruit_names() As String = {"apple", "banana", "cherry", "date"}

fruit = fruit_names(index - 1)
```

> **INTELLIGENT INDEXING**
>
> Notice that the code subtracts 1 from the index when using it to pick the right choice. The Choose statement indexes its values starting with 1, but arrays in Visual Basic .NET start with index 0. Subtracting 1 allows the program to use the same index values used in the previous example.

This version makes you think about the code in a different way. It requires that you know that the fruit_names array contains the names of the fruits that the program needs. If you understand the array's purpose, then the assignment statement is easy to understand.

The assignment code is even slightly faster than Select Case, at least if you can initialize the fruit_names array ahead of time.

If you find Choose easy to understand and it doesn't make your code more difficult to read in your particular circumstances, by all means use it. If Select Case seems clearer, use that. If you will need to perform the assignment many times and pre-building an array of values makes sense, using a value array might improve your performance.

LOOPING STATEMENTS

Looping statements make the program execute a series of statements repeatedly. The loop can run for a fixed number of repetitions, run while some condition is true, or run while some condition is false.

Broadly speaking, there are two types of looping statement. For loops execute a certain number of times that (in theory at least) is known. For example, a For loop may execute a series of statements exactly 10 times. Or, it may execute the statements once for each object in a certain collection. If you know how many items are in the collection, you know the number of times the loop will execute.

A While loop executes while a condition is true or until a condition is met. Without a lot more information about the application, it is impossible to tell how many times the code will execute. For example, suppose a program uses the InputBox function to get names from the user until the user clicks the Cancel button. In that case, there's no way for the program to guess how many values the user will enter before canceling.

The following sections describe the looping statements supported by Visual Basic .NET. The next two sections describe For loops, and the sections after those describe While loops.

> **LOTS OF LOOPS**
>
> Example program Loops, which is available for download on the book's web site, demonstrates some of these kinds of loops.

For Next

The For Next loop is the most common type of looping statement in Visual Basic. The syntax is as follows:

```
For variable [As data_type] = start_value To stop_value [Step increment]
    statements
    [Exit For]
    statements
    [Continue For]
    statements
Next [variable]
```

The value `variable` is the looping variable that controls the loop. When the program reaches the For statement, it sets `variable` equal to `start_value`. It then compares `variable` to `stop_value`. If `variable` has passed `stop_value`, the loop exits. Note that the loop may not execute even once depending on the start and stop values.

For example, the following loop runs for the values `employee_num = 1`, `employee_num = 2`, . . ., `employee_num = num_employees`. If the program has not loaded any employees so `num_employees = 0`, the code inside the loop is not executed at all.

```
For employee_num = 1 To num_employees
    ProcessEmployee(employee_num)
Next employee_num
```

After it compares `variable` to `stop_value`, the program executes the statements inside the loop. It then adds `increment` to `variable` and starts the process over, again comparing `variable` to `stop_value`. If you omit `increment`, the program uses an increment of 1.

Note that `increment` can be negative or a fractional number, as in the following example:

```
For i As Integer = 3 To 1 Step -0.5
    Debug.WriteLine(i)
Next i
```

If `increment` is positive, the program executes as long as `variable <= stop_value`. If `increment` is negative, the program executes as long as `variable >= stop_value`. This means that the loop would not execute infinitely if `increment` were to move `variable` away from `stop_value`. For example, in the following code `start_value = 1` and `increment = -1`. The variable `i` would take the values `i = 1`, `i = 0`, `i = -1`, and so forth, so `i` will never reach the `stop_value` of 2. However, because `increment` is negative, the loop only executes while `i >= 2`. Because `i` starts with the value 1, the program immediately exits and the loop doesn't execute at all.

```
For i As Integer = 1 To 2 Step -1
    Debug.WriteLine(i)
Next i
```

Visual Basic doesn't require that you include the variable's name in the Next statement, although this makes the code easier to read. If you do specify the name in the Next statement, it must match the name you use in the For statement.

If you do not specify the looping variable's data type in the For statement and Option Explicit is on and Option Infer is off, then you must declare the variable before the loop. For example, the following loop declares the variable `i` outside of the loop:

```
Dim i As Integer

For i = 1 To 10
    Debug.WriteLine(i)
Next i
```

Declaring the looping variable in the For statement is a good practice. It limits the scope of the variable so you don't need to remember what the variable is for in other pieces of code. It keeps the variable's declaration close to the code where it is used, so it's easier to remember the variable's data type. It also lets you more easily reuse counter variables without fear of confusion. If you have several loops that need an arbitrarily named looping variable, they can all declare and use the variable `i` without interfering with each other.

The program calculates its `start_value` and `stop_value` before the loop begins and it never recalculates them, even if their values change. For example, the following code loops from 1 to `this_customer.Orders(1).NumItems`. The program calculates `this_customer.Orders(1).NumItems` before executing the loop and doesn't recalculate that value even if it later changes. This saves the program time, particularly for long expressions such as this one, which could take a noticeable amount of time to reevaluate each time through a long loop.

```
For item_num As Integer = 1 To this_customer.Orders(1).NumItems
    this_customer.ProcessItem(item_num)
Next item_num
```

If you must reevaluate `stop_value` every time the loop executes, use a While loop instead of a For loop.

The Exit For statement allows the program to leave a For loop before it would normally finish. For example, the following code loops through the `employees` array. When it finds an entry with the `IsManager` property set to True, it saves the employee's index and uses Exit For to immediately stop looping.

```
Dim manager_index As Integer

For i As Integer = employees.GetLowerBound(0) To employees.GetUpperBound(0)
    If employees(i).IsManager Then
        manager_index = i
        Exit For
    End If
Next i
```

The Exit For statement exits only the For loop immediately surrounding the statement. If a For loop is nested within another For loop, the Exit For statement only exits the inner loop.

The Continue For statement makes the loop jump back to its For statement, increment its looping variable, and start the loop over again. This is particularly useful if the program doesn't need to execute the rest of the steps within the loop's body and wants to start the next iteration quickly.

OUT OF CONTROL

Your code can change the value of the control variable inside the loop, but that's generally not a good idea. The For Next loop has a very specific intent, and modifying the control variable inside the loop violates that intent, making the code more difficult to understand and debug. If you must modify the control variable in more complicated ways than are provided by a For Next loop, use a While loop instead. Then programmers reading the code won't expect a simple incrementing loop.

Non-Integer For Next Loops

Usually a For Next loop's control variable is an integral data type such as an Integer or Long, but it can be any of the fundamental Visual Basic numeric data types. For example, the following code uses a variable declared as Single to display the values 1.0, 1.5, 2.0, 2.5, and 3.0:

```
For x As Single = 1 To 3 Step 0.5
    Debug.WriteLine(x.ToString("0.0"))
Next x
```

Because floating-point numbers cannot exactly represent every possible value, these data types are subject to rounding errors that can lead to unexpected results in For Next loops. The preceding code works as you would expect, at least on my computer. The following code, however, has problems. Ideally, this code would display values between 1 and 2, incrementing them by 1/7. Because of rounding errors, however, the value of x after seven trips through the loop is approximately 1.85714316. The program adds 1/7 to this and gets 2.0000003065381731. This is greater than the stopping value 2, so the program exits the loop and the Debug statement does not execute for x = 2.

```
For x As Single = 1 To 2 Step 1 / 7
    Debug.WriteLine(x)
Next x
```

One solution to this type of problem is to convert the code into a loop that uses an Integer control variable. Integer variables do not have the same problems with rounding errors that floating-point numbers do, so you have more precise control over the values used in the loop.

The following code does roughly the same thing as the previous code. It uses an Integer control variable, however, so this loop executes exactly eight times as desired. The final value printed into the Output window by the program is 2.

```
Dim x As Single

x = 1
For i As Integer = 1 To 8
    Debug.WriteLine(x)
    x += CSng(1 / 7)
Next i
```

If you look at the value of variable x in the debugger, you will find that its real value during the last trip through the loop is roughly 2.0000001702989851. If this variable were controlling the For loop, the program would see that this value is greater than 2, so it would not display its final value.

For Each

A For Each loop iterates over the items in a collection, array, or other container class that supports For Each loops. The syntax is as follows:

```
For Each variable [As object_type] In group
    statements
    [Exit For]
    statements
    [Continue For]
    statements
Next [variable]
```

Here, group is a collection, array, or other object that supports For Each. As in For Next loops, the control variable must be declared either in or before the For statement if you have Option Explicit on and Option Infer off.

ENABLING ENUMERATORS

To support For Each, the group object must implement the System.Collections .IEnumerable interface. This interface defines a GetEnumerator method that returns an enumerator. For more information, see the next section, "Enumerators."

The control variable must be of a data type compatible with the objects contained in the group. If the group contains Employee objects, the variable could be an Employee object. It could also be a generic Object or any other class that readily converts into an Employee object. For example, if Employee inherits from the Person class, then the variable could be of type Person.

Visual Basic doesn't automatically understand what kinds of objects are stored in a collection or array until it tries to use them. If the control variable's type is not compatible with an object's type, the program generates an error when the For Each loop tries to assign the control variable to that object's value.

That means if a collection or array contains more than one type of object, the control variable must be of a type that can hold all of the objects. If the objects in a collection do not inherit from a common ancestor class, the code must use a control variable of type Object.

Like For Next loops, For Each loops support the Exit For and Continue For statements.

As is the case with For Next loops, declaring the looping variable in the For Each statement is a good practice. It limits the scope of the variable, so you don't need to remember what the variable is for in other pieces of code. It keeps the variable's declaration close to the code where it is used, so it's easier to remember the variable's data type. It also lets you more easily reuse counter variables without fear of confusion. If you have several loops that need an arbitrarily named looping variable, they can all declare and use the variable obj, person, or whatever else makes sense without interfering with each other.

Your code can change the value of the control variable inside the loop, but that has no effect on the loop's progress through the collection or array. The loop resets the variable to the next object inside the group and continues as if you had never changed the variable's value. To avoid confusion, don't bother.

Changes to a collection are immediately reflected in the loop. For example, if the statements inside the loop add a new object to the end of the collection, then the loop continues until it processes the new item. Similarly, if the loop's code removes an item from the end of the collection (that it has not yet reached), the loop does not process that item.

The exact effect on the loop depends on whether the item added or removed comes before or after the object the loop is currently processing. For example, if you remove an item before the current item, the loop has already examined that item, so there is no change to the loop's behavior. If you remove an item after the current one, the loop doesn't examine it. If you remove the current item, the loop seems to get confused and exits without raising an error.

Additions and deletions to an array are *not* reflected in the loop. If you use a ReDim statement to add items to the end of the array, the loop does not process them. If you try to access those objects, however, the program generates an "Index was outside the bounds of the array" error.

If you use ReDim to remove items from the end of the array, the loop processes those items any way! If you modify the values in the array, for example, you change an object's properties or set an array entry to an entirely new object, the loop sees the changes.

To avoid all these possible sources of confusion, don't modify a collection or array while a For Each loop is examining its contents.

CREATIVE COLLECTIONS

If you really must modify a collection while looping through it, create a new collection and modify that one instead. For example, suppose you want to loop through the original collection and remove some items. Make the new collection and then loop through the original copying the items that you want to keep into the new collection.

In really complicated situations, you may need to use a For loop and some careful indexing instead of a For Each loop.

One common scenario when dealing with collections is to examine every item in the collection and remove some of them. If you use a For Each loop, removing the loop's current item makes the loop exit prematurely.

Another approach that seems like it might work (but doesn't) is to use a For Next loop, as shown in the following code. If the code removes an object from the collection, the loop skips the next item because its index has been reduced by one and the loop has already passed that position in the collection. Worse still, the control variable i will increase until it reaches the original value of employees.Count. If the loop has removed any objects, the collection no longer holds that many items. The code tries to access an index beyond the end of the collection and throws an error.

```
Dim emp As Employee

For i As Integer = 1 To employees.Count
    emp = CType(employees(i), Employee)
    If emp.IsManager Then employees.Remove(i)
Next i
```

One solution to this problem is to use a For Next loop to examine the collection's objects in reverse order, as shown in the following example. In this version, the code never needs to use an index after it has been deleted because it is counting backward. The index of an object in the collection also doesn't change unless that object has already been examined by the loop. The loop examines every item exactly once, no matter which objects are removed.

```
For i As Integer = employees.Count To 1 Step -1
    emp = CType(employees(i), Employee)
    If emp.IsManager Then employees.Remove(i)
Next i
```

Enumerators

An *enumerator* is an object that lets you move through the objects contained by some sort of container class. For example, collections, arrays, and hash tables provide enumerators. This section discusses enumerators for collections, but the same ideas apply for these other classes.

You can use an enumerator to view the objects in a collection but not to modify the collection itself. You can use the enumerator to alter the objects in the collection, but you can generally not use it to add, remove, or rearrange the objects in the collection.

Initially, an enumerator is positioned before the first item in the collection. Your code can use the enumerator's MoveNext method to step to the next object in the collection. MoveNext returns True if it successfully moves to a new object or False if there are no more objects in the collection.

The Reset method restores the enumerator to its original position before the first object, so you can step through the collection again.

The Current method returns the object that the enumerator is currently reading. Note that Current returns a generic Object, so you will probably need to use CType to convert the result into a more specific data type before you use it. Invoking Current throws an error if the enumerator is not currently reading any object. That happens if the enumerator is before the first object or after the last object.

The following example uses an enumerator to loop through the items in a collection named m_Employees. It declares an Employee variable named `emp` and an IEnumerator object named `employee_enumerator`. It uses the collection's GetEnumerator method to obtain an enumerator for the collection. The program then enters a While loop. If `employee_enumerator.MoveNext` returns True, the enumerator has successfully moved to the next object in the collection. As long as it has read an object, the program uses CType to convert the generic object returned by Current into an Employee object, and it displays the Employee object's `Title`, `FirstName`, and `LastName` values. When it has finished processing all of the objects in the collection, `employee_enumerator.MoveNext` returns False and the While loop ends.

```
Dim emp As Employee
Dim employee_enumerator As IEnumerator
employee_enumerator = m_Employees.GetEnumerator()
```

```
Do While (employee_enumerator.MoveNext)
    emp = CType(employee_enumerator.Current, Employee)
    Debug.WriteLine(emp.Title & " " &.FirstName & " " & emp.LastName)
Loop
```

EXACT ENUMERATORS

Some containers support enumerators that use more specific data types. For example, a program can use a generic List that contains a specific kind of object such as Employee. Then it can use a generic enumerator of the correct type, in this case `IEnumerator(Of Employee)`. In that case, the enumerator's Current property returns an Employee instead of an Object so the code does not need to convert it into an Employee before using its methods.

Example program EnumerateEmployees, which is available for download on the book's web site, creates a `List(Of Employee)`. It then creates an `IEnumerator(Of Employee)` for the list and uses it to loop through the list. For more information on generics, see Chapter 29, "Generics."

A For Each loop provides roughly the same access to the items in a container class as an enumerator. Under some circumstances, however, an enumerator may provide a more natural way to loop through a container class than a For Each loop. For example, an enumerator can skip several items without examining them closely. You can also use an enumerator's Reset method to restart the enumeration. To restart a For Each loop, you would need to repeat the loop, possibly by placing it inside yet another loop that determines when to stop looping.

The Visual Basic documentation states that an enumerator is valid only as long as you do not modify the collection. If you add or remove an object to or from the collection, the enumerator throws an "invalid operation" exception the next time you use it. In at least some cases, however, this doesn't seem to be true, and an enumerator can still work even if you modify its collection. This could lead to extremely confusing situations, however. To avoid unnecessary confusion, do not modify a collection while you are accessing it with an enumerator. (If you really must modify the collection, try the techniques described in the "Creative Collections" tip earlier in this chapter.)

The IEnumerable interface defines the features needed for enumerators so any class that implements the IEnumerable interface provides enumerators. Any class that supports For Each must also implement the IEnumerable interface, so any class that supports For Each also supports enumerators. A few of the classes that implement IEnumerable include the following:

Array	HybridDictionary	SqlDataReader
ArrayList	ListDictionary	Stack
Collection	MessageQueue	String
CollectionBase	OdbcDataReader	StringCollection
ControlCollection	OleDbDataReader	StringDictionary
DataView	OracleDataReader	TableCellCollection
DictionaryBase	Queue	TableRowCollection
DictionaryEntries	ReadOnlyCollectionBase	XmlNode
Hashtable	SortedList	XmlNodeList

Iterators

An *iterator* is similar in concept to an enumerator. It also provides methods that allow you to step through the objects in some sort of container object. Iterators are more specialized than enumerators and work with a particular kind of class. Although you can use a nonspecific IEnumerator object to step through the items contained in any class that implements IEnumerable (an array, collection, hash table, or whatever), a certain iterator class is associated with a specific container class.

For example, a GraphicsPath object represents a series of connected lines and curves. A GraphicsPathIterator object can step through the line and curve data contained in a GraphicsPath object.

Iterators are much more specialized than enumerators. How you use them depends on what you need to do and on the kind of iterator, so they are not described in detail here.

Do Loop Statements

Visual Basic .NET supports three basic forms of Do Loop statements. The first form is a loop that repeats forever. The syntax is as follows:

```
Do
    statements
    [Exit Do]
    statements
    [Continue Do]
    statements
Loop
```

This kind of Do Loop executes the code it contains until the program somehow ends the loop. The following loop processes work orders. It calls the WorkOrderAvailable function to see if a work order is available. If an order is available, the code calls `ProcessWorkOrder` to process it. The code then repeats the loop to look for another work order.

```
Do
    ' See if a work order is available.
    If WorkOrderAvailable() Then
            ' Process the next work order.
        ProcessWorkOrder()
    End If
Loop
```

This example keeps checking for work orders forever. Most programs include some method for the loop to end so that the program can eventually stop. For example, the loop might use the Exit Do statement described shortly to end the loop if the user clicks a Stop button.

The second and third forms of Do Loop statements both include a test to determine whether they should continue looping. The difference between the two versions is where they place the test.

The next version of Do Loop places its test at the beginning, so the test is evaluated before the code is executed. If the test initially indicates that the loop should not continue, the statements inside the loop are never executed. The syntax is as follows:

```
Do {While | Until} condition
    statements
    [Exit Do]
    statements
    [Continue Do]
    statements
Loop
```

The final version of Do Loop places its test at the end. In this version, the statements inside the loop are executed before the loop performs its test. That means that the code is always executed at least once. The syntax is as follows:

```
Do
    statements
    [Exit Do]
    statements
    [Continue Do]
    statements
Loop {While | Until} condition
```

If the code uses the While keyword, the loop executes as long as the condition is true. If the code uses the Until keyword, the loop executes as long as the condition is false. Note that the statement Until *condition* is equivalent to While Not *condition*. Visual Basic provides these two variations so that you can pick the one that makes your code more readable. Use the one that makes the most sense to you.

The Exit Do statement allows the program to leave the nearest enclosing loop before it would normally finish. The Continue Do statement makes the loop jump back to its Do statement and start the loop over again. This is particularly useful if the program doesn't need to execute the rest of the steps within the loop and wants to quickly start the next iteration. Unlike a For loop, the Do loop does not automatically increment a looping variable or move to the next object in a collection. The code must explicitly change the loop's condition before calling Continue Do or else the loop will continue forever.

While End

A While End loop is equivalent to a Do While loop. The syntax is as follows:

```
While condition
    statements
    [Exit While]
    statements
    [Continue While]
    statements
End While
```

This is equivalent to the following Do While loop:

```
Do While condition
    statements
    [Exit Do]
    statements
    [Continue Do]
    statements
Loop
```

The Exit While statement exits a While End loop just as an Exit Do statement exits a Do While Loop. Similarly, Continue While makes the program return to the top of the loop just as Continue Do does for Do loops.

The difference between While End and Do While Loop is stylistic, and you can use whichever seems clearer to you. Because Do Loop provides more flexibility, having four different versions using While or Until at the start or finish of the loop, you might want to stick to them for consistency's sake.

Exit and Continue

The Exit and Continue statements are described in the previous sections, but they deserve a quick summary.

The Exit statement lets you end a loop early. The Continue statement lets you jump to the start of a loop before reaching its end.

Both of these statements work only on the innermost loop of the appropriate type. For example, an Exit For statement exits the innermost For loop surrounding the statement.

Example program ExitAndContinue, which is available for download on the book's web site, demonstrates the Exit and Continue statements.

GOTO

A GoTo statement unconditionally tells the program to jump to a specific location in the code. Because it tells the program what to do, it is a program control statement. The syntax is as follows:

```
    GoTo line_label
    ...
line_label:
    ...
```

Though GoTo by itself isn't a decision statement, it is often used to mimic a decision statement. For example, the following code fragment uses GoTo to mimic an If Then Else statement. It examines the purchase_total variable. If purchase_total is less than 1000, the code jumps to the line labeled SmallOrder. If purchase_total is greater than or equal to 1000, the program continues to execute the code that processes a larger order.

```
    If purchase_total < 1000 Then GoTo SmallOrder
    ' Process a large order.
    ...
    Exit Sub

SmallOrder:
    ' Process a small order.
    ...
```

The following code does roughly the same thing as the preceding version but without the GoTo statement:

```
If purchase_total < 1000 Then
    ' Process a large order.
    ...
Else
    ' Process a small order.
    ...
End If
```

Similarly, GoTo is sometimes used to build a loop. The following code uses GoTo to jump backward in the code to call subroutine DoSomething 10 times:

```
    Dim i As Integer = 1
StartLoop:
    DoSomething()
    i += 1
    If i <= 10 Then GoTo StartLoop
```

The following code does the same thing without the GoTo statement:

```
For i As Integer = 1 To 10
    DoSomething()
Next i
```

The problem with the GoTo statement is its flexibility. By using GoTo in a haphazard way, an undisciplined programmer can make the program jump all over the place with little rhyme or reason. This can lead to *spaghetti code* (so called because a diagram showing the program's flow of control can look like a pile of spaghetti) that is extremely difficult to understand, debug, and maintain.

Many programming teams prohibit any use of GoTo because it can lead to this kind of code. Some even believe GoTo should be removed from the Visual Basic language. You can always use If Then Else statements, For Next loops, While loops, and other control statements in place of GoTo statements, so GoTo is not absolutely necessary.

However, some programmers feel that GoTo simplifies code under certain very specific circumstances. The following code begins by performing some sort of initialization. It may open databases, create temporary files, connect to the Internet, and perform other startup chores. It then executes a series of tasks, each of which may fail or otherwise make it pointless for the program to continue. If any of these steps sets the variable `should_stop` to True, the program uses a GoTo statement to jump to its clean-up code. This code closes any open database, deletes temporary files, closes permanent files, and performs any other necessary clean up chores.

```
    ' Get started, open database, open files, etc.
    Initialize()

    ' Perform a long series of tasks.
    DoStuff1()
    If should_stop Then GoTo CleanUp

    DoStuff2()
    If should_stop Then GoTo CleanUp

    DoStuff3()
    If should_stop Then GoTo CleanUp

    ...

CleanUp:
    ' Close database, delete temporary files, etc.
    PerformCleanUp()
```

The GoTo statement in this code lets the program jump to the clean-up code any time it needs to stop performing its tasks. That may be because a task failed, the user canceled the operation, or all the tasks are finished.

Note that this is a very specific use of GoTo. The code only jumps forward, never backward. It also only jumps to clean-up code, not to some arbitrary point in the code. These facts help make the GoTo statement easier to understand and prevent spaghetti code.

The following code does the same thing as the preceding version without using GoTo. At each step, the program checks the value of should_stop to see if it should continue working through its tasks.

```
    ' Get started, open database, open files, etc.
    Initialize()

    ' Perform a long series of tasks.
    DoStuff1()

    If Not should_stop Then DoStuff2()

    If Not should_stop Then DoStuff3()

    ' Close database, delete temporary files, etc.
    PerformCleanUp()
```

The following code shows another version that doesn't use GoTo. This version places the code that formerly contained the GoTo statement in a new subroutine. Instead of using GoTo, this routine uses Exit Sub to stop performing tasks early if necessary.

```
Sub DoWork() '
    ' Get started, open database, open files, etc.
    Initialize()

    ' Perform all of the tasks.
    PerformTasks()

    ' Close database, delete temporary files, etc.
    PerformCleanUp()
End Sub

' Perform a long series of tasks.
Sub PerformTasks()
    DoStuff1()
    If should_stop Then Exit Sub

    DoStuff2()
    If should_stop Then Exit Sub

    DoStuff3()
    If should_stop Then Exit Sub
End Sub
```

Conceptually, an Exit Sub statement is little different from a GoTo statement. After all, it, too, is an unconditional jump command. However, Exit Sub has a very specific, well-known effect: it makes the program stop executing the current subroutine. It cannot make the program jump around arbitrarily, possibly leading to spaghetti code.

If you ever feel tempted to use GoTo, take a few moments to think about ways you might rewrite the code. If the only ways you can think of to rewrite the code are more confusing than the original version, go ahead and use GoTo. You should probably add some fairly detailed comments to ensure that the GoTo statement doesn't cause trouble later.

SUMMARY

Control statements form the heart of any program. Decision statements determine what commands are executed, and looping statements determine how many times they are executed.

Single-line and multiline If Then statements, as well as Select Case, are the most commonly used decision statements. IIf and Choose statements are often more confusing and sometimes slower, so usually you should use If Then and Select Case statements instead. Under some specific circumstances, however, IIf and Choose may make your code more readable. Use your judgment and pick the method that makes the most sense in your application.

For Next, For Each, and Do Loop are the most common looping statements. Some container classes also support enumerators that let you step through the items in the container. An enumerator can be more natural than a For Each loop under some circumstances.

A While End loop is equivalent to Do While loop. You can use whichever you think makes more sense, although you might want to use Do While because it is more consistent with the other forms of Do Loop.

Finally, the GoTo statement is often used in a decision statement or to create a loop. Unfortunately, undisciplined use of GoTo statements can lead to spaghetti code that is extremely hard to understand, debug, and maintain. To avoid later frustration, you should avoid using GoTo statements whenever possible, and provide good comments where GoTo is necessary. Some programmers use GoTo in very specialized cases, whereas others avoid it at all costs. You can always rewrite code to avoid GoTo statements, and usually that is better in the long run.

Using the control statements described in this chapter, you can build extremely complex and powerful applications. In fact, you can build applications that are so complex that it is difficult to ensure that they work correctly. Even a relatively simple application sometimes encounters errors. Chapter 19, "Error Handling," explains how you can protect an application from these and other unexpected errors and let it take action to correct any problems or at least to avoid crashing.

19

Error Handling

Although it is theoretically possible to write a program that perfectly predicts every possible situation that it might encounter, in practice that's very difficult for nontrivial programs. For large applications, it is very difficult to plan for every eventuality. Errors in the program's design and implementation can introduce bugs that give unexpected results. Users and corrupted databases may give the application values that it doesn't know how to manage.

Similarly, changing requirements over time may introduce data that the application was never intended to handle. The Y2K bug is a good example. When engineers wrote accounting, auto registration, financial, inventory, and other systems in the 1960s and 1970s, they never dreamed their programs would still be running in the year 2000. At the time, disk storage and memory were relatively expensive, so they stored years as 2-byte values (for example, 89 meant 1989). When the year 2000 rolled around, the applications couldn't tell whether the value 01 meant the year 1901 or 2001. In one humorous case, an auto registration system started issuing horseless carriage license plates to new cars because it thought cars built in 00 must be antiques.

The Y2K problem wasn't really a bug. It was a case of software used with data that wasn't part of its original design.

This chapter explains different kinds of exceptional conditions that can arise in an application. These range from unplanned data (as in the Y2K problem) to bugs where the code is just plain wrong. With some advance planning, you can build a robust application that can keep running gracefully, even when the unexpected happens.

BUGS VERSUS UNPLANNED CONDITIONS

Several different types of unplanned conditions can derail an otherwise high-quality application. How you should handle these conditions depends on their nature.

For this discussion, a *bug* is a mistake in the application code. Some bugs become apparent right away and are easy to fix. These usually include simple typographic errors and cases where you misuse an object (for example, by using the wrong control property). Other bugs are subtler and may only be detected long after they occur. For example, a data-entry routine might place invalid characters into a rarely used field in a Customer object. Only later when the program tries to access that field will you discover the problem. This kind of bug is difficult to track down and fix, but there are some proactive steps you can take to make these sorts of bugs easier to find.

BUGS THROUGHOUT HISTORY

On a historical note, the term "bug" has been used since at least the time of the telegraph to mean some sort of defect. Probably the origin of the term in computer science was an actual moth that was caught between two relays in an early computer in 1947. For a bit more information, including a picture of this first computer bug, see `www.jamesshuggins.com/h/tek1/first_computer_bug.htm`.

An *unplanned condition* is some predictable condition that you don't want to happen, but that you know could happen despite your best efforts. For example, there are many ways that a simple printing operation can fail. The printer might be unplugged, disconnected from its computer, disconnected from the network, out of toner, out of paper, experiencing a memory fault, clogged by a paper jam, or just plain broken. These are not bugs, because the application software is not at fault. There is some condition outside of the program's control that must be fixed.

Another common unplanned condition occurs when the user enters invalid data. You may want the user to enter a value between 1 and 10 in a text box, but the user might enter 0, 9999, or "lunch" instead.

Catching Bugs

By definition, bugs are unplanned. No reasonable programmer sits down and thinks, "Perhaps I'll put a bug in this variable declaration."

Because bugs are unpredictable, you cannot know ahead of time where a bug will lie. However, you can watch for behavior in the program that indicates that a bug may be present. For example, suppose that you have a subroutine that sorts a purchase order's items by cost. If the routine receives an order with 100,000 items, something is probably wrong. If one of the items is a computer keyboard with a price of $73 trillion, something is probably wrong. If the customer who placed the order doesn't exist, something is probably wrong.

This routine could go ahead and sort the 100,000 items with prices ranging from a few cents to $73 trillion. Later, the program would try to print a 5000-page invoice with no shipping or billing address. Only then would the developers realize that there is a problem.

Rather than trying to work around the problematic data, it would be better if the sorting routine immediately told developers that something is wrong so they can start trying to find the cause of the problem. Bugs are easier to find the sooner they are detected. This bug will be easier to find if the sorting routine notices it, rather than waiting until the application tries to print an invalid invoice. Your routines can protect themselves and the program as a whole by proactively validating inputs and outputs, and reporting anything suspicious to developers.

Some developers object to making routines spend considerable effort validating data that they know is correct. After all, one routine generated this data and passed it to another, so you *know* that it is correct because the first routine did its job properly. That's only true if every routine that touches the data works perfectly. Because bugs are by definition unexpected, you cannot safely assume that all the routines are perfect and that the data remains uncorrupted.

AUTOMATED BUG CATCHERS

Many companies use automated testing tools to try to flush out problems early. Regression testing tools can execute code to verify that its outcome isn't changed after you have made modifications to other parts of the application. If you build a suite of testing routines to validate data and subroutines' results, you may be able to work them into an automated testing system, too.

To prevent validation code from slowing down the application, you can use the Debug object's Assert method to check for strange conditions. When you are debugging the program, these statements throw an error if they detect something suspicious. When you make a release build to send to customers, the Debug.Assert code is removed from the application. That makes the application faster and doesn't inflict cryptic error messages on the user.

You can also use the DEBUG, TRACE, and CONFIG compiler constants to add other input and output validation code.

Example program SortOrders uses the following code to validate a subroutine's inputs. (This program doesn't actually do anything; it just shows how to write input validation code.)

```
Private Sub SortOrderItems(ByVal the_order As Order)
    ' Validate input.
    Debug.Assert(the_order.Items IsNot Nothing, "No items in order")
    Debug.Assert(the_order.Customer IsNot Nothing, "No customer in order")
    Debug.Assert(the_order.Items.Count < 100, "Too many order items")
    ...

    ' Sort the items.
    ...

    ' Validate output.
#If DEBUG Then
    ' Verify that the items are sorted.
    Dim order_item1 As OrderItem
```

```
      Dim order_item2 As OrderItem
      order_item1 = DirectCast(the_order.Items(1), OrderItem)
      For i As Integer = 2 To the_order.Items.Count
          order_item2 = DirectCast(the_order.Items(i), OrderItem)
          Debug.Assert(order_item1.Price <= order_item2.Price,
              "Order items not properly sorted")
          order_item1 = order_item2
      Next i
  #End If
  End Sub
```

code snippet SortOrders

The subroutine starts by validating its input. It verifies that the Order object that it received has an Items collection and that its Customer property is not Nothing. It also verifies that the order contains fewer than 100 items. If a larger order comes along during testing, developers can increase this number to 200 or whatever value makes sense, but there's no need to start with an unreasonably large default.

Before the subroutine exits, it loops through the sorted items to verify that they are correctly sorted. If any item has cost less than the one before, the program throws an error. Because this test is contained within an #If DEBUG Then statement, this code is removed from release builds.

After you have tested the application long enough, you should have discovered most of these types of errors. When you make the release build, the compiler automatically removes the validation code, making the finished executable smaller and faster.

Catching Unplanned Conditions

Although you don't want an unplanned condition to happen, with some careful thought, you can predict where an unplanned condition might occur. Typically, these situations arise when the program must work with something outside of its own code. For example, when the program needs to access a file, printer, web page, floppy disk, or CD-ROM, that item may be unavailable. Similarly, whenever the program takes input from the user, the user may enter invalid data.

Notice how this differs from the bugs described in the previous section. After sufficient testing, you should have found and fixed most of the bugs. No amount of testing can remove the possibility of unplanned conditions. No matter what code you use, the user may still remove a floppy disk from the drive before the program is ready.

Whenever you know that an unplanned condition might occur, you should write code to protect the program from dangerous conditions. It is generally better to test for these conditions explicitly rather than simply attempting to perform whatever action you were planning and then catching an error if one occurs. Testing for problem conditions generally gives you more complete information about what's wrong. It's also usually faster than catching an error because the structured error handling described shortly comes with considerable overhead.

For example, the following statement sets an integer variable using the value the user entered in a text box:

```
Dim num_items As Integer = Integer.Parse(txtNumItems.Text)
```

The user might enter a valid value in the text box. Unfortunately, the user may also enter something that is not a number, a value that is too big to fit in an integer, or a negative number when you are expecting a positive number. The user may even leave the field blank.

Example program ValidateInteger uses the following code to validate integer input:

Available for
download on
Wrox.com

```
' Check for blank entry.
Dim num_items_txt As String = txtNumItems.Text
If num_items_txt.Length < 1 Then
    MessageBox.Show("Please enter Num Items")
    txtNumItems.Focus()
    Exit Sub
End If

' See if it's numeric.
If Not IsNumeric(num_items_txt) Then
    MessageBox.Show("Num Items must be a number")
    txtNumItems.Select(0, num_items_txt.Length)
    txtNumItems.Focus()
    Exit Sub
End If

' Assign the value.
Dim num_items As Integer
Try
    num_items = Integer.Parse(txtNumItems.Text)
Catch ex As Exception
    MessageBox.Show("Error in Num Items." & vbCrLf & ex.Message)
    txtNumItems.Select(0, num_items_txt.Length)
    txtNumItems.Focus()
    Exit Sub
End Try

' Check that the value is between 1 and 100.
If num_items < 1 Or num_items > 100 Then
    MessageBox.Show("Num Items must be between 1 and 100")
    txtNumItems.Select(0, num_items_txt.Length)
    txtNumItems.Focus()
    Exit Sub
End If
```

code snippetValidateInteger

The code checks that the field is not blank and uses the IsNumeric function to verify that the field contains a vaguely numeric value.

Unfortunately, the IsNumeric function doesn't exactly match the behavior of functions such as Integer.Parse. IsNumeric returns False for values such as &H10, which is a valid hexadecimal value that Integer.Parse can correctly interpret. IsNumeric also returns True for values such as 123456789012345 that lie outside of the values allowed by integers and 1.2, which is numeric but not an integer. Because IsNumeric doesn't exactly match Integer.Parse, the program still needs to use a Try Catch block (bolded in the previous code) to protect itself when it actually tries to convert the string into an integer.

The code finishes by verifying that the value lies within a reasonable bound. If the value passes all of these checks, the code uses the value.

A typical subroutine might need to read and validate many values, and retyping this code would be cumbersome. A better solution is to move it into an `IsValidInteger` function and then call the function as needed.

You can write similar routines to validate other types of data fields such as phone numbers, e-mail addresses, street addresses, and so on.

Global Exception Handling

Normally, you should try to catch an error as close as possible to the place where it occurs. If an error occurs in a particular subroutine, it will be easiest to fix the bug if you catch it in that subroutine.

However, bugs often arise in unexpected places. Unless you protect every subroutine with error-handling code (a fairly common strategy), a bug may arise in code that you have not protected.

In early versions of Visual Basic, you could not catch the bug, so the application crashed. In the most recent versions of Visual Basic, however, you can define a global error handler to catch any bug that isn't caught by other error-handling code.

ERRORS, ERRORS, EVERYWHERE

In fact, some sources of errors are completely beyond your control. For example, power surges, static electricity, intermittent short circuits, or even stray radiation striking exactly the right part of a chip can make the computer's hardware misbehave so code that should work correctly fails. There's little you can do to anticipate these kinds of errors but you can use global error handling to try to recover from them.

Of course that doesn't excuse you from rigorously checking your code for errors. The vast majority of bugs are due to real mistakes in the code or data rather than to magical cosmic rays flipping a single bit on a memory chip.

To define application-level event handlers, double-click My Project in the Project Explorer. Open the Application tab and click the View Application Events button. This opens a code window for application-level events.

In the left drop-down list, select (MyApplication Events). Then in the right drop-down list, you can select one of several events including NetworkAvailabilityChanged, Shutdown, Startup, StartupNextInstance, and UnhandledException. Select the last of these commands to open the UnhandledException event handler.

In the event handler, you can take whatever action is appropriate for the error. Because you probably didn't anticipate the error, there's usually little chance that the program can correct it properly. However, you can at least log the error and possibly save data before shutting down the application.

The event parameter e has an `ExitApplication` property that you can set to True or False to tell Visual Basic whether the application should terminate.

> **KEEP RUNNING**
>
> Usually it's better for an application to do the best it can to recover and keep running instead of exiting. Even if the program must reset itself to a default state, that at least saves the user the trouble of restarting the application, reopening forms, arranging toolbars, and otherwise getting the program ready to work. Before you decide, compare the difficulty of making the program reset and continue with the trouble the user will have restarting and getting back to work.

Example program GlobalException uses the following code to display a message giving the unhandled exception's error message. It then sets e.`ExitApplication` to False, so the program keeps running.

Available for
download on
Wrox.com

```
Private Sub MyApplication_UnhandledException(
 ByVal sender As Object,
 ByVal e As Microsoft.VisualBasic.ApplicationServices.UnhandledExceptionEventArgs) _
 Handles Me.UnhandledException
     MessageBox.Show("Exception caught globally" & vbCrLf & e.Exception.Message)
     e.ExitApplication = False
 End Sub
```

code snippet GlobalException

When you run the application in the IDE, Visual Basic stops execution in the debugger when it reaches the statement that causes the error, so the UnhandledException event never executes. If you run the compiled executable, however, the UnhandledException event fires and the global error-handler runs.

STRUCTURED ERROR HANDLING

Visual Basic .NET introduced structured error handling using the Try block. The syntax is as follows:

```
Try
    try_statements ...
[Catch ex As exception_type_1
    exception_statements_1 ...
]
[Catch ex As exception_type_2
    exception_statements_2 ...
]
...
[Catch
    final_exception_statements ...
]
[Finally
    finally_statements ...
]
End Try
```

The program executes the code in the `try_statements` block. If any of that code throws an exception, the program jumps to the first Catch statement.

If the exception matches `exception_type_1`, the program executes the code in `exception_statements_1`. The exception type might match the Catch statement's exception class exactly, or it might be a subclass of the listed class. For example, suppose that the code in the `try_statements` block performs a calculation that divides by zero. That raises a DivideByZeroException. That class inherits from the ArithmeticException class, which inherits from SystemException, which inherits from Exception. That means the code would stop at the first Catch statement it finds that looks for DivideByZeroException, ArithmeticException, SystemException, or Exception.

If the raised exception does not match the first exception type, the program checks the next Catch statement. The program keeps comparing the exception to Catch statements until it finds one that applies, or it runs out of Catch statements.

CATCH CONTROL

Be sure to arrange Catch statements so the most specific come first. Otherwise, a more general statement will catch errors before a more specific statement has a chance. For example, the generic Exception class includes all other exceptions, so if the first Catch statement catches Exception, no other Catch statements will ever execute.

If two Catch statements are unrelated, neither will catch the other's exceptions, so put the exception more likely to occur first. That will make the code more efficient because it looks for the most common problems first. It also keeps the code that is most likely to execute near the top where it is easier to read.

If no Catch statement matches the exception, the exception "bubbles up" to the next level in the call stack and Visual Basic moves to the routine that called the current one. If that routine has appropriate error-handling code, it deals with the error. If that routine can't catch the error, the exception bubbles up again until Visual Basic eventually either finds error-handling code that can catch the exception, or it runs off the top of the call stack. If it runs off the call stack, Visual Basic calls the global UnhandledException event handler described in the previous section, if one exists. If there is no UnhandledException event handler, the program crashes.

If you include a Catch statement with no exception type, that block matches any exception. If the raised exception doesn't match any of the previous exception types, the program executes the `final_exception_statements` block of code. Note that the statement `Catch ex As Exception` also matches all exceptions, so it's just good as Catch by itself. It also gives you easy access to the exception object's properties and methods.

You can figure out what exception classes to use in Catch statements in several ways. First, you can spend a lot of time digging through the online help. An easier method is to let the program crash and then look at the error message it produces. Figure 19-1 shows the error message a program throws when it tries to convert the non-numeric string "Hello" into an integer with Integer.Parse. From the exception dialog's title, it's easy to see that the program should look for a FormatException.

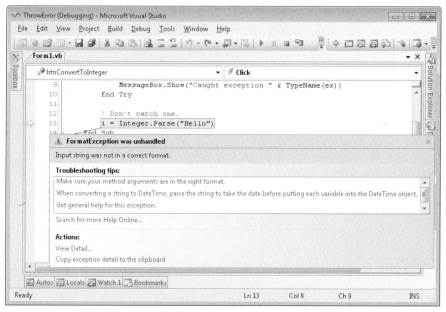

FIGURE 19-1: When a program crashes, the message it generates tells you the type of exception it raised.

Another way to decide what types of exceptions to catch is to place a final generic `Catch ex As Exception` statement at the end of the Catch list. Place code inside that Catch block that displays either the exception's type name (use TypeName) or the result of its ToString method. When you encounter new exception types, you can give them their own Catch statements and take more action that's appropriate to that exception type.

CATCH CATASTROPHES

It may not be possible to take meaningful action when you catch certain exceptions. For example, if a program uses up all of the available memory, Visual Basic throws an OutOfMemoryException. If there is no memory available, you may have trouble doing anything useful. Similarly, if there's a problem with the file system, you may be unable to write error descriptions into a log file.

After it has finished running the code in `try_statements` and it has executed any necessary exception code in a Catch block, the program executes the code in `finally_statements`. You can use the Finally section to execute code whether the code in `try_statements` succeeds or fails.

You do not need to include any Catch statements in a Try block, but leaving them all out defeats the Try block's purpose. If the `try_statements` raise an error, the program doesn't have any error code to execute, so it sends the error up the call stack. Eventually, the program finds an active error handler or the error pops off the top of the stack and the program crashes. You may as well not bother with the Try block if you aren't going to use any Catch sections.

A Try block must include at least one Catch or Finally section, although those sections do not need to contain any code. For example, the following Try block calls subroutine `DoSomething` and uses an empty Catch section to ignore any errors that occur:

```
Try
    DoSomething()
Catch
End Try
```

Using an empty Finally section is legal but not terribly useful. The following code doesn't protect the program from any exceptions and doesn't do anything in the Finally block. You may as well just omit the Try block.

```
Try
    DoSomething()
Finally
End Try
```

Example program ThrowError, which is available for download on the book's web site, shows how a program can use a Try Catch block to handle errors.

Exception Objects

When a Catch statement catches an exception, its exception variable contains information about the error that raised the exception. Different exception classes may provide different features, but they all provide the basic features defined by the Exception class from which they are all derived. The following table lists the most commonly used Exception class properties and methods.

ITEM	PURPOSE
InnerException	The exception that caused the current exception. For example, suppose that you write a tool library that catches an exception and then throws a new custom exception describing the problem in terms of your library. You should set InnerException to the exception that you caught before you throw the new exception.
Message	Returns a brief message that describes the exception.
Source	Returns the name of the application or object that threw the exception.
StackTrace	Returns a string containing a stack trace giving the program's location when the error occurred.
TargetSite	Returns the name of the method that threw the exception.
ToString	Returns a string describing the exception and including the stack trace.

Example program ShowExceptionInfo, which is available for download on the book's web site, displays an exception's Message, StackTrace, and ToString values.

At a minimum, the program should log or display the Message value for any unexpected exceptions so you know what exception occurred. It might also log the StackTrace or the result of ToString so you can see where the exception occurred.

The following text shows the results of the ToString method produced by a DivideByZeroException exception object:

```
System.DivideByZeroException: Attempted to divide by zero.
    at ShowExceptionInfo.Form1.CheckVacationPay() in C:\Documents and
Settings\Rod\Local Settings\Application Data\Temporary
Projects\ShowExceptionInfo\Form1.vb:line 25
    at ShowExceptionInfo.Form1.CalculateEmployeeSalaries() in C:\Documents and
Settings\Rod\Local Settings\Application Data\Temporary
Projects\ShowExceptionInfo\Form1.vb:line 18
    at ShowExceptionInfo.Form1.btnCalculate_Click(Object sender, EventArgs e) in
C:\Documents and Settings\Rod\Local Settings\Application Data\Temporary
Projects\ShowExceptionInfo\Form1.vb:line 5
```

The StackTrace and ToString values can help developers find a bug, but they can be intimidating to end users. Even the abbreviated format used by the exception's Message property is usually not very useful to a user. When the user clicks the "Find Outstanding Invoices" button, the message "Attempted to divide by zero" doesn't really tell the user what the problem is or what to do about it.

When a program catches an error, a good strategy is to record the full ToString message in a log file or e-mail it to a developer. Then display a message that restates the error message in terms that the user can understand. For example, the program might say the following: "Unable to total outstanding invoices. A bug report has been sent to the development team." The program should then try to continue as gracefully as possible. It may not be able to finish this calculation, but it should not crash, and it should allow the user to continue working on other tasks if possible.

StackTrace Objects

An exception object's ToString and StackTrace methods return textual representations of the program's stack trace. Your code can also use StackTrace objects to examine the program's execution position without generating an error.

The following code shows how a program can display a simple stack trace in the Immediate window:

```
Imports System.Diagnostics
...
Dim stack_trace As New System.Diagnostics.StackTrace(True)
Debug.WriteLine(stack_trave.ToString())
```

The StackTrace class also provides methods for exploring call frames in the stack. The FrameCount property and the GetFrame and GetFrames methods give you access to StackFrame objects representing the frames. StackFrame objects provide some additional detail not listed by the StackTrace object's ToString method such as each code's file name, line number, and column number. Example program ClimbStackTrace, which is available for download on the book's web site, shows how a program can climb through the layers of a stack trace and display information about each call level.

Throwing Exceptions

In addition to catching exceptions, your program may need to generate its own exceptions. Because handling an exception is called *catching* it, raising an exception is called *throwing* it. (This is just a silly pun. People also catch lions and colds, but I don't think many people throw them. It's as good a term as any, however.)

To throw an error, the program creates an instance of the type of exception it wants to generate, passing the constructor additional information describing the problem. The program can set other exception fields if you like. For example, it might set the exception's Source property to tell any other code that catches the error where it originated. The program then uses the Throw statement to raise the error. If an error handler is active somewhere in the call stack, Visual Basic jumps to that point and the error handler processes the exception.

Example program DrawableRect, which is available for download on the book's web site, uses the following code to show how the DrawableRectangle class can protect itself against invalid input:

```
Public Class DrawableRectangle
    Public Sub New(ByVal new_x As Integer, ByVal new_y As Integer,
    ByVal new_width As Integer, ByVal new_height As Integer)
        ' Verify that new_width > 0.
        If new_width <= 0 Then
            Dim ex As New ArgumentException(
                "DrawableRectangle must have a width greater than zero",
                "new_width")
            Throw ex
        End If

        ' Verify that new_height> 0.
        If new_height < = 0 Then
            Throw New ArgumentException(
                "DrawableRectangle must have a height greater than zero",
                "new_height")
        End If
        ' Save the parameter values.
        ...
    End Sub
    ...
End Class
```

code snippet DrawableRect

The class's constructor takes four arguments: an X and Y position, and a width and height. If the width is less than or equal to zero, the program creates a new ArgumentException object. It passes the exception's constructor a description string and the name of the argument that is invalid. After creating the exception object, the program uses the Throw statement to raise the error. The code checks the object's new height similarly, but it creates and throws the exception in a single statement to demonstrate another style for throwing an error.

The following code shows how a program might use a Try block to protect itself while creating a new DrawableRectangle object:

```
Try
    Dim rect As New DrawableRectangle(10, 20, 0, 100)
Catch ex As Exception
    MessageBox.Show(ex.Message)
End Try
```

When your application needs to throw an exception, it's easiest to use an existing exception class. There are a few ways to get lists of exception classes so that you can find one that makes sense for your application. First, Appendix O, "Useful Exception Classes," lists some of the more useful exception classes. The online help topic, "Introduction to Exception Handling in Visual Basic .NET" at msdn.microsoft.com/aa289505.aspx also has a good list of exception classes at the end. Microsoft's web page msdn.microsoft.com/system.exception_derivedtypelist.aspx provides a very long list of exception classes that are derived from the System.Exception class.

Another method for finding exception classes is to open the Object Browser (select the View menu's Object Browser command) and search for "Exception." Figure 19-2 shows the Object Browser displaying roughly 400 matches, many of which are exception classes. The System.FormatException class is selected, so the Object Browser is showing that class's description.

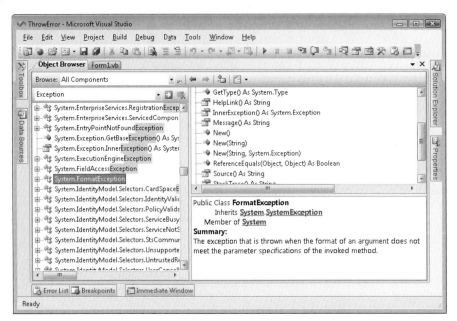

FIGURE 19-2: You can use the Object Browser to find exception classes.

When you throw exceptions, you must use your judgment about selecting these classes. For example, Visual Basic uses the System.Reflection.AmbiguousMatchException class when it tries to bind a subroutine call to an object's method, and it cannot determine which overloaded method to use. This happens at a lower level than your program will act, so you won't use that class for exactly the same purpose. It may be useful, for example, if your routine parses a string and, based on the string, cannot decide what action to take. In that case, you might use this class to represent the error, even though you're not using it exactly as it was originally intended.

Be sure to use the most specific exception class possible. Using more generic classes such as Exception makes it much harder for developers to understand and locate an error. If you cannot find a good, specific fit, create your own exception class as described in the section "Custom Exceptions" later in this chapter.

Before you use one of these classes, look it up in the online help to make sure that it fits your purpose. If there's no good fit, you can always create your own as described in the following section, "Custom Exceptions."

Specialized classes and libraries sometimes have their own particular exception classes. For example, serialization and cryptographic objects have their own sets of exception classes that make sense within their own domains. Usually, these are fairly specialized, so you won't need to throw them in your program unless you are re-raising an error you received from a serialization or cryptographic object.

Re-throwing Exceptions

Sometimes when you catch an exception, you cannot completely handle the problem. In that case, it may make sense to re-throw the exception so call higher up in the call stack can take a crack at it.

To re-throw an error exactly as you caught it, simply use the Throw keyword as in the following example.

```
Try
    ' Do something hard here.
    ...

Catch ex As ArithmeticException
    ' We can handle this exception. Fix it.
    ...

Catch ex As Exception
    ' We don't know what to do with this one. Re-throw it.
    Throw
End Try
```

If your code can figure out more or less why an error is happening but it cannot fix it, it's often a good idea to re-throw the error as a different exception type. For example, suppose a piece of code causes an ArithmeticException but the underlying cause of the exception is an invalid argument. In that case it is better to throw an ArgumentException instead of an ArithmeticException because that will provide more specific information higher up in the call stack.

At the same time, however, you don't want to lose the information contained in the original ArithmeticException.

The solution is to throw a new ArgumentException but place the original ArithmeticException in its InnerException property so code that catches the new exception has access to the original information.

The following code demonstrates this technique:

```
Try
    ' Do something hard here.
    ...

Catch ex As ArithmeticException
    ' This was caused by an invalid argument.
    ' Re-throw it as an ArgumentException.
    Throw New ArgumentException("Invalid argument X in function Whatever.", ex)

Catch ex As Exception
    ' We don't know what to do with this one. Re-throw it.
    Throw
End Try
```

Custom Exceptions

When your application needs to raise an exception, it's easiest to use an existing exception class. Reusing existing exception classes makes it easier for developers to understand what the exception means. It also prevents exception proliferation, where the developer needs to watch for dozens or hundreds of types of exceptions.

Sometimes, however, the predefined exceptions don't fit your needs. For example, suppose that you build a class that contains data that may exist for a long time. If the program tries to use an object that has not refreshed its data for a while, you want to raise some sort of "data expired" exception. You could squeeze this into the System.TimeoutException class, but that exception doesn't quite fit this use. The Expired class is a better fit, but it's part of the System.Net.Cookie namespace. Using it would require your application to include the System.Net.Cookie namespace just to define the exception class, even if the program has nothing to do with cookies. In this case, it would probably be better to create your own exception class.

Building a custom exception class is easy. Make a new class that inherits from the System. ApplicationException class. Then, provide constructor methods to let the program create instances of the class. That's all there is to it.

By convention, an exception class's name should end with the word Exception. Also by convention, you should provide at least three overloaded constructors for developers to use when creating new instances of the class. (For more information on what constructors are and how to define them, see the section "Class Instantiation Details" in Chapter 26, "Classes and Structures.")

The first constructor takes no parameters and initializes the exception with a default message describing the general type of error.

The other two versions take as parameters an error message, and an error message plus an inner exception object. These constructors pass their parameters to the base class's constructors to initialize the object appropriately.

For completeness, you can also make a constructor that takes as parameters a SerializationInfo object and a StreamingContext object. This version can also pass its parameters to a base class constructor to initialize the exception object, so you don't need to do anything special with the parameters. This constructor is useful if the exception will be serialized and deserialized. If you're not sure whether you need this constructor, you probably don't. If you do include it, however, you will need to import the System.Runtime.Serialization namespace in the exception class's file to define the SerializationInfo and StreamingContext classes.

Example program CustomException uses the following code to define the ObjectExpiredException class:

```
Imports System.Runtime.Serialization

Public Class ObjectExpiredException
    Inherits System.ApplicationException

    ' No parameters. Use a default message.
```

```
        Public Sub New()
            MyBase.New("This object has expired")
        End Sub

        ' Set the message.
        Public Sub New(ByVal new_message As String)
            MyBase.New(new_message)
        End Sub

        ' Set the message and inner exception.
        Public Sub New(ByVal new_message As String,
        ByVal inner_exception As Exception)
            MyBase.New(new_message, inner_exception)
        End Sub

        ' Include SerializationInfo object and StreamingContext objects.
        Public Sub New(ByVal info As SerializationInfo,
        ByVal context As StreamingContext)
            MyBase.New(info, context)
        End Sub
    End Class
```

code snippet CustomException

After you have defined the exception class, you can throw and catch it just as you can throw and catch any exception class defined by Visual Basic. For example, the following code throws an ObjectExpiredException error:

```
    Throw New ObjectExpiredException("This Customer object has expired.")
```

The parent class System.ApplicationException automatically handles the object's Message, StackTrace, and ToString properties so you don't need to implement them yourself.

VISUAL BASIC CLASSIC ERROR HANDLING

Structured error handling using the Try block is a relatively recent innovation, appearing in the first versions of Visual Basic .NET. Visual Basic 6 and earlier versions used a more line-oriented syntax sometimes called *Visual Basic Classic Error Handling*. Although the Try block is generally preferred, you can still use classic error handling in your Visual Basic .NET applications. In fact, you can use both styles in the same program, although not in the same routine. The section "Structured versus Classic Error Handling" later in this chapter discusses the pros and cons of each.

A classic error handler begins with an On Error statement that tells Visual Basic what it should do if it encounters an error. This statement can take one of four forms: On Error GoTo line, On Error Resume Next, On Error GoTo 0, and On Error GoTo –1.

> **CLASSIC CATCHES**
>
> Example program ClassicErrorHandling, which is available for download on the book's web site, demonstrates many of the concepts described in the following sections.

On Error GoTo Line

After the On Error GoTo *line* statement, if Visual Basic encounters an error, it enters error-handling mode and jumps to the indicated line. The error handler that begins at the indicated line can take whatever action is appropriate.

The following code executes the statement On Error GoTo LoadPayrollError and then calls subroutine LoadPayrollFile. If that routine causes an error, Visual Basic jumps to the line labeled LoadPayrollError. The error-handling code displays a message and exits the subroutine. The program then executes the statement On Error GoTo PrintPaychecksError and calls the PrintPaychecks routine. If that routine throws an error, the code starting at the PrintPaychecksError label executes. After it has finished its work, the routine uses an Exit Sub statement to end without falling into the error-handling code that follows.

```
Private Sub ProcessPayroll()
    ' Load the payroll file.
    On Error GoTo LoadPayrollError
    LoadPayrollFile()

    On Error GoTo PrintPaychecksError
    ' Print paychecks.
    PrintPaychecks()

    ' We're done.
    Exit Sub

LoadPayrollError:
    MessageBox.Show("Error loading the payroll file.")
    Exit Sub

PrintPaychecksError:
    MessageBox.Show("Error printing paychecks.")
    Exit Sub
End Sub
```

The program can leave error-handling mode using the statements Exit Sub, Exit Function, Exit Property, Resume, or Resume Next.

An Exit Sub, Exit Function, or Exit Property statement makes the program immediately leave the routine in which the error occurred, and that's the end of error-handling mode for this error.

The Resume statement makes the program resume execution with the statement that caused the error. If the problem has not been fixed, the error will occur again and the program may enter an infinite loop. You should use the Resume statement only if there is a chance that the error has been fixed. For example, if the program tries to read from a floppy disk and the drive is empty, the program could ask the user to insert the disk and then it could try to read the disk again.

The Resume Next statement makes the program resume execution with the statement after the one that caused the error. This statement is appropriate when the program cannot fix the problem but should continue anyway. For example, suppose that a program fails to read a value from a file. It might want to continue anyway so that it can close the file in the next statement.

On Error Resume Next

After the On Error Resume Next statement, if Visual Basic encounters an error, it skips the statement that caused the error and resumes execution with the following statement. If the program doesn't care whether the statement completed, On Error Resume Next lets it continue without checking for errors.

If the program needs to take action when an error occurs, it can use the Err object to check for errors after each statement. For example, the following code uses the On Error Resume Next statement and then calls subroutine DoSomething. When the subroutine returns, the program checks the Err object's Number property to see if an error occurred. If there is an error, the program displays a message and exits the subroutine. If subroutine DoSomething did not cause an error, the program calls subroutine DoSomethingElse and performs a similar check for errors.

```
On Error Resume Next
DoSomething()
If Err.Number <> 0 Then
    MessageBox.Show("Error in DoSomething")
    Exit Sub
End If

DoSomethingElse()
If Err.Number <> 0 Then
    MessageBox.Show("Error in DoSomethingElse")
    Exit Sub
End If
    ...
```

A program can also use this statement to check for different kinds of errors and take appropriate action. The following example takes no special action if there is no error. If Err.Number is 11, the program tried to divide by zero. In that case, the code sets variable X to a default value. If there is some other error, the program tells the user and exits the subroutine.

```
' Try to calculate X.
On Error Resume Next
X = CalculateValue()
```

```
Select Case Err.Number
    Case 0 ' No error. Do nothing.
    Case 11 ' Divide by zero. Set a default value.
        X = 1000
    Case Else ' Unexpected error. Tell the user.
        MessageBox.Show("Error calculating X." & vbCrLf & Err.Description)
        Exit Sub
End Select
    ...
```

On Error GoTo 0

The On Error GoTo 0 statement disables any active error handler. You should deactivate an error handler when it no longer applies to what the program is doing. The following code installs an error handler while it loads some data. When it is finished loading the data, it uses On Error GoTo 0 to deactivate the error handler before it performs other tasks.

```
    On Error GoTo LoadDataError
    ' Load the data.
    ...
    ' Done loading data.
    On Error GoTo 0
    ...
    Exit Sub

LoadDataError:
    MessageBox.Show("Error loading data." & vbCrLf & Err.Description)
    Exit Sub
End Sub
```

Deactivating the error handler stops the program from taking inappropriate action for an error. In the preceding example, it might confuse the user to say there was an error loading data when the program was doing something else. In other cases, the program might incorrectly try to fix problems that are not there if you leave an old error handler installed. For example, the program might ask the user to insert a floppy disk when it had already finished reading from the disk.

Deactivating old error handlers also lets the program fail if an unexpected error occurs. That lets developers discover and handle new types of failure, possibly by adding a new error handler.

On Error GoTo –1

The On Error GoTo –1 statement is very similar to On Error GoTo 0. It deactivates any active error handler. However, it also ends error-handling mode if it is running. Example program OnErrorGoToMinus1 uses the following code to show the difference:

```
Dim i As Integer
Dim j As Integer = 0

    On Error GoTo DivideError1
    i = 1 \ j ' This raises an error.

DivideError1: ' We enter error-handling mode here.
    On Error GoTo -1 ' This ends error-handling mode.
    On Error Resume Next ' Ignore errors in the future.
    i = 1 \ j ' This error is ignored.
    Exit Sub

    On Error GoTo DivideError2
    i = 1 \ j ' This raises an error.
    Exit Sub

DivideError2: ' We enter error-handling mode here.
    On Error GoTo 0 ' This does NOT end error-handling mode.
    On Error Resume Next ' Doesn't work in error-handling mode.
    i = 1 \ j ' This error is not caught and crashes the program.
    Exit Sub
```

code snippet OnErrorGoToMinus1

The program uses On Error GoTo DivideError1 to install an error handler and then executes a command that causes a divide-by-zero error.

The error-handling code uses On Error GoTo -1 to end error-handling mode and continue execution. It then calls On Error Resume Next to ignore further errors and performs another calculation that divides by zero. Because the On Error Resume Next statement is in effect, the program ignores this error.

Next, the code uses On Error GoTo DivideError2 to install another error handler. It divides by zero again to jump to the error handler and enter error-handling mode.

This time, the error handler uses the On Error GoTo 0 statement. This uninstalls the current error handler (On Error GoTo DivideError2) but does not end error-handling mode. The program then uses the On Error Resume Next statement. Unfortunately, this statement is ignored while the program is running in error-handling mode. If the program used a Resume statement to exit error-handling mode, this statement would then have an effect, but it does nothing until error-handling mode ends. Now, when the program divides by zero again, there is no active error handler, so the program crashes.

To avoid confusion, you should not use this style of error handling with error-handling code running through the body of a routine. Instead, place error-handling code at the end of the routine and use Exit Sub, Exit Function, Exit Property, Resume, or Resume Next to return to the routine's main body of code. The On Error GoTo -1 statement is usually more confusing than it's worth.

Error-Handling Mode

Undoubtedly, the most confusing part of classic error handling is error-handling mode. The On Error GoTo *line* statement makes the program enter a special error-handling mode that remains in effect until the error handler calls Exit Sub, Exit Function, Exit Property, Resume, Resume Next, or On Error GoTo -1.

While in error-handling mode, most other error-handling statements do not work as they normally do. Generally, their effects only take place when error-handling mode finally ends. In the example in the previous section, the final On Error Resume Next statement has no effect because it executes while the program is in error handling mode.

Trying to execute error-handling statements within error handling mode is one of the most common mistakes programmers make when working with error-handling mode. The error-handling code must be safe, or the program will crash (or at least the error will propagate up to the calling routine).

If you really need to perform operations that might crash within the error handler's code, move that code into a subroutine. That routine can use its own error-handling code to protect itself from another error. The following example demonstrates this approach. The `SetDefaultValue` subroutine uses its own `On Error Resume Next` statement to avoid crashing if it has problems of its own.

```
Private i, j As Integer

Private Sub PerformCalculation()
    On Error GoTo EquationError
    i = 1 \ j
    Exit Sub

EquationError:
    SetDefaultValue()
    Resume Next
End Sub

Private Sub SetDefaultValue()
    On Error Resume Next
    i = 2 \ j
End Sub
```

STRUCTURED VERSUS CLASSIC ERROR HANDLING

The newer structured error-handling approach provided by the Try statement has several advantages over classic error handling. First, classic error handling doesn't make it immediately obvious whether a piece of code is protected by an error handler. To determine whether a statement is protected, you must look back through the code until you find an On Error statement. If you come to a labeled line, you also must track down any places where a GoTo or a Resume *line* statement could jump to that line and see what error handler might be installed at the time.

Classic error handling also doesn't make it obvious whether the code is running in error-handling mode. In some cases, it is impossible to tell until runtime. The following code uses an On Error GoTo statement to protect itself and then initializes an integer from a value that the user enters in a text box. If the user enters a valid integer, the code works normally and keeps running in normal (not error-handling) mode. If the user enters a value that is not a valid integer, the program jumps to the label `BadFormat` and enters error-handling mode. There's no way to tell before runtime whether the program will be in error-handling mode when it reaches the following comment.

```
    Dim i As Integer
    On Error GoTo BadFormat
    i = CInt(txtNumber.Text)
BadFormat:
    ' Are we in error-handling mode here?
    ...
```

Finally, you cannot nest classic error-handling code. If you must perform a risky action in an error handler, you must place the code in a separate subroutine that contains its own error-handling code to protect itself.

Structured error handling addresses these shortcomings. By looking at the enclosing Try or Catch block, you can easily tell whether a line of code is protected (inside the Try block) or part of an error handler (in the Catch block).

You can even nest Try statements, as shown in the following code. The program tries to initialize an integer from a value that the user entered in a text box. If the user enters an invalid value, the code moves into the first Catch block. There it tries to set the value of the integer using a calculation. If that calculation fails (for example, if j is 0), the next Catch block sets the variable to a default value.

```
    ' Get the user's value.
    Try
        i = Integer.Parse(txtNumber.Text)
    Catch ex As Exception
        ' The user's value is no good.
        ' Calculate a different value.
        Try
            i = 1 \ j
        Catch ex2 As Exception
            ' The calculated value is no good.
            ' Use a default value.
            i = 3
        End Try
    End Try
```

Finally, the Try block doesn't have a bewildering error-handling mode. The potential for confusion there alone is probably worth using structured error handling.

One of the few advantages to classic error handling is that it is easier to ignore errors by using the On Error Resume Next statement. The following code uses classic error handling to execute three subroutines and ignore any errors they produce:

```
On Error Resume Next
DoSomething()
DoSomethingElse()
DoSomethingMore()
...
```

The following version shows the same code using structured error handling. This version is quite a bit more verbose and much less readable.

```
Try
    DoSomething()
Catch
End Try

Try
    DoSomethingElse()
Catch
End Try

Try
    DoSomethingMore()
Catch
End Try
...
```

THE ERR OBJECT

When an error occurs, Visual Basic initializes an object named Err. You can use this object's properties to learn more about the error. These properties correspond to those provided by the exception objects used by the Try statement's Catch sections. The following table lists these properties.

PROPERTY	PURPOSE
Description	A message describing the error.
Erl	The line number at which the error occurred.
HelpContext	The help context ID for the error.
HelpFile	The full path to the help file describing the error.
LastDLLError	A system error code generated by a call to a DLL (if appropriate).
Number	The error number. The value 0 means no error has occurred.
Source	The name of the object or application that caused the error.

The Err object also provides three useful methods for working with errors: Clear, Raise, and GetException. The Clear method clears the object's information and resets it for the next statement. If the statement following an error does not raise an error itself, the Err object may still show the previous error unless you clear it, as shown in the following code:

```
On Error Resume Next
X = Single.Parse(txtX.Text)
If Err.Number <> 0 Then
    MessageBox.Show(Err.Description) ' Display the error.
    Err.Clear ' Clear the error.
End If

Y = Single.Parse(txtY.Text)
If Err.Number <> 0 Then
    MessageBox.Show(Err.Description) ' Display the error.
    Err.Clear ' Clear the error.
End If
...
```

The Err object's Raise method generates an error. For example, the following statement raises error number 5, "Procedure call or argument is invalid":

```
Err.Raise(5)
```

Finally, the GetException method returns an Exception object representing the Err object's error. You can use this object just as you can use any other exception object. In particular, you can use its StackTrace property to get a trace showing where the error occurred.

If you use classic error handling, you can use the Err object to learn about the error. If you use structured error handling with the Try statement, you can use the Exception objects provided by Catch statements, and you can do without the Err object.

DEBUGGING

Visual Basic provides a rich set of tools for debugging an application. Using the development environment, you can stop the program at different lines of code and examine variables, change variable values, look at the call stack, and call routines to exercise different pieces of the application. You can step through the program, executing the code one statement at a time to see what it is doing. You can even make some modifications to the source code and let the program continue running.

Chapter 7, "Debugging," describes tools that the development environment provides to help you debug an application. These include tools for stepping through the code, breakpoints, and windows such as the Immediate, Locals, and Call Stack windows. See Chapter 7 for details.

In addition to setting breakpoints in the code, you can use the Stop statement to pause execution at a particular line. This can be particularly useful for detecting unexpected values during testing. For example, the following statement stops execution if the variable m_NumEmployees is less than 1 or greater than 100:

```
If (m_NumEmployees < 1) Or (m_NumEmployees > 100) Then Stop
```

SUMMARY

In practice, it's extremely difficult to anticipate every condition that can occur within a large application. You should try to predict as many incorrect situations as possible, but you should also plan for unforeseen errors. You should write error-checking code that makes bugs obvious when they occur and recovers from them if possible. You may not be able to anticipate every possible bug, but with a little thought you can make the program detect and report obviously incorrect values.

You should also look for unplanned conditions (such as the user entering a phone number in a Social Security number field) and make the program react gracefully. Your program cannot control everything in its environment (such as the user's actions, printer status, and network connectivity), but it should be prepared to act when things aren't exactly the way they should be.

When you do encounter an error, you can use tools such as breakpoints, watches, and the development environment's Locals, Auto, Immediate, and Call Stack windows to figure out where the problem begins and how to fix it. You may never be able to remove every last bug from a 100,000-line program, but you can make any remaining bugs appear so rarely that the users can do their jobs in relative safety.

Chapters 8 through 13 focus on controls, forms, and other user interface objects. Chapters 14 through 18 move the focus to the code that lies behind the user interface. Chapter 20, "Database Controls and Objects," covers database topics that fall into both the user interface and non-user interface categories. It describes database controls that you can use to build an application's user interface as well as components and other objects that you can use behind the scenes to manipulate databases.

20

Database Controls and Objects

The Windows Forms controls described in Chapter 8, "Selecting Windows Forms Controls," allow the application and the user to communicate. They let the application display data to the user, and they let the user control the application.

Visual Basic's database controls play roughly the same role between the application and a database. They move data from the database to the application, and they allow the application to send data back to the database.

Database programming is an enormous topic, and many books have been written that focus exclusively on database programming. This is such a huge field that no general Visual Basic book can adequately cover it in any real depth. However, database programming is also a very important topic, and every Visual Basic programmer should know at least something about using databases in applications.

This chapter explains how to build data sources and use drag-and-drop tasks to create simple table- and record-oriented displays. It also explains the most useful controls and objects that Visual Basic provides for working with databases. Although this chapter is far from the end of the story, it will help you get started building basic database applications.

 Note that the example programs described in this chapter refer to database locations as they are set up on my test computer. If you download them from the book's web site (www.vb-helper.com/vb_prog_ref.htm), you will have to modify many of them to work with the database locations on your computer.

AUTOMATICALLY CONNECTING TO DATA

Visual Studio provides tools that make getting started with databases remarkably easy. Although the process is relatively straightforward, it does involve a lot of steps. The steps also allow several variations, so describing every possible way to build a database connection takes a long time. To make the process more manageable, the following two sections group the steps in two pieces: connecting to the data source and adding data controls to the form.

Connecting to the Data Source

To build a simple database program, start a new application and select the Data menu's Add New Data Source command to display the Data Source Configuration Wizard shown in Figure 20-1.

FIGURE 20-1: Select the data source type for a new connection.

Visual Studio allows you to use databases, web services, and objects as data sources for your application. The most straightforward choice is Database.

Select the type of data source you want add and click Next to select a data model on the page shown in Figure 20-2.

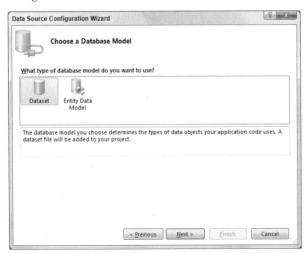

FIGURE 20-2: Pick the type of data model you want to use.

Select the type of data model that you want to use (this example assumes you pick Dataset) and click Next to select a data connection on the page shown in Figure 20-3.

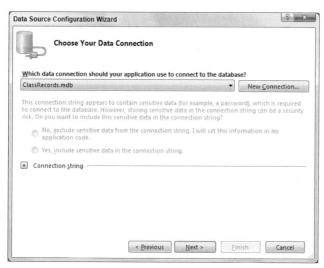

FIGURE 20-3: Pick the data connection or click New Connection to create a new one.

If you have previously created data connections, you can select one from the drop-down list. If you have not created any data connections, click the New Connection button to open the Choose Data Source dialog shown in Figure 20-4. This dialog lets you pick the type of data source you will use. For example, you can use it to select Microsoft Access databases, ODBC data sources, Microsoft SQL Server, and Oracle databases.

FIGURE 20-4: Select the data source type for a new connection.

DOWNLOADING DATABASES

You don't need to have Access to use an Access database in Visual Basic. However, if you want to give Access a try, you can download a 60-day trial version at `us20.trymicrosoftoffice.com`.

Another popular database choice is SQL Server. You can download the free Express Edition at `www.microsoft.com/express/sql`.

You can also download the open source MySQL database at `www.mysql.com`.

 If the dialog shown in Figure 20-5 appears first, you can skip the dialog in Figure 20-4 as long as it has selected the correct data source type. If you want to change the data source, click the Change button shown in Figure 20-5 to open the dialog shown in Figure 20-4.

After you select a data source type, the drop-down lists available providers for that type. The data provider acts as a bridge between the application and the data source, providing methods to move data between the two. Pick a provider and click Continue to show the dialog in Figure 20-5.

Depending on the type of database you selected in Figure 20-4, this dialog box may not look exactly like Figure 20-5. For example, if you selected the SQL Server database type, the Add Connection dialog asks for a data source and server name rather than a database file name.

FIGURE 20-5: Use the Add Connection dialog box to create a data connection.

Enter the necessary data in the Add Connection dialog box. For a SQL Server database, select the server name, authentication method, database name, and other information. For a Microsoft Access database, enter the file name or click the Browse button shown in Figure 20-5 and find the database file. Enter a user name and password if necessary.

After you enter all of the required information, click the Test Connection button to see if the wizard can open the database. If the test fails, recheck the database path (if the database is on a network, make sure the network connection is available), user name, and password and try again.

Once you can test the database connection, click OK.

When you return to the Data Source Configuration Wizard shown in Figure 20-3, the new connection should be selected in the drop-down list. If you click the plus sign next to the

"Connection string" label, the wizard shows the connection information it will use to connect the data source to the database. For example, this information might look like the following:

```
Provider=Microsoft.Jet.OLEDB.4.0;
DataSource=|DataDirectory|\ClassRecords.mdb
```

When you click Next, the wizard tells you that you have selected a local database file that is not part of the project and it asks if you want to add it to the project. If you click Yes, the wizard adds the database to the project so it shows up in Project Explorer. If you plan to distribute the database with the application, you may want to do this to make it easier to manage the database and the Visual Basic source code together.

Next, the wizard asks whether you want to save the connection string in the project's configuration file. If you leave this check box selected, the wizard adds the configuration string to the project's app.config file.

The following shows the part of the configuration file containing the connection string:

```
<connectionStrings>
    <add name="StudentTest.My.MySettings.ClassRecordsConnectionString"
connectionString="Provider=Microsoft.Jet.OLEDB.4.0;
Data Source=|DataDirectory|\ClassRecords.mdb; Persist Security Info=True;
Jet OLEDB:Database Password=MyPassword" providerName="System.Data.OleDb" />
</connectionStrings>
```

Later, the program uses the Settings.Default.ClassRecordsConnectionString values to get this value and connect to the database. You can easily make the program connect to another data source by changing this configuration setting and then restarting the application.

 You should never save real database passwords in the configuration file. The file is stored in plain text and anyone can read it. If you need to use a password, store a connection string that contains a placeholder for the real password. At runtime, load the connection string and replace the placeholder with a real password entered by the user.

Adding Data Controls to the Form

At this point you have defined the basic connection to the database. Visual Studio knows where the database is and how to build an appropriate connection string to open it. Now you must decide what data to pull out of the database and how to display it on the form.

Click Next to display the dialog box shown in Figure 20-6. This page shows the objects available in the database. In this example, the database contains two tables named Students and TestScores. By clicking the plus signs next to the objects, you can expand them to see what they contain. In Figure 20-6, the tables are expanded so you can see the fields they contain.

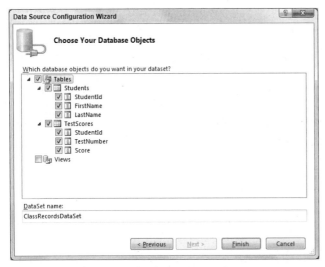

FIGURE 20-6: Select the database objects that you want included in the data source.

Select the database objects that you want to include in the data source. In Figure 20-6, both of the tables are selected.

When you click Finish, the wizard adds a couple objects to the application. The Solution Explorer, (which lists all of the solution's files, now lists the new file ClassRecordsDataSet.xsd. This is a schema definition file that describes the data source.

When you double-click the schema file, Visual Basic opens it in the editor shown in Figure 20-7. This display shows the tables defined by the schema and their fields.

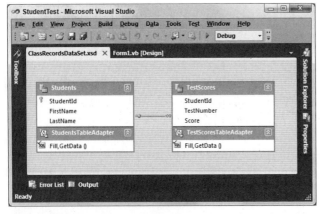

FIGURE 20-7: The Schema Editor shows the tables defined by the schema and their relationships.

The line between the files with the little key on the left and the infinity symbol on the right indicates that the tables are joined by a one-to-many relationship. In this example, the Students.StudentId field and TestScores.StudentId field form a foreign key relationship. That means every StudentId value in the TestScores table must correspond to some StudentId value in the Students table. When you double-click the relationship link or right-click it and select Edit Relation, the editor displays the dialog box shown in Figure 20-8. You can use this editor to modify the relation.

FIGURE 20-8: Use this dialog box to edit relationships among data source tables.

At the bottom of the tables shown in Figure 20-7, you can see two table adapter objects containing the labels Fill, GetData(). These represent data adapter objects that the program will later use to move data from and to the data source.

In addition to adding the schema file to Solution Explorer, the Data Source Configuration Wizard also added a new DataSet object to the Data Sources window shown in Figure 20-9. (If this window is not visible, select the Data menu's Show Data Sources command.)

FIGURE 20-9: The Data Sources window lists the new data source.

You can use the plus and minus signs to expand and collapse the objects in the DataSet. In Figure 20-9, the DataSet is expanded to show its tables, and the tables are expanded to show their fields. Notice that the TestScores table is listed below the Students table because it has a parent/child relationship with that table.

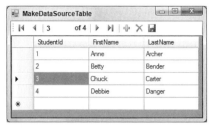

FIGURE 20-10: Drag and drop a table from the Data Sources window onto the form to create a simple DataGridView.

It takes a lot of words and pictures to describe this process, but using the wizard to build the data source is actually quite fast. After you have created the data source, you can build a simple user interface with almost no extra work. Simply drag objects from the Data Sources window onto the form.

When you click and drag a table from the Data Sources window onto the form, Visual Basic automatically creates BindingNavigator and DataGridView controls, and other components to display the data from the table. Figure 20-10 shows the result at runtime.

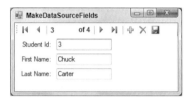

FIGURE 20-11: Drag and drop table columns onto a form to create a record-oriented view instead of a grid.

Instead of dragging an entire table onto the form, you can drag individual database columns. In that case, Visual Basic adds controls to the form to represent the column. Figure 20-11 shows the columns from the Students table dragged onto a form.

If you select a table in the Data Sources window, a drop-down arrow appears on the right. Open the drop-down to give the table a different display style, as shown in Figure 20-12. For example, if you set a table's style to Details and drag the table onto a form, Visual Basic displays the table's data using a record detail view similar to the one shown in Figure 20-11 instead of the grid shown in Figure 20-10.

Similarly, you can change the display styles for specific database columns. Select a column in the Data Sources window and click its drop-down arrow to make it display in a text box, label, link label, combo box, or other control. Now, when you drag the column onto a form, or when you drag the table onto the form to build a record view, Visual Basic uses this type of control to display the column's values.

FIGURE 20-12: Use the drop-down in the Data Sources window to give a table a different display style.

AUTOMATICALLY CREATED OBJECTS

When you drag database tables and columns from the Data Sources window onto a form, Visual Basic does a lot more than simply placing a DataGridView control on a form. It also creates about two dozen other controls and components. Five of the more important of these objects are the DataSet, TableAdapter, TableAdapterManager, BindingSource, and BindingNavigator.

The program stores data in a DataSet object. A single DataSet object can represent an entire database. It contains DataTable objects that represent database tables. Each DataTable contains DataRow objects that represent rows in a table, and each DataRow contains items representing column values for the row.

The TableAdapter object copies data between the database and the DataSet. It has methods for performing operations on the database (such as selecting, inserting, updating, and deleting records). Hidden inside the TableAdapter is a connection object that contains information on the database so that the TableAdapter knows where to find it.

The TableAdapterManager coordinates updates among different TableAdapters. This is most useful for hierarchical data sets, a topic that is outside the scope of this book. The wizard-generated code also uses the TableAdapterManager to update the single data set it creates.

The BindingSource object encapsulates all of the DataSet object's data and provides programmatic control functions. These perform such actions as moving through the data, adding and deleting items, and so forth.

The BindingNavigator provides a user interface so the user can control the BindingSource.

Figure 20-13 shows the relationships among the DataSet, TableAdapter, BindingSource, and BindingNavigator objects. The BindingNavigator is the only one of these components that has a presence on the form. It is connected to the BindingSource with a dotted arrow to indicate that it controls the BindingSource but does not actually transfer data back and forth. The other arrows represent data moving between objects.

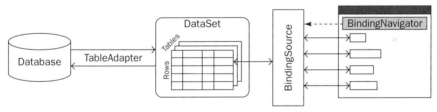

FIGURE 20-13: Visual Basic uses DataSet, TableAdapter, BindingSource, and BindingNavigator objects to display data.

Even all these objects working together don't quite do everything you need to make the program display data. When it creates these objects, Visual Basic also adds the following code to the form:

```
public Class Form1
    Private Sub StudentsBindingNavigatorSaveItem_Click(
    ByVal sender As System.Object, ByVal e As System.EventArgs) _
    Handles StudentsBindingNavigatorSaveItem.Click
        Me.Validate()
        Me.StudentsBindingSource.EndEdit()
        Me.TableAdapterManager.UpdateAll(Me.ClassRecordsDataSet)
```

```
        End Sub

        Private Sub Form1_Load(ByVal sender As System.Object,
        ByVal e As System.EventArgs) Handles MyBase.Load
            'TODO: This line of code loads data into the 'ClassRecordsDataSet.Students'
            ' table. You can move, or remove it, as needed.
            Me.StudentsTableAdapter.Fill(Me.ClassRecordsDataSet.Students)
        End Sub
    End Class
```

code snippet MakeDataSourceTable

The `StudentsBindingNavigatorSaveItem_Click` event handler fires when the user clicks the BindingNavigator object's Save tool. This routine makes the TableAdapter save any changes to the Students table to the database.

The `Form1_Load` event handler makes the TableAdapter copy data from the database into the DataSet when the form loads.

Visual Basic builds all this automatically, and if you ran the program at this point, it would display data and let you manipulate it. It's still not perfect, however. It doesn't perform any data validation, and it will let you close the application without saving any changes you have made to the data. It's a pretty good start for such a small amount of work, however.

OTHER DATA OBJECTS

If you want a simple program that can display and modify data, then the solution described in the previous sections may be good enough. In that case, you can let Visual Basic do most of the work for you, and you don't need to dig into the lower-level details of database access.

You can also use objects similar to those created by Visual Basic to build your own solutions. You can create your own DataSet, TableAdapter, BindingSource, and BindingNavigator objects to bind controls to a database. (You can even modify the controls supplied by Visual Basic by overriding their properties and methods, although that's a very advanced topic so it isn't covered here.)

If you need to manipulate the database directly with code, it doesn't necessarily make sense to create all these objects. If you simply want to modify a record programmatically, it certainly doesn't make sense to create DataGridView, BindingNavigator, and BindingSource objects.

For cases such as this, Visual Basic provides several other kinds of objects that you can use to interact with databases. These objects fall into the following four categories:

➤ **Data containers** hold data after it has been loaded from the database into the application much as a DataSet does. You can bind controls to these objects to automatically display and manipulate the data.

➤ **Connections** provide information that lets the program connect to the database.

➤ **Data adapters** move data between a database and a data container.

➤ **Command objects** provide instructions for manipulating data. A command object can select, update, insert, or delete data in the database. It can also execute stored procedures in the database.

Data container and adapter classes are generic and work with different kinds of databases, whereas different types of connection and command objects are specific to different kinds of databases. For example, the connection objects OleDbConnection, SqlConnection, OdbcConnection, and OracleConnection work with Object Linking and Embedding Database (OLE DB); SQL Server, including SQL Server Express; Open Database Connectivity (ODBC); and Oracle databases, respectively. The SQL Server and Oracle objects work only with their specific brand of database, but they are more completely optimized for those databases and may give better performance.

Aside from the different database types they support, the various objects work in more or less the same way. The following sections explain how an application uses those objects to move data to and from the database. They describe the most useful properties, methods, and events provided by the connection, transaction, data adapter, and command objects.

Later sections describe the DataSet and DataView objects and tell how you can use them to bind controls to display data automatically.

DATA OVERVIEW

An application uses three basic objects to move data to and from a database: a connection, a data adapter, and a data container such as a DataSet.

The connection object defines the connection to the database. It contains information about the database's name and location, any user name and password needed to access the data, database engine information, and flags that determine the kinds of access the program will need.

The data adapter object defines a mapping from the database to the DataSet. It determines what data is selected from the database, and which database columns are mapped to which DataSet columns.

The DataSet object stores the data within the application. It can hold more than one table and can define and enforce relationships among the tables. For example, the database used in the earlier examples in this chapter has a TestScores table that has a StudentId field. The values in this field must be values listed in the Students table. This is called a *foreign key constraint*. The DataSet can represent this constraint and raise an error if the program tries to create a TestScores record with a StudentId value that does not appear in the Students table. The section "Constraints" later in this chapter says more about constraints.

When the connection, data adapter, and DataSet objects are initialized, the program can call the data adapter's Fill method to copy data from the database into the DataSet. Later it can call the data adapter's Update method to copy any changes to the data from the DataSet back into the database. Figure 20-14 shows the process.

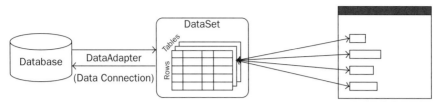

FIGURE 20-14: An application uses connection, data adapter, and DataSet objects to move data to and from the database.

If you compare Figure 20-14 to Figure 20-13, you'll see several similarities. Both approaches use an adapter to copy data between the database and a DataSet. At first glance, it may seem that Figure 20-13 doesn't use a connection object, but actually the TableAdapter contains a connection object internally that it uses to access the database.

One major difference is that Figure 20-13 uses a BindingSource to provide an extra layer between the DataSet and the program's controls. It also includes a Binding Navigator object that lets the user control the BindingSource to move through the data.

As in the previous example, a program using the objects shown in Figure 20-14 could call the data adapter's Fill method in a form's Load event handler. Later it could call the Update method when the user clicked a Save button, in the form's FormClosing event handler, or whenever you wanted to save the data.

CONNECTION OBJECTS

The connection object manages the application's connection to the database. It allows a data adapter to move data in and out of a DataSet.

The different flavors of connection object (OleDbConnection, SqlConnection, OdbcConnection, OracleConnection, and so on) provide roughly the same features, but there are some differences. Check the online help to see if a particular property, method, or event is supported by one of the flavors. The web page msdn.microsoft.com/32c5dh3b.aspx provides links to pages that explain how to connect to SQL Server, OLE DB, ODBC, and Oracle data sources. Other links lead to information on the SqlConnection, OleDbConnection, and OdbcConnection classes.

If you will be working extensively with a particular type of database (for example, SQL Server), you should also review the features provided by its type of connection object to see if it has special features for that type of database.

Some connection objects can work with more than one type of database. For example, the OleDbConnection object works with any database that has an OLE DB (Object Linking and Embedding Database) provider. Similarly the OdbcConnection object works with databases that have ODBC (Open Database Connectivity) providers such as MySQL.

Generally, connections that work with a specific kind of database (such as SqlConnection and OracleConnection) give better performance. If you think you might later need to change databases, you can minimize the amount of work required by sticking to features that are shared by all the types of connection objects.

 The Toolbox window does not automatically display tools for these objects. To add them, right-click the Toolbox tab where you want them and select Choose Items. Select the check boxes next to the tools you want to add (for example, OracleCommand or OdbcConnection) and click OK.

The following table describes the most useful properties provided by the OleDbConnection and SqlConnection classes.

PROPERTY	PURPOSE
ConnectionString	Gets or sets the string that defines the connection to the database.
ConnectionTimeout	Gets or sets the time the object waits while trying to connect to the database. If this timeout expires, the object gives up and raises an error.
Database	Returns the name of the current database.
DataSource	Returns the name of the current database file or database server.
Provider	(OleDbConnection only) Returns the name of the OLE DB database provider (for example, Microsoft.Jet.OLEDB.4.0).
ServerVersion	Returns the database server's version number. This value is available only when the connection is open and may look like 04.00.0000.
State	Returns the connection's current state. This value can be Closed, Connecting, Open, Executing (executing a command), Fetching (fetching data), and Broken (the connection was open but then broke; you can close and reopen the connection).

The ConnectionString property includes many fields separated by semicolons. The following text shows a typical ConnectionString value for an OleDbConnection object that will open an Access database. The text here shows each embedded field on a separate line, but the actual string would be all run together in one long line.

```
Jet OLEDB:Global Partial Bulk Ops=2;
Jet OLEDB:Registry Path=;
Jet OLEDB:Database Locking Mode=1;
Data Source="C:\Personnel\Data\Personnel.mdb";
Mode=Share Deny None;
Jet OLEDB:Engine Type=5;
Provider="Microsoft.Jet.OLEDB.4.0";
Jet OLEDB:System database=;
```

```
Jet OLEDB:SFP=False;
persist security info=False;
Extended Properties=;
Jet OLEDB:Compact Without Replica Repair=False;
Jet OLEDB:Encrypt Database=False;
Jet OLEDB:Create System Database=False;
Jet OLEDB:Don't Copy Locale on Compact=False;
User ID=Admin;
Jet OLEDB:Global Bulk Transactions=1"
```

> *The data source value will be different on your system. In this example, the database is at* C:\Personnel\Data\Personnel.mdb. *You would need to change it to match the location of the data on your system.*

Many of these properties are optional and you can omit them. Remembering which ones are optional (or even which fields are allowed for a particular type of connection object) is not always easy. Fortunately, it's also not necessary. Instead of typing all these fields into your code or in the connection control's ConnectString property in the Properties window, you can let Visual Basic build the string for you.

Simply follow the steps described in the section "Connecting to the Data Source" earlier in this chapter. After you build or select the database connection, click the plus sign in Figure 20-3 to see its connection string. Use the mouse to highlight the connection string and then press Ctrl+C to copy it to the clipboard.

The following code fragment shows how a program can create, open, use, and close an OleDbConnection object. The code assumes the database name is in the text box txtDatabase.

Available for
download on
Wrox.com

```
' Make the connect string.
Dim connect_string As String =
    "Provider=Microsoft.Jet.OLEDB.4.0;" &
    "Data Source=""" & txtDatabase.Text & """;" &
    "Persist Security Info=False"

' Open a database connection.
Dim conn_people As New OleDb.OleDbConnection(connect_string)
conn_people.Open()

' Do stuff with the connection.
'...

' Close the connection.
conn_people.Close()
conn_people.Dispose()
```

code snippet CommandInsert

Example program CommandInsert, which is available for download on the book's web site, uses similar code to open a connection before inserting new data into the database.

The following table describes the most useful methods provided by the OleDbConnection and SqlConnection classes.

METHOD	PURPOSE
BeginTransaction	Begins a database transaction and returns a transaction object representing it. A transaction lets the program ensure that a series of commands are either all performed or all canceled as a group. See the section "Transaction Objects" later in this chapter for more information.
ChangeDatabase	Changes the currently open database.
Close	Closes the database connection.
CreateCommand	Creates a command object that can perform some action on the database. The action might select records, create a table, update a record, and so forth.
Open	Opens the connection using the values specified in the ConnectionString property.

The connection object's most useful events are InfoMessage and StateChange. The InfoMessage event occurs when the database provider issues a warning or informational message. The program can read the message and take action or display it to the user. The StateChange event occurs when the database connection's state changes.

Note that the method for using a connection object shown in Figure 20-13 relies on the data adapter's Fill and Update methods, not on the connection object's Open and Close methods. Fill and Update automatically open the connection, perform their tasks, and then close the connection so that you don't need to manage the connection object yourself. For example, when the program calls Fill, the data adapter quickly opens the connection, copies data from the database into the DataSet, and then closes the database. When you use this model for database interaction, the data connections are open only very briefly.

TRANSACTION OBJECTS

A transaction defines a set of database actions that should be executed "atomically" as a single unit. Either all of them should occur or none of them should occur, but no action should execute without all of the others.

The classic example is a transfer of money from one account to another. Suppose that the program tries to subtract money from one account and then add it to another. After it subtracts the money from the first account, however, the program crashes. The database has lost money — a bad situation for the owners of the accounts.

On the other hand, suppose that the program performs the operations in the reverse order: first it adds money to the second account and then subtracts it from the first. This time if the program gets halfway through the operation before crashing, the database has created new money — a bad situation for the bank.

The solution is to wrap these two operations in a database transaction. If the program gets halfway through the transaction and then crashes, the database engine unwinds the transaction when the database restarts, so the data looks as if nothing had happened. This isn't as good as performing the whole transaction flawlessly, but at least the database is consistent and the money has been conserved.

To use transactions in Visual Basic, the program uses a connection object's BeginTransaction method to open a transaction. It then creates command objects associated with the connection and the transaction, and it executes them. When it has finished, the program can call the transaction object's Commit method to make all the actions occur, or it can call Rollback to cancel them all.

Example program Transactions, which is available for download on the book's web site, uses the following code to perform two operations within a single transaction. This code removes an amount of money from one account and adds the same amount to another account.

```vb
' Make a transfer.
Private Sub btnUpdate_Click() Handles btnUpdate.Click
    ' Open the connection.
    Dim connAccounts As New OleDbConnection(MakeConnectString())
    connAccounts.Open()

    ' Make the transaction.
    Dim trans As OleDbTransaction =
        connAccounts.BeginTransaction(IsolationLevel.ReadCommitted)

    ' Make a Command for this connection.
    ' and this transaction.
    Dim cmd As New OleDbCommand(
        "UPDATE Accounts SET Balance=Balance + ? WHERE AccountName=?",
        connAccounts,
        trans)

    ' Create parameters for the first command.
    cmd.Parameters.Add(New OleDbParameter("Balance",
        Decimal.Parse(txtAmount.Text)))
    cmd.Parameters.Add(New OleDbParameter("AccountName",
        "Alice's Software Emporium"))

    ' Execute the second command.
    cmd.ExecuteNonQuery()

    ' Create parameters for the second command.
    cmd.Parameters.Clear()
    cmd.Parameters.Add(New OleDbParameter("Balance",
```

```
            -Decimal.Parse(txtAmount.Text)))
        cmd.Parameters.Add(New OleDbParameter("AccountName",
            "Bob's Consulting"))

        ' Execute the second command.
        cmd.ExecuteNonQuery()

        ' Commit the transaction.
        If MessageBox.Show(
            "Commit transaction?",
            "Commit?",
            MessageBoxButtons.YesNo,
            MessageBoxIcon.Question) = indows.Forms.DialogResult.Yes _
        Then
            ' Commit the transaction.
            trans.Commit()
        Else
            ' Rollback the transaction.
            trans.Rollback()
        End If

        ' Display the current balances.
        ShowValues(connAccounts)

        ' Close the connection.
        connAccounts.Close()
    End Sub
```

code snippet Transactions

The code first creates a connection. It uses the `MakeConnectString` function to build an appropriate connection string.

Next the code uses the connection's BeginTransaction method to make the transaction object `trans`.

Next, the code defines an OleDbCommand object named `cmd`, setting its command text to the following text:

```
UPDATE Accounts SET Balance=Balance + ? WHERE AccountName=?
```

Note that it passes the transaction object into the command object's constructor to make the command part of the transaction.

The question marks in the command text represent parameters to the command. The program defines the parameters' values by adding two parameter objects to the command object. It then calls the command's ExecuteNonQuery method to perform the query.

The code clears the command's parameters, adds two parameters with different values, and calls the command's ExecuteNonQuery method again.

Now the program displays a message box asking whether you want to commit the transaction. When you click Yes, the program calls the transaction's Commit method and both of the update operations occur. When you click No, the program calls the transaction's Rollback method and both of the update operations are canceled.

The program finishes by calling ShowValues to display the updated data and by closing the connection.

Instead of clicking Yes or No when the program asks if it should commit the transaction, you can use the IDE to stop the program. When you then restart the program, you will see that neither update was processed.

In addition to the Commit and Rollback methods, transaction objects may provide other methods for performing more complex transactions. For example, the OleDbTransaction class has a Begin method that enables you to create a nested transaction. Similarly, the SqlTransaction class has a Save method that creates a "savepoint" that you can use to roll back part of the transaction. See the online help for the type of transaction object you are using to learn about these methods. The web page msdn.microsoft.com/2k2hy99x.aspx gives an overview of using transactions. Links at the bottom lead to information about the OleDbTransaction, SqlTransaction, and OdbcTransaction classes.

DATA ADAPTERS

A data adapter transfers data between a connection and a DataSet. This object's most important methods are Fill and Update, which move data from and to the database. A data adapter also provides properties and other methods that can be useful. The following table describes the object's most useful properties.

PROPERTY	PURPOSE
DeleteCommand	The command object that the adapter uses to delete rows.
InsertCommand	The command object that the adapter uses to insert rows.
SelectCommand	The command object that the adapter uses to select rows.
TableMappings	A collection of DataTableMapping objects that determine how tables in the database are mapped to tables in the DataSet. Each DataTableMapping object has a ColumnMappings collection that determines how the columns in the database table are mapped to columns in the DataSet table.
UpdateCommand	The command object that the adapter uses to update rows.

You can create the command objects in a couple of ways. For example, if you use the Data Adapter Configuration Wizard (described shortly) to build the adapter at design time, the wizard automatically creates these objects. You can select the adapter and expand these objects in the Properties window to read their properties, including the CommandText property that defines the commands.

Another way to create these commands is to use a command builder object. If you attach a command builder to a data adapter, the adapter uses the command builder to generate the commands it needs automatically.

Example program GenerateCommands uses the following code to determine the commands used by a data adapter. The code creates a new OleDbCommandBuilder, passing its constructor the data adapter. It then uses the command builder's GetDeleteCommand, GetInsertCommand, and GetUpdateCommand methods to learn about the automatically generated commands.

```
' Attach a command builder to the data adapter
' and display the generated commands.
Dim command_builder As New OleDbCommandBuilder(OleDbDataAdapter1)

Dim txt As String = ""

txt &= command_builder.GetDeleteCommand.CommandText & vbCrLf & vbCrLf
txt &= command_builder.GetInsertCommand.CommandText & vbCrLf & vbCrLf
txt &= command_builder.GetUpdateCommand.CommandText & vbCrLf & vbCrLf

txtCommands.Text = txt
txtCommands.Select(0, 0)
```

code snippet GenerateCommands

The following text shows the results of the previous Debug statements. The DELETE and UPDATE statements are wrapped across multiple lines. The command builder generated these commands based on the select statement SELECT * From Books that was used to load the DataSet.

```
DELETE FROM Books WHERE ((Title = ?) AND ((? = 1 AND URL IS NULL) OR (URL = ?))
AND ((? = 1 AND Year IS NULL) OR (Year = ?)) AND ((? = 1 AND ISBN IS NULL) OR
(ISBN = ?)) AND ((? = 1 AND Pages IS NULL) OR (Pages = ?)))

INSERT INTO Books (Title, URL, Year, ISBN, Pages) VALUES (?, ?, ?, ?, ?)

UPDATE Books SET Title = ?, URL = ?, Year = ?, ISBN = ?, Pages = ? WHERE
((Title = ?) AND ((? = 1 AND URL IS NULL) OR (URL = ?)) AND ((? = 1 AND Year IS
NULL) OR (Year = ?)) AND ((? = 1 AND ISBN IS NULL) OR (ISBN = ?)) AND ((? = 1
AND Pages IS NULL) OR (Pages = ?)))
```

A data adapter's TableMappings property enables you to change how the adapter maps data in the database to the DataSet. For example, you could make it copy the Employees table in the database into a DataSet table named People. You don't usually need to change the table and column names, however, and you can make these changes interactively at design time more easily than you can do this in code, so you will usually leave these values alone at runtime.

To create a data adapter control at design time, open a form in the Windows Forms Designer, select the Toolbox's Data tab, and double-click the appropriate data adapter control. (If the data adapter you want doesn't appear in the Toolbox, right-click the Toolbox, select Choose Items, and pick the data adapter that you want to use.)

When you create a data adapter, the Data Adapter Configuration Wizard appears. The wizard's first page lets you select or build a data connection much as the Data Source Configuration Wizard does in Figure 20-3. Select or create a connection as described in the section "Connecting to the Data Source" earlier in this chapter.

Click Next to display the page shown in Figure 20-15. Use the option buttons to select the method the adapter should use to work with the data source. This determines how the data adapter will fetch, update, delete, and insert data in the database. Your options are:

➤ **Use SQL statements** — Makes the adapter use simple SQL statements to manipulate the data.

➤ **Create new stored procedures** — Makes the wizard generate stored procedures in the database to manipulate the data.

➤ **Use existing stored procedures** — Makes the wizard use procedures you have already created to manipulate the data.

In Figure 20-15, only the first option is enabled because it is the only option available to the OleDbDataAdapter that was used in this example.

When you select the "Use SQL statements" option and click Next, the form shown in Figure 20-16 appears. If you are experienced at writing SQL statements, enter the SELECT statement that you want the data adapter to use to select its data.

If you have less experience or are not familiar with the database's structure, click the Query Builder button to use the Query Builder shown in Figure 20-17. The area in the upper left shows the tables currently selected for use by the SQL query. Check boxes indicate which fields in the tables are selected. To add new tables to the query, right-click in this area and select Add Table.

Figure 20-17 shows the Query Builder. The top part shows that the Books table is included in the query and that its Title, Year, and Pages fields are selected.

Below the table and field selection area is a grid that lists the selected fields. Columns let you specify modifiers for each field. A field's Alias indicates the name the field is known by when it is returned by the query. In Figure 20-17, the Year field will be returned with the alias PubYear.

The Output check box determines whether the field is selected. This check box does the same thing as the one in the upper field selection area.

FIGURE 20-15: Select the method the data adapter will use to manipulate database data.

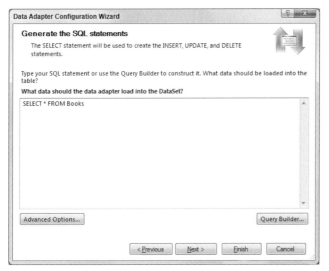

FIGURE 20-16: Enter a SQL SELECT statement or click the Query Builder button.

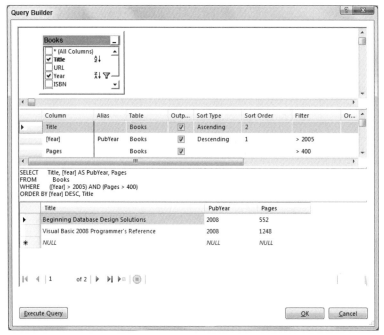

FIGURE 20-17: You can use the Query Builder to interactively define the data that a data adapter selects.

The Sort Type column lets you indicate that the results should be sorted in either ascending or descending order. Sort Order determines the order in which the fields are sorted. The query shown in Figure 20-17 sorts first by Year in descending order. If more than one book has the same Year, they are ordered by Title in ascending order.

The Filter column lets you add conditions to the fields. The values in Figure 20-17 make the query select records only where the Year is greater than 2005. Additional fields scrolled off to the right in Figure 20-17 let you add more filters combined with OR. For example, you could select books where the Year is greater than 2005 OR less than 1990.

If you place filters on more than one field, their conditions are combined with AND. For example, the values shown in Figure 20-17 select records where Year is greater than 2005 AND Pages is greater than 400.

Below the grid is a text box that shows the SQL code for the query. If you look at the query, you can see that it selects the fields checked in the field selection area at the top, uses an appropriate WHERE clause, and orders the results properly.

Click the Execute Query button to make the Query Builder run the query and display the results in the bottom grid. You can use this button to test the query to verify that it makes some sense before you finish creating the data adapter.

Click OK to close the Query Builder and return to the Data Adapter Configuration Wizard.

When you click Next, the Data Adapter Configuration Wizard displays a summary page indicating what it did and did not do while creating the data adapter. Depending on the query you use to select data, the wizard may not generate all the commands to select, update, insert, and delete data. For example, if the query joins more than one table, the wizard will be unable to figure out how to update the tables, so it won't generate insert, update, or delete commands.

Click Finish to close the wizard and see the new data adapter and its new connection object. You can see the adapter's DeleteCommand, InsertCommand, SelectCommand, and UpdateCommand objects in the Properties window. These objects' CommandText values show the corresponding SQL statements used by the objects. The wizard also generates default table mappings to transform database values into DataSet values.

COMMAND OBJECTS

The command object classes (OleDbCommand, SqlCommand, OdbcCommand, and OracleCommand) define database commands. The command can be a SQL query, or some non-query statement such as an INSERT, UPDATE, DELETE, or CREATE TABLE statement.

The object's Connection property gives the database connection object on which it will execute its command. CommandText gives the SQL text that the command represents.

The CommandType property tells the database the type of command text the command holds. This can be StoredProcedure (CommandText is the name of a stored procedure), TableDirect (CommandText is the name of one or more tables from which the database should return data), or Text (CommandText is a SQL statement).

The command object's Parameters collection contains parameter objects that define any values needed to execute the command text.

Example program CommandInsert, which is available for download on the book's web site, uses the following code to create an OleDbCommand object that executes the bolded SQL statement INSERT INTO PeopleNames (FirstName, LastName) VALUES (?, ?). The question marks are placeholders for parameters that will be added later. The code then adds two new OleDbParameter objects to the command's Parameters collection. When the code invokes the command's ExecuteNonQuery method, the adapter replaces the question marks with these parameter values in the order in which they appear in the Parameters collection. In this example, the value of txtFirstName.Text replaces the first question mark and txtLastName.Text replaces the second.

Available for download on Wrox.com

```
Private Sub btnAdd_Click() Handles btnAdd.Click
    ' Make the connect string.
    Dim connect_string As String =
        "Provider=Microsoft.Jet.OLEDB.4.0;" &
        "Data Source=""" & txtDatabase.Text & """;" &
        "Persist Security Info=False"

    ' Open a database connection.
    Dim conn_people As New OleDb.OleDbConnection(connect_string)
```

```
        conn_people.Open()

        ' Make a Command to insert data.
        Dim cmd As New OleDbCommand(
            "INSERT INTO PeopleNames (FirstName, LastName) VALUES (?, ?)",
            conn_people)

        ' Create parameters for the command.
        cmd.Parameters.Add(New OleDbParameter("FirstName", txtFirstName.Text))
        cmd.Parameters.Add(New OleDbParameter("LastName", txtLastName.Text))

        ' Execute the command.
        Try
            cmd.ExecuteNonQuery()
        Catch ex As Exception
            MessageBox.Show(ex.Message)
        End Try

        ' Show the current values.
        ShowValues(conn_people)

        ' Close the connection.
        conn_people.Close()
        conn_people.Dispose()
    End Sub
```

code snippet CommandInsert

The command object's Transaction property gives the transaction object with which it is associated. See the section "Transaction Objects" earlier in this chapter for more information about transactions.

The command object provides three methods for executing its CommandText. ExecuteNonQuery executes a command that is not a query and that doesn't return any values.

ExecuteScalar executes a command and returns the first column in the first row selected. This is useful for commands that return a single value such as SELECT COUNT * FROM Users.

ExecuteReader executes a SELECT statement and returns a data reader object (for example, OleDbDataReader). The program can use this object to navigate through the returned rows of data.

The command object's two other most useful methods are CreateParameter and Prepare. As you may be able to guess, CreateParameter adds a new object to the command's Parameters collection. The Prepare method compiles the command into a form that the database may be able to execute more quickly. It is often faster to execute a compiled command many times using different parameter values than it is to execute many new commands.

DataSet

DataSet is the flagship object when it comes to holding data in memory. It provides all the features you need to build, load, store, manipulate, and save data similar to that stored in a relational database. It can hold multiple tables related with complex parent/child relationships and uniqueness constraints. It provides methods for merging DataSet objects, searching for records that satisfy criteria, and saving data in different ways (such as into a relational database or an XML file). In many ways, it is like a complete database stored in memory rather than on a disk.

One of the most common ways to use a DataSet object is to load it from a relational database when the program starts, use various controls to display the data and let the user manipulate it interactively, and then save the changes back into the database when the program ends.

In variations on this basic theme, the program can load its data from an XML file or build a DataSet in memory without using a database. The program can use controls bound to the DataSet to let the user view and manipulate complex data with little extra programming.

Example program MemoryDataSet, which is available for download on the book's web site, uses the following code to build and initialize a DataSet from scratch. It starts by creating a new DataSet object named Scores. It creates a `DataTable` named Students and adds it to the DataSet object's Tables collection.

```vb
Private Sub Form1_Load() Handles MyBase.Load
    ' Make the DataSet.
    Dim scores_dataset As New DataSet("Scores")

    ' Make the Students table.
    Dim students_table As DataTable =
        scores_dataset.Tables.Add("Students")

    ' Add columns to the Students table.
    students_table.Columns.Add("FirstName", GetType(String))
    students_table.Columns.Add("LastName", GetType(String))
    students_table.Columns.Add("StudentId", GetType(Integer))

    ' Make the StudentId field unique.
    students_table.Columns("StudentId").Unique = True '

    ' Make the combined FirstName/LastName unique.
    Dim first_last_columns() As DataColumn = {
        students_table.Columns("FirstName"),
        students_table.Columns("LastName")
    }
    students_table.Constraints.Add(New UniqueConstraint(first_last_columns))

    ' Make the TestScores table.
    Dim test_scores_table As DataTable =
    scores_dataset.Tables.Add("TestScores")

    ' Add columns to the TestScores table.
    test_scores_table.Columns.Add("StudentId", GetType(Integer))
    test_scores_table.Columns.Add("TestNumber", GetType(Integer))
    test_scores_table.Columns.Add("Score", GetType(Integer))

    ' Make the combined StudentId/TestNumber unique.
    Dim studentid_testnumber_score_columns() As DataColumn = {
        test_scores_table.Columns("StudentId"),
        test_scores_table.Columns("TestNumber")
    }
```

```
        test_scores_table.Constraints.Add(
            New UniqueConstraint(studentid_testnumber_score_columns))

        ' Make a relationship linking the
        ' two tables' StudentId fields.
        scores_dataset.Relations.Add(
            "Student Test Scores",
            students_table.Columns("StudentId"),
            test_scores_table.Columns("StudentId"))

        ' Make some student data.
        students_table.Rows.Add(New Object() {"Art", "Ant", 1})
        students_table.Rows.Add(New Object() {"Bev", "Bug", 2})
        students_table.Rows.Add(New Object() {"Cid", "Cat", 3})
        students_table.Rows.Add(New Object() {"Deb", "Dove", 4})

        ' Make some random test scores.
        Dim score As New Random
        For id As Integer = 1 To 4
            For test_num As Integer = 1 To 10
                test_scores_table.Rows.Add(
                    New Object() {id, test_num, score.Next(65, 100)})
            Next test_num
        Next id

        ' Attach the DataSet to the DataGrid.
        grdScores.DataSource = scores_dataset
    End Sub
```

code snippet MemoryDataSet

Next, the code uses the DataTable object's `Columns.Add` method to add FirstName, LastName, and StudentId columns to the table. It then sets the StudentId column's Unique property to True to make the DataSet prohibit duplicated StudentId values.

The program then makes an array of DataColumn objects containing references to the FirstName and LastName columns. It uses the array to create a UniqueConstraint and adds it to the table's Constraints collection. This makes the DataSet ensure that each record's FirstName/LastName pair is unique.

Similarly, the program creates the TestScores table, gives it StudentId, TestNumber, and Score columns, and adds a uniqueness constraint on the StudentId/TestNumber pair of columns.

Next, the code adds a relationship linking the Students table's StudentId column and the TestScores table's StudentId column.

The program then adds some Students records and some random TestScores records.

Finally, the program attaches the DataSet to a DataGrid control to display the result. The user can use the DataGrid to examine and modify the data just as if it had been loaded from a database.

The following table describes the DataSet object's most useful properties.

PROPERTY	PURPOSE
CaseSensitive	Determines whether string comparisons inside DataTable objects are case-sensitive.
DataSetName	The DataSet object's name. Often, you don't need to use this for much. If you need to use the DataSet object's XML representation, however, this determines the name of the root element.
DefaultViewManager	Returns a DataViewManager object that you can use to determine the default settings (sort order, filter) of DataView objects you create later.
EnforceConstraints	Determines whether the DataSet should enforce constraints while updating data. For example, if you want to add records to a child table before the master records have been created, you can set EnforceConstraints to False while you add the data. You should be able to avoid this sort of problem by adding the records in the correct order.
HasErrors	Returns True if any of the DataSet object's DataTable objects contains errors.
Namespace	The DataSet's namespace. If this is nonblank, the DataSet object's XML data's root node includes an xmlns attribute as in <Scores xmlns="my_namespace">.
Prefix	Determines the XML prefix that the DataSet uses as an alias for its namespace.
Relations	A collection of DataRelation objects that represent parent/child relations among the columns in different tables.
Tables	A collection of DataTable objects representing the tables stored in the DataSet.

The DataSet object's XML properties affect the way the object reads and writes its data in XML form. For example, if the Namespace property is my_namespace and the Prefix property is pfx, the DataSet object's XML data might look like the following:

```
<pfx:Scores xmlns:pfx="my_namespace">
  <Students xmlns="my_namespace">
    <FirstName>Art</FirstName>
    <LastName>Ant</LastName>
    <StudentId>1</StudentId>
  </Students>
  <Students xmlns="my_namespace">
    <FirstName>Bev</FirstName>
    <LastName>Bug</LastName>
    <StudentId>2</StudentId>
  </Students>
  ...
```

```
<TestScores xmlns="my_namespace">
  <StudentId>1</StudentId>
  <TestNumber>1</TestNumber>
  <Score>78</Score>
</TestScores>
<TestScores xmlns="my_namespace">
  <StudentId>1</StudentId>
  <TestNumber>2</TestNumber>
  <Score>81</Score>
</TestScores>
  ...
</pfx:Scores>
```

The following table describes the DataSet object's most useful methods.

METHOD	PURPOSE
AcceptChanges	Accepts all changes to the data that were made since the data was loaded, or since the last call to AcceptChanges. When you modify a row in the DataSet, the row is flagged as modified. If you delete a row, the row is marked as deleted but not actually removed. When you call AcceptChanges, new and modified rows are marked as Unchanged instead of Added or Modified, and deleted rows are permanently removed.
Clear	Removes all rows from the DataSet object's tables.
Clone	Makes a copy of the DataSet including all tables, relations, and constraints, but not including the data.
Copy	Makes a copy of the DataSet including all tables, relations, constraints, and the data.
GetChanges	Makes a copy of the DataSet containing only the rows that have been modified. This method's optional parameter indicates the type of changes that the new DataSet should contain (added, modified, deleted, or unchanged).
GetXml	Returns a string containing the DataSet object's XML representation.
GetXmlSchema	Returns the DataSet object's XML schema definition (XSD).
HasChanges	Returns True if any of the DataSet object's tables contains new, modified, or deleted rows.
Merge	Merges a DataSet, DataTable, or array of DataRow objects into this DataSet.
ReadXml	Reads XML data from a stream or file into the DataSet.
ReadXmlSchema	Reads an XML schema from a stream or file into the DataSet.

METHOD	PURPOSE
RejectChanges	Undoes any changes made since the DataSet was loaded or since the last call to AcceptChanges.
WriteXml	Writes the DataSet object's XML data into a file or stream. It can optionally include the DataSet object's schema.
WriteXmlSchema	Writes the DataSet object's XSD schema into an XML file or stream.

Several of these methods mirror methods provided by other finer-grained data objects. For example, HasChanges returns True if any of the DataSet object's tables contain changes. The DataTable and DataRow objects also have HasChanges methods that return True if their more limited scope contains changes.

These mirrored methods include AcceptChanges, Clear, Clone, Copy, GetChanges, and RejectChanges. See the following sections that describe the DataTable and DataRow objects for more information.

DataTable

The DataTable class represents the data in one table within a DataSet. A DataTable contains DataRow objects representing its data, DataColumn objects that define the table's columns, constraint objects that define constraints on the table's data (for example, a uniqueness constraint requires that only one row may contain the same value in a particular column), and objects representing relationships between the table's columns and the columns in other tables. This object also provides methods and events for manipulating rows.

The following table describes the DataTable object's most useful properties.

PROPERTY	PURPOSE
CaseSensitive	Determines whether string comparisons inside the DataTable are case-sensitive.
ChildRelations	A collection of DataRelation objects that define parent/child relationships where this table is the parent. For example, suppose the Orders table defines order records and contains an OrderId field. Suppose that the OrderItems table lists the items for an order and it also has an OrderId field. One Orders record can correspond to many OrderItems records, all linked by the same OrderId value. In this example, Orders is the parent table and OrderItems is the child table.
Columns	A collection of DataColumn objects that define the table's columns (column name, data type, default value, maximum length, and so forth).

continues

(continued)

PROPERTY	PURPOSE
Constraints	A collection of Constraint objects represent restrictions on the table's data. A ForeignKeyConstraint requires that the values in some of the table's columns must be present in another table (for example, the Addresses record's State value must appear in the States table's StateName column). A UniqueConstraint requires that the values in a set of columns must be unique within the table (for example, only one Student record can have a given FirstName and LastName pair).
DataSet	The DataSet object that contains this DataTable.
DefaultView	Returns a DataView object that you can use to view, sort, and filter the table's rows.
HasErrors	Returns True if any of the DataTable object's rows contains an error.
MinimumCapacity	The initial capacity of the table. For example, if you know you are about to load 1000 records into the table, you can set this to 1000 to let the table allocate space all at once instead of incrementally as the records are added. That will be more efficient.
Namespace	The DataTable object's namespace. If this is nonblank, the DataTable object's XML records' root nodes include an xmlns attribute as in `<Students xmlns="my_namespace">`.
ParentRelations	A collection of DataRelation objects that define parent/child relationships where this table is the child. See the description of the ChildRelations property for more details.
Prefix	Determines the XML prefix that the DataTable uses as an alias for its namespace.
PrimaryKey	Gets or sets an array of DataColumn objects that define the table's primary key. The primary key is always unique and provides the fastest access to the records.
Rows	A collection of DataRow objects containing the table's data.
TableName	The table's name.

The DataTable object's XML properties affect the way the object reads and writes its data in XML form. For example, if the Namespace property is my_namespace and the Prefix property is tbl1, one of the DataTable object's XML records might look like the following:

```
<pfx:Students xmlns:pfx="my_namespace">
  <FirstName xmlns="my_namespace">Art</FirstName>
  <LastName xmlns="my_namespace">Ant</LastName>
  <StudentId xmlns="my_namespace">1</StudentId>
</pfx:Students>
```

The following table describes the DataTable object's most useful methods.

METHOD	PURPOSE
AcceptChanges	Accepts all changes to the table's rows that were made since the data was loaded or since the last call to AcceptChanges.
Clear	Removes all rows from the table.
Clone	Makes a copy of the DataTable, including all relations and constraints, but not including the data.
Compute	Computes the value of an expression using the rows that satisfy a filter condition. For example, the statement `tblTestScores.Compute ("SUM(Score)", "StudentId = 1")` calculates the total of the tblTestScores DataTable object's Score column where the StudentId is 1.
Copy	Makes a copy of the DataTable including all relations, constraints, and data.
GetChanges	Makes a copy of the DataTable containing only the rows that have been modified. This method's optional parameter indicates the type of changes that the new DataSet should contain (added, modified, deleted, or unchanged).
GetErrors	Gets an array of DataRow objects that contain errors.
ImportRow	Copies the data in a DataRow object into the DataTable.
LoadDataRow	This method takes an array of values as a parameter. It searches the table for a row with values that match the array's primary key values. If it doesn't find such a row, it uses the values to create the row. The method returns the DataRow object it found or creates.
NewRow	Creates a new DataRow object that matches the table's schema. To add the new row to the table, you can create a new DataRow, fill in its fields, and use the table's Rows.Add method.
RejectChanges	Undoes any changes made since the DataTable was loaded or since the last call to AcceptChanges.
Select	Returns an array of DataRow objects selected from the table. Optional parameters indicate a filter expression that the selected rows must match, sort columns and sort order, and the row states to select (new, modified, deleted, and so forth).

The DataTable object also provides several useful events, which are listed in the following table.

EVENT	PURPOSE
ColumnChanged	Occurs after a value has been changed in a column.
ColumnChanging	Occurs when a value is being changed in a column.
RowChanged	Occurs after a row has changed. A user might change several of a row's columns and ColumnChanged will fire for each one. RowChanged fires when the user moves to a new row.
RowChanging	Occurs when a row is being changed.
RowDeleted	Occurs after a row has been deleted.
RowDeleting	Occurs when a row is being deleted.

DataRow

A DataRow object represents the data in one record in a DataTable. This object is relatively simple. It basically just holds data for the DataTable, and the DataTable object does most of the interesting work.

The following table describes the DataRow object's most useful properties.

PROPERTY	PURPOSE
HasErrors	Returns True if the row's data has errors.
Item	Gets or sets one of the row's item values. Overloaded versions of this property use different parameters to identify the column. This parameter can be the column's zero-based index, its name, or a DataColumn object. An optional second parameter can indicate the version of the row so, for example, you can read the original value in a row that has been modified.
ItemArray	Gets or sets all of the row's values by using an array of generic Objects.
RowError	Gets or sets the row's error message text.
RowState	Returns the row's current state: Added, Deleted, Modified, or Unchanged.
Table	Returns a reference to the DataTable containing the row.

If a row has an error message defined by its RowError property, the DataGrid control displays a red circle containing a white exclamation point to the left of the row as an error indicator. If you hover the mouse over the error indicator, a tooltip displays the RowError text. In Figure 20-18, the third row has RowError set to "Missing registration."

Example program MemoryDataSetWithErrors, which is available for download on the book's web site, uses the following code to set errors on the second row's third column (remember, indexes start at zero) and on the third row. The result is shown in Figure 20-17.

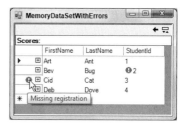

FIGURE 20-18: The DataGrid control marks a DataRow that has a nonblank RowError.

```
students_table.Rows(1).SetColumnError(2,
    "Bad name format")
students_table.Rows(2).RowError =
    "Missing registration"
```

The following table describes the DataRow object's most useful methods.

METHOD	PURPOSE
AcceptChanges	Accepts all changes to the row that were made since the data was loaded or since the last call to AcceptChanges.
BeginEdit	Puts the row in data-editing mode. This suspends events for the row, so your code or the user can change several fields without triggering validation events. BeginEdit is implicitly called when the user modifies a bound control's value and EndEdit is implicitly called when you invoke AcceptChanges. Although the row is in edit mode, it stores the original and modified values, so you can retrieve either version, accept the changes with EndEdit, or cancel the changes with CancelEdit.
CancelEdit	Cancels the current edit on the row and restores its original values.
ClearErrors	Clears the row's column and row errors.
Delete	Deletes the row from its table.
GetChildRows	Returns an array of DataRow objects representing this row's child rows as specified by a parent/child data relation.
GetColumnError	Returns the error text assigned to a column.
GetParentRow	Returns a DataRow object representing this row's parent record as specified by a parent/child data relation.
GetParentRows	Returns an array of DataRow objects representing this row's parent records as specified by a data relation.
HasVersion	Returns True if the row has a particular version (Current, Default, Original, or Proposed). For example, while a row is being edited, it has Current and Proposed versions.

continues

(continued)

METHOD	PURPOSE
IsNull	Indicates whether a particular column contains a NULL value.
RejectChanges	Removes any changes made to the row since the data was loaded or since the last call to AcceptChanges.
SetColumnError	Sets error text for one of the row's columns. If a column has an error message, then a DataGrid control displays a red circle containing a white exclamation point to the left of the column's value as an error indicator. In Figure 20-17, the second row's second column has a column error set. If you hover the mouse over the error indicator, a tooltip displays the error's text.
SetParentRow	Sets the row's parent row according to a data relation.

DataColumn

The DataColumn object represents a column in a DataTable. It defines the column's name and data type, and your code can use it to define relationships among different columns.

The following table describes the DataColumn object's most useful properties.

PROPERTY	PURPOSE
AllowDBNull	Determines whether the column allows NULL values.
AutoIncrement	Determines whether new rows automatically generate auto-incremented values for the column.
AutoIncrementSeed	Determines the starting value for an auto-increment column.
AutoIncrementStep	Determines the amount by which an auto-incrementing column's value is incremented for new rows.
Caption	Gets or sets a caption for the column. Note that some controls may not use this value. For example, the DataGrid control displays the column's ColumnName, not its Caption.
ColumnMapping	Determines how the column is saved in the table's XML data. This property can have one of the values Attribute (save the column as an attribute of the row's element), Element (save the column as a subelement), Hidden (don't save the column), and SimpleContent (save the column as XmlText inside the row's element). If a column is hidden, the DataGrid control doesn't display its value. See the text following this table for an example.

PROPERTY	PURPOSE
ColumnName	Determines the name of the column in the DataTable. Note that data adapters use the column name to map database columns to DataSet columns, so, if you change this property without updating the table mapping, the column will probably not be filled.
DataType	Determines the column's data type. Visual Basic raises an error if you change this property after the DataTable begins loading data. Visual Basic supports the data types Boolean, Byte, Char, DateTime, Decimal, Double, Int16, Int32, Int64, SByte, Single, String, TimeSpan, UInt16, UInt32, and UInt64.
DefaultValue	Determines the default value assigned to the column in new rows.
Expression	Sets an expression for the column. You can use this to create calculated columns. For example, the expression Quantity * Price makes the column display the value of the Quantity column times the value of the Price column.
MaxLength	Determines the maximum length of a text column.
Namespace	The column's namespace. If this is nonblank, the rows' XML root nodes include an xmlns attribute as in <StudentId xmlns="my_namespace">12</StudentId>.
Ordinal	Returns the column's index in the DataTable object's Columns collection.
Prefix	Determines the XML prefix that the DataColumn uses as an alias for its namespace. For example, if Namespace is my_namespace and Prefix is pfx, then a row's StudentId field might be encoded in XML as <pfx: StudentId xmlns:pfx="my_namespace">12</pfx:StudentId>.
ReadOnly	Determines whether the column allows changes after a record is created.
Table	Returns a reference to the DataTable containing the column.
Unique	Determines whether different rows in the table can have the same value for this column.

Example program MemoryDataSetXmlMappedColumns, which is available for download on the book's web site, uses the following code to define XML column mappings for the Students table. It indicates that the table's FirstName and LastName columns should be saved as attributes of the row elements, and that the StudentId column should be saved as XmlText. Note that you cannot use the SimpleContent ColumnMapping if any other column has a ColumnMapping of Element or SimpleContent.

```
students_table.Columns("FirstName").ColumnMapping = MappingType.Attribute
students_table.Columns("LastName").ColumnMapping = MappingType.Attribute
students_table.Columns("StudentId").ColumnMapping = MappingType.SimpleContent
```

code snippet MemoryDataSetXmlMappedColumns

The following text shows some of the resulting XML Students records:

```
<Students FirstName="Art" LastName="Ant">1</Students>
<Students FirstName="Bev" LastName="Bug">2</Students>
<Students FirstName="Cid" LastName="Cat">3</Students>
<Students FirstName="Deb" LastName="Dove">4</Students>
```

The following code makes the FirstName and LastName columns elements of the Students rows, and it makes the StudentId an attribute:

```
students_table.Columns("FirstName").ColumnMapping = MappingType.Element
students_table.Columns("LastName").ColumnMapping = MappingType.Element
students_table.Columns("StudentId").ColumnMapping = MappingType.Attribute
```

code snippet MemoryDataSetXmlMappedColumns

The following shows the resulting records:

```
<Students StudentId="1">
  <FirstName>Art</FirstName>
  <LastName>Ant</LastName>
</Students>
<Students StudentId="2">
  <FirstName>Bev</FirstName>
  <LastName>Bug</LastName>
</Students>
<Students StudentId="3">
  <FirstName>Cid</FirstName>
  <LastName>Cat</LastName>
</Students>
<Students StudentId="4">
  <FirstName>Deb</FirstName>
  <LastName>Dove</LastName>
</Students>
```

DataRelation

A DataRelation object represents a parent/child relationship between sets of columns in different tables. For example, suppose that a database contains a Students table containing FirstName, LastName, and StudentId fields. The TestScores table has the fields StudentId, TestNumber, and Score. The StudentId fields connect the two tables in a parent/child relationship. Each Students record may correspond to any number of TestScores records. In this example, Students is the parent table, and TestScores is the child table.

The following code defines this relationship. It uses the Students.StudentId field as the parent field and the TestScores.StudentId field as the child field.

```
' Make a relationship linking the two tables' StudentId fields.
scores_dataset.Relations.Add(
    "Student Test Scores",
    students_table.Columns("StudentId"),
    test_scores_table.Columns("StudentId"))
```

code snippet MemoryDataSet

A DataRelation can also relate more than one column in the two tables. For example, two tables might be linked by the combination of the LastName and FirstName fields.

Most programs don't need to manipulate a relation after it is created. The DataSet object's Relations .Add method shown in the previous code creates a relation and thereafter the program can usually leave it alone. However, the DataRelation object does provide properties and methods in case you do need to modify one. The following table describes the DataRelation object's most useful properties.

PROPERTY	PURPOSE
ChildColumns	Returns an array of DataColumn objects representing the child columns.
ChildKeyConstraint	Returns the ForeignKeyConstraint object for this relation. You can use this object to determine the relation's behavior when the program updates, deletes, or modifies the values used in the relationship. For example, if the StudentId field links the Students and TestScores tables and you delete a Students record, you can use this object to make the database automatically delete any corresponding TestScores records.
ChildTable	Returns a DataTable object representing the relation's child table.
DataSet	Returns a reference to the DataSet containing the relation.
Nested	Determines whether the child data should be nested within parent rows in the DataSet's XML representation. See the text following this table for more detail.
ParentColumns	Returns an array of DataColumn objects representing the parent columns.
ParentKeyConstraint	Returns the UniqueConstraint object for this relation. This object requires that the values in the parent's columns are unique within the parent table.
ParentTable	Returns a DataTable object representing the relation's parent table.
RelationName	Determines the relation's name.

Normally, tables are stored separately in a DataSet object's XML representation, but you can use the Nested property to make the XML include one table's records inside another's. For example, suppose that the Students and TestScores tables are linked by a common StudentId field. If you set this relation's Nested property to True, the XML data would include the TestScores for a student within the Students record, as shown in the following:

```
<Students>
  <FirstName>Deb</FirstName>
  <LastName>Dove</LastName>
  <StudentId>4</StudentId>
  <TestScores>
    <StudentId>4</StudentId>
    <TestNumber>1</TestNumber>
    <Score>81</Score>
  </TestScores>
  <TestScores>
    <StudentId>4</StudentId>
    <TestNumber>2</TestNumber>
    <Score>68</Score>
  </TestScores>
  ...
</Students>
```

Example program MemoryDataSetNestedXml, which is available for download on the book's web site, demonstrates this nested XML structure.

Note that in this representation the TestScores table's StudentId value is redundant because the same value is contained in the Students element's StudentId subelement. If you set the TestScores .StudentId column's ColumnMapping value to Hidden, you can remove the redundant values and get the following result:

```
<Students>
  <FirstName>Deb</FirstName>
  <LastName>Dove</LastName>
  <StudentId>4</StudentId>
  <TestScores>
    <TestNumber>1</TestNumber>
    <Score>81</Score>
  </TestScores>
  <TestScores>
    <TestNumber>2</TestNumber>
    <Score>68</Score>
  </TestScores>
  ...
</Students>
```

Constraints

A constraint imposes a restriction on the data in a table's columns. DataSets support two kinds of constraint objects:

➤ **ForeignKeyConstraint** restricts the values in one table based on the values in another table. For example, you could require that values in the Addresses table's State field must exist in the States table's StateName field. That would prevent the program from creating an Addresses record where State is XZ.

➤ **UniqueConstraint** requires that the combination of one or more fields within the same table must be unique. For example, an Employee table might require that the combination of the FirstName and LastName values be unique. That would prevent the program from creating two Employees records with the same FirstName and LastName.

The following sections describe each of these types of constraint objects in greater detail.

ForeignKeyConstraint

In addition to requiring that values in one table must exist in another table, a ForeignKeyConstraint can determine how changes to one table propagate to the other. For example, suppose that the Addresses table has a ForeignKeyConstraint requiring that its State field contain a value that is present in the States table's StateName field. If you delete the States table's record for Colorado, the constraint could automatically delete all of the Addresses records that used that state's name.

The following table describes the ForeignKeyConstraint object's most useful properties.

PROPERTY	PURPOSE
AcceptRejectRule	Determines the action taken when the AcceptChanges method executes. This value can be None (do nothing) or Cascade (update the child fields' values to match the new parent field values).
Columns	Returns an array containing references to the constraint's child columns.
ConstraintName	Determines the constraint's name.
DeleteRule	Determines the action taken when a row is deleted. This value can be Cascade (delete the child rows), None (do nothing), SetDefault (change child field values to their default values), or SetNull (change child field values to NULL).
RelatedColumns	Returns an array containing references to the constraint's parent columns.
RelatedTable	Returns a reference to the constraint's parent table.
Table	Returns a reference to the constraint's child table.
UpdateRule	Determines the action taken when a row is updated. This value can be Cascade (update the child rows' values to match), None (do nothing), SetDefault (change child field values to their default values), or SetNull (change child field values to NULL).

The following code makes a foreign key constraint relating the Students.StudentId parent field to the TestScores.StudentId child field:

```
scores_dataset.Relations.Add(
    "Student Test Scores",
    students_table.Columns("StudentId"),
    test_scores_table.Columns("StudentId"))
```

code snippet MemoryDataSet

Example program MemoryDataSet uses similar code to define a relationship between its Students and TestScores tables.

UniqueConstraint

If you want to require the values in a single column to be unique, you can set the column's Unique property to True. This automatically creates a UniqueConstraint object and adds it to the DataTable. The following code shows how a program can make the Students table's StudentId column require unique values:

```
students_table.Columns("StudentId").Unique = True
```

You can use the UniqueConstraint object's constructors to require that a group of fields has a unique combined value. The following code makes an array of DataColumn objects representing the Students table's FirstName and LastName fields. It passes the array into the UniqueConstraint object's constructor to require that the FirstName/LastName pair be unique in the table.

```
' Make the combined FirstName/LastName unique.
Dim first_last_columns() As DataColumn = {
    students_table.Columns("FirstName"),
    students_table.Columns("LastName")
}
students_table.Constraints.Add(New UniqueConstraint(first_last_columns))
```

code snippet MemoryDataSet

After executing this code, the program could add two records with the same FirstName and different LastNames or with the same LastName and different FirstNames, but it could not create two records with the same FirstName and LastName values.

The following table describes the UniqueConstraint object's properties.

PROPERTY	PURPOSE
Columns	Returns an array of DataColumn objects representing the columns that must be unique. ConstraintName determines the name of the constraint.
IsPrimaryKey	Returns True if the columns form the table's primary key.
Table	Returns a reference to the DataTable that contains the constraint.

Example program MemoryDataSet, which is available for download on the book's web site, defines several uniqueness constraints including a constraint requiring that StudentId be unique and a constraint requiring that the FirstName and LastName combination be unique.

DATAVIEW

A DataView object represents a customizable view of the data contained in a DataTable. You can use the DataView to select some or all of the DataTable's data and display it sorted in some manner without affecting the underlying DataTable.

A program can use multiple DataViews to select and order a table's data in different ways. You can then bind the DataViews to controls such as the DataGrid control to display the different views. If any of the views modifies its data, for example by adding or deleting a row, the underlying DataTable object's data is updated and any other views that need to see the change are updated as well.

Example program DataGrids, which is available for download on the book's web site, uses the following code to demonstrate DataGrid controls:

```vb
Private Sub Form1_Load() Handles MyBase.Load
    ' Make a DataTable.
    Dim contacts_table As New DataTable("Contacts")

    ' Add columns.
    contacts_table.Columns.Add("FirstName", GetType(String))
    contacts_table.Columns.Add("LastName", GetType(String))
    contacts_table.Columns.Add("Street", GetType(String))
    contacts_table.Columns.Add("City", GetType(String))
    contacts_table.Columns.Add("State", GetType(String))
    contacts_table.Columns.Add("Zip", GetType(String))

    ' Make the combined FirstName/LastName unique.
    Dim first_last_columns() As DataColumn = {
        contacts_table.Columns("FirstName"),
        contacts_table.Columns("LastName")
    }
    contacts_table.Constraints.Add(New UniqueConstraint(first_last_columns))

    ' Make some contact data.
    contacts_table.Rows.Add(New Object() {"Art", "Ant",
```

```
            "1234 Ash Pl", "Bugville", "CO", "11111"})
        contacts_table.Rows.Add(New Object() {"Bev", "Bug",
            "22 Beach St", "Bugville", "CO", "22222"})
        contacts_table.Rows.Add(New Object() {"Cid", "Cat",
            "3 Road Place Lane", "Programmeria", "KS", "33333"})
        contacts_table.Rows.Add(New Object() {"Deb", "Dove",
            "414 Debugger Way", "Programmeria", "KS", "44444"})
        contacts_table.Rows.Add(New Object() {"Ed", "Eager",
            "5746 Elm Blvd", "Bugville", "CO", "55555"})
        contacts_table.Rows.Add(New Object() {"Fran", "Fix",
            "647 Foxglove Ct", "Bugville", "CO", "66666"})
        contacts_table.Rows.Add(New Object() {"Gus", "Gantry",
            "71762-B Gooseberry Ave", "Programmeria", "KS", "77777"})
        contacts_table.Rows.Add(New Object() {"Hil", "Harris",
            "828 Hurryup St", "Programmeria", "KS", "88888"})

        ' Attach grdAll to the DataTable.
        grdAll.DataSource = contacts_table
        grdAll.CaptionText = "All Records"

        ' Make a DataView for State = CO.
        Dim dv_co As New DataView(contacts_table)
        dv_co.RowFilter = "State = 'CO'"
        grdCO.DataSource = dv_co
        grdCO.CaptionText = "CO Records"

        ' Make a DataView for FirstName >= E.
        Dim dv_name As New DataView(contacts_table)
        dv_name.RowFilter = "FirstName >= 'E'"
        grdName.DataSource = dv_name
        grdName.CaptionText = "LastName >= E"
    End Sub
```

code snippet DataGrids

The code builds a DataTable named Contacts containing the fields FirstName, LastName, Street, City, State, and Zip. It places a uniqueness constraint on the FirstName/LastName pair and adds some rows of data to the table. It then binds the DataTable to the DataGrid control named grdAll. Next the program makes a DataView named dv_co based on the table, sets its RowFilter property to make it select rows where the State field has the value CO, and binds the DataView to the DataGrid named grdCO. Finally, the code makes another DataView with RowFilter set to select records where the FirstName field is greater than or equal to E and binds that DataView to the grdName DataGrid.

Figure 20-19 shows the result. The DataGrid on the top is bound to the DataTable and shows all the table's rows. The second DataGrid is bound to the dv_co DataView and displays records where State = CO. The bottom DataGrid is bound to the dv_name DataView, so it displays records where FirstName >= E. If you use any of these DataGrid controls to modify the data, the other grids immediately show the updates.

The DataView class is geared more toward data display than toward storage. It basically refers to data stored in a DataTable object, so it doesn't provide the same features for managing relations and constraints that the DataTable does. It does, however, provide links to the DataRow objects it represents. From those objects, you can get back to the rows' DataTable objects if necessary.

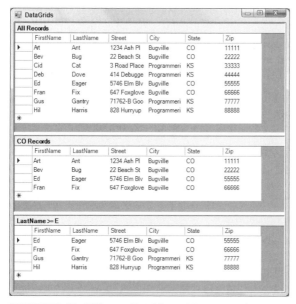

FIGURE 20-19: Different DataView objects can show different views of the same data.

The following table describes the DataView object's most useful properties.

PROPERTY	PURPOSE
AllowDelete	Determines whether the DataView allows row deletion. If this is False, any bound controls such as the DataGrid will not allow the user to delete rows.
AllowEdit	Determines whether the DataView allows row editing. If this is False, any bound controls (such as the DataGrid) will not allow the user to edit rows.
AllowNew	Determines whether the DataView allows new rows. If this is False, any bound controls (such as the DataGrid) will not allow the user to add rows.
Count	Returns the number of rows selected by the view.
Item	Returns a DataRowView object representing a row in the view.
RowFilter	A string that determines the records selected by the view.

continues

(continued)

PROPERTY	PURPOSE
RowStateFilter	The state of the records that should be selected by the view. This can be Added, CurrentRows (unchanged, new, and modified rows), Deleted, ModifiedCurrent (current version of modified rows), ModifiedOriginal (original version of modified rows), None, OriginalRows (original, unchanged, and deleted rows), and Unchanged.
Sort	A string giving the columns that should be used to sort the data. For example, "State, City, Zip" sorts by State, then City, and then Zip in descending order.
Table	Specifies the underlying DataTable object.

The following table describes some of the most useful DataView methods.

METHOD	PURPOSE
AddNew	Adds a new row to the underlying DataTable.
Delete	Deletes the row with a specific index from the underlying DataTable.
Find	Returns the index of a row that matches the view's sort key columns. This method returns −1 if no row matches the values it is passed. It raises an error if the number of values it receives does not match the number of the DataView's key values.
FindRows	Returns an array of DataRowView objects representing rows that match the view's sort key columns.

The DataView object's Sort property determines not only the fields by which the data is sorted but also the key fields used by the Find method. The following code makes the dv_name DataView sort by FirstName and LastName. It then uses the Find method to display the index of a row with FirstName = Hil and LastName = Harris.

```
dv_name.Sort = "FirstName, LastName"
MessageBox.Show(dv_name.Find(New String() {"Hil", "Harris"}).ToString)
```

DATAROWVIEW

A DataRow object can hold data for more than one state. For example, if a DataTable row has been modified, its DataRow object contains the row's original data and the new modified values.

The DataRowView object represents a view of a DataRow object in a particular state. That state can be Current (the current value), Default (if columns have defined default values), Original (the original values), or Proposed (new values during an edit before EndEdit or CancelEdit is called).

A DataView object holds DataRowView objects representing a view of a DataTable selecting particular rows in a particular state.

The DataRowView object's purpose is to represent a row in a specific state so this object is relatively simple. It basically indicates the chosen state and refers to a DataRow.

The following table describes the DataRowView object's most useful properties.

PROPERTY	PURPOSE
DataView	The DataView that contains the DataRowView.
IsEdit	Returns True if the row is in editing mode.
IsNew	Returns True if the row is new.
Item	Gets or sets the value of one of the row's fields.
Row	The DataRow object that this DataRowView represents.
RowVersion	The version of the DataRow represented by this object (Current, Default, Original, or Proposed).

SIMPLE DATA BINDING

Binding a simple property such as Text to a data source is relatively easy. First, create a DataSet, DataTable, or DataView to act as the data source. You can create this object at design time using controls or at runtime using object variables.

If you build the data source at design time, you can also bind the property at design time. Select the control that you want to bind and open the Properties window. Expand the (DataBindings) entry and find the property you want to bind (for example, Text). Click the drop-down arrow on the right, and use the pop-up display to select the data source item that you want to bind to the property.

Figure 20-20 shows the pop-up binding the txtTitle control's Text property to the dsBooks DataSet object's Books table's Title field.

At runtime, your code can bind a simple property to a data source by using the control's DataBindings collection. This collection's Add method takes as parameters the name of the property to bind, the data source, and the name of the item in the data source to bind.

The following statement binds the txtUrl control's Text property to the dsBooks DataSet object's Books table's URL field:

```
txtUrl.DataBindings.Add("Text", dsBooks.Books, "URL")
```

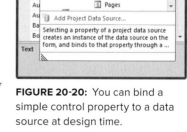

FIGURE 20-20: You can bind a simple control property to a data source at design time.

When you bind the first property, Visual Basic adds a BindingSource *to the form. You can reuse this* BindingSource *to bind other properties. When you open the dropdown shown in Figure 20–20, expand the existing* BindingSource *to reuse it rather than creating a new one.*

That's all there is to binding simple properties. By itself, however, this binding doesn't provide any form of navigation. If you were to bind the Text properties of a bunch of TextBox controls and run the program, you would see the data for the data source's first record and nothing else. To allow the user to navigate through the data source, you must use a CurrencyManager object.

CURRENCYMANAGER

Some controls such as the DataGrid control provide their own forms of navigation. If you bind a DataGrid to a DataSet, it allows the user to examine the DataSet object's tables, view and edit data, and follow links between the tables. The DataGrid provides its own methods for navigating through the data. For simpler controls, such as the TextBox, which can display only one data value at a time, you must provide some means for the program to navigate through the data source's records.

A data source manages its position within its data by using a CurrencyManager object. The CurrencyManager supervises the list of Binding objects that bind the data source to controls such as TextBoxes.

The following table describes the CurrencyManager object's most useful properties.

PROPERTY	PURPOSE
Bindings	A collection of the bindings that the object manages.
Count	Returns the number of rows associated with the CurrencyManager.
Current	Returns a reference to the current data object (row).
List	Returns an object that implements the IList interface that provides the data for the CurrencyManager. For example, if the data source is a DataSet or DataTable, this object is a DataView.
Position	Gets or sets the current position within the data. For example, in a DataTable this is the row number.

The CurrencyManager also provides some methods for manipulating the data. The following table describes the CurrencyManager object's most useful methods.

METHOD	PURPOSE
AddNew	Adds a new item to the data source.
CancelCurrentEdit	Cancels the current editing operation.
EndCurrentEdit	Ends the current editing operation, accepting any changes.
Refresh	Refills the bound controls.
RemoveAt	Removes the data source item at a specified index.

The CurrencyManager class raises a PositionChanged event when its position in the data changes.

Example program BindSimple, which is available for download on the book's web site, uses the following code to navigate through a DataSet:

```vb
Public Class Form1
    Private WithEvents m_CurrencyManager As CurrencyManager

    Private Sub Form1_Load() Handles MyBase.Load
        'TODO: This line of code loads data into the
        'BooksDataSet.Books' table. You can move, or remove it, as needed.
        Me.BooksTableAdapter.Fill(Me.BooksDataSet.Books)

        ' Get the CurrencyManager.
        m_CurrencyManager = DirectCast(Me.BindingContext(
            BooksBindingSource), CurrencyManager)

        ' Display the record number.
        m_CurrencyManager_PositionChanged()
    End Sub

    ' Move to the previous record.
    Private Sub btnPrev_Click() Handles btnPrev.Click
        If m_CurrencyManager.Position = 0 Then
            Beep()
        Else
            m_CurrencyManager.Position -= 1
        End If
    End Sub

    ' Move to the next record.
    Private Sub btnNext_Click() Handles btnNext.Click
        If m_CurrencyManager.Position >= m_CurrencyManager.Count - 1 Then
            Beep()
        Else
            m_CurrencyManager.Position += 1
        End If
    End Sub

    ' Go to the first record.
    Private Sub btnFirst_Click() Handles btnFirst.Click
```

```
            m_CurrencyManager.Position = 0
    End Sub

    ' Go to the last record.
    Private Sub btnLast_Click() Handles btnLast.Click
        m_CurrencyManager.Position = m_CurrencyManager.Count - 1
    End Sub

    Private Sub m_CurrencyManager_PositionChanged() _
    Handles m_CurrencyManager.PositionChanged
        lblPosition.Text =
            (m_CurrencyManager.Position + 1) & " of " & m_CurrencyManager.Count
    End Sub

    ' Add a record.
    Private Sub btnAdd_Click() Handles btnAdd.Click
        m_CurrencyManager.AddNew()
        txtTitle.Focus()
    End Sub

    ' Delete the current record.
    Private Sub btnDelete_Click() Handles btnDelete.Click
        If MessageBox.Show("Are you sure you want to remove this record?",
            "Confirm?", MessageBoxButtons.YesNo, MessageBoxIcon.Question) =
            Windows.Forms.DialogResult.Yes _
        Then
            m_CurrencyManager.RemoveAt(m_CurrencyManager.Position)
        End If
    End Sub
End Class
```

code snippet BindSimple

When the form loads, the program fills its data set and saves a reference to a CurrencyManager object to control the data set's Books table. It then calls subroutine `m_CurrencyManager_PositionChanged` to display the current record's index (this is described shortly).

The First, Last, Previous, and Next record buttons all work by changing the CurrencyManager's Position property. For example, the previous record button's event handler checks whether the current position is greater than zero and if it is the code decreases the position by one.

Similarly, the Next record button increases the current position by one if the CurrencyManager is not already displaying the last record.

The First and Last record buttons set the position to the indexes of the first and last records, respectively.

Whenever the CurrencyManager's position changes, its PositionChanged event handler executes. This code displays the current record's index in a label for the user to see.

When the user clicks the Add Record button, the code calls the CurrencyManager's AddNew method to make a new record. It also sets focus to the first text box to make filling in the new record easier.

Finally, when the user clicks the delete record button, the code confirms the deletion and then calls the CurrencyManager's RemoveAt method to delete the record.

Figure 20-21 shows the BindSimple program in action.

Example program BindSimpleMemoryDataSet, which is available for download on the book's web site, is similar to program BindSimple except it uses a DataSet built in memory rather than one loaded from a database.

FIGURE 20-21: This program's buttons use a CurrencyManager to let the user add, delete, and navigate through a table's records.

COMPLEX DATA BINDING

For some controls (such as the TextBox and Label) binding the Text property is good enough. Other controls, however, do not display a simple textual value.

For example, suppose that you have a database containing a Users table with fields FirstName, LastName, and UserType. The UserTypes table has fields UserTypeId and UserTypeName. The Users.UserType field contains a value that should match UserTypes.UserTypeId. The UserTypes .UserTypeName field contains values such as Programmer, Project Manager, Department Manager, Program Manager, and Lab Director.

When you build a form to display the Users table data, you would like to use a ComboBox to allow the user to select only the allowed choices Programmer, Project Manager, and so on. However, the Users table doesn't store those string values. Instead it stores the UserTypeId value corresponding to the UserTypeName value that the user selects. When the user picks a UserTypes.UserTypeName value, the ComboBox should look up the corresponding UserTypes.UserTypeId value and save it in the Users.UserType field.

Clearly, the simple binding strategy used for TextBoxes won't work here. Binding this control requires two rather complicated steps: defining the DataSet and binding the control. Each piece of the operation is easy, but you must do everything correctly. If you miss any detail, the ComboBox won't work, and Visual Basic's error messages probably won't give you enough information to figure out how to fix the problem.

Example program BindComboBox, which is available for download on the book's web site, demonstrates this technique. You may want to download this example and copy the included database ComputerUsers.mdb into a new directory so you can follow along.

The first step is building a data connection. Select the Data menu's Add New Data Source command. Use the Data Source Configuration Wizard to make a data source that selects both the Users and UserTypes tables from the database.

Next, create a ComboBox named `cboUserType` to the form. In the Properties window, select the control's DataSource property and click the drop-down arrow on the right. Select the UserTypes table as shown in Figure 20-22. This tells the ComboBox where to look up values.

When you set this property, Visual Basic also adds a DataSet, BindingSource, and TableAdapter to the form. These components provide access to the UserTypes table.

Set the ComboBox's DisplayMember property to the field in the lookup table (specified by the DataSource property) that the control will display to the user. In this example, the field is UserTypeName.

Set the ComboBox's ValueMember property to the field in the lookup table that represents the value that the ComboBox will need to read and write from the database. In this example, that's the UserTypeId field.

Next, you need to bind the ComboBox to the field that it must read and write in the database. In this example, that's the Users table's UserType field. To simplify this binding, add a new BindingSource to the form. Change its name to UsersBindingSource and set its DataSource property to the ComputerUsersDataSet as shown in Figure 20-23. Then set the BindingSource object's DataMember property to the Users table.

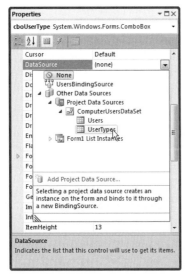

FIGURE 20-22: Set the ComboBox's DataSource property to the UserTypes table.

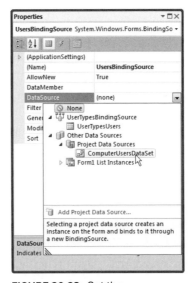

FIGURE 20-23: Set the BindingSource object's DataSource to the ComputerUsersDataSet.

The last ComboBox property you need to set is SelectedValue. Click the ComboBox, open the Properties window, and expand the (DataBindings) entry at the top. Click the drop-down arrow to the right of the SelectedValue property and select the field that the control must read and write in the database. For this example, that's the UsersBindingSource object's UserType field. Figure 20-24 shows the Property window setting this property.

Next, create TextBox controls to display the Users table's FirstName and LastName fields. In the Properties window, open their (Data Bindings) items and set their Text properties to the UsersBindingSource object's FirstName and LastName fields.

Finally, to give the user a way to navigate through the data, add a BindingNavigator to the form. Set this component's BindingSource property to UsersBindingSource and the program is ready to run. Figure 20-25 shows the BindComboBox example program, which is available for download on the book's web site, in action.

The choices allowed by the ComboBox are taken from the values in the UserTypes table's UserTypeName field. If you select a new user value from the ComboBox, the control automatically makes the appropriate change to the Users table.

The steps for binding a ListBox control are exactly the same as those for binding a ComboBox. Example program BindListBox, which is available for download on the book's web site, works much as program BindComboBox does, except it uses a ListBox instead of a ComboBox. As you move through the records, the ListBox selects the appropriate user type for each user record.

FIGURE 20-24: Set the BindingSource object's SelectedValue to the UsersBindingSource object's UserType field.

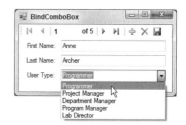

FIGURE 20-25: At runtime, the ComboBox displays the field bound to its DisplayMember property while updating the field bound to its SelectedValue property.

SUMMARY

Working with databases in Visual Basic is an enormous topic. This chapter does not cover every detail of database programming, but it does explain the basics. It tells how to build data sources and how to drag and drop tables and fields from the Data Sources window onto a form. It describes the most important database controls and objects, such as connection, data adapter, DataSet, and DataTable objects. It also explains the fundamentals of simple and complex data binding, and using CurrencyManager objects to navigate through data.

For more information on database programming in Visual Basic .NET, see one or more books about database programming. This is a very broad field so you may want to look at several books about database design, database maintenance using your particular database (for example, Access or SQL Server), Visual Basic database programming, and so forth.

Database programming has changed considerably in recent versions of Visual Basic, so be sure to get a book that's reasonably up-to-date. Older books explain many of the fundamental database objects such as DataSet, DataTable, DataRow, and CurrencyManager, but they won't cover new objects such as TableAdapter, DataConnector, and DataNavigator. Books covering Visual Basic 2005 and more recent editions should be the most useful. For example, the book *Expert One-on-One Visual Basic 2005 Database Programming* by Roger Jennings (Wrox, 2005) provides much greater depth on this topic.

If you must build and maintain large databases, you should also read books about database management. These can tell you how to design, build, and maintain a database throughout the application's lifetime. My book *Beginning Database Design Solutions* (Rod Stephens, Wrox, 2008) explains how to analyze database needs and build a robust and efficient database design.

You should also read about the particular kinds of databases that you need to use. For example, if you are working with SQL Server databases, get a good book on using SQL Server, such as *Professional Microsoft SQL Server 2008 Programming* by Robert Viera (Wrox, 2009).

Becoming an expert database developer is a big task, but the techniques described in this chapter should at least get you started.

The controls and other objects described in this chapter help a program manipulate data in a database. They help a program connect to a database, read and update data, and display the data on a form.

Chapter 21, "LINQ," explains another way to load and manipulate data. LINQ allows a program to perform complex queries similar to those provided by SQL to select data from lists, collections, arrays, and other data structures within the program's code.

21

LINQ

LINQ (Language Integrated Query, pronounced "link") is a data selection mechanism designed to give programs the ability to select data in the same way from *any* data source. Ideally the program would be able to use exactly the same method to fetch data whether it's stored in arrays, lists, relational databases, XML data, Excel worksheets, or some other data store. Currently the LINQ API supports data stored in relational databases, objects within the program stored in arrays or lists, and XML data.

LOTS OF LINQ

This chapter only covers the default LINQ providers included with Visual Basic, but you can build providers to make LINQ work with just about anything.
For a list of some third party LINQ providers to Google, Amazon, Excel, Active Directory, and more, see `rshelton.com/archive/2008/07/11/list-of-linq-providers.aspx`.

LINQ is a complex topic. LINQ provides dozens of extension methods that apply to all sorts of objects that hold data such as arrays, dictionaries, and lists. Visual Basic provides a LINQ query syntax that converts SQL-like queries into calls to LINQ functions.

LINQ tools are divided into the three categories summarized in the following list:

➤ **LINQ to Objects** refers to LINQ functions that interact with Visual Basic objects such as arrays, dictionaries, and lists. Most of this chapter presents examples using these kinds of objects to demonstrate LINQ concepts.

➤ **LINQ to XML** refers to LINQ features that read and write XML data. Using LINQ, you can easily move data between XML hierarchies and other Visual Basic objects.

➤ **LINQ to ADO.NET** refers to LINQ features that let you write LINQ-style queries to extract data from relational databases.

The first section, "Introduction to LINQ," provides an intuitive introduction to LINQ. Many of the details about LINQ functions are so complex and technical that they can be hard to understand, but the basic ideas are really quite simple. The introduction gives examples that demonstrate the essential concepts to try to give you an understanding of the basics.

The section "Basic LINQ Query Syntax" describes the most useful LINQ query commands. These let you perform complex queries that select, filter, and arrange data taken from program objects. The next section, "Advanced LINQ Query Syntax," describes additional LINQ query commands.

"LINQ Functions" describes functions that are provided by LINQ but that are not supported by Visual Basic's LINQ query syntax. To use these functions, you must apply them to the arrays, dictionaries, lists, and other objects that they extend.

"LINQ Extension Methods" explains how LINQ extends objects such as arrays, dictionaries, and lists. It describes method-based queries and explains how you can write your own extensions to increase the power of method-based queries.

After describing the tools provided by LINQ, most of the rest of the chapter describes the three main categories of LINQ usage: LINQ to Objects, LINQ to XML, and LINQ to ADO.NET. The chapter finishes by describing Parallel LINQ (PLINQ).

LINQ to Objects is a bit easier to cover effectively than LINQ to XML and LINQ to ADO.NET because it doesn't require that you have any special knowledge beyond Visual Basic itself. To understand LINQ to XML properly, you need to understand XML, which is a complex topic in its own right. Similarly, to get the most out of LINQ to ADO.NET, you need to understand relational databases such as SQL Server, a huge topic about which many books have been written.

Because LINQ to Objects is easiest to cover, this chapter focuses mostly on it, and most of the examples throughout the chapter deal with LINQ to Objects. The final sections of the chapter do provide some information about LINQ to XML and LINQ to ADO.NET, however, to give you an idea of what is possible in those arenas.

The book's web site contains 20 example programs that demonstrate the techniques described in this chapter.

INTRODUCTION TO LINQ

The LINQ API provides relatively low-level access to data in these storage formats. Visual Basic provides a higher-level layer above the LINQ API that makes querying data sources easier. This higher-level layer uses *query expressions* to define the data that should be selected from a data source. These expressions use a SQL-like syntax so they will be familiar to developers who have worked with relational databases.

For example, suppose a program defines a Customer class that provides typical customer properties such as Name, Phone, StreetAddress, AccountBalance, and so forth. Suppose also that the list all_customers holds all of the application's Customer objects. Then the following expression defines a query that selects customers with negative account balances. The results are ordered by balance in ascending order so customers with the most negative balances (who owe the most) are listed first. (Example program LinqLambda, which is available for download on the book's web site, defines a simple Customer class and performs a similar query.)

```
Dim overdue_custs =
    From cust In all_customers
    Where cust.AccountBalance < 0
    Order By cust.AccountBalance Ascending
    Select cust.Name, cust.AccountBalance
```

code snippet LinqLambda

Behind the scenes, Visual Basic transforms the query expression into calls to the LINQ API
and fetches the selected data. The program can then loop through the results as shown in the
following code:

```
For Each cust In overdue_custs
    Debug.WriteLine(cust.Name & ": " & cust.AccountBalance)
Next cust
```

There are a couple of interesting things to note about this code. First, the previous code fragments
do not declare data types for the expression or the looping variable cust in the For Each loop. The
data types for both of these variables are inferred automatically by Visual Basic. If you stop the program while it is executing and use the TypeName function to see what types these variables have,
you'll find that they have the following ungainly names:

```
<SelectIterator>d__b(Of Customer,VB$AnonymousType_0(Of String,Decimal))
VB$AnonymousType_0(Of String,Decimal)
```

The first line of this gibberish means the overdue_custs query result is an iterator that loops
through Customer objects and returns objects of an anonymous type (which is internally named
VB$AnonymousType_0) that contains String and Decimal fields. The second line indicates that the
cust variable used in the For Each loop has the same anonymous type VB$AnonymousType_0.

Because these variables have such awkward names, you don't really want to try to guess them. It's
much easier to leave Option Infer on and let Visual Basic infer them for you.

In fact, as the previous code fragments show, you never even need to know what these data types
are. The code can define the query without declaring its types, and the For Each loop can iterate
through the results without knowing the data type of the looping variable.

Because the code doesn't need to know what these data types really are, they are called
anonymous types.

A second interesting fact about this code is that the program doesn't actually fetch any data when
the query expression is defined. It only accesses the data source (in this case the all_customers
list) when the code tries to access the result in the For Each loop. Many programs don't really need
to distinguish between when the expression is declared and when it is executed. For example, if the
code iterates through the results right after defining the query, there isn't much difference. However,
if it may be a long time between defining the query and using it or if the query takes a long time to
execute, the difference may matter.

Third, if you have any experience with relational databases, you'll notice that the Select clause is
in a different position from where it would be in a SQL statement. In SQL the Select clause comes

first whereas in LINQ it comes at the end. This placement is due to implementation issues Microsoft encountered while implementing IntelliSense for LINQ. The concept is similar in SQL and LINQ. In both cases the Select clause tells which "fields" you want to select from the data. As long as you remember the difference in position (or let IntelliSense help you remember), it shouldn't be too confusing.

INTELLISENSE DEFERRED

Basically IntelliSense doesn't know what "fields" you can select until it knows what fields are available. In the preceding example, the From clause indicates that the data will be selected from `all_customers`, a list of Customer objects. It isn't until after the From clause that IntelliSense knows that the Select statement can pick from the Customer class's properties.

Though it is a new language, LINQ is quite complicated. LINQ's keywords are quite powerful and flexible, so they offer great opportunities for building powerful queries. LINQ's flexibility also offers opportunities for creating confusing code that is difficult to understand and debug. Complex LINQ queries are all the more difficult to debug because Visual Basic doesn't let you step through them while they execute as it does with code.

LINQ STEP-BY-STEP

Oddly, while Visual Basic programs cannot step through LINQ queries, C# programs can. Hopefully Visual Basic will get this feature some day.

The rest of this chapter describes LINQ in greater detail. The following sections explain the most useful LINQ keywords that are supported by Visual Basic. The next major section describes LINQ extension functions that you can use to query objects such as arrays and lists but that are not supported by LINQ queries.

BASIC LINQ QUERY SYNTAX

The following text shows the typical syntax for a LINQ query:

```
From ... Where ... Order By ... Select ...
```

The following sections describe these four basic clauses. The sections after those describe some of the other most useful LINQ clauses.

From

The From clause is the only one that is required. It tells where the data comes from and defines the name by which it is known within the LINQ query. Its basic form is:

```
From query_variable In data_source
```

Here *query_variable* is a variable that you are declaring to manipulate the items selected from the *data_source*. This is similar to declaring a looping variable in a For or For Each statement.

You can supply a data type for *query_variable* if you know its type, although due to the anonymous types used by LINQ, it's often easiest to let LINQ infer the data type automatically. For example, the following query explicitly indicates that the query variable per is from the Person class:

```
Dim query = From cust As Customer In all_customers
```

The From clause can include more than one query variable and data source. In that case, the query selects data from all of the data sources. For example, the following query selects objects from the all_customers and all_orders lists:

```
Dim query = From cust In all_customers, ord In all_orders
```

This query returns the cross-product of the objects in the two lists. In other words, for every object in the all_customers list, the query returns that object paired with every object in the all_orders list. If all_customers contains Ann, Bob, and Cindy, and all_orders contains orders numbered 1, 2, 3, then the following text shows the results returned by this query:

```
Ann        Order 1
Ann        Order 2
Ann        Order 3
Bob        Order 1
Bob        Order 2
Bob        Order 3
Cindy      Order 1
Cindy      Order 2
Cindy      Order 3
```

Usually, you will want to use a Where clause to join the objects selected from the two lists. For example, if customers and orders are related by a common CustomerId property, you might use the following query to select customers together with their orders rather than all orders:

```
Dim query = From cust In all_customers, ord In all_orders
    Where cut.CustomerId = ord.CustomerId
```

If Ann, Bob, and Cindy have CustomerId values 1, 2, 3, and the three orders have the corresponding CustomerId values, the preceding query would return the following results:

```
Ann        Order 1
Bob        Order 2
Cindy      Order 3
```

Where

The Where clause applies filters to the records selected by the From clause. It can include tests involving the objects selected and properties of those objects. The last example in the preceding section shows a particularly useful kind of query that *joins* objects from two data sources that are related by common property values. Although the Where clause is often used for simple joins, it can also execute functions on the selected objects and their properties.

For example, suppose the GoodCustomer class inherits from Customer, a class that has AccountBalance and PaymentLate properties. Also suppose the `all_customers` list contains Customer and GoodCustomer objects.

The `OwesALot` function defined in the following code returns True if a Customer owes more than $50. The query that follows selects objects from `all_customers` where the objects is not a GoodCustomer and has a PaymentLate property of True and for which function `OwesALot` returns True.

Available for
download on
Wrox.com

```
Private Function OwesALot(ByVal cust As Customer) As Boolean
    Return cust.AccountBalance < -50
End Function

Dim query = From cust In all_customers
    Where Not (TypeOf cust Is GoodCustomer)
        AndAlso cust.PaymentLate _
        AndAlso OwesALot(cust)
```

code snippet SimpleSamples

The Where clause can include just about any Boolean expression, usually involving the selected objects and their properties. As the preceding example shows, it can include Not, Is, AndAlso, and function calls. It can also include And, Or, OrElse, Mod, and Like.

Expressions can use any of the arithmetic, date, string, or other comparison operators. The following query selects Order objects from `all_orderitems` where the OrderDate property is after April 5, 2010:

```
Dim query = From ord In all_orders
    Where ord.OrderDate > #4/5/2010#
```

Order By

The Order By clause makes a query sort the objects selected according to one or more values. Usually the values are properties of the objects selected. For example, the following query selects Customer objects from the `all_customers` list and sorts them by their LastName and FirstName properties:

```
Dim query = From cust In all_customers
    Order By cust.LastName, cust.FirstName
```

In this example, customers are sorted first by last name. If two customers have the same last name, they are sorted by first name.

An Order By clause can also sort objects based on calculated values. For example, suppose some customers' names are surrounded by parentheses. Because "(" comes alphabetically before letters, those customers would normally end up at the beginning of the sorted list. The following query uses a String class's Replace method to remove parentheses from the values used in sorting so all names are positioned in the list as if they did not contain parentheses:

```
Dim query = From cust In all_customers
    Order By cust.LastName.Replace("(", "").Replace(")", ""),
        cust.FirstName.Replace("(", "").Replace(")", "")
```

code snippet OrderByExamples

Note that the values used for ordering results are not the values selected by the query. The two preceding queries do not specify what results they select so LINQ takes its default action and selects the Customer objects in the `all_customers` list. See the next section, "Select," for information on determining the values that the query selects.

To arrange items in descending order, simply add the keyword Descending after an ordering expression. Each expression can have its own Descending keyword so you can arrange them independently. The following query orders customers by LastName descending. If several customers have the same LastName, they are arranged by their FirstName values in ascending order.

```
Dim query = From cust In all_customers
    Order By cust.LastName Descending, cust.FirstName
```

Select

The Select clause lists the fields that the query should select into its result. This can be an entire record taken from a data source or it can be one or more fields taken from the data sources. It can include the results of functions and calculations on the fields. It can even include more complicated results such as the results of nested queries.

You can add an alias to any of the items that the query selects. This is particularly useful for calculated results.

The following query selects objects from `all_customers`. It gives the first selected field the alias Name. That field's value is the customer's first and last name separated by a space. The query also selects the customer's AccountBalance property, giving it the alias Balance.

```
Dim query = From cust In all_customers
    Select Name = cust.FirstName & " " & cust.LastName,
        Balance = Cust.AccountBalance
```

code snippet SimpleSamples

The result of the query is an IEnumerable that contains objects of an anonymous type that holds two fields: Name and Balance.

The following code shows how you might display the results. Notice that the code does not declare a data type for the looping variable `cust`. The objects in the query result have an anonymous type, so the code lets Visual Basic infer its data type.

```
For obj In query
    Debug.WriteLine(obj.Name & " " & FormatCurrency(obj.Balance))
Next obj
```

You can also use the New keyword to create objects of an anonymous type. The following query builds a result similar to the earlier query but uses New:

```
Dim query = From cust In all_customers
    Select New With {
        .Name = cust.FirstName & " " & cust.LastName,
        .Balance = Cust.AccountBalance}
```

This version emphasizes that you are creating new objects, but it is more verbose and doesn't seem to have any other real benefits.

The earlier queries return objects of an anonymous type. If you like, you can define a type to hold the results and then create new objects of that type in the Select clause. For example, suppose the CustInfo class has Name and Balance properties. The following query selects the same data as the preceding query but this time saves the results in a new CustInfo object:

```
Dim query = From cust In all_customers
    Select New CustInfo With {
        .Name = cust.FirstName & " " & cust.LastName,
        .Balance = Cust.AccountBalance}
```

code snippet SimpleSamples

The result of this query contains CustInfo objects, not objects of an anonymous type. The following code shows how a program can use an explicitly typed looping variable to display these results:

```
For ci As CustInfo In query
    Debug.WriteLine(ci.Name & " " & FormatCurrency(ci.Balance))
Next ci
```

code snippet SimpleSamples

If the CustInfo class provides a constructor that takes a name and account balance as parameters, you can achieve a similar result by using the constructor instead of the With keyword. The following query provides a result similar to the preceding one:

```
Dim query = From cust In all_customers
    Select New CustInfo(
        cust.FirstName & " " & cust.LastName,
        cust.AccountBalance)
```

code snippet SimpleSamples

From all of these different kinds of examples, you can see the power of LINQ. You can also see the potential for confusion. The Select clause in particular can take a number of different forms and can return a complicated set of results. If you stick to the simplest syntax, however, your code will be reasonably easy to understand.

The following example shows one of the more complicated queries that uses only basic LINQ syntax. It selects data from multiple sources, uses a common field to join them, adds an additional Where filter, uses multiple values to order the results, and returns the Customer and Order objects that meet its criteria.

```
Dim query = From cust In all_customers, ord In all_orders
    Where cust.CustId = ord.CustId AndAlso
        cust.AccountBalance < 0
    Order By cust.CustId, ord.OrderDate
    Select cust, ord
```

Note that the Select clause changes the scope of the variables involved in the query. After the query reaches the Select clause, it can only refer to items in that clause, later.

For example, the following query selects customer first and last names. The Order By clause comes after the Select clause so it can only refer to items included in the Select clause. This example orders the results by the LastName and FirstName fields picked by the Select clause.

```
Dim query = From cust In all_customers
    Select cust.FirstName, cust.LastName
    Order By LastName, FirstName
```

code snippet OrderByExamples

Because the original cust variable is not chosen by the Select clause, the Order By clause cannot refer to it.

Note also that if the Select clause gives a result an alias, then any later clause must refer to the alias. For example, the following query selects the customers' last and first names concatenated into a field known by the alias FullName so the Order By clause must use the alias FullName:

```
Dim query = From cust In all_customers
    Select FullName = cust.LastName & ", " & cust.FirstName
    Order By FullName
```

Usually, it is easiest to place Order By and other clauses before the Select clause to avoid confusion.

Using LINQ Results

A LINQ query expression returns an IEnumerable containing the query's results. A program can iterate through this result and process the items that it contains.

To determine what objects are contained in the IEnumerable result, you need to look carefully at the Select clause, bolded in the following code. If this clause chooses a simple value such as a string or integer, then the result contains those simple values.

For example, the following query selects customer first and last names concatenated into a single string. The result is a string, so the query's IEnumerable result contains strings and the For Each loop treats them as strings.

```
Dim query = From cust In all_customers
    Select cust.FirstName & " " & cust.LastName

For Each cust_name As String In query
    Debug.WriteLine(cust_name)
Next cust_name
```

Often the Select clause chooses some sort of object. The following query selects the Customer objects contained in the `all_customers` list. The result contains Customer objects, so the code can explicitly type its looping variable and treat it as a Customer.

```
Dim query = From cust In all_customers
    Select cust

For Each cust As Customer In query
    Debug.WriteLine(cust.LastName & " owes " & cust.AccountBalance)
Next cust
```

The preceding example selects objects with a known class: Customer. Many queries select objects of an anonymous type. Any time a Select clause chooses more than one item, Visual Basic defines an anonymous type to hold the results. In that case, the code should let Visual Basic infer the type of the objects in the result (and the looping variable in a For Each statement). The code can then access the fields picked by the Select clause and defined in the anonymous type.

The following query selects only the Customer objects' FirstName and LastName properties. The result is an object with an anonymous type and having those two properties. The code lets Visual Basic infer the type for the looping variable `obj`. It can then access the FirstName and LastName properties defined for the anonymous type, but no other Customer properties area available because the Select clause didn't choose them.

```
Dim query = From cust In all_customers
    Select cust.FirstName, cust.LastName

For Each obj In query
    Debug.WriteLine(obj.LastName & ", " & obj.FirstName)
Next obj
```

ADVANCED LINQ QUERY SYNTAX

The earlier sections describe the basic LINQ commands that you might expect to use regularly. Simple queries such as the following are reasonably intuitive and easy to use:

```
Dim query = From cust In all_customers, ord In all_orders
    Where cust.CustId = ord.CustId AndAlso
        cust.AccountBalance < 0
    Order By cust.CustId, ord.OrderDate
    Select cust, ord
```

However, there's much more to LINQ than these simple queries. The following sections describe some of the more advanced LINQ commands that are less intuitive and that you probably won't need to use as often.

Join

The Join keyword selects data from multiple data sources matching up corresponding fields. The following pseudo-code shows the Join command's syntax:

```
From variable1 In data source1
Join variable2 In data source2
On variable1.field1 Equals variable2.field2
```

For example, the following query selects objects from the `all_customers` list. For each object it finds, it also selects objects from the `all_orders` list where the two records have the same CustId value.

```
Dim query = From cust As Customer In all_customers
    Join ord In all_orders
    On cust.CustId Equals ord.CustId
```

code snippet JoinExamples

A LINQ Join is similar to a SQL join except the On clause only allows you to select objects where fields are equal and the Equals keyword is required.

The following query selects a similar set of objects without using the Join keyword. Here the Where clause makes the link between the `all_customer` and `all_orders` lists:

```
Dim query = From cust As Customer In all_customers, ord In all_orders
    Where cust.CustId = ord.CustId
```

code snippet JoinExamples

This is slightly more flexible because the Where clause can make tests that are more complicated than the Join statement's Equals clause.

The Group Join statement selects data much as a Join statement does, but it returns the results differently. The Join statement returns an IEnumerable object that holds whatever is selected by the query (the `cust` and `ord` objects in this example).

The Group By statement returns the same objects but in a different arrangement. Each item in the IEnumerable result contains an object of the first type (`cust` in this example) plus another IEnumerable that holds the corresponding objects of the second type (`ord` in this example).

> *Actually, the main result is a GroupJoinIterator, but that inherits from IEnumerable, so you can treat it as such.*

For example, the following query selects customers and their corresponding orders much as the earlier examples do. The new clause `Into CustomerOrders` means the IEnumerable containing the orders for each customer should be called CustomerOrders. The `= Group` part means CustomerOrders should contain the results of the grouping.

```
Dim query =
    From cust In all_customers
        Group Join ord In all_orders
        On cust.CustId Equals ord.CustId
        Into CustomerOrders = Group
```

code snippet JoinExamples

The following code shows how a program might display these results:

```
For Each c In query
    ' Display the customer.
    Debug.WriteLine(c.cust.ToString())

    ' Display the customer's orders.
    For Each o In c.CustomerOrders
        Debug.WriteLine(Space$(4) & "OrderId: " & o.OrderId &
            ", Date: " & o.OrderDate & vbCrLf
    Next o
Next c
```

code snippet JoinExamples

Each item in the main IEnumerable contains a cust object and an IEnumerable named CustomerOrders. Each CustomerOrders object contains ord objects corresponding to the cust object.

This code loops through the query's results. Each time through the loop, it displays the cust object's information and then loops through its CustomerOrders, displaying each ord object's information indented.

Example program JoinExamples, which is available for download on the book's web site, demonstrates these types of Join queries.

Group By

Like the Group Join clause, the Group By clause lets a program select data from a flat, relational style format and build a hierarchical arrangement of objects. It also returns an IEnumerable that holds objects, each containing another IEnumerable.

The following code shows the basic Group By syntax:

```
From variable1 In datasource1
Group items By value Into groupname = Group
```

Here items is a list of items whose properties you want selected into the group. In other words, the properties of the items variables are added to the objects in the nested IEnumerable.

If you omit the items parameter, the query places the objects selected by the rest of the query into the nested IEnumerable.

The value property tells LINQ on what field to group objects. This value is also stored in the top-level IEnumerable values.

The groupname parameter gives a name for the group. The objects contained in the top-level IEnumerable get a property with this name that is an IEnumerable containing the grouped values.

Finally, the = Group clause indicates that the group should contain the fields selected by the query.

If this definition seems a bit confusing, an example should help. The following query selects objects from the all_orders list. The Group By statement makes the query group orders with the same CustId value.

```
Dim query1 = From ord In all_orders
    Order By ord.CustId, ord.OrderId
    Group ord By ord.CustId Into CustOrders = Group
```

code snippet SimpleGroupBy

The result is an IEnumerable that contains objects with two fields. The first field is the CustId value used to define the groups. The second field is an IEnumerable named CustOrders that contains the group of order objects for each CustId value.

The following code shows how a program might display the results in a TreeView control:

```
Dim root1 As TreeNode = trvResults.Nodes.Add("Orders grouped by CustId")
For Each obj In query1
    ' Display the customer id.
    Dim cust_node As TreeNode = root1.Nodes.Add("Cust Id: " & obj.CustId)

    ' List this customer's orders.
    For Each ord In obj.CustOrders cust_node.Nodes.Add("OrderId: " & ord.OrderId &
        ", Date: " & ord.OrderDate)
    Next ord
Next obj
```

code snippet SimpleGroupBy

The code loops through the top-level IEnumerable. Each time through the loop, it displays the group's CustId and the loops through the group's CustOrders IEnumerable displaying each order's ID and date.

The following example is a bit more complicated. It selects objects from the all_customers and all_orders lists, and uses a Where clause to join the two. The Group By clause indicates that the results should be grouped by the customer object cust. That means results that have the same cust object are grouped together. It also means the cust object is included in the resulting top-level IEnumerable's objects much as CustId was included in the preceding example.

```
Dim query2 = From cust In all_customers, ord In all_orders
    Where cust.CustId = ord.CustId
    Order By cust.CustId, ord.OrderId
    Group ord By cust Into CustomerOrders = Group
```

code snippet SimpleGroupBy

The following code displays the results:

```
Dim root2 As TreeNode = trvResults.Nodes.Add("Orders grouped by CustId")
For Each obj In query2
    ' Display the customer info.
    Dim cust_node As TreeNode = root2.Nodes.Add("Customer: " & obj.cust.ToString())

    ' List this customer's orders.
```

```
        For Each ord In obj.CustomerOrders cust_node.Nodes.Add("OrderId: " & ord.OrderId &
            ", Date: " & ord.OrderDate)
        Next ord
    Next obj
```

The code loops through the top-level IEnumerable displaying each customer's information. Notice that the cust object is available at this level because it was used to group the results.

For each customer, the code loops through the CustomerOrders group and displays each order's information.

Example program SimpleGroupBy, which is available for download on the book's web site, demonstrates the previous two types of Group By statements.

Another common type of query uses the Group By clause to apply some aggregate function to the items selected in a group. The following query selects order and order item objects, grouping each order's items and displaying each order's total price:

```
Dim query1 = From ord In all_orders, ord_item In all_order_items
    Order By ord.CustId, ord.OrderId
    Where ord.OrderId = ord_item.OrderId
    Group ord_item By ord Into
        TotalPrice = Sum(ord_item.Quantity * ord_item.UnitPrice),
        OrderItems = Group
```

The query selects objects from the all_orders and all_order_items lists using a Where clause to join them.

The Group ord_item piece places the fields of the ord_item object in the group. The By ord piece makes each group hold items for a particular ord object.

The Into clause selects two values. The first is a sum over all of the group's ord_item objects adding up the ord_items' Quantity times UnitPrice fields. The second value selected is the group named OrderItems.

The following code shows how a program might display the results in a TreeView control named trvResults:

```
Dim root1 As TreeNode = trvResults.Nodes.Add("Orders")
For Each obj In query1
    ' Display the order id.
    Dim cust_node As TreeNode =
        root1.Nodes.Add("Order Id: " & obj.ord.OrderId &
            ", Total Price: " & FormatCurrency(obj.TotalPrice))
    ' List this order's items.
    For Each ord_item In obj.OrderItems
```

```
            cust_node.Nodes.Add(ord_item.Description & ": " &
                ord_item.Quantity & " @ " & FormatCurrency(ord_item.UnitPrice))
        Next ord_item
    Next obj
```

code snippet GroupByWithTotals

Each loop through the query results represents an order. For each order, the program creates a tree node showing the order's ID and the TotalPrice value that the query calculated for it.

Next, the code loops through the order's items stored in the OrderItems group. For each item, it creates a tree node showing the item's Description, Quantity, and TotalPrice fields.

Example program GroupByWithTotals, which is available for download on the book's web site, demonstrates this Group By statement.

Aggregate Functions

The preceding section explains how a Group By query can use the Sum aggregate function. LINQ also supports the reasonably self-explanatory aggregate functions Average, Count, LongCount, Max, and Min.

The following query selects order objects and their corresponding order items. It uses a Group By clause to calculate aggregates for each of the orders' items.

Available for
download on
Wrox.com

```
Dim query1 = From ord In all_orders, ord_item In all_order_items
    Order By ord.CustId, ord.OrderId
    Where ord.OrderId = ord_item.OrderId
    Group ord_item By ord Into
        TheAverage = Average(ord_item.UnitPrice * ord_item.Quantity),
        TheCount = Count(ord_item.UnitPrice * ord_item.Quantity),
        TheLongCount = LongCount(ord_item.UnitPrice * ord_item.Quantity),
        TheMax = Max(ord_item.UnitPrice * ord_item.Quantity),
        TheMin = Min(ord_item.UnitPrice * ord_item.Quantity),
        TheSum = Sum(ord_item.Quantity * ord_item.UnitPrice)
```

code snippet AggregateExamples

The following code loops through the query's results and adds each order's aggregate values to a string named txt. It displays the final results in a text box named txtResults.

Available for
download on
Wrox.com

```
For Each obj In query1
    ' Display the order info.
    txt &= "Order " & obj.ord.OrderId &
        ", Average: " & obj.TheAverage &
        ", Count: " & obj.TheCount &
        ", LongCount: " & obj.TheLongCount &
        ", Max: " & obj.TheMax &
        ", Min: " & obj.TheMin &
```

```
          ", Sum: " & obj.TheSum &
          vbCrLf
  Next obj
  txtResults.Text = txt
```

Set Operations

If you add the Distinct keyword to a query, LINQ keeps only one instance of each value selected. For example, the following query returns a list of IDs for customers who placed an order before 4/15/2010:

```
Dim query = From ord In all_orders
    Where ord.OrderDate < #4/15/2010#
    Select ord.CustId
    Distinct
```

The code examines objects in the `all_orders` list with OrderDate fields before 4/15/2010. It selects those objects' CustId fields and uses the Distinct keyword to remove duplicates. If a particular customer placed several orders before 4/15/2010, this query lists that customer's ID only once.

LINQ also provides Union, Intersection, and Except extension methods, but they are not supported by Visual Basic's LINQ syntax. See the section "LINQ Functions" later in this chapter for more information.

Example program SetExamples, which is available for download on the book's web site, demonstrates these set operations.

Limiting Results

LINQ includes several keywords for limiting the results returned by a query.

- ➤ **Take** makes the query keep a specified number of results and discard the rest.
- ➤ **Take While** makes the query keep selected results as long as some condition holds and then discard the rest.
- ➤ **Skip** makes the query discard a specified number of results and keep the rest.
- ➤ **Skip While** makes the query discard selected results as long as some condition holds and then keep the rest.

The following code demonstrates each of these commands:

```
Dim q1 = From cust In all_customers Take 5
Dim q2 = From cust In all_customers Take While cust.FirstName.Contains("n")
Dim q3 = From cust In all_customers Skip 3
Dim q4 = From cust In all_customers Skip While cust.FirstName.Contains("n")
```

code snippet LimitingExamples

The first query selects the first five customers and ignores the rest.

The second query selects customers as long as the FirstName field contains the letter "n." It then discards any remaining results, even if a later customer's FirstName contains an "n."

The third query discards the first three customers and then selects the rest.

The final query skips customers as long as their FirstName values contain the letter "n" and then keeps the rest.

Example program LimitingExamples, which is available for download on the book's web site, demonstrates these commands.

LINQ FUNCTIONS

LINQ provides several functions (implemented as extension methods) that are not supported by Visual Basic's LINQ syntax. Though you cannot use these in LINQ queries, you can apply them to the results of queries to perform useful operations.

For example, the following code defines a query that looks for customers named Rod Stephens. It then applies the `FirstOrDefault` extension method to the query to return either the first object selected by the query or Nothing if the query selects no objects.

```
Dim rod_query = From cust In all_customers
    Where cust.LastName = "Stephens" AndAlso cust.FirstName = "Rod"
Dim rod As Person = rod_query.FirstOrDefault()
```

code snippet FunctionExamples

The following list describes some of the more useful of these extension methods:

➤ `Aggregate` — Uses a function specified by the code to calculate a custom aggregate.

➤ `DefaultIfEmpty` — If the query's result is not empty, returns the result. If the result is empty, returns an IEnumerable containing a default value. Optionally can also specify the default value (for example, a new object rather than Nothing) to use if the query's result is empty.

➤ `Concat` — Concatenates two sequences into a new sequence.

➤ `Contains` — Determines whether the result contains a specific value.

➤ `ElementAt` — Returns an element at a specific position in the query's result. If there is no element at that position, it throws an exception.

➤ `ElementAtOrDefault` — Returns an element at a specific position in the query's result. If there is no element at that position, it returns a default value for the data type.

➤ `Empty` — This Shared IEnumerable method creates an empty IEnumerable.

➤ `Except` — Returns the items in one IEnumerable that are not in a second IEnumerable.

➤ `First` — Returns the first item in the query's result. If the query contains no results, it throws an exception.

➤ `FirstOrDefault` — Returns the first item in the query's result. If the query contains no results, it returns a default value for the data type. For example, the default value for an Integer is 0 and the default value for object references is Nothing.

➤ `Intersection` — Returns the intersection of two IEnumerable objects. In other words, it returns an IEnumerable containing items that are in both of the original IEnumerable objects.

➤ `Last` — Returns the last item in the query's result. If the query contains no results, it throws an exception.

➤ `LastOrDefault` — Returns the last item in the query's result. If the query contains no results, it returns a default value for the data type.

➤ `Range` — This Shared IEnumerable method creates an IEnumerable containing a range of integer values.

➤ `Repeat` — This Shared IEnumerable method creates an IEnumerable containing a value of a given type repeated a specific number of times.

➤ `SequenceEqual` — Returns True if two sequences are identical.

➤ `Single` — Returns the single item selected by the query. If the query does not contain exactly one result, it throws an exception.

➤ `SingleOrDefault` — Returns the single item selected by the query. If the query contains no results, it returns a default value for the data type. If the query contains more than one item, it throws an exception.

➤ `Union` — Returns the union of two IEnumerable objects. In other words, it returns an IEnumerable containing items that are in either of the original IEnumerable objects.

Example program FunctionExamples, which is available for download on the book's web site, demonstrates most of these functions. Example program SetExamples demonstrates Except, Intersection, and Union.

LINQ also provides conversion functions that convert results into new data types. The following list describes these methods:

➤ `AsEnumerable` — Converts the result into a typed IEnumerable(Of T).

➤ `AsQueryable` — Converts an IEnumerable into an IQueryable.

➤ `OfType` — Removes items that cannot be cast into a specific type.

➤ `ToArray` — Places the results in an array.

➤ `ToDictionary` — Places the results in a Dictionary using a selector function to set each item's key.

➤ `ToList` — Converts the result into a List(Of T).

➤ `ToLookup` — Places the results in a Lookup (one-to-many dictionary) using a selector function to set each item's key.

Note that the ToArray, ToDictionary, ToList, and ToLookup functions force the query to execute immediately instead of waiting until the program accesses the results.

LINQ EXTENSION METHODS

Visual Basic doesn't *really* execute LINQ queries. Instead it converts them into a series of function calls (provided by extension methods) that perform the query. Though the LINQ query syntax is generally easier to use, it is sometimes helpful to understand what those function calls look like.

The following sections explain the general form of these function calls. They explain how the function calls are built, how you can use these functions directly in your code, and how you can extend LINQ to add your own LINQ query methods.

Method-Based Queries

Suppose a program defines a List(Of Customer) named `all_customers` and then defines the following query expression. This query finds customers that have AccountBalance values less than zero, orders them by AccountBalance, and returns an IEnumerable object that can enumerate their names and balances. (Example program LinqLambda, which is available for download on the book's web site, defines a simple Customer class and performs a similar query.)

```
Dim q1 =
    From cust In all_customers
    Where cust.AccountBalance < 0
    Order By cust.AccountBalance
    Select cust.Name, cust.AccountBalance
```

code snippet LinqLambda

To perform this selection, Visual Basic converts the query into a series of function calls to form a *method-based query* that performs the same tasks as the original query. For example, the following method-based query returns roughly the same results as the original LINQ query:

```
Dim q2 = all_customers.
    Where(AddressOf OwesMoney).
    OrderBy(AddressOf OrderByAmount).
    Select(AddressOf SelectFields)
```

code snippet LinqLambda

This code calls the `all_customers` list's Where method. It passes that method the address of the function `OwesMoney`, which returns True if a Customer object has a negative account balance.

The code then calls the `OrderBy` method of the result returned by Where. It passes the OrderBy method the address of the function `OrderByAmount`, which returns a Decimal value that OrderBy can use to order the results of Where.

Finally, the code calls the Select method of the result returned by OrderBy. It passes Select the address of a function that returns a CustInfo object representing each of the selected Customer objects. The CustInfo class contains the Customer's Name and AccountBalance values.

The exact series of method calls generated by Visual Studio to evaluate the LINQ query is somewhat different from the one shown here. The version shown here uses `OwesMoney`, `OrderByAmount`, and `SelectFields` methods that I defined in the program to help pick, order, and select data. The method-based query generated by Visual Basic uses automatically generated anonymous types and lambda expressions, so it is much uglier.

The following code shows the `OwesMoney`, `OrderByAmount`, and `SelectFields` methods:

```
Private Function OwesMoney(ByVal c As Customer) As Boolean
    Return c.AccountBalance < 0
End Function

Private Function OrderByAmount(ByVal c As Customer) As Decimal
    Return c.AccountBalance
End Function

Private Function SelectFields(ByVal c As Customer, ByVal index As Integer)
As CustInfo
    Return New CustInfo() With {
        .CustName = c.Name, .Balance = c.AccountBalance}
End Function
```

code snippet LinqLambda

Function `OwesMoney` simply returns True if a Customer's balance is less than zero. The Where method calls `OwesMoney` to see if it should pick a particular Customer for output.

Function `OrderByAmount` returns a Customer's balance. The OrderBy method calls `OrderByAmount` to order Customer objects.

Function `SelectFields` returns a CustInfo object representing a Customer.

That explains where the functions passed as parameters come from, but what are Where, OrderBy, and Select? After all, Where is called as if it were a method provided by the `all_customers` object. But `all_customers` is a List(Of Customer) and that has no such method.

In fact, Where is an extension method added to the IEnumerable interface by the LINQ library. The generic List class implements IEnumerable so it gains the Where extension method.

Similarly, LINQ adds other extension methods to the IEnumerable interface such as Any, All, Average, Count, Distinct, First, GroupBy, OfType, Repeat, Sum, Union, and many more.

Method-Based Queries with Lambda Functions

Lambda functions, or anonymous functions, make building method-based queries somewhat easier. When you use lambda functions, you don't need to define separate functions to pass as parameters to LINQ methods such as Where, OrderBy, and Select. Instead you can pass a lambda function directly into the method.

The following code shows a revised version of the preceding method-based query. Here the method bodies have been included as lambda functions.

```
Dim q3 = all_customers.
    Where(Function(c As Customer) c.AccountBalance < 0).
    OrderBy(Of Decimal)(Function(c As Customer) c.AccountBalance).
    Select(Of CustInfo)(
        Function(c As Customer, index As Integer)
            Return New CustInfo() With {
                {.CustName = c.Name, .Balance = c.AccountBalance}
        End Function
    )
```

code snippet LinqLambda

Although this is more concise, not requiring you to build separate functions, it can also be a lot harder to read and understand. Passing a simple lambda function to the Where or OrderBy method may not be too confusing, but if you need to use a very complex function you may be better off making it a separate routine.

The following code shows a reasonable compromise. This code defines three lambda functions but saves them in delegate variables. It then uses the variables in the calls to the LINQ functions. This version is more concise than the original version and doesn't require separate functions, but it is easier to read than the preceding version that uses purely inline lambda functions.

```
' Query with LINQ and inline function delegates.
Dim owes_money = Function(c As Customer) c.AccountBalance < 0
Dim cust_balance = Function(c As Customer) c.AccountBalance
Dim new_custinfo = Function(c As Customer) New CustInfo() With {
    .Name = c.Name, .Balance = c.AccountBalance}
Dim q4 = all_customers.
    Where(owes_money).
    OrderBy(Of Decimal)(cust_balance).
    Select(Of CustInfo)(new_custinfo)
```

code snippet LinqLambda

Note that LINQ cannot always infer a lambda function's type exactly, so sometimes you need to give it some hints. The Of Decimal and Of CustInfo clauses in this code tell LINQ the data types returned by the cust_balance and new_custinfo functions.

HIDDEN GENERICS

The Of Decimal and Of CustInfo clauses use generic versions of the OrderBy and Select functions. Generics let a function take a data type as a parameter, allowing it to work more closely with objects of that type. For more information on generics, see Chapter 29, "Generics," or msdn.microsoft.com/w256ka79.aspx.

Instead of using these clauses, you could define the functions' return types in their declarations. The Func delegate types defined in the System namespace let you explicitly define parameters and return types for functions taking between zero and four parameters. For example, the following code shows how you might define the cust_balance function, indicating that it takes a Customer as a parameter and returns a Decimal:

```
Dim cust_balance As Func(Of Customer, Decimal) =
    Function(c As Customer) c.AccountBalance
```

If you use this version of cust_balance, you can leave out the Of Decimal clause in the previous query.

No matter which version of the method-based queries you use, the standard LINQ query syntax is usually easier to understand, so you may prefer to use that version whenever possible. Unfortunately, many references describe the LINQ extension methods as if you are going to use them in method-based queries rather than in LINQ queries. For example, the description of the OrderBy method might include the following definition:

```
<Extension()>
Public Shared Function OrderBy(Of TSource, TKey)
    (ByVal source As IEnumerable(Of TSource),
     ByVal key_selector As Func(Of TSource, TKey)) _
    As OrderedSequence(Of TSource)
```

Here the Extension attribute indicates that this is a function that extends another class. The type of the first parameter, in this case the parameter `source` has type IEnumerable(Of TSource), gives the class that this method extends. The other parameters are passed to this method. In other words, this code allows you to call the OrderBy function for an object of type IEnumerable(Of TSource), passing it a `key_selector` of type Func(Of TSource, TKey). Confusing enough for you? For more information on extension methods, see the section "Extension Methods" in Chapter 17, "Subroutines and Functions."

This description of how the method's parameters work is technically correct but may be a bit too esoteric to be intuitive. It may be easier to understand if you consider a concrete example.

If you look closely at the examples in the preceding section, you can see how this definition matches up with the use of the OrderBy method and the `OrderByAmount` function. In those examples, TSource corresponds to the Customer class and TKey corresponds to the Decimal type. In the definition of OrderBy shown here, the source parameter has type IEnumerable(Of Customer). The `key_selector` parameter is the `OrderByAmount` function, which takes a Customer (TSource) parameter and returns a Decimal (TKey). The OrderBy method itself returns an IEnumerable(Customer), corresponding to IEnumerable(TSource).

It all works but what a mess. The following syntax is much more intuitive:

```
Order By <value1> [Ascending/Descending],
         <value2> [Ascending/Descending],
         . . .
```

Generally, you should try to use the LINQ query syntax whenever possible, so most of the rest of this chapter assumes you will do so and describes LINQ methods in this manner rather than with confusing method specifications.

One time when you cannot easily use this type of syntax specification is when you want to extend the results of a LINQ query to add new features. The following section explains how you can write extension methods to provide new features for LINQ results.

Extending LINQ

LINQ queries return some sort of IEnumerable object. (Actually they return some sort of SelectIterator creature but the result implements IEnumerable.) The items in the result may be simple types such as Customer objects or strings, or they may be of some bizarre anonymous type that groups several selected fields together, but whatever the items are, the result is some sort of IEnumerable.

Because the result is an IEnumerable, you can add new methods to the result by creating extension methods for IEnumerable.

For example, the following code defines a standard deviation function. It extends the IEnumerable(Of Decimal) interface so the method applies to the results of a LINQ query that fetches Decimal values.

```
' Return the standard deviation of
' the values in an IEnumerable(Of Decimal).
<Extension()>
Public Function StdDev(ByVal source As IEnumerable(Of Decimal)) As Decimal
    ' Get the total.
    Dim total As Decimal = 0
    For Each value As Decimal In source
        total += value
    Next value

    ' Calculate the mean.
    Dim mean As Decimal = total / source.Count

    ' Calculate the sums of the deviations squared.
    Dim total_devs As Decimal = 0
    For Each value As Decimal In source
        Dim dev As Decimal = value - mean
        total_devs += dev * dev
    Next value
    ' Return the standard deviation.
    Return Math.Sqrt(total_devs / (source.Count - 1))
End Function
```

code snippet LinqFunctions

NON-STANDARD STANDARDS

There are a couple of different definitions for standard deviation. This topic is outside the scope of this book so it isn't explored here. For more information, see `mathworld.wolfram.com/StandardDeviation.html`.

Now, the program can apply this method to the result of a LINQ query that selects Decimal values. The following code uses a LINQ query to select AccountBalance values from the `all_customers` list where the AccountBalance is less than zero. It then calls the query's `StdDev` extension method and displays the result.

```
Dim bal_due =
    From cust In all_customers
    Where cust.AccountBalance < 0
    Select cust.AccountBalance
MessageBox.Show(bal_due.StdDev())
```

The following code performs the same operations without storing the query in an intermediate variable:

```
MessageBox.Show(
    (From cust In all_customers
     Where cust.AccountBalance < 0
     Select cust.AccountBalance).StdDev())
```

Similarly, you can make other extension methods for IEnumerable to perform other calculations on the results of LINQ queries.

The following version of the `StdDev` extension method extends IEnumerable(Of T). To process an IEnumerable(Of T), this version also takes as a parameter a selector function that returns a Decimal value for each of the objects in the IEnumerable(Of T).

Available for download on Wrox.com

```
<Extension()>
Public Function StdDev(Of T)(ByVal source As IEnumerable(Of T),
 ByVal selector As Func(Of T, Decimal)) As Decimal
    ' Get the total.
    Dim total As Decimal = 0
    For Each value As T In source
        total += selector(value)
    Next value
    ' Calculate the mean.
    Dim mean As Decimal = total / source.Count
    ' Calculate the sums of the deviations squared.
    Dim total_devs As Decimal = 0
    For Each value As T In source
        Dim dev As Decimal = selector(value) - mean
        total_devs += dev * dev
    Next value
    ' Return the standard deviation.
    Return Math.Sqrt(total_devs / (source.Count - 1))
End Function
```

code snippet LinqFunctions

For example, if a LINQ query selects Customer objects, the result implements IEnumerable(Of Customer). In that case, the selector function should take as a parameter a Customer object and it should return a Decimal. The following code shows a simple selector function that returns a Customer's AccountBalance:

```
Private Function TotalBalance(ByVal c As Customer) As Decimal
    Return c.AccountBalance
End Function
```

The following code shows how a program can use this version of StdDev with this selector function. The LINQ query selects Customer objects with AccountBalance values less than zero. The code then calls the query's StdDev method, passing it the address of the selector function. The new version of StdDev uses the selector to calculate the standard deviation of the selected Customer objects' AccountBalance values, and then the code displays the result.

```
Dim stddev_due =
    From cust In all_customers
    Where cust.AccountBalance < 0
    Select cust
Dim result As Decimal = stddev_due.StdDev(AddressOf TotalBalance)
MessageBox.Show(result)
```

For a final example, consider the following Randomize method, which also extends IEnumerable(Of T). It uses the IEnumerable's ToArray method to copy the values into an array, randomizes the array, and returns the array.

```
<Extension()>
Public Function Randomize(Of T) _
 (ByVal source As IEnumerable(Of T)) As IEnumerable(Of T)
    Dim rand As New Random
    Dim values() As T = source.ToArray()
    Dim num_values As Integer = values.Length
    For i As Integer = 0 To num_values - 2
        Dim j As Integer = rand.Next(i, num_values)
        Dim temp As T = values(i)
        values(i) = values(j)
        values(j) = temp
    Next i
    Return values
End Function
```

code snippet LinqFunctions

The following code shows how a program might use this method to select Customer objects from the all_customers list and then randomize the result. You could add Where and other clauses to the LINQ query without changing the way Randomize is used.

```
Dim random_custs =
    (From cust In all_customers
     Select cust).Randomize()
```

For more information on extension methods, see the section "Extension Methods" in Chapter 17, "Subroutines and Functions."

LINQ TO OBJECTS

LINQ to Objects refers to methods that let a program extract data from objects that are extended by LINQ extension methods. These methods extend IEnumerable(Of T) so that they apply to any class that implements IEnumerable(Of T) including Dictionary(Of T), HashSet(Of T), LinkedList(Of T), Queue(Of T), SortedDictionary(Of T), SortedList(Of T), Stack(Of T), and others.

For example, the following code searches the `all_customers` list for customers with negative account balances. It orders them by account balance and returns their names and balances.

```
Dim overdue_custs =
    From cust In all_customers
    Where cust.AccountBalance < 0
    Order By cust.AccountBalance Ascending
    Select cust.Name, cust.AccountBalance
```

The result of this query is an IEnumerable object that the program can iterate through to take action for the selected customers.

All of the examples shown previously in this chapter use LINQ to Objects, so this section says no more about them. See the previous sections for more information and examples.

LINQ TO XML

LINQ to XML refers to methods that let a program move data between XML objects and other data-containing objects. For example, using LINQ to XML you can select customer data and use it to build an XML document.

LINQ provides a new selection of XML elements. These classes contained in the System.Xml .Linq namespace correspond to the classes in the System.Xml namespace. The names of the new classes begin with "X" instead of "Xml." For example, the LINQ class representing an element is XElement whereas the System.Xml class is XmlElement.

The LINQ versions of the XML classes provide many of the same features as the System.Xml versions, but they also provide support for new LINQ features.

The following section describes one of the most visible features of the LINQ XML classes: XML literals. The two sections after that introduce methods for using LINQ to move data into and out of XML objects.

XML Literals

In addition to features similar to those provided by the System.Xml classes, the new System.Xml .Linq classes provide new LINQ-oriented features. One of the most visible of those features is the ability to use XML literal values. For example, the following code creates an XDocument object that contains three Customer elements:

```
Dim xml_literal As XElement = _
    <AllCustomers>
        <Customer FirstName="Ann" LastName="Archer">100.00</Customer>
        <Customer FirstName="Ben" LastName="Best">-24.54</Customer>
        <Customer FirstName="Carly" LastName="Cant">62.40</Customer>
    </AllCustomers>
```

code snippet CustomersToXml

Visual Basic LINQ translates this literal into an XML object hierarchy holding a root element named AllCustomers that contains three Customer elements. Each Customer element has two attributes, FirstName and LastName.

To build the same hierarchy using System.Xml objects would take a lot more work. The CustomersToXml example program, which is available for download on the book's web site, includes a System.Xml version in addition to the previous LINQ literal version. The System.Xml version takes 26 lines of code and is much harder to read than the LINQ literal version.

Other LINQ XML classes such as XDocument, XComment, XCdata, and XProcessingInstruction also have literal formats, although usually it's easier to use an XElement instead of an XDocument, and the others are usually contained in an XElement or XDocument.

The Visual Basic code editor also provides some extra enhancements to make writing XML literals easier. For example, if you type a new XML tag, when you type the closing "<" character the editor automatically adds a corresponding closing tag. If you type "<Customer>" the editor adds the "</Customer>" tag. Later if you change a tag's name, the code editor automatically changes the corresponding closing tag.

Together these LINQ XML literal tools make building hard-coded XML data much easier than it is using the System.Xml objects.

LINQ Into XML

To select data into XML objects, you can use syntax similar to the syntax you use to build an XML literal. You then add the special characters <%= ... %> to indicate a "hole" within the literal. Inside the hole, you replace the ellipsis with a LINQ query that extracts data from Visual Basic objects and uses them to build new XML objects.

For example, suppose the `all_customers` list contains Customer objects. The following code builds an XElement object that contains Customer XML elements for all of the Customer objects:

```
Dim x_all As XElement = _
    <AllCustomers>
        <%= From cust In all_customers
            Select New XElement("Customer",
            New XAttribute("FirstName", cust.FirstName),
            New XAttribute("LastName", cust.LastName),
            New XText(cust.Balance.ToString("0.00"))) 
        %>
    </AllCustomers>
```

code snippet CustomersToXml

The following text shows a sample of the resulting XML element:

```
<AllCustomers>
<Customer FirstName="Ann" LastName="Archer">100.00</Customer>
<Customer FirstName="Ben" LastName="Best">-24.54</Customer>
<Customer FirstName="Carly" LastName="Cant">62.40</Customer>
</AllCustomers>
```

You can have more than one hole within the XML literal. Within the hole, you can add LINQ query code as usual. For example, you can use a Where clause to filter the objects copied into the XML element.

The following code uses an XML literal that contains two holes. The first uses a Where clause to select customers with non-negative balances and the second selects customers with negative balances. It places these two groups of customers inside different sub-elements within the resulting XML.

```
' Separate customers with positive and negative balances.
Dim separated As XElement = _
    <AllCustomers>
        <PositiveBalances>
            <%= From cust In x_all.Descendants("Customer")
                Where CDec(cust.Value) <= 0
                Order By CDec(cust.Value) Descending
                Select New XElement("Customer",
                New XAttribute("FirstName",
                    CStr(cust.Attribute("FirstName"))),
                New XAttribute("LastName",
                    CStr(cust.Attribute("LastName"))),
                New XText(cust.Value))
            %>
        </PositiveBalances>
        <NegativeBalances>
            <%= From cust In x_all.Descendants("Customer")
                Where CDec(cust.Value) < 0
                Order By CDec(cust.Value) Descending
                Select New XElement("Customer",
                New XAttribute("FirstName",
                    CStr(cust.Attribute("FirstName"))),
                New XAttribute("LastName",
                    CStr(cust.Attribute("LastName"))),
                New XText(cust.Value))
            %>
        </NegativeBalances>
    </AllCustomers>
```

code snippet LinqToXml

The following text shows the resulting XML element:

```
<AllCustomers>
    <PositiveBalances>
        <Customer FirstName="Dan" LastName="Dump">117.95</Customer>
        <Customer FirstName="Ann" LastName="Archer">100.00</Customer>
        <Customer FirstName="Carly" LastName="Cant">62.40</Customer>
    </PositiveBalances>
    <NegativeBalances>
        <Customer FirstName="Ben" LastName="Best">-24.54</Customer>
        <Customer FirstName="Frank" LastName="Fix">-150.90</Customer>
        <Customer FirstName="Edna" LastName="Ever">-192.75</Customer>
    </NegativeBalances>
</AllCustomers>
```

Example program LinqToXml, which is available for download on the book's web site, demonstrates these XML literals containing holes.

LINQ Out Of XML

The LINQ XML objects provide a standard assortment of LINQ functions that make moving data from those objects into IEnumerable objects simple. Using these functions, it's about as easy to select data from the XML objects as it is from IEnumerable objects such as arrays and lists.

Because the XML objects represent special hierarchical data structures, they also provide methods to help you search those data structures. For example, the XElement object provides a Descendants function that searches the object's descendants for elements of a certain type.

The following code extracts the x_all XElement object's Customer descendants. It selects their FirstName and LastName attributes, and the balance saved as each element's value.

```
Dim select_all = From cust In x_all.Descendants("Customer")
    Order By CDec(cust.Value)
    Select FName = cust.Attribute("FirstName").Value,
           LName = cust.Attribute("LastName").Value,
           Balance = cust.Value
```

code snippet LinqToXml

The program can now loop through the select_all object just as it can loop through any other IEnumerable selected by a LINQ query.

The following query selects only customers with a negative balance:

```
Dim x_neg = From cust In x_all.Descendants("Customer")
    Where CDec(cust.Value) < 0
    Select FName = cust.Attribute("FirstName").Value,
           LName = cust.Attribute("LastName").Value,
           Balance = cust.Value
```

code snippet LinqToXml

Example program LinqToXml, which is available for download on the book's web site, demonstrates these XML literals containing holes.

The following table describes other methods supported by XElement that a program can use to navigate through an XML hierarchy. Most of the functions return IEnumerable objects that you can then use in LINQ queries.

FUNCTION	RETURNS
Ancestors	IEnumerable containing all ancestors of the element.
AncestorsAndSelf	IEnumerable containing this element followed by all ancestors of the element.
Attribute	The element's attribute with a specific name.
Attributes	IEnumerable containing the element's attributes.
Descendants	IEnumerable containing all descendants of the element.
DescendantsAndSelf	IEnumerable containing this element followed by all descendants of the element.
DescendantNodes	IEnumerable containing all descendant nodes of the element. These include all nodes such as XElement and XText.
DescendantNodesAndSelf	IEnumerable containing this element followed by all descendant nodes of the element. These include all nodes such as XElement and XText.
Element	The first child element with a specific name.
Elements	IEnumerable containing the immediate children of the element.
ElementsAfterSelf	IEnumerable containing the siblings of the element that come after this element.
ElementsBeforeSelf	IEnumerable containing the siblings of the element that come before this element.
Nodes	IEnumerable containing the nodes that are immediate children of the element. These include all nodes such as XElement and XText.
NodesAfterSelf	IEnumerable containing the sibling nodes of the element that come after this element.
NodesBeforeSelf	IEnumerable containing the sibling nodes of the element that come before this element.

Most of these functions that return an IEnumerable take an optional parameter that you can use to indicate the names of the elements to select. For example, if you pass the Descendants function the parameter "Customer," the function returns only the descendants of the element that are named Customer.

Example program LinqToXmlFunctions, which is available for download on the book's web site, demonstrates these XML functions.

In addition to these functions, Visual Basic's LINQ query syntax recognizes several axis selectors. In XML, an *axis* is a "direction" in which you can move from a particular node. These include such directions as the node's descendants, the node's immediate children, and the node's attributes.

The following table gives examples of shorthand expressions for node axes and their functional equivalents.

SHORTHAND	MEANING	EQUIVALENT
x...<Customer>	Descendants named Customer.	x.Descendants("Customer")
x.<Child>	An element named Child that is a child of this node.	x.Attributes("Child")
x.@<FirstName>	The value of the FirstName attribute.	x.Attributes("FirstName"). Value
x.@FirstName	The value of the FirstName attribute.	x.Attributes("FirstName"). Value

For example, consider the following XElement literal:

Available for download on Wrox.com

```
Dim x_all As XElement = _
    <AllCustomers>
        <PositiveBalances>
            <Customer FirstName="Dan" LastName="Dump">117.95</Customer>
            <Customer FirstName="Ann" LastName="Archer">100.00</Customer>
            <Customer FirstName="Carly" LastName="Cant">62.40</Customer>
        </PositiveBalances>
        <NegativeBalances>
            <Customer FirstName="Ben" LastName="Best">-24.54</Customer>
            <Customer FirstName="Frank" LastName="Fix">-150.90</Customer>
            <Customer FirstName="Edna" LastName="Ever">-192.75</Customer>
        </NegativeBalances>
    </AllCustomers>
```

code snippet LinqAxes

The following code uses axis shorthand to make several different selections:

Available for download on Wrox.com

```
' Select all Customer descendants of x_all.
Dim desc = x_all.Descendants("Customer") ' Functional version.
Dim desc2 = x_all.<Customer>             ' LINQ query version.

' Select Customer descendants of x_all where FirstName attribute is Ben.
Dim ben = From cust In x_all.Descendants("Customer")
    Where cust.@FirstName = "Ben"
```

```
' Select Customer descendants of x_all where FirstName attribute is Ann.
Dim ann = From cust In x_all.<Customer>
    Where cust.@<FirstName> = "Ann"

' Starting at x_all, go to the NegativeBalances node and find
' its descendants that are Customer elements. Select those with
' value less than -50.
Dim neg_desc2 = From cust In x_all.<NegativeBalances>...<Customer>
    Where CDec(cust.Value) < -50
```

code snippet LinqAxes

Example program LinqAxes, which is available for download on the book's web site, demonstrates these LINQ query XML axes.

Note that IEnumerable objects allow indexing so you can use an index to select a particular item from the results of any of these functions that returns an IEnumerable. For example, the following statement starts at element `x_all`, goes to descendants named `NegativeBalances`, gets that element's Customer children, and then selects the second of them (indexes are numbered starting with zero):

```
Dim neg_cust1 = x_all.<NegativeBalances>.<Customer>(1)
```

Together the LINQ XML functions and query axes operators let you explore XML hierarchies quite effectively.

In addition to all of these navigational features, the LINQ XML classes provide the usual assortment of methods for manipulating XML hierarchies. Those functions let you find an element's parent, add and remove elements, and so forth. For more information, see the online help or the MSDN web site.

LINQ TO ADO.NET

LINQ to ADO.NET, formerly known as DLinq, provides tools that let your applications apply LINQ-style queries to objects used by ADO.NET to store and interact with relational data.

LINQ to ADO.NET includes three components: LINQ to SQL, LINQ to Entities, and LINQ to DataSet. The following sections briefly give additional detail about these three pieces.

LINQ to SQL and LINQ to Entities

LINQ to SQL and LINQ to Entities are object-relational mapping (O/RM) tools that build strongly typed classes for modeling databases. They generate classes to represent the database and the tables that it contains. LINQ features provided by these classes allow a program to query the database model objects.

For example, to build a database model for use by LINQ to SQL, select the Project menu's Add New Item command and add a new "LINQ to SQL Classes" item to the project. This opens a designer where you can define the database's structure.

Now you can drag SQL Server database objects from the Server Explorer to build the database model. If you drag all of the database's tables onto the designer, you should be able to see all of the tables and their fields, primary keys, relationships, and other structural information.

LINQ to SQL defines a DataContext class to represent the database. Suppose a program defines a DataContext class named dcTestScores and creates an instance of it named db. Then the following code selects all of the records from the Students table ordered by first and last name:

```
Dim query = From stu In db.Students
    Order By stu.FirstName, stu.LastName
```

Microsoft intends LINQ to SQL to be a quick tool for building LINQ-enabled classes for use with SQL Server databases. The designer can quickly take a SQL Server database, build a model for it, and then create the necessary classes.

The Entity Framework that includes LINQ to Entities is designed for use in more complicated enterprise scenarios. It allows extra abstraction that decouples a data object model from the underlying database. For example, the Entity Framework allows you to store pieces of a single conceptual object in more than one database table.

Building and managing SQL Server databases and the Entity Framework are topics too large to cover in this book so LINQ to SQL and LINQ to Entities are not described in more detail here. For more information, consult the online help or Microsoft's web site. Some of Microsoft's relevant web sites include:

- ➤ The LINQ Project (msdn2.microsoft.com/netframework/aa904594.aspx)
- ➤ A LINQ to SQL overview (msdn.microsoft.com/bb425822.aspx)
- ➤ The ADO.NET Entity Framework Overview (msdn.microsoft.com/aa697427.aspx)

LINQ to DataSet

LINQ to DataSet lets a program use LINQ-style queries to select data from DataSet objects. A DataSet contains an in-memory representation of data contained in tables. Although a DataSet represents data in a more concrete format than is used by the object models used in LINQ to SQL and LINQ to Entities, DataSets are useful because they make few assumptions about how the data was loaded. A DataSet can hold data and provide query capabilities whether the data was loaded from SQL Server, some other relational database, or by the program's code.

The DataSet object itself doesn't provide many LINQ features. It is mostly useful because it holds DataTable objects that represent groupings of items, much as IEnumerable objects do.

The DataTable class does not directly support LINQ either, but it has an AsEnumerable method that converts the DataTable into an IEnumerable, which you already know supports LINQ.

> ### WHERE'S IENUMERABLE?
>
> Actually, the AsEnumerable method converts the DataTable into an EnumerableRowCollection object but that object implements IEnumerable.

Example program LinqToDataSetScores, which is available for download on the book's web site, demonstrates LINQ to DataSet concepts. This program builds a DataSet that contains two tables. The Students table has fields StudentId, FirstName, and LastName. The Scores table has fields StudentId, TestNumber, and Score.

The example program defines class-level variables `dtStudents` and `dtScores` that hold references to the two DataTable objects inside the DataSet.

The program uses the following code to select Students records where the LastName field comes before "D" alphabetically:

Available for
download on
Wrox.com

```
Dim before_d =
    From stu In dtStudents.AsEnumerable()
    Where stu!LastName < "D"
    Order By stu.Field(Of String)("LastName")
    Select First = stu!FirstName, Last = stu!LastName

dgStudentsBeforeD.DataSource = before_d.ToList
```

code snippet LinqToDataSetScores

There are only a few differences between this query and previous LINQ queries. First, the From clause calls the DataTable object's AsEnumerable method to convert the table into something that supports LINQ.

Second, the syntax `stu!LastName` lets the query access the LastName field in the `stu` object. The `stu` object is a DataRow within the DataTable.

Third, the Order By clause uses the `stu` object's Field(Of T) method. The Field(Of T) method provides strongly typed access to the DataRow object's fields. In this example the LastName field contains string values. You could just as well have used `stu!LastName` in the Order By clause, but Visual Basic wouldn't provide strong typing.

Finally, the last line of code in this example sets a DataGrid control's DataSource property equal to the result returned by the query so the control will display the results. The DataGrid control cannot display the result directly so the code calls the ToList method to convert the result into a list, which the DataGrid can use.

The following list summarizes the key differences between a LINQ to DataSet query and a normal LINQ to Objects query:

➤ The LINQ to DataSet query must use the DataTable object's AsEnumerable method to make the object queryable.

➤ The code can access the fields in a DataRow as in `stu!LastName` or as in `stu.Field(Of String)("LastName")`.

➤ If you want to display the results in a DataGrid control, use the query's ToList method.

If you understand these key differences, the rest of the query is similar to those used by LINQ to Objects. The following code shows two other examples:

```vb
' Select all students and their scores.
Dim joined =
    From stu In dtStudents.AsEnumerable()
    Join score In dtScores.AsEnumerable()
    On stu!StudentId Equals score!StudentId
    Order By stu!StudentId, score!TestNumber
    Select
        ID = stu!StudentId,
        Name = stu!FirstName & stu!LastName,
        Test = score!TestNumber,
        score!Score
dgJoined.DataSource = joined.ToList

' Select students with average scores >= 90.
Dim letter_grade =
    Function(num_score As Double)
        Return Choose(num_score \ 10,
            New Object() {"F", "F", "F", "F", "F", "D", "C", "B", "A", "A"})
    End Function

' Add Where Ave >= 90 after the Group By statement
' to select students getting an A.
Dim grade_a =
    From stu In dtStudents.AsEnumerable()
        Join score In dtScores.AsEnumerable()
        On stu!StudentId Equals score!StudentId
    Group score By stu Into
        Ave = Average(CInt(score!Score)), Group
    Order By Ave
    Select Ave,
        Name = stu!FirstName & stu!LastName,
        ID = stu!StudentId,
        Grade = letter_grade(Ave)
dgAverages.DataSource = grade_a.ToList
```

code snippet LinqToDataSetScores

The first query selects records from the Students table and joins them with the corresponding records in the Scores table. It displays the results in the `dgJoined` DataGrid control.

Next, the code defines an inline function and saves a reference to it in the variable `letter_grade`. This function returns a letter grade for numeric scores between 0 and 100.

The next LINQ query selects corresponding Students and Scores records, and groups them by the Students records, calculating each Student's average score at the same time. The query orders the results by average and selects the students' names, IDs, and averages. Finally, the code displays the result in the `dgAverages` DataGrid.

LINQ to DataSet not only allows you to pull data out of a DataSet, it also provides a way to put data into a DataSet. If the query selects DataRow objects, then its CopyToDataTable method converts the query results into a new DataTable object that you can then add to a DataSet.

The following code selects records from the Students table for students with last name less than "D." It then uses CopyToDataTable to convert the result into a DataTable and displays the results in the `dgNewTable` DataGrid control. It sets the new table's name and adds it to the `dsScores` DataSet object's collection of tables.

```
' Make a new table.
Dim before_d_rows =
    From stu In dtStudents.AsEnumerable()
    Where stu!LastName < "D"
    Select stu
Dim new_table As DataTable = before_d_rows.CopyToDataTable()
dgNewTable.DataSource = new_table

new_table.TableName = "NewTable"
dsScores.Tables.Add(new_table)
```

code snippet LinqToDataSetScores

The LinqToDataSetScores example program displays a tab control. The first tab holds a DataGrid control that uses the `dsScores` DataSet as its data source, so you can see all of the DataSet's tables including the new table.

PLINQ

PLINQ (Parallel LINQ, pronounced "plink") allows a program to execute LINQ queries across multiple processors or cores in a multi-core system. If you have a multi-core CPU and a nicely parallelizable query, PLINQ may improve your performance considerably.

So what kinds of queries are "nicely parallelizable?" The short, glib answer is, it doesn't really matter. Microsoft has gone to great lengths to minimize the overhead of PLINQ so using PLINQ may help and shouldn't hurt you too much.

Simple queries that select items from a data source often work well. If the items in the source can be examined, selected, and otherwise processed independently, then the query is parallelizable.

Queries that must use multiple items at the same time do parallelize nicely. For example, adding an OrderBy function to the query forces the program to gather all of the results before sorting them so that part of the query at least will not benefit from PLINQ.

THE NEED FOR SPEED

Some feel that adding parallelism to LINQ is kind of like giving caffeine to a snail. A snail is slow. Giving it caffeine might speed it up a bit, but you'd get a much bigger performance gain if you got rid of the snail and got a cheetah instead.

Similarly, LINQ isn't all that fast. Adding parallelism will speed it up but you will probably get a larger speed improvement by moving the data into a database or using special-purpose algorithms designed to manage your particular data.

This argument is true, but you don't use LINQ because it's fast; you use it because it's convenient, easy to use, and flexible. Adding parallelism makes it a bit faster and, as you'll see shortly, makes it so easy that it doesn't cost you much effort.

If you really need significant performance improvements, you should consider moving the data into a database or more sophisticated data structure, but if you're using LINQ anyway, you may as well take advantage of PLINQ when you can.

Adding parallelism to LINQ is remarkably simple. First, add a reference to the System.Threading library to your program. Then add a call to AsParallel to the enumerable object that you're searching. For example, the following code uses AsParallel to select the even numbers from the array `numbers`:

```
Dim evens =
    From num In numbers.AsParallel()
    Where num Mod 2 = 0
```

PUZZLING PARALLELISM

Note that for small enumerable objects (lists containing only a few items) and on computers that have only a single CPU, the overhead of using AsParallel may actually slow down execution.

SUMMARY

LINQ provides the ability to perform SQL-like queries within Visual Basic. Depending on which form of LINQ you are using, the development environment may provide strong type checking and IntelliSense support.

LINQ to Objects allows a program to query arrays, lists, and other objects that implement the IEnumerable interface. LINQ to XML and the new LINQ XML classes allow a program to extract data from XML objects and to use LINQ to generate XML hierarchies. LINQ to ADO.NET (which includes LINQ to SQL, LINQ to Entities, and LINQ to DataSet) allow a program to perform queries on objects representing data in a relational database. Together these LINQ tools allow a program to select data in powerful new ways.

Visual Basic includes many features that support LINQ. Extension methods, inline or lambda functions, anonymous types, type inference, and object initializers all help make LINQ possible. If misused, some of these features can make code harder to read and understand, but used judiciously, they give you new options for program development.

For much more information on the various LINQ technologies, see the online help and the Web. The following list includes several useful Microsoft web pages that you can follow to learn more about LINQ. Some are a bit old but they still provide invaluable information.

➤ Hooked On LINQ (a wiki with some useful information, particularly its "5 Minute Overviews") — `www.hookedonlinq.com/LINQtoSQL5MinuteOverview.ashx`.

➤ The LINQ Project — `msdn.microsoft.com/vbasic/aa904594.aspx`.

➤ 101 LINQ Samples (in C#) — `msdn.microsoft.com/vcsharp/aa336746.aspx`.

➤ LINQ jump page — `msdn.microsoft.com/bb397926.aspx`.

➤ Visual Studio 2008 Samples (including hands-on LINQ labs) — `msdn.microsoft.com/vbasic/bb330936.aspx`.

➤ Visual Studio 2010 Samples (not many now but there should be more later) — `http://msdn.microsoft.com/en-us/vstudio/dd238515.aspx`

➤ The .NET Standard Query Operators — `msdn.microsoft.com/bb394939.aspx`.

➤ LINQ to DataSet (by Erick Thompson, ADO.NET Program Manager, in the ADO.NET team blog) — `blogs.msdn.com/adonet/archive/2007/01/26/querying-datasets-introduction-to-linq-to-dataset.aspx`.

➤ LINQ to SQL overview — `msdn.microsoft.com/bb425822.aspx`.

➤ The ADO.NET Entity Framework Overview — `msdn.microsoft.com/aa697427.aspx`.

➤ PLINQ — `msdn.microsoft.com/dd460688(VS.100).aspx`.

A LINQ query returns an IEnumerable object containing a list of results. If you call the result's ToList method, you can convert the result into a form that can be displayed by a DataGrid control. That is a technique used by several of the examples described in the section "LINQ to DataSet" earlier in this chapter.

Other chapters describe other controls provided by Visual Basic. Chapter 20, "Database Controls and Objects," describes many objects and controls that you can use to display and manipulate data from a relational database. Earlier chapters describe the many controls that you can put on Windows and WPF forms.

Even all of these different kinds of controls cannot satisfy every application's needs. Chapter 22, "Custom Controls," explains how you can build controls of your own to satisfy unfulfilled needs. These controls can implement completely new features or combine existing controls to provide a tidy package that is easy to reuse.

22

Custom Controls

Visual Basic .NET provides a rich assortment of controls that you can use to build applications. Nevertheless, those controls may not always be able to do what you need. In that case, you may want to build a control of your own. Building your own control lets you get exactly the behavior and appearance that you want.

Custom controls solve three significant problems. First, they let you package a particular behavior or appearance so that you can easily reuse it later. If you need to draw one engineering diagram, you can draw it on a PictureBox. If you need to draw many engineering diagrams (possibly in different applications), it would be easier to make an EngineeringDiagram control that can make all of the diagrams.

Second, developers are familiar with controls and comfortable using them. Any experienced Visual Basic developer understands how to create instances of a control, set its properties, call its methods, and respond to its events. If you build a custom control to perform some complex task, developers already know a lot about how to use it. You just need to explain the specific features of your control.

Finally, controls can easily save and restore property information at design time. A developer can set properties for a control at design time, and the control uses those properties at runtime. This is useful for graphical controls, where properties such as Text, BackColor, and BorderStyle determine the controls' appearance. It is also useful for non-graphical controls such as database connection, data adapter, DataSet, and DataView controls that use properties to determine what data is loaded and how it is arranged.

This chapter explains how to build custom controls. There are three main approaches to building custom controls.

➤ First, you can derive a control from an existing control. If a control already does most of what you want your custom control to do, you may be able to inherit from the existing control and avoid reimplementing all of its useful features.

➤ Second, you can compose your control out of existing controls. For example, you might want to make a color selection control that enables the user to select red, green, and blue color components by using scroll bars, and then displays a sample of the resulting color. You could build this control using three scroll bars and a PictureBox. This gives you the advantages provided by the constituent controls without requiring you to reimplement their functionality.

➤ Third, you can build a custom control from scratch. This is the most work but gives you absolute control over everything that the control does.

This chapter explains the basics of building a control library project and testing its controls. It also describes the three approaches to building custom controls: deriving from an existing control, composing existing controls, and building a control from scratch.

A component is similar to a control that is invisible at runtime. Like controls, you can place components on a form at design time. Unlike controls, however, components do not sit on the form itself. Instead, they sit in the *component tray* below the form at design time, and they are invisible to the user at runtime. Most of this chapter's discussion of custom controls applies equally to custom components.

CUSTOM CONTROLS IN GENERAL

Building a custom control requires six basic steps:

1. Create the control project.

2. Make a Toolbox icon.

3. Test in the UserControl Test Container.

4. Make a test project.

5. Test the control in the test project.

6. Implement properties, methods, and events.

The following sections describe these steps.

Create the Control Project

To make a new control library in Visual Basic, select the File menu's New Project command, select the Windows Forms Control Library template, enter the project's name, and click OK. The library can contain several controls, so it may not always make sense to name the library after a single control. This example assumes that you are building a control that displays a smiley face. In that case, you might name the library FaceControls in case you want to add bored, sad, and other faces later.

Initially, Visual Basic gives the control library a single UserControl object named UserControl1. Change this file's name to something more descriptive such as SmileyFace. If you look at the file in the code editor, you should find that Visual Basic has automatically changed the control's class name to match.

Add code to the control to make it do whatever you want it to do. For a SmileyFace control, you might add properties such as FaceColor, NoseColor, and EyeColor. The control's Paint event handler will draw the smiley face.

Next use the Build menu to compile the control library. The project's bin directory contains the library's compiled .dll file.

Make a Toolbox Icon

If you add the control to the Toolbox now, you'll see a default image that looks like a gear. To make your control display something more meaningful, you must set its Toolbox icon.

You can set the control's Toolbox icon by adding a ToolboxBitmap attribute to the control's class. The constructor for the ToolboxBitmap attribute can take as parameters the name of the bitmap file, or a class that contains the bitmap resource to use, or a class and the name of a bitmap resource to use (if the class contains more than one bitmap resource). This section assumes that you will use the last method. See the online help for more information. The web page `msdn.microsoft.com/ system.drawing.toolboxbitmapattribute.aspx` describes the ToolboxBitmapAttribute class and its constructors.

Open Solution Explorer and double-click the My Project entry to view the project's property pages. Click the Resources tab and open the Add Resource drop-down list. Select the Add Existing File command, and select the bitmap file to create a new bitmap resource. Double-click the new bitmap to open it in the integrated Bitmap Editor and modify it if necessary. Use the Properties window to make the bitmap 16 × 16 pixels in size.

Set the pixel in the lower-left corner to the color that you want to use as the Toolbox bitmap's transparent color. Visual Basic will replace the pixels having this color with the Toolbox's background color. Draw and save the bitmap, and then close it.

Click the bitmap file in Solution Explorer and open the Properties window. Select the file's Build Action property, click the drop-down arrow on the right, and select Embedded Resource. Now when you compile the control library, this bitmap will be embedded as a resource inside the .dll file.

Next, open the control's module in the code editor, and insert a ToolboxBitmap attribute in front of the control's class declaration, as shown in the following code. This example tells Visual Basic that the control's Toolbox icon should come from the SmileyFaceTool.bmp resource embedded in the SmileyFace class. Note the line continuation character at the end of the first line so that the ToolboxBitmap statement is on the same code line as the class declaration.

```
<ToolboxBitmap(GetType(SmileyFace), "SmileyFaceTool.bmp")>
Public Class SmileyFace
...
End Class
```

Now when you build the control library, the SmileyFace control includes the information it needs to display its Toolbox bitmap.

Test in the UserControl Test Container

If you use the Debug menu's Start command to execute a control library project, Visual Studio displays a sample control in the UserControl Test Container shown in Figure 22-1. The drop-down list at the top lets you select different controls in the project. You can use the property grid on the right to experiment with different property values to see how the control behaves.

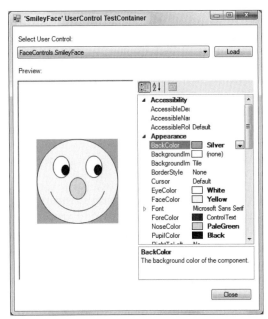

FIGURE 22-1: Visual Basic lets you preview controls in the UserControl Test Container.

Example project FaceControls, which is available for download on the book's web site, contains the SmileyFace control shown in Figure 22-1.

As its name implies, the UserControl Test Container only displays UserControls. If you create a control that inherits from the Control class or from some other control, the UserControl Test Container does not list it and will not display it. In that case, you must skip this step and move on to the next one, making a test project.

Make a Test Project

The UserControl Test Container only lets you test UserControls, not those that inherit from the Control class or some other control. It also only lets you test a control's properties. You can see the control's design-time behavior, but not how its methods and events work at runtime.

To test controls that are not UserControls and to test the control's runtime behavior, you must build a test project. You can either build a completely separate project, or you can add a new Windows application to the control's project.

To add an application to the control's project, open the File menu's Add submenu and select New Project. Select the Windows Application template, give the project a meaningful name (such as FaceControlsTest), and click OK. This adds the test project to the same solution that already contains the control library.

To make Visual Basic start execution with the test project, open the Solution Explorer, right-click the new project, and select Set as StartUp Project.

The FaceControls example solution, which is available for download on the book's web site, contains the FaceControls control library in addition to the test application FaceControlsTest.

When you open the new project's form, the Toolbox will contain a FaceControls Components section (assuming that the control project is named FaceControls) that holds icons representing the controls defined by the control library. You can use these tools just as you would use any other control tools.

Test the Control in the Test Project

After you add it to the Toolbox, you can use the control on the test project's form just as you can use any other control. Click the Toolbox icon to select the control, and click and drag to place an instance of the control on the form. Double-click the control to place an instance of the control in a default location with a default size. Initially, Visual Basic sets the controls' names to their class's name followed by a number, as in SmileyFace1, SmileyFace2, and so forth.

Use the Properties window to set the controls' properties at design time. Use code to examine and modify the controls' properties, methods, and events at runtime.

Implement Properties, Methods, and Events

At this point, you can test the control, but if you haven't given it any properties, methods, and events, you can only work with the default behavior that it inherits from its parent class. If the control is to do something useful, you must give it new properties, methods, and events.

Controls implemented from scratch often use Paint event handlers to draw the control. Composite controls often respond to events raised by their constituent controls and take actions, which may include raising new events for the form containing the control. (A *composite control* combines several other controls into a new control. For more information, see the section "Composite Controls" later in this chapter.)

When a developer places the control on a form, the Properties window automatically displays any public properties that are not read-only. This feature is remarkably intelligent. If a property has the Integer data type, the Properties window will only allow the developer to enter an integer. If a property has an enumerated type, the Properties window automatically displays a drop-down list containing the allowed values.

If a property has the Font data type, the Properties window automatically provides an ellipsis to the right of the property's value and displays a font selection dialog box if the user clicks it. Similarly, if the property is a Color, Image, or Date, the Properties window provides an appropriate dialog box or drop-down list to let the user select the property's value.

If a property's data type is OleDbDataConnection, DataSet, TextBox, Label, or some other control or component type, the Properties window provides a drop-down list that lets the developer select from any appropriate item on the form. If the data type is TextBox, the drop-down will list all of the form's TextBoxes.

In fact, the Properties window can even handle custom controls and components that you build yourself. For example, suppose that you create a control named EmployeeRegister. You can then create another control that has a property of type EmployeeRegister. If the developer selects the control, opens the Properties window, clicks that property, and clicks the drop-down arrow on the right, Visual Basic will display a list of any EmployeeRegister controls on the form.

Even more miraculously, the Properties window can handle collections of objects that you define. For example, suppose your code defines a WorkItem class. It then defines a UserControl class named WorkItemLister that has a property named WorkItems of type List(Of WorkItem).

If you add a WorkItemLister object to a form and select it, the Properties window lists the WorkItems property's value as (Collection) and displays a drop-down arrow to the right. If you click the arrow, Visual Basic displays the collection editor shown in Figure 22-2. This collection editor lets you build WorkItem objects at design time.

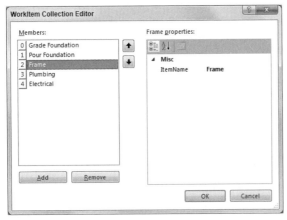

FIGURE 22-2: Visual Basic automatically provides collection editors for collection properties.

Similarly, the UserControl Test Container can let you view and edit the control's WorkItem property.

TOSTRING TIP

The WorkItem class's ToString function lets objects know what to display for an instance of the class. The collection editor uses this function to display Grade foundation, Pour foundation, and the other work item names, instead of merely the class name.

Example project WorkItemControls, which is available for download on the book's web site, includes a control project containing WorkItem controls in addition to a test project.

OTHER CUSTOM CONTROL TASKS

After you perform the six basic steps for building a custom control, there are a couple more steps you may want to take.

Add the Control to the Toolbox

When you create a control library, Visual Studio automatically adds the control to any other projects that are part of the same solution. If you create separate applications that are not part of the control library's solution, however, you must add the controls to the Toolbox manually. To add the controls, follow these steps.

1. Open a form in the form designer.

2. Right-click the Toolbox and select Choose Items.

3. On the Choose Toolbox Items dialog box shown in Figure 22-3, click the Browse button.

4. Select the .dll file in the control library's bin folder, and click Open to make the controls appear in the dialog's .NET Framework Components tab.

5. Select the check boxes next to the controls (they should be checked by default), and click OK.

If you change the control's Toolbox icon, you must rebuild the control library's .dll file. Then open the test project's form, right-click the Toolbox, select Add/Remove Items again, click the Browse button, and reselect the control library's .dll file.

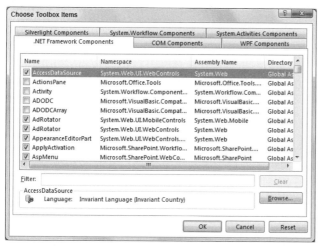

FIGURE 22-3: Use the Choose Toolbox Items dialog box to add your control to the Toolbox.

Assign Attributes

You can modify a control's behavior by adding attributes to its properties, methods, and events, and to its Class statement. The following code demonstrates some of the most useful control (or component) and property attributes for a UserControl named EmployeeRegister:

```
Imports System.ComponentModel

<ToolboxBitmap(GetType(EmployeeRegister), "EmployeeRegisterTool.bmp"),
 DefaultProperty("TextValue"),
 DefaultEvent("TheEvent"),
 DesignTimeVisible(True)>
Public Class EmployeeRegister
    ' Declare a public event.
    Public Event TheEvent()
    ' The TextValue property.
    Private m_TextValue As String = "Default Value"
    <Description("The object's text value."),
     Category("String Values"),
     Browsable(True),
     DefaultValue("Default Value")>
    Public Property TextValue() As String
        Get
            Return m_TextValue
        End Get
        Set(ByVal value As String)
            m_TextValue = value
        End Set
    End Property
End Class
```

code snippet EmployeeRegisterTest

The ToolboxBitmap attribute tells Visual Basic that it can find a Toolbox bitmap for the class in the assembly containing the EmployeeRegister type, and that the bitmap resource's name is EmployeeRegisterTool.bmp.

The DefaultProperty attribute sets the component's default property. If you click an EmployeeRegister control in the form designer, the property named TextValue is initially selected in the Properties window.

> ### DEFECTIVE DEFAULTS
>
> The DefaultProperty doesn't always work as advertised because the Properties window tries to display the same property when you select different controls. For example, suppose that you click a TextBox control and select its Name property in the Properties window. If you then click an EmployeeRegister control, the Properties window shows its Name property because EmployeeRegister also has a Name property. On the other hand, if you select a TextBox's MultiLine property and then click an EmployeeRegister control, the Properties window selects the TextValue property because EmployeeRegister doesn't have a MultiLine property.

The DefaultEvent attribute indicates the component's default event. If you double-click an EmployeeRegister control in the form designer, Visual Basic opens the code editor and displays the control's default event handler.

The DesignTimeVisible attribute determines whether the component is visible on the form designer at design time. If you set this to False, the control or component does not appear in the Toolbox. You can use this attribute to build a control that the program can create and manipulate at runtime but that the developer cannot create at design time.

The TextValue property's Description attribute gives the text displayed at the bottom of the Properties window when you select the property.

The Category attribute determines the category that contains the property when you select the Property window's Categorized button. This attribute's value can be any string. The Property window will make a new category with this name if it doesn't name an existing category.

The Browsable attribute determines whether the Property window displays the property. If you set this value to False, developers cannot set the property's value at design time.

Finally, the DefaultValue property determines the default value for the property. If you set a control's property to this value, Visual Basic does not store the property's value with the form. Later, when it reloads the form, Visual Basic does not load any value for the property. This code shows one way to initialize a property's value when it declares Private m_TextValue As String = "Default Value". To avoid confusion, you should generally initialize the private variable representing a property to the same value you set with DefaultValue attribute.

When you right-click a property in the Properties window and select the Reset command, Visual Basic sets the property to the value defined by the DefaultValue attribute. This is particularly useful for images and other objects where you might want to make the default value Nothing.

Example project EmployeeRegisterTest, which is available for download on the book's web site, includes the EmployeeRegister control.

You can learn more about the ToolboxBitmap attribute at `msdn.microsoft.com/system .drawing.toolboxbitmapattribute.aspx`. You can learn more about other attribute classes at `msdn2.microsoft.com/library/2e39z096.aspx`.

Manage Design Time and Runtime

A control or component can use its predefined DesignMode property to determine whether it is running at design time or runtime and take different actions if that is appropriate. For example, a control might allow the developer to manipulate its data directly at design time but prevent the user from changing the data at runtime.

The following code shows how the control can check whether it is running at design or runtime:

```
If Me.DesignMode Then
    ' Let the developer manipulate the data at design time.
    ...
Else
    ' Don't let the user change the data at run time.
    ...
End If
```

Example project ShowModeTest, which is available for download on the book's web site, includes a simple control that displays a label indicating whether it is running in design mode or run mode.

DERIVED CONTROLS

If an existing control does almost what you need to do, you can derive a new control from the existing one. That enables you to take advantage of all of the existing control's features while adding new ones of your own.

To make a derived control, start a control library project as usual and give the library a meaningful name. Discard the default UserControl1 class, add a new class, and give it an appropriate Inherits statement. For example, the following code derives the RowSortingListView class from the ListView class:

```
Public Class RowSortingListView
    Inherits ListView

End Class
```

That's about all there is to building a derived control. Now you just need to write code that implements new features and modifies inherited features. One particularly common task for derived controls is overriding the functionality provided by the parent control class. The RowSortingListView control provides a good example.

The standard ListView control lets a program display data items with subitems in a variety of ways. The control can display items as large icons, small icons, a list showing the items' names, or a detail list showing the items and their subitems. The list and detail displays even allow you to sort the items in ascending and descending order. Unfortunately, the ListView control doesn't use the subitems in the sort even to break ties. It sorts only on the main items' names.

For example, suppose that several items all have the item value Book and their first subitems contain book titles. If you set the ListView control's Sorting property to Ascending or Descending, the control will group these items together because they all have the same item value: Book. Unfortunately, the items' order in the list is arbitrary. The control does not sort the Book items by their titles.

Fortunately, the ListView control provides a back door for implementing custom sort orders. To implement a custom sort order, you set the ListView control's ListViewItemSorter property to an object that implements the IComparer interface. To satisfy the interface, this object must provide a Compare function that compares two ListView items and returns -1, 0, or 1 to indicate whether the first item should be considered less than, equal to, or greater than the second item.

The ListViewComparerAllColumns class shown in the following code implements the IComparer interface. Its private m_SortOrder variable tells the object whether to sort in ascending or descending order. The class's constructor takes a parameter that sets this value. The Compare function converts the generic Objects that it is passed into ListViewItems. It calls the ListViewItemValue helper function to get strings containing the items and their subitems separated by Tab characters. It then uses the String class's Compare method to determine which value should come first in the sort order.

```
' Implements a ListViewItem comparer
' that sorts on all columns.
Private Class ListViewComparerAllColumns
    Implements IComparer

    ' Ascending or Descending.
    Private m_SortOrder As SortOrder

    ' Initialize with a sort order.
    Public Sub New(ByVal sort_order As SortOrder)
        m_SortOrder = sort_order
    End Sub

    ' Compare two items' subitems.
    Public Function Compare(ByVal x As Object, ByVal y As Object) As Integer _
      Implements System.Collections.IComparer.Compare
        ' Get the ListViewItems.
        Dim item_x As ListViewItem = DirectCast(x, ListViewItem)
        Dim item_y As ListViewItem = DirectCast(y, ListViewItem)
        ' Get the ListViewItems' values.
        Dim values_x As String = ListViewItemValue(item_x)
        Dim values_y As String = ListViewItemValue(item_y)

        ' Compare the values.
        If m_SortOrder = SortOrder.Ascending Then
            Return String.Compare(values_x, values_y)
        Else
            Return String.Compare(values_y, values_x)
        End If
    End Function
    ' Return a delimited string containing all of
    ' the ListViewItem's values.
    Private Function ListViewItemValue(ByVal lvi As ListViewItem, _
      Optional ByVal delimiter As String = vbTab) As String
        Dim txt As String = ""
        For i As Integer = 0 To lvi.SubItems.Count - 1
            txt &= delimiter & lvi.SubItems(i).Text
        Next i
        Return txt.Substring(delimiter.Length)
    End Function
End Class
```

code snippet RowSortingListViewTest

The RowSortingListView control uses the ListViewComparerAllColumns class and the following code to sort its data using all of the items' values and their subitems' values. To provide the new sorting behavior, the control must override the Sorting property defined by the parent ListView class.

```
' Reimplement the Sorting property.
Private m_Sorting As SortOrder
Public Shadows Property Sorting() As SortOrder
    Get
        Return m_Sorting
    End Get
    Set(ByVal Value As SortOrder)
        ' Save the new value.
        m_Sorting = Value
        ' Make a new ListViewItemSorter if necessary.
        If m_Sorting = SortOrder.None Then
            MyBase.ListViewItemSorter = Nothing
        Else
            MyBase.ListViewItemSorter =
                New ListViewComparerAllColumns(m_Sorting)
        End If
    End Set
End Property
```

code snippet RowSortingListViewTest

The control defines a private `m_Sorting` variable to store the property's value and declares property procedures to let the program get and set it. The property is declared with the Shadows keyword, so it hides the definition of the parent class's Sorting property. That prevents the developer or a program that uses the RowSortingListView control from using the original ListView version of the property.

The Sorting Property Get procedure simply returns the value of `m_Sorting`.

The Property Set procedure saves the new value. Then if the new Sorting value is None, the code sets the control's inherited ListViewItemSorter property to Nothing to remove any previously installed sorter object. If Sorting is not None, the code sets the control's ListViewItemSorter property to a new ListViewComparerAllColumns object configured to sort the items in the proper order.

Adding new properties and methods that don't shadow those of the base class is even easier. Simply declare the property or method as you would for any other class. You can also create new events for the derived control just as you would add events to any other class.

Example program RowSortingListViewTest, which is available for download on the book's web site, demonstrates the RowSortingListView control.

Shadowing Parent Features

The RowSortingListView control's code implements a Sorting property that shadows the property in its parent class. You can provide new versions of methods and events in the same way.

For example, normally, the ListView control raises a ColumnClick event when the user clicks a column header. By default, the RowSortingListView control inherits that behavior, so it also raises the event when the user clicks a column header.

The following code replaces the parent class's ColumnClick event with a new version. The event declaration uses the Shadows keyword so this version hides the parent's version from the program that uses the RowSortingListView control so the program cannot receive the original version of the event.

The inherited version of ColumnClick passes the event handler a parameter that gives information about the event. The new version just returns the index of the column clicked. The control's ColumnClick event handler (which handles the MyBase.ColumnClick event) raises the new event handler. The control could also raise the event from some other code or not at all.

```
Public Shadows Event ColumnClick(ByVal column_number As Integer)

Private Sub RowSortingListView_ColumnClick(ByVal sender As Object,
 ByVal e As System.Windows.Forms.ColumnClickEventArgs) _
 Handles MyBase.ColumnClick
    RaiseEvent ColumnClick(e.Column)
End Sub
```

code snippet RowSortingListViewTest

The following code shows how a program could handle the new event. This code simply displays the column number that the user clicked.

```
Private Sub RowSortingListView1_ColumnClick(ByVal column_number As Integer) _
 Handles RowSortingListView1.ColumnClick
    MessageBox.Show(column_number)
End Sub
```

code snippet RowSortingListViewTest

Example program RowSortingListViewTest demonstrates this technique.

In the same way, you can shadow a method provided by the parent class. The following code shows how the RowSortingListView class can replace its parent's Clear method. Instead of removing all of the data from the control, this version removes only items with text value "Book."

```
Public Shadows Sub Clear()
    For Each item As ListViewItem In Me.Items
        If item.Text = "Book" Then item.Remove()
    Next item
End Sub
```

code snippet RowSortingListViewTest

Hiding Parent Features

Sometimes you might want to completely hide a parent feature rather than replace it with a new version. For example, suppose you want to make a grid-like control that uses some of the special features of the ListView control. You decide to derive your control from the ListView control, but you don't want to write code to handle any of the control's display modes except the detail view. You can rely on developers' common sense and ask them not to use features that involve other display modes, or you can hide those features to prevent the developers who use your control from doing something stupid. In that case, you need to hide the properties, methods, and events that deal with the other display modes.

Hiding an event is easy. Declare a new event with the Shadows keyword as described in the previous section and then never raise the event. A program using the control can write an event handler for the event, but it will never be called.

Unfortunately, you cannot completely hide inherited properties and methods from the program using the control, but you can shadow them and make the new version do nothing or throw an exception. The following code declares a shadowing version of the ListView control's Clear method. If the program invokes this method, the control throws the MissingMethodException.

```
Public Shadows Sub Clear()
    Throw New System.MissingMethodException("RowSortingListView", "Clear")
End Sub
```

The following code defines a shadowing version of the Tag property. It gives the property the BrowsableAttribute with the value False. This prevents the property from appearing in the Properties window at design time. If the program tries to read or set the control's Tag property at runtime, the control throws a MissingFieldException.

```
<System.ComponentModel.BrowsableAttribute(False)>
Public Shadows Property Tag() As Object
    Get
        Throw New System.MissingFieldException("RowSortingListView", "Tag")
    End Get
    Set(ByVal Value As Object)
        Throw New System.MissingFieldException("RowSortingListView", "Tag")
    End Set
End Property
```

COMPOSITE CONTROLS

A *composite control* combines several existing controls into one new control. For example, the ColorScrollerTest program, which is available for download on the book's web site and shown in Figure 22-4, defines a ColorScroller control that contains three labels, three scroll bars, and a panel. At runtime, the user can drag the scroll bars to select a color's red, green, and blue components. The control displays a sample of the color in the panel on the right.

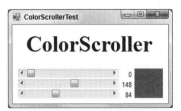

FIGURE 22-4: The ColorScroller control lets the user select a color interactively by dragging scroll bars.

To build a composite control, start a new control library project as usual. Give the library a meaningful name, and change the name of the default control UserControl1 to something more descriptive.

Next, in Solution Explorer, double-click the control to open it in the form designer. Use the Toolbox to add constituent controls to the UserControl just as you would add controls to a form. Set the controls' design-time properties using the Properties window.

Edit the code of the UserControl to make the constituent controls work together to provide the behavior that you want. For the ColorScroller control shown in Figure 22-4, you would make the scroll bars' events adjust the color displayed in the sample area on the right. You can handle the constituent controls' events, get and set their property values, and invoke their methods. You can also define new properties, methods, and events for the composite control.

The following code shows how the ColorScroller control works. It starts by declaring the ColorChanged event to tell the program when the user changes the control's selected color. It then includes property procedures that define the SelectedColor property. The Property Get procedure uses the Color class's FromArgb to convert the scroll bars' values into a color. The Property Set procedure sets the control's Red, Green, and Blue properties to the components of the new Color value. The Red Property Get procedure returns the value of the red scroll bar. The Property Set procedure sets the red scroll bar's value, displays the value in the red label, displays a sample of the current color, and raises the ColorChanged event. The Green and Blue property procedures are basically the same so they are not shown here. When the user changes the red scroll bar's value, the hbarRed_Scroll event handler sets the control's new Red property value. The event handlers for the Green and Blue scroll bars are similar, so they are not shown here.

```
Public Class ColorScroller
    ' Tell the program that the color has changed.
    Public Event ColorChanged(ByVal new_color As Color)

    ' Get or set the currently selected Color.
    Public Property SelectedColor() As Color
        Get
            Return Color.FromArgb(
                255,
                hbarRed.Value,
                hbarGreen.Value,
                hbarBlue.Value)
        End Get
        Set(ByVal value As Color)
            Red = value.R
            Green = value.G
            Blue = value.B
        End Set
    End Property
    ' Get: Return the color component value.
    ' Set: Set the scroll bar value,
    '      display the color, and
```

```
'        raise the ColorChanged event.
Public Property Red() As Byte
    Get
        Return CByte(hbarRed.Value)
    End Get
    Set(ByVal Value As Byte)
        hbarRed.Value = Value
        lblRed.Text = hbarRed.Value.ToString
        panSample.BackColor = SelectedColor
        RaiseEvent ColorChanged(SelectedColor)
    End Set
End Property
' Green and Blue property procedures omitted...

' The user has changed a color value.
' Set the appropriate color component value.
Private Sub hbarRed_Scroll() Handles hbarRed.Scroll
    Red = CByte(hbarRed.Value)
End Sub

' Green and Blue scroll bar Scroll event handlers omitted..
End Class
```

code snippet ColorScrollerTest

Composite controls are useful when you can build the behavior you want by using existing controls. They are most useful when you will need to use the combined controls many times, either in the same application or in several applications. If you need to implement these features only once, you can simply place the constituent controls right on a form and include code to handle their events.

Composite controls are also useful for keeping the related controls and their code together. This keeps the details of the controls and their code separate from the rest of the application. If the interactions among the controls are complex, it may make sense to build a separate UserControl to simplify the project.

Composite controls (or any control, for that matter) also provide a nice, clean separation between developers. If you build a complex control and add it to a large project, other developers can interact with the control only through the properties, methods, and events that it exposes. They cannot access the constituent controls directly, and that removes a potential source of bugs.

CONTROLS BUILT FROM SCRATCH

If no existing control or group of controls can provide the behavior that you want, you can build a control completely from scratch.

EXTRA WORK WARNING

Building a control from scratch is more work than building one by one of the other methods. You'll need to provide more features in your code and that means you'll need to perform a lot more testing and debugging to make sure the code works. It you build a composite control using some scrollbars, you have some reason to believe the scrollbars work. If you build a scrollbar-like control from scratch, you need to provide all of the scrollbar functionality yourself.

To build a control from scratch, start a new control library project as usual. Give the library a meaningful name and remove the default control UserControl1.

Add a new class, open it in the code editor, and add the statement Inherits Control. Then add whatever code you need to make the control do what you want.

The following code shows how the SimpleSmiley control works. When the control receives a Paint or Resize event, it calls subroutine DrawFace, passing it the Graphics object on which it should draw. Subroutine DrawFace clears the control using the parent's background color. It then calls a series of Graphics object methods to draw a smiley face on the control's surface. This drawing code isn't terribly relevant for this discussion, so it is omitted here to save space.

Available for download on Wrox.com

```
<ToolboxBitmap(GetType(SimpleSmiley), "SmileyFaceTool.bmp")>
Public Class SimpleSmiley
    Inherits Control
    Private Sub SimpleSmiley_Paint(ByVal sender As Object,
     ByVal e As System.Windows.Forms.PaintEventArgs) Handles Me.Paint
        DrawFace(e.Graphics)
    End Sub
    Private Sub SimpleSmiley_Resize(ByVal sender As Object,
     ByVal e As System.EventArgs) Handles Me.Resize
        Me.Invalidate()
    End Sub
    ' Draw the smiley face.
    Private Sub DrawFace(ByVal gr As Graphics)
        If (Me.ClientSize.Width = 0) Or
           (Me.ClientSize.Height = 0) Then Exit Sub

        gr.Clear(Me.BackColor)
        gr.SmoothingMode = Drawing2D.SmoothingMode.HighQuality
    ' Drawing code omitted...
    End Sub
End Class
```

code snippet SimpleSmileyControls

Example solution SimpleSmileyControls uses similar code to build a SimpleSmiley control. The test program SimpleSmileyControls demonstrates the control.

When you build your own control from scratch, you can make it do just about anything that you like. The obvious drawback is that you need to write code to make it do everything that you want. If there's already a control that does almost what you need, it is generally easier to derive a control from that one rather than building one from scratch.

If you can display the data in standard controls such as Label, TextBox, or TreeView controls, it would be easier to build a composite control. If you must display information by drawing it yourself anyway, a composite control won't help, so you might want to use this kind of control. For example, if you are building a mapping or drafting system, you might want to build a control from scratch to load and display maps and architectural drawings.

COMPONENTS

A *component* is basically a control with no visible appearance at runtime. Instead of appearing on the form at design time, a component appears in the component tray below the form. Figure 22-5 shows a form containing several components.

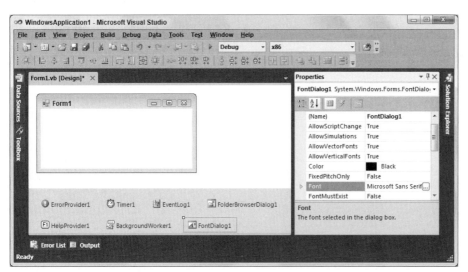

FIGURE 22-5: The form designer displays components in the component tray below the form.

You can select a component in the component tray and then view and modify its properties in the Properties window. In Figure 22-5, the FontDialog1 component is selected, so the Properties window is displaying that component's properties.

Building a component is just as easy as building a control. In fact, components are often easier to build because they don't have any visible components to implement and debug.

To make a new component, open the Project menu and select Add Component. Leave the Component Class template selected, enter the name you want to give the component, and click OK.

Because a component is invisible at runtime, the component designer (the component's equivalent of the form designer) does not display a visible area. The designer does have a component tray, however, and you can place other components there to build composite components much as you can build composite controls.

You can add properties, methods, and events to the component just as you would add them to a control. You can also use the same attributes to modify the component and its properties and events. For example, you can give the component a Toolbox bitmap, a default property and event, add descriptions to properties, and assign properties to categories. In addition to displaying the bitmap in the Toolbox, Visual Basic also displays it in the component tray below the form when you add an instance of the component to the form.

INVISIBLE CONTROLS

You can make a control invisible at runtime by setting its Visible property to False. For example, the following code shows how the InvisibleControl class works. Whenever it needs to draw itself, the control's DrawControl method sets the control's Visible property equal to its DesignMode property, so the control is visible at design time and hidden at runtime.

Available for download on Wrox.com

```
Public Class InvisibleControl
    Private Sub InvisibleControl_Paint(ByVal sender As Object,
     ByVal e As System.Windows.Forms.PaintEventArgs) Handles Me.Paint
        DrawControl(e.Graphics)
    End Sub

    Private Sub InvisibleControl_Resize() Handles Me.Resize
        Me.Invalidate()
    End Sub

    Private Sub DrawControl(ByVal gr As Graphics)
        Me.Visible = Me.DesignMode

        gr.Clear(Me.BackColor)
        Dim pen_wid As Integer =
            (Me.ClientSize.Width + Me.ClientSize.Height) \ 20
        Using the_pen As New Pen(Me.ForeColor, pen_wid)
            gr.DrawEllipse(the_pen,
                pen_wid \ 2, pen_wid \ 2,
                Me.ClientSize.Width — pen_wid,
                Me.ClientSize.Height — pen_wid)
        End Using
    End Sub
End Class
```

code snippet InvisibleControlTest

Example program InvisibleControlTest, which is available for download on the book's web site, uses similar code in its InvisibleControl.

If you want a control to be invisible at runtime, you should consider making it a component instead of a control. Components take fewer resources and don't take up space on the form at design time. The only reason you should use the Visible property to make a control invisible is if you want it to display some sort of complex data at design time, instead of an icon in the component tray, and you want the data hidden from the user at runtime.

PICKING A CONTROL CLASS

There are several ways you can build objects that sit on a form at design time. Depending on the features you need, these objects can inherit from the Component, Control, and UserControl classes. They can also inherit from an existing control class such as a Button, TextBox, or ListView.

The Component class is the simplest of these classes. It doesn't take up space on the form at design time, so it is appropriate when you don't want an object that is visible to the user. If you want a class with properties that you can set at design time, but that should be invisible at runtime, build a Component.

The Control class is visible on the form at design and runtime but it is simpler than the UserControl class and uses fewer resources. Unlike a UserControl, it cannot contain constituent controls. If you want a control that draws itself without using any constituent controls, make your control inherit from the Control class.

The UserControl class is visible on the form at design and runtime. Unlike the Control class, it can contain constituent controls. If you want a control that uses constituent controls, make your control inherit from the UserControl class.

Finally, if some existing class provides some of the features that you need to use, make your control inherit from that class. The standard Visual Basic controls are very powerful and extensively tested, so you can save yourself a considerable amount of time by taking advantage of their existing features.

CONTROLS AND COMPONENTS IN EXECUTABLE PROJECTS

Most of this chapter explains how to build a control library containing any number of controls and components. You can compile the library into a .dll file and use it in executable applications.

You can also build custom controls or components within an executable project. In that case, the controls or components are compiled into the executable rather than a separate .dll file, so you cannot use them in other applications. If these are very specialized objects that you probably won't need to use in other applications, this is not a major disadvantage and saves you the trouble of installing an extra .dll file with the application.

UserControls in Executable Projects

To add a custom UserControl to a project, open the Project menu and select Add User Control. Leave the User Control template selected, enter a name for the control, and click Add. Add constituent controls to the UserControl as usual.

Initially, the control does not appear in the Toolbox, so you cannot use it on a form. Select the Build menu's Build command to compile the control and the rest of the project. Visual Basic places the new control in a Toolbox section named after the project. If the project's name is Billing, it places the control in a Toolbox section named Billing Components. Now you can use the control as usual.

Inherited UserControls in Executable Projects

To build a UserControl that inherits from an existing UserControl class, select the Project menu's Add New Item command. In the resulting dialog, select the Inherited User Control template, enter a name for the control, and click Add. The Inheritance Picker dialog box shown in Figure 22-6 lists compiled components in the current project. Select the control from which you want to inherit and click OK.

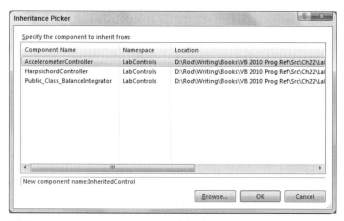

FIGURE 22-6: Use the Inheritance Picker to make a control that inherits from an existing UserControl.

> **TEMPLATE HUNT**
>
> You may need to hunt a bit to find the Inherited User Control template in the Add New Item dialog. If you can't find it, type "Inherited" in the "Search Installed Templates" box in the Add New Item dialog's upper right corner.

Add properties, methods, and events to the control as usual. Select the Build menu's Build command to compile the control and add it to the Toolbox.

Alternatively, you can create a new class and add an Inherits statement that makes the class inherit from the previously built UserControl.

Controls in Executable Projects

To build a control that inherits from the Control class in an executable project, select the Project menu's Add Class command. Leave the Class template selected, enter a name for the control, and click Add. Add the statement Inherits Control to the control's code.

Add properties, methods, and events to the control as usual. For example, you may want to give the control Paint and Resize event handlers so that it can draw itself. Select the Build menu's Build command to compile the control and add it to the Toolbox.

Inherited Controls in Executable Projects

To build a control that inherits from a predefined control, select the Project menu's Add Class command. Leave the Class template selected, enter a name for the control, and click Add. Add an Inherits statement that makes the class inherit from another control.

Add properties, methods, and events to the control as usual. For example, you may want to override the parent class's behaviors. Select the Build menu's Build command to compile the control and add it to the Toolbox.

Components in Executable Projects

To add a component to an executable project, select the Project menu's Add Component command. Leave the Component Class template selected, enter a name for the component, and click Add.

Add properties, methods, and events to the component as usual. Then select the Build menu's Build command to compile the component and add it to the Toolbox.

CUSTOM COMPONENT SECURITY

This chapter implicitly assumes that any custom controls or components that you build are safe and trustworthy. It assumes that you don't need to worry about a control installing a virus on your computer or deleting a bunch of files. That's certainly true when you use a control that you write yourself (unless for some reason you want to destroy your operating system).

It's also true when you build a custom component inside an executable application. If a project's files include a custom control that the program uses, you know that the control is as safe as you write it.

In contrast, suppose you download a control library DLL from the Internet. If you use the controls in the DLL in your application, you cannot tell if the controls are safe. You can't even always tell if the DLL you download is the one that the author originally posted. It is possible that some scofflaw replaced the original DLL with a virus-infested version. In fact, it's possible that a prankster has replaced a DLL that you built yourself with another version that looks similar but that has malicious side effects.

Visual Studio provides two approaches for combating these problems: making a strongly named assembly and using a signature authority.

Strongly Named Assemblies

A *strongly named assembly* includes a manifest identifying the files that the assembly contains and a digital signature. Another program can verify the digital signature to verify that the assembly has not been tampered with since it was created.

Unfortunately, that doesn't guarantee that the assembly is actually what you think it is. An attacker could make a new assembly and then strongly sign it. If you verify the signature, you can tell that the attacker's version of the assembly hasn't been tampered with since it was written and that the viruses it contains are the original ones. The Microsoft web page Code Security and Signing in Components at `msdn2.microsoft.com/txzh776x(vs.71).aspx` says:

> *Although providing a strong name for your assembly guarantees its identity, it is by no means a guarantee that the code can be trusted. Put another way, the strong name uniquely identifies and guarantees the identity of the assembly, but does not guarantee that you wrote it. Nevertheless, a trust decision can reasonably be made based on strong-name identity alone, provided that the assembly is a well-known assembly.*

(Go to `msdn.microsoft.com/en-us/library/txzh776x.aspx` for the most recent version of this Web page.)

Although this is a pretty big loophole, it's still better than nothing.

To sign an assembly, start a new Visual Basic project as usual. Typically the assembly will be a DLL, control library, or other code project rather than a main program such as a Windows Forms or WPF application.

In Project Explorer, double-click My Project to open the project's Property pages and select the Signing tab, as shown in Figure 22-7.

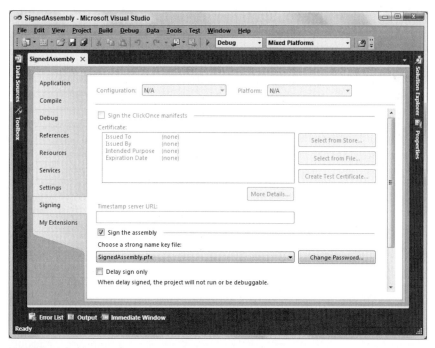

FIGURE 22-7: Use the Signing tab to sign an assembly.

Select the "Sign the assembly" check box. Then, open the key file drop-down list and select <New . . . >. On the resulting dialog box, enter the name that you want to give the file and optionally enter a password to protect the file. Then click OK.

At this point, Visual Studio builds the key file. It looks like gibberish, but contains all the ingredients needed to sign the assembly. When you build the assembly, Visual Studio uses the key file to sign the result. Build a main program, reference the assembly, and use its methods as you normally would.

When the executable program needs to use the assembly, it loads the assembly, hashes it, and verifies that the hash matches the signature. If the hash doesn't match, the program assumes the assembly has been corrupted and refuses to use it.

Using a Signature Authority

Signing an assembly ensures that some villain hasn't meddled with the assembly since it was signed. If you built the assembly yourself, that gives you some assurance that the code is safe.

However, if someone else built the assembly and posted it on the Web, the signature only guarantees that the assembly contains whatever the original author put in it. It doesn't guarantee that that author didn't insert a virus. In fact, it doesn't guarantee that a hacker didn't replace the original author's assembly with a spoofed version signed by the hacker.

If you write an assembly that you want to share with others, you can make using your assembly safer by using a certificate authority.

A *certificate authority* is a company that sells digital certificates that guarantee the authenticity of a piece of signed code. The company verifies your identity, so it is certain that you are who you claim you are. It then gives you a certificate that you can use to sign assemblies. Later, when someone uses your assembly, they cannot only verify that it has been signed and that it has not been corrupted since you wrote it, but they can also verify that *you* wrote it.

Hackers won't use certificate authorities to spread viruses because they would have to identify themselves to the authority, and that would give you a way to track them down and sue them. The certificate still doesn't guarantee that the code is safe, but it does establish accountability if the code turns out to be dangerous.

For information on signing assemblies and using certificate authorities, see the Microsoft web pages Signing an Assembly with a Strong Name at `msdn2.microsoft.com/library/aa719592.aspx` and Code Security and Signing in Components at `msdn2.microsoft.com/library/txzh776x.aspx`.

SUMMARY

Visual Basic provides a large assortment of controls that you can use on your forms. When they don't do exactly what you need, you can build others.

If an existing control does most of what you need, derive a new control from that one. If a group of controls together with their properties, methods, and events can do what you need, combine them into a composite control that inherits from the UserControl class. If you want to build a new control from scratch, make a class that inherits from the Control class. Finally, if you want an object that is available at design time but invisible at runtime, build a component.

When you build a control or component, you can use attributes to give extra information to Visual Studio. The ToolboxBitmap, DefaultProperty, DefaultEvent, DesignTimeVisible, Description, Category, Browsable, and DefaultValue attributes are some of the more useful attributes for control and component classes.

Visual Basic provides many other features that you can use to build other kinds of control-related classes and their properties. An *extender provider* class adds new properties to the other controls on a form much as the ErrorProvider and ToolTip controls do. A *type converter* (which translates data from one type to another) can translate between values and text for display in the Properties window and can generate a customized list of choices for a property drop-down list. A *UI type editor* enables you to build a graphical editor that the developer can use to view and manipulate special property values. These are more advanced topics that lie beyond the scope of this book. My book *Expert One-on-One Visual Basic 2005 Design and Development* (Stephens, Wrox, 2006) explains these techniques. For more information, see the book's web pages on `Wrox.com` or `www`
`.vb-helper.com/one_on_one.htm`.

Controls provide an interface between the user and the program. The user views controls to get information from the program and manipulates the controls to provide information to the program. Chapter 23, "Drag and Drop, and the Clipboard," covers another important way for the user to move data in and out of the program. It explains how the user can use drag and drop and the clipboard to move data between the program and other applications.

23

Drag and Drop, and the Clipboard

The clipboard is an object where programs can save and restore data. A program can save data in multiple formats and retrieve it later, or another program might retrieve the data. Windows, rather than Visual Basic, provides the clipboard, so it is available to every application running on the system, and any program can save or fetch data from the clipboard.

The clipboard can store remarkably complex data types. For example, an application can store a representation of a complete object in the clipboard for use by other applications that know how to use that kind of object.

Drag-and-drop support enables the user to drag information from one control to another. The controls may be in the same application or in different applications. For example, your program could let the user drag items from one list to another, or it could let the user drag files from Windows Explorer into a file list inside your program.

A drag occurs in three main steps. First, a *drag source* control starts the drag, usually when the user presses the mouse down on the control. The control starts the drag, indicating the data that it wants to drag and the type of drag operations it wants to perform (such as Copy, Link, or Move).

When the user drags over a control, that control is a possible *drop target*. The control examines the kind of data being dragged and the type of drag operation requested (such as Copy, Link, or Move). The drop target then decides whether it will allow the drop and what type of feedback it should give to the user. For example, if the user drags a picture over a label control, the label might refuse the drop and display a no drop icon (a circle with a line through it). If the user drags the picture over a PictureBox that the program is using to display images, it might display a drop link icon (a box with a curved arrow in it).

Finally, when the user releases the mouse, the current drop target receives the data and does whatever is appropriate. For example, if the drop target is a TextBox control and the data is a string, the TextBox control might display the string. If the same TextBox control receives a file name, it might read the file and display its contents.

The following sections describe drag-and-drop events in more detail and give several examples of common drag-and-drop tasks. The section "Using the Clipboard" near the end of the chapter explains how to use the clipboard. Using it is very similar to using drag and drop, although it doesn't require as much user feedback, so it is considerably simpler.

DRAG-AND-DROP EVENTS

The drag source control starts a drag operation by calling its DoDragDrop method. It passes this method the data to be dragged and the type of drag operation that the control wants to perform. The drag type can be Copy, Link, or Move.

If you are dragging to other general applications, the data should be a standard data type such as a String or Bitmap so that the other application can understand it. If you are dragging data within a single application or between two applications that you have written, you can drag any type of data. This won't necessarily work with general objects and arbitrary applications. For example, WordPad doesn't know what an Employee object is, so you can't drop an Employee on it.

As the user drags the data around the screen, Visual Basic sends events to the controls it moves over. Those controls can indicate whether they will accept the data and how they can accept it. For example, a control might indicate that it will allow a Copy, but not a Move. The following table describes the events that a drop target receives as data is dragged over it.

EVENT	PURPOSE
DragEnter	The drag is entering the control. The control can examine the type of data available and set e.Effect to indicate the types of drops it can handle. These can include All, Copy, Move, Link, and None. The control can also display some sort of highlighting to indicate that the data is over it. For example, it might display a dark border or shade the area where the new data would be placed.
DragLeave	The drag has left the control. If the control displays some sort of highlighting or other indication that the drag is over it in the DragEnter event, it should remove that highlight now.
DragOver	The drag is over the control. This event continues to fire a few times per second until the drag is no longer over the control. The control may take action to indicate how the drop will be processed much as the DragEnter event handler does. For example, as the user moves the mouse over a ListBox, the control might highlight the list item that is under the mouse to show that this item will receive the data. The program can also check for changes to the mouse or keyboard. For example, it might allow a Copy if the Ctrl key is pressed and a Move if the Ctrl key is not pressed.
DragDrop	The user has dropped the data on the control. The control should process the data.

A drop target with simple needs can specify the drop actions it will allow in its DragEnter event handler and not provide a DragOver event handler. It knows whether it will allow a drop based solely on the type of item being dropped. For example, a graphical application might allow the user to drop a bitmap on it, but not a string.

A more complex target that must track such items as the keyboard state, mouse position, and mouse button state can provide a DragOver event handler and skip the DragEnter event handler. For example, a circuit design application might check the drag's position over its drawing surface, and highlight the location where the dragged item would be positioned. As the user moves the object around, the DragOver event would continue to fire so the program could update the drop highlighting.

After the drag and drop finishes, the drag source's DoDragDrop method returns the last type of action that was displayed when the user dropped the data. That lets the drag source know what the drop target expects the source to do with the data. For example, if the drop target accepted a Move, the drag source should remove the data from its control. If the drop target accepted a Copy, the drag source should not remove the data from its control.

The following table describes the two events that the drag source control receives to help it control the drop.

EVENT	PURPOSE
GiveFeedback	The drag has entered a valid drop target. The source can take action to indicate the type of drop allowed. For example, it might allow a Copy if the target is a Label and allow Move or Copy if the target is a TextBox.
QueryContinueDrag	The keyboard or mouse button state has changed. The drag source can decide whether to continue the drag, cancel the drag, or drop the data immediately.

The following sections describe some examples that demonstrate common drag-and-drop scenarios.

A Simple Example

The following code shows one of the simplest examples possible that contains both a drag source and a drop target. To build this example, start a new project and add two Label controls named lblDragSource and lblDropTarget.

```
Public Class Form1
    ' Start a drag.
    Private Sub lblDragSource_MouseDown() Handles lblDragSource.MouseDown
        lblDragSource.DoDragDrop("Here's the drag data!",
            DragDropEffects.Copy)
    End Sub

    ' Make sure the drag is coming from lblDragSource.
    Private Sub lblDropTarget_DragEnter(ByVal sender As Object,
```

```
            ByVal e As System.Windows.Forms.DragEventArgs) _
            Handles lblDropTarget.DragEnter
                e.Effect = DragDropEffects.Copy
        End Sub

        ' Display the dropped data.
        Private Sub lblDropTarget_DragDrop(ByVal sender As Object,
         ByVal e As System.Windows.Forms.DragEventArgs) _
         Handles lblDropTarget.DragDrop
            MessageBox.Show(e.Data.GetData("Text").ToString)
        End Sub
    End Class
```

code snippet LabelDrag

Note that the lblDropTarget control must have its AllowDrop property set to True either at design time or at runtime or it will not receive any drag-and-drop events. When the user presses a mouse button down over the lblDragSource control, the MouseDown event handler calls that control's DoDragDrop method, passing it the text ("Here's the drag data!") and indicating that it wants to perform a Copy. When the user drags the data over the lblDropTarget control, its DragEnter event handler executes. The event handler sets the routine's e.Effect value to indicate that the control will allow a Copy operation. If the user drops the data over the lblDropTarget control, its DragDrop event handler executes. This routine uses the e.Data.GetData method to get a text data value and displays it in a message box.

Example program LabelDrag uses this code to demonstrate a simple drag-and-drop operation.

As it is, this program lets you drag and drop data from the lblDragSource control to the lblDropTarget control. You can also drag data from the lblDragSource control into Word, WordPad, and any other application that can accept a drop of text data.

Similarly, the lblDropTarget control can act as a drop target for any application that provides drag sources. For example, if you open WordPad, enter some text, select it, and then click and drag it onto the lblDropTarget control, the application will display the text you dropped in a message box.

This example is a bit too simple to be really useful. If the drop target does nothing more, it should check the data it will receive and ensure that it is text. When you drag a file from Windows Explorer and drop it onto the lblDropTarget control, the e.Data.GetData method returns Nothing so the program cannot display its value. Because the program cannot display a file, it is misleading for the lblDropTarget control to display a Copy cursor when the user drags a file over it.

Example program LabelDrag2 uses the following code to make drag-and-drop a bit safer. The new lblDropTarget_DragEnter event handler uses the e.Data.GetDataPresent method to see if the data being dragged has a textual format. If a text format is available, the control allows a Copy operation. If the data does not come in a textual form, the control doesn't allow a drop.

```
' Make sure the drag is coming from lblDragSource.
Private Sub lblDropTarget_DragEnter(ByVal sender As Object,
 ByVal e As System.Windows.Forms.DragEventArgs) Handles lblDropTarget.DragEnter
    ' See if the drag data includes text.
    If e.Data.GetDataPresent("Text") Then
        e.Effect = DragDropEffects.Copy
    Else
        e.Effect = DragDropEffects.None
    End If
End Sub
```

code snippet LabelDrag

Now, if you drag a file from Windows Explorer onto lblDropTarget, the control displays a no drop icon.

The lblDropTarget_DragDrop event handler doesn't need to change because Visual Basic doesn't raise the event if the control does not allow any drop operation. For example, if the user drags a file from Windows Explorer onto lblDropTarget, that control's DragEnter event handler sets e.Effect to DragDropEffects.None, so Visual Basic doesn't raise the DragDrop event handler if the user drops the file there.

Example program DragBetweenListBoxes, which is also available for download, provides a more complete example than program LabelDrag2 and demonstrates many of the drag-and-drop events. It allows the user to drag items between two ListBoxes. It also allows the user to drag an item to a specific position in its new ListBox and to drag an item from one position to another within the same ListBox.

Example program DragBetweenListBoxes2, which is also available for download, adds the ability to make copies of items. If the user holds down the Ctrl key while dragging an item, the program displays a plus sign drag icon to indicate that dropping the item will make a copy. If the user drops the item while pressing the Ctrl key, the program copies the item and leaves the original item where it started.

Learning Data Types Available

When the user drags data over a drop target, the target's DragEnter event handler decides which kinds of drop to allow. The event handler can use the e.GetDataPresent method to see whether the data is available in a particular format and then decide whether it should allow a drop accordingly.

GetDataPresent takes as a parameter a string giving the desired data type. An optional second parameter indicates whether the program will accept another format if the system can derive it from the original format. For example, the system can convert Text data into System.String data so you can decide whether to allow the system to make this conversion.

The DataFormats class provides standardized string values specifying various data types. For example, DataFormats.Text returns the string Text representing the text data type.

If you use a DataFormats value, you don't need to worry about misspelling one of these formats. Some of the most commonly used DataFormats include Bitmap, Html, StringFormat, and Text. See

the online help for other formats. The web page msdn2.microsoft.com//system.windows.forms
.dataformats_members.aspx lists the DataFormats class's supported formats.

GetDataPresent can also take as a parameter a data type. For example, the following code fragment
uses GetDataPresent to allow a Copy operation if the drag data contains an Employee object:

```
if e.Data.GetDataPresent(GetType(Employee)) Then
    ' Allow Copy.
    e.Effect = DragDropEffects.Copy
Else
    ' Allow no other drops.
    e.Effect = DragDropEffects.None
End if
```

In addition to GetDataPresent, you can use the e.Data.GetFormats method to get an array of strings
giving the names of the available formats. The following code shows how a program can list the
formats available. It clears its lstWithoutConversion ListBox and then loops through the values
returned by e.Data.GetFormats, adding them to the ListBox. It passes GetFormats the parameter
False to indicate that it should return only data formats that are directly available, not those that
can be derived from others. The program then repeats these steps, this time passing GetFormats the
parameter True to include derived formats.

```
Private Sub lblDropTarget_DragEnter(ByVal sender As Object,
 ByVal e As System.Windows.Forms.DragEventArgs) Handles lblDropTarget.DragEnter
    lstWithoutConversion.Items.Clear()
    For Each fmt As String In e.Data.GetFormats(False)
        lstWithoutConversion.Items.Add(fmt)
    Next fmt

    lstWithConversion.Items.Clear()
    For Each fmt As String In e.Data.GetFormats(True)
        lstWithConversion.Items.Add(fmt)
    Next fmt
End Sub
```

Dragging within an Application

Sometimes, you may want a drop target to accept only data dragged from within the same
application. The following code shows one way to handle this. Before it calls DoDragDrop, the
program sets its m_Dragging variable to True. The lblDropTarget control's DragEnter event checks
m_Dragging. If the user drags data from a program other than this one, m_Dragging will be False
and the program sets e.Effect to DragDropEffects.None, prohibiting a drop. If m_Dragging is True,
that means this program started the drag, so the program allows a Copy operation. After the drag
and drop finishes, the lblDragSource control's MouseDown event handler sets m_Dragging to False,
so the drop target will refuse future drags from other applications.

```
Public Class Form1
    ' True while we are dragging.
    Private m_Dragging As Boolean

    ' Start a drag.
    Private Sub lblDragSource_MouseDown() _
     Handles lblDragSource.MouseDown
        m_Dragging = True
        lblDragSource.DoDragDrop("Some text", DragDropEffects.Copy)
        m_Dragging = False
    End Sub
    ' Only allow Copy if we are dragging.
    Private Sub lblDropTarget_DragEnter(ByVal sender As Object, _
     ByVal e As System.Windows.Forms.DragEventArgs) _
     Handles lblDropTarget.DragEnter
        If m_Dragging Then
            e.Effect = DragDropEffects.Copy
        Else
            e.Effect = DragDropEffects.None
        End If
    End Sub

    ' Display the dropped text.
    Private Sub lblDropTarget_DragDrop(ByVal sender As Object, _
     ByVal e As System.Windows.Forms.DragEventArgs) _
     Handles lblDropTarget.DragDrop
        MessageBox.Show(e.Data.GetData(DataFormats.Text).ToString)
    End Sub
End Class
```

code snippet DragWithinApp

Example program DragWithinApp uses this code to provide restricted drag-and-drop.

There is no easy way to allow your program to drag data to its own controls, but not allow it to drag data to another program. The philosophy is that a drag source provides data for any application that can handle it, not just for its own use.

If you don't want other applications to read data dragged from your application, you can package the data in an object and drag the object as described in the section "Dragging Serializable Objects" later in this chapter. This will make it very difficult for most applications to understand the data, even if they try to accept it.

Accepting Dropped Files

Many applications let you drop files onto them. When you drag files over a drop target, the data object contains data of several types, including FileDrop. This data is an array of strings containing the names of the files being dragged.

Example program AcceptDroppedFiles uses the following code to process files dragged onto it. The lblDropTarget control's DragEnter event handler uses the GetDataPresent method to see if the drag contains FileDrop data, and allows the Copy operation if it does. The control's DragDrop event handler uses GetData to get the data in FileDrop format. It converts the data from a generic object into an array of strings, and then loops through the entries, adding each to the lstFiles ListBox.

```vb
Public Class Form1
    ' Allow Copy if there is FileDrop data.
    Private Sub lblDropTarget_DragEnter(ByVal sender As Object,
     ByVal e As System.Windows.Forms.DragEventArgs) _
     Handles lblDropTarget.DragEnter
        If e.Data.GetDataPresent(DataFormats.FileDrop) Then
            e.Effect = DragDropEffects.Copy
        Else
            e.Effect = DragDropEffects.None
        End If
    End Sub

    ' Display the dropped file names.
    Private Sub lblDropTarget_DragDrop(ByVal sender As Object,
     ByVal e As System.Windows.Forms.DragEventArgs) _
     Handles lblDropTarget.DragDrop
        lstFiles.Items.Clear()
        Dim file_names As String() =
            DirectCast(e.Data.GetData(DataFormats.FileDrop), String())
        For Each file_name As String In file_names
            lstFiles.Items.Add(file_name)
        Next file_name
    End Sub
End Class
```

code snippet AcceptDroppedFiles

A more realistic application would do something more useful than simply listing the files. For example, it might delete them, move them into the wastebasket, copy them to a backup directory, display thumbnails of image files, and so forth.

Dragging Serializable Objects

Dragging text is simple enough. Simply pass the text into the DoDragDrop method and you're finished.

You can drag an arbitrary object in a similar manner, as long as the drag source and drop target are within the same application. If you want to drag objects between applications, however, you must use serializable objects. A *serializable* object is one that provides methods for translating the object into and out of a stream-like format. Usually, this format is text, and lately XML is the preferred method for storing text streams.

> **XML XPLAINED**
>
> XML (eXtensible Markup Language) is language that uses matching opening and closing tokens to delimit pieces of data in a hierarchical data structure. XML is a simple, flexible, and powerful way to store data so it makes an ideal medium for serializing objects. For more information on XML, see msdn.microsoft.com/xml and en.wikipedia.org/wiki/XML.

You can use drag and drop to move a serializable object between applications. The drag source converts the object into its serialization and sends the resulting text to the drop target. The drop target uses the serialization to re-create the object.

You might think it would be hard to make an object serializable. Fortunately, Visual Basic .NET can serialize and deserialize many classes automatically. In most cases, all you need to do is add the Serializable attribute to the class, as shown in the following code:

```
<Serializable()>
Public Class Employee
    ...
End Class
```

The drag source can pass objects of this type to the DoDragDrop method.

Example program DragEmployee allows you to drag and drop Employee objects. The program's code starts by defining the constant DATA_EMPLOYEE. This value, DragEmployee.frmDragEmployee+Employee, is the name of the data format type assigned to the Employee class. This name combines the project name, the module name where the class is defined, and the class name.

```
Public Const DATA_EMPLOYEE As String =
    "DragEmployee.frmDragEmployee+Employee"
```

The following code shows the program's serializable Employee class:

```
<Serializable()>
Public Class Employee
    Public FirstName As String
    Public LastName As String
    Public Sub New()
    End Sub
    Public Sub New(ByVal first_name As String, ByVal last_name As String)
        FirstName = first_name
        LastName = last_name
    End Sub
End Class
```

code snippet DragEmployee

The following code shows how an application can act as a drag source and a drop target for objects of the Employee class. It starts by defining the Employee class. It also defines the string constant DATA_EMPLOYEE. This value, DragEmployee.frmDragEmployee+Employee, is the name of the data format type assigned to the Employee class. This name combines the project name, the module name where the class is defined, and the class name.

When the user presses the mouse down over the lblDragSource control, the following Mouse-Down event handler creates an Employee object, initializing it with the values contained in the txtFirstName and txtLastName text boxes. It then calls the lblDragSource control's DoDragDrop method, passing it the Employee object and allowing the Move and Copy operations. If DoDrag-Drop returns the value Move, the user performed a Move rather than a Copy, so the program removes the values from the text boxes.

```
' Start dragging the Employee.
Private Sub lblDragSource_MouseDown() Handles lblDragSource.MouseDown
    Dim emp As New Employee(txtFirstName.Text, txtLastName.Text)

    If lblDragSource.DoDragDrop(emp,
        DragDropEffects.Copy Or DragDropEffects.Move) =
            DragDropEffects.Move _
    Then
        ' A Move succeeded. Clear the TextBoxes.
        txtFirstName.Text = ""
        txtLastName.Text = ""
    End If
End Sub
```

code snippet DragEmployee

When the user drags over the lblDropTarget control, the following DragOver event handler executes.
The routine first uses the GetDataPresent method to verify that the dragged data contains an Employee
object. It then checks the Ctrl key's state and allows a Copy or Move operation as appropriate.

```
' If an Employee object is available, allow a Move
' or Copy depending on whether the Ctrl key is pressed.
Private Sub lblDropTarget_DragOver(ByVal sender As Object,
 ByVal e As System.Windows.Forms.DragEventArgs) _
 Handles lblDropTarget.DragOver
    If e.Data.GetDataPresent(DATA_EMPLOYEE) Then
        ' Display the Move or Copy cursor.
        Const KEY_CTRL As Integer = 8
        If (e.KeyState And KEY_CTRL) <> 0 Then
            e.Effect = DragDropEffects.Copy
        Else
            e.Effect = DragDropEffects.Move
        End If
    End If
End Sub
```

code snippet DragEmployee

If the user drops the data on the lblDropTarget control, the following DragDrop event handler
executes. It uses the GetData method to retrieve the Employee object. GetData returns a generic
Object, so the program uses DirectCast to convert the result into an Employee object. The event
handler finishes by displaying the object's FirstName and LastName properties in its text boxes.

```
' Display the dropped Employee object.
Private Sub lblDropTarget_DragDrop(ByVal sender As Object,
 ByVal e As System.Windows.Forms.DragEventArgs) _
 Handles lblDropTarget.DragDrop
    Dim emp As Employee =
        DirectCast(e.Data.GetData(DATA_EMPLOYEE), Employee)
    lblFirstName.Text = emp.FirstName
    lblLastName.Text = emp.LastName
End Sub
```

code snippet DragEmployee

If you compile this program, you can run two copies of the executable program and drag from the drag source in one to the drop target in the other.

If you remove the Serializable attribute from the Employees class, the program still works if you drag from the drag source to the drop target within the same instance of the application. If you run two instances and drag from one to the other, however, the drop target gets the value Nothing from the GetData method, so the drag and drop fails.

Changing Format Names

The previous example dragged data with the rather unwieldy data format name DragEmployee .frmDragEmployee+Employee. This name identifies the class reasonably well, so it is unlikely that another application will try to load this data if it has some other definition for the Employee class.

On the other hand, the name is rather awkward. It is also problematic if you want to drag objects between two different applications, because each will use its project and module name to define the data format type. If you want to drag Employee objects between the TimeSheet program and the EmployeePayroll program, the names of the data formats generated by the two programs won't match.

The DataObject class provides more control over how the data is represented. Instead of dragging an Employee object directly, you create a DataObject, store the Employee object inside it with the data format name of your choosing, and then drag the DataObject.

Example program DragEmployee2 uses the following code fragment to demonstrate this technique. It creates an Employee object as before and then creates a DataObject. It calls the DataObject object's SetData method, passing it the Employee object and the data format name.

Available for download on Wrox.com

```
Dim emp As New Employee(txtFirstName.Text, txtLastName.Text)
Dim data_object As New DataObject()
data_object.SetData("Employee", emp)

If lblDragSource.DoDragDrop(data_object,
    DragDropEffects.Copy Or DragDropEffects.Move) = DragDropEffects.Move _
Then
    ' A Move succeeded. Clear the TextBoxes.
    txtFirstName.Text = ""
    txtLastName.Text = ""
End if
```

code snippet DragEmployee2

In general, you should try to avoid very generic names such as Employee for data types. Using such a simple name increases the chances that another application will use the same name for a different class. Another program will not be able to convert your Employee data into a different type of Employee class.

To ensure consistency across applications, you must define a naming convention that can identify objects across projects. To ensure that different applications use exactly the same object definitions, you might also want to define the objects in a separate DLL used by all of the applications. That simplifies the naming problem, because you can use the DLL's name as part of the object's name.

For example, suppose that you build an assortment of billing database objects such as Employee, Customer, Order, OrderItem, and so forth. If the objects are defined in the module BillingObjects. dll, you could give the objects names such as BillingObjects.Employee, BillingObjects.Customer, and so forth.

Dragging Multiple Data Formats

The DataObject not only allows you to pick the data form name used by a drag; it also allows you to associate more than one piece of data with a drag. To do this, the program simply calls the object's SetData method more than once, passing it data in different formats.

Example program DragRichText uses the following code to drag the text in a RichTextBox control in three data formats: RTF, plain text, and HTML. (RTF, the Rich Text Format, allows text to include different fonts, sizes, styles, and colors.) The lblDragSource control's MouseDown event handler makes a DataObject and calls its SetData method, passing it the rchSource control's contents in the RTF and Text formats. It then builds an HTML string and passes that to the SetData method as well.

```vb
' Start a drag.
Private Sub lblDragSource_MouseDown() Handles lblDragSource.MouseDown
    ' Make a DataObject.
    Dim data_object As New DataObject
    ' Add the data in various formats.
    data_object.SetData(DataFormats.Rtf, rchSource.Rtf)
    data_object.SetData(DataFormats.Text, rchSource.Text)

    ' Build the HTML version.
    Dim html_text As String
    html_text = "<HTML>" & vbCrLf
    html_text &= " <HEAD>The Quick Brown Fox</HEAD>" & vbCrLf
    html_text &= " <BODY>" & vbCrLf
    html_text &= rchSource.Text & vbCrLf
    html_text &= " </BODY>" & vbCrLf & "</HTML>"
    data_object.SetData(DataFormats.Html, html_text)

    ' Start the drag.
    lblDragSource.DoDragDrop(data_object, DragDropEffects.Copy)
End Sub
```

code snippet DragRichText

The following code shows the lblDropTarget control's DragEnter event handler. If the data includes the RTF, Text, or HTML data formats, the control allows a Copy operation.

```
' Allow drop of Rtf, Text, and HTML.
Private Sub lblDropTarget_DragEnter(ByVal sender As Object,
 ByVal e As System.Windows.Forms.DragEventArgs) _
 Handles lblDropTarget.DragEnter
    If e.Data.GetDataPresent(DataFormats.Rtf) Or
        e.Data.GetDataPresent(DataFormats.Text) Or
        e.Data.GetDataPresent(DataFormats.Html) _
    Then
        e.Effect = DragDropEffects.Copy
    End If
End Sub
```

code snippet DragRichText

The following code shows how a program can read these formats. If the dropped data includes the DataFormats.Rtf format, the code displays it in the RichTextControl rchTarget. It also displays the RTF data in the lblRtf Label. This lets you see the Rich Text codes. If the data includes the Text format, the program displays it in the lblTarget label. Finally, if the data includes HTML, the program displays it in the lblHtml label.

```
' Display whatever data we can.
Private Sub lblDropTarget_DragDrop(ByVal sender As Object,
 ByVal e As System.Windows.Forms.DragEventArgs) Handles lblDropTarget.DragDrop
    If e.Data.GetDataPresent(DataFormats.Rtf) Then
        rchTarget.Rtf = e.Data.GetData(DataFormats.Rtf).ToString
        lblRtf.Text = e.Data.GetData(DataFormats.Rtf).ToString
    Else
        rchTarget.Text = ""
        lblRtf.Text = ""
    End If

    If e.Data.GetDataPresent(DataFormats.Text) Then
        lblTarget.Text = e.Data.GetData(DataFormats.Text).ToString
    Else
        lblTarget.Text = ""
    End If

    If e.Data.GetDataPresent(DataFormats.Html) Then
        lblHtml.Text = e.Data.GetData(DataFormats.Html).ToString
    Else
        lblHtml.Text = ""
    End If
End Sub
```

code snippet DragRichText

Figure 23-1 shows the DragRichText program in action. The RichTextBox on the top shows the original data in rchSource. Below the drag source and drop target labels, other controls show the dropped results. The first control is a RichTextBox that shows the RTF data. The second control is a label displaying the Rich Text codes. The third control is a label showing the Text data, and the final control is a label showing the HTML data.

If you drag data from another application onto the drop target, this program displays only the data that is available. For example, if you drag data from WordPad, this program will display only RTF and Text data, because those are the only compatible formats provided by WordPad.

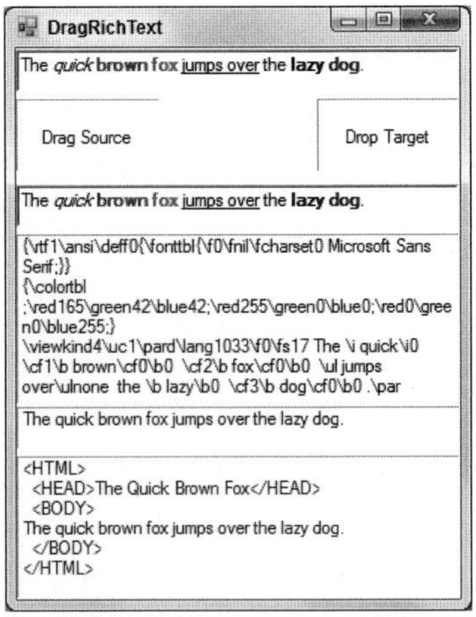

USING THE CLIPBOARD

Using the clipboard is very similar to using drag and drop. To save a single piece of data, call the Clipboard object's SetDataObject method, passing it the data that you want to save. For example, the following code copies the text in the txtLastName control to the clipboard:

FIGURE 23-1: This program drags and drops data in Text, RTF, and HTML formats.

```
Clipboard.SetDataObject(txtLastName.Text)
```

Copying data to the clipboard in multiple formats is very similar to dragging and dropping multiple data formats. First, create a DataObject and use its SetData method to store the data exactly as before. Then call the Clipboard object's SetDataObject method, passing it the DataObject.

The following code adds RTF, plain text, and HTML data to the clipboard:

Available for download on Wrox.com

```
' Copy data to the clipboard.
Private Sub btnCopy_Click() Handles btnCopy.Click
    ' Make a DataObject.
    Dim data_object As New DataObject

    ' Add the data in various formats.
    data_object.SetData(DataFormats.Rtf, rchSource.Rtf)
    data_object.SetData(DataFormats.Text, rchSource.Text)

    ' Build the HTML version.
    Dim html_text As String
    html_text = "<HTML>" & vbCrLf
    html_text &= " <HEAD>The Quick Brown Fox</HEAD>" & vbCrLf
    html_text &= " <BODY>" & vbCrLf
    html_text &= rchSource.Text & vbCrLf
    html_text &= " </BODY>" & vbCrLf & "</HTML>"
    data_object.SetData(DataFormats.Html, html_text)

    ' Copy data to the clipboard.
    Clipboard.SetDataObject(data_object)
End Sub
```

code snippet CopyPasteRichText

To retrieve data from the clipboard, use the GetDataObject method to get an IDataObject representing the data. Use that object's GetDataPresent method to see if a data type is present, and use its GetData method to get data with a particular format.

The following code displays RTF, plain text, and HTML data from the clipboard:

```
' Paste data from the clipboard.
Private Sub btnPaste_Click() Handles btnPaste.Click
    Dim data_object As IDataObject = Clipboard.GetDataObject()

    If data_object.GetDataPresent(DataFormats.Rtf) Then
        rchTarget.Rtf = data_object.GetData(DataFormats.Rtf).ToString
        lblRtf.Text = data_object.GetData(DataFormats.Rtf).ToString
    Else
        rchTarget.Text = ""
        lblRtf.Text = ""
    End If

    If data_object.GetDataPresent(DataFormats.Text) Then
        lblTarget.Text = data_object.GetData(DataFormats.Text).ToString
    Else
        lblTarget.Text = ""
    End If

    If data_object.GetDataPresent(DataFormats.Html) Then
        lblHtml.Text = data_object.GetData(DataFormats.Html).ToString
    Else
        lblHtml.Text = ""
    End If
End Sub
```

code snippet CopyPasteRichText

Example program CopyPasteRichText uses similar code to copy and paste data in RTF, HTML, and plain text formats.

The IDataObject returned by the GetDataObject method also provides a GetFormats method that returns an array of the data formats available. This array is very similar to the one returned by the GetFormats method provided by the DragEnter event described earlier in this chapter.

You can copy and paste objects using the clipboard much as you drag and drop objects. Simply make the object's class serializable and add an instance of the class to the DataObject.

Example program CopyPasteEmployee uses the following code to copy and paste an Employee object. The btnCopy_Click event handler makes an Employee object and a DataObject. It passes the Employee object to the DataObject object's SetData method, giving it the data format name Employee. The program then passes the DataObject to the Clipboard object's SetDataObject method. The btnPaste_Click event handler retrieves the clipboard's data object and uses its GetDataPresent method to see if the clipboard is holding data with the Employee format. If the data is present, the program uses the data object's GetData method to fetch the data, casts it into an Employee object, and displays the object's property values.

```vb
' Copy the Employee to the clipboard.
Private Sub btnCopy_Click() Handles btnCopy.Click
    Dim emp As New Employee(txtFirstName.Text, txtLastName.Text)
    Dim data_object As New DataObject
    data_object.SetData("Employee", emp)
    Clipboard.SetDataObject(data_object)
End Sub

' Paste data from the clipboard.
Private Sub btnPaste_Click() Handles btnPaste.Click
    Dim data_object As IDataObject = Clipboard.GetDataObject()
    If data_object.GetDataPresent("Employee") Then
        Dim emp As Employee =
            DirectCast(data_object.GetData("Employee"), Employee)
        txtPasteFirstName.Text = emp.FirstName
        txtPasteLastName.Text = emp.LastName
    End If
End Sub
```

code snippet CopyPasteEmployee

The following table lists the most useful methods provided by the Clipboard object, including several that make working with common data types easier.

METHOD	PURPOSE
Clear	Removes all data from the clipboard.
ContainsAudio	Returns True if the clipboard contains audio data.
ContainsData	Returns True if the clipboard contains data in a particular format.
ContainsFileDropList	Returns True if the clipboard contains a file drop list.
ContainsImage	Returns True if the clipboard contains an image.
ContainsText	Returns True if the clipboard contains text.
GetAudioStream	Returns the audio stream contained in the clipboard.
GetData	Returns data in a specific format.
GetDataObject	Returns the clipboard's DataObject.
GetFileDropList	Returns the file drop list contained in the clipboard.
GetImage	Returns the image contained in the clipboard.
GetText	Returns the text contained in the clipboard.
SetAudio	Saves audio bytes or an audio stream in the clipboard.
SetData	Saves data in a particular format in the clipboard.
SetDataObject	Saves the data defined by a DataObject in the clipboard.

METHOD	PURPOSE
SetFileDropList	Saves a file drop list in the clipboard. The data should be a StringCollection containing the file names.
SetImage	Saves an image in the clipboard.
SetText	Saves text in the clipboard.

Example program PasteFileList uses the following code to retrieve file drop list data from the clipboard:

```
Private Sub btnPaste_Click() Handles btnPaste.Click
    lstFiles.Items.Clear()
    If Clipboard.ContainsFileDropList() Then
        Dim file_names As StringCollection = Clipboard.GetFileDropList()
        For Each file_name As String In file_names
            lstFiles.Items.Add(file_name)
        Next file_name
    End If
End Sub
```

code snippet PasteFileList

SUMMARY

Drag-and-drop events and the clipboard both move data from a source to a destination. The source and destination can be in the same program or in two different applications.

The clipboard lets a program save and retrieve data in a central, shared location. Data copied to the clipboard may remain in the clipboard for a long time so that the user can paste it into the same or another application later.

Providing drag-and-drop support with appropriate feedback is more work than using the clipboard, but it provides the user with more direct control, and it doesn't replace whatever data currently sits in the clipboard.

Together, these two tools let you provide the user with more control over the application's data. They let the user move data between different parts of an application and between different applications. Although drag-and-drop support and the clipboard are usually not the main purpose of an application, they can give the user an extra dimension of hands-on control.

The chapters in the book so far focus on specific Visual Basic programming details. They explain the Visual Basic development environment, language syntax, standard controls and forms, custom controls, drag and drop, and the clipboard.

Chapter 24, "UAC Security," examines applications at a slightly higher level in the context of the operating system. It explains the User Account Control (UAC) security system provided by the Windows 7 operating system and tells how UAC can prevent your application from running properly. Unless you understand how UAC works and how to interact with it, the operating system may not allow your program to perform the tasks that it should.

24

UAC Security

The previous chapters have dealt with general Visual Basic programming tasks. They show how to write the Visual Basic code needed to build an application.

This chapter discusses User Account Control (UAC) security issues. UAC is a system implemented by recent versions of Windows operating systems that allows programs to elevate their privileges only when they absolutely must.

In earlier operating systems that don't have UAC, users often logged in with administrator privileges to perform fairly routine tasks because the programs they used might need administrator privileges. Now, with UAC, users can run with normal user privileges and only elevate their privileges to perform the specific tasks that need them.

UAC OVERVIEW

In general, a program cannot perform actions that require privileges that the user doesn't have. If the user doesn't have permission to delete files in the Windows directory, a program that the user can run should not be able to delete those files either. Otherwise, the user could perform actions that are supposed to be prohibited.

Developers have long known that an application should require the fewest privileges possible to get its job done. If a program needs a lot of privileges, only the users who have those privileges can use it.

Unfortunately, many applications occasionally perform some fairly powerful operations. They may sometimes need to create or delete a file in the Windows directory, access system-related parts of the Registry, or modify environment settings. If the program needs those privileges, the users running the program must have those privileges. That means that many users run programs while logged in as a system administrator so that they have the necessary permissions.

Carrying around all of those permissions comes with some additional risk. If the program misbehaves, it could wreak havoc on the operating system. Even if the program itself works properly, the user might accidentally do something disastrous while logged on as an administrator. An inadvertent keystroke or mouse click could delete important files or drag them into oblivion, making it difficult to restore the system.

A better solution would be to allow a program to temporarily increase its privileges while it performs these powerful operations. If the program made a mistake while running some other part of its code, it would not have enough privileges to do serious harm. The user would not need to constantly have administrative privileges, so system-destroying accidents would be much less likely.

This chapter describes some of the new tools that you can use to minimize the user's exposure to administrator privileges. It explains how to write applications that normally run with normal user privileges, but can use more powerful administrative privileges when necessary.

In older versions of the Windows operating system, when you logged in, the system gave you an access token that later determined the kinds of operations you were allowed to perform. If you logged in as an administrator, your token would let you do just about everything.

The Windows 7 operating system's UAC system takes a slightly different approach. Now, when you log in as an administrator, the system creates two tokens. The first token has only standard user privileges, and the second has full administrative privileges. You begin running using the first token, and the second is saved in case it is needed later.

When you try to perform a task that requires extra privileges, UAC displays a dialog box asking for your approval. If you approve the action, your privileges are elevated to the full administrator token until you finish the action. Then your privileges return to the normal user-level token.

If you are a logged in as a normal user without administrative privileges, you may still be able to perform administrative tasks. When you try to execute a command that requires elevated privileges, UAC presents a dialog box warning you and allowing you to log in as an administrator. If you log in successfully, you are granted administrator privileges until you finish the action.

The difference between these two scenarios is small. If you are logged in as an administrator, UAC only asks you to confirm that you want elevated privileges. If you are logged in as another user, UAC requires you to enter an administrator's password.

DESIGNING FOR UAC

UAC will not elevate an application's privileges after it is running. UAC assigns privileges when the application starts, and will not change the privileges after that. If an application needs to run with elevated privileges, it must obtain those privileges when it starts.

To avoid giving your application more privileges than necessary, you should separate your code into the pieces that require elevated privileges and those that do not. The main program should run with normal user privileges. Later, it should execute other applications that run with elevated privileges when necessary.

For example, a program that saves data into its local database or into a SQL Server database doesn't need administrator privileges. However, the Windows directory is protected, so a program that creates a summary file in that directory needs administrator privileges. You could separate this program into a piece that performs most of the work and another program that writes the summary information into the log file. Before closing, the first program would run the second to write into the file.

If possible, it's better to rewrite an application slightly to avoid requiring special privileges. For example, consider that many applications are installed in the Program Files directory. That directory is protected, so an application requires special privileges to write into it. That means if the application saves information into a file located where its executable is, it will need extra privileges. You can work around this problem by making the program write to a file located in the current user's directory hierarchy.

Other operations that require elevated privileges include writing into other protected directories, interacting directly with hardware, and modifying protected sections of the Registry such as HKEY_LOCAL_MACHINE.

Breaking an application into privileged and non-privileged parts not only lets the main program run with the fewest privileges possible, but separating the application into high- and low-privileges sections will probably help you reduce the number of places that you need extra privileges. That should simplify the riskiest parts of your code and make them easier to debug. It will also improve the separation between the two pieces, making them even easier to debug.

Example programs ShellUAC and ExecuteMe, which are available for download on the book's web site, demonstrate this handoff. Program ShellUAC uses the following code to run the ExecuteMe program, which is flagged for execution with elevated privileges. (How to flag an application in this way is described in the following sections.)

Available for download on Wrox.com

```
Private Sub btnRun_Click() Handles btnRun.Click
    Try
        ' Start the process.
        Dim pro As System.Diagnostics.Process
        pro = System.Diagnostics.Process.Start(
            txtProgram.Text, txtArguments.Text)

        ' Wait for the process to exit.
        pro.WaitForExit()

        ' Display the process's exit code.
        MessageBox.Show("Exit code: " & pro.ExitCode)

    Catch ex As System.ComponentModel.Win32Exception
        ' This happens if the user fails to elevate to Administrator.
        MessageBox.Show("Operation canceled",
            "Canceled", MessageBoxButtons.OK,
            MessageBoxIcon.Information)
    End Try
End Sub
```

code snippet ShellUAC

The code uses the System.Diagnostics.Process.Start function to execute the application. It passes the function the path to the program to execute, and the command-line parameters for the program that are entered in text boxes.

The code calls the returned object's WaitForExit method, so it waits until the other program has finished. It then checks the process's ExitCode property to see what value the ExecuteMe application returned.

The following code shows the ExecuteMe program's Main subroutine:

Available for download on Wrox.com

```
Function Main(ByVal cmdArgs() As String) As Integer
    Dim frm As New frmChoices
    ' Display the arguments.
    For Each str As String In cmdArgs
        frm.lstArguments.Items.Add(str)
    Next str

    ' Select the first item.
    If frm.lstArguments.Items.Count > 0 Then
        frm.lstArguments.SelectedIndex = 0
    End If

    ' Return the index of the selected item.
    If frm.ShowDialog() = DialogResult.Cancel Then
        Return -1
    Else
        Return frm.lstArguments.SelectedIndex
    End If
End function
```

code snippet ExecuteMe

The program starts by creating a frmChoices form and adding its command-line arguments to the form's lstArguments list box. It selects the first item in the list and displays the form modally.

If the user clicks the form's Cancel button, the program returns –1. If the user clicks OK, the program returns the index of the selected list item. The Process object in calling program ShellUAC receives the return value in its ExitCode parameter.

SAFETY FIRST

Remember that the program that runs with elevated privileges can potentially do a lot of damage to the system. To make this program as safe as possible, you should try to restrict its capabilities as much as you can and still get the job done. If you make the program too general, a bug in the calling program or a malicious program written by a hacker might be able to use it to cause a lot of damage. For example, if the program's command-line arguments give it the names of files to delete, a bug in the caller can delete important system files.

As part of the UAC user experience, any action that requires privilege elevation (and, therefore, a UAC dialog box) should be marked with the standard UAC shield. Figure 24-1 shows the ShellUAC example program displaying a button with this shield. The button displays the UAC shield to warn the user that clicking it launches an application that requires privilege elevation.

Unfortunately, there currently isn't a really simple way to display the UAC shield in Visual Basic applications. However, you can use an API call to make a button display the shield. The ShellUAC program uses the AddShieldToButton subroutine shown in the following code to make a button display the shield:

FIGURE 24-1: Buttons that launch actions that require privilege elevation should display the UAC shield.

```
Imports System.Runtime.InteropServices

Module UacStuff
    Declare Auto Function SendMessage Lib "user32.dll" _
        (ByVal hWnd As HandleRef, ByVal msg As Int32, _
        ByVal wParam As IntPtr, ByVal lParam As IntPtr) As Int32
    ' Make the button display the UAC shield.
    Public Sub AddShieldToButton(ByVal btn As Button)
        Const BCM_SETSHIELD As Int32 = &H160C

        btn.FlatStyle = Windows.Forms.FlatStyle.System
        SendMessage(New HandleRef(btn, btn.Handle),
            BCM_SETSHIELD, IntPtr.Zero, CType(1, IntPtr))
    End Sub
End Module
```

code snippet ShellUAC

The module declares the SendMessage API function. Subroutine AddShieldToButton sets the button's FlatStyle property to System, and then uses SendMessage to send the button the BCM_SHIELD message. Example programs RunStartAs and ShellUAC, which are available for download on the book's web site, demonstrate this code to add the UAC shield to their buttons.

Microsoft provides no method for adding the UAC shield to controls other than buttons. For example, if you want to add a shield to a menu item or link label, you're on your own. You could make a shield image and simply place it on your controls, but the image would not change when the system's version of the image changes. If the user changes the system's font size, the standard shield may grow smaller or larger on the system.

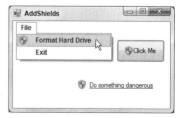

Example program AddShields, which is also available for download on the book's web site, works around this problem. It uses the previously described method to add a UAC shield to a button. It then makes the button draw itself onto a bitmap and extracts the shield graphic from the bitmap. You Can see the result in Figure 24-2. Download the example to see the details.

FIGURE 24-2: The AddShields program adds UAC shields to Button, PictureBox, and menu item.

ELEVATING PROGRAMS

The following sections describe three methods for running a program with elevated privileges. These methods differ in who decides that the called program should be elevated: the user, the calling program, or the called program.

User

To elevate an application by using the Run As command, the user can right-click the executable and select the "Run as administrator" command. The operating system displays the UAC dialog box and, after the user enters an administrator password, the program executes with elevated privileges.

This method is simple and requires no extra action on your part, but it does require the user to perform an extra step, so it is not always the best solution. Nevertheless, if the user runs the program only very rarely, it may make sense to require this extra step. This will discourage the user from using the program too often.

Calling Program

Just as a user can start a program with elevated privileges, another application can start a program with elevated privileges. This technique is similar to the one used by the user: the program executes the program, asking the operating system to run the program as an administrator.

The StartRunAs example program uses the following code to execute another program. This program is intended for use with program NoPrivs, which is also available for download. Program NoPrivs does not request privilege elevation itself so the StartRunAs program uses the following code to do so:

```
Try
    ' Use the runas verb to start the process.
    Dim psi As New ProcessStartInfo
    psi.Verb = "runas"
    psi.UseShellExecute = True
    psi.FileName = txtProgram.Text
    psi.Arguments = txtArguments.Text

    Dim pro As System.Diagnostics.Process
    pro = System.Diagnostics.Process.Start(psi)

    ' Wait for the process to exit.
    pro.WaitForExit()

    ' Display the process's exit code.
    MessageBox.Show("Exit code: " & pro.ExitCode)

Catch ex As System.ComponentModel.Win32Exception
    ' This happens if the user fails to elevate to Administrator.
```

```
        MessageBox.Show("Operation canceled",
            "Canceled", MessageBoxButtons.OK,
            MessageBoxIcon.Information)
    End Try
```

This code builds a ProcessStartInfo object describing the program that the code needs to start. The code sets the object's Verb property to "runas" to indicate that the program should run as an administrator. The code also sets the name of the program and arguments to pass to it, and then calls Process.Start to start the program. The code then waits for the called program to finish and displays its exit status.

Called Program

If you always know that a program must run with elevated permissions, you can make the program request its own elevation so the user and calling program don't need to do it. This technique uses a manifest embedded within the application to request elevation.

To create the manifest, open Solution Explorer and double-click My Project. On the Application tab, click the View UAC Settings button to open the file app.manifest. The following code shows the initial manifest (with comments slightly reformatted to fit on the page):

Available for
download on
Wrox.com

```xml
<?xml version="1.0" encoding="utf-8"?>
<asmv1:assembly manifestVersion="1.0" xmlns="urn:schemas-microsoft-com:asm.v1"
    xmlns:asmv1="urn:schemas-microsoft-com:asm.v1"
    xmlns:asmv2="urn:schemas-microsoft-com:asm.v2"
    xmlns:xsi="http://www.w3.org/2001/XMLSchema-instance">
    <assemblyIdentity version="1.0.0.0" name="MyApplication.app"/>
    <trustInfo xmlns="urn:schemas-microsoft-com:asm.v2">
        <security>
            <requestedPrivileges xmlns="urn:schemas-microsoft-com:asm.v3">
                <-- UAC Manifest Options
                    If you want to change the Windows User Account Control level
                    replace the requestedExecutionLevel node with one of
                    the following.
                <requestedExecutionLevel level="asInvoker" uiAccess="false" />
                <requestedExecutionLevel level="requireAdministrator" uiAccess="false"/ >
                <requestedExecutionLevel level="highestAvailable" uiAccess="false" />

                    If you want to utilize File and Registry Virtualization
                    for backward compatibility then delete the
                    requestedExecutionLevel node.
                -->
                <requestedExecutionLevel level="asInvoker" uiAccess="false" />
            </requestedPrivileges>
        </security>
    </trustInfo>
</asmv1:assembly>
```

To make the program request UAC elevation, change the uncommented requestedExecutionLevel so the level is requireAdministrator. Now when you compile the program, Visual Studio flags the executable as requiring administrator privilege. When the user or another program executes this program, the system automatically tries to elevate it to administrator privileges and displays the UAC elevation dialog.

SUMMARY

The UAC programming standards require an application to use the fewest privileges necessary to get the job done. An application should run with normal user privileges if possible.

If the application must perform some task that requires greater privileges, it can execute a separate application that has elevated privileges.

This chapter shows three methods for running a program with elevated privileges. First, you can ask the user to right-click the executable program and select "Run as administrator." This is not the most convenient strategy, but should be acceptable for programs that the user only needs to run rarely, or that only rarely need administrator privileges.

Second, you can make the calling application start the new one with elevated privileges. This is more convenient for the user because he or she doesn't need to right-click the program and select "Run as administrator," but this still allows you to run the called program with or without privileges as needed.

Third, you can embed a manifest inside the called application that makes it always request privilege elevation. This is most appropriate when the called program should never run without elevated privileges.

The chapters in the book so far focus on specific Visual Basic programming details that you need to understand to write Visual Basic applications. They explain the Visual Basic development environment, language syntax, standard controls and forms, custom controls, drag and drop, and the clipboard. This chapter describes some UAC security issues that you need to be aware of if you want to perform tasks that require elevated user privileges.

The chapters in the next part of the book deal with higher-level object-oriented programming (OOP) issues. They explain fundamental concepts in object-oriented development and how they apply to Visual Basic. They tell how to build and use classes and objects, and they describe some of the standard classes that Visual Basic and the .NET Framework provide to perform common programming tasks.

Chapter 25 starts by explaining fundamental ideas behind object-oriented programming, such as the three main features of OOP: encapsulation, polymorphism, and inheritance. It explains the benefits of these features and tells how you can take advantage of them in Visual Basic.

PART III
Object-Oriented Programming

25

OOP Concepts

This chapter explains the fundamental ideas behind object-oriented programming (OOP). It describes the three main features of OOP languages: encapsulation, inheritance, and polymorphism. It explains the benefits of these features and describes how you can take advantage of them in Visual Basic.

This chapter also describes method overloading. In a sense, overloading provides another form of polymorphism. It lets you create more than one definition of the same class method, and Visual Basic decides which version to use based on the parameters the program passes to the method.

Many of the techniques described in this chapter help you define a new class, but extension methods let you modify an existing class. For example, you could use extension methods to add new features to the String class, perhaps to make it encrypt and decrypt text.

Many of the ideas described in this chapter will be familiar to you from your experiences with forms, controls, and other building blocks of the Visual Basic language. Those building blocks are object-oriented constructs in their own rights, so they provide you with the benefits of encapsulation, inheritance, and polymorphism whether you knew about them or not.

CLASSES

A *class* is a programming entity that gathers all the data and behavior that characterizes some sort of programming abstraction. It wraps the abstraction in a nice, neat package with well-defined interfaces to outside code. Those interfaces determine exactly how code outside of the class can interact with the class. A class determines which data values are visible outside of the class and which are hidden. It determines the routines that the class supports and their availability (visible or hidden).

A class defines properties, methods, and events that let the program work with the class:

➤   A *property* is some sort of data value. It may be a simple value (such as a name or number), or it may be a more complex item (such as an array, collection, or object containing its own properties, methods, and events).

➤   A *method* is a subroutine or function. It is a piece of code that makes the object defined by the class do something.

➤   An *event* is an action notification defined by the class. An event calls some other piece of code to tell it that some condition in a class object has occurred.

For a concrete example, imagine a Job class that represents a piece of work to be done by an employee. This class might have the properties shown in the following table.

PROPERTY	PURPOSE
JobDescription	A string describing the job
EstimatedHours	The number of hours initially estimated for the job
ActualHours	The actual number of hours spent on the job
Status	The job's status (New, Assigned, In Progress, or Done)
ActionTaken	A string describing the work performed, parts installed, and so forth
JobCustomer	An object of the Customer class that describes the customer (name, address, phone number, service contract number, and so on)
AssignedEmployee	An object of the Employee class that describes the employee assigned to the job (name, employee ID, Social Security number, and so on)

The JobDescription, EstimatedHours, ActualHours, Status, and ActionTaken properties are relatively simple string and numeric values. The JobCustomer and AssignedEmployee properties are objects themselves with their own properties, methods, and events.

This class might provide the methods shown in the following table.

METHOD	PURPOSE
AssignJob	Assign the job to an employee
BillJob	Print an invoice for the customer after the job is finished
EstimatedCost	Returns an estimated cost based on the customer's service contract type and EstimatedHours

The class could provide the events shown in the following table to keep the main program informed about the job's progress.

EVENT	PURPOSE
Created	Occurs when the job is first created
Assigned	Occurs when the job is assigned to an employee
Rejected	Occurs if an employee refuses to do the job, perhaps because the employee doesn't have the right skills or equipment to do the work
Canceled	Occurs if the customer cancels the job before it is worked
Finished	Occurs when the job is finished

In a nutshell, a class is an entity that encapsulates the data and behavior of some programming abstraction such as a Job, Employee, Customer, LegalAction, TestResult, Report, or just about anything else you could reasonably want to manipulate as a single entity.

After you have defined a class, you can create instances of the class. An *instance* of the class is an object of the class type. For example, if you define a Job class, you can then make an instance of the class that represents the specific job of installing a new computer for a particular customer. The process of creating an instance is called *instantiation*.

There are a couple of common analogies to describe instantiation. One compares the class to a blueprint. After you define the class, you can use it to create any number of instances of the class, much as you can use the blueprint to make any number of similar houses (instances).

Another analogy compares a class definition to a cookie cutter. When you define the cookie cutter, you can use it to make any number of cookies (instances).

Note that Visual Basic is jam-packed with classes. Every type of control and component (Form, TextBox, Label, Timer, ErrorProvider, and so forth) is a class. The parent classes Control and Component are classes. Even Object, from which all other classes derive, is a class. Whenever you work with any of these (getting or setting properties, calling methods, and responding to events), you are working with instances of classes.

Because all of these ultimately derive from the Object class, they are often simply called *objects*. If you don't know or don't care about an item's class, you can simply refer to it as an object.

OUTSTANDING OBJECTS

When you read the section "Polymorphism" later in this chapter, you'll see that this makes technical as well as intuitive sense. Because all classes eventually derive from the Object class, all instances of all classes are in fact Objects.

The following sections describe some of the features that OOP languages in general, and Visual Basic in particular, add to this bare-bones definition of a class.

ENCAPSULATION

A class's *public interface* is the set of properties, methods, and events that are visible to code outside of the class. The class may also have private properties, methods, and events that it uses to do its job. For example, the Job class described in the previous section provides an AssignJob method. That method might call a private FindQualifiedEmployee function, which looks through an employee database to find someone who has the skills and equipment necessary to do the job. That routine is not used outside of the class, so it can be declared private.

The class may also include properties and events hidden from code outside of the class. These hidden properties, methods, and events are not part of the class's public interface.

The class *encapsulates* the programming abstraction that it represents (a Job in this ongoing example). Its public interface determines what is visible to the application outside of the class. It hides the ugly details of the class's implementation from the rest of the world. Because the class hides its internals in this way, encapsulation is also sometimes called *information hiding*.

By hiding its internals from the outside world, a class prevents exterior code from messing around with those internals. It reduces the dependencies between different parts of the application, allowing only those dependencies that are explicitly permitted by its public interface.

Removing dependencies between different pieces of code makes the code easier to modify and maintain. If you must change the way the Job class assigns a job to an employee, you can modify the AssignJob method appropriately. The code that calls the AssignJob routine doesn't need to know that the details have changed. It simply continues to call the method and leaves the details up to the Job class.

Removing dependencies also helps break the application into smaller, more manageable pieces. A developer who calls the AssignJob method can concentrate on the job at hand, rather than on how the routine works. This makes developers more productive and less likely to make mistakes while modifying the encapsulated code.

The simpler and cleaner a class's public interface is, the easier it is to use. You should try to hide as much information and behavior inside a class as possible while still allowing the rest of the program to do its job. Keep properties, methods, and events as simple and focused as possible. When you write code that the class needs to use to perform its tasks, do not expose that code to the outside program unless it is really necessary. Adding extra features complicates the class's public interface and makes the programmer's job more difficult.

This can be a troublesome concept for beginning programmers. Exposing more features for developers to use gives them more power, so you might think it would make their jobs easier. Actually, it makes development more difficult. Rather than thinking in terms of giving the developer more power, you should think about giving the developer more things to worry about and more ways to make mistakes. Ideally, you should not expose any more features than the developer will actually need.

Note that you can achieve many of the benefits of encapsulation without classes. Decades before the invention of object-oriented languages, programmers were making code libraries that encapsulated functionality. For example, a library of trigonometry functions would expose public function calls to calculate sines, cosines, tangents, arctangents, and so forth. To perform its calculations, the library might contain private lookup tables and helper functions that calculate series expansions. The tables and helper functions were hidden from the main program calling the library functions.

One big benefit of classes over this sort of library encapsulation is intuitiveness. When you make a class named Job, Customer, or Employee, anyone familiar with your business can make a lot of assumptions about what the class represents. Even if you don't know how the Job class works, you can probably guess what a new ReassignJob method would do. As long as everyone has a common vision of what the class does, you get an extra level of *intuitive encapsulation* that you don't necessarily get with a more procedural approach.

INHERITANCE

Inheritance is the process of deriving a child class from a parent class. The child class inherits all of the properties, methods, and events of the parent class. It can then modify, add to, or subtract from the parent class. Making a child class inherit from a parent class is also called *deriving* the child class from the parent, and *subclassing* the parent class to form the child class.

For example, you might define a Person class that includes variables named FirstName, LastName, Street, City, State, Zip, Phone, and Email. It might also include a DialPhone method that dials the person's phone number on the phone attached to the computer's modem.

You could then derive the Employee class from the Person class. The Employee class inherits the FirstName, LastName, Street, City, State, Zip, Phone, and Email variables. It then adds new EmployeeId, SocialSecurityNumber, OfficeNumber, Extension, and Salary variables. This class might override the Person class's DialPhone method, so it dials the employee's office extension instead of the home phone number.

You can continue deriving classes from these classes to make as many types of objects as you need. For example, you could derive the Manager class from the Employee class and add fields such as Secretary, which is another Employee object that represents the manager's secretary. Similarly, you could derive a Secretary class that includes a reference to a Manager object. You could derive ProjectManager, DepartmentManager, and DivisionManager from the Manager class, Customer from the Person class, and so on for other types of people that the application needed to use. Figure 25-1 shows these inheritance relationships.

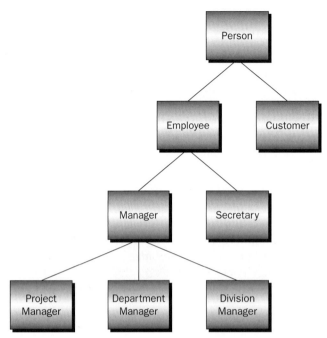

FIGURE 25-1: You can derive classes from other classes to form quite complex inheritance relationships.

Inheritance Hierarchies

One of the key benefits of inheritance is code reuse. When you derive a class from a parent class, the child class inherits the parent's properties, methods, and events, so the child class gets to reuse the parent's code. That means you don't need to implement separate FirstName and LastName properties for the Person, Employee, Manager, Secretary, and other classes shown in Figure 25-1. These properties are defined only in the Person class, and all of the other classes inherit them.

Code reuse not only saves you the trouble of writing more code but also makes maintenance of the code easier. Suppose that you build the hierarchy shown in Figure 25-1 and then decide that everyone needs a new BirthDate property. Instead of adding a new property to every class, you can simply add it to the Person class and all of the other classes inherit it.

Similarly, if you need to modify or delete a property or method, you only need to make the change in the class where it is defined, not in all of the classes that inherit it. If the Person class defines a SendEmail method and you must modify it so that it uses a particular e-mail protocol, you only need to change the routine in the Person class, not in all the classes that inherit it.

MULTIPLE INHERITANCE

Some languages allow multiple inheritance, where one class can be derived from more than one parent class. For example, suppose that you create a Vehicle class that defines properties of vehicles (number of wheels, horsepower, maximum speed, acceleration, and so forth) and a House class that defines properties of living spaces (square feet, number of bedrooms, number of bathrooms, and so forth). Using multiple inheritance, you could derive a MotorHome class from both the Vehicle and House classes. This class would have the features of both Vehicles and Houses.

Visual Basic does not allow multiple inheritance, so a class can have at most one parent class. That means relationships such as those shown in Figure 25-1 are treelike and form an inheritance hierarchy.

If you think you need multiple inheritance, you can use interface inheritance. Instead of defining multiple parent classes, define parent interfaces. Then you can make the child class implement as many interfaces as you like. The class doesn't inherit any code from the interfaces, but at least its behavior is defined by the interfaces. See the section "Implements interface" in Chapter 26, "Classes and Structures," for more information on interfaces.

Refinement and Abstraction

You can think about the relationship between a parent class and its child classes in two different ways. First, using a top-down view of inheritance, you can think of the child classes as *refining* the parent class. They provide extra detail that differentiates among different types of the parent class.

For example, suppose that you start with a broadly defined class such as Person. The Person class would need general fields such as name, address, and phone number. It would also need more specific fields that do not apply to all types of person. For example, employees would need employee ID, Social Security number, office number, and department fields. Customers would need customer ID, company name, and discount code fields. You could dump all these fields in the Person class, but that would mean stretching the class to make it play two very different roles. A Person acting as an Employee would not use the Customer fields, and vice versa.

A better solution is to derive new Employee and Customer classes that refine the Person class and differentiate between the types of Person.

A bottom-up view of inheritance considers the parent class as *abstracting* common features out of the child classes into the parent class. Common elements in the child classes are removed and placed in the parent class. Because the parent class is more general than the child classes (it includes a larger group of objects), abstraction is sometimes called *generalization*.

Suppose that you are building a drawing application and you define classes to represent various drawing objects such as Circle, Ellipse, Polygon, Rectangle, and DrawingGroup (a group of objects that should be drawn together). After you work with the code for a while, you may discover that these classes share a lot of functionality. Some, such as Ellipse, Circle, and Rectangle, are defined by bounding rectangles. All the classes need methods for drawing the object with different pens and brushes on the screen or on a printer.

You could abstract these classes and create a new parent class named Drawable. That class might provide basic functionality such as a simple variable to hold a bounding rectangle. This class would also define a DrawObject routine for drawing the object on the screen or printer. It would declare that routine with the MustOverride keyword, so each child class would need to provide its own DrawObject implementation, but the Drawable class would define its parameters.

Sometimes you can pull variables and methods from the child classes into the parent class. In this example, the Drawable class might include Pen and Brush variables that the objects would use to draw themselves. Putting code in the parent class reduces the amount of redundant code in the child classes, making debugging and maintenance easier.

To make the classes more consistent, you could even change their names to reflect their shared ancestry. You might change their names to DrawableEllipse, DrawablePolygon, and so forth. This not only makes it easier to remember that they are all related to the Drawable class but also helps avoid confusion with class names such as Rectangle that are already used by Visual Basic.

The Drawable parent class also allows the program to handle the drawing objects more uniformly. It can define a collection named AllObjects that contains references to all the current drawing's objects. It could then loop through the collection, treating the objects as Drawables, and calling their DrawObject methods. The section "Polymorphism" later in this chapter provides more details.

Usually application architects define class hierarchies using refinement. They start with broad general classes and then refine them as necessary to differentiate among the kinds of objects that the application will need to use. These classes tend to be relatively intuitive, so you can easily imagine their relationships.

Abstraction often arises during development. As you build the application's classes, you notice that some have common features. You abstract the classes and pull the common features into a parent class to reduce redundant code and make the application more maintainable.

Refinement and abstraction are useful techniques for building inheritance hierarchies, but they have their dangers. Designers should be careful not to get carried away with *unnecessary refinement* or *overrefinement*. For example, suppose that you define a Vehicle class. You then refine this class by creating Auto, Truck, and Boat classes. You refine the Auto class into Wagon and Sedan classes and further refine those for different drive types (four-wheel drive, automatic, and so forth). If you really go crazy, you could define classes for specific manufacturers, body styles, and color.

The problem with this hierarchy is that it captures more detail than the application needs. If the program is a repair dispatch application, it might need to know whether a vehicle is a car or truck. It will not need to differentiate between wagons and sedans, different manufacturers, or colors. Vehicles with different colors have the same behaviors as far as this application is concerned. Creating many unnecessary classes makes the object model harder to understand and can lead to confusion and mistakes. (I even worked on one project that failed due to an overly complicated object model.)

Avoid unnecessary refinement by only refining a class when doing so lets you capture new information that the application actually needs to know.

Just as you can take refinement to ridiculous extremes, you can also overdo class abstraction. Because abstraction is driven by code rather than intuition, it sometimes leads to unintuitive inheritance hierarchies. For example, suppose that your application needs to mail work orders to remote employees and invoices to customers. If the WorkOrder and Invoice classes have enough code in common, you might decide to give them a common parent class named MailableItem that contains the code needed to mail a document to someone.

This type of unintuitive relationship can confuse developers. Because Visual Basic doesn't allow multiple inheritance, it can also cause problems if the classes are already members of other inheritance hierarchies. You can avoid some of those problems by moving the common code into a library and having the classes call the library code. In this example, the WorkOrder and Invoice classes would call a common set of routines for mailing documents and would not be derived from a common parent class.

Unnecessary refinement and overabstracted classes lead to overinflated inheritance hierarchies. Sometimes the hierarchy grows very tall and thin. Other times, it may include several root classes (with no parents) on top of only one or two small classes each. Either of these can be symptoms of poor designs that include more classes than necessary. If your inheritance hierarchy starts to take on one of these forms, you should spend some time reevaluating the classes. Ensure that each adds something meaningful to the application and that the relationships are reasonably intuitive. Too many classes with confusing relationships can drag a project to a halt as developers spend more time trying to understand the hierarchy than they spend implementing the individual classes.

If you are unsure whether to add a new class, leave it out. It's usually easier to add a new class later if you discover that it is necessary than it is to remove a class after developers start using it.

"Has-a" and "Is-a" Relationships

Refinement and abstraction are two useful techniques for generating inheritance hierarchies. The "has-a" and "is-a" relationships can help you understand whether it makes sense to make a new class using refinement or abstraction.

The "is-a" relationship means one object is a specific type of another class. For example, an Employee "is-a" specific type of Person object. The "is-a" relation maps naturally into inheritance hierarchies. Because an Employee "is-a" Person, it makes sense to derive the Employee class from the Person class.

The "has-a" relationship means that one object has some item as an attribute. For example, a Person object "has-a" street address, city, state, and ZIP code. The "has-a" relation maps most naturally to embedded objects. For example, you could give the Person class Street, City, State, and Zip properties.

Suppose that the program also works with WorkOrder, Invoice, and other classes that also have street, city, state, and ZIP code information. Using abstraction, you might make a HasPostalAddress class that contains those values. Then you could derive Person, WorkOrder, and Invoice as child classes. Unfortunately, that makes a rather unintuitive inheritance hierarchy. Deriving the Person, WorkOrder, and Invoice classes from HasPostalAddress makes those classes seem closely related when they are actually related almost coincidentally.

A better solution would be to encapsulate the postal address data in its own PostalAddress class and then include an instance of that class in the Person, WorkOrder, and Invoice classes. The following code shows how the Person class would include an instance of the PostalAddress class:

```
Public Class Person
    Public MailingAddress As PostalAddress
    ...
End Class
```

You make a parent class through abstraction in part to avoid duplication of code. The parent class contains a single copy of the common variables and code, so the child classes don't need to have their own separate versions for you to debug and maintain. Placing an instance of the PostalAddress class in each of the other classes provides the same benefit without confusing the inheritance hierarchy.

You can often view a particular relationship as either an "is-a" or "has-a" relationship. A Person "has-a" postal address. At the same time, a Person "is-a" thing that has a postal address. Use your intuition to decide which view makes more sense. One hint is that *postal address* is easy to describe whereas *thing that has a postal address* is more awkward and ill-defined. Also, think about how the relationship might affect other classes. Do you really want Person, WorkOrder, and Invoice to be siblings in the inheritance hierarchy? Or would it make more sense for them to just share an embedded class?

Adding and Modifying Class Features

Adding new properties, methods, and events to a child class is easy. You simply declare them as you would in any other class. The parent class knows nothing about them, so the new items are added only to the child class.

The following code shows how you could implement the Person and Employee classes in Visual Basic. The Person class includes variables that define the FirstName, LastName, Street, City, State, Zip, Phone, and Email values. It also defines the DialPhone method. The version shown here simply displays the Person object's Phone value. A real application could connect to the computer's modem and dial the number.

The Employee class inherits from the Person class. It declares its own EmployeeId, SocialSecurityNumber, OfficeNumber, Extension, and Salary variables. It also defines a new version of the DialPhone method that displays the Employee object's Extension value rather than its Phone value. The DialPhone method in the Person class is declared with the Overridable keyword to allow derived classes to override it. The version defined in the Employee class is declared with the Overrides keyword to indicate that it should replace the version defined by the parent class.

```
Public Class Person
    Public FirstName As String
    Public LastName As String
    Public Street As String
    Public City As String
    Public State As String
    Public Zip As String
```

```
        Public Phone As String
        Public Email As String

        ' Dial the phone using Phone property.
        Public Overridable Sub DialPhone()
            MessageBox.Show("Dial " & Me.Phone)
        End Sub
End Class

Public Class Employee
    Inherits Person
    Public EmployeeId As Integer
    Public SocialSecurityNumber As String
    Public OfficeNumber As String
    Public Extension As String
    Public Salary As Single

    ' Dial the phone using Extension property.
    Public Overrides Sub DialPhone()
        MessageBox.Show("Dial " & Me.Extension)
    End Sub
End Class
```

A class can also *shadow* a feature defined in a parent class. When you declare a property, method, or event with the Shadows keyword, it hides any item in the parent that has the same name. This is very similar to overriding, except that the parent class does not have to declare the item as overridable and the child item needs only to match the parent item's name.

For example, the parent might define a SendMail subroutine that takes no parameters. If the child class defines a SendMail method that takes some parameters and uses the Shadows keyword, the child's version hides the parent's version.

In fact, the child and parent items don't even need to be the same kind of item. For example, the child class could make a subroutine named FirstName that shadows the parent class's FirstName variable. This type of change can be confusing, however, so usually you should only shadow items with similar items.

The following code shows how the Employee class might shadow the Person class's SendMail subroutine. The Person class displays the mailing address where it would send a letter. A real application might print a letter on a specific printer for someone to mail. The Employee class shadows this routine with one of its own, which displays the employee's office number instead of a mailing address.

```
Public Class Person
    ...
    ' Send some mail to the person's address.
    Public Sub SendMail()
        MessageBox.Show("Mail " & Street & ", " & City & ", " &
            State & " " & Zip)
    End Sub
End Class
```

```
Public Class Employee
    Inherits Person
    ...
    ' Send some mail to the person's office.
    Public Shadows Sub SendMail()
        MessageBox.Show("Mail " & OfficeNumber)
    End Sub
End Class
```

Interface Inheritance

When you derive one class from another, the child class inherits the properties, methods, and events defined by the parent class. It inherits both the definition of those items as well as the code that implements them.

Visual Basic also enables you to define an interface. An *interface* defines a class's behaviors, but does not provide an implementation. After you have defined an interface, a class can use the Implements keyword to indicate that it provides the behaviors specified by the interface. It's then up to you to provide the code that implements the interface.

For example, consider again the MotorHome class. Visual Basic does not allow a class to inherit from more than one parent class, but a class can implement as many interfaces as you like. You could define an IVehicle interface (by convention, interface names begin with the capital letter I) that defines properties of vehicles (number of wheels, horsepower, maximum speed, acceleration, and so forth) and an IHouse interface that defines properties of living spaces (square feet, number of bedrooms, number of bathrooms, and so forth). Now, you can make the MotorHome class implement both of those interfaces. The interfaces do not provide any code, but they do declare that the MotorHome class implements the interface's features.

Like true inheritance, interface inheritance provides polymorphism (see the next section, "Polymorphism," for more details on this topic). You can use a variable having the type of the interface to refer to objects that define the interface. For example, suppose that the Employee class implements the IPerson interface. Then you can use a variable of type IPerson to refer to an object of type Employee.

Suppose that the people collection contains Employee objects. The following code uses a variable of type IPerson to display the objects' names:

```
For Each person As IPerson In people
    Debug.WriteLine(person.FirstName & " " & person.LastName)
Next person
```

POLYMORPHISM

Roughly speaking, *polymorphism* means treating one object as another. In OOP terms, it means that you can treat an object of one class as if it were from a parent class.

For example, suppose that Employee and Customer are both derived from the Person class. Then you can treat Employee and Customer objects as if they were Person objects because in a sense they are Person objects. They are specific types of Person objects. After all, they provide all of the properties, methods, and events of a Person object.

Visual Basic enables you to assign a value from a child class to a variable of the parent class. In this example, you can place an Employee or Customer object in a Person variable, as shown in the following code:

```
Dim emp As New Employee      ' Create an Employee.
Dim cust As New Customer     ' Create a Customer.
Dim per As Person            ' Declare a Person variable.
per = emp                    ' Okay. An Employee is a Person.
per = cust                   ' Okay. A Customer is a Person.
emp = per                    ' Not okay. A Person is not necessarily an Employee.
```

One common reason to use polymorphism is to treat a collection of objects in a uniform way that makes sense in the parent class. For example, suppose that the Person class defines the FirstName and LastName fields. The program could define a collection named AllPeople and add references to Customer and Employee objects to represent all the people that the program needs to work with. The code could then iterate through the collection, treating each object as a Person, as shown in the following code:

```
For Each per As Person In AllPeople
    Debug.WriteLine(per.FirstName & " " & per.LastName)
Next Per
```

You can only access the features defined for the type of variable you actually use to refer to an object. For example, if you use a Person variable to refer to an Employee object, you can only use the features defined by the Person class, not those added by the Employee class.

If you know that a particular object is of a specific subclass, you can convert the variable into a more specific variable type. The following code loops through the AllPeople collection and uses the TypeOf statement to test each object's type. If the object is an Employee, the code uses DirectCast to convert the object into an Employee object. It can then use the Employee object to perform Employee-specific tasks.

Similarly, the code determines whether the object is a Customer object. If it is, the code converts the generic Person variable into a Customer variable and uses the new variable to perform Customer-specific tasks, as shown here:

```
For Each per As Person In AllPeople
    If TypeOf per Is Employee Then
        Dim emp As Employee = DirectCast(per, Employee)
        ' Do something Employee-specific.
        ...
    ElseIf TypeOf per Is Customer Then
        Dim cust As Customer = DirectCast(per, Customer)
        ' Do something Customer-specific.
        ...
    End If
Next per
```

METHOD OVERLOADING

Visual Basic .NET enables you to give a class more than one method with the same name but with different parameters. The program decides which version of the method to use based on the parameters being passed to the method.

For example, the Person class shown in the following code has two constructors named New. The first takes no parameters and initializes the object's FirstName and LastName variables to default values. The second overloaded constructor takes two strings as parameters and uses them to initialize FirstName and LastName.

```
Public Class Person
    Public FirstName As String
    Public LastName As String

    Public Sub New()
        FirstName = "<first>"
        LastName = "<last>"
    End Sub

    Public Sub New(ByVal first_name As String, ByVal last_name As String)
        FirstName = first_name
        LastName = last_name
    End Sub
End Class
```

The following code uses these constructors. The first statement passes no parameters to the constructor, so Visual Basic uses the first version of the New method. The second statement passes two strings to the constructor, so Visual Basic uses the second constructor.

```
Dim person1 As New Person()
Dim person2 As New Person("Rod", "Stephens")
```

A common technique for providing constructors that take different numbers of arguments is to make the simpler constructors call those with more parameters. In the following code, the empty constructor calls a constructor that takes two parameters, passing it default values:

```
Public Class Person
    Public FirstName As String
    Public LastName As String

    Public Sub New()
        Me.New("<first>", "<last>")
    End Sub

    Public Sub New(ByVal first_name As String, ByVal last_name As String)
        FirstName = first_name
        LastName = last_name
    End Sub
End Class
```

Two overloaded methods cannot differ only by optional parameters. For example, the first_name and last_name parameters in the previous constructor could not both be optional. If they were, Visual Basic .NET could not tell which version of the New subroutine to call if the program passed it no parameters. Although you cannot make the parameters optional in the second constructor, you can get a similar result by combining the two constructors, as shown in the following code:

```
Public Class Person
    Public FirstName As String
    Public LastName As String

    Public Sub New(
     Optional ByVal first_name As String = "<first>",
     Optional ByVal last_name As String = "<last>")
        FirstName = first_name
        LastName = last_name
    End Sub
End Class
```

Overloaded functions also cannot differ only in their return types. For example, you cannot have two versions of a function with the same name and parameters but different return types.

If you have Option Strict set to Off, there are many circumstances where Visual Basic performs automatic type conversion. In that case, it might not be able to decide which of two functions to use if they differ only in return type. For example, suppose that one version of the TotalCost function returns an Integer and another version returns a Double. If you set a string variable equal to the result of the function, Visual Basic wouldn't know whether to use the Integer version or the Double version.

EXTENSION METHODS

Extension methods let you add new subroutines or functions to an existing class without rewriting it or deriving a new class from it even if you don't have access to the class's source code.

To make an extension method, place the System.Runtime.CompilerServices.Extension attribute before the method's declaration. Then make a normal subroutine or function that takes one or more parameters. The first parameter determines the class that the method extends. The method can use that parameter to learn about the item for which them method was called. The other parameters are passed into the method so it can use them to perform its chores.

For example, the following code adds a MatchesRegexp subroutine to the String class. The Extension attribute tells Visual Basic that this is an extension method. The method's first parameter is a String so this method extends the String class. The second parameter is a regular expression. The method returns True if the String matches the regular expression.

```
' Return True if a String matches a regular expression.
<Extension()>
Public Function MatchesRegexp(ByVal the_string As String,
 ByVal regular_expression As String) As Boolean
    Dim reg_exp As New Regex(regular_expression)
    Return reg_exp.IsMatch(the_string)
End Function
```

The program can use the extension methods just as if they were part of the String class. The following code uses the MatchesRegexp method to decide whether the phone_number variable contains a value that looks like a valid United States phone number:

```
If Not phone_number.MatchesRegexp("^[2-9]\d{2}-\d{4}$") Then
    MessageBox.Show("Not a valid phone number")
End If
```

If used haphazardly, extension methods can blur the purpose of a class. They can make the class do things for which it was never intended. They add behaviors that the class's original authors did not have in mind. The result may be a class that does too many poorly defined or unrelated things, and that is confusing and hard to use properly. They weaken the class's encapsulation by adding new features that are not hidden within the control's code.

If you have access to the class's source code, make changes to the class within that code. Then if there is a problem, at least all of the code is together within the class. If you really need to add new methods to a class that is outside of your control, such as adding new methods to String and other classes defined by Visual Basic and the .NET Framework, you can use extension methods.

SUMMARY

Classes are programming abstractions that group data and related behavior in nicely encapsulated packages. After you define a class, you can instantiate it to create an instance of the class. You can interact with the new object by using its properties, methods, and events.

Inheritance enables you to derive one class from another. You can then add, remove, or modify the behavior that the child class inherits from the parent class. Sometimes it makes sense to think of the classes in inheritance hierarchies in a top-down manner, so child classes refine the features of their parents. At other times, it makes sense to use a bottom-up view and think of a parent class as abstracting the features of its children.

Interface inheritance lets you define some of the features of a class without using true class inheritance. This gives you another method for using polymorphism and lets you build classes that, in a sense, appear to inherit from multiple parents.

Polymorphism enables you to treat an object as if it were of an ancestor's type. For example, if the Manager class inherits from Employee and Employee inherits from Person, then you can treat a Manager object as if it were a Manager, Employee, or Person.

In addition to these features, Visual Basic .NET enables you to overload a class's subroutines, functions, and operators. It lets you create different methods with the same name but different parameters. The compiler selects the right version of the method based on the parameters you pass to it. Extension methods even let you add new subroutines and functions to existing classes when you don't have access to the class's source code.

These object-oriented concepts provide the general background you need to understand classes in Visual Basic. Chapter 26, "Classes and Structures," describes the specifics of classes and structures in Visual Basic .NET. It shows how to declare and instantiate classes and structures and explains the differences between the two.

26

Classes and Structures

A variable holds a single value. It may be a simple value such as an Integer or String, or a reference that points to a more complex entity. Two kinds of more complex entities are classes and structures.

Classes and structures are both *container types*. They group several related data values into a convenient package that you can manipulate as a group.

For example, an EmployeeInfo structure might contain fields that hold information about an employee (such as first name, last name, employee ID, office number, extension, and so on). If you make an EmployeeInfo structure and fill it with the data for a particular employee, you can then move the structure around as a single unit instead of passing around a bunch of separate variables holding the first name, last name, and the rest.

This chapter explains how to declare classes and structures, and how to create instances of them (*instantiate* them). It explains the differences between classes and structures and provides some advice about which to use under different circumstances.

Finally, this chapter describes some of the mechanical issues that you'll face when building classes. It explains how garbage collection affects objects. It finishes by explaining how to implement some of the most basic features of classes: constants, properties, methods, and events.

CLASSES

A class packages data and related behavior. For example, a WorkOrder class might store data describing a customer's work order in its properties. It could contain methods (subroutines and functions) for manipulating the work order. It might provide methods for scheduling the work, modifying the order's requirements, and setting the order's priority.

Here is the syntax for declaring a class:

```
[attribute_list] [Partial] [accessibility] [Shadows] [inheritance] _
  Class name[(Of type_list)]
      [Inherits parent_class]
      [Implements interface]
      statements
End Class
```

The only things that all class declarations must include are the Class clause (including the class's name) and the End Class statement. Everything else is optional. The following code describes a valid (albeit not very interesting) class:

```
Class EmptyClass
End Class
```

The following sections describe the pieces of the general declaration in detail.

Attribute_list

The optional *attribute_list* is a comma-separated list of attributes that apply to the class. An attribute further refines the definition of a class to give more information to the compiler and the runtime system.

AVOID COMMA DRAMA

Instead of using commas to separate multiple attributes inside one set of brackets, you can place each attribute inside its own brackets. For example, the two code snippet defines two classes that each has two attributes: Serializable and Obsolete.

```
<Serializable(),
 Obsolete("No longer supported. Use Sku instead")>
Public Class SkuNumber
   ...
End Class

<Serializable()>
<Obsolete("No longer supported. Use ProductType instead")>
Public Class Product
   ...
End Class
```

Which style you should use is a matter of personal preference, although it's slightly easier to insert or remove attributes with the second style because you can add or remove whole lines at a time without messing up the commas.

Attributes are rather specialized. They address issues that arise when you perform very specific programming tasks. For example, if your application must use drag-and-drop support to copy instances of the class from one application to another, you must mark the class as serializable, as shown in the following code:

```
<Serializable()>
Class Employee
     Public FirstName As String
     Public LastName As String
End Class
```

Some attributes are particular to specific kinds of classes. For example, the DefaultEvent attribute gives the form designer extra information about component classes. If you double-click a component on a form, the code designer opens to the component's default event.

Because attributes are so specialized, they are not described in more detail here. For more information, see the sections in the online help that are related to the tasks you need to perform.

For more information on attributes, see Microsoft's "Attributes in Visual Basic" web page at `msdn.microsoft.com/39967861.aspx`. For a list of attributes that you can use, go to Microsoft's "Attribute Class" web page at `msdn.microsoft.com/system.attribute.aspx` and look at the "Inheritance Hierarchy" section.

Partial

The Partial keyword tells Visual Basic that the current declaration defines only part of the class. The following code shows the Employee class broken into two pieces:

```
Partial Public Class Employee
    Public FirstName As String
    Public LastName As String
    ...
End Class

... other code, possibly unrelated to the Employee class ...

Partial Public Class Employee
    Public Email As String
    ...
End Class
```

The program could contain any number of other pieces of the Employee class, possibly in different code modules. At compile time, Visual Basic finds these pieces and combines them to define the class.

One of the primary benefits of classes is that they hold the code and data associated with the class together in a nice package. Scattering the pieces of a class in this way makes the package less self-contained and may lead to confusion. To prevent confusion, you should avoid splitting a class unless you have a good reason to (for example, to allow different developers to work on different pieces of the class at the same time or if one piece must have Option Strict turned off).

At least one of the pieces of the class must be declared with the Partial keyword, but in the other pieces it is optional. Explicitly providing the keyword in all of the class's partial definitions emphasizes the fact that the class is broken into pieces and may minimize confusion.

Accessibility

A class's *accessibility* clause can take one of the following values: Public, Protected, Friend, Protected Friend, or Private.

Public indicates that the class should be available to all code inside or outside of the class's module. This enables the most access to the class. Any code can create and manipulate instances of the class.

You can use the Protected keyword only if the class you are declaring is contained inside another class. For example, the following code defines an Employee class that contains a protected EmployeeAddress class:

```
Public Class Employee
    Public FirstName As String
    Public LastName As String
    Protected Address As EmployeeAddress

    Protected Class EmployeeAddress
        Public Street As String
        Public City As String
        Public State As String
        Public Zip As String
    End Class

    ... other code ...
End Class
```

Because the EmployeeAddress class is declared with the Protected keyword, it is visible only within the enclosing Employee class and any derived classes. For example, if the Manager class inherits from the Employee class, code within the Manager class can access the Address variable.

The Friend keyword indicates that the class should be available to all code inside or outside of the class's module *within the same project*. The difference between this and Public is that Public allows code outside of the project to access the class. This is generally only an issue for code libraries (.dll files) and control libraries. For example, suppose that you build a code library containing dozens of routines and then you write a program that uses the library. If the library declares a class with the Public keyword, the code in the library and the code in the main program can use the class. If the library declares a class with the Friend keyword, only the code in the library can access the class, not the code in the main program.

Protected Friend is the union of the Protected and Friend keywords. A class declared Protected Friend is accessible only to code within the enclosing class or a derived class and only within the same project.

A class declared Private is accessible only to code in the enclosing module, class, or structure. If the EmployeeAddress class were declared Private, only code within the Employee class could use that class.

If you do not specify an accessibility level, it defaults to Friend.

Shadows

The Shadows keyword indicates that the class hides the definition of some other entity in the enclosing class's base class.

The following code shows an Employee class that declares a public class OfficeInfo and defines an instance of that class named Office. The derived class Manager inherits from Employee. It declares a new version of the OfficeInfo class with the Shadows keyword. It defines an instance of this class named ManagerOffice.

```
Public Class Employee
    Public Class OfficeInfo
        Public OfficeNumber As String
        Public Extension As String
    End Class

    Public FirstName As String
    Public LastName As String
    Public Office As New OfficeInfo
End Class

Public Class Manager
    Inherits Employee

    Public Shadows Class OfficeInfo
    Public OfficeNumber As String
    Public Extension As String
    Public SecretaryOfficeNumber As String
    Public SecretaryExtension As String
    End Class

    Public ManagerOffice As New OfficeInfo
End Class
```

The following code uses the Employee and Manager classes. It creates instances of the two classes and sets their Office.Extension properties. Both of those values are part of the Employee class's version of the OfficeInfo class. Next, the code sets the Manager object's ManagerOffice .SecretaryExtension value.

```
Dim emp As New Employee
Dim mgr As New Manager
emp.Office.Extension = "1111"
mgr.Office.Extension = "2222"
mgr.ManagerOffice.SecretaryExtension = "3333"
```

Note that the Manager class contains two different objects of type OfficeInfo. Its Office property is the Employee class's flavor of OfficeInfo class. Its ManagerOffice value is the Manager class's version of OfficeInfo.

The presence of these different classes with the same name can be confusing. Usually, you are better off not using the Shadows keyword in the declarations and giving the classes different names. In this case, you could call the Manager class's included class ManagerOfficeInfo.

Inheritance

A class's *inheritance* clause can take the value MustInherit or NotInheritable.

MustInherit prohibits the program from creating instances of the class. The program should create an instance of a derived class instead. This kind of class is sometimes called an *abstract class*.

By using MustInherit, you can make a parent class that defines some of the behavior that should be implemented by derived classes without implementing the functionality itself. The parent class is not intended to be used itself, just to help define the derived classes.

For example, the following code defines the Vehicle class with the MustInherit keyword. This class defines features that are common to all vehicles. It defines a NumWheels variable and a Drive subroutine declared with the MustOverride keyword. The real world doesn't contain generic vehicles, however. Instead, it contains cars, trucks, and other specific kinds of vehicles. The code defines a Car class that inherits from the Vehicle class. When you enter the Inherits statement and press Enter, Visual Basic automatically adds the empty Drive subroutine required by the Vehicle class.

```
Public MustInherit Class Vehicle
    Public NumWheels As Integer
    Public MustOverride Sub Drive()
End Class

Public Class Car
    Inherits Vehicle

    Public Overrides Sub Drive()

    End Sub
End Class
```

The following code uses these classes. It declares a Vehicle and a Car variable. The first assignment statement causes an error because it tries to make a new Vehicle object. This is not allowed, because Vehicle is declared with the MustInherit keyword. The program sets variable a_car to a new Car variable and then sets variable a_vehicle to a_car. This works because a Car is a type of Vehicle, so the a_vehicle variable can refer to a Car object. In its last line, the code assigns a_vehicle directly to a new Car object.

```
Dim a_vehicle As Vehicle
Dim a_car As Car

a_vehicle = New vehicle ' Error. Vehicle is MustInherit.
a_car = New Car         ' This works.
a_vehicle = a_car       ' This works.
a_vehicle = New Car     ' This works.
```

The NotInheritable keyword does the opposite of the MustInherit keyword. MustInherit says that a class must be inherited to be instantiated. NotInheritable says no class can inherit from this one.

You can use NotInheritable to stop other developers from making new versions of the classes you have built. This isn't really necessary if you design a well-defined object model before you start programming and if everyone obeys it. NotInheritable can prevent unnecessary proliferation of classes if developers don't pay attention, however. For example, declaring the Car class NotInheritable would prevent overeager developers from deriving FrontWheelDriveCar, RedCar, and Subaru classes from the Car class.

> **EXTENSION TENSION**
>
> Extension methods allow developers to add new subroutines and functions to a class even if it is marked NotInheritable. This can ruin the class's focus of purpose, making it harder to understand and use safely. It also violates the intent of the NotInheritable keyword so you should avoid it if possible. For more information, see the section "Extension Methods" in Chapter 25, "OOP Concepts."

Of type_list

The Of type_list clause makes the class generic. It allows the program to create instances of the class that work with specific data types. For example, the following code defines a generic Tree class. The class includes a public variable named RootObject that has the data type given in the class's Of data_type clause.

```
Public Class Tree(Of data_type)
    Public RootObject As data_type
    ...
End Class
```

When you read this declaration, you should think "Tree of *something*," where *something* is defined later when you make an instance of the class.

The following code fragment declares the variable my_tree to be a "Tree of Employee." It then instantiates my_tree and sets its RootObject variable to an Employee object.

```
Dim my_tree As Tree(Of Employee)
my_tree = New Tree(Of Employee)
my_tree.RootObject = New Employee
...
```

Chapter 29, "Generics," discusses generic classes further.

Inherits parent_class

The Inherits statement indicates that the class (the child class) is derived from another class (the parent class). The child class automatically inherits the parent's properties, methods, and events.

The following code defines an Employee class that contains LastName, FirstName, OfficeNumber, and Phone variables. It then derives the Manager class from the Employee class. Because it inherits from the Employee class, the Manager class automatically has LastName, FirstName, OfficeNumber, and Phone variables. It also adds new SecretaryOfficeNumber and SecretaryPhone variables. These are available to instances of the Manager class but not to the Employee class.

```
Public Class Employee
    Public FirstName As String
    Public LastName As String
    Public OfficeNumber As String
    Public Phone As String
End Class

Public Class Manager
    Inherits Employee

    Public SecretaryOfficeNumber As String
    Public SecretaryPhone As String
End Class
```

If a class inherits from another class, the Inherits statement must be the first statement after the Class statement that is not blank or a comment. Also note that a class can inherit from at most one parent class, so a class definition can include at most one Inherits statement.

For more information on inheritance, see the section "Inheritance" in Chapter 25.

Implements interface

The Implements keyword indicates that a class will implement an interface. An interface defines behaviors that the implementing class must provide, but it does not provide any implementation for the behaviors.

For example, the following code defines the IDomicile interface. By convention, the names of interfaces should begin with the capital letter I. This interface defines the SquareFeet, NumBedrooms, and NumBathrooms properties, and the Clean subroutine.

```
Public Interface IDomicile
    Property SquareFeet() As Integer
    Property NumBedrooms() As Integer
    Property NumBathrooms() As Integer
    ReadOnly Property NeedsFireSystem() As Boolean
    Sub Clean()
End Interface
```

The interface also defines the read-only property NeedsFireSystem. Usually, a read-only property calculates its return value from other property values. For example, NeedsFireSystem might return True if a house has more than a certain number of square feet.

The House class shown in the following code implements the IDomicile interface. When you type the Implements statement and press Enter, Visual Basic automatically generates empty routines to provide the features defined by the interface.

```
Public Class House
    Implements IDomicile

    Public Sub Clean() Implements IDomicile.Clean

    End Sub

    Public Property NumBathrooms() As Integer Implements IDomicile.NumBathrooms
        Get

        End Get
        Set(ByVal Value As Integer)

        End Set
    End Property

    Public Property NumBedrooms() As Integer Implements IDomicile.NumBedrooms
        Get

        End Get
        Set(ByVal Value As Integer)

        End Set
```

```
        End Property

    Public Property SquareFeet() As Integer Implements IDomicile.SquareFeet
        Get

        End Get
        Set(ByVal Value As Integer)

        End Set
    End Property

    Public ReadOnly Property NeedsFireSystem() As Boolean _
     Implements IDomicile.NeedsFireSystem
        Get

        End Get
    End Property
End Class
```

An interface defines behaviors but does not supply them. When you derive a class from a parent class, the derived class inherits all the code that the parent class uses to implement its features. When you implement an interface, the behavior is defined, but not supplied for you. That makes interfaces more difficult to use than inheritance, so inheritance is generally preferred whenever it is possible.

One case where the inheritance of Visual Basic is insufficient is when you need to implement multiple inheritance. In *multiple inheritance,* one child class can inherit from more than one parent class. For example, you might define a Domicile class and a Boat class, and then make the HouseBoat class inherit from both. You can do this in some languages but not in Visual Basic. However, you can make a class implement more than one interface. Simply define IDomicile and IBoat interfaces and then have the HouseBoat class implement them both.

The IDomicile interface was shown earlier. The following code defines the IBoat interface:

```
Public Interface IBoat
    Property HasMotor() As Boolean
    Property HorsePower() As Integer
    Property Capacity() As Integer
    Sub Sail()
End Interface
```

The following code shows parts of the HouseBoat class. It begins with two Implements statements that indicate that the class implements both the IDomicile and IBoat interfaces. It then includes implementations of the methods specified by IDomicile and IBoat.

```
Public Class HouseBoat
    Implements IDomicile
    Implements IBoat

    Public Sub Clean() Implements IDomicile.Clean

    End Sub

    Public ReadOnly Property NeedsFireSystem() As Boolean Implements _
     IDomicile.NeedsFireSystem
        Get

        End Get
    End Property

    Public Property NumBathrooms() As Integer Implements IDomicile.NumBathrooms
        Get

        End Get
        Set(ByVal Value As Integer)

        End Set
    End Property

    Public Property NumBedrooms() As Integer Implements IDomicile.NumBedrooms
        Get

        End Get
        Set(ByVal Value As Integer)

        End Set
    End Property

    Public Property SquareFeet() As Integer Implements IDomicile.SquareFeet
        Get

        End Get
        Set(ByVal Value As Integer)

        End Set
    End Property

    Public Property Capacity() As Integer Implements IBoat.Capacity
        Get

        End Get
        Set(ByVal Value As Integer)

        End Set
    End Property

    Public Property HasMotor() As Boolean Implements IBoat.HasMotor
        Get
```

```
            End Get
            Set(ByVal Value As Boolean)

            End Set
      End Property

      Public Property HorsePower() As Integer Implements IBoat.HorsePower
            Get

            End Get
            Set(ByVal Value As Integer)

            End Set
      End Property

      Public Sub Sail() Implements IBoat.Sail

      End Sub
   End Class
```

Using an interface in place of inheritance is sometimes called *interface inheritance*. The class doesn't inherit a parent class's code, but it does inherit the definition of the features that it must provide.

Note that a class can inherit from one class and also implement one or more interfaces. To save coding, you could make one of the parent interfaces into a class. For example, if the IDomicile interface defines more behaviors than the IBoat interface, and if those behaviors are generic enough to provide help for derived classes, you can turn IDomicile into a Domicile class that provides those features. Then the HouseBoat class could inherit the Domicile class's features and implement the IBoat interface.

If a class declaration uses any Implements statements, they must come after any Inherits statement and before any other statements (other than blank lines and comments).

For more information on interfaces and how you can use them to mimic inheritance, see the section "Interface Inheritance" in Chapter 25.

STRUCTURES

Structures are very similar to classes. The syntax for declaring a structure is as follows:

```
[attribute_list] [Partial] [accessibility] [Shadows] _
Structure name[(Of type_list)]
    [Implements interface]
    Statements
End Structure
```

The only thing that all structure declarations must include is the Structure clause (including the structure's name) and the End Structure statement. The rest is optional.

Unlike a class, however, a structure cannot be empty. It must contain at least one variable or event declaration. The following code describes a valid structure. Its only member is a Private variable, so this structure wouldn't be of much use, but it is valid.

```
Structure EmptyStructure
     Private m_Num As Integer
End Structure
```

The structure's *attribute_list* and *accessibility* clauses, Shadows and Partial keywords, and the Implements statement are the same as those for classes. See the earlier sections discussing these keywords for details.

There are two main differences between a structure and a class: structures cannot inherit and structures are value types rather than reference types.

Structures Cannot Inherit

Unlike a class, a structure cannot inherit so it cannot use the MustInherit, NotInheritable, or Inherits keywords; however, like a class, a structure can implement any number of interfaces. You can use interface inheritance to define inheritance-mimicking hierarchies of structures, and you can simulate multiple inheritance by making a structure implement multiple interfaces.

Structures Are Value Types

The biggest difference between a structure and a class is in how each allocates memory for its data. Classes are *reference types*. That means an instance of a class is actually a reference to the object's storage in memory. When you create an instance of a class, Visual Basic actually creates a reference that points to the object's actual location in memory.

On the other hand, structures are *value types*. An instance of a structure contains the data inside the structure rather than simply pointing to it. Figure 26-1 illustrates the difference.

The difference between reference and value type has several important consequences that are described in the following sections.

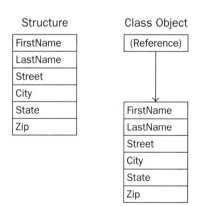

FIGURE 26-1: A structure contains the data, whereas a class object contains a reference that points to data.

Memory Required

The difference in memory required by classes and structures is small when you consider only a single object. If you look at an array, however, the distinction is more important. An array of class objects contains references to data in some other part of memory. When you first declare the array, the references all have the value Nothing, so they don't point to any data and no memory is allocated for the data. The references take 4 bytes each, so the array uses only 4 bytes per array entry.

> **ONE SIZE DOESN'T FIT ALL**
>
> Actually, the size of a reference is not necessarily 4 bytes. On a 64-bit system, references are larger. In general, you should not assume a reference has a particular size. Just be aware that references take relatively little memory.

An array of structure instances, on the other hand, allocates space for the data inside the array. If each structure object takes up 1000 bytes of memory, then an array containing N items uses 1000 * N bytes of memory. Each structure object's memory is allocated, whether or not its fields contain meaningful data.

Figure 26-2 illustrates this situation. The array of class objects on the left uses very little memory when the references are Nothing. The array of structure objects on the right uses a lot of memory even if its elements have not been initialized.

If you must use a large array of objects where only a few at a time will have values other than Nothing, using a class may save the program a considerable amount of memory. If you will need most of the objects to have values other than Nothing at the same time, it may be faster to allocate all the memory at once using a structure. This will also use slightly less memory, because an array of class references requires 4 extra bytes per entry to hold the references.

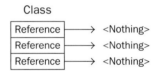

FIGURE 26-2: An array of class objects contains small references to data, many of which may be Nothing. An array of structures takes up a significant amount of memory.

PERFORMANCE ANXIETY

In theory, you may see a slight performance benefit to using an array of structures if you want them initialized to default values. The array will be allocated and later freed in a single step, and its memory will be contiguous, so for some applications, this kind of array may reduce paging.

The garbage collector can also mark the array's memory as in use in a single step, whereas it must follow the references to class objects separately.

In practice, however, the differences are so small that you should not use performance to decide which approach to use. Usually, you are best off picking the method that makes the most logical sense, and not worrying too much about the slight performance difference.

Heap and Stack Performance

Visual Basic programs allocate variables from two pools of memory called the *stack* and the *heap*. They take memory for value types (such as integers and dates) from the stack.

Space for reference types comes from the heap. More than one reference can point to the same chunk of memory allocated on the heap. That makes garbage collection and other heap-management issues more complex than using the stack, so using the heap is generally slower than using the stack.

Because structures are value types and classes are reference types, structures are allocated on the stack and class objects are allocated from the heap. That makes structures faster than classes. The exact difference for a particular program depends on the application.

Note that arrays are themselves reference types, so all arrays are allocated from the heap whether they contain structures or references to class objects. The memory for an array of structures is allocated all at once, however, so there is still some benefit to using structures. All the memory in an array of structures is contiguous, so the program can access its elements more quickly than it would if the memory were scattered throughout the heap.

Object Assignment

When you assign one reference type variable to another, you make a new reference to an existing object. When you are finished, the two variables point to the same object. If you change the object's fields using one variable, the fields shown by the other are also changed.

On the other hand, if you set one value type variable equal to another, Visual Basic copies the data from one to the other. If you change the fields in one object, the fields in the other remain unchanged. Figure 26-3 illustrates the difference for classes and structures.

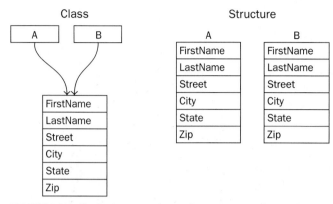

FIGURE 26-3: Assigning one class reference to another makes them both point to the same object. Assigning one structure variable to another makes a new copy of the data.

Example program StructuresAndClasses uses the following code to demonstrate this difference:

```
Dim cperson1 As New CPerson
Dim cperson2 As CPerson
cperson1.FirstName = "Alice"
cperson2 = cperson1
cperson2.FirstName = "Ben"
MessageBox.Show(cperson1.FirstName & vbCrLf & cperson2.FirstName)

Dim sperson1 As New SPerson
Dim sperson2 As SPerson
sperson1.FirstName = "Alice"
sperson2 = sperson1
sperson2.FirstName = "Ben"
MessageBox.Show(sperson1.FirstName & vbCrLf & sperson2.FirstName)
```

code snippet StructuresAndClasses

The code creates a CPerson object and sets its first name value. It then assigns another CPerson variable to the same object. Because CPerson is a class, the two variables refer to the same piece of memory so when the code sets the new variable's first name value it overwrites the previous variable's first name value. The message box displays the name Ben twice.

The code performs the same steps again but this time it uses structure variables instead of class variables. The code makes an SPerson structure and sets its first name value. When it sets the second SPerson variable equal to the first one, it makes a copy of the structure. Now when the code sets the second variable's first name to Ben, it does not overwrite the previous variable's first name value. The message box displays the names Alice and Ben.

Parameter Passing

When you pass a parameter to a function or subroutine, you can pass it by reference using the ByRef keyword, or by value using the ByVal keyword. If you pass a parameter by reference, any changes that the routine makes are reflected in the original parameter passed into the routine.

For example, consider the following code. Subroutine TestByRef creates an integer named i and sets its value to 1. It then calls subroutine PassByVal. That routine declares its parameter with the ByVal keyword, so i is passed by value. PassByVal multiplies its parameter by 2 and ends. Because the parameter was declared ByVal, the original variable i is unchanged, so the message box displays the value 1. Next the program calls subroutine PassByRef, passing it the variable i. Subroutine PassByRef declares its parameter with the ByRef keyword, so a reference to the variable is passed into the routine. PassByRef doubles its parameter and ends. Because the parameter is declared with the ByRef keyword, the value of variable i is modified so the message box displays the value 2.

```
Public Sub TestByRef()
Dim i As Integer = 1

    PassByVal(i)
    MessageBox.Show(i.ToString) ' i = 1.

    PassByRef(i)
    MessageBox.Show(i.ToString) ' i = 2.
End Sub

Public Sub PassByVal(ByVal the_value As Integer)
    the_value *= 2
End Sub

Public Sub PassByRef(ByRef the_value As Integer)
    the_value *= 2
End Sub
```

When you work with class references and structures, you must think a bit harder about how ByRef and ByVal work. There are four possible combinations: reference ByVal, structure ByVal, reference ByRef, and structure ByRef.

If you pass a class reference to a routine by value, the routine receives a copy *of the reference*. If it changes the reference (perhaps making it point to a new object), the original reference passed into the routine remains unchanged. It still points to the same object it did when it was passed to the routine. However, the routine can change the values in the object to which the reference points. If the reference points to a Person object, the routine can change the object's FirstName, LastName, and other fields. It cannot change the reference itself to make it point to a different Person object, but it can change the object's data.

On the other hand, suppose that you pass a structure into a routine by value. In that case, the routine receives a *copy* of the entire structure. The routine can change the values contained in its copy of the structure, but the original structure's values remain unchanged. It cannot change the original structure's fields the way it could if the parameter were a reference type.

If you pass a class reference variable by reference, the routine can not only modify the values in the reference's object but it can also make the reference point to a different object. For example, the routine could use the New keyword to make the variable point to a completely new object.

If you pass a structure by reference, the routine receives a pointer to the structure's data. If it changes the structure's data, the fields in the original variable passed into the routine are modified.

In addition to these differences in behavior, passing class references and structures by reference or by value can make differences in performance. When you pass a reference to data, Visual Basic only needs to send the routine a 4-byte value. If you pass a structure into a routine by value, Visual Basic must duplicate the entire structure, so the routine can use its own copy. If the structure is very large, that may take a little extra time.

Boxing and Unboxing

Visual Basic allows a program to treat any variable as an object. For example, a collection class stores objects. If you add a simple value type such as an Integer to a collection, Visual Basic wraps the Integer in an object and adds that object to the collection.

The process of wrapping the Integer in an object is called *boxing*. Later, if you need to use the Integer as a value type again, the program *unboxes* it. Because structures are value types, the program must box and unbox them whenever it treats them as objects, and that adds some extra overhead.

Some operations that require boxing and possibly unboxing include assigning a structure to an Object variable, passing a structure to a routine that takes an Object as a parameter, or adding a structure to a collection class. Note that this last operation includes adding a structure to a collection used by a control or other object. For example, adding a structure to a ListBox control's Items collection requires boxing.

Note that arrays are themselves reference types, so treating an array as an object doesn't require boxing.

CLASS INSTANTIATION DETAILS

When you declare a reference variable, Visual Basic allocates space for the reference. Initially, that reference is set to Nothing, so it doesn't point to anything and no memory is allocated for an actual object.

You create an object by using the New keyword. Creating an actual object is called *instantiating* the class.

The following code shows a simple object declaration and instantiation. The first line declares the reference variable. The second line makes the variable point to a new Employee object.

```
Dim emp As Employee ' Declare a reference to an Employee object.
emp = New Employee   ' Make a new Employee object and make emp point to it.
```

Visual Basic also enables you to declare and initialize a variable in a single statement. The following code shows how to declare and initialize an object reference in one statement:

```
Dim emp As Employee = New Employee ' Declare and instantiate an object.
```

Visual Basic lets you declare a variable to be of a new object type, as shown in the following statement. This version has the same effect as the preceding one but is slightly more compact.

```
Dim emp As New Employee ' Declare and instantiate an object.
```

Both of these versions that define and initialize an object in a single statement ensure that the variable is initialized right away. They guarantee that the object is instantiated before you try to use it. If you place these kinds of declarations immediately before the code where the object is used, they also make it easy to see where the object is defined.

Although you can declare and instantiate a reference variable separately, value type variables are allocated when they are declared. Because structures are value types, when you declare one you also allocate space for its data, so you don't need to use the New keyword to initialize a structure variable.

Both classes and structures can provide special subroutines called *constructors*. A constructor is a special subroutine named New that Visual Basic calls when a new instance of the class or structure is created. The constructor can perform initialization tasks to get the new object ready for use.

A constructor can optionally take parameters to help in initializing the object. For example, the Person class shown in the following code has a constructor that takes as parameters first and last names and saves them in the control's FirstName and LastName variables:

```
Public Class Person
    Public FirstName As String
    Public LastName As String

    Public Sub New(ByVal first_name As String, ByVal last_name As String)
        FirstName = first_name
        LastName = last_name
    End Sub
End Class
```

The following code shows how a program might use this constructor to create a new Person object:

```
Dim author As New Person("Rod", "Stephens")
```

You can overload the New method just as you can overload other class methods. The different overloaded versions of the constructor must have different parameter lists so that Visual Basic can decide which one to use when it creates a new object.

The following code shows a Person class that provides two constructors. The first takes no parameters and sets the object's FirstName and LastName values to <unknown>. The second version takes two strings as parameters and copies them into the object's FirstName and LastName values.

```
Public Class Person
    Public FirstName As String
    Public LastName As String

    Public Sub New()
        Me.New("<unknown>", "<unknown>")
    End Sub

    Public Sub New(ByVal first_name As String, ByVal last_name As String)
        FirstName = first_name
        LastName = last_name
    End Sub
End Class
```

The following code uses each of these constructors:

```
Dim person1 As New Person                      ' <unknown> <unknown>.
Dim person2 As New Person("Olga", "O'Toole") ' Olga O'Toole.
```

If you do not provide any constructors for a class, Visual Basic allows the program to use the New keyword with no parameters. If you create any constructor, however, Visual Basic does not allow the program to use this default empty constructor (without parameters) unless you build one explicitly. For example, if the previous version of the Person class did not include an empty constructor, the program could not use the first declaration in the previous code that doesn't include any parameters.

You can use this feature to ensure that the program assigns required values to an object. In this case, it would mean that the program could not create a Person object without assigning FirstName and LastName values.

If you want to allow an empty constructor in addition to other constructors, an alternative is to create a single constructor with optional parameters. The following code shows this approach. With this class, the program could create a new Person object, passing its constructor zero, one, or two parameters.

```
Public Class Person
    Public FirstName As String
    Public LastName As String

    Public Sub New(
     Optional ByVal first_name As String = "<unknown>",
     Optional ByVal last_name As String = "<unknown>")
        FirstName = first_name
```

```
        LastName = last_name
    End Sub
End Class
```

When you use a class's empty constructor to create an object, you can also include a With clause to initialize the object's properties. The following code uses the Person class's parameter-less constructor to make a new Person object. The With statement then sets values for the object's FirstName and LastName values.

```
Dim author As New Person() With {.FirstName = "Rod", .LastName = "Stephens"}
```

STRUCTURE INSTANTIATION DETAILS

Structures handle instantiation somewhat differently from object references. When you declare a reference variable, Visual Basic does not automatically allocate the object to which the variable points. In contrast, when you declare a value type such as a structure, Visual Basic automatically allocates space for the variable's data. That means you never need to use the New keyword to instantiate a structure.

However, the Visual Basic compiler warns you if you do not explicitly initialize a structure variable before using it. To satisfy the compiler, you can use the New keyword to initialize the variable when you declare it.

A structure can also provide constructors, and you can use those constructors to initialize the structure. The following code defines the SPerson structure and gives it a constructor that takes two parameters, the second optional:

```
Public Structure SPerson
    Public FirstName As String
    Public LastName As String

    Public Sub New(
     ByVal first_name As String,
     Optional ByVal last_name As String = "<unknown>")
        FirstName = first_name
        LastName = last_name
    End Sub
End Structure
```

To use a structure's constructor, you initialize the structure with the New keyword much as you initialize a reference variable. The following code allocates an SPerson structure variable using the two-parameter constructor:

```
Dim artist As New SPerson("Sergio", "Aragones")
```

You can also use structure constructors later to reinitialize a variable or set its values, as shown here:

```
' Allocate the artist variable.
Dim artist As SPerson

' Do something with artist.
...

' Reset FirstName and LastName to Nothing.
artist = New SPerson
...

' Set FirstName and LastName to Bill Amend.
artist = New SPerson("Bill", "Amend")
```

As is the case with classes, you can use a With clause to set structure values when you initialize a structure variable. For example, the following code creates a new SPerson structure and sets its FirstName and LastName values:

```
Dim artist As New SPerson() With {.FirstName = "Anna", .LastName = "Aux"}
```

> **NEW NEEDED**
>
> Although you can create a structure without using the New keyword, you cannot include a With clause unless you use New.

Structure and class constructors are very similar, but there are some major differences.

➤ A structure cannot declare a constructor that takes no parameters.

➤ A structure cannot provide a constructor with all optional parameters, because that would allow the program to call it with no parameters.

➤ Visual Basic always allows the program to use a default empty constructor to declare a structure variable, but you cannot make it use *your* empty constructor. Unfortunately, that means you cannot use a default constructor to guarantee that the program always initializes the structure's values as you can with a class. If you need that feature, you should use a class instead of a structure.

➤ You also cannot provide initialization values for variables declared within a structure as you can with a class. That means you cannot use this technique to provide default values for the structure's variables.

The following code demonstrates these differences. The CPerson class defines initial values for its FirstName and LastName variables, provides an empty constructor, and provides a two-parameter constructor. The SPerson structure cannot define initial values for FirstName and LastName and cannot provide an empty constructor.

```
' Class.
Public Class CPerson
    Public FirstName As String = "<unknown>" ' Initialization value allowed.
    Public LastName As String = "<unknown>"  ' Initialization value allowed.

    ' Empty constructor allowed.
    Public Sub New()
    End Sub

    ' Two-parameter constructor allowed.
    Public Sub New(ByVal first_name As String, ByVal last_name As String)
        FirstName = first_name
        LastName = last_name
    End Sub
End Class

' Structure.
Public Structure SPerson
    Public FirstName As String ' = "<unknown>" ' Initialization NOT allowed.
    Public LastName As String ' = "<unknown>" ' Initialization NOT allowed.

    '' Empty constructor NOT allowed.
    'Public Sub New()
    'End Sub

    ' Two-parameter constructor allowed.
    Public Sub New(ByVal first_name As String, ByVal last_name As String)
        FirstName = first_name
        LastName = last_name
    End Sub
End Structure
```

GARBAGE COLLECTION

When a program starts, the system allocates a chunk of memory for the program called the *managed heap*. When it allocates data for reference types (class objects), Visual Basic uses memory from this heap. (For more information about the stack and heap and their relative performance, see the section "Heap and Stack Performance" earlier in this chapter.)

When the program no longer needs to use a reference object, Visual Basic does *not* mark the heap memory as free for later use. If you set a reference variable to Nothing so that no variable points to the object, the object's memory is no longer available to the program, but Visual Basic does not reuse the object's heap memory, at least not right away.

The optimizing engine of the *garbage collector* determines when it needs to clean up the heap. If the program allocates and frees many reference objects, a lot of the heap may be full of memory that is no longer used. In that case, the garbage collector will decide to clean house.

When it runs, the garbage collector examines all the program's reference variables, parameters that are object references, CPU registers, and other items that might point to heap objects. It uses those values to build a graph describing the heap memory that the program can still access. It then compacts the objects in the heap and updates the program's references so they can find any moved items. The garbage collector then updates the heap itself so that the program can allocate memory from the unused portion.

When it destroys an object, the garbage collector frees the object's memory and any managed resources it contains. It may not free unmanaged resources, however. You can determine when and how an object frees its managed and unmanaged resources by using the Finalize and Dispose methods.

Finalize

When it destroys an object, the garbage collector frees any managed resources used by that object. For example, suppose that an unused object contains a reference to an open file stream. When the garbage collector runs, it notices that the file stream is inaccessible to the program, so it destroys the file stream as well as the object that contains its reference.

However, suppose that the object uses an *unmanaged resource* that is outside of the scope of objects that Visual Basic understands. For example, suppose the object holds an integer representing a file handle, network connection, or channel to a hardware device that Visual Basic doesn't understand. In that case, the garbage collector doesn't know how to free that resource.

You can tell the garbage collector what to do by overriding the class's Finalize method, which is inherited from the Object class. The garbage collector calls an object's Finalize method before permanently removing the object from the heap. Note that there are no guarantees about exactly when the garbage collector calls this method, or the order in which different objects' methods are called. Two objects' Finalize methods may be called in either order even if one contains a reference to the other or if one was freed long before the other. If you must guarantee a specific order, you must provide more specific clean-up methods of your own.

Example program GarbageCollection uses the following code to demonstrate the Finalize method:

```
Public Class Form1
    Public Running As Boolean

    Private Class Junk
        Public MyForm As Form1

        Public Sub New(ByVal my_form As Form1)
            MyForm = my_form
        End Sub

        ' Garbage collection started.
        Protected Overrides Sub Finalize()
            ' Stop making objects.
            MyForm.Running = False
```

```
        End Sub
    End Class

    ' Make objects until garbage collection starts.
    Private Sub btnCreateObjects_Click() Handles btnCreateObjects.Click
        Running = True

        Dim new_obj As Junk
        Dim max_i As Long
        For i As Long = 1 To 100000
            new_obj = New Junk(Me)

            If Not Running Then
                max_i = i
                Exit For
            End If
        Next i
        MessageBox.Show("Allocated " & max_i.ToString & " objects")
    End Sub
End Class
```

code snippet GarbageCollection

The Form1 class defines the public variable Running. It then defines the Junk class, which contains a variable referring to the Form1 class. This class's constructor saves a reference to the Form1 object that created it. Its Finalize method sets the Form1 object's Running value to False.

When the user clicks the form's Create Objects button, the btnCreateObjects_Click event handler sets Running to True and starts creating Junk objects, passing the constructor this form as a parameter. The routine keeps creating new objects as long as Running is True. Note that each time it creates a new object, the old object that the variable new_obj used to point to becomes inaccessible to the program so it is available for garbage collection.

Eventually the program's heap runs low, so the garbage collector executes. When it destroys one of the Junk objects, the object's Finalize subroutine executes and sets the form's Running value to False. When the garbage collector finishes, the btnCreateObjects_Click event handler sees that Running is False, so it stops creating new Junk objects. It displays the number of the last Junk object it created and is done.

In one test, this program created 30,456 Junk objects before the garbage collector ran. In a second trial run immediately after the first, the program created 59,150 objects, and in a third it created 26,191. The garbage collector gives you little control over when it finalizes objects.

Visual Basic also calls every object's Finalize method when the program ends. Again, there are no guarantees about the exact timing or order of the calls to different objects' Finalize methods.

Example program FinalizeObjects, which is available for download on the book's web site, uses the following code to test the Finalize method when the program ends:

```
Public Class Form1
    Private Class Numbered
        Private m_Number As Integer
        Public Sub New(ByVal my_number As Integer)
            m_Number = my_number
        End Sub

        ' Garbage collection started.
        Protected Overrides Sub Finalize()
            ' Display the object's number.
            Debug.WriteLine("Finalized object " & m_Number)
        End Sub
    End Class

    ' Make objects until garbage collection starts.
    Private Sub btnGo_Click() Handles btnGo.Click
        Static i As Integer = 0
        i += 1
        Dim new_numbered As New Numbered(i)
        Debug.WriteLine("Created object " & i.ToString)
    End Sub
End Class
```

code snippet FinalizeObjects

The Numbered class contains a variable m_Number and initializes that value in its constructor. Its Finalize method writes the object's number in the Output window.

The btnGo_Click event handler creates a new Numbered object, giving it a new number. When the event handler ends, the new_numbered variable referring to the Numbered object goes out of scope, so the object is no longer available to the program. If you look at the Output window at this time, you will probably find that the program has not bothered to finalize the object yet. If you click the button several times and then close the application, Visual Basic calls each object's Finalize method. If you click the button five times, you should see five messages displayed by the objects' Finalize methods.

If your class allocates unmanaged resources, you should give it a Finalize method to free them.

> **MEMORY MADNESS**
>
> Better still, use and free unmanaged resources as quickly as possible, not even waiting for finalization if you can. Unmanaged resources, in particular memory allocated in strange ways such as by using Marshal, can cause strange behaviors and leaks if you don't free them properly and promptly.

Dispose

Because Visual Basic doesn't keep track of whether an object is reachable at any given moment, it doesn't know when it can permanently destroy an object until the program ends or the garbage collector reclaims it. That means the object's memory and resources may remain unused for quite a while. The memory itself isn't a big issue. If the program's heap runs out of space, the garbage collector runs to reclaim some of the unused memory.

If the object contains a reference to a resource, however, that resource is not freed until the object is finalized. That can have dire consequences. You generally don't want control of a file, network connection, scanner, or other scarce system resource left to the whims of the garbage collector.

By convention, the Dispose subroutine frees an object's resources. Before a program frees an object that contains important resources, it can call that object's Dispose method to free the resources explicitly.

To handle the case where the program does not call Dispose, the class should also free any unmanaged resources that it holds in its Finalize subroutine. Because Finalize is executed whether or not the program calls Dispose, it must also be able to execute both the Dispose and Finalize subroutines without harm. For example, if the program shuts down some piece of unusual hardware, it probably should not shut down the device twice.

To make building a Dispose method a little easier, Visual Basic defines the IDisposable interface, which declares the Dispose method. If you enter the statement Implements IDisposable and press Enter, Visual Basic creates an empty Dispose method for you.

Example program UseDispose, which is available for download on the book's web site, uses the following code to demonstrate the Dispose and Finalize methods:

```
Public Class Form1
    Private Class Named
        Implements IDisposable

        ' Save our name.
        Public Name As String
        Public Sub New(ByVal new_name As String)
            Name = new_name
        End Sub

        ' Free resources.
        Protected Overrides Sub Finalize()
            Dispose()
        End Sub

        ' Display our name.
        Public Sub Dispose() Implements System.IDisposable.Dispose
            Static done_before As Boolean = False
            If done_before Then Exit Sub
            done_before = True

            Debug.WriteLine(Name)
        End Sub
    End Class

    ' Make an object and dispose it.
    Private Sub btnDispose_Click() Handles btnDispose.Click
        Static i As Integer = 0
        i += 1
        Dim obj As New Named("Dispose " & i)
```

```
            obj.Dispose()
        End Sub

        ' Make an object and do not dispose it.
        Private Sub btnNoDispose_Click() Handles btnNoDispose.Click
            Static i As Integer = 0
            i += 1
            Dim obj As New Named("No Dispose " & i)
        End Sub
    End Class
```

code snippet UseDispose

The Named class has a Name variable that contains a string identifying an object. Its Finalize method simply calls its Dispose method. Dispose uses a static variable named done_before to ensure that it performs its task only once. If it has not already run, the Dispose method displays the object's name. In a real application, this method would free whatever resources the object holds. Whether the program explicitly calls Dispose, or whether the garbage collector calls the object's Finalize method, this code is executed exactly once.

The main program has two buttons labeled Dispose and No Dispose. When you click the Dispose button, the btnDispose_Click event handler makes a Named object, giving it a new name, and then calls the object's Dispose method, which immediately displays the object's name.

When you click the No Dispose button, the btnNoDispose_Click event handler makes a new Named object with a new name and then ends without calling the object's Dispose method. Later, when the garbage collector runs or when the program ends, the object's Finalize method executes and calls Dispose, which displays the object's name.

If your class allocates managed or unmanaged resources and you don't want to wait for the garbage collector to get around to freeing them, you should implement a Dispose method and use it when you no longer need an object.

CONSTANTS, PROPERTIES, AND METHODS

Declaring constants, properties, and methods within a class is the same as declaring them outside a class. The main difference is that the context of the declaration is the class rather than a namespace. For example, a variable declared Private within a class is available only to code within the class.

For information on declaring variables and constants, see Chapter 15, "Data Types, Variables, and Constants." For information on declaring methods, see Chapter 17, "Subroutines and Functions," which also describes property procedures, special routines that implement a property for a class.

One issue that is sometimes confusing is that the unit scope of a class is the class's *code*, not the code within a specific instance of the class. If you declare a variable within a class Private, then all code within the class can access the variable, whether or not that code belongs to the instance of the object that contains the variable.

For example, consider the following Student class. The m_Scores array is Private to the class, so you might think that a Student object could only access its own scores. In fact, any Student object can access any other Student object's m_Scores array as well. The CompareToStudent subroutine calculates the total score for the current Student object. It then calculates the total score for another student and displays the results.

```
Public Class Student
    Public FirstName As String
    Public LastName As String
    Private m_Scores() As Integer
    ...
    Public Sub CompareToStudent(ByVal other_student As Student)
        Dim my_score As Integer = 0
        For i As Integer = 0 To m_Scores.GetUpperBound(0)
            my_score += m_Scores(i)
        Next i

        Dim other_score As Integer = 0
        For i As Integer = 0 To other_student.m_Scores.GetUpperBound(0)
            other_score += other_student.m_Scores(i)
        Next i

        Debug.WriteLine("My score: " & my_score)
        Debug.WriteLine("Other score: " & other_score)
    End Sub
    ...
End Class
```

Breaking the encapsulation provided by the objects in this way can lead to unnecessary confusion. It is generally better to try to access an object's Private data only from within that object. You can provide access routines that make using the object's data easier.

The following version of the Student class includes a TotalScore function that returns the total of a Student object's scores. This function works only with its own object's scores, so it does not pry into another object's data. The CompareToStudent subroutine uses the TotalScore function to display the total score for its object and for a comparison object.

```
Public Class Student
    Public FirstName As String
    Public LastName As String
    Private m_Scores() As Integer
    ...
    Public Sub CompareToStudent(ByVal other_student As Student)
        Debug.WriteLine("My score: " & TotalScore())
        Debug.WriteLine("Other score: " & other_student.TotalScore())
    End Sub

    ' Return the total of this student's scores.
    Private Function TotalScore() As Integer
        Dim total_score As Integer = 0
        For i As Integer = 0 To m_Scores.GetUpperBound(0)
            total_score += m_Scores(i)
        Next i
```

```
            Return total_score
        End Function
        ...
    End Class
```

Function TotalScore is itself declared Private, so only code within the class can use it. In this example, the CompareToStudent subroutine calls another object's Private TotalScore function, so the separation between the two objects is not absolute, but at least CompareToStudent doesn't need to look directly at the other object's data.

EVENTS

Properties let the application view and modify an object's data. Methods let the program invoke the object's behaviors and perform actions. Together, properties and methods let the program send information (data values or commands) to the object.

In a sense, events do the reverse: They let the object send information to the program. When something noteworthy occurs in the object's code, it can raise an event to tell the main program about it. The main program can then decide what to do about the event.

The following sections describe events. They explain how a class declares events and how other parts of the program can catch events.

Declaring Events

A class object can raise events whenever it needs to notify to the program of changing circumstances. Normally, the class declares the event using the Event keyword. The following text shows the Event statement's syntax:

```
[attribute_list] [accessibility] [Shadows] _
Event event_name([parameters]) [Implements interface.event]
```

The following sections describe the pieces of this declaration. Some of these are similar to earlier sections that describe constant, variable, and class declarations. By now, you should notice some familiarity in the use of the *attribute_list* and *accessibility* clauses. For more information on constant and variable declarations, see Chapter 15. For more information on class declarations, refer to the section "Classes" earlier in this chapter.

attribute_list

The *attribute_list* defines attributes that apply to the event. For example, the following declaration defines a description that the code editor should display for the ScoreAdded event:

```
Imports System.ComponentModel

Public Class Student
```

```
            <Description("Occurs when a score is added to the object")>
            Public Event ScoreAdded(ByVal test_number As Integer)
            ...
    End Class
```

accessibility

The *accessibility* value can take one of the following values: Public, Protected, Friend, Protected Friend, or Private. These values determine which pieces of code can catch the event.

The meanings of these keywords is very similar to that of the class accessibility keywords described earlier in this chapter. See the subsection "Accessibility" inside the "Classes" section earlier in this chapter for details.

Shadows

The Shadows keyword indicates that this event replaces an event in the parent class that has the same name but not necessarily the same parameters.

parameters

The *parameters* clause gives the parameters that the event will pass to event handlers. The syntax for the parameter list is the same as the syntax for declaring the parameter list for a subroutine or function.

If an event declares a parameter with the ByRef keyword, the code that catches the event can modify that parameter's value. When the event handler ends, the class code that raised the event can read the new parameter value.

Implements interface.event

If the class implements an interface and the interface defines an event, this clause identifies this event as the one defined by the interface. For example, the IStudent interface shown in the following code defines the ScoreChanged event handler. The Student class implements the IStudent interface. The declaration of the ScoreChanged event handler uses the Implements keyword to indicate that this event handler provides the event handler defined by the IStudent interface.

```
    Public Interface IStudent
        Event ScoreChanged()
        ...

    End Interface

    Public Class Student
        Implements IStudent

        Public Event ScoreChanged() Implements IStudent.ScoreChanged
        ...
    End Class
```

Raising Events

After it has declared an event, a class raises it with the RaiseEvent keyword. It should pass the event whatever parameters were defined in the Event statement.

For example, the Student class shown in the following code declares a ScoreChange event. Its AddScore method makes room for a new score, adds the score to the Scores array, and then raises the ScoreChanged event, passing the event handler the index of the score in the Scores array.

```
Public Class Student
    Private Scores() As Integer
    ...
    Public Event ScoreChanged(ByVal test_number As Integer)
    ...
    Public Sub AddScore(ByVal new_score As Integer)
        ReDim Preserve Scores(Scores.Length)
        Scores(Scores.Length - 1) = new_score
        RaiseEvent ScoreChanged(Scores.Length - 1)
    End Sub
    ...
End Class
```

Catching Events

You can catch an object's events in two ways. First, you can declare the object variable using the WithEvents keyword, as shown in the following code:

```
Private WithEvents TopStudent As Student
```

In the code editor, click the left drop-down list and select the variable's name. In the right drop-down list, select the event. This makes the code editor create an empty event handler similar to the following one. When the object raises its ScoreChanged event, the event handler executes.

```
Private Sub TopStudent_ScoreChanged(ByVal test_number As Integer) _
 Handles TopStudent.ScoreChanged

End Sub
```

The second method for catching events is to use the AddHandler statement to define an event handler for the event. First, write the event handler subroutine. This subroutine must take parameters of the proper type to match those defined by the event's declaration in the class. The following code shows a subroutine that can handle the ScoreChanged event. Note that the parameter's name has been changed, but its accessibility (ByRef or ByVal) and data type must match those declared for the ScoreChanged event.

```
Private Sub HandleScoreChanged(ByVal quiz_num As Integer)

End Sub
```

If the event handler's parameter list is long and complicated, writing an event handler can be tedious. To make this easier, you can declare an object using the WithEvents keyword and use the drop-down lists to give it an event handler. Then you can edit the event handler to suit your needs (change its name, remove the Handles clause, change parameter names, and so forth).

After you build the event handler routine, use the AddHandler statement to assign the routine to a particular object's event. The following statement makes the HandleScoreChanged event handler catch the TopStudent object's ScoreChanged event:

```
AddHandler TopStudent.ScoreChanged, AddressOf HandleScoreChanged
```

Using AddHandler is particularly handy when you want to use the same event handler with more than one object. For example, you might write an event handler that validates a TextBox control's contents to ensure that it contains a valid phone number. By repeatedly using the AddHandler statement, you can make the same event handler validate any number of TextBox controls.

AddHandler is also convenient if you want to work with an array of objects. The following code shows how a program might create an array of Student objects and then use the HandleScoreChanged subroutine to catch the ScoreChanged event for all of them:

```
' Create an array of Student objects.
Const MAX_STUDENT As Integer = 30
Dim students(MAX_STUDENT) As Student
For i As Integer = 0 To MAX_STUDENT
    students(i) = New Student
Next i

' Add ScoreChanged event handlers.
For i As Integer = 0 To MAX_STUDENT
    AddHandler students(i).ScoreChanged, AddressOf HandleScoreChanged
Next i
...
```

If you plan to use AddHandler in this way, you may want to ensure that the events provide enough information for the event handler to figure out which object raised the event. For example, you might modify the ScoreChanged event so that it passes a reference to the object raising the event into the event handler. Then the shared event handler can determine which Student object had a score change.

If you add an event handler with AddHandler, you can later remove it with the RemoveHandler statement. The syntax is the same as the syntax for AddHandler, as shown here:

```
RemoveHandler TopStudent.ScoreChanged, AddressOf HandleScoreChanged
```

Note that relaxed delegates allow an event handler to declare its parameters to have different data types from those provided by the event, as long as the new data types are compatible, or to omit the parameters entirely.

For example, suppose the Student class defines a ScoreChanged event that takes an Integer parameter. The following three subroutines could all catch this event. The first matches the event's parameters precisely. The second version declares its quiz_num parameter to be a Long. Long is compatible with Integer so, when it invokes the event handler, Visual Basic can convert the Integer value into a Long parameter safely. The third version of the event handler declares no parameters so the event's Integer value is ignored.

```
Private Sub HandleScoreChanged1(ByVal quiz_num As Integer)

End Sub

Private Sub HandleScoreChanged2(ByVal quiz_num As Long)

End Sub

Private Sub HandleScoreChanged3()

End Sub
```

STRICTLY SPEAKING

The second version works because you can always store an Integer value in a Long parameter. The reverse is not always true: a Long value won't necessarily fit in an Integer. If the event is declared with a Long parameter but the event handler is declared with an Integer parameter, the result depends on the Option Strict setting. If Option Strict is off, Visual Basic allows the code and tries to convert the Long value into an Integer parameter, possibly crashing at runtime. If Option Strict is on, Visual Basic flags this as an error.

For more information, see the section "Relaxed Delegates" in Chapter 17.

Declaring Custom Events

A second form of event declaration provides more control over the event. This version is quite a bit more complicated and at first can seem very confusing. Skim through the syntax and description that follow and then look at the example. Then if you go back and look at the syntax and description again, they should make more sense. This version is also more advanced and you may not need it often (if ever), so you can skip it for now if you get bogged down.

This version enables you to define routines that are executed when the event is bound to an event handler, removed from an event handler, and called. The syntax is as follows:

```
[attribute_list] [accessibility] [Shadows] _
  Custom Event event_name As delegate_name [Implements interface.event]
    [attribute_list] AddHandler(ByVal value As delegate_name)
      ...
    End AddHandler
```

```
    [attribute_list] RemoveHandler(ByVal value As delegate_name)
        ...
    End RemoveHandler
    [attribute_list] RaiseEvent(delegate_signature)
        ...
    End RaiseEvent
End Event
```

The *attribute_list*, *accessibility*, Shadows, and Implements *interface.event* parts have the same meaning as in the previous, simpler event declaration. See the section, "Declaring Events," earlier in this chapter for information on these pieces.

The *delegate_name* tells Visual Basic the type of event handler that will catch the event. For example, the delegate might indicate a subroutine that takes as a parameter a String variable named new_name. The following code shows a simple delegate for this routine. The delegate's name is NameChangedDelegate. It takes a String parameter named new_name.

```
    Public Delegate Sub NameChangedDelegate(ByVal new_name As String)
```

For more information on delegates, see the section "Delegates" in Chapter 15.

The main body of the custom event declaration defines three routines named AddHandler, RemoveHandler, and RaiseEvent. You can use these three routines to keep track of the event handlers assigned to an object (remember that the event declaration is declaring an event for a class) and to call the event handlers when appropriate.

The AddHandler routine executes when the program adds an event handler to the object. It takes as a parameter a delegate variable named value. This is a reference to a routine that matches the delegate defined for the event handler. For example, if the main program uses the AddHandler statement to add the subroutine Employee_NameChanged as an event handler for this object, the parameter to AddHandler is a reference to the Employee_NameChanged subroutine.

Normally, the AddHandler subroutine saves the delegate in some sort of collection so the RaiseEvent subroutine described shortly can invoke it.

The RemoveHandler subroutine executes when the program removes an event handler from the object. It takes as a parameter a delegate variable indicating the event handler that should be removed. Normally, the RemoveHandler subroutine deletes the delegate from the collection that AddHandler used to originally store the delegate.

Finally, the RaiseEvent subroutine executes when the object's code uses the RaiseEvent statement to raise the event. For example, suppose that the Employee class defines the NameChanged event. When the class's FirstName or LastName property procedure changes an Employee object's name, it uses the RaiseEvent statement to raise the NameChanged event. At that point, the custom RaiseEvent subroutine executes.

Normally, the RaiseEvent subroutine calls the delegates stored by the AddHandler subroutine in the class's collection of event delegates.

Example program CustomEvent, which is available for download on the book's web site, uses the following code to implement a custom NameChanged event. It begins with the FirstName and

LastName property procedures. The Property Set procedures both use the RaiseEvent statement to raise the NameChanged event. This is fairly straightforward and works just as it would if the class used the simpler event declaration.

```vb
Public Class Employee
    ' The FirstName property.
    Private m_FirstName As String
    Public Property FirstName() As String
        Get
            Return m_FirstName
        End Get
        Set(ByVal value As String)
            m_FirstName = value
            RaiseEvent NameChanged(m_FirstName & " " & m_LastName)
        End Set
    End Property

    ' The LastName property.
    Private m_LastName As String
    Public Property LastName() As String
        Get
            Return m_LastName
        End Get
        Set(ByVal value As String)
            m_LastName = value
            RaiseEvent NameChanged(m_FirstName & " " & m_LastName)
        End Set
    End Property

    ' List to hold the event handler delegates.
    Private m_EventDelegates As New ArrayList

    ' Defines the event handler signature.
    Public Delegate Sub NameChangedDelegate(ByVal new_name As String)

    ' Define the custom NameChanged event.
    Public Custom Event NameChanged As NameChangedDelegate
        AddHandler(ByVal value As NameChangedDelegate)
            Debug.WriteLine("AddHandler")
            m_EventDelegates.Add(value)
        End AddHandler

        RemoveHandler(ByVal value As NameChangedDelegate)
            Debug.WriteLine("RemoveHandler")
            m_EventDelegates.Remove(value)
        End RemoveHandler

        RaiseEvent(ByVal new_name As String)
            Debug.WriteLine("RaiseEvent (" & new_name & ")")
            For Each a_delegate As NameChangedDelegate In m_EventDelegates
                a_delegate(new_name.Replace(" ", "+"))
            Next a_delegate
```

```
        End RaiseEvent
    End Event
End Class
```

code snippet CustomEvent

Next, the code defines an ArrayList named m_EventDelegates that it will use to store the event handler delegates. It then uses a Delegate statement to define the types of event handlers that this event will call. In this example, the event handler must be a subroutine that takes a String parameter passed by value.

Now, the code defines the NameChanged custom event. Notice that the Custom Event statement ends with the delegate NameChangedDelegate. If you type this first line and press Enter, Visual Basic creates empty AddHandler, RemoveHandler, and RaiseEvent subroutines for you.

Subroutine AddHandler displays a message and saves the delegate in the m_EventDelegates list. When AddHandler is called, the value parameter refers to an event handler routine that has the proper type.

The subroutine RemoveHandler displays a message and removes a delegate from the m_EventDelegates list. In a real application, this routine would need some error-handling code in case the delegate is not in m_EventDelegates.

When the FirstName and LastName property set procedures use the RaiseEvent statement, the RaiseEvent subroutine executes. This routine's parameter takes whatever value the class used when it used the RaiseEvent statement. This subroutine displays a message and then loops through all the delegates stored in the m_EventDelegates list, invoking each. It passes each delegate the new_name value it received in its parameter, with spaces replaced by plus signs.

The following code demonstrates the NameChanged event handler. It creates a new Employee object and then uses two AddHandler statements to assign the event Employee_NameChanged handler to the object's NameChanged event. This makes the custom AddHandler subroutine execute twice and save two references to the Employee_NameChanged subroutine in the delegate list.

Next, the program sets the Employee object's FirstName. The FirstName property set procedure raises the NameChanged event so the RaiseEvent subroutine executes. RaiseEvent loops through the delegate list and calls the delegates. In this example, that means the subroutine Employee_NameChanged executes twice.

The program then uses a RemoveHandler statement to remove an Employee_NameChanged event handler. The custom RemoveHandler subroutine executes and removes one instance of the Employee_NameChanged subroutine from the delegate list. Next the program sets the Employee object's LastName. The LastName property set procedure uses the RaiseEvent statement so the RaiseEvent subroutine executes. Now there is only one instance of the Employee_NameChanged subroutine in the delegate list, so it is called once. Finally, the code uses the RemoveHandler statement to remove the remaining instance of Employee_NameChanged from the delegate list. The RemoveHandler subroutine executes and removes the instance from the delegate list.

```
Dim emp As New Employee
AddHandler emp.NameChanged, AddressOf Employee_NameChanged
AddHandler emp.NameChanged, AddressOf Employee_NameChanged
emp.FirstName = "Rod"
RemoveHandler emp.NameChanged, AddressOf Employee_NameChanged
emp.LastName = "Stephens"
RemoveHandler emp.NameChanged, AddressOf Employee_NameChanged
```

code snippet CustomEvent

The following text shows the result in the Debug window. It shows where the AddHandler, RaiseEvent, and RemoveHandler subroutines execute. You can also see where the Employee_ NameChanged event handler executes and displays its name.

```
AddHandler
AddHandler
RaiseEvent (Rod )
Employee_NameChanged: Rod+
Employee_NameChanged: Rod+
RemoveHandler
RaiseEvent (Rod Stephens)
Employee_NameChanged: Rod+Stephens
RemoveHandler
```

Shared Variables

If you declare a variable in a class with the Shared keyword, all objects of the class share a single instance of that variable. You can get or set the variable's value through any instance of the class.

For example, suppose the Student class declares a shared NumStudents variable, as shown in the following code:

```
Public Class Student
    Shared NumStudents As Integer
    ...
End Class
```

In this case, all instances of the Student class share the same NumStudents value. The following code creates two Student objects. It uses one to set the shared NumStudents value and uses the other to display the result.

```
Dim student1 As New Student
Dim student2 As New Student
student1.NumStudents = 100
MessageBox.Show(student2.NumStudents)
```

Because all instances of the class share the same variable, any changes to the value that you make using one object are visible to all the others. Figure 26-4 illustrates this idea. Each Student class instance has its own FirstName, LastName, Scores, and other individual data values, but they all share the same NumStudents value.

Because a shared variable is associated with the class as a whole and not a specific instance of the class, Visual Basic lets you refer to it using the class's name in addition to using specific instance variables. In fact, if you try to access a shared variable through a specific instance rather than through the class, Visual Basic flags the code with a warning, although it will run the code.

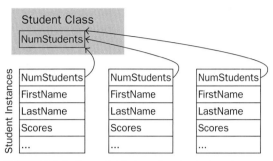

FIGURE 26-4: If a variable in a class is declared Shared, all instances of a class share the same value.

The following code defines a new Student object and uses it to set NumStudents to 100. It then uses the class name to display the NumStudents value.

```
Dim student1 As New Student
student1.NumStudents = 100
MessageBox.Show(Student.NumStudents)
```

Shared Methods

Shared methods are a little less intuitive than shared variables. Like shared variables, shared methods are accessible using the class's name. For example, the NewStudent function shown in the following code is declared with the Shared keyword. This function creates a new Student object, initializes it by adding it to some sort of database, and then returns the new object.

```
Public Class Student
    ...
    ' Return a new Student.
    Public Shared Function NewStudent() As Student
        ' Instantiate the Student.
        Dim new_student As New Student

        ' Add the new student to the database.
        ' ...

        ' Return the new student.
        Return new_student
    End Function
    ...
End Class
```

This type of function that creates a new instance of a class is sometimes called a *factory method*. In some cases, you can use an appropriate constructor instead of a factory method. One time when a factory method is useful is when object creation might fail. If data passed to the method is invalid, some resource (such as a database) prohibits the new object (perhaps a new Student has the same name as an existing Student), or the object may come from more than one place (for example, it may be either a new object or one taken from a pool of existing objects). In those cases, a factory method can return Nothing. A constructor could raise an error, but it cannot return Nothing if it fails.

If you want to force the program to use a factory method rather than creating an instance of the object directly, give the class a private constructor. Code that lies outside of the class cannot use the constructor because it is private. It also cannot use the default constructor associated with the New statement because the class has an explicit constructor. The code must create new objects by using the factory method, which can use the private constructor because it's inside the class.

As is the case with shared variables, you can access a shared method by using any instance of the class or by using the class's name. As is also the case with shared variables, if you access a shared method from an instance of the class, Visual Basic flags it with a warning.

The following code declares the student1 variable and initializes it by calling the NewStudent factory method using the class's name. Next, the code declares student2 and uses the student1 object's NewStudent method to initialize it.

```
Dim student1 As Student = Student.NewStudent()
Dim student2 As Student = student1.NewStudent()
```

One oddity of shared methods is that they can use class variables and methods only if they are also shared. If you think about accessing a shared method through the class name rather than an instance of the class, this makes sense. If you don't use an instance of the class, there is no instance to give the method data.

In the following code, the Student class declares the variable NumStudents with the Shared keyword so shared methods can use that value. It declares the instance variables FirstName and LastName without the Shared keyword, so shared methods cannot use those values. The shared NewStudent method starts by incrementing the shared NumStudents value. It then creates a new Student object and initializes its FirstName and LastName values. It can initialize those values because it is using a specific instance of the class and that instance has FirstName and LastName values.

```
Public Class Student
    Public Shared NumStudents As Integer
    Public FirstName As String
    Public LastName As String
    ...
    ' Return a new Student.
    Public Shared Function NewStudent() As Student
        ' Increment the number of Students loaded.
        NumStudents += 1

        ' Instantiate the Student.
        Dim new_student As New Student
        new_student.FirstName = "<unknown>"
        new_student.LastName = "<unknown>"

        ' Add the new student to the database.
        ...

        ' Return the new student.
```

```
        Return new_student
    End Function
    ...
End Class
```

Figure 26-5 illustrates the situation. The shared NewStudent method is contained within the class itself and has access to the NumStudents variable. If it wanted to use a FirstName, LastName, or Scores value, however, it needs to use an instance of the class.

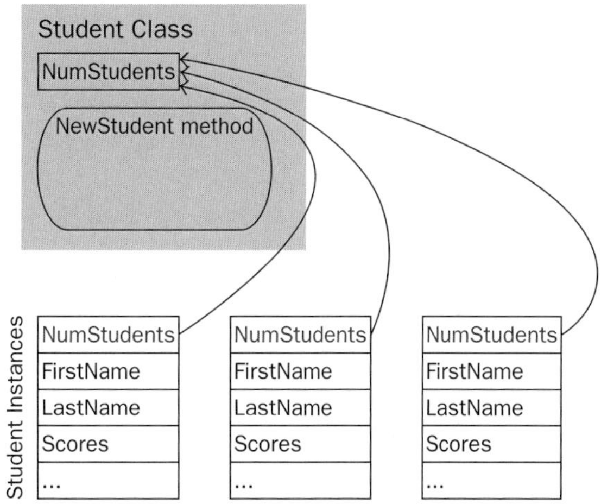

FIGURE 26-5: A shared method can only access other shared variables and methods.

SUMMARY

Classes and structures are very similar. Both are container types that group related variables, methods, and events in a single entity.

Most developers use classes exclusively, primarily because structures are relatively new and developers are more familiar with classes. Structures also cannot take advantage of inheritance.

Another significant factor when picking between classes and structures, however, is their difference in type. Classes are reference types, whereas structures are value types. This gives them different behaviors when defining and initializing objects, and when passing objects to routines by value and by reference.

When you understand the differences between classes and structures, you can select the one that is more appropriate for your application.

If you build enough classes and structures, you may start to have naming collisions. It is common for developers working on different projects to define similar business classes such as Employee, Customer, Order, and InventoryItem. Although these objects may be similar, they may differ in important details. The Customer class defined for a billing application might include lots of account and billing address information, whereas a repair assignment application might focus on the customer's equipment and needs.

Having two Customer classes around can result in confusion and programs that cannot easily interact with each other. Namespaces can help categorize code and differentiate among classes. You can define separate namespaces for the billing and repair assignment applications, and use them to tell which version of the Customer class you need for a particular purpose.

Chapter 27, "Namespaces," describes namespaces in detail. It explains how to create namespaces and how to use them to refer to classes created in other modules.

27

Namespaces

In large applications, it is fairly common to have name collisions. One developer might create an Employee class, while another makes a function named Employee that returns the employee ID for a particular person's name. Or two developers might build different Employee classes that have different properties and different purposes. When multiple items have the same name, this is called a *namespace collision* or *namespace pollution.*

These sorts of name conflicts are most common when programmers are not working closely together. For example, different developers working on the payroll and human resources systems might both define Employee classes with slightly different purposes.

Namespaces enable you to classify and distinguish among programming entities that have the same name. For example, you might build the payroll system in the Payroll namespace and the human resources system in the HumanResources namespace. Then, the two Employee classes would have the fully qualified names Payroll.Employee and HumanResources.Employee, so they could coexist peacefully and the program could tell them apart.

The following code shows how an application would declare these two types of Employee objects:

```
Dim payroll_emp As Payroll.Employee
Dim hr_emp As HumanResources.Employee
```

Namespaces can contain other namespaces, so you can build a hierarchical structure that groups different entities. You can divide the Payroll namespace into pieces to give developers working on that project some isolation from each other.

Namespaces can be confusing at first, but they are really fairly simple. They just break up the code into manageable pieces so that you can group parts of the program and tell different parts from each other.

This chapter describes namespaces. It explains how to use namespaces to categorize programming items and how to use them to select the right versions of items with the same name.

THE IMPORTS STATEMENT

Visual Studio defines thousands of variables, classes, routines, and other entities to provide tools for your applications. It categorizes them in namespaces to prevent name collisions and to make it easier for you to find the items you need.

The Visual Studio root namespaces are named Microsoft and System. The Microsoft namespace includes namespaces that support different programming languages and tools. For example, typical namespaces include CSharp, JScript, and VisualBasic, which contain types and other tools that support the C#, JScript, and Visual Basic languages. The Microsoft namespace also includes the Win32 namespace, which provides classes that handle operating system events and that manipulate the Registry.

The System namespace contains a huge number of useful programming items, including many nested namespaces. For example, the System.Drawing namespace contains classes related to drawing, System.Data contains classes related to databases, System.Threading holds classes dealing with multithreading, and System.Security includes classes for working with security and cryptography.

Note that these namespaces are not necessarily available to your program at all times. For example, by default, the Microsoft.JScript namespace is not available to Visual Basic programs. To use it, you must first add a reference to the Microsoft.JScript.dll library.

Visual Studio includes so many programming tools that the namespace hierarchy is truly enormous. Namespaces are refined into sub-namespaces, which may be further broken into more namespaces until they reach a manageable size. Although this makes it easier to differentiate among all of the different programming entities, it makes the fully qualified names of some classes rather cumbersome.

Example program DrawDashes uses the following code to draw a rectangle inside its form. Fully qualified names such as `System.Drawing.Drawing2D.DashStyle.DashDotDot` are so long that they make the code hard to read.

Available for download on Wrox.com

```
Private Sub DrawDashedBox(ByVal gr As System.Drawing.Graphics)
    gr.Clear(Me.BackColor)

    Dim rect As System.Drawing.Rectangle = Me.ClientRectangle
    rect.X += 10
    rect.Y += 10
    rect.Width -= 20
    rect.Height -= 20

    Using my_pen As New System.Drawing.Pen(System.Drawing.Color.Blue, 5)
        my_pen.DashStyle = System.Drawing.Drawing2D.DashStyle.DashDotDot
        gr.DrawRectangle(my_pen, rect)
    End Using
End Sub
```

code snippet DrawDashes

You can use the Imports statement at the top of the file to make using namespaces easier. After you import a namespace, your code can use the items it contains without specifying the namespace.

Example program DrawDashesWithImports uses the following code. It imports the System.Drawing and System.Drawing.Drawing2D namespaces so it doesn't need to mention the namespaces in its object declarations. This version is much easier to read.

```
Imports System.Drawing
Imports System.Drawing.Drawing2D
. . .
Private Sub DrawDashedBox(ByVal gr As Graphics)
    gr.Clear(Me.BackColor)

    Dim rect As Rectangle = Me.ClientRectangle
    rect.X += 10
    rect.Y += 10
    rect.Width -= 20
    rect.Height -= 20

    Using my_pen As New Pen(Color.Blue, 5)
        my_pen.DashStyle = DashStyle.DashDotDot
        gr.DrawRectangle(my_pen, rect)
    End Using
End Sub
```

code snippet DrawDashesWithImports

DRAWING DEFAULTS

System.Drawing is automatically imported by default in Windows Forms applications so you normally don't need to import it. See the following section for more information on automatic imports.

A file can include any number of Imports statements. The statements must appear at the beginning of the file, and they define namespace shortcuts for the entire file. If you want different pieces of code to use different sets of Imports statements, you must place the pieces of code in different files. If the pieces of code are in the same class, use the Partial keyword so you can split the class into multiple files.

COLLISION PROVISION

If a program imports two namespaces that define classes with the same names, Visual Basic may become confused and give you an *ambiguous reference* error. To fix the problem, the code must use fully qualified names to select the right versions.

For example, suppose that the Payroll and HumanResources modules both define Employee classes. Then you must use the fully qualified names Payroll.Employee and HumanResources.Employee to differentiate between the two within the same file.

Sometimes this problem occurs even with namespaces built by Microsoft. For example, both the System.Windows.Forms and System.Web.UI.Controls namespaces define a CheckBox class, so if your program includes both namespaces, you may encounter an ambiguous reference.

The complete syntax for the Imports statement is as follows:

```
Imports [alias =] namespace[.element]
```

Later sections in this chapter describe namespace aliases and elements in detail.

Automatic Imports

Visual Basic lets you quickly import a namespace for all of the modules in a project. In Solution Explorer, double-click My Project. Click the References tab to display the page shown in Figure 27-1.

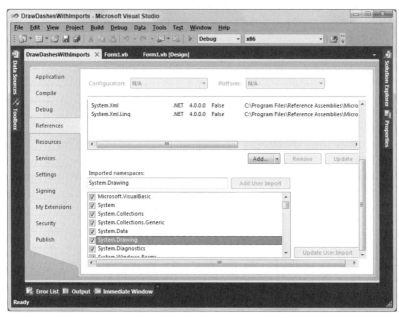

FIGURE 27-1: Use the My Project References tab to import namespaces for every module in a project.

In the Imported namespaces list at the bottom, select the check box next to the namespaces that you want to import. The program's files will be able to use the objects defined in these namespaces, even though they do not include Imports statements.

This is most useful when most of the program's modules need to import the same namespaces. Including the Imports statement in the files makes it easier for developers to see which namespaces are available, however, so you might want to do this instead, particularly if you use unusual namespaces.

By default, Visual Basic loads imports for the type of application you are building. For example, when you start a Windows Form application, Visual Basic imports the following namespaces:

- ➤ Microsoft.VisualBasic
- ➤ System
- ➤ System.Collections
- ➤ System.Collections.Generic
- ➤ System.Data
- ➤ System.Drawing
- ➤ System.Diagnostics
- ➤ System.Windows.Forms

You can use the upper half of the References property page to manage project references. Use the Add and Remove buttons (scrolled off to the right in Figure 27-1) to add and remove references.

Click the Unused References button (scrolled off to the right in Figure 27-1) to see a list of referenced libraries not currently used by the project. Before you distribute the program, you can remove the unused references.

Namespace Aliases

You can use the *alias* clause to define a shorthand notation for the namespace. For instance, the following code imports the System.Drawing.Drawing2D namespace and gives it the alias D2. Later, it uses D2 as shorthand for the fully qualified namespace.

```
Imports D2 = System.Drawing.Drawing2D
...
Dim dash_style As D2.DashStyle = D2.DashStyle.DashDotDot
```

This technique is handy if you need to use two namespaces that define different classes with the same name. Normally, if two namespaces define classes with the same name, you must use the fully qualified class names so that Visual Basic can tell them apart. You can use aliases to indicate the namespaces more concisely.

Suppose that the JobClasses and FinanceStuff namespaces both define an Employee class. If you declare a variable using the unqualified class Employee, Visual Basic would not know which version to use. The following code shows how you can declare fully qualified versions of the Employee class in the JobNamespaces application:

```
Imports JobNamespaces.JobClasses
Imports JobNamespaces.FinanceStuff
...
Dim job_emp As JobNamespaces.JobClasses.Employee
Dim finance_emp As JobNamespaces.FinanceStuff.Employee
...
```

Example program JobNamespaces uses aliases to simplify these declarations. This program uses Job as an alias for MyApplication.JobClasses and Finance as an alias for MyApplication.FinanceStuff.

Now suppose that the JobClasses namespace also defines the Dispatcher class. The FinanceStuff namespace does not define a Dispatcher class, so there is no name conflict between the namespaces. You could use the Job alias to refer to the Dispatcher class, or you could import the JobClasses namespace again without an alias as shown in the following code:

```
Imports JobNamespaces.JobClasses
Imports Job = JobNamespaces.JobClasses
Imports Finance = JobNamespaces.FinanceStuff
...
Dim job_emp As Job.Employee
Dim finance_emp As Finance.Employee
Dim job_dispatcher As Dispatcher
...
```

code snippet JobNamespaces

Namespace Elements

In addition to importing a namespace, you can import an element within the namespace. This is particularly useful for enumerated types.

For example, the following code imports the System.Drawing.Drawing2D namespace, which defines the DrawStyle enumeration. It declares the variable dash_style to be of the DashStyle type and sets its value to DashStyle.DashDotDot.

```
Imports System.Drawing.Drawing2D
...
Dim dash_style As DashStyle = DashStyle.DashDotDot
...
```

Example program DrawDashesImportsDashStyle, which is available for download on the book's web site, uses the following code to import the System.Drawing.Drawing2D.DashStyle enumeration. That allows it to set the value of my_pen.DashStyle to DashDotDot without needing to specify the name of the enumeration (DashStyle).

```
Imports System.Drawing.Drawing2D
Imports System.Drawing.Drawing2D.DashStyle
...
my_pen.DashStyle = DashDotDot
...
```

code snippet DrawDashesImportsDashStyle

THE ROOT NAMESPACE

Every project has a root namespace, and every item in the project is contained directly or indirectly within that namespace. To view or change the project's root namespace, open Solution Explorer and double-click the My Projects entry. View or modify the root namespace on the Application tab's "Root namespace" text box.

MAKING NAMESPACES

You can create new namespaces nested within the root namespace to further categorize your code. The easiest way to create a namespace is by using the Namespace statement. The following code declares a namespace called SchedulingClasses. It includes the definition of the TimeSlot class and possibly other classes.

```
Namespace SchedulingClasses
     Public Class TimeSlot
          ...
     End Class
     ...
End Namespace
```

Code inside the namespace can refer to the TimeSlot class as simply TimeSlot. Code outside of the namespace can refer to the class using the namespace as shown in the following code (assuming MyApplication is the project's root namespace):

```
Dim time_slot As New MyApplication.SchedulingClasses.TimeSlot
```

You can nest namespaces within other namespaces to any depth. In fact, because all of your application's code is contained within the root namespace, any namespace you create is already contained within another namespace. There is no way to make a namespace that is not contained within the root namespace.

If you want to make a namespace that lies outside of the application's root namespace, you must create a library project. Then the code in that project lies within its own root namespace.

The following code defines the DispatchClasses namespace. That namespace contains the AppointmentClasses and JobClasses namespaces, each of which defines some classes.

```
Namespace DispatchClasses
    Namespace AppointmentClasses
        Public Class AppointmentWindow
            ...
        End Class
        ...
    End Namespace

    Namespace JobClasses
        Public Class SkilledJob
            ...
        End Class
        ...
    End Namespace
End Namespace
```

The following code shows how an application could create references to AppointmentWindow and SkilledJob objects using the class's fully qualified names:

```
Dim appt As New MyApplication.DispatchClasses.AppointmentClasses.AppointmentWindow
Dim job As New MyApplication.DispatchClasses.JobClasses.SkilledJob
```

A Namespace statement can only appear at the namespace level. You cannot create a namespace within a module, class, structure, or method.

Inside a namespace, you can define other namespaces, classes, structures, modules, enumerated types, and interfaces. You cannot directly define variables, properties, subroutines, functions, or events. Those items must be contained within some other entity (such as a class, structure, module, or interface).

You can use more than one Namespace statement to define pieces of the same namespace. For example, the following code uses a Namespace statement to make the OrderEntryClasses namespace, and it defines the Employee class inside it. Later, the code uses another Namespace statement to add the Customer class to the same namespace. In this case, the single namespace contains both classes.

```
Namespace OrderEntryClasses
    Public Class Employee
        ...
    End Class
End Namespace
  ...
Namespace OrderEntryClasses
    Public Class Customer
        ...
    End Class
End Namespace
```

Example program NamespaceHierarchy, which is available for download on the book's web site, defines several nested namespaces.

Scattering pieces of a namespace throughout your code will probably confuse other developers. One case where it might make sense to break a namespace into pieces would be if you want to put different classes in different code files, either to prevent any one file from becoming too big or to allow different programmers to work on the files at the same time. In that case, it might make sense to place related pieces of the application in the same namespace but in different files.

CLASSES, STRUCTURES, AND MODULES

Classes, structures, and modules create their own name contexts that are similar in some ways to namespaces. For example, a class or structure can contain the definition of another class or structure, as shown in the following code:

```
Public Class Class1
    Public Class Class2
        ...
    End Class

    Public Structure Struct1
        Public Name As String

        Public Structure Struct2
            Public Name As String
        End Structure
    End Structure
End Class
```

You can access public module members and shared class or structure members using a fully qualified syntax similar to the one used by namespaces. For example, the following code creates the GlobalValues module and defines the public variable MaxJobs within it. Later, the program can set MaxJobs using its fully qualified name.

```
Module GlobalValues
    Public MaxJobs As Integer
    ...
End Module
...
MyApplication.GlobalValues.MaxJobs = 100
```

Although these cases look very similar to namespaces, they really are not. One big difference is that you cannot use a Namespace statement inside a class, structure, or module.

IntelliSense gives another clue that Visual Basic treats classes, structures, and modules differently from namespaces. The IntelliSense popup shown in Figure 27-2 displays curly braces ({}) next to the FinanceStuff and JobClasses namespaces, but it displays different icons for the classes Employer and Form1, and the module Module1. When you select a namespace, IntelliSense also displays a tooltip (on the right in Figure 27-2) giving the namespace's name.

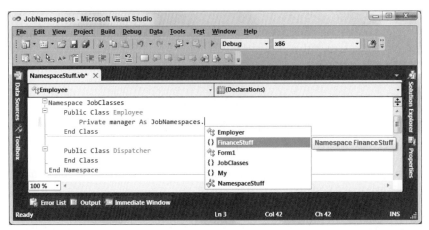

FIGURE 27-2: IntelliSense displays curly braces (({)}) to the left of namespaces such as FinanceStuff and JobClasses.

RESOLVING NAMESPACES

Normally, Visual Basic does a pretty good job of resolving namespaces, and you don't need to worry too much about the process. If you import a namespace, you can omit the namespace in any declarations that you use. If you have not imported a namespace, you can fully qualify declarations that use the namespace and you're done. There are some in-between cases, however, that can be confusing. To understand them, it helps to know a bit more about how Visual Basic resolves namespaces.

When Visual Basic sees a reference that uses a fully qualified namespace, it looks in that namespace for the item it needs and that's that. It either succeeds or fails. For example, the following code declares a variable of type System.Collections.Hashtable. Visual Basic looks in the System.Collections namespace and tries to find the Hashtable class. If the class is not there, the declaration fails.

```
Dim hash_table As New System.Collections.Hashtable
```

When Visual Basic encounters a qualified namespace, it first assumes that it is fully qualified. If it cannot resolve the reference as described in the previous paragraph, it tries to treat the reference as partially qualified and it looks in the current namespace for a resolution. For example, suppose you declare a variable as shown in the following code:

```
Dim emp As JobClasses.Employee
```

In this case, Visual Basic searches the current namespace for a nested namespace called JobClasses. If it finds such a namespace, it looks for the Employee class in that namespace.

If Visual Basic cannot resolve a namespace using these methods, it moves up the namespace hierarchy and tries again. For example, suppose that the current code is in the MyApplication .JobStuff.EmployeeClasses.TimeSheetRoutines namespace. Now, suppose that the SalaryLevel class is defined in the MyApplication.JobStuff namespace and consider the following code:

```
Dim salary_level As New SalaryLevel
```

Visual Basic examines the current namespace MyApplication.JobStuff.EmployeeClasses .TimeSheetRoutines and doesn't find a definition for SalaryLevel. It moves up the namespace hierarchy and searches the MyApplication.JobStuff.EmployeeClasses namespace, again failing to find SalaryLevel. It moves up the hierarchy again to the MyApplication.JobStuff namespace, and there it finally finds the SalaryLevel class.

Movement up the namespace hierarchy can sometimes be a bit confusing. It may lead Visual Basic to resolve references in an ancestor of the current namespace, in some sort of "uncle/aunt" namespace, or in a "cousin" namespace.

For example, consider the namespace hierarchy shown in Figure 27-3. The root namespace MyApplication contains the namespaces BusinessClasses and AssignmentStuff .BusinessClasses defines the Employee and Customer classes. AssignmentStuff contains the AssignmentGlobals module, which defines the MakeAssignment subroutine and a different version of the Employee class.

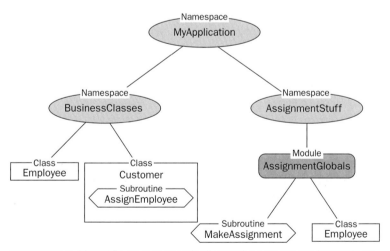

FIGURE 27-3: Visual Basic may search all over the namespace hierarchy to resolve a declaration.

Now, suppose that the Customer class contains the following subroutine:

```
Public Sub AssignEmployee()
    AssignmentStuff.AssignmentGlobals.MakeAssignment(Me)
    ...
End Sub
```

This code lies in the MyApplication.BusinessClasses namespace. Visual Basic cannot find a meaning for the AssignmentStuff namespace locally in that context, so it moves up the namespace hierarchy to MyApplication, where it finds the AssignmentStuff namespace. Within that namespace, it finds the AssignmentGlobals module and the MakeAssignment subroutine that it contains.

Visual Basic can also peer into modules as if their public contents were part of the namespace itself. That means you can rewrite the previous code in the following slightly simpler version:

```
Public Sub AssignEmployee()
    AssignmentStuff.MakeAssignment(Me)
    ...
End Sub
```

In this example, there is only one MakeAssignment subroutine, so there's little doubt that Visual Basic has found the correct one. If different namespaces define items with the same names, the situation can be somewhat more confusing. Suppose that the Customer class declares an object that is from the Employee class defined in the MyApplication.AssignmentStuff namespace, as shown in the following code:

```
Dim emp As New AssignmentStuff.Employee
```

If you understand how Visual Basic performs namespace resolution, you can figure out that the object is of the Employee class defined in the MyApplication.AssignmentStuff namespace. This isn't completely obvious, however.

If you add an Imports statements to the program, the situation gets more confusing. Suppose that the program imports the AssignmentStuff namespace and then the Customer class declares a variable of type Employee. Because this code is in the BusinessClasses namespace, Visual Basic uses that namespace's version of Employee. If the code is in some other namespace (such as MyApplication), the program uses the imported AssignmentStuff version of the class.

Finally, suppose that the program imports both BusinessClasses and AssignmentStuff .AssignmentGlobals and then makes the following declaration in another namespace. In this case, Visual Basic cannot decide which version of the class to use, so it generates an error.

```
Dim emp As Employee
```

This example is so confusing, however, that you would probably be better off restructuring the namespaces and possibly renaming one of the versions of the Employee class rather than trying to figure out how Visual Basic is resolving the namespaces.

You can simplify these issues by avoiding duplicate names across all namespaces. When you do use duplicate names, you can use fully qualified namespaces to avoid ambiguity. You can also use Imports statements to make namespace aliases and then use the aliases to avoid ambiguity more concisely.

SUMMARY

Namespaces are everywhere in Visual Basic. Every piece of code you write is contained in some namespace, even if it is only the application's root namespace. Despite their pervasiveness, many developers never need to use namespaces explicitly, so they find them somewhat mystifying.

Namespaces are really quite simple, however. They merely divide programming items into a hierarchy. They enable you to categorize related items and resolve name collisions in different parts of the application.

You can use the Imports statement to allow the program to refer to items in a namespace without giving fully qualified names. A namespace alias lets you explicitly specify an item's namespace in an abbreviated form. This is particularly useful to resolve ambiguous names that appear in more than one namespace included in Imports statements.

This chapter describes namespaces in general. Chapter 28 "Collection Classes," describes some of the useful classes for grouping object classes, including those in the System.Collections and System.Collections.Generic namespaces.

28

Collection Classes

Visual Basic .NET includes a large assortment of pre-built classes that store and manage groups of objects. These collection classes provide a wide variety of different features, so the right class for a particular purpose depends on your application.

For example, an array is good for storing objects in a particular fixed order. An ArrayList enables you to add, remove, and rearrange its objects much more easily than an array does. A Queue lets a program easily add items and remove them in first in, first out order. In contrast, a Stack lets the program remove items in last in, first out order.

This chapter describes these different kinds of collection classes and provides tips for selecting the right one for various purposes.

WHAT IS A COLLECTION?

The word *collection* means a group of objects that should be kept together. For example, a coin collection is a group of coins that you keep together because they are rare, valuable, or otherwise interesting.

Unfortunately, the idea of a collection is such a useful concept that Visual Basic adopted the word and made a specific class named Collection. The Collection class *does* keep a group of objects together, but it reserves for its own use the perfect word for other similar kinds of groups of objects.

That leads to some semantic ambiguity when you talk about collection classes. Do you mean the Collection class? Or do you mean some other class that groups objects? Even the Visual Basic documentation has this problem and sometimes uses *collection classes* to mean classes that group things together.

This chapter describes the Collection class as well as other collection classes.

One of the most basic Visual Basic entities that groups objects is an *array*. An array stores data values or references to objects in a simple block of memory with one entry directly following another. The Array *class* provides some special methods for manipulating arrays (such as reversing, sorting, or searching an array).

The Collection class provides a few specific features for working with its group of objects. It enables you to add an item to the Collection, optionally specifying a key for the item. You can then search for the item or remove the item using its key or its index in the Collection.

One of the most useful features of the Collection class is that it supports enumerators and For Each loops. That lets you easily loop over the objects in a Collection without worrying about the number of objects it contains.

Other classes derived from the Collection class provide additional features. For example, the Hashtable class can store a large number of objects with associated keys very efficiently. Dictionary is essentially a strongly-typed generic Hashtable so, although the Hashtable uses the Object data type for its key/value pairs, the Dictionary uses more specific data types that you specify such as Strings or Employees. The section "Dictionaries" later in this chapter describes the Dictionary class in more detail.

The Queue class makes it easy to work with objects on a first in, first out (FIFO) basis, whereas the Stack class helps you work with objects in a last in, first out order (LIFO).

The remainder of this chapter describes these classes in detail.

ARRAYS

Visual Basic .NET provides two basic kinds of arrays. First, it provides the normal arrays that you get when you declare a variable by using parentheses. For example, the following code declares an array of Integers named "squares." The array contains 11 items with indexes ranging from 0 to 10. The code loops over the items, setting each one's value. Next, it loops over the values again, adding them to a string. When it has finished building the string, the program displays the result.

```
Private Sub ShowSquaresNormalArray()
    Dim squares(10) As Integer

    For i As Integer = 0 To 10
        squares(i) = i * i
    Next i

    Dim txt As String = ""
    For i As Integer = 0 To 10
        txt &= squares(i).ToString & vbCrLf
    Next i
    MessageBox.Show(txt)
End Sub
```

code snippet ShowSquares

INITIALIZING ARRAYS

You can initialize an array as in the following code:

```
Dim fibonacci() As Integer = {1, 1, 2, 3, 5, 8, 13, 21, 33, 54, 87}
```

If you have Option Infer turned on, you can omit the data type as in the following:

```
Dim numbers() = {1, 2, 3}
```

For more information on array initialization, see the section "Initializing Arrays" in Chapter 15, "Data Types, Variables, and Constants."

The Visual Basic Array class provides another kind of array. This kind of array is actually an object that provides methods for managing the items stored in the array.

The following code shows the previous version of the code rewritten to use an Array object. This version creates the array by using the Array class's shared CreateInstance method, passing it the data type that the array should contain and the number of items that it should hold. The code then loops over the items using the array's SetValue method to set the items' values. If you have Option Strict turned off, the code can set the items' values exactly as before by using the statement squares(i) = i * i. If Option Strict is on, you need to use SetValue. Next, the program loops over the items again, using the array's GetValue method to add the item values to a string. If Option Strict is off, you can use the same syntax as before: txt &= squares(i).ToString & vbCrLf. If Option Strict is on, you need to use the array's GetValue method. After building the string, the program displays it in a message box as before.

```
Private Sub ShowSquaresArrayObject()
    Dim squares As Array =
        Array.CreateInstance(GetType(Integer), 11)

    For i As Integer = 0 To 10
        squares.SetValue(i * i, i)
    Next i

    Dim txt As String = ""
    For i As Integer = 0 To 10
        txt &= squares.GetValue(i).ToString & vbCrLf
    Next i
    MessageBox.Show(txt)
End Sub
```

code snippet ShowSquares

Example program ShowSquares uses similar code to build a list of squares by using a normal array and by using an Array object.

The following sections describe the similarities and differences between normal arrays and Array objects.

Array Dimensions

Both normal variable arrays and Array objects can support multiple dimensions. The following statement declares a three-dimensional array with 11 items in the first dimension, 11 in the second, and 21 in the third. It then sets the value for the item in position (1, 2, 3).

```
Dim values(10, 10, 20) As Integer
values(1, 2, 3) = 100
```

The following code does the same thing with an Array object:

```
Dim values As Array =
    Array.CreateInstance(GetType(Integer), 11, 21, 31)
values.SetValue(100, 1, 2, 3)
```

If Option Strict is off, the code can use the same syntax for getting and setting the Array item's value. The following code sets the (1, 2, 3) item's value to 100 and then displays its value (100):

```
Option Strict Off
. . .
values(1, 2, 3) = 100
Debug.WriteLine(values(1, 2, 3))
```

Lower Bounds

A normal array of variables always has lower bound 0 in every dimension. The following code declares an array with indexes ranging from 0 to 10:

```
Dim values(10) As Integer
```

You can fake a variable array that has nonzero lower bounds, but it requires extra work on your part. You must add or subtract an appropriate amount from each index to map the indexes you want to use to the underlying zero-based indexes.

Array objects can handle nonzero lower bounds for you. The following code creates a two-dimensional array with indexes ranging from 1 to 10 in the first dimension, and 101 to 120 in the second dimension:

```
Dim dimension_lengths() As Integer = {10, 20}
Dim lower_bounds() As Integer = {1, 101}
Dim values As Array =
    Array.CreateInstance(GetType(Integer), dimension_lengths, lower_bounds)
```

The code first defines an array containing the number of elements it wants for each dimension (10 in the first dimension and 20 in the second dimension). It then creates an array containing the lower bounds it wants to use for each dimension (the first dimension starts with index 1 and the second dimension starts with index 101).

The code then calls the Array class's shared CreateInstance method, passing it the data type of the array's objects, the array of dimension lengths, and the array of lower bounds. The CreateInstance method uses the arrays of lower bounds and dimensions to create an Array object with the appropriate bounds.

The following code sets the values in this array. The last two parameters in the call to SetValue give the items' positions in the Array.

```
For i As Integer = 1 To 10
    For j As Integer = 101 To 120
        values.SetValue(i * 100 + j, i, j)
    Next j
Next i
```

If Option Strict is off, the program can use the following simpler syntax:

```
For i As Integer = 1 To 10
    For j As Integer = 101 To 120
        values(i, j) = i * 100 + j
    Next j
Next i
```

Resizing

You can use the ReDim statement to change a normal array's dimensions. Add the Preserve keyword if you want the array to keep its existing values, as shown here:

```
Dim values(100) As Integer
. . .
ReDim Preserve values(200)
```

An Array object cannot resize itself, but it is relatively easy to copy an Array object's items to another Array object. The following code creates a values array containing 101 items with indexes ranging from 0 to 100. Later, it creates a new Array object containing 201 items and uses the values array's CopyTo method to copy its values into the new array. The second parameter to CopyTo gives the index in the destination array where the copy should start placing values.

```
Dim values As Array =
    Array.CreateInstance(GetType(Integer), 101)
. . .
Dim new_array As Array =
    Array.CreateInstance(GetType(Integer), 201)
values.CopyTo(new_array, 0)
values = new_array
```

The Array class's shared Copy method allows you greater control. It lets you specify the index in the source array where the copy should start, the index in the destination array where the items should be copied, and the number of items to be copied.

Although building a new Array object and copying items into it is more cumbersome than using ReDim to resize a variable array, the process is surprisingly fast.

Speed

There's no doubt that arrays of variables are much faster than Array objects. In one test, setting and getting values in an Array object took more than 100 times as long as performing the same operations in a variable array.

If your application performs only a few hundred or a thousand array operations, the difference is unimportant. If your application must access array values many millions of times, you may need to consider using an array of variables even if the Array class would be more convenient for other reasons (such as nonzero lower bounds).

> **THE NEED FOR SPEED**
>
> Normally I don't recommend that you focus too much on speed issues until you're certain there will be a problem. Usually it's much more important to make the program work correctly than it is to squeeze the last iota of performance out of it. Many applications fail because they don't work reliably or correctly, but I've only seen a few fail because they weren't fast enough.
>
> However, the difference in speed between arrays and the Array class is huge. If you know your program is array-intensive, you can save some effort by using normal arrays instead of the Array class from the beginning.

Microsoft has also optimized one-dimensional variable arrays, so they are faster than multidimensional arrays. The difference is much less dramatic than the difference between variable arrays and Array classes, however.

Example program ArraySpeeds, which is available for download on the book's web site, compares the speeds of variable arrays and Array objects. Enter the number of items that you want to use in the arrays and click Go. The program builds one- and two-dimensional arrays and Array objects holding integers. It then fills the arrays and displays the elapsed time.

Figure 28-1 shows the results. Variable arrays are much faster than array classes. One-dimensional variable arrays generally seem to be slightly faster than two-dimensional arrays.

FIGURE 28-1: Variable arrays are faster than array classes.

Other Array Class Features

The Array class provides several other useful shared methods. For example, the IndexOf and LastIndexOf methods return the position of a particular item in an Array.

Methods such as IndexOf and LastIndexOf would be a strong argument supporting Array objects over normal arrays of variables if it weren't for one somewhat surprising fact: Those same methods work with regular arrays of variables, too! The following code fills an array of integers and then uses Array methods to display the indexes of the first item with value 6 and the last item with value 3:

```
Dim values(10) As Integer
For i As Integer = 0 To 10
    values(i) = i
Next i

MessageBox.Show(Array.IndexOf(values, 6).ToString)
MessageBox.Show(Array.LastIndexOf(values, 3).ToString)
```

The following sections describe some of the Array class's other useful shared methods. All of these work both for arrays of variables and Array objects.

Example program ArrayTests, which is available for download on the book's web site, demonstrates the Array class's IndexOf, LastIndexOf, Reverse, and BinarySearch methods. It also demonstrates the Sort method for arrays containing integers, objects that implement the IComparable interface, and objects that can be sorted with IComparer objects.

Array.Reverse

The Array.Reverse method reverses the order of the items in an array. There's nothing particularly confusing about this method. It can easily reverse its items even if the items are not things that you can reasonably compare. For example, it can reverse an array of integers, strings, StockOption objects, or TreeView controls.

Array.Sort

The Array.Sort method sorts the items in the array. To sort the items, this method must compare them to each other. That means the items must be things that can be reasonably compared, such as integers, strings, or dates. More precisely, the method can sort the items if they implement the IComparable interface, meaning they contain the means to compare themselves to each other.

The following code shows a Person class that implements the IComparable interface. The class defines two public strings, FirstName and LastName. For convenience, it also defines a constructor and a ToString function. The code then defines the CompareTo function that is required by the IComparable interface. This function should compare the value of the current object to the value of the object passed as a parameter. It should return –1 if the current object should come before the parameter, 0 if neither object must come before the other, and 1 if the parameter should come before the current object. The String.Compare function makes exactly that calculation for two strings, so the CompareTo function uses it to compare the two Person objects' names. You could use a more complicated CompareTo function to order just about anything.

```
Public Class Person
    Implements IComparable

    Public FirstName As String
    Public LastName As String

    Public Sub New(ByVal first_name As String, ByVal last_name As String)
        FirstName = first_name
        LastName = last_name
    End Sub

    Public Overrides Function ToString() As String
        Return LastName & ", " & FirstName
    End Function

    Public Function CompareTo(ByVal obj As Object) As Integer _
     Implements System.IComparable.CompareTo
        Dim other_Person As Person = DirectCast(obj, Person)
        Return String.Compare(Me.ToString, other_Person.ToString)
    End Function
End Class
```

code snippet ArrayTests

If a program has an array of Person objects, the Array.Sort method will sort the objects by last name followed by first name.

You can sort objects that do not implement the IComparable interface if you pass the Sort method an object that can sort them. For example, suppose you define a Manager class that does not implement the IComparable interface. The following code shows a ManagerComparer class that implements the IComparer interface. Its Compare method compares two Manager objects and returns –1, 0, or 1 to indicate the one that should come first. The call to DirectCast converts the Compare method's parameters from Objects (specified by the IComparer interface) to Managers.

```
Public Class ManagerComparer
    Implements IComparer

    Public Function Compare(ByVal x As Object, ByVal y As Object) As Integer _
     Implements System.Collections.IComparer.Compare
        Dim mgr1 As Manager = DirectCast(x, Manager)
        Dim mgr2 As Manager = DirectCast(y, Manager)

        Return String.Compare(mgr1.ToString, mgr2.ToString)
    End Function
End Class
```

code snippet ArrayTests

The following code uses a ManagerComparer object to sort an array of Manager objects named dept_managers:

```
' Sort.
Array.Sort(dept_managers, New ManagerComparer)

' Display the results.
Dim txt As String = ""
For i As Integer = 0 To dept_managers.GetUpperBound(0)
    txt &= dept_managers(i).ToString() & vbCrLf
Next i
MessageBox.Show(txt)
```

code snippet ArrayTests

Other overloaded versions of the Sort method let you sort two arrays (one containing keys and the other values) in tandem or sort only parts of the array.

Array.BinarySearch

If the array contains items that are sorted, and the items implement the IComparable interface, then the Array.BinarySearch method uses a binary search algorithm to locate a specific item within the array.

For example, suppose that the array contains Person objects as defined in the previous section. Then you could use the following code to find the object representing Rod Stephens in the people array. The code starts by using Array.Sort to sort the array. Next the program makes a new Person object that has the name Rod Stephens to represent the target value. The program calls the Array. BinarySearch method to find the index of the object with the target name.

```
' Sort the array.
Array.Sort(people)

' Find Rod Stephens.
Dim target_person As New Person("Rod", "Stephens")
Dim target_index As Integer = Array.BinarySearch(people, target_person)
MessageBox.Show(people(target_index).ToString)
```

code snippet ArrayTests

Binary search is extremely fast, so it works well if you need to find an item within a sorted array. If the items are not sorted, you should consider using a database or Hashtable object to store and find items. See the section "Hashtable" later in this chapter for more information.

COLLECTIONS

The Visual Basic collection classes basically hold items and don't provide a lot of extra functionality. Other classes described later in this chapter provide more features.

The following sections describe the simple collection classes in Visual Basic: ArrayList, StringCollection, and NameValueCollection. They also describe strongly typed collections that you can build to make code that uses these classes a bit easier to debug and maintain.

ArrayList

The *ArrayList* class is a resizable array. You can add and remove items from any position in the list and it resizes itself accordingly. The following table describes some of the class's more useful properties and methods.

PROPERTY/METHOD	PURPOSE
Add	Adds an item at the end of the list.
AddRange	Adds the items in an object implementing the ICollection interface to the end of the list.
BinarySearch	Returns the index of an item in the list. The items must implement the IComparable interface, or you must provide the Sort method with an IComparer object.
Capacity	Gets or sets the number of items that the list can hold. For example, if you know that you will need to add 1000 items to the list, you may get better performance by setting Capacity to 1000 before starting, rather than letting the object grow incrementally as you add the items.
Clear	Removes all of the items from the list. The Capacity property remains unchanged, so the ArrayList keeps any space it has previously allocated to improve performance.
Contains	Returns True if a specified item is in the list.
CopyTo	Copies some or the entire list into a one-dimensional Array object.
Count	Returns the number of items currently in the list. This is always less than or equal to Capacity.
GetRange	Returns an ArrayList containing the items in part of the list.
IndexOf	Returns the zero-based index of the first occurrence of a specified item in the list.
Insert	Adds an item at a particular position in the list.
InsertRange	Adds the items in an object implementing the ICollection interface to a particular position in the list.
Item	Returns the item at a particular position in the list.
LastIndexOf	Returns the zero-based index of the last occurrence of a specified item in the list.
Remove	Removes the first occurrence of a specified item from the list.

PROPERTY/METHOD	PURPOSE
RemoveAt	Removes the item at the specified position in the list.
RemoveRange	Removes the items in the specified positions from the list.
Reverse	Reverses the order of the items in the list.
SetRange	Replaces the items in part of the list with new items taken from an ICollection object.
Sort	Sorts the items in the list. The items must implement the IComparable interface, or you must provide the Sort method with an IComparer object.
ToArray	Copies the list's items into a one-dimensional array. The array can be an array of objects, an array of a specific type, or an Array object (holding objects).
TrimToSize	Reduces the list's allocated space so that it is just big enough to hold its items. This sets Capacity = Count.

A single ArrayList object can hold objects of many different kinds. The following code creates an ArrayList and adds a string, Form object, integer, and Bitmap to it. It then loops through the items in the list and displays their types.

```
Dim array_list As New ArrayList
array_list.Add("What?")
array_list.Add(Me)
array_list.Add(1001)
array_list.Add(New Bitmap(10, 10))
For Each obj As Object In array_list
    Debug.WriteLine(obj.GetType.ToString)
Next obj
```

code snippet UseArrayList

The following text shows the results:

```
System.String
UseArrayList.Form1
System.Int32
System.Drawing.Bitmap
```

The value displayed for the second item depends on the name of the project (in this case, UseArrayList).

Example program UseArrayList demonstrates several ArrayList methods.

StringCollection

A *StringCollection* is similar to an ArrayList, except that it can hold only strings. Because it works only with strings, this class provides some extra type checking that the ArrayList does not. If your program tries to add an Employee object to a StringCollection, the collection raises an error.

To take advantage of this extra error checking, you should always use a StringCollection instead of an ArrayList if you are working with strings. Of course, if you need other features (such as the fast lookups provided by a Hashtable), you should use one of the classes described in the following sections.

Strongly Typed Collections

A *strongly typed collection* is a collection class built to work with a particular data type. An ArrayList can store objects of any data type. A StringCollection is strongly typed to work only with strings. That gives you extra error checking that makes finding and fixing programming mistakes easier. If the program tries to insert an IncidentReport object into a StringCollection, the collection immediately raises an error and the problem is relatively easy to find.

Similarly, you can define your own collection classes that are strongly typed. For example, you could make an OrderCollection class that holds Order items. If the program tries to add a Manager or Secretary object to it, the collection raises an error.

To build a strongly typed collection from scratch, create a new class that inherits from System. Collections.CollectionBase. Inheriting from this class automatically gives your class an ArrayList object named List. It also gives your class some inherited routines that do not depend on the type of object you want the collection to hold. For example, the RemoveAt method removes the object at a specific index in the list.

Your class can implement other methods for adding and retrieving items in the collection. For example, it can implement the Add, Remove, and Item methods.

Fortunately, you don't need to build these methods from scratch. You can simply delegate them to the inherited List object. For example, the Add method can simply call List.Add, as shown in the following code:

```
' Add an Employee.
Public Sub Add(ByVal value As Employee)
    List.Add(value)
End Sub
```

This code does nothing other than call the List object's methods. The only magic here is that the EmployeeCollection class's Add method takes a parameter of a particular type (Employee), whereas the List object's Add method takes a generic Object as a parameter. It is the EmployeeCollection class's insistence on Employee objects that makes the collection strongly typed.

The Add and Item methods are about the minimum useful feature set you can provide for a strongly typed collection class.

The following table lists the standard methods provided by a strongly typed collection class. The third column indicates whether the CollectionBase parent class automatically provides the method, or whether you must delegate the method to the List object.

METHOD	PURPOSE	PROVIDED BY
Add	Adds an item to the collection	List
Capacity	Returns the amount of space in the collection	CollectionBase
Clear	Removes all items from the collection	CollectionBase
Contains	Returns True if the collection contains a particular item	List
CopyTo	Copies items from the collection into an array	List
Count	Returns the number of items in the collection	CollectionBase
IndexOf	Returns the index of an item	List
InnerList	Returns an ArrayList holding the collection's objects	CollectionBase
Insert	Inserts an item at a specific position	List
Item	Returns the item at a specific position	List
List	Returns an IList holding the collection's objects	CollectionBase
Remove	Removes an item	List
RemoveAt	Removes the item at a specific position	CollectionBase

You can also add other more specialized methods if they would be useful in your application. For example, you could add methods for working with object field values rather than with the objects themselves. You might make an overloaded version of the Item method that takes as parameters a first and last name and returns the corresponding Employee object if it is in the list. You could also modify the simple Add method shown previously so that it doesn't allow duplicates. And you could make an Add function that takes first and last names as parameters, creates a new Employee object using those names, and returns the new object.

Example program EmployeeCollection, which is available for download on the book's web site, builds a strongly typed collection of Employee objects that inherits from the CollectionBase class.

An additional benefit that comes with inheriting from the CollectionBase class is For Each support. The following code shows how a program might use an EmployeeCollection class named emp_list. It creates the collection and adds some Employee objects to the list. It then uses a For Each loop to display the Employees.

```
Dim emp_list As New EmployeeCollection
emp_list.Add(New Employee("Ann", "Anderson"))
emp_list.Add(New Employee("Bart", "Baskerville"))
```

```
. . .

For Each emp As Employee In emp_list
    Debug.WriteLine(emp.ToString)
Next emp
```

code snippet MakeEmployeeCollection

Generics provide another method for building strongly typed collections. Refer to the section "Generics" later in this chapter for more information on generic collections. For more general information on generics, see Chapter 29, "Generics."

Read-Only Strongly Typed Collections

The CollectionBase class enables you to build a strongly typed collection class that allows a program to store and retrieve values. In some cases, you might want a function to return a collection of objects that the calling program cannot modify. For example, suppose that your function returns a list of your company's production locations. You don't want the program to modify the list because it cannot change the locations. In this case, you can build a read-only strongly typed collection.

You can do this much as you build a strongly typed collection. Instead of deriving the new collection class from CollectionBase, however, derive it from the ReadOnlyCollectionBase class. Provide read-only Item methods, but do not provide any Add or Remove methods. The class itself can access its inherited InnerList object to add and remove items, but it must not give the program using your class access to that object.

Your program still needs a way to get objects into the collection, however. One method is to build the collection class in a separate library project and give it initialization methods declared with the Friend keyword. Other code in the library project could use those methods while the main program could not.

Another technique is to pass initialization data to the class's constructor. Your code creates the collection and returns it to the main program. The main program cannot change the collection's contents. It can create an instance of the collection of its own, but it cannot modify the one you built.

NameValueCollection

The *NameValueCollection* class is a collection that can hold more than one string value for a particular key (name). For example, you might use employee names as keys. The string values associated with a particular key could include extension, job title, employee ID, and so forth. Of course, you could also store the same information by putting extension, job title, employee ID, and the other fields in an object or structure, and then storing the objects or structures in some sort of collection class such as an ArrayList. A NameValueCollection, however, is very useful if you don't know ahead of time how many strings will be associated with each key.

The following table describes some of the NameValueCollection's most useful properties and methods.

PROPERTY/METHOD	DESCRIPTION
Add	Adds a new name/value pair to the collection. If the collection already holds an entry for the name, it adds the new value to that name's values.
AllKeys	Returns a string array holding all of the key values.
Clear	Removes all names and values from the collection.
CopyTo	Copies items starting at a particular index into a one-dimensional Array object. This copies only the items (see the Item property), not the keys.
Count	Returns the number of key/value pairs in the collection.
Get	Gets the item for a particular index or name as a comma-separated list of values.
GetKey	Returns the key for a specific index.
GetValues	Returns a string array containing the values for a specific name or index.
HasKeys	Returns True if the collection contains any non-null keys.
Item	Gets or sets the item for a particular index or name as a comma-separated list of values.
Keys	Returns a collection containing the keys.
Remove	Removes a particular name and all of its values.
Set	Sets the item for a particular index or name as a comma-separated list of values.

Note that there is no easy way to remove a particular value from a name. For example, if a person's name is associated with extension, job title, and employee ID, it is not easy to remove only the job title.

The following statement shows one approach to removing a person's JobTitle entry, although you would need to modify it slightly if you didn't know whether the JobTitle entry was last in the list (so it might or might not be followed by a comma):

```
nvc.Item("RodStephens") = nvc.Item("RodStephens").Replace("JobTitle,", "")
```

Example program UseNameValueCollection, which is available for download on the book's web site, demonstrates NameValueCollection class features.

DICTIONARIES

A *dictionary* is a collection that associates keys with values. You look up a key, and the dictionary provides you with the corresponding value. This is similar to the way a NameValueCollection works, except that a dictionary's keys and values need not be strings, and a dictionary associates each key with a single value object.

Visual Studio provides several different kinds of dictionary classes that are optimized for different uses. Their differences come largely from the ways in which they store data internally. Though you don't need to understand the details of how the dictionaries work internally, you do need to know how they behave so that you can pick the best one for a particular purpose.

Because all of the dictionary classes provide the same service (associating keys with values), they have roughly the same properties and methods. The following table describes some of the most useful of these.

PROPERTY/METHOD	DESCRIPTION
Add	Adds a key/value pair to the dictionary.
Clear	Removes all key/value pairs from the dictionary.
Contains	Returns True if the dictionary contains a specific key.
CopyTo	Copies the dictionary's data starting at a particular position into a one-dimensional array of DictionaryEntry objects. The DictionaryEntry class has Key and Value properties.
Count	Returns the number of key/value pairs in the dictionary.
Item	Gets or sets the value associated with a key.
Keys	Returns a collection containing all of the dictionary's keys.
Remove	Removes the key/value pair with a specific key.
Values	Returns a collection containing all of the dictionary's values.

The following sections describe different Visual Studio dictionary classes in more detail.

ListDictionary

A *ListDictionary* stores its data in a linked list. In a linked list, each item is held in an object that contains its data plus a reference or *link* to the next item in the list. Figure 28-2 illustrates a linked list. This list contains the key/value pairs Appetizer/Salad, Entrée/Sandwich, Drink/Water, and Dessert/Cupcake. The link out of the Dessert/Cupcake item is set to Nothing, so the program can tell when it has reached the end of the list. A reference variable inside the ListDictionary class, labeled Top in Figure 28-2, points to the first item in the list.

The links in a linked list make adding and removing items relatively easy. The ListDictionary simply moves the links to point to new objects, add objects, remove objects, or insert objects between two others. For example, to add a new item at the top of the list, you create the new item, set its link to point to the item that is currently at the top, and then make the list's Top variable point to the new item. Other rearrangements are almost as easy. For more information on how linked lists work, see a book on algorithms and data structures such as *Data Structures and Algorithms Using Visual Basic.NET* (McMillan, Cambridge University Press, 2005).

Unfortunately, if the list grows long, finding items in it can take a long time. To find an item in the list, the program starts at the top and works its way down, following the links between items, until it finds the one it wants. If the list is short, that doesn't take very long. If the list holds 100,000 items, this means potentially a 100,000-item crawl from top to bottom. That means a ListDictionary object's performance degrades if it contains too many items.

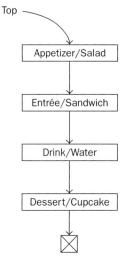

FIGURE 28-2: Each item in a linked list keeps a reference to the next item in the list.

If you only need to store a few hundred items in the dictionary and you don't need to access them frequently, a ListDictionary is fine. If you need to store 100,000 entries, or if you need to access the dictionary's entries a huge number of times, you may get better performance using a "heavier" object such as a Hashtable. A Hashtable has more overhead than a ListDictionary but is faster at accessing its entries.

Hashtable

A *Hashtable* looks a lot like a ListDictionary on the outside, but internally it stores its data in a very different way. Rather than using a linked list, this class uses a hash table to hold data.

A hash table is a data structure that allows extremely fast access to items using their keys. It works by mapping an object's key into a bucket by calculating the key's *hash value*.

For example, suppose that you want to make a dictionary associating Employee objects with their Social Security numbers. You could make an array holding 10 buckets and then map employees to bucket numbers using the last digit of their Social Security numbers. Employee 123-45-6789 goes in bucket 9, employee 111-22-3333 goes in bucket 3, and employee 865-29-8361 goes in bucket 1.

This kind of hash table is easy to enlarge. If you add a few dozen employees, you might use 100 buckets and map Social Security numbers using their last two digits. Then employee 123-45-6789 goes in bucket 89, employee 111-22-3333 goes in bucket 33, and employee 865-29-8361 goes in bucket 61.

More employees? Make more buckets! You can use 1000, 10,000, or more buckets if necessary.

To find an employee's data in the dictionary, you only need to calculate the hash value (last digits of Social Security number) and then look in that bucket. For a large dictionary, this is much faster than digging through a linked list. If you have 10,000 employees perfectly divided one to a bucket in a table of 10,000 buckets, you only need to look in one bucket to find the data you want. That's a lot faster than slogging through a 10,000-item linked list.

Of course, there is a catch. Actually, there are two catches.

First, if you have too many employees, you are eventually going to find two that map to the same bucket. Suppose that you have 10 buckets and two employees with Social Security numbers 732-45-7653 and 145-76-4583. These both map to bucket 3. This is called a *key collision,* and the hash table must use some sort of *collision resolution policy* to figure out what to do when two keys map to the same bucket. This policy is generally some simple method such as making a linked list in the bucket or letting the second item spill over into the following bucket. Whatever collision resolution scheme you use, it takes a little extra time to search through full buckets.

You can make the buckets less full if you use more of them. In this example, if you switched to 100 buckets, the two employees would map to buckets 53 and 83, so no collision occurs. That makes looking up these items faster.

The second catch is that you can make a hash table faster by adding more buckets, but using more buckets means using more space. When a hash table starts to fill up, collisions are common, so performance suffers. Add more space and performance improves, but there may be a lot of wasted space not occupied by any data. If the table grows too big, it may start to use up all of the system's memory and starve the application for memory. The application must then page memory to disk when it needs more room, a process that can make the program extremely slow.

Those are the advantages and disadvantages of the Hashtable class. A Hashtable gives better performance than a ListDictionary, but takes more space.

In addition to the usual dictionary properties and methods, the Hashtable has a few that help manage the internal hash table that it uses to store its items.

One overloaded version of the Hashtable class's constructor takes a parameter that tells how many items the table should initially be able to hold. If you know you are going to load 1000 items, you might make the table initially hold room for 1500. Then the program could add all the items without filling the table too much, so it would still give good performance. If you don't set an initial size, the hash table might start out too small and need to resize itself many times before it could hold 1000 items, and that will slow it down.

Another version of the constructor lets you specify the hash table's *load factor.* The load factor is a number between 0.1 and 1.0 that gives the largest ratio of elements to buckets that the Hashtable will allow before it enlarges its internal table. For example, suppose that the hash table's capacity is 100 and its load factor is 0.8. Then when it holds 80 elements, the Hashtable will enlarge its internal table.

For high-performance lookups, the Hashtable class is a great solution.

HybridDictionary

A *HybridDictionary* is a cross between a ListDictionary and a Hashtable. If the dictionary is small, the HybridDictionary stores its data in a ListDictionary. If the dictionary grows too large, HybridDictionary switches to a Hashtable.

If you know that you will only need a few items, you can use a ListDictionary. If you know you will need to use a very large number of items, you can use a Hashtable. If you are unsure whether you will have few or many items, you can hedge your bet with a HybridDictionary. It'll take a bit of extra time to switch from a list to a Hashtable if you add a lot of items, but you'll save time in the long run if the list does turn out to be enormous.

Strongly Typed Dictionaries

Just as you can make strongly typed collections, you can also make strongly typed dictionaries. The idea is exactly the same. You derive your strongly typed class from a class that supports basic dictionary functionality. In this case, that parent class is DictionaryBase, and it provides a Dictionary object that your class can use to implement its dictionary features.

Next, you implement dictionary methods such as Add, Item, Keys, and so forth. Your code requires specific data types and uses the parent class's Dictionary variable to do all the hard work through delegation.

The following table lists the standard methods provided by a strongly typed dictionary class. The third column indicates whether the DictionaryBase parent class automatically provides the method or whether you must delegate the method to the Dictionary object.

METHOD	PURPOSE	PROVIDED BY
Add	Adds a key/value pair to the dictionary	Dictionary
Clear	Removes all key/value pairs from the dictionary	DictionaryBase
Contains	Returns True if the dictionary contains a specific key	Dictionary
CopyTo	Copies elements from the dictionary into an array of DictionaryEntry objects	DictionaryBase
Count	Returns the number of key/value pairs in the dictionary	DictionaryBase
Dictionary	Returns a Dictionary holding the dictionary's key/value pairs	DictionaryBase
InnerHashtable	Returns a Hashtable holding the dictionary's key/value pairs	DictionaryBase
Item	Returns the value corresponding to a specific key	Dictionary
Keys	Returns an ICollection containing the dictionary's keys	Dictionary
Remove	Removes the key/value pair for a specific key	Dictionary
Values	Returns an ICollection containing the dictionary's values	Dictionary

As is the case with strongly typed collections, you can add other, more specialized methods if they would be useful in your application.

Example program MakeEmployeeDictionary, which is available for download on the book's web site, shows how to build a strongly typed dictionary of Employee objects that inherits from the DictionaryBase class.

Other Strongly Typed Derived Classes

How a class stores its data internally is generally not a developer's concern. As long as it does its job, you shouldn't care whether the DictionaryBase class stores its data in a linked list, hash table, or some other data structure. (Although the DictionaryBase class has an InnerHashtable method that returns its data in a Hashtable form, so perhaps that's a hint.)

However, if you really want a strongly typed class that you know uses a ListDictionary instead of a hash table (or whatever CollectionBase uses), you could derive a strongly typed class from the ListDictionary class.

The following code shows the EmployeeListDictionary class, which is derived from the ListDictionary class. It uses the Shadows keyword to replace the ListDictionary class's Add, Item, Contains, and Remove methods with new strongly typed versions. Those methods simply pass their requests along to the base class ListDictionary.

Available for download on Wrox.com

```
Public Class EmployeeListDictionary
    Inherits ListDictionary

    ' Add a Dictionary entry.
    Public Shadows Sub Add(ByVal new_key As String,
     ByVal new_employee As Employee)
        MyBase.Add(new_key, new_employee)
    End Sub

    ' Return an object with the given key.
    Default Public Shadows Property Item(ByVal key As String) As Employee
        Get
            Return DirectCast(MyBase.Item(key), Employee)
        End Get
        Set(ByVal Value As Employee)
            MyBase.Item(key) = Value
        End Set
    End Property

    ' Return True if the Dictionary contains this Employee.
    Public Shadows Function Contains(ByVal key As String) As Boolean
        Return MyBase.Contains(key)
    End Function

    ' Remove this entry.
    Public Shadows Sub Remove(ByVal key As String)
        MyBase.Remove(key)
    End Sub
End Class
```

code snippet MakeEmployeeListDictionary

Example program MakeEmployeeListDictionary, which is available for download on the book's web site, builds a strongly typed ListDictionary that holds Employee objects.

StringDictionary

The *StringDictionary* class uses a hash table to manage keys and values that are all strings. Because it uses a hash table, it can handle very large data sets quickly.

Its methods are strongly typed to require strings, so they provide extra type checking that can make finding potential bugs easier. For that reason, you should use a StringDictionary instead of a generic ListDictionary or Hashtable if you want to work exclusively with strings.

SortedList

The *SortedList* class acts as a Hashtable/Array hybrid. When you access a value by key, it acts as a hash table. When you access a value by index, it acts as an array containing items sorted by key value. For example, suppose that you add a number of Job objects to a SortedList named jobs using their priorities as keys. Then jobs(0) always returns the job with the smallest priority value.

Example program UseSortedList, which is available for download on the book's web site, demonstrates the SortedList class.

A SortedList is more complicated than a Hashtable or an array, so you should only use it if you need its special properties.

COLLECTIONSUTIL

Normally Hashtables and SortedLists are case-sensitive. The CollectionsUtil class provides two shared methods, CreateCaseInsensitiveHashtable and CreateCaseInsensitiveSortedList, that create Hashtables and SortedLists objects that are case-insensitive.

Example program UseCaseInsensitiveSortedList, which is available for download on the book's web site, uses code similar to the following to create a normal case-sensitive SortedList. It then adds two items with keys that differ only in their capitalization. This works because a case-sensitive SortedList treats the two keys as different values. The code then creates a case-insensitive SortedList. When it tries to add the same two items, the list raises an exception, complaining that it already has an object with key value Sport.

```
Dim sorted_list As SortedList

' Use a normal, case-sensitive SortedList.
sorted_list = New SortedList
sorted_list.Add("Sport", "Volleyball")
sorted_list.Add("sport", "Golf") ' Okay because Sport <> sport.

' Use a case-insensitive SortedList.
sorted_list = CollectionsUtil.CreateCaseInsensitiveSortedList()
sorted_list.Add("Sport", "Volleyball")
sorted_list.Add("sport", "Golf") ' Error because Sport = sport.
```

code snippet UseCaseInsensitiveSortedList

If you can use case-insensitive Hashtables and SortedLists, you should generally do so. This prevents the program from adding two entries that are supposed to be the same but have different capitalization. For example, if one routine spells a key value "Law Suit" and another spells it "law suit," the case-insensitive Hashtable or SortedList will quickly catch the error. Neither will notice an error if part of your program spells this "LawSuit." (You could also add extra logic to remove spaces and special symbols to increase the chances of finding similar terms that should be the same, but a discussion of these sorts of methods is beyond the scope of this book.)

STACKS AND QUEUES

Stacks and queues are specialized data structures that are useful in many programming applications that need to add and remove items in a particular order. The Visual Basic Stack and Queue classes implement stacks and queues.

The difference between a stack and a queue is the order in which they return the items stored in them. The following two sections describe stacks and queues and explain the ways in which they return items.

Stack

A *stack* returns items in last-in, first-out (LIFO, pronounced *life-o*) order. Because of the LIFO behavior, a stack is sometimes called a *LIFO list* or simply a *LIFO*.

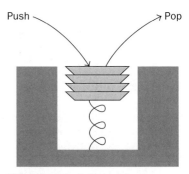

Adding an item to the stack is called *pushing the item onto the stack* and removing an item is called *popping the item off of the stack*. These operations have the names push and pop because a stack is like a spring-loaded stack of plates in a cafeteria or buffet. You push new plates down onto the top of the stack and the plates sink into the counter. You pop the top plate off and the stack rises to give you the next plate.

FIGURE 28-3: A Stack lets you remove items in last-in, first-out (LIFO) order.

Figure 28-3 illustrates this kind of stack. If you haven't seen this sort of thing before, don't worry about it. Just remember that push adds an item and pop removes the top item.

Normally, you use a Stack object's Push and Pop methods to add and remove items, but the Stack class also provides some cheating methods that let you peek at the Stack's top object or convert the Stack into an array. The following table describes the Stack class's most useful properties and methods.

PROPERTY/METHOD	PURPOSE
Clear	Removes all items from the Stack.
Contains	Returns True if the Stack contains a particular object.
CopyTo	Copies some or all of the Stack class's objects into a one-dimensional array.

PROPERTY/METHOD	PURPOSE
Count	Returns the number of items in the Stack.
Peek	Returns a reference to the Stack class's top item without removing it from the Stack.
Pop	Returns the Stack class's top item and removes it from the Stack.
Push	Adds an item to the top of the Stack.
ToArray	Returns a one-dimensional array containing references to the objects in the Stack. The Stack class's top item is placed first in the array.

A Stack allocates memory to store its items. If you Push an object onto a Stack that is completely full, the Stack must resize itself to make more room and that slows down the operation.

To make memory management more efficient, the Stack class provides three overloaded constructors. The first takes no parameters and allocates a default initial capacity. The second takes as a parameter the number of items it should initially be able to hold. If you know that you will add 10,000 items to the Stack, you can avoid a lot of resizing by initially allocating room for 10,000 items.

The third version of the constructor takes as a parameter an object that implements the ICollection interface. The constructor allocates enough room to hold the items in the collection and copies them into the Stack.

Example program UseStack, which is available for download on the book's web site, uses a Stack to reverse the characters in a string.

Queue

A *queue* returns items in first-in, first-out (FIFO, pronounced *fife-o*) order. Because of the FIFO behavior, a queue is sometimes called a *FIFO list* or simply a *FIFO*.

A queue is similar to a line at a customer service desk. The first person in line is the first person to leave it when the service desk is free. Figure 28-4 shows the idea graphically.

Customer enters queue here

FIGURE 28-4: Customers leave a queue in first-in, first-out (FIFO) order.

Queues are particularly useful for processing items in the order in which they were created. For example, an order-processing application might keep orders in a queue so that customers who place orders first are satisfied first (or at least their order is shipped first, whether they are satisfied or not).

Historically, the routines that add and remove items from a queue are called Enqueue and Dequeue. The following table describes these methods and the Queue class's other most useful properties and methods.

PROPERTY/METHOD	PURPOSE
Clear	Removes all items from the Queue.
Contains	Returns True if the Queue contains a particular object.
CopyTo	Copies some or all of the Queue class's objects into a one-dimensional array.
Count	Returns the number of items in the Queue.
Dequeue	Returns the item that has been in the Queue the longest and removes it from the Queue.
Enqueue	Adds an item to the back of the Queue.
Peek	Returns a reference to the Queue class's oldest item without removing it from the Queue.
ToArray	Returns a one-dimensional array containing references to the objects in the Queue. The Queue class's oldest item is placed first in the array.
TrimToSize	Frees empty space in the Queue to set its capacity equal to the number of items it actually contains.

A Queue allocates memory to store its items. If you Enqueue an object while the queue's memory is full, the Queue must resize itself to make more room, and that slows down the operation.

To make memory management more efficient, the Queue class provides four overloaded constructors. The first takes no parameters and allocates a default initial capacity. If the Queue is full, it enlarges itself by a default growth factor.

The second constructor takes as a parameter its initial capacity. If you know that you will add 600 items to the Queue, you can save some time by initially allocating room for 600 items. With this constructor, the Queue also uses a default growth factor.

The third constructor takes as a parameter an object that implements the ICollection interface. The constructor allocates enough room to hold the items in the collection and copies them into the Queue. It also uses a default growth factor.

The final version of the constructor takes as parameters an initial capacity and a growth factor between 1.0 and 10.0. A larger growth factor will mean that the Queue resizes itself less often, but it may contain a lot of unused space.

Queues are useful for scheduling items in a FIFO order. For example, a shared network computer uses a queue. Users on different computers send jobs to the printer, and they are printed in FIFO order.

Example program UseQueue, which is available for download on the book's web site, demonstrates a Queue.

GENERICS

Chapter 29 explains how you can build and use generic classes to perform similar actions for objects of various types. For example, you could build a Tree class that can build a tree of any specific kind of object. Your program could then make a tree of Employees, a tree of Customers, a tree of Punchlines, or even a tree of trees. Visual Basic comes with a useful assortment of pre-built generic collection classes.

The System.Collections.Generic namespace provides several generic collection classes that you can use to build strongly typed collections. These collections work with a specific data type that you supply in a variable's declaration. For example, the following code makes a List that holds strings:

```
Imports System.Collections.Generic

. . .
Dim places As New List(Of String)
places.Add("Chicago")
```

The places object's methods are strongly typed and work only with strings, so they provide extra error protection that a less specialized collection doesn't provide. To take advantage of this extra protection, you should use generic collections or strongly typed collections derived from the CollectionBase class whenever possible.

When you derive a strongly typed collection from the CollectionBase class, you can add extra convenience functions to it. For example, an EmployeeCollection class could include an overloaded version of the Add method that accepts first and last names as parameters, makes a new Employee object, and adds it to the collection.

You cannot directly modify a generic collection class, but you can add extension methods to it. For example, the following code adds an AddPerson method to the generic List(Of Person) class. This method takes as parameters a first and last name, uses those values to make a Person object, and adds it to the list.

```
Module PersonListExtensions
    <Extension()>
    Public Sub AddPerson(ByVal person_list As List(Of Person),
     ByVal first_name As String, ByVal last_name As String)
        Dim per As New Person() With _
            {.FirstName = first_name, .LastName = last_name}
        person_list.Add(per)
    End Sub
End Module
```

For more information on extension methods, see the section "Extension Methods" in Chapter 17, "Subroutines and Functions."

In addition to adding extension methods to a generic class, you can also derive an enhanced collection from a generic class. For example, the following code defines an EmployeeCollection class that inherits from the generic Collection(Of Employee). It then adds an overloaded version of the Add method that takes first and last names as parameters.

```
Imports System.Collections.Generic

Public Class EmployeeList
    Inherits List(Of Employee)

    Public Overloads Sub Add(
      ByVal first_name As String, ByVal last_name As String)
        Dim emp As New Employee(first_name, last_name)
        MyBase.Add(emp)
    End Sub
End Class
```

code snippet GenericEmployeeList

NO OVERLOADS ALLOWED

Note that extension methods cannot overload a class's methods. If you want multiple versions of the Add method as in this example, you need to use a derived class.

The following table lists the some of the most useful collection classes defined by the System. Collections.Generic namespace.

COLLECTION	PURPOSE
Comparer	Compares two objects of the specific type and returns −1, 0, or 1 to indicate whether the first is less than, equal to, or greater than the second
Dictionary	A strongly typed dictionary
LinkedList	A strongly typed linked list
LinkedListNode	A strongly typed node in a linked list
List	A strongly typed list
Queue	A strongly typed queue

COLLECTION	PURPOSE
SortedDictionary	A strongly typed sorted dictionary
SortedList	A strongly typed sorted list
Stack	A strongly typed stack

Example program GenericStringList, which is available for download on the book's web site, demonstrates a generic List(Of String). Example program GenericEmployeeList, which is also available for download, derives a strongly typed EmployeeList class from a generic List(Of Employee).

For more information on generics (including instructions for writing your own generic classes), see Chapter 29.

COLLECTION INITIALIZERS

A new feature in Visual Basic 2010 allows you to easily initialize collection classes that have an Add method. To initialize a collection, follow the variable's instantiation with the keyword From and then a series of comma-separated values inside braces.

For example, the following code snippet initializes an ArrayList, StringCollection, and generic List(Of Person). Notice how the generic List's initializer includes a series of new Person objects that are initialized with the With keyword.

```
Dim numbers As New ArrayList() From {1, 2, 3}
Dim names As New StringCollection() From {"Alice", "Bob", "Cynthia"}
Dim authors As New List(Of Person) From {
    New Person() With {.FirstName = "Simon", .LastName = "Green"},
    New Person() With {.FirstName = "Christopher", .LastName = "Moore"},
    New Person() With {.FirstName = "Terry", .LastName = "Pratchett"}
}
```

If a collection's Add method takes more than one parameter, simply include the appropriate values for each item inside their own sets of braces. The following code uses this method to initialize a NameValueCollection and a Dictionary with Integer keys and String values:

```
Dim phone_numbers As New NameValueCollection() From {
    {"Ashley", "502-253-3748"},
    {"Jane", "505-847-2984"},
    {"Mike", "505-847-3984"},
    {"Shebly", "502-487-4939"}
}
Dim greetings As New Dictionary(Of Integer, String) From {
    {1, "Hi"},
    {2, "Hello"},
    {3, "Holla"}
}
```

The same technique works for other collections that need two values such as ListDictionary, Hashtable, HybridDiction, StringDictionary, and SortedList.

Unfortunately, you cannot use this method to initialize the Stack and Queue classes. For historical reasons, the methods in those classes that add new items are called Push and Enqueue rather than Add, and this method requires the class to have an Add method.

Fortunately, you can write extension methods to give those classes Add methods. The following code creates Add methods for the Stack and Queue classes:

```
Module Extensions
    <Extension()>
    Public Sub Add(ByVal the_stack As Stack, ByVal value As Object)
        the_stack.Push(value)
    End Sub

    <Extension()>
    Public Sub Add(ByVal the_queue As Queue, ByVal value As Object)
        the_queue.Enqueue(value)
    End Sub
End Module
```

After you create these extension methods, you can initialize Stacks and Queues as in the following code:

```
Dim people_stack As New Stack() From {"Electra", "Storm", "Rogue"}
Dim people_queue As New Queue() From {"Xavier", "Anakin", "Zaphod"}
```

SUMMARY

This chapter describes five types of objects: arrays, collections, dictionaries, stacks, and queues. It also explains how to convert any of these into strongly typed classes and how to use generic collections.

Arrays store objects sequentially. They allow fast access at any point in the array. The Array class lets you make arrays indexed with nonzero lower bounds, although they provide slower performance than arrays of variables, which require lower bounds of zero. The Array class provides several useful methods for working with Array objects and normal variable arrays, including Sort, Reverse, IndexOf, LastIndexOf, and BinarySearch.

Collections store data in ways that are different from those used by arrays. An ArrayList stores items in a linked list. That works well for short lists, but slows down when the list grows large. A StringCollection holds a collection of strings. StringCollection is an example of a strongly typed collection (it holds only strings). The NameValueCollection class is a specialized collection that can hold more than one string value for a given key value.

Dictionaries associate key values with corresponding data values. You look up the key to find the data much as you might look up a word in the dictionary to find its definition. The ListDictionary class stores its data in a linked list. It is fast for small data sets but slow when it contains too much data. A Hashtable, on the other hand, has substantial overhead, but is extremely fast for large dictionaries. A HybridDictionary acts as a ListDictionary if it doesn't contain too much data, and switches to a Hashtable when it gets too big. The StringDictionary class is basically a Hashtable that is strongly typed to work with strings. The SortedList class is a Hashtable/Array hybrid that lets you access values by key or in sorted order.

Stack classes provide access to items in last-in, first-out (LIFO) order, whereas Queue classes give access to their items in first-in, first-out (FIFO) order.

The generic Dictionary, LinkedList, List, Queue, SortedDictionary, SortedList, and Stack classes enable you to use strongly typed data structures without going to the trouble of building your own strongly typed classes.

Although these classes have very different features for adding, removing, finding, and ordering objects, they share some common traits. For example, those that provide an Add method support collection initialization, a feature new in Visual Basic 2010.

All of these classes, plus other strongly typed collections that you can derive from the CollectionBase, DictionaryBase, and other classes, provide significant flexibility and options, so you can pick the class that best satisfies your needs. Deciding which class is best can be tricky, but making the right choice can mean the difference between a program that processes a large data set in seconds, hours, or not at all. Spend some time reviewing the different characteristics of the class so that you can make the best choice possible.

This chapter explains how you can use the generic collection classes provided by the System .Collections.Generic namespace to build strongly typed collection classes of several useful types. Chapter 29, "Generics," explains how you can build generic classes of your own. Using generics, you can build strongly typed classes that manipulate all sorts of objects in any way you can imagine.

29

Generics

Classes are often described as cookie cutters for creating objects. You define a class, and then you can use it to make any number of objects that are instances of the class.

Similarly, a *generic* is like a cookie cutter for creating classes. You define a generic, and then you can use it to create any number of classes that have similar features.

For example, Visual Basic comes with a generic List class. You can use it to make lists of strings, lists of integers, lists of Employee objects, or lists of just about anything else.

This chapter explains generics. It shows how you define generics of your own and how you can use them.

ADVANTAGES OF GENERICS

A generic class takes one or more data types as parameters. An instance of a generic class has those parameters filled in with specific data types such as String, TextBox, or Employee.

For example, you can build a list of OrderItem objects, a hash table containing PurchaseOrders identified by number, or a Queue that contains Customer objects.

Tying generics to specific data types gives them a few advantages over more traditional classes:

➤ **Strong typing** — Methods can take parameters and return values that have the class's instance type. For example, a List(Of String) can hold only string values, and its Item method returns string values. This makes it more difficult to accidentally add the wrong type of object to the collection.

➤ **IntelliSense** — By providing strong typing, a class built from a generic lets Visual Studio provide IntelliSense. If you make a List(Of Employee), Visual Studio knows that the items in the collection are Employee objects, so it can give you appropriate IntelliSense.

➤ **No boxing** — Because the class manipulates objects with a specific data type, Visual Basic doesn't need to convert items to and from the plain Object data type. For example, if a program stores TextBox controls in a normal collection, the program must convert the TextBox controls to and from the Object class when it adds and uses items in the collection. Avoiding these steps makes the code more efficient.

➤ **Code reuse** — You can use a generic class with more than one data type. For example, if you have built a generic PriorityQueue class, you can make a PriorityQueue holding Employee, Customer, Order, or Objection objects. Without generics, you would need to build four separate classes to build strongly typed priority queues for each of these types of objects. Reusing this code makes it easier to write, test, debug, and maintain the code.

The main disadvantage to generics is that they are slightly more complicated and confusing than non-generic classes. If you know that you will only ever need to provide a class that works with a single type, you can simplify things slightly by not using a generic class. If you think you might want to reuse the code later for another data type, it's easier to just build the class generically from the start.

DEFINING GENERICS

Visual Basic allows you to define generic classes, structures, interfaces, procedures, and delegates. The basic syntax is similar, so when you understand how to make generic classes, the others should be fairly easy.

To define a generic class, make a class declaration as usual. After the class name, add a parenthesis, the keyword Of, and a placeholder for a data type. For example, the following code shows the outline of a generic MostRecentList class. Its declaration takes one type that the class internally names ItemType. This is similar to a parameter name that you would give to a subroutine. The class's code can use the name ItemType to refer to the type associated with the instance of the generic class.

```
Public Class MostRecentList(Of ItemType)
    ...
End Class
```

For example, suppose that you want to make a list that can act as a most recently used (MRU) file list. It should be able to hold at most four items. New items are added at the top of the list, and the others are bumped down one position with the last item being dropped if the list contains too many items. If you add an existing item to the list, it jumps to the top of the list.

Example program GenericMruList uses the following code to build a generic MostRecentList class:

```
' A list of at most MaxItems items.
Public Class MostRecentList(Of ItemType)
    ' The Item property.
    Private m_Items As New List(Of ItemType)
    Public Property Item(ByVal index As Integer) As ItemType
        Get
            Return m_Items(index)
        End Get
```

```vb
        Set(ByVal value As ItemType)
            m_Items(index) = value
        End Set
    End Property

    ' The MaxItems property.
    Private m_MaxItems As Integer = 4
    Public Property MaxItems() As Integer
        Get
            Return m_MaxItems
        End Get
        Set(ByVal value As Integer)
            m_MaxItems = value

            ' Resize appropriately.
            Do While m_Items.Count > m_MaxItems
                m_Items.RemoveAt(m_Items.Count - 1)
            Loop
        End Set
    End Property

    ' The current number of items.
    Public ReadOnly Property Count() As Integer
        Get
            Return m_Items.Count
        End Get
    End Property

    ' Add an item to the top of the list.
    Public Sub Add(ByVal value As ItemType)
        ' Remove the item if it is present.
        If m_Items.Contains(value) Then m_Items.Remove(value)

        ' Add the item to the top of the list.
        m_Items.Insert(0, value)

        ' Make sure there are at most MaxItems items.
        If m_Items.Count > m_MaxItems Then m_Items.RemoveAt(m_Items.Count - 1)
    End Sub

    ' Remove an item.
    Public Sub Remove(ByVal value As ItemType)
        m_Items.Remove(value)
    End Sub

    ' Remove an item at a specific position.
    Public Sub RemoveAt(ByVal index As Integer)
        m_Items.RemoveAt(index)
    End Sub
End Class
```

code snippet GenericMruList

The Of ItemType clause indicates that the class will take a single type that it internally names ItemType. The class stores its items in a private list named m_Items. It declares this list using the generic list class defined in the System.Collections.Generic namespace, and it indicates that this is a list that will hold ItemType objects. This refers to the ItemType parameter used in the generic MostRecentList class's declaration. If the program makes a MostRecentList of strings, then m_Items is a list of strings.

In this code, the Item property procedures simply let the main program get and set the values in the m_Items list. The MaxItems property lets the program determine the number of items that the list can hold. The property Set routine saves the new size and then resizes the m_Items list appropriately if necessary. The Count property returns the number of items currently in the list. The subroutine Add first removes the new item if it is already in the list. It then adds the new item at the top of the list and removes the last item if the list now contains too many items. The Remove and RemoveAt routines simply call the m_Items list's Remove and RemoveAt methods.

The following code creates a new MostRecentList of strings and then adds some values to it:

```
Dim the_items As New MostRecentList(Of String)
the_items.Add("Apple")
the_items.Add("Banana")
the_items.Add("Cherry")
the_items.Add("Date")
the_items.Add("Banana")
the_items.Add("Fig")
```

After this code executes, the list contains the values in the following order: Fig, Banana, Date, Cherry.

Generic Constructors

Generic classes can have constructors just as any other class can. For example, the following constructor initializes the MostRecentList class's MaxItem property:

```
' Initialize MaxItems for the new list.
Public Sub New(ByVal max_items As Integer)
    MaxItems = max_items
End Sub
```

To use the constructor, the main program adds normal parameters after the type parameters in the object declaration. The following statement creates a new MostRecentList of strings, passing its constructor the value 4:

```
Dim the_items As New MostRecentList(Of String)(4)
```

Multiple Types

If you want the class to work with more than one type, you can add other types to the declaration separated by commas. For example, suppose that you want to create a list of items where each key is associated with a pair of data items. Example program GenericPairDictionary uses the following code to define the generic PairDictionary class. This class acts as a dictionary that associates a key value with a pair of data values. Notice how the class declaration includes three data types named KeyType, DataType1, and DataType2.

```vb
' A Dictionary that associates
' a pair of data values with each key.
Public Class PairDictionary(Of KeyType, DataType1, DataType2)
    ' A structure to hold paired data.
    Private Structure DataPair
        Public Data1 As DataType1
        Public Data2 As DataType2
        Public Sub New(ByVal data_value1 As DataType1,
         ByVal data_value2 As DataType2)
            Data1 = data_value1
            Data2 = data_value2
    End Sub
End Structure

    ' A Dictionary to hold the paired data.
    Private m_Dictionary As New Dictionary(Of KeyType, DataPair)

    ' Return the number of data pairs.
    Public ReadOnly roperty Count() As Integer
        Get
            Return m_Dictionary.Count
        End Get
    End Property

    ' Add a key and data pair.
    Public Sub Add(ByVal key As KeyType,
     ByVal data_value1 As DataType1,
     ByVal data_value2 As DataType2)
        m_Dictionary.Add(key, New DataPair(data_value1, data_value2))
    End Sub

    ' Remove all data.
    Public Sub Clear()
        m_Dictionary.Clear()
    End Sub

    ' Return True if the PairDictionary contains this key.
    Public Function ContainsKey(ByVal key As KeyType) As Boolean
        Return m_Dictionary.ContainsKey(key)
    End Function

    ' Return a data pair.
    Public Sub GetItem(ByVal key As KeyType,
     ByRef data_value1 As DataType1,
     ByRef data_value2 As DataType2)
        Dim data_pair As DataPair = m_Dictionary.Item(key)
        data_value1 = data_pair.Data1
        data_value2 = data_pair.Data2
    End Sub
```

```
' Set a data pair.
Public Sub SetItem(ByVal key As KeyType,
 ByVal data_value1 As DataType1,
 ByVal data_value2 As DataType2)
    m_Dictionary.Item(key) = New DataPair(data_value1, data_value2)
End Sub

' Return a collection containing the keys.
Public ReadOnly Property Keys() As System.Collections.ICollection
    Get
        Return m_Dictionary.Keys()
    End Get
End Property

' Remove a particular entry.
    Public Sub Remove(ByVal key As KeyType) m_Dictionary.Remove(key)
End Sub
End Class
```

code snippet GenericPairDictionary

The PairDictionary class defines its own private DataPair class to hold data pairs. The DataPair class has two public variables of types DataType1 and DataType2. Its only method is a constructor that makes initializing the two variables easier.

After defining the DataPair class, the PairDictionary class declares a generic Dictionary object named m_Dictionary using the key type KeyType and data type DataPair.

PairDictionary provides Count, Add, Clear, ContainsKey, GetItem, SetItem, Keys, and Remove methods. Notice how it delegates these to the m_Dictionary object and how it uses the DataPair class to store values in m_Dictionary.

The following code creates an instance of the generic PairDictionary class that uses integers as keys and strings for both data values. It adds three entries to the PairDictionary and then retrieves and displays the entry with key value 32.

```
' Create the PairDictionary and add some data.
Dim pair_dictionary As New PairDictionary(Of Integer, String, String)
pair_dictionary.Add(10, "Ann", "Archer")
pair_dictionary.Add(32, "Bill", "Beach")
pair_dictionary.Add(17, "Cynthia", "Campos")

' Print the values for index 32.
Dim value1 As String = ""
Dim value2 As String = ""
pair_dictionary.GetItem(32, value1, value2)
Debug.WriteLine(value1 & ", " & value2)
```

Constrained Types

To get the most out of your generic classes, you should make them as flexible as possible. Depending on what the class will do, however, you may need to constrain the types used to create instances of the generic.

For example, consider the generic MostRecentList class described earlier in this chapter. It stores at most a certain number of objects in a list. When you add an object to the list, the class first removes the object from the list if it is already present.

That works with simple data types such as integers and strings. However, suppose that you want the list to hold Employee objects. When you add a new Employee object, the list tries to remove the item if it is already present in its m_Items list. However, you are adding a *new* instance of the Employee class. The object may have the same values as an object that is already in the list, but the list won't know that because the values are stored in two different objects.

What the list needs is a way to compare objects in the list to see if they are equal. It can then look through the list and remove an existing item if it matches the new one.

One way to allow the list to compare items is to guarantee that the items implement the IComparable interface. Then the program can use their CompareTo methods to see if two objects match.

Example program GenericMruList2 uses the following code to make a new version of the MostRecentList class. Instead of calling the m_Items list's Remove method directly, the Add method now calls the class's Remove method. That method loops through the list using each item's CompareTo method to see if the item matches the target item. If there is a match, the program removes the item from the list.

```vb
Public Class MostRecentList(Of ItemType As IComparable)
    ...
    ' Add an item to the top of the list.
    Public Sub Add(ByVal value As ItemType)
        ' Remove the item if it is present.
        Remove(value)

        ' Add the item to the top of the list.
        m_Items.Insert(0, value)

        ' Make sure there are at most MaxItems items.
        If m_Items.Count >> m_MaxItems Then m_Items.RemoveAt(m_Items.Count - 1)
    End Sub

    ' Remove an item.
    Public Sub Remove(ByVal value As ItemType)
        ' Find the item.
        For i As Integer = m_Items.Count - 1 To 0 Step -1
            If value.CompareTo(m_Items(i)) = 0 Then
                m_Items.RemoveAt(i)
            End If
        Next i
    End Sub
    ...
End Sub
```

code snippet GenericMruList2

A type's As clause can specify any number of interfaces and at most one class from which the type must be derived. It can also include the keyword New to indicate that the type used must provide a constructor that takes no parameters. If you include more than one constraint, the constraints should be separated by commas and enclosed in brackets.

The following code defines the StrangeGeneric class that takes three type parameters. The first type must implement the IComparable interface and must provide an empty constructor. The second type has no constraints, and the third type must be a class that inherits from Control.

```
Public Class StrangeGeneric(Of Type1 As {IComparable, New}, Type2,
  Type3 As Control)
    ...
End Class
```

The following code declares an instance of the StrangeGeneric class:

```
Dim my_strange_generic As New StrangeGeneric(Of Integer, Employee, Button)
```

Constraining a type gives Visual Basic more information about that type, so it lets you use the properties and methods defined by the type. In the previous code, for example, if a variable is of type Type3, then Visual Basic knows that it inherits from the Control class, so you can use Control properties and methods such as Anchor, BackColor, Font, and so forth.

USING GENERICS

The previous sections have already shown a few examples of how to use a generic class. The program declares the class and includes whatever data types are required in parentheses. The following code shows how a program might create a generic list of strings:

```
Imports System.Collections.Generic
...
Dim names As New List(Of String)
```

To use a generic class's constructor, add a second set of parentheses and any parameters after the type specifications. The following statement creates an IntStringList object, passing it the types Integer, String, and Employee. It calls the class's constructor, passing it the value 100.

```
Dim the_employees As New IntStringList(Of Integer, String, Employee)(100)
```

If the program needs to use only a few generic classes (for example, a single collection of strings), this isn't too bad. If the program needs to use many instances of the class, however, the code becomes cluttered.

For example, suppose that the TreeNode class shown in the following code represents a node in a tree. Its MyData field holds some piece of data and its Children list holds references to child nodes.

```
Public Class TreeNode(Of DataType)
    Public MyData As DataType
    Public Children As New List(Of TreeNode(Of DataType))

    Public Sub New(ByVal new_data As DataType)
        MyData = new_data
    End Sub
End Class
```

The following code uses this class to build a small tree of Employee objects:

```
Dim root As New TreeNode(Of Employee)(New Employee("Annabelle", "Ant"))
Dim child1 As New TreeNode(Of Employee)(New Employee("Bert", "Bear"))
Dim child2 As New TreeNode(Of Employee)(New Employee("Candice", "Cat"))

root.Children.Add(child1)
root.Children.Add(child2)
```

Example program GenericTree, which is available for download on the book's web site, uses similar code to build a generic Tree(Of DataType) class.

Repeating the nodes' data types in the first three lines makes the code rather cluttered. Two techniques that you can use to make the code a bit simpler are using an imports alias and deriving a new class. Both of these let you create a simpler name for the awkward class name TreeNode(Of Employee).

Imports Aliases

Normally, you use an Imports statement to make it easier to refer to namespaces and the symbols they contain. However, the Imports statement also lets you define an alias for a namespace entity. To use this to make using generics easier, create an Imports statement that refers to the type of generic class you want to use and give it a simple alias.

For example, the following code is in the DataTreeTest namespace. It uses an Imports statement to refer to a TreeNode of Employee. It gives this entity the alias EmployeeNode. Later, the program can use the name EmployeeNode to create a TreeNode of Employee.

```
Imports EmployeeNode = DataTreeTest.TreeNode(Of DataTreeTest.Employee)
    . . .
Dim root As New EmployeeNode(New Employee("Annabelle", "Ant"))
Dim child1 As New EmployeeNode(New Employee("Bert", "Bear"))
Dim child2 As New EmployeeNode(New Employee("Candice", "Cat"))

root.Children.Add(child1)
root.Children.Add(child2)
    . . .
```

code snippet GenericTreeImportsAlias

Example program GenericTreeImportsAlias demonstrates this approach.

Derived Classes

A second method that simplifies using generics is to derive a class from the generic class. The following code derives the EmployeeNode class from TreeNode(Of Employee). Later, it creates instances of this class to build the tree.

```
Public Class EmployeeNode
    Inherits TreeNode(Of Employee)
    Public Sub New(ByVal new_data As Employee)
        MyBase.New(new_data)
    End Sub
End Class
...
Dim root As New EmployeeNode(New Employee("Annabelle", "Ant"))
Dim child1 As New EmployeeNode(New Employee("Bert", "Bear"))
Dim child2 As New EmployeeNode(New Employee("Candice", "Cat"))

root.Children.Add(child1)
root.Children.Add(child2)
...
```

code snippet GenericTreeSubclass

Example program GenericTreeSubclass demonstrates this approach.

If you use this technique, you can also add extra convenience functions to the derived class. For example, the following code shows a new EmployeeNode constructor that creates the Employee object that it holds:

```
Public Sub New(ByVal first_name As String, ByVal last_name As String)
    MyBase.New(New Employee(first_name, last_name))
End Sub
```

PREDEFINED GENERIC CLASSES

The System.Collections.Generic namespace defines several generic classes. These are basically collection classes that use generics to work with the data type you specify. See the section "Generics" near the end of Chapter 28, "Collection Classes," for more information and a list of the predefined generic collection classes.

GENERIC METHODS

Generics are usually used to build classes that are not data type–specific such as the generic collection classes. You can also give a class (generic or otherwise) a generic method. Just as a generic class is not tied to a particular data type, the parameters of a generic method are not tied to a specific data type.

The method's declaration includes an Of clause similar to the one used by generic classes, followed by the method's parameter list.

Example program UseSwitcher uses the following code to define a generic Switch subroutine. This subroutine defines the type T and takes two parameters of type T. If this were a function, you could use the type T for its return value if you wanted. Subroutine Switch declares a variable temp of type T and uses it to switch the values of its parameters.

Available for
download on
Wrox.com

```
Public Class Switcher
    Public Sub Switch(Of T)(ByRef thing1 As T, ByRef thing2 As T)
        Dim temp As T = thing1
        thing1 = thing2
        thing2 = temp
    End Sub
End Class
```

code snippet UseSwitcher

> ### GENERIC CLASSES AND METHODS
>
> The Switcher class is not generic but it contains a generic method. Note that a generic class can also contain generic and non-generic methods.

The following code uses a Switcher object to switch the values of two Person variables. In the call to the Switch method, Visual Basic uses the first parameter to infer that the type T is Person and then requires the second parameter to have the same type.

```
Dim person1 As New Person("Anna")
Dim person2 As New Person("Bill")
Dim a_switcher As New Switcher
a_switcher.Switch(person1, person2)
```

GENERICS AND EXTENSION METHODS

Just as extension methods allow you to add new features to existing classes, they also allow you to add new features to generic classes. For example, suppose you have an application that uses a List(Of Person). This List class is a generic collection class defined in the System.Collections.Generic namespace.

The generic class is not defined in your code so you cannot modify it, but you can add extension methods to it. The following code adds an AddPerson method to List(Of Person) that takes as parameters a first and last name, uses those values to make a Person object, and adds it to the list:

```
Module PersonListExtensions
    <Extension()>
    Public Sub AddPerson(ByVal person_list As List(Of Person),
     ByVal first_name As String, ByVal last_name As String)
        Dim per As New Person() With _
            {.FirstName = first_name, .LastName = last_name}
        person_list.Add(per)
    End Sub
End Module
```

This example adds an extension method to a specific instance of a generic class. In this example, the code adds the method to List(Of Person). With a little more work, you can add a generic extension method to a generic class itself instead of adding it to an instance of the class.

Example program GenericNumDistinct uses the following code to add a NumDistinct function to the generic List(Of T) class for any type T. The declaration identifies its generic type T. The first parameter has type List(Of T) so this method extends List(Of T). The function has an Integer return type.

```
Module ListExtensions
    <Extension()>
    Public Function NumDistinct(Of T)(ByVal the_list As List(Of T)) As Integer
        Return the_list.Distinct().Count()
    End Function
End Module
```

code snippet GenericNumDistinct

The generic List(Of T) class provides a Distinct method that returns a new list containing the distinct objects in the original list. The NumDistinct function calls that method and returns the new list's Count value.

The following code shows how a program could call this function. It creates a new List(Of String) and gives it some data. It then calls the list's NumDistinct function.

```
Dim name_list As New List(Of String)
name_list.Add("Llamaar Aarchibald")
name_list.Add("Dudley Eversol")
...

MessageBox.Show("The list contains " & name_list.NumDistinct() &
 " distinct entries")
```

For more information on extension methods, see the section "Extension Methods" in Chapter 17, "Subroutines and Functions."

SUMMARY

A class abstracts the properties and behaviors of a set of objects to form a template that you can use to make objects that implement those properties and behaviors. After you define the class, you can make many instances of it, and they will all have the features defined by the class.

Generics take abstraction one level higher. A generic class abstracts the features of a set of classes defined for specific data types. It determines the properties and methods that any class in the generic group provides. After you define the generic class, you can easily make classes that work with different data types but that all provide the common set of features defined by the generic.

By defining common functionality, generic classes let you reuse code to perform similar actions for different data types. By allowing you to parameterize the class instances with a data type, they let you build strongly typed classes quickly and easily. That, in turn, lets Visual Basic provide IntelliSense to make programming faster and easier.

Together these benefits — easier code reuse, strong typing, and IntelliSense support — help you write, test, debug, and maintain code more easily.

Up to this point, the book's chapters describe fairly general Visual Basic programming topics such as building forms, using controls, using loops to repeat a series of instructions, and building classes. The chapters in the next part of the book move to a slightly more specific topic: graphics programming. They explain how to draw lines, ellipses, curves, and text. They show how to use different colors, line styles, and brush types. They also explain how to manipulate bitmapped images, print, and generate reports. Though the techniques are not needed in as many situations as are the techniques described in previous chapters, they are still useful under a wide variety of circumstances.

Chapter 30 explains the fundamentals of drawing graphics in Visual Basic. It provides the information you need to start drawing simple shapes and curves. The chapters that follow build on these techniques and use them to carry out more specific graphical tasks.

PART IV
Graphics

30

Drawing Basics

Visual Basic .NET provides a large assortment of objects for drawing and for controlling drawing attributes. The Graphics object provides methods that enable you to draw and fill rectangles, ellipses, polygons, curves, lines, and other shapes. Pen and Brush objects determine the appearance of lines (solid, dashed, dotted) and filled areas (solid colors, hatched, filled with a color gradient).

This chapter provides an overview of the drawing process and a survey of the most important drawing namespaces and their classes. It describes in detail the most central of these classes, the Graphics object, and provides examples showing how to use it. You can download example programs demonstrating most of the methods described in this chapter on the book's web site. The examples also include code to draw the figures in this chapter.

Chapter 31, "Brushes, Pens, and Paths," describes some of the other important drawing classes in greater detail.

> **FOR MORE INFORMATION**
>
> If you are new to graphics, this chapter and those that follow may involve a lot of new concepts and unfamiliar terms. The examples available on the book's web site will help make many of the concepts more concrete. If you find some terms confusing, you can find additional details by using the advanced Microsoft search page search.microsoft.com/AdvancedSearch.aspx. The advanced Google search page www.google.com/advanced_search also returns excellent results and you can enter one of the Microsoft sites www.microsoft.com, msdn.microsoft .com, or support.microsoft.com in the "Search within a site or domain" field if you want to restrict the search to Microsoft sites. You can also consult online glossaries such as the Webopedia (www.webopedia.com) and Wikipedia (www.wikipedia.org) for basic definitions.

DRAWING OVERVIEW

Whenever you draw something in Visual Basic, you must use a Graphics object. This object represents the surface where you are drawing, whether it is a PictureBox, Form, or PrintDocument. Sometimes you will have to create a Graphics object, and other times (as in a Paint event handler) one is provided for you.

The Graphics Device Interface+ (GDI+), or the .NET version of GDI drawing routines, uses two classes, Pen and Brush, to determine the appearance of lines and filled shapes.

A Pen object determines how lines are drawn. A Pen sets a line's color, thickness, dash style, end cap style, and other properties. The Pen applies to all lines drawn by a GDI+ routine. For example, the DrawPolygon subroutine draws a series of lines, and its Pen parameter determines how all the lines are drawn.

A Brush object determines how areas are filled. A Brush sets the area's fill color, hatch pattern, color gradient, and texture. Chapter 31 provides more advanced details of these and provides figures showing examples. The Brush applies to GDI+ routines that fill closed areas such as FillRectangle, FillEllipse, and FillPolygon.

The basic steps for drawing a simple shape are:

1. Obtain a Graphics object.
2. Define a Brush object and fill with it.
3. Define a Pen object and draw with it.

For example, the Paint event handler shown in the following code runs when the form needs to redraw itself. The Paint event handler's e.Graphics parameter gives the Graphics object on which the program should draw. When the event handler is finished, Visual Basic copies the contents drawn in this Graphics object onto the parts of the form that must be redrawn. The event handler creates an orange SolidBrush object. SolidBrush is a class derived from the Brush class, so it will serve as a Brush. The program uses the brush to fill the circle bounded by the square with upper-left corners at (10, 10) and 100 pixels wide and 100 pixels tall. The code then creates a pen representing a 10-pixel wide blue line and uses it to draw the outline of the same circle. The result is an orange filled circle with a thick blue border.

```
Private Sub Form1_Paint(ByVal sender As Object,
 ByVal e As System.Windows.Forms.PaintEventArgs) Handles MyBase.Paint
    Using circle_brush As New SolidBrush(Color.Orange)
        e.Graphics.FillEllipse(circle_brush, 10, 10, 100, 100)
    End Using

    Using circle_pen As New Pen(Color.Blue, 10)
        e.Graphics.DrawEllipse(circle_pen, 10, 10, 100, 100)
    End Using
End Sub
```

Whenever the form is hidden and exposed, partially covered and exposed, minimized and restored or maximized, or resized to expose a new part of the form, the Paint event handler executes and redraws the circle.

The Graphics object's filling and drawing methods provide several overloaded versions. Most can take an object parameter that defines the shape to draw. For example, the FillEllipse and DrawEllipse methods can take a Rectangle as a parameter to define the ellipse's bounding rectangle.

This provides a convenient method for ensuring that a filled area and its outline match exactly. The following code draws the same circle as the previous example, but it uses a Rectangle method to define the circle. It uses the same Rectangle for its calls to FillEllipse and DrawEllipse, so it's easy to tell that they define exactly the same circle. If you modify this code to change the circle, you don't need to remember to change its coordinates everywhere they occur, because the circle is defined in only one place (the Rectangle).

```
Private Sub Form1_Paint(ByVal sender As Object,
 ByVal e As System.Windows.Forms.PaintEventArgs) Handles MyBase.Paint
    Dim rect As New Rectangle(10, 10, 100, 100)
    Using circle_brush As New SolidBrush(Color.Orange)
        e.Graphics.FillEllipse(circle_brush, rect)
    End Using

    Using circle_pen As New Pen(Color.Blue, 10)
        e.Graphics.DrawEllipse(circle_pen, rect)
    End Using
End Sub
```

All GDI+ drawing is based on these simple steps, but there are a lot of variations. Pens and brushes can be much more complicated. For example, you can fill a polygon with a color gradient that follows a path you define and then outline it with a custom dash pattern. The Graphics object also provides some fairly exotic drawing routines such as DrawBezier, which draws a Bézier curve.

BEAUTIFUL BÉZIERS

A Bézier curve is a smooth curve guided by a set of four control points. The curve starts at the first point and ends at the last. The middle two points control the curve's direction and curvature. The section "DrawBezier" later in this chapter gives more information on Bézier curves, and Figure 30-4 shows an example.

The following sections describe the namespaces containing the most useful GDI+ objects. Chapter 31 provides additional details and contains pictures of the results produced by many of these objects.

DRAWING NAMESPACES

Before jumping into GDI+ graphics, it's worth taking a moment to learn which namespaces contain which objects. By default, the System.Drawing namespace is imported into new Windows Forms applications, so you don't need to import it explicitly to work with Graphics, Pen, Brush, and the other basic drawing objects. However, if you want to create custom dash patterns, linear gradient color fills, or advanced image files, you must know which namespaces to import into your application.

System.Drawing

The System.Drawing namespace contains the most important and basic GDI+ classes. These classes include Graphics, Pen, Brush, Font, FontFamily, Bitmap, Icon, and Image. The following table describes the most useful System.Drawing classes.

CLASS	DESCRIPTION
Graphics	This is without doubt the most important class you'll use when creating graphics. An object of this class represents the surface you're going to draw on. That could be a PictureBox, form, bitmap in memory, or whatever. The class provides the methods for drawing lines, rectangles, ellipses, and so forth.
Pen	This class represents the drawing characteristics of a line, including the line's color, thickness, dash style, and so forth.
Pens	This class provides a large number of predefined pens with different colors and width 1. For example, you can use Pens.Blue as a standard blue pen.
Brush	This class represents how solid areas are filled. It determines whether the area is solidly colored, hatched, filled with a pattern, and so on.
Brushes	This class provides a large number of predefined solid brushes with different colors. For example, you can use Brushes.Green to fill an area with green.
SolidBrush	This class represents a solid brush. When you want to fill an object with a solid color, you use a SolidBrush class. This is by far the most common type of fill for most applications.
Bitmap	This class represents a bitmap image defined by pixel data rather than drawn lines.
Icon	This class represents a Windows icon similar to a bitmap.
Metafile	This class represents a graphic metafile that contains graphical operations that a program can record, save to a file, load from a file, and play back later.

CLASS	DESCRIPTION
Image	This is an abstract base class from which Bitmap, Icon, and Metafile inherit. Some routines can work with any of these kinds of objects, so they take an Image parameter. (In brief, a *bitmap* is a typical picture. An *icon* has additional transparency and possibly hot-spot information so it can act as a form or application icon or mouse pointer. A *metafile* defines a drawing in terms of lines, curves, and filled areas rather than using pixels in a bitmap. This lets the program later redraw the image scaled, rotated, or otherwise transformed smoothly without the distortion that would occur in a bitmapped image.)
Font	This class represents a particular font. It defines the font's name, size, and style (such as italic or bold).
FontFamily	This class represents a group of typefaces with similar characteristics.
Region	This class defines a shape created from rectangles and paths. You can fill a region, use it to perform hit testing, or clip a drawing to a region.

The System.Drawing namespace also defines some structures that a program can use for drawing. The following table describes the most useful of these structures.

STRUCTURE	DESCRIPTION
Color	This object defines a color's red, green, and blue components as values between 0 and 255, plus an *alpha* value that indicates the color's transparency. An alpha value of 0 means the object is completely transparent, and a value of 255 means it is totally opaque.
Point	This object defines a point's X and Y coordinates.
Size	This object defines a width and height.
Rectangle	This object defines a rectangle using a Point and a Size.

GDI+ routines work in pixels on the screen, printer, or whatever object they are drawing on, so the Point, Size, and Rectangle structures hold integral coordinates and sizes. However, the System .Drawing namespace also defines PointF, SizeF, and RectangleF classes to work with floating-point values.

The Color class provides a large number of predefined color values. For example, Color.PaleGreen defines a light green color. You can use these predefined colors instead of creating a new color object.

System.Drawing.Drawing2D

The System.Drawing.Drawing2D namespace contains most of the other objects you'll need to draw more advanced two-dimensional graphics. Some of these classes refine the more basic drawing classes, or define values for those classes. For example, the HatchBrush class represents a specialized type of Brush that fills with a hatch pattern. The following table describes this namespace's most useful classes.

CLASS	DESCRIPTION
HatchBrush	This class defines a Brush that fills an area with a hatch pattern. It defines the pattern, a foreground color, and a background color.
LinearGradientBrush	This class defines a Brush that fills an area with a linear color gradient. By default the fill shades smoothly from one color to another along a line that you define, but it can also represent multicolor gradients.
Blend	This class represents a blend pattern for a LinearGradientBrush or PathGradientBrush. For example, suppose that you define a gradient running from red to yellow. Normally the gradient is smooth and linear, but you can use a Blend to change this. For example, you might want the color to change from red to yellow very quickly, so it is 80 percent yellow only 20 percent of the way across the gradient.
PathGradientBrush	This class is similar to a LinearGradientBrush except its gradient follows a path rather than a line.
ColorBlend	This class defines colors and positions for LinearGradientBrush or PathGradientBrush. This lets you make the colors vary between several different colors along the brush's path.
GraphicsPath	This class represents a series of connected lines and curves. You can draw, fill, or clip to a GraphicsPath. For example, you could add text to a GraphicsPath and then draw its outline or clip a drawing so that it only shows within the text's path.
Matrix	This class represents a 3 × 3 transformation matrix. You can use matrixes to translate, scale, and rotate graphics operations. See the section "Transformation Basics" later in this chapter for more information.

Chapter 31 has more to say about the gradient brushes. It includes sample images.

The System.Drawing.Drawing2D namespace also defines some enumerations that are useful for more advanced drawing. The following table describes the most useful of these enumerations.

ENUMERATION	DESCRIPTION
DashCap	These values determine how the ends of a dash in a dashed line are drawn. DashCap values include Flat, Round, and Triangle. These give the same appearance as the Flat, Round, and Triangle LineCap enumerations shown in Figure 30-1.

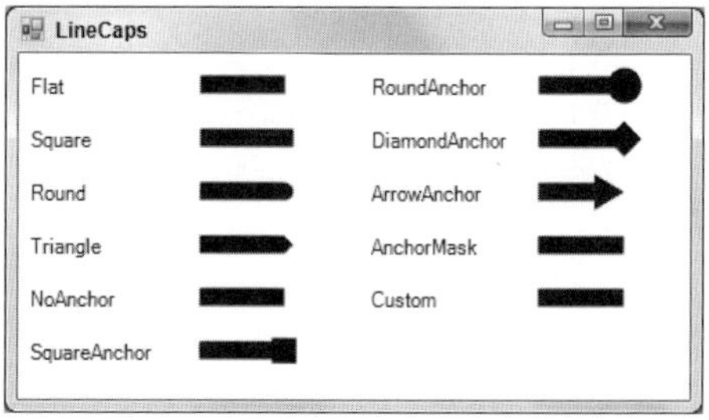

FIGURE 30-1: The LineCap enumeration determines how a line's end point is drawn.

ENUMERATION	DESCRIPTION
DashStyle	These values determine how a dashed line is drawn. DashStyle values include Dash, DashDot, DashDotDot, Dot, Solid, and Custom. If you set a Pen's DashStyle property to DashStyle.Custom, you should also set its DashPattern property to an array telling the Pen how many to pixels to draw and skip. For example, the array {10, 20, 5, 2} means draw 10, skip 2, draw 5, skip 2, and then repeat as necessary.
LineCap	These values determine how the ends of a line are drawn. Values include ArrowAnchor, DiamondAnchor, Flat, NoAnchor, Round, RoundAnchor, Square, SquareAnchor, Triangle, and Custom. If LineCap is Custom, you should use a CustomLineCap object to define the cap. Figure 30-1 shows the standard LineCaps.
LineJoin	These values determine how lines are joined by a GDI+ method that draws connected lines. For example, the DrawPolygon and DrawLines methods use this property. Figure 30-2 shows the possible values Bevel, Miter, Round, and MiterClipped. MiterClipped produces either a mitered or beveled corner, depending on whether the miter's length exceeds a certain limit determined by the Pen class's MiterLimit property. The MiterClipped example in Figure 30-2 shows one join that exceeds this limit and one that does not.

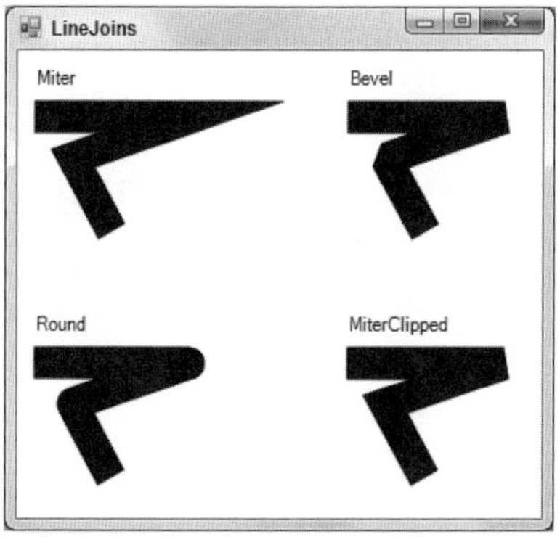

FIGURE 30-2: The LineJoin enumeration determines how lines are joined.

continues

(continued)

ENUMERATION	DESCRIPTION
HatchStyle	These values define the hatch style used by a HatchBrush object to fill an area. This enumeration includes 54 values, so they are not all listed here. Example program HatchStyles, which is available for download on the book's web site and shown in Figure 30-3, lists them and shows samples.

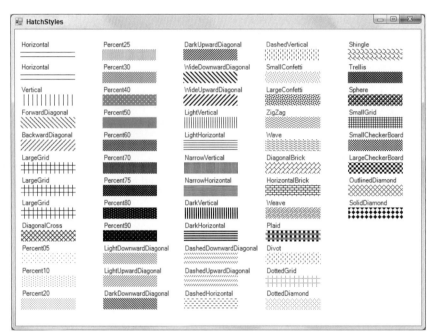

FIGURE 30-3: The HatchStyle enumeration determines how HatchBrush objects fill areas.

System.Drawing.Imaging

The System.Drawing.Imaging namespace contains classes that deal with more advanced bitmap graphics. It includes classes that define image file formats such as GIF and JPG, classes that manage color palettes, and classes that define metafiles. The following table describes this namespace's most useful classes.

CLASS	DESCRIPTION
ImageFormat	This class specifies an image's format. This can be one of BMP, EMF, EXIF, GIF, ICON, JPEG, memory bitmap, PNG, TIFF, or WMF. For descriptions of these image format types, try searching for them at web sites such as Webopedia (`www.webopedia.com`). The page `www.webopedia.com/DidYouKnow/Internet/2002/JPG_GIF_PNG.asp` discusses the differences between the three most common web image formats: GIF, JPEG, and PNG. The Microsoft web site has a comparison of the BMP, GIF, JPEG, Exif, PNG, and TIFF formats at `msdn.microsoft.com/ms536393.aspx`.
ColorMap	This class defines a mapping from old color values to new ones. You can use the ColorMap class to change some colors in an image to others.
ColorPalette	This class represents a palette of color values. (A *palette* is a collection of color values that are used in a particular image. For example, 8-bit color images can contain only 256 different colors. The image's color palette lists the colors used, and an 8-bit numeric value gives each pixel's color index in the palette. Recently, higher color models such as 16-, 24-, and 32-bit color have become more common. In those color models, the bits give each pixel's red, green, and blue color components directly rather than referring to a color palette, so no palette is needed.)
Metafile	This class represents a graphic metafile that contains drawing instructions. You can create, save, reload, and play back metafile information.
MetafileHeader	This class defines the attributes of a Metafile object.
MetaHeader	This class contains information about a Windows metafile (WMF).
WmfPlaceableFileHeader	This class defines how a metafile should be mapped to an output device. You can use this to ensure that the metafile is properly sized when you import it into a drawing program such as CorelDRAW.

System.Drawing.Text

The System.Drawing.Text namespace contains only three classes. These three classes provide a somewhat awkward method for learning about the fonts installed on the system or the fonts installed for an application. The following table describes these three classes.

CLASS	DESCRIPTION
FontCollection	A base class for the derived InstalledFontCollection and PrivateFontCollection classes. It provides a method that returns an array of FontFamily objects.
InstalledFontCollection	This is derived from the FontCollection class. This class's Families method returns an array containing FontFamily objects representing the fonts installed on the system.
PrivateFontCollection	This is also derived from the FontCollection class. Objects from this class represent fonts installed by an application from font files. The program can use this object to install fonts just for the use of the application and not for the rest of the system. This class provides methods for installing and listing the application's fonts.

It is rather odd that this class is defined just to provide one method that returns an array of FontFamily objects. It would have made more sense to give the FontCollection class a method such as ListInstalledFonts or to give the InstalledFontCollection class a shared method that creates such a FontCollection object. That's not the way these classes work, however.

Example program ListInstalledFonts uses the following code to list the system's installed fonts. The program creates an instance of the InstalledFontCollection and uses that object's Families method to get an array of the installed FontFamily objects. The program then loops through the array to list the fonts.

Available for download on Wrox.com

```
Private Sub Form1_Load(ByVal sender As System.Object,
 ByVal e As System.EventArgs) Handles MyBase.Load
    ' Get the installed fonts collection.
    Dim installed_fonts As New InstalledFontCollection

    ' Get an array of the system's font families.
    Dim font_families() As FontFamily = installed_fonts.Families()

    ' Display the font families.
    For Each font_family As FontFamily In font_families
        lstFonts.Items.Add(font_family.Name)
    Next font_family
    lstFonts.SelectedIndex = 0
End Sub
```

code snippet ListInstalledFonts

The System.Drawing.Text namespace also defines the TextRenderingHint enumeration. *Anti-aliasing* is a process that uses pixels of different shades to make jagged edges and curves appear smoother. You can set a Graphics object's TextRenderingHint property to tell Visual Basic whether it should use anti-aliasing to smooth the text.

HELPFUL HINTS

Some fonts include extra hints to help the system produce smoother text. If you set TextRenderingHint to include hints, you'll get smoother text but possibly with slight performance cost. Unless you're drawing a lot of text, however, you may not notice the difference in speed. For more information on font hinting, see en.wikipedia.org/wiki/Font_hinting and damieng .com/blog/2009/05/07/font-hinting-and-instructing-a-primer.

The following table describes the TextRenderingHint enumeration values.

ENUMERATION VALUE	DESCRIPTION
AntiAlias	Characters are drawn anti-aliased without hinting.
AntiAliasGridFit	Characters are drawn anti-aliased with hinting to improve stems and curves.
ClearTypeGridFit	Characters are drawn using ClearType glyphs with hinting. This takes advantage of ClearType font features. (In this context, a glyph is the image of a letter. Some fonts are drawn as glyphs and others such as TrueType fonts are drawn as outlines. TrueType was developed jointly by Microsoft and Apple. ClearType is a newer type of glyph font developed by Microsoft.)
SingleBitPerPixel	Characters are drawn without anti-aliasing or hinting. This is the fastest and lowest-quality setting.
SingleBitPerPixelGridFit	Characters are drawn without anti-aliasing, but with hinting.
SystemDefault	Characters are drawn using the system default setting.

The following code shows how a program can display text with and without anti-aliasing. First it creates a large font. It sets the Graphics object's TextRenderingHint property to AntiAliasGridFit and draws some text. Then it sets TextRenderingHint to SingleBitPerPixel and draws the text again.

Available for download on Wrox.com

```
Private Sub Form1_Paint(ByVal sender As Object,
 ByVal e As System.Windows.Forms.PaintEventArgs) Handles MyBase.Paint
    ' Make a big font.
    Using the_font As New Font(Me.Font.FontFamily,
        40, FontStyle.Bold, GraphicsUnit.Pixel)

        ' Draw without anti-aliasing.
        e.Graphics.TextRenderingHint = TextRenderingHint.AntiAliasGridFit
        e.Graphics.DrawString("Alias", the_font, Brushes.Black, 5, 5)
```

```
        ' Draw with anti-aliasing.
        e.Graphics.TextRenderingHint = TextRenderingHint.SingleBitPerPixel
        e.Graphics.DrawString("Alias", the_font, Brushes.Black, 5, 50)
    End Using
End Sub
```

code snippet AntiAliasing

Figure 30-4 shows the result, greatly enlarged to emphasize the difference. Notice how the anti-aliased version uses different shades of gray to make the text appear smoother.

For information on anti-aliasing as it applies to shapes other than text, see the section "Anti-Aliasing" later in this chapter.

System.Drawing.Printing

The System.Drawing.Printing namespace contains objects for printing and managing the printer's characteristics.

Normally, to generate a printed document, you create a PrintDocument object. You set the object's properties to define printing

FIGURE 30-4: Anti-aliasing (top) makes characters appear smoother.

attributes and then call its Print method. As it prints, the PrintDocument object generates PrintPage events that let you draw on the printout's pages.

Other classes in this namespace define properties for the PrintDocument object. The following table describes the most useful of these property objects.

CLASS	DESCRIPTION
PageSettings	This class defines the page settings for either an entire PrintDocument or for a particular page. This object has properties that are Margins, PaperSize, PaperSource, PrinterResolution, and PrinterSettings objects.
Margins	This class defines the margins for the printed page through its Top, Bottom, Left, and Right properties.
PaperSize	This class defines the paper's size. You can set the object's Kind property to a standard value such as A2, Legal, or Letter. Alternatively, you can set the object's Height and Width properties explicitly.
PaperSource	This class defines the printer's paper source. You can set this object's Kind property to such values as AutomaticFeed, Upper, Middle, Lower, Envelope, and ManualFeed.

CLASS	DESCRIPTION
PrinterResolution	This class defines the printer's resolution.
PrinterSettings	This class defines the printer's settings. You can use this class to get setting values such as whether the printer can print double-sided (CanDuplex), the names of the installed printers (InstalledPrinters), and the printer's supported resolutions (PrinterResolutions). You can use other properties to control the printer. For example, you can set the number of copies (Copies), set the minimum and maximum page number the user can select in a print dialog (MinimumPage and MaximumPage), and determine whether the printer collates its output (Collate).

GRAPHICS

Whenever you draw in Visual Basic .NET, you need a Graphics object. A Graphics object represents a drawing surface, whether it is a Form, PictureBox, Bitmap in memory, metafile, or printer surface.

The Graphics class provides many methods for drawing shapes and filling areas. It also includes properties and methods that modify the graphics results. For example, its transformation methods enable you to scale, translate, and rotate the drawing output.

The following sections describe the Graphics object's properties and methods for drawing, filling, and otherwise modifying the drawing.

Drawing Methods

The Graphics object provides many methods for drawing lines, rectangles, curves, and other shapes. The following table describes these methods.

METHOD	DESCRIPTION
DrawArc	Draws an arc of an ellipse.
DrawBezier	Draws a Bézier curve. See the section "DrawBezier" later in this chapter for an example.
DrawBeziers	Draws a series of Bézier curves. See the section "DrawBezier" later in this chapter for an example.
DrawClosedCurve	Draws a closed curve that joins a series of points, connecting the final point to the first point. See the section "DrawClosedCurve" later in this chapter for an example.

continues

(continued)

METHOD	DESCRIPTION
DrawCurve	Draws a smooth curve that joins a series of points. This is similar to a DrawClosedCurve, except that it doesn't connect the final point to the first point.
DrawEllipse	Draws an ellipse. To draw a circle, draw an ellipse with a width equal to its height.
DrawIcon	Draws an Icon onto the Graphics object's drawing surface.
DrawIconUnstretched	Draws an Icon object onto the Graphics object's drawing surface without scaling. If you know that you will not resize the icon, this may be faster than the DrawIcon method.
DrawImage	Draws an Image object onto the Graphics object's drawing surface. Note that Bitmap is a subclass of Image, so you can use this method to draw a Bitmap on the surface.
DrawImageUnscaled	Draws an Image object onto the drawing surface without scaling. If you know that you will not resize the image, this may be faster than the DrawImage method.
DrawLine	Draws a line.
DrawLines	Draws a series of connected lines. If you need to draw a series of connected lines, this is much faster than using DrawLine repeatedly.
DrawPath	Draws a GraphicsPath object. See the section "DrawPath" later in this chapter for an example.
DrawPie	Draws a pie slice taken from an ellipse.
DrawPolygon	Draws a polygon. This is similar to DrawLines, except that it connects the last point to the first point.
DrawRectangle	Draws a rectangle.
DrawRectangles	Draws a series of rectangles. If you need to draw a series of rectangles, this is much faster than using DrawRectangle repeatedly.
DrawString	Draws text on the drawing surface.

The following sections provide examples of some of the more complicated of these drawing methods.

DrawBezier

The DrawBezier method draws a Bézier curve. A Bézier curve is a smooth curve defined by four control points. The curve starts at the first point and ends at the last point. The line between the first and second points gives the curve's initial direction. The line connecting the third and fourth points gives its final direction as it enters the final point.

The following code draws a Bézier curve. It starts by defining the curve's control points. It then draws dashed lines connecting the points, so you can see where the control points are in the final drawing. You would omit this step if you just wanted to draw the curve. Next the program sets the Graphics object's SmoothingMode property to HighQuality, so the program draws a smooth, anti-aliased curve. The SmoothingMode property is described in the section "SmoothingMode" later in this chapter. The program creates a black pen three pixels wide and draws the Bézier curve.

```vb
Private Sub Form1_Paint(ByVal sender As Object,
  ByVal e As System.Windows.Forms.PaintEventArgs) Handles MyBase.Paint
    ' Define the Bezier curve's control points.
    Dim pts() As Point = {
        New Point(10, 10),
        New Point(200, 10),
        New Point(50, 200),
        New Point(200, 150)
    }
    ' Connect the points with dashed lines.
    Using dashed_pen As New Pen(Color.Black, 0)
        dashed_pen.DashStyle = Drawing2D.DashStyle.Dash
        For i As Integer = 0 To 2
            e.Graphics.DrawLine(dashed_pen, pts(i), pts(i + 1))
        Next i
    End Using

    ' Draw the Bezier curve.
    e.Graphics.SmoothingMode = Drawing2D.SmoothingMode.HighQuality
    Using bez_pen As New Pen(Color.Black, 3)
        e.Graphics.DrawBezier(bez_pen, pts(0), pts(1), pts(2), pts(3))
    End Using
End Sub
```

code snippet Bezier

Figure 30-5 shows the result. You can see in the picture how the control points determine the curve's end points and the direction it takes at them.

DrawBeziers

The DrawBeziers method draws a series of Bézier curves with common end points. It takes as parameters an array of points that determine the curves' end points and interior control points. The first four entries in the array represent the first curve's starting point, its two interior control points, and the curve's end point. The next curve uses the first curve's end point as its starting point, provides two interior control points, and its own end point. This pattern repeats for each of the curves. To draw N curves, the array should contain $3 * N + 1$ points.

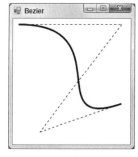

FIGURE 30-5 The DrawBezier method draws a smooth curve defined by four control points.

Figure 30-6 shows two Bézier curves drawn by the DrawBeziers method. Notice that the two curves share a common end point, but they do not meet smoothly. To make them meet smoothly, you would need to ensure that the last two points in the first curve and the first two points in the second curve (one of which is the same as the last point in the first curve) all lie along the same line.

DrawClosedCurve

Using the DrawBeziers method, you can draw a series of connected curves, but joining them smoothly is difficult. The DrawClosedCurve method connects a series of points with a smooth curve.

DrawClosedCurve takes as parameters a pen and an array of points to connect. Figure 30-7 shows an example. Notice that the curve is smooth and that it passes through each of the control points exactly. If you just want to connect a series of points smoothly, it is easier to use a closed curve than Bézier curves.

The DrawCurve method is similar to DrawClosedCurve, except that it doesn't connect the last point to the first.

Overloaded versions of the DrawClosedCurve method take a tension parameter that indicates how tightly the curve bends. Usually this value is between 0 and 1. The value 0 makes the method connect the curve's points with straight lines. The value 1 draws a nicely rounded curve. Tension values greater than 1 produce some strange (but sometimes interesting) results.

Figure 30-8 shows closed curves drawn with tension set to 0.0, 0.25, 0.5, 0.75, and 1.0. It uses progressively thicker lines so you can see which curves are which. You can see the curves growing smoother as the tension parameter increases and the pen thickens.

Overloaded versions of the DrawCurve method also take tension parameters.

DrawPath

The DrawPath method draws a GraphicsPath object as shown in the following code. The program creates a new, empty GraphicsPath object and uses its AddString method to add a string to the path. This method takes as parameters a string, FontFamily, font style, font size, point where the text should start, and a string format. The code sets the Graphics object's SmoothingMode property to draw anti-aliased curves. It then calls the FillPath method to fill the area defined by the GraphicsPath object with white and uses the DrawPath method to draw the path's outline in black.

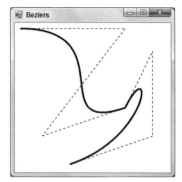

FIGURE 30-6: The DrawBeziers method draws a series of Bézier curves with common end points.

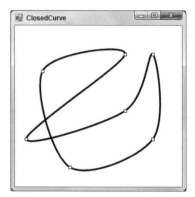

FIGURE 30-7: The DrawClosedCurve method draws a smooth curve connecting a series of points.

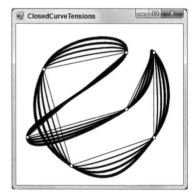

FIGURE 30-8: The DrawClosedCurve method's tension parameter determines how tightly the curve bends.

```
Private Sub Form1_Paint(ByVal sender As Object,
 ByVal e As System.Windows.Forms.PaintEventArgs) Handles MyBase.Paint
    ' Create a GraphicsPath.
    Using graphics_path As New Drawing2D.GraphicsPath
        ' Add some text to the path.
        graphics_path.AddString("GraphicsPath",
            New FontFamily("Times New Roman"),
            CInt(FontStyle.Bold),
            80, New Point(10, 10),
            StringFormat.GenericTypographic)

        ' Draw the path.
        e.Graphics.SmoothingMode = SmoothingMode.AntiAlias
        e.Graphics.FillPath(Brushes.White, graphics_path)
        Using thick_pen As New Pen(Color.Black, 3)
            e.Graphics.DrawPath(thick_pen, graphics_path)
        End Using
    End Using
End Sub
```

code snippet DrawTextPath

Figure 30-9 shows the result.

FIGURE 30-9: The DrawPath method draws the outline
defined by a GraphicsPath object.

You can use GraphicsPath objects to make all sorts of interesting effects. For example, you could fill
a GraphicsPath with a color gradient, hatch pattern, or bitmap.

Filling Methods

The Graphics object provides many methods for filling areas. These correspond exactly to the
drawing methods that define a closed shape. For example, DrawRectangle draws a rectangle and
FillRectangle fills one.

Corresponding draw and fill methods take exactly the same parameters, except that the filling methods use a Brush object instead of a Pen object. For example, the following statements fill and draw a GraphicsPath object. The only difference in the parameters is the Pen or Brush.

```
e.Graphics.FillPath(Brushes.White, graphics_path)
e.Graphics.DrawPath(Pens.Black, graphics_path)
```

The Graphics object provides the following methods for filling areas: FillClosedCurve, FillEllipse, FillPath, FillPie, FillPolygon, FillRectangle, and FillRectangles. These methods work the same way as the corresponding drawing methods (DrawClosedCurve, DrawEllipse, DrawPath, DrawPie, DrawPolygon, DrawRectangle, and DrawRectangles), except they fill an area with a brush rather than drawing it with a pen. See the section "Drawing Methods" earlier in this chapter for descriptions of these methods.

Other Graphics Properties and Methods

The following table describes the Graphics object's most useful properties and methods, other than those that draw or fill shapes.

PROPERTIES/METHODS	DESCRIPTION
AddMetafileComment	If the Graphics object is attached to a metafile, this adds a comment to it. Later, if an application enumerates the metafile's records, it can view the comments.
Clear	Clears the Graphics object and fills it with a specific color. For example, a form's Paint event handler might use the statement e.Graphics .Clear(Me.BackColor) to clear the form using its background color.
Clip	Determines the Region object used to clip a drawing on the Graphics surface. Any drawing command that falls outside of this Region is clipped off and not shown in the output.
Dispose	Releases the resources held by the Graphics object. You can use this method to free the resources of an object that you no longer need sooner than they would be freed by garbage collection. For a more detailed discussion, see the section "Dispose" in Chapter 26, "Classes and Structures."
DpiX	Returns the horizontal number of dots per inch (DPI) for this Graphics object's surface.
DpiY	Returns the vertical number of DPI for this Graphics object's surface.
EnumerateMetafile	If the Graphics object is attached to a metafile, this sends the metafile's records to a specified callback subroutine one at a time.
ExcludeClip	Updates the Graphics object's clipping region to exclude the area defined by a Region or Rectangle.

(continued)

`FromHdc`	Creates a new Graphics object from a handle to a device context (DC). (A *device context* is a structure that defines an object's graphic attributes: pen, color, fill, and so forth.)
`FromHwnd`	Creates a new Graphics object from a window handle (hWnd).

HANDLING HANDLES

The device context handle (hDC) and window handle (hWnd) have been around since the dawn of Windows. They were originally used by C and C++ programmers so they have a very different feel from modern .NET programming objects.

Usually, you can use the GDI+ drawing routines and ignore DCs. They're most useful when you need to use the older GDI functions or when using P/Invoke. These are advanced topics so they aren't covered here.

`FromImage`	Creates a new Graphics object from an Image object. This is a very common way to make a new Graphics object to manipulate a bitmap.
`InterpolationMode`	Determines whether drawing routines use anti-aliasing when drawing images. See the section "InterpolationMode" later in this chapter for an example.
`IntersectClip`	Updates the Graphics object's clipping region to be the intersection of the current clipping region and the area defined by a Region or Rectangle. (The *clipping region* determines where GDI+ will draw output. If a line falls outside of the clipping region, GDI+ doesn't draw the part that sticks out. Normally, an image's clipping region includes its whole visible area, but you can redefine it so that, for example, parts of the visible area are not drawn.)
`IsVisible`	Returns True if a specified point is within the Graphics object's visible clipping region.
`MeasureCharacterRanges`	Returns an array of Region objects that show where each character in a string will be drawn.
`MeasureString`	Returns a SizeF structure that gives the size of a string drawn on the Graphics object with a particular font.
`MultiplyTransform`	Multiplies the Graphics object's current transformation matrix by another transformation matrix.

continues

(continued)

PageScale	Determines the amount by which drawing commands are scaled. For example, if you set this to 2, every coordinate and measurement is scaled by a factor of 2 from the origin.
PageUnits	Determines the units of measurement. This can be Display (1/75 inch), Document (1/300 inch), Inch, Millimeter, Pixel, or Point (1/72 inch).
RenderingOrigin	Determines the point used as a reference when hatching. Normally this is (0, 0), so all HatchBrushes use the same RenderingOrigin and, if you draw two overlapping hatched areas, their hatch patterns line up. If you change this property, you can make their hatch patterns not line up.
ResetClip	Resets the object's clipping region, so the drawing is not clipped.
ResetTransformation	Resets the object's transformation matrix to the identity matrix, so the drawing is not transformed.
Restore	Restores the Graphics object to a state saved by the Save method. See the section "Saving and Restoring Graphics State" later in this chapter for an example.
RotateTransform	Adds a rotation to the object's current transformation. This rotates all drawing by a specified amount. See the section "Transformation Basics" later in this chapter for an example.
Save	Saves the object's current state in a GraphicsState object, so you can later restore it by calling the Restore method. See the section "Saving and Restoring Graphics State" later in this chapter for an example.
ScaleTransform	Adds a scaling transformation to the Graphics object's current transformation. This scales all drawing by a specified factor in the X and Y directions. See the section "Transformation Basics" later in this chapter for an example.
SetClip	Sets or merges the Graphics object's clipping area to another Graphics object, a GraphicsPath object, or a Rectangle. Only parts of drawing commands that lie within the clipping region are displayed.
SmoothingMode	Determines whether drawing routines use anti-aliasing when drawing lines and curves. See the section "SmoothingMode" later in this chapter for an example.
TextRenderingHint	Determines whether text is drawn with anti-aliasing and hinting. See the section "TextRenderingHint" later in this chapter and the section "System.Drawing.Text" earlier in this chapter for more details.

Transform	Gets or sets the Graphics object's transformation matrix. This matrix represents all scaling, translation, and rotation applied to the object.
TransformPoints	Applies the object's current transformation to an array of points.
TranslateTransform	Adds a translation transformation to the Graphics object's current transformation. This offsets all drawing a specified distance in the X and Y directions. See the section "Transformation Basics" later in this chapter for an example.

The following sections give examples of some of the more important (but confusing) Graphics properties and methods.

Anti-Aliasing

Aliasing is an effect caused when you draw lines, curves, and text that do not line up exactly with the screen's pixels. For example, if you draw a vertical line, it neatly fills in a column of pixels. If you draw a line at a 45-degree angle, it also fills a series of pixels that are nicely lined up, but the pixels are a bit farther apart and that makes the line appear lighter on the screen. If you draw a line at some other angle (for example, 30 degrees), the line does not line up exactly with the pixels. The line will contain some runs of two or three pixels in a horizontal group. The result is a line that is lighter than the vertical line and that is noticeably jagged.

A similar effect occurs when you resize a bitmap or other image. If you enlarge an image by simply drawing each pixel as a larger block of the same color, the result is blocky. If you shrink an image by removing some pixels, the result may have tears and gaps.

Anti-aliasing is a process that smoothes out lines, text, and images. Instead of drawing a series of pixels that all have the same color, the drawing routines give pixels different shades of color to make the result smoother.

The Graphics object provides three properties that control anti-aliasing for lines and curves, text, and images: SmoothingMode, TextRenderingHint, and InterpolationMode.

SmoothingMode

The SmoothingMode property controls anti-aliasing for drawn lines and curves, and for filled shapes. This property can take the values AntiAlias, Default, HighQuality, HighSpeed, and None. The following code shows how a program might draw a circle's outline and a filled circle using the HighQuality SmoothingMode:

```
gr.SmoothingMode = SmoothingMode.HighQuality
gr.DrawEllipse(Pens.Black, 10, 10, 20, 20)
gr.FillEllipse(Brushes.Black, 30, 10, 20, 20)
```

It's hard to see any difference in a book, although the difference is clear on the screen. It's not clear whether there's any difference between the Default, HighSpeed, and None modes, or between HighQuality and AntiAlias, at least on this computer. The HighQuality and AntiAlias modes are noticeably smoother than the others, however.

TextRenderingHint

The TextRenderingHint property controls anti-aliasing for text. This property can take the values AntiAlias, AntiAliasGridFit, ClearTypeGridFit, SingleBitPerPixel, SingleBitPerPixelGridFit, and SystemDefault. The following code shows how a program can draw text using the TextRenderingHint value AntiAliasGridFit:

```
gr.TextRenderingHint = TextRenderingHint.AntiAliasGridFit
gr.DrawString("TextRenderingHint", Me.Font, Brushes.Black, 10, 10)
```

As is the case with SmoothingMode values, it's hard to see any difference in a book, but the difference is clear on the screen. The TextRenderingHint value SingleBitPerPixel produces a poor result. SystemDefault and SingleBitPerPixelGridFit give an acceptable result (the default appears to be AntiAliasGridFit on this computer). AntiAlias and AntiAliasGridFit give the best results.

Most of the differences are quite subtle. The "grid fit" versions use hinting about where the characters are positioned to try to improve stems and curves. If you look extremely closely (perhaps with a magnifying glass), you can see that the base of a T is a bit cleaner and more solid in the AntiAliasGridFit and ClearTypeGridFit modes than in the AntiAlias mode. The "grid fit" modes also provide text that is slightly more compact horizontally than the AntiAlias mode.

InterpolationMode

The InterpolationMode property controls anti-aliasing when a program shrinks or enlarges an image. This property can take the values Bicubic, Bilinear, Default, High, HighQualityBicubic, HighQualityBilinear, Low, and NearestNeighbor.

Example program InterpolationModes, which is available for download on the book's web site, draws a smiley face in a bitmap. It then draws the bitmap's image at enlarged and reduced scales using InterpolationMode values. The differences are hard to see in a book but are obvious on the screen.

For enlarged images, the NearestNeighbor interpolation mode gives a sharply blocky result. All of the other modes give a slightly fuzzier image that looks a little smoother but that is still somewhat blocky.

For reduced images, the three high-quality modes (High, HighQualityBilinear, and HighQualityBicubic) produce very nice results. The other modes cause gaps in the lines in the reduced images.

All of the interpolation modes produce better results on photographic images instead of the line drawings used in this example.

Speed Considerations

The anti-aliasing settings for all three of these properties provide smoother results, but they are slower. For a few lines, strings, and images, the difference in performance won't be an issue. However, if you build a more intensive application (such as a mapping program that draws several thousand street segments on the form), you may notice a difference in speed. In that case, you may be willing to accept slightly worse appearance in exchange for better performance.

Transformation Basics

Graphical transformations modify the coordinates and sizes you use to draw graphics to produce a result that is scaled, translated, or rotated. For example, you could apply a scaling transformation that multiplies by 2 in the X direction and 3 in the Y direction. If you then drew a line between the points (10, 10) and (20, 20), the result drawn on the screen would connect the points (10 * 2, 10 * 3) = (20, 30) and (20 * 2, 20 * 3) = (40, 60). This stretches the line so it is larger overall, but it stretches its height more than its width (a factor of 3 versus a factor of 2). Notice that this also moves the line farther from the origin [from (10, 10) to (20, 30)]. In general, a scaling transformation moves an object farther from the origin unless it lies on the origin.

You don't really need to understand all the details of the mathematics of transformations to use them, but a little background is quite helpful.

Transformation Mathematics

In two dimensions, you can represent scaling, translation, and rotation with 3 x 3 matrixes. You represent a point with a vector of three entries, two for the X and Y coordinates and a final 1 that gives the vector three entries so that it matches the matrices.

When you multiply a point's coordinates by a transformation matrix, the result is the transformed point.

To multiply a point by a matrix, you multiply the point's coordinates by the corresponding entries in the matrix's columns. The first transformed coordinate is the point's coordinates times the first column, the second transformed coordinate is the point's coordinates times the second column, and the third transformed coordinate is the point's coordinates times the third column.

The following calculation shows the result when you multiply a generic vector <A, B, C> by a matrix. When you work with two-dimensional transformations, the value C is always 1.

```
                 | m11 m12 m13 |
   < A, B, C > * | m21 m22 m23 |
                 | m31 m32 m33 |

 = < A * m11 + B * m21 + C * m31,
     A * m12 + B * m22 + C * m32,
     A * m13 + B * m23 + C * m33 >
```

The following matrix represents scaling by a factor of *Sx* in the X direction and a factor of *Sy* in the Y direction:

```
| Sx  0  0 |
| 0  Sy  0 |
| 0   0  1 |
```

The following example shows the point (10, 20) multiplied by a matrix that represents scaling by a factor of 2 in the X direction and 3 in the Y direction. The result is the vector <20, 60, 1>, which represents the point (20, 60) as you should expect.

```
                | 2 0 0 |
< 10, 20, 1 > * | 0 3 0 |
                | 0 0 1 |
= < 10 * 2 + 20 * 0 + 1 * 0,
    10 * 0 + 20 * 3 + 1 * 0,
    10 * 0 + 20 * 0 + 1 * 1 >
= < 20, 60, 1 >
```

The following matrix represents translation through the distance *Tx* in the X direction and *Ty* in the Y direction:

```
|  1  0  0 |
|  0  1  0 |
| Tx Ty  1 |
```

The following matrix represents rotation through the angle *t*:

```
|  Cos(t) Sin(t) 0 |
| -Sin(t) Cos(t) 0 |
|    0      0    1 |
```

Finally, the following transformation, called the *identity transformation*, leaves the point unchanged. If you multiply a point by this matrix, the result is the same as the original point.

```
| 1 0 0 |
| 0 1 0 |
| 0 0 1 |
```

You can work through some examples to verify that these matrices represent translation, scaling, rotation, and the identity, or consult an advanced graphics programming book for proofs.

One of the most useful and remarkable properties of matrix/point multiplication is that it is associative. If *p* is a point and *T1* and *T2* are transformation matrices, p * *T1* * *T2* = (p * *T1*) * *T2* = p * (*T1* * *T2*).

This result means that you can multiply any number of transformation matrices together to create a single combined matrix that represents all of the transformations applied one after the other. You can then apply this single matrix to all the points that you need to draw. This can save a considerable amount of time over multiplying each point by a long series of matrices one at a time.

Transformation Code

The Graphics object maintains a current transformation matrix at all times, and it provides several methods that let you add more transformations to that matrix. The ScaleTransform, TranslateTransform, and RotateTransform methods add a new transformation to the current transformation. These methods take parameters that specify the amount by which points should be scaled, translated, or rotated.

A final parameter indicates whether you want to prepend the new transformation on the left (MatrixOrder.Prepend) or append it on the right (MatrixOrder.Append) of the current transformation. If you prepend the new transformation on the left, that transformation is applied before any that are already part of the current transformation. If you append the new transformation on the right, that transformation is applied after any that are already part of the current transformation.

Strangely, the default if you omit this parameter is to prepend the new transformation on the left. That means transformations that you add last are applied first. That, in turn, means that you must compose a combined transformation backward. If you want to rotate, then scale, then translate, you need to prepend the translation first, the scaling second, and the rotation last. That seems very counterintuitive.

A more natural approach is to explicitly set this final parameter to MatrixOrder.Append so that later transformations are applied after existing ones.

The following code shows how a program can use transformations to draw a complex result with a simple drawing routine. Subroutine DrawArrow draws an arrow within the rectangle 0 <= X <= 4, 0 <= Y <= 4. If you were to call this routine without any transformations, you would see a tiny arrow four pixels long and four pixels wide drawn in the upper-left corner of the form.

```vb
' Draw an arrow outline.
Private Sub DrawArrow(ByVal gr As Graphics, ByVal hatch_style As HatchStyle)
    Dim pts() As Point = {
        New Point(0, 1),
        New Point(2, 1),
        New Point(2, 0),
        New Point(4, 2),
        New Point(2, 4),
        New Point(2, 3),
        New Point(0, 3)
    }
    Using hatch_brush As New HatchBrush(hatch_style, Color.Black, Color.White)
        gr.FillPolygon(hatch_brush, pts)
    End Using

    Using black_pen As New Pen(Color.Black, 0)
        gr.DrawPolygon(black_pen, pts)
    End Using
End Sub

Private Sub Form1_Paint(ByVal sender As Object,
  ByVal e As System.Windows.Forms.PaintEventArgs) Handles MyBase.Paint
    ' Scale by a factor of 30.
```

```
    e.Graphics.ScaleTransform(30, 30, MatrixOrder.Append)
    DrawArrow(e.Graphics, HatchStyle.Horizontal)

    ' Translate 150 horizontally and 60 vertically.
    e.Graphics.TranslateTransform(150, 60, MatrixOrder.Append)
    DrawArrow(e.Graphics, HatchStyle.Vertical)

    ' Rotate 30 degrees.
    e.Graphics.RotateTransform(30, MatrixOrder.Append)
    DrawArrow(e.Graphics, HatchStyle.Cross)
End Sub
```

code snippet TransformArrow

This form's Paint event handler uses the ScaleTransform method to give the Graphics object a transformation that scales by a factor of 30 in both the X and Y directions. It then calls the DrawArrow routine, passing it the parameter HatchStyle.Horizontal. The result is an arrow near the upper-left corner but 30 times larger than the original arrow and filled with a horizontal hatch pattern.

Next the program uses the TranslateTransform method to add a transformation that translates 150 pixels in the X direction and 60 pixels vertically. It appends this transformation so that the drawing is first scaled (the scaling transformation is still part of the Graphics object's current transformation) and then translated. It calls DrawArrow again, passing it the parameter HatchStyle. Vertical, so the result is an arrow 30 times larger than the original, moved 150 pixels to the right and 60 pixels down, and filled with a vertical hatch pattern.

Finally, the program uses the RotateTransform method to add a transformation that rotates the drawing by 30 degrees clockwise around the origin in the upper-left corner. It again appends the transformation so that the drawing is first scaled, then translated, and then rotated. It calls DrawArrow, passing it the parameter HatchStyle.Cross, so the result is an arrow 30 times larger than the original, moved 150 pixels to the right and 60 pixels down, rotated 30 degrees, and filled with a crosshatch pattern.

Figure 30-10 shows the result.

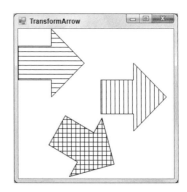

The Graphics object's methods for working with transformations include MultiplyTransform, PageScale, PageUnits, ResetTransformation, RotateTransform, ScaleTransform, Transform, TransformPoints, and TranslateTransform. See the section "Other Graphics Properties and Methods" earlier in this chapter for descriptions of those methods.

Note also that the transformations apply to text as well as drawn lines and filled shapes so a program can easily draw text that is stretched, scaled, and rotated.

FIGURE 30-10: This program draws arrows scaled, translated, and rotated.

Advanced Transformations

You can build very complex transformations by combining simple ones. For example, you can scale around an arbitrary point by combining simple translation and scaling transformations.

A normal scaling transformation moves an object farther away from the origin. If you scale the point (10, 20) by a factor of 20 in the X and Y directions, you get the point (200, 400), which is much farther from the origin. Similarly, if you scale all the points in a shape, all the points move farther from the origin.

To scale the object around some point other than the origin, first translate it so the point of rotation is centered at the origin. Then scale it and translate it back to its original position.

The following code scales a diamond around its center. The DrawDiamond subroutine draws a diamond centered at the point (125, 125). The form's Paint event handler calls DrawDiamond to draw the original diamond. It then translates to move the diamond's center to the origin, scales by a factor of 2 vertically and horizontally, and then reverses the first translation to move the origin back to the diamond's original center.

```vb
Private Sub DrawDiamond(ByVal gr As Graphics)
    Dim pts() As Point = {
        New Point(75, 125),
        New Point(125, 75),
        New Point(175, 125),
        New Point(125, 175)
    }
    gr.DrawPolygon(Pens.Black, pts)
End Sub

Private Sub Form1_Paint(ByVal sender As Object,
 ByVal e As System.Windows.Forms.PaintEventArgs) Handles MyBase.Paint
    ' Draw the original diamond.
    DrawDiamond(e.Graphics)

    ' Translate to center at the origin.
    e.Graphics.TranslateTransform(-125, -125, MatrixOrder.Append)

    ' Scale by a factor of 2.
    e.Graphics.ScaleTransform(2, 2, MatrixOrder.Append)

    ' Translate the center back to where it was.
    e.Graphics.TranslateTransform(125, 125, MatrixOrder.Append)

    ' Draw the diamond.
    DrawDiamond(e.Graphics)
End Sub
```

code snippet ScaleDiamond

Notice that line widths are also scaled by scaling transformations, so in this example, the enlarged diamond's borders are two pixels wide. The Pen object's Width property is a Single, so you can use fractional pen widths if necessary. For example, if you want to scale an object by a factor of 4 and you want the result to have a line width of 2, you can set the Pen's Width to 0.5 and let it scale.

If you want the final result to have a line width of 1, you can also set the Pen's Width to 0. This value tells the GDI+ routines to use a single pixel line width, no matter how the drawing is scaled.

Note also that the line width will not go below 1 if you use a scaling transformation to reduce the size of the drawing.

A particularly useful transformation maps a specific rectangle in world coordinates (the coordinates in which you draw) to a specific rectangle in device coordinates (the coordinates on the drawing surface). For example, you might graph a function in the world coordinates $-1 <= X <= 1$, $-1 <= Y <= 1$ and want to map it to the drawing surface rectangle $10 <= X <= 200$, $10 <= Y <= 200$.

To do this, you can first translate to center the world coordinate rectangle at the origin, scale to resize the rectangle to match the size of the device coordinate rectangle, and then translate to move the origin to the center of the device coordinate rectangle.

The MapRectangles subroutine shown in the following code maps a world coordinate rectangle into a device coordinate rectangle for a Graphics object. It begins by resetting the Graphics object's transformation to clear out anything that may already be in there. Next, the routine translates the center of the world coordinate rectangle to the origin, scales to stretch the world coordinate rectangle to the device coordinate rectangle's size, and then translates to move the origin to the center of the device-coordinate rectangle.

```
' Map a world coordinate rectangle to a device coordinate rectangle.
Private Sub MapRectangles(ByVal gr As Graphics,
 ByVal world_rect As Rectangle, ByVal device_rect As Rectangle)
    ' Reset the transformation.
    gr.ResetTransform()

    ' Translate to center the world coordinate
    ' rectangle at the origin.
    gr.TranslateTransform(
        CSng(-(world_rect.X + world_rect.Width / 2)),
        CSng(-(world_rect.Y + world_rect.Height / 2)),
        MatrixOrder.Append)

    ' Scale.
    gr.ScaleTransform(
        CSng(device_rect.Width / world_rect.Width),
        CSng(device_rect.Height / world_rect.Height),
        MatrixOrder.Append)

    ' Translate to move the origin to the center
    ' of the device coordinate rectangle.
    gr.TranslateTransform(
        CSng(device_rect.X + device_rect.Width / 2),
        CSng(device_rect.Y + device_rect.Height / 2),
        MatrixOrder.Append)
End Sub
```

code snippet MapRectangle

The following code shows how a program can use this subroutine to position a drawing. The DrawSmiley subroutine draws a smiley face within the area $0 <= X <= 1$, $0 <= Y <= 1$. The Paint event handler creates a Rectangle representing the device coordinates where it wants to draw the smiley face. It draws the rectangle so that you can see where the target is. The code then creates a world coordinate rectangle representing the area where the DrawSmiley subroutine draws the face.

```
' Draw a smiley face in the rectangle
' 0 < = X < = 1, 0 < = Y < = 1.
Private Sub DrawSmiley(ByVal gr As Graphics)
    Using the_pen As New Pen(Color.Black, 0)
        gr.FillEllipse(Brushes.Yellow, 0, 0, 1, 1) ' Face.
        gr.DrawEllipse(the_pen, 0, 0, 1, 1)
        gr.DrawArc(the_pen, 0.2, 0.2, 0.6, 0.6, 0, 180) ' Smile.
        gr.FillEllipse(Brushes.Black, 0.4, 0.4, 0.2, 0.25) ' Nose
        gr.FillEllipse(Brushes.White, 0.25, 0.15, 0.2, 0.25) ' Left eye.
        gr.DrawEllipse(the_pen, 0.25, 0.15, 0.2, 0.25)
        gr.FillEllipse(Brushes.Black, 0.35, 0.2, 0.1, 0.15)
        gr.FillEllipse(Brushes.White, 0.55, 0.15, 0.2, 0.25) ' Right eye.
        gr.DrawEllipse(the_pen, 0.55, 0.15, 0.2, 0.25)
        gr.FillEllipse(Brushes.Black, 0.65, 0.2, 0.1, 0.15)
    End Using
End Sub

Private Sub Form1_Paint(ByVal sender As Object,
 ByVal e As System.Windows.Forms.PaintEventArgs) Handles MyBase.Paint
    ' Draw the target rectangle.
    Dim device_rect As New Rectangle(50, 50, 150, 150)
    e.Graphics.DrawRectangle(Pens.Black, device_rect)

    ' Map between world and device coordinate rectangles.
    Dim world_rect As New Rectangle(0, 0, 1, 1)
    MapRectangles(e.Graphics, world_rect, device_rect)

    ' Draw the smiley face.
    DrawSmiley(e.Graphics)
End Sub
```

code snippet MapRectangle

Figure 30-11 shows the result. Note that the smiley face fits the target device coordinate rectangle nicely.

The preceding example uses subroutine MapRectangles to scale and translate a drawing, but the routine can also stretch or flip the drawing. For example, if the previous code used the following statement to define the device rectangle, the result has width 50 and height 150 so it is tall and thin:

```
Dim device_rect As New Rectangle(50, 50, 50, 150)
```

Subroutine MapRectangles can be particularly handy if you need to graph an equation. Normally, in device coordinates, the origin is in the upper-left corner and Y values increase downward. When you draw a graph, however, the origin is in the lower-left corner and Y values increase upward. You could work out how to modify the

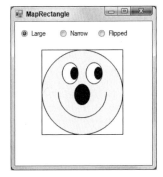

FIGURE 30-11: This program uses the MapRectangles subroutine to map a smiley face in world coordinates into a rectangle in device coordinates.

equation you are trying to draw so that it comes out in the proper orientation, but it's much easier to use subroutine MapRectangles to flip the Y coordinates.

To invert the Y coordinates, set the device coordinate Rectangle structure's Y property to the largest Y coordinate you want to use, and set its height to the negative of the height you really want to use. For example, suppose that you want the graph to fill the device coordinate rectangle 50 <= X <= 200, 50 <= Y <= 200. The rectangle has width and height 150, so you would use the following statement to map the coordinate windows:

```
Dim device_rect As New Rectangle(50, 200, 150, -150)
```

You could also use subroutine MapRectangles to flip a drawing's X coordinates, although the need for that is much less common.

Saving and Restoring Graphics State

The Graphics object's Save method takes a snapshot of the object's state and stores it in a GraphicsState object. Later, you can pass this GraphicsState object to the Graphics object's Restore method to return to the saved state.

Note that you can pass a particular GraphicsState object to the Restore method only once. If you want to use the same state again, you can call the Save method to save it again right after you restore it. That's the approach used by the following code. The program creates transformations that scale by a factor of 90 and then translate to move the origin to the center of the form. It then starts a loop to draw a rectangle rotated by angles between 5 degrees and 90 degrees.

Available for download on Wrox.com

```
Private Sub Form1_Paint(ByVal sender As Object,
  ByVal e As System.Windows.Forms.PaintEventArgs) Handles MyBase.Paint
    Using black_pen As New Pen(Color.Black, 0)
        ' Scale by a factor of 90.
        e.Graphics.ScaleTransform(90, 90, MatrixOrder.Append)

        ' Translate to center on the form.
        e.Graphics.TranslateTransform(
            Me.ClientRectangle.Width \ 2,
            Me.ClientRectangle.Height \ 2,
            MatrixOrder.Append)

        For i As Integer = 5 To 90 Step 5
            ' Save the state.
            Dim graphics_state As GraphicsState = e.Graphics.Save()

            ' Rotate i degrees.
            e.Graphics.RotateTransform(i, MatrixOrder.Prepend)

            ' Draw a rectangle.
            e.Graphics.DrawRectangle(black_pen, -1, -1, 2, 2)

            ' Restore the saved state.
            e.Graphics.Restore(graphics_state)
        Next i
    End Using
End Sub
```

code snippet SaveRestore

Within the loop it calls the Save method to record the Graphics object's current state. That state includes the initial scaling and translation. The loop then adds a rotation transformation to the Graphics object. It passes the RotateTransform method the value MatrixOrder.Prepend, so the rotation is added to the *front* of the transformation matrix. That makes the combined transformation apply the rotation before the scaling and translation. In other words, drawings are rotated, then scaled, and then translated.

The loop then draws the rectangle –1 <= X <= 1, –1 <= Y <= 1, and then calls Restore to restore the saved graphics state that holds just the scaling and translation.

Figure 30-12 shows the result.

There are usually many other ways to achieve the same effect in graphics programming. Though changing the order of transformations generally does not give the same result, you can always use different sets of transformations to produce the same outcome.

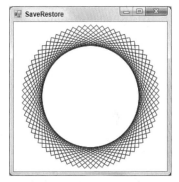

FIGURE 30-12: This program saves and restores the Graphics object's state containing a scaling and translation, adding an extra rotation as needed.

The following code shows a simpler For loop that creates the same result as the previous version. Rather than using Restore to remove the Graphics object's current rotation and replacing it with a new one, this version simply adds another 5-degree rotation to the current rotation. For example, a single 10-degree rotation is the same as two 5-degree rotations.

Available for download on Wrox.com

```
For i As Integer = 5 To 90 Step 5
    ' Rotate 5 degrees.
    e.Graphics.RotateTransform(5, MatrixOrder.Prepend)

    ' Draw a rectangle.
    Using black_pen As New Pen(Color.Black, 0)
        e.Graphics.DrawRectangle(black_pen, -1, -1, 2, 2)
    End Using
Next i
```

code snippet SaveRestore

Normally, you would not use Save and Restore if such a simple solution is available without them. Save and Restore are more useful when you want to perform several operations using the same transformation and other transformations are interspersed.

DRAWING EVENTS

When part of a control must be redrawn, it generates a Paint event. For example, if you minimize a form and then restore it, partially cover a form with another form, or enlarge a form, parts of the form must be redrawn.

The Paint event handler provides a parameter e of type PaintEventArgs. That parameter's Graphics property holds a reference to a Graphics object that the event handler should use to redraw the control. This Graphics object has its clipping region set to the part of the control that must be redrawn. For example, if you make a form wider, the Graphics object is clipped, so it only draws on the new piece of form on the right that was just exposed. Clipping the Graphics object makes drawing faster because the GDI+ routines can ignore drawing commands outside of the clipping region more quickly than they can draw them.

Clipping the Graphics object sometimes leads to unexpected results, particularly if the Paint event handler draws something that depends on the form's size. The following code draws a rectangle with an X in it, filling the form whenever the form resizes:

```
Private Sub Form1_Paint(ByVal sender As Object,
 ByVal e As System.Windows.Forms.PaintEventArgs) Handles MyBase.Paint
    e.Graphics.Clear(Me.BackColor)
    e.Graphics.DrawRectangle(Pens.Black, 0, 0,
        Me.ClientSize.Width - 1,
        Me.ClientSize.Height - 1)
    e.Graphics.DrawLine(Pens.Black, 0, 0,
        Me.ClientSize.Width - 1,
        Me.ClientSize.Height - 1)
    e.Graphics.DrawLine(Pens.Black,
        Me.ClientSize.Width - 1, 0,
        0, Me.ClientSize.Height - 1)
End Sub
```

code snippet PaintResizeX

Figure 30-13 shows the result after the form has been resized several times. Each time the form resizes, the Paint event handler draws the newly exposed region, but the existing drawing remains, giving the appearance of stacked envelopes.

Some computers generate Paint events every time the mouse moves during a resize, so the newly exposed areas are filled with a densely packed series of lines.

Paint event handlers also don't execute when the form shrinks. If the form shrinks, no new areas are exposed, so no Paint events fire.

Paint event handlers work well if the image on the control does not depend on the control's size. For example, if you want to draw an ellipse with bounds 10 <= X <= 300, 10 <= Y <= 10, then a Paint event handler works nicely. If a drawing depends on the control's size, you must also draw the picture in the control's Resize event handler.

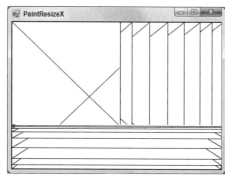

FIGURE 30-13: Paint event handlers that adjust their drawings based on the form's size may produce unexpected results.

You could implement the drawing code in the Paint and Resize event handlers, or call a drawing subroutine from those event handlers, but Visual Basic provides an easier way to deal with these issues. The following code shows how to make the form use its Paint event handler to draw itself whenever it is exposed or resized.

When the form loads, its Load event handler sets the form's ResizeRedraw property to True to indicate that the form should redraw itself when it is resized. Next the code calls the form's SetStyle method to set the AllPaintingInWmPaint style to True. This tells Visual Basic that the form does all of its drawing in its Paint event handler. Now, when the form resizes, Visual Basic raises the Paint event, so the program can do all of its drawing in the Paint event and not worry about the Resize event.

```vb
Private Sub Form1_Load() Handles MyBase.Load
    Me.ResizeRedraw = True
    Me.SetStyle(ControlStyles.AllPaintingInWmPaint, True)
End Sub

Private Sub Form1_Paint(ByVal sender As Object,
 ByVal e As System.Windows.Forms.PaintEventArgs) Handles Me.Paint
    e.Graphics.Clear(Me.BackColor)
    e.Graphics.DrawRectangle(Pens.Black, 0, 0,
        Me.ClientSize.Width - 1,
        Me.ClientSize.Height - 1)
    e.Graphics.DrawLine(Pens.Black, 0, 0,
        Me.ClientSize.Width - 1,
        Me.ClientSize.Height - 1)
    e.Graphics.DrawLine(Pens.Black,
        Me.ClientSize.Width - 1, 0,
        0, Me.ClientSize.Height - 1)
End Sub
```

code snippet PaintResizeX

SUMMARY

Visual Basic .NET provides a huge number of graphical classes. This chapter provides an overview of these classes. It also focuses on the most important graphics class: Graphics. The Graphics class provides methods that let you draw and fill rectangles, ellipses, polygons, curves, lines, and other shapes. Pen and Brush objects determine the appearance of lines and filled areas. Other Graphics properties and methods let you determine the types of anti-aliasing used when drawing different kinds of objects, and how drawings are transformed.

Chapter 31 describes the next two most important graphics classes: Brush and Pen. It also explains the GraphicsPath object that you can use to draw and fill paths consisting of lines, shapes, curves, and text.

31

Brushes, Pens, and Paths

After Graphics, Pen and Brush are the two most important graphics classes. Whenever you perform any drawing operation that does not manipulate an image's pixels directly, you use a Pen or a Brush.

➤ Pen classes control the appearance of lines. They determine a line's color, thickness, dash style, and caps.

➤ Brush classes control the appearance of filled areas. They can fill an area with solid colors, hatched colors, a tiled image, or different kinds of color gradients.

This chapter describes the Pen and Brush classes in detail. It shows how to use these classes to draw and fill all sorts of interesting shapes.

This chapter also describes the GraphicsPath class that represents a series of lines, shapes, curves, and text. You can fill a GraphicsPath using Pen and Brush classes.

> **EXAMPLES GALORE!**
>
> You can download example programs demonstrating most of the methods described in this chapter on the book's web site. The examples also include code to draw the figures in this chapter.

PEN

The Pen object determines how lines are drawn. It determines the lines' color, thickness, dash style, join style, and end cap style.

A program can explicitly create Pen objects, but often it can simply use one of the more than 280 pens that are predefined by the Pens class. For example, the following code draws a rectangle using a hot pink line that's one pixel wide:

```
gr.DrawRectangle(Pens.HotPink, 10, 10, 50, 50)
```

Pen objects are scaled by transformations applied to a Graphics object, however, so the result is not necessarily one pixel thick. If the Graphics object applies a transformation that scales by a factor of 10, the resulting line will have thickness 10.

One solution to this problem is to create a new Pen object setting its thickness to 0.1, as shown in the following code. The thickness is scaled to 0.1 * 10 = 1.

```
gr.DrawRectangle(New Pen(Color.HotPink, 0.1), 10, 10, 50, 50)
```

Another solution is to create a pen with thickness 0. The GDI + routines always draw lines that have 0 thickness as one pixel wide.

The Pen class provides several overloaded constructors, which are described in the following table.

CONSTRUCTORS	DESCRIPTION
Pen(brush)	Creates a pen of thickness 1 using the indicated Brush. Lines are drawn as rectangles filled with the Brush. This makes the most sense for relatively thick lines, so the fill is visible. It produces sometimes irregular dashed or dotted results for thin lines.
Pen(color)	Creates a pen of thickness 1 using the indicated color.
Pen(brush, thickness)	Creates a pen with the indicated thickness (a Single) using a Brush.
Pen(color, thickness)	Creates a pen with the indicated thickness (a Single) using the indicated color.

The following table describes some of the Pen class's most useful properties and methods.

PROPERTY OR METHOD	PURPOSE
Alignment	Determines whether the line is drawn inside or centered on the theoretical perfectly thin line specified by the drawing routine. See the section "Alignment" later in this chapter for examples.
Brush	Determines the Brush used to fill lines.
Color	Determines the lines' color.
CompoundArray	Lets you draw lines that are striped lengthwise. See the section "CompoundArray" later in this chapter for examples.
CustomEndCap	Determines the line's end cap. See the section "Custom Line Caps" later in this chapter for examples.
CustomStartCap	Determines the line's start cap. See the section "Custom Line Caps" later in this chapter for examples.

PROPERTY OR METHOD	PURPOSE
DashCap	Determines the cap drawn at the ends of dashes. This can be Flat, Round, or Triangle.
DashOffset	Determines the distance from the start of the line to the start of the first dash.
DashPattern	An array of Singles that specifies a custom dash pattern. The array entries tell how many pixels to draw, skip, draw, skip, and so forth. Note that these values are scaled if the pen is not one pixel wide.
DashStyle	Determines the line's dash style. This value can be Dash, DashDot, DashDotDot, Dot, Solid, or Custom. If you set the DashPattern property, this value is set to Custom. Note that the dashes and gaps between them are scaled if the pen is not one pixel wide.
EndCap	Determines the cap used at the end of the line. This value can be ArrowAnchor, DiamondAnchor, Flat, NoAnchor, Round, RoundAnchor, Square, SquareAnchor, Triangle, and Custom. If LineCap is Custom, you should use a CustomLineCap object to define the cap. Figure 30-1 in Chapter 30 shows the standard LineCap values.
LineJoin	Determines how lines are joined by a GDI+ method that draws connected lines. For example, the DrawPolygon and DrawLines methods use this property. This value can be Bevel, Miter, and Round. Figure 30-2 in Chapter 30 shows these values.
MultiplyTransform	Multiplies the Pen class's current transformation by another transformation matrix. See the section "Pen Transformations" later in this chapter for more information and examples.
ResetTransform	Resets the Pen class's transformation to the identity transformation. See the section "Pen Transformations" later in this chapter for more information and examples.
RotateTransform	Adds a rotation transformation to the Pen class's current transformation. See the section "Pen Transformations" later in this chapter for more information and examples.
ScaleTransform	Adds a scaling transformation to the Pen class's current transformation. See the section "Pen Transformations" later in this chapter for more information and examples.
SetLineCap	This method takes parameters that let you specify the Pen class's StartCap, EndCap, and LineJoin properties at the same time.
StartCap	Determines the cap used at the start of the line. See the EndCap property for details.

continues

(continued)

PROPERTY OR METHOD	PURPOSE
Transform	Determines the transformation applied to the initially circular "pen tip" used to draw lines. The transformation lets you draw with an elliptical tip. See the section "Pen Transformations" later in this chapter for more information and examples.
TranslateTransform	Adds a translation transformation to the Pen class's current transformation. Pen objects ignore any translation component in their transformations, so this method has no effect on the Pen class's final appearance and was probably added for consistency and completeness. See the section "Pen Transformations" later in this chapter for more information and examples.
Width	The width of the pen. This value is scaled if the pen is transformed either by its own transformation or by the transformation of the Graphics object that uses it.

The following sections describe some of the Pen class's more confusing properties and methods.

Alignment

The Alignment property determines whether thick lines for closed curves are drawn inside or centered on the theoretical perfectly thin line specified by the drawing routine. This property can take the values Center or Inset.

The following code draws a circle with a thick white line and its pen's Alignment set to Center. It then draws the same circle with a thin black line. Next, the code repeats these steps, drawing its thick white circle with Alignment set to Inset.

Available for
download on
Wrox.com

```
Private Sub Form1_Paint(ByVal sender As Object,
 ByVal e As System.Windows.Forms.PaintEventArgs) Handles MyBase.Paint
    Using the_pen As New Pen(Color.LightGray, 20)
        the_pen.Alignment = PenAlignment.Center
        e.Graphics.DrawEllipse(the_pen, 25, 25, 100, 100)
        e.Graphics.DrawEllipse(Pens.Black, 25, 25, 100, 100)

        the_pen.Alignment = PenAlignment.Inset
        e.Graphics.DrawEllipse(the_pen, 150, 25, 100, 100)
        e.Graphics.DrawEllipse(Pens.Black, 150, 25, 100, 100)
    End Using
End Sub
```

code snippet PenAlignments

Figure 31-1 shows a more elaborate program that draws samples of all of the Alignment values. Notice that all of the Alignment values produce the same result as Center, except for the value Inset.

The Alignment property applies only to closed figures such as ellipses, rectangles, and polygons. Open figures such as line segments, arcs, and unclosed curves are always drawn centered.

CompoundArray

The CompoundArray property lets a program draw lines that are striped lengthwise. This property is an array of Single values that determine where the solid and empty parts of the line lie as a fraction of the line's

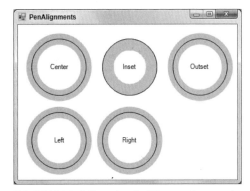

FIGURE 31-1: A Pen class's Alignment property determines whether the line is drawn on or inside its theoretical perfectly thin line.

width. For example, an array containing the values {0.0, 0.25, 0.75, 1.0} makes the first quarter of the line solid (0.0–0.25), the next half of the line not drawn (0.25–0.75), and the last quarter of the line solid (0.75–1.0).

The following code demonstrates the CompoundArray property. It creates a thick pen, sets its CompoundArray property to draw a line with a thin empty stripe down the middle, and draws a line. Next, the code sets the CompoundArray property to draw three equally sized and spaced stripes, and draws a rectangle and circle. Finally, the code sets the Graphics object's SmoothingMode property to AntiAlias, resets CompoundArray to draw a line with two thin empty stripes, and draws another circle.

```
Private Sub Form1_Paint(ByVal sender As Object,
  ByVal e As System.Windows.Forms.PaintEventArgs) Handles MyBase.Paint
    e.Graphics.SmoothingMode = Drawing2D.SmoothingMode.AntiAlias

    Using the_pen As New Pen(Color.Black, 10)
        the_pen.CompoundArray = New Single() {0.0, 0.45, 0.55, 1.0}
        e.Graphics.DrawLine(the_pen, 10, 20, 400, 20)

        the_pen.CompoundArray = New Single() {0.0, 0.2, 0.4, 0.6, 0.8, 1.0}
        e.Graphics.DrawRectangle(the_pen, 20, 50, 100, 100)
        e.Graphics.DrawEllipse(the_pen, 150, 50, 100, 100)

        the_pen.CompoundArray = New Single() {0.0, 0.1, 0.2, 0.8, 0.9, 1.0}
        e.Graphics.SmoothingMode = Drawing2D.SmoothingMode.AntiAlias
        e.Graphics.DrawEllipse(the_pen, 300, 50, 100, 100)
    End Using
End Sub
```

code snippet CompoundArrays

Figure 31-2 shows the result.

Custom Line Caps

The Pen class's CustomEndCap and CustomStartCap properties let you define your own end caps for lines. To make a custom cap, make a GraphicsPath object that defines the cap's drawing commands. This object should use a coordinate system where X increases to the left of the line, and Y increases in the direction of the line, as shown in Figure 31-3.

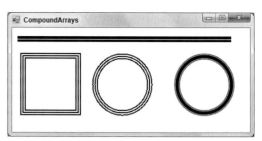

FIGURE 31-2: A Pen class's CompoundArray property lets you draw line that are striped lengthwise.

Next, create a CustomLineCap object, passing its constructor the GraphicsPath object. Pass the GraphicsPath as the first parameter if it defines a fill for the cap. Pass it as the second parameter if it defines drawn lines for the cap. Pass Nothing for the other parameter.

You can use the CustomLineCap object's properties and methods to modify its appearance. For example, its StrokeJoin property determines the style used to join the lines in the GraphicsPath, and its SetStrokeCaps method lets you specify the end caps for the lines in the GraphicsPath.

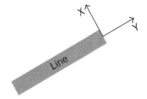

FIGURE 31-3: When building a custom line cap, X increases to the line's left and Y increases in the line's direction.

The following code shows an example. It defines an array of points that defines lines that make an X. It makes a GraphicsPath object and uses its AddLines method to add the lines to it. It then creates a CustomLineCap object, passing its constructor this GraphicsPath. The code makes a Pen and sets its CustomStartCap and CustomEndCap properties to the CustomLineCap object. It then draws four lines with different widths.

```
Private Sub Form1_Paint(ByVal sender As Object,
  ByVal e As System.Windows.Forms.PaintEventArgs) Handles MyBase.Paint
    ' Make a GraphicsPath that draws an X.
    Dim pts() As Point = {
        New Point(-2, -2),
        New Point(0, 0),
        New Point(-2, 2),
        New Point(0, 0),
        New Point(2, 2),
        New Point(0, 0),
        New Point(2, -2)
    }

    Using cap_path As New GraphicsPath
    cap_path.AddLines(pts)

    ' Make the CustomLineCap.
    Using x_cap As New CustomLineCap(Nothing, cap_path)
        ' Draw some lines with x_cap.
        Using the_pen As New Pen(Color.Black, 1)
            the_pen.CustomStartCap = x_cap
```

```
                the_pen.CustomEndCap = x_cap
                e.Graphics.DrawLine(the_pen, 50, 10, 200, 10)

                the_pen.Width = 5
                e.Graphics.DrawLine(the_pen, 50, 40, 200, 40)

                the_pen.Width = 10
                e.Graphics.DrawLine(the_pen, 50, 100, 200, 100)

                the_pen.Width = 20
                e.Graphics.DrawLine(the_pen, 50, 200, 200, 200)
            End Using
        End Using
    End Sub
```

code snippet CompoundArrays

Figure 31-4 shows the result.

Pen Transformations

The Pen class has properties and methods that let you define a transformation. The Pen class applies this transformation to its initially circular tip when drawing lines. (For basic information on transformations, see the section "Transformation Basics" in Chapter 30, "Drawing Basics.")

The Pen class ignores any translation component in the transformation, so the result is always an ellipse. (With some thought, you can probably convince yourself that any combination of scaling and rotation applied to a circle always gives an ellipse.) When the program draws with the transformed pen, its lines may have thick and thin elements similar to the ones you get when you draw with a calligraphy pen.

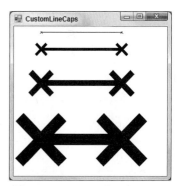

FIGURE 31-4: This program uses a CustomLineCap that draws an X at the end of lines.

The following code uses a transformed Pen to draw a circle. It begins by defining some constants to make working with the circle easier. It defines the circle's center (Cx, Cy) and its radius R. It also defines a constant to represent the Pen's Width. Next, the program creates a new Pen with the desired width. It applies a scaling transformation to the pen, scaling by a factor of 4 in the Y direction. For the purposes of scaling Pens, the X and Y directions match those on the screen. This transformation stretches the Pen class's tip vertically on the screen. Next, the program rotates the Pen's tip by 45 degrees.

```
Private Sub Form1_Paint(ByVal sender As Object,
 ByVal e As System.Windows.Forms.PaintEventArgs) Handles MyBase.Paint
    Const Cx As Integer = 120
    Const Cy As Integer = 120
    Const R As Integer = 100
    Const PEN_WID As Integer = 10

    ' Draw a circle with a transformed Pen.
    Using the_pen As New Pen(Color.Black, PEN_WID)
```

```
            the_pen.ScaleTransform(1, 4, MatrixOrder.Append)
            the_pen.RotateTransform(45, MatrixOrder.Append)
            e.Graphics.SmoothingMode = SmoothingMode.AntiAlias
            e.Graphics.DrawEllipse(the_pen, Cx - R, Cx - R, R * 2, R * 2)
        End Using

        ' Draw "Pen tips" on the circle.
        e.Graphics.ScaleTransform(1, 4, MatrixOrder.Append)
        e.Graphics.RotateTransform(45, MatrixOrder.Append)

        For angle As Single = 0 To 2 * PI Step PI / 8
            Dim graphics_state As GraphicsState = e.Graphics.Save
            e.Graphics.TranslateTransform(
                CSng(Cx + R * Cos(angle)),
                CSng(Cy + R * Sin(angle)),
                MatrixOrder.Append)
            e.Graphics.DrawEllipse(Pens.White,
                -PEN_WID / 2, -PEN_WID / 2, PEN_WID, PEN_WID)
            e.Graphics.Restore(graphics_state)
        Next angle
    End Sub
```

code snippet TransformedPen

The program sets the Graphics object's SmoothingMode property to AntiAlias and draws a circle centered at (Cx, Cy) with radius R.

Next, the program draws some ellipses showing where the Pen's tip was while it was drawing the circle. It starts by applying the same scaling and rotation transformations to the Graphics object. The program will later draw a circle with a diameter equal to the line's thickness and centered at the origin. These transformations give the circle the same shape as the Pen class's transformed tip. The final step is to translate these ellipses so that they lie along the path of the circle drawn earlier with the transformed Pen class.

The program uses a loop to make an angle vary from 0 to 2 *PI radians in steps of PI / 8. For each angle, the code saves the Graphics object's state so it doesn't lose the scaling and rotation it already applied. It then applies a translation transformation to move the origin to a point on the circle drawn earlier. The center of the circle is at (Cx, Cy). The points on the circle are offset from that point by R * Cos(angle) in the X direction and R * Sin(angle) in the Y direction.

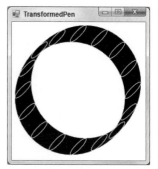

Having defined all these transformations, the program draws a white ellipse centered at the origin and with diameter matching the Pen class's width. The transformations scale, rotate, and translate the ellipse to match one of the Pen class's tip positions while it drew the large ellipse. Finally, the code restores the saved graphics state so it is ready for the next trip through the loop.

FIGURE 31-5: The white ellipses show where the Pen object's transformed tip was as it drew the large black circle.

Figure 31-5 shows the result. The small white ellipses show the positions that the Pen object's tip took while drawing the large black circle. This picture should give you a good intuition for how transformed Pens work.

BRUSH

The Brush object determines how areas are filled when you draw them using the Graphics object's methods FillClosedCurve, FillEllipse, FillPath, FillPie, FillPolygon, FillRectangle, and FillRectangles. Different types of Brushes fill areas with solid colors, hatch patterns, and color gradients.

The Brush class itself is an abstract or MustInherit class, so you cannot make instances of the Brush class itself. Instead, you can create instances of one of the derived classes SolidBrush, TextureBrush, HatchBrush, LinearGradientBrush, and PathGradientBrush. The following table briefly describes these classes.

CLASS	PURPOSE
SolidBrush	Fills areas with a single solid color
TextureBrush	Fills areas with a repeating image
HatchBrush	Fills areas with a repeating hatch pattern
LinearGradientBrush	Fills areas with a linear gradient of two or more colors
PathGradientBrush	Fills areas with a color gradient that follows a path

The following sections describe these classes in more detail and provide examples.

SolidBrush

A SolidBrush class fills areas with a single solid color. This class is extremely simple. It provides a single constructor that takes a parameter giving the brush's color. Its only commonly useful property is Color, which determines the brush's color.

A program can create a SolidBrush using its constructor, or it can use one of the 280+ predefined solid brushes defined by the Brushes class. The following code demonstrates both techniques. First, it creates a red SolidBrush and uses it to fill a rectangle. Then, it uses the Brushes class's Blue property to get a standard blue solid brush and fills another rectangle with that brush.

```
Private Sub Form1_Paint(ByVal sender As Object,
 ByVal e As System.Windows.Forms.PaintEventArgs) Handles MyBase.Paint
    Dim red_brush As New SolidBrush(Color.Red)
    e.Graphics.FillRectangle(red_brush, 10, 10, 200, 100)

    Dim blue_brush As Brush = Brushes.Blue
    e.Graphics.FillRectangle(blue_brush, 10, 120, 200, 100)
End Sub
```

code snippet UseSolidBrush

TextureBrush

A TextureBrush class fills areas with an image, usually a Bitmap. The following table describes this class's most useful properties and methods.

PROPERTY OR METHOD	PURPOSE
Image	The image that the brush uses to fill areas.
MultiplyTransform	Multiplies the brush's current transformation by another transformation matrix.
ResetTransform	Resets the brush's transformation to the identity transformation.
RotateTransform	Adds a rotation transformation to the brush's current transformation.
ScaleTransform	Adds a scaling transformation to the brush's current transformation.
Transform	A transformation that the brush applies to its image before using it to fill areas.
TranslateTransform	Adds a translation transformation to the brush's current transformation.
WrapMode	Determines how the brush wraps the image. This property can take the values Clamp (use a single copy that overlaps the origin of the shape's bounding rectangle), Tile (tile normally), TileFlipX (tile flipping every other column of images over horizontally), TileFlipY (tile flipping every other row of images over vertically), and TileFlipXY (tile flipping every other column horizontally and every other row vertically). Figure 31-6 shows examples of these settings.

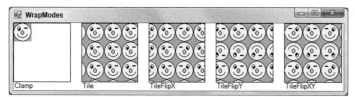

FIGURE 31-6: The TextureBrush class's WrapMode property determines how the brush tiles its image.

If you look closely at Figure 31-6, you'll see that the images do not always begin in the upper-left corner of the shape being filled. The brush essentially sets its tiling origin to the form's upper-left corner and then spaces its images accordingly.

If you want to move the tiling origin, you can apply a translation transformation to the brush to move the image to the new origin. The following code creates a TextureBrush using a PictureBox's Image property to define its image and sets WrapMode to TileFlipXY. It translates the brush to the point (50, 100) and then fills a rectangle with its upper-left corner at this same point. This ensures that the first copy of the brush's image is placed exactly in the rectangle's upper-left corner. It also ensures that the first image is not flipped vertically or horizontally.

```
' Make a TextureBrush using the smiley face.
Using texture_brush As New TextureBrush(picSmiley.Image)
    texture_brush.WrapMode = System.Drawing.Drawing2D.WrapMode.TileFlipXY
```

```
      texture_brush.TranslateTransform(50, 100)
      DrawSample(e.Graphics, texture_brush, 50, 100)
   End Using
```

The following code uses a transformed TextureBrush. First, it generates points to define a star-shaped polygon and creates a TextureBrush using a PictureBox Image property to define its image. Next, the program scales the brush by a factor of 2 in the X direction, making the smiley face wider than normal. It then rotates the brush by 30 degrees, fills the star-shaped polygon with the brush, and then outlines the polygon in black.

```
Private Sub Form1_Paint(ByVal sender As Object,
 ByVal e As System.Windows.Forms.PaintEventArgs) Handles MyBase.Paint
    ' Generate points to draw a star shape.
    Dim cx As Integer = Me.ClientSize.Width \ 2
    Dim cy As Integer = Me.ClientSize.Height \ 2
    Dim r1 As Integer = Min(cx, cy) - 10
    Dim r2 As Integer = Min(cx, cy) \ 2
    Dim pts(9) As Point
    For i As Integer = 0 To 9 Step 2
        pts(i).X = cx + CInt(r1 * Cos(i * PI / 5 - PI / 2))
        pts(i).Y = cy + CInt(r1 * Sin(i * PI / 5 - PI / 2))
        pts(i + 1).X = cx + CInt(r2 * Cos((i + 1) * PI / 5 - PI / 2))
        pts(i + 1).Y = cy + CInt(r2 * Sin((i + 1) * PI / 5 - PI / 2))
    Next i

    ' Make a TextureBrush using the smiley face.
    Using texture_brush As New TextureBrush(picSmiley.Image)
        texture_brush.ScaleTransform(2, 1, MatrixOrder.Append)
        texture_brush.RotateTransform(30, MatrixOrder.Append)
        e.Graphics.FillPolygon(texture_brush, pts)
    End Using

    e.Graphics.DrawPolygon(Pens.Black, pts)
End Sub
```

code snippet UseSolidBrush

Figure 31-7 shows the result. Note that not only is the image transformed, but the tiled rows and columns are also transformed.

HatchBrush

A *hatch pattern* fills an area with a simple pattern of lines, dots, or other shapes. For example, you could fill a rectangle with a series of black lines drawn at a 45 degree angle.

A TextureBrush class gives you complete control over every pixel in the filled area so you could use a simple image to build hatch patterns. However, for standard hatch patterns it's a lot easier to use the HatchBrush class.

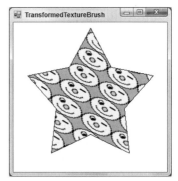

FIGURE 31-7: This star is filled with a TextureBrush that is scaled and rotated.

HatchBrush is a relatively simple class. Its three most useful properties are BackgroundColor, ForegroundColor, and HatchStyle. ForegroundColor and BackgroundColor determine the colors the brush uses. HatchStyle can take one of 54 values. Example program HatchStyles, which is available for download on the book's web site, lists the HatchStyle values and shows samples.

The following code shows how a program can fill a rectangle with a HatchBrush. It makes a brush using the LargeConfetti style with a blue foreground and light blue background. It calls a Graphics object's FillRectangle method to fill a rectangle with this brush, and then calls DrawRectangle to outline the rectangle in black.

```
Using the_brush As New HatchBrush(HatchStyle.LargeConfetti, Color.Blue, _
  Color.LightBlue)
    gr.FillRectangle(the_brush, 10, 10, 200, 200)
    gr.DrawRectangle(Pens.Black, 10, 10, 200, 200)
End Using
```

Figure 30-3 in Chapter 30 shows the available hatch patterns.

LinearGradientBrush

A LinearGradientBrush class fills areas with a linear gradient of two or more colors. The simplest of these brushes shades an area smoothly from one color to another along a specified direction. For example, a rectangle might be red at one end and shade smoothly to blue at the other.

With some extra work, you can specify exactly how the colors blend from one to the other. For example, you could make the colors blend quickly at the start and then slowly across the rest of the rectangle.

You can also specify more than two colors for the brush. You could make the colors blend from red to green to blue.

The following table describes the LinearGradientBrush class's most useful properties and methods.

PROPERTY OR METHOD	PURPOSE
Blend	A Blend object that determines how quickly the colors blend across the brush. By default, this is a simple linear blending.
InterpolationColors	A ColorBlend object that determines the colors (possibly more than two) that the brush blends and their positions within the blend.
LinearColors	An array of two colors that determines the starting and ending colors for a simple linear blend.
MultiplyTransform	Multiplies the brush's current transformation by another transformation matrix.
ResetTransform	Resets the brush's transformation to the identity transformation.

PROPERTY OR METHOD	PURPOSE
RotateTransform	Adds a rotation transformation to the brush's current transformation.
ScaleTransform	Adds a scaling transformation to the brush's current transformation.
SetBlendTriangularShape	Makes the brush use a midpoint gradient where the color blends from the start color to the end color, and then back to the start color. You could do something similar with the Blend property, but this is easier.
SetSigmaBellShape	Makes the brush's color gradient change according to a bell curve instead of linearly.
Transform	A transformation that the brush applies to its gradient before using it to fill areas.
TranslateTransform	Adds a translation transformation to the brush's current transformation.
WrapMode	Determines how the brush wraps when it doesn't completely fill the area. This property can take the values Clamp, Tile, TileFlipX, TileFlipY, and TileFlipXY. Because the brush is infinitely tall in the direction perpendicular to the line that determines its direction, not all of these values make a difference for all brushes.

The following code draws the assortment of filled rectangles shown in Figure 31-8. As you step through the code, refer to the figure to see the result.

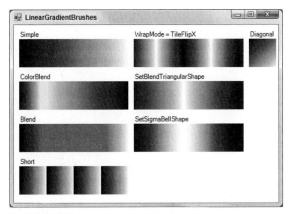

FIGURE 31-8: LinearGradientBrush objects can produce all these effects and more.

```vb
Private Sub Form1_Paint(ByVal sender As Object,
 ByVal e As System.Windows.Forms.PaintEventArgs) Handles MyBase.Paint
    Dim y As Integer = 10
    Dim x As Integer = 10
    Dim wid As Integer = 200
    Dim hgt As Integer = 50

    ' Make a rectangle that shades from black to white.

    e.Graphics.DrawString("Simple", Me.Font, Brushes.Black, x, y)
    y += 15
    Using black_white_brush As New LinearGradientBrush(
     New Point(x, y), New Point(x + wid, y), Color.Black, Color.White)
        e.Graphics.FillRectangle(black_white_brush, x, y, wid, hgt)
        y += hgt + 10

        ' ColorBlend.
        e.Graphics.DrawString("ColorBlend", Me.Font, Brushes.Black, x, y)
        y += 15
        Dim color_blend As New ColorBlend(3)
        color_blend.Colors = New Color() {Color.Red, Color.Green, Color.Blue}
        color_blend.Colors = New Color() _
            {Color.Black, Color.White, Color.Black}
        color_blend.Positions = New Single() {0.0, 0.2, 1.0}
        black_white_brush.InterpolationColors = color_blend
        e.Graphics.FillRectangle(black_white_brush, x, y, wid, hgt)
        y += hgt + 10

        ' Make a brush that makes 50 percent of the color change
        ' in the first 20 percent of the distance, stays there
        ' until 80 percent of the distance, and then finishes
        ' in the remaining distance.
        e.Graphics.DrawString("Blend", Me.Font, Brushes.Black, x, y)
        y += 15
        Dim the_blend As New Blend(4)
        the_blend.Factors = New Single() {0.0, 0.5, 0.5, 1.0}
        the_blend.Positions = New Single() {0.0, 0.2, 0.8, 1.0}
        black_white_brush.Blend = the_blend
        e.Graphics.FillRectangle(black_white_brush, x, y, wid, hgt)
        y += hgt + 10

        ' This brush's line is too short to cross the whole rectangle.
        e.Graphics.DrawString("Short", Me.Font, Brushes.Black, x, y)
        y += 15
        Using short_brush As New LinearGradientBrush(
         New Point(x, y), New Point(x + 50, y),
         Color.Black, Color.White)
            e.Graphics.FillRectangle(short_brush, x, y, wid, hgt)
            y += hgt + 10

            x += wid + 10
            y = 10

            ' Change the brush's WrapMode.
            e.Graphics.DrawString("WrapMode = TileFlipX", Me.Font,
                Brushes.Black, x, y)
```

```
                y += 15
                short_brush.WrapMode = WrapMode.TileFlipX
                e.Graphics.FillRectangle(short_brush, x, y, wid, hgt)
                y += hgt + 10
            End Using ' short_brush

            ' Trangular brush.
            e.Graphics.DrawString("SetBlendTriangularShape", Me.Font,
                Brushes.Black, x, y)
            y += 15
            black_white_brush.SetBlendTriangularShape(0.5)
            e.Graphics.FillRectangle(black_white_brush, x, y, wid, hgt)
            y += hgt + 10
        End Using ' black_white_brush

        ' Sigma bell shape.
        e.Graphics.DrawString("SetSigmaBellShape", Me.Font, Brushes.Black, x, y)
        y += 15
        black_white_brush.SetSigmaBellShape(0.5, 1)
        e.Graphics.FillRectangle(black_white_brush, x, y, wid, hgt)
        y += hgt + 10

        ' A diagonal brush.
        x += wid + 10
        y = 10
        wid = hgt
        e.Graphics.DrawString("Diagonal", Me.Font, Brushes.Black, x, y)
        y += 15
        Dim diag_brush As New LinearGradientBrush(
            New Point(x, y), New Point(x + wid, y + hgt), Color.Black, Color.White)
        e.Graphics.FillRectangle(diag_brush, x, y, wid, hgt)
        y += hgt + 10
    End Sub
```

code snippet LinearGradientBrushes

The code begins by making a relatively straightforward LinearGradientBrush shading from black to white along the line starting at (9, 10) and ending at (210, 10). It then fills a rectangle with the brush. Notice that the points defining the brush determine the brush's drawing origin. The rectangle's X coordinates cover the same range as those of the brush, so the brush's origin lines up nicely with the rectangle. If the two did not line up, the brush would finish its gradient before it reached the end of the rectangle and it would need to wrap. Usually, you will want the brush to line up with the object it is filling. You can arrange that by carefully defining the brush to fit over the object or by using a transformation to make it fit.

Next, the code creates a ColorBlend object. It passes the object's constructor the value 3 to indicate that it will use three colors. The code sets the ColorBlend object's Colors property to an array containing the three colors black, white, and black. This example uses black and white, so the result will show up well in the book, but you could use any colors here such as orange, hot pink, and blue. Next, the code sets the ColorBlend object's Positions property to an array of Singles that define the positions within the blend where the colors should be located. In this example, the first color (black) begins 0.0 of the way through the blend, the second color (white) sits 0.2 or 20 percent of the distance through the blend, and the third color (black again) sits at the end of the blend. You can see in Figure 31-8 that the white area is to the left of the center in this rectangle.

The code then creates a Blend object, passing its constructor the parameter 4 to indicate that the program will set four blend points. It sets the object's Factors property to an array of Singles that determine the fraction of the blend that should occur at the four points. It then sets the object's Positions property to an array that sets the positions of the blend points. In this example, the point 0.0 of the distance through the blend has factor 0.0, so the blend has not begun and that point has the start color. The point 0.2 of the distance through the blend has a factor of 0.5, so the blend should be half done at that point. The point 0.8 of the distance through the blend has a factor of 0.5, so the blend should still be only half done at that point. Finally, the point at the end of the blend should have the end color. The result is a blend that changes quickly initially, remains fixed for a stretch in the middle, and then finishes quickly. (An optical illusion makes the area on the left of the flat region in the middle appear brighter than it really is, and the area on the right appears darker than it really is.)

Next, the program makes a LinearGradientBrush that is defined by points too close together to cover its whole rectangle. The brush repeats its gradient as many times as necessary to cover the rectangle.

The program then changes the previous brush's WrapMode property to TileFlipX. When the brush must repeat its gradient to fill the rectangle, it reverses the start and end colors to produce a series of gradient bands.

Next, the program calls a brush's SetBlendTriangularShape method. This makes the gradient shade from the start color to the end color and back. The SetBlendTriangularShape method's parameter gives the position in the gradient where the end color should occur. You could get a similar effect using a Blend, but this method is easier for this kind of fill.

The program then calls the brush's SetSigmaBellShape method. It uses the same position parameter 0.5 as the previous call to SetBlendTriangularShape, so it places the end color in the middle of the gradient. The effect is similar to the triangular brush, except that the colors vary according to a bell curve instead of linear relationship. These two rectangles are lined up vertically in Figure 31-8, so it is easy to see the difference.

The code defines the final brush with a line that is not horizontal, so its gradient moves diagonally across its rectangle.

PathGradientBrush

A PathGradientBrush object fills areas with a color gradient that blends colors from a center point to the points along a path. For example, you might shade from white in the middle of an ellipse to blue along its edges.

The Blend, InterpolationColors, SetBlendTriangularShape, SetSigmaBellShape, and other properties and methods that deal with the characteristics of the blend work along lines running from the center point to the points on the path. For example, you can use this object's Blend property to determine how quickly colors blend across the brush. In the LinearGradientBrush class, this property determines how the colors blend from one side of the brush to the other. In a PathGradientBrush, it controls how the colors blend from the center point to the path's points.

The following table describes the PathGradientBrush object's most useful properties and methods.

PROPERTY OR METHOD	PURPOSE
Blend	A Blend object that determines how quickly the colors blend across the brush. By default, this is a simple linear blending.
CenterColor	Determines the color at the center point.
CenterPoint	Determines the location of the center point. By default, this point is set to the center of the path.
InterpolationColors	A ColorBlend object that determines the colors (possibly more than two) that the brush blends and their positions within the blend.
MultiplyTransform	Multiplies the brush's current transformation by another transformation matrix.
ResetTransform	Resets the brush's transformation to the identity transformation.
RotateTransform	Adds a rotation transformation to the brush's current transformation.
ScaleTransform	Adds a scaling transformation to the brush's current transformation.
SetBlendTriangularShape	Makes the brush use a midpoint gradient where the color blends from the start color to the end color and then back to the start color. You could do something similar with the Blend property, but this is easier.
SetSigmaBellShape	Makes the brush's color gradient change according to a bell curve instead of linearly.
SurroundColors	An array of Colors that correspond to the points on the path. The color gradient blends from the CenterColor to these colors around the edge of the path. If there are more points in the path than colors, the final color is repeated as needed. Note that curves such as ellipses define a large number of colors that you do not explicitly specify, so making these colors match up with points on the curve can be difficult. This property is easier to understand for polygons.
Transform	A transformation that the brush applies to its gradient before using it to fill areas.

continues

(continued)

PROPERTY OR METHOD	PURPOSE
TranslateTransform	Adds a translation transformation to the brush's current transformation.
WrapMode	Determines how the brush wraps when it doesn't completely fill the area. This property can take the values Clamp, Tile, TileFlipX, TileFlipY, and TileFlipXY. Because the brush is infinitely tall in the direction perpendicular to the line that determines its direction, not all of these values make a difference for all brushes.

Example program PathGradientBrushes, which is available for download on the book's web site, uses PathGradientBrush objects to draw the shapes shown in Figure 31-9.

The following code fills the shapes shown in Figure 31-9. As you step through the code, refer to the figure to see the result.

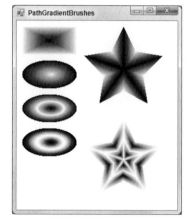

FIGURE 31-9: PathGradientBrush objects can produce all these effects and more.

```
Private Sub Form1_Paint(ByVal sender As Object,
 ByVal e As System.Windows.Forms.PaintEventArgs) _
 Handles MyBase.Paint
    e.Graphics.SmoothingMode = SmoothingMode.AntiAlias

    Dim x As Integer = 10
    Dim y As Integer = 10
    Dim wid As Integer = 50
    Dim hgt As Integer = 100

    ' Fill a rectangle.
    Dim rect_pts() As Point = {
        New Point(x, y),
        New Point(x + wid, y),
        New Point(x + wid, y + hgt),
        New Point(x, y + hgt)
    }
    Dim path_brush As New PathGradientBrush(rect_pts)
    e.Graphics.FillPolygon(path_brush, rect_pts)
    x += wid + 10

    ' Fill an ellipse setting CenterColor and SurroundColors.
    Dim ellipse_path As New GraphicsPath
    ellipse_path.AddEllipse(x, y, wid, hgt)
    path_brush = New PathGradientBrush(ellipse_path)
    path_brush.CenterColor = Color.White
    path_brush.SurroundColors = New Color() {Color.Black}
    e.Graphics.FillEllipse(path_brush, x, y, wid, hgt)
    x += wid + 10

    ' Fill an ellipse using SetBlendTriangularShape.
    ellipse_path = New GraphicsPath
```

```
ellipse_path.AddEllipse(x, y, wid, hgt)
path_brush = New PathGradientBrush(ellipse_path)
path_brush.CenterColor = Color.White
path_brush.SurroundColors = New Color() {Color.Black}
path_brush.SetBlendTriangularShape(0.5)
e.Graphics.FillEllipse(path_brush, x, y, wid, hgt)
x += wid + 10

' Fill an ellipse using SetSigmaBellShape.
ellipse_path = New GraphicsPath
ellipse_path.AddEllipse(x, y, wid, hgt)
path_brush = New PathGradientBrush(ellipse_path)
path_brush.CenterColor = Color.White
path_brush.SurroundColors = New Color() {Color.Black}
path_brush.SetSigmaBellShape(0.5, 1)
e.Graphics.FillEllipse(path_brush, x, y, wid, hgt)
x += wid + 10

' Fill a star shape.
wid = 150
hgt = 150
Dim cx As Integer = x + wid \ 2
Dim cy As Integer = y + hgt \ 2
Dim r1 As Integer = CInt(wid * 0.5)
Dim r2 As Integer = CInt(hgt * 0.25)
Dim star_pts(9) As Point
For i As Integer = 0 To 9 Step 2
    star_pts(i).X = cx + CInt(r1 * Cos(i * PI / 5 - PI / 2))
    star_pts(i).Y = cy + CInt(r1 * Sin(i * PI / 5 - PI / 2))
    star_pts(i + 1).X = cx + CInt(r2 * Cos((i + 1) * PI / 5 - PI / 2))
    star_pts(i + 1).Y = cy + CInt(r2 * Sin((i + 1) * PI / 5 - PI / 2))
Next i
Dim star_path As New GraphicsPath
star_path.AddPolygon(star_pts)
Dim star_brush As New PathGradientBrush(star_pts)
star_brush.CenterColor = Color.Black
star_brush.SurroundColors = New Color() {
    Color.Black, Color.White,
    Color.Black, Color.White,
    Color.Black, Color.White,
    Color.Black, Color.White,
    Color.Black, Color.White
}

e.Graphics.FillPolygon(star_brush, star_pts)
x += wid + 10

' Fill a star shape.
cx = x + wid \ 2
cy = y + hgt \ 2
r1 = CInt(wid * 0.5)
r2 = CInt(hgt * 0.25)
For i As Integer = 0 To 9 Step 2
    star_pts(i).X = cx + CInt(r1 * Cos(i * PI / 5 - PI / 2))
```

```
          star_pts(i).Y = cy + CInt(r1 * Sin(i * PI / 5 - PI / 2))
          star_pts(i + 1).X = cx + CInt(r2 * Cos((i + 1) * PI / 5 - PI / 2))
          star_pts(i + 1).Y = cy + CInt(r2 * Sin((i + 1) * PI / 5 - PI / 2))
     Next i
     star_path = New GraphicsPath
     star_path.AddPolygon(star_pts)
     star_brush = New PathGradientBrush(star_pts)
     star_brush.CenterColor = Color.White
     star_brush.SurroundColors = New Color() {
          Color.White, Color.Black,
          Color.White, Color.Black,
          Color.White, Color.Black,
          Color.White, Color.Black,
          Color.White, Color.Black
     }
     Dim star_blend As New Blend
     star_blend.Positions = New Single() {0.0, 0.25, 0.5, 0.75, 1.0}
     star_blend.Factors = New Single() {0.0, 1.0, 0.0, 1.0, 0.0}
     star_brush.Blend = star_blend
     e.Graphics.FillPolygon(star_brush, star_pts)

     ' Draw the outline in white to remove some
     ' incorrectly drawn pixels.
     e.Graphics.DrawPolygon(Pens.White, star_pts)

     path_brush.Dispose()
     ellipse_path.Dispose()
     star_brush.Dispose()
     star_path.Dispose()
End Sub
```

code snippet PathGradientBrushes

The code first creates an array of Point objects initialized to form a rectangle. It passes those points to the constructor for a PathGradientBrush and then uses the brush to fill that rectangle. This is about the simplest PathGradientBrush you can build, so it's worth studying a bit before moving on to more confusing examples. Notice that the color shades smoothly from black in the center to white on the rectangle's edges (those are the default colors).

Next, the program makes a GraphicsPath object and adds an ellipse to it. It passes the GraphicsPath to the PathGradientBrush object's constructor. It then sets the brush's CenterColor and SurroundColors properties. The SurroundColors array doesn't contain enough values for every point on the elliptical path, so the last color (black) is repeated as much as necessary. The program fills the ellipse with this brush.

The code then creates a new GraphicsPath object, adds a new ellipse, and uses it to make a PathGradientBrush as before. It also sets the brush's CenterColor and SurroundColors properties as before. The program then calls the brush's SetBlendTriangularShape method to make the colors along the lines from the center point to the path's edges blend from the end color to the start color and back. The parameter 0.5 makes the start color appear halfway from the center point to the edge.

Next, the program repeats these same steps, except that it calls the brush's SetSigmaBellShape method instead of SetBlendTriangularShape. The result is similar to the previous result, except that the colors vary according to a bell curve instead of a linear relationship.

The code then generates an array of points that defines a star shape. It creates a new GraphicsPath object and calls its AddPolygon method to add the star. It passes this GraphicsPath object to the PathGradientBrush object's constructor to make the brush use the star as its path. The program then sets the brush's SurroundPoints property to an array containing the Colors it should use for each of the star's points. The code fills the star using this brush to draw a star where the tips of the star are black and the rest of the shape's points vary from white to black.

Finally, the program repeats the previous steps to define a new star-shaped brush. It creates a new Blend object and sets its Position and Factors properties to indicate how the gradient should progress from the center point to the shape's edges. The Positions values give locations along a line from the center to an edge point. The Factors values indicate how far the blend should have progressed for the corresponding point. For example, this code's second entries for those arrays are 0.25 and 1.0 to indicate that the point one quarter of the distance from the center point to an edge point should have blended completely to the end color. This example sets its Factors values so the color blends from the start color to the end color several times.

GRAPHICSPATH OBJECTS

A GraphicsPath object represents a path defined by lines, curves, text, and other drawing commands. A GraphicsPath can even include other GraphicsPath objects.

You can use a Graphics object's DrawPath and FillPath methods to draw or fill a GraphicsPath. For example, the following code creates a GraphicsPath object and adds a string to it. It creates a TextureBrush from a PictureBox image and uses the FillPath method to fill the path with the TextureBrush. It finishes by calling the DrawPath method to outline the path in black.

Available for download on Wrox.com

```
Private Sub Form1_Paint(ByVal sender As Object,
 ByVal e As System.Windows.Forms.PaintEventArgs) Handles MyBase.Paint
    ' Make a GraphicsPath containing text.
    Dim txt As String = "Path"
    Using graphics_path As New GraphicsPath()
        graphics_path.AddString(txt,
            New FontFamily("Times New Roman"),
            FontStyle.Bold, 150,
            New Point(0, 0),
            New StringFormat)

        ' Fill the path with an image.
        Using smiley_brush As New TextureBrush(picSmiley.Image)
            e.Graphics.FillPath(smiley_brush, graphics_path)
        End Using
        e.Graphics.DrawPath(Pens.Black, graphics_path)
    End Using
End Sub
```

code snippet GraphicsPathTextureBrush

Figure 31-10 shows the result.

In addition to drawing and filling a GraphicsPath, you can also use one to define a region. The following code creates a GraphicsPath representing text much as the previous example does. It then sets the form's Region property equal to a new Region object created from the GraphicsPath. This restricts the form to the region. Any pieces of the form that lie outside of the textual path are chopped off, so they are not drawn and mouse events in those areas fall through to whatever lies below the form.

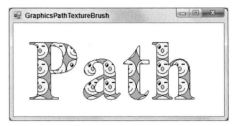

FIGURE 31-10: A program can use a Graphics object's FillPath and DrawPath methods to fill and draw a GraphicsPath object.

When you use a path to define a form's region, the path is taken relative to the form's origin, which is not the same as the origin of the form's client area. The form's origin is at the upper-left corner of the form, including its borders and title bar. To allow for this difference in origins, the code uses the PointToScreen method to get the screen coordinates of the client area's origin.

The code applies a translation transformation to the Graphics object so the client area origin is mapped to the form's origin. It then sets the Graphics object's SmoothingMode, fills the path with light gray, and then outlines the path with a thick black pen. Because the 5-pixel-wide line around the path is centered on the edge of the form's region, half of it is cut off.

```
Private Sub Form1_Paint(ByVal sender As Object,
  ByVal e As System.Windows.Forms.PaintEventArgs) Handles MyBase.Paint
    ' Make a GraphicsPath containing text.
    Dim txt As String = "Path"
    Using graphics_path As New GraphicsPath()
        graphics_path.AddString(txt,
            New FontFamily("Times New Roman"),
            FontStyle.Bold, 150,
            New Point(0, 0),
            New StringFormat)

        ' Set the form's region to the path.
        Me.Region = New Region(graphics_path)

        ' Fill the path with white and outline it in black.
        Dim origin As Point = Me.PointToScreen(New Point(0, 0))
        e.Graphics.TranslateTransform(Me.Left - origin.X, Me.Top - origin.Y)
        e.Graphics.SmoothingMode = SmoothingMode.AntiAlias
        e.Graphics.FillPath(Brushes.LightGray, graphics_path)

        Using black_pen As New Pen(Color.Black, 5)
            e.Graphics.DrawPath(black_pen, graphics_path)
        End Using
    End Using
End Sub
```

code snippet GraphicsPathTextRegion

The result is a form shaped to fit the text in the GraphicsPath. Note that the path used in this example cuts the form's borders and title bar off, so the user has no way to resize, move, or close this form. If you use this technique in an application, be sure to at least provide some method for the user to close the form such as a button or context menu.

One more use for GraphicsPath objects is to define clipping regions. The following code creates a GraphicsPath containing text much as the previous examples do. It then calls the Graphics object's SetClip method to make this path the form's clipping region. Next, the program draws 200 lines between randomly generated points on the form. Only the parts of the lines inside the clipping region are drawn.

```
Private Sub Form1_Paint(ByVal sender As Object,
 ByVal e As System.Windows.Forms.PaintEventArgs) Handles MyBase.Paint
    ' Make a GraphicsPath containing text.
    Dim txt As String = "Path"
    Using graphics_path As New GraphicsPath
        graphics_path.AddString(txt,
            New FontFamily("Times New Roman"),
            FontStyle.Bold, 150,
            New Point(0, 0),
            New StringFormat)
        e.Graphics.SetClip(graphics_path)
    End Using

    ' Fill the ClientRectangle with white.
    e.Graphics.FillRectangle(Brushes.White, Me.ClientRectangle)

    ' Draw a bunch of random lines on the form.
    Dim rnd As New Random
    Dim x1, y1, x2, y2 As Integer
    For i As Integer = 1 To 200
        x1 = rnd.Next(0, Me.ClientSize.Width - 1)
        y1 = rnd.Next(0, Me.ClientSize.Height - 1)
        x2 = rnd.Next(0, Me.ClientSize.Width - 1)
        y2 = rnd.Next(0, Me.ClientSize.Height - 1)
        e.Graphics.DrawLine(Pens.Black, x1, y1, x2, y2)
    Next i
End Sub
```

code snippet GraphicsPathClip

The GraphicsPath class provides many methods for adding lines, curves, text, and other shapes to the path. These methods include AddArc, AddBezier, AddBeziers, AddClosedCurve, AddCurve, AddEllipse, AddLine, AddLines, AddPath, AddPie, AddPolygon, AddRectangle, AddRectangles, and AddString. These are roughly analogous to the Draw and Fill methods provided by the Graphics object. For example, DrawEllipse draws an ellipse, FillEllipse fills an ellipse, and AddEllipse adds an ellipse to a path.

The following table describes the GraphicsPath object's other most useful properties and methods.

PROPERTY OR METHOD	PURPOSE
CloseAllFigures	Closes all open figures by connecting their last points with their first points, and then starts a new figure.
CloseFigure	Closes the current figure by connecting its last point with its first point, and then starts a new figure. For example, if you draw a series of lines and arcs, this method closes the figure.
FillMode	Determines how the path handles overlaps when you fill it. This property can take the values Alternate and Winding. Figure 31-11 shows the difference. **FIGURE 31-11:** The GraphicsPath object's FillMode property determines how areas between the lines are filled.
Flatten	Converts any curves in the path into a sequence of lines. For example, this lets you explicitly calculate colors for every point in the path when setting a PathGradientBrush object's SurroundColors property.
GetBounds	Returns a RectangleF structure representing the path's bounding box.
GetLastPoint	Returns the last PointF structure in the PathPoints array.
IsOutlineVisible	Returns True if the indicated point lies beneath the path's outline.
IsVisible	Returns True if the indicated point lies within the path's interior.
PathData	Returns a PathData object that encapsulates the path's graphical data. It holds arrays similar to those returned by the PathPoints and PathTypes properties.
PathPoints	Returns an array of PointF structures giving the points in the path.
PathTypes	Returns an array of Bytes representing the types of the points in the path.
PointCount	Returns the number of points in the path.
Reset	Clears the path data and resets FillMode to Alternate.

PROPERTY OR METHOD	PURPOSE
Reverse	Reverses the order of the path's data.
StartFigure	Starts a new figure so future data is added to the new figure. Later, calling CloseFigure will close this figure, but not the previous one.
Transform	Applies a transformation matrix to the path.
Warp	Applies a warping transformation to the path. The transformation is defined by mapping a parallelogram to a rectangle.
Widen	Enlarges the curves in the path to enclose a line drawn by a specific pen.

GARBAGE-COLLECTION ISSUES

Objects such as brushes contain references to memory and graphics resources. If you allocate a lot of brushes and then let them go out of scope, they become candidates for garbage collection. Later, when the system decides it needs to free some memory, it walks through all of the objects that you have previously allocated and determines which ones are not reachable by your code. It frees those objects and makes their memory available for future use.

Unfortunately, if those objects contain references to other objects, the garbage collector may think those second-hand objects are still referenced by the original object, so it will not collect them until it runs a second time.

For example, suppose that your program allocates a brush, uses it, and lets it fall out of scope. When the garbage collector runs, it sees that the brush refers to some resources, so it doesn't reclaim them. It sees that your program is no longer using the brush, however, so it frees that memory. The next time the garbage collector runs, the brush is gone, so nothing refers to the brush's secondary resources and the garbage collector can free those, too.

Although the garbage collector eventually frees all of the memory, it takes longer than necessary. It ties up memory longer and that may force more frequent garbage collection.

You can speed up the process greatly by explicitly calling the brush object's Dispose method. Dispose makes the brush free its internal resources and prepare for garbage collection. Now, when the garbage collector runs, it frees both the brush and its secondary resources in a single pass.

The following code shows how to use the Dispose method. When the form loads, this code makes a new Bitmap object to fit the form. It attaches a Graphics object to the Bitmap, makes a HatchBrush and Pen, and uses them to draw a filled ellipse on the Bitmap. The program then sets the form's BackgroundImage property to the Bitmap. Finally, the code calls the Dispose method for the HatchBrush, Pen, and Graphics objects.

```vbnet
Private Sub Form1_Load() Handles MyBase.Load
    ' Make a new bitmap to fit the form.
    Dim bm As New Bitmap(Me.ClientRectangle.Width, Me.ClientRectangle.Height)
    Dim gr As Graphics = Graphics.FromImage(bm)
    gr.Clear(Me.BackColor)

    ' Fill an ellipse.
    Dim hatch_brush As New HatchBrush(HatchStyle.LargeConfetti,
        Color.Blue, Color.Yellow)
    Dim rect As New Rectangle(10, 10,
        Me.ClientRectangle.Width - 20,
        Me.ClientRectangle.Height - 20)
    gr.FillEllipse(hatch_brush, rect)

    ' Outline the ellipse.
    Dim thick_pen As New Pen(Color.Black, 5)
    gr.DrawEllipse(thick_pen, rect)

    ' Set the result as the form's BackgroundImage.
    Me.BackgroundImage = bm

    ' Free resources.
    hatch_brush.Dispose()
    thick_pen.Dispose()
    gr.Dispose()
End Sub
```

code snippet UseDispose

Whenever you can call an object's Dispose method, you should do so. This lets the garbage collector reclaim memory more efficiently.

You cannot always call Dispose, however. If you call Dispose on an object that is still needed by some other object, the program will crash. For example, the preceding code uses a Bitmap object. It's not obvious from the code, but the form's BackgroundImage property continues to reference that object after this subroutine exits. If the program calls the Bitmap object's Dispose method, the form will later be unable to redraw itself and will either crash or display a panicked error message depending on your operating system and .NET Framework version.

Instead of calling Dispose explicitly, you can use the Using statement. Declare the variable that you must dispose of with a Using statement. When you have finished with the variable, end the Using block with an End Using statement. When Visual Basic reaches the End Using statement, it automatically calls the variable's Dispose method.

The following code is similar to the previous version, except that it uses Using statements instead of calling the Dispose method explicitly:

```vbnet
Private Sub Form1_Load() Handles MyBase.Load
    ' Make a new bitmap to fit the form.
    Dim bm As New Bitmap(Me.ClientRectangle.Width, Me.ClientRectangle.Height)
    Using gr As Graphics = Graphics.FromImage(bm)
        gr.Clear(Me.BackColor)
        Dim rect As New Rectangle(10, 10,
```

```
        Me.ClientRectangle.Width - 20,
        Me.ClientRectangle.Height - 20)

    ' Fill an ellipse.
    Using hatch_brush As New HatchBrush(HatchStyle.LargeConfetti,
     Color.Blue, Color.Yellow)
        gr.FillEllipse(hatch_brush, rect)
    End Using

    ' Outline the ellipse.
    Using thick_pen As New Pen(Color.Black, 5)
        gr.DrawEllipse(thick_pen, rect)
    End Using

    ' Set the result as the form's BackgroundImage.
    Me.BackgroundImage = bm
    End Using ' gr
End Sub
```

code snippet UseUsing

The Using statement increases the nesting depth of the code. In this example, the FillEllipse and DrawEllipse calls are contained in two nested Using blocks, so they are indented twice. That makes the code a little harder to read, but it makes it less likely that you will forget to call the objects' Dispose methods. In most cases, the increase is a small price to pay, particularly for graphics programs that may use hundreds or thousands of pens and brushes very quickly.

SUMMARY

Visual Basic .NET provides a huge variety of objects for drawing graphics. The three most important drawing classes are Graphics, Pen, and Brush.

The Graphics object represents the canvas on which you will draw. It provides methods that let you draw and fill all sorts of shapes including lines, rectangles, ellipses, polygons, text, and curves. It also provides methods for transforming those commands to translate, scale, and rotate the results.

The Pen object determines the appearance of lines. It sets the lines' color, thickness, dash style, fill pattern, and caps.

Various kinds of brush objects determine the appearance of filled areas. They can fill areas with solid colors, tiled images, hatch patterns, linear color gradients, and color gradients that follow a path.

These classes and the others described in this chapter give you powerful tools for drawing graphics of practically unlimited complexity and sophistication.

This chapter discusses the brushes, pens, and paths that you use to draw lines, curves, and other shapes. Chapter 32, "Text," explains how to draw text. Although you can display simple text in a Label, TextBox, or other control, when you draw text using GDI+ routines you have greater control over exactly how the text appears.

32

Text

Text is different from the lines, rectangles, ellipses, and other kinds of shapes that a program typically draws. A program normally draws and fills a rectangle in separate steps. On the other hand, a program typically draws text in a single step, usually with a solid color.

Text also differs in the way it is drawn by the GDI+ routines. To draw a line, rectangle, or ellipse, the program specifies the shape's location, and the GDI+ routines draw it accordingly. Text is not specified by simple location data. A program can specify the text's general location but has only limited control over its size. Different characters may have different widths in a particular font, so strings containing the same number of characters may have different sizes when displayed.

Even if you know every character's nominal size, you may not be able to add them up to calculate the size of a string. Fonts sometimes use special algorithms that adjust the spacing between certain pairs of letters to make the result look better. For example, a font might decrease the spacing between the characters A and W when they appear next to each other (as in AW) to allow the W to lean over the A.

HINTING HINTS

Adjusting the spacing between characters is a form of "hinting" used to make text look better. For more information on font hinting, see `en.wikipedia.org/wiki/Font_hinting` and `damieng.com/blog/2009/05/07/font-hinting-and-instructing-a-primer`.

This chapter describes some of the tools that Visual Basic provides for controlling text. It explains how to draw text aligned and formatted in various ways, and how to measure text so that you can figure out more exactly where it will appear.

Note that several examples use the Graphics object's TextRenderingHint property to make text appear smoother. For more information on this property, see the section "System.Drawing.Text" in Chapter 30, "Drawing Basics."

DRAWING TEXT

The Graphics object's DrawString method draws text. It provides several overloaded versions that let you specify the string, font, positioning, and alignment information.

One of the simplest versions of DrawString takes only four parameters: the text to draw, the font to use, the brush to use when filling the text, and the position where the text should start. The following code draws some text starting at the point (10, 10) on the form. It then draws a circle around this point.

```
Private Sub Form1_Paint(ByVal sender As Object,
 ByVal e As System.Windows.Forms.PaintEventArgs) Handles MyBase.Paint
    Dim txt As String = "The quick brown fox jumps over the lazy dog."
    Using big_font As New Font("Times New Roman", 30, FontStyle.Bold)
        e.Graphics.TextRenderingHint =
            System.Drawing.Text.TextRenderingHint.AntiAliasGridFit
        e.Graphics.DrawString(txt, big_font, Brushes.Black, 10, 10)
        e.Graphics.DrawEllipse(Pens.Black, 8, 8, 4, 4)
    End Using
End Sub
```

code snippet DrawSimpleString

Figure 32-1 shows the result. Note that the text doesn't begin exactly at the point (10, 10). The text contains some leading space on the top and bottom that moves it slightly right and downward from the starting point.

Note also that the text runs blithely off the edge of the form. The following section describes ways you can format text so it automatically provides alignment and wrapping as necessary.

FIGURE 32-1: Text doesn't begin exactly at the starting point passed to the DrawString method.

DrawString automatically starts a new line when it encounters a Carriage Return/Line Feed pair in the text. It also advances to the next tab stop when it encounters a Tab character, making it slightly easier to align text in rows and columns.

TEXT FORMATTING

Some of the overloaded versions of the Graphics object's DrawString method take additional parameters that help format the text. The first of these parameters is a layout rectangle. This is a RectangleF structure that indicates the area where the text should be drawn. The second parameter is a StringFormat object that determines how the text is formatted.

The following code draws text inside a rectangle. It begins by defining the layout rectangle, text, and font. It then creates a StringFormat object. It sets the object's Alignment property to Center so it is centered horizontally in the layout rectangle. It sets the object's LineAlignment property to Near so text is aligned vertically at the top of the rectangle. The program calls DrawString to draw the text and then uses DrawRectangle to display the layout rectangle.

```
Private Sub Form1_Paint(ByVal sender As Object,
 ByVal e As System.Windows.Forms.PaintEventArgs) Handles MyBase.Paint
    Dim layout_rect As New RectangleF(10, 10,
        Me.ClientSize.Width - 20, Me.ClientSize.Height - 20)
    Dim txt As String = "The quick brown fox jumps over the lazy dog."
    Using big_font As New Font("Times New Roman", 30, FontStyle.Bold)
        Using string_format As New StringFormat
            string_format.Alignment = StringAlignment.Center
            string_format.LineAlignment = StringAlignment.Near

            e.Graphics.DrawString(txt, big_font,
            Brushes.Black,
                layout_rect, string_format)
            e.Graphics.DrawRectangle(Pens.Black,
                Rectangle.Round(layout_rect))
        End Using ' string_format
    End Using ' big_font
End Sub
```

FIGURE 32-2: The DrawString method can use a layout rectangle and a StringFormat object to format text.

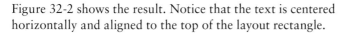
code snippet DrawSimpleLayoutRect

Figure 32-2 shows the result. Notice that the text is centered horizontally and aligned to the top of the layout rectangle.

The StringFormat object provides several other properties and methods that you can use to position text. The following table describes the most useful of these.

PROPERTY OR METHOD	PURPOSE
Alignment	Determines the text's horizontal alignment. This can be Near (left), Center (middle), or Far (right).
FormatFlags	Gets or sets flags that modify the StringFormat object's behavior. See the section "FormatFlags" later in this chapter for more information.
GetTabStops	Returns an array of Singles, giving the positions of tab stops. See the section "Tab Stops" later in this chapter for more information.

continues

(continued)

PROPERTY OR METHOD	PURPOSE
HotkeyPrefix	Determines how the hotkey prefix character is displayed. (In a menu caption or label, the *hotkey* is underlined to show that pressing Alt+<hotkey> performs some special action. For example, in most applications Alt+F opens the File menu. A program specifies a control's hotkey character by placing an ampersand in front of it. For example, "& File" is displayed as "File.") If HotkeyPrefix is Show, any character that follows an ampersand is drawn as an underlined hotkey (a double ampersand is drawn as a single ampersand). If this is None, any ampersands are drawn as ampersands. If this is Hide, hotkey ampersands are hidden.
LineAlignment	Determines the text's vertical alignment. This can be Near (top), Center (middle), or Far (bottom).
SetMeasureableCharacterRanges	Sets an array of CharacterRange structures representing ranges of characters that will later be measured by the Graphics object's MeasureCharacterRanges method.
SetTabStops	Sets an array of Singles giving the positions of tab stops. See the section "Tab Stops" later in this chapter for more information.
Trimming	Determines how the text is trimmed if it cannot fit in the layout rectangle. See the section "Trimming" later in this chapter for more information.

The following sections describe some of the more complex formatting issues in greater detail.

FormatFlags

The StringFormat object's FormatFlags property determines the object's behavior. This property can take a bitwise combination of the values described in the following table.

FORMATFLAGS VALUE	PURPOSE
DirectionRightToLeft	Indicates that the text is drawn from right to left.
DirectionVertical	Indicates that the text is drawn vertically.
FitBlackBox	Indicates that no character should extend beyond the layout rectangle. If this is not set, some characters in certain fonts may stick out a bit.

FORMATFLAGS VALUE	PURPOSE
`LineLimit`	If the last line displayed in the layout rectangle is too tall to fit, this flag indicates that it should be omitted. By default, that line is clipped to show whatever parts will fit.
`MeasureTrailingSpaces`	Indicates that the Graphics object's MeasureString method should include spaces at the ends of lines. By default, it does not.
`NoClip`	Indicates that parts of characters that hang over the layout rectangle are not clipped.
`NoFontFallback`	If a character is missing from the selected font, the GDI+ normally looks for an equivalent character in another font. This flag prevents that and forces the character to be displayed as the font's missing character glyph (usually an open square).
`NoWrap`	Indicates that text should not be wrapped.

Figure 32-3 shows the difference between the FitBlackBox, NoClip, and LineLimit flags. If the last visible line won't fit within the layout rectangle, the default behavior is to clip the line to show whatever fits. If FormatFlags is NoClip, that line is displayed entirely. If FormatFlags is LineLimit, the line is omitted entirely.

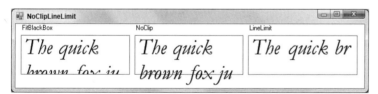

FIGURE 32-3: The FitBlackBox, NoClip, and LineLimit flags change how a StringFormat object handles the text's last displayed line.

The following code fragment sets a StringFormat object's DirectionVertical flag and then draws some text. Example program DirectionVertical uses this code to produce the picture shown in Figure 32-4.

```
string_format.FormatFlags =
    StringFormatFlags.DirectionVertical Or
    StringFormatFlags.DirectionRightToLeft
e.Graphics.DrawString(txt, the_font, Brushes.Black, layout_rect, string_format)
```

code snippet DirectionVertical

This code fragment sets the FormatFlags property to DirectionVertical plus DirectionRightToLeft. If you omit the second flag, the lines of text are drawn left to right. That means the line "The quick" appears on the left and the subsequent lines appear moving to the right, so the lines are drawn in the reverse of the order that you might expect.

Note that you can also draw vertical text by applying a transformation to the Graphics object that translates the text to the origin, rotates it, and translates the text back to where it belongs.

The following code demonstrates this technique. It defines its layout rectangle, text, and font. It uses the form's width to define the rectangle's height and the form's height to define the rectangle's width, so the rectangle will fit the form after it is rotated. The code creates a StringFormat object to center the text and applies the transformations to the Graphics object. Finally, the code draws the text. The result is similar to the text produced by the previous example.

FIGURE 32-4: Setting the StringFormat object's FormatFlags property to DirectionVertical produces vertical text.

Available for download on Wrox.com

```vb
Private Sub Form1_Paint(ByVal sender As Object,
  ByVal e As System.Windows.Forms.PaintEventArgs) Handles MyBase.Paint
    ' Define the layout rectangle. It's slightly smaller
    ' than the form rotated 90 degrees so the rotated
    ' text will fit the form nicely.
    Dim rect_wid As Integer = Me.ClientSize.Height - 20
    Dim rect_hgt As Integer = Me.ClientSize.Width - 20
    Dim layout_rect As New RectangleF(
        (Me.ClientSize.Width - rect_wid) \ 2,
        (Me.ClientSize.Height - rect_hgt) \ 2,
        rect_wid, rect_hgt)
    ' Define the text and font.
    Dim txt As String = "The quick brown fox jumps over the lazy dog."
    Using the_font As New Font("Times New Roman", 30,
        FontStyle.Bold, GraphicsUnit.Pixel)

        ' Set the StringFormat to center the text.
        Using string_format As New StringFormat
            string_format.Alignment = StringAlignment.Center
            string_format.LineAlignment = StringAlignment.Center

            ' Translate to the origin, rotate, and translate back.
            e.Graphics.TranslateTransform(
                -Me.ClientSize.Width \ 2,
                -Me.ClientSize.Height \ 2,
              MatrixOrder.Append)
            e.Graphics.RotateTransform(90, Matri xOrder.Append)
             e.Graphics.TranslateTransform(
                Me.ClientSize.Width \ 2,
                Me.ClientSize.Height \ 2,
                MatrixOrder.Append)
            ' Draw the text and layout rectangle.
            e.Graphics.TextRenderingHint =
                System.Drawing.Text.TextRenderingHint.AntiAliasGridFit
```

```
            e.Graphics.DrawString(txt, the_font, Brushes.Black,
                layout_rect, string_format)
            e.Graphics.DrawRectangle(Pens.Black, Rectangle.Round(layout_rect))
        End Using ' string_format
    End Using ' the_font
End Sub
```

code snippet TransformedText

This approach is a bit more complicated than the previous method of setting the StringFormat object's FormatFlags property to DirectionVertical, but it gives you more flexibility. Simply by changing the rotation transformation, you can draw text at any angle, not just rotated 90 degrees. Figure 32-5 shows this program with the angle of rotation changed from 90 to 60 degrees.

FIGURE 32-5: Transformations can produce text rotated at any angle.

Tab Stops

The StringFormat object's GetTabStops and SetTabStops methods let you get and set an array of Singles that determine the position of the layout rectangle's tab stops. Each entry in the array gives the distance between two tab stops. For example, the values {50, 50, 50} specify tab stops 50, 100, and 150 pixels from the left edge of the layout rectangle.

The following code fragment sets two tab stops for a StringFormat object named string_format. It sets two tab stops 60 and 140 (60 + 80) pixels from the left edge of the layout rectangle.

```
Dim tab_stops() As Single = {60, 80}
string_format.SetTabStops(0, tab_stops)
```

code snippet SetTabs

Example program SetTabs uses this code to display some randomly generated data aligned in columns. The code simply builds a string that uses vbTab to move characters horizontally to the next tab stop and that uses vbCrLf to start a new line. Figure 32-6 shows the result.

Alpha	Gamma	Value
73	0.951139	0.45
21	0.814464	0.02
34	0.566147	0.80
17	0.757784	0.93
67	0.346777	0.85
19	0.453600	0.61
15	0.917264	0.67
17	0.066652	0.72
92	0.981094	0.24
87	0.993788	0.76

Trimming

Normally, a string is wrapped as necessary until its layout rectangle is full. If there is still text that has not been displayed, the Trimming property determines how that text is handled. The following table describes the values this property can take.

FIGURE 32-6: The SetTabStops method lets you easily align text.

TRIMMING VALUE	PURPOSE
Character	The text is trimmed to the nearest character.
EllipsisCharacter	The text is trimmed to the nearest character and an ellipsis is displayed at the end of the line.
EllipsisPath	The center of the line is removed and replaced with an ellipsis. This is sometimes a good choice when displaying file paths because it shows the beginning of the path and the file name. This method keeps as much of the last backslash (\) delimited part of the text as possible (it assumes that this is a file name).
EllipsisWord	The text is trimmed to the nearest word and an ellipsis is displayed at the end of the line.
None	The text is not trimmed. Instead, it is wrapped to the next line, which is hidden because it is below the bottom of the layout rectangle. If the last visible line contains a word break, the line will wrap after the last word that fits. That makes this seem similar to the Word setting.
Word	The text is trimmed to the nearest word.

Example program Trimming, available for download on the book's web site, draws samples of each of the Trimming values. Figure 32-7 shows the program in action. Each sample contains the letters A through Z in groups of three separated by backslashes (left column) or spaces (right column).

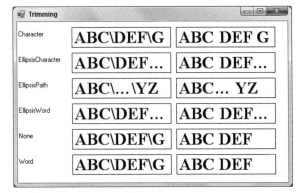

FIGURE 32-7: The StringFormat object's Trimming property determines how text is trimmed.

MEASURESTRING

The Graphics object's MeasureString method returns a SizeF structure holding the string's width and height drawn in a particular font. You can use that information to arrange the text and other drawn objects on the form.

The following code shows how a program might center text on its form. It starts by defining the text it will draw and the font it will use (in this case, a bold, 40-pixel-tall, Times New Roman font). Next, the program uses the Graphics object's MeasureString method to get the string's size in that font. It uses the size to determine where it needs to draw the text to center it, and then draws the text. The code then makes a Rectangle object using the text's position and the size it got from MeasureString. It finishes by drawing the rectangle around the string.

```
Private Sub Form1_Paint(ByVal sender As Object,
 ByVal e As System.Windows.Forms.PaintEventArgs) Handles MyBase.Paint
    Dim the_string As String = "MeasureString"
    ' Define the font and text we will use.
    Using the_font As New Font("Times New Roman", 40,
        FontStyle.Bold, GraphicsUnit.Pixel)

        ' Get the text's size.
        Dim string_size As SizeF =
            e.Graphics.MeasureString("MeasureString", the_font)
        ' Draw the text centered on the form.
        Dim x As Integer = (Me.ClientSize.Width - CInt(string_size.Width)) \ 2
        Dim y As Integer =
            (Me.ClientSize.Height - CInt(string_size.Height)) \ 2
        e.Graphics.DrawString(the_string, the_font, Brushes.Black, x, y)
        ' Draw a rectangle around the text.
        Dim string_rect As New Rectangle(x, y,
            CInt(string_size.Width), CInt(string_size.Height))
        e.Graphics.DrawRectangle(Pens.Black,
        string_rect)
    End Using
End Sub
```

code snippet MeasureString

Figure 32-8 shows the result. Notice that the rectangle includes some extra space above, below, and to the sides of the string. The section "Font Metrics" later in this chapter has more to say about this extra space.

FIGURE 32-8: You can use the Graphics object's MeasureString method to see how big a string will be when drawn in a particular font.

EASIER ALIGNMENT

An easier way to center text on a form is to use a StringFormat object with Alignment and LineAlignment properties set to Center. Then use the form's client area for the formatting rectangle.

Occasionally, it is useful to know where parts of a string will be drawn. For example, you might want to draw a box around certain words or know when the user has clicked a particular letter.

The Graphics object provides a MeasureCharacterRanges method that returns an array of Regions representing the positions of ranges of characters within a string. To use MeasureCharacterRanges, the program must first create an array of CharacterRange objects defining the ranges of interest. It calls a StringFormat object's SetMeasurableCharacterRanges method, passing it this array. Finally, it calls MeasureCharacterRanges.

The following code uses MeasureCharacterRanges to show the positions of all of the characters in a short string. It begins by defining its text, layout rectangle, font, and StringFormat object as usual. It then creates an array of CharacterRange objects, one for each character in the string. It loops through this array, filling it with new CharacterRange objects, each of which represents a single character. When it has filled the array, the code passes it to the StringFormat object's SetMeasurableCharacterRanges method. The program then calls the Graphics object's MeasureCharacterRanges method to get Region objects representing the characters' positions. It loops through this array, calling each Region object's GetBounds method to convert the region into a RectangleF structure. It transforms the RectangleF into a Rectangle and draws it. Finally, the program draws the string.

```vb
Private Sub Form1_Paint(ByVal sender As Object,
 ByVal e As System.Windows.Forms.PaintEventArgs) Handles MyBase.Paint
    Dim txt As String = "Great Galloping Giraffes"
    Dim layout_rect As New RectangleF(0, 0,
        Me.ClientSize.Width, Me.ClientSize.Height)
    e.Graphics.TextRenderingHint =
        System.Drawing.Text.TextRenderingHint.AntiAliasGridFit

    Using the_font As New Font("Times New Roman", 50,
      FontStyle.Bold Or FontStyle.Italic, GraphicsUnit.Pixel)
        Using string_format As New StringFormat
            string_format.LineAlignment = StringAlignment.Center
            string_format.Alignment = StringAlignment.Center

            ' Define an array of CharacterRange objects,
            ' one for each character.
            Dim character_ranges(txt.Length - 1) As CharacterRange
            For i As Integer = 0 To txt.Length - 1
                character_ranges(i) = New CharacterRange(i, 1)
            Next i '
            Set the ranges in the StringFormat object.
            string_format.SetMeasurableCharacterRanges(character_ranges)
            ' Get the character range regions.
            Dim character_regions() As Region =
                e.Graphics.MeasureCharacterRanges(txt,
                the_font, layout_rect, string_format)
            ' Draw each region's bounds.
            For Each rgn As Region In character_regions
                ' Convert the region into a Rectangle.
                Dim character_bounds As RectangleF = rgn.GetBounds(e.Graphics)
                Dim character_rect As Rectangle =
                    Rectangle.Round(character_bounds)
                ' Draw the bounds.
                e.Graphics.DrawRectangle(Pens.White,
                character_rect)
            Next rgn

            ' Draw the text.
            e.Graphics.DrawString(txt, the_font,
            Brushes.Black,
                layout_rect, string_format)
        End Using ' string_format
    End Using ' the_font
End Sub
```

code snippet MeasureCharacterRanges

FIGURE 32-9: The Graphics object's MeasureCharacterRanges method shows where ranges of characters will be drawn in a string.

Figure 32-9 shows the result.

CHALLENGING CHARACTERS

For some reason, the array of CharacterRange objects you pass to the SetMeasurableCharacterRanges method can hold at most 32 items. If the array is larger, SetMeasurableCharacterRanges throws an overflow error. Microsoft says this behavior is by design and doesn't plan to change it. If you need to measure the positions of individual characters in a longer string, you should break the string into pieces smaller than 32 characters, probably at word boundaries, and arrange the pieces yourself.

Note that characters do not necessarily stay within their assigned regions. Depending on the font, they may stick out slightly. In Figure 32-9, the ff pair is particularly shameless in its trespassing, overlapping both the previous and following characters.

FONT METRICS

The Graphics object's MeasureString method tells you approximately how big a string will be when drawn on that object. Its MeasureCharacterRanges method enables you to get more information about the positioning of ranges within a string.

The FontFamily class provides some additional methods that a program can use to get even more information about how characters are drawn. Before you can use these values, you must understand a bit of extra character anatomy.

Figure 32-10 shows how a font's internal leading, ascent, descent, and external leading values help determine a character's position.

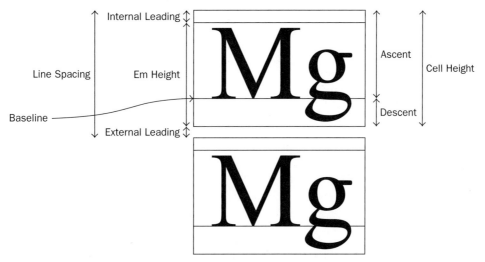

FIGURE 32-10: How text is positioned depends on many font metrics, including internal leading, ascent, descent, and external leading.

The following table describes these font metrics.

VALUE	MEANING
Internal Leading	Extra space left above the characters but considered part of the string.
Em Height	The height within which the characters are drawn.
Ascent	The part of the character cell above the baseline.
Baseline	The line on which the character sits. Normally a font lines up all the characters in a string so their baselines align.
Descent	The part of the character cell below the baseline.
Cell Height	The height of the character area including internal leading.
External Leading	Extra space left below one line and above the next.
Line Spacing	The distance between one line and the next.

MISLEADING LEADING

In the terms "internal leading" and "external leading," the word "leading" is pronounced "led-ing" not "leed-ing." It comes from a printer term that meant a thin strip of metal called lead or leading, (you guessed it, pronounced "led" or "led-ing") used to increase the spacing between lines.

From the figure, you can verify the following relationships:

```
Cell Height = Ascent + Descent = Internal Leading + Em Height
Line Spacing = Cell Height + External Leading
```

The FontFamily object provides several methods for determining font metric values. These methods include GetCellAscent, GetCellDescent, GetEmHeight, and GetLineSpacing.

All of these methods return values in *font design units*. The key to converting them into some other unit is to realize that the Font object's Size property returns the font's em size in whatever units the font is currently using. For example, if you specify the font's size in pixels, then Font.Size returns the em size in pixels.

Traditionally, em size was the height of the metal block used to hold a letter. Sometimes an em is said to be the width of the letter "M," although this isn't strictly true, particularly in modern computerized fonts in which the M tends to be less than an em wide. An en is half an em. For more information, see en.wikipedia.org/wiki/Em_(typography).

Using Font.Size and the value returned by the FontFamily class's GetEmHeight method, you can convert the other values into pixels. For example, the following equation shows how to calculate a font family's ascent in pixels:

```
Ascent Pixels = FontFamily.GetCellAscent * Font.Size / FontFamily.GetEmHeight
```

Example program FontMetrics calls the MeasureCharacters subroutine shown in the following code to display the font metrics for text in three different fonts:

```
Public Sub MeasureCharacters(ByVal gr As Graphics, ByVal the_font As Font, _
 ByVal txt As String, ByVal layout_rect As RectangleF, _
 ByVal string_format As StringFormat)
    ' Define an array of CharacterRange objects,
    ' one for each character.
    Dim character_ranges(txt.Length - 1) As CharacterRange
    For i As Integer = 0 To txt.Length - 1
        character_ranges(i) = New CharacterRange(i, 1)
    Next i
    ' Set the ranges in the StringFormat object.
    string_format.SetMeasurableCharacterRanges(character_ranges)

    ' Get the character range regions.
    Dim character_regions() As Region =
        gr.MeasureCharacterRanges(txt,
            the_font, layout_rect, string_format)

    ' Get the font's ascent.
    Dim em_height As Integer = the_font.FontFamily.GetEmHeight(FontStyle.Bold)
    Dim em_height_pix As Single = the_font.Size
    Dim design_to_pixels As Single = the_font.Size / em_height
    Dim ascent As Integer = the_font.FontFamily.GetCellAscent(FontStyle.Bold)
    Dim ascent_pix As Single = ascent * design_to_pixels
    Dim descent As Integer = the_font.FontFamily.GetCellDescent(FontStyle.Bold)
    Dim descent_pix As Single = descent * design_to_pixels
    Dim cell_height_pix As Single = ascent_pix + descent_pix
    Dim internal_leading_pix As Single = cell_height_pix - em_height_pix
    Dim line_spacing As Integer = the_font.FontFamily.GetLineSpacing(FontStyle.Bold)
    Dim line_spacing_pix As Single = line_spacing * design_to_pixels
    Dim external_leading_pix As Single = line_spacing_pix - cell_height_pix
```

```
    ' Draw each region's bounds.
    For Each rgn As Region In character_regions
        ' Convert the region into a Rectangle.
        Dim character_bounds As RectangleF = rgn.GetBounds(gr)
        Dim character_rect As Rectangle =
            Rectangle.Round(character_bounds)
        ' Draw the bounds.
        gr.DrawRectangle(Pens.Black, character_rect)

        ' Draw the internal leading.
        gr.DrawLine(Pens.Black,
            character_rect.X,
            character_rect.Y + internal_leading_pix,
            character_rect.Right,
            character_rect.Y + internal_leading_pix)

        ' Draw the ascent.
        gr.DrawLine(Pens.Black,
            character_rect.X,
            character_rect.Y + ascent_pix,
            character_rect.Right,
            character_rect.Y + ascent_pix)

        ' Draw the descent.
        gr.DrawLine(Pens.Orange,
            character_rect.X,
            character_rect.Y + ascent_pix + descent_pix,
            character_rect.Right,
            character_rect.Y + ascent_pix + descent_pix)

        ' Draw the external leading.
        gr.FillRectangle(Brushes.Red,
            character_rect.X,
            character_rect.Y + ascent_pix + descent_pix,
            character_rect.Width,
            external_leading_pix)
    Next rgn
    ' Draw the text.
    gr.DrawString(txt, the_font, Brushes.Black,
        layout_rect, string_format)
End Sub
```

code snippet FontMetrics

MeasureCharacters defines an array of CharacterRange objects and initializes them so that they each refer to a single character in the string. The program calls SetMeasurableCharacterRanges and then MeasureCharacterRanges, as described in the section "MeasureString" earlier in this chapter.

Next, the code calculates the font's em height, ascent, descent, cell height, internal leading, line spacing, and external leading. The subroutine then loops through the Regions returned by MeasureCharacterRanges, converting each Region into a Rectangle and drawing it.

The program then draws lines showing the internal leading, ascent, and descent values, and fills an area representing the external leading space. It draws the descent in orange and fills the external leading in red so you can tell them apart where they overlap in the left font.

The subroutine finishes by drawing the text. Figure 32-11 shows the result.

Note that the font metrics are not always rigidly followed. For example, sometimes a character may extend into the external leading space.

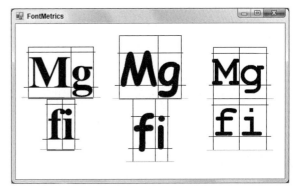

FIGURE 32-11: The FontFamily and Font classes provide the methods you need to calculate font metrics.

SUMMARY

When you draw lines, rectangles, and other shapes, you can completely define the shape by giving its size and position. Text is different. Different fonts may produce very different results, even for the same text. A single font sometimes even produces different results for a character, depending on the characters that surround it and the area in which it is drawn.

This chapter describes some of the methods you can use to position and measure text in Visual Basic. Layout rectangles and StringFormat objects let you easily draw text that is centered or aligned vertically and horizontally. The DrawString method automatically wraps text if necessary and can understand Tabs and Carriage Return/Line Feed characters contained in the text.

The StringFormat object's flags let you determine how text is aligned, wrapped, and trimmed. The StringFormat object's methods let you read and define tab stops.

The Graphics object's MeasureString method lets you determine roughly how big a string will be when drawn on the object. Its MeasureCharacterRanges method lets you determine the placement of regions of text within a string.

With all of these methods at your disposal, you can position text almost exactly where you want it.

Chapters 30 through 32 explain how to draw objects such as lines, ellipses, and text at a relatively high level. When you draw a line from one point to another, you don't need to specify exactly how the pixels on the screen should be colored. You set values for higher-level properties such as the pen color and dash style, brush color and style, and so forth. Then Visual Basic figures out the details.

Chapter 33, "Image Processing," explains how you can read and manipulate images on a pixel-by-pixel basis. It tells how to load and save image files in different formats (such as BMP, GIF, JPEG, and PNG) and how to get and set the colors of individual pixels.

33

Image Processing

The Graphics class represents a drawing surface at a logical level. Below that level, a Graphics object is attached to a Bitmap or Metafile object. Those objects understand the slightly lower-level needs of managing more physical data structures. For example, a Bitmap object maps abstract drawing commands such as DrawLine and DrawEllipse to colored pixels that can be displayed on a PictureBox or saved into a file. Similarly, a Metafile maps the Graphics object's abstract commands into metafile records that you can play back on a drawing surface, or save in a graphical metafile.

This chapter describes the more down-to-earth Bitmap and Metafile classes. It explains methods for building, modifying, and manipulating these objects. It shows how to load and save them from graphics files and, in the case of Bitmap classes, how to work with files saved in a variety of graphic formats such as BMP, GIF, JPEG, TIFF, and PNG.

IMAGE

An Image object represents some sort of picture that you can draw on, copy, transform, and display. Image is an abstract (MustInherit) class, so you cannot create instances of this class directly. Instead you must make instances of its derived classes Bitmap and Metafile.

 You can also derive your own class from Image if you want, although that's a fairly advanced technique, so it isn't covered here.

The Image class provides useful graphical methods that the Bitmap and Metafile classes inherit. Many other objects can work with any type of Image object, so you can pass them either a Bitmap or a Metafile. For example, the Graphics object's FromImage method takes an Image object as a parameter and returns a Graphics object attached to that Image. This parameter can be either a Bitmap or a Metafile. The following code creates a new Bitmap object, attaches a Graphics object to it, and then uses the Graphics object to draw a rectangle on the Bitmap:

```
Dim bm As New Bitmap(100, 100)
Using gr As Graphics = Graphics.FromImage(bm)
    gr.DrawRectangle(Pens.Black, 10, 10, 80, 80)
End Using
```

The Image class itself provides several useful methods, particularly Load and Save. The following table describes these and some of the class's other useful properties and methods.

PROPERTY OR METHOD	PURPOSE
Dispose	Frees the resources associated with this image. See the sections "Loading Bitmaps" and "Saving Bitmaps" later in this chapter for more information.
Flags	Returns attribute flags for the image. These provide information such as whether the pixel data contains alpha values and whether the image is a gray scale. For more information, see msdn.microsoft .com/system.drawing.imaging.imageflags.aspx.
FromFile	This shared function loads an image from a file as in bm = Bitmap .FromFile(file-name).
FromHbitmap	This shared function loads a Bitmap image from a Windows bitmap handle. (A *bitmap handle* is a 32-bit integer that gives a value associated with the bitmap in the GDI environment. Windows uses the handle to refer to the bitmap when it needs to manipulate it. In the .NET environment, you generally work with Bitmap and Image objects and don't need to worry about bitmap handles. It's useful to know about this method, however, in case you need to manipulate a bitmap loaded using older GDI routines.)
FromStream	This shared function loads an image from a data stream.
GetBounds	Returns a RectangleF structure representing the rectangle's bounds.
GetPixelFormatSize	Returns the color resolution (bits per pixel) for a specified PixelFormat.
GetThumbnailImage	Returns a thumbnail representation of the image.
Height	Returns the image's height.
HorizontalResolution	Returns the horizontal resolution of the image in pixels per inch.
IsAlphaPixelFormat	Returns True if the specified PixelFormat contains alpha information.
Palette	Determines the ColorPalette object used by the image.

PROPERTY OR METHOD	PURPOSE
PhysicalDimension	Returns a SizeF structure giving the image's dimensions in pixels for Bitmaps and 0.01 millimeter units for Metafiles.
PixelFormat	Returns the image's pixel format. This property can take such values as Format24bppRgb (24-bit red/green/blue data), Format32bppArgb (32-bit alpha/red/green/blue data), and Format8bppIndexed (8-bit index into a 256-color table). For more information, see `msdn` `.microsoft.com/system.drawing.imaging.pixelformat.aspx`.
RawFormat	Returns an ImageFormat object representing the image's raw format. The ImageFormat class has shared members for each of the standard image types. For example, the following code checks whether the Bitmap bm was loaded from a JPEG file: `If bm.RawFormat` `.Equals(ImageFormat.Jpeg) Then . . .`
RotateFlip	Rotates, flips, or rotates and flips the image. The parameter indicates which combination of flips (vertical, horizontal, or both) and rotation (0, 90, 180, or 270 degrees) to use.
Save	Saves the image in a file or stream with a given data format (BMP, GIF, JPEG, and so on). See the sections "Loading Bitmaps" and "Saving Bitmaps" later in this chapter for more information.
Size	Returns a Size structure containing the image's width and height in pixels.
VerticalResolution	Returns the vertical resolution of the image in pixels per inch.
Width	Returns the image's width.

BITMAP

The Bitmap class represents an image defined by pixel data. You can use a Bitmap to create, load, modify, and save image data to sources that display pixel data such as screen objects (PictureBoxes, Forms, UserControls, and so on) and image files (BMP, GIF, JPEG, PNG, TIFF, and so on).

Many of the Bitmap class's most useful properties and methods are inherited from the Image class. These include Height, HorizontalResolution, Palette, RawFormat, Size, Width, GetThumbnailImage, RotateFlip, and Save. See the section "Image" earlier in this chapter for information about those and other inherited properties and methods.

The following table describes some of the most useful methods that the Bitmap class adds to those inherited from the Image class.

METHOD	PURPOSE
FromHicon	This shared function loads a Bitmap image from a Windows icon handle. (An *icon handle* is a 32-bit integer that gives a value associated with the icon in the GDI environment. Windows uses the handle to refer to the icon when it needs to manipulate it. In the .NET environment, you generally work with Icon objects and don't need to worry about icon handles. It's useful to know about this method, however, in case you need to manipulate an icon loaded using older GDI routines.)
FromResource	This shared function loads a Bitmap image from a Windows resource.
GetPixel	Returns a specified pixel's Color.
LockBits	Locks the Bitmap class's data in memory, so it cannot move until the program calls UnlockBits.
MakeTransparent	Makes all pixels with a specified color transparent by setting their alpha components to 0.
SetPixel	Sets a specified pixel's Color value.
SetResolution	Sets the Bitmap class's horizontal and vertical resolution in dots per inch (DPI).
UnlockBits	Unlocks the Bitmap class's data in memory so the system can relocate it if necessary.

For most applications, the GetPixel and SetPixel methods provide adequate performance when manipulating pixels, but there is some overhead in moving through the different layers between the program's code and the actual pixel data. For applications that work with very large images or that need to process pixel data on many images very quickly, performance may be an issue.

In cases where speed is an issue, you can access the pixel data more directly using so-called unsafe access. The program locks the Bitmap class's data, reads and updates the pixel values, and then unlocks the data. See the section "Pixel-by-Pixel Operations" later in this chapter for more information and examples.

Loading Bitmaps

Loading a Bitmap from a file is simple. Simply pass the file's name into the Bitmap class's constructor. The following code loads the bitmap file whose name is stored in the variable file_name, and then displays it in the PictureBox control named picImage:

```
Dim bm As New Bitmap(file_name)
picImage.Image = bm
```

After you have loaded a Bitmap, you can attach a Graphics object to it, draw on it, display it, and save the results in a new bitmap file. The following code loads the bitmap file, attaches a Graphics object to it, uses that object to draw an ellipse, and displays the result in the picImage control:

```
Dim bm As New Bitmap(file_name)
Using gr As Graphics = Graphics.FromImage(bm)
    gr.DrawEllipse(Pens.White, 0, 0, bm.Width - 1, bm.Height - 1)
End Using
picImage.Image = bm
```

Unfortunately, the Bitmap object holds some sort of attachment to the bitmap file. If you try to delete the file while the program is running and still using the Bitmap, the operating system complains that the file is locked by another process. Similarly, if you open the file in a program such as Microsoft Paint, make some changes, and try to save the file, the operating system complains about a sharing violation.

To release the file for other programs to use, you must dispose of the Bitmap object that opened it. However, if you assign the Bitmap to a property (such as Image property of a PictureBox), the property keeps a reference to the Bitmap and will later generate an error when it tries to use the Bitmap that you have disposed.

One solution to this problem is to create a second Bitmap that is a copy of the first Bitmap, as shown in the following code. Then you can safely dispose of the first Bitmap. Because the second Bitmap was never associated with the bitmap file, the file is not locked.

```
' Load the bitmap file.
Dim bm As New Bitmap(file_name)

' Make a copy.
Dim new_bm As New Bitmap(bm)

' Dispose of the original Bitmap.
bm.Dispose

' Draw on the new Bitmap and display the result.
Using gr As Graphics = Graphics.FromImage(new_bm)
    gr.DrawEllipse(Pens.White, 0, 0, new_bm.Width - 1, new_bm.Height - 1)
End Using
picImage.Image = new_bm
```

code snippet LoadPicture

Saving Bitmaps

You can use a Bitmap object's Save method to save the bitmap into a file or data stream. By default the image is saved in PNG format, so if you want to use the PNG format you only need to pass Save the name of the file. To save the image in some other format, pass the format as the Save method's second parameter.

> *The Save method uses its second parameter, not the file name's extension, to determine the file format. For example, if you pass the Save method only the string "Test.bmp," you'll get a PNG file with a .bmp extension. To avoid confusion, explicitly specify the data type that matches the file name's extension.*

The following code generates a 256 × 256 pixel bitmap from scratch and saves it in a JPEG file. Because the program doesn't specify a path for the file, it is created in the program's current directory.

```
' Make a 256x256 pixel Bitmap.
Dim bm As New Bitmap(256, 256)

' Draw on it.
Using gr As Graphics = Graphics.FromImage(bm)
    gr.Clear(Color.White)
    gr.DrawEllipse(Pens.Red, 0, 0, bm.Width - 1, bm.Height - 1)
    gr.DrawLine(Pens.Green, 0, 0, bm.Width - 1, bm.Height - 1)
    gr.DrawLine(Pens.Blue, bm.Width - 1, 0, 0, bm.Height - 1)
End Using

' Save the result as a JPEG file.
bm.Save("test.jpg", ImageFormat.Jpeg)
```

code snippet SaveJpeg

The ImageFormat enumeration defines the values Bmp, Emf, Exif, Icon, Jpeg, MemoryBmp, Png, Tiff, and Wmf.

METAFILE MIX-UP

ImageFormat's Wmf (Windows Metafile) and Emf (Enhanced Metafile) formats don't really work. If you try to save in those formats, you get the Png format instead. See the "Remarks" section at `msdn.microsoft.com/system.drawing.imaging .metafile.aspx` for details.

You can still produce a metafile, it's just more work. See the section "Metafile Objects" later in this chapter for more information.

You can find information about the different file formats on the Web. For example, you can find some general descriptions of various formats at `en.wikipedia.org/wiki/Graphics_file_format`. Also see Microsoft's article "Guidelines for selecting the appropriate picture format" at `support .microsoft.com/kb/272399`.

If you save a Bitmap image in the Wmf (Windows metafile) or Emf (Enhanced metafile) format, the Save method creates a metafile that contains a bitmapped image. If you create a metafile by using a Metafile object, on the other hand, the result is a metafile that contains records that draw lines, curves, text, and so forth. The difference can have a couple of important consequences.

First, if the image is large, the bitmapped version may take up a lot more space than the version that records only drawing commands. It may also take a lot longer to draw a large bitmap than it would to draw a few circles and lines.

Second, you can transform a metafile that contains commands more readily than you can transform a metafile that contains a bitmap. If you enlarge a metafile containing commands, the result contains enlarged lines, curves, and other output. If you enlarge a metafile containing a bitmap, the result is a relatively blocky enlarged bitmap. Anti-aliasing may help a little, but the metafile containing drawing commands will produce a much better result.

On the other hand, not all programs understand all metafile commands. You may load a metafile containing drawing commands into another application and find that your ellipses and text don't work. Although a metafile containing a bitmap won't resize nicely, at least it should look similar to what you created.

See the section "Metafile Objects" later in this chapter for more information on metafiles.

Implementing AutoRedraw

In Visual Basic 6 and earlier versions, the Form and PictureBox objects had an AutoRedraw property. If you set this property to True, anything you drew on the object was automatically saved. If the object was later obscured and redrawn, the drawing was automatically restored.

This method required Visual Basic to allocate a chunk of internal memory to store the image, so it was not free. However, it could be a lot easier and faster than redrawing a complex image from scratch every time the drawing is exposed. For example, drawing a Mandelbrot set or other complex fractal may take 10 or 20 seconds even on a relatively fast computer. Some of the complex images used in modern computer animated movies take hours or days to build. Redrawing these images from scratch every time a form was exposed would be impractical.

The bad news is that Visual Basic .NET has no AutoRedraw property. If you want similar functionality, you must implement it yourself. The good news is that Visual Basic .NET has a couple of controls that can display a persistent image, and they can do a lot of the work for you.

The Form object's BackgroundImage property holds an image that covers the form's background. If the image is too big to fit, it is cropped. If the image is too small to cover the whole form, it is repeated to tile the form.

The PictureBox object's Image property also displays a persistent image. The control's SizeMode property determines how Visual Basic uses the image to cover the control. This property can take the values Normal (the image is drawn at full scale in the upper-left corner of the PictureBox and is cropped if it is too big), StretchImage (the image is stretched or squashed to fit the control, possibly changing its shape), AutoSize (the PictureBox resizes to fit the image), and CenterImage (the image is drawn at full scale in the center of the PictureBox and is cropped if it is too big).

One relatively easy method for implementing AutoRedraw is to make a Bitmap and assign it to a PictureBox object's Image property. Then the PictureBox automatically redisplays the image whenever it is exposed.

Some programs don't need to redraw their images when the form resizes. For example, a mapping application might display its map at a specific size. In that case, you don't need to redraw the map in the form's Resize event handler. Instead, you would probably add menus and buttons to let the user zoom in and out, and scroll to different parts of the map. In an application such as that one, the code would need to draw images only when the content changed. The rest is automatic.

Other applications draw in several routines and not just in the form's Load and Resize event handlers. For example, a drawing program might let the user draw various shapes (such as lines, rectangles, ellipses, and free-form curves). The program would add these shapes to a Bitmap as they were drawn and then display the result.

In programs such as this, you can create Bitmap and Graphics objects at a module or application level and then use them whenever the user modifies the image.

The Scribble example program, which is available for download on the book's web site, uses this approach to allow the user to draw free-form curves. When it starts and when the user selects the File menu's Clear command, the program makes Bitmap and Graphics objects at the module level. It displays the Bitmap in a PictureBox control's Image property.

The program's MouseDown, MouseMove, and MouseUp event handlers allow the user to draw lines on the Bitmap. Each time the program makes a change it re-displays the Bitmap in the PictureBox.

Figure 33-1 shows program Scribble in action.

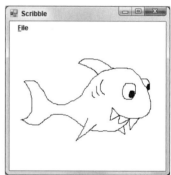

A final issue related to AutoRedraw is resizing. If the user makes the form larger or smaller, you need to figure out what to do about the AutoRedraw image. There are several approaches you can take, depending on your application.

The simplest approach is to not allow the user to resize the form or at least not to resize the PictureBox that displays the AutoRedraw image. Then you can ignore the whole issue.

A second approach is to create a new Bitmap of the new correct size. Use a Graphics object's Clear method to erase the new Bitmap. Then use the object's DrawImage method to copy the contents of the old Bitmap into the new one.

FIGURE 33-1: Program Scribble automatically redisplays its image when the form is hidden and exposed.

In this approach, if the new Bitmap is larger than the old one, all of its data is saved. If the new Bitmap is smaller, some of the old drawing is lost. You can preserve that information if you only allow the Bitmap to grow and never shrink. When the user resizes the form, you make the new Bitmap object's width and height the larger of the old Bitmap object's size and the form's new size.

Finally, if you think the program will often run maximized, you could just allocate a really big Bitmap when the program begins and forget the whole resizing issue.

Pixel-by-Pixel Operations

The Bitmap object provides two methods, GetPixel and SetPixel, that let a program easily read and write pixel values in the image. The following discussion describes an example that uses these methods to invert an image.

GetPixel and SetPixel are easy to use and fast enough for many applications. For high-performance graphics, however, they are relatively slow. The section "Unsafe Pixel Manipulation" later in this chapter explains how you can use unsafe methods to access pixel data more directly. This is a bit more difficult, but it is much faster for large images.

GetPixel and SetPixel

The Bitmap object's GetPixel method returns a Color structure for a pixel in a specific X and Y location. SetPixel sets the Color of a pixel at a particular position. These two methods are quite easy to use and provide good enough performance for many applications.

Example program InvertImageGetSetPixels uses the InvertImage subroutine shown in the following code to invert the pixel colors in a Bitmap:

```
Private Sub InvertImage(ByVal bm As Bitmap)
    ' Process the image's pixels.
    For y As Integer = 0 To bm.Height - 1
        For x As Integer = 0 To bm.Width - 1
            ' Get this pixel's color.
            Dim clr As Color = bm.GetPixel(x, y)

            ' Invert the color's components.
            clr = Color.FromArgb(255,
                255 - clr.R,
                255 - clr.G,
                255 - clr.B)
            ' Set the result pixel's color.
            bm.SetPixel(x, y, clr)
        Next x
    Next y
End Sub
```

code snippet InvertImageGetSetPixels

Subroutine InvertImage loops over all of the pixels in the image. It uses the bitmap's GetPixel function to get the color of each pixel. It inverts the red, green, and blue components of the pixel's color by subtracting them from the maximum allowed value 255. It then calls the destination Bitmap's SetPixel method to set the result pixel's value.

The first argument to the SetPixel method is the new color's alpha value, which gives the color's opacity. Setting alpha = 0 means the color should be completely transparent. Setting alpha = 255 means the color should be completely opaque. Subroutine InvertImage sets alpha to 255 for each pixel so the result is completely opaque.

Figure 33-2 shows the program in action. The output image on the right is essentially the photographic negative of the original image on the left.

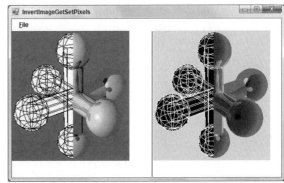

FIGURE 33-2: This program uses GetPixel and SetPixel to invert an image's pixel values.

Unsafe Pixel Manipulation

The GetPixel and SetPixel methods are very easy to use, and they are fast enough for many applications. For example, a program that generates fractals such as the Mandelbrot set spends a considerable amount of time calculating colors for each individual pixel. If it takes the program 5 seconds to generate the image and a tenth of a second of that time is spent by the SetPixel method, then SetPixel is probably fast enough. Using unsafe array methods may shave a few hundredths of a second off the total time, but the program's time is dominated by the code that calculates the pixels' colors, so it's hardly worth the extra complication.

However, suppose that you need to transform a series of images very quickly to display an animated sequence. In that case, the time spent by GetPixel and SetPixel may be significant. In that case, you may get much better performance using unsafe methods.

The basic idea is to directly access the array of bytes containing the red, green, and blue component values for the image's pixels. The Bitmap object's LockBits method copies the pixel data for a rectangular part of the image into a temporary buffer where you can manipulate it. Later, you call the UnlockBits method to copy any changes you made back into the bitmap.

Unfortunately, the LockBits method returns the buffer of data as a pointer to memory and Visual Basic cannot work directly with that kind of pointer. To resolve this problem, you can use the Marshal class's Copy method to move the data into a Visual Basic array. You can then modify the data and, when you are finished, use Marshal.Copy to move the results back into the buffer.

The following code shows the BitmapBytesRGB24 class that makes this somewhat simpler for the main program. This class works with 24-bit image representations. Your call to LockBits can specify other formats, but this one is particularly easy to work with because it uses one byte for each of the pixels' red, green, and blue components.

```
Imports System.Drawing.Imaging
Imports System.Runtime.InteropServices

Public Class BitmapBytesRGB24
    ' Provide public access to the picture's byte data.
    Public ImageBytes() As Byte
    Public RowSizeBytes As Integer
    Public Const PixelDataSize As Integer = 24

    ' A reference to the Bitmap.
    Private m_Bitmap As Bitmap

    ' Save a reference to the bitmap.
    Public Sub New(ByVal bm As Bitmap)
        m_Bitmap = bm
    End Sub
    ' Bitmap data.
    Private m_BitmapData As BitmapData

    ' Lock the bitmap's data.
    Public Sub LockBitmap()
        ' Lock the bitmap data.
        Dim bounds As Rectangle = New Rectangle(
```

```
            0, 0, m_Bitmap.Width, m_Bitmap.Height)
        m_BitmapData = m_Bitmap.LockBits(bounds, _
            Imaging.ImageLockMode.ReadWrite, _
            Imaging.PixelFormat.Format24bppRgb)
        RowSizeBytes = m_BitmapData.Stride

        ' Allocate room for the data.
        Dim total_size As Integer = m_BitmapData.Stride * m_BitmapData.Height
        ReDim ImageBytes(total_size)

        ' Copy the data into the ImageBytes array.
        Marshal.Copy(m_BitmapData.Scan0, ImageBytes, 0, total_size)
    End Sub

    ' Copy the data back into the Bitmap
    ' and release resources.
    Public Sub UnlockBitmap()
        ' Copy the data back into the bitmap.
        Dim total_size As Integer = m_BitmapData.Stride * m_BitmapData.Height
        Marshal.Copy(ImageBytes, 0, _
            m_BitmapData.Scan0, total_size)

        ' Unlock the bitmap.
        m_Bitmap.UnlockBits(m_BitmapData)

        ' Release resources.

        ImageBytes = Nothing
        m_BitmapData = Nothing
    End Sub
End Class
```

code snippet InvertImageUnsafe

The class's ImageBytes array will contain the pixel data stored as a one-dimensional array. Each pixel is represented by a byte for its blue component, a byte for its green component, and a byte for its red component, in that order.

The RowSizeBytes property tells how many bytes are stored in the array per row of pixels. The system may pad the array, so the number of bytes in each row is a multiple of four or some other number that is convenient for the operating system. Thus, RowSizeBytes may not always be three times the number of pixels in each row.

The constant PixelDataSize is 24 for this class because it works with 24-bit (3-byte) pixel data.

The class's constructor takes as a parameter a reference to a Bitmap and saves that reference for later use.

The class next declares a BitmapData object named m_BitmapData. This object will contain data describing the bitmap.

The LockBitmap method creates a Rectangle bounding the bitmap. This is the area in the bitmap that the routine will lock. This class doesn't mess around with pieces of the image, so it simply locks the entire bitmap.

LockBitmap calls the Bitmap object's LockBits method, passing it the bounding Rectangle, a flag indicating that it wants to lock the data for reading and writing, and a flag indicating that we want to work with 24-bit pixel data. LockBits returns information about the bitmap in a BitmapData object, which the routine saves in m_BitmapData. The routine sets the RowSizeBytes value so that it is easy for the main program to use.

LockBitmap then calculates the total number of bytes needed to hold the pixel data, makes the ImageBytes array big enough, and calls Marshal.Copy to copy the pixel data into the array.

The class's UnlockBitmap method copies the modified pixel data back into the bitmap. It recalculates the size of the array and uses Marshal.Copy to copy the data from the ImageBytes array back into the buffer allocated by LockBits. Finally, it calls the Bitmap object's UnlockBits method.

The following code shows how a main program can use the BitmapBytesRGB24 class to invert an image's pixels. The code creates a new BitmapBytesRGB24 object, passing the constructor the Bitmap that it wants to modify. It then calls the object's LockBitmap method to copy the pixel data into the object's ImageBytes array. Next, the program loops over the rows in the image. For each row, the code calculates the position in the pixel data that holds the row's first pixel's information. It then loops over the pixels in the row, modifying each pixel's blue, green, and red components. Remember that the components are in stored in the order blue, green, red. When it has finished modifying the pixel data, the program calls the BitmapBytesRGB24 object's UnlockBitmap method to copy the results back into the bitmap.

```vb
' Invert the pixel values in this Bitmap.
Private Sub InvertImage(ByVal bm As Bitmap)
    ' Make a BitmapBytesRGB24 object.
    Dim bm_bytes As New BitmapBytesRGB24(bm)

    ' Lock the bitmap.
    bm_bytes.LockBitmap()

    Dim pix As Integer
    For y As Integer = 0 To bm.Height - 1
        pix = y * bm_bytes.RowSizeBytes
        For x As Integer = 0 To bm.Width - 1
            ' Blue component.
            bm_bytes.ImageBytes(pix) = CByte(255) - bm_bytes.ImageBytes(pix)
            pix += 1
            ' Green component.
            bm_bytes.ImageBytes(pix) = CByte(255) - bm_bytes.ImageBytes(pix)
            pix += 1
            ' Red component.
            bm_bytes.ImageBytes(pix) = CByte(255) - bm_bytes.ImageBytes(pix)
            pix += 1
        Next x
    Next y
    ' Unlock the bitmap.
    bm_bytes.UnlockBitmap()
End Sub
```

code snippet InvertImageUnsafe

This is quite a bit more complicated than the previous program that uses GetPixel and SetPixel, so it's not the best method for simple applications. For high-performance image processing, however, the extra complication is sometimes worth it. In one set of tests on a 798-MHz Athlon 64 processor, the previous version using GetPixel and SetPixel took roughly 1.109 seconds to invert an 800 × 600 pixel image, while the version using the BitmapBytesRGB24 class took only 0.047 seconds.

METAFILE OBJECTS

The Metafile class represents image data defined by metafile records. These records encapsulate typical graphics commands that scale, rotate, draw lines, display text, and so forth. Using a Metafile object, you can build the metafile records and save them into a metafile, load a metafile, and play the metafile records on a display surface such as a Bitmap.

Many of the Metafile's most useful properties and methods are inherited from the Image class. These include Height, HorizontalResolution, Palette, RawFormat, Size, Width, GetThumbnailImage, RotateFlip, and Save. See the section "Image" earlier in this chapter for information about those and other inherited properties and methods.

The following table describes some of the most useful methods that the Metafile class adds to those inherited from the Image class.

METHOD	PURPOSE
GetMetafileHeader	Returns the MetafileHeader object associated with this Metafile. See the following text for more information on the MetafileHeader class.
PlayRecord	Plays a metafile record. To play the whole metafile, you can use a Graphics object's DrawImage method to copy the metafile's image onto a Bitmap and then display the Bitmap. PlayRecord lets you selectively play metafile records.

To build a Metafile, you create a Metafile object, attach a Graphics object to it, and then use drawing methods to draw into the metafile. In that respect, the Metafile behaves just like a Bitmap does.

The Graphics object also provides two special methods for working with its Metafile. AddMetafileComment adds a comment to the metafile. EnumerateMetafile sends the metafile's records to a callback subroutine one at a time. You can use that routine if you want to play back only some of the Metafile's records.

Example program MakeMetafile uses the following code to make and use a metafile. It starts by building a file name for the metafile. If the file already exists, the program deletes it. Next the program makes a Graphics object to get a handle to its device context. It uses that handle as a parameter to the Metafile object's constructor. It also passes the constructor the name of the file, a RectangleF that defines the metafile's bounds, and the units used by the bounds.

```
Private Sub Form1_Load() Handles MyBase.Load
    ' Make a bitmap.
    Const WID As Integer = 200
    Dim bm As New Bitmap(WID, WID)

    ' Find the WMF file's path and delete the file if it exists.
    Dim path_name As String = Application.StartupPath
    If path_name.EndsWith("\bin") Then
        path_name = path_name.Substring(0, path_name.Length - 4)
    End If
    Dim file_name As String = path_name & "\test.wmf"
    If Len(Dir$(file_name)) > 0 Then Kill(file_name)

    ' Make a Graphics object so we can use its hDC as a reference.
    Using me_gr As Graphics = Me.CreateGraphics
        Dim me_hdc As IntPtr = me_gr.GetHdc

        ' Make the Metafile, using the reference hDC.
        Dim bounds As New RectangleF(0, 0, WID, WID)
        Using mf As New Metafile(file_name, me_hdc,
         bounds, MetafileFrameUnit.Pixel)
            me_gr.ReleaseHdc(me_hdc)

            ' Make a Graphics object and draw.
            Using gr As Graphics = Graphics.FromImage(mf)
                gr.PageUnit = GraphicsUnit.Pixel
                gr.Clear(Color.White)
                gr.SmoothingMode = Drawing2D.SmoothingMode.AntiAlias
                Using thick_pen As New Pen(Color.Red, 5)
                    gr.DrawEllipse(thick_pen, bounds)
                    thick_pen.Color = Color.Green
                    gr.DrawLine(thick_pen, 0, 0, WID, WID)
                    thick_pen.Color = Color.Blue
                    gr.DrawLine(thick_pen, WID, 0, 0, WID)
                End Using
            End Using ' gr
        End Using ' mf

    ' Reload the metafile and copy it into a Bitmap.
    Using mf As New Metafile(file_name)
        Using gr As Graphics = Graphics.FromImage(bm)
            Dim dest_bounds As New RectangleF(0, 0, WID, WID)
            Dim source_bounds As New RectangleF(0, 0, WID + 1, WID + 1)
            gr.DrawImage(mf, bounds, source_bounds, GraphicsUnit.Pixel)
            picOrig.SizeMode = PictureBoxSizeMode.AutoSize
            picOrig.Image = bm
        End Using ' gr
    End Using ' mf

    ' Redisplay the result shrunk by 50%.
    Using mf As New Metafile(file_name)
        picSmall.SetBounds(
            picOrig.Right + 10, picOrig.Top,
            picOrig.Width \ 2, picOrig.Height \ 2)
```

```
        bm = New Bitmap(
            picSmall.ClientSize.Width,
            picSmall.ClientSize.Height)
        Using gr As Graphics = Graphics.FromImage(bm)
            Dim source_bounds As New RectangleF(0, 0, WID + 1, WID + 1)
            gr.ScaleTransform(0.5, 0.5)
            gr.DrawImage(mf, bounds, source_bounds, GraphicsUnit.Pixel)
            picSmall.Image = bm
            gr.Dispose()
        End Using ' gr
    End Using ' mf
End Using ' me_gr
End Sub
```

code snippet MakeMetafile

After creating the Metafile object, the program attaches a Graphics object to it. It uses the Graphics object to clear the metafile in white and to draw a circle and two lines.

The program then disposes of the Graphics and Metafile objects. That closes the metafile.

The program then calls the Metafile constructor again, passing it the file's name. It makes a Bitmap and associated Graphics object, and defines source and destination RectangleF structures to use when copying the image. It enlarges the source rectangle slightly so the metafile doesn't crop off the circle's right and bottom pixels.

Next, the code uses the Graphics object's DrawImage method to copy the metafile onto the Bitmap. It then sets the picOrig control's Image property to the Bitmap to display the result.

The program then repeats these steps to display the metafile on the picSmall control. This time it makes the control half as large as the full-scale image and uses a scaling transformation to shrink the metafile data when it calls DrawImage.

Figure 33-3 shows program MakeMetafile in action.

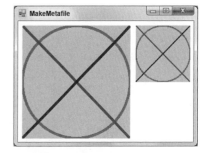

FIGURE 33-3: Program MakeMetafile creates a metafile and then draws two copies of it.

SUMMARY

The Image class represents a generic image. Its two child classes, Bitmap and Metafile, represent specific file types.

The Bitmap class lets you manipulate pixel-oriented image data. Its GetPixel and SetPixel methods let you get and set a pixel's color. Those methods are fast enough for most applications, but when performance is really critical, you can use unsafe methods to access the pixel data more directly and manipulate pixels much faster. When you are finished, you can use the Bitmap object's Save method to save the result in many different kinds of graphics files including Bmp, Emf, Exif, Icon, Jpeg, MemoryBmp, Png, Tiff, and Wmf.

The Metafile class represents a collection of drawing commands. Metafiles are reasonably standardized, so you can use them to import and export graphic data between your application and external programs (such as Microsoft Word and CorelDRAW).

Chapters 30 through 33 explain how to draw shapes, text, and images on the screen. Chapter 34, "Printing," shows how to generate similar output on a printer. The basic approach you use for printing shapes, text, and images is the same as it is for displaying those objects on the screen, but when and where you generate printed output requires some new techniques.

34

Printing

Visual Basic .NET provides several good tools for printing. String formatting objects enable you to determine how text is wrapped and truncated if it won't fit in a printing area. Methods provided by Graphics objects enable you to easily scale, rotate, and translate drawing commands.

The basic process, however, seems somewhat backward to many programmers. Rather than issuing commands to a printer object, a program responds to requests to draw pages generated by a PrintDocument object. Instead of telling the printer what to do, the program responds to the PrintDocument object's requests for data.

In some cases, generating a printout using only Visual Basic commands can be difficult. The following section explains alternative methods for generating a printout and tells when you might want to use those methods. If you just want to print several pages of text, it's often easier to pull the text into Microsoft Word or some other application that specializes in formatting text rather than writing your own.

Another option used by many developers is to purchase a third-party printing application. Some of these tools help with certain kinds of printing such as report generation. Chapter 35, "Reporting," provides an introduction to Crystal Reports, a report generation and printing tool that is available with some versions of Visual Basic and that you can purchase separately.

In some cases, however, you cannot take an easy way out. If the program generates very complex images and graphs, or produces text that is positioned and formatted in a complex manner, you probably need to work through the Visual Basic printing system. The rest of this chapter explains the techniques that you use to generate printouts in Visual Basic. It shows how to draw graphics and text on the printer and how to scale and center the results.

HOW NOT TO PRINT

Although Visual Basic provides many tools for arranging graphics on a printout, it does not always provide the best approach to printing. The general method for printing in Visual Basic requires you to generate each page of output in turn. For simple documents (such as a line drawing containing a few lines and circles on a single page), this is easy.

On the other hand, suppose you want to print several dozen pages of text interspersed with tables and pictures. Figuring out where to put line breaks, page breaks, tables, and figures could be a huge undertaking. To do the job right, you might need to consider orphan lines (when the first line of a paragraph sits at the bottom of a page), widow lines (the last line of a paragraph sits at the top of a page), orphan and widow words (when the first or last word in a sentence sits on a separate line), inserting extra space between words to make a line look nicer, page numbers, headers and footers, hyphenation, different left and right margins, mirrored margins, page gutters, bulleted and numbered lists, indentation and justification, different font sizes and styles, and a host of other issues.

Word processing and text-formatting applications such as Microsoft Word spend a great deal of effort on these issues — effort that you probably don't want to duplicate. In fact, Word is so good at handling these issues that you should consider using it to print your output instead of writing an elaborate Visual Basic program to do it.

If your output is simple text, your program can write it into a text file so you can use Word to open, format, and print it. For printouts that you don't need to generate too frequently, and for printouts where the user may want to edit the results before printing anyway, this is a simple, flexible solution that doesn't require you to write, debug, and maintain a lot of complicated formatting code.

For more elaborate printouts, programs such as Word may still be useful. Using Visual Studio Tools for Office (VSTO), you can open a Microsoft Word application and control it from your Visual Basic program. Your program can use the Word object model to add text, insert pictures, build tables, set page printing options, and even print the result. You can then save the document for later use or discard it.

Using VSTO, not only can you control Microsoft Word, but you can also use the other Microsoft Office applications. For example, you can load information into Excel so that you can use its tools to analyze and graph the data, copy information into Access for analysis by other database applications, or compose e-mail messages in Outlook.

VSTO is relatively complicated and outside of the scope of this book, so it isn't described here. For more information, see the VTSO web site at `msdn2.microsoft.com/office/aa905533.aspx`. You can also learn more in a book about VSTO such as *Professional VSTO 2005: Visual Studio 2005 Tools for Office* by Alvin Bruney (Wiley, 2006).

BASIC PRINTING

The PrintDocument class sits at the heart of the printing process in Visual Basic. The program creates an instance of this class and installs event handlers to catch its events. When the object must perform printing-related tasks, it raises events to ask the program for help.

The PrintDocument object raises four key events:

➤ `BeginPrint` — The PrintDocument raises its BeginPrint event when it is about to start printing. The program can initialize data structures, load data, connect to databases, and perform any other chores it must do to get ready to print.

➤ `QueryPageSettings` — Before it prints a page, the PrintDocument object raises its QueryPageSettings event. A program can catch this event and modify the document's margins for the page that it is about to print.

➤ `PrintPage` — The PrintDocument object raises its PrintPage event to generate a page. The program must catch this event and use the Graphics object provided by the event handler's parameters to generate output. When it is finished, the event handler should set the value e.HasMorePages to True or False to tell the PrintDocument whether there are more pages to generate.

➤ `EndPrint` — Finally, when it has finished printing, the PrintDocument object raises its EndPrint event. The program can catch this event to clean up any resources it used while printing. It can free data structures, close data files and database connections, and perform any other necessary cleanup chores.

Having created a PrintDocument object and its event handlers, you can do three things with it. First you can call the object's Print method to immediately send a printout to the currently selected printer. The PrintDocument object raises its events as necessary as it generates the printout.

Second, you can set a PrintPreviewDialog control's Document property to the PrintDocument object and then call the dialog's ShowDialog method. The PrintPreviewDialog displays the print preview window shown in Figure 34-1, using the PrintDocument object to generate the output it displays.

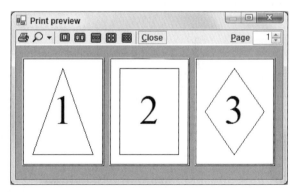

FIGURE 34-1: The PrintPreviewDialog control lets the user zoom in and out, and view the printout's various pages.

The preview dialog box's printer button on the left sends the printout to the printer. Note that this makes the PrintDocument object regenerate the printout using its events, this time sending the results to the printer instead of to the print preview dialog box. The magnifying glass button displays a drop-down list where the user can select various scales for viewing the printout. The next five buttons let the user display one, two, three, four, or six of the printout's pages at the same time. The Close button closes the dialog box and the Page up/down arrows let the user move through the printout's pages.

The PrintPreviewControl displays a print preview much as the PrintPreviewDialog control does, except that it sits on your form. It does not provide all the buttons that the dialog box does, but it does provide methods that let you implement similar features. For example, it lets your program set the zoom level, number of columns in the display, and so forth.

The third task you can do with a PrintDocument is assign it to a PrintDialog object's Document property and then call the dialog box's ShowDialog method to display the dialog box shown in Figure 34-2. The user can select the

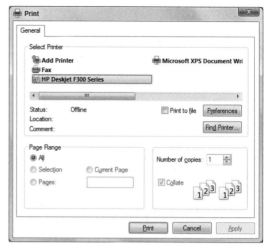

FIGURE 34-2: The PrintDialog control lets the user send a printout to a printer.

printer and set its properties (for example, selecting landscape or portrait orientation). When the user clicks Print, the dialog box uses the PrintDocument object to send the printout to the printer.

PREVIEW POSSIBILITIES

Your results could look different from those shown here. The print preview adjusts its appearance based on such factors as the type of printer you are using, its settings, the size of the paper you are using, and the paper's orientation.

Example program UsePrintPreviewDialog uses the following code to preview and print a page showing the page's bounds and margin bounds. This is just about the smallest program that demonstrates all three uses for a PrintDocument object: printing immediately, displaying a print preview dialog box, and displaying a print dialog box.

```
Imports System.Drawing.Printing

Public Class Form1
    Private WithEvents m_PrintDocument As PrintDocument

    ' Print now.
    Private Sub btnPrintNow_Click() Handles btnPrintNow.Click
        m_PrintDocument = New PrintDocument
        m_PrintDocument.Print()
    End Sub

    ' Display a print preview dialog.
```

```
        Private Sub btnPrintPreview_Click() Handles btnPrintPreview.Click
            m_PrintDocument = New PrintDocument
            dlgPrintPreview.Text = "UsePrintPreviewDialog"
            dlgPrintPreview.Document = m_PrintDocument
            dlgPrintPreview.ShowDialog()
        End Sub

        ' Display a print dialog.
        Private Sub btnPrintDialog_Click() Handles btnPrintDialog.Click
            m_PrintDocument = New PrintDocument
            dlgPrint.Document = m_PrintDocument
            dlgPrint.ShowDialog()
        End Sub

        ' Print a page with a diamond on it.
        Private Sub m_PrintDocument_PrintPage(ByVal sender As Object, _
         ByVal e As System.Drawing.Printing.PrintPageEventArgs) _
         Handles m_PrintDocument.PrintPage
            Using the_pen As New Pen(Color.Black, 20)
                e.Graphics.DrawRectangle(the_pen, e.MarginBounds)

                the_pen.DashStyle = Drawing2D.DashStyle.Dash
                the_pen.Alignment = Drawing2D.PenAlignment.Inset
                e.Graphics.DrawRectangle(the_pen, e.PageBounds)
            End Using

            e.HasMorePages = False
        End Sub
    End Class
```

code snippet UsePrintPreviewDialog

The code declares a PrintDocument object named m_PrintDocument. It uses the WithEvents keyword, so it can easily catch the object's events.

When the user clicks the Print Now button, the btnPrintNow_Click event handler assigns m_PrintDocument to a new PrintDocument object and calls its Print method.

If the user clicks the Print Preview button, the btnPrintPreview_Click event handler assigns m_PrintDocument to a new PrintDocument object, sets the PrintPreviewDialog object's Document property equal to the new object, and invokes the dialog box's ShowDialog method.

When the user clicks the Print Dialog button, the btnPrintDialog_Click event handler assigns m_PrintDocument to a new PrintDocument object, sets the PrintDialog object's Document property equal to the new object, and calls the dialog box's ShowDialog method.

In all three cases, the PrintDocument object raises its PrintPage event when it is ready to print a page. The program's event handler creates a 20-pixel-wide pen and uses it to draw a rectangle around the page's margin bounds. It changes the pen so that it is dashed and inset (so it draws inside the borders of a rectangle), and then draws a rectangle around the page's bounds. It finishes by setting e.HasMorePages to False to tell the PrintDocument that the printout is complete.

The PrintDocument object's PrintPage event handler provides a parameter of type PrintPageEventArgs to let the program control the printout and to give information about the printer. This object's PageBounds and MarginBounds properties give the location of the printer's printable surface and the page's margins, respectively. Typically, the printable area might be a quarter inch smaller than the paper's physical size, and the margins might be an inch or more inside the paper's physical size.

Figure 34-3 shows these rectangles in a print preview. The MarginBounds are drawn with a thick line, and the PageBounds are shown with a thick dashed line.

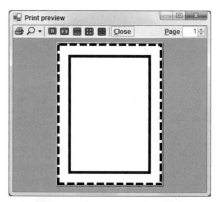

FIGURE 34-3: The e.PageBounds and e.MarginBounds parameters give the paper's printable area and margins.

PRINTING TEXT

The printing application described in the previous section is extremely simple. It prints a very straightforward shape on a single page. You know the positions of the diamond before starting, so the program needs to perform little arranging and formatting. The only formatting it does is to make its diamond fit the page's margins.

This section describes a more useful example that prints a long series of paragraphs using different font sizes. The PrintBooklet example program, which is available for download on the book's web site, must figure out how to break the text into pages. It also assumes that you will print the pages double-sided and then later bind the results into a booklet. To allow extra room for the binding, the program adds a *gutter* to the margin of edge on each page on the side where the binding will be. The program assumes that you will place the first page on the outside of the booklet, so it adds the gutter to the left margin on odd-numbered pages and to the right margin on even-numbered pages. Finally, the program displays a page number in the upper corner opposite the gutter.

Figure 34-4 shows the PrintBooklet program's print preview dialog box, so you can understand the goals. If you look closely, you can see that the left margins on the first and third pages and the right margin on the second page are enlarged to allow room for the gutter. You can also see that the page numbers are in the upper corner on the side that doesn't have the gutter. Imagine the second page printed on the back of the first, so their gutters lie on the same edge of the paper.

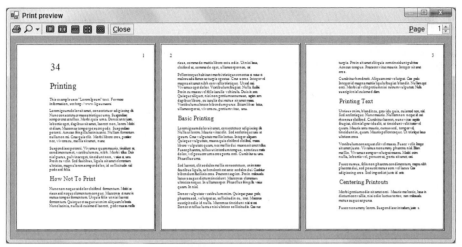

FIGURE 34-4: This preview shows text broken across pages with a gutter and displaying page numbers along the outside edges.

The program's Print Preview, Print Dialog, and Print Now buttons work much as the previous program's does, displaying the appropriate dialog boxes or calling the PrintDocument object's Print method. The most interesting differences between this program and the previous one are in how it stores its text to print and how it generates pages of printout.

The program uses the following ParagraphInfo structure to store information about the text it will print:

Available for
download on
Wrox.com

```
' Information about the paragraphs to print.
Private Structure ParagraphInfo
    Public FontSize As Integer
    Public Text As String
    Public Sub New(ByVal font_size As Integer, ByVal txt As String)
        FontSize = font_size
        Text = txt
    End Sub
End Structure
```

code snippet PrintBooklet

In the following code, the program declares its PrintDocument object. It uses the WithEvents keyword so it will be easy to catch the object's events. The code also declares collections to hold all of the ParagraphInfo structures that it will print and those that have not yet been printed. When the program's form loads, the code initializes these variables and adds a series of ParagraphInfo structures containing the text it will print to the m_Paragraphs collection.

Available for
download on
Wrox.com

```
' The PrintDocument.
Private WithEvents m_PrintDocument As New PrintDocument

' The paragraphs.
Private m_Paragraphs As Collection
```

```
Private m_ParagraphsToPrint As Collection
Private m_PagesPrinted As Integer

' Load the paragraph info.
Private Sub Form1_Load() Handles MyBase.Load
    ' Attach the PrintDocument to the
    ' PrintDialog and PrintPreviewDialog.
    dlgPrint.Document = m_PrintDocument
    dlgPrintPreview.Document = m_PrintDocument

    ' Make the text to print.
    m_Paragraphs = New Collection
    m_Paragraphs.Add(New ParagraphInfo(45, "23"))
    m_Paragraphs.Add(New ParagraphInfo(27, "Printing"))
    ... Code omitted...
End Sub
```

code snippet PrintBooklet

When the PrintDocument object starts drawing a printout, the BeginPrint event handler shown in the following code executes. This code resets the page number variable m_PagesPrinted. It then copies the ParagraphInfo structures from the m_Paragraphs collection (which holds all of the data) into the m_ParagraphsToPrint collection (which holds those that have not yet been printed).

```
' Get ready to print pages.
Private Sub m_PrintDocument_BeginPrint() _
 Handles m_PrintDocument.BeginPrint
    ' We have not yet printed any pages.
    m_PagesPrinted = 0

    ' Make a copy of the text to print.
    m_ParagraphsToPrint = New Collection
    For Each para_info As ParagraphInfo In m_Paragraphs
        m_ParagraphsToPrint.Add(
            New ParagraphInfo(para_info.FontSize, para_info.Text))
    Next para_info
End Sub
```

code snippet PrintBooklet

After the BeginPrint event handler finishes, the PrintDocument object starts printing pages. Before it prints each page, the object raises its QueryPageSettings event. The program uses the following code to catch this event and prepare the next page for printing. This code determines whether the next page will be odd or even numbered and adjusts the page's margin appropriately to create the gutter.

```
' Set the margins for the following page.
Private Sub m_PrintDocument_QueryPageSettings(ByVal sender As Object,
 ByVal e As System.Drawing.Printing.QueryPageSettingsEventArgs) _
 Handles m_PrintDocument.QueryPageSettings
    ' Use a 1 inch gutter (printer units are 100 per inch).
    Const gutter As Integer = 100

    ' See if the next page will be the first, odd, or even.
```

```
        If m_PagesPrinted = 0 Then
            ' The next page is the first.
            ' Increase the left margin.
            e.PageSettings.Margins.Left += gutter
        ElseIf (m_PagesPrinted Mod 2) = 0 Then
            ' The next page will be odd.
            ' Shift the margins right.
            e.PageSettings.Margins.Left += gutter
            e.PageSettings.Margins.Right -= gutter
        Else
            ' The next page will be even.
            ' Shift the margins left.
            e.PageSettings.Margins.Left -= gutter
            e.PageSettings.Margins.Right += gutter
        End If
    End Sub
```

code snippet PrintBooklet

After each QueryPageSettings event, the PrintDocument object raises its PrintPage event to generate the corresponding page. The following code shows the most complicated part of the program, the PrintPage event handler:

```
' Print the next page.
Private Sub m_PrintDocument_PrintPage(ByVal sender As Object,
 ByVal e As System.Drawing.Printing.PrintPageEventArgs) _
 Handles m_PrintDocument.PrintPage
    ' Increment the page number.
    m_PagesPrinted += 1

    ' Draw the margins (for debugging).
    'e.Graphics.DrawRectangle(Pens.Red, e.MarginBounds)

    ' Print the page number right justified
    ' in the upper corner opposite the gutter
    ' and outside of the margin.
    Dim x As Integer
    Using string_format As New StringFormat
        ' See if this is an odd or even page.
        If (m_PagesPrinted Mod 2) = 0 Then
            ' This is an even page.
            ' The gutter is on the right and
            ' the page number is on the left.
            x = (e.MarginBounds.Left + e.PageBounds.Left) \ 2
            string_format.Alignment = StringAlignment.Near
        Else
            ' This is an odd page.
            ' The gutter is on the left and
            ' the page number is on the right.
            x = (e.MarginBounds.Right + e.PageBounds.Right) \ 2
            string_format.Alignment = StringAlignment.Far
        End If

        ' Print the page number.
        Using the_font As New Font("Times New Roman", 20,
```

```vbnet
                FontStyle.Regular, GraphicsUnit.Point)
            e.Graphics.DrawString(m_PagesPrinted.ToString,
                the_font, Brushes.Black, x,
                (e.MarginBounds.Top + e.PageBounds.Top) \ 2,
                string_format)
        End Using ' the_font

        ' Draw the rest of the text left justified,
        ' wrap at words, and don't draw partial lines.
        string_format.Alignment = StringAlignment.Near
        string_format.FormatFlags = StringFormatFlags.LineLimit
        string_format.Trimming = StringTrimming.Word

        ' Draw some text.
        Dim paragraph_info As ParagraphInfo
        Dim ymin As Integer = e.MarginBounds.Top
        Dim layout_rect As RectangleF
        Dim text_size As SizeF
        Dim characters_fitted As Integer
        Dim lines_filled As Integer
        Do While m_ParagraphsToPrint.Count > 0
            ' Print the next paragraph.
            paragraph_info = DirectCast(m_ParagraphsToPrint(1), ParagraphInfo)
            m_ParagraphsToPrint.Remove(1)

            ' Get the area available for this paragraph.
            layout_rect = New RectangleF(
                e.MarginBounds.Left, ymin,
                e.MarginBounds.Width,
                e.MarginBounds.Bottom - ymin)

            ' See how big the text will be and
            ' how many characters will fit.
            ' Get the font.
            Using the_font As New Font("Times New Roman",
             paragraph_info.FontSize, FontStyle.Regular, GraphicsUnit.Point)
                text_size = e.Graphics.MeasureString(
                    paragraph_info.Text, the_font,
                    New SizeF(layout_rect.Width, layout_rect.Height),
                    string_format, characters_fitted, lines_filled)

                ' See if any characters will fit.
                If characters_fitted > 0 Then
                    ' Draw the text.
                    e.Graphics.DrawString(paragraph_info.Text,
                        the_font, Brushes.Black,
                        layout_rect, string_format)

                    ' Debugging: Draw a rectangle around the text.
                    'e.Graphics.DrawRectangle(Pens.Green,
                    '     layout_rect.Left,
                    '     layout_rect.Top,
                    '     text_size.Width,
                    '     text_size.Height)

                    ' Increase the location where we can start.
```

```
                      ' Add a little interparagraph spacing.
                      ymin += CInt(text_size.Height +
                          e.Graphics.MeasureString("M", the_font).Height / 2)
                  End If
              End Using ' the_font

              ' See if some of the paragraph didn't fit on the page.
              If characters_fitted < Len(paragraph_info.Text) Then
                  ' Some of the paragraph didn't fit.
                  ' Prepare to print the rest on the next page.
                  paragraph_info.Text = paragraph_info.Text.
                      Substring(characters_fitted)
                  m_ParagraphsToPrint.Add(paragraph_info, Before:=1)

                  ' That's all that will fit on this page.
                  Exit Do
              End If
          Loop
      End Using ' string_format

      ' If we have more paragraphs, we have more pages.
      e.HasMorePages = (m_ParagraphsToPrint.Count > 0)
  End Sub
```

code snippet PrintBooklet

The PrintPage event handler starts by incrementing the number of pages printed. It then includes commented code to draw a rectangle around the page's margins. When you are debugging a printing routine, drawing this rectangle can help you see where your drawing is in relation to the page's margins.

Next, the routine creates a font for the page number. Depending on whether this page is odd or even numbered, it calculates an X coordinate halfway between the non-gutter margin and the edge of the printable page. It sets a StringFormat object's Alignment property to make numbers in the left margin left-justified and to make numbers in the right margin right-justified. It then draws the page number at the calculated X position, halfway between the top margin and the paper's top printable boundary.

The program then prepares to draw the text for this page. It sets the StringFormat object's properties so that the text is left-justified and lines wrap at word boundaries instead of in the middle of words. It sets the FormatFlags property to LineLimit. If only part of a line of text would fit vertically on the page, this makes Visual Basic not draw the line rather than drawing just the top halves of its letters.

After this preparation, the program sets variable ymin to the minimum Y coordinate where the routine can draw text. Initially, this is the top margin. It then enters a Do loop to process as much text as will fit on the page.

Inside the loop, the program takes the first ParagraphInfo structure from the m_ParagraphsToPrint collection and makes a font that has the right size for that paragraph. It creates a RectangleF representing the remaining area on the page. This includes the area between the left and right margins horizontally, and between ymin and the bottom margin vertically.

The program then uses the e.Graphics object's MeasureString method to see how much space the next piece of text will need. It passes MeasureString the layout rectangle's size and the StringFormat object so Visual Basic can decide how it will need to wrap the paragraph's text when it prints it. The code also passes in the variables characters_fitted and lines_filled. These parameters are passed by reference, so MeasureString can fill in the number of characters and lines it could draw within the allowed size.

The routine then checks characters_fitted to see if any characters will fit in the available area. If any characters can fit, the program draws the paragraph. Commented code draws a rectangle around the text to help with debugging. The program increases ymin by the paragraph's printed height plus half of the font's height to provide a break between paragraphs.

Next, the program determines whether the entire paragraph fits in the allowed area. If some of the paragraph did not fit, the program stores the remaining text in the ParagraphInfo structure and puts the structure back at the beginning of the m_ParagraphsToPrint collection so it can be printed on the next page. It then exits the Do loop because the current page is full.

When the page is full or the m_ParagraphsToPrint collection is empty, the PrintPage event handler is finished. It sets e.HasMorePages to True if m_ParagraphsToPrint is not empty.

Finally, when the PrintDocument has finished printing the whole document, the following EndPrint event handler executes. This routine cleans up by setting the m_ParagraphsToPrint variable to Nothing, freeing up the collection object's memory. In this program, freeing the collection is a small matter. In a program that allocated more elaborate data structures, cleaning up in this event handler would be more important.

```
' Clean up.
Private Sub m_PrintDocument_EndPrint() Handles m_PrintDocument.EndPrint
    m_ParagraphsToPrint = Nothing
End Sub
```

CENTERING PRINTOUTS

The previous section explained how to handle a common scenario: printing large amounts of text. Another common scenario is printing a picture centered on the printed page. To do that, you must move the drawing vertically and horizontally to put it at the correct position. You can do this by using the Graphics object's TranslateTransform method. That method defines a translation transformation for all the graphics drawn by the object. After you set the transformation, you can draw any graphics as usual, and the Graphics object automatically moves them to the correct position.

The CenterPictureInMargins subroutine shown in the following code defines a translation transformation that centers an area within some specified bounds. The routine begins by calling the Graphics object's ResetTransform method to remove any transformations that may already be defined. Next, the routine calculates the horizontal and vertical offsets by which it must translate the rectangle picture_bounds so it will be centered within the rectangle margin_bounds. It calls the Graphics object's TranslateTransform method to make the translation.

```
' Transform the Graphics object to center the rectangle
' picture_bounds within margin_bounds.
Private Sub CenterPictureInMargins(ByVal gr As Graphics,
 ByVal picture_bounds As RectangleF, ByVal margin_bounds As RectangleF)
    ' Remove any existing transformation.
    gr.ResetTransform()

    ' Apply the transformation.
    Dim dx As Single =
        margin_bounds.Left - picture_bounds.Left +
        (margin_bounds.Width - picture_bounds.Width) / 2
    Dim dy As Single =
        margin_bounds.Top - picture_bounds.Top +
        (margin_bounds.Height - picture_bounds.Height) / 2
    gr.TranslateTransform(dx, dy)
End Sub
```

code snippet CenterPicture

You can use subroutine CenterPictureInMargins to prepare the e.Graphics object provided by the
PrintPage event handler to center a drawing on a printout. For example, the CenterPicture example
program uses the following PrintPage event handler code to draw a bar chart in the coordinate
space 100 <= X <= 600, 100 <= Y <= 400. It begins with commented code that draws the page's
margins for debugging purposes.

```
' Print the page.
Private Sub Print_PrintPage(ByVal sender As Object,
 ByVal e As System.Drawing.Printing.PrintPageEventArgs)
    ' Draw the margins (for debugging). Be sure
    ' to do this before transforming the Graphics object.
    e.Graphics.DrawRectangle(Pens.Red, e.MarginBounds)

    ' This routine draws a bar chart for 5 values
    ' in printer coordinates between
    ' (100, 100) - (600, 400).
    ' Transform the Graphics object to center the results.
    Dim picture_rect As New RectangleF(100, 100, 600, 400)
    Dim margin_rect As New RectangleF(
        e.MarginBounds.X,
        e.MarginBounds.Y,
        e.MarginBounds.Width,
        e.MarginBounds.Height)
    CenterPictureInMargins(e.Graphics, picture_rect, margin_rect)

    ' Draw a rectangle around the chart.
    e.Graphics.FillRectangle(Brushes.LightGray, picture_rect)
    e.Graphics.DrawRectangle(Pens.Black, Rectangle.Round(picture_rect))

    ' Draw the values.
    Dim x As Integer = 100
    DrawBar(e.Graphics, x, 200, HatchStyle.BackwardDiagonal)
    DrawBar(e.Graphics, x, 280, HatchStyle.Vertical)
    DrawBar(e.Graphics, x, 240, HatchStyle.ForwardDiagonal)
```

```
        DrawBar(e.Graphics, x, 170, HatchStyle.Horizontal)
        DrawBar(e.Graphics, x, 290, HatchStyle.DiagonalCross)

        ' There are no more pages.
        e.HasMorePages = False
    End Sub

    ' Draw a bar in (x, 400)-(x + 100, 400 - hgt).
    Private Sub DrawBar(ByVal gr As Graphics, ByRef x As Integer, _
     ByVal hgt As Integer, ByVal hatch_style As HatchStyle)
        Dim rect As New Rectangle(x, 400 - hgt, 100, hgt)
        Using hatch_brush As New HatchBrush(hatch_style, Color.Black, Color.White)
            gr.FillRectangle(hatch_brush, rect)
        End Using
        gr.DrawRectangle(Pens.Black, rect)
        x += 100
    End Sub
```

code snippet CenterPicture

The code defines rectangles representing the area in which it will draw and the printed page's margin bounds. It passes those rectangles to the CenterPictureInMargins subroutine to prepare the Graphics object for centering.

Next, the program fills the picture area's rectangle with light gray and outlines it in black. It then calls subroutine DrawBar several times to draw five values for the bar chart. The event handler sets e.HasMorePages to False, and then it ends.

Subroutine DrawBar draws a rectangle for the bar chart. It draws its rectangle at the X coordinate passed as a parameter, making it 100 units wide and hgt units tall. It fills the rectangle with a hatch pattern and then outlines it in black. The subroutine finishes by adding 100 to x, so the next call to DrawBar draws a rectangle to the right.

Figure 34-5 shows program CenterPicture in action. You can see in the picture that the bar chart is centered within the margins.

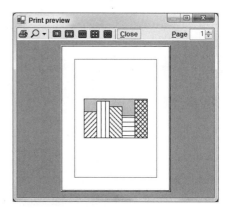

FIGURE 34-5: Subroutine CenterPictureInMargins makes it easy to center a picture within a printed page.

FITTING PICTURES TO THE PAGE

Another common scenario is drawing a picture as large as possible on the page without distorting it. You can use the same approach to this problem that was described in the previous section: Apply a transformation to the PrintPage event handler's Graphics object to make the picture fit the printed page.

The subroutine FitPictureToMargins shown in the following code makes this transformation. It begins by calling the Graphics object's ResetTransform method to remove any existing transformation. Next the subroutine translates to center the picture_bounds rectangle at the origin. Scaling an object centered at the origin is relatively simple because the object's center remains at the origin, so the program starts by centering picture_bounds.

```vb
' Transform the Graphics object to fit the rectangle
' picture_bounds to margin_bounds and center it.
Private Sub FitPictureToMargins(ByVal gr As Graphics,
    ByVal picture_bounds As RectangleF, ByVal margin_bounds As RectangleF)
        ' Remove any existing transformation.
        gr.ResetTransform()

        ' Translate to center picture_bounds at the origin.
        gr.TranslateTransform(
            -(picture_bounds.Left + picture_bounds.Width / 2),
            -(picture_bounds.Top + picture_bounds.Height / 2))

        ' Scale to make picture_bounds fit margin_bounds.
        ' Compare the aspect ratios.
        Dim margin_aspect As Single = margin_bounds.Height / margin_bounds.Width
        Dim picture_aspect As Single =
            picture_bounds.Height / picture_bounds.Width
        Dim scale As Single
        If picture_aspect > margin_aspect Then
            ' picture_bounds is relatively tall and thin.
            ' Make it as tall as possible.
            scale = margin_bounds.Height / picture_bounds.Height
        Else
            ' picture_bounds is relatively short and wide.
            ' Make it as wide as possible.
            scale = margin_bounds.Width / picture_bounds.Width
        End If
        ' Scale.
        gr.ScaleTransform(scale, scale, MatrixOrder.Append)

        ' Translate to move the origin to the center of margin_bounds.
        gr.TranslateTransform(
            margin_bounds.Left + margin_bounds.Width / 2,
            margin_bounds.Top + margin_bounds.Height / 2,
            MatrixOrder.Append)
    End Sub
```

code snippet FitToMargins

The program compares aspect ratios (ratios of height/width) of the picture_bounds and margin_bounds rectangles. If picture_bounds has the greater aspect ratio, it is relatively taller and thinner than margin_bounds. In that case, the program scales to make picture_bounds the same height as margin_bounds and sets its width appropriately.

If picture_bounds has the smaller aspect ratio, it is relatively wider and shorter than margin_bounds. In that case, the program scales to make picture_bounds the same width as margin_bounds and sets its height accordingly.

After calculating the scale factor it needs, the program calls the Graphics object's ScaleTransform method to add it to the Graphics object's transformation. It uses the MatrixOrder.Append parameter to make the object apply the scaling transformation after its first translation.

Finally, the subroutine applies another translation to move the center of the scaled picture_bounds rectangle from the origin to the center of margin_bounds. It again uses the MatrixOrder.Append parameter, so the new transformation is applied after the previous ones.

A program can use subroutine FitPictureToMargins exactly as it can use subroutine CenterPictureInMargins. Example program FitToMargins uses this subroutine to draw the bar chart shown in Figure 34-6. This routine works whether the drawing's area is relatively short and wide (as in this case) or tall and thin. It will also shrink a picture that is bigger than the page.

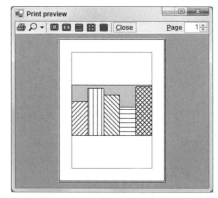

FIGURE 34-6: Subroutine FitPictureToMargins makes it easy to center a picture within a printed page, making it as large as possible without distortion.

SIMPLIFYING DRAWING AND PRINTING

Many applications draw some graphics, possibly with some user interaction, and then later print the same graphics, perhaps centered and scaled to fit the page.

You can make this process easier if you move all of the program's drawing code into subroutines that are independent of the drawing or printing surface. These drawing routines should take as a parameter a Graphics object on which to draw. Then it doesn't matter whether the program passes these routines the Graphics object provided by a PrintPage event handler or a control's Paint event handler. They can even use a Graphics object generated by the control's CreateGraphics method.

The DrawGraphics subroutine shown in the following code encapsulates the drawing code used in the previous sections. It takes a Graphics object as a parameter, draws a background on it, and calls DrawBar to draw five hatched rectangles to form a bar chart.

```
' Draw the bar chart with world coordinate bounds (100, 100)-(600, 400).
Private Sub DrawGraphics(ByVal gr As Graphics)
    ' Draw a rectangle around the chart.
    Dim picture_rect As New Rectangle(100, 100, 500, 300)
    gr.FillRectangle(Brushes.LightGray, picture_rect)
    gr.DrawRectangle(Pens.Black, picture_rect)

    ' Draw the values.
    Dim x As Integer = 100
    DrawBar(gr, x, 200, HatchStyle.BackwardDiagonal)
```

```
        DrawBar(gr, x, 280, HatchStyle.Vertical)
        DrawBar(gr, x, 240, HatchStyle.ForwardDiagonal)
        DrawBar(gr, x, 170, HatchStyle.Horizontal)
        DrawBar(gr, x, 290, HatchStyle.DiagonalCross)
    End Sub
```

Now the PrintPage event handler and other code can call this subroutine to draw the program's graphics. The following code shows how a program can use this routine to draw the bar chart on a PictureBox named picCanvas. The control's Resize event handler invalidates the control, so the Paint event handler can redraw the entire surface. The control's Paint event handler clears the PictureBox, calls FitPictureToMargins to fit the bar chart to the PictureBox's surface (minus a 3-pixel margin), and calls DrawGraphics to draw the bar chart.

```
    Private Sub picCanvas_Resize() Handles picCanvas.Resize
        picCanvas.Invalidate()
    End Sub

    Private Sub picCanvas_Paint(ByVal sender As Object,
     ByVal e As System.Windows.Forms.PaintEventArgs) Handles picCanvas.Paint
        ' Clear the picture.
        e.Graphics.Clear(picCanvas.BackColor)

        ' This routine draws a bar chart for 5 values
        ' in printer coordinates between
        ' (100, 100) - (600, 400).
        ' Transform the Graphics object to center the results.
        Dim picture_rect As New RectangleF(100, 100, 500, 300)
        Dim margin_rect As New RectangleF(
            picCanvas.ClientRectangle.X + 3,
            picCanvas.ClientRectangle.Y + 3,
            picCanvas.ClientRectangle.Width - 6,
            picCanvas.ClientRectangle.Height - 6)
        FitPictureToMargins(e.Graphics, picture_rect, margin_rect)
        ' Draw the bar chart.
        DrawGraphics(e.Graphics)
    End Sub
```

Example program PictureBoxPrint, shown in Figure 34-7 uses this code to draw a bar chart in a PictureBox and in a print preview dialog.

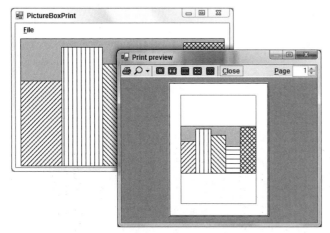

FIGURE 34-7: A program can use subroutine FitPictureToMargins to make a picture fit a PictureBox as well as a printed page.

This technique minimizes the amount of drawing code. It lets the program share the same code for drawing, printing, and print previewing. That means less code to debug and maintain. It also means that you need only to modify the code in one place if you need to change it later.

By calling FitPictureToMargins, the program makes the bar chart fill the PictureBox as much as possible without distorting it. If the control is anchored or docked so that it resizes when the form does, the bar chart also resizes so that it is as big as possible, a fairly impressive feat at the cost of a single subroutine call.

Although very useful, the technique of using a common routine to draw and print graphics is not appropriate for every application. Sometimes a program must take advantage of the particular characteristics of a printer or screen object, and the results may not make sense for other types of devices.

For example, suppose that a program draws fractals by performing time-consuming calculations for each pixel. It may make sense to show the results as the pixels are calculated on the screen. That would take advantage of the fact that the user can immediately see the results of pixels drawn on the screen. On the printer, however, the results aren't visible until the complete page is printed, so sending pixels to the printer one at a time doesn't particularly help the user and may slow printing. It would make more sense to draw the complete image on a Bitmap in memory and then send the result to the printer all at once by using the Graphics object's DrawImage method.

Similarly, the text-printing example described earlier in this chapter prints a long series of paragraphs broken across several pages. It takes advantage of the printed page's exact size and margins. You might be able to display the same page data in a scrolling window on the screen, but that probably wouldn't make much sense. In that application, trying to force screen drawing and page printing routines to produce exactly the same result would probably be a waste of time. It would be much easier and just as effective to display the text on the screen in a print preview control or dialog.

SUMMARY

The PrintDocument object sits at the heart of the standard Visual Basic printing process. A program makes a PrintDocument object and then responds to its BeginPrint, QueryPageSettings, PrintPage, and EndPrint events to generate a printout.

The PrintDocument object's Print method immediately generates a printout. You can also attach the PrintDocument to a PrintDialog, PrintPreviewDialog, or PrintPreviewControl and use those objects to display previews and generate printouts.

This chapter describes printing in general. Using the Graphics object provided by the PrintDocument object's PrintPage event, you can print lines, curves, text, images, and anything else you can draw to the screen.

Appendix I, "Visual Basic Power Packs," describes some additional tools that you can download for free. The Printer Compatibility Library and the PrintForm component give you new options for printing. See Appendix I for more information.

My book *Expert One-on-One Visual Basic Design and Development* (Stephens, Wrox, 2005) includes a chapter on printing that explains how to print images of forms much as the PrintForm Power Pack component does. It also shows how to wrap text so it flows around images on a printed page and how to use metafiles to let a program print procedurally rather than by responding to events. For more information, see the book's web site at www.wrox.com or www.vb-helper.com/one_on_one.htm.

Most of the programs described in this book so far are relatively self-contained. They take input from the user, perform some calculations, and display the results. Only a few chapters have interacted much with the outside system. The two exceptions are Chapter 23, which explains how to use drag and drop and the clipboard to interact with other programs, and this chapter, which explains how to interact with printers.

The chapters in the next part of the book explain more ways a program can interact with the system. Chapter 36, "Configuration and Resources," describes some of the ways that a Visual Basic program can store configuration and resource values for use at runtime. Some of the most useful of these methods include environment variables, the Registry, configuration files, and resource files.

PART V
Interacting with the Environment

35

Configuration and Resources

A very simple application performs a well-defined task that changes minimally over time. You may not need to configure such an application for different circumstances.

Many more complex applications, however, must be configured to meet different conditions. For example, the application might display different data for different kinds of users (such as data-entry clerks, supervisors, managers, and developers). Similarly, you might configure an application for various levels of support. You might have different configurations for trial, basic, professional, and enterprise versions.

The application may also need to save state information between sessions. It might remember the types of forms that were last running, their positions, and their contents. The next time the program runs, it can restore those forms so the user can get back to work as quickly as possible.

Visual Studio provides many ways to store and use application configuration and resource information. This chapter describes some of these tools. It starts by describing the My namespace that was invented to make these tools easier to find. It then tells how an application can use environment variables, the Registry, configuration files, resource files, and the Application object.

This chapter does not explain how to work with disk files more directly. Databases, XML files, text files, and other disk files are generally intended for storage of larger amounts of data, rather than simple configuration and resource information. Those topics are described more thoroughly in Chapters 20, "Database Controls and Objects," and 38, "File-System Objects."

MY

In older versions of Visual Basic .NET, programmers discovered that many common tasks were difficult to perform. For example, many programs get the name of the user logged on to the computer, read a text file into a string, get the program's version number, or examine all of the application's currently loaded forms. Although you can accomplish all of these tasks in early versions of Visual Basic .NET, doing so is awkward.

To make these common tasks easier, the My namespace was introduced to provide shortcuts for basic chores. For example, to read the text in a file in Visual Basic .NET 2003, you must create some sort of object that can work with a file such as a StreamReader, use the object to read the file (the ReadToEnd method for a StreamReader), and then dispose of the object. The following code shows how you might do this in Visual Basic .NET 2003:

```
Dim stream_reader As New IO.StreamReader(file_name)
Dim file_contents As String = stream_reader.ReadToEnd()
stream_reader.Close()
```

This isn't too difficult, but it does seem more complicated than such a simple everyday task should be.

The My namespace provides a simpler method for reading a file's contents. The Computer .FileSystem.ReadAllText method reads a text file in a single statement. The following statement reads the text in the file C:\Temp\Test.txt and displays it in a message box:

```
Dim file_contents As String =
    My.Computer.FileSystem.ReadAllText("C:\Temp\Test.txt")
```

There is nothing new in the My namespace. All the tasks it performs you can already handle using existing methods. The My namespace just makes some things easier.

This section describes the My namespace and the shortcuts it provides.

Me and My

Some programmers confuse the Me object and the My namespace. Me is a reference to the object that is currently executing code. If a piece of code is inside a particular class, Me is a reference to the class object that is running.

For example, if the class is a form, then within the form's code, Me returns a reference to the running form. If the form's code must change the form's BackColor property, it can use the Me object to explicitly refer to its own form. It can also omit the keyword to refer to its form implicitly. That means the following two statements are equivalent:

```
Me.BackColor = SystemColors.Control
BackColor = SystemColors.Control
```

If you build several instances of a class, the code in each instance gets a different value for Me. Each instance's Me object returns a reference to that instance.

On the other hand, My isn't an object at all. It is a namespace that contains objects, values, routines, and other namespaces that implement common functions. The My namespace is a single unique entity shared by all of the code throughout the application.

It may help if you try not to think of the My namespace as a thing in and of itself. The My namespace doesn't do anything all alone. It needs to be paired with something within the namespace. Think of My.Application, My.User, My.Computer, and so forth. It makes sense to think of My.Computer as representing the computer.

My Sections

The following table briefly outlines the major sections within the My namespace. Other sections of this chapter and Appendix S, "The My Namespace," describe these sections in greater detail.

SECTION	PURPOSE
My.Application	Provides information about the current application: current directory, culture, and assembly information (such as program version number, log, splash screen, and forms)
My.Computer	Controls the computer hardware and system software: audio, clock, keyboard, clipboard, mouse, network, printers, Registry, and file system
My.Forms	Provides access to an instance of each type of Windows Form defined in the application
My.Resources	Provides access to the application's resources: strings, images, audio, and so forth
My.Settings	Provides access to the application's settings
My.User	Provides access to information about the current user
My.WebServices	Provides access to an instance of each XML web service referenced by the application

ENVIRONMENT

Environment variables are values that a program can use to learn information about the system. There are three types of environment variables that apply at the system, user, and process levels. As you may guess from their names, system-level variables apply to all processes started on the system, user-level variables apply to processes started by a particular user, and process-level variables apply to a particular process and any other processes that it starts.

Environment variables may indicate such things as the name of the operating system, the location of temporary directories, the user's name, and the number of processors the system has. You can also store configuration in environment variables for your programs to use.

Environment variables are loaded when a process starts, and they are inherited by any process launched by the initial process. For Visual Basic development, that means the variables are loaded when you start Visual Studio and they are inherited by the program you are working on when you start it. If you make changes to the system's environment variables, you need to close and reopen Visual Studio before your program will see the changes.

A program can also create temporary process-level variables that are inherited by launched processes and that disappear when the original process ends.

Visual Basic provides a couple of tools for working with the application's environment. The following sections describe two: the Environ function and the System.Environment object. Before you can read environment variables, however, you should know how to set their values.

Setting Environment Variables

Environment variables are normally set on a system-wide basis before the program begins. In older operating systems, batch files such as autoexec.bat set these values. More recent systems provide Control Panel tools to set environment variables.

Newer systems also use an autoexec.nt file to set environment variables that apply only to command-line (console) applications so they don't affect GUI applications. Sometimes you can use this fact to your advantage by giving different kinds of applications different environment settings.

To set environment variables in Windows XP, open the Control Panel, run the System applet, and select the Advanced tab. Alternatively, you can right-click My Computer or Computer in newer versions of Windows and select Properties from the context menu. Click the Environment Variables button to display the Environment Variables dialog box. Use the dialog's Add, Edit, and Delete buttons to add, modify, or remove environment variables.

To set environment variables in Windows Vista, open the Control Panel, open the System and Maintenance applet, and then open its System applet. On the left, click the "Advanced system settings" link. That link requires administrator privileges so Vista displays a UAC privilege elevation dialog. Enter an administrator's password and click OK to get to the System Properties dialog. Select the Advanced tab and click the Environment Variables button to display the Environment Variables dialog box. Use the dialog's Add, Edit, and Delete buttons to add, modify, or remove environment variables.

Be careful to use the variables properly. Use system variables when a value should apply to all processes started by all users, user variables when a value should apply to all processes started by a particular user, and process variables when a value should apply to a process and any processes that it starts.

REFRESH REMINDER

Remember that Visual Studio won't see environment variable changes that you make after it is running. You need to close and reopen Visual Studio before your program will see the changes.

Using Environ

At runtime, a Visual Basic application can use the Environ function to retrieve environment variable values. If you pass this function a number, it returns a string giving the statement that assigns the corresponding environment variable. For example, Environ(1) might return the following string:

```
ALLUSERSPROFILE=C:\ProgramData
```

You should pass the function a number between 1 and 255. Environ returns a zero-length string if the number does not correspond to an environment variable. The following code uses this fact to list all the application's environment variables. When it finds a variable that has zero length, it knows it has read all of the variables with values.

Available for
download on
Wrox.com

```
For i As Integer = 1 To 255
    If Environ(i).Length = 0 Then Exit For
    Debug.WriteLine(Environ(i))
Next i
```

code snippet ListEnviron

Example program ListEnviron uses similar code to display all of the environment variables' assignment statements. Example program ListEnvironValues, which is also available for download, uses the String class's Split method to separate the environment variables' names and values and displays them in separate columns in a ListView control.

If you pass the Environ function the name of an environment variable, the function returns the variable's value or Nothing if the variable does not exist. The following code displays the value assigned to the USERNAME variable:

```
MessageBox.Show(Environ("USERNAME"))
```

Using System.Environment

The Environ function is easy to use, but it's not very flexible; it cannot create or modify variable values.

Of course sometimes that lack of flexibility can be an asset. A malicious program cannot use Environ to mess up the system's environment variables so it gives you one less potential problem.

The System.Environment object provides methods for getting and setting process-level environment variables. It also provides properties and methods for working with many other items in the application's environment. The following table describes the Environment object's most useful properties.

PROPERTY	PURPOSE
CommandLine	Returns the process's command line.
CurrentDirectory	Gets or sets the fully qualified path to the current directory.
ExitCode	Gets or sets the process's exit code. If the program starts from a Main function, that function's return value also sets the exit code.
HasShutdownStarted	Returns True if the common language runtime is shutting down.
MachineName	Returns the computer's NetBIOS name.
NewLine	Returns the environment's defined new line string. For example, this might be a carriage return followed by a line feed.
OSVersion	Returns an OperatingSystem object containing information about the operating system. This object provides the properties ServicePack (name of the most recent service pack installed), Version (includes Major, Minor, Build, and Revision; ToString combines them all), VersionString (combines the operating system name, version, and most recent service pack), and Platform, which can be Unix, Win32NT (Windows NT or later), Win32S (runs on 16-bit Windows to provide access to 32-bit applications), Win32Windows (Windows 95 or later), or WinCE.
ProcessorCount	Returns the number of processors on the computer.
StackTrace	Returns a string describing the current stack trace.
SystemDirectory	Returns the system directory's fully qualified path.
TickCount	Returns the number of milliseconds that have elapsed since the system started.
UserDomainName	Returns the current user's network domain name.
UserInteractive	Returns True if the process is interactive. This only returns False if the application is a service process or web service.
UserName	Returns the name of the user who started the process.
Version	Returns a Version object describing the Common Language Runtime. This object provides the properties Major, Minor, Build, and Revision. Its ToString method combines them all.
WorkingSet	Returns the amount of physical memory mapped to this process in bytes.

Example program SystemEnvironment, which is available for download on the book's web site, displays the values of many of the Environment object's properties.

The following table describes the Environment object's most useful methods.

METHOD	PURPOSE
Exit	Ends the process immediately. Form Closing and Closed event handlers do not execute.
ExpandEnvironment-Variables	Replaces environment variable names in a string with their values. For example, the following code displays the current user's name: `MessageBox.Show(Environment.ExpandEnvironment Variables("I am %username%."))`
GetCommandLineArgs	Returns an array of strings containing the application's command-line arguments. The first entry (with index 0) is the name of the program's executable file.
GetEnvironmentVariable	Returns an environment variable's value.
GetEnvironmentVariables	Returns an IDictionary object containing the names and values of all environment variables.
GetFolderPath	Returns the path to a system folder. This method's parameter is a SpecialFolder enumeration value such as Cookies, Desktop, SendTo, or Recent. See the online help for a complete list of available folders.
GetLogicalDrives	Returns an array of strings containing the names of the logical drives on the current computer.
SetEnvironmentVariable	Creates, modifies, or deletes an environment variable.

The SetEnvironmentVariable method lets you set environment variables at the system, user, and process level. If you set a variable's value to Nothing, this method deletes the variable. For system and user values, it updates the Registry appropriately to set the values. Example program EnvironmentVariableLevels, which is available for download on the book's web site, uses SetEnvironmentVariable to get and set variable values. For more information on the SetEnvironmentVariable method, see `msdn2.microsoft.com/library/96xafkes.aspx`.

PERMISSION REQUIRED

Note that a program needs privilege to write to the Registry to set a system-level environment variable.

REGISTRY

The System Registry is a hierarchical database that stores values for applications on the system. The hierarchy's root is named MyComputer and is divided into the several subtrees that are also called *hives*. Which hives are available depends on your operating system. The following table summarizes the most commonly available hives. (The "HKEY" part of each name stands for "hive key.")

REGISTRY BRANCH	CONTAINS
HKEY_CLASSES_ROOT	Definitions of types or classes, and properties associated with those types.
HKEY_CURRENT_CONFIG	Information about the system's current hardware configuration.
HKEY_CURRENT_USER	The current user's preferences (such as environment variable settings, program group information, desktop settings, colors, printers, network connections, and preferences specific to applications). Each user has separate HKEY_CURRENT_USER values. This is usually the subtree where a Visual Basic application stores and retrieves its settings.
HKEY_DYN_DATA	Performance data for Windows 95, 98, and Me. (Yes, this is a bit outdated but this hive is still there.)
HKEY_LOCAL_MACHINE	Information about the computer's physical state, including bus type, system memory, installed hardware and software, and network logon and security information.
HKEY_USERS	Default configuration information for new users and the current user's configuration.

Depending on your operating system, the Registry may also contain the unsupported keys HKEY_PERFORMANCE_DATA, HKEY_PERFORMANCE_NLSTEXT, and HKEY_PERFORMANCE_TEXT.

Many applications store information in the Registry. The HKEY_CURRENT_USER subtree is particularly useful for storing individual users' preferences and other configuration information.

Lately, the Registry has gone out of style for saving configuration information. Microsoft now recommends that you store this kind of data locally within a user's data storage area. This makes sense because it makes it easier to copy the settings (they're just files) and helps reduce clutter in the Registry. You can use the configuration files settings (see the section "Configuration Files" later in this chapter) or you can store data in XML files.

Visual Basic provides two main ways to access the Registry. First, you can use the Visual Basic native Registry methods. Second, you can use the tools in the My.Computer.Registry namespace. These two methods are described in the following sections.

You can also use API functions to manipulate the Registry. These are more complicated and not generally necessary (the My.Computer.Registry namespace contains some very powerful tools), so they are not described here.

Native Visual Basic Registry Methods

Visual Basic provides four methods for saving and reading Registry values for a particular application: SaveSetting, GetSetting, GetAllSettings, and DeleteSetting.

The SaveSetting method saves a value into a Registry key. This routine takes as parameters the name of the application, a section name, the setting's name, and the setting's value. For example, the following code saves the value stored in the m_CurrentDirectory variable in the RegistrySettings application's Config section with the name CurrentDirectory:

```
SaveSetting("RegistrySettings", "Config", "CurrentDirectory",
    m_CurrentDirectory)
```

SaveSetting automatically creates the application and section areas in the Registry if they don't already exist.

This value is saved at the following Registry location. This is all one name; it just doesn't fit on one line here:

```
HKEY_CURRENT_USER\Software\VB and VBA Program Settings\
    RegistrySettings\Config\CurrentDirectory
```

If you use the Visual Basic SaveSetting, GetSetting, GetAllSettings, and DeleteSetting methods, you don't need to worry about the first part of this Registry path. You need only to remember the application name, section name, and setting name.

POWERFUL PRIVILEGES

Windows protects the Registry so that you cannot inadvertently damage critical values. If you mess up some values, you can wreak havoc on the operating system, and even make the system unbootable.

To prevent possible chaos, newer versions of Windows don't let you edit some parts of the Registry without elevated privileges. Fortunately, the part of the Registry used by these routines is accessible to normal users, so you don't need elevated privileges to use SaveSetting, GetSetting, GetAllSettings, or DeleteSetting.

The GetSetting function retrieves a Registry value. It takes as parameters the application name, section name, and setting name you used to save the value. It can optionally take a default value to return if the setting doesn't exist in the Registry. The following code displays the value saved by the previous call to SaveSetting. If no value is saved in the Registry, it displays the string <none>.

```
MessageBox.Show(GetSetting("RegistrySettings", "Config", "CurrentDirectory",
    "<none>"))
```

The GetAllSettings function returns a two-dimensional array of name and value pairs for a Registry section. The following code uses GetAllSettings to fetch the values stored in the RegistrySettings application's Config section. It loops through the results, displaying the setting names and values.

```
Dim settings As String(,) = GetAllSettings("RegistrySettings", "Config")
For i As Integer = 0 To settings.GetUpperBound(0)
    Debug.WriteLine(settings(i, 0) & " = " & settings(i, 1))
Next i
```

If an application needs to use all of the settings in a section, GetAllSettings may be faster than using GetSetting repeatedly.

The DeleteSetting method removes a setting, section, or an entire application's setting area from the Registry. The following code shows how to remove each of those kinds of items:

```
' Remove the RegistrySettingsRegistrySettings/Config/CurrentDirectory setting.
DeleteSetting("RegistrySettings", "Config", "CurrentDirectory")

' Remove the RegistrySettings/Config section.
DeleteSetting("RegistrySettings", "Config")

' Remove all of the RegistrySettings application's settings.
DeleteSetting("RegistrySettings")
```

NEATNESS COUNTS

As part of its uninstallation procedure, a program should remove any Registry entries it has made. All too often, programs leave the Registry cluttered with garbage. This not only makes it harder to figure out what real values the Registry contains, but it can also slow the system down.

In an attempt to combat this problem, Microsoft is promoting XCopy compatibility, where applications store values in configuration files instead of the Registry. Then you can easily copy and remove these files rather than modifying the Registry.

Example program RegistrySettings, which is available for download on the book's web site, demonstrates each of Visual Basic's Registry commands.

My.Computer.Registry

The My.Computer.Registry namespace provides objects that manipulate the Registry . My.Computer.Registry has seven properties that refer to objects of type RegistryKey. The following table lists these objects and the corresponding Registry subtrees.

MY.COMPUTER.REGISTRY PROPERTY	REGISTRY SUBTREE
ClassesRoot	HKEY_CLASSES_ROOT
CurrentConfig	HKEY_CURRENT_CONFIG
CurrentUser	HKEY_CURRENT_USER
DynData	HKEY_DYNAMIC_DATA
LocalMachine	HKEY_LOCAL_MACHINE
PerformanceData	HKEY_PERFORMANCE_DATA
Users	HKEY_USERS

REGISTRY RESTRICTIONS

Note that some parts of the Registry are off limits to programs running as normal users in recent versions of Windows. Normal users can modify values in HKEY_CURRENT_USER, but to do more than look in other areas, a program would probably need to run with elevated privileges. For more information on privilege elevation, see Chapter 24, "UAC Security."

The program can use these RegistryKey objects to work with the corresponding Registry subtree. The following table describes the most useful properties and methods provided by the RegistryKey class.

PROPERTY OR METHOD	PURPOSE
Name	Returns the key's Registry path.
Close	Closes the key and writes it to disk if it has been modified.
CreateSubKey	Creates a new subkey or opens an existing subkey within this key.

DeleteSubKey	Deletes the specified subkey. This method will delete the subkey if it contains values, but not if it contains other subkeys. The subkey to be deleted need not be a direct child of this key. For example, the following code uses the CurrentUser RegistryKey object to delete the descendant key Software\VB and VBA Program Settings\MyComputerRegistry\Config:
	
	`My.Computer.Registry.CurrentUser.DeleteSubKey("Software\`
	`VB and VBA Program Settings\RegistrySettings\Config")`

DeleteSubKeyTree	Recursively deletes a subkey and any child subkeys it contains. The subkey to be deleted need not be a direct child of this key. For example, the following code uses the CurrentUser RegistryKey object to delete all of the settings for the RegistrySettings application:
	
	`My.Computer.Registry.CurrentUser.DeleteSubKeyTree`
	`("Software\VB and VBA Program Settings\RegistrySettings")`

DeleteValue	Deletes a value from the key.
Flush	Writes any changes to the key into the Registry.
GetSubKeyNames	Returns an array of strings giving subkey names.
GetValue	Returns the value of a specified value within this key.
GetValueKind	Returns the type of a specified value within this key. This can be Binary, DWord, ExpandString, MultiString, QWord, String, or Unknown.

PROPERTY OR METHOD	PURPOSE
GetValueNames	Returns an array of strings giving the names of all of the values contained within the key.
OpenSubKey	Returns a RegistryKey object representing a descendant key. Parameters give the subkey name, and indicate whether the returned RegistryKey should allow you to modify the subkey.
SetValue	Sets a value within the key.
SubKeyCount	Returns the number of subkeys that are this key's direct children.
ToString	Returns the key's name.
ValueCount	Returns the number of values stored in this key.

The following example opens the HKEY_CURRENT_USER\Software\VB and VBA Program Settings\RegistrySettings\Config key. It reads the CurrentDirectory value from that key using the default value "C:\" and saves the result in the variable current_directory. It closes the key and then uses the DeleteSubKey method to delete the RegistrySettings application's Config section.

```
' Open the application's Config subkey.
Dim config_section As Microsoft.Win32.RegistryKey =
    My.Computer.Registry.CurrentUser.OpenSubKey(
        "Software\VB and VBA Program Settings\RegistrySettings\Config\")

' Get the CurrentDirectory value.
Dim current_directory As String =
    CType(config_section.GetValue("CurrentDirectory", "C:\"), String)

' Close the subkey.
config_section.Close()

' Delete the application's whole Config section.
My.Computer.Registry.CurrentUser. DeleteSubKey DeleteSubKey (
    "Software\VB and VBA Program Settings\RegistrySettings\Config")
```

The following code shows the equivalent operations using the native Registry methods of Visual Basic:

```
 ' Get the CurrentDirectory value.
Dim current_directory As String =
GetSetting("RegistrySettings", "Config", "CurrentDirectory", "C:\")

 ' Delete the application's whole Config section.
DeleteSetting("RegistrySettings", "Config")
```

It is generally easier to use the native Registry methods of Visual Basic. Those methods work only with values in the HKEY_CURRENT_USER\Software\VB and VBA Program Settings Registry subtree, however. If you need to access keys and values outside of this subtree, you must use the My.Computer.Registry objects.

Example program MyComputerRegistry, which is available for download on the book's web site, demonstrates many useful My.Computer.Registry operations. It does the same things as program RegistrySettings mentioned in the previous section except it uses My.Computer.Registry instead of Visual Basic's native Registry methods.

CONFIGURATION FILES

Configuration files let you store information for a program to use at runtime in a standardized external file. You can change the values in the configuration file, and the program will use the new value the next time it starts. That enables you to change some of the application's behavior without needing to recompile the executable program.

One way to use configuration files is through dynamic properties. Dynamic properties are automatically loaded from the configuration file at runtime by Visual Basic.

Start by defining the settings you will bind to the dynamic properties. In Solution Explorer, double-click My Project and select the Settings tab to see the property page shown in Figure 35-1. Use this page to define the settings that you will load at runtime.

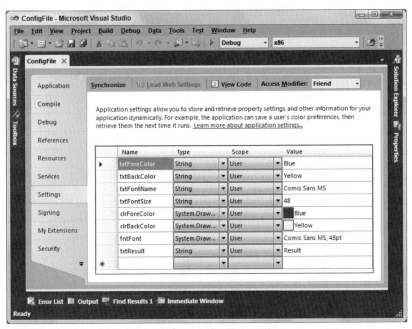

FIGURE 35-1: Use this page to define application settings.

A setting's scope can be Application or User. A setting with Application scope is shared by all of the program's users. Settings with User scope are stored separately for each user so different users can use and modify their own values.

Next, add a control to a form and select it. In the Properties window, open the ApplicationSettings entry, click the PropertyBinding subitem, and click the ellipsis to the right to display a list of the control's properties.

Select the property that you want to load dynamically and click the drop-down arrow on the right to see a list of defined settings that you might assign to the property. Figure 35-2 shows the Application Setting dialog box with this drop-down list displayed for a control's Text property. From the list, select the setting that you want to assign to the property.

FIGURE 35-2: Use the drop-down list to assign a setting to the dynamic property.

Visual Studio adds the setting to the program's configuration file. If you open Solution Explorer and double-click the app .config entry, you'll see the new dynamic property.

The following text shows the configuration setting sections of an App.config file. The applicationSettings section defines the settings shown in Figure 35-1.

```xml
<?xml version="1.0" encoding="utf-8" ?>
<configuration>
    ...
    <userSettings>
        <ConfigFile.My.MySettings>
            <setting name="txtBackColor" serializeAs="String">
                <value>Yellow</value>
            </setting>
            <setting name="txtForeColor" serializeAs="String">
                <value>Blue</value>
            </setting>
            <setting name="txtFontName" serializeAs="String">
                <value>Comic Sans MS</value>
            </setting>
            <setting name="txtFontSize" serializeAs="String">
                <value>50</value>
            </setting>
            <setting name="clrForeColor" serializeAs="String">
                <value>Blue</value>
            </setting>
            <setting name="clrBackColor" serializeAs="String">
                <value>Yellow</value>
            </setting>
            <setting name="fntFont" serializeAs="String">
                <value>Comic Sans MS, 48pt</value>
            </setting>
        </ConfigFile.My.MySettings>
    </userSettings>
</configuration>
```

code snippet ConfigFile

When the application starts, Visual Basic loads the app.config file, reads the settings, and assigns their values to any properties bound to them.

So far, this is just a very roundabout way to set the control's property value. The real benefit of this method comes later when you want to change this setting. If you look in the compiled application's directory (normally the bin\Debug directory when you're developing the program), you'll find a file with the same name as the application but with a .config extension. If the application is called ConfigFile.exe, then this file is called ConfigFile.exe.config.

If you open this file with any text editor and change the value of a setting, the program uses the new value the next time it runs. For example, if you change the value of clrBackColor from Yellow to Orange, then the next time the program runs, any controls that use that color for their backgrounds will now be orange. Instead of recompiling the whole application, you only need to change this simple text file. If you have distributed the application to a large number of users, you need only to give them the revised configuration file and not a whole new executable.

When you make a new setting, Visual Basic automatically generates code that adds the setting to the My.Settings namespace, so the program can easily get their values. The following code displays the values of the txtFontSize and txtFontName settings:

```
MessageBox.Show(My.Settings.txtFontSize & "pt " & My.Settings.txtFontName)
```

The My.Settings namespace provides several other properties and methods that make working with settings easy. The following table summarizes the most useful My.Settings properties and methods.

PROPERTY OR METHOD	PURPOSE
Item	A name-indexed collection of the values for the settings.
Properties	A name-indexed collection of SettingsProperty objects that contain information about the settings, including their names and default values.
Reload	Reloads the settings from the configuration file.
Save	Saves any modified settings into the configuration file. The program can modify settings with user scope. Settings with application scope are read-only.

Example program ShowSettings uses the following code to display the settings listed in the My.Settings.Properties collection:

```
Imports System.Configuration

Public Class Form1
    Private Sub Form1_Load() Handles MyBase.Load
        For Each settings_property As SettingsProperty In
         My.Settings.Properties
            Dim new_item As New ListViewItem(settings_property.Name)
            new_item.SubItems.Add(settings_property.DefaultValue.ToString)
            lvSettings.Items.Add(new_item)
        Next settings_property
```

```
          lvSettings.Columns(0).Width = -2
          lvSettings.Columns(1).Width = -2
      End Sub
  End Class
```

code snippet ShowSettings

SAVE RESTRICTIONS

The security features in newer versions of Windows make saving configuration information more difficult to manage. If an application is installed in a protected part of the file system, a normal user won't be able to save configuration settings there. If the program saves settings on a per-user basis in the user's own directories, the changes won't affect other users. Similarly, the SaveSettings command saves values into the Registry separately for each user, so changes made with SaveSettings don't affect other users. One solution is to save user-specific settings in the user's directories, and save application-wide settings in a file stored in a common directory that all users can access.

When a program closes, it automatically saves any changes to User scope settings. However, if the program crashes, it does not have a chance to save any changes. If you want to be sure changes are saved, call My.Settings.Save after the user changes settings.

Example program SaveSettings, which is also available for download, uses two settings: a User scope color named clrForm that determines the form's background color and an Application scope color named clrButton that determines the background colors of the program's two buttons. The program provides Form Color and Button Color buttons to let you change the two color settings. If you change the colors, close the program, and restart it, you'll see that the User scope form color is saved, but the Application scope button color is not.

RESOURCE FILES

Resource files contain text, images, and other data for the application to load at runtime. The intent of resource files is to let you easily replace one set of resources with another.

One of the most common reasons for using resource files is to provide different resources for different languages. To create installation packages for different languages, you simply ship the executable and a resource file that uses the right language. Alternatively, you can ship resource files for all of the languages you support and then let the application pick the appropriate file at runtime based on the user's computer settings.

Resource files are not intended to store application configuration information and settings. They are intended to hold values that you might want to change, but only infrequently. Configurations and settings, on the other hand, may change relatively often. You should store frequently changing data in configuration files or the System Registry rather than in resource files.

The distinction is small and frankly somewhat artificial. Both configuration files and resource files store data that you can swap without recompiling the application. Rebuilding resource files can be a little more complex, however, so perhaps the distinction that configuration and setting data changes more frequently makes some sense.

Resource files can also be embedded within a compiled application. In that case, you cannot swap the resource file without recompiling the application. Although this makes embedded resource files less useful for storing frequently changing information, they still give you a convenient place to group resource data within the application. This is particularly useful if several parts of the application must use the same pieces of data. For example, if every form should display the same background image, it makes sense to store the image in a common resource file that they can all use.

The following sections describe the four most common types of resources: application, embedded, satellite, and localization.

Application Resources

To create application resources in Visual Basic, open Solution Explorer, double-click the My Project entry, and select the Resources tab. Use the dropdown on the left to select one of the resource categories: Strings, Images, Icons, Audio, Files, or Other. Figure 35-3 shows the application's Resources tab displaying the application's images.

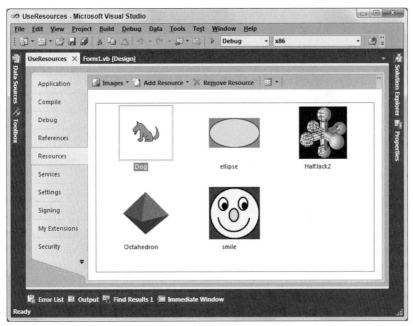

FIGURE 35-3: The Resources tab contains image and other resources used by the application.

If you double-click an item, Visual Studio opens an appropriate editor. For example, if you double-click a bitmap resource, Visual Studio opens the image in an integrated bitmap editor.

Click the Add Resource dropdown list and select Add Existing File to add a file from the disk to the program's resources. Use the dropdown's Add New String, Add New Icon, or Add New Text File commands to add new items to the resource file. The dropdown's New Image item opens a cascading submenu that lets you create new PNG, bitmap, GIF, JPEG, and TIFF images.

Using Application Resources

When you create application resources, Visual Studio automatically generates code that adds strongly typed resource properties to the My.Resources namespace. If you open Solution Explorer and click the Show All Files button, you can see the Resources.Designer.vb file that contains this code. The Solution Explorer path to this file is My Project/Resources.resx/Resources.Designer.vb.

For example, the following code shows the property that Resources.Designer.vb contains to retrieve the Octahedron image resource:

Available for download on Wrox.com

```
Friend ReadOnly Property Octahedron() As System.Drawing.Bitmap
    Get
        Dim obj As Object =
            ResourceManager.GetObject("Octahedron", resourceCulture)
        Return CType(obj, System.Drawing.Bitmap)
    End Get
End Property
```

code snippet UseResources

The following code shows how a program can use these My.Resources properties. It sets the lblGreeting control's Text property to the string returned by the My.Resources.Greeting property. Then it sets the form's BackgroundImage property to the image resource named Dog.

Available for download on Wrox.com

```
Private Sub Form1_Load() Handles MyBase.Load
    lblGreeting.Text = My.Resources.Greeting
    Me.BackgroundImage = My.Resources.Dog
End Sub
```

code snippet UseResources

Because these property procedures are strongly typed, IntelliSense can offer support for them. If you type My.Resources, IntelliSense lists the values defined in the application's resource file.

The strongly typed resource properties use a ResourceManager object to fetch the application's resources. The My.Resources namespace exposes that object through its ResourceManager property, so you can use that object directly to retrieve the application's resources. The following code does the same things as the previous version, except it uses the ResourceManager directly. Note that the ResourceManager property's GetObject method returns a generic Object, so the code uses CType to convert the result into an Image before assigning it to the form's BackgroundImage property.

Available for download on Wrox.com

```
Private Sub Form1_Load() Handles MyBase.Load
    lblGreeting.Text = My.Resources.ResourceManager.GetString("Greeting")
    Me.BackgroundImage = CType(
        My.Resources.ResourceManager.GetObject("Dog"), Image)
End Sub
```

code snippet UseResources

Example program UseResources uses similar code to set a label's text and to display an image. Commented-out code does the same thing by using the strongly typed resource properties.

Generally, you should use the automatically generated resource properties in the My.Resources namespace because they are easier to use and they are strongly typed. The ResourceManager class is much more useful when you use other embedded resource files as described in the following section.

Embedded Resources

In addition to storing resources in the application's resource file Resources.resx, you can add other resources files to the application. Open the Project menu and select the Add New Item command. Pick the Resources File template, give the file a meaningful name, and click OK.

After you add a resource file to the project, you can double-click it in Solution Explorer to open it in the resource editor. Then you can add resources to the file exactly as you do for the application's resource file.

At runtime, you can use a ResourceManager object to fetch the resources from the embedded file. The following code loads the Dog image from the file Images.resx and the string Greeting from the file Strings.resx.

It starts by declaring a ResourceManager variable. It then initializes the variable, passing its constructor the resource file's path and the assembly containing the file. The file's path consists of the application's root namespace EmbeddedResources followed by the file's name Images.

The program then uses the ResourceManager object's GetObject method to fetch the Dog image, converts the generic Object returned into an Image, and assigns the result to the form's BackgroundImage property.

Next, the code reinitializes the ResourceManager object so it represents the Strings resource file. It calls the manager's GetString method to get the value of the Greeting resource and saves the result in the lblGreeting control's Text property.

Available for download on Wrox.com

```
Private Sub Form1_Load() Handles MyBase.Load
    Dim resource_manager As ResourceManager

    ' Get the Dog image from Images.resx.
    resource_manager = New ResourceManager(
        "EmbeddedResources.Images",
        Me.GetType.Assembly)
    Me.BackgroundImage = CType(
        resource_manager.GetObject("Dog"), Image)

    ' Get the Greeting from StringResources.resx.
    resource_manager = New ResourceManager(
        "EmbeddedResources.Strings", Me.GetType.Assembly)
    lblGreeting.Text = resource_manager.GetString("Greeting")
End Sub
```

code snippet EmbeddedResources

Just as it generates strongly typed properties for application resources, Visual Studio generates similar code for other embedded resource files. You can access these properties by adding the resource file's name after My.Settings and before the resource name. For example, to get the image resource named Dog from the Images resource file, the program would use My.Settings.Images.Dog.

Example program EmbeddedResources, which is available for download on the book's web site, contains code to load embedded resources both with a resource manager and by using the strongly typed resource properties.

Satellite Resources

Embedded resource files enable you to organize data in central locations. For example, you can keep all the images used by the application in a single resource file, and all of the program's forms can fetch the images from that file.

Rather than embedding a resource file in the application, you can load it at runtime. Then if you must make changes to the resources, you can replace the resource file and the program will load the new resources the next time it runs.

To make switching resources easy, you can place them in a resource-only assembly. This *satellite assembly* contains data for the application but doesn't contain any program logic.

To make a resource-only satellite assembly, start a new Visual Basic project, selecting the Class Library template. Delete the project's initial class. Then, add resources to the project as you would add them to any other project. You can add resources to the project's application resources or to embedded resource files. When you are finished adding resources, compile the project to build a .dll file.

You can then build an executable Windows application that loads resources from the assembly as shown in the following code:

Available for
download on
Wrox.com

```
Private Sub Form1_Load() Handles MyBase.Load
    ' Get the resource Assembly.
    Dim satellite_assembly As Assembly
    satellite_assembly = Assembly.LoadFrom("SatelliteResourcesDll.dll")

    ' Create a ResourceManager for the satellite's
    ' main resource file.
    Dim resource_manager As ResourceManager
    resource_manager = New ResourceManager(
        "SatelliteResourcesDll.Resources", satellite_assembly)
    ' Get the string resource from the satellite's
    ' main resource file.
    lblGreeting.Text = resource_manager.GetString("Greeting")

    ' Create a ResourceManager for the satellite's
    ' Images resource file.
    resource_manager = New ResourceManager(
        "SatelliteResourcesDll.Images", satellite_assembly)

    ' Get the form's background image from the satellite's
    ' Images resource file.
    Me.BackgroundImage = CType(resource_manager.GetObject("Dog"), Image)
End Sub
```

code snippet SatelliteMain

The program declares an Assembly object and uses the shared Assembly.LoadForm method to load information about the resource-only assembly SatelliteResourcesDll.dll. In this example, the file was copied into the executable program's startup directory so the program does not need to pass a complete path to the LoadFrom method.

Next, the program uses the Assembly object to create a ResourceManager. For the resource file's name, it passes the ResourceManager object's constructor to the assembly's root namespace SatelliteResourcesDll, followed by the name of the resource file within the satellite project. In this case, the first resource is stored in the project's resources, so the file is MyResources.resx. Now the program uses the ResourceManager object's GetString method to fetch the Greeting resource.

The program then creates a new ResourceManager using the same Assembly object, this time using the resource file named ImageResources.resx. It uses the GetObject method to fetch the image named Dog, converts the result into an Image, and saves the result in the form's BackgroundImage property.

Later, if you must change the value of the Greeting string or the Dog image, you can update the satellite project, build a new DLL file, and copy the DLL file into the executable program's startup directory. The next time you run the program, it will load the new resources.

Example projects SatelliteResourcesDll and SatelliteMain, which are both available for download on the book's web site, contain the satellite resource DLL and an executable program that uses it, respectively.

Localization Resources

One of the most important reasons for inventing resource files was to allow localization: supporting different text, images, and other items for different languages and cultures. In Visual Studio .NET, localization is easy.

First, create a form using whatever language you typically use from day to day. For me, that's English as spoken in the United States. Open the form in the form designer and give it whatever controls you need. Set the form's and controls' properties as usual.

Next, set the form's Localizable property to True. Then set the form's Language property to the first language you want to support other than the default language that you have been working with so far. Modify the controls' properties for the new language.

As you modify a form, Visual Studio saves the changes you make to a new resource file attached to the form. If you open Solution Explorer and click the Show All Files button, you can see these resource files below the form's file.

Example program Localized, which is available for download on the book's web site, uses default settings for United States English. It also includes localizations for generic German (as opposed to German as spoken in Switzerland, Germany, Liechtenstein, or some other country). If you expand the form's entry in Solution Explorer, you'll find the files Form1.resx holding the default settings and Form1.de.resx holding the German settings.

At runtime, the application automatically checks the user's computer and selects the best resource file based on the system's regional settings.

Normally, you should let the application pick the appropriate resource file automatically, but you can explicitly select a resource file for testing purposes. To do that, open the Solution Explorer and click the Show All Files button. Find the form's design file (for example, Form1.Designer.vb) and open it.

Give the form an empty constructor that sets the current thread's CurrentCulture and CurrentUICulture properties to the culture that you want to use. See the online help for the CultureInfo class to get a list of possible cultures such as en-US (United States English) or de-DE (German in Germany, as opposed to in Austria, Switzerland, or some other locale). The result should look something like the following code:

```
Imports System.Threading
Imports System.Globalization

Public Class Form1
    Public Sub New()
        MyBase.New()

        ' Set the culture and UI culture to German.
        Thread.CurrentThread.CurrentCulture = New CultureInfo("de-DE")
        Thread.CurrentThread.CurrentUICulture = New CultureInfo("de-DE")

        'This call is required by the Windows Forms Designer.
        InitializeComponent()
    End Sub
End Class
```

code snippet LocalizedUseGerman

> **CULTURE COMES FIRST**
>
> Note that the program must set the culture and user interface culture before it calls InitializeComponent because InitializeComponent is where the program sets the form and control properties.

The rest is automatic. When the form's InitializeComponent method executes, it loads the resources it needs for the culture you selected.

Example program LocalizedUseGerman, which is available for download on the book's web site, uses this code to open the form localized for German even if your system would not normally select that version.

ComponentResourceManager

Like the ResourceManager class, the ComponentResourceManager class provides GetString and GetObject methods for loading resources from a resource file one at a time.

ComponentResourceManager also provides the ApplyResources method, which makes applying resources to an object easier. ApplyResources searches a resource file for items with a particular object name. It then applies any resources it finds to an object's properties.

For example, you could use ApplyResources to search for resources with the object name ExitButton and apply them to the btnExit control. If the resource file contained an item named ExitButton.Text, ApplyResources would apply it to the btnExit control's Text property. If the method found other resources (such as ExitButton.Location and ExitButton.Size), it would apply those properties to the control, too.

When you localize a form, Visual Studio automatically creates entries in the appropriate resource files for the form's controls. If you set the form's Language to German and set the btnYes button's Text property to Ja, Visual Studio adds a string entry named btnYes.Text with value Ja to the form's German resource file.

Visual Studio uses the special name $this to represent the form's properties. For example, if you set the form's Text property, the IDE adds a string resource named $this.Text to the appropriate resource file.

Example program LocalizedPickLanguage uses ComponentResourceManager objects in the following code to load different localized resources while it is running:

```vb
' Select English.
Private Sub radEnglish_CheckedChanged() Handles radEnglish.CheckedChanged
    If Not radEnglish.Checked Then Exit Sub
    LoadAllResources(New CultureInfo("en-US"))
End Sub

' Select German.
Private Sub radGerman_CheckedChanged() Handles radGerman.CheckedChanged
    If Not radGerman.Checked Then Exit Sub
    LoadAllResources(New CultureInfo("de-DE"))
End Sub

' Load resources for the form and all controls.
Private Sub LoadAllResources(ByVal culture_info As CultureInfo)
    ' Make a ComponentResourceManager.
    Dim component_resource_manager As New ComponentResourceManager(Me.GetType)

    ' Load the form's resources.
    LoadResources(Me, "$this", component_resource_manager, culture_info)
End Sub

 ' Load appropriate resources for an object and its contained controls.
Private Sub LoadResources(ByVal parent As Control,
 ByVal parent_name As String,
 ByVal component_resource_manager As ComponentResourceManager,
 ByVal culture_info As CultureInfo)
    ' Load the parent's resources.
    component_resource_manager.ApplyResources(
        parent, parent_name, culture_info)
```

```
    ToolTip1.SetToolTip(parent, component_resource_manager.GetString(
        parent_name & ".ToolTip", culture_info))

    ' Load each contained control's resources.
    For Each ctl As Control In parent.Controls
        LoadResources(ctl, ctl.Name, component_resource_manager, culture_info)
    Next ctl
End Sub
```

code snippet LocalizedPickLanguage

When the user clicks the radEnglish radio button, the code calls subroutine LoadAllResources, passing it a new CultureInfo object representing United States English. Similarly, when the user clicks the radGerman radio button, the code calls LoadAllResources passing it a CultureInfo object representing German.

Subroutine LoadAllResources creates a ComponentResourceManager for the form's type and calls subroutine LoadResources, passing it the form, the special form resource named $this, the component resource manager, and the CultureInfo object.

Subroutine LoadResources loads the resources for an object and all of the controls it contains. First, it uses the component resource manager's ApplyResources to load the object's resources.

Next, it sets the object's tooltip if it has one. Recall that a control's tooltip is actually not a property of the control. Instead it is an extender provider property provided by a ToolTip control. To load the form's tooltip, the code explicitly calls the Tooltip1 control's SetToolTip method, passing to it the object being loaded and the object's name with ".ToolTip" appended.

Finally, the code loops through the object's contained controls and performs calls LoadResources for each. This makes the code recursively call subroutine LoadResources for every control in the application.

Example program LocalizedPickLanguage2 uses the following slightly modified code to accomplish the same tasks. Instead of passing a CultureInfo object into the ApplyResources method, the program sets the current thread's CurrentCulture and CurrentUICulture properties. It then lets the calls to ApplyResources figure out which resource file to use.

Available for download on Wrox.com

```
' Load resources for the form and all controls.
Private Sub LoadAllResources(ByVal culture_info As CultureInfo)
    ' Set the current culture and UI culture.
    Thread.CurrentThread.CurrentCulture = culture_info
    Thread.CurrentThread.CurrentUICulture = culture_info

    ' Make a ComponentResourceManager.
    Dim component_resource_manager As New ComponentResourceManager(Me.GetType)

    ' Load the form's resources.
    LoadResources(Me, "$this", component_resource_manager)
End Sub

' Load appropriate resources for an object and its contained controls.
```

```
Private Sub LoadResources(ByVal parent As Control,
 ByVal parent_name As String,
 ByVal component_resource_manager As ComponentResourceManager)
    ' Load the parent's resources.
    component_resource_manager.ApplyResources(parent, parent_name)
    ToolTip1.SetToolTip(parent,
        component_resource_manager.GetString(parent_name & ".ToolTip"))

    ' Load each contained control's resources.
    For Each ctl As Control In parent.Controls
        LoadResources(ctl, ctl.Name, component_resource_manager)
    Next ctl
End Sub
```

code snippet LocalizedPickLanguage2

The program can later check the CurrentCulture and CurrentUICulture properties if it needs to remember which culture it is currently using.

APPLICATION

The Application object represents the running application at a very high level. It provides properties and methods for starting an event loop to process Windows messages, possibly for a form. It also provides methods for controlling and stopping the event loop.

Don't confuse the Application object with the My.Application namespace. The two have somewhat similar purposes but very different features.

The following sections describe the Application object's most useful properties, methods, and events.

Application Properties

The following table describes the Application object's most useful properties.

PROPERTY	PURPOSE
CommonAppDataPath	Returns the path where the program should store application data shared by all users. By default, this path has the form base_path\ company_name\product_name\product_version. The base_path is typically C:\Documents and Settings\All Users\Application Data.
CommonAppDataRegistry	Returns the Registry key where the program should store application data shared by all users. By default, this path has the form HKEY_ LOCAL_MACHINE\Software\company_name\product_name\product_ version.
CompanyName	Returns the application's company name.

PROPERTY	PURPOSE
`CurrentCulture`	Gets or sets the CultureInfo object for this thread.
`CurrentInputLanguage`	Gets or sets the InputLanguage for this thread.
`ExecutablePath`	Returns the fully qualified path to the file that started the execution, including the file name.
`LocalUserAppDataPath`	Returns the path where the program should store data for this local, nonroaming user. By default, this path has the form base_path\company_name\product_name\product_version. The base_path is typically `C:\Documents and Settings\user_name\Local Settings\Application Data`.
`MessageLoop`	Returns True if the thread has a message loop. If the program begins with a startup form, this loop is created automatically. If it starts with a custom Sub Main, the loop doesn't initially exist and the program must start it by calling Application.Run.
`OpenForms`	Returns a collection holding references to all of the application's open forms.
`ProductName`	Returns the application's product name.
`ProductVersion`	Gets the product version associated with this application.
`StartupPath`	Returns the fully qualified path to the directory where the program starts.
`UserAppDataPath`	Returns the path where the program should store data for this user. By default, this path has the form base_path\company_name\product_name\product_version. The base_path is typically `C:\Documents and Settings\user_name\Application Data`.
`UserAppDataRegistry`	Returns the Registry key where the program should store application data for this user. By default, this path has the form HKEY_CURRENT_USER\Software\company_name\product_name\product_version.
`UseWaitCursor`	Determines whether this thread's forms display a wait cursor. Set this to True before performing a long operation, and set it to False when the operation is finished.

Example program ListForms, which is available for download on the book's web site, uses the Application.OpenForms collection to list its running forms.

To set the CompanyName, ProductName, and ProductVersion, open Solution Explorer, double-click the My Project entry, and select the Application tab. Then click the Assembly Information button and enter the values on the Assembly Information dialog box. Example program ShowProductInfo displays these three values.

Application Methods

The following table describes the Application object's most useful methods.

METHOD	PURPOSE
AddMessageFilter	Adds a message filter to monitor the event loop's Windows messages. See the following text for an example.
DoEvents	Processes Windows messages that are currently in the message queue. If the thread is performing a long calculation, it would normally prevent the rest of the thread from taking action such as processing these messages. Calling DoEvents lets the user interface catch up with the user's actions. Note that you can often avoid the need for DoEvents if you perform the long task on a separate thread.
Exit	Ends the whole application. This is a rather abrupt halt and any forms that are loaded do not execute their FormClosing or FormClosed event handlers, so be certain that the application has executed any necessary clean-up code before calling Application.Exit.
ExitThread	Ends the current thread. This is a rather abrupt halt, and any forms running on the thread do not execute their FormClosing or FormClosed event handlers.
OnThreadException	Raises the Application object's ThreadException event, passing it an exception. If your application throws an uncaught exception in the IDE, the IDE halts. That makes it hard to test Application. ThreadException event handlers. You can call OnThreadException to invoke the event handler.
RemoveMessageFilter	Removes a message filter.
Run	Runs a message loop for the current thread. If you pass this method a form object, it displays the form and processes its messages until the form closes.
SetSuspendState	Makes the system suspend operation or hibernate. When the system hibernates, it writes its memory contents to disk. When you restart the system, it resumes with its previous desktop and applications running. When the system suspends operation, it enters low-power mode. It can resume more quickly than a hibernated system, but memory contents are not saved, so they will be lost if the computer loses power.

Example program FilterMessages uses the following code to filter messages and ignore left mouse button down messages:

```
Public Class Form1
    ' Filter out left mouse button down messages.
    Private Class NoLeftDownMessageFilter
        Implements IMessageFilter

        Public Function PreFilterMessage(
          ByRef m As System.Windows.Forms.Message) _
          As Boolean Implements IMessageFilter.PreFilterMessage
            ' If the message is left mouse down, return True
            ' to indicate that the message should be ignored.
            Const WM_LBUTTONDOWN As Long = & H201
            Return (m.Msg = WM_LBUTTONDOWN)
        End Function
    End Class

    ' Install the message filter.
    Private Sub Form1_Load() Handles MyBase.Load
        Dim no_left_down_message_filter As New NoLeftDownMessageFilter
        Application.AddMessageFilter(no_left_down_message_filter)
    End Sub

    ' Toggle the wait cursor.
    Private Sub Form1_Click() Handles Me.Click
        Application.UseWaitCursor = Not Application.UseWaitCursor
    End Sub
End Class
```

code snippet FilterMessages

The NoLeftDownMessageFilter class implements the IMessageFilter interface, which specifies the PreFilterMessage function. That function examines a message and returns True if it wants to filter the message out of the form's message queue. In this example, the function returns True if the message is WM_LBUTTONDOWN, indicating that the left button has been pressed.

The form's Load event handler creates a new instance of the filter class and uses the Application object's AddMessageFilter method to install the filter.

The form's Click event handler toggles the state of the Application object's UseWaitCursor property. This displays or hides the wait cursor.

When you left-click the form, the message filter intercepts the left button down message, so the Click event doesn't occur. If you right-click the form, the filter allows all messages through so the Click event occurs and the form displays or hides the wait cursor.

Application Events

The Application object provides a few events that give you information about the application's state. The following table describes these events.

EVENT	PURPOSE
`ApplicationExit`	Occurs when the application is about to shut down.
`Idle`	Occurs when the application finishes executing some code and is about to enter an idle state to wait for events.
`ThreadException`	Occurs when the application throws an unhandled exception. See the following code for an example.
`ThreadExit`	Occurs when a thread is about to exit.

When you end an application by unloading its form, the program receives the events FormClosing, FormClosed, ThreadExit, and ApplicationExit, in that order.

If you end the application by calling the Application object's Exit method, the program only receives the ThreadExit and ApplicationExit events. If more than one thread is running, they each receive ThreadExit events, and then they each receive ApplicationExit events.

Example program CatchThreadException uses the following code to catch all exceptions thrown by the application:

Available for download on Wrox.com

```
Imports System.IO

Public Class Form1
    ' Install the ThreadException event handler.
    Private Sub Form1_Load() Handles Me.Load
        AddHandler Application.ThreadException,AddressOf Me.app_ThreadException
    End Sub

    ' Catch a ThreadException event.
    Private Sub app_ThreadException(ByVal sender As Object,
     ByVal e As System.Threading.ThreadExceptionEventArgs)
        MessageBox.Show("Caught unhandled exception:" &
            vbCrLf & vbCrLf & e.Exception.Message)
    End Sub

    ' Throw an InvalidDataException.
    Private Sub btnThrow_Click() Handles btnThrow.Click
        Throw New InvalidDataException("Bad data! Bad!")
    End Sub

    ' Call the OnThreadException method.
    Private Sub btnOnThreadException_Click() Handles btnOnThreadException.Click
        Application.OnThreadException(New InvalidDataException("Bad data! Bad!"))
    End Sub
End Class
```

code snippet CatchThreadException

When it starts, the form's Load event handler uses the Application object's AddHandler method to add the app_ThreadException subroutine as a handler for the Application's ThreadException event.

The app_ThreadException subroutine simply displays an error message describing the exception that it caught. A real application would take different actions such as logging the error and a stack trace, restarting the application, and so forth.

When the user clicks the Throw button, the program throws an exception. If you are running the program in the development environment, Visual Studio halts at the Throw statement and tells you that it encountered an unhandled exception. If you run the compiled executable outside of the development environment, the application's ThreadException event occurs. The app_ThreadException routine catches the event and displays its message.

When the user clicks the OnThreadException button, the program calls the Application object's OnThreadException method, passing it an exception object. Whether you are running in the development environment or running the compiled executable, the application's ThreadException event occurs and the app_ThreadException routine catches it. You can use OnThreadException to throw the exception without the IDE's interference, so you can catch it and debug the exception handling code.

SUMMARY

Visual Studio provides many ways to store and use application configuration and resource information. Some of the most useful of these include environment variables, the Registry, configuration files, and resource files. The My namespace and the Application object make working with some of these easier.

Store configuration information that changes relatively often in configuration files. Store resources that determine the application's appearance in resource files. If you will distribute the application in multiple languages, use localized resource files to manage the different languages. If necessary, you can change the data stored in configuration and resource files and redistribute them to your users without rebuilding the entire application.

You can store small pieces of information between program runs in the System Registry. Use databases, XML files, and other files to store larger amounts of data.

Using all of these techniques, you can make your application easily configurable. You can satisfy the needs of different kinds of users and customize the application without recompiling it.

This chapter explained ways that a program can save configuration and resource information using tools such as the Registry, environment variables, and resource files. Generally, these kinds of data are of relatively limited size. If an application needs to store larger amounts of data, it generally uses a database or file.

Chapter 37, "Streams," explains classes that a Visual Basic application can use to work with stream data in general, and files in particular. Using streams attached to files, a program can read and write large amounts of data without cluttering up the Registry, environment variables, or resource files.

36

Streams

At some very primitive level, all pieces of data are just piles of bytes. The computer doesn't really store invoices, employee records, and recipes. At its most basic level, the computer stores bytes of data (or even bits, but the computer naturally groups them in bytes). It is only when a program interprets those bytes that they acquire a higher-level meaning that is valuable to the user.

Although you generally don't want to treat high-level data as undifferentiated bytes, there are times when thinking of the data as bytes lets you handle it in more uniform ways.

One type of byte-like data is the *stream*, an ordered series of bytes. Files, data flowing across a network, messages moving through a queue, and even the memory in an array all fit this description.

Defining the abstract idea of a stream lets applications handle these different types of objects uniformly. If an encryption or serialization routine manipulates a generic stream of bytes, it doesn't need to know whether the stream represents a file, a chunk of memory, plain text, encrypted text, or data flowing across a network.

Visual Studio provides several classes for manipulating different kinds of streams. It also provides higher-level classes for working with this kind of data at a more abstract level. For example, it provides classes for working with streams that happen to represent files and directories.

This chapter describes some of the classes you can use to manipulate streams. It explains lower-level classes that you may use only rarely and higher-level classes that let you read and write strings and files relatively easily.

The following table summarizes the most useful stream classes.

CLASS	USE
FileStream	Read and write bytes in a file.
MemoryStream	Read and write bytes in memory.
BinaryReader, BinaryWriter	Read and write specific data types in a stream.
StringReader, StringWriter	Read and write text with or without new lines in a string.
StreamReader, StreamWriter	Read and write text with or without new lines in a stream (usually a file stream).

STREAM

The Stream class defines properties and methods that derived stream classes must provide. These let the program perform relatively generic tasks with streams such as determining whether the stream allows writing.

The following table describes the Stream class's most useful properties.

PROPERTY	PURPOSE
CanRead	Returns True if the stream supports reading.
CanSeek	Returns True if the stream supports seeking to a particular position in the stream.
CanTimeout	Returns True if the stream supports timing out of read and write operations.
CanWrite	Returns True if the stream supports writing.
Length	Returns the number of bytes in the stream.
Position	Returns the stream's current position in its bytes. For a stream that supports seeking, the program can set this value to move to a particular position.
ReadTimeout	Determines the number of milliseconds that a read operation will wait before timing out.
WriteTimeout	Determines the number of milliseconds that a write operation will wait before timing out.

The following table describes the Stream class's most useful methods.

METHOD	PURPOSE
BeginRead	Begins an asynchronous read.
BeginWrite	Begins an asynchronous write.
Close	Closes the stream and releases any resources it uses (such as file handles).
EndRead	Waits for an asynchronous read to finish.
EndWrite	Ends an asynchronous write.
Flush	Flushes data from the stream's buffers into the underlying storage medium (device, file, memory, and so forth).
Read	Reads bytes from the stream and advances its position by that number of bytes.
ReadByte	Reads a byte from the stream and advances its position by one byte.
Seek	If the stream supports seeking, sets the stream's position.
SetLength	Sets the stream's length. If the stream is currently longer than the new length, it is truncated. If the stream is shorter than the new length, it is enlarged. The stream must support both writing and seeking for this method to work.
Write	Writes bytes into the stream and advances the current position by this number of bytes.
WriteByte	Writes one byte into the stream and advances the current position by one byte.

You can learn about the other members of the Stream class at `msdn.microsoft.com/system.io.stream.aspx`.

FILESTREAM

The FileStream class provides a stream representation of a file.

The FileStream class's parent class Stream defines most of its properties and methods. See the preceding section "Stream" for descriptions of those properties and methods.

FileStream adds two useful new properties to those it inherits from Stream. First, IsAsync returns True if the FileStream was opened asynchronously. Second, the Name property returns the file name passed into the object's constructor.

The class also adds two new useful methods to those it inherits from Stream. The Lock method locks the file, so other processes can read it but not modify it. Unlock removes a previous lock.

Overloaded versions of the FileStream class's constructor let you specify the following:

➤ A file name or handle, the file mode (Append, Create, CreateNew, Open, OpenOrCreate, or Truncate)

➤ Access mode (Read, Write, or ReadWrite)

➤ File sharing (Inheritable, which allows child processes to inherit the file handle, None, Read, Write, or ReadWrite)

➤ A buffer size

➤ File options (Asynchronous, DeleteOnClose, Encrypted, None, RandomAccess, SequentialScane, or WriteThrough)

Example program FileStreamWrite uses the following code to create a file. It creates a file and uses a Universal Transformation Format (UTF) UTF8Encoding object to convert a string into an array of bytes. It writes the bytes into the file and then closes the FileStream.

```
Dim file_name As String = Application.StartupPath & "\test.txt"
Using file_stream As New FileStream(file_name, FileMode.Create)
    Dim bytes As Byte() = New UTF8Encoding().GetBytes("Hello world!")

    file_stream.Write(bytes, 0, bytes.Length)
    file_stream.Close()
End Using
```

code snippet FileStreamWrite

CHARACTER SETS

The 8-bit UTF encoding is the most popular type on the Web, although there are other encoding formats such as UTF-7 and UTF-16. For additional information, see zsigri.tripod.com/fontboard/cjk/unicode.html or www.i18nguy.com/unicode/codepages.html.

As this example demonstrates, the FileStream class provides only low-level methods for reading and writing files. These methods let you read and write bytes, but not integers, strings, or the other types of data that you are more likely to want to use.

The BinaryReader and BinaryWriter classes let you read and write binary data more easily than the FileStream class does. The StringReader and StringWriter classes let you read and write string data more easily than the other classes. See the section "StringReader and StringWriter" describing these classes later in this chapter for more information.

MEMORYSTREAM

Like FileStream, the MemoryStream class inherits from the Stream class. This class represents a stream with data stored in memory. Like the FileStream, it provides only relatively simple methods for reading and writing data. Usually, you will want to attach a higher-level object to the MemoryStream to make using it easier.

Example program MemoryStreamWrite uses the following code to write and read from a MemoryStream object. It first creates the MemoryStream. It then creates a BinaryWriter attached to the MemoryStream and uses it to write some text into the stream. Next, the program creates a BinaryReader object attached to the same MemoryStream. It uses the stream's Seek method to rewind the stream to its beginning, and then uses the BinaryReader object's ReadString method to read the string out of the MemoryStream.

```
Dim memory_stream As New MemoryStream()
Dim binary_writer As New BinaryWriter(memory_stream)
binary_writer.Write("Peter Piper picked a peck of pickled peppers.")

Dim binary_reader As New BinaryReader(memory_stream)
memory_stream.Seek(0, SeekOrigin.Begin)
MessageBox.Show(binary_reader.ReadString())
binary_reader.Close()
```

code snippet MemoryStreamWrite

The following example does the same things as the previous example, except that it uses the StreamWriter and StreamReader classes instead of BinaryWriter and BinaryReader. Note that this version must call the StreamWriter class's Flush method to ensure that all of the text is written into the MemoryStream before it can read the memory using the StreamReader.

```
Using memory_stream As New MemoryStream()
    Dim stream_writer As New StreamWriter(memory_stream)
    stream_writer.Write("Peter Piper picked a peck of pickled peppers.")
    stream_writer.Flush()

    Dim stream_reader As New StreamReader(memory_stream)
    memory_stream.Seek(0, SeekOrigin.Begin)
    MessageBox.Show(stream_reader.ReadToEnd())
    stream_reader.Close()
End Using
```

BUFFEREDSTREAM

The BufferedStream class adds buffering to another stream class. For example, you can create a BufferedStream class attached to a network stream that communicates with another application through sockets. The BufferedStream class buffers data passing through the network connection.

Most programs don't need to explicitly create their own buffered streams, so this class isn't described further here. See the online help for more information.

BINARYREADER AND BINARYWRITER

The BinaryReader and BinaryWriter classes are not stream classes. Instead, they are helper classes that work with stream classes. They let you read and write data in files using a specific encoding. For example, the BinaryReader object's ReadInt32 method reads a 4-byte (32-bit) signed integer from the stream. Similarly, the ReadUInt16 method reads a 2-byte (16-bit) unsigned integer.

These classes still work at a relatively low level, and you should generally use higher-level classes to read and write data. For example, you shouldn't tie yourself to a particular representation of an integer unless you really must.

BinaryReader and BinaryWriter objects are attached to stream objects that provide access to the underlying bytes. Both of these classes have a BaseStream property that returns a reference to the underlying stream. Note also that the Close method provided by each of these classes automatically closes the underlying stream.

The following table describes the BinaryReader class's most useful methods.

METHOD	PURPOSE
Close	Closes the BinaryReader and its underlying stream.
PeekChar	Reads the stream's next character but does not advance the reader's position, so other methods can still read the character later.
Read	Reads characters from the stream and advances the reader's position.
ReadBoolean	Reads a Boolean from the stream and advances the reader's position by 1 byte.
ReadByte	Reads a byte from the stream and advances the reader's position by 1 byte.
ReadBytes	Reads a number of bytes from the stream into a byte array and advances the reader's position by that number of bytes.
ReadChar	Reads a character from the stream, and advances the reader's position according to the stream's encoding and the character.
ReadChars	Reads a number of characters from the stream, returns the results in a character array, and advances the reader's position according to the stream's encoding and the characters.
ReadDecimal	Reads a decimal value from the stream and advances the reader's position by 16 bytes.

METHOD	PURPOSE
ReadDouble	Reads an 8-byte floating-point value from the stream and advances the reader's position by 8 bytes.
ReadInt16	Reads a 2-byte signed integer from the stream and advances the reader's position by 2 bytes.
ReadInt32	Reads a 4-byte signed integer from the stream and advances the reader's position by 4 bytes.
ReadInt64	Reads an 8-byte signed integer from the stream and advances the reader's position by 8 bytes.
ReadSByte	Reads a signed byte from the stream and advances the reader's position by 1 byte.
ReadSingle	Reads a 4-byte floating-point value from the stream and advances the reader's position by 4 bytes.
ReadString	Reads a string from the current stream and advances the reader's position past it. The string begins with its length.
ReadUInt16	Reads a 2-byte unsigned integer from the stream and advances the reader's position by 2 bytes.
ReadUInt32	Reads a 4-byte unsigned integer from the stream and advances the reader's position by 4 bytes.
ReadUInt64	Reads an 8-byte unsigned integer from the stream and advances the reader's position by 8 bytes.

The following table describes the BinaryWriter class's most useful methods.

METHOD	PURPOSE
Close	Closes the BinaryWriter and its underlying stream.
Flush	Writes any buffered data into the underlying stream.
Seek	Sets the position within the stream.
Write	Writes a value into the stream. This method has many overloaded versions that write characters, arrays of characters, integers, strings, unsigned 64-bit integers, and so forth.

You can learn about the other members of the BinaryWriter and BinaryReader classes at
`msdn.microsoft.com/system.io.binarywriter.aspx` and `msdn.microsoft.com/system`
`.io.binaryreader.aspx`, respectively.

TEXTREADER AND TEXTWRITER

The TextReader and TextWriter classes are also not stream classes, but they provide properties
and methods for working with text, which is stream-related. In particular, the StreamWriter and
StreamReader classes derived from TextReader and TextWriter are associated with streams.

TextReader and TextWriter are abstract (MustInherit) classes that define behaviors for derived
classes that read or write text characters. For example, the StringWriter and StreamWriter classes
derived from TextWriter let a program write characters into a string or stream, respectively.
Normally, you would use these derived classes to read and write text, but you might want to use
the TextReader or TextWriter classes to manipulate the underlying classes more generically. You
may also encounter a method that requires a TextReader or TextWriter object as a parameter.
In that case, you could pass the method either a StringReader/StringWriter or a StreamReader/
StreamWriter. For more information on these, see the sections "StringReader and StringWriter" and
"StreamReader and StreamWriter" later in this chapter.

The following table describes the TextReader object's most useful methods.

METHOD	PURPOSE
Close	Closes the reader and releases any resources that it is using.
Peek	Reads the next character from the text without changing the reader's state, so other methods can read the character later.
Read	Reads data from the input. Overloaded versions of this method read a single character or an array of characters up to a specified length.
ReadBlock	Reads data from the input into an array of characters.
ReadLine	Reads a line of characters from the input and returns the data in a string.
ReadToEnd	Reads any remaining characters in the input and returns them in a string.

The TextWriter class has three useful properties. Encoding specifies the text's encoding (ASCII,
UTF-8, Unicode, and so forth).

FormatProvider returns an object that controls formatting. For example, you can build
a FormatProvider object that knows how to display numbers in different bases (such as hexadecimal
or octal).

The NewLine property gets or sets the string used by the writer to end lines. Usually, this value is
something similar to a carriage return or a carriage return plus a line feed.

The following table describes the TextWriter object's most useful methods.

METHOD	PURPOSE
Close	Closes the writer and releases any resources it uses.
Flush	Writes any buffered data into the underlying output.
Write	Writes a value into the output. This method has many overloaded versions that write characters, arrays of characters, integers, strings, unsigned 64-bit integers, and so forth.
WriteLine	Writes data into the output followed by the new line sequence.

You can learn about the other members of the TextWriter and TextReader classes at `msdn.microsoft.com/system.io.textwriter.aspx` and `msdn.microsoft.com/system` `.io.textreader.aspx`, respectively.

STRINGREADER AND STRINGWRITER

The StringReader and StringWriter classes let a program read and write text in a string.

These classes are derived from TextReader and TextWriter and inherit the definitions of most of their properties and methods from those classes. See the preceding section "TextReader and TextWriter" for details.

The StringReader provides methods for reading lines, characters, or blocks of characters from the string. Its ReadToEnd method returns any of the string that has not already been read. The StringReader class's constructor takes as a parameter the string that it should process.

The StringWriter class lets an application build a string. It provides methods to write text into the string with or without a new-line character. Its ToString method returns the StringWriter class's string.

The StringWriter stores its string in an underlying StringBuilder class. StringBuilder is designed to make incrementally building a string more efficient. For example, if an application needs to build a very large string by concatenating a series of long substrings, it may be more efficient to use a StringBuilder rather than adding the strings to a normal String variable. StringWriter provides a simple interface to the StringBuilder class.

The most useful method provided by StringWriter that is not defined by the TextWriter parent class is GetStringBuilder. This method returns a reference to the underlying StringBuilder object that holds the class's data.

Example program StringWriterReader uses the following code to demonstrate the StringWriter and StringReader classes. It creates a StringWriter object and uses its WriteLine method to add two lines to the string. It then displays the result of the writer's ToString method. This method returns the writer's current contents. Next, the program creates a StringReader, passing its constructor the string from which it will read. It closes the StringWriter because it is no longer needed. The code displays the result of the StringReader class's ReadLine method. Because the StringWriter created the string as two separate lines, this displays only the first line, "The quick brown fox." Next, the code uses the StringReader class's ReadToEnd method to read and display the rest of the text, "jumps over the lazy dog." The code finishes by closing the StringReader.

```
' Use a StringWriter to write into a string.
Using string_writer As New StringWriter()
    string_writer.WriteLine("The quick brown fox")
    string_writer.WriteLine("jumps over the lazy dog.")
    MessageBox.Show(string_writer.ToString)

    Use a StringReader to read from the string.
    Using string_reader As New StringReader(string_writer.ToString)
        string_writer.Close()
        MessageBox.Show(string_reader.ReadLine())
        MessageBox.Show(string_reader.ReadToEnd())
        string_reader.Close()
    End Using
End Using
```

code snippet StringWriterReader

STREAMREADER AND STREAMWRITER

The StreamReader and StreamWriter classes let a program read and write data in a stream. The underlying stream is usually a FileStream. You can pass a FileStream into these classes' constructors, or you can pass a file name and the object will create a FileStream automatically.

The StreamReader provides methods for reading lines, characters, or blocks of characters from the stream. Its ReadToEnd method returns any of the stream that has not already been read. The EndOfStream method returns True when the StreamReader has reached the end of the stream.

Example program ReadLines uses the following code fragment to read the lines from a file and add them to the a ListBox control:

```
Do Until stream_reader.EndOfStream()
    lstValues.Items.Add(stream_reader.ReadLine())
Loop
```

code snippet ReadLines

The StreamWriter class provides methods to write text into the stream with or without a new-line character.

StreamReader and StreamWriter are derived from the TextReader and TextWriter classes and inherit the definitions of most of their properties and methods from those classes. See the section "TextReader and TextWriter" earlier in this chapter for a description of these properties and methods.

The StreamWriter class adds a new AutoFlush property that determines whether the writer flushes its buffer after every write.

Example program StreamWriterReader uses the following code to demonstrate the StreamReader and StreamWriter classes. It generates a file name and passes it into a StreamWriter class's constructor. It uses the StreamWriter class's Write and WriteLine methods to place two lines of text in the file. It then closes the file. If you were to open the file now with a text editor, you would see the text. The program then creates a new StreamReader, passing its constructor the same file name. It uses the reader's ReadToEnd method to grab the file's contents and displays the results.

```
Dim file_name As String = Application.StartupPath & "\test.txt"
Using stream_writer As New StreamWriter(file_name)
    stream_writer.Write("The quick brown fox")
    stream_writer.WriteLine(" jumps over the lazy dog.")
    stream_writer.Close()
End Using

Using stream_reader As New StreamReader(file_name)
    MessageBox.Show(stream_reader.ReadToEnd())
    stream_reader.Close()
End Using
```

code snippet StreamWriterReader

This example would have been much more awkward using a FileStream object's lower-level Write and Read methods to manipulate byte arrays. Compare this code to the example in the "FileStream" section earlier in this chapter.

OPENTEXT, CREATETEXT, AND APPENDTEXT

The File class in the System.IO namespace provides four shared methods that are particularly useful for working with StreamReader and StreamWriter objects associated with text files. The following table summarizes these four methods.

METHOD	PURPOSE
Exists	Returns True if a file with a given path exists.
OpenText	Returns a StreamReader that lets you read from an existing text file.
CreateText	Creates a new text file, overwriting any existing file at the given path, and returns a StreamWriter that lets you write into the new file.
AppendText	If the indicated file does not exist, creates the file. Whether the file is new or previously existing, returns a StreamWriter that lets you append text at the end of the file.

The following code demonstrates the Exists and OpenText methods. First, it uses Exists to see if the file exists. If the file does exist, the code uses OpenText to open the file and get a StreamReader associated with it. It uses the StreamReader class's ReadToEnd method to display the file's text in the text box txtData.

```
Dim file_name As String = Application.StartupPath & "\test.txt"
If Not Exists(file_name) Then
    txtData.Text = " < File not found > "
Else
    Using sr As StreamReader = OpenText(file_name)
        txtData.Text = sr.ReadToEnd()
        sr.Close()
    End Using
End If
```

code snippet OpenCreateAppendText

The following code demonstrates the CreateText method. The code uses CreateText to create a new text file named test.txt. If test.txt already exists, CreateText overwrites it without warning. The program uses the StreamWriter returned by CreateText to write the contents of the txtData text box into the file and closes the file.

```
Dim file_name As String = Application.StartupPath & "\test.txt"
Using sw As StreamWriter = CreateText(file_name)
    sw.Write(txtData.Text)
    sw.Close()
End Using
```

code snippet OpenCreateAppendText

The following code demonstrates the AppendText method. The AppendText method creates the file if it doesn't already exist, or opens it for appending if it does exist. The program uses the StreamWriter returned by AppendText to write into the file and then closes the file.

```
Dim file_name As String = Application.StartupPath & "\test.txt"
Using sw As StreamWriter = AppendText(file_name)
    sw.Write(txtData.Text)
    sw.Close()
End Using
```

code snippet OpenCreateAppendText

Example program OpenCreateAppendText uses these code snippets to see if a file exists, create a new file, open an existing file, append to an existing file, and read from a file.

CUSTOM STREAM CLASSES

Visual Studio provides a few other stream classes with more specialized uses.

The CryptoStream class applies a cryptographic transformation to data that passes through it. For example, if you attach a CryptoStream to a file using a particular cryptographic transformation and then use it to write data, the CryptoStream automatically transforms the data and produces an encrypted file. Similarly, you can use a CryptoStream to read an encrypted file and recover the original text.

The NetworkStream class represents a socket-based stream over a network connection. You can use this class to make different applications communicate over a network.

Three other special uses of streams are standard input, standard output, and standard error. Console applications define these streams for reading and writing information to and from the console. An application can interact directly with these streams by accessing the Console.In, Console.Out, and Console.Error properties. It can change these streams to new stream objects such as StreamReaders and StreamWriters by calling the Console.SetIn, Console.SetOut, and Console .SetError methods.

SUMMARY

Streams let a program consider a wide variety of data sources in a uniform way. If a subroutine takes a stream as a parameter, it doesn't need to worry about whether the stream is attached to a string, file, block of memory, or network connection.

Many applications use the StringReader and StringWriter classes to read and write text in strings, and the StreamReader and StreamWriter classes to read and write text in streams (usually files). The Exists, OpenText, CreateText, and AppendText methods are particularly useful for working with StreamReader and StreamWriter objects associated with text files.

The other stream classes are often used at lower levels or as more abstract classes to allow a routine to process different kinds of streams in a uniform way. If you focus on these four classes (StringReader, StringWriter, StreamReader, and StreamWriter), you will quickly learn how to perform the most common stream operations.

Programs often use the StreamReader and StreamWriter classes to read and write files. Chapter 38, "File-System Objects," describes classes that let a Visual Basic application interact with the file system in other ways. These classes let a program examine, rename, move, and delete files and directories.

37

File-System Objects

Visual Basic includes a bewildering assortment of objects that you can use to manipulate drives, directories, and files. The stream classes described in Chapter 36 enable you to read and write files, but they don't really capture any of the special structure of the file system.

A Visual Basic application has two main choices for working with the file system: Visual Basic methods and .NET Framework classes. This chapter describes these two approaches and the classes that they use. It finishes by describing some of the My namespace properties and methods that you can use to access file-system tools more easily. For more information on the My namespace, see the section "My" in Chapter 35, "Configuration and Resources," and Appendix S, "The My Namespace."

PERMISSIONS

An application cannot perform a task if the user running it doesn't have the appropriate permissions. Although this is true of any operation a program must perform, permission issues are particularly common when working with files, and recent versions of the Windows operating system are particularly strict about enforcing permission requirements.

A common mistake is for developers to build and test an application while logged in as a user who has a lot of privileges. Sometimes, developers even have system administrator privileges, so their programs can do pretty much anything on the computer. To ensure that users will have the permissions needed by an application, develop or at least test the code using an account with the privileges that typical users will have.

Chapter 24, "UAC Security," describes permissions in greater detail.

VISUAL BASIC METHODS

Visual Basic provides a number of commands for manipulating the file system. These commands are relatively flexible and easy to understand. Most of them have been around since the early days of Visual Basic, so many long-time Visual Basic developers prefer to use them rather than the newer .NET Framework methods.

One disadvantage to these methods is that they do not natively allow you to read and write nonstandard data types. They can handle string, date, integer, long, single, double, and decimal data. They can also handle structures and arrays of those types. They cannot, however, handle classes themselves. You can use XML serialization to convert a class object into a string and then use these methods to read and write the result, but that requires an extra step with some added complexity.

The section "File-System Methods" later in this chapter describes the native file-system methods of Visual Basic. The sections "Sequential-File Access," "Random-File Access," and "Binary-File Access" later in this chapter describe specific issues for working with sequential, random, and binary files.

File Methods

The following table describes the methods Visual Basic provides for working with files.

METHOD	PURPOSE
EOF	Returns True if a file open for reading is at the end of file. (EOF stands for End Of File.)
FileClose	Closes an open file.
FileGet	Reads data from a file opened in Random and Binary mode into a variable.
FileGetObject	Reads data as an object from a file opened in Random and Binary mode into a variable.
FileOpen	Opens a file for reading or writing. Parameters indicate the mode (Append, Binary, Input, Output, or Random), access type (Read, Write, or ReadWrite), and sharing (Shared, LockRead, LockWrite, or LockReadWrite).
FilePut	Writes data from a variable into a file opened for Random or Binary access.
FilePutObject	Writes an object from a variable into a file opened for Random or Binary access.
FreeFile	Returns a file number that is not currently associated with any file in this application. You should use FreeFile to get file numbers rather than using arbitrary numbers such as 1.
Input	Reads data written into a file by the Write method back into a variable.
InputString	Reads a specific number of characters from the file.

METHOD	PURPOSE
LineInput	Returns the next line of text from the file.
Loc	Returns the current position within the file.
LOF	Returns the file's length in bytes. ("LOF" stands for Length Of File.)
Print	Prints values into the file. Multiple values separated by commas are aligned at tab boundaries.
PrintLine	Prints values followed by a new line into the file. Multiple values separated by commas are aligned at tab boundaries.
Seek	Moves to the indicated position within the file.
Write	Writes values into the file, delimited appropriately so that they can later be read by the Input method.
WriteLine	Writes values followed by a new line into the file, delimited appropriately so that they can later be read by the Input method.

Many of the Visual Basic file methods use a file number to represent an open file. The file number is just a number used to identify the file. There's nothing magic about it. You just need to be sure not to use the same file number for more than one file at a time. The FreeFile method returns a number that is not in use so that you know it is safe to use as a file number.

The following example uses FreeFile to get an available file number. It uses FileOpen to open a file for reading. Then, while the EOF method indicates that the code hasn't reached the end of the file, the program uses LineInput to read a line from the file and it displays the line. When it finishes reading the file, the program uses FileClose to close it.

```
' Get an available file number.
Dim file_num As Integer = FreeFile()

' Open the file.
FileOpen(file_num, "C:\Temp\test.txt",
    OpenMode.Input, OpenAccess.Read, OpenShare.Shared)

' Read the file's lines.
Do While Not EOF(file_num)
    ' Read a line.
    Dim txt As String = LineInput(file_num)
    Debug.WriteLine(txt)
Loop

' Close the file.
FileClose(file_num)
```

DIRECTORY RESTRICTIONS

Note that Windows restricts access to certain directories by normal non-administrator users. In general, you need the correct permissions to work with files. For example, you would need increased permissions to write into the system's root directory (for example, C:\) and the Windows directory. This example reads a file in the Temp directory, which should be accessible to all users, so it should work for everyone.

File-System Methods

Visual Basic also provides several methods for working with the file system. The following table describes methods that manipulate directories and files.

METHOD	PURPOSE
ChDir	Changes the application's current working directory.
ChDrive	Changes the application's current working drive.
CurDir	Returns the application's current working directory.
Dir	Returns a file matching a directory path specification that may include wildcards, and matching certain file properties such as ReadOnly, Hidden, or Directory. The first call to Dir should include a path. Subsequent calls can omit the path to fetch the next matching file for the initial path. Dir returns file names without the path and returns Nothing when no more files match.
FileCopy	Copies a file to a new location.
FileDateTime	Returns the date and time when the file was created or last modified.
FileLen	Returns the length of a file in bytes.
GetAttr	Returns a value indicating the file's attributes. The value is a combination of the values vbNormal, vbReadOnly, vbHidden, vbSystem, vbDirectory, vbArchive, and vbAlias.
Kill	Permanently deletes a file.
MkDir	Creates a new directory.
Rename	Renames a directory or file.
RmDir	Deletes an empty directory.
SetAttr	Sets the file's attributes. The attribute value is a combination of the values vbNormal, vbReadOnly, vbHidden, vbSystem, vbDirectory, vbArchive, and vbAlias.

Sequential-File Access

With sequential file access, a program reads or writes the contents of a file byte-by-byte from start to finish with no jumping around. In contrast, in a random-access file, the program can jump freely to any position in the file and write data wherever it likes.

A text file is a typical sequential file. The program can read the text in order, and read it one line at a time, but it cannot easily jump around within the file.

The Input, InputString, LineInput, Print, PrintLine, Write, and WriteLine methods provide sequential access to files.

The Print and PrintLine methods provide mostly unformatted results. If you pass these methods multiple parameters separated by commas, they align the results on tab boundaries. Write and WriteLine, on the other hand, delimit their output so that it can be easily read by the Input method.

A program cannot directly modify only part of a sequential file. For example, it cannot modify, add, or remove a sentence in the middle of a paragraph. If you must modify the file, you should read it into a string, make the changes you want, and then rewrite the file.

If you must frequently modify text in the middle of a file, you should consider using random or binary access, or storing the data in a database.

Random-File Access

A random-access file contains a series of fixed-length records. For example, you could create an employee file that contains a series of values defining an employee. Each record would have fixed-length fields to hold an employee's ID, first name, last name, street address, and so forth, as shown in the following structure definition:

```
Structure Employee
    Public Id As Long
    <VBFixedString(20) > Public FirstName As String
    <VBFixedString(20) > Public LastName As String
    <VBFixedString(40) > Public Street As String
    ...
End Structure
```

When you open a file for random access, you can jump to any record in the file. That makes certain kinds of file manipulation easier. For example, if the file is sorted, you can use a binary search to locate records in it.

You can overwrite the values in a record within the file, but you cannot add or remove records in the middle of the file. If you must make those sorts of changes, you must load the file into memory and then rewrite it from scratch.

The FileGet, FileGetObject, FilePut, and FilePutObject methods read and write records in random-access files. Example program RandomAccessEmployees uses the following code to demonstrate the FilePut and FileGet methods:

```vb
Public Class Form1
    Public Structure Employee
        Public ID As Integer
        <VBFixedString(15) > Public FirstName As String
        <VBFixedString(15) > Public LastName As String

        Public Sub New(ByVal new_id As Integer, ByVal first_name As String,
         ByVal last_name As String)
            ID = new_id
            FirstName = first_name
            LastName = last_name
        End Sub

        Public Overrides Function ToString() As String
            Return ID & ": " & FirstName & " " & LastName
        End Function
    End Structure

    Private Sub btnMakeRecords_Click() Handles btnMakeRecords.Click
        ' Declare a record variable.
        Dim emp As New Employee

        ' Get an available file number.
        Dim file_num As Integer = FreeFile()

        ' Open the file.
        FileOpen(file_num, "MYFILE.DAT", OpenMode.Random,
            OpenAccess.ReadWrite, OpenShare.Shared, Len(emp))

        ' Make some records.
        FilePut(file_num, New Employee(1, "Alice", "Altanta"))
        FilePut(file_num, New Employee(2, "Bob", "Bakersfield"))
        FilePut(file_num, New Employee(3, "Cindy", "Chicago"))
        FilePut(file_num, New Employee(4, "Dan", "Denver"))
        FilePut(file_num, New Employee(5, "Erma", "Eagle"))
        FilePut(file_num, New Employee(6, "Fred", "Frisco"))

        ' Fetch and display the records.
        Dim obj As ValueType = DirectCast(emp, ValueType)
        For Each i As Integer In New Integer() {3, 1, 5, 2, 6}
            FileGet(file_num, obj, i)
            emp = DirectCast(obj, Employee)
            Debug.WriteLine("[" & emp.ToString() & "]")
        Next i

        ' Close the file.
        FileClose(file_num)
    End Sub
End Class
```

code snippet RandomAccessEmployees

First, the code defines a structure named Employee to hold the data in a record. Notice how the code uses the `VBFixedString` attribute to flag the strings as fixed length. The structure must have a fixed length if you want to jump randomly through the file because Visual Basic calculates a record's position by multiplying a record's size by its index in the file. If records contained strings of unknown length, the calculation wouldn't work.

When the user clicks the Make Records button, the btnMakeRecords_Click event handler executes. This code declares a variable of the record type, Employee. It uses the FreeFile method to get an available file number and uses FileOpen to open the file for random access. The final parameter to FileOpen is the length of the file's records. To calculate this length, the program uses the Len function, passing it the Employee instance emp.

Next, the program uses the FilePut method to write six records into the file. It passes FilePut the file number and a new Employee structure. The structure's constructor makes initializing the new records easy.

The program then uses FileGet to retrieve the six records using their indexes as keys, fetching them out of numeric order to demonstrate random access. It then displays each record's data in the Output window surrounded by brackets so you can see where the data starts and ends.

There are two key points to notice here. First, the file numbers records starting with 1 not 0, so the first record in the file has index 1.

Second, the FileGet method does not have an overloaded version that takes an Employee structure as a parameter. Because this example has Option Strict set to On, the code must perform some shenanigans to pass FileGet a ValueType variable and then later convert it into an Employee.

If you set Option Strict to Off, you can pass an Employee object directly into FileGet. Turning off Option Strict is generally a bad idea, however, because it can hide implicit data type conversions that may indicate a mistake. You can minimize the danger by placing as little code as possible in the file with Option Strict Off. For example, if the code that uses FileGet is in a class, you can use the Partial keyword to move that code into a separate module. Then that module can turn off Option Strict whereas the rest of the class's code keeps Option Strict On.

After it has read and displayed the records, the program uses FileClose to close the file.

The following text shows the result. Notice that the first and last names are padded with spaces to 15 characters, the length of the Employee structure's fixed-length strings. The last names are also padded to 15 characters.

```
[3: Cindy        Chicago        ]
[1: Alice        Altanta        ]
[5: Erma         Eagle          ]
[2: Bob          Bakersfield    ]
[6: Fred         Frisco         ]
```

Binary-File Access

Binary access is similar to random access, except that it does not require its data to fit into neat records. You get control over pretty much every byte in the file, and you can jump to an arbitrary byte number in the file. If the items in the file are not fixed-length records, however, you cannot jump to a particular record because you cannot calculate where that record would begin.

.NET FRAMEWORK CLASSES

The System.IO namespace provides several classes for working with the file system. The Directory and File classes provide shared methods that you can use to manipulate the file system without creating instances of helper objects.

The DirectoryInfo and FileInfo classes let you work with specific relevant file system objects. For example, a FileInfo object represents a particular file and provides methods to create, rename, delete, and get information about that file.

The following sections describe these and the other classes that the Framework provides to help you work with the file system.

Directory

The Directory class provides shared methods for working with directories. These methods let you create, rename, move, and delete directories. They let you enumerate the files and subdirectories within a directory, and get and set directory information such as the directory's creation and last access time.

The following table describes the Directory class's shared methods.

METHOD	PURPOSE
CreateDirectory	Creates a directory and any missing ancestors (parent, grandparent, and so on).
Delete	Deletes a directory and its contents. It can delete all subdirectories, their subdirectories, and so forth to remove the entire directory tree.
Exists	Returns True if the path points to an existing directory.
GetCreationTime	Returns a directory's creation date and time.
GetCreationTimeUtc	Returns a directory's creation date and time in Coordinated Universal Time (UTC).
GetCurrentDirectory	Returns the application's current working directory.
GetDirectories	Returns an array of strings holding the fully qualified names of a directory's subdirectories.

QUALIFIED AND RELATIVE PATHS

A "fully qualified name" or "fully qualified path" is one that starts at a disk's root directory as in "C:\Whatever\Someplace\Expenses.txt."

A "relative path" starts at the program's current directory and doesn't include the root as in "standards.txt" or "Data\Pictures\Smiley.bmp."

METHOD	PURPOSE
GetDirectoryRoot	Returns the directory root for a path (the path need not exist). For example, C:\.
GetFiles	Returns an array of strings holding the fully qualified names of a directory's files.
GetFileSystemEntries	Returns an array of strings holding the fully qualified names of a directory's files and subdirectories.
GetLastAccessTime	Returns a directory's last access date and time.
GetLastAccessTimeUtc	Returns a directory's last access date and time in UTC.
GetLastWriteTime	Returns the date and time when a directory was last modified.
GetLastWriteTimeUtc	Returns the date and time in UTC when a directory was last modified.
GetLogicalDrives	Returns an array of strings listing the system's logical drives as in A:\. The list only includes drives that are attached. For example, it lists an empty floppy drive and a connected flash disk but doesn't list a flash disk after you disconnect it.
GetParent	Returns a DirectoryInfo object representing a directory's parent.
Move	Moves a directory and its contents to a new location on the same disk volume.
SetCreationTime	Sets a directory's creation date and time.
SetCreationTimeUtc	Sets a directory's creation date and time in UTC.
SetCurrentDirectory	Sets the application's current working directory.
SetLastAccessTime	Sets a directory's last access date and time.
SetLastAccessTimeUtc	Sets a directory's last access date and time in UTC.
SetLastWriteTime	Sets a directory's last write date and time.
SetLastWriteTimeUtc	Sets a directory's last write date and time in UTC.

File

The File class provides shared methods for working with files. These methods let you create, rename, move, and delete files. They also make working with file streams a bit easier.

The following table describes the File class's most useful shared methods.

METHOD	PURPOSE
AppendAll	Adds text to the end of a file, creating it if it doesn't exist, and then closes the file.
AppendText	Opens a file for appending UTF-8 encoded text and returns a StreamWriter class attached to it.
Copy	Copies a file.
Create	Creates a new file and returns a FileStream attached to it.
CreateText	Creates or opens a file for writing UTF-8 encoded text and returns a StreamWriter class attached to it.
Delete	Permanently deletes a file.
Exists	Returns True if the specified file exists.
GetAttributes	Gets a file's attributes. This is a combination of flags defined by the FileAttributes enumeration: Archive, Compressed, Device, Directory, Encrypted, Hidden, Normal, NotContextIndexed, Offline, ReadOnly, ReparsePoint, SparseFile, System, and Temporary.
GetCreationTime	Returns a file's creation date and time.
GetCreationTimeUtc	Returns a file's creation date and time in UTC.
GetLastAccessTime	Returns a file's last access date and time.
GetLastAccessTimeUtc	Returns a file's last access date and time in UTC.
GetLastWriteTime	Returns a file's last write date and time.
GetLastWriteTimeUtc	Returns a file's last write date and time in UTC.
Move	Moves a file to a new location.
Open	Opens a file and returns a FileStream attached to it. Parameters let you specify the mode (Append, Create, CreateNew, Open, OpenOrCreate, or Truncate), access (Read, Write, or ReadWrite), and sharing (Read, Write, ReadWrite, or None) settings.
OpenRead	Opens a file for reading and returns a FileStream attached to it.

METHOD	PURPOSE
OpenText	Opens a UTF-8-encoded text file for reading and returns a StreamReader attached to it.
OpenWrite	Opens a file for writing and returns a FileStream attached to it.
ReadAllBytes	Returns a file's contents in an array of bytes.
ReadAllLines	Returns a file's lines in an array of strings.
ReadAllText	Returns a file's contents in a string.
Replace	Takes three file paths as parameters, representing a source file, a destination file, and a backup file. If the backup file exists, this method permanently deletes it. It then moves the destination file to the backup file, and moves the source file to the destination file. For example, imagine a program that writes a log file every time it runs. It could use this method to keep three versions of the log: the current log (the method's source file), the most recent backup (the method's destination file), and a second backup (the method's backup file). This method throws an error if either the source or destination file doesn't exist.
SetAttributes	Sets a file's attributes. This is a combination of flags defined by the FileAttributes enumeration: Archive, Compressed, Device, Directory, Encrypted, Hidden, Normal, NotContextIndexed, Offline, ReadOnly, ReparsePoint, SparseFile, System, and Temporary.
SetCreationTime	Sets a file's creation date and time.
SetCreationTimeUtc	Sets a file's creation date and time in UTC.
SetLastAccessTime	Sets a file's last access date and time.
SetLastAccessTimeUtc	Sets a file's last access date and time in UTC.
SetLastWriteTime	Sets a file's last write date and time.
SetLastWriteTimeUtc	Sets a file's last write date and time in UTC.
WriteAllBytes	Creates or replaces a file, writes an array of bytes into it, and closes the file.
WriteAllLines	Creates or replaces a file, writes an array of strings into it, and closes the file.
WriteAllText	Creates or replaces a file, writes a string into it, and closes the file.

DriveInfo

A DriveInfo object represents one of the computer's drives. The following table describes the properties provided by this class. Note that some of these properties are available only when the drive is ready, as indicated in the Must Be Ready column. If you try to access them when the drive is not ready, Visual Basic throws an exception. The program should check the IsReady property to determine whether the drive is ready before trying to use the AvailableFreeSpace, DriveFormat, TotalFreeSpace, or VolumeLabel properties.

DRIVEINFO PROPERTY	PURPOSE	MUST BE READY
AvailableFreeSpace	Returns the amount of free space available on the drive in bytes.	True
DriveFormat	Returns the name of the file-system type such as NTFS (NT File System) or FAT32 (32-bit File Allocation Table). (For a comparison of these, see `www.ntfs.com/ntfs_vs_fat.htm`.)	True
DriveType	Returns a DriveType enumeration value indicating the drive type. This value can be CDRom, Fixed, Network, NoRootDirectory, Ram, Removable, or Unknown.	False
IsReady	Returns True if the drive is ready. Many DriveInfo properties are unavailable and raise exceptions if you try to access them while the drive is not ready.	False
Name	Return's the drive's name. This is the drive's root name (as in A:\ or C:\).	
RootDirectory	Returns a DirectoryInfo object representing the drive's root directory. See the following section "DirectoryInfo" for more information on this class.	False
TotalFreeSpace	Returns the total amount of free space on the drive in bytes.	True
VolumeLabel	Gets or sets the drive's volume label.	True

The DriveInfo class also has a public shared method GetDrives that returns an array of DriveInfo objects describing the system's drives.

DirectoryInfo

A DirectoryInfo object represents a directory. You can use its properties and methods to create and delete directories and to move through a directory hierarchy.

The following table describes the most useful public properties and methods provided by the DirectoryInfo class.

PROPERTY OR METHOD	PURPOSE
Attributes	Gets or sets flags for the directory from the FileAttributes enumeration: Archive, Compressed, Device, Directory, Encrypted, Hidden, Normal, NotContentIndexed, Offline, ReadOnly, ReparsePoint, SparseFile, System, and Temporary.
Create	Creates the directory. You can create a DirectoryInfo object, passing its constructor the fully qualified name of a directory that doesn't exist. You can then call the object's Create method to create the directory.
CreateSubdirectory	Creates a subdirectory within the directory and returns a DirectoryInfo object representing it. The subdirectory's path must be relative to the DirectoryInfo object's directory, but can contain intermediate subdirectories. For example, the following code creates the Tools subdirectory and the Bin directory inside that: `dir_info.CreateSubdirectory("Tools\Bin")`
CreationTime	Gets or sets the directory's creation time.
CreationTimeUtc	Gets or sets the directory's creation time in UTC.
Delete	Deletes the directory if it is empty. A parameter lets you tell the object to delete its contents, too, if it isn't empty.
Exists	Returns True if the directory exists.
Extension	Returns the extension part of the directory's name. Normally, this is an empty string for directories.
FullName	Returns the directory's fully qualified path.
GetDirectories	Returns an array of DirectoryInfo objects representing the directory's subdirectories. An optional parameter gives a pattern to match. This method does not recursively search the subdirectories.
GetFiles	Returns an array of FileInfo objects representing files inside the directory. An optional parameter gives a pattern to match. This method does not recursively search subdirectories.
GetFileSystemInfos	Returns a strongly typed array of FileSystemInfo objects, representing subdirectories and files inside the directory. The items in the array are DirectoryInfo and FileInfo objects, both of which inherit from FileSystemInfo. An optional parameter gives a pattern to match. This method does not recursively search subdirectories.

continues

(continued)

PROPERTY OR METHOD	PURPOSE
LastAccessTime	Gets or sets the directory's last access time.
LastAccessTimeUtc	Gets or sets the directory's last access time in UTC.
LastWriteTime	Gets or sets the directory's last write time.
LastWriteTimeUtc	Gets or sets directory's last write time in UTC.
MoveTo	Moves the directory and its contents to a new path.
Name	The directory's name without the path information.
Parent	Returns a DirectoryInfo object, representing the directory's parent. If the directory is its file system's root (for example, C:\), this returns Nothing.
Refresh	Refreshes the DirectoryInfo object's data. For example, if the directory has been accessed since the object was created, you must call Refresh to load the new LastAccessTime value.
Root	Returns a DirectoryInfo object representing the root of the directory's file system.
ToString	Returns the directory's fully qualified path and name.

FileInfo

A FileInfo object represents a file. You can use its properties and methods to create and delete directories and to move through a directory hierarchy.

The following table describes the most useful public properties and methods provided by the FileInfo class.

PROPERTY OR METHOD	PURPOSE
AppendText	Returns a StreamWriter that appends text to the file.
Attributes	Gets or sets flags for the file from the FileAttributes enumeration: Archive, Compressed, Device, Directory, Encrypted, Hidden, Normal, NotContentIndexed, Offline, ReadOnly, ReparsePoint, SparseFile, System, and Temporary.
CopyTo	Copies the file and returns a FileInfo object, representing the new file. A parameter lets you indicate whether the copy should overwrite an existing file. If the destination path is relative, it is relative to the application's current directory, not to the FileInfo object's directory.

PROPERTY OR METHOD	PURPOSE
Create	Creates the file and returns a FileStream object attached to it. For example, you can create a FileInfo object, passing its constructor the name of a file that doesn't exist. Then you can call the Create method to create the file.
CreateText	Creates the file and returns a StreamWriter attached to it. For example, you can create a FileInfo object passing its constructor the name of a file that doesn't exist. Then you can call the CreateText method to create the file.
CreationTime	Gets or sets the file's creation time.
CreationTimeUtc	Gets or sets the file's creation time in UTC.
Delete	Deletes the file.
Directory	Returns a DirectoryInfo object representing the file's directory.
DirectoryName	Returns the name of the file's directory.
Exists	Returns True if the file exists.
Extension	Returns the extension part of the file's name, including the period. For example, the extension for game.txt is .txt.
FullName	Returns the file's fully qualified path and name.
IsReadOnly	Returns True if the file is marked read-only.
LastAccessTime	Gets or sets the file's last access time.
LastAccessTimeUtc	Gets or sets the file's last access time in UTC.
LastWriteTime	Gets or sets the file's last write time.
LastWriteTimeUtc	Gets or sets the file's last write time in UTC.
Length	Returns the number of bytes in the file.
MoveTo	Moves the file to a new location. If the destination uses a relative path, it is relative to the application's current directory, not to the FileInfo object's directory. When this method finishes, the FileInfo object is updated to refer to the file's new location.
Name	The file's name without the path information.

continues

(continued)

PROPERTY OR METHOD	PURPOSE
Open	Opens the file with various mode (Append, Create, CreateNew, Open, OpenOrCreate, or Truncate), access (Read, Write, or ReadWrite), and sharing (Read, Write, ReadWrite, or None) settings. This method returns a FileStream object attached to the file.
OpenRead	Returns a read-only FileStream attached to the file.
OpenText	Returns a StreamReader with UTF-8 encoding attached to the file for reading.
OpenWrite	Returns a write-only FileStream attached to the file.
Refresh	Refreshes the FileInfo object's data. For example, if the file has been accessed since the object was created, you must call Refresh to load the new LastAccessTime value.
Replace	Replaces a target file with this one, renaming the old target as a backup copy. If the backup file already exists, it is deleted and replaced with the target. You can use this method to save backups of logs and other periodically updated files.
ToString	Returns the file's fully qualified name.

FileSystemInfo

The FileSystemInfo class is the parent class for the FileInfo and DirectoryInfo classes. It is a MustInherit class, so you cannot create instances of it directly, but some routines return this class rather than the more specific child classes. For example, the DirectoryInfo class's GetFileSystemInfos method returns an array of FileSystemInfo objects describing the files in the directory.

FileSystemWatcher

The FileSystemWatcher class keeps an eye on part of the file system and raises events to let your program know if something changes. For example, you could make a FileSystemWatcher monitor a work directory. When a new file with a .job extension arrives, the watcher could raise an event and your application could process the file.

WATCHER WARNING

The FileSystemWatcher seems to have a few problems. Sometimes it is overwhelmed and misses changes that it should see and it seems to get confused under some circumstances and either stop raising events or raise duplicate events. The control will hopefully improve over time but for now, use it cautiously.

The FileSystemWatcher class's constructor takes parameters that tell it which directory to watch and that give it a filter for selecting files to watch. For example, the filter might be "*.txt" to watch for changes to text files. The default filter is "*.*", which catches changes to all files that have an extension. Set the filter to the empty string "" to catch changes to all files including those without extensions.

The following table describes the FileSystemWatcher class's most useful properties.

PROPERTY	PURPOSE
EnableRaisingEvents	Determines whether the component is enabled. Note that this property is False by default, so the watcher will not raise any events until you set it to True.
Filter	Determines the files for which the watcher reports events. You cannot watch for multiple file types as in *.txt and *.dat. Instead use multiple FileSystemWatcher classes. If you like, you can use AddHandler to make all of the FileSystemWatcher classes use the same event handlers.
IncludeSubdirectories	Determines whether the object watches subdirectories within the main path.
InternalBufferSize	Determines the size of the internal buffer. If the watcher is monitoring a very active directory, a small buffer may overflow.
NotifyFilter	Determines the types of changes that the watcher reports. This is a combination of values defined by the NotifyFilters enumeration and can include the values Attributes, CreationTime, DirectoryName, FileName, LastAccess, LastWrite, Security, and Size.
Path	Determines the path to watch.

The FileSystemWatcher class provides only two really useful methods. First, Dispose releases resources used by the component. When you are finished using a watcher, call its Dispose method to allow garbage collection to reclaim its resources more efficiently.

Second, the WaitForChanged method waits for a change synchronously (with an optional timeout). When a change occurs, the method returns a WaitForChangedResult object, giving information about the change that occurred.

When the FileSystemWatcher detects a change asynchronously, it raises an event to let the program know what has happened. The following table describes the class's events.

NAME	DESCRIPTION
Changed	A file or subdirectory has changed.
Created	A file or subdirectory was created.
Deleted	A file or subdirectory was deleted.
Error	The watcher's internal buffer overflowed.
Renamed	A file or subdirectory was renamed.

The following simple example shows how to use a FileSystemWatcher to look for new files in a directory:

```
Private WithEvents fswJobFiles As FileSystemWatcher

Private Sub Form1_Load() Handles MyBase.Load
    Dim watch_path As String =
        FileSystem.GetParentPath(Application.StartupPath)
    fswJobFiles = New FileSystemWatcher(watch_path, "*.job")
    fswJobFiles.NotifyFilter = NotifyFilters.FileName
    fswJobFiles.EnableRaisingEvents = True
End Sub

Private Sub fswJobFiles_Created(ByVal sender As Object,
 ByVal e As System.IO.FileSystemEventArgs) Handles fswJobFiles.Created
    ' Process the new file.
    MessageBox.Show("Process new job: " & e.FullPath)

    File.Delete(e.FullPath)
End Sub
```

The program uses the WithEvents keyword to declare a FileSystemWatcher object. When the program's main form loads, the Form1_Load event handler allocates this object. Its constructor sets the object's path to the program's startup directory's parent. It sets the object's filter to "*.job" so that the object will watch for changes to files that end with a .job extension.

The event handler sets the watcher's NotifyFilter to FileName, so it will raise its Created event if a new file name appears in the target directory. Unfortunately, the NotifyFilter values (Attributes,

CreationTime, DirectoryName, FileName, LastAccess, LastWrite, Security, and Size) do not match up well with the events provided by the FileSystemWatcher, so you need to figure out which NotifyFilter values to set to raise different kinds of events.

The Form1_Load event handler finishes by setting the watcher's EnableRaisingEvents property to True so the object starts watching.

When a .job file is created in the watcher's target directory, the program's fswJobFiles_Created executes. The program processes and then deletes the file. In this example, the program processes the file by displaying a message giving its fully qualified name. A more realistic example might read the file; parse fields, indicating the type of job this is; assign it to an employee for handling; and then e-mail it to that employee.

The UseFileSystemWatcher example program, which is available for download on the book's web site, uses similar code without the filter to look for any new file in the program's startup directory.

Path

The Path class provides shared properties and methods that you can use to manipulate paths. Its methods return the path's file name, extension, directory name, and so forth. Other methods provide values that do not relate to a specific path. For example, they can give you the system's temporary directory path, or the name of a temporary file.

The following table describes the Path class's most useful public properties.

PROPERTY	PURPOSE
AltDirectorySeparatorChar	Returns the alternate character used to separate directory levels in a hierarchical path. Typically this is /.
DirectorySeparatorChar	Returns the character used to separate directory levels in a hierarchical path. Typically this is \ (as in C:\Tests\Billing\2008q2.dat).
InvalidPathChars	Returns a character array that holds characters that are not allowed in a path string. Typically, this array includes characters such as ", <, >, and I, as well as nonprintable characters such as those with ASCII values between 0 and 31.
PathSeparator	Returns the character used to separate path strings in environment variables. Typically this is a semi-colon (;).
VolumeSeparatorChar	Returns the character placed between a volume letter and the rest of the path. Typically this is a colon (:).

The following table describes the Path class's most useful methods.

METHOD	PURPOSE
`ChangeExtension`	Changes a path's extension.
`Combine`	Returns two path strings concatenated.
`GetDirectoryName`	Returns a path's directory.
`GetExtension`	Returns a path's extension.
`GetFileName`	Returns a path's file name and extension.
`GetFileNameWithoutExtension`	Returns a path's file name without the extension.

`GetFullPath`	Returns a path's fully qualified value. This can be particularly useful for converting a partially relative path into an absolute path. For example, the following statement returns the string `"C:\Tests\New\Code"`:
	
	`Path.GetFullPath("C:\Tests\OldTests\`
	`Software\..\..\New\Code")`

`GetInvalidFileNameChars`	Returns an array listing characters that are invalid in file names.
`GetInvalidPathChars`	Returns an array listing characters that are invalid in file paths.
`GetPathRoot`	Returns a path's root directory string. For example, the following statement returns the string `"C:\"`: `Path.GetPathRoot("C:\Invoices\Unpaid\Deadbeats")`
`GetRandomFileName`	Returns a random file name.
`GetTempFileName`	Creates a uniquely named, empty temporary file and returns its fully qualified path. Your program can open that file for scratch space, do whatever it needs to do, close the file, and then delete it. A typical file name might be `C:\Documents and Settings\Rod\Local Settings\Temp\tmp19D.tmp`.
`GetTempPath`	Returns the path to the system's temporary folder. This is the path part of the file names returned by GetTempFileName.
`HasExtension`	Returns True if a path includes an extension.
`IsPathRooted`	Returns True if a path is an absolute path. This includes `\Temp\Wherever` and `C:\Clients\Litigation`, but not `Temp\Wherever` or `.\Uncle`.

MY.COMPUTER.FILESYSTEM

The My.Computer.FileSystem object provides tools for working with drives, directories, and files. The following table summarizes this object's properties.

PROPERTY	DESCRIPTION
CurrentDirectory	Gets or sets the fully qualified path to the application's current directory.
Drives	Returns a read-only collection of DriveInfo objects describing the system's drives. See the section "DriveInfo" earlier in this chapter for information about the DriveInfo class.
SpecialDirectories	Returns a SpecialDirectoriesProxy object that has properties giving the locations of various special directories (such as the system's temporary directory and the user's MyDocuments directory). See the following section "My.Computer.FileSystem.SpecialDirectories" for more information.

The following list describes the My.Computer.FileSystem object's methods:

METHOD	PURPOSE

CombinePath	Combines a base path with a relative path reference and returns a properly formatted fully qualified path. For example, the following code displays the name of the directory that is the parent of the application's current directory:
	
	`MessageBox.Show(My.Computer.FileSystem.CombinePath`
	`(My.Computer.FileSystem.CurrentDirectory(), ".")`

CopyDirectory	Copies a directory. Parameters indicate whether to overwrite existing files, whether to display a progress indicator, and what to do if the user presses Cancel during the operation.
CopyFile	Copies a file. Parameters indicate whether to overwrite existing files, whether to display a progress indicator, and what to do if the user presses Cancel during the operation.
CreateDirectory	Creates a directory. This method will create ancestor directories if necessary. For example, if the C:\Temp directory contains no subdirectories, creating C:\Temp\Project\Data will automatically create C:\Temp\Project and C:\Temp\Project\Data.

continues

(continued)

METHOD	PURPOSE
DeleteDirectory	Deletes a directory. Parameters indicate whether to recursively delete subdirectories, prompt the user for confirmation, or move the directory into the Recycle Bin.
DeleteFile	Deletes a file. Parameters indicate whether to prompt the user for confirmation or move the file into the Recycle Bin, and what to do if the user presses Cancel while the deletion is in progress.
DirectoryExists	Returns True if a specified directory exists.
FileExists	Returns True if a specified file exists.
FindInFiles	Returns a read-only collection of strings listing files that contain a target string.
GetDirectories	Returns a string collection listing subdirectories of a given directory. Parameters tell whether to recursively search the subdirectories, and the wildcards to match.
GetDirectoryInfo	Returns a DirectoryInfo object for a directory. See the section "DirectoryInfo" earlier in this chapter for more information.
GetDriveInfo	Returns a DriveInfo object for a drive. See the section "DriveInfo" earlier in this chapter for more information.
GetFileInfo	Returns a FileInfo object for a file. See the section "FileInfo" earlier in this chapter for more information.
GetFiles	Returns a string collection holding the names of files within a directory. Parameters indicate whether the search should recursively search subdirectories, and give wildcards to match.
GetParentPath	Returns the fully qualified path of a path's parent. For example, this returns a file's or directory's parent directory.
MoveDirectory	Moves a directory. Parameters indicate whether to overwrite files that have the same name in the destination directory and whether to prompt the user when such a collision occurs.
MoveFile	Moves a file. Parameters indicate whether to overwrite a file that has the same name as the file's destination and whether to prompt the user when such a collision occurs.
OpenTextFieldParser	Opens a TextFieldParser object attached to a delimited or fixed-field file such as a log file. You can use the object to parse the file.

METHOD	PURPOSE
OpenTextFileReader	Opens a StreamReader object attached to a file. You can use the object to read the file.
OpenTextFileWriter	Opens a StreamReader object attached to a file. You can use the object to write into the file.
ReadAllBytes	Reads all of the bytes from a binary file into an array.
ReadAllText	Reads all of the text from a text file into a string.
RenameDirectory	Renames a directory within its parent directory.
RenameFile	Renames a file with its directory.
WriteAllBytes	Writes an array of bytes into a binary file. A parameter tells whether to append the data or rewrite the file.
WriteAllText	Writes a string into a text file. A parameter tells whether to append the string or rewrite the file.

MY.COMPUTER.FILESYSTEM.SPECIALDIRECTORIES

The My.Computer.FileSystem.SpecialDirectories property returns a SpecialDirectoriesProxy object that has properties giving the locations of various special directories such as the system's temporary directory and the user's MyDocuments directory.

The following table describes these special directory properties.

PROPERTY	PURPOSE
AllUsersApplicationData	Application settings for all users.
CurrentUserApplicationData	Application settings for the current user.
Desktop	The current user's desktop directory.
MyDocuments	The current user's MyDocuments directory.
MyMusic	The current user's MyMusic directory.
MyPictures	The current user's MyPictures directory.
Programs	The current user's Start Menu\Programs directory.
ProgramFiles	The current user's Start Menu\Programs directory.
Temp	The current user's temporary directory.

> **DIRECTORY DEFICIENCIES**
>
> Note that these directories may not all exist on a particular system. For example, it may not define the MyMusic or MyPictures directories. Trying to access the values of a missing directory causes a DirectoryNotFoundException. You can use a Try Catch block to protect the program from the exception.

SUMMARY

Visual Basic provides a native set of methods for reading and writing files, including FreeFile, FileOpen, Input, LineInput, Print, Write, and FileClose. It also provides method for working with the file system (such as ChDir, MkDir, Kill, and RmDir). If you have a lot of previous experience with Visual Basic, you may prefer these familiar methods.

The System.IO namespace offers many objects that provide even more powerful capabilities than the native methods of Visual Basic. Classes such as Directory, DirectoryInfo, File, and FileInfo make it easy to create, examine, move, rename, and delete directories and files. The File class's methods make it particularly easy to read or write an entire file and to create streams attached to files for reading or writing.

The FileSystemWatcher class lets an application keep an eye on a file or directory and take action when it is changed. For example, a program can watch a spooling directory and take action when a new file appears in it.

The Path class provides miscellaneous support for working with paths. For example, it provides methods for examining a path's file name or extension.

The My.Computer.FileSystem namespace provides shortcuts to some of the more useful of the methods offered by the other file system classes. Its methods let you create, examine, and delete files and directories. The SpecialDirectories object also provides information about the locations of system directories.

There is considerable overlap among all of these tools, so you don't need to feel that you have to use them all. Take a good look so you know what's there, and then pick the tools that you find the most comfortable.

The tools that this chapter describes allow you fairly unstructured access to files. These classes and methods let you do just about anything you want to a file. That flexibility, however, means that you must know exactly what you want to do to the file. By letting you do anything, these tools make you do everything.

One of the most important ways an application can interact with the computer that is running it is through the file system. The classes and methods that this chapter describes allow an application to interact with the local computer's file system relatively easily.

Interacting with other computers is much more complicated. Chapter 38, "Windows Communication Foundation," describes tools that the .NET Framework provides to make interacting with remote computers easier.

38

Windows Communication Foundation

Programmers have long been able to have one program to call routines provided by another program that is running either on the local computer or some other computer on the same network. The omnipresent Internet extended this capability to new and greater levels, allowing a *client* program to call service routines provided by a *server* that could be physically on the other side of the world.

New web technologies such as Simple Object Access Protocol (SOAP) made it easy enough to build web services for use by other programs over the Internet. This gave rise to a whole new type of application that implements a significant amount of its functionality by calling services. Because these programs focus on the use of services, this design is called service-oriented architecture (SOA).

Windows Communication Foundation (WCF) is a set of classes and tools in .NET Framework 3.0 that make it easier to build SOA applications. It includes attribute classes that let you easily mark pieces of a server application to publish services for use by clients. It also includes tools to automatically generate the Visual Basic code you need to use or consume the services.

WCF is quite large and very flexible. It gives you the ability to write secure, reliable services that support transactions and can use a variety of transport methods. For example, clients and services can communicate using HTTP or TCP network protocols, or named pipes or message queues on the local computer.

Because WCF is so flexible, there isn't space to cover it all here. Instead, this chapter provides an overview of the main concepts behind WCF, and describes a simple example client and server implementation.

WCF CONCEPTS

WCF is based on the concept of messages. A *message* contains some sort of communication between a client and a service. Note that the program doesn't need to deal directly with messages. It can issue subroutine and function calls just as if it were calling a local object's methods. The WCF library routines convert the call into a message and send it to the recipient transparently.

An *endpoint* is a place where messages are sent or received. Typically, a service creates endpoints to receive request messages from clients and clients create endpoints to initiate those requests.

Endpoints define the characteristics of the communication. They determine the number and types of parameters passed to a request and the type of any returned data. They determine whether the communication uses a request-reply, one-way, or duplex style of communication. The definition of the message format is called its *service contract*.

The message definitions at the endpoints at the two ends of a communication must agree. They must satisfy the same service contract. If a client sends a message in one format, but the service expects the message in a different format, the communication won't work. WCF provides tools that help you define service endpoints and automatically generate Visual Basic code to properly use corresponding client endpoints.

After you have built the client and server, the two pass messages between their endpoints following the rules of the service contract. For example, if the contract indicates that the communication is one-way, the client invokes service subroutines that do not return any data. If the communication has a request-reply style, the client invokes service functions that return some sort of reply. If the contract indicates duplex communication, then the client can call service subroutines and the server can invoke client callbacks. For example, the client can tell the service that it is interested in certain events such as stock price updates, and then the service can call the client as the updates are available.

The following sections describe a concrete example that implements a simple client and server.

WCF EXAMPLE

To build a service from scratch, you follow the steps outlined in the following list:

1. Define the service contract in a Visual Basic interface.
2. Implement the service contract in a service class.
3. Build the host application to run the service.
4. Configure the service to specify bindings and endpoints.
5. Run the service.

After you build the service, you follow these steps to build a client:

1. Use the SvcUtil tool to discover information about the service contract and build Visual Basic code to implement a client class.

2. Write the client application that uses the client class.

These steps are somewhat involved and require that you know a lot about service configuration files and tools such as SvcUtil.exe. Fortunately, Visual Basic provides some application templates that make building a simple service much easier.

BUILDING THE INITIAL SERVICE

To build a service, open the File menu and select New Project. Under the Visual Basic project type, select the WCF category. Click the WCF Service Library template, enter a meaningful project name, and click OK.

Initially, Visual Basic creates an interface named IService1 shown in the following code to define the service's contract:

```
' NOTE: You can use the "Rename" command on the "Refactor" menu to
' change the interface name "IService1" in both code and config file together.
<ServiceContract()>
Public Interface IService1

    <OperationContract()>
    Function GetData(ByVal value As Integer) As String

    <OperationContract()>
    Function GetDataUsingDataContract(ByVal composite As CompositeType)
        As CompositeType

    ' TODO: Add your service operations here
End Interface
```

This interface defines two methods decorated by OperationContract attributes to identify them as methods that the service will expose to clients.

The GetData function takes an integer parameter and returns a string result. This function demonstrates a simple service method that uses standard Visual Basic data types.

The GetDataUsingDataContract function takes an object of class CompositeType as a parameter and returns another object of the same class. This function demonstrates a slightly more complicated function that works with a program-defined data type.

The following code shows the initial implementation of the service class:

```
' NOTE: You can use the "Rename" command on the "Refactor" menu to
' change the class name "Service1" in both code and config file together.
Public Class Service1
    Implements IService1

    Public Function GetData(ByVal value As Integer) As String _
    Implements IService1.GetData
        Return String.Format("You entered: {0}", value)
    End Function

    Public Function GetDataUsingDataContract(
     ByVal composite As CompositeType) As CompositeType _
     Implements IService1.GetDataUsingDataContract
        If composite Is Nothing Then
            Throw New ArgumentNullException("composite")
        End If
        If composite.BoolValue Then
            composite.StringValue &= "Suffix"
        End If
        Return composite
    End Function
End Class
```

The class Service1 implements the IService1 interface. The GetData method simply returns a string echoing its numeric parameter. The GetDataUsingDataContract method modifies its CompositeType parameter's StringValue property and returns its parameter object.

The final piece to the service is its configuration file. The following code shows the App.config file initially built by Visual Basic for the service class, slightly reformatted to make it easier to read:

```
<?xml version="1.0" encoding="utf-8" ?>
<configuration>

  <system.web>
    <compilation debug="true" />
  </system.web>
  <!-- When deploying the service library project, the content of the
       config file must be added to the host's app.config file.
       System.Configuration does not support config files for libraries. -->
  <system.serviceModel>
    <services>
      <service name="QuoteServiceLib.Service1">
        <host>
          <baseAddresses>
            <add baseAddress =
"http://localhost:8732/Design_Time_Addresses/QuoteServiceLib/Service1/" />
          </baseAddresses>
        </host>
        <!-- Service Endpoints -->
        <!-- Unless fully qualified, address is relative to base address
             supplied above -->
```

```xml
<endpoint address ="" binding="wsHttpBinding"
 contract="QuoteServiceLib.IService1">
  <!--
      Upon deployment, the following identity element
      should be removed or replaced to reflect the
      identity under which the deployed service runs.
      If removed, WCF will infer an appropriate identity
      automatically.
  -->
  <identity>
    <dns value="localhost"/>
  </identity>
</endpoint>
<!-- Metadata Endpoints -->
<!-- The Metadata Exchange endpoint is used by the service
     to describe itself to clients. -->
<!-- This endpoint does not use a secure binding and should
     be secured or removed before deployment -->
<endpoint address="mex" binding="mexHttpBinding"
 contract="IMetadataExchange"/>
  </service>
</services>
<behaviors>
  <serviceBehaviors>
    <behavior>
      <!-- To avoid disclosing metadata information,
           set the value below to false and remove the
           metadata endpoint above before deployment -->
      <serviceMetadata httpGetEnabled="True"/>
      <!-- To receive exception details in faults for debugging purposes,
      set the value below to true.  Set to false before deployment
      to avoid disclosing exception information -->
      <serviceDebug includeExceptionDetailInFaults="False" />
    </behavior>
  </serviceBehaviors>
</behaviors>
</system.serviceModel>

</configuration>
```

The <services> element contains service definitions. Each service gives its name and the names of the behaviors it provides. This example defines the service library WcfServiceLibrary1.Service1. The <host> element tells where the service will listen for requests.

The <service> element contains endpoint definitions. These definitions set the addresses, bindings, and contracts for the endpoints. The binding attribute gives the name of the binding that the endpoint uses. This example implements the contract defined by WcfServiceLibrary1 .IService1.

The last endpoint in this example is a Metadata Exchange (MEX) endpoint. It exposes metadata that describes the service to potential clients. A client can use a tool such as SvcUtil to query this endpoint to learn about the service.

The configuration file's `<serviceBehaviors>` section describes the service's behaviors. In this example, the behavior elements indicate that the service allows clients to look up information about the service and that the service provides details when it has an error.

BUILDING QUOTESERVICE

Modifying the initial service definition to implement the QuoteService isn't too hard. The following code shows the revised interface that defines the service contract. The differences between this version and the initial version are highlighted in bold, so they are easy to see.

```
<ServiceContract()>
Public Interface IQuoteService

    <OperationContract()>
    Function GetData(ByVal value As Integer) As String

    <OperationContract()>
    Function GetDataUsingDataContract(ByVal composite As CompositeType) _
        As CompositeType

    ' TODO: Add your service operations here
    <OperationContract()>
    Function GetQuote() As String

End Interface
```

code snippet QuoteServiceLib

This example changes the name of the interface to IQuoteService. To change the interface's name to IQuoteService, right-click on the original name, select Rename, enter the new name, and click OK.

The code leaves the initial GetData and GetDataUsingDataContract methods alone and adds a new GetQuote function that takes no parameters and that returns a string.

The following code shows the revised service class that implements this contract. The differences between this version and the initial version are again shown in bold.

```
Public Class QuoteService
    Implements IQuoteService

    ' Methods GetData and GetDataUsingDataContract omitted.
    ' ...

    ' Return a random quote.
    Public Function GetQuote() As String Implements IQuoteService.GetQuote
        Dim quotes() As String = {
```

```
        "I stand by all the misstatements that I've made.--Dan Quayle",
        "You can observe a lot just by watching.--Yogi Berra",
        ...
        "Two nations divided by a common language.--Winston Churchill"
    }

    ' Return a random quote.
    Dim rand As New Random
    Return quotes(rand.Next(0, quotes.Length))
  End Function
End Class
```

code snippet QuoteServiceLib

Again right-click and use Rename to change the service class's name to QuoteService. The GetData and GetDataUsingDataContract are the same as before, so they are not shown here.

This code adds the new GetQuote method. That method simply contains an array of quote strings, picks one randomly, and returns it.

The last change needed to build QuoteService is in the configuration file. The Rename tool updated the App.config file so you only need to change the baseAddress line to the following.

```
<add baseAddress="http://localhost:8732/Design_Time_Addresses/QuoteServiceLib/
QuoteService/" />
```

TESTING QUOTESERVICE

After you have built a server, you should test it. Visual Studio provides integrated support for a test service host named WCF Service Host and a test client named WCF Test Client. If you press F5 to run the service library, those programs automatically start so you can test the service.

When you run the program, the WCF Service Host starts and runs the service. Next, the WCF Test Client shown in Figure 38-1 starts. Find the service on the left and expand it to see a list of its behaviors. Double-click a behavior to open it in a tab on the right. In Figure 38-1 the Get Quote behavior is shown on the right.

If the GetQuote method required parameters, they would be listed in the upper grid. You could click a parameter's Value entry and type in a new value.

When you click the Invoke button, the client uses your parameter values to build a request and send it to the service. It displays the results in the lower grid. In Figure 38-1, the GetQuote method returned the quote "You can observe a lot just by watching. — Yogi Berra."

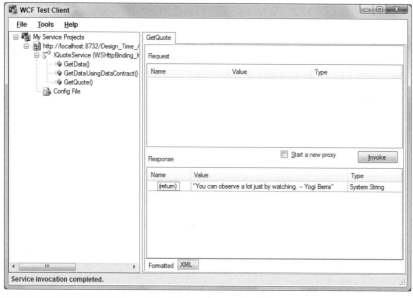

FIGURE 38-1: The WCF Test Client lets you test a WCF service.

BUILDING QUOTECLIENT

The client for the QuoteService can be any Windows application. Keeping the service project loaded, open the File menu, expand its Add submenu, and select New Project. In the New Project dialog, select the Windows Forms Application template, name the project QuoteClient, and click OK.

Now, in Solution Explorer, right-click the QuoteClient entry and select Add Service Reference. In the resulting dialog, click the Discover button to find the service, and then click OK to add the reference to the program.

Next, add code to the client application. The example client available for download displays a Get Quote button that executes the following code:

Available for download on Wrox.com

```
Private Sub btnGetQuote_Click() Handles btnGetQuote.Click
    Me.Cursor = Cursors.WaitCursor

    Dim quote_service As New ServiceReference1.QuoteServiceClient
    lblQuote.Text = quote_service.GetQuote()

    Me.Cursor = Cursors.Default
End Sub
```

code snippet QuoteClient

This code creates a new ServiceReference1.QuoteServiceClient object, calls its GetQuote method, and displays the result in a label.

When you add the service reference, Visual Studio automatically generates a lot of code including the QuoteServiceClient class. This class includes methods that automatically configure service endpoints and that call the methods exposed by the service.

VIEW SERVICE DEFINITIONS

To see the definition of the QuoteServiceClient class, open Solution Explorer, click the Show All Files button, drill down to Service References/ServiceReference/Reference.svcmap, and open the file Reference.vb. Alternatively, after you have entered the previous code in the client program, right-click the QuoteServiceClient data type and select Go To Definition.

Right-click the QuoteClient program and make it the startup program. Then press F5 to run the client. When you click the Get Quote button, the program uses the service to display a random quote.

SUMMARY

The idea behind WCF is relatively simple: Allow a client application to call methods provided by a service. Although the idea is simple, WCF is a complicated topic because it provides so much flexibility. It lets clients and services communicate through a variety of transport mechanisms using an assortment of security protocols. WCF provides attributes that make defining service contracts easy, but the great flexibility it provides makes configuring services more difficult.

For more information on WCF, search the Microsoft online help and the Web. A good starting point is the Microsoft WCF home page at `msdn.microsoft.com/aa388579.aspx`. Several books are also available that cover WCF in depth such as *Professional WCF Programming: .NET Development with the Windows Communication Foundation* (Klein, Wrox, 2007).

WCF is huge but the .NET Framework is even larger, containing thousands of classes, types, enumerations, interfaces, and other items. To make finding and using all of this material easier, the .NET Framework divides groups of useful files into namespaces. For example, WCF classes are in the System.ServiceModel namespace.

Chapter 40, "Useful Namespaces," describes some other useful namespaces defined by the .NET Framework. It provides a brief overview of some of the most important System namespaces and gives more detailed examples that demonstrate regular expressions, XML, cryptography, reflection, threading, and Direct3D.

39

Useful Namespaces

The .NET Framework is a library of classes, interfaces, and types that add extra power to Visual Studio .NET. These features go beyond what is normally provided by a programming language such as Visual Basic.

The .NET Framework is truly enormous. To make it more manageable, Microsoft has broken it into namespaces. The namespaces form a hierarchical catalog that groups related classes and functions in a meaningful way.

For example, the System namespace contains basic classes and methods that an application can use to perform common tasks. The System.Drawing namespace is the part of the System namespace that holds graphical tools. The System.Drawing.Design, System.Drawing .Drawing2D, System.Drawing.Imaging, System.Drawing.Printing, and System.Drawing .Text namespaces further subdivide System.Drawing into finer groupings.

Many of the .NET Framework namespaces are essential for day-to-day programming. For example, many Visual Basic applications need to produce printouts, so they use the System .Drawing.Printing namespace. Different applications draw graphics or images on the screen, so they need to use other System.Drawing namespaces.

Because so much of the .NET Framework is used in everyday programming tasks, this book doesn't strongly differentiate between Visual Basic and .NET Framework functionality. Presumably, the book could have focused solely on the Visual Basic language and ignored the .NET Framework, but it would have been a much less useful book.

Although the book covers many useful .NET Framework features, there's a huge amount that it doesn't cover. The .NET Framework includes hundreds of namespaces that define a huge number of classes, types, enumerated values, and other paraphernalia.

The following sections describe some of the highest-level and most useful namespaces provided by the .NET Framework.

ROOT NAMESPACES

Initially a Windows application includes two root namespaces: Microsoft and System.

> **NAMESPACES GALORE**
>
> Your program may include references to many other namespaces. If you add references to development libraries, your program will have access to their namespaces. For example, you might have Amazon.com, Google, eBay, and other development toolkits installed, and they come with their own namespaces. Later versions of Windows will also provide namespaces that you may want to reference.
>
> Also note that the My namespace provides shortcuts that make common programming tasks easier. For more information on the My namespace, see the section "My" in Chapter 36, "Configuration and Resources," and Appendix S, "The My Namespace."

The Microsoft Namespace

The Microsoft root namespace contains Microsoft-specific items. In theory, any vendor can implement .NET languages that translate into Intermediate Language (IL) code. If you were to build such a language, the items in the Microsoft namespace would generally not apply to your language. Items in the System namespace described next would be as useful to users of your language as they are to programmers who use the Microsoft languages, but the items in the Microsoft namespace would probably not be as helpful.

The following table describes the most important second-level namespaces contained in the Microsoft root namespace.

NAMESPACE	CONTAINS
Microsoft.Csharp	Items supporting compilation and code generation for C#.
Microsoft.JScript	Items supporting compilation and code generation for JScript.
Microsoft.VisualBasic	Items supporting compilation and code generation for Visual Basic. Some of the items in this namespace are useful to Visual Basic programmers, mostly for compatibility with previous versions of Visual Basic.
Microsoft.Vsa	Items supporting Visual Studio for Applications (VSA), which lets you include scripting in your application.
Microsoft.WindowsCE	Items supporting Pocket PC and Smartphone applications using the .NET Compact Framework.
Microsoft.Win32	Classes that handle operating system events and that manipulate the System Registry.

The System Namespace

The System namespace contains basic classes used to define fundamental data types. It also defines important event handlers, interfaces, and exceptions.

The following table describes the second-level namespaces contained in the System root namespace.

NAMESPACE	CONTAINS
System.CodeDom	Classes for representing and manipulating source-code documents.
System.Collections	Interfaces and classes for defining various collection classes, lists, queues, hash tables, and dictionaries.
System.ComponentModel	Classes that control design time and runtime behavior of components and controls. Defines several useful code attributes such as Description, DefaultEvent, DefaultProperty, and DefaultValue. Also defines some useful classes such as ComponentResourceManager.
System.Configuration	Classes and interfaces for working with configuration files.
System.Data	Mostly classes for ADO.NET (the .NET version of ADO — ActiveX Data Objects). Sub-namespaces include features for specific kinds of databases and database technologies such as SQL Server, Oracle, OLE DB (Object Linking and Embedding), and so forth.
System.Deployment	Classes that let you programmatically update ClickOnce deployments.
System.Diagnostics	Classes for working with system processes, performance counters, and event logs.
System.DirectoryServices	Classes for working with Active Directory.
System.Drawing	Classes for using GDI+ graphics routines to draw two-dimensional graphics, text, and images.
System.EnterpriseServices	Tools for working with COM+ and building enterprise applications.
System.Globalization	Classes that help with internationalization. Includes tools for customizing an application's language and resources, and for using localized formats such as date, currency, and number formats.
System.IO	Classes for reading and writing streams and files.
System.Linq	Classes for LINQ. See Chapter 21, "LINQ," for more information.

continues

(continued)

NAMESPACE	CONTAINS
System.Management	Classes for system management and monitoring.
System.Media	Classes for playing sounds. For example, you can use the following code to play the system's "hand" sound: `System.Media.SystemSounds.Hand.Play()` Example program SystemSounds, which is available for download on the book's web site, uses this namespace to play the system sounds.
System.Messaging	Classes for working with message queues to send and receive messages across the network.
System.Net	Classes for working with network protocols.
System.Reflection	Classes for working with loaded types. A program can use these to learn about classes and their capabilities, and to invoke an object's methods.
System.Resources	Classes to create and manage culture-specific resources programmatically.
System.Runtime	Classes for working with metadata for compilers, interop services (interoperating with unmanaged code), marshalling, remoting, and serialization.
System.Security	Classes for security and cryptography.
System.ServiceProcess	Classes that let you implement, install, and control Windows service processes.
System.Text	Classes representing various character encodings. Also contains the StringBuilder class, which lets you build large strings quickly, and classes for working with regular expressions.
System.Threading	Classes for multithreading.
System.Timers	Timer class.
System.Transactions	Classes for working with transactions involving multiple distributed components and multiphase notifications.
System.Web	Classes for web programming and browser/server interactions.
System.Windows.Forms	Classes that define Windows forms controls (including the Form class itself).
System.Xml	Classes that let you manipulate XML files.

You can find more detailed information on these namespaces on Microsoft's web pages. The URL for a namespace's web page is "msdn.microsoft.com/" followed by the namespace followed by ".aspx" as in:

```
msdn.microsoft.com/system.codedom.aspx
msdn.microsoft.com/system.reflection.aspx
msdn.microsoft.com/system.windows.forms.aspx
```

ADVANCED EXAMPLES

Several chapters in this book cover pieces of the .NET Framework namespaces. For example, Chapter 36 describes many of the most useful tools provided by the System.Globalization and System.Resources namespaces. Similarly, Chapters 30 through 34 explain many of the most useful drawing tools provided by the System.Drawing namespace.

Other parts of the .NET Framework namespaces are quite specialized, and you may never need to use them. For example, many developers can use fairly standard installation techniques, so they will never need to use the System.Deployment classes to programmatically update ClickOnce deployments.

A few namespaces bear some special mention here, however. They are quite useful in many situations but they tend to stand separately rather than fitting nicely into one of the book's major parts such as IDE, Object-Oriented Programming, or Graphics.

The following sections give a few examples that demonstrate some of the more useful of these namespaces.

Regular Expressions

A *regular expression* is a series of symbols that represents a class of strings. A program can use regular expression tools to determine whether a string matches a regular expression or to extract pieces of a string that match an expression. For example, a program can use regular expressions to see if a string has the format of a valid phone number, Social Security number, ZIP code or other postal code, e-mail address, and so forth.

The following regular expression represents a 7- or 10-digit phone number in the United States:

```
^([2-9]\d{2}-)?[2-9]\d{2}-\d{4}$
```

The following table describes the pieces of this expression.

SUBEXPRESSION	MEANING
^	(The caret symbol.) Matches the beginning of the string.
[2-9]	Matches the characters 2 through 9 (United States phone numbers cannot begin with 0 or 1).
\d	Matches any digit 0 through 9.
{2}	Repeats the previous group ([0-9]) exactly two times.

continues

(continued)

SUBEXPRESSION	MEANING
-	Matches a dash.
([2-9]\d{2}-)?	The parentheses group the items inside. The ? matches the previous item exactly zero or one times. Thus the subexpression matches three digits and a dash, all repeated zero or one times.
[2-9]\d{2}-	Matches one digit 2 through 9 followed by two digits 0 through 9 followed by a dash.
\d{4}	Matches any digit exactly four times.
$	Matches the end of the string.

Taken together, this regular expression matches strings of the form NXX-XXXX and NXX-NXX-XXXX where N is a digit 2 through 9 and X is any digit.

A complete discussion of regular expressions is outside the scope of this book. Search the online help or the Microsoft web site to learn about the rules for building regular expressions. The web page msdn.microsoft.com/az24scfc.aspx provides useful links to information about regular expression language elements. Another useful page is www.regexlib.com/RETester.aspx, which provides a regular expression tester and a library of useful regular expressions.

As you read the rest of this section and when visiting regular expression web sites, be aware that there are a couple different types of regular expression languages, which won't all work with every regular expression class.

The following code shows how a program can validate a text field against a regular expression. When the user changes the text in the txtTestExp control, its Changed event handler creates a new Regex object, passing its constructor the regular expression held in the txtRegExp text box. It then calls the Regex object's IsMatch method to see if the text matches the regular expression. If the text matches, the program sets the txtTestExp control's background color to white. If the text doesn't match the expression, the program makes the control's background yellow to indicate an error.

```vb
Private Sub txtTestExp_TextChanged() Handles txtTestExp.TextChanged
    Dim reg_exp As New Regex(txtRegExp.Text)
    If reg_exp.IsMatch(txtTestExp.Text) Then
        txtTestExp.BackColor = Color.White
    Else
        txtTestExp.BackColor = Color.Yellow
    End If
End Sub
```

code snippet RegExValidate

The following example uses a Regex object's Matches method to retrieve a collection of Match objects that describe the places where a string matches a regular expression. It then loops through the collection, highlighting the matches in a Rich Text Box.

```
Private Sub btnGo_Click() Handles btnGo.Click
    Dim reg_exp As New Regex(txtPattern.Text)
    Dim matches As MatchCollection
    matches = reg_exp.Matches(txtTestString.Text)

    rchResults.Text = txtTestString.Text
    For Each a_match As Match In matches
        rchResults.Select(a_match.Index, a_match.Length)
        rchResults.SelectionBackColor = Color.Black
        rchResults.SelectionColor = Color.White
    Next a_match
End Sub
```

code snippet RegExHighlight

In this example, the regular expression is (in|or), so the program finds matches where the string contains in or or.

The following code uses a Regex object to make replacements in a string. It creates a Regex object, passing its constructor the IgnoreCase option to tell the object to ignore capitalization in the string. It then calls the object's Replace method, passing it the string to modify and the pattern that it should use to make the replacement.

```
Dim reg_exp As New Regex(txtPattern.Text, RegexOptions.IgnoreCase)
lblResult.Text = reg_exp.Replace(Me.txtTestString.Text,
txtReplacementPattern.Text)
```

code snippet RegExReplace

The Regex class can perform much more complicated matches. For example, you can use it to find fields within each line in a multiline string and then build a string containing the fields reformatted or reordered. See the online help for more details.

XML

Extensible Markup Language (XML) is a simple language for storing data in a text format. It encloses data within tags that delimit the data. You can give those tags any names that you want. For example, the following text shows an XML file containing three Employee records:

```xml
<?xml version="1.0" encoding="utf-8" standalone="yes"?>
<Employees>
    <Employee>
        <FirstName>Albert</FirstName>
        <LastName>Anders</LastName>
        <EmployeeId>11111</EmployeeId>
    </Employee>
    <Employee>
        <FirstName>Betty</FirstName>
        <LastName>Beach</LastName>
        <EmployeeId>22222</EmployeeId>
    </Employee>
```

```
        <Employee>
            <FirstName>Chuck</FirstName>
            <LastName>Cinder</LastName>
            <EmployeeId>33333</EmployeeId>
        </Employee>
    </Employees>
```

The System.Xml namespace contains classes for reading, writing, and manipulating XML data. Different classes let you process XML files in different ways. For example, the XmlDocument class lets you represent an XML document completely within memory. Using this class, you can perform complex manipulations of an XML file, adding and removing elements, searching for elements with particular attributes, and merging XML documents.

The XmlTextReader and XmlTextWriter classes let you read and write XML data in a fast, forward-only fashion. These classes can be more efficient than XmlDocument when you must quickly build or scan very large XML files that might not easily fit in memory all at once.

The following code shows one way a program can use the System.Xml namespace to generate the previous employee XML file:

```
Private Sub btnGo_Click() Handles btnGo.Click
    Dim xml_text_writer As _
        New XmlTextWriter("employees.xml", System.Text.Encoding.UTF8)

    ' Use indentation to make the result look nice.
    xml_text_writer.Formatting = Formatting.Indented
    xml_text_writer.Indentation = 4

    ' Write the XML declaration.
    xml_text_writer.WriteStartDocument(True)

    ' Start the Employees node.
    xml_text_writer.WriteStartElement("Employees")

    ' Write some Employee elements.
    MakeEmployee(xml_text_writer, "Albert", "Anders", 11111)
    MakeEmployee(xml_text_writer, "Betty", "Beach", 22222)
    MakeEmployee(xml_text_writer, "Chuck", "Cinder", 33333)

    ' End the Employees node.
    xml_text_writer.WriteEndElement()

    ' End the document.
    xml_text_writer.WriteEndDocument()

    ' Close the XmlTextWriter.
    xml_text_writer.Close()
End Sub

' Add an Employee node to the document.
```

```
Private Sub MakeEmployee(ByVal xml_text_writer As XmlTextWriter,
 ByVal first_name As String, ByVal last_name As String,
 ByVal emp_id As Integer)
    ' Start the Employee element.
    xml_text_writer.WriteStartElement("Employee")

    ' Write the FirstName.
    xml_text_writer.WriteStartElement("FirstName")
    xml_text_writer.WriteString(first_name)
    xml_text_writer.WriteEndElement()

    ' Write the LastName.
    xml_text_writer.WriteStartElement("LastName")
    xml_text_writer.WriteString(last_name)
    xml_text_writer.WriteEndElement()

    ' Write the EmployeeId.
    xml_text_writer.WriteStartElement("EmployeeId")
    xml_text_writer.WriteString(emp_id.ToString)
    xml_text_writer.WriteEndElement()

    ' Close the Employee element.
    xml_text_writer.WriteEndElement()
End Sub
```

code snippet BuildMemoryXml

The code starts by creating an XmlTextWriter object. This class provides methods for efficiently writing items into an XML file. The code sets the writer's Formatting and Indentation properties to make the object indent the resulting XML file nicely. If you don't set these properties, the file comes out all run together on a single line. That's fine for programs that process XML files but makes the file hard for humans to read.

The program calls the WriteStartDocument method to write the file's XML declaration, including the XML version, encoding, and standalone attribute. It calls WriteStartElement to write the starting <Employees> XML tag and then calls subroutine MakeEmployee to generate three Employee items. It calls the WriteEndElement method to write the </Employees> end tag, and calls WriteEndDocument to end the document. The program then closes the XmlTextWriter to close the file.

Subroutine MakeEmployee writes a starting <Employee> element into the file. It then uses the WriteStartElement, WriteString, and WriteEndElement methods to add the employee's FirstName, LastName, and EmployeeId elements to the document. The routine finishes by calling WriteEndElement to create the </Employee> end tag.

Other classes within the System.Xml namespace let you load and manipulate XML data in memory, read XML data in a fast forward–only manner, and search XML documents for elements matching certain criteria. XML is quickly becoming a common language that allows unrelated applications to communicate with each other. Using the XML tools provided by the System.Xml namespace, your application can read, write, and manipulate XML data, too.

Cryptography

The System.Security namespace includes objects for performing various cryptographic operations. The four main scenarios supported by these objects include the following:

➤   **Secret-key encryption** — This technique encrypts data so you cannot read it unless you know the secret key. This is also called *symmetric cryptography.*

➤   **Public-key encryption** — This technique encrypts data using a public key that everyone knows. Only the person with a secret private key can read the data. This is useful if you want to be the only one able to read messages anyone sends to you. This is also called *asymmetric cryptography.*

➤   **Signing** — This technique signs data to guarantee that it really came from a specific party. For example, you can sign an executable program to prove that it's really your program and not a virus substituted by some hacker.

➤   **Hashing** — This technique maps a piece of data such as a document into a hash value so it's very unlikely that two different documents will map to the same hash value. If you know a document's hash value, you can later hash the document again and compare the values. If the calculated value matches the previously known value, it is very unlikely that anyone has modified the file since the first hashing.

The example described later in this section encrypts and decrypts files. The basic idea is to create a CryptoStream object attached to a file stream opened for writing. As you write data into the CryptoStream, it encrypts or decrypts the data and sends the result to the output file stream.

Although the classes provided by Visual Studio are easier to use than the routines contained in the underlying cryptography API, the details are still somewhat involved. To encrypt and decrypt files, you must first select an encryption algorithm. You need to pick key and block sizes that are supported by the corresponding encryption provider.

To use an encryption provider, you must pass it a key and initialization vector (IV). Each of these is a series of bytes that the encryption provider uses to initialize its internal state before it encrypts or decrypts files.

If you want to control the encryption with a textual password, you must convert it into a series of bytes that you can use for the key and initialization vector. You can do that with a PasswordDeriveBytes object, but that object also requires the name of the hashing algorithm that it should use to convert the password into the key and initialization vector bytes.

Working through the following example should make this less confusing. Example program AesFile, which is available for download on the book's web site, uses the AES (Advanced Encryption Standard) algorithm to encrypt and decrypt files. The program uses the SHA384 hashing algorithm to convert a text password into key and initialization vector bytes. (For information on AES, see `en.wikipedia.org/wiki/Advanced_Encryption_Standard`. For information on SHA384, see `en.wikipedia.org/wiki/Sha_hash`.)

```vb
' Encrypt or decrypt a file, saving the results
' in another file.
Private Sub CryptFile(ByVal password As String, ByVal in_file As String, _
ByVal out_file As String, ByVal encrypt As Boolean)
    ' Create input and output file streams.
    Dim in_stream As New FileStream(in_file, FileMode.Open, FileAccess.Read)
    Dim out_stream As New FileStream(out_file, FileMode.Create, FileAccess.Write)

    ' Make an AES service provider.
    Dim aes_provider As New AesCryptoServiceProvider()

    ' Find a valid key size for this provider.
    Dim key_size_bits As Integer = 0
    For i As Integer = 1024 To 1 Step -1
        If aes_provider.ValidKeySize(i) Then
            key_size_bits = i
            Exit For
        End If
    Next i
    Debug.Assert(key_size_bits > 0)

    ' Get the block size for this provider.
    Dim block_size_bits As Integer = aes_provider.BlockSize

    ' Generate the key and initialization vector.
    Dim key As Byte() = Nothing
    Dim iv As Byte() = Nothing
    Dim salt As Byte() = {&H0, &H0, &H1, &H2, &H3, &H4, &H5, _
        &H6, &HF1, &HF0, &HEE, &H21, &H22, &H45}
    MakeKeyAndIV(password, salt, key_size_bits, block_size_bits, key, iv)
    ' Make the encryptor or decryptor.
    Dim crypto_transform As ICryptoTransform
    If encrypt Then
        crypto_transform = aes_provider.CreateEncryptor(key, iv)
    Else
        crypto_transform = aes_provider.CreateDecryptor(key, iv)
    End If

    ' Attach a crypto stream to the output stream.
    Dim crypto_stream As New CryptoStream(out_stream, crypto_transform, _
        CryptoStreamMode.Write)

    ' Encrypt or decrypt the file.
    Const BLOCK_SIZE As Integer = 1024
    Dim buffer(BLOCK_SIZE) As Byte
    Dim bytes_read As Integer
    Do
        ' Read some bytes.
        bytes_read = in_stream.Read(buffer, 0, BLOCK_SIZE)
        If bytes_read = 0 Then Exit Do

        ' Write the bytes into the CryptoStream.
        crypto_stream.Write(buffer, 0, bytes_read)
```

```
        Loop

        ' Close the streams.
        crypto_stream.Close()
        in_stream.Close()
        out_stream.Close()
    End Sub

    ' Use the password to generate key bytes.
    Private Sub MakeKeyAndIV(ByVal password As String, ByVal salt() As Byte,
     ByVal key_size_bits As Integer, ByVal block_size_bits As Integer,
     ByRef key As Byte(), ByRef iv As Byte())
        Dim derive_bytes As New Rfc2898DeriveBytes(txtPassword.Text, salt, 1000)

        key = derive_bytes.GetBytes(key_size_bits \ 8)
        iv = derive_bytes.GetBytes(block_size_bits \ 8
    End Sub
```

code snippet AesFile

Subroutine CryptFile encrypts or decrypts a file, saving the result in a new file. It takes as parameters a password string, the names of the input and output files, and a Boolean indicating whether it should perform encryption or decryption.

The routine starts by opening the input and output files. It then makes an AesCryptoServiceProvider object to provide the encryption and decryption algorithms using AES. The program must find a key length that is supported by the encryption service provider. This code counts backward from 1,024 until it finds a value that the provider's ValidKeySize method approves. On my computer, the largest key size the provider supports is 192 bits.

The AES algorithm encrypts data in blocks. The program uses the provider's BlockSize property to see how big those blocks are. The program must generate an initialization vector that has this same size.

The program calls the MakeKeyAndIV subroutine. This routine, which is described shortly, converts a text password into arrays of bytes for use as the key and initialization vector. The salt array contains a series of random bytes to make guessing the password harder for an attacker. The Rfc2898DeriveBytes class used by subroutine MakeKeyAndIV can generate a random salt for the program, but this example uses a salt array written into the code to make reading the code easier.

After obtaining the key and initialization vector, the program makes an object to perform the encryption or decryption transformation, depending on whether the subroutine's encrypt parameter is True or False. The program uses the encryption provider's CreateEncryptor or CreateDecryptor method, passing it the key and initialization vector.

Now, the program makes a CryptoStream object attached to its output file stream. It passes the object's constructor and output file stream, the cryptographic transformation object, and a flag indicating that the program will write to the stream.

At this point, the program has set the stage and can finally begin processing data. It allocates a buffer to hold data and then enters a Do loop. In the loop, it reads data from the input file into the buffer. If it reads no bytes, the program has reached the end of the input file, so it exits the loop. If it reads some bytes, the program writes them into the CryptoStream. The CryptoStream uses its cryptographic transformation object to encrypt or decrypt the data and sends the result to its attached output file stream.

When it has finished processing the input file, the subroutine closes its streams.

Subroutine MakeKeyAndIV uses a text password to generate arrays of bytes to use as a key and initialization vector. It begins by creating an Rfc2898DeriveBytes object, passing to its constructor the password text, the salt, and the number of iterations the object should use to generate the random bytes. The salt can be any array of bytes as long as it's the same when encrypting and decrypting the file. The salt makes it harder for an attacker to build a dictionary of key and initialization vector values for every possible password string.

Having built the PasswordDeriveBytes object, the subroutine calls its GetBytes method to get the proper number of bytes for the key and initialization vector.

HOW EASY WAS THAT?

Previous editions of this book used the triple DES (Data Encryption Standard) algorithm to encrypt and decrypt files. However, DES is an old standard and cryptographers now recommend using AES instead.

The only thing I had to do to update this example was change the single statement that created the cryptographic service provider to

```
Dim aes_provider As New AesCryptoServiceProvider()
```

For clarity I also renamed the provider variable from des_provider to aes_provider but the update really only required changing a single statement. Setting up and using the cryptographic library takes a bit of work but the pieces are fairly interchangeable so switching algorithms is easy.

(Both the original program DesFile and new program AesFile are available for download on the book's web site.)

The following code uses the CryptFile subroutine to encrypt and then decrypt a file. First it calls CryptFile, passing it a password, input and output file names, and the value True to indicate that the routine should encrypt the file. Next, the code calls CryptFile again, this time to decrypt the encrypted file.

```
' Encrypt the file.
CryptFile(txtPassword.Text, txtPlaintextFile.Text, txtCyphertextFile.Text, True)

' Decrypt the file.
CryptFile(txtPassword.Text, txtCyphertextFile.Text, txtDecypheredFile.Text, False)
```

The DesFile example program, which is available for download on the book's web site, demonstrates the CryptFile subroutine. Enter some text and a password, and then click the left > button to encrypt the file. Click the right > button to decrypt the encrypted file and see if it matches the original text.

If you change the password by even a single character, the decryption returns gibberish. Figure 39-1 shows the program trying to decrypt a message incorrectly. Before the program tried to decrypt the file, I added an "s" to the end of the password. The result is completely unreadable.

FIGURE 39-1: Changing even a single character in the password makes decryption produce an unintelligible result.

See the online help for information about the other main cryptographic operations (secret-key encryption, public-key encryption, signing, and hashing). Other books may also provide additional insights into cryptography. For example, the book *Applied Cryptography: Protocols, Algorithms, and Source Code in C, Second Edition* (Schneier, Wiley Publishing, Inc., 1996) provides an excellent overview of modern cryptography and describes many important algorithms in detail. *Practical Cryptography* (Ferguson and Schneier, Wiley, 2003) provides a higher level executive summary of the algorithms and how to use them without covering implementation details. *Cryptography for Dummies* (Cobb, For Dummies, 2004) provides another high-level introduction to basic cryptographic concepts such as hashing and public key encryption.

Reflection

Reflection lets a program learn about itself and other programming entities. It includes objects that tell the program about assemblies, modules, and types.

Example program ReflectionFormProperties uses the following code to examine the program's form and display a list of its properties, their types, and their values:

```
Private Sub Form1_Load() Handles MyBase.Load
    ' Make column headers.
    lvwProperties.View = View.Details
    lvwProperties.Columns.Clear()
    lvwProperties.Columns.Add("Property", 10,
        HorizontalAlignment.Left)
    lvwProperties.Columns.Add("Type", 10,
        HorizontalAlignment.Left)
    lvwProperties.Columns.Add("Value", 10,
        HorizontalAlignment.Left)

    ' List the properties.
    Dim property_value As Object
    Dim properties_info As PropertyInfo() =
        GetType(Form1).GetProperties()
```

```
        lvwProperties.Items.Clear()
        For i As Integer = 0 To properties_info.Length - 1
            With properties_info(i)
                If .GetIndexParameters().Length = 0 Then
                    property_value = .GetValue(Me, Nothing)
                    If property_value Is Nothing Then
                        ListViewMakeRow(lvwProperties,
                            .Name,
                            .PropertyType.ToString,
                            " < Nothing > ")
                    Else
                        ListViewMakeRow(lvwProperties,
                            .Name,
                            .PropertyType.ToString,
                          property_value.ToString)
                    End If
                Else
                    ListViewMakeRow(lvwProperties,
                        .Name,
                        .PropertyType.ToString,
                        " < array > ")
                End If
            End With
        Next i

        ' Size the columns to fit the data.
        lvwProperties.Columns(0).Width = -2
        lvwProperties.Columns(1).Width = -2
        lvwProperties.Columns(2).Width = -2
    End Sub

    ' Make a ListView row.
    Private Sub ListViewMakeRow(ByVal lvw As ListView,
     ByVal item_title As String, ByVal ParamArray subitem_titles() As String)
        ' Make the item.
        Dim new_item As ListViewItem = lvw.Items.Add(item_title)

        ' Make the subitems.
        For i As Integer = subitem_titles.GetLowerBound(0) To _
         subitem_titles.GetUpperBound(0)
            new_item.SubItems.Add(subitem_titles(i))
        Next i
    End Sub
```

code snippet ReflectionFormProperties

The program starts by formatting the ListView control named lvwProperties. Next, it defines an array of PropertyInfo objects named properties_info. It uses GetType to get type information about the Form1 class and then uses the type's GetProperties method to get information about the properties. The program then loops through the PropertyInfo objects.

If the object's GetIndexParameters array contains no entries, the property is not an array. In that case, the program uses the PropertyInfo object's GetValue method to get the property's value. The code then displays the property's name, type, and value.

If the PropertyInfo object's GetIndexParameters array contains entries, the property is an array. In that case, the program displays the property's name and type, and the string <array>.

The subroutine finishes by sizing the ListView control's columns and then making the form fit the columns.

The helper subroutine ListViewMakeRow adds a row of values to the ListView control. It adds a new item to the control and then adds subitems to the item. The item appears in the control's first column and the subitems appear in the other columns.

Using reflection to learn about your application is interesting, but not always necessary. After all, if you build an object, you probably know what its properties are.

Reflection can also tell you a lot about other applications. The ReflectionGetResources example program uses the following code to learn about another application. This program reads the assembly information in a file (example ReflectionHasResources is a resource-only DLL that this program can examine) and lists the embedded resources that it contains. The user can then select a resource to view it.

```vb
Private m_TargetAssembly As Assembly

' List the target assembly's resources.
Private Sub btnList_Click() Handles btnList.Click
    ' Get the target assembly.
    m_TargetAssembly = Assembly.LoadFile(txtFile.Text)

    ' List the target's manifest resource names.
    lstResourceFiles.Items.Clear()
    For Each str As String In m_TargetAssembly.GetManifestResourceNames()
        lstResourceFiles.Items.Add(str)
    Next str
End Sub

' List this file's resources.
Private Sub lstResourceFiles_SelectedIndexChanged()
 Handles lstResourceFiles.SelectedIndexChanged
    lstResources.Items.Clear()

    Dim resource_reader As ResourceReader
    resource_reader = New ResourceReader(
        m_TargetAssembly.GetManifestResourceStream(lstResourceFiles.Text))
    Dim dict_enumerator As IDictionaryEnumerator =
        resource_reader.GetEnumerator()
    While dict_enumerator.MoveNext()
        lstResources.Items.Add(New ResourceInfo(
            dict_enumerator.Key,
            dict_enumerator.Value))
    End While
    resource_reader.Close()
End Sub
```

```
' Display the selected resource.
Private Sub lstResources_SelectedIndexChanged() _
 Handles lstResources.SelectedIndexChanged
    lblString.Text = ""
    picImage.Image = Nothing
    Me.Cursor = Cursors.WaitCursor
    Refresh()

    Dim resource_info As ResourceInfo =
        DirectCast(lstResources.SelectedItem, ResourceInfo)
    Select Case resource_info.Value.GetType.Name
        Case "Bitmap"
            picImage.Image = CType(resource_info.Value, Bitmap)
            lblString.Text = ""
        Case "String"
            picImage.Image = Nothing
            lblString.Text = CType(resource_info.Value, String)
        Case Else
            ' Try to play it as audio.
            Try
                My.Computer.Audio.Play(resource_info.Value,
                    AudioPlayMode.WaitToComplete)
            Catch ex As Exception
                MessageBox.Show(resource_info.Key &
                    " has an unkown resource type",
                    "Unknown Resource Type", MessageBoxButtons.OK)
            End Try
    End Select

    Me.Cursor = Cursors.Default
End Sub

Private Class ResourceInfo
    Public Key As Object
    Public Value As Object
    Public Sub New(ByVal new_key As Object, ByVal new_value As Object)
        Key = new_key
        Value = new_value
    End Sub
    Public Overrides Function ToString() As String
        Return Key.ToString & " (" & Value.ToString & ")"
    End Function
End Class
```

code snippet ReflectionGetResources

The user enters the name of the assembly to load the txtFile text box. For example, this can be the name of a .NET executable program.

When the user clicks the List button, the btnList_Click event handler uses the Assembly class's shared LoadFile method to load an Assembly object representing the indicated assembly. It then loops through the array of strings returned by the Assembly object's GetManifestResourceNames method, adding the resource file names to the ListBox named lstResourceFiles.

When the user selects a resource file from the list, the lstResourceFiles_SelectedIndexChanged event handler displays a list of resources in the file. It uses the Assembly object's GetManifestResourceStream method to get a stream for the resources. It uses the stream to make a ResourceReader object and then enumerates the items found by the ResourceReader. It saves each object in a new ResourceInfo object (this class is described shortly) and adds it to the lstResources list.

When the user selects a resource from lstResources, its SelectedIndexChanged event handler retrieves the selected ResourceInfo object, converts its Value property into an appropriate data type, and displays the result. The ResourceInfo class stores Key and Value information for a resource enumerated by a ResourceReader object's enumerator. It provides an overloaded ToString that the lstResources list uses to represent the items.

This is admittedly a fairly complex example, but it performs the fairly remarkable feat of pulling resources out of another compile application.

Reflection can provide a lot of information about applications, modules, types, methods, properties, events, parameters, and so forth. It lets a program discover and invoke methods at runtime and build types at runtime.

An application also uses reflection indirectly when it performs such actions as serialization, which uses reflection to learn how to serialize and deserialize objects.

Reflection is a very advanced and somewhat arcane topic, but it is extremely powerful.

TPL

The *Task Parallel Library*, or *TPL*, is a set of tools that make building parallel programs easier. It provides a set of relatively simple method calls that launch multiple routines simultaneously on whatever processors are available.

Not long ago, only supercomputers contained multiple processing units, so only they could truly perform more than one task at the same time. Desktop operating systems switched rapidly back and forth between applications so it appeared as if the computer was performing a lot of tasks simultaneously, but in fact it was only doing one thing at a time.

More recently multi-processor computers are becoming quite common and relatively inexpensive. Practically any computer vendor sells computers with two or four processors. Soon it's likely that you'll be able to buy affordable computers with 8, 16, or possibly even dozens of processors.

The operating system can use some of this extra computing power transparently to make your system run more quickly, but if you have a computationally intensive application that hogs the processor, you must take special action if you want to get the full benefits of all of your processors.

To improve performance, you can launch multiple *threads of execution* to perform different tasks. If you run the threads on separate processors, they can do their work at the same time.

Unfortunately, writing safe and effective multi-threaded applications can be tricky. If you do it wrong, the threads will interfere with each other, possibly making the application crash or even take longer than it would on a single thread.

TPL is intended to make writing safe and effective multi-threaded applications easier. The TPL methods are lightweight and don't add too much overhead to an application so, if you need to perform several tasks at once and you have multiple processors available, your program will probably run faster. TPL overhead is fairly low, so even if you run the program on a single-processor system, you don't pay a huge penalty for trying to use multiple threads.

Getting Started

TPL is part of the System.Threading namespace. To make working with the namespace easier, you can add the following Imports statement at the top of your program files.

```
Imports System.Threading.Tasks
```

Now you're ready to use TPL. The following sections describe some of the most useful TPL methods: Parallel.Invoke, Parallel.For, and Parallel.ForEach.

Parallel.Invoke

The Parallel class contains methods for launching parallel threads. The Parallel.Invoke takes as parameters a series of System.Action objects that give it information about the tasks it should launch.

The System.Action class is actually just a named delegate representing a subroutine that takes no parameters so you can use the address of any subroutine.

Example program ParallelInvoke shown in Figure 39-2 demonstrates the Parallel.Invoke method. As you can see, the parallel version was significantly faster on my dual-core system.

The following code shows how program ParallelInvoke uses Parallel.Invoke:

```
Parallel.Invoke(
    AddressOf Fibonacci0,
    AddressOf Fibonacci1,
    AddressOf Fibonacci2,
    AddressOf Fibonacci3)
```

FIGURE 39-2: Parallel.Invoke runs several subroutines on multiple threads.

The four Fibonacci routines simply evaluate the Fibonacci number for various values. For example, the Fibonacci0 function shown in the following code gets the first text box's value stored in the Numbers array, calls the Fibonacci function, and saves the result in the Results array.

```
Private Sub Fibonacci0()
    Results(0) = Fibonacci(Numbers(0))
End Sub
```

FIBONACCI FUN

The Fibonacci sequence is defined recursively by Fibonacci(0) = 1, Fibonacci(1) = 1, and for larger values of N Fibonacci(N) = Fibonacci(N − 1) + Fibonacci(N − 2). The first 10 values are 1, 1, 2, 3, 5, 8, 13, 21, 34, 55, and 89.

The function grows fairly quickly so, as you can see in Figure 39-2, Fibonacci(36) = 24,157,817.

More importantly for this example is the fact that the recursive definition is an inefficient way to calculate Fibonacci numbers. To see why, consider that calculating Fibonacci(N) requires calculating Fibonacci(N − 1) and Fibonacci (N − 2). But calculating Fibonacci(N − 1) also requires calculating Fibonacci (N − 2), so that value is calculated twice. During the course of a calculation, intermediate values are calculated a huge number of times so the code takes a while and the example has some nice long routines to parallelize.

The following code shows the Fibonacci function.

```
Private Function Fibonacci(ByVal N As Long) As Long
    If N <= 1 Then Return 1

    Return Fibonacci(N - 1) + Fibonacci(N - 2)
End Function
```

Before calling ParallelInvoke, this example stores the values N in an array. Each of the routines looks only at its array entry and places its result in its own separate variable, which is also stored in an array. That means the routines never read or write each other's values. This is important because parallel routines that work with the same variables may interfere with each other.

For example, suppose one routine sets a variable's value to 10 and another routine sets the same variable's value to 20. If the routines are running at the same time, you can't tell which routine gets there first, so you don't know what value the variable holds at the end.

The following list summarizes some of the details you need to consider when working with multiple threads:

➤ Two threads trying to access the same variables can interfere with each other.

➤ Two threads trying to lock several shared resources can form a deadlock where neither can continue until the other finishes.

➤ Parallel threads cannot directly access the user interface thread, so they cannot safely use control properties.

➤ Some classes are not "thread-safe" so you cannot safely use them in multiple threads at the same time.

As long as separate threads use only their own variables and don't try to interact with the user interface thread, Parallel.Invoke is remarkably easy to use.

Parallel.For

The Parallel.For method lets you invoke a single subroutine while passing it a series of numeric values.

Example program ParallelFor performs calculations similar to those performed by program Parallel. Invoke except it uses the Parallel.For method.

This version calls the FindFibonacci subroutine shown in the following code:

```
Private Sub FindFibonacci(ByVal index As Integer)
    Results(index) = Fibonacci(Numbers(index))
End Sub
```

The index parameter tells which entry in the Numbers array is the Fibonacci number that the routine should calculate. The Numbers array holds the numbers entered in the text boxes shown in Figure 39-2. The code calls the Fibonacci function and saves the results in the Results array.

The following code shows how the program calls subroutine FindFibonacci sequentially, passing it the values 0 through 3:

```
For i As Integer = 0 To 3
    FindFibonacci(i)
Next i
```

The program uses the following code to make the same subroutine calls in parallel:

```
    Parallel.For(0, 3, AddressOf FindFibonacci)
```
The results of the two calculations are the same but the parallel version takes only about 41% as long on my dual-core system.

Parallel.For is most useful when you need to call a routine many times with different numeric inputs.

Parallel.ForEach

As you may be able to guess, the Parallel.ForEach method is similar to Parallel.For except it passes a series of objects from a collection into the subroutine instead of a series of sequential values.

Example program ParallelForEach performs the same Fibonacci calculations as the previous examples except it uses the Parallel.ForEach method. The following code shows the FiboInfo class that it passes in the parallel subroutine calls:

```
Private Class FiboInfo
    Public N As Long
    Public Result As Long
End Class
```

The following code shows the new FindFibonacci subroutine. The FiboInfo parameter both tells the routine which Fibonacci number to calculate and holds the result.

```
Private Sub FindFibonacci(ByVal fibo_info As FiboInfo)
    fibo_info.Result = Fibonacci(fibo_info.N)
End Sub
```

The following code shows the key parallel pieces of example program ParallelForEach. This code first initializes the fibo_info array and then uses Parallel.ForEach to pass its values to different calls to subroutine FindFibonacci.

```
Dim fibo_info() As FiboInfo = {
    New FiboInfo() With {.N = CLng(txtNum0.Text)},
    New FiboInfo() With {.N = CLng(txtNum1.Text)},
    New FiboInfo() With {.N = CLng(txtNum2.Text)},
    New FiboInfo() With {.N = CLng(txtNum3.Text)}
}

Parallel.ForEach(fibo_info, AddressOf FindFibonacci)
```

Once again, the results are the same as in the previous examples, but the parallel version takes less time than the sequential version.

There are still plenty of TPL details that I don't have room to cover here. The library provides other classes and methods for executing tasks in parallel and there are many ways you can coordinate among different threads. For more information on TPL, search the Web for articles such as these two of mine posted by DevX.com:

➤ Getting Started with the .NET Task Parallel Library (www.devx .com/dotnet/Article/39204)

➤ Getting Started with the .NET Task Parallel Library: Multi-Core Case Studies (www.devx .com/dotnet/Article/39219)

These articles contain more detailed information and other examples.

SUMMARY

The .NET Framework defines hundreds of namespaces, and this chapter described only a few. It provided a brief overview of some of the most important System namespaces and gave more detailed examples that demonstrated regular expressions, XML, cryptography, reflection, and TPL.

Even in these somewhat specialized areas, the examples can cover only a tiny fraction of the capabilities of the namespaces; however, the examples should give you an idea of the types of features that these namespaces can add to your application. If you need to do something similar, they will hopefully inspire you to do more in-depth research so that you can take full advantage of these powerful tools.

The chapters in this book cover a wide variety of Visual Basic programming topics. In the first part of the book, Chapters 1 through 7 describe the Visual Studio integrated development environment and many of the tools that you use to build Visual Basic programs. In the second part of the book, Chapters 8 through 24 explained basic topics of Visual Basic programming (such as the language itself, using standard controls, and drag and drop). In the third part of the book, Chapters 25 through 29 describe object-oriented concepts (such as class and structure declaration, namespaces, and generics). In the fourth part of the book, Chapters 30 through 35 cover graphical topics (such as how to draw shapes and text, image manipulation, printing, and report generation). In the fifth part of the book, Chapters 36 through 40 explain ways a program can interact with its environment by using techniques such as configuration files, the Registry, streams, and file-system objects.

The rest of this book contains appendices that provide a categorized reference for Visual Basic .NET. You can use them to review quickly the syntax of a particular command, select from among several overloaded versions of a routine, or refresh your memory of what a particular class can do.

PART VI
Appendices

▶ **APPENDIX O: Useful Exception Classes**

▶ **APPENDIX P: Date and Time Format Specifiers**

▶ **APPENDIX Q: Other Format Specifiers**

▶ **APPENDIX R: The Application Class**

▶ **APPENDIX S: The My Namespace**

▶ **APPENDIX T: Streams**

▶ **APPENDIX U: File-System Classes**

▶ **APPENDIX V: Index of Examples**

Useful Control Properties, Methods, and Events

A control interacts with a program or the user through properties, methods, and events. Although each type of control provides different features, they are all derived from the Control class. This class provides many useful properties, methods, and events that other controls inherit, if they don't take special action to override them. The following sections describe some of the most useful of these inherited features.

> **CLASSY CONTROLS**
>
> You can learn more about the Control class at msdn.microsoft.com/system .windows.forms.control.aspx.

PROPERTIES

The following table lists properties implemented by the Control class. All controls that inherit from this class inherit these properties unless they override the Control class's behavior.

PROPERTY	PURPOSE
AllowDrop	Determines whether the control allows drag-and-drop operations.
Anchor	Determines which of the control's edges are anchored to the edges of the control's container.
AutoSize	Determines whether the control automatically resizes to fit its contents.

continues

(continued)

PROPERTY	PURPOSE
BackColor	Determines the control's background color.
BackgroundImage	Determines the control's background image.
BackgroundImageLayout	Determines how the control's background image is used to fill the control. This can be Center, None, Tile, Stretch, and Zoom.
Bottom	Returns the distance between the top edge of the control's container and the bottom edge of the control. This is read-only. Modify the Top and Height properties to change this value.
Bounds	Determines the control's size and location, including nonclient areas.
CanFocus	Determines whether the control can receive the input focus. See also the Focus method.
CanSelect	Determines whether the control can select. For example, a TextBox can select some or all of its text. See also the Select method.
Capture	Determines whether the control has captured the mouse.
CausesValidation	Determines whether the control makes other controls validate when it receives the focus.
ClientRectangle	This Rectangle structure represents the control's client area.
ClientSize	This Size structure represents the control's height and width.
ContainsFocus	Indicates whether the control or one of its child controls has the input focus. This is read-only.
ContextMenu	Determines the context menu associated with the control.
ContextMenuStrip	Determines the context menu strip associated with the control.
Controls	This collection contains references to the controls contained within this control.
Cursor	Determines the cursor that the control displays when the mouse is over it.
DataBindings	Gets the control's DataBindings, used to bind the control to a data source.
DefaultBackColor	Returns the control's default background color.
DefaultFont	Returns the control's default font.
DefaultForeColor	Returns the control's default foreground color.

PROPERTY	PURPOSE
DisplayRectangle	Returns a Rectangle structure giving the control's display area. Figure A-1 shows two GroupBoxes with the same size. The GroupBox on the right contains two labels that cover its ClientRectangle and DisplayRectangle.
Dock	Determines the edge of the control's parent to which the control is docked.
Enabled	Determines whether the control will interact with the user.
Focused	Indicates whether the control has the input focus. This is read-only.
Font	Determines the control's font.
ForeColor	Determines the control's foreground color.
Handle	Returns the control's window handle. This is read-only.
HasChildren	Indicates whether the control holds any child controls. This is read-only. Also see the Controls property.
Height	Determines the control's height.
InvokeRequired	Returns True if the calling code is running on a thread different from the control's thread and therefore must use an invoke method to interact with the control.
Left	Determines the X coordinate of the control's left edge.
Location	This Point structure determines the position of the control's upper-left corner.
Margin	Determines the spacing between this control and another control's margin within an arranging container.
MaximumSize	Determines the control's largest allowed size.
MinimumSize	Determines the control's smallest allowed size.
ModifierKeys	Indicates what modifier keys (Shift, Ctrl, and Alt) are pressed. This is read-only.
MouseButtons	Indicates what mouse buttons (Left, Right, Middle, None) are pressed. This is read-only.
MousePosition	Returns a Point structure giving the mouse's current position in screen coordinates (the point (0, 0) is in the screen's upper-left corner). This is read-only.
Name	Determines the control's name.

continues

(continued)

PROPERTY	PURPOSE
Padding	Determines the spacing of the control's contents.
Parent	Determines the parent containing the control.
PreferredSize	Returns a size that is big enough to hold the control's contents.
Region	Determines the control's window region. This is the area in which the control may draw.
Right	Returns the distance between the left edge of the control's container and the right edge of the control. This is read-only. Modify the Left and Width properties to change this value.
Size	This Size structure determines the control's size including client and nonclient areas.
TabIndex	Determines the control's position in its container's tab order. If more than one control has the same TabIndex, they are traversed front to back using the stacking order.
TabStop	Determines whether the user can tab to the control.
Tag	This property can hold an object that you want to associate with the control.
Text	Determines the control's text.
Top	Determines the Y coordinate of the control's top edge.
TopLevelControl	Returns the control's top-level ancestor. Usually that is the outermost Form containing the control. This is read-only.
Visible	Determines whether the control is visible.
Width	Determines the control's width.

FIGURE A-1 The DisplayRectangle property gives the area in which you should normally place items within a control.

METHODS

The following table lists useful methods implemented by the Control class. All controls that inherit from this class inherit these properties unless they override the Control class's behavior.

> **WATCH WRAPPING**
>
> Many of the entries in the Method column wrap across multiple lines. In Visual Basic code, each would be all on a single line.

METHOD	PURPOSE
`Sub BringToFront()`	Brings the control to the front of the stacking order.
`Function Contains(ByVal child As Control) As Boolean`	Returns True if the control child is contained by this control.
`Function CreateGraphics() As Graphic`	Creates a Graphic object that you can use to draw on the control's surface.
`Function DoDragDrop(ByVal dragging_ object As Object, ByVal allowed_ effects As DragDropEffects)`	Starts a drag-and-drop operation.
`Sub DrawToBitmap(ByVal bm As Bitmap, ByVal rect As Rectangle)`	Draws an image of the control including contained controls onto the Bitmap in the indicated Rectangle.
`Function FindForm() As Form`	Returns the Form that contains this control.
`Function Focus() As Boolean`	Gives the control the input focus.
`Function GetChildAtPoint (ByVal pt As Point) As Control`	Returns the control's child that contains the indicated point. If more than one control contains the point, the method returns the control that is higher in the stacking order.
`Function GetNextControl (ByVal ctl As Control, ByVal next As Boolean) As Control`	If next is True, returns the next control in the tab order of this control's children after control ctl. If next is False, returns the previous control in the tab order. Set ctl=Nothing to start from the start/end of the tab order. Returns Nothing when you reach the start/end.
`Function GetPreferredSize (ByVal proposed_size) As Size`	Returns a size that is big enough to hold the control's contents.
`Function GetType() As Type`	Returns a Type object representing the control's class. You can use this object to get information about the class.

continues

(continued)

METHOD	PURPOSE
`Sub Hide()`	Hides the control by setting its Visible property to False.
`Sub Invalidate()`	Invalidates some or all of the control and sends it a Paint event so that it redraws itself.
`Sub Invoke(ByVal delegate As Delegate)`	Invokes a delegate on the thread that owns the control.
`Function PointToClient (ByVal screen_point Point) As Point`	Converts a Point in screen coordinates into the control's coordinate system.
`Function PointToScreen (ByVal control_point As Point) As Point`	Converts a Point in control coordinates into the screen coordinate system.
`Function RectangleToClient (ByVal screen_rect As Rectangle) As Rectangle`	Converts a Rectangle in screen coordinates into the control's coordinate system.
`Function RectangleToScreen (ByVal control_rect As Rectangle) As Rectangle`	Converts a Rectangle in control coordinates into the screen coordinate system.
`Sub Refresh()`	Invalidates the control's client area, so the control redraws itself and its child controls.
`Sub ResetBackColor()`	Resets the control's background color to its default value.
`Sub ResetCursor()`	Resets the control's cursor to its default value.
`Sub ResetFont()`	Resets the control's font to its default value.
`Sub ResetForeColor()`	Resets the control's foreground color to its default value.
`Sub ResetText()`	Resets the control's text to its default value.
`Sub Scale(ByVal scale_factor As Single)`	Scales the control and any contained controls by multiplying the Left, Top, Width, and Height properties by scale_factor.
`Sub Select()`	Moves the input focus to the control. Some controls have overloaded versions.
`Function SelectNextControl (ByVal ctl As Control, ByVal forward As Boolean, ByVal tab_stop_only As Boolean, ByVal include_nested As Boolean, ByVal wrap As Boolean) As Boolean`	Moves the input focus to the next control contained within this one.

METHOD	PURPOSE
Sub SendToBack()	Sends the control to the back of the stacking order.
Sub SetBounds(ByVal x As Integer, ByVal y As Integer, ByVal width As Integer, ByVal height As Integer)	Sets the control's position and size.
Sub Show()	Displays the control by setting its Visible property to True.
Function ToString() As String	Returns a textual representation of the control. This is generally the type of the control followed by its most commonly used property.
Sub Update()	Makes the control redraw any invalidated areas.

EVENTS

The following table lists useful events implemented by the Control class. All controls that inherit from this class inherit these properties unless they override the Control class's behavior.

EVENT	PURPOSE
AutoSizeChanged	Occurs when the control's AutoSize property changes.
BackColorChanged	Occurs when the control's BackColor property changes.
BackgroundImageChanged	Occurs when the control's BackgroundImage property changes.
BackgroundImageLayoutChanged	Occurs when the control's BackgroundImageLayout property changes.
Click	Occurs when the user clicks the control. This event is at a higher logical level than the MouseClick event, and it can be triggered by other actions than a mouse click (such as pressing the Enter key or a shortcut key).
ContextMenuChanged	Occurs when the control's ContextMenu property changes.
ContextMenuStripChanged	Occurs when the control's ContextMenuStrip property changes.
ControlAdded	Occurs when a new control is added to the control's contained child controls.

continues

(continued)

EVENT	PURPOSE
ControlRemoved	Occurs when a control is removed from the control's contained child controls.
CursorChanged	Occurs when the control's Cursor property changes.
DockChanged	Occurs when the control's Dock property changes.
DoubleClick	Occurs when the user double-clicks the control.
DragDrop	Occurs when the user drops something on the control in a drag-and-drop operation. This event handler should process the dropped information appropriately.
DragEnter	Occurs when the user drags something over the control in a drag-and-drop operation.
DragLeave	Occurs when the user drags something off of the control in a drag-and-drop operation.
DragOver	Occurs when the user has dragged something over the control in a drag-and-drop operation. This event fires repeatedly until the user drags off of the control, drops on the control, or cancels the drop.
EnabledChanged	Occurs when the control's Enabled property changes.
Enter	Occurs when the control is entered. This event fires before the GotFocus event.
FontChanged	Occurs when the control's Font property changes.
ForeColorChanged	Occurs when the control's ForeColor property changes.
GiveFeedback	Occurs during a drag-and-drop operation to let the drag source control take action.
GotFocus	Occurs when the control receives the input focus. This event fires after the Enter event. Generally, the Enter event is preferred.
HelpRequested	Occurs when the user requests help for the control. For example, if the user moves the focus to a TextBox and presses F1, the TextBox raises this event.
Invalidated	Occurs when part of the control is invalidated.
KeyDown	Occurs when the user presses a key while the control has the input focus.

EVENT	PURPOSE
KeyPress	Occurs when the user presses and releases a key while the control has the input focus.
KeyUp	Occurs when the user releases a key while the control has the input focus.
Layout	Occurs when the control should arrange its child controls. This event occurs before the Resize and SizeChanged events and is preferred for arranging child controls.
Leave	Occurs when the input focus leaves the control. This event fires before the LostFocus event.
LocationChanged	Occurs when the control's Location property changes. This event fires after the Move event fires.
LostFocus	Occurs when the input focus leaves the control. This event fires after the Leave event. Generally, the Leave event is preferred.
MarginChanged	Occurs when the control's Margin property changes.
MouseCaptureChanged	Occurs when the control loses a mouse capture.
MouseClick	Occurs when the user clicks the mouse on the control.
MouseDoubleClick	Occurs when the user double-clicks the mouse on the control.
MouseDown	Occurs when the user presses a mouse button down over the control.
MouseEnter	Occurs when the mouse enters the control.
MouseHover	Occurs when the mouse hovers over the control.
MouseLeave	Occurs when the mouse leaves the control.
MouseMove	Occurs when the mouse moves over the control.
MouseUp	Occurs when the user releases a mouse button over the control.
MouseWheel	Occurs when the user moves the mouse wheel while the control has the input focus.
Move	Occurs when the control is moved. This event fires before the LocationChanged event fires.

continues

(continued)

EVENT	PURPOSE
PaddingChanged	Occurs when the control's Padding property changes.
Paint	Occurs when the control must redraw itself. Normally the program draws on the control during this event (if it draws on the control at all).
ParentChanged	Occurs when the control's Parent property changes.
QueryContinueDrag	Occurs when something changes during a drag-and-drop operation so that the drag source can decide whether to modify or cancel the drag.
RegionChanged	Occurs when the control's Region property changes.
Resize	Occurs while the control is resizing. This event occurs after the Layout event, but before the SizeChanged event.
SizeChanged	Occurs while the control is resizing. This event occurs after the Layout and Move events.
SystemColorsChanged	Occurs when the system colors change. For instance, you might want to draw something using the same color that the operating system uses for active forms. If the user changes the system's color for borders, you can use this event to update your application.
TabIndexChanged	Occurs when the control's TabIndex property changes.
TabStopChanged	Occurs when the control's TabStop property changes.
TextChanged	Occurs when the control's Text property changes.
Validated	Occurs when the control has successfully finished validating its data.
Validating	Occurs when the control should validate its data.
VisibleChanged	Occurs when the control's Visible property changes.

EVENT SEQUENCES

Several situations generate a series of events in a precise order.

UNDERSTANDING EVENTS

There are a couple ways you can discover event sequences such as these. One is to place Debug.WriteLine statements in the event handlers so that you can see the events as they occur. Another method is to use the Spy++ tool to track events. For more information on that technique, see the article "Working with Windows Messages in .NET" by John Mueller at `www.devsource.com/article2/0,1895,1961574,00.asp`.

Mouse Events

When you click a control, the following events are raised in the order shown. The first instance of the MouseMove event can occur any number of times if you move the mouse while holding the mouse button down. The final MouseMove event occurs whether or not you move the mouse.

```
MouseDown

    [MouseMove]

Click

MouseClick

MouseUp

MouseCaptureChanged

MouseMove
```

When you double-click a control, the following events are raised in the order shown:

```
MouseDown

    [MouseMove]

Click

MouseClick

MouseUp

MouseCaptureChanged

MouseMove

MouseDown

DoubleClick

MouseDoubleClick

MouseUp

MouseCaptureChanged

MouseMove
```

Resize Events

When you resize a control, the following events are raised in this order. These events are repeated as long as you are resizing the control.

```
Layout

Resize

SizeChanged
```

Form controls also provide ResizeBegin and ResizeEnd events that occur before and after the other events, respectively.

Move Events

When you move a control, the following events are raised in this order. These events are repeated as long as you are moving the control.

```
Move

LocationChanged
```

Form controls also provide ResizeBegin and ResizeEnd events that occur before and after the other events, respectively.

Variable Declarations and Data Types

This appendix provides information about variable declarations and data types.

VARIABLE DECLARATIONS

The following code shows a standard variable declaration:

```
[attribute_list] [accessibility] [Shared] [Shadows] [ReadOnly] _
Dim [WithEvents] name[?] [(bounds_list)] [As [New] type[?]] _
[= initialization_expression]
```

The following list describes the pieces of this declaration:

➤ attribute_list — A comma-separated list of attributes specific to a particular task. For example, <XmlAttributeAttribute(AttributeName:="Cost")>.

➤ accessibility — Public, Protected, Friend, Protected Friend, Private, or Static.

➤ Shared — Means that all instances of the class or structure containing the variable share the same variable.

➤ Shadows — Indicates that the variable hides a variable with the same name in a base class.

➤ ReadOnly — Indicates that the program can read, but not modify, the variable's value. You can set the value in an initialization statement or in an object constructor.

➤ Dim — Officially tells Visual Basic that you want to create a variable. You can omit the Dim keyword if you specify Public, Protected, Friend, Protected Friend, Private, Static, or ReadOnly.

➤ `WithEvents` — Tells Visual Basic that the variable is of a specific object type that may raise events that you will want to catch.

➤ `name` — Gives the name of the variable.

➤ `?` — Indicates this should be a nullable variable. For more information, see the section "Nullable Types" in Chapter 15, "Data Types, Variables, and Constants."

➤ `bounds_list` — Bounds for an array.

➤ `New` — Use New to make a new instance of an object variable. Include parameters for the class's constructor if appropriate.

➤ `type` — The variable's data type.

➤ `initialization_expression` — An expression that sets the initial value for the variable.

Visual Basic enables you to declare and initialize more than one variable in a single declaration statement, but that can make the code more difficult to read. To avoid possible later confusion, declare only variables of one type in a single statement.

INITIALIZATION EXPRESSIONS

Initialization expressions assign a value to a new variable. Simple expressions assign a literal value to a simple data type. The following example sets the value of a new string variable:

```
Dim txt As String = "Test"
```

The assignment expression can also initialize a variable to the result of a function or constructor, as in the following example:

```
Dim a_person As Person = New Person("Rod", "Stephens") ' Constructor.
Dim num_tools As Integer = CountTools() ' Function.
```

An initialization expression for an object can use the With keyword to specify values for the object's public properties as in the following example, which sets the object's FirstName and LastName properties:

```
Dim emp As New Employee With {.FirstName = "Rod", .LastName = "Stephens"}
```

To initialize a one-dimensional array, put the array's values inside curly braces separated by commas as in the following code:

```
Dim fibonacci() As Integer = {1, 1, 2, 3, 5, 8, 13, 21, 33, 54, 87}
```

To initialize higher-dimensional arrays, place lower-dimensional array values inside curly brackets and separate them with commas as in the following example, which initializes a two-dimensional array:

```
Dim int_values(,) As Integer = _
{ _
    {1, 2, 3}, _
    {4, 5, 6} _
}
```

Note that Visual Basic's automatic line continuation knows when an array initializer is open so you can omit the underscores in this statement as in the following code:

```
Dim int_values(,) As Integer =
{
    {1, 2, 3},
    {4, 5, 6}
}
```

Visual Basic's type inference system can guess the data type of an array from its initialization if Option Strict is Off. For example, in the following code, Visual Basic concludes that the array values hold Integers:

```
Dim values() = {1, 2, 3} ' Integer
```

If an array initializer holds values of more than one compatible data type, Visual Basic assumes the array holds the more general type. For example, the following array holds Doubles:

```
Dim values() = {1, 2, 3.4} ' Double
```

If an array holds values of multiple incompatible data types, Visual Basic makes the array hold Objects, as in the following example:

```
Dim values() = {1, 2.3, "three"} ' Object
```

WITH

When you create a new object variable, you can include a With clause to initialize the object's properties. The following code uses the Person class's parameterless constructor to make a new Person object. The With statement then sets values for the object's FirstName and LastName values.

```
Dim author As New Person() With {.FirstName = "Rod", .LastName = "Stephens"}
```

FROM

When you declare a collection, you can use the From keyword to initialize the collection. For example, the following code creates a collection of strings:

```
Dim fruits As New Collection() From {"Apple", "Banana", "Cherry"}
```

This works for any collection class that has an Add method.

If the collection's Add method takes more than one parameter, group parameters in brackets, as in the following example:

```
Dim fruits As New Dictionary(Of Integer, String)() From {
    {1, "Apple"}, {2, "Banana"}, {2, "Cherry"}}
```

If a class does not provide an Add method, you can create one with extension methods. The following code creates Add methods for the Stack and Queue classes:

```
Module CollectionExtensions
  ' Add method for the Stack class.
    <Extension()>
    Public Sub Add(ByVal the_stack As Stack, ByVal value As Object)
        the_stack.Push(value)
    End Sub

  ' Add method for the Queue class.
    <Extension()>
    Public Sub Add(ByVal the_queue As Queue, ByVal value As Object)
        the_queue.Enqueue(value)
    End Sub
End Module
```

USING

To make it easy to call an object's Dispose method, you can declare a variable in a Using statement. When the code reaches the corresponding End Using statement, Visual Basic automatically calls the object's Dispose method.

You can only place Using statements inside code blocks, not at the module level, so the syntax is somewhat simpler than the syntax for declaring a variable in general. The following code shows the syntax for declaring a variable in a Using statement:

```
Using name [(bounds_list)] [As [New] type] [= initialization_expression]
...
End Using
```

The parts of this statement are described in the previous section.

If it declares the variable, the Using statement must also initialize either with the As New syntax or with an initialization expression.

Note that you can also use a Using statement to make it easier to call a previously created object's Dispose method. The following code defines the thick_pen object, and then is used in a Using statement:

```
Dim thick_pen As New Pen(Color.Red, 10)
Using thick_pen
...
End Using
```

With this technique, the variable is available outside of the Using block, which may occasionally lead to confusion, so I recommend declaring variables in their Using blocks whenever possible.

ENUMERATED TYPE DECLARATIONS

The syntax for declaring an enumerated type is as follows:

```
[attribute_list] [accessibility] [Shadows] Enum name [As type]
    [attribute_list] value_name [= initialization_expression
    [attribute_list] value_name [= initialization_expression]
    ...
End Enum
```

Most of these terms (including *attribute_list* and *accessibility*) are similar to those used by variable declarations. See the section "Variable Declarations" earlier in this appendix for more information.

XML VARIABLES

To initialize XML data, declare an XElement variable and set it equal to properly formatted XML code. For example, the following code declares a variable named book_node that contains XML data representing a book:

```
Dim book_node As XElement = _
    <Book>
        <Title>The Bug That Was</Title>
        <Year>2010</Year>
        <Pages>376</Year>
    </Book>
```

OPTION EXPLICIT AND OPTION STRICT

When Option Explicit is on, you must explicitly declare all variables before using them. When Option Explicit is off, Visual Basic creates a variable the first time it is encountered if is has not yet been declared. To make your code easier to understand, and to avoid problems such as Visual Basic creating a new variable because of a typographical error, you should always turn Option Explicit on.

When Option Strict is on, Visual Basic will not implicitly perform narrowing type conversions. For example, if you set an Integer variable equal to a String value, Visual Basic will raise an error because the String might not contain an Integer value. When Option Strict is off, Visual Basic will silently attempt narrowing conversions. It tries to convert the String value into an Integer and raises an error if the String doesn't contain an integral value. To avoid confusion and potentially slow conversions, always turn Option Strict on.

OPTION INFER

When Option Infer is on, Visual Basic can infer the data type of a variable from its initialization expression. For example, Visual Basic would infer that the variable txt in the following code has data type String:

```
Dim message = "Hello!"
```

INFERENCE INHIBITED

Type inference only works on local variables declared within a subroutine, function, property, or other local context. It doesn't work for variables declared at the class level or in code modules.

Because inferred data types do not explicitly give the variable's data type, they can make the code harder to understand. To avoid confusion, leave Option Infer off unless you really need it.

For example, LINQ (Language Integrated Query) lets a program generate results that have an *anonymous* type. LINQ creates an object data type to hold results but the type is not given a name for the program to use. Instead type inference allows the program to manipulate the results without ever referring to the type by name. In this case, Option Infer must be on. For more information on LINQ, see Chapter 21, "LINQ."

DATA TYPES

The following table summarizes the Visual Basic data types.

TYPE	SIZE	VALUES
Boolean	2 bytes	True or False
Byte	1 byte	0 to 255 (unsigned byte)
SByte	1 byte	–128 to 127 (signed byte)
Char	2 bytes	0 to 65,535 (unsigned character)
Short	2 bytes	–32,768 to 32,767
UShort	2 bytes	0 through 65,535 (unsigned short)
Integer	4 bytes	–2,147,483,648 to 2,147,483,647
UInteger	4 bytes	0 through 4,294,967,295 (unsigned integer)
Long	8 bytes	–9,223,372,036,854,775,808 to 9,223,372,036,854,775,807
ULong	8 bytes	0 through 18,446,744,073,709,551,615 (unsigned long)
Decimal	16 bytes	0 to +/–79,228,162,514,264,337,593,543,950,335 with no decimal point 0 to +/–7.9228162514264337593543950335 with 28 places
Single	4 bytes	–3.4028235E+38 to –1.401298E-45 (negative values) 1.401298E-45 to 3.4028235E+38 (positive values)

continues

(continued)

TYPE	SIZE	VALUES
Double	8 bytes	−1.79769313486231570E+308 to −4.94065645841246544E-324 (negative values) 4.94065645841246544E-324 through 1.79769313486231570E+308 (positive values)
String	variable	Depending on the platform, approximately 0 to 2 billion Unicode characters
Date	8 bytes	January 1, 0001 0:0:00 to December 31, 9999 11:59:59 pm
Object	4 bytes	Points to any type of data
Structure	variable	Structure members have their own ranges

DATA TYPE CHARACTERS

The following table lists the Visual Basic data type characters.

CHARACTER	DATA TYPE
%	Integer
&	Long
@	Decimal
!	Single
#	Double
$	String

Using data type characters alone to determine a variable's data type can be confusing, so I recommend that you use an As clause instead. For example, the following code defines two integer variables and then uses them in nested loops. The declaration of j is more explicit and easier to understand.

```
Dim i%
Dim j As Integer

For i = 1 To 10
    For j = 1 To 10
        Debug.WriteLine(i * 100 1 j)
    Next j
Next i
```

LITERAL TYPE CHARACTERS

The following table lists the Visual Basic literal type characters.

CHARACTER	DATA TYPE
S	Short
US	UShort
I	Integer
UI	UInteger
L	Long
UL	ULong
D	Decimal
F	Single (F for "floating point")
R	Double (R for "real")
c	Char (note that this is a lowercase "c")

DATA TYPE CONVERSION FUNCTIONS

The following table lists the Visual Basic data type conversion functions.

FUNCTION	CONVERTS TO
CBool	Boolean
CByte	Byte
CChar	Char
CDate	Date
CDbl	Double
CDec	Decimal
CInt	Integer
CLng	Long
CObj	Object

continues

(continued)

FUNCTION	CONVERTS TO
CSByte	SByte
CShort	Short
CSng	Single
CStr	String
CUInt	UInteger
CULng	ULong
CUShort	UShort

Remember that data types have their own parsing methods in addition to these data type conversion functions. For example, the following code converts the String variable a_string into an Integer value:

```
an_integer = Integer.Parse(a_string)
```

These methods are faster than the corresponding data type conversion function (in this case, CInt).

The Convert class also provides methods for converting from one data type to another. The following table lists the most useful Convert class functions.

FUNCTION	FUNCTION
ToBoolean	ToInt64
ToByte	ToSByte
ToChar	ToSingle
ToDateTime	ToString
ToDecimal	ToUInt16
ToDouble	ToUInt32
ToInt16	ToUInt64
ToInt32	

All of the Convert class functions provide many overloaded versions to convert different kinds of values. For example, ToInt32 has different versions that take parameters that are Boolean, Byte, String, and other data types.

The integer functions ToInt16, ToInt32, ToInt64, ToUInt16, ToUInt32, and ToUInt64 also provide an overloaded version that takes as parameters a string value and a base, which can be 2, 8, 10, or 16 to if the string is in binary, octal, decimal, or hexadecimal. For example, the following statement converts the binary value 00100100 into the integer value 36.

```
Dim value As Integer = Convert.ToInt32("00100100",2)
```

CTYPE AND DIRECTCAST

The CType and DirectCast statements also perform type conversion. CType converts data from one type to another type if the types are compatible. For example, the following code converts the string "1234" into an integer:

```
Dim value As Integer = CType("1234", Integer)
```

DirectCast converts an object reference into a reference of another type provided the reference is actually of the second type. For example, suppose the Employee class inherits from the Person class, and consider the following code:

```
Dim emp1 As New Employee

' Works because emp1 is an Employee and a Person.
Dim per1 As Person = DirectCast(emp1, Person)

' Works because per1 happens to point to an Employee object.
Dim emp2 As Employee = DirectCast(per1, Employee)

Dim per2 As New Person

' Fails because per2 is a Person but not an Employee.
Dim emp3 As Employee = DirectCast(per2, Employee)
```

The code creates an Employee object. It then uses DirectCast to convert the Employee into a Person and then to convert the new Person back into an Employee. This works because this object is both an Employee and a Person.

Next, the code creates a Person object and tries to use DirectCast to convert it into an Employee. This fails because this Person is not an Employee.

Operators

The Visual Basic operators fall into five main categories: arithmetic, concatenation, comparison, logical, and bitwise. The following sections explain these categories and the operators they contain. The end of this appendix describes special Date and TimeSpan operators, as well as operator overloading.

ARITHMETIC OPERATORS

The following table lists the arithmetic operators provided by Visual Basic.

OPERATOR	PURPOSE	EXAMPLE	RESULT
^	Exponentiation	2 ^ 3	(2 to the power 3) = 2 * 2 * 2 = 8.
–	Negation	-2	-2
*	Multiplication	2 * 3	6
/	Division	3 / 2	1.5
\	Integer division	17\5	3
Mod	Modulus	17 Mod 5	2
+	Addition	2 + 3	5
–	Subtraction	3 - 2	1
<<	Bit left shift	&H57 << 1	&HAE
>>	Bit right shift	&H57 << 1	&H2B

The bit shift operators deserve a little extra discussion. These operators shift the binary representation of a number by a given number of bits either left or right. Unfortunately, Visual Basic doesn't understand binary so you must manually translate between binary and decimal, octal, or hexadecimal.

For example, the hexadecimal value &H57 is 01010111 in binary. If you shift this one bit to the left, you get 10101110, which is &HAE in hexadecimal. If you shift the original value one bit to the right, you get 00101011, which is &H2B in hexadecimal.

When working with binary values, many developers prefer to work in hexadecimal because each hexadecimal digit corresponds to four binary bits so you can work with each group of four bits separately.

CONCATENATION OPERATORS

Visual Basic provides two concatenation operators: + and &. Both join two strings together. Because the + symbol also represents an arithmetic operator, your code will be easier to read if you use the & symbol for concatenation.

COMPARISON OPERATORS

The following table lists the comparison operators provided by Visual Basic.

OPERATOR	PURPOSE	EXAMPLE	RESULT
=	Equals	A = B	True if A equals B
<>	Not equals	A <> B	True if A does not equal B
<	Less than	A < B	True if A is less than B
<=	Less than or equal to	A <= B	True if A is less than or equal to B
>	Greater than	A > B	True if A is greater than B
>=	Greater than or equal to	A >= B	True if A is greater than or equal to B
Is	Equality of two objects	emp Is mgr	True if emp and mgr refer to the same object
IsNot	Inequality of two objects	emp IsNot mgr	True if emp and mgr refer to different objects
TypeOf ... Is ...	Object is of a certain type	TypeOf obj Is Manager	True if obj points to a Manager object
Like	Matches a text pattern	value Like "###-####"	True if value contains three digits, a dash, and four digits

The following table lists characters that have special meanings to the Like operator.

CHARACTER(S)	MEANING
?	Matches any single character
*	Matches any zero or more characters
#	Matches any single digit
[characters]	Matches any of the characters between the brackets
[!characters]	Matches any character not between the brackets
A-Z	When inside brackets, matches any character in the range A to Z

The following table lists some useful Like patterns.

PATTERN	MEANING
[2–9]##-####	Seven–digit U.S. phone number
[2–9]##-[2–9]##-####	Ten-digit U.S. phone number including area code
1-[2–9]##-[2–9]##-####	Eleven-digit U.S. phone number beginning with 1 and area code
#####	Five-digit U.S. ZIP code
#####-####	Nine-digit U.S. ZIP+4 code
?*@?*.?*	e-mail address
[A–Z][0–9][A–Z] [0–9][A–Z][0–9]	Canadian postal code

LOGICAL OPERATORS

The following table summarizes the Visual Basic logical operators.

OPERATOR	PURPOSE	EXAMPLE	RESULT
Not	Logical or bitwise negation	Not A	True if A is false
And	Logical or bitwise And	A And B	True if A and B are both true
Or	Logical or bitwise Or	A Or B	True if A or B or both are true

continues

(continued)

OPERATOR	PURPOSE	EXAMPLE	RESULT
Xor	Logical or bitwise exclusive Or	A Xor B	True if A or B but not both is true
AndAlso	Logical or bitwise And with short-circuit evaluation	A AndAlso B	True if A and B are both true
OrElse	Logical or bitwise Or with short-circuit evaluation	A OrElse B	True if A or B or both are true

BITWISE OPERATORS

Bitwise operators work much as logical operators do, except that they compare values one bit at a time. Visual Basic provides bitwise versions of Not, And, Or, and Xor but not bitwise versions of AndAlso or OrElse.

OPERATOR PRECEDENCE

The following table lists the operators in order of precedence. When evaluating an expression, the program evaluates an operator before it evaluates those lower than it in the list. When operators are on the same line, the program evaluates them from left to right.

OPERATOR	DESCRIPTION
^	Exponentiation
-	Negation
*, /	Multiplication and division
\	Integer division
Mod	Modulus
+, -, +	Addition, subtraction, and concatenation
&	Concatenation
<<, >>	Bit shift

OPERATOR	DESCRIPTION
=, <>, <, <=, >, >=, Like, Is, IsNot, TypeOf ... Is ...	All comparisons
Not	Logical and bitwise negation
And, AndAlso	Logical and bitwise And with and without short-circuit evaluation
Xor, Or, OrElse	Logical and bitwise Xor, and Or with and without short-circuit evaluation

Use parentheses to change the order of evaluation and to make expressions easier to read.

ASSIGNMENT OPERATORS

The following table summarizes the Visual Basic assignment operators.

OPERATOR	EXAMPLE	ORIGINAL SYNTAX EQUIVALENT
=	A = B	A = B
^=	A ^= B	A = A ^ B
*=	A *= B	A = A * B
/=	A /= B	A = A / B
\=	A \= B	A = A \ B
+=	A += B	A = A + B
-=	A -= B	A = A - B
&=	A &= B	A = A & B
<<=	A <<= B	A = A << B
>>=	A >>= B	A = A >> B

There are no assignment operators corresponding to Mod or the Boolean operators.

CHOOSE, IF, AND IIF

The Choose, If, and IIf statements return values that you can assign to a variable. These statements are not really assignment operators (you need to use = to assign their results to a variable) and they perform decisions so they are described in Appendix E, "Control Statements."

DATE AND TIMESPAN OPERATORS

The Date and TimeSpan data types are related through their operators. The following list shows the relationships between these two data types:

- ➤ Date – Date = TimeSpan
- ➤ Date + TimeSpan = Date
- ➤ TimeSpan + TimeSpan = TimeSpan
- ➤ TimeSpan – TimeSpan = TimeSpan

The following table lists convenient methods provided by the Date data type.

SYNTAX	MEANING
`result_date = date1.Add(timespan1)`	Returns date1 plus timespan1
`result_date = date1` `.AddYears(num_years)`	Returns the date plus the indicated number of years
`result_date = date1` `.AddMonths(num_months)`	Returns the date plus the indicated number of months
`result_date = date1.AddDays(num_days)`	Returns the date plus the indicated number of days
`result_date = date1` `.AddHours(num_hours)`	Returns the date plus the indicated number of hours
`result_date = date1` `.AddMinutes(num_minutes)`	Returns the date plus the indicated number of minutes
`result_date = date1` `.AddSeconds(num_seconds)`	Returns the date plus the indicated number of seconds
`result_date = date1.AddMilliseconds` `(num_milliseconds)`	Returns the date plus the indicated number of milliseconds
`result_date = date1` `.AddTicks(num_ticks)`	Returns the date plus the indicated number of ticks (100 nanosecond units)
`result_timespan = date1` `.Subtract(date2)`	Returns the time span between date2 and date1
`result_integer = date1` `.CompareTo(date2)`	Returns a value indicating whether date1 is greater than, less than, or equal to date2
`result_boolean = date1.Equals(date2)`	Returns True if date1 equals date2

OPERATOR OVERLOADING

The syntax for defining an operator for a class is as follows:

```
[ <attributes> ] Public [ Overloads ] Shared [ Shadows ] _
[ Widening | Narrowing ] Operator symbol ( operands ) As type
    ...
End Operator
```

The operator's symbol can be +, -, *, /, \, ^, &, <<, >>, =, <>, <, >, <=, >=, Mod, Not, And, Or, Xor, Like, IsTrue, IsFalse, or CType.

For example, the following code defines the + operator for the ComplexNumber class. This class has two public properties, Re and Im, that give the number's real and imaginary parts.

```
Public Shared Operator +(
  ByVal c1 As ComplexNumber,
  ByVal c2 As ComplexNumber) As ComplexNumber
     Return New ComplexNumber With {
          .Re = c1.Re + c2.Re,
          .Im = c1.Im + c2.Im}
End Operator
```

Some operands come in pairs, and if you define one, you must define the other. The pairs are = and <>, < and >, <= and >=, and IsTrue and IsFalse.

If you define And and IsFalse, Visual Basic uses them to define the AndAlso operator. Similarly, if you define Or and IsTrue, Visual Basic automatically provides the OrElse operator.

Subroutine and Function Declarations

This appendix provides information about subroutine, function, and generic declarations. A property procedure includes a subroutine and function pair, so they are also described here.

SUBROUTINES

The syntax for writing a subroutine is as follows:

```
[attribute_list] [interitance_mode] [accessibility]
Sub subroutine_name [(parameters)] [ Implements interface.procedure ]
    [ statements ]
End Sub
```

The *inheritance_mode* can be one of the following values: Overloads, Overrides, Overridable, NotOverridable, MustOverride, Shadows, or Shared. These values determine how a subroutine declared within a class inherits from the parent class or how it allows inheritance in derived classes.

The *accessibility* clause can take one of the following values: Public, Protected, Friend, Protected Friend, or Private. These values determine which pieces of code can invoke the subroutine.

FUNCTIONS

The syntax for writing a function is as follows:

```
[attribute_list] [interitance_mode] [accessibility] _
Function function_name([parameters]) [As return_type] [ Implements interface.
function ]
    [ statements ]
End Function
```

This is the same as the syntax used for declaring a subroutine, except that a function includes a return type and ends with End Function.

The *inheritance_mode* can be one of the values Overloads, Overrides, Overridable, NotOverridable, MustOverride, Shadows, or Shared. These values determine how a subroutine declared within a class inherits from the parent class or how it allows inheritance in derived classes.

The *accessibility* clause can take one of the following values: Public, Protected, Friend, Protected Friend, or Private. These values determine which pieces of code can invoke the subroutine.

A function assigns its return value either by setting its name equal to the value or by using the Return statement. Using the Return statement may allow the compiler to optimize the code more, so it is generally preferred.

PROPERTY PROCEDURES

The syntax for read/write property procedures is as follows:

```
Property property_name () As data_type
    Get
        . . .
    End Get
    Set(ByVal Value As data_type)
        . . .
    End Set
End Property
```

The syntax for a read-only property procedure is as follows:

```
Public ReadOnly Property property_name () As data_type
    Get
        . . .
    End Get
End Property
```

The syntax for a write-only property procedure is as follows:

```
Public WriteOnly Property property_name () As data_type
    Set(ByVal Value As data_type)
        . . .
    End Set
End Property
```

In all three of these cases, you don't need to remember all the declaration details. If you type the first line (including the ReadOnly or WriteOnly keywords if you want them) and press Enter, Visual Basic creates blank property procedures for you.

The Property Get procedures should all assign return values, as in `property_name = return_value` or by using the Return statement, as in `Return return_value`.

Auto-implemented properties let you create simple read/write properties without providing Get and Set. The following code shows the syntax:

```
Property property_name () As data_type [= initial_value]
```

Visual Basic automatically makes a backing variable to hold the property's value, and Get and Set routines to access the value.

Note that Visual Basic cannot provide auto-implemented ReadOnly or WriteOnly properties.

LAMBDA FUNCTIONS AND EXPRESSIONS

A *lambda function* (also called an *inline function*) is a function declared within another routine. You can use lambda functions to initialize a delegate or to pass the function to a method that takes a delegate as a parameter.

For example, the following code creates an inline delegate named F. It then displays the value of F(12).

```
Dim F = Function(x As Integer) Sin(x / 2) + 2 * Cos(x / 3)
Debug.WriteLine(F(12))
```

The following code calls subroutine ApplyFunction. This function takes as parameters an array of values and a function that it should apply to each of the values. The code passes an inline delegate that doubles a number into ApplyFunction to double each of the values.

```
ApplyFunction(values, Function(x As Single) 2 * x)
```

A *lambda subroutine* is similar to a lambda function except it doesn't return a value. The syntax is similar to the syntax for lambda functions except you use the type Action instead of Function. You would also use a lambda subroutine where no return value is required. The following code creates and invokes a lambda subroutine:

```
Dim echo As Action(Of Integer) =
    Sub(x As Integer) Debug.WriteLine(x)
echo(123)
```

The following code creates a lambda subroutine inline as a parameter to a call to the Array.ForEach method:

```
Dim states() As String 5 {"CO", "UT", "KS", "WY"}
Array.ForEach(Of String)(states,
    Sub(str As String) MessageBox.Show(str))
```

You can make multiline lambda functions or subroutines. Start a new line after the Sub or Function statement, include the lines of code that you need, and finish with End Sub of End Function.

The following code shows a call to Array.ForEach that uses a multiline lambda subroutine:

```
Array.ForEach(Of String)(states,
    Sub(str As String)
        Debug.WriteLine(str)
        MessageBox.Show(str)
    End Sub
)
```

EXTENSION METHODS

To make an extension method, place a method in a code module and decorate it with the Extension attribute. The first parameter to the method determines the class that the method extends. For example, the following code gives the String class a MatchesRegexp method that returns True if the String matches a regular expression:

```
Module StringExtensions
    <Extension()>
    Public Function MatchesRegexp(ByVal the_string As String,
     ByVal regular_expression As String) As Boolean
        Dim reg_exp As New Regex(regular_expression)
        Return reg_exp.IsMatch(the_string)
    End Function
End Module
```

PARTIAL METHODS

A partial method is a private subroutine that is declared in one place and implemented in another. The following code defines the signature of the RecordException subroutine and then later defines its body:

```
Public Class PathAlgorithm
    Partial Private Sub RecordException(ByVal ex As Exception)
    End Sub
    ...
    Private Sub RecordException(ByVal ex As Exception)
        Debug.WriteLine("Error: " & ex.Message)
    End Sub
    ...
End Class
```

Partial methods are mainly intended for use by code generators. In your code, you can usually use events instead. It's useful to understand what they do in case you need to read generated code.

Control Statements

Control statements tell an application which other statements to execute under a particular set of circumstances.

The two main categories of control statements are decision statements and looping statements. The following sections describe the decision and looping statements provided by Visual Basic .NET.

DECISION STATEMENTS

A decision statement represents a branch in the program. It marks a place where the program can execute one set of statements or another or possibly no statements at all. These include If, Choose, and Select Case statements.

Single-Line If Then

A single-line If Then statement tests a condition and, if the condition is true, executes a piece of code. The code may include more than one simple statement separated by a colon.

Optional Else If clauses let the program evaluate other conditions and execute corresponding pieces of code. A final optional Else clause lets the program execute a piece of code if none of the previous conditions is true.

The syntax is as follows:

```
If condition Then statement
If condition Then statement1 Else statement2
If condition1 Then statement1 Else If condition2 Then statement2 _
    Else statement3
If condition Then statement1: statement2
If condition Then statement1: statement2 Else statement3: statement4
```

Complicated single-line If Then statements can be confusing and difficult to read, so I recommend using the multiline versions if the statement includes an Else clause or executes more than one statement.

Multiline If Then

A multiline If Then statement is similar to the single-line version, except the pieces of code executed by each part of the statement can include multiple lines. Each piece of code ends before the following ElseIf, Else, or End If keywords. In complex code, this format is often easier to read than a complicated single-line If Then statement.

The syntax is as follows:

```
If condition1 Then
    statements1...
ElseIf condition2
    statements2...
Else
    statements3...
End If
```

The statement can contain any number of ElseIf sections.

Select Case

A Select Case statement lets a program execute one of several pieces of code based on a test value. Select Case is equivalent to a long If Then Else statement.

The syntax is as follows:

```
Select Case test_value
    Case comparison_expression1
        statements1
    Case comparison_expression2
        statements2
    Case comparison_expression3
        statements3
        ...
    Case Else
        else_statements
End Select
```

A comparison expression can contain multiple expressions separated by commas, can use the To keyword to specify a range of values, and can use the Is keyword to evaluate a logical expression using the test value. The following example's first case looks for a string in the range "A" to "Z" or "a" to "z." Its second and third cases look for values less than "A" and greater than "Z," respectively.

```
Select Case key_pressed
    Case "A" To "Z", "a" To "z"
        . . .
    Case Is < "A"
        . . .
    Case Is > "Z"
        . . .
End Select
```

Many developers always include a Case Else section to catch unexpected situations. If every possible situation should be covered by other cases, some developers throw an exception inside the Case Else section to make it easier to find errors.

If and IIf

IIf takes a Boolean value as its first parameter. It returns its second parameter if the value is true, and it returns its third parameter if the value is false.

The syntax is as follows:

```
variable = IIf(condition, value_if_false, value_if_true)
```

Note that IIf always evaluates all of its arguments. For example, if the condition is true, IIf only returns the second argument, but it evaluates both the second and third arguments.

The If function does the same thing as IIf except it uses short-circuit evaluation, so it only evaluates the second and third arguments if necessary. If the condition is true in the following code, If evaluates the second argument but not the third:

```
variable = If(condition, value_if_false, value_if_true)
```

A second form if the If function takes two parameters: an object reference or a nullable type and a return value. The If function returns the first parameter if it is not Nothing and the second argument if it is Nothing. The following code shows the syntax:

```
variable = If(nullable_value, default_if_nothing)
```

IIf is sometimes used when the code must evaluate both results so short-circuiting would cause problems. For example, suppose the value_if_true and value_if_false parts have *side effects*. In other words, they perform actions that may not be obvious in addition to returning their results. They may open databases, initialize network connections, and perform other actions that the program will need finished for later tasks.

Side effects are often confusing, however, because it's not always obvious what side effects a particular function call has. That can make the code harder to understand, debug, and maintain. To avoid potential trouble, I recommend always using functions without side effects and moving any other necessary code into a subroutine that the program can call before the call to IIf or If. In that case, IIf has no advantage over If.

> **THE CASE FOR IIF**
>
> I have yet to see a convincing case for using IIf and functions with side effects. If you think you can make that case, let me know at RodStephens@vb-heleper.com and I'll post your comments on the book's web site.

IIf and If are often confusing and IIf at least is slower than an If Then Else statement, so you may want to use If Then Else instead.

Choose

Choose takes an index value as its first parameter and returns the corresponding one of its other parameters.

The syntax is as follows:

```
variable = Choose(index, value1, value2, value3, value4, ...)
```

Choose is rarely used by many programmers, so it can be confusing. To avoid unnecessary confusion, you may want to use a Select Case statement instead.

LOOPING STATEMENTS

A looping statement makes the program execute a series of statements repeatedly. The loop can run for a fixed number of repetitions, run while some condition holds true, run until some condition holds true, or run indefinitely.

For Next

A For Next loop executes a piece of code while a loop control variable ranges from one value to another.

The syntax is as follows:

```
For variable [As data_type] = start_value To stop_value [Step increment]
    statements
    [Exit For]
    statements
Next [variable]
```

For Each

A For Each loop executes a piece of code while a loop control variable ranges over all of the items contained in a group class such as a collection or array.

The syntax is as follows:

```
For Each variable [As object_type] In group
    statements
    [Exit For]
    statements
Next [variable]
```

The *group* in this code can also be a LINQ (Language Integrated Query) query. The following code creates a LINQ query to select information from the book_data array, and then uses a For Each loop to display the results:

```
Dim book_query = From book_info In book_data
    Select book_info
    Where book_info.Year > = 2000
    Order By book_info.Year
For Each bi In book_query
    Debug.WriteLine(bi.Title)
Next bi
```

For more information about LINQ, see Chapter 21, "LINQ."

Do Loop

Do Loop statements come in three forms. First, if the statement has no While or Until clause, the loop repeats infinitely or until the code uses an Exit Do, Exit Sub, GoTo, or some other statement to break out of the loop.

The syntax is as follows:

```
Do
    statements
    [Exit Do]
    statements
Loop
```

The other two forms of Do Loop statements execute as long as a condition is true (Do While condition) or until a condition is true (Do Until condition).

The second form of Do Loop statement tests its condition before it executes, so the code it contains is not executed even once if the condition is initially false.

The syntax is as follows:

```
Do {While | Until} condition
    statements
    [Exit Do]
    statements
Loop
```

The third form of Do Loop statement tests its condition after it executes, so the code it contains is executed at least once even if the condition is initially false.

The syntax is as follows:

```
Do
    statements
    [Exit Do]
    statements
Loop {While | Until} condition
```

While End

The While End loop executes a series of statements as long as a condition is true. It tests its condition before it executes, so the code it contains is not executed even once if the condition is initially false.

The syntax is as follows:

```
While condition
    statements
    [Exit While]
    statements
End While
```

This statement is equivalent to the Do Loop:

```
Do While condition
    statements
    [Exit Do]
    statements
Loop
```

GOTO

GoTo performs an unconditional jump to a specified line.

The syntax is as follows:

```
    GoTo line_label
    ...
line_label:
    ...
```

Because undisciplined use of GoTo can lead to "spaghetti code," which is difficult to understand, debug, and maintain, you should generally avoid using GoTo.

Error Handling

This appendix provides information on error handling.

STRUCTURED ERROR HANDLING

A Try block tries to execute some code and reacts to errors. The syntax is as follows:

```
Try
    try_statements...
[Catch ex As exception_type_1
    exception_statements_1...]
[Catch ex As exception_type_2
    exception_statements_2...]
...
[Catch
    final_exception_statements...]
[Finally
    finally_statements...]
End Try
```

When an error occurs, the program examines the Catch statements until it finds one that matches the current exception. The program executes the *finally_statements* after the *try_statements* succeed or after any Catch block is done executing.

THROWING EXCEPTIONS

Use the Throw statement to throw an exception, as in the following code:

```
Throw New ArgumentException("Width must be greater than zero")
```

Exception classes provide several overloaded constructors so you can indicate such things as the basic error message, the name of the variable that caused the exception, and an inner exception.

For information on useful exception classes and custom exception classes, see Appendix O, "Useful Exception Classes."

CLASSIC ERROR HANDLING

The On Error statement controls error handlers in Visual Basic classic error handling. You can use structured and classic error handling in the same program but not in the same routine.

The following list briefly describes the On Error statement's four variations:

➤   `On Error GoTo` *line* — If an error occurs, the program enters error-handling mode and control jumps to the indicated line.

➤   `On Error Resume Next` — If an error occurs, the program ignores it. The code can use the Err object to see whether an error occurred and what error it was.

➤   `On Error GoTo 0` — This command disables any currently active error handler. If the program encounters an error after this statement, the routine fails and control passes up the call stack until the program finds an active error handler or the program crashes.

➤   `On Error GoTo -1` — This command is similar to On Error GoTo 0, except that it also ends error-handling mode if the program is in error-handling mode.

Visual Basic provides four ways to exit error-handling mode:

➤   `Exit Sub` (*or* `Exit Function` *or* `Exit Property`) — Ends error-handling mode and exits the current routine.

➤   `Resume` — Makes the program resume execution with the statement that caused the error. If the program has not taken some action to correct the problem, the error will occur again, triggering the error handler and possibly entering an infinite loop.

➤   `Resume Next` — Makes the program resume execution with the statement after the one that caused the error.

➤   `On Error GoTo -1` — Ends error-handling mode and lets execution continue with the statement that follows.

Using On Error GoTo −1 to end error-handling mode can be very confusing because it's hard to tell when the program is in error-handling mode and when it isn't. Usually, the code is easier to understand if all of the error-handling code is grouped at the end of the routine and if each block of error-handling code ends with one of the other methods (Exit Sub, Exit Function, Resume, or Resume Next).

Windows Forms Controls and Components

This appendix describes the standard controls and components provided by Visual Basic .NET. Some of these are quite complicated, providing dozens or even hundreds of properties, methods, and events, so it would be impractical to describe them all completely here. However, it's still worthwhile having a concise guide to the most important properties, methods, and events provided by the Windows Forms controls.

The sections in this appendix describe the components' general purposes and give examples of what I believe to be their simplest, most common, and most helpful usages. The idea is to help you decide which components to use for which purposes, and to give you some idea about the components' most commonly used properties, methods, and events. To learn more about a particular component, see the online help.

> **MORE INFORMATION**
>
> You can find information about most of these controls under the "System.Windows .Forms Namespace" topic in the MSDN help at `msdn.microsoft.com/system .windows.forms.aspx`. Use the navigation tree in the left pane to find the controls you want to study.

You can also learn more by studying this appendix's example programs, which are available for download on the book's web site.

Note that all of these components inherit from the Component class, and the controls inherit from the Control class. Except where overridden, the components and controls inherit the properties, methods, and events defined by the Component and Control classes. Chapter 9, "Using Windows Forms Controls," discusses some of the more useful properties, methods, and events provided by the Control class, and many of those apply to these controls as well. Appendix A, "Useful Control Properties, Methods, and Events," summarizes the Control class's most useful properties.

Figure G-1 shows the Visual Basic Toolbox displaying the standard Windows Forms controls.

> ### TUNING THE TOOLBOX
>
> You can add and remove controls from the Toolbox. You can add controls built by Microsoft, other companies, yourself, or other Visual Basic programmers. Some extra controls even come installed with Visual Basic but not displayed by default in the Toolbox. Right-click the Toolbox and select Choose Items to add or remove items.

The following table lists the components shown in Figure G-1 in the same order in which they appear in the figure. Read the table by rows. For example, the first several entries (Pointer, BackgroundWorker, BindingNavigator, BindingSource, Button, and so on) correspond to the first controls in the first row in Figure G-1.

FIGURE G-1: Visual Basic provides a large number of standard components and controls for Windows Forms.

Pointer	BackgroundWorker	BindingNavigator	BindingSource
Button	CheckBox	CheckedListBox	ColorDialog
ComboBox	ContextMenuStrip	DataGridView	DataSet
DateTimePicker	DirectoryEntry	DirectorySearcher	DomainUpDown
ErrorProvider	EventLog	FileSystemWatcher	FlowLayoutPanel
FolderBrowserDialog	FontDialog	GroupBox	HelpProvider
HScrollBar	ImageList	Label	LinkLabel
ListBox	ListView	MaskedTextBox	MenuStrip
MessageQueue	MonthCalendar	NotifyIcon	NumericUpDown

OpenFileDialog	PageSetupDialog	Panel	PerformanceCounter
PictureBox	PrintDialog	PrintDocument	PrintPreviewControl
PrintPreviewDialog	Process	ProgressBar	PropertyGrid
RadioButton		RichTextBox	SaveFileDialog
SerialPort	ServiceController	SplitContainer	Splitter
StatusStrip	TabControl	TableLayoutPanel	TextBox
Timer	ToolStrip	ToolStripContainer	ToolTip
TrackBar	TreeView	VScrollBar	WebBrowser

COMPONENTS' PURPOSES

By default, the Toolbox provides several tabs that group related components together. With such a large number of components at your fingertips, having categorized tabs sometimes makes finding a particular tool easier. Each tab also contains a Pointer tool.

The following table lists the tools in various Toolbox tabs. You can use this table to help decide which tool to use for a particular purpose.

COMMON CONTROLS			
Button	CheckBox	CheckedListBox	ComboBox
DateTimePicker	Label	LinkLabel	ListBox
ListView	MaskedTextBox	MonthCalendar	NotifyIcon
NumericUpDown	PictureBox	ProgressBar	RadioButton
RichTextBox	TextBox	ToolTip	TreeView
WebBrowser			
Containers			
FlowLayoutPanel	GroupBox	Panel	SplitContainer
TabControl	TableLayoutPanel		
Menus and Toolbars			
ContextMenuStrip	MenuStrip	StatusStrip	ToolStrip
ToolStripContainer			

continues

(continued)

Data

DataSet	DataGridView	BindingSource	BindingNavigator

Components

BackgroundWorker	DirectoryEntry	Directory Searcher	ErrorProvider
EventLog	FileSystemWatcher	HelpProvider	ImageList
MessageQueue	PerformanceCounter	Process	SerialPort
ServiceController	Timer		

Printing

PageSetupDialog	PrintDialog	PrintDocument	PrintPreview Control
PrintPreviewDialog			

Dialogs

ColorDialog	FolderBrowser Dialog	FontDialog	OpenFileDialog
SaveFileDialog			

WPF Interoperability

ElementHost

Reporting

MicrosoftReport Viewer	CrystalReport Viewer	CrystalReport Document

Visual Basic Power Packs

PrintForm

One other section, General, is initially empty.

The following sections describe the tools shown in Figure G-1. Except for the generic pointer tool, all tools are presented in alphabetical order.

POINTER

Each of the Toolbox's sections begins with an arrow in its upper-left corner. This is the only tool shown in Figure G-1 that does not represent a type of control or component. Selecting the pointer deselects any other currently selected tool. You can then click the controls on the form to select them without creating a new control.

BACKGROUNDWORKER

The BackgroundWorker component simplifies multi-threading. When a program invokes its RunWorkerAsync method, the component starts running on a new thread. It raises its DoWork method on the new thread, and the corresponding event handler should perform the necessary work. While it runs, the worker can call the component's ReportProgress method to raise a ProgressChanged event on the main thread to let the program know how it is progressing.

When the worker thread finishes, the component receives a RunWorkerCompleted event on the main thread.

The UseBackgroundWorker example program, which is available for download on the book's web site, demonstrates the BackgroundWorker component. It allows the user to start a BackgroundWorker that simulates a long task. The program displays the worker's progress and lets the user cancel the task, stopping the worker before it finishes.

BINDINGNAVIGATOR

A BindingNavigator provides a user interface so the user can control a data source. It initially appears as a toolbar docked to the top of the form, although you can move it if you like. It contains navigation buttons that move to the beginning, previous record, next record, and end of the data source. It also contains a text box where you can enter a record number to jump to, a label showing the current record number, and buttons to add and delete records.

See Chapter 20, "Database Controls and Objects," for more information on BindingNavigator and other database controls.

BINDINGSOURCE

A BindingSource provides control of bound data on a form. It provides programmatic methods for navigating through the data, adding items, deleting items, and otherwise managing the data at the code level.

Typically you attach the BindingSource to a data source. You then bind controls to the BindingSource. When the BindingSource changes its position in the data source, it automatically updates the bound controls. If you attach a BindingNavigator to the BindingSource, the user can use the BindingNavigator to control the BindingSource.

See Chapter 20 for more information on BindingNavigator and other database controls.

BUTTON

The Button control is a simple push button. You can use it to let the user tell the program to do something.

A Button can display a textual caption, a picture, or both. Use the ImageAlign and TextAlign properties to determine where the caption and picture appear on the Button.

When the user clicks the Button, it raises its Click event. The program can take the appropriate action in the Button control's Click event handler, as shown in the following code:

```
Private Sub btnValidatePhoneNumber_Click(ByVal sender As System.Object,
 ByVal e As System.EventArgs) Handles btnValidatePhoneNumber.Click
    ValidatePhoneNumber(txtPhoneNumber.Text)
End Sub
```

Note that most button Click event handlers are assigned to a single button so they don't need to use their sender and e parameters. In that case, you can use relaxed delegates to omit the parameters completely, significantly simplifying the event handler as shown in the following code:

```
Private Sub btnValidatePhoneNumber_Click() Handles btnValidatePhoneNumber.Click
    ValidatePhoneNumber(txtPhoneNumber.Text)
End Sub
```

For more information on relaxed delegates, see the section "Relaxed Delegates" in Chapter 17, "Subroutines and Functions."

You can use the control's ImageList and ImageIndex properties to assign an image to the Button.

If you set a form's AcceptButton property to a Button, the Button control's Click event handler runs when the user presses the Enter key while the form has focus. Similarly, if you set a form's CancelButton property to a Button, the Button control's Click event handler runs when the user presses the Escape key while the form has focus.

CHECKBOX

A CheckBox displays a box that enables the user to select or clear an option.

A CheckBox can display a textual caption, a picture, or both. Use the ImageAlign and TextAlign properties to determine where the caption and picture appear in the CheckBox.

You can also use the control's ImageList and ImageIndex properties to assign an image to the CheckBox.

Use the control's CheckAlign property to determine where the check box appears. Normally the box appears on the left, but you can make it appear on the right, center, upper-left corner, and so forth.

Usually a program uses the CheckBox control's Checked property to tell if it is checked. This property returns True if the CheckBox is checked and False if it is not. Your program can also set this property to True or False to check or uncheck the control.

Although a CheckBox usually is either checked or not, this control also has a third indeterminate state. This state is represented as a grayed-out check in the box. Some applications use this state to represent a partial or unknown selection.

If you want to allow the user to cycle through the three values (checked, indeterminate, and unchecked), set the control's ThreeState property to True.

Most programs use CheckBoxes to gather information and only process the information when the user clicks a button or selects a menu item, so they don't need to process any CheckBox events. The control does provide a CheckedChanged event, however, that fires whenever the control's value changes, either because the user clicked it or because your program's code changed the value. For example, the program could hide and display extra information that only applies when the box is checked, as shown in the following code:

```
Private Sub chkExtraInfo_CheckedChanged() Handles chkExtraInfo.CheckedChanged
    grpExtraInfo.Visible = chkExtraInfo.Checked
End Sub
```

CHECKEDLISTBOX

A CheckedListBox control displays a series of items with check boxes in a list format. This enables the user to pick and choose similar items from a list of choices. You can also use a ListBox to allow the user to select items in a list, but there are some important differences between the two controls' behaviors.

First, in a CheckedListBox, previously checked items remain checked when the user clicks another item. If the user clicks an item in a ListBox, the control deselects any previously selected items. Though you can use the Shift and Ctrl keys to modify this behavior, making complex selections can be tricky.

Second, the user must click each CheckedListBox item individually to select it. You can make a ListBox allow simple or extended selections. That means, for example, the user could Shift+click to select all of the items in a range. If the user is likely to want that type of selection, consider using a ListBox instead of a CheckedListBox.

If a CheckedListBox isn't big enough to display all of its items at once, it displays a vertical scroll bar to let the user see all the items. If some of the items are too wide to fit, set the control's HorizontalScrollBar property to True to display a horizontal scroll bar.

If you set the MultiColumn property to True, the control displays items in multiple columns.

By default, the user must click an item and then click its box to check the item. To allow the user to select an item with a single click, set the control's CheckOnClick property to True. This usually makes selection easier.

If the control's IntegralHeight property is True, the control will not display a partial item. For example, if the control is tall enough to display 10.7 items, it will make itself slightly shorter so that it can only display 10 items.

Set the control's Sorted property to True to make the control display its items in sorted order.

Use the control's Items.Add method to add an item to the list. This method has three overloaded versions. All three take a generic Object as the first parameter. The control uses this object's ToString method to generate the text that it displays to the user. The first overloaded version takes no extra parameters. The second version takes a Boolean parameter indicating whether the new item should be checked. The last version takes a parameter that indicates whether the new item should be checked, unchecked, or indeterminate.

For example, suppose that a program defines the following Employee class. The important part here is the ToString method, which tells the CheckedListBox how to display an Employee object, as shown in the following code:

```
Public Class Employee
    Public FirstName As String
    Public LastName As String

    Public Sub New(ByVal first_name As String, ByVal last_name As String)
        FirstName = first_name
        LastName = last_name
    End Sub

    Public Overrides Function ToString() As String
        Return FirstName & " " & LastName
    End Function
End Class
```

code snippet UseCheckedListBox

The CheckedListBox item's CheckedItems property returns a collection containing the objects that are checked, including those that are in the indeterminate state. The control's CheckedIndices property returns a collection of integers representing the items that are selected or indeterminate (numbered starting with zero).

COLORDIALOG

The ColorDialog component displays a dialog that enables the user to select a color from a standard palette or from a custom color palette. A program calls its ShowDialog method to display a color selection dialog. ShowDialog returns DialogResult.OK if the user selects a color and clicks OK. It returns DialogResult.Cancel if the user cancels.

The following code sets the dialog box's Color property to the btnPickColor control's current background color. It displays the dialog box and, if the user clicks OK, it sets the btnPickColor control's background color to the user's selection.

```
Private Sub btnPickColor_Click() Handles btnPickColor.Click
    dlgColor.Color = btnPickColor.BackColor
    If dlgColor.ShowDialog() = DialogResult.OK Then
        btnPickColor.BackColor = dlgColor.Color
    End If
End Sub
```

code snippet UseColorDialog

The dialog box provides an area on the right where the user can define custom colors. Set the component's AllowFullOpen property to True to allow the user to access this area. Set the FullOpen property to True to make the dialog appear with this area already open (otherwise the user must click the Define Custom Colors button to show this area).

If you set the SolidColorOnly property to True, the dialog box only allows the user to select solid colors. This applies only to systems using 256 or fewer colors, where some colors are dithered combinations of other colors. All colors are solid on systems using more than 256 colors.

DITHER FOR COLOR

Dithering is the process of using dots or other shapes of various sizes to create the illusion of another color. For example, you can make orange by displaying a red area sprinkled with tiny yellow dots or checks. On a system that uses a higher color model such as 24-bit color, the system can display every color directly. If you're using a lower color model system such as 8-bit color (256 colors), the system might dither to simulate colors that it cannot display directly.

The component's CustomColors property is an array of integers that determine the colors that the dialog displays in its custom colors area. These color values are a combination of red, green, and blue values between 0 and 255. In hexadecimal, the form of a value is *BBGGRR,* where *BB* is the blue component, *GG* is the green component, and *RR* is the red component.

For example, the color &HFF8000 has a blue component of &HFF = 255, a green component of &H80 = 128, and a red component of 0. This color is light blue. Unfortunately, the Color object's ToArgb method returns the color in the reversed format RRGGBB, so you cannot use that method to calculate these values. Instead, you need to calculate them yourself.

Example program UseColorDialog demonstrates a simple color dialog. Example program CustomColorDialog displays a dialog initialized with a custom color palette. Both of these programs are available for download on the book's web site.

COMBOBOX

The ComboBox control contains a text box where the user can enter a value. It also provides a list box or drop-down list where the user can select a value. How the text box, list box, and drop-down list work depends on the control's DropDownStyle property. Figure G-2 shows the three styles.

When DropDownStyle is Simple, the ComboBox displays a text box and a list, as shown on the left in Figure G-2. The user can type a value in the text box, or select one from the list. The user can enter any text in the text box, even if it does not appear in the list.

When DropDownStyle is DropDown, the ComboBox displays a text box and a drop-down list, as shown in the middle in Figure G-2. The user can type a value in the text box. If the user clicks the drop-down arrow to the right of the text box, the control displays the list where the user

FIGURE G-2: The ComboBox provides three different styles: Simple, DropDown, and DropDownList.

can select an item. The user can enter any text in the text box, even if it does not appear in the list. In Figure G-2, the middle ComboBox control's text box contains the value Persimmon, which does not appear in the list.

When DropDownStyle is DropDownList, the ComboBox displays a non-editable text box and a drop-down list. If the user clicks the control, the ComboBox displays a drop-down list exactly as it does when DropDownStyle is DropDown. The difference is that the user must select an item from the list. If the user sets focus to the control and types a letter, the control selects the next item in the list that begins with that letter. If the user presses the same letter again, the control moves to the next choice beginning with that letter.

Setting DropDownStyle to DropDownList restricts the user's choices the most and allows the least room for error. So, if you know all of the user's choices, you should use the DropDownList style. If you must allow the user to enter new values, you should use one of the other styles. The DropDown style takes less room on the form and is more familiar to most users, so that is often the better choice.

The control's DropDownWidth property determines how wide the drop-down list should be.

The ComboBox control's MaxDropDownItems property determines how many items the control displays in its drop-down list. For example, if you set this to 10 and the list contains more than 10 items, the drop-down list displays a scroll bar to let the user find the additional items.

The MaxLength property lets you specify the maximum number of characters the user can type into the control's text box. Note, however, that the control will display a longer value if the user selects it from the control's list box or drop-down list. Set MaxLength to 0 to allow entries of any length.

If you set the control's Sorted property to True, the ComboBox lists its choices in sorted order.

The ComboBox control's Text property gets or sets the value displayed by the control's text box. If the control's DropDownStyle is DropDownList, this property does nothing at design time and the program can only set it to values that are in the control's list of allowed values at runtime. Many programs use this property to see what value is selected in the control.

Like the CheckedListBox described earlier in this appendix, the items in a ComboBox can be any type of object and the control uses the objects' ToString methods to figure out what text to display to the user. As is the case with the CheckedListBox, you can use the ComboBox control's Items.Add method to add new objects to the control. See the "CheckedListBox" section earlier in this appendix for more information and an example Employee class that will also work with ComboBox controls.

If an item is selected, the ComboBox control's SelectedItem property returns the item's object. If no item is selected, this property returns Nothing.

If an item is selected, the ComboBox control's SelectedIndex property returns the item's index, numbered starting with zero. If no item is selected, this property returns –1.

Note that the SelectedItem and SelectedIndex properties return Nothing and –1, respectively, if the user types a new value into the text area, even if the user types a value that appears in the control's item list. If you want the user to select an item rather than typing some text, you should set the control's DropDownStyle property to DropDownList.

CONTEXTMENUSTRIP

The ContextMenuStrip component represents a context menu. When you select it on the form at design time, the development environment displays the menu at the top of the form. Enter the menu's items, use the Property window to set their names and other properties, and double-click the items to edit their event handlers. See the section "MenuStrip" later in this appendix for information on menu item properties and events.

To use a ContextMenuStrip, you need to attach it to a control. Use the Properties window to set the control's ContextMenuStrip property to your ContextMenuStrip component. The rest is automatic. When the user right-clicks this control at runtime, Visual Basic automatically displays the ContextMenuStrip. If the user selects one of the menu's items, Visual Basic triggers the menu item's event handler.

DATAGRIDVIEW

The DataGridView control displays a table-like grid display. The control's underlying data can come from a data source such as a DataSet or BindingSource, or the program can add rows and columns directly to the control. The DataGridView provides many properties for customizing the grid's appearance. For example, it lets you change column header styles and cell border styles, determine whether rows and columns are resizable, and determine whether the control displays tooltips and errors in data cells.

Visual Basic can automatically create a DataGridView bound to a BindingSource and associated with a BindingNavigator. To do this, create a data source and drag a table from the Data Sources window onto a form. For more information on this technique, or for information on using the control in general, see Chapter 20.

DATASET

The DataSet component holds data in a relational format. It provides all the features you need to build, load, store, manipulate, and save data similar to that stored in a relational database. It can hold multiple tables related with complex parent/child relationships and uniqueness constraints.

It provides methods for merging DataSets, searching for records that satisfy criteria, and saving data in different ways (such as into a relational database or an XML file).

One of the most common ways to use a DataSet is to load it from a relational database when the program starts, use various controls to display the data and let the user manipulate it interactively, and then save the changes back into the database when the program ends.

For more information on the DataSet component, see the online help (`msdn.microsoft.com/system.data.dataset.aspx`) and Chapter 20.

DATETIMEPICKER

The DateTimePicker control allows the user to select a date and time. The control can display one of several styles, depending on its property values.

If the ShowUpDown property is True, the control displays small up and down arrows on its right, as shown at the top of Figure G-3. Click a date field (month, date, year) to select it, and use the up and down arrow buttons to adjust that field.

If ShowUpDown is False (the default), the control displays a drop-down arrow on its right, as shown in the second DateTimePicker in Figure G-3. If you click this arrow, the control displays the calendar shown under the control in Figure G-3. The right and left arrows at the top of the calendar let you move through months. If you click the calendar's month, the control displays a pop-up menu listing the months so that you can quickly select one. If you click the year, the control displays small up and down arrows that you can use to change the year. When you have found the month and year you want, click a date to select it and close the calendar.

If you get lost while scrolling through the calendar's months, you can click the Today entry at the bottom of the calendar to jump back to the current date. You can also right-click the calendar and select the "Go to today" command.

FIGURE G-3: The DateTimePicker control lets the user select a date and time.

Whether ShowUpDown is True or False, you can click a date field (month, date, year) and then use the up and down arrow keys to adjust the field's value. You can also type a new value into numeric fields (such as the date and year).

The control's Format property determines the way in which the control displays dates and times. This property can take the values Long, Short, Time, and Custom. The results depend on the regional settings on the computer. The following table shows typical results for the Long, Short, and Time settings in the United States.

FORMAT PROPERTY	EXAMPLE
Long	Saturday, February 20, 2010
Short	2/20/2010
Time	3:12:45 PM

When the Format property is set to Custom, the control uses the date and time format string stored in the control's CustomFormat property. For example, the DateTimePicker on the bottom in Figure G-3 has CustomFormat set to h:mm tt, MMM d, yyyy to display the time, abbreviated month, date, and year. See Appendix P, "Date and Time Format Specifiers," for more information.

If the control displays time (either because Format is set to Time or because a CustomFormat value includes time fields), the user can click a time field and use the arrow keys to adjust its value. You can also click a numeric field or AM/PM designator and type a new value.

The DateTimePicker control's MinDate and MaxDate properties determine the first and last dates that the control will let the user select.

The control has several properties that determine the appearance of the calendar, if it displays one. These include CalendarFont, CalendarForeColor, CalendarMonthBackground, CalendarTitleBackColor, CalendarTitleForeColor, and CalendarTrailingForeColor.

The program can use the control's Value property to get or set the control's date and time.

DIRECTORYENTRY

The DirectoryEntry component represents a node or object in an Active Directory hierarchy. Active Directory is a service that provides a common, hierarchical view of distributed resources and services on a network.

Active Directory is really a Windows operating system topic, not a Visual Basic topic, so it is not covered further here. For more information, see the DirectoryEntry class's web page at msdn .microsoft.com/system.directoryservices.directoryentry.aspx.

DIRECTORYSEARCHER

The DirectorySearcher component performs searches on an Active Directory hierarchy. See the online help for more information on Active Directory (msdn.microsoft.com/aa286486.aspx) and the DirectorySearcher component (msdn.microsoft.com/system.directoryservices .directorysearcher.aspx).

DOMAINUPDOWN

The DomainUpDown control displays a list of items that the user can select by clicking the up and down arrow buttons beside the control. For example, the control might let the user select one of the values High, Medium, and Low.

If the control's InterceptArrowKeys property is True, the user can also scroll through the items by using the up and down arrow keys. If InterceptArrowKeys is False, the user must click the arrow buttons to change the value.

Normally, the control's ReadOnly property is set to False so the user can type text into the control's text area much as you can enter text in a ComboBox. If ReadOnly is True, the user cannot type in this area and must use the arrow keys or buttons to pick one of the control's items. Unfortunately, setting ReadOnly to True gives the control a gray background, so it appears disabled unless you look closely and notice that the text is black rather than dark gray.

Like the CheckedListBox control, the DomainUpDown control can hold arbitrary objects as items. It displays the string returned by an object's ToString method. See the "CheckedListBox" section earlier in this appendix for more information about displaying objects in the control.

The control's SelectedItem property returns the object representing the item that is currently selected. Note that there may be no item selected if the user typed a value in the text area, rather than selecting a value from the list of items. The SelectedIndex property returns the index of the currently selected item or -1 if no choice is selected.

The control's Text property returns the text that the control is currently displaying. This property returns something meaningful whether the user typed a value or selected an item from the list.

When the control is first displayed, no item is selected. You can use the Properties window to give the control a Text value at design time, but you cannot make it select an item, even if the Text value matches an item's text. If you want the control to begin with an item selected, you can use code similar to the following in the form's Load event handler:

```
' Select the first Priority value.
dudPriority.SelectedIndex = 0
```

If you set the control's Sorted property to True, the control displays its items in sorted order.

If you set the Wrap property to True, the control wraps its list of items around if the user moves past the beginning or end of the list.

ERRORPROVIDER

The ErrorProvider component indicates to the user that another control has an error associated with it. ErrorProvider is an extender provider, so it adds a new Error property to the other controls on its form. For example, if the ErrorProvider is named ErrorProvider1, each control on the form gets a new property named "Error on ErrorProvider1." At design time, use the Properties window to set or clear this value.

To associate an error with a control at runtime, use the ErrorProvider's SetError method. The ErrorProvider automatically displays a red circle containing an exclamation mark next to the control. If the user hovers the mouse over the circle, the ErrorProvider displays a tooltip giving the error text.

To remove an error on a control at runtime, use the ErrorProvider's SetError method to set the control's error message to an empty string.

Many programs set or clear errors on a control in the control's Validating event. Example program UseErrorProvider, which is available for download on the book's web site, uses a Validating event to validate a ZIP code text box.

The component's BlinkRate property determines how quickly the error icon blinks. The BlinkStyle property determines how it blinks.

If BlinkStyle is BlinkIfDifferentError, the component makes the icon blink several times whenever the program sets a control's error message to a new nonblank value.

If BlinkStyle is AlwaysBlink, the component makes the icon blink as long as the control has an associated error. The icon continues blinking, even if another application has the focus, until the user fixes the error and moves to a new field to trigger the Validating event handler again.

If BlinkStyle is NeverBlink, the component displays the error icon without blinking.

The component's Icon property gives the icon that the component displays for an error. You can change this icon if you want to use a special error image.

ANNOYANCE ALERT

Blinking text can be extremely irritating to users, so don't abuse it. The default behavior of blinking a couple of times and then stopping is reasonable, but a message that is constantly blinking very quickly is a bad idea.

Note that the United States Accessibility code prohibits objects that blink between 2 Hz and 55 Hz (see www.hhs.gov/od/topics/it/final_section_508_policy .html#1211SubpartBTechnicalStandards) at least in part because blinking can cause seizures and other life-threatening reactions in some people.

EVENTLOG

The EventLog component enables an application to manipulate event logs. It provides methods to create logs, write and read log messages, and clear logs. Event logs are a more advanced topic. For detailed information, see the MSDN topic "Logging Application, Server, and Security Events" at msdn.microsoft.com/e6t4tk09.aspx.

FILESYSTEMWATCHER

The FileSystemWatcher component keeps an eye on part of the file system and raises events to let your program know if something changes. For example, it can notify your program if a file is created in a particular directory.

For more information on the FileSystemWatcher component, see Chapter 37, "File-System Objects," and Appendix U, "File-System Classes."

FLOWLAYOUTPANEL

The FlowLayoutPanel control displays the controls that it contains in rows or columns. For example, when laying out rows, it places controls next to each other horizontally in a row until it runs out of room, and then it starts a new row.

The FlowLayoutPanel is particularly useful for Toolboxes and in situations where the goal is to display as many of the contained controls as possible at one time, and the exact arrangement of the controls isn't too important.

The control's FlowDirection property determines the manner in which the control arranges its contained controls. This property can take the values LeftToRight, RightToLeft, TopDown, and BottomUp. Example program FlowDirections, which is available for download on the book's web site, demonstrates these different arrangements.

The control's AutoScroll property determines whether the control automatically provides scroll bars if its contents won't fit within the control all at once.

The Padding property determines how much space the control leaves between its edges and the controls that it contains. Use the Margin properties of the contained controls to specify the spacing between the controls.

The TableLayoutPanel control also arranges its contained controls, but in a grid. For information on that control, see the section "TableLayoutPanel" later in this appendix.

FOLDERBROWSERDIALOG

The FolderBrowserDialog component displays a dialog box that lets the user select a folder (directory) in the file system. The program displays the dialog box by calling the component's ShowDialog method.

The component's SelectedPath property not only returns the path selected by the user, but it also determines where the dialog begins browsing. If your code uses the dialog box, does not change this value, and then uses the dialog box again later, the dialog box starts the second time where it left off the first time.

The program can also explicitly set the SelectedPath value to start browsing at a particular folder. For example, the following code makes the dialog begin browsing in the C:\Temp directory:

```
dlgFolder.SelectedPath = "C:\Temp"
```

Alternatively, you can use the component's RootFolder property to make the component start in one of the system folders. Set this property to one of the Environment.SpecialFolder values. For example, to start browsing in the MyPictures directory, set RootFolder to Environment. SpecialFolder.MyPictures.

The dialog box will not allow the user to leave the root folder. For example, if you set the RootFolder property to Environment.SpecialFolder.ProgramFiles, the user will be able to browse through the Program Files hierarchy (normally, C:\Program Files), but will not be able to move to other parts of the system.

If you want to start browsing at a particular directory but want to allow the user to move to other parts of the directory hierarchy, leave the RootFolder with its default value of Environment .SpecialFolder.Desktop and then set the SelectedPath property appropriately. For example, the following code uses the Environment object's SpecialFolder method to make the browser start browsing at the Program Files folder:

```
dlgFolder.RootFolder = Environment.SpecialFolder.Desktop
dlgFolder.SelectedPath =
    Environment.GetFolderPath(Environment.SpecialFolder.ProgramFiles)
```

FONTDIALOG

The FontDialog component displays a font selection dialog. If the user selects a font and clicks OK, the ShowDialog method returns DialogResult.OK.

The component has several properties that determine the options that the dialog displays and the types of fonts it will allow the user to select. The following table describes some of the most important of the component's properties.

PROPERTY	PURPOSE
AllowScriptChange	Determines whether the component allows the user to change the character set shown in the Script combo box. If this is False, the dropdown is still visible, but it only contains one choice.
AllowSimulations	Determines whether the component allows graphics device font simulations. For example, many fonts do not include bold or italics, but the graphics device interface (GDI) can simulate them.
AllowVectorFonts	Determines whether the component allows vector fonts. (Characters in a raster font are drawn as bitmaps. Characters in a vector font are drawn as a series of lines and curves. Vector fonts may provide a nicer look because they scale more easily than raster fonts, but vector fonts may take longer to draw.)
AllowVerticalFonts	Determines whether the component allows vertical fonts (such as Chinese).

Color	Sets or gets the font's color. Note that this is not part of the Font property, so if you want to let the user set a control's font and color, you must handle them separately, as shown in the following code:
	
	`dlgFont.Font = Me.Font`
	`dlgFont.Color = Me.ForeColor`
	`dlgFont.ShowColor = True`
	`If dlgFont.ShowDialog() = DialogResult.OK Then`
	    `Me.Font = dlgFont.Font`
	    `Me.ForeColor = dlgFont.Color`
	`End If`

FixedPitchOnly	Determines whether the dialog box only allows fixed-pitch (fixed-width) fonts. (In a fixed-width font, all characters have the same width. `For example, this sentence is in the Courier font, which is fixed-width.` In a variable-width font, some characters such as I and i are thinner than other characters such as W. This sentence is in the Times New Roman font, which has variable width.
Font	Sets or gets the font described by the dialog box.
FontMustExist	Determines whether the component raises an error if the user tries to select a font that doesn't exist.
MaxSize	Determines the maximum allowed point size.
MinSize	Determines the minimum allowed point size.

PROPERTY	PURPOSE
ShowApply	Determines whether the dialog box displays the Apply button. If you set this to True, you should catch the component's Apply event and apply the currently selected font.
ShowColor	Determines whether the component allows the user to select a color.
ShowEffects	Determines whether the component displays the Effects group box that includes the Strikeout and Underline boxes and the Color dropdown.
ShowHelp	Determines whether the dialog box displays the Help button. If you set this to True, you should catch the component's HelpRequest event. The event handler might explain to the user how the font will be used. For example, "Select the font to be used for item descriptions."

Example program UseFontDialog demonstrates a simple font selection dialog. Example program UseFontDialogWithShowEffects shows how to respond when the user clicks the font dialog's Apply button. Both of these examples are available for download on the book's web site.

GROUPBOX

The GroupBox control displays a caption and a border. This control is mostly for decoration and provides a visually appealing method for grouping related controls on the form.

The GroupBox is also a control container, so you can place other controls inside it. If a GroupBox contains RadioButton controls, those buttons form a group separate from any other RadioButton controls on the form. If you click one of those buttons, the other buttons in the GroupBox deselect, but any selected RadioButton controls outside of the GroupBox remain unchanged. This is important if you need to create more than one group of RadioButton controls.

If you want to create multiple RadioButton groups, but you don't want to display a caption and border, use a Panel control instead of a GroupBox.

The GroupBox control provides a typical assortment of properties that determine its appearance (such as BackColor, BackgroundImage, and Font). These properties are straightforward.

If you set the control's Enabled property to False, its caption is grayed out and any controls it contains are also disabled. This is a convenient way for a program to enable or disable a group of controls all at once.

The GroupBox control's Controls property returns a collection containing references to the controls inside the GroupBox.

One of the few confusing aspects to working with GroupBox controls in code is figuring out where to position controls within the GroupBox. The control's borders and caption take up room inside the control's client area, so deciding how to position controls without covering those decorations is not obvious. Fortunately, the control's DisplayRectangle property returns a Rectangle object that you can use to position items. This rectangle fills most of the control's area that isn't occupied by the caption and borders.

HELPPROVIDER

The HelpProvider component displays help for other controls. You can associate a HelpProvider with a control. Then, if the user sets focus to the control and presses the F1 key, the HelpProvider displays help for the control. The HelpProvider either displays a small tooltip-like pop-up displaying a help string, or it opens a help file.

To assign a help string to a control at design time, open the form in the form designer and select the control. In the Properties window, look for a property named "HelpString on HelpProvider1," where HelpProvider1 is the name of your HelpProvider component. If the form contains more than one HelpProvider, the control should have more than one "HelpString on" property.

Enter the text you want the HelpProvider to display in this property and you're finished. When the user sets focus to the control and presses F1, the HelpProvider displays the string automatically.

To set the help string programmatically, call the HelpProvider component's SetHelpString method passing it the control and the help string that it should display for the control.

To provide help using a help file, set the HelpProvider component's HelpNamespace property to the full name and path to the help file. Set the other control's "HelpNavigator on HelpProvider1" property to one of the values shown in the following table to tell the HelpProvider how to use the help file when the user asks for help on this control.

HELPNAVIGATOR VALUE	PURPOSE
AssociateIndex	Opens the help file's Index page and goes to the first entry that begins with the same letter as the control's "HelpKeyword on HelpProvider1" property.
Find	Opens the help file's Index tab.
Index	Opens the help file's Index tab and searches for the value entered in the control's "HelpKeyword on HelpProvider1" property.
KeywordIndex	Opens the help file's Index tab and searches for the value entered in the control's "HelpKeyword on HelpProvider1" property.
TableOfContents	Opens the help file's Table of Contents tab.
Topic	Displays the topic in the help file that has URL stored in the control's "HelpKeyword on HelpProvider1" property. For example, the URL street_name.htm might contain the help file's page for the Street field.

To set a control's HelpNavigator value in code, call the HelpProvider component's SetHelpNavigator method passing it the control and the navigator method that you want to use.

A control's "ShowHelp on HelpProvider1" property indicates whether the control should use the HelpProvider to display its help.

HSCROLLBAR

The HScrollBar control represents a horizontal scroll bar. The user can drag the scroll bar's "thumb" to select a number.

The control's Value property gets and sets its current numeric value. The Minimum and Maximum properties determine the range of values that the control can display. These are integer values, so the HScrollBar control is not ideal for letting the user select a nonintegral value such as 1.25. (You can multiply the values by 100 to get finer grained resolution but the user still can't select truly nonintegral values.)

The control's SmallChange property determines how much the control's Value property changes when the user clicks the arrows at the scroll bar's ends. The LargeChange property determines how much the Value changes when the user clicks the scroll bar between the thumb and the arrows.

Strangely, the control does not let the user actually select the value given by its Maximum property. The program can select that value using code, but the largest value the user can select is Maximum − LargeChange + 1. For example, if Maximum is 100 and LargeChange is 10 (the default values), the user can select values up to $100 - 10 + 1 = 91$.

If you set the control's TabStop property to True, the control can hold the input focus. While the control has the focus, you can use the arrow keys to change its value by the SmallChange amount.

The control's Scroll event fires when the user changes the control's value interactively. The ValueChanged event occurs when the control's value changes either because the user changed it interactively, or because the program changed it with code. The following code shows how a program can display the hbarDays control's Value property when the user or program changes it:

```
Private Sub hbarDays_ValueChanged() Handles hbarDays.ValueChanged
    lblDays.Text = hbarDays.Value.ToString
End Sub
```

Note that many controls that might otherwise require scroll bars can provide their own. For example, the ListBox, TextBox, and Panel controls can display their own scroll bars when necessary, so you don't need to add your own.

IMAGELIST

The ImageList component stores a series of images for use by other controls or by the program's code. For example, one way to display an image on a Button control is to create an ImageList component holding the image. Set the Button's ImageList property to the ImageList component and set its ImageIndex property to the index of the image in the ImageList.

To add images to the component at design time, open the form designer, select the component, click the Images property in the Properties window, and click the ellipsis (. . .) on the right. The Image Collection Editor that appears has buttons that let you add, remove, and rearrange the images.

The ImageList component's ImageSize property determines the size of the images. The component stretches any images of different sizes to fit the ImageSize. This means that a single ImageList component cannot provide images of different sizes. If you must store images of different sizes in the application, use another method such as multiple ImageList components, PictureBox controls (possibly with the Visible property set to False), or resources.

LABEL

The Label control displays some read-only text. Note that you cannot even select the text at runtime so, for example, you cannot copy it to the clipboard. If you want to allow the user to select and copy text, but not modify it, use a TextBox with the ReadOnly property set to True.

The Label control can display an image in addition to text. To display an image, either set the control's Image property to the image or set the control's ImageList and ImageIndex properties. Use the ImageAlign and TextAlign properties to determine where the image and text are positioned within the control.

If you set the Label control's AutoSize property to True (the default), the control resizes itself to fit its text. This can be particularly useful for controls that contain text that changes at runtime because it ensures that the control is always big enough to hold the text. Note that the control does not automatically make itself big enough to display any image it contains.

The Label control automatically breaks lines that contain embedded carriage returns. The following code makes a label display text on four lines:

```
lblInstructions.Text = "Print this message and either:" & vbCrLf &
    "     - Mail it to the recipient" & vbCrLf &
    "     - Fax it to the recipient" & vbCrLf &
    "     - Throw it away"
```

Text that contains carriage returns confuses the control's AutoSize capabilities, however, so you should not use AutoSize with multiline text.

The Label control also automatically wraps to a new line if the text it contains is too long to fit within the control's width.

LINKLABEL

The LinkLabel control displays a label that is associated with a hyperlink. By default, the label is blue and underlined, so it is easy to recognize as a link. It also displays a pointing hand cursor when the mouse moves over it, so it looks more or less like a link on a web page.

When the user clicks a LinkLabel, the control raises its LinkClicked event. The program can catch the event and take whatever action is appropriate. For example, it could display another form, open a document, or open a web page.

The LinkLabel control provides all the formatting properties that the Label control does. See the section "Label" earlier in this appendix for more information on formatting the control's label.

The control also provides several properties for determining the appearance of its link. The following table describes some of the most useful.

PROPERTY	PURPOSE
ActiveLinkColor	The color of an active link.
DisabledLinkColor	The color of a disabled link.
LinkArea	The piece of the control's text that is represented as a link. This includes a start position and a length in characters.
LinkBehavior	Determines when the link is underlined. This can take the values AlwaysUnderline, HoverUnderline, NeverUnderline, and SystemDefault.
LinkColor	The color of a normal link.
Links	A collection of objects representing the link(s) within the control's text.
LinkVisited	A Boolean that indicates whether the link should be displayed as visited.
VisitedLinkColor	The color of a visited link.

A LinkLabel can display more than one link within its text. For example, in the text "The quick brown fox jumps over the lazy dog," the control might display the words *fox* and *dog* as links and the rest as normal text. At design time, you can use the LinkArea property to specify only one link. To make *fox* the link, the program would set LinkArea to 16, 3 to start with the seventeenth character (remember indexing starts at 0) and include 3 letters.

At runtime, the program can add other links to the control. The following code clears the llblPangram control's Links collection and then adds two new link areas. The program sets each of the new Link objects' LinkData property to a URL that the program should display when the user clicks that link.

```
Dim new_link As System.Windows.Forms.LinkLabel.Link

llblPangram.Links.Clear()
new_link = llblPangram.Links.Add(16, 3)
new_link.LinkData = "http://www.somewhere.com/fox.htm"
new_link = llblPangram.Links.Add(40, 3)
new_link.LinkData = "http://www.somewhere.com/dog.htm"
```

The following code shows how the program displays the URL corresponding to the link the user clicked. The code gets the appropriate Link object from the event handler's event arguments, converts the Link object's LinkData property into a string, and uses System.Diagnostics.Process .Start to open it with the system's default browser.

```
' Display the URL associated with the clicked link.
Private Sub llblPangram_LinkClicked(ByVal sender As System.Object,
 ByVal e As System.Windows.Forms.LinkLabelLinkClickedEventArgs) _
 Handles llblPangram.LinkClicked
    System.Diagnostics.Process.Start(e.Link.LinkData.ToString)
End Sub
```

LISTBOX

The ListBox control displays a list of items that the user can select. The following table describes some of the control's most useful properties.

PROPERTY	PURPOSE
SelectionMode	Determines how the user can select text. See the following text for details.
MultiColumn	If this is True, the control does not display a vertical scroll bar. Instead, if there are too many items to fit, the control displays them in multiple columns. If the columns will not all fit, the control displays a horizontal scroll bar to let you see them all. The control's ColumnWidth property determines the width of the columns.
IntegralHeight	If this is True, the control will not display a partial item. For example, if the control is tall enough to display 10.7 items, it will shrink slightly so it can only display 10 items.
ScrollAlwaysVisible	If this is True, the control displays its vertical scroll bar even if all of its items fit. This can be useful if the program will add and remove items to and from the list at runtime and you don't want the control to change size depending on whether the items all fit.
Sorted	Determines whether the control displays its items in sorted order.
SelectedItem	Returns a reference to the first selected item or Nothing if no item is selected. This is particularly useful if the control's SelectionMode is One.
SelectedIndex	Returns the zero-based index of the first selected item or –1 if no item is selected. This is particularly useful if the control's SelectionMode is One.
Text	Returns the text displayed for the first currently selected item, or an empty string if no item is selected. Your code can set this property to a string to make the control select the item that displays exactly that string.

PROPERTY	PURPOSE
SelectedItems	A collection containing references to all the items that are currently selected.
SelectedIndices	A collection containing the indices of all the items that are currently selected.
UseTabStops	Determines whether the control recognizes tabs embedded within its items' text. If UseTabStops is True, the control replaces tab characters with empty space. If UseTabStops is False, the control displays tab characters as thin black boxes.

The control's SelectionMode property determines how the user can select items. This property can take the value None, One, MultiSimple, or MultiExtended.

When SelectionMode is None, the user cannot select any items. This mode can be useful for displaying a read-only list. It can be particularly handy when the list is very long and the control's automatic scrolling is useful, allowing the user see all of the list's items.

When SelectionMode is One, the user can select a single item. When the user clicks an item, any previously selected item is deselected.

When SelectionMode is MultiSimple, the user can select multiple items by clicking them one at a time. When the user clicks an item, the other items keep their current selection status. This mode is useful when the user needs to select multiple items that are not necessarily near each other in the list. It is less useful if the user must select a large number of items. For example, clicking 100 items individually would be tedious.

When SelectionMode is MultiExtended, the user can select multiple items in several ways. The user can click and drag to manipulate several items at once. If the first item clicked is not selected, all of the items are selected. If the first item is already selected, all of the items are deselected. If the user holds down the Ctrl key and clicks an item, the other items' selection status remains unchanged. If the user doesn't hold down the Ctrl key, any other items are deselected when the user selects new items. If the user clicks an item and then clicks another item while holding down the Shift key, all of the items between those two are selected. If the user holds down the Ctrl key at the same time, those items are selected and the other items' selection status remains unchanged.

The MultiExtended mode is useful when the user needs to select many items, some of which may be next to each other. This mode is quite complicated, however, so MultiSimple may be a better choice if the user doesn't need to select ranges of items or too many items. The CheckedListBox control is often a good alternative when the user must make many complicated selections.

Use the control's Items.Add method to add an object to the list. If the object isn't a string, the control uses the object's ToString method to determine the value it displays to the user.

The ListBox control's FindString method returns the index of the first item that begins with a given string. For example, the following code selects the first item that begins with the string Code:

```
lstTask.SelectedIndex = lstTask.FindString("Code")
```

The FindStringExact method returns the index of the first item that matches a given string exactly.

LISTVIEW

The ListView control displays a list of items in one of five possible views, determined by the control's View property. The View property can take the following values:

➤   `Details` — For each item, displays a small icon, the item's text, and the sub-items' text on a row.

➤   `LargeIcon` — Displays large icons above the item's text. Entries are arranged from left to right until they wrap to the next row.

➤   `List` — Displays small icons to the left of the item's text. Each entry is placed on its own row.

➤   `SmallIcon` — Displays small icons to the left of the item's text. Entries are arranged from left to right until they wrap to the next row.

➤   `Tile` — Displays large icons to the left of the item's text. Entries are arranged from left to right until they wrap to the next row.

Figure G-4 shows each of these views for the same list of items. The second tiled view shown in the lower-right corner uses the control's CheckBoxes and StateImageList properties, and is described shortly.

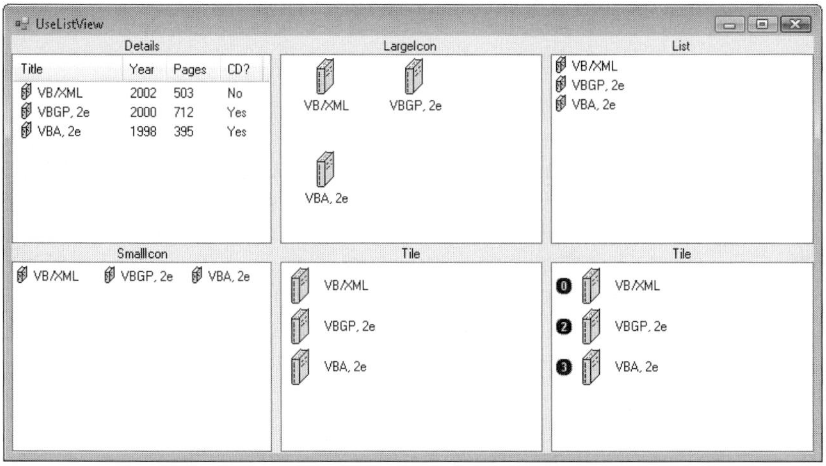

FIGURE G-4: The ListView control can display five views.

Set the control's LargeImageList and SmallImageList properties to ImageList controls containing the images that you want to use for the LargeIcon and SmallIcon views.

Each of the ListView control's items may contain one or more sub-items that are displayed in the Details view. To create the items and sub-items, open the form designer, select the ListView control, click the Items property in the Properties window, and click the ellipsis (. . .) button to the right to display the ListViewItem Collection Editor.

Click the Add button to make a new item. Set the item's Text property to the string you want the control to display. If you have attached ImageList controls to the ListView, set the new item's ImageIndex property to the index of the image you want to display for this item in the LargeIcon and SmallIcon views.

For example, the program in Figure G-4 contains two ImageList controls. The imlBig control contains 32 × 32 pixel images and the imlSmall control contains 16 × 16 pixel images. Each holds one image of a book. All of the items in the ListView items have ImageIndex set to 0, so they all display the first images in the imlBig and imlSmall controls.

To give an item sub-items at design time, select it in the ListViewItem Collection Editor, click its SubItems property, and then click the ellipsis (. . .) button to the right to display the ListViewSubItem Collection Editor. Use the Add button to make sub-items. Set the sub-items' Text properties to determine what the Details view displays.

If you set the ListView control's CheckBoxes property to True, the control displays check boxes next to its items. If you set the control's StateImageList property to an ImageList control, the control displays the images in that list. When the user double-clicks an item, the control toggles the image index between 0 and 1 and displays the first or second image in the ImageList control. In Figure G-4, the ListView on the lower-right uses check box images that look like circles with numbers inside. If you set CheckBoxes to True but do not set the ListView control's StateImageList property, the control displays simple boxes containing check marks.

If CheckBoxes is True, the program can use the CheckedIndices or CheckedItems collections to see which items the user has selected. If the StateImageList control holds more than two images, an item is considered checked if it is displaying any picture other than the first one. The following code lists the currently checked items in the lvwMeals ListView control:

```
For Each checked_item As ListViewItem In lvwMeals.CheckedItems
    Debug.WriteLine(checked_item.ToString)
Next checked_item
```

The control's SelectedIndices and SelectedItems collections let the program see which items the user has currently selected. The user can select items by clicking them. If the user holds down the Ctrl key while clicking, any items that are already selected remain selected. If the user clicks an item, holds down the Shift key, and then clicks another item, the control selects all of the items in between the two.

If you are using the ListView in Details mode, you must define the control's columns. Open the form designer, select the control, click the Columns property in the Properties window, and click the ellipsis (. . .) button to the right to display the ColumnHeader Collection Editor.

Use the Add button to create column headers and then set each header's text. If you don't define enough columns for all of the sub-items, some of the sub-items will not be visible to the user. This is one way you can include data for an item but hide it from the user.

The LabelEdit control has several other properties that determine its appearance and how the control interacts with the user. The following table describes some of the most important of these.

PROPERTY	PURPOSE
AllowColumnReorder	If True, the user can rearrange the columns by dragging their column headers while in Detail mode.
FullRowSelect	If True, clicking an item or any of its sub-items selects the item. If False, the user must click the item, not a sub-item, to select the item. If AllowColumnReorder is True, you may want to set FullRowSelect to True also so the user doesn't need to figure out which rearranged column contains the item itself.
GridLines	If True, the control displays gray lines between the rows and columns while in Detail mode.
HeaderStyle	When in Detail mode, this can be None to not display column headers, Clickable to allow the user to click column headers, or Nonclickable to not let the user click column headers. If this is Clickable, the program can catch the control's ColumnClick event to learn the index of the column clicked. For example, you may want to sort the ListView control's items using the clicked column.
LabelEdit	If True, the user can modify the items' labels. The user can never change the sub-items' labels.
MultiSelect	If True, the user can use the Ctrl and Shift keys to select multiple items.
Sorting	Indicates whether the control displays its items sorted ascending, sorted descending, or not sorted.

Example program UseListView, shown in Figure G-4 and available for download on the book's web site, uses these techniques to initialize its ListView controls at design time.

ListView Helper Code

In addition to using the ListView control's collection property editors at design time, you can manipulate the control's items and sub-items at runtime using code.

The control's Columns collection contains ColumnHeader objects representing the control's column headers. You can use the collection's Add, Count, Remove, RemoveAt, and other methods to manage the text displayed above the columns.

The ListViewMakeColumnHeaders subroutine shown in the following code uses the Columns collection to define a ListView control's column headers. The routine takes as parameters a ListView control and a ParamArray of values that contain title strings, alignment values, and widths. The code clears the control's Columns collection and then loops through the ParamArray. For each triple of array entries, the control creates a column header using the title string, alignment value, and width.

```
' Make the ListView's column headers.
' The ParamArray entries should be triples holding
' column title, HorizontalAlignment value, and width.
Private Sub ListViewMakeColumnHeaders(ByVal lvw As ListView, _
 ByVal ParamArray header_info() As Object)
    ' Remove any existing headers.
    lvw.Columns.Clear()

    ' Make the column headers.
    For i As Integer = header_info.GetLowerBound(0) To _
                       header_info.GetUpperBound(0) Step 3
        Dim col_header As ColumnHeader = lvw.Columns.Add(
            DirectCast(header_info(i), String),
            -1,
            DirectCast(header_info(i + 1), HorizontalAlignment))
        col_header.Width = DirectCast(header_info(i + 2), Integer)
    Next i
End Sub
```

The following code shows how a program might use subroutine ListViewMakeColumnHeaders to define the lvwBooks control's column headers. Because the Pages and Year columns contain numeric values, the control aligns them on the right of their columns.

```
' Make the ListView column headers.
ListViewMakeColumnHeaders(lvwBooks,
    "Title", HorizontalAlignment.Left, 120,
    "URL", HorizontalAlignment.Left, 120,
    "ISBN", HorizontalAlignment.Left, 90,
    "Picture", HorizontalAlignment.Left, 120,
    "Pages", HorizontalAlignment.Right, 50,
    "Year", HorizontalAlignment.Right, 40)
```

The ListView control's Items collection contains ListViewItem objects that represent the control's items. Each ListViewItem has a SubItems collection that represents the item's sub-items. These collections provide the usual assortment of methods for managing collections: Count, Add, Remove, RemoveAt, and so forth.

The ListViewMakeRow subroutine shown in the following code uses these collections to add an item and its sub-items to a ListView. The routine takes as parameters the ListView control, the name of the item, and a ParamArray containing the names of any number of sub-items. The code uses the ListView control's Items.Add method to make the new item. It then loops through the sub-item names, using the new item's SubItems.Add method to make the sub-items.

```
' Make a ListView row.
Private Sub ListViewMakeRow(ByVal lvw As ListView, ByVal image_index As Integer, _
 ByVal item_title As String, ByVal ParamArray subitem_titles() As String)
    ' Make the item.
    Dim new_item As ListViewItem = lvw.Items.Add(item_title)
    new_item.ImageIndex = image_index

    ' Make the subitems.
```

```
      For i As Integer = subitem_titles.GetLowerBound(0) To _
                          subitem_titles.GetUpperBound(0)
          new_item.SubItems.Add(subitem_titles(i))
      Next i
  End Sub
```

If you set a ListView column's width to –1, the control automatically resizes the column so it is wide enough to display all of its data. If you set a column's width to –2, the control makes the column wide enough to display all of its data and its header text.

The ListViewSizeColumns subroutine shown in the following code sizes all of a ListView control's columns so that they fit their data. If the allow_room_for_header parameter is True, it also allows room for the column headers.

```
  ' Set column widths to -1 to fit data, -2 to fit data and header.
  Private Sub ListViewSizeColumns(ByVal lvw As ListView,
   ByVal allow_room_for_header As Boolean)
      Dim new_wid As Integer = -1
      If allow_room_for_header Then new_wid = -2

      ' Set the width for each column.
      For i As Integer = 0 To lvw.Columns.Count-1
          lvw.Columns(i).Width = new_wid
      Next i
  End Sub
```

These helper routines make working with ListView controls a bit easier.

Custom ListView Sorting

The ListView control's Sorting property enables you to sort items in ascending or descending order, but it only considers the items, not the sub-items. It doesn't even use the sub-items to break ties when two items have the same value.

Fortunately, the ListView control's ListViewItemSorter property provides the flexibility to change the sort order in any way you like. To use this property, you must create a class that implements the IComparer interface. The ListView control will use an object of this type to decide which items to place before other items.

The key to the IComparer interface is its Compare function. This function takes two ListViewItem objects as parameters and returns –1, 0, or 1 to indicate whether the first should be considered less than, equal to, or greater than the second object in the sort order.

To implement a custom sort order, the program should set the ListView control's ListViewItemSorter property to an object that implements IComparer and then call the control's Sort method. The control then uses the IComparer object to put the items in the proper order.

CREATIVE COMPARERS

You can find other uses of the IComparer interface in the section "Array.Sort" in Chapter 28, "Collection Classes," and in the section "Derived Controls" in Chapter 22, "Custom Controls."

Example program ListViewCustomSort, which is available for download on the book's web site, uses an IComparer class to allow the user to sort ascending or descending on any of the ListView control's item or sub-item columns in the control's Details view. The code is fairly involved so it is not shown here. Download the example from the book's web site to see the details.

MASKEDTEXTBOX

The MaskedTextBox control is a text box that provides a mask that helps guide the user in entering a value in a particular format. The mask determines which characters are allowed at different positions in the text. It displays placeholder characters to help prompt the user and underscores where the user can enter characters. For example, an empty United States phone number field would appear as (___)___-____ in the MaskedTextBox.

The control's Mask property uses the characters shown in the following table.

CHARACTER	MEANING
0	A required digit between 0 and 9.
9	An optional digit or space.
#	An optional digit, space, +, or −. If the user leaves this blank, this character appears as a space in the control's Text, InputText, and OutputText properties.
L	A required letter a–z or A–Z.
?	An optional letter a–z or A–Z.
&	A required nonspace character.
C	An optional character.
A	A required alphanumeric character a–z, A–Z, or 0–9.
a	An optional alphanumeric character a–z, A–Z, or 0–9.
.	A decimal separator placeholder. The control automatically displays the appropriate decimal separator character for the current UI culture.
,	A thousands separator placeholder. The control automatically displays the appropriate thousands separator character for the current UI culture.

continues

(continued)

CHARACTER	MEANING
:	A time separator placeholder. The control automatically displays the appropriate time separator character for the current UI culture.
/	A date separator placeholder. The control automatically displays the appropriate date separator character for the current UI culture.
$	A currency symbol placeholder. The control automatically displays the appropriate currency symbol character for the current UI culture.
<	Automatically converts the characters that the user types after this point into lowercase.
>	Automatically converts the characters that the user types after this point into uppercase.
|	Disables the previous < or > character.
\	Escapes a character so it is displayed literally by the control even if the character would otherwise have special meaning. For example, \9 places a 9 in the output and \\ displays a \.

All other characters appear as literals within the mask. Dashes and parentheses are common literal characters. For example, the Social Security number mask 000-00-0000 displays dashes as in "___-__-___."

The following table shows the MaskTextBox control's most useful properties. Note that this control inherits from the TextBox control, so it inherits most of that control's properties, methods, and events. See the section "TextBox" later in this appendix for more information.

PROPERTY	PURPOSE
AllowPromptAsInput	Determines whether the user can enter the prompt character determined by the PromptChar property (normally an underscore).
AsciiOnly	Determines whether the control allows non-ASCII Unicode characters.
BeepOnError	Determines whether the control beeps whenever the user types an invalid keystroke.
EnableCutCopyLiterals	Determines whether literal characters such as the parentheses in the mask (999)000-0000 are included when the user copies and pastes the control's text.
HidePromptOnLeave	Determines whether the control hides its prompt characters when it loses the focus.

PROPERTY	PURPOSE
IncludeLiterals	Determines whether the control includes literal characters in the Text and OutputText properties.
IncludePrompt	Determines whether the control includes the PromptChar character in the OutputText property.
InputText	Gets or sets the characters input by the user. This doesn't include any literal mask characters.
Mask	Gets or sets the mask.
MaskCompleted	Returns True if the user's input satisfies the required mask characters.
MaskFull	Returns True if the user has entered characters for all of the mask's required and optional elements.
OutputText	Returns the user's text modified by the IncludeLiterals and IncludePrompt properties.
PromptChar	Determines the character that the control uses as a placeholder for user input.
Text	Gets or sets the text as it is currently displayed to the user, including prompt and literal characters.

The following table describes the control's most useful events.

EVENT	OCCURS WHEN
InputTextChanged	The control's text has been modified.
MaskChanged	The control's mask changed.
MaskInputRejected	The user's input does not satisfy the mask at the current position.
OutputTextChanged	The control's text has been modified.
TextChanged	The control's text has been modified.

Unfortunately, the MaskedTextBox control is relatively inflexible. It requires the user to enter exactly the right characters at the right positions, and there can be no variation in the format. For example, a single mask cannot let the user enter a telephone number in either of the formats 456-7890 or (123)456-7890. The mask (999)000-0000 makes the first three digits optional, but the user must enter spaces in those positions or skip over them. The mask also considers each character separately, so this mask accepts the value (3)456-7890.

This inflexibility means the MaskedTextBox control is most useful when you know *exactly* what the user will need to enter. If you want the user to type a four-digit telephone extension, a seven-digit phone number, or a five-digit ZIP code, then the control works well. If the user might enter either a seven- or ten-digit phone number, a five-digit ZIP code or a nine-digit ZIP+4 code, or an arbitrary e-mail address, the control is much less useful. In these cases, you might want to use regular expressions to validate the user's input more precisely. For more information on regular expressions, see the "Regular Expressions" section in Chapter 39, "Useful Namespaces."

MENUSTRIP

The MenuStrip control represents a form's menus, submenus, and menu items. To make the form display the menu, its Menu property must be set to the MenuStrip control. The first time you add a MenuStrip control to the form, Visual Basic automatically sets the form's Menu property to the new control, so you usually don't need to worry about this. If you later delete the control and create a new MenuStrip, you may need to set this property yourself.

At design time, the MenuStrip control is visible both at the top of the form and in the component tray. Click a menu entry and type to change the caption it displays. Place an ampersand in front of the character that you want to use as a keyboard accelerator. For example, to make the caption of the File menu display as File, set the menu's text to &File. If you type Alt+F at runtime, the program opens this menu.

> **MISSING MENUS**
>
> If the form also contains a ContextMenuStrip control and you select that control, then that control appears at the top of the form instead of the MenuStrip. Click the MenuStrip in the component tray to make it reappear at the top of the form.

To make a cascading submenu, click a menu item and enter its caption. A ghostly text box appears to the right containing the text "Type Here." Click this text and enter the submenu's name.

When you select a menu item, the Properties window displays the menu item's properties. The following table describes the most useful menu item properties.

PROPERTY	PURPOSE
Checked	Indicates whether the item is checked. You can use this property to let the user check and uncheck menu items.
CheckOnClick	Determines whether the item should automatically check and uncheck when the user clicks it.
CheckState	Determines whether the item is checked, unchecked, or displayed as in an indeterminate state.

PROPERTY	PURPOSE
DisplayStyle	Determines whether the item displays text, an image, both, or neither. The image appears on the left where a check box would otherwise go. If the item displays an image, it draws a box around the image when the item is checked.
Enabled	Determines whether the menu item is enabled. If an item is disabled, its shortcut is also disabled and the user cannot open its submenu if it contains one.
Font	Determines the font used to draw the item.
MergeAction	Determines how Visual Basic merges MDI child and parent form menus. See the online help for more information.
MergeIndex	Determines the order in which Visual Basic merges MDI child and parent form menus. See the online help for more information.
Name	Gives the menu item's name.
ShortcutKeys	Determines the item's keyboard shortcut. For instance, if you set an item's shortcut to F5, the user can instantly invoke the item at runtime by pressing the F5 key.
ShowShortcutKeys	Determines whether the menu displays its shortcut to the right at runtime. Usually this should be True, so users can learn about the items' shortcuts.
Text	Gives the caption displayed by the item. Place an ampersand in front of the character you want to use as a keyboard accelerator as already described.
Visible	Determines whether the item is visible. An item's shortcut will still work even if the item is not visible. You can use that feature to provide keyboard shortcuts for functions that are not available in any menu.

TRICKY TYPING

When you select a menu item and start typing, your text always goes into the menu item's Text property. To change some other property, such as the menu item's name, you must click the property in the Properties window before typing.

This behavior is different from that of other controls. Usually if you select a control and start typing, your text goes to the previously selected property. For example, if you select one control's Name property and then click another control, any text you type goes into the new control's Name property. That lets you quickly set the names of many controls. If you try this same technique for menu items, you'll end up changing their Text values instead.

When the user selects a menu item, the item raises a Click event. You can write an event handler to take whatever action is appropriate. For example, the following code shows how the File menu's Exit item closes the form:

```
Private Sub mnuFileExit_Click() Handles mnuFileExit.Click
    Me.Close()
End Sub
```

To create a menu item event handler, open the item in the form editor and double-click it.

For online help about the MenuStrip control, go to `msdn.microsoft.com/system.windows.forms .menustrip.aspx`.

MESSAGEQUEUE

The MessageQueue component provides access to a queue on a message-queuing server. An application can use a message queue to communicate with other applications. This is a fairly advanced and specialized topic, so it is not covered in detail here. See the online help at `msdn .microsoft.com/system.messaging.messagequeue.aspx` for more information.

MONTHCALENDAR

The MonthCalendar control displays a calendar that allows the user to select a range of dates. This calendar is similar to the one that the DateTimePicker control displays when its ShowUpDown property is False and you click the control's drop-down arrow (on the bottom in Figure G-3). See the section "DateTimePicker" earlier in this appendix for more information on that control.

The DateTimePicker control is designed to let the user select a single date. The MonthCalendar control is a bit more powerful. For example, this control can allow the user to select a range of dates by clicking and dragging across the calendar. The program can use the control's SelectionRange, SelectionStart, and SelectionEnd properties to see what dates the user has selected.

The following table describes the control's most useful properties for controlling its more advanced features.

PROPERTY	PURPOSE
AnnuallyBoldedDates	An array that specifies dates that should be bolded every year. For example, you can bold April 1 for every year displayed.
BoldedDates	An array that specifies specific dates that should be displayed in bold.
CalendarDimensions	Sets the number of columns and rows of months the control displays. Figure G-5 shows a MonthCalendar control with Calendar Dimensions = 3, 2 (three columns and two rows).
FirstDayOfWeek	Sets the day of the week shown in the leftmost column of each month. Figure G-5 uses the default value Sunday.

PROPERTY	PURPOSE
MaxDate	The last date the user is allowed to select.
MaxSelectionCount	The maximum number of days the user can select.
MinDate	The first date the user is allowed to select.
MonthlyBoldedDates	An array that specifies dates that should be bolded every month. For example, you can bold the 13th of every month displayed.
SelectionEnd	A DateTime object representing the control's last selected date.
SelectionRange	A SelectionRange object representing the control's selected range of dates.
SelectionStart	A DateTime object representing the control's first selected date.
ShowToday	Determines whether the control displays today's date at the bottom.
ShowTodayCircle	Determines whether the control circles today's date (April 1, 2010 in Figure G-5). (Although on this system at least the date is "circled" with a rectangle.)
ShowWeekNumbers	Determines whether the control displays the number of each week in the year to the left of each week.
SingleMonthSize	Returns the minimum size needed to display a single month.
TodayDate	Determines the date displayed as today's date (April 1, 2010 in Figure G-5).
TodayDateSet	Boolean that indicates whether the control's TodayDate property has been explicitly set.

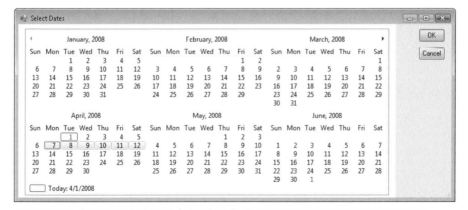

FIGURE G-5: Program UseMonthCalendarInDialog displays several months at a time.

DIFFICULT DATES

The TodayDate property has an annoying side effect. If you set this value at design time and then set it back to the current day's date, the control's TodayDateSet property still returns True, indicating that you have set the TodayDate property. To clear TodayDate so that TodayDateSet returns False, right-click the name (not the value) of the TodayDate property in the Properties window and select Reset.

The MonthCalendar control provides several handy methods. The following table describes the most useful.

METHOD	PURPOSE
AddAnnuallyBoldedDate	Adds a date to the control's array of annually bolded dates. You must call UpdateBoldedDates after using this method.
AddBoldedDate	Adds a date to the control's array of bolded dates. You must call UpdateBoldedDates after using this method.
AddMonthlyBoldedDate	Adds a date to the control's array of monthly bolded dates. You must call UpdateBoldedDates after using this method.
GetDisplayRange	Returns a SelectionRange object that indicates the range of dates currently displayed by the control. If this method's visible parameter is True, the SelectionRange includes only dates that are included in the months that are completely visible (1/1/2010 to 6/30/2010 in Figure G-5). If this parameter is False, the SelectionRange includes all of the displayed dates even if they are in the partially displayed months.
RemoveAllAnnuallyBoldedDates	Empties the control's array of annually bolded dates. You must call UpdateBoldedDates after using this method.
RemoveAllBoldedDates	Empties the control's array of bolded dates. You must call UpdateBoldedDates after using this method.
RemoveAllMonthlyBoldedDates	Empties the control's array of monthly bolded dates. You must call UpdateBoldedDates after using this method.
RemoveAnnuallyBoldedDate	Removes a specific annually bolded date. You must call UpdateBoldedDates after using this method.
RemoveBoldedDate	Removes a specific bolded date. You must call UpdateBoldedDates after using this method.
RemoveMonthlyBoldedDate	Removes a specific monthly bolded date. You must call UpdateBoldedDates after using this method.
SetCalendarDimensions	Sets the control's CalendarDimensions property.

METHOD	PURPOSE
SetDate	Selects the specified date.
SetSelectionRange	Selects the range defined by two dates.
UpdateBoldedDates	Makes the control update itself to show changes to its bolded dates.

The control's bolded dates, monthly bolded dates, and annually bolded dates are all tracked separately and the control displays any date that is listed in any of those groups as bold. That means, for instance, that the RemoveAllBoldedDates subroutine does not change the monthly bolded dates or annually bolded dates.

For example, the following code sets April 1 as an annually bolded date and January 13 as a monthly bolded date. It then removes all of the nonspecific bolded dates and calls UpdateBoldedDates. The result is that April 1 in every year is bold and that the 13th of every month is bold.

```
calStartDate.AddAnnuallyBoldedDate(#4/1/2010#)
calStartDate.AddMonthlyBoldedDate(#1/13/2010#)
calStartDate.RemoveAllBoldedDates()
calStartDate.UpdateBoldedDates()
```

Example program UseMonthCalendar uses a MonthCalendar control to display a single month at a time and lets the user select a date range. Example program UseMonthCalendarInDialog also lets the user select a range of dates, but it displays six months at a time. Both of these programs are available for download on the book's web site.

NOTIFYICON

The NotifyIcon component is invisible at runtime. A program can use the NotifyIcon to display an icon in the system tray. The system tray (also called the *status area*) is the little area holding small icons in the lower-right part of the taskbar. The program can use this icon to indicate the application's state.

Figure G-6 shows part of the desktop while the UseNotifyIcon example program is running. The program's NotifyIcon is displaying a happy face icon in the system tray on the lower right. When you click the program's Happy or Sad radio buttons, the NotifyIcon component displays the corresponding icon.

Figure G-6 also shows the program and the program's icon in the taskbar. These (and the Task Manager, too, although it isn't shown in Figure G-6) also display happy and sad icons. The pictures used for these come from the form's Icon property, not

FIGURE G-6: The NotifyIcon component displays an icon in the system tray.

from the NotifyIcon component, so you can display different images for these and the one in the system tray, if you like. Download the UseNotifyIcon example program from the book's web site to see how it sets the icons.

Notification icons are particularly useful for programs that have no user interface or that run in the background. For example, a program that monitors the system's load could use its system tray icon to give the user an idea of the current load.

These sorts of programs, particularly those without normal user interfaces, often add a context menu to their tray icons so that the user can interact with them. This menu might include commands to minimize or restore the application if it has a user interface, or to close the application.

The NotifyIcon component only has a few interesting properties. Its Icon property determines the icon that the component displays. Its Text property sets the tooltip text that the component displays when the user hovers the mouse over the icon. The Visible property determines whether the icon is visible. Finally, the component's ContextMenuStrip property sets the ContextMenuStrip control that displays when the user right-clicks the icon.

NUMERICUPDOWN

The NumericUpDown control displays a number with up and down arrows that you can use to change the number. If you click an arrow and hold it down, the number changes repeatedly. After a small delay, the changes start happening faster, so you can make some fairly large changes in a reasonable amount of time. You can also change the number by clicking it and typing in a new value.

The following table lists the control's most interesting properties.

PROPERTY	PURPOSE
DecimalPlaces	Determines the number of decimal places that the control displays. This has no effect when Hexadecimal is True.
Hexadecimal	Determines whether the control displays the number using a hexadecimal format as in A1C when the control's value is 2588 (decimal).
Increment	Determines the amount by which the values are modified when the user clicks an arrow.
InterceptArrowKeys	If this is True, the user can also adjust the number's value using the up and down arrow keys.

PROPERTY	PURPOSE
Maximum	Determines the largest value that the control allows.
Minimum	Determines the smallest value that the control allows.
ReadOnly	Determines whether the user can type in a new value. Note that the arrow keys and arrow buttons still work when ReadOnly is True. You can disable them by setting InterceptArrowKeys to False and Increment to 0.
TextAlign	Determines whether the number is aligned on the left, right, or center of the control.
ThousandsSeparator	If this is True, the control displays thousands separators when the value is greater than 999. This has no effect when Hexadecimal is True.
UpDownAlign	Determines whether the up and down arrows are positioned on the left or right.
Value	The control's numeric value.

The control's more important event, ValueChanged, fires whenever the control's numeric value changes, whether because the user changed it or because the program's code changed it.

The Click event handler is not as useful for deciding when the control's value has changed. It executes when the user changes the value by clicking an arrow button, but it does not execute if the user types a new value into the field or uses the arrow keys. It also fires if the user clicks the control's number but doesn't make any changes.

OPENFILEDIALOG

The OpenFileDialog component displays a standard dialog box that lets the user select a file to open. A program calls the component's ShowDialog method to display a file selection dialog. ShowDialog returns DialogResult.OK if the user selects a file and clicks OK, and it returns DialogResult.Cancel if the user cancels.

This component provides many properties for determining the kinds of files the user can select. The following table describes the most useful of these.

PROPERTY	PURPOSE
AddExtension	If True, the component adds the default extension specified in the DefaultExt property to the file name if the user does not include an extension.
CheckFileExists	If True, the component verifies that the file exists. If the user types in the name of a nonexistent file, the component warns the user and refuses to close.
CheckPathExists	If True, the component verifies that the file's directory path exists. If the user types in a file and path and the path doesn't exist, the component warns the user and refuses to close.
DefaultExt	The default extension that the component adds to the file's name if the user omits the extension. This property should have a value such as txt.
DereferenceLinks	If this is True and the user selects a shortcut file (.lnk), the component returns the name of the file referenced by the shortcut rather than the link file.
FileName	Sets the first file selected when the dialog is initially displayed. When the user closes the dialog box, this property returns the name of the file selected. The dialog box retains this value so the next time it is displayed it begins with this file selected.
FileNames	Gets an array of all of the files selected (if the dialog box allows multiple selections).
Filter	A string giving the filter that the dialog box should use. This string holds pairs of display names (such as Bitmaps) and their corresponding filter expressions (such as *.bmp) separated by vertical bar characters (|). Separate multiple expressions within a filter entry with semicolons. For example, the following value lets the user search for GIF files, JPG files, both GIFs and JPGs, or all files: `GIFs|*.gif|JPGs|*.jpg;*.jpeg|Both|*.gif;*.jpg;*.jpeg|All Files|*.*`
FilterIndex	Gives the index of the filter entry that the dialog box initially displays. The indexes start with 1.
InitialDirectory	Determines the path where the dialog box starts when it is displayed. If you later redisplay the same dialog box, it will start at the path determined by its FileName property, so it continues where it last left off. If you want to change InitialDirectory to start in some other directory, you also need to set FileName = "".
MultiSelect	Determines whether the user can select multiple files.

PROPERTY	PURPOSE
ReadOnlyChecked	Determines whether the dialog box's Open as read-only check box is initially selected. This has no effect unless ShowReadOnly is True. The dialog box retains this value so that the next time it is displayed it has the value that the user selected. If you want the box checked every time the dialog box appears, you must set ReadOnlyChecked to True before you display the dialog each time.
RestoreDirectory	If this value is True, the dialog box restores its initial directory after the user closes it, if the user has navigated to some other directory. However, if you later redisplay the same dialog box, it will start at the path determined by its FileName property, so it continues where it last left off. That means if you want to restore the initial directory, you must also set FileName = "" before redisplaying the dialog.
ShowHelp	Determines whether the dialog box displays a Help button. If you set this to True, the application should catch the dialog box's HelpRequest event and give the user some help.
ShowReadOnly	Determines whether the dialog box displays an Open as read-only check box.
Title	Determines the dialog's title text.

The OpenFileDialog component raises its FileOk event when the user tries to accept a file. You can use an event handler to catch the event and perform extra validation. Set the event's e.Cancel value to True to stop the dialog box from accepting the selection.

The following code allows the dlgBitmapFile dialog box to accept only bitmap files. The code loops through the dialog box's selected files. If it finds one with a name that doesn't end in .bmp, the program displays an error message, sets e.Cancel to True, and exits the function.

```
' Ensure that the user only selects bitmap files.
Private Sub dlgBitmapFile_FileOk() Handles dlgBitmapFile.FileOk
    For Each file_name As String In dlgBitmapFile.FileNames
        ' See if this file name ends with .bmp.
        If Not file_name.EndsWith(".bmp") Then
            MessageBox.Show("File "" & file_name & "" is not a bitmap file",
                "Invalid File Type",
                MessageBoxButtons.OK,
                MessageBoxIcon.Exclamation)
            e.Cancel = True
            Exit Sub
        End If
    Next file_name
End Sub
```

PAGESETUPDIALOG

The PageSetupDialog component displays a dialog box that lets the user specify properties for printed pages. For example, the user can specify the printer's paper tray, page size, margins, and orientation (portrait or landscape).

Before you can display the dialog box, you must assign it a PageSetting object to modify. You can do this in two ways. First, you can set the component's Document property to a PrintDocument object. If the user clicks OK, the dialog box modifies the PrintDocument's settings. This method is preferred because a PrintDocument object defines both page settings and printer settings.

Second, you can set the dialog box's PageSettings property to a PageSettings object. If the user clicks OK, the dialog modifies that object's settings.

Your program calls the component's ShowDialog method to display the dialog. ShowDialog returns DialogResult.OK if the user clicks OK and it returns DialogResult.Cancel if the user cancels. Often, the program doesn't need to know whether the user accepted or canceled the dialog box, however, because the dialog box modifies a PageSettings object automatically if the user clicks OK. The program can use that object when printing later, so it doesn't need to keep track of whether the user accepted or canceled the dialog box.

The following code displays a PageSetupDialog attached to a PrintDocument object:

```
PageSetupDialog1.Document = New PrintDocument
PageSetupDialog1.ShowDialog()
```

The following table describes the PageSetupDialog component's most useful properties.

PROPERTY	PURPOSE
AllowMargins	Determines whether the dialog box lets the user modify its margin settings.
AllowOrientation	Determines whether the dialog box lets the user modify its orientation settings.
AllowPaper	Determines whether the dialog box lets the user modify its paper settings.
AllowPrinter	Determines whether the dialog box lets the user modify its printer settings.
Document	The PrinterDocument object that the dialog box will modify.
MinMargins	Gives the smallest allowed margin values. MinMargins is a reference to a Margins object that has Left, Right, Top, and Bottom properties that you can use to specify each margin separately.
PageSettings	The PageSettings object that the dialog box will modify.

PROPERTY	PURPOSE
PrinterSettings	The PrinterSettings object that the dialog box will modify when the user clicks the Printer button. If you set the Document property, the PrinterDocument object includes a PrinterSettings object.
ShowHelp	Determines whether the dialog box displays a Help button. If you set this to True, the application should catch the dialog box's HelpRequest event and give the user some help.
ShowNetwork	Determines whether the dialog box displays a Network button on the Printer setup dialog box when the user clicks the Printer button.

PANEL

The Panel control is a container of other controls. By setting the Anchor and Dock properties of the contained controls, you can make those controls arrange themselves when the Panel is resized.

You can use a Panel to make it easy to manipulate the controls it contains as a group. If you move the Panel, the controls it contains move also. If you set the Panel control's Visible property to False, the controls it contains are hidden. If you set the Panel control's Enabled property to False, the controls it contains are also disabled.

Similarly, you can set the Panel control's other style properties such as BackColor, ForeColor, and Font and any controls contained in the Panel inherit these values (although a few controls insist on keeping their own values for some properties, such as the TextBox control's ForeColor and BackColor properties).

A Panel also defines a separate group for radio buttons. If you have two Panel controls, each containing several radio buttons, then the two groups of buttons work independently, so clicking a button in one Panel doesn't deselect the buttons in the other Panel.

The most advanced feature of the Panel control is its auto-scroll capability. If you set the AutoScroll property to True, the control automatically provides working scroll bars if the controls that it contains don't fit. The AutoScrollMargin property lets you define extra space that the control should add around its contents when it is auto-scrolling.

Use the AutoScrollMinSize property to ensure that the control's scrolling area is at least a certain minimum size. For example, suppose that the Panel contains controls with coordinates between 0 and 100 in both the X and Y directions. Normally, the control would let you scroll over the area $0 <= X <= 100, 0 <= Y <= 100$ so that you can see all of the controls. If you set AutoScrollMinSize to 200, 50, the control would let you scroll over the area $0 <= X <= 200, 0 <= Y <= 100$ so that you can see the controls plus the area defined by AutoScrollMinSize.

The AutoScrollPosition property lets your program get or set the scroll bars' position at runtime. For example, the following code makes the panMap control scroll to make the upper-left corner of its contents visible:

```
panMap.AutoScrollPosition = New Point(0, 0)
```

If you set AutoScrollPosition to a point that is outside of the Panel's display area, the control adjusts the point so that it lies within the area.

Although a program often uses a Panel control as an invisible container for other controls, you can use its BackColor and BorderStyle properties to make it visible if you like.

PERFORMANCECOUNTER

The PerformanceCounter component represents a Windows NT-style performance counter. You can use the component's methods to read, increment, and decrement the counters. This is a fairly advanced and specialized topic, so it is not covered in detail here. See the online help at `msdn .microsoft.com/system.diagnostics.performancecounter.aspx` for more information.

> **PERFORMANCE PROBLEMS**
>
> If you're interested in performance counters, you may also find the second part of the article "Detecting DDOS and Other Security Problems" at `www.informit.com/ articles/article.asp?p=169493&seqNum=2&rl=1` useful. This part explains how to create a custom performance counter.

PICTUREBOX

The PictureBox control displays images. It also provides a Graphics object that you can use to draw lines, rectangles, ellipses, and other shapes at runtime.

The control's Image property determines the picture that the control displays. Its SizeMode property determines how the image is sized to fit into the control. The following table describes the allowed SizeMode values.

VALUE	MEANING
Normal	The image is not resized. If it sticks off the edge of the PictureBox, the image is clipped.
StretchImage	The image is stretched to fill the control. This may change the image's shape, making it shorter and wider or taller and thinner than it should be.
AutoSize	The PictureBox adjusts its size to fit the image. If the control is displaying borders, it allows extra room for them.
CenterImage	The image is centered in the PictureBox at its normal size. If it sticks off the edge of the PictureBox, the image is clipped.

If you set the control's BackgroundImage property to a picture, the control tiles itself completely with copies of the picture. If you also set the Image property, the background shows behind the image. If you have SizeMode set to StretchImage or AutoSize, the image fills the entire control, so you will not see the background image.

The PictureBox control has several properties that deal with its size internally and externally. Its Size, Width, and Height properties give information about the size of the control, including its border if it has one. The ClientRectangle, ClientSize, and DisplayRectangle properties give information about the area inside the control, not including its border. You should use these properties when you draw on the control.

The PictureBox control's CreateGraphics method returns a Graphics object that represents the control's client area. Your code can use that object's methods to draw on the control.

Although you can draw on the object returned by the control's CreateGraphics method, that does not ensure that the drawing will remain. If you hide the PictureBox with another form and then bring it back to the top, the drawing is gone. There are two main approaches to keeping a drawing visible on a PictureBox.

First, you can place the drawing commands in the PictureBox control's Paint event handler. The Paint event occurs any time part of the control needs to be refreshed. That happens if the control is covered and then uncovered, when its form is minimized and then restored, and when the control is enlarged so that a new part of its display area is exposed.

The second approach is to make a Bitmap that fits the PictureBox, draw on the Bitmap, and then set the control's Image property equal to the Bitmap. After that, the control automatically displays its image.

This method takes more memory than the previous method of drawing in the control's Paint event handler. If the drawing is very complicated and takes a long time, however, it may be faster to generate the Bitmap once rather than redrawing the picture every time the control raises its Paint event.

The final PictureBox feature that is relevant to drawing is its Invalidate method. This method invalidates some or all of the control's display area and generates a Paint event. You can use this method to redraw the control if you have changed some data that will affect the drawing's appearance.

PRINTDIALOG

The PrintDialog component displays a dialog box that lets the user prepare to print. The dialog lets the user select a printer, modify printer properties, select the pages to print, and determine the number of copies to print. A program calls the component's ShowDialog method to display the dialog.

The following table describes the PrintDialog's most useful properties.

PROPERTY	PURPOSE
AllowPrintToFile	Determines whether the Print to file button is enabled.
AllowSelection	Determines whether the Selection radio button is enabled.
AllowSomePages	Determines whether the Pages radio button, as well as the From and To text boxes, are enabled.
Document	The PrintDocument object that provides the dialog with a PrinterSettings object.
PrinterSettings	The PrinterSettings object that the dialog modifies.
PrintToFile	Determines whether the Print to file box is checked.
ShowHelp	Determines whether the Help button is visible. If this is True, you should catch the component's HelpRequest event and give the user some help.
ShowNetwork	Determines whether the Network button is visible.

If the user clicks Print, the dialog returns DialogResult.OK. If the user clicks Cancel, the dialog box returns DialogResult.Cancel. The program can use the dialog box's PrintToFile property to see if the user checked the Print to file box, and it can use the PrinterSettings object to learn about the user's other selections.

The following table lists the PrinterSettings object's properties that are most useful for learning about the user's selections. You can set many of these properties before displaying the dialog box to give it initial values. After the dialog box closes, the properties indicate the user's selections.

PROPERTY	PURPOSE
CanDuplex	Indicates whether the printer can print in duplex.
Collate	Indicates whether the user checked the Collate box.
Copies	The number of copies the user selected.
Duplex	Indicates whether the user asked for duplex printing.
FromPage	The number the user entered in the From text box.
InstalledPrinters	Returns a collection listing the system's installed printers.
IsDefaultPrinter	True if the printer given by the PrinterName property is the default printer.
IsPlotter	True if the printer is a plotter device.
IsValid	True if the printer given by the PrinterName property is a valid printer.

PROPERTY	PURPOSE
LandscapeAngle	The angle at which the printout is rotated to produce landscape printing. The valid angles are 90 and 270 degrees, or 0 if the printer doesn't support landscape printing.
MaximumCopies	The maximum number of copies that the printer will let you print at a time.
MaximumPage	The largest value that the user is allowed to enter in the To and From boxes.
MinimumPage	The smallest value that the user is allowed to enter in the To and From boxes.
PaperSizes	Returns a collection of objects describing the paper sizes supported by the printer. These PaperSize objects have the properties Height, Width, PaperName, and Kind (for example, Letter).
PaperSources	Returns a collection of objects describing the paper trays provided by the printer. These PaperSource objects have the properties SourceName (for example, Default tray) and Kind (for example, Upper).
PrinterName	Gets or sets the name of the printer to use.
PrinterResolutions	Returns a collection of PrinterResolution objects that describe the resolutions supported by the printer. PrinterResolution objects have the properties Kind (High, Medium, Low, Draft, or Custom), X, and Y. The X and Y properties return negative values for standard resolutions and the number of dots per inch (dpi) for custom resolutions.
PrintRange	Indicates the pages that the user wants to print. This can have the value AllPages (print everything), Selection (print the current selection), or SomePages (print the pages between FromPage and ToPage).
PrintToFile	Indicates whether the Print to file check box is selected.
SupportsColor	True if the printer supports color.
ToPage	The number the user entered in the To text box.

The FromPage and ToPage properties must lie between the MinimumPage and MaximumPage values before you display the dialog box or the dialog box throws an error. If the user enters a value outside of the range MinimumPage to MaximumPage and clicks Print, the dialog box displays a message similar to "This value is not within the page range. Enter a number between 10 and 30." It then refuses to close.

Usually a program associates a PrintDialog with a PrintDocument object and that object provides the PrinterSettings object. You can either create the PrintDialog object at runtime, or you can use the PrintDocument component described in the following section at design time. If you create a PrintDocument component at design time, you can also set the PrintDialog's Document property to that component at design time.

Example program UsePrintDialog uses the following code to print a document. In this example, the pdlgRectangle and pdlgRectangle components were created and pdlgRectangle.Document was set to pdlgRectangle at design time. When the user clicks the Print button, the program displays the PrintDialog. If the user clicks the dialog box's Print button, the code calls the PrintDocument object's Print method. When the PrintDocument object needs to generate a page for printing, it raises its PrintPage event. In this example, the event handler draws a rectangle and indicates that the document has no more pages to draw.

```
Imports System.Drawing.Printing

Public Class Form1
    ' Display the print dialog.
    Private Sub btnPrint_Click() Handles btnPrint.Click
        If pdlgRectangle.ShowDialog() = Windows.Forms.DialogResult.OK Then
            ' Print the document.
            pdocRectangle.Print()
        End If
    End Sub

    ' Print a page of the document.
    Private Sub PrintDocument1_PrintPage(ByVal sender As Object, _
     ByVal e As System.Drawing.Printing.PrintPageEventArgs) _
     Handles pdocRectangle.PrintPage
        e.Graphics.DrawRectangle(Pens.Black, 100, 100, 600, 300)
        e.HasMorePages = False
    End Sub
End Class
```

code snippet UsePrintDialog

For more information on the PrintDocument object, see the following section.

PRINTDOCUMENT

The PrintDocument component represents an object that will be printed. Your program can use this object to send output to a printer.

The general procedure for printing using this object is to create the object, set its properties to determine how the printout is generated (the printer's name, paper tray, and so forth), and then call the object's Print method.

When the object needs to generate a page of output, it raises its PrintPage event. Your code catches that event, draws the page, and then sets the event handler's e.HasMorePages value to indicate whether that was the last page of output. See the previous section, "PrintDialog," for a small example.

The PrintDocument object provides only a few important properties itself. You set most of the values that describe the printing operation using the PrinterSettings object referenced by the component's PrinterSettings property. See the previous section, "PrintDialog," for information on the PrinterSettings object.

In addition to its PrinterSettings property, the PrintDocument object provides a DocumentName property that determines the name displayed for the document in printing-related dialog boxes such as the printer queue display.

This component also provides an OriginAtMargins property that determines whether each page's graphical origin begins at the page's margins. Setting OriginAtMargins to True makes it easier to draw relative to the left and top margins, rather than the upper-left corner of the physical page.

PRINTPREVIEWCONTROL

The PrintPreviewControl control (and yes, the word *Control* is part of the control's name, possibly to differentiate it from the PrintPreviewDialog control) displays a print preview within one of your forms. Usually, it is easier to use the PrintPreviewDialog control described in the next section to display a print preview dialog box, but you can use this control to display a preview integrated into some other part of your application.

Example program UsePrintPreviewControl uses the following code to display three printed pages inside a PrintPreviewControl. The module-level variable m_PageNum indicates the next page that the pdocShapes PrintDocument component should draw. When it needs to generate a page, pdocShapes raises its PrintPage event. The event handler uses a Select Case statement to see which page it should generate and it draws an appropriate shape. It sets e.HasMorePages appropriately and increments the page number.

```
Public Class Form1
    ' The number of the current page.
    Private m_PageNum As Integer = 1

    ' Generate the print document.
    Private Sub pdocShapes_PrintPage(ByVal sender As System.Object,
     ByVal e As System.Drawing.Printing.PrintPageEventArgs) _
     Handles pdocShapes.PrintPage
        Select Case m_PageNum
            Case 1 ' Page 1. Draw a triangle.
                Dim pts() As Point = {
                    New Point(e.MarginBounds.X + e.MarginBounds.Width \ 2,
                              e.MarginBounds.Y),
                    New Point(e.MarginBounds.X + e.MarginBounds.Width,
                              e.MarginBounds.Y + e.MarginBounds.Height),
                    New Point(e.MarginBounds.X,
                              e.MarginBounds.Y + e.MarginBounds.Height)
                }
                e.Graphics.DrawPolygon(Pens.Red, pts)
                e.HasMorePages = True
                m_PageNum += 1
            Case 2 ' Page 2. Draw a rectangle.
                e.Graphics.DrawRectangle(Pens.Green, e.MarginBounds())
                e.HasMorePages = True
                m_PageNum += 1
```

```
        Case 3 ' Page 3. Draw an ellipse.
            e.Graphics.DrawEllipse(Pens.Blue, e.MarginBounds())
            e.HasMorePages = False
            m_PageNum = 1
        End Select
    End Sub
End Class
```

code snippet UsePrintPreviewControl

That's all the code that the program needs. When the program starts, the PrintPreviewControl control uses pdocShapes to generate the pages it needs and it displays them.

The following table describes some of the PrintPreviewControl control's most useful properties.

PROPERTY	PURPOSE
AutoZoom	Determines whether the control automatically adjusts its Zoom property to make the display fill the control.
Columns	The number of columns of pages that the control displays. In Figure G-7, Columns = 3.
Document	The PrintDocument object that the control previews.
Rows	The number of rows of pages that the control displays. In Figure G-7, Rows = 1.
StartPage	The page number (starting with 0) displayed in the control's first page. Your code can use this property to change the pages displayed.
UseAntiAlias	Determines whether the control uses the system's anti-aliasing features to smooth the preview image. Setting this to True may make the image smoother, but it may also slow down the display.
Zoom	Determines the size of the pages within the control. The value 1.0 is full size, 0.5 is half-size, 2.0 is double size, and so forth. It's usually easier to just set AutoZoom to True and let the control make the pages as large as possible. If you set the scale so large that the page(s) won't fit, the control adds scroll bars so the user can see the results.

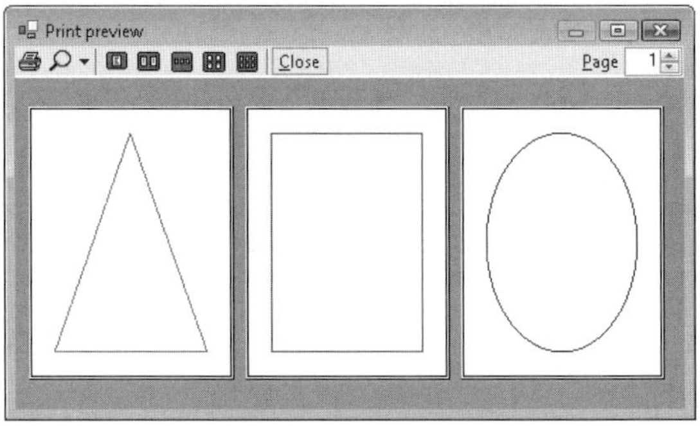

FIGURE G-7: The PrintPreviewDialog component lets you easily display a full-featured print preview dialog box.

The control's InvalidatePreview method makes the control regenerate the print preview.

See the following section for information about the PrintPreviewDialog control. You can use that control to display a print preview without needing to build your own dialog.

PRINTPREVIEWDIALOG

The PrintPreviewDialog component displays a dialog box that shows what a print document will look like when it is printed. You can use this component to display a print preview dialog similar to the one shown in Figure G-7. This dialog box contains a PrintPreviewControl, plus some extra tools to let the user control the preview.

The tools that run from left to right across the top of the dialog box automatically give the user the following features:

➤ A Print button that prints the document

➤ A Zoom menu that lets the user zoom to scales between 10% and 500%, or to select Auto zoom

➤ Buttons that make the dialog box display one, two, three, four, or six pages at a time

➤ A button that closes the dialog box

➤ A text box and numeric up/down control that let the user select the number of the page to display

The dialog box's most important property is Document. This property determines the PrintDocument object that the dialog box previews. See the section "PrintDocument" earlier in this appendix for more information about this class.

The component's most important methods are Show, which displays the dialog box, and ShowDialog, which displays the dialog box modally.

Using this component is remarkably simple. Set its Document property and catch the PrintDocument object's PrintPage event as shown in the previous section. Then display the dialog box as in the following code:

```
dlgPrintPreview.ShowDialog()
```

The rest is automatic. The dialog box lets the user move through the document's pages, zoom in and out, and even print the document.

PROCESS

The Process component provides access to the processes running on the computer. You can use this object to start, stop, and monitor processes. You can use the object to get information about a running process such as its threads, the modules it has loaded, and the amount of memory it is using.

The UseProcess example program, which is available for download on the book's web site, uses the following code to start an executable program. It creates a new Process object and sets values in its StartInfo property to define the application to run. This example sets the executable file name to the string contained in the txtFileName text box and sets the component's Verb to Open ("opening" an executable file makes it run). The program then calls the object's Start method.

```
' Start the process.
Private Sub btnRun_Click() Handles btnRun.Click
    Dim new_process As New Process
    new_process.StartInfo.FileName = txtFileName.Text
    new_process.StartInfo.Verb = "Open"
    new_process.Start()
End Sub
```

code snippet UseProcess

The Process object's StartInfo property contains several values that tell the object how to start the new process. These values indicate whether the new process should be created without a window; what environment variables it should use; whether the new process's standard input, output, and error streams should be redirected; and the new process's working directory.

The Process object itself provides only a few properties at design time. Other than the StartInfo property, the most useful of these is EnableRaisingEvents. If this property is True, the component monitors the new process and raises an Exited event when the process ends.

At runtime, the Process object provides read-only StandardInput, StandardOutput, and StandardError properties that the program can use to interact with the new process. It also provides methods for reading and writing with these streams, and properties for monitoring the process. For example, it lets you learn about the process's working set size, paged memory size, and total processor time.

This is a fairly advanced and specialized topic, so it is not covered in greater detail here. For more information, see the Process component's web page at `msdn.microsoft.com/system .diagnostics.process.aspx`.

PROGRESSBAR

The ProgressBar control lets a program display a visible indication of its progress during a long task. As the task proceeds, the ProgressBar fills in from the left to the right. Ideally, the ProgressBar is completely full just as the task finishes.

The control's Minimum and Maximum properties determine the integers over which the ProgressBar control's values will range. When the control's Value property equals its Minimum property, the control is completely blank. When its Value property equals its Maximum property, the control is completely filled.

By default, Minimum and Maximum are set to 0 and 100, respectively, so the Value property indicates the percentage of the task that is complete. However, you can set Minimum and Maximum to any values that make sense for the application. For example, if a program must back up some data by copying 173 files from one directory to another, you could set these properties to 0 and 173. As it copies each file, the program would set the ProgressBar control's Value property to the number of files it has copied.

Instead of setting the control's Value property to indicate the task's status, you can set the Step property to indicate how much the control should update at each step. Then you can call the ProgressBar control's PerformStep method to increment the Value by that amount.

Note that the Minimum, Maximum, Value, and Step properties are all integers. If the value you want to display has some other data type (such as Double or TimeSpan), you must convert the values into integers before you use them with the ProgressBar.

PROPERTYGRID

The PropertyGrid control displays information about an object in a format similar to the one used by the Properties window at design time. The control lets the user organize the properties alphabetically or by category, and lets the user edit the property values. Figure G-8 shows a PropertyGrid displaying information about an Employee object.

The control's two most important properties are SelectedObject and SelectedObjects, which get or set the object(s) associated with the PropertyGrid.

The PropertyGrid control displays only object properties, not public variables. It also displays only properties that are browsable. If you give a property the Browsable(False) attribute, the PropertyGrid will not display it.

For more information, refer to the PropertyGrid class's web page at msdn.microsoft.com/ system.windows.forms.propertygrid.aspx.

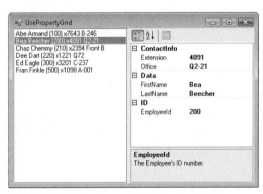

FIGURE G-8: The PropertyGrid control displays an object's properties.

RADIOBUTTON

A RadioButton control represents one of an exclusive set of options. For example, suppose that you want to let the user select between the choices Small, Medium, and Large. You could add three RadioButtons to a form with those captions. When the user clicks one button, Visual Basic selects it and deselects the others.

All the RadioButton controls within a particular container are part of the same RadioButton group. If the user clicks a RadioButton, Visual Basic automatically deselects the others in the same group.

If you want to make more than one group on the same form, you must place the controls in separate containers (such as GroupBox or Panel controls). For example, you could put the Small, Medium, and Large buttons in one GroupBox and then put the Red, Green, and Blue buttons in another GroupBox. Then, when the user selects a size button, the other size buttons are deselected, but the color buttons are unaffected. When the user selects a color, the other colors are deselected, but the size buttons are unaffected.

RadioButton groups provide special navigation for the user. If one of the buttons in the group has the focus, the user can press the arrow keys to move forward and backward through the group. If the user presses the Tab key, focus moves out of the group to the next control in the tab sequence.

The following table describes the RadioButton control's most useful properties.

PROPERTY	PURPOSE
Appearance	Determines whether the control displays with its default appearance of a selection circle containing a black dot (Appearance = Normal) or a raised button (Appearance = Button).
AutoCheck	Determines whether the control automatically selects itself when the user clicks it. If this is False, the code must check and uncheck the control and any other controls in the RadioButton group. Usually it's better to use a CheckBox control instead if you don't want the button to behave like a normal RadioButton.
CheckAlign	Determines whether the control's selection circle is positioned in the bottom center, top center, middle right, and so forth.
Checked	Determines whether the control is selected.
Image	Determines the image that the control displays.
ImageAlign	Determines whether the control's image is positioned in the bottom center, top center, middle right, and so forth.
Text	Determines the text that the control displays.
TextAlign	Determines whether the control's text is positioned in the bottom center, top center, middle right, and so forth.

The RadioButton control's most useful events are Click, which occurs when the user clicks the control, and CheckedChanged, which occurs when the control is checked or unchecked either because the user clicked a RadioButton in the group or because the code changed the button's state.

RICHTEXTBOX

The RichTextBox control is a text box that supports rich text extensions. Those extensions let the control display text that is bold, underlined, italicized, indented, in different fonts, and has other special visual properties.

The control can load and save its contents in plain-text files (in which case the formatting is lost) or in Rich Text Format (RTF) files (which preserve formatting).

A program can use the RichTextBox control's Select method to select some of its text. It can then use one of the control's properties to change the appearance of the selected text. For example, the following code selects the 10 characters starting with character 50 (the first character is number 0). It then sets the selection's color to red and makes its font bold.

```
rchNotes.Select(50, 10)
rchNotes.SelectionColor = Color.Red
rchNotes.SelectionFont = New Font(RichTextBox1.SelectionFont, FontStyle.Bold)
```

The following table lists the RichTextBox control's most useful properties.

PROPERTY	PURPOSE
AcceptsTab	For multiline controls, determines whether pressing the Tab key adds a Tab to the text, rather than moving to the next control in the tab sequence.
AutoSize	For single-line controls, determines whether the control automatically sets its height for the fonts it contains.
BulletIndent	Determines the number of pixels added after a bullet as indentation. If you make the selection a bulleted paragraph and then change this value, the paragraph's indentation is adjusted accordingly.
CanRedo	Indicates whether the control has any redo information that it can apply. See the discussion later in this section for an example.
CanUndo	Indicates whether the control has any undo information that it can apply. See the discussion later in this section for an example.
DetectUrls	Determines whether the control automatically recognizes web URLs when they are typed. If some text looks like a URL, the control displays it in blue, underlines it, and displays a hyperlink cursor (pointing hand) when the mouse hovers over the text. If the user clicks a recognized link, the control raises its LinkClicked event.
Lines	An array of strings giving the lines of text (separated by carriage returns) that are displayed by the control. You can use this property to give the control more than one paragraph at design time.

continues

(continued)

PROPERTY	PURPOSE
MaxLength	The maximum number of characters the user can enter into the control.
MultiLine	Determines whether the control displays multiple lines.
PreferredHeight	Returns the height a single-line control would want for the font size.
ReadOnly	Determines whether the user can modify the control's text.
RedoActionName	The name of the action that will be redone if the program calls the control's Redo method (for example, Typing or Delete). You can use this property to show the user what the next redo action is.
RightMargin	Determines the control's right margin in pixels. The value 0 means there is no right margin.
Rtf	Determines the RTF codes for the control's text. This includes the text itself, font information, and paragraph information (such as indentation, bulleting, and so forth).
ScrollBars	Determines which scroll bars the control displays. The values Horizontal, Vertical, and Both make the control display the corresponding scroll bars only when they are needed. The values ForcedHorizontal, ForcedVertical, and ForcedBoth make the control display the corresponding scroll bars always. The value None makes the control display no scroll bars. Note that some of these values may not always be honored. For example, if WordWrap is True or RightMargin is nonzero, the control never displays horizontal scroll bars.
SelectedRtf	Determines the selected text's value and RTF formatting code.
SelectedText	Determines the selected text's value without RTF formatting codes.
SelectionAlignment	Determines the selected text's alignment (Left, Center, or Right).
SelectionBullet	Determines whether the selected text's paragraph is bulleted.
SelectionCharOffset	Determines the selected text's character offset above or below the baseline in pixels.
SelectionColor	Determines the selected text's color.

PROPERTY	PURPOSE
SelectionFont	Determines the selected text's font.
SelectionHangingIndent	Determines the selected text's hanging indent.
SelectionIndent	Determines the number of pixels by which subsequent lines are indented in the selected text's paragraph.
SelectionLength	Determines the length of the selected text. You can use SelectionStart and SelectionLength to select text, or you can use the Select method.
SelectionProtected	Determines whether the selected text is protected so that the user cannot modify it.
SelectionRightIndent	Determines the number of pixels by which the selected text's paragraph is indented on the right.
SelectionStart	Determines the start of the selection. You can use SelectionStart and SelectionLength to select text, or you can use the Select method.
SelectionTabs	Determines the tabs for the selected text's paragraph. For example, the array {20, 40, 60} sets tabs 20, 40, and 60 pixels from the left margin.
ShowSelectionMargin	If True, the control adds a selection margin on the left. If the user clicks inside this margin, the control selects the text to the right.
Text	Determines the control's text, not including any formatting information. If you want to preserve formatting information, use the SelectedRtf property.
TextLength	Returns the length of the control's text.
UndoActionName	The name of the action that will be undone if the program calls the control's Undo method (for example, Typing or Delete). You can use this property to show the user what the next undo action is.
WordWrap	For multiline controls, determines whether the control wraps text to a new line if it is too long to fit.

The control also provides several important methods, as shown in the following table.

METHOD	PURPOSE
AppendText	Adds text to the end of the control's text.
CanPaste	Determines whether you can paste data of a specified format from the clipboard into the control.
Clear	Clears the control's text.
ClearUndo	Empties the control's undo list.
Copy	Copies the control's selection to the clipboard.
Cut	Copies the control's selection to the clipboard and removes it from the control's text.
Find	Finds and selects text. Overloaded versions let you search for one of a group of characters or a string, possibly with options (MatchCase, NoHighlight, Reverse, or WholeWord), and possibly within a range of characters.
GetCharFromPosition	Finds the character closest to a specified (X, Y) position.
GetCharIndexFromPosition	Finds the index of the character closest to a specified (X, Y) position.
GetLineFromCharIndex	Returns the number of the line containing the specified character index.
GetPositionFromCharIndex	Returns the (X, Y) position of the character at a specified index.
LoadFile	Loads an RTF or text file or a stream into the control.
Paste	Pastes the clipboard's contents into the control, replacing the current selection.
Redo	Reapplies the last action that was undone.
SaveFile	Saves the control's text into an RTF or text file or stream.
ScrollToCaret	Scrolls the text so the insertion position is visible.
Select	Selects the indicated text.
SelectAll	Selects all of the control's text.
Undo	Undoes the most recent action.

A program can use the CanUndo and CanRedo properties to determine when it should enable Undo and Redo buttons and menu items. The following code shows how a program can manage Undo and Redo buttons for the rchNotes control. When the control's contents change, the TextChanged event handler enables or disables the buttons, depending on which information the control has. The buttons simply call the control's Undo and Redo methods.

```vb
Private Sub rchNotes_TextChanged() Handles rchNotes.TextChanged
    btnUndo.Enabled = rchNotes.CanUndo
    btnRedo.Enabled = rchNotes.CanRedo
End Sub

Private Sub btnUndo_Click() Handles btnUndo.Click
    rchNotes.Undo()
End Sub

Private Sub btnRedo_Click() Handles btnRedo.Click
    rchNotes.Redo()
End Sub
```

code snippet UseRichTextBox

The following version of the TextChanged event handler adds the values returned by the UndoActionName and RedoActionName methods to the buttons' captions. For example, after the user deletes some text, the undo button's caption says "Undo Delete."

```vb
Private Sub rchNotes_TextChanged() Handles rchNotes.TextChanged
    btnUndo.Enabled = rchNotes.CanUndo
    btnRedo.Enabled = rchNotes.CanRedo

    If btnUndo.Enabled Then
        btnUndo.Text = "Undo " & rchNotes.UndoActionName
    Else
        btnUndo.Text = "Undo"
    End If

    If btnRedo.Enabled Then
        If btnRedo.Enabled Then btnRedo.Text = "Redo " & rchNotes.RedoActionName
    Else
        If btnRedo.Enabled Then btnRedo.Text = "Redo"
    End If
End Sub
```

code snippet UseRichTextBox

The RichTextBox control's most useful event is TextChanged. You can use this event to take action when the user changes the control's text. For example, you can display a visible indication that the data has been modified or, as the previous examples show, you can enable and disable Undo and Redo buttons.

SAVEFILEDIALOG

The SaveFileDialog component displays a dialog box that lets the user select a file for saving. The ShowDialog method returns DialogResult.OK if the user selects a file and clicks OK. It returns DialogResult.Cancel if the user cancels.

This component provides many properties for determining the kinds of files the user can specify. Most of these properties are the same as those provided by the OpenFileDialog component described earlier in this appendix. See the section "OpenFileDialog" earlier in this appendix for more information about those properties.

Unlike OpenFileDialog, this component does not provide the properties MultiSelect, ReadOnlyChecked, and ShowReadOnly because those properties don't make sense when the user is selecting a file for saving. The FileNames collection is also less useful for this component because the user will always select only one file, so you can use the FileName property instead.

The SaveFileDialog component provides one additional property not provided by the OpenFileDialog: CreatePrompt. If this property is True and the user enters the name of a file that doesn't exist, the dialog asks the user if it should create the file. If the user clicks No, the dialog box continues letting the user select a different file.

Like the OpenFileDialog, this component raises its FileOk event when the user tries to accept a file. You can use an event handler to catch the event and perform extra validation. Set the event's e.Cancel value to True to stop the dialog box from accepting the selection.

Note that the dialog box adds its default extension if applicable before it raises the FileOk event. If the component has DefaultExt = "dat" and AddExtension = True, this example would accept a file name with no extension.

SERIALPORT

The SerialPort component represents one of the computer's physical serial ports. It provides properties and methods for reading and configuring the port's baud rate, break signal, Data Set Ready (DSR) state, port name, parity, and stop bits. The class has methods to write data to the port and to read synchronously or asynchronously.

Serial communications is a fairly advanced and specialized topic that depends on your particular application, so it is not covered in detail here. See the online help at `msdn.microsoft.com/system .io.ports.serialport.aspx` for more information. You may also find these articles useful:

➤ Programming Serial Ports Using Visual Basic 2005 (`www.devx .com/dotnet/Article/31001`)

➤ RS232 Serial Communication in .NET (`http://www.freevbcode.com/ShowCode .asp?ID=4666`)

If you plan to work extensively with serial communication, you might want to find a good book on the topic such as *Visual Basic Programmer's Guide to Serial Communications, 4th Edition* by Richard Grier (Mabry Software, 2004).

Unfortunately all of these resources are fairly old but the basic concepts shouldn't have changed much in the last couple of Visual Basic releases.

SERVICECONTROLLER

The ServiceController component represents a Windows service process. It provides methods that let you connect to a running or stopped service to control it or get information about it.

The ServiceController component's ServiceName property gets or sets the name of the service associated with the component. To set this value at design time, select a ServiceController in the form designer. Then, click the ServiceName property in the Properties window and click the drop-down arrow on the right to see a list of available services on the system. The class's methods let you start, pause, continue, or stop the service.

Windows services and their control is a relatively advanced topic, so it is not covered in detail here. For more information, see the ServiceController class's web page at msdn.microsoft.com/system .serviceprocess.servicecontroller.aspx. For an introduction to Windows service applications, refer to msdn.microsoft.com/y817hyb6.aspx. For a walkthrough that creates a Windows service application, see msdn.microsoft.com/zt39148a.aspx.

SPLITCONTAINER

The SplitContainer control represents an area divided into two regions either vertically or horizontally. The control contains a bar (called the splitter) that the user can drag to adjust the amount of space given to each region.

Each of the SplitContainer control's regions holds a Panel control and you can place other controls inside the Panels. You can also use the Panel control's properties to affect their behavior. For example, you can set their AutoScroll properties to True so the Panels display scroll bars when their contents don't fit.

The following table describes the SplitContainer control's most useful properties.

PROPERTY	PURPOSE
BorderStyle	Determines the control's border style.
FixedPanel	Determines which panel keeps the same size when the control is resized.
IsSplitterFixed	Determines whether the user can drag the splitter.
Orientation	Determines whether the Panels are arranged vertically or horizontally.
Panel1	Returns a reference to the first panel (left or top depending on Orientation).
Panel1Collapsed	Determines whether the first Panel is collapsed. When collapsed, a Panel is completely hidden and the user cannot get it back by dragging the splitter.

continues

(continued)

PROPERTY	PURPOSE
Panel1MinSize	Determines the minimum size (width or height depending on Orientation) of the first Panel.
Panel2	Returns a reference to the second panel (right or bottom depending on Orientation).
Panel2Collapsed	Determines whether the second Panel is collapsed. When collapsed, a Panel is completely hidden and the user cannot get it back by dragging the splitter.
Panel2MinSize	Determines the minimum size (width or height depending on Orientation) of the second Panel.
SplitterDistance	Determines the distance from the control's left or top edge (depending on Orientation) to the splitter.
SplitterIncrement	Determines the number of pixels by which the splitter will move when dragged. For example, if SplitterIncrement is 10, the splitter jumps in 10-pixel increments are you drag it. The default is 1.
SplitterRectangle	Returns a Rectangle representing the splitter's current size and location within the SplitContainer.
SplitterWidth	Determines the splitter's width in pixels. The default is 4.

The SplitterContainer control's most interesting events are SplitterMoving and SplitterMoved. You can catch these events if you need to take action when the user drags the splitter. You can also use the Panel controls' sizing events Resize, ResizeBegin, ResizeEnd, and SizeChanged to take action when the Panel controls resize.

One rather confusing feature of the SplitterContainer is the way its contained Panel controls behave in the form designer. The drop-down list at the top of the Properties window lets you select the controls on the form, including the SplitterContainer. The Panel controls are contained inside the SplitterContainer, so they are not always listed in this dropdown. If you click one of the Panel controls, the dropdown lists the Panel and the Properties window lets you view and edit the control's properties. If some other control is selected, however, the SplitterContainer is listed in the dropdown, but not its Panel controls.

SPLITTER

The Splitter control provides the thin strip that users can grab to resize the two panes of a SplitContainer. In addition to using the Splitter within a SplitContainer control, you can also use it directly to separate any two other controls.

Visual Basic uses the Dock properties and stacking order of the two controls and the Splitter to determine how the Splitter behaves. To build a simple vertical splitter between two Panel controls, add the first Panel to the form and set its Dock property to Left so that it fills the left side of the form.

Next, add a Splitter control. By default, its Dock property is also Left, so it attaches to the right side of the Panel. Finally, add a second Panel control, and set its Dock property to Fill so that it fills the rest of the form. Now, when you drag the Splitter back and forth, Visual Basic adjusts the Panel controls accordingly.

You can use multiple Splitters to separate more than two controls. For example, you could add a Panel with Dock set to Left, a Splitter, another Panel with Dock set to Left, another Splitter, and a final Panel with Dock set to Fill. This would let the user divide the form between the three Panel controls.

The Splitter control uses the controls' stacking order to determine the order of the controls. When you initially create controls, their stacking order is the same as their order of creation. Unfortunately, if the stacking order changes, the positions of the controls can become very confusing very quickly. In some cases, it's easier to delete all of the controls and start over than it is to fix the stacking order.

It's far easier to use the SplitContainer control than it is to use Splitters directly, so you should use the SplitContainer when you have fairly straightforward needs. Only use Splitters directly if you need to provide unusual configurations such as dividing a form among three Panel controls.

STATUSSTRIP

The StatusStrip control provides an area where the application can display brief status information, usually at the bottom of the form.

The StatusStrip can contain several kinds of objects such as drop-down buttons, progress bars, and panels. These objects are represented by different kinds of controls contained in the form. For example, a progress bar is represented by a ToolStripProgressBar control.

You can edit a StatusStrip much as you edit a MenuStrip. When you click the StatusStrip, a box appears that contains the text "Type Here." Enter the text that you want to display on this object and press Enter. Click an object and then click the little action arrow on the object's right edge to change the object's type (progress bar, panel, and so forth) and to configure the item.

You can also edit an object's properties in the Properties window. Simply click the object and then use the Properties window to change its appearance.

The StatusStrip control provides access to the objects it contains through its Items collection. If you click the ellipsis to the right of this property in the Properties window, the Items Collection Editor appears. To make new items, select the type of object you want to add from the editor's dropdown and click the Add button. Click an item and use the other buttons to move or delete it. Use the properties grid on the editor's right to modify the object's appearance.

The following list shows the types of objects you can add to a StatusStrip control:

➤ `ToolStripStatusLabel` — A simple label.

➤ `ToolStripProgressBar` — A Progress bar.

➤ `ToolStripDropDownButton` — A button that displays text in the StatusStrip. When you click its drop-down arrow, a list of buttons appears.

➤ `ToolStripSplitButton` — A button that displays an image in the StatusStrip. When you click its drop-down arrow, a list of buttons appears.

See the online help at `msdn.microsoft.com/system.windows.forms.statusstrip.aspx` for more information about these classes and the StatusStrip control.

TABCONTROL

The TabControl control (for some reason, the word *Control* is part of the class's name) displays a series of tabs attached to separate pages. Each page is a control container, holding whatever controls you want for that tab. When you click a tab at design time or the user clicks one at runtime, the control displays the corresponding page.

The control's tabs are represented programmatically by TabPage objects contained in the control's TabPages collection. To edit these objects at design time, select the control's TabPages property and click the ellipsis on the right to display the collection editor.

The following table describes the TabPage object's most useful properties.

PROPERTY	PURPOSE
AutoScroll	If True, the tab page automatically provides scroll bars if it is not big enough to display all of its contents.
BackColor	Determines the tab page's background color. This affects the tab's page, not the tab itself.
BackgroundImage	Determines the background image that tiles the tab's page. This affects the tab's page, not the tab itself.
BorderStyle	Determines the style of border around the tab's page. This can be None, FixedSingle, or Fixed3D.
Font	Determines the font used by the controls contained in the tab's page. To change the font used to draw the tabs, set the TabControl control's Font property.
ImageIndex	If the TabControl control's ImageList property is set to an ImageList control, this property determines the image within that list that the tab displays.
Text	Determines the text displayed on the tab.
ToolTipText	Determines the tooltip text displayed when the user hovers the mouse over the tab. This is ignored unless the TabControl control's ShowToolTips property is True.

The TabPage object provides several events of its own. These include the usual assortment of events for a control container such as Click, Layout, Resize, Paint, and various mouse events.

The TabControl provides several properties that are useful for arranging the tabs. The following table describes the most useful of these properties.

PROPERTY	PURPOSE
Alignment	Determines whether the control places its tabs on the Top, Bottom, Left, or Right. If you set this to Left or Right, the control rotates its tabs' text sideways. If a tab contains an image, the image is not rotated.
Appearance	Determines how the control displays its tabs. This property can take the value Normal, Buttons, or FlatButtons.
DrawMode	Determines whether the control draws the tabs automatically (DrawMode = Normal) or whether the code draws them (DrawMode = OwnerDrawFixed). See the discussion later in this section for an example.
Enabled	Determines whether the TabControl is enabled. If Enabled is False, none of the tabs will respond to the user (although the tabs do not look disabled) and all of the controls on the tab pages are disabled.
Font	Determines the font that the control uses to draw its tabs. This does not affect the font used within the tab pages.
HotTrack	If this is True, the tabs visually change when the mouse moves over them. For example, the tabs' text may change color.
ImageList	Determines the ImageList control that provides images for the tabs.
ItemSize	Determines the height of all of the tabs. Also determines the width of fixed-width tabs (see the SizeMode property) and owner-drawn tabs (see the DrawMode property).
MultiLine	Determines whether the control allows more than one line of tabs. If MultiLine is False and the tabs won't all fit, the control displays left-arrow and right-arrow buttons on the right to let the user scroll through the tabs.
Padding	Determines the horizontal and vertical space added around the tabs' text and images.
RowCount	Returns the current number of tab rows.
SelectedIndex	Sets or gets the index of the currently selected tab. At design time, you can simply click the tab you want to select.
SelectedTab	Sets or gets the currently selected TabPage object. At design time, you can simply click the tab you want to select.
ShowToolTips	Determines whether the control displays the TabPage controls' ToolTip values when the user hovers the mouse over the tabs.

continues

(continued)

PROPERTY	PURPOSE
SizeMode	Determines how the control sizes its tabs. This property can take the values Normal (tabs fit their contents), FillToRight (if the control needs more than one row of tabs, the tabs resize so each row fills the width of the control), and Fixed (all tabs have the same width).
TabCount	Returns the number of tabs.
TabPages	The collection of TabPage objects.

The TabControl control's most useful event is SelectedIndexChanged, which fires when the control's selected tab index changes either because the user clicked a new tab, or because the code set the SelectedIndex or SelectedTab property.

If you set the TabControl control's DrawMode property to OwnerDrawFixed, your code must draw the tabs in the control's DrawItem event. Example program UseTabControlOwnerDrawn uses the following code to draw colored ellipses on its tabs:

```
' Draw ellipses in the tabs.
Private Sub tabProject_DrawItem(ByVal sender As Object,
  ByVal e As System.Windows.Forms.DrawItemEventArgs) Handles tabProject.DrawItem
    ' Decide how thick to draw the outline.
    Dim line_wid As Integer = 1
    If (e.State And DrawItemState.Selected) = DrawItemState.Selected Then
        line_wid = 3
    End If

    ' Get the drawing bounds.
    Dim rect As New Rectangle(
        e.Bounds.Left + (line_wid + 1) \ 2,
        e.Bounds.Top + (line_wid + 1) \ 2 + 1,
        e.Bounds.Width—line_wid - 2,
        e.Bounds.Height—line_wid - 2)

    ' Get the fill colors.
    Dim fill_colors() As Color = {Color.Red, Color.Green, Color.Blue}

    ' Fill.
    Using the_brush As New SolidBrush(fill_colors(e.Index))
        e.Graphics.FillEllipse(the_brush, rect)
    End Using

    ' Outline.
    Using the_pen As New Pen(Color.Black, line_wid)
        e.Graphics.DrawEllipse(the_pen, rect)
    End Using
End Sub
```

code snippet UseTabControlOwnerDrawn

The DrawItem event handler starts by setting the line_wid variable to the pen width it will use to draw the ellipse. It makes the line width larger for the selected tab.

The code then builds a rectangle to define the ellipse. It starts with the event handler's e.Bounds property and then shrinks the area slightly to make room for the ellipse's border.

The code makes a brush of the appropriate color for each tab and fills the ellipse. It finishes by making a black pen of the correct thickness and outlining the ellipse.

The TabControl is ideal for displaying multiple pages of related information in a limited amount of space. It works particularly well when the information is naturally categorized and each tab represents a category of data. It doesn't work as well if different tabs contain data that the user might want to compare to each other.

TABLELAYOUTPANEL

The TableLayoutPanel control displays the controls that it contains in rows and columns. This makes it easy to build grids of regularly spaced controls.

The following table describes the TableLayoutPanel control's most useful properties.

PROPERTY	PURPOSE
AutoScroll	Determines whether the control automatically provides scroll bars if the controls it contains won't fit.
CellBorderStyle	Determines the cell border style. This can be None, NotSet (an appropriate style is selected based on the row and column styles), Inset (single sunken line), InsetDouble (double sunken line), Outset (single raised line), OutsetDouble (double raised line), OutsetPartial (single line containing a raised area), and Single (single line).
ColumnCount	Determines the number of columns.
ColumnStyles	A collection giving column styles.
ColumnWidths	An array of column widths.
Controls	A collection of controls contained within the control.
Enabled	Determines whether the control is enabled. If the TableLayoutPanel is disabled, the controls it contains are also disabled.
GrowStyle	Determines how the control grows when you add new child controls to it. This can be AddRows, AddColumns, or FixedSize (the control throws an exception if you add more controls).
RowCount	Determines the number of rows.
RowHeights	An array of row heights.
RowStyles	A collection of row styles.
Visible	Determines whether the control and its contents are visible.

The following table describes the TableLayoutPanel control's most useful methods.

METHOD	PURPOSE
GetColumn	Returns a child control's column number.
GetColumnSpan	Returns the number of columns that a child control spans.
GetRow	Returns a child control's row number.
GetRowSpan	Returns the number of rows that a child control spans.
ScrollControlIntoView	If the TableLayoutPanel control has AutoScroll set to True, this scrolls an indicated child control into view.
SetColumn	Sets a child control's column number.
SetColumnSpan	Sets a child control's column span.
SetRow	Sets a child control's row number.
SetRowSpan	Sets a child control's row span.

In addition to providing its own properties, the TableLayoutPanel acts as a property provider for its child controls. These properties include Column, ColumnSpan, Row, and RowSpan. For example, if you add a button to the TableLayoutPanel control named TableLayoutPanel1, the button's Properties window will contain an entry labeled "Column on TableLayoutPanel1" that determines the button's column.

The TableLayoutPanel control also changes the meaning of its child controls' Anchor property. By default, a child control has Anchor property set to None, so it is centered in its table cell. If you set Anchor to Left, the control is moved to the left edge of the cell. If you set Anchor to "Left, Right," both of the control's edges are attached to the cell's edges, so the control stretches to fit the cell's width. The Top and Bottom Anchor settings work similarly.

The FlowLayoutPanel control also arranges contained controls, but not in a grid. Instead it places controls one after another to fill either rows or columns. For information on that control, see the section "FlowLayoutPanel" earlier in this appendix.

TEXTBOX

The TextBox control is a typical everyday text box. The user can enter and modify text, click and drag to select text, press Ctrl+C to copy the selected text to the clipboard, and so forth.

The TextBox control is much simpler than the RichTextBox control described earlier in this appendix. It can use only one font, background color, and foreground color for all of its text. It also cannot provide special formatting such as bullets, hanging indentation, and margins the way the RichTextBox control can. If you need those extra features, use a RichTextBox instead of a TextBox control.

The following table describes the TextBox control's most useful properties.

PROPERTY	PURPOSE
AcceptsReturn	For multiline controls, determines whether pressing the Enter key adds a new line to the text rather than triggering the form's Accept button.
AcceptsTab	For multiline controls, determines whether pressing the Tab key adds a Tab to the text rather than moving to the next control in the tab sequence.
AutoSize	For single-line controls, determines whether the control automatically sets its height for the fonts it contains.
CharacterCasing	Determines whether the control automatically changes the case of text as it is entered. This property can take the values Normal (leave the case alone), Upper (uppercase), and Lower (lowercase). The control changes the text's case whether the user types or pastes it into the control, or if the program sets the control's text.
Lines	An array of strings giving the lines of text (separated by carriage returns) displayed by the control. You can use this property to give the control more than one paragraph at design time.
MaxLength	The maximum number of characters the user can enter into the control.
MultiLine	Determines whether the control displays multiple lines.
PasswordChar	Determines the password character displayed by a single-line TextBox control for each character it contains. For example, if you set PasswordChar to *, each character the user types appears as a * in the text box. The control's Text property returns the actual text to the program.
PreferredHeight	Returns the height a single-line control would want to use for the font size.
ReadOnly	Determines whether the user can modify the control's text. You can display read-only text in a label, but then the user cannot select it and copy it to the clipboard. If you want to display information that the user might want to copy, place it in a TextBox control and set ReadOnly to True.
ScrollBars	Determines which scroll bars the control displays. This property can take the values None, Vertical, Horizontal, and Both. The appropriate scroll bars are always displayed, although they are disabled when they are not needed. Note that some of these values may not always be honored. For example, if WordWrap is True, the control never displays horizontal scroll bars.
SelectedText	Gets or sets the selected text's value.
SelectionLength	Gets the length of the selected text, or selects this number of letters. You can use SelectionStart and SelectionLength to select text, or you can use the Select method.

continues

(continued)

PROPERTY	PURPOSE
SelectionStart	Gets or sets the start of the selection. You can use SelectionStart and SelectionLength to select text, or you can use the Select method.
Text	Gets or sets the control's text.
TextAlign	Determines the text's alignment within the control. This can be Left, Right, or Center.
TextLength	Returns the length of the control's text.
WordWrap	For multiline controls, determines whether the control wraps text to a new line if it is too long to fit.

The TextBox control also provides several important methods, described in the following table.

METHOD	PURPOSE
AppendText	Adds text to the end of the control's text.
Clear	Clears the control's text.
ClearUndo	Empties the control's undo list.
Copy	Copies the control's selection to the clipboard.
Cut	Copies the control's selection to the clipboard and removes it from the control's text.
Paste	Pastes the clipboard's contents into the control, replacing the current selection. This method does nothing if the clipboard doesn't contain textual data.
ScrollToCaret	Scrolls the text so the insertion position is visible.
Select	Selects the indicated text.
SelectAll	Selects all of the control's text.
Undo	Undoes the most recent action. The TextBox stores information for only one undo action, so calling Undo again undoes the undo. That also means that the TextBox doesn't need a Redo method because it would do the same thing as Undo.

The TextBox control's most useful event is TextChanged. You can use this event to take action when the user changes the control's text. For example, you can display a visible indication that the data has been modified.

TIMER

The Timer component periodically raises a Tick event so the program can take action at specific intervals.

The component's Interval property determines the number of milliseconds (1000ths of a second) between events. This property is a 32-bit integer that must be greater than zero, so it can hold values between 1 and 2,147,483,647. If you set Interval to its maximum value, the component raises its Tick event roughly every 24.86 days.

The Timer component's Enabled property determines whether the Timer generates Tick events. The component continues raising its event as long as Enabled is True.

The component's Start and Stop methods simply set its Enabled property to True and False, respectively.

TOOLSTRIP

The ToolStrip control displays a series of buttons, dropdowns, and other tools. The user can access these tools quickly without navigating through a series of menus, so they are most useful for performing frequently needed tasks. Menus are more appropriate for commands that are needed less often.

The following list shows the types of items that a ToolStrip may contain:

ToolStripButton	ToolStripProgressBar
ToolStripComboBox	ToolStripSeparator
ToolStripDropDownButton	ToolStripSplitButton
ToolStripLabel	ToolStripTextBox

These tools are relatively straightforward. ToolStripButton is a button that sits on a ToolStrip, ToolStripComboBox is a combo box that sits on a ToolStrip, and so forth.

The only tool that doesn't correspond to another type of control is the SplitButton. This control is a button with a drop-down area. If the user clicks the button, it raises a Click event. If the user clicks the drop-down arrow, the control displays a drop-down menu containing menu items that the user can select as usual. See the online help at msdn.microsoft.com/system.windows.forms .toolstrip.aspx for more information on SplitButton and the other tool control classes.

The ToolStrip control stores its tools in its Items collection. At runtime, a program can access the controls inside this collection, or it can refer to the tools directly by name. At design time, you can select a ToolStrip, click its Items property in the Properties window, and click the ellipsis to the right to display an Items Collection Editor.

You can also click the ToolStrip and add items to it much as you edit a MenuStrip control.

The following table describes the ToolStrip control's most useful properties.

PROPERTY	PURPOSE
AllowItemReorder	Determines whether the user can drag and drop items to reorder them.
AllowMerge	Determines whether the ToolStrip can merge with others.
CanOverflow	Determines whether items can be sent to an overflow menu if the ToolStrip doesn't fit completely on the form.
GripDisplayStyle	Gets the orientation of the control's move handle.
GripMargin	Determines the space around the control's move handle.
GripRectangle	Gets the boundaries of the control's move handle.
GripStyle	Determines whether the control's move handle is visible or hidden.
Items	Returns a collection of ToolStripItem objects representing the control's tools.
OverflowButton	Returns a ToolStripItem representing the control's overflow button.
ShowItemToolTips	Determines whether the control's tools display their tooltips.

TOOLSTRIPCONTAINER

The ToolStripContainer control contains a ToolStripPanel along each of its edges where a ToolStrip control can dock. The control's center is filled with another ToolStripPanel that can contain other controls that are not part of the tool strips.

The user can drag the ToolStrips around and position them inside of any of the ToolStripPanel controls much as you can move the toolbars in the Visual Basic development environment. The user can drag the ToolStrips into multiple rows or columns within the panels.

Figure G-9 shows a form containing a ToolStripContainer with its Dock property set to Fill, so it fills the form. The lighter area in the middle is a PictureBox sitting inside the middle ToolStripPanel, also with its Dock property set to Fill.

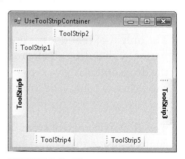

The ToolStripContainer in Figure G-9 holds five ToolStrip controls positioned in the container's various edge panels. Each ToolStrip contains a label identifying the ToolStrip. The ToolStrip3 control's TextDirection property is set to Vertical90, so it sits along the right edge of the form. The ToolStrip1 and ToolStrip2 controls have been dragged into two rows at the top of the form. The ToolStrip1 and ToolStrip2 controls share a row at the bottom.

FIGURE G-9: The ToolStripContainer control lets the user rearrange ToolStrip controls at runtime.

The ToolStripContainer control's LeftToolStripPanel, RightToolStripPanel, TopToolStripPanel, BottomToolStripPanel, and ContentPanel properties contain references to the ToolStripPanel controls that the control contains. Its LeftToolStripPanelVisible, RightToolStripPanelVisible, TopToolStripPanelVisible, and BottomToolStripPanelVisible properties let you show or hide specific panels. For example, you can hide the bottom or side panels if you don't want the user to drag ToolStrips there.

The ToolStripContainer control's other properties are relatively straightforward. See the online help at `msdn.microsoft.com/system.windows.forms.toolstripcontainer.aspx` for more information.

TOOLTIP

The ToolTip component allows you to provide tooltip help when the user hovers the mouse over another control. After you add a ToolTip component to a form, the other controls on the form get a special ToolTip property. For example, suppose that you create a ToolTip component named ttHint. Then a button on the form would have a new property named "ToolTip on ttHint." Set that property to the text you want the ToolTip to display, and you are all set.

The following table describes the ToolTip component's most useful properties.

PROPERTY	PURPOSE
Active	Determines whether the component displays tooltips.
AutomaticDelay	Sets the AutoPopDelay, InitialDelay, and ReshowDelay properties to values that are appropriate for this value.
AutoPopDelay	The number of milliseconds before the tooltip disappears if the mouse remains stationary in the tooltip's area.
BackColor	Determines the tooltip's background color.
ForeColor	Determines the tooltip's foreground color.
InitialDelay	The number of milliseconds that the mouse must remain stationary inside the tooltip's area before the component displays the tooltip.
IsBalloon	Determines whether the tooltip is displayed as a balloon rather than a rectangle.
OwnerDraw	Determines whether your code will draw the tooltip. If you set this to True, catch the ToolTip component's Draw method and draw the tooltip. Parameters to the method give the Graphics object to use, the bounds of the area to draw, and the tooltip text. This property is ignored if IsBalloon is True.
ReshowDelay	The number of milliseconds before the next tooltip will display when the mouse moves from one tooltip area to another. The idea is that subsequent tooltips display more quickly if one is already visible.

continues

(continued)

PROPERTY	PURPOSE
ShowAlways	Determines whether the component still displays tooltips, even if the form does not have the focus. The mouse still must hover over the tooltip area as usual if ShowAlways is True.
StripAmpersands	Determines whether the component removes ampersand characters from tooltip text. This can be useful if the tooltip text looks like menu and label captions where ampersands are converted into underscores.
UseAnimation	Determines whether animation effects are used to show and hide the tooltip.
UseFading	Determines whether fading effects are used to show and hide the tooltip.

The ToolTip component's SetToolTip method lets a program associate a tooltip with a control at runtime. The following code adds tooltip text to several address controls:

```
ttHint.SetToolTip(txtFirstName, "Customer first name")
ttHint.SetToolTip(txtLastName, "Customer last name")
ttHint.SetToolTip(txtStreet, "Mailing address street number and name")
ttHint.SetToolTip(txtCity, "Mailing address city")
ttHint.SetToolTip(cboState, "Mailing address state")
ttHint.SetToolTip(txtZip, "Mailing address ZIP code")
```

The following table lists the ToolTip component's most useful methods.

METHOD	PURPOSE
GetToolTip	Returns a control's associated tooltip text.
RemoveAll	Removes all tooltip text associated with this ToolTip component.
SetToolTip	Sets a control's associated tooltip text. Set the text to Nothing or an empty string to remove that control's tooltip text.
Show	Displays a tooltip over a specific control. Different overloaded versions let you specify the tooltip's location and duration.

TRACKBAR

The TrackBar control allows the user to drag a pointer along a bar to select a numeric value. This control is very similar to a horizontal scroll bar, but with a different appearance.

The following table describes the control's most useful properties.

PROPERTY	PURPOSE
AutoSize	Determines whether the control automatically sets its height or width, depending on its Orientation property. For example, if the control's orientation is horizontal, setting AutoSize to True makes the control pick a height that is appropriate for the control's width.
LargeChange	The amount by which the control's value changes when the user clicks the TrackBar, but not on its pointer.
Maximum	The largest value that the user can select.
Minimum	The smallest value that the user can select.
Orientation	Determines the control's orientation. This can be Horizontal or Vertical.
SmallChange	The amount by which the control's value changes when the user presses an arrow key.
TickFrequency	The number of values between tick marks on the control.
TickStyle	Determines the position of tick marks on the control. This can be TopLeft (on the top if Orientation is Horizontal; on the left if Orientation is Vertical), BottomRight (on the bottom if Orientation is Horizontal; on the right if Orientation is Vertical), Both, or None.
Value	The control's current numeric value.

The control's Value, Minimum, Maximum, and TickFrequency properties are integer values, so the TrackBar control is not ideal for letting the user select a nonintegral value such as 1.25. (You can multiply the values by 100 to get finer grained resolution but the user still can't select truly nonintegral values.)

The control's Scroll event fires when the user changes the control's value interactively. The ValueChanged event occurs when the control's value changes either because the user changed it interactively or because the program changed it with code.

TREEVIEW

The TreeView control displays a hierarchical data set graphically, as shown in Figure G-10.

The TreeView control uses TreeNode objects to represent the items it contains. The control's Nodes collection contains references to the top-level objects called its *root nodes*. In Figure G-10, the R & D and Sales & Support items are the root nodes.

Each TreeNode object has a Nodes collection of its own that contains references to its child nodes. For example, in Figure G-10

FIGURE G-10: The TreeView control displays hierarchical data graphically.

the R & D root node has children labeled Engineering and Test. Each of those nodes has child nodes representing employees.

You can assign each of the TreeNode objects an icon to display. In Figure G-10, the nodes display images representing factories, workgroups, and people.

Your program can manipulate the TreeNode objects at runtime, but you can also edit the tree data at design time. Select the TreeView control, select its Nodes property in the Properties window, and click the ellipsis to the right to make Visual Basic display the TreeNode Editor.

Click Add Root to add a new root node to the tree. Select a node and click Add Child to give the node a new child. Select a node and click Delete to remove the node and any descendants it contains.

If the TreeView control's ImageList property is set to an ImageList control, you can set a node's ImageIndex property to the index of the image in the ImageList that the node should display. Set the node's SelectedImageIndex to the index of the image that the control should display when the node is selected.

The following table describes the TreeView control's most useful properties.

PROPERTY	PURPOSE
BorderStyle	Determines the control's border style.
CheckBoxes	Determines whether the control displays check boxes next to the nodes.
DrawMode	Determines whether your code draws nothing (the default), the nodes' text, or the nodes' text and lines.
FullRowSelect	Determines whether selection highlights span the whole width of the control.
HideSelection	Determines whether the selected node remains visibly highlighted even when the TreeView control loses the focus.
HotTracking	Determines whether node labels look like hyperlinks when the mouse moves over them.
ImageIndex	Determines the default image index for the nodes.
ImageList	Determines the ImageList control that contains the images used by the nodes.
Indent	Determines the indentation distance for each level in the tree.
ItemHeight	Determines the height of each node.
LabelEdit	Determines whether the user can edit the nodes' labels.
LineColor	Determines the color of the lines connecting the nodes.

PROPERTY	PURPOSE
Nodes	Returns the collection of tree nodes.
PathSeparator	Determines the delimiter string used to represent paths in the tree. For example, using the default separator \, the path to the first person in Figure G-10 is "R & D\Engineering\Cameron, Charlie."
Scrollable	Determines whether the control displays scroll bars when necessary.
SelectedImageIndex	Determines the default image index for the selected nodes.
SelectedNode	Determines the currently selected node.
ShowLines	Determines whether the control draws lines connecting the nodes.
ShowNodeToolTips	Determines whether the control displays tooltips when the mouse hovers over a node. Use the TreeNode objects' ToolTipText properties to set the tooltip text.
ShowPlusMinus	Determines whether the control displays plus and minus signs next to tree nodes. The user can click the plus and minus signs or double-click the nodes to expand and collapse them.
ShowRootLines	Determines whether the control draws lines between the root nodes. In Figure G-10, ShowRootLines is True.
Sorted	Determines whether the control displays the nodes in sorted order.
TopNode	Returns the first node that is currently completely visible.
VisibleCount	Returns the number of nodes that could be fully visible. Fewer nodes may actually be visible if some are collapsed.

The TreeView control provides several methods that let your code manage the data at runtime. The following table describes the most useful of these methods.

METHOD	PURPOSE
CollapseAll	Collapses all of the control's nodes.
ExpandAll	Expands all of the control's nodes. In the process, the control scrolls down, so the last node is visible and selects the topmost visible control. To select some other control, such as the topmost root node, set the control's SelectedNode property as in: `trvOrgChart.SelectedNode = trvOrg.Nodes(0)`
GetNodeAt	Returns the TreeNode object at a specific (X, Y) location.
GetNodeCount	Returns the number of the tree's nodes. If the method's includeSubTrees parameter is False, the routine returns only the number of root nodes. If includeSubTrees is True, the routine returns the total number of nodes in the tree.

The control provides a series of events that fire before and after the user takes certain actions. For example, when the user clicks a node's check box, the control raises its BeforeCheck event, changes the node's checked state, and then raises its AfterCheck event. The other actions that have similar Before and After event handlers are Collapse, Expand, LabelEdit, and Select.

Each of the Before event handlers provides a parameter that the code can set to cancel the event. For example, the UseTreeView example program, which is available for download on the book's web site, uses the following code to prevent the user from editing the labels of the tree's root nodes:

```
Private Sub trvOrgChart_BeforeLabelEdit(ByVal sender As Object,
  ByVal e As System.Windows.Forms.NodeLabelEditEventArgs) _
  Handles trvOrgChart.BeforeLabelEdit
    e.CancelEdit = Not e.Node.FullPath.Contains(trvOrgChart.PathSeparator)
End Sub
```

code snippet UseTreeView

When the user tries to edit a node's label, the BeforeLabelEdit event fires. The value e.Node represents the node that the user is about to edit. Its FullPath property returns a delimited path showing the node's position in the tree.

The code searches this path for the path separator character (normally \). If the node is a root node, the separator is not in the path so the Contains method returns False and the code sets e.CancelEdit to True so the edit never occurs. If Contains finds the path separator in the node's FullPath, the code sets e.CancelEdit to False so the edit takes place as usual.

The TreeNode object also provides properties and methods if its own. The following table describes the TreeNode object's most useful properties.

PROPERTY	PURPOSE
Checked	Determines whether the node is checked, assuming that the TreeView control's CheckBoxes property is True.
FirstNode	Returns the node's first child node.
FullPath	Returns a string representing the node and its ancestors in the tree, delimited by the character specified by the TreeView control's PathSeparator property.
ImageIndex	Determines the index of the node's image in the ImageList control specified by the TreeView control's ImageList property.
Index	Returns the node's index within its parent node's collection of children.
IsEditing	Indicates whether the user is editing the node's label.
IsExpanded	Indicates whether the node is expanded.

PROPERTY	PURPOSE
IsSelected	Indicates whether the node is selected.
IsVisible	Indicates whether the node is at least partly visible.
LastNode	Returns the node's last child node.
Level	Returns the node's level in the tree. Root nodes have level 0, their children have level 1, the children of those nodes have level 2, and so forth.
NextNode	Returns the node's next sibling node.
NextVisibleNode	Returns the next node that is not hidden because of a collapse. This may be a sibling, child, or some other node, depending on which nodes are expanded at the time. Note that this node may lie below the visible scrolling area, so it may not really be visible.
NodeFont	The font used to draw the node's text. If the node's font makes the text bigger than the TreeView control's Font property does, the text is clipped.
Nodes	The collection of this node's child nodes.
Parent	Returns a reference to the node's parent node in the tree.
PrevNode	Returns the node's previous sibling node.
PrevVisibleNode	Returns the previous node that is not hidden because of a collapse. This may be a sibling, parent, or some other node, depending on which nodes are expanded at the time. Note that this node may be above the visible scrolling area, so it may not really be visible.
SelectedImageIndex	Determines the index of the node's selected image in the ImageList control specified by the TreeView control's ImageList property. The node displays this image while it is selected.
Text	Determines the text displayed in the node's label.
ToolTipText	Determines the node's tooltip text.
TreeView	Returns a reference to the TreeView control that contains the node.

The TreeNode object also provides several methods. The following table describes the most useful of these.

METHOD	PURPOSE
BeginEdit	Begins editing of the node's label. This raises an error if the TreeView control's LabelEdit property is False.
Clone	Copies the node and its entire subtree.
Collapse	Collapses the node's subtree.
EndEdit	Ends editing of the node's label.
EnsureVisible	Expands nodes and scrolls the TreeView as necessary to ensure that the node is visible.
Expand	Expands the node to display its children.
ExpandAll	Expands the node's whole subtree.
GetNodeCount	Returns the number of child nodes.
Remove	Removes the node and its subtree.
Toggle	Toggles the node between expanded and collapsed.

VSCROLLBAR

The VScrollBar control is similar to the HScrollBar control, except that it is oriented vertically instead of horizontally. See the section "HScrollBar" earlier in this appendix for more information on the control.

WEBBROWSER

The WebBrowser control displays the contents of web pages, XML documents, text files, and other documents understood by the browser. The control can automatically follow links that the user clicks in the document and provides a standard web browser context menu, containing commands such as Back, Forward, Save Background As, and Print.

Using this control, you can easily add Web-based hypertext to your applications. For example, you could display an HTML help system or tutorial pages within the control.

The control provides several properties and methods for navigating to different documents. The following table describes the most useful of these.

PROPERTY/METHOD	PURPOSE
Url	Gets or sets the control's current web address.
Navigate	Makes the control open a specific URL.
GoBack	Makes the control move to the URL it previously displayed.
GoForward	After a call to GoBack, makes the control move forward to the next URL it displayed.
GoHome	Makes the control go to the current user's home page.
GoSearch	Makes the control go to the current user's search page.

Whenever the control moves to a new document, it fires three events. The Navigating event fires before the control moves to the new document. The Navigated event occurs after the control has navigated to the new document and is loading it. The DocumentCompleted event occurs when the control has finished loading the new document.

The control also supports a variety of other events that tell a program when something has changed. Some of the more useful of these notification events include CanGoBackChanged, CanGoForwardChanged, DocumentTitleChanged, NewWindow (the browser is about to open a new window), ProgressChanged (gives progress information on the download of a document), and StatusTextChanged.

After the control loads a document, the program can manipulate the document through the control's Document property. This property contains a reference to an HtmlDocument object that gives access to the document's images, forms, links, and other HTML document elements.

In addition to opening existing documents, a program can make the WebBrowser display a file generated within the application by setting its DocumentText or DocumentStream properties.

The WebBrowser control provides all of the power and flexibility of Internet Explorer. Unfortunately, that power and flexibility makes the control quite complicated, so it is not described further here. Refer to the online help at msdn.microsoft.com/system.windows.forms.webbrowser.aspx for more information.

H

WPF Controls

This appendix lists the most useful Windows Presentation Foundation (WPF) controls that are available in the .NET Framework 4, and briefly describes their purposes. This list does not include all of the hundreds of classes that WPF defines; it lists only the tools most likely to appear in the window designer's Toolbox.

These controls are part of the System.Windows.Controls namespace. In contrast, the controls used in Windows Forms are contained in the System.Windows.Forms namespace. Many of the controls in the two namespaces serve very similar purposes, although they have different capabilities. For example, both namespaces have buttons, labels, combo boxes, and check boxes but only the System.Windows.Controls classes provide foreground and background brushes, render transformations, complex content, and XAML-defined triggers.

This appendix describes the WPF controls in far less detail than Appendix G describes the Windows Forms controls. This is mostly due to space constraints, not because the WPF controls are inferior. These controls can do some amazing things that the Windows Forms controls cannot, such as containing other controls as content and applying transformations while drawing. Unfortunately, these new features would take at least a few hundred pages to cover in depth, and there just isn't room in this edition of the book to do them justice.

For much more information about WPF controls and WPF in general, see my book *WPF Programmer's Reference* (Stephens, Wrox 2010). You can learn more about the book at www .vb-helper.com/wpf.htm.

Note that not all of the controls described here are available by default when you create a new WPF application. You need to add some of these controls to the Toolbox before you can use them. To add a control that is missing, right-click a Toolbox section and select Choose Items. On the Choose Toolbox Items dialog, select the WPF Components tab to display the dialog shown in Figure H-1. Check the boxes next to the controls that you want, and click OK.

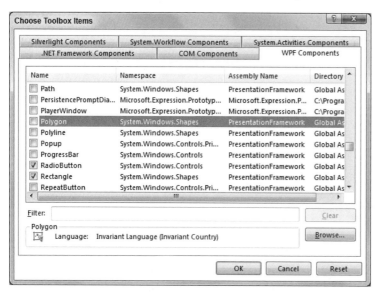

FIGURE H-1: Use this dialog to add new WPF controls to the Toolbox.

Controls in the following table are marked with superscripts [0], [1,] or [2] to indicate whether they can hold 0, 1, or 2 children. Controls with no superscripts can hold any number of children.

CONTROL	PURPOSE
Border[1]	Provides a visible border around or background behind its contents.
BulletDecorator[2]	Contains two children. The first is used as a bullet and the second is aligned with the first. For example, you can use this to align bullet images next to labels.
Button[1]	Displays a button that the user can click. Raises a Click event that the program can catch to perform an action.
Canvas	Creates an area in which you can explicitly position children by specifying their Width, Height, Canvas.Left, and Canvas.Top properties.
CheckBox[1]	Allows the user to select or deselect an item. Each CheckBox choice is independent of all others.
ComboBox	Allows the user to select an item from a drop-down list. The list can contain all sorts of objects, but typically holds a series of ComboBoxItems.
ComboBoxItem[1]	Represents an item in a ComboBox control's list.

CONTROL	PURPOSE
ContentControl[1]	Represents a control that contains a single piece of content. Note, however, that the content may, in turn, contain other objects.
ContextMenu	Builds a popup menu for a control. This element should be inside the control's ContextMenu property (for example, inside a <Button.ContextMenu> element). Normally the ContextMenu contains MenuItem controls.
DockPanel	Docks its children to its left, right, top, or bottom much as the Dock property does in a Windows Forms application. If the control's LastChildFill property is True, the control makes its last child control fill the remaining space.
DocumentViewer[1]	Displays a FixedDocument. See the section "Fixed Documents" in Chapter 12, "Using WPF Controls."
Ellipse[0]	Displays an ellipse.
Expander[1]	Displays a header and lets the user expand and contract a single detail item. The <Expander.Header> sub-element contains the content displayed in the header.
FlowDocumentPageViewer[1]	Displays a FlowDocument one page at a time. If the control is wide enough, it may display multiple columns although it still only displays one page at a time. See the section "Flow Documents" in Chapter 12.
FlowDocumentReader[1]	Displays a FlowDocument in one of three modes. When in *single page* mode, it acts as a FlowDocumentPageViewer. When in *scrolling* mode, it acts as a FlowDocumentScrollViewer. In *book reading mode*, it displays two pages side-by-side much as a real book does. See the section "Flow Documents" in Chapter 12.
FlowDocumentScrollViewer[1]	Displays a FlowDocument as a single, long, vertically scrolling page. See the section "Flow Documents" in Chapter 12.
Frame[0]	Supports navigation and content display. The control can navigate to a .NET Framework object or to HTML content.
Grid	Displays children in rows and columns. This is similar to the Windows Forms TableLayoutPanel control.
GridSplitter[0]	Acts as a splitter that allows the user to resize rows or columns in a Grid.
GridView	Displays data in columns within a ListView control.

continues

(continued)

CONTROL	PURPOSE
GridViewColumnHeader[1]	Represents a column header for a GridViewColumn.
GroupBox[1]	Displays a visible border with a header. The Header property determines the content displayed in the header. The control also forms a grouping for any RadioButtons that it contains.
GroupItem[1]	Used to group items in other controls such as a TreeView.
HeaderedContentControl[2]	This is the base class for controls that have a single content element and a header. Although you can create one directly, usually it's better use a subclass such as GroupBox.
HeaderedItemsControl	Displays a header and multiple content elements.
Image[0]	Displays an image. Can optionally stretch the image with or without distortion.
InkCanvas	Displays or captures ink strokes.
InkPresenter[0]	Displays ink strokes.
ItemsControl	Displays a collection of content items.
Label[1]	Displays non-editable text.
Line[0]	Draws a line segment.
ListBox	Lets the user select items from a list. ListBoxItem objects hold the items. The control automatically displays scroll bars when needed.
ListBoxItem[1]	Holds content for display by a ListBox object.
ListView	Displays a group of items in various display modes.
ListViewItem[1]	Contains the content for an item displayed in a ListView.
MediaElement[0]	Presents audio and video. To let you control the media, it provides Play, Pause, and Stop methods, and Volume and SpeedRatio properties.
Menu	Builds a menu that is visible, in contrast to a ContextMenu, which is hidden until displayed. Normally, the Menu contains MenuItem controls representing the top-level menus. Those items contain other MenuItem controls representing commands.
MenuItem	Defines a top-level menu, submenu, or menu item for a ContextMenu or Menu.
NavigationWindow[0]	Navigates to content and displays it, keeping a navigation history. Similar to Frame.

CONTROL	PURPOSE
Panel	Panel is the parent class for Canvas, DockPanel, Grid, TabPanel, ToolbarOverflowPanel, UniformGrid, StackPanel, VirtualizingPanel, and WrapPanel. Usually, you should use one of those classes instead of Panel, but you can use Panel to implement your own custom panel controls.
PasswordBox[0]	A text box where the user can enter sensitive information such as passwords. The control's PasswordChar property determines the character displays for each character the user types. By default, this is a solid black circle.
Path[0]	Contains a series of drawing instructions that make line segments, arcs, curves, ellipses, and so forth. For more information, see the section "Path" in Chapter 12.
Polygon[0]	Draws a closed polygon.
Polyline[0]	Draws a series of connected line segments.
Popup[1]	Displays content in a window above another control. Usually, you can use the Tooltip and ContextMenu controls instead of a Popup.
PrintDialog[0]	Displays a standard Windows print dialog. You shouldn't place a PrintDialog on a window. Instead use code to build and display the PrintDialog.
ProgressBar[0]	Indicates the fraction of a long task that has been completed. Usually, the task is performed synchronously, so the user is left staring at the form while it completes. The ProgressBar lets the user know that the operation is not stuck.
RadioButton[1]	Lets the user pick from among a set of options. If the user checks one RadioButton, all others with the same parent become unchecked.
Rectangle[0]	Draws a rectangle, optionally with rounded corners.
RepeatButton[1]	Acts as a Button that raises its Click event repeatedly when it is pressed and held down.
ResizeGrip[0]	Displays a resize grip similar to the one used on the lower-right corner of a window.
RichTextBox[1]	Similar to a TextBox but contains text in the form of a document object. See the section "Managing Documents" in Chapter 11, "Selecting WPF Controls," for more information on documents.

continues

(continued)

CONTROL	PURPOSE
ScrollBar[0]	Allows the user to drag a "thumb" to select a numeric value. Usually scroll bars are used internally by other controls such as the ScrollViewer and your applications should use a Slider instead.
ScrollViewer[1]	Provides vertical and horizontal scroll bars for a single content element. Makes a scrollable area that can contain other controls.
Separator[0]	Draws a vertical or horizontal separator in controls that contain other controls, such as StatusBar, Menu, ListBox, or ToolBar.
Slider[0]	Enables the user to select a value from a range by sliding a Thumb along a Track. Similar to the Windows Forms TrackBar control.
StackPanel	Arranges children in a single row or column. If there are too many controls, those that don't fit are clipped.
StatusBar	Displays a container at the bottom of the form where you can place controls holding status information. Though you can place anything inside a StatusBar, this control is intended to hold summary status information not tools. Generally, menus, combo boxes, buttons, toolbars, and other controls that let the user manipulate the application do not belong in a SatusBar.
StatusBarItem[1]	Contains an item in a StatusBar.
TabControl	Arranges children in tabs. TabItem controls contain the items that should be displayed in the tabs.
TabItem[1]	Represents an item in a TabControl. The Header property determines the content displayed on the tab, and the Content property determines what's displayed on the tab's body.
TextBlock	Displays more complex non-editable text. This control's contents can include inline tags to indicate special formatting. Tags can include AnchoredBlock, Bold, Hyperlink, InlineUIContainer, Italic, LineBreak, Run, Span, and Underline.
TextBox[0]	Allows the user to enter simple text. Optionally can allow carriage returns and tabs, and can wrap text.
Thumb[0]	Represents an area that the user can grab and drag as in a ScrollBar or Slider.
ToggleButton[1]	This is the base class for controls that toggle between two states such as a CheckBox or RadioButton. You can make one directly, but it's easier to use CheckBox or RadioButton.

CONTROL	PURPOSE
`ToolBar`	Contains a series of tools, typically Button controls, ComboBox controls, and other small controls. The Header property gives the ToolBar a header.
`ToolBarTray`	Contains ToolBars and allows the user to drag them into new positions.
`ToolTip`[1]	Displays a tooltip. To give a control a simple textual tooltip, set its Tooltip property. Use the Tooltip control to build more complex tooltips. For example, a Tooltip control might contain a StackPanel that holds other controls.
`TreeView`	Displays hierarchical data with a series of nested collapsible nodes. TreeViewItems contain the items displayed in the hierarchy.
`TreeViewItem`	Represents an item within a TreeView. The Header attribute or sub-element determines the content displayed for the item.
`UserControl`[1]	A container that you can use to create a simple compound control. Note, however, that classes derived from UserControl do not support templates.
`Viewbox`[1]	Stretches its single child to fill the Viewbox. The Stretch property determines whether the control stretches its child uniformly (without changing the width-to-height ratio).
`VirtualizingStackPanel`	Generates child items to hold items that can fit in the available area. For example, when working with a ListBox bound to a data source, the VirtualizingStackPanel generates only the items that will fit within the ListBox. If the control is not bound to a data source, this control behaves like a StackPanel.
`Window`[1]	Represents a window, the WPF equivalent of a form. The Window includes two areas: the client area where you normally put controls and the non-client area where the window displays borders, title bar, caption, system menus, and so on. Normally, you add a Window to an application by using the Project menu's Add New Item command.
`WrapPanel`	Arranges children in rows or columns depending on its Orientation property. When a row or column is full, the next child moves to a new row or column. This is similar to the Windows Forms FlowLayoutPanel control.

For more detailed descriptions plus examples using these and other controls, see the Microsoft online help. You can find a reference for System.Windows.Controls classes at `msdn.microsoft.com/system.windows.controls.aspx`. You can find a reference for the System.Windows.Controls.Primitives classes, which include base classes used by other controls, at `msdn.microsoft.com/system.windows.controls.primitives.aspx`.

For much more information about WPF controls and WPF in general, see my book *WPF Programmer's Reference*. You can learn more about the book at `www.vb-helper.com/wpf.htm`

I

Visual Basic Power Packs

When Visual Basic .NET first appeared, it was missing many features that developers had found extremely useful in Visual Basic 6. Power Packs were invented to provide objects and tools to fill the need for these missing tools and to make programming easier and more productive in general.

This appendix describes Visual Basic Power Packs provided by Microsoft and others that you make find useful.

It also briefly describes some older Power Packs that were available from the GotDotNet web site. Although these were written in an older version of Visual Basic .NET, they may still be useful, at least as inspiration for tools you may want to build.

Finally, this appendix explains where you can find the Power Toys Pack Installer, a tool that lets you view, download, and install the latest Power Toys for Visual Studio.

MICROSOFT POWER PACKS

Originally Microsoft provided its Power Packs as a download but in Visual Basic 2010 they are included within Visual Basic. That doesn't mean you can instantly use them, however. By default, the Power Pack is installed but its tools are not included in new Visual Basic projects.

To use these tools, start a new project, open Solution Explorer, and double-click My Project to open the project property pages. On the References tab, click the Add button and add a reference to Microsoft.VisualBasic.PowerPacks.vs. This allows you to use the tools in your code and places the tools on the Windows Forms Designer's Toolbox with the other controls.

The Microsoft Visual Basic Power Packs 3.0 download includes DataRepeater, line and shape controls, plus a PrintForm and Printer Compatibility Library. The printer tools are mostly intended to help developers upgrade applications from Visual Basic 6 to Visual Basic .NET but they can be useful for new Visual Basic 2010 programs, too. The following sections describe the Power Pack tools in greater detail. For more information about these tools, go to the Microsoft Power Packs home page msdn.microsoft.com/vbasic/aa701257.aspx.

> Instead of going directly to the Power Packs home page, you may want to start at the Visual Basic Developer Center (msdn.microsoft.com/vbasic). It should always contain a link to the latest Power Packs home page in addition to other useful Visual Basic resources.

DataRepeater

The DataRepeater control allows you to define a template of controls to display a piece of data. The repeater then repeats your template for each row in a data source and displays the result in a scrollable container.

Line and Shape Controls

The LineShape, OvalShape, and RectangleShape controls let you easily place lines, ovals, and rectangles on a form without using pens, brushes, and Graphics objects.

Properties let you set the controls' pens and brushes at design time. The controls support events such as Click and DoubleClick, and many of the graphical methods provided in the System.Drawing namespace. The OvalShape and RectangleShape controls even support linear gradient brushes that let you add interesting graphical effects at design time.

Printer Compatibility Library

In Visual Basic 6 and earlier versions, programs used the Printer object to generate printouts. Programs used the object's properties to define printing characteristics, and called its methods to draw on the printed page. Methods let you draw shapes, text, and images. Other methods let you start a new page, cancel the print document, or finish printing and send the results to the printer.

Visual Basic .NET uses a very different printing model. Instead of calling a Printer object's methods, the program creates a PrintDocument object and then responds to that object's events. When the object needs to generate a page, it raises an event and the program responds. Instead of actively telling the Printer object what to do, the program reactively responds to requests from the PrintDocument object.

The Printer Compatibility Library provides a way for Visual Basic .NET applications to print in a manner that is similar to the one used by Visual Basic 6. The library defines a Printer class. You can create a new Printer object and then use it much as you would use Visual Basic 6's Printer object.

See Chapter 34 for more information on printing in Visual Basic 2010.

My book *Expert One-on-One Visual Basic Design and Development* (Stephens, Wrox, 2005) includes a chapter on printing that explains how to print images of forms much as the PrintForm Power Pack component does. It also shows how to wrap text so it flows around images on a printed page and how to use metafiles to let a program print procedurally rather than by responding to events. For more information, see the book's web site at www.wrox.com or www.vb-helper.com/one_on_one.htm.

PrintForm Component

In Visual Basic 6 and earlier versions, the Form control have a PrintForm method that sends an image of the form to the printer. The result is a bitmap image that usually looks grainy on the printout. It does not take full advantage of the printer's high resolution, and it doesn't add extra data that can't fit on the monitor but that can fit on a printout.

However, PrintForm is extremely easy to use. The program simply calls the form's PrintForm method. This is much simpler than generating a high-resolution printout, so developers often use it to give early versions of an application a printing capability. For many applications, PrintForm is good enough, and it gives users a WYSIWYG (what you see is what you get) printing tool, so that's all the program needs.

The PrintForm component enables a Visual Basic .NET application to print a form's image quickly and easily.

> **CAPTURE OR PRINT**
>
> Note also that you can use the Form object's DrawToBitmap method to capture an image of the form in a bitmap. You can then print the image, display a print preview, save it into a file, or do anything else that you can do with a bitmap. For an example, see `www.vb-helper.com/howto_2005_drawtobitmap.html`. That example was written in Visual Basic 2005 but works in later versions, too.

GOTDOTNET POWER PACK

The GotDotNet Visual Basic Power Pack includes seven useful controls. While they were written in Visual Basic 2003, they can still be useful. The Power Pack comes with source code so you can upgrade them to Visual Basic 2010 or use their code as a starting point for building your own controls.

The following list summarizes the seven controls:

➤ `BlendPanel` — Provides a background with linear gradient shading. Note that the WPF LinearGradientBrush class provides a similar, but more flexible, effect. Other WPF classes such as RadialGradientBrush provide even more shading features.

➤ `UtilityToolbar` — A toolbar that has a look and feel similar to the Microsoft Internet Explorer toolbar.

➤ `ImageButton` — A button with a transparent background. You can use it, for example, to display a round button over a gradient shaded, or complex background, without messing up the background.

➤ `NotificationWindow` — Displays text and graphics in a popup notification window.

➤ `TaskPane` — A container that provides collapsible panes similar to the WPF Expander control.

➤ `FolderViewer` — Displays a hierarchical view of a directory tree.

➤ `FileViewer` — Displays a list of the files in a directory.

Unfortunately, Microsoft closed the GotDotNet web site in 2007. Before the site disappeared, however, I saved a copy of the Power Pack. You can get more information and download it at `www.vb-helper.com/tip_gotdotnet_powerpack.html`.

POWER TOYS PACK INSTALLER

The Power Toys Pack Installer is a tool that lets you view, download, and install the latest Power Toys for Visual Studio. The "toys" include code snippets, starter kits, examples, and other tools divided into categories such as Visual Basic 2005, Visual Basic 6.0, C#, Printing, Interop, and Debugging.

You can learn more about the installer and download it at `www.codeplex.com/PackInstaller`.

REFACTOR!

Refactor! is a free plug-in developed by Developer Express Inc. that provides refactoring tools that can help you rearrange and restructure your code. For example, they can extract a section of code into a new routine, reorder a routine's parameters, or convert methods to properties and vice versa.

You can find a link to information about Refactor! at the Basic Developer Center. You can also learn about it on Developer Express's Refactor! web page `www.devexpress.com/Products/Visual_Studio_Add-in/VBRefactor`.

> **EXPRESS STRESS**
>
> Unfortunately Refactor! doesn't work with the free Visual Basic Express Edition. If you're using the Express Edition, you'll have to look for other refactoring tools.

J
Form Objects

This appendix describes the most useful properties, methods, and events provided by the Windows Form class.

The Form class inherits indirectly from the Control class (Control is the Form class's "great-grandparent"), so in many ways, a form is just another type of control. Except where overridden, Form inherits the properties, methods, and events defined by the Control class. Chapter 9, "Using Windows Forms Controls," discusses some of the more useful properties, methods, and events provided by the Control class and most of those apply to the Form class as well. Appendix A, "Useful Control Properties, Methods, and Events," summarizes the Control class's most useful properties.

PROPERTIES

The following table describes some of the most useful Form properties.

PROPERTY	DESCRIPTION
AcceptButton	Determines the button that clicks when the user presses the Enter key. This button basically gives the form a default action. Most forms used as dialog boxes should have an Accept button and a Cancel button (see the CancelButton property described shortly). This makes the form more accessible to the visually impaired and is more efficient for users who prefer to use the keyboard.
ActiveControl	Gets the form's currently active control.
ActiveForm	Gets the application's currently active form. If an MDI (Multiple Document Interface) child form is active, this returns the active form's MDI parent.

continues

(continued)

PROPERTY	DESCRIPTION
ActiveMdiChild	Gets the MDI parent form's currently active MDI child form.
AllowDrop	Determines whether the form processes drag-and-drop events. See Chapter 23, "Drag and Drop, and the Clipboard," for more information on drag-and-drop tasks.
Anchor	Determines which edges of the form are anchored to the edges of its container. This lets MDI child forms resize with their MDI parents.
AutoScroll	Determines whether the form automatically provides scroll bars when it is too small to display all of the controls it contains.
AutoScrollMargin	If AutoScroll is True, the control will provide scroll bars if necessary to display its controls plus this much margin.
AutoScrollPosition	Adjusts the AutoScroll scroll bars so this point on the form is placed at the upper-left corner of the visible area (if possible). For example, if a button has location (100, 20), the statement `AutoScrollPosition = New Point(100, 20)` scrolls the form so the button is in the upper-left corner of the visible area.
BackColor	Determines the form's background color.
BackgroundImage	Determines the image displayed in the form's background.
BackgroundImageLayout	Determines how the BackgroundImage is displayed. This can be None (the image is displayed at up to normal scale, or compressed, if necessary, to make it fit vertically or horizontally), Tile (the image is tiled to fill the form), Center (the image is centered on the form at up to normal scale, or compressed, if necessary, to make it fit vertically or horizontally), Stretch (the image is resized to fill the form exactly), or Zoom (the image is resized to fill the form as much as possible without distorting it).
Bottom	Returns the distance between the form's bottom edge and the top edge of its container.
Bounds	Determines the form's size and location within its container. These bounds include the form's client and non-client areas (such as the borders and caption area).
CancelButton	Determines the button that clicks when the user presses the Escape key. This button basically gives the form a cancel action. If the form is being displayed modally, clicking this button either manually or by pressing Escape automatically closes the form.

PROPERTY	DESCRIPTION
Capture	Determines whether the form has captured mouse events. While this is True, all mouse events go to the form's event handlers. For example, pressing the mouse button sends the form a MouseDown event even if the mouse is over a control on the form or even if it is off of the form completely.
ClientRectangle	Returns a Rectangle object representing the form's client area.
ClientSize	Gets or sets a Size object representing the client area's size. If you set this value, the form automatically adjusts to make the client area this size while allowing room for its non-client areas (such as borders and title bar). For example, the following statement makes the form just big enough to display the txtNotes control within the client area: ```Me.ClientSize = New Size(` ` lblNotes.Left + lblNotes.Width,` ` lblNotes.Top + lblNotes.Height)```
ContainsFocus	Returns True if the form or one of its controls has the input focus.
ContextMenuStrip	Gets or sets the form's context menu. If the user right-clicks the form, Visual Basic automatically displays this menu. Note that controls on the form share this menu unless they have context menus of their own. Also note that some controls have their own context menus by default. For example, a TextBox displays a Copy, Cut, Paste menu, unless you explicitly set its ContextMenu property.
ControlBox	Determines whether the form displays a control box (the Minimize, Maximize, Restore, and Close buttons) on the right side of its caption area.
Controls	Returns a collection containing references to all the controls on the form. This includes only the controls contained directly within the form, and not controls contained within other controls. For example, if a form contains a GroupBox that holds several TextBox controls, only the GroupBox is listed in the form's Controls collection. You would need to search the GroupBox control's Controls collection to find the TextBox controls.
Cursor	Determines the cursor displayed by the mouse when it is over the form.
DesktopBounds	Determines the form's location and size as a Rectangle.
DesktopLocation	Determines the form's location as a Point.

continues

(continued)

PROPERTY	DESCRIPTION
DialogResult	Gets or sets the form's dialog box result. If code displays the form modally using its ShowDialog method, the method returns the DialogResult value the form has when it closes. Setting the form's DialogResult value automatically closes the dialog box. Triggering the form's CancelButton automatically sets DialogResult to Cancel and closes the dialog box.
DisplayRectangle	Gets a Rectangle representing the form's display area. This is the area where you should display things on the form. In theory, this might not include all of the client area and could exclude form decorations, although in practice it seems to be the same as ClientRectangle.
Enabled	Determines whether the form will respond to user events. If the form is disabled, all of its controls are disabled and drawn grayed out. The user can still resize the form and its controls' Anchor and Dock properties still rearrange the controls accordingly. The user can also click the form's Minimize, Maximize, Restore, and Close buttons. Note that you cannot display a form modally using ShowDialog if it is disabled.
Font	Determines the form's font.
ForeColor	Determines the foreground color defined for the form.
FormBorderStyle	Determines the form's border style. This can be None, FixedSingle, Fixed3D, FixedDialog, Sizeable, FixedToolWindow, or SizeableToolWindow.
Handle	Returns the form's integer window handle (hWnd). You can pass this value to API functions that work with window handles. Many of the API functions that are necessary in Visual Basic 6 are no longer needed in Visual Basic .NET because their functions have been incorporated into the .NET Framework, but there are still occasions when the form's handle is useful.
HasChildren	Returns True if the form contains child controls.
Height	Determines the form's height.
HelpButton	Determines whether the form displays a Help button with a question mark in the caption area to the left of the close button. The button is only visible if the MaximizeBox and MinimizeBox properties are both False. If the user clicks the Help button, the mouse pointer turns into a question mark arrow. When the user clicks the form, Visual Basic raises the form's HelpRequested event. The form can provide help based on the location of the click and, if it provides help, it should set the event handler's hlpevent.Handled parameter to True.

PROPERTY	DESCRIPTION
Icon	Determines the form's icon displayed in the left of the form's caption area, in the taskbar, and by the Task Manager. Typically, this icon should contain images at the sizes 16 × 16 pixels and 32 × 32 pixels, so different displays can use an image with the correct size without resizing.

IsMdiChild	Returns True if the form is an MDI child form. To make an MDI application, set IsMdiContainer = True for the MDI parent form. Then display a child form, as shown in the following code. In the child form, IsMdiChild will return True.
	
	`Dim child_form As New MyChildForm ()`
	`child_form.MdiParent = MdiParentForm`
	`child_form.Show`

IsMdiContainer	Returns True if the form is an MDI parent form. See the description of IsMdiChild for more information.
KeyPreview	Determines whether the form receives key events before they are passed to the control with the input focus. If KeyPreview is True, the form's key event handlers can see the key, take action, and hide the key from the control that would normally receive it, if necessary. For example, the following statement in a KeyDown event handler would close the form if the user presses Escape, no matter what control has the focus: `If e.Keys = Keys.Escape Then Me.Close`
Left	Determines the distance between the form's left edge and the left edge of its container.
Location	Determines the coordinates of the form's upper-left corner.
MainMenuStrip	Gets or sets the form's main menu.
MaximizeBox	Determines whether the form displays a Maximize button on the right of its caption area.
MaximumSize	This Size object determines the maximum size the form can take.
MdiChildren	Returns an array of forms that are this form's MDI children.
MdiParent	Gets or sets the form's MDI parent form.
MinimizeBox	Determines whether the form displays a Minimize button on the right of its caption area.
MinimumSize	This Size object determines the minimum size the form can take.

continues

(continued)

PROPERTY	DESCRIPTION
Modal	Returns True if the form is displayed modally.
Name	Gets or sets the form's name. Initially, this is the form's class name, but your code can change it to anything, possibly even duplicating another form's name.
Opacity	Determines the form's opacity level between 0.0 (transparent) and 1.0 (opaque).
OwnedForms	Returns an array listing this form's owned forms. To make this form own another form, call this form's AddOwnedForm method, passing it the other form. Owned forms are minimized and restored with the owner and can never lie behind the owner. Typically, they are used for things like Toolboxes and search forms that should remain above the owner form.
Region	Gets or sets the region that defines the area that the form can occupy. Pieces of the form that lie outside of the region are clipped. For more information on regions, see Chapter 31, "Brushes, Pens, and Paths."
Right	Returns the distance between the form's right edge and the left edge of its container.
ShowIcon	Determines whether the form displays an icon in its title bar. If this is False, the system displays a default icon in the taskbar and Task Manager if ShowInTaskbar is True.
ShowInTaskbar	Determines whether the form is displayed in the taskbar and Task Manager.
Size	Gets or sets a Size object representing the form's size, including client and non-client areas.
SizeGripStyle	Determines how the resize grip is shown in the form's lower-right corner. This can be Show, Hide, or Auto.
StartPosition	Determines the form's position when it is first displayed at runtime. This can be Manual (use the size and position specified by the form's properties), CenterScreen (center the form on the screen taking the taskbar into account), WindowsDefaultLocation (use a default position defined by Windows and use the form's specified size), and WindowsDefaultBounds (use Windows default position and size).
Tag	Gets or sets an object associated with the form. You can use this for whatever purpose you see fit.

PROPERTY	DESCRIPTION
Text	Determines the text displayed in the form's caption.
Top	Determines the distance between the form's top edge and the top edge of its container.
TopMost	Determines whether the form is a topmost form. A topmost form always sits above all other non-topmost forms, even when the other forms have the input focus.
TransparencyKey	Gets or sets a color that determines the areas of the form that are shown as transparent. This applies to the form itself and any controls it contains. For example, if you set TransparencyKey to the default form and control color Colors.Control, the whole form and the bodies of many of its controls are invisible, so you will see text and borders floating above whatever forms lie behind.
UseWaitCursor	Determines whether the form is currently displaying the wait cursor.
Visible	Determines whether the form is visible. If the form is not visible, the user cannot interact with it. If you set Visible = False, the form's icon is also removed from the taskbar and Task Manager.
Width	Determines the form's width.
WindowState	Gets or sets the form's state. This can be Normal, Minimized, or Maximized.

METHODS

The following table describes some of the most useful Form methods.

METHOD	DESCRIPTION
Activate	Activates the form and gives it the focus. Normally, this pops the form to the top. Note that forcing a form to the top takes control of the desktop away from the user, so you should use this method sparingly. For example, if the user dismisses one form, you might activate the next form in a logical sequence. You should not activate a form to get the user's attention every few minutes.
AddOwnedForm	Adds an owned form to this form. Owned forms are minimized and restored with the owner and can never lie behind the owner. Typically, they are used for things like Toolboxes and search forms that should remain above the owner form.

continues

(continued)

METHOD	DESCRIPTION
BringToFront	Brings the form to the top of the z-order. This applies only to other forms in the application. This form will pop to the top of other forms in this program, but not forms in other applications.
Close	Closes the form. The program can still prevent the form from closing by catching the FormClosing event and setting e.Cancel to True.
Contains	Returns True if a specified control is contained in the form. This includes controls inside GroupBox controls, Panel controls, and other containers, which are not listed in the form's Controls collection.

CreateGraphics	Creates a Graphics object that the program can use to draw on the form's surface. For example, the following code draws a circle when the user presses a button:
	
	`Private Sub Button1_Click(`
	`  ByVal sender As System.Object,`
	`  ByVal e As System.EventArgs) _`
	`  Handles Button1.Click`
	`      Dim gr As Graphics =`
	`          Me.CreateGraphics()`
	`      gr.FillEllipse(Brushes.Orange,`
	`          10, 10, 210, 220)`
	`      gr.DrawEllipse(Pens.Red,`
	`          10, 10, 210, 220)`
	`End Sub`
	
	Note that the Paint event handler provides a Graphics object in its e.Graphics parameter when the form needs to be redrawn. You should use that object rather than a new one returned by CreateGraphics while inside a Paint event handler. Otherwise, the Paint event handler's version will draw over anything that you draw using the object returned by CreateGraphics.

DoDragDrop	Begins a drag-and-drop operation. For more information on drag and drop, see Chapter 23.

METHOD	DESCRIPTION
GetChildAtPoint	Returns a reference to the child control at a specific point. Note that the control is the outermost control at that point. For example, if a GroupBox contains a Button and you call GetChildAtPoint for a point above the Button, GetChildAtPoint returns the GroupBox. To find the Button, you would need to use the GroupBox control's GetChildAtPoint method. Note also that the position of the Button within the GroupBox is relative to the GroupBox control's origin, so you would need to subtract the GroupBox control's position from the X and Y coordinates of the point relative to the form's origin.
GetNextControl	Returns the next control in the tab order. Parameters indicate the control to start from and whether the search should move forward or backward through the tab order.
Hide	Hides the form. This sets the form's Visible property to False.
Invalidate	Invalidates some or all of the form's area and generates a Paint event.
LayoutMdi	If this form is an MDI parent form, arranges its MDI child forms. This method can take the parameters ArrangeIcons, Cascade, TileHorizontal, and TileVertical. Typically, this command is used in a menu titled Window.
PointToClient	Converts a point from screen coordinates into the form's coordinate system.
PointToScreen	Converts a point from the form's coordinate system into screen coordinates.
RectangleToClient	Converts a rectangle from screen coordinates into the form's coordinate system.
RectangleToScreen	Converts a rectangle from the form's coordinate system into screen coordinates.
Refresh	Invalidates the form's client area and forces it to redraw itself and its controls.
RemoveOwnedForm	Removes an owned form from this form's OwnedForms collection.
ResetBackColor	Resets the form's BackColor property to its default value (Control). This change is adopted by any controls on the form that do not have their BackColor properties explicitly set.
ResetCursor	Resets the form's Cursor property to its default value (Default). This change is adopted by any controls on the form that do not have their Cursor properties explicitly set.

continues

(continued)

METHOD	DESCRIPTION
ResetFont	Resets the form's Font property to its default value (8-point regular Microsoft Sans Serif). This change is adopted by any controls on the form that do not have their Font properties explicitly set.
ResetForeColor	Resets the form's ForeColor property to its default value (ControlText). This change is adopted by any controls on the form that do not have their ForeColor properties explicitly set.
ResetText	Resets the form's Text property to its default value (an empty string).
Scale	Resizes the form and the controls it contains by a scale factor. A second overloaded version scales by different amounts in the X and Y directions. Note that this doesn't change the controls' font sizes, just their dimensions.
ScrollControlIntoView	If the form has AutoScroll set to True, this scrolls to make the indicated control visible.
SelectNextControl	Activates the next control in the tab order. Parameters indicate the control to start at, whether the search should move forward or backward through the tab order, whether the search should include only controls with TabStop set to True or all controls, whether to include controls nested inside other controls, and whether to wrap around to the first/last control if the search passes the last/first control.
SendToBack	Sends the form to the back of the z-order. This puts the form behind all other forms in all applications, although it *does not remove the focus from this form.*
SetAutoScrollMargin	If AutoScroll is True, this method sets the AutoScroll margin. The control will provide scroll bars if necessary to display its controls plus this much margin.
SetBounds	Sets some or all of the form's bounds: X, Y, Width, and Height.
SetDesktopBounds	Sets the form's position and size in desktop coordinates. See SetDesktopLocation for more information.
SetDesktopLocation	Sets the form's position in desktop coordinates. Desktop coordinates include only the screen's working area and do not include the area occupied by the taskbar. For example, if the taskbar is attached to the left edge of the screen, the point (0, 0) in *screen coordinates* is *beneath the taskbar.* However, the point (0, 0) in *desktop coordinates* is just *to the right of the taskbar.* If you set the form's location to (0, 0), part of the form is hidden by the taskbar. If you set the form's desktop location to (0, 0), the form is visible just to the right of the taskbar.

METHOD	DESCRIPTION
Show	Displays the form. This has the same effect as setting the form's Visible property to True.
ShowDialog	Displays the form as a modal dialog box. The user cannot interact with other parts of the application before this form closes. Note that some other processes may still be running. For example, a Timer control on another form still raises Tick events and the program can still respond to them.

EVENTS

The following table describes some of the most useful Form events.

EVENT	DESCRIPTION
Activated	Occurs when the form activates.
Click	Occurs when the user clicks the form. Normally, if the user clicks a control, the control rather than the form receives the Click event. If the form's Capture property is set to True, however, the event goes to the form.
ControlAdded	Occurs when a new control is added to the form.
ControlRemoved	Occurs when a control is removed from the form.
Deactivate	Occurs when the form deactivates.
DoubleClick	Occurs when the user double-clicks the form. Normally, if the user double-clicks a control, the control rather than the form receives the DoubleClick event. If the form's Capture property is set to True, however, the first click goes to the form and the second goes to the control.
DragDrop	Occurs when the user drops data onto the form. The form should process the data in an appropriate way. See Chapter 23 for more information on drag-and-drop operations.
DragEnter	Occurs when a drag-and-drop operation moves over the form. The form should indicate what drag operations it will allow and optionally display a visible indication that the drag is over it. Refer to Chapter 23 for more information on drag-and-drop operations.
DragLeave	Occurs when a drag-and-drop operation leaves the form. If the form is displaying a visible indicator of the pending drop, it should remove that indicator now. See Chapter 23 for more information on drag-and-drop operations.

continues

(continued)

EVENT	DESCRIPTION
DragOver	Occurs repeatedly as long as a drag-and-drop operation is being performed over the form. The form can use this event to display a more complex visible indicator of the pending drop. For example, it might show where on the form the data will be dropped or it might highlight the area on the form under the mouse. See Chapter 23 for more information on drag-and-drop operations.
FormClosed	Occurs when the form is closed. The program can still access the form's properties, methods, and controls, but it is going away. See also the FormClosing event. Note that if the program calls Application.Exit, the form's FormClosed and FormClosing events do not occur. If you want the program to free resources before the form disappears, it should do so before calling Application.Exit.
FormClosing	Occurs when the form is about to close. The program can cancel the close (for example, if some data has not been saved) by setting the even handler's e.Cancel parameter to True.
GiveFeedback	Occurs when a drag moves over a valid drop target. The source can take action to indicate the type of drop allowed. For example, it might change the drag cursor displayed. See Chapter 23 for more information on drag-and-drop operations.
GotFocus	Occurs when focus moves into the form.
HelpRequested	Occurs when the user requests help from the form, usually by pressing F1 or by pressing a context-sensitive Help button (see the HelpButton property) and then clicking a control on the form. Help requests move up through control containers until a HelpRequested event sets its hlpevent .Handled parameter to True. For example, suppose that the user sets focus to a TextBox contained in the form and presses F1. The TextBox control's HelpRequested event handler executes. If that routine doesn't set hlpevent .Handled to True, the event bubbles up to the TextBox control's container, the form, and its HelpRequested event handler executes.
KeyDown	Occurs when the user presses a keyboard key down.
KeyPress	Occurs when the user presses and releases a keyboard key.
KeyUp	Occurs when the user releases a keyboard key.
Layout	Occurs when the form should reposition its child controls. If your code needs to perform custom repositioning, this is the event where it should do so.
Load	Occurs after the form is loaded but before it is displayed. You can perform one-time initialization tasks here.

EVENT	DESCRIPTION
LostFocus	Occurs when the focus moves out of the form.
MdiChildActivate	Occurs when an MDI child form contained in this MDI parent form is activated or closed. This activation only applies to the MDI children within this form. For example, setting focus to a different form or application and then back to the MDI child does not raise this event, but switching back and forth between two MDI children does. This event basically occurs when the MDI parent's active MDI child changes. You can catch the event to update the MDI parent's menus or perform other actions when the active child changes.
MouseClick	Occurs when the user clicks the form. You should consider the Click event to be on a logically higher level than MouseClick. For example, the Click event may be triggered by actions other than an actual mouse click (such as the user pressing the Enter key).
MouseDoubleClick	Occurs when the user double-clicks the form. You should consider the DoubleClick event to be on a logically higher level than MouseDoubleClick.
MouseDown	Occurs when the user presses the mouse down over the form. Also see the Capture property.
MouseEnter	Occurs when the mouse first moves so it is over the form. If the mouse moves over one of the form's controls, that counts as leaving the form, so when it moves back over an unoccupied part of the form, it raises a MouseEnter event.
MouseHover	Occurs when the mouse remains stationary over the form for a while. This event is raised once when the mouse first hovers and then is not raised again until the mouse leaves the form and returns. Note that the mouse moving over one of the form's controls counts as leaving.
MouseLeave	Occurs when the mouse leaves the form. Note that the mouse moving over one of the form's controls counts as leaving.
MouseMove	Occurs when the mouse moves while over the form.
MouseUp	Occurs when the user releases the mouse button. When the user presses a mouse button down, the form will capture subsequent mouse events until the user releases the button. While the capture is in place, the form receives MouseMove events, even if the mouse is moving off of the form. It will receive a MouseHover event, even if the mouse is off of the form, if no such event has been raised since the last time the mouse moved over the form. When the user finally releases the button, the form receives a MouseUp event and then, if the mouse is no longer over the form, a MouseLeave event.

continues

(continued)

EVENT	DESCRIPTION
MouseWheel	Occurs when the user moves the mouse wheel. The event's e.X and e.Y parameters give the mouse's current position. The e.Delta parameter gives the signed distance by which the wheel has been rotated. Currently, this is defined as 120 *detents* per notch of the wheel. (A detent is a unit of the wheel's rotation. A notch is the amount by which the wheel rotates with a discrete click. So every time you turn the wheel 1 notch, e.Delta changes by 120 detents.) Standards dictate that you should scroll data when the accumulated delta reaches plus or minus 120 detents, and that you should then scroll the data by the number of lines given by SystemInformation .MouseWheelScrollLines (currently this is 3). If higher-resolution mouse wheels are added some day, a notch might send a value smaller than 120, and you could update the data more often, but you should keep the same ratio: SystemInformation.MouseWheelScrollLines lines per 120 detents.
Move	Occurs when the form is moved.
Paint	Occurs when part of the form must be redrawn. You can use the e.ClipRectangle parameter to see what area needs to be drawn. For very complicated drawings, you may be able to draw more quickly if you only draw the area indicated by e.ClipRectangle. Note also that Visual Basic clips drawings outside of this rectangle and may clip some areas inside this rectangle that do not need to be redrawn. That makes drawing faster in some cases. The idea here is that part of the form has been covered and exposed so only that part must be redrawn. If you need to adjust the drawing when the form is resized, you should invalidate the form in the Resize event handler to force a redraw of the whole form.
QueryContinueDrag	Occurs during a drag-and-drop operation (with this form as the drag source) when the keyboard or mouse button state has changed. The form can decide to continue the drag, cancel the drag, or drop the data immediately. See Chapter 23 for more information on drag-and-drop operations.
Resize	Occurs when the form is resized.
ResizeBegin	Occurs when the user starts resizing the form.
ResizeEnd	Occurs when the user has finished resizing the form.
SizeChanged	Occurs when the form is resized.

When focus moves into and out of a form, the sequence of events is: Activated, GotFocus, Deactivate, Validating, Validated, LostFocus.

Typically, when the user clicks the form, the sequence of events is: MouseDown, Click, MouseClick, MouseUp.

Typically, when the user double-clicks the form, the sequence of events is: MouseDown, Click, MouseClick, MouseUp, MouseDown, DoubleClick, MouseDoubleClick, MouseUp.

When code resizes the form, the sequence of events is: Resize, SizeChanged.

When the user resizes the form, the sequence of events is: ResizeBegin, Resize, SizeChanged, Resize, SizeChanged, . . . , ResizeEnd.

PROPERTY-CHANGED EVENTS

The Form class provides several events that fire when certain form properties change. The name of each of these events has the form *PropertyName*Changed where *PropertyName* is the name of the corresponding property. For example, the BackColorChanged event fires when the form's BackColor property changes.

The following is a list of these events.

BackColorChanged	MaximumSizeChanged
BackgroundImageChanged	MinimumSizeChanged
ContextMenuChanged	ParentChanged
CursorChanged	SizeChanged
DockChanged	StyleChanged
EnabledChanged	SystemColorsChanged
FontChanged	TextChanged
ForeColorChanged	VisibleChanged
LocationChanged	

The names of most of these controls are self-explanatory, so they are not described here. The exception is the SystemColorsChanged event. This occurs when the system's colors are changed either by the user or programmatically.

For example, suppose that you want the form to draw using its ForeColor property and you want that property to match the active title bar text color. Then, you could use the following code to update ForeColor when the user changed the system colors:

```
Private Sub Form2_SystemColorsChanged(ByVal sender As Object,
  ByVal e As System.EventArgs) Handles MyBase.SystemColorsChanged
    Me.ForeColor = SystemColors.ActiveCaptionText
End Sub
```

Note that Visual Basic invalidates the form after raising the SystemColorsChanged event, so the form immediately repaints itself using the new settings.

Classes and Structures

This appendix provides information about class and structure declarations.

CLASSES

The syntax for declaring a class is:

```
[attribute_list] [Partial] [accessibility] [Shadows] [inheritance] _
Class name [(Of type_list)]
    [Inherits parent_class]
    [Implements interface]
    statements
End Class
```

The *attribute_list* can include any number of attribute specifiers separated by commas.

The *accessibility* clause can take one of the following values: Public, Protected, Friend, Protected Friend, and Private.

The Partial keyword indicates that this is only part of the class declaration and that the program may include other partial declarations for this class.

The Shadows keyword indicates that the class hides the definition of some other entity in the enclosing class's base class.

The *inheritance* clause can take the value MustInherit or NotInheritable.

The *type_list* clause defines type parameters for a generic class. For information on generics, see Chapter 29, "Generics."

The Inherits statement tells which class this class inherits from. A class can include at most one Inherits statement and, if present, this must be the first non-comment statement after the Class statement.

The Implements statement specifies an interface that the class implements. A class can implement any number of interfaces. You can specify interfaces in separate Interface statements or in a single statement separated by commas.

The following example declares a simple Person class and an Employee class that inherits from it:

```
Public Class Person

End Class

Public Class Employee
    Inherits Person

End Class
```

STRUCTURES

The syntax for writing a structure is as follows:

```
[attribute_list] [Partial] [accessibility] [Shadows] _
Structure name [(Of type_list)]
    [Implements interface]
    statements
End Structure
```

The structure's *attribute_list*, Partial, *accessibility*, Shadows, *type_list*, and Implements statements are the same as those for classes. See the previous section for details.

The differences between a structure and a class are:

➤ Structures cannot use the MustInherit or NotInheritable keyword (because you cannot inherit from a structure).

➤ Structures cannot use the Inherits clause.

➤ Structures must contain at least one instance variable or event, which may be private. Strangely, a property procedure is not enough.

➤ Structures are *value types*, whereas classes are *reference types*. See Chapter 26, "Classes and Structures," for information on the consequences of this difference.

CONSTRUCTORS

A *constructor* is a special subroutine named New.

Class constructors can take any number of parameters. If you provide no constructors, Visual Basic allows a default empty constructor that takes no parameters. If you provide *any* constructor, Visual Basic does not provide a default empty constructor. If you want to allow the program to use an empty constructor in that case, you must either provide one or provide a constructor with all optional parameters.

Example program Constructors, which is available for download on the book's web site, defines a Person class that includes both empty and non-empty constructors, and demonstrates different ways of creating and initializing objects.

Structure constructors are very similar to class constructors with two major exceptions. First, you cannot make an empty structure constructor. Second, Visual Basic always provides a default empty constructor, even if you give the structure other constructors.

EVENTS

The syntax for declaring an event is:

```
[accessibility] [Shadows] Event event_name(parameters)
```

The *accessibility* clause can take one of the following values: Public, Protected, Friend, Protected Friend, or Private.

Use the Shadows keyword to indicate that the event shadows an item with the same name in the parent class. Any type of item can shadow any other type of item. For example, an event can shadow a subroutine, function, or variable. This would be rather bizarre and confusing, but it is possible.

The *parameters* clause specifies the parameters that you will pass when raising the event. An event handler catching the event will receive those parameters. Use ByRef parameters to allow the event handler to provide feedback to the code that raises the event.

The syntax for raising an event is as follows:

```
RaiseEvent event_name(parameters)
```

The parameters that you pass to the event handler must match those declared in the Event statement.

The following code shows pieces of a SeatAssignment class that raises a NameChanged event when its Name property changes:

```
Public Class SeatAssignment
    Public Event NameChanged()
    ...
    Private m_Name As String
    Public Property Name() As String
        Get
            Return m_Name
        End Get
        Set(ByVal value As String)
            m_Name=value
            RaiseEvent NameChanged()
        End Set
    End Property
    ...
End Class
```

LINQ

This appendix provides syntax summaries for the most useful LINQ methods. For more detailed information, see Chapter 21, "LINQ."

BASIC LINQ QUERY SYNTAX

The following text shows the typical syntax for a LINQ query:

```
From ... Where ... Order By ... Select ...
```

The following sections describe these four basic clauses. The sections after those describe some of the other most useful LINQ clauses.

From

The From clause tells where the data comes from and defines the name by which it is known within the LINQ query.

```
From var1 In data_source1, var2 In data_source2, ...
```

Examples:

```
Dim query1 = From cust As Customer In all_customers
Dim query2 = From stu In students, score In TestScores
```

Usually, if you select data from multiple sources, you will want to use a Where clause to join the results from the sources.

Where

The Where clause applies filters to the records selected by the From clause. The syntax is:

```
Where conditions
```

Use comparison operators (>, <, =), logical operators (Not, Or, AndAlso), object methods (ToString, Length), and functions to build complex conditions.

For example, the following query selects student and test score data, matching students to their test scores:

```
Dim query = From stu In students, score In TestScores
    Where stu.StudentId = score.StudentId
```

The following example selects only students with last names starting with S:

```
Dim query = From stu In students, score In TestScores
    Where stu.StudentId = score.StudentId AndAlso
        stu.LastName.ToUpper.StartsWith("S")
```

Order By

The Order By clause makes a query sort the selected objects. For example, the following query selects students and their scores and orders the results by student last name followed by first name:

```
Dim query = From stu In students, score In TestScores
    Where stu.StudentId = score.StudentId
    Order By stu.LastName, stu.FirstName
```

Add the Descending keyword to sort a field in descending order. The following example orders the results by descending TestAverage value:

```
Dim query = From stu In students, score In TestScores
    Where stu.StudentId = score.StudentId
    Order By stu.TestAverage Descending
```

Select

The Select clause lists the fields that the query should select into its result. If this is omitted, the query selects all of the data in the data sources. You can add an alias to the result.

The following query selects customers' FirstName and LastName values concatenated and gives the result the alias Name. It also selects the customers' AccountBalance value and gives it the alias Balance.

```
Dim query = From cust In all_customers
    Select Name = cust.FirstName & " " & cust.LastName,
        Balance = Cust.AccountBalance
```

You can pass values form the data sources into functions or constructors. For example, suppose the Person class has a constructor that takes first and last names as parameters. Then the following query returns a group of Person objects created from the selected customer data:

```
Dim query = From cust In all_customers
    Select New Person(cust.FirstName, cust.LastName)
```

Distinct

The Distinct keyword makes a query return only one copy of each result. The following example selects the distinct CustId values from the all_orders list:

```
Dim query = From ord In all_orders
    Select ord.CustId
    Distinct
```

Join

The Join keyword selects data from multiple data sources matching up corresponding fields. The following pseudo-code shows the Join command's syntax:

```
From variable1 In datasource1
Join variable2 In datasource2
On variable1.field1 Equals variable2.field2
```

For example, the following query selects corresponding objects from the all_customers and all_orders lists:

```
Dim query = From cust As Customer In all_customers
    Join ord In all_orders
    On cust.CustId Equals ord.CustId
```

Note that you can get a similar result by using a Where clause. The following query selects a similar set of objects without using the Join keyword:

```
Dim query = From cust As Customer In all_customers, ord In all_orders
    Where cust.CustId = ord.CustId
```

Group By

The Group By clause lets a program select data from a flat, relational style format and build a hierarchical arrangement of objects. The following code shows the basic Group By syntax:

```
Group items By value Into groupname = Group
```

Here, *items* is a list of items whose properties you want selected into the group, *value* tells LINQ on what field to group objects, and *groupname* gives a name for the group.

The following query selects objects from the all_orders list. The Group By statement makes the query group orders with the same CustId value.

```
Dim query1 = From ord In all_orders
    Order By ord.CustId, ord.OrderId
    Group ord By ord.CustId Into CustOrders = Group
```

The result is an IEnumerable that contains objects with two fields. The first field is the CustId value used to define the groups (the value part in the syntax shown earlier). The second field is an IEnumerable named CustOrders that contains the group of order objects for each CustId value.

The following code shows how a program might display the results in a TreeView control:

```
Dim root1 As TreeNode = trvResults.Nodes.Add("Orders grouped by CustId")
For Each obj In query1
    ' Display the customer id.
    Dim cust_node As TreeNode = root1.Nodes.Add("Cust Id: " & obj.CustId)

    ' List this customer's orders.
    For Each ord In obj.CustOrders
        cust_node.Nodes.Add("OrderId: " & ord.OrderId &
            ", Date: " & ord.OrderDate)
    Next ord
Next obj
```

Another common type of query uses the Group By clause to apply some aggregate function to the items selected in a group. The following query selects order and order item objects, grouping each order's items and displaying each order's total price:

```
Dim query1 = From ord In all_orders, ord_item In all_order_items
    Order By ord.CustId, ord.OrderId
    Where ord.OrderId = ord_item.OrderId
    Group ord_item By ord Into
        TotalPrice = Sum(ord_item.Quantity * ord_item.UnitPrice),
        OrderItems = Group
```

The following code shows how a program might display the results in a TreeView control named trvResults:

```
Dim root1 As TreeNode = trvResults.Nodes.Add("Orders")
For Each obj In query1
    ' Display the customer id.
    Dim cust_node As TreeNode =
        root1.Nodes.Add("Order Id: " & obj.ord.OrderId &
            ", Total Price: " & FormatCurrency(obj.TotalPrice))

    ' List this customer's orders.
    For Each ord_item In obj.OrderItems
        cust_node.Nodes.Add(ord_item.Description & ": " &
            ord_item.Quantity & " @ " &
            FormatCurrency(ord_item.UnitPrice))
    Next ord_item
Next obj
```

Limiting Results

LINQ includes several keywords for limiting the results returned by a query.

Take makes the query keep a specified number of results and discard the rest.

Take While makes the query keep selected results as long as some condition holds and then discard the rest.

Skip makes the query discard a specified number of results and keep the rest.

Skip While makes the query discard selected results as long as some condition holds and then keep the rest.

The following code demonstrates each of these commands:

```
Dim q1 = From cust In all_customers Take 5
Dim q2 = From cust In all_customers Take While cust.FirstName.Contains("n")
Dim q3 = From cust In all_customers Skip 3
Dim q4 = From cust In all_customers Skip While cust.FirstName.Contains("n")
```

USING QUERY RESULTS

A LINQ query expression returns an IEnumerable containing the query's results. A program can iterate through this result and process the items that it contains.

If the selected data has a well-understood data type, such as strings or objects from a known class, you can iterate through the result by using an explicitly typed looping variable. The following example selects customer names and then displays them. The looping variable is explicitly typed as a string.

```
Dim query = From cust In all_customers
    Select Name = cust.FirstName, cust.LastName
For Each cust_name As String In query
    Debug.WriteLine(cust_name)
Next cust_name
```

If the returned data type is less well understood, you can use a looping variable with inferred data type. The following code selects customers and their orders. It then loops through the results displaying order dates and numbers, together with the names of the customers who placed the orders. The looping variable obj has an inferred type.

```
Dim query = From cust In all_customers, ord In all_orders
    Where cust.CustId = ord.CustId
    Order By ord.OrderDate

For Each obj In query
    Debug.WriteLine(obj.ord.OrderDate & vbTab & obj.ord.OrderId &
        vbTab & obj.cust.Name)
Next obj
```

LINQ FUNCTIONS

The following table summarizes LINQ extension methods that are not available from Visual Basic LINQ query syntax.

FUNCTION	PURPOSE
Aggregate	Uses a function specified by the code to calculate a custom aggregate.
DefaultIfEmpty	Returns the query's result or a default value if the query returns an empty result.
Concat	Concatenates two sequences into a new sequence.
Contains	Returns True if the result contains a specific value.
ElementAt	Returns an element at a specific position in the query's result.
ElementAtOrDefault	Returns an element at a specific position in the query's result or a default value if there is no such position.
Empty	Creates an empty IEnumerable.
Except	Returns the items in one IEnumerable that are not in a second IEnumerable.
First	Returns the first item in the query's result.
FirstOrDefault	Returns the first item in the query's result or a default value if the query contains no results.
Intersection	Returns the intersection of two IEnumerable objects.
Last	Returns the last item in the query's result.
LastOrDefault	Returns the last item in the query's result or a default value if the query contains no results.
Range	Creates an IEnumerable containing a range of integer values.
Repeat	Creates an IEnumerable containing a value repeated a specific number of times.
SequenceEqual	Returns True if two sequences are identical.
Single	Returns the single item selected by the query.
SingleOrDefault	Returns the single item selected by the query or a default value if the query contains no results.
Union	Returns the union of two IEnumerable objects.

The following table summarizes LINQ data type conversion functions.

FUNCTION	PURPOSE
AsEnumerable	Converts the result to IEnumerable(Of T).
AsQueryable	Converts an IEnumerable to IQueryable.
OfType	Removes items that cannot be cast into a specific type.
ToArray	Places the results in an array.
ToDictionary	Places the results in a Dictionary.
ToList	Converts the result to List(Of T).
ToLookup	Places the results in a Lookup (one-to-many dictionary).

LINQ TO XML

LINQ provides methods to move data in and out of XML.

LINQ Into XML

To select data into XML objects, use the special characters <%= and %> to indicate a "hole" within the XML literal. Inside the hole, place a LINQ query.

For example, the following code builds an XElement object that contains Customer XML elements for objects in the all_customers list:

```
Dim x_all As XElement =
    <AllCustomers>
        <%= From cust In all_customers
            Select New XElement("Customer",
            New XAttribute("FirstName", cust.FirstName),
            New XAttribute("LastName", cust.LastName),
            New XText(cust.Balance.ToString("0.00")))
        %>
    </AllCustomers>
```

LINQ Out Of XML

XML classes such as XElement provide LINQ functions that allow you to use LINQ queries on them just as you can select data from IEnumerable objects.

The following code extracts the descendants of the x_all XElement object that have negative balances. It selects each XML element's FirstName and LastName attributes, and balance (saved in the element's value).

```
Dim select_all = From cust In x_all.Descendants("Customer")
    Where CDec(cust.Value) < 0
    Select FName = cust.Attribute("FirstName").Value,
           LName = cust.Attribute("LastName").Value,
           Balance = cust.Value
```

The following table summarizes LINQ methods supported by XElement.

FUNCTION	RETURNS
Ancestors	IEnumerable containing all ancestors of the element.
AncestorsAndSelf	IEnumerable containing this element followed by all ancestors of the element.
Attribute	The element's attribute with a specific name.
Attributes	IEnumerable containing the element's attributes.
Descendants	IEnumerable containing all descendants of the element.
DescendantsAndSelf	IEnumerable containing this element followed by all descendants of the element.
DescendantNodes	IEnumerable containing all descendant nodes of the element. These include all nodes such as XElement and XText.
DescendantNodesAndSelf	IEnumerable containing this element followed by all descendant nodes of the element. These include all nodes such as XElement and XText.
Element	The first child element with a specific name.
Elements	IEnumerable containing the immediate children of the element.
ElementsAfterSelf	IEnumerable containing the siblings of the element that come after this element.
ElementsBeforeSelf	IEnumerable containing the siblings of the element that come before this element.
Nodes	IEnumerable containing the nodes that are immediate children of the element. These include all nodes such as XElement and XText.
NodesAfterSelf	IEnumerable containing the sibling nodes of the element that come after this element.
NodesBeforeSelf	IEnumerable containing the sibling nodes of the element that come before this element.

The following table gives examples of shorthand expressions for node axes and their functional equivalents.

SHORTHAND	MEANING	EQUIVALENT
`x...<Customer>`	Descendants named Customer.	`x.Descendants("Customer")`
`x.<Child>`	An element named Child that is a child of this node.	`x.Attributes("Child")`

`x.@<FirstName>`
Or:
`x.@FirstName`
	The value of the FirstName attribute.	`x.Attributes("FirstName").Value`

LINQ TO DATASET

LINQ to DataSet refers to methods provided by database objects that support LINQ queries.

The DataSet class itself doesn't provide many LINQ features, but the DataTable objects that it holds do. The DataTable has an AsEnumerable method that converts the DataTable into an IEnumerable, which supports LINQ.

The following list summarizes the key differences between a DataTable query and a normal LINQ to Objects query:

➤ The code must use the DataTable object's AsEnumerable method to make the object queryable.

➤ The code can access the fields in a DataRow as in `stu!LastName` or as in `stu.Field(Of String)("LastName")`.

➤ If you want to display the results in a DataGrid control, use the query's ToList method.

The following example shows a query that selects student data from the dtStudents DataTable where the LastName comes before D. It selects the students' FirstName and LastName fields, and displays the result in a DataGrid control.

```
Dim before_d =
    From stu In dtStudents.AsEnumerable()
    Where stu!LastName < "D"
    Order By stu.Field(Of String)("LastName")
    Select First = stu!FirstName, Last = stu!LastName

dgStudentsBeforeD.DataSource = before_d.ToList
```

Method-Based Queries

LINQ query keywords including Where, Order By, and Select actually correspond to methods that take parameters giving the functions they should use to perform their tasks. For example, the Where method takes as a parameter the address of a function that returns True if an item should be selected in the query result.

In addition to using standard LINQ query syntax, you can use method-based queries to select data. The following example selects data from all_customers where the OwesMoney function returns True. The OrderByAmount function returns values that can be used to order the results and SelectFields returns an object that contains selected fields for a selected item.

```
Dim q2 = all_customers.
    Where(AddressOf OwesMoney).
    OrderBy(AddressOf OrderByAmount).
    Select(AddressOf SelectFields)
```

Instead of passing the address of a function to these methods, you can pass lambda functions. The following code returns a result similar to the preceding query but using lambda functions instead of addresses of functions:

```
Dim q3 = all_customers.
    Where(Function(c As Customer) c.AccountBalance < 0).
    OrderBy(Of Decimal)(Function(c As Customer) c.AccountBalance).
    Select(Of CustInfo)(
        Function(c As Customer, index As Integer)
            Return New CustInfo() With
                {.CustName = c.Name, .Balance = c.AccountBalance}
    )
```

PLINQ

Adding parallelism to LINQ is remarkably simple. First, add a reference to the System.Threading library to your program. Then add a call to the AsParallel to the enumerable object that you're searching. For example, the following code uses AsParallel to select the even numbers from the array numbers:

```
Dim evens =
    From num In numbers.AsParallel()
    Where num Mod 2 = 0
```

Generics

This appendix summarizes generic classes, extensions, and methods. Example program GenericExamples, which is available for download on the book's web site, demonstrates each of these.

The final section in this appendix describes items that you cannot make generic.

GENERIC CLASSES

The syntax for declaring a generic class is as follows:

```
[attribute_list] [Partial] [accessibility] [Shadows] [inheritance] _
Class name [(Of type_list)]
    [Inherits parent_class]
    [Implements interface]
    statements
End Class
```

All of these parts of the declaration are the same as those used by a normal (non-generic) class. See Chapter 26, "Classes and Structures," and Appendix K for information about non-generic classes.

The key to a generic class is the (Of *type_list*) clause. Here, *type_list* is a list of data types separated by commas that form the generic's parameter types. Each type can be optionally followed by the keyword As and a list of constraints that the corresponding type must satisfy. The constraint list can contain any number of interfaces and, at most, one class. It can also contain the New keyword to indicate that the corresponding type must provide an empty constructor. If a constraint list contains more than one item, the list must be surrounded by braces.

The following code defines the generic MyGeneric class. It takes three type parameters. The first is named Type1 within the generic's code and has no constraints. The second type, named

Type2, must satisfy the IComparable interface. The third parameter, named Type3, must provide an empty constructor, must satisfy the IDisposable interface, and must inherit directly or indirectly from the Person class.

```
Public Class MyGeneric(Of _
 Type1,
 Type2 As IComparable,
 Type3 As {New, IDisposable, Person})
```

GENERIC EXTENSIONS

Due to their somewhat idiosyncratic nature, extension methods add an extra level of complexity to generics.

Normally, a generic class declaration includes the types on which it depends and what code within the class can use those types. For example, consider the Schedule class shown in the following code, which represents a schedule of tasks:

```
' Represents a schedule of Tasks.
Public Class Schedule(Of Task)
    Public Sub AddTask(ByVal new_task As Task)
        ...
    End Sub
    ...
End Class
```

The type list for the Schedule class includes a type named Task and the class's code can use the type Task. In this example, the AddTask subroutine takes a parameter of this type.

Now suppose you want to add an extension method named Prioritize to the generic Schedule class. The first parameter in the extension method's declaration indicates the class that the method extends. In this case, that should be Schedule(Of Task), but the extension method itself must also be generic, so it must use a type list just as any other generic method does.

The result is the following declaration. The Prioritize method first includes a type list indicating that it generically depends on a type named T within this method. It then includes the extension method parameter list. The first parameter (the only parameter in this example) gives the class that the method extends: Schedule(Of T).

```
Public Module ScheduleExtensions
    ' Prioritizes the schedule.
    <Extension()>
    Sub Prioritize(Of T)(ByVal sched As Schedule(Of T))
        Debug.WriteLine("Prioritizing Schedule of " & GetType(T).Name)
        ...
    End Sub
End Module
```

The following code fragment shows how a program could create a Schedule of Job objects and then call the Prioritize extension:

```
Dim sched As New Schedule(Of Job)
...
sched.Prioritize()
```

Generic extension methods can become extremely complicated. For more detailed information about extension methods in general, see Chapter 17, "Subroutines and Functions," and the Microsoft Visual Basic Team blog post at `blogs.msdn.com/vbteam/pages/articles-about-extension-methods.aspx`, paying special attention to Part 5, "Generics and Extension Methods."

GENERIC METHODS

In addition to generic classes and extension methods, you can create generic methods. This is simply a method that takes generic parameters. The following code shows a Switcher class that has a shared generic Switch method:

```
Public Class Switcher
    Public Shared Sub Switch(Of T)(ByRef thing1 As T, ByRef thing2 As T)
        Dim temp As T = thing1
        thing1 = thing2
        thing2 = temp
    End Sub
End Class
```

The Switcher class is not generic, but it contains a generic method. Both generic and non-generic classes can define both generic and non-generic methods.

PROHIBITED GENERICS

Unfortunately (or perhaps fortunately because this could be extremely complicated and confusing), you cannot make generic lambda functions. The following code shows a lambda function that is allowed and a generic lambda function that is not allowed:

```
' Allowed.
Dim max_index1 = Function(lst As List(Of Integer)) lst.Count - 1

' Prohibited.
Dim max_index2 = Function(Of T)(lst As List(Of T)) lst.Count - 1
```

You also cannot make generic properties, operators, events, or constructors.

Graphics

This appendix provides information about graphics classes.

GRAPHICS NAMESPACES

This section describes the most important graphics namespaces and their most useful classes, structures, and enumerated values.

System.Drawing

This namespace defines the most important graphics objects such as Graphics, Pen, Brush, Font, FontFamily, Bitmap, Icon, and Image. The following table describes the namespace's most useful classes and structures.

CLASSES AND STRUCTURES	PURPOSE
Bitmap	Represents a bitmap image defined by pixel data.
Brush	Represents area fill characteristics.
Color	Defines a color's red, green, blue, and alpha components as values between 0 and 255. Alpha = 0 means the object is transparent; alpha = 255 means it is opaque.
Font	Represents a particular font (name, size, and style, such as italic or bold).
FontFamily	Represents a group of typefaces with similar characteristics.

continues

(continued)

CLASSES AND STRUCTURES	PURPOSE
Graphics	Represents a drawing surface. Provides methods to draw on the surface.
Icon	Represents a Windows icon.
Image	Abstract base class from which Bitmap, Icon, and Metafile inherit.
Metafile	Represents a graphic metafile.
Pen	Represents line drawing characteristics (such as color, thickness, and dash style).
Pens	Provides a large number of predefined pens with different colors and width 1.
Point	Defines a point's X and Y coordinates.
PointF	Defines a point's X and Y coordinates with floating-point values.
Rectangle	Defines a rectangle using a Point and a Size.
RectangleF	Defines a rectangle using a PointF and a SizeF (with floating-point values).
Region	Defines a shape created from rectangles and paths for filling, hit testing, or clipping.
Size	Defines a width and height.
SizeF	Defines a width and height with floating-point values.
SolidBrush	Represents a solid brush.

System.Drawing.Drawing2D

This namespace contains classes for more advanced two-dimensional drawing. Some of these classes refine more basic drawing classes. For example, the HatchBrush class represents a specialized type of Brush that fills with a hatch pattern. Other classes define values for use by other graphics classes. For example, the Blend class defines color-blending parameters for a LinearGradientBrush.

The following table describes this namespace's most useful classes and enumerations.

CLASSES AND ENUMERATIONS	PURPOSE
Blend	Defines blend characteristics for a LinearGradientBrush.
ColorBlend	Defines blend characteristics for a PathGradientBrush.
DashCap	Enumeration that determines how the ends of a dash in a dashed line are drawn.
DashStyle	Enumeration that determines how a dashed line is drawn.
GraphicsPath	Represents a series of connected lines and curves for drawing, filling, or clipping.
HatchBrush	Defines a Brush that fills an area with a hatch pattern.
HatchStyle	Enumeration that determines the hatch style used by a HatchBrush object.
LinearGradientBrush	Defines a Brush that fills an area with a linear color gradient.
LineCap	Enumeration that determines how the ends of a line are drawn.
LineJoin	Enumeration that determines how lines are joined by a GDI method that draws connected lines.
Matrix	Represents a transformation matrix.
PathGradientBrush	Defines a Brush that fills an area with a color gradient that follows a path.

System.Drawing.Imaging

This namespace contains objects that deal with more advanced bitmap graphics. It includes classes that define image file formats such as GIF and JPG, classes that manage color palettes, and classes that define metafiles. The following table describes this namespace's most useful classes.

CLASS	PURPOSE
ColorMap	Defines a mapping from old color values to new ones.
ColorPalette	Represents a palette of color values.
ImageFormat	Specifies an image's format (bmp, emf, gif, jpeg, and so on).
Metafile	Represents a graphic metafile that contains drawing instructions.
MetafileHeader	Defines the attributes of a Metafile object.
MetaHeader	Contains information about a Windows metafile (WMF).
WmfPlaceableFileHeader	Specifies how a metafile should be mapped to an output device.

System.Drawing.Printing

This namespace contains objects for printing and managing the printer's characteristics. The following table describes the most useful of these classes.

CLASS	PURPOSE
PageSettings	Defines the page settings for either an entire PrintDocument or for a particular page. This object has properties that are Margins, PaperSize, PaperSource, PrinterResolution, and PrinterSettings objects.
Margins	Defines the margins for the printed page.
PaperSize	Defines the paper's size.
PaperSource	Defines the printer's paper source.
PrinterResolution	Defines the printer's resolution.
PrinterSettings	Defines the printer's settings.

System.Drawing.Text

This namespace contains only three classes for working with installed fonts. The following table describes these classes.

CLASS	PURPOSE
FontCollection	Base class for the derived InstalledFontCollection and PrivateFontCollection classes.
InstalledFontCollection	Provides a list of the system's installed fonts.
PrivateFontCollection	Provides a list of the application's privately installed fonts.

DRAWING CLASSES

The following sections describe the most useful properties and methods provided by key drawing classes.

Graphics

The Graphics object represents a drawing surface. It provides many methods for drawing shapes, filling areas, and determining the appearance of drawing results. All of these methods except DrawString take a Pen object as a parameter to determine the lines' color, thickness, dash style, and other properties. DrawString takes a Brush object instead of a Pen object as a parameter.

The following table lists the Graphics object's drawing methods.

DRAWING METHOD	PURPOSE
DrawArc	Draws an arc of an ellipse.
DrawBezier	Draws a Bézier curve.
DrawBeziers	Draws a series of connected Bézier curves.
DrawClosedCurve	Draws a closed curve that connects a series of points, joining the final point to the first point.
DrawCurve	Draws a smooth curve that connects a series of points.
DrawEllipse	Draws an ellipse.
DrawIcon	Draws an Icon onto the Graphics object's drawing surface.
DrawIconUnstretched	Draws an Icon object onto the Graphics object's drawing surface without scaling.
DrawImage	Draws an Image object onto the Graphics object's drawing surface.
DrawImageUnscaled	Draws an Image object onto the drawing surface without scaling.
DrawLine	Draws a line.
DrawLines	Draws a series of connected lines.
DrawPath	Draws a GraphicsPath object.
DrawPie	Draws a pie slice taken from an ellipse.
DrawPolygon	Draws a polygon.
DrawRectangle	Draws a rectangle.
DrawRectangles	Draws a series of rectangles.
DrawString	Draws text on the drawing surface.

The following table lists the Graphics object's area filling methods. These methods take Brush objects as parameters to determine the filled shape's color, hatch pattern, gradient colors, and other fill characteristics.

FILLING METHOD	PURPOSE
FillClosedCurve	Fills a smooth curve that connects a series of points.
FillEllipse	Fills an ellipse.
FillPath	Fills a GraphicsPath object.
FillPie	Fills a pie slice taken from an ellipse.
FillPolygon	Fills a polygon.
FillRectangle	Fills a rectangle.
FillRectangles	Fills a series of rectangles.
FillRegion	Fills a Region object.

The following table lists other useful Graphics object properties and methods.

PROPERTIES AND METHODS	PURPOSE
AddMetafileComment	Adds a comment to a metafile.
Clear	Clears the Graphics object and fills it with a specific color.
Clip	Determines the Region object used to clip drawing on the Graphics surface.
Dispose	Releases the resources held by the Graphics object.
DpiX	Returns the horizontal number of dots per inch (DPI) for this object's surface.
DpiY	Returns the vertical number of dots per inch (DPI) for this object's surface.
ExcludeClip	Updates the Graphics object's clipping region to exclude the area defined by a Region or Rectangle.
FromHdc	Creates a new Graphics object from a device context handle (hDC).
FromHwnd	Creates a new Graphics object from a window handle (hWnd).
FromImage	Creates a new Graphics object from an Image object.
InterpolationMode	Controls anti-aliasing when drawing images.

PROPERTIES AND METHODS	PURPOSE
IntersectClip	Updates the Graphics object's clipping region to be the intersection of the current clipping region and the area defined by a Region or Rectangle.
IsVisible	Returns True if a specified point is within the Graphics object's visible clipping region.
MeasureCharacterRanges	Returns an array of Region objects that show where each character in a string will be drawn.
MeasureString	Returns a SizeF structure that gives the size of a string drawn on the Graphics object with a particular font.
MultiplyTransform	Multiplies the Graphics object's current transformation matrix by another transformation matrix.
PageScale	Determines the amount by which drawing commands are scaled.
PageUnit	Determines the units of measurement: Display (depends on the device, typically pixel for monitors and 1/100 inch for printers), Document (1/300 inch), Inch, Millimeter, Pixel, or Point (1/72 inch).
RenderingOrigin	Determines the point used as a reference when hatching.
ResetClip	Resets the object's clipping region so that the drawing is not clipped.
ResetTransformation	Resets the object's transformation matrix to the identity matrix.
Restore	Restores the Graphics object to a state saved by the Save method.
RotateTransform	Adds a rotation to the object's current transformation.
Save	Saves the object's current state.
ScaleTransform	Adds a scaling transformation to the Graphics object's current transformation.
SetClip	Sets or merges the Graphics object's clipping area to another Graphics object, a GraphicsPath object, or a Rectangle.
SmoothingMode	Controls anti-aliasing when drawing lines, curves, or filled areas.
TextRenderingHint	Controls anti-aliasing and hinting when drawing text.
Transform	Gets or sets the Graphics object's transformation matrix.
TransformPoints	Applies the object's current transformation to an array of points.
TranslateTransform	Adds a translation transformation to the Graphics object's current transformation.

Pen

The Pen object determines the appearance of drawn lines. It determines such properties as a line's width, color, and dash style. The following table lists the Pen object's most useful properties and methods.

PROPERTIES AND METHODS	PURPOSE
Alignment	Determines whether the line is drawn inside or centered on the theoretical perfectly thin line specified by the drawing routine.
Brush	Determines the Brush used to fill the line.
Color	Determines the line's color.
CompoundArray	Lets you draw a line that is striped lengthwise.
CustomEndCap	Determines the line's end cap.
CustomStartCap	Determines the line's start cap.
DashCap	Determines the cap drawn at the ends of dashes.
DashOffset	Determines the distance from the start of the line to the start of the first dash.
DashPattern	An array of Singles that specifies a custom dash pattern.
DashStyle	Determines the line's dash style.
EndCap	Determines the cap used at the end of the line.
LineJoin	Determines how lines are joined by a GDI method that draws connected lines such as DrawPolygon.
MultiplyTransform	Multiplies the Pen object's current transformation by another transformation matrix.
ResetTransform	Resets the Pen object's transformation to the identity transformation.
RotateTransform	Adds a rotation transformation to the Pen object's current transformation.
ScaleTransform	Adds a scaling transformation to the Pen object's current transformation.
SetLineCap	This method takes parameters that let you specify the Pen object's StartCap, EndCap, and LineJoin properties at the same time.
StartCap	Determines the cap used at the start of the line.
Transform	Determines the transformation applied to the initially circular "pen tip" used to draw lines.
Width	The width of the pen.

Brushes

The Brush class is an abstract class, so you cannot make instances of it. Instead, you must make instances of one of its derived classes: SolidBrush, TextureBrush, HatchBrush, LinearGradientBrush, or PathGradientBrush. The following table briefly describes these classes.

CLASS	PURPOSE
SolidBrush	Fills areas with a single solid color.
TextureBrush	Fills areas with a repeating image.
HatchBrush	Fills areas with a repeating hatch pattern.
LinearGradientBrush	Fills areas with a linear gradient of two or more colors.
PathGradientBrush	Fills areas with a color gradient that follows a path.

GraphicsPath

The GraphicsPath object represents a path defined by lines, curves, text, and other drawing commands. You can use Graphics object methods to fill and draw a GraphicsPath, and you can use a GraphicsPath to define a clipping region. The following table lists the GraphicsPath object's most useful properties and methods.

PROPERTIES AND METHODS	PURPOSE
CloseAllFigures	Closes all open figures by connecting their last points with their first points and then starts a new figure.
CloseFigure	Closes the current figure by connecting its last point with its first point and then starts a new figure.
FillMode	Determines how the path handles overlaps when you fill it. This property can take the values Alternate and Winding.
Flatten	Converts any curves in the path into a sequence of lines.
GetBounds	Returns a RectangleF structure representing the path's bounding box.
GetLastPoint	Returns the last PointF structure in the PathPoints array.
IsOutlineVisible	Returns True if the indicated point lies beneath the path's outline.
IsVisible	Returns True if the indicated point lies in the path's interior.
PathData	Returns a PathData object that encapsulates the path's graphical data.
PathPoints	Returns an array of PointF structures giving the points in the path.

continues

(continued)

PROPERTIES AND METHODS	PURPOSE
PathTypes	Returns an array of Bytes representing the types of the points in the path.
PointCount	Returns the number of points in the path.
Reset	Clears the path data and resets FillMode to Alternate.
Reverse	Reverses the order of the path's data.
StartFigure	Starts a new figure, so future data is added to the new figure.
Transform	Applies a transformation matrix to the path.
Warp	Applies a warping transformation defined by mapping a parallelogram onto a rectangle to the path.
Widen	Enlarges the curves in the path to enclose a line drawn by a specific pen.

StringFormat

The StringFormat object determines how text is formatted. It enables you to draw text that is centered vertically or horizontally, aligned on the left or right, and wrapped or truncated. The following table lists the StringFormat object's most useful properties and methods.

PROPERTIES AND METHODS	PURPOSE
Alignment	Determines the text's horizontal alignment. This can be Near (left), Center (middle), or Far (right).
FormatFlags	Gets or sets flags that modify the StringFormat object's behavior.
GetTabStops	Returns an array of Singles giving the positions of tab stops.
HotkeyPrefix	Determines how the hotkey prefix character is displayed. This can be Show, Hide, or None.
LineAlignment	Determines the text's vertical alignment. This can be Near (top), Center (middle), or Far (bottom).
SetMeasureable-CharacterRanges	Sets an array of CharacterRange structures representing ranges of characters that will later be measured by the Graphics object's MeasureCharacterRanges method.
SetTabStops	Sets an array of Singles giving the positions of tab stops.
Trimming	Determines how the text is trimmed if it cannot fit within the layout rectangle.

Image

The Image class represents the underlying physical drawing surface hidden below the logical layer created by the Graphics class. Image is an abstract class, so you cannot directly create instances of it. Instead, you must create instances of its child classes Bitmap and Metafile.

The following table describes the Image class's most useful properties and methods, which are inherited by the Bitmap and Metafile classes.

PROPERTIES AND METHODS	PURPOSE
Dispose	Frees the resources associated with this image.
Flags	Returns attribute flags for the image.
FromFile	Loads an image from a file.
FromHbitmap	Loads a Bitmap image from a Windows bitmap handle.
FromStream	Loads an image from a data stream.
GetBounds	Returns a RectangleF structure representing the rectangle's bounds.
GetPixelFormatSize	Returns the color resolution (bits per pixel) for a specified PixelFormat.
GetThumbnailImage	Returns a thumbnail representation of the image.
Height	Returns the image's height.
HorizontalResolution	Returns the horizontal resolution of the image in pixels per inch.
IsAlphaPixelFormat	Returns True if the specified PixelFormat contains alpha information.
Palette	Determines the ColorPalette object used by the image.
PhysicalDimension	Returns a SizeF structure giving the image's dimensions in pixels for Bitmaps and 0.01 millimeters for Metafile classes.
PixelFormat	Returns the image's pixel format.
RawFormat	Returns an ImageFormat object representing the image's raw format.
RotateFlip	Rotates, flips, or rotates and flips the image.
Save	Saves the image in a file or stream with a given data format.
Size	Returns a Size structure containing the image's width and height in pixels.
VerticalResolution	Returns the vertical resolution of the image in pixels per inch.
Width	Returns the image's width.

Bitmap

The Bitmap class represents an image defined by pixel data. It inherits the Image class's properties and methods described in the previous section. The following table describes some of the most useful new methods added by the Bitmap class.

METHOD	PURPOSE
FromHicon	Loads a Bitmap image from a Windows icon handle.
FromResource	Loads a Bitmap image from a Windows resource.
GetPixel	Returns a Color representing a specified pixel.
LockBits	Locks the Bitmap image's data in memory, so it cannot move until the program calls UnlockBits.
MakeTransparent	Makes all pixels with a specified color transparent by setting the alpha component of those pixels to 0.
SetPixel	Sets a specified pixel's Color value.
SetResolution	Sets the Bitmap image's horizontal and vertical resolution in DPI.
UnlockBits	Unlocks the Bitmap image's data in memory so that the system can relocate it, if necessary.

Metafile

The Metafile class represents an image defined by metafile records. It inherits the Image class's properties and methods described in the section "Image" earlier in this appendix. The following table describes some of the most useful new methods added by the Metafile class.

METHOD	PURPOSE
GetMetafileHeader	Returns the MetafileHeader object associated with this Metafile.
PlayRecord	Plays a metafile record.

Useful Exception Classes

When your program throws an exception, it's easy enough to use a TryCatch block to catch the exception and examine it to determine its class. When you want to throw your own exception, however, you must know what exception classes are available so that you can pick the right one.

For more information on error handling, see Chapter 19, "Error Handling," and Appendix F.

STANDARD EXCEPTION CLASSES

The following table lists some of the most useful exception classes in Visual Basic .NET. You can raise one of these when you need to throw an error.

CLASS	PURPOSE
AmbiguousMatchException	The program could not figure out which overloaded object method to use.
ApplicationException	This is the ancestor class for all nonfatal application errors. When you build custom exception classes, you should inherit from this class, or from one of its descendants.
ArgumentException	An argument is invalid.
ArgumentNullException	An argument that cannot be Nothing has value Nothing.
ArgumentOutOfRangeException	An argument is out of its allowed range.
ArithmeticException	An arithmetic, casting, or conversion operation has occurred.

continues

(continued)

CLASS	PURPOSE
ArrayTypeMismatchException	The program tried to store the wrong type of item in an array.
ConfigurationException	A configuration setting is invalid.
ConstraintException	A data operation violates a database constraint.
DataException	The ancestor class for ADO.NET exception classes.
DirectoryNotFoundException	A needed directory is missing.
DivideByZeroException	The program tried to divide by zero.
DuplicateNameException	An ADO.NET operation encountered a duplicate name (for example, it tried to create a second table with the same name).
EvaluateException	Occurs when a DataColumn's Expression property cannot be evaluated.
FieldAccessException	The program tried to access a class property improperly.
FormatException	An argument's format doesn't match its required format.
IndexOutofRangeException	The program tried to access an item outside of the bounds of an array or other container.
InvalidCastException	The program tried to make an invalid conversion. For example, Integer.Parse("oops").
InvalidOperationException	The operation is not currently allowed.
IOException	The ancestor class for input/output (I/O) exception classes. A generic I/O error occurred.
EndOfStreamException	A stream reached its end.
FileLoadException	Error loading a file.
FileNotFoundException	Error finding a file.
InternalBufferOverflow-Exception	An internal buffer overflowed.
MemberAccessException	The program tried to access a class member improperly.
MethodAccessException	The program tried to access a class method improperly.
MissingFieldException	The program tried to access a class field that doesn't exist.
MissingMemberException	The program tried to access a class member that doesn't exist.

CLASS	PURPOSE
MissingMethodException	The program tried to access a class method that doesn't exist.
NotFiniteNumberException	A floating-point number is PositiveInfinity, NegativeInfinity, or NaN (Not a Number). You can get these values from the floating-point classes (as in Single.Nan or Double.PositiveInfinity).
NotImplementedException	The requested operation is not implemented.
NotSupportedException	The requested operation is not supported. For example, the program might be asking a routine to modify data that was opened as read-only.
NullReferenceException	The program tried to use an object reference that is Nothing.
OutOfMemoryException	There isn't enough memory. Note that sometimes a program cannot recover from an OutOfMemoryException because it doesn't have enough memory to do anything useful. This exception is most useful if you can predict beforehand that you will run out of memory before you actually use up all of the memory and crash the program. For example, if the user wants to generate a really huge data set, you may be able to predict how much memory the program will need, see if it is available, and throw this error without actually allocating the data set.
OverflowException	An arithmetic, casting, or conversion operation created an overflow. For example, the program tried to assign a large Integer value to a Byte variable.
PolicyException	Policy prevents the code from running.
RankException	A routine is trying to use an array with the wrong number of dimensions.
ReadOnlyException	The program tried to modify read-only data.
SecurityException	A security violation occurred.
SyntaxErrorException	A DataColumn's Expression property contains invalid syntax.
UnauthorizedAccessException	The system is denying access because of an I/O or security error.

Use the Throw statement to raise an exception. The following code throws a DivideByZeroException. It passes the exception class's constructor a message describing the exception. In this case, the divide by zero exception occurred because the application did not have any employees defined. Notice that the message explains the reason for the exception, not the mere fact that a division by zero occurred.

```
Throw New DivideByZeroException("No employees are defined.")
```

CUSTOM EXCEPTION CLASSES

To define a custom exception class, make a class that inherits from Exception. To give developers who use the class the most flexibility, provide four constructors that delegate their work to the Exception class's corresponding constructors.

The following code shows the InvalidWorkAssignmentException class. The empty constructor passes the Exception class's constructor a default error message. The other constructors simply pass their arguments to the Exception class's other constructors.

```
Public Class InvalidWorkAssignmentException
    Inherits Exception

    Public Sub New()
        MyBase.New("This work assignment is invalid")
    End Sub

    Public Sub New(ByVal msg As String)
        MyBase.New(msg)
    End Sub

    Public Sub New(ByVal msg As String, ByVal inner_exception As Exception)
        MyBase.New(msg, inner_exception)
    End Sub

    Public Sub New(ByVal info As SerializationInfo,
     ByVal context As StreamingContext)
        MyBase.New(info, context)
    End Sub
End Class
```

For more information on custom exception classes, see Chapter 19 and the online documentation for topics such as "Designing Custom Exceptions" (msdn.microsoft.com/ms229064.aspx) and "Design Guidelines for Exceptions" (msdn.microsoft.com/ms229014.aspx), or search the Web for articles such as "Custom Exceptions in VB 2005" by Josh Fitzgerald (www.developer.com/net/vb/article.php/3590931).

Date and Time Format Specifiers

A program uses date and time format specifiers to determine how dates and times are represented as strings. For example, the Date object's ToString method returns a string representing a date and time. An optional parameter to this method tells the object whether to format itself as in 2/20/2010, 02.20.10 A.D or Saturday, February 20, 2010 2:37:18 PM.

Visual Basic provides two kinds of specifiers that you can use to determine a date and time value's format: standard format specifiers and custom format specifiers.

STANDARD FORMAT SPECIFIERS

A standard format specifier is a single character that you use alone to indicate a standardized format. For example, the format string d indicates a short date format (as in 2/20/2010).

The following table lists standard format specifiers that you can use to format date and time strings. The results depend on the regional settings on the computer. The examples shown in this table are for a typical computer in the United States.

SPECIFIER	MEANING	EXAMPLE
d	Short date.	2/20/2010
D	Long date.	Saturday, February 20, 2010
t	Short time.	2:37 PM

continues

(continued)

SPECIFIER	MEANING	EXAMPLE
T	Long time.	2:37:18 PM
f	Full date/time with short time.	Saturday, February 20, 2010 2:37 PM
F	Full date/time with long time.	Saturday, February 20, 2010 2:37:18 PM
g	General date/time with short time.	2/20/2010 2:37 PM
G	General date/time with long time.	2/20/2010 2:37:18 PM
m or M	Month and date.	February 20
r or R	RFC1123 pattern. Formatting does not convert the time to Greenwich Mean Time (GMT), so you should convert local times to GMT before formatting.	Sat, 20 Feb 2010 14:37:18 GMT
s	Sortable ISO 8601 date/time.	2010-02-20T14:37:18
u	Universal sortable date/time. Formatting does not convert the time to universal time, so you should convert local times to universal time before formatting.	2010-02-20 14:37:18Z
U	Universal full date/time. This is the full universal time, not the local time.	Saturday, February 20, 2010 9:37:18 PM
y or Y	Year and month.	February, 2010

You can learn more about RFC1123 at `www.faqs.org/rfcs/rfc1123.html`. You can learn more about ISO 8601 at `www.iso.org/iso/support/faqs/faqs_widely_used_standards/widely_used_standards_other/date_and_time_format.htm`.

CUSTOM FORMAT SPECIFIERS

Custom format specifiers describe pieces of a date or time that you can use to build your own customized formats. For example, the specifier ddd indicates the abbreviated day of the week, as in Wed.

The following table lists characters that you can use to build custom formats for date and time strings.

SPECIFIER	MEANING	EXAMPLE
d	Date of the month.	3
dd	Date of the month with two digits.	03
ddd	Abbreviated day of the week.	Wed
dddd	Full day of the week.	Wednesday
f	Fractions of seconds, one digit. Add additional f's for up to seven digits (fffffff).	8
g	Era.	A.D.
h	Hour, 12-hour clock with one digit, if possible.	1
hh	Hour, 12-hour clock with two digits.	01
H	Hour, 24-hour clock with one digit, if possible.	13
HH	Hour, 24-hour clock with two digits.	07
m	Minutes with one digit, if possible.	9
mm	Minutes with two digits.	09
M	Month number (1–12) with one digit, if possible.	2
MM	Month number (1–12) with two digits.	02
MMM	Month abbreviation.	Feb
MMMM	Full month name.	February
s	Seconds with one digit, if possible.	3
ss	Seconds with two digits.	03
t	am/pm designator with one character.	A
tt	am/pm designator with two characters.	am
y	Year with up to two digits, not zero-padded.	10
yy	Year with two digits.	10
yyyy	Year with four digits.	2010
z	Time zone offset (hours from GMT in the range –12 to +13).	–7
zz	Time zone offset with two digits.	–07
zzz	Time zone offset with two digits of hours and minutes.	–07:00
:	Time separator.	

continues

(continued)

SPECIFIER	MEANING	EXAMPLE
/	Date separator.	
" . . . "	Quoted string. Displays the enclosed characters without trying to interpret them.	
' . . . '	Quoted string. Displays the enclosed characters without trying to interpret them.	
%	Displays the following character as a custom specifier. (See the following discussion.)	
\	Displays the next character without trying to interpret it.	

Some of the custom specifier characters in this table are the same as characters used by standard specifiers. For example, if you use the character d alone, Visual Basic interprets it as the standard specifier for a short date. If you use the character d in a custom specifier, Visual Basic interprets it as the date of the month.

If you want to use a custom specifier alone, precede it with the % character. The following shows two queries and their results executed in the Immediate window:

```
?Now.ToString("d")
"2/20/2010"
?Now.ToString("%d")
"20"
```

Custom specifiers are somewhat sensitive to the computer's regional settings. For example, they at least know the local names and abbreviations of the months and days of the week.

The standard specifiers have even more information about the local culture, however. For example, the date specifiers know whether the local culture places months before or after days. The d specifier gives the result 2/20/2010 for the en-US culture (English, United States), and it returns 20/02/2010 for the culture en-NZ (English, New Zealand).

To simplify cultural differences, you should use the standard specifiers whenever they will satisfy your needs rather than building your own custom format specifiers. For example, use d instead of M/d/yyyy.

Other Format Specifiers

A program uses format specifiers to determine how objects are represented as strings. For example, by using different format specifiers, you can make an integer's ToString method return a value as −12345, −12,345, (12,345), or 012,345−.

Visual Basic provides standard format specifiers in addition to custom specifiers. The standard specifiers make it easy to display values in often-used formats (such as currency or scientific notation). Custom specifiers provide more control over how results are composed.

STANDARD NUMERIC FORMAT SPECIFIERS

Standard numeric format specifiers enable you to easily display commonly used numeric formats. The following table lists the standard numeric specifiers.

SPECIFIER	MEANING
C or c	Currency. The exact format depends on the computer's internationalization settings. If a precision specifier follows the C, it indicates the number of digits that should follow the decimal point. On a standard system in the United States, the value −1234.5678 with the specifier C produces ($1,234.57).
D or d	Decimal. This specifier works only with integer types. It simply displays the number's digits. If a precision specifier follows the D, it indicates the number of digits the result should have, padding on the left with zeros, if necessary. If the value is negative, the result has a minus sign on the left. The value −1234 with the specifier D6 produces −001234.

continues

(continued)

SPECIFIER	MEANING
E or e	Scientific notation. The result always has exactly one digit to the left of the decimal point, followed by more digits, an E or e, a plus or minus sign, and at least three digits of exponent (padded on the left with zeros, if necessary). If a precision specifier follows the E, it indicates the number of digits the result should have after the decimal point. The value –1234.5678 with the specifier e2 produces –1.23e+003.
F or f	Fixed point. The result contains a minus sign if the value is negative, digits, a decimal point, and then more digits. If a precision specifier follows the F, it indicates the number of digits the result should have after the decimal point. The value –1234.5678 with the specifier f3 produces –1234.568.
G or g	General. Either scientific or fixed point notation depending on which is more compact.
N or n	Number. The result has a minus sign if the value is negative, digits with thousands separators, a decimal point, and more digits. If a precision specifier follows the N, it indicates the number of digits the result should have after the decimal point. The value –1234.5678 with the specifier N3 produces –1,234.568.
P or p	Percentage. The value is multiplied by 100 and then formatted according to the computer's settings. If a precision specifier follows the P, it indicates the number of digits that should follow the decimal point. On a typical computer, the value 1.2345678 with the specifier P produces 123.46%.
R or r	Round trip. The value is formatted in such a way that the result can be converted back into its original value. Depending on the data type and value, this may require 17 digits of precision. The value 1/7 with the specifier R produces 0.14285714285714285.
X or x	Hexadecimal. This works for integer types only. The value is converted into hexadecimal. The case of the X or x determines whether hexadecimal digits above 9 are written in uppercase or lowercase. If a precision specifier follows the X, it indicates the number of digits the result should have, padding on the left with zeros, if necessary. The value 183 with the specifier x4 produces 00b7.

CUSTOM NUMERIC FORMAT SPECIFIERS

Custom numeric format specifiers describe how a number should be formatted. The following table lists characters that you can use to build custom numeric formats.

SPECIFIER	MEANING
0	A digit or zero. If the number doesn't have a digit in this position, the specifier adds a 0. The value 12 with the specifier 000.00 produces 012.00.
#	A digit. If the number doesn't have a digit in this position, nothing is printed.
,	If used between two digits (either 0 or #), adds thousands separators to the result. Note that it will add many comma separators if necessary. The value 1234567 with the specifier #,# produces 1,234,567.
,	If used immediately to the left of the decimal point, the number is divided by 1000 for each comma. The value 1234567 with the specifier #,#,. produces 1,235.
%	Multiplies the number by 100 and inserts the % symbol where it appears in the specifier. The value 0.123 with the specifier .00% produces 12.30%.
E0 or e0	Displays the number in scientific notation inserting an E or e between the number and its exponent. Use # and 0 to format the number before the exponent. The number of 0s after the E determines the number of digits in the exponent. If you place a + sign between the E and 0, the result's exponent includes a + or − sign. If you omit the + sign, the exponent only includes a sign if it is negative. The value 1234.5678 with the specifier 00.000E+000 produces 12.346E+002.
\	Displays the following character literally without interpreting it. Use \\ to display the \ character. The value 12 with the specifier #\% produces 12%, and the same value with the specifier #% produces 1200%.
'ABC' or "ABC"	Displays the characters in the quotes literally. The value 12 with the specifier #'%' (single quotes around the % symbol) produces 12%.

NUMERIC FORMATTING SECTIONS

A numeric format specifier may contain one, two, or three sections separated by semicolons. If the specifier contains one section, the specifier is used for all numeric values.

If the specifier contains two sections, the first is used to format values that are positive or zero, and the second is used to format negative values.

If the specifier contains three sections, the first is used to format positive values, the second is used to format negative values, and the third is used to format values that are zero.

The following text shows output from the Immediate window for three values using the format specifier #,#.00;<#,#.00>;ZERO:

```
?(1234.5678).ToString("#,#.00; <#,#.00>;ZERO")
1,234.57
?(-1234.5678).ToString("#,#.00; <#,#.00>;ZERO")
<1,234.57>
?(0).ToString("#,#.00; <#,#.00>;ZERO")
ZERO
```

COMPOSITE FORMATTING

The String.Format, Console.WriteLine, and TextWriter.WriteLine methods provide a different method for formatting strings. These routines can take a composite formatting string parameter that contains literal characters plus placeholders for values. Other parameters to the methods give the values.

The value placeholders have the following format:

```
{index[,alignment][:format_specifier]}
```

The *index* value gives the index numbered from 0 of the parameter that should be inserted in this placeholder's position.

The optional *alignment* value tells the minimum number of spaces the item should use and the result is padded with spaces, if necessary. If this value is negative, the result is left-justified. If the value is positive, the result is right-justified.

The *format_specifier* indicates how the item should be formatted.

For example, consider the following code:

```
Dim emp As String = "Crazy Bob":
Dim sales As Single = -12345.67
MessageBox.Show(String.Format("{0} {1:earned;lost} {1:c} this year", emp, sales))
```

The first placeholder refers to parameter number 0, which has the value "Crazy Bob." The second placeholder refers to parameter number 1 and includes a two-part format specifier that displays "earned" if the value is positive or zero, and "lost" of the value is negative. The third placeholder refers to parameter number 1 again, this time formatted as currency.

The following code shows the result:

```
Crazy Bob lost ($12,345.67) this year
```

ENUMERATED TYPE FORMATTING

Visual Basic provides special formatting capabilities that can display the values of enumerated variables. For example, consider the following code:

```
Private Enum Dessert
    Cake = 1
    Pie = 2
    Cookie = 3
    IceCream = 4
End Enum
. . .
Dim dessert_choice As Dessert = Dessert.Cake
MessageBox.Show(dessert_choice.ToString)
```

This code displays the string "Cake."

For variables of an enumerated type such as dessert_choice, the ToString method can take a specifier that determines how the value is formatted.

The specifier G or g formats the value as a string if possible. If the value is not a valid entry in the Enum's definition, the result is the variable's numeric value. For example, the previous code does not define a Dessert enumeration for the value 7 so, if you set dessert_choice to 7, then `dessert_choice.ToString("G")` returns the value 7.

If you define an enumerated type with the Flags attribute, variables of that type can be a combination of the Enum's values, as shown in the following code:

```
<Flags()>
Private Enum Dessert
    Cake = 1
    Pie = 2
    Cookie = 4
    IceCream = 8
End Enum
. . .
Dim dessert_choice As Dessert = Dessert.IceCream Or Dessert.Cake
MessageBox.Show(dessert_choice.ToString("G"))
```

In this case, the G format specifier returns a string that contains all of the flag values separated by commas. In this example, the result is "Cake, IceCream." Note that the values are returned in the order in which they are defined by the enumeration, not the order in which they are assigned to the variable.

If you do not use the Flags attribute when defining an enumerated type, the G format specifier always returns the variable's numeric value if it is a combination of values rather than a single value from the list. On the other hand, the F specifier returns a list of comma-separated values if it makes sense. If you omit the Flags attribute from the previous code, `dessert_choice.ToString("G")` would return 9, but `dessert_choice.ToString("F")` would return "Cake, IceCream."

The D or d specifier always formats the variable as a number.

The specifier X or x formats the value as a hexadecimal number.

The Application Class

The Application class provides static properties and methods for controlling the application. This appendix contains a summary of the Application class's most useful properties, methods, and events. Chapter 36, "Configuration and Resources," has a bit more to say about the Application class and provides some example code.

PROPERTIES

The following table describes the Application class's most useful properties.

PROPERTY	PURPOSE
CommonAppDataPath	Returns the path where the program should store application data that is shared by all users. By default, this path has the form base_path\company_name\product_name\product_version. The base_path is typically C:\Documents and Settings\All Users\Application Data (here "C" may be replaced with a different drive letter depending on how your system is set up).
CommonAppDataRegistry	Returns the Registry key where the program should store application data that is shared by all users. By default, this path has the form HKEY_LOCAL_MACHINE\Software\company_name\product_name\product_version.
CompanyName	Returns the application's company name.

continues

(continued)

PROPERTY	PURPOSE
CurrentCulture	Gets or sets the CultureInfo object for this thread. The CultureInfo object specifies information about a specific culture (such as its name, writing system, and calendar, and its formats for dates, times, and numbers).
CurrentInputLanguage	Gets or sets the InputLanguage for this thread. The InputLanguage object defines the layout of the keyboard for the culture. It determines how the keyboard keys are mapped to the characters in the culture's language.
ExecutablePath	Returns the fully qualified path to the file that started the execution, including the file name.
LocalUserAppDataPath	Returns the path where the program should store data for this local, non-roaming user. By default, this path has the form base_path\ company_name\product_name\product_version. The base_path is typically C:\Documents and Settings\user_name\Local Settings\ Application Data.
MessageLoop	Returns True if the thread has a message loop. If the program begins with a startup form, this loop is created automatically. If it starts with a custom Sub Main, then the loop doesn't initially exist, and the program must start it by calling Application.Run.
OpenForms	Returns a collection holding references to all of the application's open forms.
ProductName	Returns the application's product name.
ProductVersion	Gets the product version associated with this application.
StartupPath	Returns the fully qualified path to the file that started the execution, including the file name.
UserAppDataPath	Returns the path where the program should store data for this user. By default, this path has the form base_path\company_name\ product_name\product_version. The base_path is typically C:\Documents and Settings\user_name\Application Data.
UserAppDataRegistry	Returns the Registry key where the program should store application data for this user. By default, this path has the form HKEY_ CURRENT_USER\Software\company_name\product_name\ product_version.
UseWaitCursor	Determines whether this thread's forms display a wait cursor. Set this to True before performing a long operation, and set it to False when the operation is finished.

METHODS

The following table describes the Application class's most useful methods.

METHOD	PURPOSE
AddMessageFilter	Adds a message filter to monitor the event loop's Windows messages.
DoEvents	Processes Windows messages that are currently in the message queue. If the thread is performing a long calculation, it would normally prevent the rest of the thread from taking action (such as processing these messages). Calling DoEvents lets the user interface catch up with the user's actions. Note that you can often avoid the need for DoEvents if you perform the long task on a separate thread.
Exit	Ends the whole application. This is a rather abrupt halt, and any forms do not execute their FormClosing or FormClosed event handlers, so be sure the application has executed any necessary clean-up code before calling Application.Exit.
ExitThread	Ends the current thread. This is a rather abrupt halt, and any forms on the thread do not execute their FormClosing or FormClosed event handlers.
OnThreadException	Raises the Application object's ThreadException event, passing it an exception. If your application throws an uncaught exception in the IDE, the IDE halts. That makes it hard to test Application.ThreadException event handlers. You can call OnThreadException to invoke the event handler.
RemoveMessageFilter	Removes a message filter.
Run	Runs a message loop for the current thread. If you pass this method a form object, it displays the form and processes its messages until the form closes.
SetSuspendState	Makes the system suspend operation or hibernate. When the system *hibernates*, it writes its memory contents to disk. When you restart the system, it resumes with its previous desktop and applications running. When the system *suspends* operation, it enters low-power mode. It can resume more quickly than a hibernated system, but memory contents are not saved, so they will be lost if the computer loses power.

EVENTS

The following table describes the Application object's events.

EVENT	PURPOSE
ApplicationExit	Occurs when the application is about to shut down.
Idle	Occurs when the application finishes executing some code and is about to enter an idle state to wait for events.
ThreadException	Occurs when the application throws an unhandled exception.
ThreadExit	Occurs when a thread is about to exit.

The My Namespace

The My namespace provides shortcuts to make performing common tasks easier. The following sections describe the major items within the My namespace and describe the tools that they make available.

MY.APPLICATION

My.Application provides information about the current application. It includes properties that tell you the program's current directory, culture, Log object, and splash screen. It also includes information about the application's assembly, including the program's version numbering.

The following table describes the most useful My.Application properties, methods, and events.

ITEM	PURPOSE
ApplicationContext	Returns an ApplicationContext object for the currently executing thread. It provides a reference to the thread's form. Its ExitThread method terminates the thread and its ThreadExit event fires when the thread is exiting.
ChangeCurrentCulture	Changes the thread's culture used for string manipulation and formatting.
ChangeCurrentUICulture	Changes the thread's culture used for retrieving resources.
CommandLineArgs	Returns a collection containing the command-line argument strings used when the application was started. The first entry (with index 0) is the fully qualified name of the executable application.

continues

(continued)

ITEM	PURPOSE
CurrentCulture	Returns a CultureInfo object that represents the settings used for culture-specific string manipulation and formatting. This includes calendar information, date and time specifications, the culture's name, keyboard layout, number formats for general numbers (for example, the thousands separator character and decimal character), currency, and percentages.
CurrentUICulture	Returns a CultureInfo object that represents the culture-specific settings used by the thread to retrieve resources. It determines the culture used by the Resource Manager and My.Resources.
Deployment	Returns the application's current ApplicationDeployment object used for ClickOnce deployment. Normally, you don't need to manage deployment yourself, but this object lets you check for updates, start an update synchronously or asynchronously, download files, and restart the updated application.
DoEvents	Makes the application process all of the Windows messages currently waiting in the message queue. Doing this allows controls to process messages and update their appearances while the program is performing a long calculation. Often, you can avoid using DoEvents by performing long calculations on a separate thread, so the user interface can continue running normally.
GetEnvironment-Variable	Returns the value of the specified environment variable. For example, the following code displays the value of the PATH environment variable: ```\n MessageBox.Show(\n My.Application.GetEnvironmentVariable("PATH"))\n``` This method raises an exception if the named environment variable doesn't exist. The method Environment.GetEnvironmentVariable performs the same function, except that it returns Nothing if the variable doesn't exist.
Info	Returns an AssemblyInfo object that provides information about the assembly such as assembly name, company name, copyright, trademark, and version.
IsNetworkDeployed	Returns True if the application was deployed over the network. You should check this property and only try to use the My.Application. Deployment object if it returns True.
Log	An object of the class MyLog. You can use this object's WriteEntry and WriteException methods to log messages and exceptions.
MainForm	Gets or sets the application's main form.
NetworkAvailability-Changed	The application raises this event when the network's availability changes.

ITEM	PURPOSE
OpenForms	Returns a collection containing references to all of the application's open forms.
Shutdown	The application raises this event when it is shutting down. This event occurs after all forms' FormClosing and FormClosed event handlers have finished. Note that it only fires if the program shuts down normally. If it exits, these events don't fire.
SplashScreen	Gets or sets the application's splash screen.
Startup	The application raises this event when it is starting up before it creates any forms.
StartupNextInstance	The application raises this event when the user tries to start a second instance of a single-instance application.
UICulture	Gets the thread's culture used for retrieving resources.
UnhandledException	The application raises this event if it encounters an unhandled exception.

The following table lists the Info object's properties. Note that these properties have default blank values unless you set them by opening the project's property pages, selecting the Application tab, and clicking the Assembly Information button.

PROPERTY	PURPOSE
AssemblyName	Gets the assembly's name.
CompanyName	Gets the assembly's company name.
Copyright	Gets the assembly's copyright information.
Description	Gets the assembly's description.
DirectoryPath	Gets the directory where the assembly is stored.
LoadedAssemblies	Returns a collection of Assembly objects for the application's currently loaded assemblies.
ProductName	Gets the assembly's product name.
StackTrace	Gets a stack trace.
Title	Gets the assembly's title.
Trademark	Gets the assembly's trademark information.
Version	Gets the assembly's version number.
WorkingSet	Gets the number of bytes mapped to the process context.

The project's Application property page gives you access to most of the Info values at design time. To open the Application property page, open Solution Explorer, double-click the My Project entry, and select the Application tab.

To set Info values at design time, open the Application property page and click the Assembly Information button, and then enter the assembly information in the dialog shown in Figure S-1, and click OK.

To place code in the My.Application object's NetworkAvailabilityChanged, Shutdown, Startup, StartupNextInstance, or UnhandledException event handlers, open the Application property page and click the View Application Events button.

Alternatively, you can open Solution Explorer, click the Show All Files button, expand the My Project entry, and open the file ApplicationEvents.vb.

FIGURE S-1: Use this dialog box to enter information that the program can later retrieve using My.Application.AssemblyInfo.

To make the application a single-instance application, open the Application property page and check the "Make single instance application" box.

MY.COMPUTER

My.Computer provides methods to understand and control the computer's hardware and the system software. It lets you work with the audio system, clock, keyboard, clipboard, mouse, network, printers, Registry, and file system.

The following sections describe the properties, methods, and events available through My.Computer in detail.

Audio

This object provides access to the computer's audio system. Its methods let you play a .wav file synchronously or asynchronously, stop a file playing asynchronously, or play a system sound. For example, the following code plays the system's exclamation sound:

```
My.Computer.Audio.PlaySystemSound(SystemSounds.Exclamation)
```

The following table describes the Audio object's methods.

METHOD	PURPOSE
Play	Plays .wav data from a file, byte array, or stream. The second parameter can be Background (play asynchronously in the background), BackgroundLoop (play asynchronously in the background and repeat when it ends), or WaitToComplete (play synchronously).
PlaySystem-Sound	Plays a system sound. The parameter should be a member of the SystemSounds enumeration and can have the value Asterisk, Beep, Exclamation, Hand, or Question.
Stop	Stops the sound currently playing asynchronously.

Clipboard

The Clipboard object described in Chapter 23, "Drag and Drop, and the Clipboard," enables you to move data in and out of the system's clipboard. The My.Computer.Clipboard object provides extra tools that simplify some clipboard operations. The following table briefly summarizes the My.Computer.Clipboard object's methods.

METHOD	PURPOSE
Clear	Removes all data from the clipboard.
ContainsAudio	Returns True if the clipboard contains audio data.
ContainsData	Returns True if the clipboard contains data in a specific custom format.
ContainsFileDropList	Returns True if the clipboard contains a file drop list.
ContainsImage	Returns True if the clipboard contains image data.
ContainsText	Returns True if the clipboard contains textual data.
GetAudioStream	Gets audio data from the clipboard.
GetData	Gets data in a specific custom format from the clipboard.
GetDataObject	Gets a DataObject from the clipboard.
GetFileDropList	Gets a StringCollection holding the names of the files selected for drop from the clipboard.
GetImage	Gets image data from the clipboard.
GetText	Gets textual data from the clipboard.
SetAudio	Saves audio data to the clipboard.
SetData	Saves data in a specific custom format to the clipboard.

continues

(continued)

METHOD	PURPOSE
SetDataObject	Saves a DataObject to the clipboard.
SetFileDropList	Saves a StringCollection containing a series of fully qualified file names to the clipboard.
SetImage	Saves an image to the clipboard.
SetText	Saves textual data to the clipboard.

See Chapter 23 for more information about using the clipboard.

Clock

This property returns an object of type MyClock that you can use to learn about the current time. The following table describes this object's properties.

PROPERTY	PURPOSE
GmtTime	Returns a Date object that gives the current local date and time converted into Coordinated Universal Time (UTC) or Greenwich Mean Time (GMT).
LocalTime	Returns a Date object that gives the current local date and time.
TickCount	Returns the number of milliseconds since the computer started.

For example, suppose that you live in Colorado, which uses Mountain Standard Time (MST), seven hours behind Greenwich Mean Time. If My.Computer.Clock.LocalTime returns 2:03 PM, then My.Computer.Clock.GmtTime returns 9:03 PM.

If you must store a date and time for later use (for example, in a database), you should generally store it in UTC. Then you can meaningfully compare that value with other times stored on other computers in different time zones such as those across the Internet.

FileSystem

The FileSystem object provides tools for working with drives, directories, and files. The following table summarizes this object's properties and methods.

ITEM	DESCRIPTION
CombinePath	Returns a properly formatted combined path as a string.
CopyDirectory	Copies a directory.
CopyFile	Copies a file.

ITEM	DESCRIPTION
CreateDirectory	Creates a directory.
CurrentDirectory	Determines the fully qualified path to the application's current directory.
DeleteDirectory	Deletes a directory.
DeleteFile	Deletes a file.
DirectoryExists	Returns a Boolean indicating whether a directory exists.
Drives	Returns a read-only collection of DriveInfo objects describing the system's drives. See Chapter 38, "File-System Objects," for information about the DriveInfo class.
FileExists	Returns a Boolean indicating whether a file exists.
FindInFiles	Returns a collection holding names of files that contain a search string.
GetDirectories	Returns a String collection representing the path names of subdirectories within a directory.
GetDirectoryInfo	Returns a DirectoryInfo object for the specified path.
GetDriveInfo	Returns a DriveInfo object for the specified path.
GetFileInfo	Returns a FileInfo object for the specified path.
GetFiles	Returns a read-only String collection representing the names of files within a directory.
GetParentPath	Returns a string representing the absolute path of the parent of the provided path.
MoveDirectory	Moves a directory.
MoveFile	Moves a file.
OpenTextFieldParser	Opens a TextFieldParser.
OpenTextFileReader	Opens a TextReader.
OpenTextFileWriter	Opens a TextWriter.
ReadAllBytes	Reads from a binary file.
ReadAllText	Reads from a text file.
RenameDirectory	Renames a directory.
RenameFile	Renames a file.

continues

(continued)

ITEM	DESCRIPTION
SpecialDirectories	Returns a SpecialDirectoriesProxy object that has properties giving the locations of various special directories such as the system's temporary directory and the user's MyDocuments directory. See Chapter 38 for more information.
WriteAllBytes	Writes to a binary file.
WriteAllText	Writes to a text file.

Info

The My.Computer.Info object provides information about the computer's memory and operating system. The following list describes this object's properties:

PROPERTY	PURPOSE
AvailablePhysicalMemory	Returns the computer's total amount of free physical memory in bytes.
AvailableVirtualMemory	Returns the computer's total amount of free virtual address space in bytes.
InstalledUICulture	Returns the current user-interface culture.
LoadedAssemblies	Returns a collection of the assemblies loaded by the application.
OSFullName	Returns the computer's full operating-system name as in Microsoft Windows XP Home Edition.
OSPlatform	Returns the platform identifier for the operating system of the computer. This can be Unix, Win32NT (Windows NT or later), Win32S (runs on 16-bit Windows to provide access to 32-bit applications), Win32Windows (Windows 95 or later), or WinCE.
OSVersion	Returns the operating system's version in a string with the format major.minor.build.revision.
StackTrace	Returns a string containing the application's current stack trace.
TotalPhysicalMemory	Returns the computer's total amount of physical memory in bytes.
TotalVirtualMemory	Returns the computer's total amount of virtual address space in bytes.
WorkingSet	Returns the amount of physical memory mapped to the process context in bytes.

Keyboard

This object returns information about the current keyboard state. The following table describes this object's properties.

PROPERTY	PURPOSE
AltKeyDown	Returns True if the Alt key is down.
CapsLock	Returns True if Caps Lock is on.
CtrlKeyDown	Returns True if the Ctrl key is down.
NumLock	Returns True if Num Lock is on.
ScrollLock	Returns True if Scroll Lock is on.
ShiftKeyDown	Returns True if the Shift key is down.

The My.Computer.Keyboard object also provides one method named SendKeys. This method sends keystrokes to the currently active window just as if the user had typed them. You can use this method to provide some automated control over applications.

Mouse

The My.Computer.Mouse object provides information about the computer's mouse. The following table describes this object's properties.

PROPERTY	DESCRIPTION
ButtonsSwapped	Returns True if the functions of the mouse's left and right buttons have been switched. This can make using the mouse easier for left-handed users.
WheelExists	Returns True if the mouse has a scroll wheel.
WheelScrollLines	Returns a number indicating how much to scroll when the mouse wheel rotates one notch.

Name

The My.Computer.Name property simply returns the computer's name.

Network

The My.Computer.Network object provides a few simple properties and methods for working with the network. Its single property, IsAvailable, returns True if the network is available.

The following table describes the object's methods.

METHOD	DESCRIPTION
DownloadFile	Downloads a file from a remote computer. Parameters give such values as the file name, user name, password, and connection timeout.
IsAvailable	Returns True if the network is available.
Ping	Pings a remote computer to see if it is connected to the network.
UploadFile	Uploads a file to a remote computer. Parameters give such values as the file name, user name, password, and connection timeout.

This object also provides one event, NetworkAvailabilityChanged, that you can catch to learn when the network becomes available or unavailable.

Ports

This object provides one property and a single method. Its SerialPortNames property returns an array of strings listing the names of the computer's serial ports.

The OpenSerialPort method opens the serial port with a particular name (optional parameters give the baud rate, parity, and other port configuration information) and returns a reference to a SerialPort object.

The SerialPort class is much more complex than the My.Computer.Ports object. The following table describes the SerialPort class's most useful properties.

PROPERTY	PURPOSE
BaseStream	Returns the underlying Stream object.
BaudRate	Gets or sets the port's baud rate.
BreakState	Gets or sets the break signal state.
BytesToRead	Returns the number of bytes of data in the receive buffer.
BytesToWrite	Returns the number of bytes of data in the send buffer.
CDHolding	Returns the state of the port's Carrier Detect (CD) line.
CtsHolding	Returns the state of the port's Clear-to-Send (CTS) line.
DataBits	Gets or sets the standard length of data bits per byte.
DiscardNull	Determines whether null characters are ignored.
DsrHolding	Returns the state of the Data Set Ready (DSR) signal.

PROPERTY	PURPOSE
DtrEnable	Determines enabling of the Data Terminal Ready (DTR) signal.
Encoding	Determines the character encoding for text conversion.
Handshake	Determines the handshaking protocol.
IsOpen	Returns True if the port is open.
NewLine	Determines the end-of-line sequence for the ReadLine and WriteLine methods. This is a linefeed by default.
Parity	Determines the parity-checking protocol.
ParityReplace	Determines the character used to replace invalid characters when a parity error occurs.
PortName	Gets or selects the port.
ReadBufferSize	Determines the port's read buffer size.
ReadTimeout	Determines the read timeout in milliseconds.
ReceivedBytesThreshold	Determines the number of bytes in the input buffer before a ReceivedEvent is raised.
RtsEnable	Determines whether the Request to Transmit (RTS) signal is enabled.
StopBits	Determines the standard number of stop bits per byte.
WriteBufferSize	Determines the port's write buffer size.
WriteTimeout	Determines the write timeout in milliseconds.

The following table describes the SerialPort object's most useful methods.

METHOD	PURPOSE
Close	Closes the port.
DiscardInBuffer	Discards any data that is currently in the read buffer.
DiscardOutBuffer	Discards any data that is currently in the write buffer.
GetPortNames	Returns an array of strings holding the serial ports' names.
Open	Opens the port's connection.
Read	Reads data from the read buffer.
ReadByte	Synchronously reads one byte from the read buffer.

continues

(continued)

METHOD	PURPOSE
ReadChar	Synchronously reads one character from the read buffer.
ReadExisting	Reads all immediately available characters in both the stream and the read buffer.
ReadLine	Reads up to the next NewLine value in the read buffer.
ReadTo	Reads a string up to the specified value in the read buffer.
Write	Writes data into the port's write buffer.
WriteLine	Writes a string and a NewLine into the write buffer.

The SerialPort object also has a few events that you can use to learn about changes in the port's status. The following table describes the object's most useful events.

EVENT	PURPOSE
DataReceived	Occurs when the port receives data. The e.EventType parameter indicates the type of data and can be SerialData.Eof (end of file received) or SerialData.Chars (characters were received).
ErrorEvent	Occurs when the port encounters an error. The e.EventType parameter indicates the type of error and can be Frame (framing error), Overrun (character buffer overrun), RxOver (input buffer overrun), RxParity (hardware detected parity error), or TxFull (output buffer full).
PinChangedEvent	Occurs when the port's serial pin changes. The e.EventType parameter indicates the type of change and can be Break (break in the input), CDChanged (Receive Line Signal Detect, or RLSD, signal changed state), CtsChanged (CTS signal changed state), DsrChanged (DSR signal changed state), and Ring (detected a ring indicator).

Registry

My.Computer.Registry provides objects that manipulate the Registry. My.Computer.Registry has seven properties that refer to objects of type RegistryKey that represent the Registry's main subtrees or "hives."

The following table lists these objects and the corresponding Registry hives.

MY.COMPUTER.REGISTRY PROPERTY	REGISTRY SUBTREE
ClassesRoot	HKEY_CLASSES_ROOT
CurrentConfig	HKEY_CURRENT_CONFIG
CurrentUser	HKEY_CURRENT_USER
DynData	HKEY_DYNAMIC_DATA
LocalMachine	HKEY_LOCAL_MACHINE
PerformanceData	HKEY_PERFORMANCE_DATA
Users	HKEY_USERS

My.Computer.Registry also provides two methods, GetValue and SetValue, that get and set Registry values.

The program can use the RegistryKey objects to work with the corresponding Registry subtrees. The following table describes the most useful properties and methods provided by the RegistryKey class.

PROPERTY OR METHOD	PURPOSE
Close	Closes the key and writes it to disk if it has been modified.
CreateSubKey	Creates a new subkey or opens an existing subkey within this key.
DeleteSubKey	Deletes the specified subkey.
DeleteSubKeyTree	Recursively deletes a subkey and any child subkeys it contains.
DeleteValue	Deletes a value from the key.
Flush	Writes any changes to the key into the Registry.
GetSubKeyNames	Returns an array of strings giving subkey names.
GetValue	Returns the value of a specified value within this key.
GetValueKind	Returns the type of a specified value within this key. This can be Binary, DWord, ExpandString, MultiString, QWord, String, or Unknown. (Unknown is particularly important because the Registry can contain just about any custom data type.)
GetValueNames	Returns an array of strings giving the names of all of the values contained within the key.
Name	Returns the key's Registry path.
OpenSubKey	Returns a RegistryKey object representing a descendant key. A parameter indicates whether you need write access to the key.

continues

(continued)

PROPERTY OR METHOD	PURPOSE
SetValue	Sets a value within the key.
SubKeyCount	Returns the number of subkeys that are this key's direct children.
ToString	Returns the key's name.
ValueCount	Returns the number of values stored in this key.

Visual Basic's native Registry methods SaveSetting and GetSetting are generally easier to use than My.Computer.Registry, although they provide access to only part of the Registry.

Screen

The My.Computer.Screen property returns a Screen object representing the computer's main display. The following table describes the Screen object's most useful properties.

PROPERTY	PURPOSE
AllScreens	Returns an array of Screen objects representing all of the system's screens.
BitsPerPixel	Returns the screen's color depth in bits per pixel.
Bounds	Returns a Rectangle giving the screen's bounds in pixels.
DeviceName	Returns the screen's device name as in \\.\DISPLAY1.
Primary	Returns True if the screen is the computer's primary screen.
PrimaryScreen	Returns a reference to a Screen object representing the system's primary display. For a single display system, the primary display is the only display.
WorkingArea	Returns a Rectangle giving the screen's working area bounds in pixels. This is the desktop area excluding taskbars, docked windows, and docked toolbars.

The following table describes the Screen class's most useful methods.

METHOD	PURPOSE
FromControl	Returns a Screen object representing the display that contains the largest piece of a specific control.
FromHandle	Returns a Screen object representing the display that contains the largest piece of the object with a given handle.

METHOD	PURPOSE
FromPoint	Returns a Screen object representing the display that contains a given point.
FromRectangle	Returns a Screen object representing the display that contains the largest piece of a given Rectangle.
GetBounds	Returns a Rectangle giving the bounds of the screen that contains the largest piece of a control, rectangle, or point.
GetWorkingArea	Returns a Rectangle giving the working area of the screen that contains the largest piece of a control, rectangle, or point.

The AllScreens and PrimaryScreen properties, and all of these methods, are shared members of the Windows.Forms.Screen class. If you refer to them using an instance of the class such as My.Computer.Screen, the IDE flags the code with a warning. You can avoid the warning by using the class itself (System.Windows.Forms.Screen) rather than an instance to refer to these properties, as in the following code:

```
Debug.WriteLine(System.Windows.Forms.Screen.AllScreens(0).DeviceName)
Debug.WriteLine(System.Windows.Forms.Screen.PrimaryScreen.DeviceName)
```

The WorkingArea property does not update after you access the Screen object. If the user moves the system taskbar, the WorkingArea property does not show the new values.

The GetWorkingArea method retrieves the screen's current working area, however. If you must be certain that the user has not moved the taskbar or a docked object, use the GetWorkingArea method.

MY.FORMS

My.Forms provides properties that give references to an instance of each of the types of forms defined by the application. If the program begins with a startup form, the corresponding My.Forms entry refers to that form. For example, suppose the program begins by displaying Form1. Then, My.Forms.Form1 refers to the startup instance of the Form1 class.

You can also refer to these forms directly. For example, the following two statements set the text and display the predefined instance of the Form2 class:

```
My.Forms.Form2.Text = "Hello!"
Form2.Show()
```

Other forms that you create using the New keyword are separate instances from those provided by My.Forms.

If you know you will only want one instance of a particular form, for example if the form is a dialog box, you can use this instance instead of creating new instances of the class. If you will need to use more than one instance of the form at the same time, you must use New to create them.

You can set these properties to Nothing to dispose of the forms, but you can never set them to anything else. In particular, you cannot set them to new instances of their form classes later. When you destroy one of these instances, it is gone forever. If you will need to reuse the form later, set its Visible property to False rather than setting it equal to Nothing. Alternatively, you can just create new instances of the class when you need them and ignore the forms in My.Forms.

MY.RESOURCES

My.Resources provides access to the application's resources. Its ResourceManager property returns a reference to a ResourceManager object attached to the project's resources. You can use this object to retrieve the application's resources.

My.Resources also provides strongly typed properties that return the application's resources. For example, if you create a string resource named Greeting, the following code sets the form's caption to that string's value:

```
Me.Text = My.Resources.Greeting
```

See Chapter 36, "Configuration and Resources," for more information on using My.Resources to access the application's resources.

MY.USER

My.User returns information about the current user. The following table describes the My.User object's most useful properties.

PROPERTY OR METHOD	PURPOSE
CurrentPrincipal	Gets or sets an IPrincipal object used for role-based security.
InitializeWithWindowsUser	Sets the thread's principal to the Windows user who started it.
IsAuthenticated	Returns True if the user's identity has been authenticated.
IsInRole	Returns True if the user belongs to a certain role.
Name	Returns the current user's name in the format domain\user_name.

Streams

Visual Studio provides several classes that treat data as a stream, a series of bytes. These classes are not difficult to use, but they are similar enough to be confusing. This appendix summarizes the stream classes and describes their properties and their methods. See Chapter 37, "Streams," for more information on streams.

STREAM CLASS SUMMARY

The following table lists the Visual Studio stream classes. It can provide you with some guidance for selecting a stream class.

CLASS	PURPOSE
Stream	A generic stream class. This is a virtual (MustInherit) class, so you cannot create one directly. Instead, you must instantiate one of its subclasses.
FileStream	Represents a file as a stream. Usually, you can use a helper class such as BinaryReader or TextWriter to make working with a FileStream easier.
MemoryStream	Lets you read and write stream data in memory. This is useful when you need a stream but don't want to read or write a file.
BufferedStream	Adds buffering to another stream type. This sometimes improves performance on relatively slow underlying devices.
BinaryReader, BinaryWriter	Read and write data from an underlying stream using routines that manage specific data types (such as ReadDouble and ReadUInt16).

continues

(continued)

CLASS	PURPOSE
`TextReader,` `TextWriter`	These virtual (MustInherit) classes define methods that make working with text on an underlying stream easier.
`StringReader,` `StringWriter`	These classes inherit from TextReader and TextWriter. They provide methods for reading and writing text into an underlying string.
`StreamReader,` `StreamWriter`	These classes inherit from TextReader and TextWriter. They provide methods for reading and writing text into an underlying stream, usually a FileStream.
`CryptoStream`	Applies a cryptographic transformation to its data.
`NetworkStream`	Sends and receives data across a network connection.

STREAM

The following table describes the Stream class's most useful properties.

PROPERTY	PURPOSE
`CanRead`	Returns True if the stream supports reading.
`CanSeek`	Returns True if the stream supports seeking to a particular position in the stream.
`CanTimeout`	Returns True if the stream supports timeouts.
`CanWrite`	Returns True if the stream supports writing.
`Length`	Returns the number of bytes in the stream.
`Position`	Returns the stream's current position in its bytes. For a stream that supports seeking, the program can set this value to move to a particular position.
`ReadTimeout`	Determines the stream's read timeout in milliseconds.
`WriteTimeout`	Determines the stream's write timeout in milliseconds.

The following table describes the Stream class's most useful methods.

METHOD	PURPOSE
BeginRead	Begins an asynchronous read.
BeginWrite	Begins an asynchronous write.
Close	Closes the stream and releases any resources it uses (such as file handles).
EndRead	Waits for an asynchronous read to finish.
EndWrite	Ends an asynchronous write.
Flush	Flushes data from the stream's buffers into the underlying storage medium (device, file, and so on).
Read	Reads bytes from the stream and advances its position by that number of bytes.
ReadByte	Reads a byte from the stream and advances its position by 1 byte.
Seek	If the stream supports seeking, sets the stream's position.
SetLength	Sets the stream's length. If the stream is currently longer than the new length, it is truncated. If the stream is shorter than the new length, it is enlarged. The stream must support both writing and seeking for this method to work.
Write	Writes bytes into the stream and advances the current position by this number of bytes.
WriteByte	Writes 1 byte into the stream and advances the current position by 1 byte.

The FileStream and MemoryStream classes add only few methods to those defined by the Stream class. The most important of those are new constructors specific to the type of stream. For example, the FileStream class provides constructors for opening files in various modes (append, new, and so forth).

BINARYREADER AND BINARYWRITER

These are stream helper classes that make it easier to read and write data in specific formats onto an underlying stream. The following table describes the BinaryReader class's most useful methods.

METHOD	PURPOSE
Close	Closes the BinaryReader and its underlying stream.
PeekChar	Reads the reader's next character, but does not advance the reader's position, so other methods can still read the character later.
Read	Reads characters from the stream and advances the reader's position.
ReadBoolean	Reads a Boolean from the stream and advances the reader's position by 1 byte.
ReadByte	Reads a byte from the stream and advances the reader's position by 1 byte.
ReadBytes	Reads a number of bytes from the stream into a byte array and advances the reader's position by that number of bytes.
ReadChar	Reads a character from the stream and advances the reader's position according to the stream's encoding and the character.
ReadChars	Reads a number of characters from the stream, returns the results in a character array, and advances the reader's position according to the stream's encoding and the number of characters.
ReadDecimal	Reads a decimal value from the stream and advances the reader's position by 16 bytes.
ReadDouble	Reads an 8-byte floating-point value from the stream and advances the reader's position by 8 bytes.
ReadInt16	Reads a 2-byte signed integer from the stream and advances the reader's position by 2 bytes.
ReadInt32	Reads a 4-byte signed integer from the stream and advances the reader's position by 4 bytes.
ReadInt64	Reads an 8-byte signed integer from the stream and advances the reader's position by 8 bytes.
ReadSByte	Reads a signed byte from the stream and advances the reader's position by 1 byte.
ReadSingle	Reads a 4-byte floating-point value from the stream and advances the reader's position by 4 bytes.
ReadString	Reads a string from the current stream and advances the reader's position past it. The string begins with its length.
ReadUInt16	Reads a 2-byte unsigned integer from the stream and advances the reader's position by 2 bytes.
ReadUInt32	Reads a 4-byte unsigned integer from the stream and advances the reader's position by 4 bytes.
ReadUInt64	Reads an 8-byte unsigned integer from the stream and advances the reader's position by 8 bytes.

The following table describes the BinaryWriter class's most useful methods.

METHOD	DESCRIPTION
Close	Closes the BinaryWriter and its underlying stream.
Flush	Writes any buffered data into the underlying stream.
Seek	Sets the position within the stream.
Write	Writes a value into the stream. This method has many overloaded versions that write characters, arrays of characters, integers, strings, unsigned 64-bit integers, and so on.

TEXTREADER AND TEXTWRITER

These are stream helper classes that make it easier to read and write text data onto an underlying stream. The following table describes the TextReader class's most useful methods.

METHOD	PURPOSE
Close	Closes the reader and releases any resources that it is using.
Peek	Reads the next character from the text without changing the reader's state so other methods can read the character later.
Read	Reads data from the input. Overloaded versions of this method read a single character, or an array of characters up to a specified length.
ReadBlock	Reads data from the input into an array of characters.
ReadLine	Reads a line of characters from the input and returns the data in a string.
ReadToEnd	Reads any remaining characters in the input and returns them in a string.

The following table describes the TextWriter class's most useful properties.

PROPERTY	PURPOSE
Encoding	Specifies the data's encoding (ASCII, UTF-8, Unicode, and so forth).
FormatProvider	Returns an object that controls formatting.
NewLine	Gets or sets the stream's new-line sequence.

The following table describes the TextWriter class's most useful methods.

METHOD	PURPOSE
Close	Closes the writer and releases any resources it uses.
Flush	Writes any buffered data into the underlying output.
Write	Writes a value into the output. This method has many overloaded versions that write characters, arrays of characters, integers, strings, unsigned 64-bit integers, and so forth.
WriteLine	Writes data into the output followed by the new-line sequence.

STRINGREADER AND STRINGWRITER

The StringReader and StringWriter classes let a program read and write text in a string. They implement the features defined by their parent classes TextReader and TextWriter. See the section "TextReader and TextWriter" earlier in this appendix for a list of those features.

STREAMREADER AND STREAMWRITER

The StreamReader and StreamWriter classes let a program read and write data in an underlying stream, often a FileStream. They implement the features defined by their parent classes TextReader and TextWriter. See the section "TextReader and TextWriter" earlier in this appendix for a list of the features.

TEXT FILE STREAM METHODS

The System.IO.File class provides several handy methods for working with text files. The following table summarizes these methods.

METHOD	PURPOSE
AppendText	Creates a text file or opens it for appending if it already exists. Returns a StreamWriter for writing into the file.
CreateText	Creates a text file, overwriting it if it already exists. Returns a StreamWriter for writing into the file.
Exists	Returns True if a file exists. It is better practice (and much faster) to only try to open the file if Exists returns True, rather than just trying to open the file and catching errors with a Try Catch block.
OpenText	Opens an existing text file and returns a StreamReader to read from it. This method throws a FileNotFoundException if the file doesn't exist.

U

File-System Classes

A Visual Basic application can take three basic approaches to file system manipulation: Visual Basic methods, System.IO Framework classes, and the My.Computer.FileSystem namespace. This appendix summarizes the properties, methods, and events provided by these approaches. For more information on file system objects, see Chapter 38, "File-System Objects."

VISUAL BASIC METHODS

The following table summarizes the Visual Basic methods for working with files. They let a program create, open, read, write, and learn about files.

METHOD	PURPOSE
Method	Purpose
EOF	Returns True if the file is at the end of file.
FileClose	Closes an open file.
FileGet	Reads data from a file opened in Random and Binary mode into a variable.
FileGetObject	Reads data as an object from a file opened in Random and Binary mode into a variable.
FileOpen	Opens a file for reading or writing. Parameters indicate the mode (Append, Binary, Input, Output, or Random), access type (Read, Write, or ReadWrite), and sharing (Shared, LockRead, LockWrite, or LockReadWrite).
FilePut	Writes data from a variable into a file opened for Random or Binary access.

continues

(continued)

METHOD	PURPOSE
FilePutObject	Writes an object from a variable into a file opened for Random or Binary access.
FreeFile	Returns a file number that is not currently associated with any file in this application. You should use FreeFile to get file numbers rather than using arbitrary numbers such as 1.
Input	Reads data written into a file by the Write method back into a variable.
InputString	Reads a specific number of characters from the file.
LineInput	Returns the next line of text from the file.
Loc	Returns the current position within the file.
LOF	Returns the file's length in bytes.
Print	Prints values into the file. Multiple values separated by commas are aligned at tab boundaries.
PrintLine	Prints values followed by a new line into the file. Multiple values separated by commas are aligned at tab boundaries.
Seek	Moves to the indicated position within the file.
Write	Writes values into the file, delimited appropriately so that they can later be read by the Input method.
WriteLine	Writes values followed by a new line into the file, delimited appropriately so that they can later be read by the Input method.

The following table describes Visual Basic methods that manipulate directories and files. They let an application list, rename, move, copy, and delete files and directories.

METHOD	PURPOSE
ChDir	Changes the application's current working directory.
ChDrive	Changes the application's current working drive.
CurDir	Returns the application's current working directory.
Dir	Returns a file matching a directory path specification that may include wildcards, and matching certain file properties such as ReadOnly, Hidden, or Directory. The first call to Dir should include a path. Subsequent calls can omit the path to fetch the next matching file for the initial path. Dir returns file names without the path and returns Nothing when no more files match.

METHOD	PURPOSE
FileCopy	Copies a file to a new location.
FileDateTime	Returns the date and time when the file was created or last modified.
FileLen	Returns the length of a file in bytes.
GetAttr	Returns a value indicating the file's attributes. The value is a combination of the values vbNormal, vbReadOnly, vbHidden, vbSystem, vbDirectory, vbArchive, and vbAlias.
Kill	Permanently deletes a file.
MkDir	Creates a new directory.
Rename	Renames a directory or file.
RmDir	Deletes an empty directory.
SetAttr	Sets the file's attributes The value is a combination of the values vbNormal, vbReadOnly, vbHidden, vbSystem, vbDirectory, vbArchive, and vbAlias.

FRAMEWORK CLASSES

The System.IO namespace provides several classes for working with the file system. The following sections describe the properties, methods, and events provided by these classes.

FileSystem

The FileSystem class provides shared methods for working with the file system at a large scale. The following table describes its most useful properties and methods.

PROPERTY OR METHOD	PURPOSE
CombinePath	Combines a base path with a relative child path and returns the resulting path. For example, the statement FileSystem.CombinePath("C:\Someplace\Lost", "..\Else") returns C:\Someplace\Else.
CopyDirectory	Copies a directory and its contents to a new location. A parameter indicates whether you want to overwrite existing files that have the same names.
CopyFile	Copies a file to a new location, possibly overwriting an existing file.
CreateDirectory	Creates a new directory.
DeleteDirectory	Deletes an existing directory. Parameters indicate whether the method should recursively delete the directory's contents and whether the deleted files should be placed in the Recycle Bin or deleted permanently.

continues

(continued)

PROPERTY OR METHOD	PURPOSE
DeleteFile	Deletes a file. A parameter indicates whether the file should be placed in the Recycle Bin or deleted permanently.
DirectoryExists	Returns True if the specified directory exists.
FileExists	Returns True if the specified file exists.
FindInFiles	Returns a collection holding names of files that contain a search string.
GetDirectories	Returns a read-only collection of strings giving the subdirectories within a specific directory. Parameters indicate whether the method should recursively search the subdirectories and whether the routine should allow wildcards.
GetDirectoryInfo	Returns a DirectoryInfo object representing a directory. Note that the directory need not exist yet. For example, you can create a DirectoryInfo object and then use its Create method to create the directory.
GetDriveInfo	Returns a DriveInfo object representing a drive.
GetFileInfo	Returns a FileInfo object representing a file. Note that the file need not exist yet. For example, you can create a FileInfo object and then use its Create method to create the file.
GetFiles	Returns a read-only collection of strings giving the names of files within a specific directory. Parameters indicate whether the method should recursively search the subdirectories and whether the routine should allow wildcards.
GetName	Returns the name portion of a file path.
GetParentPath	Returns a directory's parent directory path.
GetTempFileName	Creates a uniquely named empty file and returns its full path.
MoveDirectory	Moves a directory to a new parent directory. A parameter indicates whether you want to overwrite existing files with the same names.
MoveFile	Moves a file to a new directory. Parameters indicate whether the file should overwrite an existing file at the new location.
OpenTextFieldParser	Returns a TextFieldParser for a file. A TextFieldParser makes it easy to read fields from a delimited file or from a file with fixed-width field columns.
OpenTextFileReader	Returns a StreamReader attached to a file.
OpenTextFileWriter	Returns a StreamWriter attached to a file. A parameter indicates whether the StreamWriter should append to the file or create a new file.
ReadAllBytes	Returns a file's contents as an array of bytes.

PROPERTY OR METHOD	PURPOSE
ReadAllText	Returns a file's contents as a string.
RenameDirectory	Changes a directory's name within its current parent directory.
RenameFile	Changes a file's name within its current directory.
WriteAllBytes	Writes a byte array into a file. A parameter indicates whether the method should append the bytes to the file or create a new file.
WriteAllText	Writes a string into a file. A parameter indicates whether the method should append the string to the file or create a new file.

Directory

The Directory class provides shared methods for working with directories. The following table summarizes its shared methods.

METHOD	PURPOSE
CreateDirectory	Creates all of the directories along a path.
Delete	Deletes a directory and its contents. It can recursively delete all subdirectories.
Exists	Returns True if the path points to an existing directory.
GetCreationTime	Returns a directory's creation date and time.
GetCreationTimeUtc	Returns a directory's creation date and time in Coordinated Universal Time (UTC).
GetCurrentDirectory	Returns the application's current working directory.
GetDirectories	Returns an array of strings holding the fully qualified names of a directory's subdirectories.
GetDirectoryRoot	Returns the directory root for a path, which need not exist (for example, C:\).
GetFiles	Returns an array of strings holding the fully qualified names of a directory's files.
GetFileSystemEntries	Returns an array of strings holding the fully qualified names of a directory's files and subdirectories.
GetLastAccessTime	Returns a directory's last access date and time.
GetLastAccessTimeUtc	Returns a directory's last access date and time in UTC.

continues

(continued)

METHOD	PURPOSE
GetLastWriteTime	Returns the date and time when a directory was last modified.
GetLastWriteTimeUtc	Returns the date and time when a directory was last modified in UTC.
GetLogicalDrives	Returns an array of strings listing the system's logical drives as in A:\. The list includes drives that are attached. For example, it lists an empty floppy drive and a connected flash disk but doesn't list a flash disk after you disconnect it.
GetParent	Returns a DirectoryInfo object representing a directory's parent directory.
Move	Moves a directory and its contents to a new location on the same disk volume.
SetCreationTime	Sets a directory's creation date and time.
SetCreationTimeUtc	Sets a directory's creation date and time in UTC.
SetCurrentDirectory	Sets the application's current working directory.
SetLastAccessTime	Sets a directory's last access date and time.
SetLastAccessTimeUtc	Sets a directory's last access date and time in UTC.
SetLastWriteTime	Sets a directory's last write date and time.
SetLastWriteTimeUtc	Sets a directory's last write date and time in UTC.

File

The File class provides shared methods for working with files. The following table summarizes its most useful shared methods.

METHOD	PURPOSE
AppendAllText	Adds text to the end of a file, creating it if it doesn't exist, and then closes the file.
AppendText	Opens a file for appending UTF-8 encoded text and returns a StreamWriter attached to it. (For more information on UTF-8, see en.wikipedia.org/wiki/UTF-8).
Copy	Copies a file.

METHOD	PURPOSE
Create	Creates a new file and returns a FileStream attached to it.
CreateText	Creates or opens a file for writing UTF-8 encoded text and returns a StreamWriter attached to it.
Delete	Permanently deletes a file.
Exists	Returns True if the specified file exists.
GetAttributes	Gets a file's attributes. This is a combination of flags defined by the FileAttributes enumeration, which defines the values Archive, Compressed, Device, Directory, Encrypted, Hidden, Normal, NotContextIndexed, Offline, ReadOnly, ReparsePoint, SparseFile, System, and Temporary.
GetCreationTime	Returns a file's creation date and time.
GetCreationTimeUtc	Returns a file's creation date and time in UTC.
GetLastAccessTime	Returns a file's last access date and time.
GetLastAccessTimeUtc	Returns a file's last access date and time in UTC.
GetLastWriteTime	Returns a file's last write date and time.
GetLastWriteTimeUtc	Returns a file's last write date and time in UTC.
Move	Moves a file to a new location.
Open	Opens a file and returns a FileStream attached to it. Parameters let you specify the mode (Append, Create, CreateNew, Open, OpenOrCreate, or Truncate), access (Read, Write, or ReadWrite), and sharing (Read, Write, ReadWrite, or None) settings.
OpenRead	Opens a file for reading and returns a FileStream attached to it.
OpenText	Opens a UTF-8 encoded text file for reading and returns a StreamReader attached to it.
OpenWrite	Opens a file for writing and returns a FileStream attached to it.
ReadAllBytes	Returns a file's contents in an array of bytes.
ReadAllLines	Returns a file's lines in an array of strings.
ReadAllText	Returns a file's contents in a string.

continues

(continued)

METHOD	PURPOSE
Replace	This method takes three file paths as parameters representing a source file, a destination file, and a backup file. If the backup file exists, the method permanently deletes it. It then moves the destination file to the backup file, and moves the source file to the destination file. For example, imagine a program that writes a log file every time it runs. It could use this method to keep three versions of the log: the current log (the method's source file), the most recent backup (the method's destination file), and a second backup (the method's backup file). This method throws an error if either the source or destination file doesn't exist.
SetAttributes	Sets a file's attributes. This is a combination of flags defined by the FileAttributes enumeration, which defines the values Archive, Compressed, Device, Directory, Encrypted, Hidden, Normal, NotContextIndexed, Offline, ReadOnly, ReparsePoint, SparseFile, System, and Temporary.
SetCreationTime	Sets a file's creation date and time.
SetCreationTimeUtc	Sets a file's creation date and time in UTC.
SetLastAccessTime	Sets a file's last access date and time.
SetLastAccessTimeUtc	Sets a file's last access date and time in UTC.
SetLastWriteTime	Sets a file's last write date and time.
SetLastWriteTimeUtc	Sets a file's last write date and time in UTC.
WriteAllBytes	Creates or replaces a file, writes an array of bytes into it, and closes the file.
WriteAllLines	Creates or replaces a file, writes an array of strings into it, and closes the file.
WriteAllText	Creates or replaces a file, writes a string into it, and closes the file.

DriveInfo

A DriveInfo object represents one of the computer's drives. The following table describes the properties provided by this class. The final column in the table indicates whether a drive must be ready for the property to work without throwing an exception. Use the IsReady property to see whether the drive is ready before using those properties.

PROPERTY	PURPOSE	MUST BE READY?
AvailableFreeSpace	Returns the amount of free space available on the drive in bytes. This value takes quotas into account, so it may not match TotalFreeSpace.	True
DriveFormat	Returns the name of the file system type such as NTFS or FAT32. (For more information on NTFS and FAT file systems, search the Web. For example, the page www.ntfs.com/ntfs_vs_fat.htm compares the FAT, FAT32, and NTFS file systems.)	True
DriveType	Returns a DriveType enumeration value indicating the drive type. This value can be CDRom, Fixed, Network, NoRootDirectory, Ram, Removable, or Unknown.	False
IsReady	Returns True if the drive is ready. Many DriveInfo properties are unavailable and raise exceptions if you try to access them while the drive is not ready.	False
Name	Return's the drive's name. This is the drive's root name as in A:\ or C:\.	False
RootDirectory	Returns a DirectoryInfo object representing the drive's root directory. See the section "DirectoryInfo" later in this appendix for more information.	False
TotalFreeSpace	Returns the total amount of free space on the drive in bytes.	True
TotalSize	Returns the total amount of space on the drive in bytes.	True
VolumeLabel	Gets or sets the drive's volume label.	True

FINDING NTFS FEATURES

Different NTFS versions support different features. You can learn which version a volume is using by opening a command window and executing the command `fsutil fsinfo ntfsinfo d:`.

DirectoryInfo

A DirectoryInfo object represents a directory. The following table summarizes its most useful properties and methods.

PROPERTY OR METHOD	PURPOSE
Attributes	Gets or sets flags from the FileAttributes enumeration for the directory. These flags can include Archive, Compressed, Device, Directory, Encrypted, Hidden, Normal, NotContentIndexed, Offline, ReadOnly, ReparsePoint, SparseFile, System, and Temporary.
Create	Creates the directory. You can create a DirectoryInfo object, passing its constructor the fully qualified name of a directory that doesn't exist. You can then call the object's Create method to create the directory.
CreateSubdirectory	Creates a subdirectory within the directory and returns a DirectoryInfo object representing it. The subdirectory's path must be relative to the DirectoryInfo object's directory but can contain intermediate subdirectories. For example, the statement `dir_info.CreateSubdirectory("Tools\Bin")` creates the Tools subdirectory and the Bin directory inside that.
CreationTime	Gets or sets the directory's creation time.
CreationTimeUtc	Gets or sets the directory's creation time in UTC.
Delete	Deletes the directory if it is empty. A parameter lets you tell the object to delete its contents, too, if it isn't empty.
Exists	Returns True if the directory exists.
Extension	Returns the extension part of the directory's name. Normally, this is an empty string for directories.
FullName	Returns the directory's fully qualified path.
GetDirectories	Returns an array of DirectoryInfo objects representing the directory's subdirectories. An optional parameter gives a pattern to match. This method does not recursively search the subdirectories.
GetFiles	Returns an array of FileInfo objects representing files inside the directory. An optional parameter gives a pattern to match. This method does not recursively search subdirectories.
GetFileSystemInfos	Returns a strongly typed array of FileSystemInfo objects representing subdirectories and files inside the directory. The items in the array are DirectoryInfo and FileInfo objects, both of which inherit from FileSystemInfo. An optional parameter gives a pattern to match. This method does not recursively search subdirectories.

PROPERTY OR METHOD	PURPOSE
LastAccessTime	Gets or sets the directory's last access time.
LastAccessTimeUtc	Gets or sets the directory's last access time in UTC.
LastWriteTime	Gets or sets the directory's last write time.
LastWriteTimeUtc	Gets or sets the directory's last write time in UTC.
MoveTo	Moves the directory and its contents to a new path.
Name	Returns the directory's name without the path information.
Parent	Returns a DirectoryInfo object representing the directory's parent. If the directory is its file system's root (for example, C:\), this returns Nothing.
Refresh	Refreshes the DirectoryInfo object's data. For example, if the directory has been accessed since the object was created, you must call Refresh to load the new LastAccessTime value.
Root	Returns a DirectoryInfo object representing the root of the directory's file system.
ToString	Returns the directory's fully qualified path and name.

FileInfo

A FileInfo object represents a file. The following table summarizes its most useful properties and methods.

PROPERTY OR METHOD	PURPOSE
AppendText	Returns a StreamWriter that appends text to the file.
Attributes	Gets or sets flags from the FileAttributes enumeration for the file. These flags can include Archive, Compressed, Device, Directory, Encrypted, Hidden, Normal, NotContentIndexed, Offline, ReadOnly, ReparsePoint, SparseFile, System, and Temporary.
CopyTo	Copies the file and returns a FileInfo object representing the new file. A parameter lets you indicate whether the copy should overwrite an existing file if it already exists. If the destination path is relative, it is relative to the application's current directory, not to the FileInfo object's directory.
Create	Creates the file and returns a FileStream object attached to it. For example, you can create a FileInfo object passing its constructor the name of a file that doesn't exist. Then you can call the Create method to create the file.

continues

(continued)

PROPERTY OR METHOD	PURPOSE
CreateText	Creates the file and returns a StreamWriter attached to it. For example, you can create a FileInfo object passing its constructor the name of a file that doesn't exist. Then you can call the CreateText method to create the file.
CreationTime	Gets or sets the file's creation time.
CreationTimeUtc	Gets or sets the file's creation time in UTC.
Delete	Deletes the file.
Directory	Returns a DirectoryInfo object representing the file's directory.
DirectoryName	Returns the name of the file's directory.
Exists	Returns True if the file exists.
Extension	Returns the extension part of the file's name including the period. For example, the extension for game.txt is .txt.
FullName	Returns the file's fully qualified path and name.
IsReadOnly	Returns True if the file is marked read-only.
LastAccessTime	Gets or sets the file's last access time.
LastAccessTimeUtc	Gets or sets the file's last access time in UTC.
LastWriteTime	Gets or sets the file's last write time.
LastWriteTimeUtc	Gets or sets the file's last write time in UTC.
Length	Returns the number of bytes in the file.
MoveTo	Moves the file to a new location. If the destination uses a relative path, it is relative to the application's current directory, not to the FileInfo object's directory. When this method finishes, the FileInfo object is updated to refer to the file's new location.
Name	The file's name without the path information.
Open	Opens the file with different mode (Append, Create, CreateNew, Open, OpenOrCreate, or Truncate), access (Read, Write, or ReadWrite), and sharing (Read, Write, ReadWrite, or None) settings. This method returns a FileStream object attached to the file.
OpenRead	Returns a read-only FileStream attached to the file.
OpenText	Returns a StreamReader with UTF-8 encoding attached to the file for reading.

PROPERTY OR METHOD	PURPOSE
OpenWrite	Returns a write-only FileStream attached to the file.
Refresh	Refreshes the FileInfo object's data. For example, if the file has been accessed since the object was created, you must call Refresh to load the new LastAccessTime value.
Replace	Replaces a target file with this one, renaming the old target as a backup copy. If the backup file already exists, it is deleted and replaced with the target. You can use this method to save backups of logs and other periodically updated files.
ToString	Returns the file's fully qualified name.

FileSystemWatcher

The FileSystemWatcher class lets an application watch for changes to a file or directory. The following table summarizes its most useful properties.

PROPERTY	PURPOSE
EnableRaisingEvents	Determines whether the component is enabled. Note that this property is False by default, so the watcher will not raise any events until you set it to True.
Filter	Determines the files for which the watcher reports events. You cannot watch for multiple file types as in *.txt and *.dat. Instead, use multiple FileSystemWatchers. If you like, you can use AddHandler to make all of the FileSystemWatchers use the same event handlers.
IncludeSubdirectories	Determines whether the object watches subdirectories within the main path.
InternalBufferSize	Determines the size of the internal buffer. If the watcher is monitoring a very active directory, a small buffer may overflow.
NotifyFilter	Determines the types of changes that the watcher reports. This is a combination of values defined by the NotifyFilters enumeration and can include the values Attributes, CreationTime, DirectoryName, FileName, LastAccess, LastWrite, Security, and Size.
Path	Determines the path to watch.

The following table summarizes the FileSystemWatcher class's two most useful methods.

METHOD	PURPOSE
Dispose	Releases resources used by the object.
WaitForChanged	Synchronously waits for a change to the target file or directory.

The following table summarizes the class's events.

NAME	DESCRIPTION
Changed	A file or subdirectory has changed.
Created	A file or subdirectory was created.
Deleted	A file or subdirectory was deleted.
Error	The watcher's internal buffer overflowed.
Renamed	A file or subdirectory was renamed.

Path

The Path class provides shared properties and methods that you can use to manipulate paths. The following table summarizes its most useful public properties.

PROPERTY	PURPOSE
AltDirectorySeparatorChar	Returns the alternate character used to separate directory levels in a hierarchical path (typically, /).
DirectorySeparatorChar	Returns the character used to separate directory levels in a hierarchical path (typically, \, as in C:\Tests\Billing\2010q2 .dat).
InvalidPathChars	Returns a character array that holds characters that are not allowed in a path string. Typically, this array will include characters such as ", <, >, and |, as well as nonprintable characters such as those with ASCII values between 0 and 31.
PathSeparator	Returns the character used to separate path strings in environment variables (typically, ;).
VolumeSeparatorChar	Returns the character placed between a volume letter and the rest of the path (typically, :, as in C:\Tests\Billing\2010q2 .dat).

The following table summarizes the Path class's most useful methods.

METHOD	PURPOSE
ChangeExtension	Changes a path's extension.
Combine	Returns two path strings concatenated. This does not simplify the result as the FileSystem.CombinePath method does.
GetDirectoryName	Returns a path's directory.
GetExtension	Returns a path's extension.
GetFileName	Returns a path's file name and extension.
GetFileNameWithoutExtension	Returns a path's file name without the extension.
GetFullPath	Returns a path's fully qualified value. This can be particularly useful for converting a partially relative path into an absolute path. For example, the statement `Path.GetFullPath("C:\Tests\OldTests\Software\..\..\New\Code")` returns "C:\Tests\New\Code."
GetInvalidFileNameChars	Returns a character array that holds characters that are not allowed in a file names.
GetPathRoot	Returns a path's root directory string. For example, the statement `Path.GetPathRoot("C:\Invoices\Unpaid\Deadbeats")` returns "C:\."
GetRandomFileName	Returns a random file name.
GetTempFileName	Creates a uniquely named, empty temporary file, and returns its fully qualified path. Your program can open that file for scratch space, do whatever it needs to do, close the file, and then delete it. A typical file name might be "C:\Documents and Settings\Rod\Local Settings\Temp\tmp19D.tmp."
GetTempPath	Returns the path to the system's temporary folder. This is the path part of the file name returned by GetTempFileName.
HasExtension	Returns True if a path includes an extension.
IsPathRooted	Returns True if a path is an absolute path. This includes \Temp\Wherever and C:\Clients\Litigation, but not Temp\Wherever or ..\Uncle.

MY.COMPUTER.FILESYSTEM

The My.Computer.FileSystem object provides tools for working with drives, directories, and files. The following table summarizes this object's properties.

PROPERTY	DESCRIPTION
CurrentDirectory	Gets or sets the fully qualified path to the application's current directory.
Drives	Returns a read-only collection of DriveInfo objects describing the system's drives. See Chapter 38, "File-System Objects," for information about the DriveInfo class.
SpecialDirectories	Returns a SpecialDirectoriesProxy object that has properties giving the locations of various special directories such as the system's temporary directory and the user's My Documents directory. See the section "My.Computer.FileSystem .SpecialDirectories" later in this appendix for more information.

The following list summarizes the My.Computer.FileSystem object's methods:

METHOD	PURPOSE
CombinePath	Combines a base path with a relative path reference and returns a properly formatted fully qualified path.
CopyDirectory	Copies a directory. Parameters indicate whether to overwrite existing files, whether to display a progress indicator, and what to do if the user presses Cancel during the operation.
CopyFile	Copies a file. Parameters indicate whether to overwrite existing files, whether to display a progress indicator, and what to do if the user presses Cancel during the operation.
CreateDirectory	Creates all of the directories along a path.
DeleteDirectory	Deletes a directory. Parameters indicate whether to recursively delete subdirectories, prompt the user for confirmation, or move the directory into the Recycle Bin.
DeleteFile	Deletes a file. Parameters indicate whether to prompt the user for confirmation, or move the file into the Recycle Bin, and what to do if the user presses Cancel while the deletion is in progress.
DirectoryExists	Returns True if a specified directory exists.
FileExists	Returns True if a specified file exists.

METHOD	PURPOSE
FindInFiles	Returns a collection holding names of files that contain a search string.
GetDirectories	Returns a string collection listing subdirectories of a given directory. Parameters tell whether to recursively search the subdirectories, and wildcards to match.
GetDirectoryInfo	Returns a DirectoryInfo object for a directory. See the section "DirectoryInfo" earlier in this appendix for more information.
GetDriveInfo	Returns a DriveInfo object for a drive. See the section "DriveInfo" earlier in this appendix for more information.
GetFileInfo	Returns a FileInfo object for a file. See the section "FileInfo" earlier in this appendix for more information.
GetFiles	Returns a string collection holding the names of files within a directory. Parameters indicate whether the search should recursively search subdirectories and give wildcards to match.
GetParentPath	Returns the fully qualified path of a path's parent. For example, this returns a file's or directory's parent directory.
MoveDirectory	Moves a directory. Parameters indicate whether to overwrite files that have the same name in the destination directory and whether to prompt the user when such a collision occurs.
MoveFile	Moves a file. Parameters indicate whether to overwrite a file that has the same name as the file's destination and whether to prompt the user when such a collision occurs.
OpenTextFieldParser	Opens a TextFieldParser object attached to a delimited or fixed-field file (such as a log file). You can use the object to parse the file.
OpenTextFileReader	Opens a StreamReader object attached to a file. You can use the object to read the file.
OpenTextFileWriter	Opens a StreamReader object attached to a file. You can use the object to write into the file.
ReadAllBytes	Reads all the bytes from a binary file into an array.
ReadAllText	Reads all the text from a text file into a string.
RenameDirectory	Renames a directory within its parent directory.
RenameFile	Renames a file with its directory.

continues

(continued)

METHOD	PURPOSE
WriteAllBytes	Writes an array of bytes into a binary file. A parameter tells whether to append the data or rewrite the file.
WriteAllText	Writes a string into a text file. A parameter tells whether to append the string or rewrite the file.

MY.COMPUTER.FILESYSTEM.SPECIALDIRECTORIES

The My.Computer.FileSystem.SpecialDirectories property returns a SpecialDirectoriesProxy object that has properties giving the locations of various special directories (such as the system's temporary directory and the user's My Documents directory). The following table summarizes these special directory properties.

PROPERTY	PURPOSE
AllUsersApplicationData	The directory where applications should store settings for all users (typically, something like C:\ProgramData\ WindowsApplication1\WindowsApplication1\1.0.0.0).
CurrentUserApplicationData	The directory where applications should store settings for the current user (typically, something like C:\Users\ CrazyBob\AppData\Roaming\WindowsApplication1\ WindowsApplication1\1.0.0.0).
Desktop	The current user's desktop directory (typically, C:\Users\CrazyBob\Desktop).
MyDocuments	The current user's My Documents directory (typically, C:\Users\CrazyBob\Documents).
MyMusic	The current user's My Music directory (typically, C:\Users\CrazyBob\Music).
MyPictures	The current user's My Pictures directory (typically, C:\Users\CrazyBob\Pictures).
ProgramFiles	The Program Files directory (typically, C:\Program Files).
Programs	The current user's Programs directory (typically, C:\Users\ CrazyBob\AppData\Roaming\Microsoft\Windows\Start Menu\Programs).
Temp	The current user's temporary directory (typically, C:\Users\CrazyBob\AppData\Local\Temp).

V

Index of Examples

This book includes more than 400 example programs that are available for download from the book's web site. This appendix briefly describes the examples in each chapter so you know which programs to look at for a particular topic.

Most of the chapters include example applications, so the following list includes entries for every chapter. Only Appendixes A, G, and K have examples, so only they are listed here (although many of the chapters have examples covering material in the other appendixes).

- ➤ Chapter 1
  - ➤ There are no example programs for this chapter.
- ➤ Chapter 2
  - ➤ There are no example programs for this chapter.
- ➤ Chapter 3
  - ➤ There are no example programs for this chapter.
- ➤ Chapter 4
  - ➤ There are no example programs for this chapter.
- ➤ Chapter 5
  - ➤ There are no example programs for this chapter.
- ➤ Chapter 6
  - ➤ Fibonacci — Calculates Fibonacci numbers. [page 82]
- ➤ Chapter 7
  - ➤ There are no example programs for this chapter.

➤ Chapter 13

➤ Chapter 14

➤ Chapter 15

➤ Appendix A

➤ DisplayRectangles — Shows a GroupBox's DisplayRectangle and ClientRectangle. [page 918]

See the chapter listings for more examples that demonstrate control properties, methods, and events. In particular, see Chapter 8, "Selecting Windows Forms Controls," and Chapter 9, "Using Windows Forms Controls."

➤ Appendix G

➤ CustomColorDialog — Displays a color dialog with custom colors. [page 957]

➤ FlowDirections — Demonstrates the FlowLayoutPanel control's FlowDirection property values LeftToRight, RightToLeft, TopDown, and BottomUp. [page 964]

➤ ListViewCustomSort — Uses an IComparer class to implement a custom sort for the ListView control. Also shows how to let the user select different display modes. [page 979]

➤ MultiLineLabel — Uses a multiline label.

➤ RunTimeListView — Inserts data into a ListView control at runtime.

➤ UseBackgroundWorker — Demonstrates a BackgroundWorker component controlling a simulated long task. [page 953]

➤ UseButton — Demonstrates a button.

➤ UseCheckedListBox — Displays a CheckedListBox that displays Employee objects (shows how to display objects in a ListBox or ComboBox). Shows how to enumerate the selected items. [page 956]

➤ UseColorDialog — Shows how to let the user select a color. [page 957]

➤ UseComboBox — Demonstrates the ComboBox control and its different DropDownStyle values. [page 966]

➤ UseDataGridView — Demonstrates a DataGridView control attached to a database.

➤ UseDateTimePicker — Demonstrates the DateTimePicker control. [page 968]

➤ UseDomainUpDown — Uses the DomainUpDown control to let the user select a month by name.

➤ UseErrorProvider — Use an ErrorProvider component to display an error indicator if the user doesn't enter a five-digit ZIP code. [page 963]

➤ UseFolderBrowserDialog — Demonstrates the FolderBrowserDialog component.

➤ UseFontDialog — Demonstrates the FontDialog. [page 967]

➤ UseFontDialogWithShowEffects — Demonstrates the FontDialog. Allows the user to click the Apply button to show the new font on the form, and then cancel or okay the changes. [page 967]

➤ UseGroupBox — Demonstrates GroupBoxes containing RadioButtons.

➤ UseHelpProvider — Uses a HelpProvider to display a help popup if the user selects a field and presses F1.

➤ UseHScrollBar — Demonstrates the HScrollBar control.

➤ UseLinkLabel — Demonstrates the LinkLabel control and shows how to open a web site when the user clicks a link.

➤ UseListView — Demonstrates the ListView control and its display modes. [page 976]

➤ UseMonthCalendar — Demonstrates the MonthCalendar control. Sets the control's minimum, maximum, and current dates; selects date range; and bolds Mondays. [page 987]

➤ UseMonthCalendarInDialog — Shows how to make a dialog that displays a MonthCalendar control that shows two rows of three months. The dialog lets the user pick a date range and returns OK or Cancel. [page 987]

➤ UseNotifyIcon — Demonstrates the NotifyIcon component and shows how to add a ContextMenu to the notification icon. [page 987]

➤ UseNumericUpDown — Demonstrates the NumericUpDown control.

➤ UseOpenFileDialog — Demonstrates the OpenFileDialog component. Shows how to catch the FileOk event to validate the user's selection.

➤ UsePageSetupDialog — Demonstrates the PageSetupDialog.

➤ UsePanel — Demonstrates a Panel with AutoScroll. Lets the user set the control's AutoScrollPosition.

➤ UsePictureBox — Shows three ways to draw on PictureBoxes: by assigning an image to a PictureBox's Image property, by drawing in the PictureBox's Paint event handler, and when the code executes so the image is not refreshed later.

➤ UsePrintDialog — Demonstrates the PrintDialog component.

➤ UsePrintPreviewControl — Uses a PrintPreviewControl control to display three pages of printout inside a form. [page 1000]

➤ UsePrintPreviewDialog — Uses a PrintPreviewDialog to display three pages of printout in a dialog.

➤ UseProcess — Demonstrates the Process component by using it to start a new process running this program. [page 1002]

➤ UseProgressBar — Demonstrates the ProgressBar control.

➤ UsePropertyGrid — Displays Employee object data in a ListBox and a PropertyGrid. [page 1011]

➤ UseRadioButton — Demonstrates RadioButton controls inside GroupBoxes.

INDEX

N

Q

R

Y